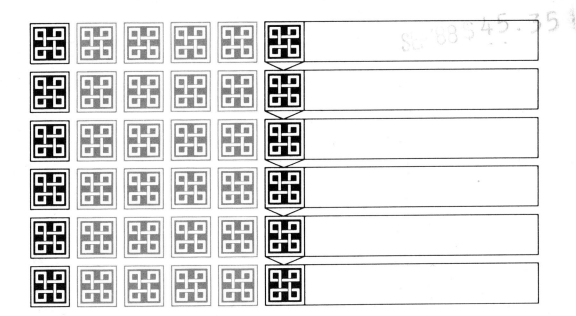

MARKETING RESEARCH

METHODOLOGICAL FOUNDATIONS

Fourth Edition

GILBERT A. CHURCHILL, Jr.
University of Wisconsin

The Dryden Press
*Chicago   New York   Philadelphia   San Francisco
Montreal   Toronto   London   Sydney
Tokyo   Mexico City   Rio de Janeiro   Madrid*

To my parents, wife, and children; and in memory of my grandmother and our son, John.

Acquisitions Editor: Rob Zwettler
Developmental Editor: Judy Sarwark
Project Editor: Cate Rzasa
Production Manager: Mary Jarvis
Permissions Editor: Doris Milligan
Director of Editing, Design, and Production: Jane Perkins

Text and Cover Designer: Alan Wendt
Copy Editor: Judy Lary
Indexer: Sheila Ary
Compositor: The Clarinda Company
Text Type: 10/12 Times Roman

Library of Congress Cataloging-in-Publication Data
Churchill, Gilbert A.
　Marketing research.

　Includes bibliographical references and index.
　1. Marketing research.　I. Title.
　HF5415.2.C5　1987　　658.8′3　　85-31138
　ISBN 0-03-005532-6

Printed in the United States of America
789-039-9876543

Address orders:
383 Madison Avenue
New York, NY 10017

Address editorial correspondence:
One Salt Creek Lane
Hinsdale, IL 60521

The Dryden Press
Holt, Rinehart and Winston
Saunders College Publishing

Preface

Intended Market

The basic objective that motivated the first three editions of this book serves as the impetus for the fourth edition as well. The book, which is designed for the introductory sequence in marketing research, attempts to structure the discipline of marketing research for students.

The topic of marketing research is a complex one. It involves a number of questions that need to be answered and a number of decisions that need to be made with respect to the choice of technique or techniques to be used to solve a research problem. Without some overriding framework, it is easy for students to "fail to see the forest for the trees," that is, to become so overwhelmed by the bits and pieces that they fail to see the interrelationships of the parts to the whole. Distorted vision like this can be detrimental to both the aspiring manager and the aspiring researcher, for in a very real sense marketing research is one big trade-off. Decisions made with respect to one stage in the research process have consequences for the other stages. Managers need an appreciation of the subtle and pervasive interactions among the parts of the research process so that they can have the appropriate degree of confidence in a particular research result. Researchers also need to appreciate the interactions among the parts. While the parts serve as the "pegs" upon which to hang the knowledge they accumulate about research methods, researchers need to avoid becoming enamored of the parts to the detriment of the whole.

This book attempts to serve both of these masters—the aspiring manager and the aspiring researcher—through its basic organization around the stages of the research process. The research process is a sequence of steps, most typically traveled with much iteration, which reflects the stages that must be completed in answering a research question. The specific stages are

1. Formulate the problem
2. Determine the research design
3. Design the data collection method and forms
4. Design the sample and collect the data
5. Analyze and interpret the data
6. Prepare the research report

The organization of the book parallels these stages in the process. More specifically, the book is organized into six parts, with each part corresponding to one of the stages. Moreover, the stages are broken into smaller parts, so that a given stage is typically discussed in multiple chapters and appendixes. Not only does this allow students to see the forest for the trees but it also provides instructors a great deal of latitude with respect to what is covered. An instructor's decision on what to cover will depend, of course, on the background, interests, and maturity of the students and on the time provided in the curriculum for marketing research. Because of the flexibility the book provides instructors when choosing the level of depth with which to cover any particular stage in the research process, *Marketing Research: Methodological Foundations,* Fourth Edition, can be used in a variety of introductory marketing research course sequences. It can be used effectively, for example, either in one- or two-quarter sequences or in semester courses either at the undergraduate or graduate levels. I have used the first three editions of the book to advantage at both the undergraduate and graduate levels by simply covering more material at a higher level of sophistication in the graduate course.

Organization

As mentioned, the book is organized into six parts, with each part corresponding to one of the stages in the process.

Part 1, on formulating the problem, consists of two chapters. Chapter 1 provides an overview of marketing research, including the kinds of problems for which it is used, who is doing research, and how it is organized. It also discusses some of the career opportunities available in marketing research. Chapter 2 overviews the process in terms of the kinds of decisions that need to be made at each stage and then discusses in some detail the problem formulation stage of the research process. One question that needs to be asked whenever research is being considered is whether the research is likely to be worth the money it will cost. The appendix to Chapter 2 discusses how Bayesian analysis can be used to make this judgment.

Part 2 also consists of two chapters and deals with the nature of the research design, to ensure that the research addresses the appropriate questions and treats them in an efficient manner. Chapter 3 overviews the role of various research designs and also discusses two of the basic designs, the exploratory and the descriptive, at some length. Chapter 4 discusses the role and conceptual logic of experiments.

The four chapters in Part 3 delve into methods of data collection and design of data collection forms. Chapter 5 focuses on secondary data as an information resource and includes a discussion of commercial marketing information services, while the appendix to Chapter 5 discusses the many sources of published secondary data. Chapter 6 discusses the two main methods of data collection—observation and communication—while Chapter 7 covers the construction of questionnaires and observation data collection forms. Chapter 8 explains the general topic of attitude measurement using scales and discusses some of the more common types of attitude scales. The important but often neglected topic of how one develops measures for marketing constructs of interest is discussed in one of the three appendixes to Chapter 8, and multidimensional scaling and conjoint analysis are explained in the other two.

Part 4, which consists of three chapters, is concerned with the actual collection of data needed to answer questions. Chapter 9 discusses the various types of sampling plans that can be used to determine the population elements from which data should be collected. Chapter 10 treats the question of how many of these elements are needed, so that the problem can be answered with the required precision and confidence in the results. Chapter 11 discusses the many errors that can arise in completing this data collection task from a perspective that allows managers the opportunity to better assess the quality of the information they receive from research.

Once data have been collected, emphasis in the research process logically turns to analysis, which amounts to searching for meaning in the collected information. The search for meaning involves many questions and several steps, and the five chapters, as well as the several appendixes, in Part 5 attempt to overview these steps and questions. Chapter 12 reviews the preliminary analysis steps of editing, coding, and tabulating the data. The main questions that must be resolved before the statistical examination of the data can begin are covered in Chapter 13. Next, Chapters 14, 15, and 16 review the statistical techniques most useful in the analysis of marketing data. Chapter 14 discusses the procedures appropriate for examining the differences among and between groups; Chapter 15 covers the assessment of association; and Chapter 16 examines the multivariate techniques of discriminant, factor, and cluster analysis.

Part 6 consists of two chapters. Chapter 17 discusses one of the most critically important parts in the whole research process: the research report. Because it often becomes the standard by which the research effort is assessed, it is important that the research report contribute positively to that evaluation. Chapter 17 discusses the criteria a research report should satisfy and the form it can follow so that it does contribute positively to the research effort. This chapter also discusses some of the graphical means that can be used to communicate the important findings more forcefully. Chapter 18 then goes on to discuss the relationship between a decision support system approach to the gathering of marketing intelligence and the project emphasis stressed in this book. It also discusses some of the more important issues that must be addressed in designing a decision support system.

The organization of the material in this book around the stages in the research process produces several significant benefits. First, it demonstrates and continually reinforces how the "bits" of research technique fit into a larger whole. Students can see readily, for example, the relationship between statistics and marketing research, or where they might pursue additional study to become research specialists.

Second, the organization permits great flexibility. For example, instructors with only a single, one-quarter introductory course in marketing research faced with the need to develop some appreciation for the basic questions addressed in research might choose to overview the research process at an elementary level. One way this could be accomplished would be by omitting Chapter 4 on causal research designs, Chapter 8 on attitude measurement, and Chapter 10 on sample size and by covering only Chapter 12 from among the five analysis chapters. This approach would serve to present the process while at the same time avoiding some of the more technical questions of research design, measurement, sampling, and the statistical analysis of the collected data.

On the other hand, instructors who wish to emphasize, say, the questions of analysis or measurement, would have ample materials to do so. There is, for example, one data base in the text itself and a number of other data bases in the *Instructor's Manual* that instructors can have students analyze using one of the standard statistical packages. Each of these data bases is available both in hard copy and on computer disk to all who adopt the book. The data base in the book involves buying through catalogs. It is used to demonstrate everything from the coding of data to the most involved statistical techniques. The appendixes to appropriate chapters contain sample computer output and discuss the interpretation of that output in light of the notions discussed in the chapter. One of the appendixes also lists and describes the deck set-up for an SPSS run. These appendixes provide students a direct connection between statistical concepts and the application of these concepts. The data base is rich enough for students to perform their own analyses, thereby increasing their comfort level with the statistical techniques discussed. The specific portions of the book that should be used to produce this emphasis or several other emphases are discussed in the *Instructor's Manual,* which contains suggested outlines for organizing courses to achieve different emphases in different time frames.

All of the parts except Part 6 conclude with cases that illustrate many of the major issues raised in the section. The cases represent actual situations, although many of them have disguised names and locations to protect the identity of the sponsors. The cases afford students the opportunity to apply what they have learned by critically evaluating what others have done, thereby increasing their analytic skills.

Changes in the Fourth Edition

Although this edition looks very much like the first three editions, there have been some major changes. For one thing, there has been a major revision of the cases. There are 20 percent more cases in the fourth edition than in the third. Further, over one-half of the cases are new, and several of the old cases have been revised and updated.

Another major change concerns the analysis chapters. There is much greater emphasis on confidence interval estimation in this edition in keeping with the changing emphasis in the philosophy of science and statistics literatures. The new treatment is also less imposing quantitatively while revealing more of the quality of the research results. The data set on catalog buying mentioned above is brand new, as are the descriptions in the appendixes interpreting the SPSS output. Furthermore, the discussion of the multivariate analysis techniques of discriminant, factor, and cluster analyses has been completely revised. The new discussion is not only more extensive but clearer.

The two measurement appendixes covering multidimensional scaling and conjoint analysis have also been revised extensively to reflect recent developments for securing perceptual and preference judgments.

In addition, all of the chapters have been subjected to thorough scrutiny and rewrite. There has been a major updating of the examples, for instance. There are many more examples than were found in the third edition, and the examples are as up-to-date as possible. Chapter references have also been updated. Both of these changes help the book reflect what is happening in the world of marketing research as it is practiced today. The discussion in some chapters has been expanded while in other places it has been streamlined, always with the intent of making it as clear as possible. Some of the more significant chapter-by-chapter changes include:

Chapter 1 An extensive, completely new set of examples outlining the scope and thrust of marketing research.

Chapter 2   Greater elaboration of the distinction between program and project strategies to research; new discussion describing a process that helps ensure that the decision problem and the aspects of the decision problem that research is to address are accurately stated; a new section on the preparation of a research proposal; relocation of the material on the use of Bayesian decision theory to assess the potential value of research to an appendix.

Chapter 3   Greater emphasis on how one can ensure that the questions asked in a survey are appropriate and important given the objectives motivating the study; a number of new examples that illustrate the objectives of productive exploratory and descriptive research; new discussion on cohort analysis for analyzing data from sets of surveys.

Chapter 4   New discussion of two recent variations in new product testing (use of controlled test markets and simulated test marketing); new examples reflecting firms' recent experiences when test marketing new products; elimination of the appendix on statistical experimental design and the incorporation of the more important elements of that discussion in the analysis section.

Chapter 5   New discussion of how to search the many sources of secondary data to locate published information on a particular topic; new discussion of Information Resources' BehaviorScan and Nielsen's Scantrak systems; inclusion of a number of additional general sources of marketing research information in the appendix.

Chapter 6   New section on psychological/life-style characteristics; new data on the cost and problems encountered with random digit dialing; new data on the popularity of various data collection techniques among practitioners; new examples reflecting the technologies currently being used by firms doing marketing research.

Chapter 7   New summary table offering specific advice on the things to do at each stage of the process when constructing questionnaires.

Chapter 8   New evidence with respect to the impact various features of rating scales have on the reliability of those scales; comparison of nonattribute-based versus attribute-based approaches to the development of perceptual maps; new step-by-step flow diagram and its discussion outlining the stages analysts have to complete to do a multidimensional scaling analysis; new step-by-step process model analysts can follow when doing a conjoint analysis.

Chapter 11   New discussion summarizing the evidence regarding the impact various response-generating techniques have on response rates; new summary table that highlights the things that can be done to handle nonsampling errors.

Chapter 12   New discussion describing how analysts can use cross-tabulation analysis to determine which of several variables exerts the greatest impact on a dependent variable.

Chapter 13   Greater emphasis on proper interpretation and common misinterpretations of what a statistical test of significance means.

Chapter 14   Incorporation of confidence interval estimates for all the statistics discussed.

Chapter 16   Completely rewritten discussion of discriminant analysis including a new example and greater elaboration on how to interpret the output of a discriminant analysis; completely rewritten discussion of factor analysis, with a new example to motivate the discussion, and expanded discussion on the decision rules for choosing the number of factors, how to interpret factor loadings, and how to name the factors, all of which is summarized in a flow diagram that outlines the key decisions to be made when conducting a factor analysis; completely rewritten discussion of cluster analysis, including a new example, procedures for determining the number of clusters when linkage procedures are used, and new discussion on how to choose the attributes on which objects are to be clustered, all of which is summarized in a step-by-step flow diagram with surrounding explanation that outlines the decisions analysts have to make to conduct a cluster analysis.

Chapter 17   New discussion on how to present the information in a table most effectively; new section on the preparation of oral reports; expanded discussion on how to write clear reports.

Chapter 18   Completely rewritten discussion regarding the role and design of marketing information systems (MIS) in supplying marketing intelligence; new discussion of decision support systems (DSS), including the description of their basic components and how they differ from marketing information systems.

Special Features

As readers might suspect from the above chapter descriptions, there is variation in the level and difficulty of the material. Certain parts, such as the discussion of commercial information services in the secondary data chapter, are purely descriptive. Others, such as the notion of measurement, are by their nature abstract and, as such, are difficult for students not used to thinking in abstract terms. This, though, is the nature of marketing research, and this book does not avoid topics simply because they are difficult to grasp. Rather, the posture has been to include those topics that are vital to understanding the nature of the research process while attempting to simplify the complex ideas into their basic elements. Throughout, the emphasis is placed on conceptual understanding of the material rather than on mathematical niceties or discussion of interesting but unimportant tangents. The purpose here is to walk the middle ground between the two kinds of introductory texts currently available. One type discusses the concepts of marketing research without providing sufficient detail about some of the important, but perhaps more difficult, stages in the process. The other kind goes to the opposite extreme of discussing some technically difficult stages in great detail while omitting the basic structure of the process, and at other stages providing only cursory coverage of some of the more elementary, but critically important, methods. *Marketing Research: Methodologi-*

cal Foundations, Fourth Edition, is designed to avoid such extremes by providing the student with a thorough treatment of the important concepts, both simple and complex.

The general approach employed throughout is not only to provide the student with the pros and cons of the various methods with which a research problem could be addressed but also to develop an appreciation of why these advantages and disadvantages arise. The hope is that through this appreciation, students will be able to creatively apply and critically evaluate the procedures of marketing research. The cases are included to assist students in developing their evaluation and analytical skills. The cases are also useful in demonstrating the universal application of marketing research techniques. The methods of marketing research can be used not only by manufacturers and distributors of products, as is commonly assumed, but also to address other issues in the private and public sectors. The cases include such diverse entities or issues as the Big Brothers program, computerized bibliographic data services, an electric utility, rent control, generic drugs, banking services, legal services, and university extension programs, among others.

A new feature in the fourth edition is the addition of problems at the end of each chapter, allowing students the opportunity to apply the chapter notions to very focused situations. Another new feature is the inclusion of student exercises for each chapter that direct students to do small-scale research using particular techniques to thereby develop first-hand knowledge of the strengths and weaknesses of the technique. These are contained in the *Instructor's Manual.* Still a third new feature is the addition of "Research Realities" to each chapter. These boxed inserts show what is going on generally in the world of marketing research today or specifically at companies such as General Mills, Gillette, and others.

Ancillaries

The *Instructor's Manual (IM)* to the text completes a comprehensive teaching package. The *IM* includes a preface that offers suggestions on how the book and *IM* can be used most effectively. The preface is followed by suggested outlines on how to teach the course to achieve desired emphases within different time frames. Next are the chapter-by-chapter resource materials, which include the following for each chapter:

1. Learning objectives
2. List of key terms
3. A detailed outline
4. Lecture and discussion suggestions
5. Suggested supplementary readings
6. Answers to the application questions and/or problems in the book
7. Student exercises and answers
8. Suggested cases for the chapter
9. Suggested ethical scenarios for the chapter

The individual chapter materials are followed by a section on marketing research ethics, including some scenarios that will stimulate class discussion. Next are the analyses for the cases included in the book. Six of the cases ask students to perform their own analysis to answer the questions posed. The raw data for these cases are listed for the convenience of those who find it easier to enter the data directly rather than using the computer disk that is available to adopters. The disk, though, allows those who have statistical packages available on microcomputers to use them for analysis. Others may find it more convenient to upload the data from the disk onto the school's mainframe computer and to have students use the larger system for their analyses. To obtain a copy of the disk, which is available for the IBM microcomputer, adopters must send the insert card in the *IM* to the nearest Dryden regional sales office.

The next section of the *Instructor's Manual* contains an extensive set (over 1,600 in all) of objective examination questions. Both multiple-choice and true–false questions are included, and the questions are organized by chapter. Many of the questions are new for this edition. Finally, there are over 100 transparencies that illustrate major points. While some of these transparencies are enlargements of the more important figures or tables in the book, many of them are original.

Acknowledgments

While writing a book is never the work of a single person, when attempting to acknowledge the contributions of others, one always runs the risk that he will omit some important contributions. Nonetheless, the attempt must be made because this book has been helped immensely by the many helpful comments I have received along the way from users and interested colleagues. I especially wish to acknowledge those people who reviewed the manuscript for this or for one of the earlier editions of this book. While much of the credit for the strengths of the book is theirs, the blame for any weaknesses is strictly mine. Thank you one and all for your most perceptive and helpful comments.

Mark I. Alpert
University of Texas at Austin

Robert L. Anderson
University of South Florida

Gary M. Armstrong
University of North Carolina

Frank J. Carmone, Jr.
Drexel University

Imran S. Currim
University of California

Albert J. DellaBitta
University of Rhode Island

James F. Engel
Wheaton College

Claes Fornell
University of Michigan

James W. Harvey
University of Maryland

Vince Howe
University of Kentucky

Roy Howell
Texas Tech University

G. David Hughes
University of North Carolina

H. Bruce Lammers
California State University,
    Northridge

C. P. Rao
University of Arkansas

Kenneth J. Roering
University of Minnesota

William Rudelius
University of Minnesota

Alan G. Sawyer
University of Florida

Randall L. Schultz	Sandra Teel
University of Texas-Dallas	University of South Carolina
Subrata K. Sen	David J. Urban
Yale University	Georgia State University
Allan D. Shocker	William G. Zikmund
University of Washington	Oklahoma State University

My colleagues at the University of Wisconsin have my thanks for the intellectual stimulation they have always provided. Dr. B. Venkatesh, who is now with the Burke Marketing Services, Inc., was particularly instrumental in getting the first edition off the ground. My discussions with him were important in determining the scope and structure of the book.

I wish to thank the many secretaries at the University of Wisconsin who participated in the typing of one or more versions of the manuscript. A special thank you goes to Janet Christopher, who again did most of the typing on the fourth edition and who assumed responsibility for other activities as well. I also wish to thank students Annette Drummond, Margaret Friedman, Larry Hogue, Joseph Kuester, Jayashree Mahajan, and David Szymanski for their help with many of the miscellaneous tasks involved in completing a book such as this. I would like to thank the editorial and production staff of The Dryden Press for their professional effort. I am grateful to the Literary Executor of the late Sir Ronald A. Fisher, F.R.S., to Dr. Frank Yates, F.R.S., and to Longman Group Ltd, for permission to reprint Table III from their book *Statistical Tables for Biological, Agricultural and Medical Research* (6th Edition, 1974).

Finally, I owe a special debt of thanks to my wife, Helen, and our four children, Carol, Elizabeth, David, and Thomas. Their understanding, cooperation, and support through all four editions of this book are sincerely appreciated.

Gilbert A. Churchill, Jr.
Madison, Wisconsin
September 1986

About the Author

Gilbert A. Churchill, Jr., DBA (Indiana University), is the Donald C. Slichter Professor in Business Research at the University of Wisconsin—Madison. He joined the Wisconsin faculty in 1966 and has taught there since, except for one year that he spent as a visiting professor at Bedriftsokonomisk Institutt in Oslo, Norway. Professor Churchill was named Distinguished Marketing Educator by the American Marketing Association in 1986, only the second individual so honored. The award recognizes and honors a living marketing educator for distinguished service and outstanding contributions in the field of marketing education.

Professor Churchill is a past recipient of the William O'Dell Award for the outstanding article appearing in the *Journal of Marketing Research* during the year. He has also been a finalist for the award three other times. He was named Marketer of the Year by the South Central Wisconsin Chapter of the American Marketing Association in 1981. He is a member of the American Marketing Association and has served as vice-president of publications and on its board of directors as well as on the association's Advisory Committee to the Bureau of the Census. In addition, he has served as consultant to a number of companies, including Oscar Mayer, Western Publishing Company, and Parker Pen.

Professor Churchill's articles have appeared in such publications as the *Journal of Marketing Research,* the *Journal of Marketing,* the *Journal of Consumer Research,* the *Journal of Retailing,* the *Journal of Business Research, Decision Sciences, Technometrics, Organizational Behavior,* and *Human Performance,* among others. He is a co-author of several other books, including *Sales Force Management: Planning, Implementation, and Control,* Second Edition (Homewood, Ill.: Irwin, 1985) and *Salesforce Performance* (Lexington, Mass.: Lexington Books, 1984). He is a former editor of the *Journal of Marketing Research* and has served on the editorial boards of the *Journal of Marketing Research,* the *Journal of Marketing,* the *Journal of Business Research,* and the *Journal of Health Care Marketing.* Professor Churchill currently teaches undergraduate and graduate courses in marketing research and sales management.

Contents

Part 2
Determination of Sources of Information and Research Design   69

Part 3
Design Data Collection Method and Forms   177

Chapter 5
Data Collection: Secondary Data   179

Chapter 6
Data Collection: Primary Data   217

Chapter 7
Data Collection Forms   271

Part 4
Sample Design and Data Collection   429

Chapter 9
Sampling Procedures   431

Part 5
Analysis and Interpretation of Data   561

Part 6
The Research Report and the Firm's
Marketing Information System   833

Part 1

Marketing Research, the Research Process, and Problem Definition

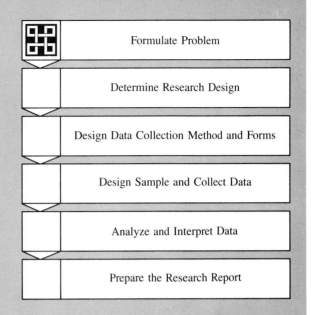

Formulate Problem
Determine Research Design
Design Data Collection Method and Forms
Design Sample and Collect Data
Analyze and Interpret Data
Prepare the Research Report

Part 1 gives an overview of marketing research. Chapter 1 overviews the kinds of problems for which it is used, who is doing it, and how it is organized. Chapter 2 provides an overview of the research process and contains detailed discussion of the problem formulation stage in the research process.

Chapter 1
Introduction

Marketing research is a pervasive activity. Consider the following examples.[1]

Example In an attempt to determine the proper weight for its candy bars, M&M/Mars conducted a 12-month test in 150 stores. For the test it altered the size of its products across the stores but kept the prices constant. It found that in those stores where the dimensions were increased, sales went up almost 20% to 30%. As a result of this test, the company decided to change almost its entire product line.[2]

Example In an attempt to expand their product line, Fisher-Price, the very successful toy maker, had some of their executives peer through a one-way mirror and eavesdrop for four hours as a dozen women in Cleveland complained about their battles with the zippers, buckles, buttons, and snaps on kids' clothing. The subsidiary of Quaker Oats used this information and the results of other similar focus groups to design a line of preschool playwear that did not include a button or zipper; rather, just about all of the fasteners are Velcro. The new line is consistent with the company's philosophy of identifying areas in which small children are not being well served and then designing a nearly indestructible product that is easy to use.[3]

Example For evidence that could be used to convince bottlers to switch to Nutra-Sweet, G. D. Searle's NutraSweet division interviewed 5,000 users of low-calorie soft drinks. The company found that when given a choice between a saccharine-NutraSweet blend and 100% NutraSweet, 70% of them chose NutraSweet. Further, among users of nondiet soft drinks, 40% preferred NutraSweet over sugar-sweetened formulas. The evi-

---

[1]Do not worry if some of the terms and data collection methods mentioned in the examples, such as scanners, focus groups, panels, and so on, are unfamiliar, as they are described later in the book. The intent in the examples is simply to provide some flavor of the types of problems that marketing research is used to address and some of the approaches that are used.

[2]John Koten, ''Why Do Hot Dogs Come in Packs of 10 and Buns in 8s or 12s?'' *Wall Street Journal,* 64 (September 21, 1984), pp. 1 and 25.

[3]Ronald Alsop, ''Fisher-Price Banks on Name, Design in Foray Into Playwear,'' *Wall Street Journal,* 64 (August 2, 1984), p. 27.

dence played a key role in getting a number of bottlers to switch to 100% NutraSweet formulation; several of the early switchers even used that fact in their advertising.[4]

Example   The Eastman Kodak Company, interested in altering a relatively flat sales curve and knowing that amateur photographers goof on more than two billion pictures a year, had its technical researchers look at 10,000 photos to see what kinds of things users were doing wrong. The study led to a number of design ideas for the Kodak disc camera that helped eliminate almost one-half of the out-of-focus and underexposed shots. First introduced in 1982, the disc camera has been one of the most successful new products in Kodak history.[5]

Example   Executives at Hoover became suspicious sometime ago when their surveys showed that people claimed they vacuumed their houses for an hour a week. They consequently decided to hook up timers to some models and exchanged these models with vacuums in homes. The subsequent analysis of the timers showed that people actually spend about 35 minutes a week vacuuming.[6]

Example   When Mercedes Benz made its initial foray into the U.S. market, it felt it needed some basic data. It consequently conducted surveys of nonowners and owners and also gathered market-by-market sales data. The sales data revealed that Mercedes's strongest market on a per capita basis was Anchorage, Alaska, and that the majority of new owners were not trading in Cadillacs or other expensive cars but rather Chevrolets and other inexpensive cars. The survey data indicated that people wanted a no-nonsense car with distinct quality, engineering, design, and performance. This research not only served as the basis for the products that Mercedes introduced into the U.S. market but also served as the prime mover for the print ads they have run since that time, which are heavy in copy with lots of facts and relatively devoid of gimmickry.[7]

Example   Safeway Stores, in its constant endeavor to improve its merchandising efforts, conducts a number of in-store experiments. The experiments involve such things as the effectiveness of merchandising efforts suggested by manufacturers, the impact of in-store advertising in the way of posterboards, aisle markers, grocery-cart signs and so on, the effects of end-of-aisle displays on sales, the price elasticity of certain products, the sales impact of alternative placements of products in the stores, and every other conceivable element of the marketing mix. The company is able to engage in such an extensive assessment program because it uses optical scanners to monitor sales by item.[8]

---

[4]Kevin Higgins, ''Conversion of Diet Soft Drinks to 100% NutraSweet Is Latest Coup in Searle's Long-range Marketing Strategy,'' *Marketing News*, 19 (February 15, 1985), p. 10.

[5]John Koten, ''You Aren't Paranoid If You Feel Someone Eyes You Constantly,'' *Wall Street Journal*, 65 (March 29, 1985), pp. 1 and 21. See also ''Credit Success of Kodak Disc Camera to Research,'' *Marketing News*, 17 (January 21, 1983), pp. 8 and 9.

[6]*Ibid*.

[7]''Research Played Role in Launch of 'Baby Benz','' *Marketing News*, 19 (January 4, 1985), pp. 20 and 21.

[8]''Merchandising Ploys Effective? Scanners Know,'' *Marketing News*, 19 (January 4, 1985), p. 17.

Example   Columbia Pictures, in an attempt to assess the effectiveness of its advertising, decided to find out how much it would cost in national advertising dollars to increase a show's ratings by three to five share points. Using the show "T. J. Hooker" as a test case, the company ran an ad campaign in three undisclosed test markets. The ad campaign utilized 30-second ad spots that showed action scenes from the next episode. The company, using monitors hooked up to cable TV households that record everything a household watches, can determine whether the households that see the ads also watch the program.[9]

Example   A number of companies, in an attempt to find out which packages and package colors will stand out most on cluttered shelves and in advertising, are turning to perception researchers for advice. Microsoft Corporation, for example, is counting on a new, flashy, crimson red and royal blue package to attract browsers' attention in the crowded computer software market. To find which packages garner the most attention, perception researchers rely on slides of package displays that are shown to people while a camera and computer track their eye movements to detect what they see first.[10]

Example   The Toy Manufacturers of America, the industry trade group, uses National Panel Diary data to assess the changing distribution patterns for toys. The data indicate there is a fundamental shift occurring from the toy departments in department and discount stores to the toy supermarkets like Toys "R" Us and Child World with respect to where people are buying toys.[11]

Example   Loctite Corporation, the Newington, Connecticut, manufacturer of industrial sealants and adhesives, believed that psychological fears and inaccurate perceptions among engineers rather than objective qualities of its products might be standing in the way of rapid sales growth. The company consequently hired an independent research firm to conduct 90-minute depth interviews with 450 design, maintenance, and production engineers. As part of the interview, the engineers were given self-administered personality and activity-interest-opinion (AIO) tests. The sample of engineers was subsequently divided into users and nonusers, and use patterns were related to the engineers personality characteristics. The results served as the foundation for a new promotion campaign aimed at nonusers.[12]

Example   The Chevrolet Division of General Motors is increasingly turning to computer interviewing at trade shows to assess attendees' reactions to its new models. The company used to hire field interviewers to ask passerbys about the new models. In a recent trade show, though, nearly 800 prospective customers were recruited and asked

---

[9]Laura Landro, "Movie Studio Is Marketing Own TV Series," *Wall Street Journal,* 64 (November 28, 1984), p. 29.

[10]Ronald Alsop, "Color Grows More Important in Catching Consumers' Eyes," *Wall Street Journal,* 64 (November 29, 1984), p. 33.

[11]"Toy Departments Are Fading Away," *Wisconsin State Journal,* (December 16, 1984), p. 12.

[12]Bob Donath, "What Loctite Learned with Psychographic Insights," *Business Marketing,* 69 (July 1984), pp. 100, 101, 134.

to complete the self-administered questionnaire displayed on the monitor of an IBM PC microcomputer. One of the biggest benefits realized by the company from the switch in procedures was that the tabulation of the results was ready one day after the show ended. This was made possible by the fact that as the respondents tapped in their answers on the keyboard, the results were transmitted by phone lines to a central computer for processing.[13]

Example   Studies of the garbage gathered from its various flights recently prompted United Airlines to discontinue serving butter on many of its short-range flights because few people were eating it. United is currently watching butter consumption on many of its other flights.[14]

Example   Frustrated with its inability to attract female cardholders, American Express recently had a group of its executives listen to a group of Atlanta women who were participants in a market research panel discuss credit cards. The session indicated that the women were very familiar with American Express and quite laudatory about the card, but few saw it as something for them. It seems that the prestige image promoted for years using various celebrities who had American Express cards appealed more to men than to women. Based on this insight, the company developed a new ad campaign that does away with celebrities and emphasizes instead that American Express is ''part of a lot of interesting lives.''[15]

Example   Burger King Corporation, before deciding to switch from Coke to Pepsi in 1983 in all of its outlets, spent two years studying data from the soft-drink industry and doing its own research. One part of that research involved Burger King sending some of its employees to Jack-in-the-Box franchises to find out how much time was wasted informing customers who asked for Coke that the chain only served Pepsi instead.[16]

Example   National Car Rental Systems, in an attempt to cultivate consumer loyalty at an early age, recently developed a plan to offer its credit cards to college students. The company test marketed the plan in five cities (Boston, Philadelphia, Minneapolis, Dallas, and San Francisco) and tracked applications by area to assess its success.[17]

The previous examples should provide some idea of the scope of marketing research activities. Note that it is much more than simply asking individual consumers for their

---

[13]Bernie Whalen, ''On-site Computer Interviewing Yields Research Data Instantly,'' *Marketing News,* 18 (November 9, 1984), pp. 1 and 17.

[14]''Business Bulletin,'' *Wall Street Journal,* 63 (August 11, 1983), p. 1.

[15]Bill Abrams, ''American Express Is Gearing New Ad Campaign to Women,'' *Wall Street Journal,* 63 (August 4, 1983), p. 19.

[16]John Koten, ''Fast-Food Firms' New Items Undergo Exhaustive Testing,'' *Wall Street Journal,* 64 (January 5, 1984), p. 21.

[17]Kevin Higgins, ''Marketers Cultivate Youth Loyalty with Credit Card Programs,'' *Marketing News,* 18 (November 23, 1984), pp. 1, 17, and 18.

likes and dislikes. To be sure, a consumer survey of the kind used by NutraSweet is a very important marketing research activity. Note, though, that observation, either personal observation as was done by the Kodak engineers, Burger King, and United Airlines personnel or mechanical observation using scanners à la Safeway or timers à la Hoover, is also a very legitimate marketing research activity. Note further that surveys do not have to be done one-on-one or with consumers. Rather, they can sometimes be more productive when done with groups of people at one time, such as with Fisher-Price or American Express, or when done with persons other than the ultimate consumers, such as with Loctite. There can also be advantages to conducting consumer surveys by machine rather than in person, as the Chevrolet example indicates. Some very productive research involves no more than the study of readily available data, such as the use of market-by-market sales data by Mercedes Benz. Note finally that some of the research examples involve the assessment of marketing opportunities, some the evaluation of the impact of manipulations in the marketing mix, and some control of the marketing effort.

The examples are by no means exhaustive. The list of activities could be expanded considerably, since the basic purpose of marketing research is to help marketing managers make better decisions in any of their areas of responsibility.

Marketing Manager's Role Revisited

The marketing concept suggests that the central focus of the firm should be the customer's satisfaction. The marketing manager can control a number of factors in attempting to satisfy consumer desires. Labeled the marketing mix, these factors have been categorized in various ways. One of the better-known classifications is the four P's of product, price, place, and promotion.[18] The marketing manager's essential task is to combine these variables into an effective and profitable marketing program, a program in which all the elements of the marketing mix are conceived and implemented as part of a cohesive and interrelated whole.

The marketing manager's task would be much simpler if all the elements that potentially affect customer satisfaction were under the manager's control and if consumer reaction to any contemplated change could be predicted. Unfortunately, neither of these things usually happens. The behavior of individual consumers is largely unpredictable. Further, a number of factors affecting the success of the marketing effort are beyond the marketing manager's control, including the internal resources and objectives of the firm and the competitive, technological, economic, cultural and social, and political and legal environments.

Figure 1.1 summarizes the task of marketing management. Customers are at the center because they are the focus of the firm's activities. Their satisfaction is achieved through simultaneous adjustments in the elements of the marketing mix, but the results of these adjustments are uncertain because the marketing task takes place within an

---

[18]E. Jerome McCarthy and William D. Perreault, Jr., *Basic Marketing: A Managerial Approach,* 8th ed. (Homewood, Ill.: Richard D. Irwin, 1984), pp. 46–49.

Figure 1.1
Task of Marketing Management

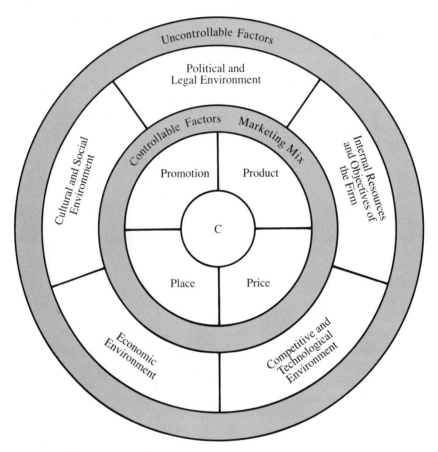

Source: Adapted from E. Jerome McCarthy and William D. Perreault, Jr., *Basic Marketing: A Managerial Approach,* 8th ed. (Homewood, Ill.: Richard D. Irwin, 1984), p. 59. Used with permission.

uncontrollable environment. Thus, as director of the firm's marketing activities, the marketing manager has an urgent need for information; marketing research is traditionally responsible for this intelligence function. Marketing research is the firm's formal communication link with the environment. It generates, transmits, and interprets feedback information originating in the environment relating to the success of the firm's marketing plans and the strategies employed in implementing those plans.

Marketing Research Role

Marketing research can help the manager with each of the sectors of Figure 1.1. Table 1.1, for example, summarizes the latest survey of marketing research activities con-

Table 1.1

Research Activities of Respondent Companies

	Percent Doing	Done by Marketing Research Department	Done by Another Department	Done by Outside Firm
Advertising Research				
A. Motivation research	47	30	2	15
B. Copy research	61	30	6	25
C. Media research	68	22	14	32
D. Studies of ad effectiveness	76	42	5	29
Business Economics and Corporate Research				
A. Short-range forecasting (up to one year)	89	51	36	2
B. Long-range forecasting (over one year)	87	49	34	4
C. Studies of business trends	91	68	20	3
D. Pricing studies	83	34	47	2
E. Plant and warehouse location studies	68	29	35	4
F. Acquisition studies	73	33	38	2
G. Export and international studies	49	22	25	2
H. MIS (Management Information System)	80	25	53	2
I. Operations research	65	14	50	1
J. Internal company employees	76	25	45	6
Corporate Responsibility Research				
A. Consumers' "right to know" studies	18	7	9	2
B. Ecological impact studies	23	2	17	4
C. Studies of legal constraints on advertising and promotion	46	10	31	5
D. Social values and policies studies	39	19	13	7
Product Research				
A. New product acceptance and potential	76	59	11	6
B. Competitive product studies	87	71	10	6
C. Testing of existing products	80	55	19	6
D. Packaging research: design or physical characteristics	65	44	12	9
Sales and Market Research				
A. Measurement of market potentials	97	88	4	5
B. Market share analysis	97	85	6	6
C. Determination of market characteristics	97	88	3	6
D. Sales analyses	92	67	23	2
E. Establishment of sales quotas, territories	78	23	54	1
F. Distribution channel studies	71	32	38	1
G. Test markets, store audits	59	43	7	9
H. Consumer panel operations	63	46	2	15
I. Sales compensation studies	60	13	43	4
J. Promotional studies of premiums, coupons, sampling, deals, etc.	58	38	14	6

Source: Reprinted from Dik Warren Twedt, *1983 Survey of Marketing Research* (Chicago: American Marketing Association, 1983), p. 41.

ducted by the American Marketing Association.[19] While the table is organized around problem areas, the ties between the research activity descriptions and Figure 1.1 are evident. Much research is done to measure consumer wants and needs, for example, or to assess the impact of past or contemplated adjustments in the marketing mix, the two inner rings of Figure 1.1. Some of the research, though, deals directly with the environment; for example, studies of legal constraints on advertising and promotion,[20] social values and policy studies, and studies of business trends.

Another way to view the types of marketing intelligence that research provides is to assess the use to which management puts the information. Some marketing research is used for planning, some for problem solving, and some for control. Marketing research, when used for planning, deals largely with marketing opportunities. The emphasis is on determining those opportunities that are viable and those that are not promising for the firm, and on providing estimates of the viable opportunities so that marketing management can better assess the resources needed to develop them. Problem-solving marketing research focuses on the short- or long-term decisions that the firm must make with respect to the elements of the marketing mix, while control-oriented marketing research helps management to isolate trouble spots and to keep abreast of current operations. The kinds of questions addressed by marketing research with regard to the planning, problem-solving, and control decision functions are listed in Table 1.2. The ties between the marketing manager's responsibilities and the typical questions dealt with by marketing research are again evident.

Definition of Marketing Research

The American Marketing Association has defined **marketing research** as the "systematic gathering, recording, and analyzing of data about problems relating to the marketing of goods and services."[21]

There are least three important elements of this definition. First, the definition is rather broad. Marketing research deals with all phases of the marketing of either goods or services. Second, the definition emphasizes the *systematic* gathering, recording, and analysis of data. One does not simply secure those data that are convenient or easily accessible. Rather, the problem is approached systematically so that a comprehensive picture of the situation is obtained. Third, and closely allied to the second point, is the implicit requirement that the data are *objectively* and *accurately* gathered, recorded, and analyzed. One does not simply generate those data or perform those analyses that sub-

[19]Dik Warren Twedt, *1983 Survey of Marketing Research* (Chicago: American Marketing Association, 1983). This survey is the seventh in a series begun in 1947. This latest survey was sent to 2,153 marketing research executives, and the tabulation in Table 1.1 is based on the returns from the 650 usable questionnaires.
[20]Marketing research is also increasingly being employed in legal suits and to assist in the formulation of new regulations. See Michael T. Brandt and Ivan L. Preston, "The Federal Trade Commission's Use of Evidence to Determine Deception," *Journal of Marketing,* 41 (January 1977), pp. 54–62; Robert F. Dyer and Terence A. Shimp, "Enhancing the Role of Marketing Research in Public Policy Decision Making," *Journal of Marketing,* 41 (January 1977), pp. 63–67; and John Koten, "More Firms File Challenges to Rivals' Comparative Ads," *Wall Street Journal,* 64 (January 12, 1984), p. 21.
[21]*Report of Definitions Committee of the American Marketing Association* (Chicago: American Marketing Association, 1961).

stantiate one's preconceived view. Researchers do no one any favors by looking at the problem through biased eyes. Their stance should be objective, and the research should reflect this objectivity at each step.

Who Does Marketing Research?

Marketing research, as a significant business activity, owes its existence to the shift from a production-oriented to a consumption-oriented economy that occurred in this country at the end of World War II. However, some marketing research was conducted before the war, and the origins of formal marketing research predate the war by a good number of years.

More by accident than foresight, N. W. Ayer & Son applied marketing research to marketing and advertising problems. In 1879, in attempting to fit a proposed advertising schedule to the needs of the Nichols-Shepard Company, manufacturers of agricultural machinery, the agency wired state officials and publishers throughout the country requesting information on expected grain production. As a result, the agency was able to construct a crude but formal market survey by states and counties. This attempt to construct a market survey is probably the first real instance of marketing research in the United States.[22]

There were even formal marketing research departments and marketing research firms before World War II.[23] However, marketing research really began to grow when firms found they could no longer sell all they could produce but rather had to gauge market needs and produce accordingly. Marketing research was called upon to estimate these needs. As consumer discretion became more important, there was a concurrent shift in the orientation of many firms. Marketing began to assume a more dominant role and production a less important one. The marketing concept emerged and along with it a reorganization of the marketing effort. Many marketing research departments were born in these reorganizations. The growth of these departments was stimulated by a number of factors, including past successes, increased management sophistication, and the data revolution created by the computer. The success of firms with marketing research departments caused still other firms to establish departments.

The growth in the formation of new marketing research departments has abated somewhat recently. Yet the firm that does not have a formal department, or at least a person assigned specifically to the marketing research activity, is now the exception

---

[22]From Lawrence C. Lockley, "History and Development of Marketing Research," pp. 1–4, in Robert Ferber, ed., *Handbook of Marketing Research*. Copyright © 1974 by McGraw-Hill, 1974. Used with permission of McGraw-Hill Book Company.

[23]The Curtis Publishing Company is generally conceded to have formed the first formal marketing research department with the appointment of Charles Parlin as manager of the Commercial Research Division of the Advertising Department in 1911, while the A. C. Nielsen Company, the largest marketing research firm in the world, began operation in 1934. For a detailed treatment of the development of marketing research, see Robert Bartels, *The Development of Marketing Thought* (Homewood, Ill.: Richard D. Irwin, 1962), pp. 106–124, or Jack J. Honomichl, *Marketing Research People: Their Behind-the-Scenes Stories* (Chicago: Crain Books, 1984), especially Part II on pages 95–184, which deals with the evolution and status of the marketing research industry.

Table 1.2

Typical Questions Addressed by Marketing Research with Respect to Each of the Decision Areas of Planning, Problem Solving, and Control

---

Planning

1. What are the basic trends in the domestic economy? How, specifically, will these affect the market for our products?

2. What changes can we expect in customer purchasing patterns? Will these be based upon changes in real income, upon changing tastes and values, or upon changes in patterns of distribution?

3. What will our needs be over the next three years in terms of sales representatives? Branch offices? Distribution centers (warehouses)?

4. What new markets are likely to open up? What types of products or services will be needed to serve them? Are there promising markets we are not now serving?

5. Are there more efficient channels of distribution for our products? What new types of marketing institutions are likely to evolve?

6. What opportunities exist for our products or services in other countries? Are our international marketing efforts intensive enough?

Problem Solving

1. Product
   a. Which of several alternative new product designs is most likely to be successful? What specific features should the final product have?
   b. Should we offer the product in cans, bottles, plastic containers, or aerosol spray cans? What color should the container be?
   c. What is the reason for our poor sales performance? The product itself? Our service facilities? What changes are necessary?
   d. What action should we take to counter a new product offering by competitors?

2. Price
   a. How should we price new products? Should we employ a penetration (low) price or a skimming (high) price?
   b. What about product-line pricing and pricing variations within a single product?
   c. Should we strive for lower prices or improved quality as production costs decline?
   d. What is the shape of our "demand curve"?

Source: Adapted from pages 23–46 in the *Management of Marketing Research* by James H. Myers and Richard R. Mead. Copyright © 1969 by Harper & Row, Publishers, Inc. Reprinted by permission of Harper & Row, Publishers, Inc.

---

rather than the rule (see Figure 1.2).[24] While marketing research departments are most prevalent among industrial and consumer manufacturing companies, they also exist in other types of companies. Publishers and broadcasters, for example, also do a good deal of research. Most of this research involves the generation of market coverage statistics to measure the size of the audience reached by the message, and to provide a demo-

---

[24]Twedt, *1983 Survey*, p. 23. A plot of the number of departments on the Y-axis and time on the X-axis using semilogarithmic graph paper indicates the number of marketing research departments increased at a relatively constant rate between 1918 and 1978, but the growth rate now may be leveling off.

Problem Solving (continued)

3. Place
   a. What types of intermediate dealers should be used at the agent, wholesale, or retail levels? How intensive should this coverage be?
   b. What level of discounts or commissions should be made available to the firm's intermediate agents?
   c. What decisions should the firm make with respect to consignment sales, sales of its products under private labels, and cooperative advertising arrangements?
   d. What special inducements are necessary to encourage intermediate agents to handle and push the firm's offerings?
   e. How many manufacturing and/or warehousing facilities should the firm operate and in what locations?
   f. What forms of transportation should be used to ship the firm's products to company warehouses, to intermediate agents, and to customers buying direct?
   g. Where and in what quantities should various stocks of goods be warehoused?

4. Promotion
   a. What should the total promotion budget be and how should it be allocated among products, among geographic areas, and among the various forms of promotion (advertising, personal selling, and so on)?
   b. What specific product attributes and consumer benefits should be featured in advertising and sales presentations? How can these be converted into effective appeals, themes, and formats?
   c. To what extent should we use such sales stimulants as coupons, premiums, deals, and contests to increase customer traffic in retail stores?
   d. Which one or combination of existing media (TV, radio, magazines, newspapers, and so on) is most suitable for our product or service?
   e. How effective have our previous advertising programs been in making consumers aware of our offerings, in stimulating increased sales, and in enhancing the image of the firm?

Control

1. What are current sales and/or market shares for each of our product lines? Each geographical area? Each major customer type?

2. Are we covering our various markets or geographical areas as well as we should? Are we getting what we should from each segment relative to the *potential* in that segment?

3. What is our "corporate image" among present customers? Potential customers? Our distributors?

4. Is the product catching on? Are the plans for our new product entry being followed?

---

graphic profile of this audience. These data are then used by the communication medium to sell advertising space or time.

Financial service companies use marketing research less than do manufacturers, although almost three-fourths of those responding did have formal departments. Much of the research done by these departments involves forecasting, measurement of market potentials, determination of market characteristics, market share analyses, sales analyses, location analyses, and product mix studies.[25]

---

[25]*Ibid.*, p. 43.

Figure 1.2
Organization for Marketing Research

	Number Answering	Percent Having Formal Department	One Person	No One Assigned
Manufacturers of Consumer Products	142	83	14	3
Publishing and Broadcasting	69	93	7	0
Manufacturers of Industrial Products	124	69	22	9
Financial Services	105	71	26	3
Advertising Agencies	60	85	12	3
All Others	97	65	32	3
All Companies* Answering This Question	597	77	20	3

*Excludes marketing research and consulting firms.

Source: Dik Warren Twedt, *1983 Survey of Marketing Research* (Chicago: American Marketing Association, 1983), p. 11.

All except one of the large advertising agencies that reported (those with billings of over $25 million) have formal marketing research departments; 69 percent of the reporting medium-sized agencies (billings between $5 and $25 million) also have formal research departments. Much of the research conducted by these agencies deals directly with the advertising function, involving such things as studying the effectiveness of alternative copy or alternative advertisements. However, many of them also do marketing research for their clients; for example, measuring the market potential of a product or the client firm's market share.

The enterprises included in the "all other" category shown in Figure 1.2 include public utilities, transportation companies, and trade associations, among others. Public utilities and transportation companies often provide their customers with useful marketing information, particularly statistics dealing with area growth and potential. Trade associations often collect and disseminate operating data gathered from members.

The entire spectrum of marketing research activity also includes specialized marketing research and consulting firms, government agencies, and universities. While most specialized research firms are small, a few are large.[26] Some of these firms provide

---

[26]For a list of the 40 largest, see Jack J. Honomichl, "Top Research Companies' Revenues Rise 13.7%," *Advertising Age,* 56 (May 23, 1985), p. 16.

syndicated research; they collect certain information on a regular basis, which they then sell to interested clients. The syndicated services would include such operations as the A. C. Nielsen store audit and the National Panel Diary consumer panel. The syndicated services are distinguished by the fact that their research is not custom designed, except in the limited sense that the firm will perform special analyses for the client from the data it regularly collects. Other research firms, though, specialize in custom-designed research. Some of these provide only a field service; they collect data and return the data-collection instruments directly to the research sponsor. Some are limited-service firms that not only collect the data, but also analyze them for the client. And some are full-service research suppliers that help the client in the design of the research, as well as in collecting and analyzing data.

Government agencies provide much marketing information in the form of published statistics. As a matter of fact, the federal government is the largest producer of marketing facts through its various censuses and other publications.[27]

Much university-sponsored research of interest to marketers is produced by the marketing faculty or by the bureaus of business research found in many schools of business. Faculty research is often reported in marketing journals, while research bureaus often publish monographs on various topics of interest.

Organization of Marketing Research

The marketing research function has no single form of organization. Rather, organizational form depends very much on the size and organizational structure of the company itself. Small firms are much less likely to have a research department, and it is much more likely to be a one-person operation than a full department.[28] In these cases, of course, there are few organizational questions other than determining to whom the research director shall report. Most often this will be the sales or marketing manager, although some marketing research managers report directly to the president or the executive vice-president.

Larger research units present internal organizational problems with which to contend. Once again, there appears to be no general form of organization, although three types are common:

1. by area of application, such as by product line, by brand, by market segment, or by geographic area;

2. by marketing function performed, such as field sales analysis, advertising research, or product planning;

3. by research technique or approach, such as sales analysis, mathematical and/or statistical analysis, field interviewing, or questionnaire design.

Many firms with very large marketing research departments combine still further these "pure" organizational structures into a hybrid approach.

---

[27]Some government publications containing useful marketing information are reviewed in the appendix to Chapter 5.

[28]Twedt, *1983 Survey*, p. 13.

Figure 1.3
Share of Marketing Budgets Allocated to Research

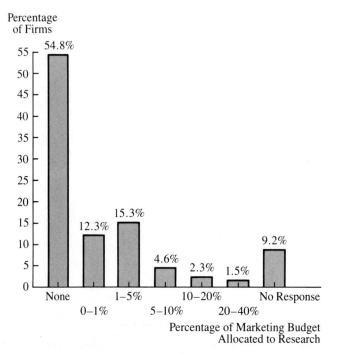

Source: Developed from data in A. Parasuraman, ''Research's Place in the Marketing Budget,'' *Business Horizons,* 26 (March-April 1983), pp. 25–29.

The organizational structure of the firm itself—particularly whether it is centralized or decentralized—also affects the organization of the marketing research function.[29] With decentralized companies, the fundamental question is whether each division or operating unit should have its own marketing research department, whether a single department in central headquarters should serve all operating divisions, or whether there should be research departments at both levels. The primary advantages of a corporate-level location are greater coordination and control of corporate research activity, economy, increased capability from an information system perspective, and greater usefulness to corporate management in planning. The primary advantage of a division or group-level location is that it allows research personnel to acquire valuable knowledge about divisional markets, products, practices, and problems. While shifting between the corporate and divisional structures occurs quite frequently, the recent trend is toward a mixed arrangement, in an attempt to secure the advantages of each.

---

[29]For a discussion of management of the research function, see Lee Adler and Charles S. Mayer, eds., *Readings in Managing the Marketing Research Function* (Chicago: American Marketing Association, 1980).

Perhaps the most appropriate summary comment about the organization of the marketing research function is that this organization might be expected to be dynamic and ever-changing. It will depend on the relative importance of the marketing research function within the firm and on the scale and complexity of the research activities to be undertaken. The data indicate that large firms, for example, are likely to spend a larger proportion of the marketing budget on research than are small firms. Among firms with sales of $25 million and over, approximately 3½ percent of the average marketing budget is spent on research, while among smaller firms only about 1½ percent of the average marketing budget is spent on research.[30] As Figure 1.3 indicates, a few firms spend a very large proportion of their total marketing budget on research. As the firm's size and market position change, the emphasis and organization of the marketing research function must change also, so that it is continually tailored to suit the firm's information needs.

One important change that has been occurring in marketing research in recent years is the transition from a specific problem perspective to a total marketing intelligence perspective. This perspective is usually called a marketing information system (**MIS**) or decision support system (**DSS**). The emphasis in those systems is on diagnosing the information needs of each of the marketing decision makers so that they have the kinds of information they need, when they need it, to make the kinds of decisions they must make. We shall have more to say on marketing intelligence systems in the final chapter of this book.

Job Opportunities in Marketing Research

It is hard to generalize about the kinds of tasks a marketing researcher might perform. As previously suggested, the tasks will depend upon the type, size, and organizational structure of the firm with which the individual is employed. They will also depend upon whether the person works for a research supplier or for a consumer of research information. The responsibilities of a marketing researcher could range from the simple tabulation of questionnaire responses to the management of a large research department. Research Realities 1.1, for example, lists some common job titles and the functions typically performed by occupants of these positions. Figure 1.4 illustrates what they are likely to be paid and how that compares with salaries of those in similar positions in 1978.[31]

As you can tell from these job descriptions, there are opportunities in marketing research for people with a variety of skills. One could find a career as a technical specialist, such as a statistician, or as a research generalist managing others, such as a research director. The skills required to perform each job satisfactorily will, of course, vary.

---

[30]A. Parasuraman, "Research's Place in the Marketing Budget," *Business Horizons,* 26 (March–April 1983), pp. 25–29.

[31]For further discussion of the opportunities in marketing research, see Linden A. Davis, Jr., "What's Ahead in Marketing Research," *Journal of Advertising Research,* 21 (June 1981), pp. 49–51. For a discussion of threats to the future of marketing research, see Stephen W. McDaniel, Perry Verille, and Charles S. Madden, "The Threats to Marketing Research: An Empirical Reappraisal," *Journal of Marketing Research,* 22 (February 1985), pp. 74–80.

Research Realities 1.1

Marketing Research Job Titles and Responsibilities

1. **Research Director:** This is the senior position in research. The Director is responsible for the entire research program of the company. Accepts assignments from superiors or from clients or may, on own initiative, develop and propose research undertakings to company executives. Employs personnel and exercises general supervision of research department. Presents research findings to clients or to company executives.

2. **Assistant Director of Research:** This position usually represents a defined "second in command," a senior staff member having responsibilities above those of other staff members.

3. **Statistician/Data Processing Specialist:** Duties are usually those of an expert consultant on theory and application of statistical technique to specific research problems. Usually responsible for experimental design and data processing.

4. **Senior Analyst:** Usually found in larger research departments. Participates with superior in initial planning of research projects and directs execution of projects assigned. Operates with minimum supervision. Prepares, or works with analysts in preparing, questionnaires. Selects research techniques, makes analyses, and writes final report. Budgetary control over projects and primary responsibility for meeting time schedules rest with the Senior Analyst.

5. **Analyst:** The Analyst usually handles the bulk of the work required for execution of research projects. Often works under Senior Analyst's supervision.

The Analyst assists in questionnaire preparation, pre-tests them, and makes preliminary analyses of results. Most of the library research or work with company data is handled by the Analyst.

6. **Junior Analyst:** Working under rather close supervision, Junior Analysts handle routine assignments. Editing and coding of questionnaires, statistical calculations above the clerical level, simpler forms of library research are among the duties. A large portion of the Junior Analyst's time is spent on tasks assigned by superiors.

7. **Librarians:** The Librarian builds and maintains a library of reference sources adequate to the needs of the research department.

8. **Clerical Supervisor:** In larger departments, the central handling and processing of statistical data are the responsibility of one or more Clerical Supervisors. Duties include work scheduling and responsibility for accuracy.

9. **Field Work Director:** Usually only larger departments have a Field Work Director who hires, trains, and supervises field interviewers.

10. **Full-time Interviewer:** The interviewer conducts personal interviews and works under direct supervision of the Field Work Director. Few companies employ full-time interviewers.

11. **Tabulating and Clerical Help:** The routine, day-to-day work of the department is performed by these individuals.

Source: Dik Warren Twedt, *1983 Survey of Marketing Research* (Chicago: American Marketing Association, 1983), p. 4. of the Appendix.

The typical entry-level position in consumer goods companies is analyst, most usually for a specific brand. While learning the characteristics and details of the industry, the analyst will receive on-the-job training from a research manager. The usual progression of responsibilities is senior analyst, research supervisor, and research manager for a specific brand, after which time the researcher's responsibilities broaden to include a group of brands.

The typical entry-level position among research suppliers is that of research trainee, a position in which the person will get exposed to the types of studies in which the

Figure 1.4
Mean Compensation for Research Positions

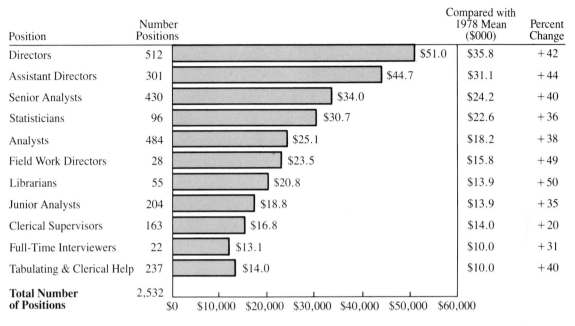

Position	Number Positions		Compared with 1978 Mean ($000)	Percent Change
Directors	512	$51.0	$35.8	+42
Assistant Directors	301	$44.7	$31.1	+44
Senior Analysts	430	$34.0	$24.2	+40
Statisticians	96	$30.7	$22.6	+36
Analysts	484	$25.1	$18.2	+38
Field Work Directors	28	$23.5	$15.8	+49
Librarians	55	$20.8	$13.9	+50
Junior Analysts	204	$18.8	$13.9	+35
Clerical Supervisors	163	$16.8	$14.0	+20
Full-Time Interviewers	22	$13.1	$10.0	+31
Tabulating & Clerical Help	237	$14.0	$10.0	+40
Total Number of Positions	2,532			

$0 $10,000 $20,000 $30,000 $40,000 $50,000 $60,000

Source: Dik Warren Twedt, *1983 Survey of Marketing Research* (Chicago: American Marketing Association, 1983), p. 57.

supplier specializes and procedures that are followed in completing them. Quite often, trainees will spend some time actually conducting interviews or coding completed data collection forms or possibly even assisting with the analysis. The idea is to expose trainees to the processes that are followed in the firm so that when they become account representatives, they will be sufficiently familiar with the firm's capabilities to be able to develop intelligent responses, perhaps in the form of formal quotations, to client needs for research information.

The requirements to enter marketing research include analytical, communication, and human relation skills.[32] Marketing researchers also should have some basic statistical skills, or at least they should have the capacity to develop those skills. They must be

---

[32]For discussion of the characteristics of successful researchers and typical career paths, see John R. Blair, "Marketing Research Offers Highly Visible Action-Oriented Career with Growth Potential," Emanuel H. Demby, "The Marketing Researcher: A Professional Statistician, Social Scientist—Not Just Another Business Practitioner," and Lawrence D. Gibson, "Confused New Marketing Researchers Soon Feel Confidence, Then Challenge," *Student Edition Marketing News,* 2 (March 1984), pp. 1, 3, and 7. For some suggestions for preparing for a career in marketing research, see Michale Boudreaux, "Prepare for Your Future in Marketing, Your Interviews, and Something 'Extra'," *Student Edition Marketing News,* 2 (March 1984), p. 3.

comfortable with numbers and with the techniques and technologies of marketing research. Successful marketing researchers tend to be proactive rather than reactive; that is, they tend to identify and lead the direction in which the individual studies and overall programs go rather than simply responding to the explicit requests for information given them. Successful marketing researchers realize that marketing research is conducted for only one reason—to help make better marketing decisions. Thus, they are comfortable in the role of staff person making recommendations to others rather than having responsibility for the decisions themselves.

Summary

This chapter sought to present an overview of marketing research with respect to its nature, its usefulness in marketing decision making, the extent to which it is currently being used and by what types of companies, and the organization of the research function. By definition, marketing research is the systematic gathering, recording, and analyzing of data about problems relating to the marketing of goods and services.

Marketing research was indeed found to be a pervasive activity. Marketing research departments exist in most larger firms and among most types of companies. Marketing research was shown to have been employed, at least by some companies, in each of the domains of the marketing manager's responsibility.

No dominant form of organization was found for the marketing research function. Rather, the research activity is typically organized to reflect the specific firm's unique needs. Two factors that bear heavily on this organization are the firm's size and the degree of centralization/decentralization of its operations.

Job opportunities in marketing research are good and are getting better. While there is variety in the positions available and in the skills needed for them, most positions require analytical, communication, and human-relations skills. Marketing researchers must be comfortable working with numbers and statistical techniques and must be familiar with a great variety of marketing research methods and techniques.

Questions

1. What is marketing management's task? What is marketing research's task? Is there any relationship between the two tasks?

2. How is marketing research defined? What does the definition imply?

3. Who does marketing research? What are the primary kinds of research done by each?

4. How would you explain the fact that production research started in the 1860s but that marketing research did not develop formally until the 1910s and did not experience real growth until after World War II?

5. What factors influence the internal organization of the marketing research department and its reporting location within the company?

6. In a large research department, who would be responsible for specifying the objective of a research project? For deciding on specific procedures to be followed? For designing the questionnaire? For analyzing results? For reporting results to top management?

Applications and Problems

1. Indicate whether marketing research is relevant to the following. If relevant, briefly explain how each might use marketing research.
    (a) Diet Pepsi Cola
    (b) Your university
    (c) The Chase Manhattan Bank
    (d) The American Cancer Society
    (e) A small dry-cleaner

2. What do the following two research situations have in common?

    Situation I: The SprayIt Company marketed a successful insect repellent. The product was effective and a leader in the market. The product was available in blue aerosol cans with red caps. The instructions were clearly specified on the container in addition to a warning to keep the product away from children. Most of the company's range of products were also produced by competitors in similar containers. The CEO was worried because of declining sales and shrinking profit margins. Another issue that perturbed him was that companies such as his were being severely criticized by government and consumer groups for their use of aerosol cans. The CEO contacted the company's advertising agency and requested it to do the necessary research to find out what was happening.

    Situation II: In early 1986 the directors of University Z were considering the expansion of the business school due to increasing enrollments over the past ten years. Their plans included constructing a new wing, hiring five new faculty members and increasing the number of scholarships from 100 to 120. The funding for this ambitious project was to be provided by some private sources, internally generated funds, and the state and federal government. A prior research study (completed in 1978), using the Box-Jenkins forecasting methodology, indicated that student enrollment would peak in 1985. Another study conducted in November 1980 indicated universities could expect gradual declining enrollments during the late 1980s. The directors were concerned about the results of the later study and the talk it stimulated about budget cuts by the government. A decision to conduct a third and final study was made to determine likely student enrollment.

3. What do the two following research situations have in common?

    Situation I: The sales manager of CanAl, an aluminum can manufacturing company, was delighted with the increase in sales over the past few months. He was wondering whether the new cans, which would be on the market in two months, should be priced higher than the traditional products. He confidently commented to the vice-president of marketing, ''Nobody in the market is selling aluminum cans with screw-on tops, we can get a small portion of the market and yet make substantial profits.'' The product manager disagreed with this strategy. In fact, he was opposed to marketing these new cans. The cans might present problems in preserving the contents. He thought to himself, ''Aluminum cans are re-cycled so nobody is going to keep them as containers.'' There was little he could do formally because these cans were the president's own idea. He strongly recommended to the vice-president that the cans should be priced in line with the other products. The vice-president thought a marketing research study would resolve this issue.

    Situation II: A large toy manufacturer was in the process of developing a tool kit for children in the 5–10 year age group. The tool kit included a small saw, screwdriver, hammer, chisel, and drill. This tool kit was different from the competitors' as it included an instruction manual with "101 things to do." The product manager was concerned about the safety of the kit and recommended the inclusion of a separate booklet for parents. The sales manager recommended that the tool kit be made available in a small case, as this would increase its marketability. The advertising manager recommended a special promotional campaign be launched in order to distinguish it from the competitors. The vice-president thought that all the recommendations were worthwhile but the costs would increase drastically. He consulted the market research manager who further recommended that a study be conducted.

4. In light of the definition of marketing research, evaluate the research situation in the following example.

The HiFlyer Airline company was interested in altering the interior layout of its aircrafts to suite the tastes and needs of an increasing segment of their market—business people. Management was planning to reduce the number of seats and install small tables to enable business people to work during long flights. Prior to the renovation, management decided to do some research to ensure that these changes would suit the needs of their passengers. To keep expenses to a minimum the following strategy was employed.

The questionnaires were completed by passengers during a flight. Due to the ease of administration and collection, the questionnaires were distributed only on the short flights (those less than one hour). The study was conducted during the second and third week of December, as that was when flights were full. To increase the response rate, each steward and stewardess on the flight was responsible for a certain number of questionnaires. The management thought this was a good time to acquire as much information as possible, hence the questionnaire included issues apart from the new seating arrangement. As a result, the questionnaire took 20 minutes to complete. After the study, management decided that the study would not be repeated as the information was insightful enough.

Chapter 2
The Research Process and Problem Formulation

Chapter 1 highlighted the many kinds of problems that marketing research can be used to solve. It emphasized that marketing research is the firm's communication link with the environment and can help the marketing manager in planning, problem solving, and control, although few companies use marketing research for exactly the same activities. It is not even unusual for different firms within the same industry to have different philosophies regarding the role of research in marketing decision making. Within the beer industry, for example, Heileman uses research very sparingly, and then typically to confirm the wisdom of a decision that has already been made. Anheuser-Busch, on the other hand, places a strong emphasis on research and uses it to support the entire marketing program.[1]

A company's philosophy of how marketing research fits into its marketing plan determines its *program strategy* for marketing research.[2] Some companies may use marketing research on a continuous basis to track sales or to monitor the firm's market share. Others may resort to marketing research only when a problem arises or an important decision—such as the launching of a new product—needs to be made. A program strategy specifies the types of studies that are to be conducted and for what purposes. Research Realities 2.1, for example, outlines the types and purposes of the various studies that are conducted by Gillette Company in its constant endeavor to maintain its 60% share of the blade and razor market. The design of the individual studies themselves defines the firm's *project strategy;* for example, the use of personal interviews in the national consumer studies, mail questionnaires in the brand tracking studies, and telephone interviews when measuring brand awareness.

Wendy's restaurants' experience is helpful in distinguishing between a program strategy and a project strategy. To help with positioning questions, Wendy's annually conducts in-store surveys. These are conducted in each restaurant in the chain and involve interviews, conducted over a four-day period, with 200 customers who are asked 20 questions each. The questions cover such things as "demographics, what the customer

---

[1]Marj Charlier, ''Heileman Again Goes to Battle, This Time to Capture the Low-Alcohol Beer Market,'' *Wall Street Journal,* 64 (July 5, 1984), p. 15.

[2]Walter B. Wentz, *Marketing Research: Management and Methods* (New York: Harper and Row Publishers, 1972), pp. 19–24.

Research Realities 2.1

Major Thrusts of Marketing Research at Gillette Company

1. **Annual National Consumer Studies**
    The objectives of these annual studies are to determine what brand of razor and blade was used for the respondents' last shave, to collect demographic data, and to examine consumer attitudes toward the various blade and razor manufacturers. These studies rely on personal interviews with national panels of male and female respondents, who are selected using probability sampling methods.

2. **National Brand Tracking Studies**
    The purpose of these studies is to track the use of razors and blades so as to monitor brand loyalty and brand switching tendencies over time. These studies are also conducted annually and use panels of male and female shavers. However, the information for them is collected via mail questionnaires.

3. **Annual Brand Awareness Studies**
    These studies are aimed at determining the "share of mind" Gillette products have. This information is collected by annual telephone surveys that employ unaided as well as aided recall of brand names and advertising campaigns.

4. **Consumer Use Tests**
    The key objectives of the use-testing studies are to ensure that "Gillette remains state of the art in the competitive arena, that our products are up to our desired performance standards, and that no claims in our advertising, packaging, or display materials are made without substantiation." At least two consumer use tests are conducted each month by Gillette. In these tests, consumers are asked to use a single variation of a product for an extended period of time, at the end of which their evaluation of the product is secured.

5. **Continuous Retail Audits**
    The purpose of the retail audits is to provide top management with monthly market share data, along with information regarding distribution, out-of-stock, and inventory levels of the various Gillette products. This information is purchased from the commercial information services providing syndicated retail audit data. The information is supplemented by special retail audits which Gillette conducts itself that look at product displays and the extent to which Gillette blades and razors are featured in retailer advertisements.

Source: Adapted from "Mature Products Remain as the Mainstays in the Gillette Company," *Marketing News,* 17 (June 10, 1983), p. 17. Published by the American Marketing Association.

would order, how often they come to Wendy's, how often they come to a competitors establishment, and what they like and dislike about Wendy's and its competitors."[3] The *program strategy* issue is whether or not the assessment of these various customer characteristics is worthwhile and should be continued. If the answer is yes, the *project strategy* issue is how, specifically, to go about this. Should the emphasis in data collection, for example, continue to be in-store surveys using personal interviews? Or should it be switched to self-administered printed questionnaires or perhaps one of the newer electronic interviewing devices? Should a larger or smaller sample be taken within each store? Should the period of time during which the data are collected be changed? In sum, project strategy deals with how a study should be conducted, whereas program

---

[3]"Wendy's to Use Research Positioning to Direct Growth," *Marketing News,* 14 (January 25, 1980), p. 7.

Figure 2.1

Relationship among the Stages in the Research Process

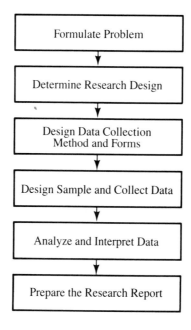

strategy addresses the question of what type of studies the firm should conduct and for what purposes.

All research problems require their own special emphases and approaches. Since every marketing research problem is unique in some ways, the research procedure typically is custom tailored. Nonetheless, there is a sequence of steps, called the **research process** (see Figure 2.1),[4] that can be followed when designing the research project. This chapter reviews the research process and discusses the first step—formulating the problem.

Marketing Research—Sequence of Steps

Formulate Problem

One of the more valuable roles marketing research can perform is helping to define the problem to be solved. Only when the problem is carefully and precisely defined can research be designed to provide pertinent information. Part of the process of problem

---

[4]Our diagram of the research process is similar to the statement of Claire Selltiz, Lawrence S. Wrightsman, and Stuart W. Cook, *Research Methods in Social Relations,* 3rd ed. (New York: Holt, Rinehart and Winston, 1976), p. 13, and also to that of Harper W. Boyd, Jr., Ralph Westfall, and Stanley F. Stasch, *Marketing Research: Text and Cases,* 6th ed. (Homewood, Ill.: Richard D. Irwin, 1985), pp. 235–249.

definition includes specifying the *objectives* of the specific research project or projects that might be undertaken. Each project should have one or more objectives, and the next step in the process should not be taken until these can be explicitly stated.

Determine Research Design

The sources of information for a study and the research design go hand in hand. They both depend on how much is known about the problem. If relatively little is known about the phenomenon to be investigated, exploratory research will be warranted. Exploratory research may involve reviewing published data, interviewing knowledgeable people, or investigating trade literature that discusses similar cases. One of the most important characteristics of exploratory research is its flexibility. Since researchers know little about the problem at this point, they must be ready to follow their intuition about possible areas of investigation or tactics to adopt. If, on the other hand, the problem is precisely and unambiguously formulated, descriptive or causal research is needed. In these research designs, data collection is not flexible but is rigidly specified, both with respect to the data-collection forms and the sample design.

Design Data Collection Method and Forms

Quite often, the information needed to solve the problem cannot be found in the firm's own sales data or other internal records or in published documents such as government census reports or industry sales trends. The research then must depend on **primary data,** which are collected specifically for the study. The research questions here are several. Should the data be collected by observation or questionnaire? Should the form be structured as a fixed set of alternative answers or should the responses be open-ended? Should the purpose be made clear to the respondent or should the study objectives be disguised? There are more questions, but these should serve to illustrate the basic concerns at this stage of the research process.

Design Sample and Collect Data

In designing the sample, the researcher must specify, among other things (1) the sampling frame, (2) the sample selection process, and (3) the size of the sample. The **sampling frame** is the list of population elements from which the sample will be drawn. While we often assume the frame is implicit in the research problem and thus take it for granted, the assumption can be dangerous.

Take the case of the manufacturer of dog food . . . who went out and did an intensive market study. He tested the demand for dog food; he tested the package size, the design, the whole advertising program. Then he launched the product with a big campaign, got the proper distribution channels, put it on the market and had tremendous sales. But two months later, the bottom dropped out—no follow-up sales. So he called in an expert, who took the dog food out to the local pound, put it in front of the dogs—and they would not touch it. For all the big marketing study, no one had tried the product on the dogs.[5]

As this old but classic example illustrates, the dog population was not part of the sampling frame, probably because it is people who buy dog food and not the dogs themselves. Nevertheless, the careless specification of population elements had dire consequences. While the results may not be as severe, we need to realize that when we sample from, say, a phone book or a mailing list, we are not sampling from the population as a whole but are only sampling from people whose names appear in the phone book or on the mailing list.

The sample selection process requires that the form of the sample be specified. Will it be a probability sample, in which each population element has a known chance of being selected, or will it be a nonprobability sample? Will the probability sample, if one is indicated, be simple or complex? If a nonprobability sample is used, will it be one of convenience, judgment, or some kind of quota system?

The decision on sample size involves determining how many people, households, business firms, or whatever it is necessary to study in order to get answers to the problem that are sufficiently accurate and reliable for the decision being made, without exceeding the time and money budgeted for the project.

Once the dimensions of the sample design are specified, data collection can commence. Data collection will require a field force of some type, although field methods will be largely dictated by the kinds of information to be obtained and the sampling requirements. The use of personnel to collect data raises a host of questions with respect to selection, training, and control of the field staff—questions that must be anticipated in designing the research.

Analyze and Interpret the Data

Researchers may amass a mountain of data, but it is useless unless the findings are analyzed and the results interpreted in light of the problem at hand. Data analysis generally involves several steps. First, the data collection forms must be scanned to be sure that they are complete and consistent and that the instructions were followed. This process is called **editing.** Once the forms have been edited, they must be coded. **Coding** involves assigning numbers to each of the answers so that they may be analyzed, typically by computer. The final step in analyzing the data is **tabulation.** This refers to the orderly arrangement of data in a table or other summary format achieved by counting the frequency of responses to each question. It is common to also cross classify the data against other variables. For example, researchers may have asked women if they liked a certain kind of new cosmetic. Their responses could be analyzed by age group, income level, and other characteristics.

---

[5]Joseph R. Hochstim, "Practical Uses of Sampling Surveys in the Field of Labor Relations," *Proceedings of the Conference on Business Application of Statistical Sampling Methods* (Monticello, Ill.: The Bureau of Business Management, University of Illinois, 1950), pp. 181–182.

The coding, editing, and tabulation functions are common to most research studies. The statistical tests applied to the data, if any, are somewhat unique to the particular sampling procedures and data collection instruments used in the research. These tests should be anticipated before data collection is begun, if possible, to assure that the data and analyses will be appropriate to the problem as specified.

Prepare the Research Report

The research report is the document submitted to management that summarizes the research results and conclusions. It is all that many executives will see of the research effort, and it becomes the standard by which that research is judged. Thus, it is imperative that the research report be clear and accurate, since no matter how well all previous steps have been completed, the project will be no more successful than the research report. One empirical study that investigated the factors determining the extent to which research results are used by firms found that the research report was one of the five most important determinants.[6]

Additional Comments

While this discussion should provide some understanding of the steps in the research process, four points need be made. First, the stages in the research process serve to structure the remainder of this book. The remainder of this chapter, for example, deals with stage 1, problem formulation, while each of the remaining stages warrants a special section in the book.

Second, the stages in the research process can also be used to direct additional study in research method. The aspiring research student needs more sophistication in at least some of the stages than this book could possibly provide. The sections and chapters should provide some indication of where in-depth study might be most useful.

Third, the stages have been presented as if one would proceed through them in a lockstep fashion when designing a research project. Nothing could be further from the truth. Rather, Figure 2.1 could be drawn with a number of feedback loops suggesting a possible need to rethink and revise the various elements in the process as the study proceeds. The process would begin with problem formulation, but after that anything can happen. The problem may not be specified explicitly enough to allow the development of the research design, in which case the researcher would need to return to stage 1 to delineate the research objectives more clearly. Alternatively, the process may proceed smoothly to the design of the data-collection forms, the pretest of which may require a revision of the research objectives or the research design. Still further, the sample necessary to answer the problem as specified may be prohibitively costly, again requiring a revision of the earlier steps. Once the data are collected, no revision of the procedure is possible. It is possible, though, to revise the earlier steps on the basis of the *anticipated* analysis, and it is imperative that the methods used to analyze the data be determined before the data are collected. Although it is hard for beginning research-

---

[6]Rohit Deshpande and Gerald Zaltman, ''A Comparison of Factors Affecting Researcher and Manager Perceptions of Market Research Use,'' *Journal of Marketing Research*, 21 (February 1984), pp. 32–38.

ers to understand, the steps in the research process are highly interrelated. A decision made at one stage affects decisions at each of the other stages, and a revision of the procedure at any stage often requires modifications of procedures at each of the other stages. Unfortunately, it seems that this lesson is only understood by those who have experienced the frustrations and satisfactions of being involved in an actual research project.

Fourth, the important error to note when designing a research project is the *total error* likely to be associated with the project. All the steps are necessary and vital, and it is dangerous to emphasize one to the exclusion of one or more others. Many beginning students of research, for example, argue for large sample sizes so as to reduce sampling error. What they fail to realize is that sample size is a decision with respect to one subset of one stage in the process. Further, and more important, an increase in the sample size to reduce sampling error can often lead to an *increase* in the *total error* of the research effort, since other errors increase more than proportionately with sample size. The larger sample size, for example, may dictate fewer follow-ups with those who did not respond to the initial contact so as to keep the study within budget. The larger this nonresponse problem is, the greater is the question of whether the responses that are secured are representative of the selected sample. Response errors can also increase when the sample size is increased. The larger sample will typically mean the use of more interviewers if the study is being done by phone or in person. This raises a host of issues with respect to the selection and training of the interviewers so that they all handle the interviews in the same way. Otherwise the different responses that are secured can be as much a function of the interviewers collecting the data as they are differences in respondents. Thus, researchers frequently face a dilemma because of normal budget and time constraints. Should they select a large sample to minimize sampling error, or should they select a smaller sample, thereby ensuring better interviewer controls, more accurate responses, and a higher response rate among those contacted? In one study that investigated the incidence of sampling and nonsampling errors by comparing respondent replies against known data, the consistent finding was "that nonsampling error is the major contributor to total survey error, while random sampling error is minimal."[7] The fact that nonsampling error far outweighed sampling error led the authors to conclude that the "emphasis on methods to reduce random sampling error by emphasizing large samples may be misplaced."[8] The fundamental point is that total error is the important error in research work and not the error incurred in any of the stages, except insofar as this error affects total error. Quite often, part or stage error will be increased so that total error may be decreased.

Problem Formulation

An old adage says, "A problem well defined is half-solved." This is especially true in marketing research, for it is only when the problem has been clearly defined and the objectives of the research precisely stated that research can be designed properly.

---

[7]Henry Assael and John Keon, "Nonsampling vs. Sampling Errors in Survey Research," *Journal of Marketing,* 46 (Spring 1982), p. 114.

[8]*Ibid.,* p. 121.

"Properly" here means not only that the research will generate the kinds of answers needed but that it will do so efficiently.

Problem formulation requires good communication between decision maker and marketing researcher. The decision maker needs to understand what research can and cannot accomplish. The researcher needs to understand the nature of the decision managers face and what they hope to learn from research, i.e., the project objectives.

Nothing in marketing research requires more creativity and insight than the definition of the research problem and the establishment of project objectives. In many ways the marketing researcher is like a doctor. A patient who is not feeling well describes his symptoms to the doctor. The patient may or may not be able to diagnose his own case. A broken arm can easily be identified. In most instances, however, the patient has several complaints (symptoms) resulting from underlying disorders (causal factors). The source of the disorder may not be as easy to pinpoint. The creative challenge for the doctor is in diagnosis. Once an accurate diagnosis has been made, the doctor can ascertain whether the fundamental problem is curable and take appropriate measures. . . .

The marketing researcher, like the doctor, is responsible for an accurate diagnosis. Again like the doctor, the marketing researcher normally cannot fulfill his responsibility without some help from the client. It is with respect to this issue that one of the most frequent and crucial errors made in marketing research often occurs. When the research director allows the project to be based on a client's request for specific information he not only allows the client to diagnose the cause of the problem but to specify a prescription for the cure as well. The doctor's responsibility is to cure the patient; the marketing researcher's responsibility is to solve the client's problem. In each case the cure may or may not have any relationship to the information presented by the patient.[9]

A proper understanding of the basic structure of the problems involved in reaching a decision can help a researcher reach a diagnosis. The simplest of decision situations can be characterized by the following conditions.

1. A decision maker *(D)* is operating in some environment *(E)* in which there is a problem.

2. There are at least two courses of action, A_1 and A_2, that *D* can follow.

3. If *D* chooses to follow A_1, for example, there are at least two possible outcomes of that choice (O_1 and O_2), and *D* prefers one of these outcomes to the other.

4. There is a chance, but not an equal chance, that each course of action will lead to the desired outcome. If the chances are equal, the choice does not matter.[10]

In sum, a person faces a decision situation if he or she has a problem, has several good, but not equally good, ways of solving it, and thus is unsure about which course of action to select. Research can assist in clarifying any of these characteristics of the decision situation. Let us briefly consider how.

---

[9]Robert W. Joselyn, *Designing the Marketing Research Project* (New York: Petrocelli/Charter, 1977), pp. 25–26.

[10]See Russell L. Ackoff, *The Art of Problem Solving* (New York: John Wiley & Sons, Inc., 1978).

The Decision Maker and the Environment

One of the more important tasks facing the researcher in defining the problem is understanding the individual making the decision and the environment in which that person operates. For example, when the decision maker is uncertain about the state of the environment, part of the task of research is to reduce this uncertainty.

If the decision maker's original posture will not change regardless of what is found, the research will be wasted. Surprisingly, research is sometimes simply "conscience money"; the research results are readily accepted when they are consistent with the decision the individual "wants to make" or with the person's perceptions of the environment or the consequences of alternative actions. When the research results conflict, though, with the decision maker's original position, the results are questioned, at best, and at worst discarded as being inaccurate. The reason, of course, is that the individual's view of the decision problem is so strongly held that research will do little to change it. When this situation prevails, research will be a waste of the firm's resources. The researcher's task is to find this out before, rather than after, by determining the decision maker's objectives, view of how the decision might change if so and so were found, and so on.

A rather surprising example of such pointless research was cited in a survey of financial service companies that had been undertaken by the Advertising Research Foundation. Financial service companies—banks, brokers, insurers, and so forth—have begun to advertise on television almost as much as beer and wine marketers. However, unlike brewers and other consumer goods industries, who routinely spend upwards of $500,000 annually to test the effectiveness of their ads, financial service companies have paid surprisingly little attention to advertising research. In fact, the Advertising Research Foundation found that the median annual research budget was $28,300 at banks, $45,800 at diversified financial companies, and only $22,500 at insurance companies. What is even more startling was the finding that, of the 60% of this group who bothered to test at all, fully 58% admitted that the results of such research did not play an important part in their marketing decision making.[11] Unless financial service advertisers come to value the insights that advertising research might offer, even the small sums that they currently allot to such research could be considered money down the drain.

Often the task of determining how the management decision might change with research information is complicated by the fact that the researcher's contact is not the final decision maker, but a liaison. Yet, this determination must be made if the researcher is to design a cost-effective attack on the problem.

The researcher also needs to understand the environment in which the decision maker operates. What are the constraints on that person's actions? What are the resources at the decision maker's disposal? What is the time frame in which the manager is operating? It does little good to design a study, however accurate, that costs $20,000 and takes six months to complete when the decision maker needs the results within one month and has only $2,000 for the research. Obviously, some compromises must be

---

[11]Bill Abrams, "Financial Service Advertisers Seen Neglecting Ad Research," *Wall Street Journal,* 63 (August 8, 1983), p. 23.

made, and it is the researcher's responsibility to anticipate them by carefully examining the decision environment.

Researchers also need to be aware that the corporate culture can affect decision making and, consequently, research that supports that decision making. Things simply happen differently at different institutions. In some firms, the process by which decisions are made is dominant while in other firms the personality of management might be more important. At General Mills, for example, the emphasis is on research that evaluates alternatives, and the culture at General Mills tries to force all information requests into action alternatives. Instead of focusing on the question "What proportion of potato chips are eaten at meals?", the emphasis would be on translating the question into "How can I advertise my potato chips for meal consumption?" or "Will a 'meal commercial' sell more chips than my present commercial?" To design the most effective research, researchers need to be aware of the general corporate culture regarding how decisions are made and what role research plays when making those decisions.[12]

Alternative Courses of Action

Research can be properly designed only when the alternative courses of action being considered are known. The more obvious ones are typically given to the researcher by the decision maker, and the researcher's main task here is to determine whether the list provided indeed exhausts the alternatives. Quite often, some of the options will remain unstated. Yet, if the research is to be germane to all the alternatives, implicit options must be made explicit. Thus, it is important that the decision maker and the researcher work together to come up with a complete list of the alternative courses of action being considered.

Objectives of the Decision Maker

One of the more basic facts of decision making is that individuals differ in their attitudes toward risk and these differences influence their choices. Some people are risk takers; they are willing to assume a good deal of risk for the chance of a big gain.[13] Some are risk evaders; they are willing to assume little risk, even when the size of the potential gain is large, if the chance of loss also exists. Some individuals simply walk a middle ground. A person's attitude towards risk is not always consistent. It changes with the situation and the magnitude of the potential consequences. Thus, a person may be a risk taker, even when the chances of things turning out badly are reasonably high, if that person feels secure and if the consequences of his or her actions would not be cata-

[12]Joel Levine, the vice president of marketing research at The Pillsbury Company in Minneapolis suggests that awareness of the corporate culture is one of the most important factors that distinguishes researchers who affect strategic marketing decisions from those who do not. See "Six Factors Mark Researchers Who Sway Strategic Decisions," *Marketing News,* 17 (February 4, 1983), p. 1. See also Bernie Whalen, "Researchers Stymied by 'Adversary Culture' in Firms," *Marketing News,* 16 (September 17, 1982), pp. 1 and 7.

[13]The types of decision makers are more formally defined in decision theory literature. See, for example, the classic work by Howard Raiffa, *Decision Analysis: Introductory Lectures on Choices under Uncertainty* (Reading, Mass.: Addison-Wesley, 1968), pp. 51–101.

strophic. That same person may avoid risks if his or her position in the company is insecure or if the consequences would be disastrous if things were to turn out wrong.

Consider the case of Jimmy Spradley, young president of Standard Candy of Nashville, manufacturers of Goo Goo Clusters—a gooey confection dear to the hearts of Southerners. When Spradley took over Standard Candy, it was close to bankruptcy. The new president immediately turned his focus to marketing, offering brokers trips as incentives for improved sales performance and enticing retailers to stock the brand by offering appealing discounts. By the summer of 1983, sales were strong, and the company's debts were being paid off. It was then that Spradley took a big risk.

Impatient to boost sales even further, he doubled his discounts for certain customers. Sales soared, but profits plummeted, and the company began to lose money. Spradley quickly stopped the practice, admitting ruefully, ''I've learned there's more to my company's health than fast growth.''

Spradley could afford to take risks. After all, his father owned 50% of the company's stock, sales were on the upswing, and his decision could easily be reversed if things turned out badly. A year earlier, with the wolves at the door, Spradley's tactics were more conventional and less risky. He knew that at that point, one serious slip meant there would be no tomorrow.[14]

It is the researchers' task to discover as best they can the type of decision maker with whom they are dealing. Very often some hint of the decision maker's posture can be gained from intensive probing, using ''what-if'' hypothetical outcomes of the research.

Closely allied to the need to determine the decision maker's attitude toward risk is the need to determine the decision maker's specific objectives. It is unfortunate, but true, that these are rarely explicitly stated.

Despite a popular misconception to the contrary, objectives are seldom given to the researcher. The decision maker seldom formulates his objectives accurately. He is likely to state his objectives in the form of platitudes which have no operational significance. Consequently, objectives usually have to be extracted by the researcher. In so doing, the researcher may well be performing his most useful service to the decision maker.[15]

The researcher must transform the platitudes into specific operational objectives that the research can be designed to serve.

One effective technique for uncovering these objectives consists of confronting the decision-maker with each of the possible solutions to a problem and asking him whether he would follow that course of action. Where he says ''no,'' further probing will usually reveal objectives which are not served by the course of action.[16]

Once the objectives for the research are finally decided upon, they should be committed to writing. This often produces additional clarity in communication and thinking. The decision maker and researcher should then agree formally on their written expression (by each initialing each statement of purpose, by initialing the entire document, or by

---

[14]John F. Persinos, ''Sugar Baby,'' *Inc.,* (May 1984), pp. 85–92.

[15]Russell L. Ackoff, *Scientific Method* (New York: John Wiley, 1962), p. 71.

[16]*Ibid.,* p. 71.

some other means). This tends to prevent later misunderstandings. The formal endorsement of objectives also helps to ensure that the research will not treat symptoms but rather the problem that produced the symptoms.

Consequences of Alternative Courses of Action

A great deal of marketing research is intended to determine the consequences of various courses of action. Much of the research highlighted in Tables 1.1 and 1.2, for example, deals with the impact of manipulating one of the P's in the marketing mix. This is not surprising since, as we have seen, the marketing manager's task basically involves manipulating the elements of the mix to achieve customer satisfaction. What is a more natural marketing research activity than seeking answers to such questions as: What will be the change in sales produced by a change in the product's package? If we change the sales compensation plan, what will be the effect on the sales representatives' performance and on their attitudes toward the job and company? Which ad is likely to generate the most favorable customer response?

Researchers are primarily responsible for designing research that accurately assesses the outcomes of past or contemplated marketing actions. In this capacity, they must gauge the actions against all the outcomes management deems relevant. Management, for example, may want to know the impact of the proposed change on sales as well as on consumer attitudes. If the research addresses only consumer attitudes, management will most assuredly ask for the relationship between attitudes and sales. Embarrassing questions of this nature can only be avoided if researchers painstakingly probe for all relevant outcomes before designing the research.

Decision Problem to Research Problem

A detailed understanding of the total decision situation described above should enable researchers to translate the decision problem into a research problem. A research problem is essentially a restatement of the decision problem in research terms. Consider, for example, the new product introduction for which sales are below target. The decision problem faced by the marketing manager is deciding what to do about the shortfall. Should the target be revised? Was it too optimistic? Should the product be withdrawn? Should one of the other elements in the marketing mix, such as advertising, be altered? Suppose the manager suspects that the advertising campaign supporting the new product introduction has been ineffective. This suspicion could serve as the basis for a research problem. For example, a product manager who felt that advertising was not creating sufficient customer awareness for a successful new product launch might wish to have some evidence that either confirmed or disconfirmed that suspicion before changing the advertising program. The research problem would then become the assessment of product awareness among potential customers.

Some illustrations of the distinctions between decision problems and research problems can be found in Table 2.1. Though it should be apparent that the two problems are related, it should also be apparent that they are not the same. The decision problem involves what needs to be done. Research can provide the necessary information to make an informed choice, and the research problem essentially involves determining what information to provide and how that information can best be secured.

Table 2.1
Examples of the Relationship between Decision Problems and Research Problems

Decision Problems	Research Problems
Develop package for a new product	Evaluate effectiveness of alternative package designs
Increase market penetration through the opening of new stores	Evaluate prospective locations
Increase store traffic	Measure current image of the store
Increase amount of repeat purchasing behavior	Assess current amount of repeat purchasing behavior
Develop more equitable sales territories	Assess current and proposed territories with respect to their potential and workload
Allocate advertising budget geographically	Determine current level of market penetration in the respective areas
Introduce new product	Design a test market through which the likely acceptance of the new product can be assessed

In making this determination, the researcher must make certain that the real decision problem, not just the symptoms, is being addressed. The plight of the *Chicago Daily News,* which folded during the 1970s, is interesting in this regard. The *Chicago Daily News* was historically one of the most intellectual and best written of the Chicago daily papers. By the time it ceased publishing, it had won more Pulitzer prizes than any other newspaper in the country except *The New York Times.* Marketing research seems to have been one of the more important factors that contributed to its demise. "Yes, it was market research that ultimately killed the *Chicago Daily News.* But, oddly enough, it wasn't bad research that did it. The research was right on target."[17] Apparently, the decision problem was incorrectly defined. It seems that the basic decision problem was defined as how to stimulate circulation, rather than how to appeal better to the basic market segment that the *Daily News* served. As a result, the *Daily News* shifted its emphasis, which led to its demise.

How does one avoid the trap of researching the wrong decision problem? The main way is by refusing to respond to requests for information without developing a proper appreciation for the decision problem. The difference in response perspectives is highlighted in the Parkay margarine example in Research Realities 2.2. There is an old saying, "If you do not know where you want to go, any road will get you there." It is the same in decision making. If you do not know what you want to accomplish, any alternative will be satisfactory. If the decision maker does not know what he or she wants to achieve, the research study won't accomplish it. Instead of going off to prepare a research proposal outlining the methods to be used when a research request first comes in, which is the typical procedure, researchers are well advised to take the time to probe the situation carefully until they have acquired the necessary appreciation for (1) the decision maker and the environment, (2) the alternative courses of action, (3) the objectives of the decision maker, and (4) the consequences of alternative actions.

---

[17]Joe Cappo, "The Failure to Properly Interpret Market Research Ruins Many Firms," *Marketing News,* 13 (January 11, 1980), pp. 1 and 18.

Research Realities 2.2

Alternative Responses to an Information Request and Their Likely Impacts

I would like you to meet someone—research analyst X, . . . (who has) been at Kraft for a little more than two years now and he's well regarded by the marketing group he works with.

One morning analyst X receives a phone call from the marketing manager on Parkay margarine. The marketing manager tells our analyst that the R & D lab has been working on a new improved flavor for Parkay margarine and that they've finally come up with one that he thinks is acceptable.

Before he authorizes full production with the new formula, he thinks it would be prudent to conduct a taste test to determine if consumers will react favorably to the new flavor. Actually, he is calling to find out how much product would be required for such a test. He adds that it's very important that this research be initiated quickly since a competitor, Blue Bonnet, has just come out with a new improved version of its product.

Analyst X decided to conduct personal interviews in central location mall facilities. Basically, these will be blind taste tests.

Then analyst X determines that he wants to use a triangular discrimination taste test to determine if respondents can detect differences between the products. That will be followed by a sequential monadic evaluation of each product to obtain additional diagnostic rating data and preference.

You might be saying that this design sounds pretty good. . . . Sequential approach so you don't waste time and money if the new flavor is not as good as everyone thinks, adequate sample sizes for both stick and soft versions, two phases for the evaluation, a triangle discrimination to see if respondents can detect differences between the formulas, and sequential monadic to obtain diagnostic evaluations.

But let me introduce research analyst Y. She has the same credentials as analyst X and is faced with the same initial phone call. The marketing manager asks how much product is needed for a taste test?

Analyst Y responds before she can design any research, she needs a little more information. Sounds like analyst X, right? Just listen. Analyst Y is not sure a taste test is exactly what is needed. She suggests they discuss the project.

Analyst Y begins to review the information she has been given and lists some of the questions she will want to ask the marketing manager when they get together. She looks up the most recent SAMI information to see how well Blue Bonnet has been performing since the introduction of its new flavor. She checks to see if Parkay has been affected by this change. She reviews the historical project files to review any prior test research for Parkay.

When analyst Y meets the marketing manager she asks the following questions:

- Why are we considering a new formula? Blue Bonnet doesn't seem to have hurt our franchise with its new flavor.

- If we do utilize the new flavor, what do we hope to accomplish? Do we expect to pull in new users or do we want to minimize the chances of our consumers converting over to Blue Bonnet?

Source: Larry P. Stanek, "Bad Design Leads Managers to Doubt Value of Research," *Marketing News*, 11 (January 1980), p. 12. Published by the American Marketing Association.

One useful mechanism for making sure that the real decision problem will be addressed by the research is to execute a "research request step" before preparing the research proposal.[18] The research request step requires that the decision maker and re-

---

[18]Paul W. Conner, "'Research Request Step' Can Enhance Use of Results," *Marketing News*, 19 (January 4, 1985), p. 41. See also Paul D. Boughton, "Marketing Research and Small Business: Pitfalls and Potential," *Journal of Small Business Management*, 21 (July 1983), pp. 36–42, for a list of questions small business managers (any decision maker, actually) can ask so as to make sure they are getting the most from their research.

- How will we announce the new flavor?
- Does the new formula taste more like butter or affect aftertaste, spreadability, or cooking uses?
- Can we obtain product from a regular facility? So often R & D's controls are much more stringent than those of our production plants. I would rather use product for this test that closely resembles the product consumers would receive.

Analyst Y then works out a research design. She also recommends a two-phase study, but her objectives are to determine Parkay users' responses to the new flavor in terms of usage and preference and to determine competitive users' response to the new flavor versus the new Blue Bonnet flavor.

Analyst Y also will interview 600 respondents who are female heads of household, primary grocery shoppers, between 18 and 60, and who have used Parkay in the past month. Respondents in the first phase of the research must be regular users of Parkay. In the second phase, they must be regular users of competitive margarines.

The research will involve personal sequential monadic in-home placements. In the first phase, 300 respondents will evaluate Parkay's current formula and the new one. In the second, 300 respondents will compare Parkay's new formula and Blue Bonnet's formula. In both phases, half the sample will evaluate sticks, the other half will evaluate soft products.

There are several clear differences between this research design and the first example, all the differences being dependent on the problem definition phase.

Analyst X is a research taker or research technician. He basically responded to the marketing manager's request for a taste test without considering the marketing situation that prompted the request.

His research design was quite sound given the information he had. He would have obtained answers and those answers would probably have been correct. Unfortunately, both he and the marketing manager would be wondering why they were receiving consumer complaint letters about the new flavor from long-time Parkay users.

Research analyst Y is an internal marketing consultant—a true marketing research professional. Her approach was to attempt to clearly understand the marketing situation, understand marketing decisions that would be based on this research.

Her research design was fundamentally sound as well, but it was a more costly and time-consuming approach than that of analyst X. Why? Because she understood the risks involved as well as the potential gains that could be realized.

In both instances, the marketing manager could make a decision based on data obtained from a research study. The difference is that one manager now suspects marketing research because it failed to predict some Parkay users' negative responses. The other is even more confident in using marketing research.

We marketing research professionals must strive to go beyond simple problem solving. We must insist on being internal marketing consultants. That is the only way we can be assured that our research designs, techniques, and statistical analyses will continue to be valid. It is the only way marketing management will become more confident in its use of marketing research.

searcher have a meeting in which the decision maker describes the problem and the information that is needed. The researcher then drafts a statement describing his or her understanding of the problem. The statement should include, but is not limited to, the following items:

1. **Action**—the actions that are contemplated on the basis of the research.
2. **Origin**—the events that led to a need for the decision to act; while the events may not directly affect the research that is conducted, they help the researcher understand more deeply the nature of the research problem.

3. **Information**—the questions that the decision maker needs to have answered in order to take one of the contemplated courses of action.

4. **Use**—a section that explains how each piece of information will be used to help make the action decision; supplying logical reasons for each piece of the research ensures that the questions make sense in light of the action to be taken.

5. **Targets and subgroups**—a section that describes from whom the information must be gathered; specifying the target groups helps the researcher design an appropriate sample for the research project.

6. **Logistics**—a section that gives approximate estimates of the time and money that are available to conduct the research; both of these factors will affect the techniques finally chosen.

This written statement should be submitted to the decision maker for his or her approval. The approval should be formalized by having the decision maker initial and date the entire document or each section. Following a procedure like this helps ensure that the *purpose* of the research is agreed upon before the research is designed.

The Research Proposal

Once the purpose and scope of the research are agreed upon, researchers can turn their attention to choosing the *techniques* that will be used to conduct the research. The techniques decided upon should also be communicated to the decision maker before the research begins. Typically this is done via a formal research proposal, which allows the researcher another opportunity to make sure that the research being contemplated will provide the information necessary to answer the decision maker's problem.

Research proposals can take many forms. Some will be very long and detailed, running 20 pages or more. Others will be short and to the point. Much depends on the detail with which the various parts are described. Table 2.2 contains a sample form that can be followed in preparing a research proposal or plan. Again, the decision maker's approval for the plan should be sought and formalized by having him or her sign and date the proposal.

Research Realities 2.3 contains portions of an actual research plan, with some authorization and budget information removed, that was prepared by the research department at General Mills. Note the clearly stated criteria that will be used to interpret the results and the carefully crafted action standards specifying what will be done depending upon what the research results indicate. The effort expended by the marketing research department in translating information requests into specific, action-oriented statements like this helps account for the wide acceptance of and enthusiastic support for the research function at General Mills.

Is Marketing Research Justified?

While the benefits of marketing research are many, it is not without its drawbacks, and the question of whether the research costs are likely to exceed the research benefits always needs to be asked. There is no denying that the research process is often time-consuming and expensive, and, if done incorrectly (as in the case of the *Chicago Daily News*), it can hurt more than help a company. There are also cases where even the best

Table 2.2
Sample Research Proposal

I. Tentative Project Title

II. Statement of the Problem

One or two sentences to outline or to describe the general problem under consideration.

III. Define and Delimit the Project

Here the writer states the purpose(s) and scope of the project. *Purpose* refers to goals or objectives. Closely related to this is *justification*. Sometimes this is a separate step, depending upon the urgency of the task. *Scope* refers to the actual limitations of the research effort; in other words, what is *not* going to be investigated. Here is the point where the writer spells out the various hypotheses to be investigated or the questions to be answered.

IV. Outline

Generally, this is a tentative framework for the entire project by topics. It should be flexible enough to accommodate unforeseen difficulties. Show statistical tables in outline form and also show graphs planned. Tables should reflect the hypotheses.

V. Method and Data Sources

The types of data to be sought (primary, secondary) are briefly identified. A brief explanation of how the necessary information or data will be gathered (e.g., surveys, experiments, library sources) is given. *Sources* refer to the actual depositories for the information, whether from government publications, company records, actual people, and so forth. If measurements are involved, such as consumers' attitudes, the techniques for making such measurements are stated. All of the techniques (statistical and nonstatistical) should be mentioned and discussed about their relevance for the task at hand. The nature of the problem will probably indicate the types of techniques to be employed, such as factor analysis, depth interviews, or focus groups.

VI. Sample Design

This provides the limits of the universe or population to be studied and how it will be listed (or prepared). The writer specifies the population, states the sample size, whether sample stratification will be employed, and how. If a nonrandom sample is to be used, the justification and the type of sampling strategy to be employed, such as a convenience sample, are stated.

VII. Data Collection Forms

The forms to be employed in gathering the data should be discussed and, if possible, included in the plan. For surveys this will involve either a questionnaire or an interview schedule. For other types of methods the forms could include inventory forms, psychological tests, and so forth. The plan should state how these instruments have been or will be validated and the reader should be given some indication of their reliability and validity.

VIII. Personnel Requirements

This provides a complete list of all personnel who will be required, indicating exact jobs, time duration, and expected rate of pay. Assignments should be made indicating each person's responsibility and authority.

IX. Phases of the Study with a Time Schedule

This is a detailed outline of the plan to complete the study. The entire study should be broken down into workable pieces. Then, considering the person who will be employed in each phase, their qualifications and experience and so forth, the time in months for the job is estimated. Some jobs may overlap. This will help in estimating the work months required. The overall time for the project should allow for time overlaps on some jobs.

Illustration:
1. Preliminary investigation—two months.
2. Final test of questionnaire—one month.
3. Sample selection—one month.
4. Mail questionnaires, field follow-up, and so forth—four months.
5. Additional phases. . . .

X. Tabulation Plans

This is a discussion of editing and proof of questionnaires, coding and entering the data, and the type of computer analysis. An outline of some of the major tables required is very important.

XI. Cost Estimate for Doing the Study

Personnel requirements are combined with time on different phases to estimate total personnel costs. Estimates on travel, materials, supplies, drafting, computer charges, and printing and mailing costs must also be included. If an overhead charge is required by the administration, it should be calculated and added to the subtotal of the above items.

Source: J. Paul Peter and James H. Donnelly, Jr., *A Preface to Marketing Management*, 3rd ed. (Plano, Tex.: Business Publications, Inc., 1985), pp. 48–49. Reprinted with permission.

Research Realities 2.3

A Sample Proposal at General Mills for Research on *Protein Plus* Cereal[1]

1. *Problem and Background.* Protein Plus has performed below objectives in test market. New product and copy alternatives are being readied for testing. Three alternative formulations—Hi Graham (A), Nut (B), and Cinnamon (C)—which retain the basic identity of current Protein Plus but which have been judged to be sufficiently different and of sufficient potential, have been developed for testing against current (D).

2. *Decision Involved.* Which product formulations should be carried into the concept fulfillment test?

3. *Method and Design.* Monadic in-home product test will be conducted. Each of the four test products will be tested by a separate panel of 150 households. Each household will have purchased adult ready-to-eat (RTE) cereal within the past month and will be interested in the test product as measured by the selection of Protein Plus as one or more of their next ten cereal packages they would like to buy. They will be exposed to Protein Plus in a booklet that will also contain an ad for several competitive products, such as Product 19, Special K, Nature Valley, and Grape Nuts. A Protein Plus ad will be constructed for each of the four test products, differing primarily on the kind of taste reassurance provided. Exposure to these various executions will be rotated so that each of the four test panels are matched on RTE cereal usage.

The study will be conducted in eight markets. Product will be packaged in current Protein Plus package flagged with the particular flavor reassurance for that product.

The criterion measure will be the homemakers weighted post share, adjusted to reflect the breadth of interest in the various Protein Plus communications strategies.

Rather than trust a random sampling procedure to represent the population at large, a quota will be established to insure that the sample of people initially contacted for each panel will conform as closely as possible to the division of housewives under 45 (56%) and over 45 (44%) in the U.S. population.

4. *Criteria for Interpretation.* Each formulation generating a higher weighted homemaker share than standard will be considered for subsequent testing. If more than one formulation beats standard, each will be placed in concept fulfillment test unless one is better than the other(s) at odds of 2:1 or more.

5. *Estimated Project Expense:* Within ±500: $22,000.

6. Individual who must finally approve recommended action: _____.

7. Report to be delivered by _____ if authorized by _____ and test materials shipped by _____.

[1]Used with permission of General Mills, Inc.

marketing research either cannot provide answers a company seeks or poses risks that outweigh its possible advantages. The benefits of testing a new product, for example, must be weighed against the risk of tipping off a competitor, who can then rush into the market with a similar product at perhaps a better price or some other added product advantage. Similarly, it may be worthwhile to forego research if there is little financial risk associated with the decision. The expense and effort of marketing research may also not be worthwhile if the results will not influence subsequent decisions. Such was the case in our earlier example of financial service advertisers.

The appendix to this chapter outlines a formal process by which the potential value of research can be determined and a comparison with its costs made. Whether or not the formal process is followed is immaterial. What matters is that the fundamental question be asked and answered before research is begun: Will the research be worth it? Do potential benefits exceed anticipated costs? These questions demand that the "criterion of adequacy" be applied: By what standard will the research be judged? Will the objective be to explore the impact of a prespecified set of alternatives or to discover which decision options are potentially viable? The objectives of the research very much depend on what is known about the decision problem, a question explored more fully in Part 2.

Summary

A company's philosophy of how marketing research fits into its marketing plan determines its program strategy for marketing research. A program strategy specifies the types of studies that are to be conducted and for what purposes. The design of the individual studies themselves defines the firm's project strategy.

Although each research problem imposes its own special requirements, a marketing research project can be productively viewed as a sequence of steps—the research process—that includes: (1) formulate problem, (2) determine research design, (3) design data collection method and forms, (4) design sample and collect data, (5) analyze and interpret the data, and (6) prepare the research report. These steps are so highly interrelated that they can rarely be performed consecutively but rather require a good deal of iteration between and among the various steps. The steps organize the remainder of this book, since each section elaborates a stage. The stages also indicate the potential areas of expertise needed by the aspiring researcher. Finally, and most importantly, the research process highlights the key error in designing a research project, which is total error. This means that a larger error may have to be accepted at some specific stage, such as sampling, so that the total error associated with the project may be minimized.

The first stage in the research process is problem formulation. The second part of this chapter focuses on the role the researcher can perform in defining the decision problem. The simplest decision problem is characterized by an individual operating in an environment who wants something, has alternative ways of pursuing it, and is in doubt about which course of action to take, since the available options will not be equally efficient. The decision problem is what to do in this situation. To determine whether research can assist the decision maker in making the choice, it is necessary to translate the decision problem into a research problem and to address the questions of what information to provide for the decision problem and how that information can best be secured.

It is absolutely imperative that the research address the "real" decision problem and not some visible, but incorrect, specification of it. In order for this to happen, it is necessary that the researcher working on the problem develop sufficient understanding of the decision maker and the environment, the alternative courses of action being considered, the objectives of the decision maker (including the person's attitude toward risk), and the potential consequences of the alternative courses of action. One useful mechanism for ensuring that the actual decision problem will be addressed by the research is for the researcher to prepare a written statement of the problem after meeting with the decision maker and to secure signed agreement from him or her that the written statement correctly captures the situation. After such agreement is obtained, the researcher should prepare a research proposal, which describes the techniques that will be used to address the problem. The research proposal should include some perspective on how each stage in the research process will be handled as well as the time and cost estimates.

Before going ahead with the research, the potential gains to be derived should always be specified explicitly and a comparison made to the costs to ensure that the research is likely to be worthwhile.

Questions

1. What is the research process?
2. What is the most important error in research?
3. What is the basic nature of a decision problem?
4. What are the fundamental characteristics of decision problems?
5. What is the difference between a decision problem and a research problem?
6. What is involved in a research request step? What is included in the written statement?
7. What is the purpose of a research proposal? What goes into the various parts?
8. What is the criterion of adequacy?

Applications and Problems

1. Go to the library and refer to the following article: ''Japanese Heat on the Watch Indus-try,'' *Business Week,* May 5, 1980, p. 92+. Now assume that you are head of the marketing research department of the Texas Instrument consumer products group. The vice-president of the TI consumer products group requests you to undertake the necessary research to explore the issues raised in this article regarding *the watch industry*.
    (a) What should be the objective(s) of the research?
    (b) Briefly describe the major environmental factors you should be aware of.
    (c) What are the alternative courses of action available to Texas Instruments?
    (d) What are the consequences of these alternatives?

2. Given the following decision problems, identify the research problems.
    (a) the pricing strategy to follow for a new product
    (b) whether to increase the level of advertising expenditures on print
    (c) whether to increase in-store promotion of existing products
    (d) whether to expand current warehouse facilities
    (e) whether to change the sales force compensation package

3. Given the following research problems, identify corresponding decision problems for which they might provide useful information.
    (a) design a test market to assess the impact on sales volume of a particular discount theme
    (b) evaluate the stock level at the different warehouses
    (c) evaluate the sales and market share of grocery stores in a particular location
    (d) develop sales forecasts for a particular product line

4. Briefly discuss the difference between a decision problem and research problem.

Appendix 2A
Bayesian Decision Theory

It was suggested in the chapter that once the decision problem has been defined, the manager or researcher must determine whether research will or will not be employed to help solve it. Bayesian decision theory is a particularly useful scheme for structuring the research decision so that the proper choice can be made; further, when research is the indicated choice, Bayesian analysis also provides for the systematic evaluation of alternative research strategies. While the rudiments of the Bayesian statistical method are quite old, the technique has only recently become popular. It is the purpose of this appendix to indicate how Bayesian decision theory can be employed to determine whether research should be conducted or the decision should be made with the available information.[1] A proper discussion of this question requires that we first review some basic notions associated with decision making and probability, a task to which we now turn.

Basic Notions of Decision Making

Probability

Suppose I was holding a coin in my hand and I asked you, "What is the probability of getting a head when I toss this coin?" You might reply, "Fifty percent, or one-half." Would it make any difference to you, though, if I told you the coin was not a fair coin? According to classical probability theory, you could not provide the probability of a head turning up if the coin was not fair. In classical statistics, probability refers to relative frequency in the long run. If the coin was fair, one could extrapolate from past experience. If the coin was not fair, though, one would have to toss the coin a great number of times under controlled conditions and record the relative proportion of heads. **Classical probabilities** are thus seen to be limited in cases where one can safely extrapolate from past information or where one can run a controlled experiment.

Bayesians assume a different perspective on probabilities. Instead of viewing them as long-run relative frequencies, they view them as more akin to betting odds. Thus, when asked for the probability of getting a head in one toss of the coin, you would have to judge for yourself whether the coin is fair or not, and if you do consider it likely to be biased, by how much.

---

[1]The technique has its origins in a paper by Reverend Thomas Bayes, "An Essay Toward Solving a Problem in the Doctrine of Chance," *Philosophical Transactions of the Royal Society,* 1763. Bayes suggested that probability judgments based on hunches can and should be combined with traditional probabilities based on relative frequencies through the use of a theorem he designed. Robert Schlaifer's book, *Probability and Statistics for Business Decisions* (New York: McGraw-Hill, 1959), probably did more than any other work to popularize Bayesian decision theory. For a number of interesting case studies regarding its potential usefulness, see Robert D. Behn and James W. Vaupel, *Quick Analysis for Busy Decision Makers* (New York: Basic Books, Inc., 1982).

Bayesians hold that this view of probability is more appropriate to the problems the business decision maker faces than is classical probability. When introducing a new product, for example, the decision maker cannot simply argue that the chance of success for this product is 60 percent, since historically 60 percent of all the products introduced have been successful. At a minimum, the economic environment, consumer demand, and the competitive frame will be different, and these factors must be taken into account in assessing the likelihood of success. Certainly the decision maker can rely on past experience in making probability judgments, much as you might rely on your knowledge about me and the likelihood of my cheating you when tossing the coin. The fact remains, though, that each new product introduction is unique, and the probability estimates associated with the product's success must be **personal** or **subjective** probabilities, since they cannot be generated in the classical sense.

Each of us makes these subjective judgments all the time, although we most often do it implicitly. Poker players, for example, well recognize the need for subjective judgments. While good poker players may know the objective probability of getting four of a kind in a game of five-card stud, when they are betting they must decide whether the person sitting across the table actually has the four of a kind necessary to beat their own full house. It is doubtful that they would simply use objective probabilities. Rather, they will take into account the other cards that are showing on the table and the way the person is betting and what they know about that person's betting behavior. Does the other player bluff? Or only bet heavily on a good hand? While the particular hand in question is a unique event, poker players need to form, and will form, some personal estimate of their chances of winning the hand. Similarly, many of you are probably already assessing the likelihood of getting an A, B, and so on in each of your courses. One can, and most of us do, assign personal probabilities to events, and Bayesians hold that these probability judgments need to be made explicit in framing our decisions.

Payoff Table

Another important ingredient in the decision theory approach to problem solving is the **payoff table.** The payoff table and the important role played by Bayesian analysis in marketing research are best illustrated by an example.

Consider the problem facing the marketing manager who is responsible for pricing a new product. Suppose the manager is considering whether to use a skim- or penetration-pricing strategy or whether to price the product somewhere in between the two extremes. That is, suppose three price alternatives are under consideration:

- A_1—skim-pricing strategy (price per unit is \$12.50);
- A_2—intermediate price (\$10.00 per unit);
- A_3—penetration strategy (price per unit, \$7.50).

The marketing manager recognizes that the desirability of each price depends on the demand that develops for the product. Suppose that the possible levels of product demand and associated consequences are as depicted in Table 2A.1.

Table 2A.1 is a payoff table depicting the decision situation. The example is somewhat limited; it contains only three alternatives and three possible states of nature. Either

Table 2A.1
Payoff Table for Pricing Decision

| | State of Nature | | |
Alternative	Light Demand, S_1	Moderate Demand, S_2	Heavy Demand, S_3
Skimming price—A_1	100	50	−50
Intermediate price—A_2	50	100	−25
Penetration price—A_3	−50	0	80

the alternatives or the states of nature, or both, could have been expanded. The only difference this would have made would have been an increase in the amount of computation.

Note that the payoff table contains three elements: alternatives, states of nature, and consequences. The alternatives, sometimes called acts, are options open to the decision maker. The states of nature are uncontrollable elements in the environment in which the manager operates. These elements may be of two types—those beyond the decision maker's influence and those that can be influenced. General economic conditions are typically a given for most firms and are of the first type. Competitive reactions, on the other hand, are often influenced by the decisions of the firm and illustrate the second type. Since both types are beyond the decision maker's control, though, they are logically considered states of nature or environmental variables and not decision options. The example treats the demand materializing for the product, not the decision maker's brand, as the states of nature. There is a consequence associated with each decision alternative, given each potential state of nature.

Table 2A.1 is read as follows. If the decision maker selects the skimming price (A_1), and low demand for the product actually results, the company can be expected to realize a profit of $100.[2] If there is intermediate demand, the resulting profits could be expected to be $50, while with high demand the firm could be expected to incur a loss of −$50. You may wonder why the example is cast in this way; that is, why the firm could be expected to lose money under conditions of high product demand and to make money under conditions of low product demand. Note two things. First, the entries themselves are unimportant for illustrating the Bayesian approach. They will affect the computations and possibly the decision, but not the procedure. If you take issue with the numbers, rest assured that any other numbers could serve as well in illustrating the technique. Second, the numbers do reflect some traditional wisdom as to when skim-pricing and penetration-pricing strategies are warranted. For example, it is generally held that all other things being equal, a penetration strategy is better when there is high potential

---

[2]The entries in the table should be, or at least could be, considered as discounted future returns reflecting the cost of capital. They could also be treated as thousands or millions of dollars, or whatever unit is appropriate. The example is framed in dollars to keep the mathematics simple.

demand for the product, as this gives the firm some opportunity to keep out competition and thereby get a larger share of the market. A skimming strategy under conditions of high product demand would be an enticement for competitors. With low product demand, on the other hand, a penetration strategy could be disastrous. It might not allow the firm to recover its investment, while a skimming strategy would afford the possibility of quicker capital recovery. The numbers used for the consequences are designed to reflect these kinds of considerations. In practice, they would be generated from the best available information. The important thing for now is to note that a payoff table contains alternatives, states of nature, and the consequences of each alternative given each state of nature—the essential elements in decision problems. The payoff table, then, provides a formal structure for the traditional decision problem. The structure is productive in determining the best course of action.

Which pricing decision is optimal? If the marketing manager is 100 percent certain that there will be low product demand, then clearly alternative A_1 (skimming price) is the preferable choice, since it provides higher profits than either A_2 or A_3. If the manager is 100 percent certain that there will be high product demand, then the penetration strategy A_3 is best, while the intermediate price A_2 is best if the decision maker expects a moderate level of demand. Clearly, then, the individual's choice of alternatives depends upon which state of nature is expected. This suggests the assignment of probabilities to the various states of nature.

Suppose, on the basis of the company's past experience, some past marketing research, and the company's knowledge of available substitute products, that the decision maker expects this product to attract a limited market segment. In particular, the probabilities associated with each state of nature are assessed to be[3]

- light demand (S_1): $P(S_1) = 0.6$;
- moderate demand (S_2): $P(S_2) = 0.3$;
- heavy demand (S_3): $P(S_3) = 0.1$.

Different decision makers, given the same information, might assess these probabilities differently, just as two experienced poker players might assess the likelihood of the same player having four of a kind differently. This is why these probabilities are personal or subjective. In all other ways, though, they follow the normal rules and definitions of probabilities.

Prior Analysis

Now that the preliminary notions connected with payoff tables and probability have been reviewed, we are in a position to address the question of whether research should or should not be conducted. In essence, this question can be reduced to a comparison of the value of the decision without research to the anticipated value of the decision assum-

---

[3]One could argue that the numbers actually assigned to the probabilities for the states of nature should depend upon the action considered, since economic theory would suggest that product demand is influenced by the price charged. This presents no new conceptual difficulties, although it does make the discussion and calculations somewhat more cumbersome. We will assume, for discussion purposes, that the probabilities for the states of nature and the alternatives being considered are independent.

ing research were to be conducted. If the anticipated value is higher with research, then by all means research is warranted. Conversely, if the cost of research exceeds its potential contribution to the managerial decision, research is not justified.

Expected Value

A criterion that has been used for comparing the potential value of the decision with research to the potential value without research is that of expected value. **Expected value** is nothing more than a weighted average of the various consequences in the payoff table, where the weights are the probabilities assigned to each of the possible states of nature. Expected value is defined for each alternative or act i. Further, when (1) the alternative has n outcomes, (2) the probability of the jth outcomes is p_j, and (3) the value of the jth outcome given the ith alternative is V_{ij}, then the expected value of the ith alternative is

$$EV_i = \sum_{j=1}^{n} p_j V_{ij}.$$

The expected value of the three pricing alternatives is thus determined to be

$$EV(A_1) = (0.6)(100) + (0.3)(50) + (0.1)(-50) = 70.0.$$

$$EV(A_2) = (0.6)(50) + (0.3)(100) + (0.1)(-25) = 57.5.$$

$$EV(A_3) = (0.6)(-50) + (0.3)(0) + (0.1)(80) = -22.0.$$

Alternative A_1—the skim-pricing strategy—offers the highest expected value. It would be the best choice assuming the decision maker's goal is to maximize expected returns. The decision maker, to be sure, may have other goals. He or she might, for example, be interested in minimizing any potential loss, in which case alternative A_2, with a maximum loss of $25, would be preferred. The decision theory apparatus can be adapted to reflect other decision criteria.

Let us assume, though, that the decision maker does desire to maximize expected return, in which case the expected value of the optimal act without research is $70. This means that in the absence of any further information, the decision maker would choose a skim-pricing strategy with an expected return of $70.

Preposterior Analysis

Suppose that, before making the pricing decision, the decision maker has the opportunity to commission a marketing research study. Should that be done, or should the pricing decision be made with the present information? To make the choice between research and no research, it seems reasonable *to compare the expected value of the optimal act before the research and the expected value of the optimal act after the research, taking account of the cost of the research itself.*

Value of Perfect Information

One way of generating a quick comparison is to determine the greatest possible increase in expected value. This would occur, of course, if the research information perfectly predicted the state of nature—level of product demand—that would actually result. The decision maker could then simply price the product accordingly.

For instance, if the research indicated that the demand for the product would be light, the decision maker would choose the skimming price with a return of $100, since this return is higher than the $50 return associated with an intermediate price and the $50 loss associated with the penetration price. Similarly, if the research indicated that the demand for the product would be moderate, the intermediate price would be optimal, and if product demand should be indicated to be heavy, the penetration price would be best.

How likely is it that the decision maker would select each alternative price and realize the gain associated with that price? This likelihood is given by the probability that the individual will be told a given state of nature will result; for if S_1 results, the manager makes decision A_1; if S_2 results, decision A_2; and if S_3 results, decision A_3. The best estimates of these probabilities are the probabilities assigned to each state of nature, since the individual is not given a choice as to which state of nature will result but is only told in advance which one will happen. Once the decision maker is told this, though, there is no question about its validity, since the information is perfect. One can proceed with certainty in the choice of alternatives.

Expected value under certainty is found by multiplying the probability the decision maker will be told a given state of nature will occur by the value associated with the *optimal act* given that particular state of nature. Expected value under certainty for the example problem is

$$EV(C) = (0.6)(100) + (0.3)(100) + (0.1)(80) = 98,$$

where the consequences reflect, respectively, alternative A_1 with S_1, alternative A_2 with S_2, and alternative A_3 with S_3.

The difference between the expected value under certainty and the expected value of the optimal act under uncertainty (recall this was A_1) is the **expected value of perfect information;** that is,

$$
\begin{aligned}
EV(PI) &= EV(C) - EV \text{ (optimal act under uncertainty)} \\
&= \$98 - \$70 \\
&= \$28.
\end{aligned}
$$

The perfect information calculation indicates that the cost of the contemplated research cannot exceed $28, since this is the net benefit that results with perfect information, a result the research is unlikely to produce. If the research project costs more than $28, it should not be undertaken, and the pricing decision should be made with the information currently available. This means that the skimming price would be selected.

Value of Sample Information

It would be extremely helpful if the decision maker could buy research information that would allow the pricing decision to be made under conditions of certainty. It is also true that such information is generally unavailable. However, the decision maker does usually have the option of buying imperfect sample information. Should this be done? This is the question to which we now turn.

Disregarding the cost of the research for the moment, suppose the firm is considering test marketing the product. It intends to use test market results to predict eventual prod-

Table 2A.2
Conditional Probabilities of Getting Each Test Market
Result Given Each State of Nature

Test Market Result	Light Demand, S_1	Moderate Demand, S_2	Heavy Demand, S_3
Disappointing or only slightly successful—Z_1	0.7	0.2	0.1
Moderately successful—Z_2	0.2	0.6	0.3
Highly successful—Z_3	0.1	0.2	0.6
	1.0	1.0	1.0

uct demand, although it recognizes the hazards associated with test marketing. Sometimes the product will sell poorly in a test market and yet be highly successful when introduced nationally. The reverse may also be true. Suppose, on the basis of past product performances, the company is able to anticipate certain correlations between test market results and product performance nationally. Let

■ Z_1—disappointing or only slightly successful test market,

■ Z_2—moderately successful test market, and

■ Z_3—highly successful test market,

and suppose past experience provided the estimates contained in Table 2A.2.

Table 2A.2 is read by row within column. This means, for example, that 0.7 of those products that eventually produced only light demand nationally also performed poorly in the test market, whereas 0.2 of them were moderately successful in the test market, and 0.1 were highly successful in the text market. On the other hand, most products that were successful nationally (generated heavy demand) also had highly successful test markets (0.6), while a few national successes had moderately successful test markets (0.3), and a small percentage even had disappointing test markets (0.1). In other words, the test market was a relatively good but not perfect barometer of success. Products that performed poorly in the test market generally performed poorly nationally and vice versa, although there were exceptions.

One of the key factors in deciding whether or not to conduct research is finding out how the managerial decision might change as a result of the research. If the managerial decision will be the same regardless of the research findings, the research is not worthwhile. There must be some research results, perhaps extreme, that would alter the managerial decision. This means that the first step in evaluating the worth of sample information (research results) must be revision of the initial probabilities on the basis of the research results that might occur. Someone, usually the research director, must directly assess the question of how the probabilities surrounding the various states of nature would change if the results of the contemplated test market are disappointing (Z_1), moderately successful (Z_2), or highly successful (Z_3).

The revision of prior probabilities in the light of additional information is the very essence of **Bayes' rule.** The right-hand column of Table 2A.3 contains the revised

Table 2A.3

Revision of Prior Probabilities in the Light of Possible Test Market Results

j (1)	State of Nature S_j (2)	Prior Probability $P(S_j)$ (3)	Conditional Probability $P(Z_k\|S_j)$ (4)	Joint Probability $P(Z_k S_j)$ (5) = (3) × (4)	Posterior Probability $P(S_j\|Z_k)$ (6) = (5) ÷ sum of (5)
Z_1—*Disappointing or Only Slightly Successful Test Market*					
1 Light demand—S_1	0.6	0.7	0.42	0.858
2 Moderate demand—S_2	0.3	0.2	0.06	0.122
3 Heavy demand—S_3	0.1	0.1	0.01	0.020
			0.49	1.000
Z_2—*Moderately Successful Test Market*					
1 Light demand—S_1	0.6	0.2	0.12	0.364
2 Moderate demand—S_2	0.3	0.6	0.18	0.545
3 Heavy demand—S_3	0.1	0.3	0.03	0.091
			0.33	1.000
Z_3—*Highly Successful Test Market*					
1 Light demand—S_1	0.6	0.1	0.06	0.333
2 Moderate demand—S_2	0.3	0.2	0.06	0.333
3 Heavy Demand—S_3	0.1	0.6	0.06	0.333
			0.18	1.000

probabilities associated with each state of nature.[4] There are three sets of these probabilities, one for each possible test market result.

The top section of Table 2A.3, for example, contains the revised probabilities for each of the states of nature, given that the test market results were disappointing. A disappointing performance of the product in the test market would imply (1) that the probability of light demand for the product should be revised upward to 0.858 from its initial value of 0.6, (2) that the probability of moderate demand should be revised downward to 0.122 from its initial value of 0.3, and (3) that the probability of heavy demand should be revised downward to 0.020 from its initial value of 0.1.

Note two things about these calculations. First, the calculations can be performed before doing the research. The possible research results are simply *anticipated,* and the prior probabilities are revised systematically employing Bayes' rule on the basis of what might happen. Second, two people given the same test market results might arrive at different final probabilities for the states of nature. This is because the posterior probabilities depend on both the test market results and the initial assessment of the prior probabilities. There is nothing very unusual about different people arriving at different

---

[4]See Schlaifer, *Probability and Statistics,* for the development of the logic and calculations as to how prior probabilities are systematically revised with new information.

conclusions on the basis of the same set of evidence. Most experienced researchers have met the decision maker who argues, "I don't care what your research says, I know better. We have been doing things this way successfully for ten years and I do not see any reason to change, particularly on the basis of one research study, which must be in error anyway." What this decision maker is really saying is that his or her prior probabilities are such (for example, so close to 1) that the research is not substantial enough to warrant any significant change in them.

One interesting example of the impact of prior probabilities on the desirability of doing research involves the Allied Mills Company. In this instance, the product manager and the research manager disagreed about whether a market test should be run before introducing a new product. The research manager favored a market test, while the product manager did not. The disagreement became so heated that "the research manager accused the product manager of misleading management. The product manager in turn accused the research manager of not recognizing a sound new product idea when he saw one."[5] The disagreement finally narrowed down to a difference in their prior assessments about the likely success of the new product. Given this basic difference, the research made sense to the research manager but did not make sense to the product manager. It is only when the two parties agreed to commit these prior estimates to paper that the basis for the dispute became clear. Whenever a decision maker's prior probabilities are so strong that research will do little to change them, the research will be wasted. If this is anticipated before the research is begun, unnecessary research costs can be avoided.

These arguments demonstrate that the first step in evaluating the worth of some proposed research is to calculate how the prior probabilities would be revised on the basis of the possible anticipated research results. The second step involves calculation of the value of the research on the basis of the optimal decision, given each possible research result and the likelihood that the result will indeed occur. In other words, the second step requires that *the optimal decision be determined for each potential research outcome.*

The expected value of each alternative pricing strategy is calculated for each sample result in Table 2A.4. If the test market is unsuccessful, the skim-pricing strategy A_1 is optimal because it offers the highest expected return. On the other hand, if the test market is either moderately or highly successful, the intermediate pricing strategy (A_2) would be optimal. The penetration strategy (A_3) would not be called for regardless of the test market outcome. Although this finding may at first be surprising, the explanation is straightforward. The only time the penetration strategy is optimal is when heavy product demand can be expected. The prior probability of heavy product demand materializing was initially so low that heavy demand would never become the dominant state of nature regardless of the test market results. Consequently, the penetration strategy would never be optimal, at least on the basis of the proposed research.

Given a choice, the decision maker would prefer test market result Z_1 because this allows the opportunity to maximize the expected return. Given a Z_1 result, the individual

---

[5]Donald S. Tull and Del I. Hawkins, *Marketing Research: Measurement and Method,* 3rd ed. (New York: Macmillan, 1984), p. 47.

Table 2A.4

Expected Value of Each Alternative Given Each Research Outcome

Z_1—*Disappointing or Only Slightly Successful Test Market*

Revised probabilities: $P(S_1) = 0.858$; $P(S_2) = 0.122$; $P(S_3) = 0.020$

$EV(A_1) = 100(0.858) + 50(0.122) + (-50)(0.020) = 90.9$

$EV(A_2) = 50(0.858) + 100(0.122) + (-25)(0.020) = 54.6$

$EV(A_3) = (-50)(0.858) + 0(0.122) + 80(0.020) = -41.3$

Z_2—*Moderately Successful Test Market*

Revised probabilities: $P(S_1) = 0.364$, $P(S_2) = 0.545$; $P(S_3) = 0.091$

$EV(A_1) = 100(0.364) + 50(0.545) + (-50)(0.091) = 59.1$

$EV(A_2) = 50(0.364) + 100(0.545) + (-25)(0.091) = 70.4$

$EV(A_3) = (-50)(0.364) + 0(0.545) + 80(0.091) = -10.9$

Z_3—*Highly Successful Test Market*

Revised probabilities: $P(S_1) = 0.333$; $P(S_2) = 0.333$; $P(S_3) = 0.333$

$EV(A_1) = 100(0.333) + 50(0.333) + (-50)(0.333) = 33.3$

$EV(A_2) = 50(0.333) + 100(0.333) + (-25)(0.333) = 41.6$

$EV(A_3) = (-50)(0.333) + 0(0.333) + 80(0.333) = 10.0$

would simply choose A_1 with a return of $90.90. Unfortunately the decision maker will not have a choice of test market results, since these will be governed by consumer response to the product. The decision maker can, however, anticipate the *likelihood of getting each possible test market result*. These projections can then be used in conjunction with the optimal acts to determine the potential value of the proposed research.

The probability of obtaining each test market result, that is, the probability of each Z_k, is given as

$$P(Z_k) = \sum_{j=1}^{n} P(S_j)P(Z_k|S_j),$$

and for $k = 1$, for example, the probability is found to be

$$P(Z_1) = P(S_1)P(Z_1|S_1) + P(S_2)P(Z_1|S_2) + P(S_3)P(Z_1|S_3)$$

$$= (0.6)(0.7) + (0.3)(0.2) + (0.1)(0.1)$$

$$= 0.49.$$

This probability is given in the tabular computation form as the sum of the elements in Column 5, Table 2A.3. Table 2A.3 thus indicates that the probabilities associated with each test market outcome are $P(Z_1) = 0.49$, $P(Z_2) = 0.33$, and $P(Z_3) = 0.18$.[6]

---

[6]The probabilities sum to 1, as they should, because one of the three test market outcomes must result.

The expected value of the test-marketing procedure is found by weighting each expected value of the optimal act given each research result by the probability of receiving that expected value. Thus, although the decision maker cannot necessarily fulfill a desire to obtain a Z_1 test market result, the probability of receiving the $90.90 expected value from making decision A_1 is 0.49. Similarly, the manager can anticipate the $70.40 associated with making decision A_2, given test market result Z_2, 33 percent of the time and the $41.60 associated with making decision A_2, given test market result Z_3, 18 percent of the time. The expected value of the proposed research is thus found to be

$$EV(\text{research}) = (90.90)(0.49) + (70.40)(0.33) + (41.60)(0.18)$$
$$= 75.26,$$

since in general **the expected value of a research procedure** *is the sum of the products of the probability of obtaining the* kth *research result and the expected value of the preferred decision given the* kth *research result.*

Should the research be undertaken? The answer is yes as long as it costs less than $5.26. The $5.26 represents the *increment* in expected value with the research. The expected value of the best decision in the absence of research was $70, while the expected value with the proposed research was $75.26. If the expected value with the research were less than $70, the research would not be warranted.

Review of Procedure

Since determining the value of research involves a number of steps and calculations, a review of the overall procedure is helpful. We have essentially calculated three quantities: (1) the expected value of the decision without research, (2) the expected value of perfect information, and (3) the expected value of some proposed research. The first two quantities provide ready benchmarks to which the value of the research can be compared. The benefits of the research must exceed (1), and the cost must be less than (2).

Figure 2A.1 diagrams the situation. Assuming the benefits and costs are both measured in the same units, the 45-degree line separates the area into situations where research is beneficial and those where it is undesirable. The value of the decision with present information is given by the expected value of the optimal act without research. The expected value of each act is in turn determined by weighting the consequences by the probabilities of obtaining each consequence.

Perfect information provides an easily calculated upper benchmark of the value of research. The ease with which it can be calculated is its primary value because research does not produce perfect information. The value of perfect information is given by the difference between the expected value under certainty and the expected value of the optimal decision without research. The expected value under certainty is in turn determined by weighting the value of the optimal act under each assumed state of nature by the probability of obtaining that value, that is, by the probability associated with the state of nature.

Figure 2A.1
Value of Research Information

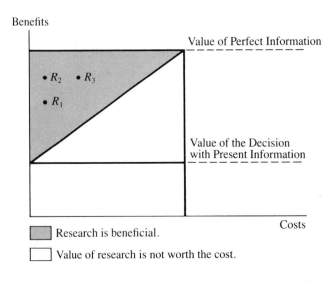

Determining the value of proposed research requires the calculation of several quantities, including:

1. how the prior probabilities would be revised on the basis of the research results;
2. the expected value of the optimal act, given each potential research result, and the revised probabilities surrounding the states of nature;
3. the probability of obtaining each research result and thereby realizing the return associated with the optimal act.

These calculations were all made on the basis of what might be expected to happen and, as such, are anticipated quantities.

The anticipated results of the research can be used to compare alternative research strategies as well as to determine whether research should or should not be conducted. Figure 2A.1 contains three hypothetical research strategies, labeled R_1, R_2, and R_3. All these are beneficial in that the assumed value of the research exceeds the value of the decision without research. R_2 is best; it costs the same as R_1 but has greater benefits and has the same benefits as R_3 but costs less.

Decision Tree

An alternative way of approaching what we have been doing is by using a decision tree. A **decision tree** is simply a decision flow diagram, in which the problem is structured in chronological order. The tree has branches, which are connected by decision forks or chance forks. A decision fork or node is typically depicted as a small square and a chance fork as a small circle. The important thing in decision tree analysis is to lay out the problem completely before attempting to solve it by pruning or crossing off the undesirable branches.

Figure 2A.2 shows a decision tree for the pricing decision. All numbers have been left off on purpose so as to throw the basic structure of the tree into bolder relief. The decision maker's initial decision, reading from left to right, is whether to conduct research or to select a pricing strategy on the basis of the data at hand. The choice will depend on the expected value of the two options, quantities that can be determined by solving the tree. Disregarding the solution for a moment, if the decision maker decides to make the decision with the data at hand, he or she is immediately confronted with another decision, shown by the square fork—the particular price to use. If research is the indicated option, the next node is a chance fork representing the various research results that might occur, since the decision maker cannot control the test market results. Given any of the three possible test market results, the decision maker will then have to choose a particular price, and thus the next junction in each case is a square representing a decision fork. The decision can be good or bad in any case. It depends on the product demand that actually results, and this, of course, is beyond the decision maker's control.

The decision tree is solved from right to left. The solution involves determining the expected value associated with each alternative. The alternative that is optimal at each decision node is then carried backward, and the nonoptimal ones are simply crossed off, most commonly by putting a double line through each undesirable alternative.

Consider the upper branch. The expected value of each alternative is calculated as before, by weighting the consequences by the probabilities associated with attaining each consequence. Since we already have all the necessary numbers, we need not repeat the calculations. Decision A_1 is optimal, and alternatives A_2 and A_3 are pruned. Since decision A_1 had an expected value of $70, the value of the decision without research is also $70. Figure 2A.3 contains the entries.

Consider the lower branch. The expected value of each pricing alternative would now change, since the probabilities associated with each state of nature would change, depending on the test market results. Proceeding as before, we first enter the expected value of each pricing option reflecting the *new probabilities* at the right-hand side of the tree, and the undesirable alternatives are deleted. The value of the optimal act is then carried back to the decision node. All that remains then is the weighting of each value at the decision node by the probability that the value will be attained, that is, by the probability of going down the branch in question. The sum of the products of probabilities and values, 75.26, is entered at the chance node to indicate the value of the decision with research. Since this quantity exceeds that associated with the upper branch, the upper branch would be crossed off, and the decision would be to go ahead with the research, assuming it costs no more than $5.26. Although the whole analysis could have been carried out with the cost of the research entered directly as a net subtraction from the values in the payoff table, it was done this way so as to demonstrate the maximum value of the research, given the potential research outcomes.

It is not necessary to formally solve the decision tree to benefit from it. The decision tree is a most useful device for conceptualizing a problem and communicating its basic

Figure 2A.2
Decision Tree for Pricing Decision Problem

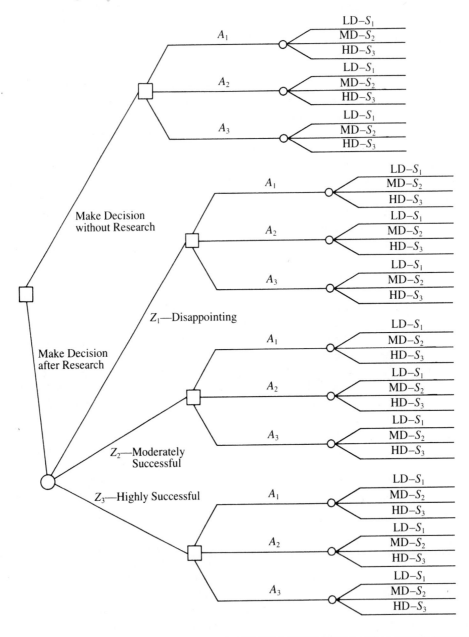

Figure 2A.3
Solution to the Decision Tree for the Pricing Decision Problem

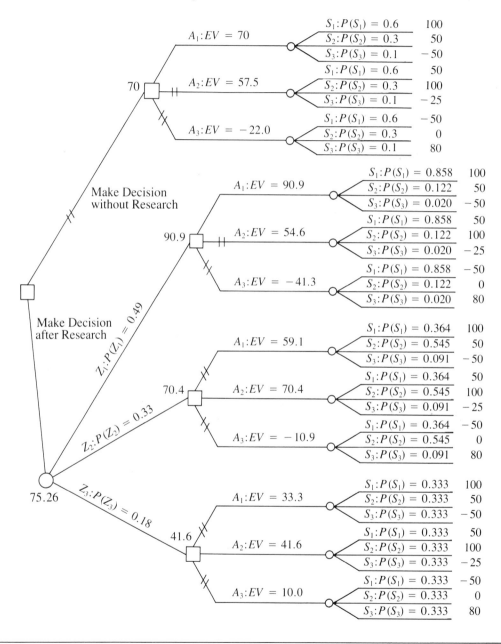

structure to others. Diagramming the problem forces a focus on the interrelationship of the decisions that need be made. This helps illuminate the role of research in the decision and encourages communication between decision maker and researcher. Whether or not a formal Bayesian analysis is undertaken to determine whether potential research benefits justify the costs, constructing a tree of the decision problem can cast such problems in bold relief.

Additional Considerations

While the basic concept behind the decison theory approach is simple enough—compare the expected value of the optimal decision without research to the expected value of the research results—calculations for even the simplest of examples can get tedious. The previous example was basic in several respects, not the least of which are (1) the limited states of nature and alternatives it considered, (2) the assumption that the decision maker possessed a "linear utility function," and (3) the certainty associated with the payoffs. There is no conceptual problem in introducing refinements. The basic approach remains the same, although there are more calculations to perform.

Additional States of Nature and/or Alternatives

Only three pricing alternatives and three states of nature were treated in the example. This is unreal in actual decision problems. At a very minimum, the states of nature could be expanded to include the economic environment, competitive reaction, and consumer demand. This expansion could create problems in the assignment of prior probabilities. Probabilities for states of nature such as "competitor introduces product at lower price when demand is strong and economy is booming" or "at same price" under these conditions would have to be assessed. These probability assignments could become complex, involving, as they do, joint probabilities. Someone would have to take special pains to ensure that the states of nature were indeed mutually exclusive and exhaustive.

The expansion of alternatives would simply entail a greater number of expected value calculations. The problem here is again one of ensuring that all viable alternatives are entered in the decision calculations and that they are expressed as mutually exclusive options.

Nonlinear Utility Functions

The example was framed using an expected value criterion. The expected value criterion is appropriate when potential gains or losses are "within bounds," that is, when none of the returns is psychologically overwhelming to the decision maker.

If the decision maker in the example could not tolerate the loss of $50, since it would ruin the business or produce great financial strain, the expected value criterion would not apply. The expected value criterion is an average, and averages obscure. The decision maker who could not tolerate a loss of $50 could never be expected to select pricing strategies A_1 or A_3 because of the probability that each of these could result in such a loss.

There are alternatives to the expected value criterion. One of the more popular approaches is to construct an index that reflects the decision maker's attitude toward risk and to employ the index values in the payoff table. All calculations then proceed as before, but now the criterion is one of expected utility, taking account of the riskiness of the situation rather than of expected value.[7]

Uncertain Payoffs

The consequences in the payoff table were shown as single numbers. Thus, if the skimming price was selected and light demand materialized, the payoff was $100, no more, no less. The more likely situation is that the payoffs would be estimated with some uncertainty, and rather than the single figure of $100, the estimate might be that there is a 50-percent chance of realizing a $100 return, but the return may also go as low as $75 or as high as $125.

An estimate with a range of values can be incorporated in the decision structure. However, such an estimate entails an assessment of the likely returns and the probability associated with each return. The average return, which is then calculated by weighting the returns by the respective probabilities, is entered in the payoff table, and the calculations proceed as before.

Bayesian Analysis and Marketing Research

It is clear from this simplified example that Bayesian analysis has much to offer the decision and research analysts. It facilitates communication between them because of the conceptual structuring of the decision problem it provides, particularly when the tree diagram is constructed. Bayesian analysis is demanding of each of them as well. It demands that decision makers make their judgments clear, both with respect to what they anticipate might happen and also with respect to the probabilities they attach to the states of nature. It also requires that decision makers clarify the alternatives they are considering and the consequences they anticipate for each of the alternatives, given their assessment of the environment. Not all decision makers will be willing to expose their decision calculus in detail.

Bayesian analysis also demands much of the researcher. It requires taking on a computational burden, demonstrating finesse in extracting the decision maker's judgments

---

[7]A number of authors discuss the construction of these utility indices. See, for example, Howard Raiffa, *Decision Analysis: Introductory Lectures on Choices under Uncertainty* (Reading, Mass.: Addison-Wesley, 1968), pp. 51–101, for a particularly helpful discussion. See also Paul J. H. Schoemaker, "The Expected Utility Model: Its Variants, Purposes, Evidence, and Limitations," *Journal of Economic Literature*, 20 (July 1982), pp. 529–563 and Paul J. H. Schoemaker, *Experiments on Decisions Under Risk: The Expected Utility Hypotheses* (Boston: Kluwer-Nijhoff Publishing, 1980).

so that the implicit alternatives and states of nature are completely enumerated and the appropriate decision criterion is used, and paying attention to detail so that the problem is correctly structured and the decision maker's subjective judgments are correctly translated into probabilistic statements.[8]

These problems are not insurmountable, as reported applications attest.[9] While some decision makers might not be willing to employ the entire decision theory apparatus, the fundamental question needs to be asked and answered before research is begun: "Will the research be worth it? Do potential benefits exceed anticipated costs?"

Questions

1. What is the basic nature of a payoff table?

2. What is the role of marketing research with respect to the elements of a payoff table?

3. How is the maximum value of any contemplated research determined?

4. What is meant by perfect information? How is the value of such information determined?

5. Outline the procedure necessary to determine the value of imperfect research information.

6. What is Bayesian analysis? What role does it play in evaluating the contribution of research to the decision problem?

7. What is the difference between objective and subjective probabilities? How is the difference important for business decision making?

8. What is a decision tree? How is it constructed? How is it "solved"?

Applications and Problems

1. Mr. Ventura decided that he was ready to enter into the retail business and was considering opening a shoe store. He was hesitant because the economy was in a recession with high interest rates on loans and low consumer purchasing power. Mrs. Ventura was sure that the store would be successful and convinced her husband that the probability of the store being successful was 70%. Mr. Ventura agreed but was wondering whether he should do some marketing research. If he did the research with the aid of

---

[8]For a review of the evidence regarding the elicitation of subjective probabilities, see Thomas S. Wallsten and David V. Budescu, "Encoding Subjective Probabilities: A Psychological and Psychometric Review," *Management Science,* 29 (February 1983), pp. 151–173.

[9]For specific assessments of the use of decision theory in evaluating contemplated marketing research, see Gert Assmus, "Bayesian Analysis for the Evaluation of Marketing Research Expenditures," *Journal of Marketing Research,* 14 (November 1977), pp. 562–568, and G. S. Albaum, D. S. Tull, and J. Hansen, "The Expected Value of Information: How Widely Is It Used in Marketing Research?" in Neil Beckwith, Michael Houston, Robert Mittelstaedt, Kent B. Monroe, and Scott Ward, eds., *1979 Educators' Conference Proceedings,* (Chicago: American Marketing Association, 1979), pp. 32–34. For a general review of decision theory in decison making, see Robert P. Abelson and Ariel Levi, "Decision Making and Decision Theory" in G. Lindzey and E. Aronson, eds., *Handbook of Social Psychology* (New York: Random House, 1985), pp. 231–309.

some students the cost would be only $500. On the other hand, he could get reliable results from a research agency but this would cost him $2,000.

Assume the following payoff table:

	State of Nature	
	Successful (High Demand)	Not Successful (Low Demand)
Alternative	1	2
Open the Store (A1)	250,000	− 120,000
Do Not Open the Store (A2)	0	0

Also assume the following conditional probabilities of survey results:

Research By:	Conditional Probabilities
Mr. Ventura	$P(Z1/S1) = P(Z2/S2) = .8$
	$P(Z1/S2) = P(Z2/S1) = .2$
Research Agency	$P(Z1/S1) = P(Z2/S2) = .9$
	$P(Z1/S2) = P(Z2/S1) = .1$

*Where Z1: research results indicate high demand or success.
Where Z2: research results indicate low demand or failure.

(a) What is the expected value of each alternative without research? Which alternative is preferred assuming Mr. Ventura wants to maximize expected returns?

(b) What is the expected value of perfect information? What does this indicate?

(c) Revise the prior probabilities to capture the anticipated results by completing the following table.

State of Nature	Prior Probabilities	Conditional Probabilities	Joint Probabilities	Posterior Probabilities

Mr. Ventura's Research

Z1: Research results indicate high demand or success.
  S1: successful
     (high demand)
  S2: unsuccessful
     (low demand)
Z2: Research results indicate low demand or failure.
  S1: successful
     (high demand)
  S2: unsuccessful
     (low demand)

Research Agency

Z1: Research results indicate high demand or success.
  S1: successful
     (high demand)
  S2: unsuccessful
     (low demand)
Z2: Research results indicate low demand or failure.
  S1: successful
     (high demand)
  S2: unsuccessful
     (low demand)

(d) Compute the expected value for the two research options.

(e) Would Mr. Ventura do any research? If yes, which research option would he choose? If no, why not?

2. For Problem 1 prepare the appropriate decision trees for the three options (i) do not do any research, (ii) Mr. Ventura does the necessary research, and (iii) the agency does the necessary research.

3. The Pokerbridge Manufacturing Company, a maker of card table sets, is considering raising the price of one of the company's more popular sets from $34.95 to $39.95. Mr. Deal, the marketing manager, recently attended a conference at which several papers on Bayesian decision theory were presented. Mr. Deal was quite enamored with the technique and thinks it might be appropriate for the pricing decision now facing him. He has called upon you to help him with his analysis. He particularly wants help in determining

    1. whether he should make the price change decision on the basis of the information he now has, or
    2. whether he should secure some marketing research information before making the above decision.

    The company's best projection of the future discounted profits of this item is $300,000 if the price is not changed. If the price is changed, the estimated return is much more uncertain, in that it depends on consumer reaction to the change. If there is little negative reaction, the discounted future returns are projected at $800,000 while they are projected at $400,000 if there is some negative reaction, and $100,000 if there is a strong negative reaction.

    Mr. Deal feels that the most likely state of affairs will be some consumer resistance to the price hike, but that consumer reaction will not be strongly negative and that there is even a possibility of no negative reaction at all to the price increase. When pressed, Mr. Deal attached these probabilities to the various consumer reactions.

    - S1: little or no negative reaction   probability = 0.3
    - S2: some negative reaction   probability = 0.5
    - S3: strong negative reaction   probability = 0.2

    The research being considered by Mr. Deal for reducing the uncertainty surrounding the decision is a small test market, in which the price of the product would be raised to $39.95 and the change in sales monitored. The company has had some previous experience with research of this kind, and although the results are not directly generalizable, they do provide a good indication of what might happen. There have been instances, though, where the test-market results overestimated and other cases where the test market underestimated what happened nationally. Prior experience suggested the following contingencies in particular between eventual market demand and the test-market results.

General Reaction

Test Market Result	S1 Little or None	S2 Some Negative Reaction	S3 Strong Negative Reaction
T1: little change in sales	0.5	0.1	0.1
T2: some sales decrease	0.4	0.7	0.3
T3: significant sales decrease	0.1	0.2	0.6

The entry 0.7 in the second row, second column, suggests, for instance, that 70 percent of the time in which there was some negative reaction to the price boost nationally, there was also some decrease in the quantity sold in the test market; the entry in the third row, second column indicates that 20 percent of the time in which there was some negative reaction nationally, there was a significant sales decrease in the test market; and the entry in the first row, second column indicates that 10 percent of the time there was little change in sales of the product in the test market, although the price boost did occasion some negative reaction when implemented nationally. The costs associated with market-testing the price change total $100,000.

(a) Should Mr. Deal make the price change decision on the basis of the information he has now, or should he pay to have the market-test experiment conducted?

(b) Diagram Mr. Deal's dilemma in the form of a decision tree.

(c) Calculate the value of perfect information to Mr. Deal.

(d) Calculate the value of the market test information to Mr. Deal.

Cases to Part 1

Case 1.1
Big Brothers of Fairfax County

Big Brothers of America is a social service program designed to meet the needs of boys ages six to eighteen from single-parent homes. Most of the boys served by the program live with their mothers and rarely see or hear from their fathers. The purpose of the program is to give these boys the chance to establish a friendship with an interested adult male. Big Brothers of America was founded on the belief that an association with a responsible adult can help program participants become more responsible citizens and better adjusted young men.

The program was started in Cincinnati in 1903. Two years later, the organization was granted its first charter in New York State through the efforts of Mrs. Cornelius Vanderbilt. By the end of World War II, there were 30 Big Brothers agencies. Today there are 300 agencies across the United States, and 120,000 boys currently are matched with Big Brothers.

The Fairfax County chapter of Big Brothers of America was founded in Fairfax in 1966. In 1971, United Way of Fairfax County accepted the program as part of its umbrella organization and now provides about 85 percent of its funding. The remaining 15 percent is raised by the local Big Brothers agency.

Information about the Big Brothers program in Fairfax County reaches the public primarily through newspapers (feature stories and classified advertisements), radio, public service announcements, posters (on buses and in windows of local establishments), and word-of-mouth advertising. The need for volunteers is a key message emanating from these sources. The agency phone number is always included so that people wanting to know more about the program can call for information. Those calling in are given basic information over the telephone and are invited to attend one of the monthly orientation sessions organized by the Big Brothers program staff. At these meetings, men get the chance to talk to other volunteers and to find out what will be expected of them should they decide to join the program. At the end of the session, prospective volunteers are asked to complete two forms. One is an application form and the other is a questionnaire in which the person is asked to describe the type of boy he would prefer to be matched with, as well as his own interests.

The files on potential Little Brothers are then reviewed in an attempt to match boys with the volunteers. A match is made only if both partners agree. The agency stays in close contact with the pair and monitors their progress. The three counselors for the Big Brothers program serve as resources for the volunteer.

The majority of the inquiry calls received by the Fairfax County agency are from women who are interested in becoming Big Sisters or from people desiring information on the Couples Program. Both programs are similar to the Big Brothers program and are administered by it. In fact, of fifty-five calls concerning a recent orientation meeting, only five were from males. Only three of the five callers actually attended the meeting, a typical response.

While the informational campaigns and personal appeals thus seemed to have some impact, the results were also generally disappointing and did little to alleviate the problem of a shortage of volunteer Big Brothers. There are currently 250 boys waiting to be matched with Big Brothers, and the shortage grows weekly.

Big Brothers of Fairfax County believed a lack of awareness and accurate knolwedge could be the cause of the shortage of volunteers. Are there men who would volunteer if only they were made aware of the program and its needs? Or is the difficulty a negative program image? Do people think of Little Brothers as problem children, boys who have been in trouble with the law or who have severe behavioral problems? Or could there be a misconception of the type of man who would make a good Big Brother? Do people have stereotypes with respect to the volunteers—for example, that the typical volunteer is a young, single, professional male?

Questions

1. What is (are) the marketing decision problem(s)?
2. What is (are) the marketing research problem(s)?
3. What types of information would be useful to answer these questions?
4. How would you go about securing this information?

Case 1.2
Supervisory Training at the Management Institute

University of Wisconsin-Extension is the outreach campus of the University of Wisconsin System. Its mission is to extend high-quality education to people who are not necessarily "college students" in the normal sense. The Management Institute (MI) is one of the departments within UW-Extension. It conducts programs aimed at providing education and training in at least a dozen areas of business and not-for-profit management.

The supervisory training area within the Management Institute designs and conducts continuing education training programs for first-level supervisors. The training programs are designed to improve a trainee's managerial, communication, decision-making, and human relation skills. They consequently cover a broad range of topics.

A continuing decline in enrollments in the various programs during the past several years had become a problem of increasing concern to the three supervisory program directors. They were at a loss to explain why, although informal discussions among the supervisors raised a number of questions to which they did not know the answers. Have people's reasons for attending supervisory training programs changed? What are their reasons for attending them? Was the decline caused by economic factors? Was it because of increased competition among continuing education providers? Was it due to the content or structure of MI's programs themselves? Was it due to the way the programs were structured or promoted? Were the programs targeted at the right level of supervisor?

Typically, the major promotion for any program involved mailed brochures that described the content and structure of the course. The mailing list for the brochures was all past attendees of any supervisory training program conducted by the Management Institute.

Questions

1. What is the decision problem?
2. What is (are) the research problem(s)?
3. How would you recommend MI go about addressing the research problem(s)? That is, what data would you collect and how might that data be used to answer the research question(s) posed?

Case 1.3
Bonita Baking Company (A)[1]

Frank Fortunada, Jr, is the sales manager of Bonita Baking Company. Bonita is a moderate-size regional bakery in southern California, specializing in breads and bread products for markets, restaurants, and institutional accounts. Established in 1910 by Frank's grandfather, Vito Fortunada, Bonita bakes and sells a number of well-known brands of bread under licensing agreements. Among these brands are Holsum, Butter-top, and Hillbilly bread and rolls. Since his grandfather's retirement many years ago, Bonita has been run by Frank's father. To this day, everyone refers to them as Frank and Frank, Jr. (except in the latter's presence).

Frank Fortunada, Jr., has been involved in the bread business all of his life. As a boy he cleaned up at the bakery and later drove a route truck while attending high school. After serving four years in the U.S. Navy (as a baker), Frank, Jr., continued to work as a routeman while attending college on a part-time basis. A year after graduating with a degree in marketing from the local state college, Frank's father appointed him retail sales manager, in charge of 65 driver salespeople. Within two years, he was put in charge of both retail and commercial accounts. As such, Fortunada was the ranking marketing person at Bonita Baking, with his father in charge of operations of the bakery.

The Marketing Problem

About ten years ago, Bonita Baking introduced a line of specialty bread under the brand name of Bonita Health Bread. Specialty bread is made from special or mixed grain flour and is heavier than regular bread. National brands that have gained popularity include

---

[1]Source: From: *Cases in Marketing Research* by William G. Zikmund, William J. Lundstrom, and Donald Sciglimpaglia, pp. 3–4 (Chicago: Dryden). Copyright © 1982 by CBS College Publishing. Reprinted by permission of CBS College Publishing.

Roman Meal, Millbrook, and Pepperidge Farm. Not only has specialty breads been a rapidly growing segment of the bread market, but it is a higher gross margin product. Industry trade publications identified the specialty bread consumer as coming from higher income households and as more highly educated than the typical bread consumer.

Fortunada knew that Bonita's specialty breads were high quality and that they should be selling well, but sales figures indicated otherwise. The Bonita Health line was apparently losing market share rapidly to the national brands and to another regional brand, Orowheat, which was the market leader. All, including Bonita Health, were actively promoted with consumer advertising, coupons, and price deals. Also bothersome was the fact that many supermarket chains were also selling their own private brands of specialty bread. Fortunada's salespeople could offer no real insight as to why Bonita Health was doing poorly.

Fortunada decided to do something that had never been attempted at Bonita—to undertake some marketing research. He knew he would have trouble selling the idea to his father, but he also knew that he needed more information. Taking out a pad of paper, Fortunada began making notes as to what he would like to know about Bonita Health's position. Except for his own sales records and the trade publication reports, he decided that he knew very little.

Fortunada knew almost nothing about the size or growth rates of the specialty bread market in his area. He had no idea who bought his brand or those of his competitors, or how much consumers bought and how often. Except for his own experience, he really didn't even know who in the household requested specialty bread or who selected the brand. Another point that troubled him was not knowing the relative awareness of Bonita Health and its image among consumers. Lastly, since he hadn't been on a bread route in some time, Fortunada thought that he had better get to know retailers' attitudes toward the brands and the associated marketing practices.

Questions

1. How would you define the problem at Bonita Baking Company?

2. What are some of the major objectives of any research to be conducted with consumers?

3. What are some major objectives of any research to be conducted with retailers?

4. Why do you think that research has not been done previously at Bonita? Why will Fortunada have difficulty convincing his father of the need for research now?

Case 1.4
The Williams Company

The Williams Company is a regional manufacturer of soft drinks in flavors such as grape, cherry, and orange. Top management has recently become concerned about the erosion of its competitive position and is now considering plans for a summer promotional campaign. The special promotion would cost $100,000, and management is concerned about whether it should contract for an expenditure of this magnitude, since it has little past experience against which to measure the possible success of these efforts. If consumer reaction is extremely favorable (over a 10 percent increase in market share), the company stands to make an incremental profit of $400,000; if it is favorable (5 to 10 percent increase in market share), the projected profits are $100,000; while if it is unfavorable (no appreciable change in market share), the company stands to incur an incremental loss of $100,000—the cost of the campaign. The marketing manager's best estimates of the likelihood of these occurrences are, respectively,

■ S_1: extremely favorable consumer reaction   probability = 0.3

■ S_2: favorable consumer reaction   probability = 0.4

■ S_3: unfavorable consumer reaction   probability = 0.3

The Williams Company is considering contracting for a marketing research study to assess the potential effectiveness of the planned campaign. The research study would cost $25,000 and would include laboratory copy tests to measure attention-getting power and field studies to assess consumer attitudes toward the advertisements. On the basis of its past experience, the Surveys Unlimited research company has suggested the following relationship between its assessments of an ad's effectiveness and the ultimate success of the advertisement.

	Consumer Reaction		
Surveys Unlimited's Experience	**Extremely Favorable**	Favorable	Unfavorable
Strongly positive	0.7	0.2	0.0
Moderately positive	0.3	0.6	0.2
Slightly positive	0.0	0.2	0.8

The table is read row within column. Thus, for example, the entry in the first row, first column indicates that 70 percent of those advertisements that created an extremely favorable customer reaction also elicited a strongly positive reaction in the research.

Questions

1. Should the decision on the special promotion be made without the research, or should the proposed research be conducted? Construct a payoff table for the promotion decision option without the research.

2. Diagram the total decision, including the research option, in the form of a decision tree.

3. Evaluate the value of perfect research information. Evaluate the value of the research information to be provided by Surveys Unlimited.

Part 2

Determination of Sources of Information and Research Design

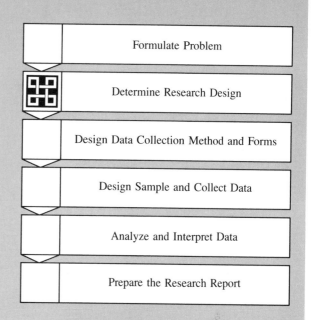

	Formulate Problem
	Determine Research Design
	Design Data Collection Method and Forms
	Design Sample and Collect Data
	Analyze and Interpret Data
	Prepare the Research Report

Part 2 deals with the general nature of designing research so that it addresses the appropriate questions efficiently. Chapter 3 is an overview of the role of the various research designs and also discusses two of the basic designs—the exploratory and the descriptive—at some length, while Chapter 4 discusses the role of experiments in marketing research.

Chapter 3
Research Design

Chapter 1 showed the many problems to which marketing research has been and can be applied. The problems differed in their specificity. Some were clearly of the "if–then" variety, others were more general. This chapter will introduce the notion of research design and discuss basic design types and their interrelationships. Two design types—the exploratory and the descriptive—will be discussed in some detail. Chapter 4 will deal with the nature of causal or experimental designs.

Plan of Action

A **research design** is simply the framework or plan for a study used as a guide in collecting and analyzing data. It is the blueprint that is followed in completing a study. It resembles the architect's blueprint for a house. While it is possible to build a house without a detailed blueprint, doing so will more than likely produce a final product that is somewhat different from what was originally envisioned by the buyer. A certain room is too small; the traffic pattern is poor; some things really wanted are omitted, other less important things are included, and so on. It is also possible to conduct research without a detailed blueprint. The research findings, too, will likely differ widely from what was desired by the consumer or user of the research. "These results are interesting, but they do not solve the basic problem" is a common lament. Further, just as the house built without a blueprint is likely to cost more because of midstream alterations in construction, research conducted without a research design is likely to cost more than research properly executed using a research design.

Thus a research design ensures that the study (1) will be relevant to the problem and (2) will use economical procedures. It would help the student learning research methods if there were a single procedure to follow in developing the framework or if there were a single framework to be learned. Unfortunately, this is not the case.

There is never a single, standard, correct method of carrying out research. Do not wait to start your research until you find out the proper approach, because there are many ways to tackle a problem—some good, some bad, but probably several good ways. There is no single perfect design. A research method for a given problem is not like the solution to a problem in algebra. It is more like a recipe for beef stroganoff; there is no one best recipe.[1]

Rather, there are many research design frameworks, just as there are many unique house designs. Fortunately, though, just as house designs can be broken into basic types (for example, ranch, split level, two-story), research designs can be classified into some basic types. One very useful classification is in terms of the fundamental objective of the research: exploratory, descriptive, or causal.[2]

Types of Research Design

The major emphasis in **exploratory research** is on the discovery of *ideas* and *insights*.[3] The soft drink manufacturer faced with decreased sales might conduct an exploratory study to generate possible explanations. The **descriptive research** study is typically concerned with determining the *frequency* with which something occurs or the relationship between two variables. The descriptive study is typically guided by an initial hypothesis. An investigation of the trends in the consumption of soft drinks with respect to such characteristics as age, sex, geographic location, and so on, would be a descriptive study. A **causal research** design is concerned with determining *cause-and-effect* relationships. Causal studies typically take the form of experiments, since experiments are best suited to determine cause and effect. For instance, our soft drink manufacturer may be interested in ascertaining the effectiveness of different advertising appeals. One way for the company to proceed would be to use different ads in different geographic areas and investigate which ad generated the highest sales. In effect, the company would perform an experiment, and if it was designed properly, the company would be in a position to conclude that one specific appeal caused the higher rate of sales.

Having stated the basic general purpose of each major type of research design, three important caveats are in order. First, although the suggested classification of design types is useful for gaining insight into the research process, the distinctions are not absolute. Any given study may serve several purposes. Nevertheless, certain types of research designs are better suited for some purposes than others. The crucial tenet of research is that *the design of the investigation should stem from the problem.* Each of these types is appropriate to specific kinds of problems.

Second, in the remainder of this chapter and in the next chapter, we shall discuss in more detail each of the design types. The emphasis will be on their *basic characteristics* and *generally fruitful approaches.* Whether or not the designs are useful in a given problem setting depends on how imaginatively they are applied. Architects can be taught basic design principles; whether they then design attractive, well-built houses depends on how they apply these principles. So it is with research. The general characteristics of each design can be taught. Whether they are productive in a given situation depends

---

[1] Julian L. Simon, *Basic Research Methods in Social Science: The Art of Empirical Investigation* (New York: Random House, 1969), p. 4.

[2] Claire Selltiz, Lawrence S. Wrightsman, and Stuart W. Cook, *Research Methods in Social Relations,* 3rd ed. (New York: Holt, Rinehart and Winston, 1976), pp. 90–91.

[3] The basic purposes are those suggested by Selltiz, Wrightsman, and Cook, *Research Methods.*

Figure 3.1
Relationship among the Research Designs

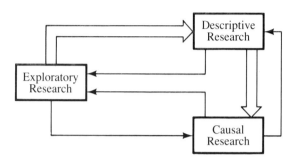

on how skillfully they are applied. There is no single best way to proceed, just as there is no single best floor plan for, say, a ranch-type house. It all depends on the specific problem to be solved. Research analysts, then, need an understanding of the basic designs so that they can modify them to suit specific purposes.

Third, the three basic designs can be looked at as stages in a continuous process. Figure 3.1 shows the interrelationships. Exploratory or formulative studies are often seen as the initial step. When researchers begin an investigation, it stands to reason that they lack a great deal of knowledge about the problem. Consider: ''Market share of Brand X bourbon has been decreasing; why?'' This statement is too broad to serve as a guide for research. To narrow and refine it would logically be accomplished with exploratory research, in which the emphasis would be on finding tentative explanations for the sales decrease. These tentative explanations or hypotheses would then serve as specific guides for descriptive or causal studies. Suppose the tentative explanation that emerged was, ''Brand X is a heavy bourbon. More people are drinking socially, and a lighter taste is preferred by the social drinker. It stands to reason that our market share would decrease.'' The hypothesis that there are now more social drinkers could be examined in a descriptive study of trends in the consumption of alcoholic beverages.

Suppose the descriptive study did support the hypothesis. The company might then wish to determine whether the social drinker did, in fact, prefer a lighter taste in alcoholic beverages through some kind of taste test, a causal design. Each stage in the process thus represents the investigation of a more detailed statement of the problem, and although we have suggested that the sequence would be from exploratory to descriptive to causal research, alternative sequences might occur. The ''social drinkers prefer lighter taste beverages'' hypothesis might be so generally accepted that the sequence would be from exploratory directly to causal. The potential for the reverse flow also exists. A causal hypothesis, say, might be disproved, at which point the analyst might need another descriptive study or even another exploratory study. Also, not every research problem will begin with an exploratory study. It depends on the specificity with which the research problem can be formulated. A general, vague statement leads naturally to exploratory work, while a specific cause-and-effect hypothesis opts for experimental work.

Research Realities 3.1, for instance, lists some of the individual projects that were conducted by PepsiCo to support the conception and introduction of its very successful O'Grady's potato chips. In this instance, the examination of the potato chip category with respect to market shares and trends, the ideation sessions, and the focus groups to help develop meaningful ways to describe a thick potato chip could all be classified as exploratory research. The diary panel that was set up to measure trial and repeat purchase behavior would be considered descriptive, while the market simulation test and the test of the commercial would be considered causal.

Exploratory Research

As previously stated, the general objective in exploratory research is to gain insights and ideas. The exploratory study is particularly helpful in breaking broad, vague problem statements into smaller, more precise subproblem statements, hopefully in the form of specific hypotheses. A **hypothesis** is a statement that specifies how two or more measurable variables are related.[4] A good hypothesis carries clear implications for testing stated relationships. In the early stages of research, we usually lack sufficient understanding of the problem to formulate a specific hypothesis. Further, there are often several tentative explanations for a given marketing phenomenon. For example: sales are off because our price is too high; our dealers or sales representatives are not doing the job they should; our advertising is weak, and so on. Exploratory research can be used to establish priorities in studying these competing explanations. The priorities would be established because a particular hypothesis discovered in the exploratory study appeared to be promising. They might also arise because the exploratory study generates information about the practical possibilities of researching specific, conjectural statements.

The exploratory study is also used to increase the analyst's familiarity with the problem. This is particularly true when the analyst is new to the problem arena (for example, a marketing research consultant going to work for a company for the first time).

The exploratory study may be used to clarify concepts. For instance, management is considering a change in service policy that will, hopefully, result in improved dealer satisfaction. An exploratory study could be used to clarify the notion of dealer satisfaction and to develop a method by which dealer satisfaction could appropriately be measured.

One problem with which the Reagan administration had to contend when it tried to change the tax code to make it more fair, for example, was to determine what fairness in the tax code means. Several studies had supported the notion that a majority of Americans believed the system then in place was unfair; 82 percent responding to an Internal Revenue Service–sponsored survey felt this way, and two-thirds responding to

---

[4]See Fred N. Kerlinger, *Foundations of Behavioral Research*, 3rd ed. (New York: Holt, Rinehart and Winston, 1986), pp. 17–20, for a discussion of the criteria of good hypotheses and of the value of hypotheses in guiding research.

Research Realities 3.1

Research Supporting the Development and Introduction of O'Grady's Potato Chips

As a first step, Frito-Lay examined whether or not a consumer need existed. An inventory was made of the potato chip category. There were relatively few options out there. Potato chips on the market were either flat or ridged, unflavored or cheese flavor or sour cream and onion. Yet, Frito-Lay knew that consumers seek variety and they often differentiate between products on a textural basis.

At the corporate level, a number of hurdle criteria were set: a $100 million-plus business, it had to add incremental volume, it had to have broad national appeal, and it had to be a unique, not easily replicated product.

To start with, new product ideas were developed through a number of sources; ideation sessions were conducted with scientists, the marketing department, home economists, and consumers. Recipe books were collected, and the industry's packaged potato snack products were purchased from stores and studied for differentiation opportunities, for needs that weren't being filled.

Four distinct product ideas resulted from this exercise: a "better Pringles," which was dropped on judgment due to Pringles' lack of success; a "potato Frito," a thicker, processed chip that later became "crunch chips"; a super-crispy chip that became Ta-Tos; and a bite-sized, latticed chip—a small, thin, fragile O'Grady's forerunner. The ideas were exposed to consumers through product evaluation groups, which provided direction on product refinement and positioning issues. The results suggested that development should continue on all three, although the crunch chips and the Ta-Tos were the most well received at this stage. The O'Grady's product was de-emphasized because consumers saw it as too light and thin.

While the Ta-Tos and Crunchy's were well received and eventually went to test market, they did not fit with the business objective of being a new potato chip. Despite its consumer rejection, the lattice chip, which was to become O'Grady's, offered the most differentiable

potato chip. O'Grady's was then taken from thin and crispy to the other end of the spectrum—thicker, heavier, and crunchier. The lattice cut gave it a unique appearance. The thickness gave it a unique texture (crunchiness) and taste (more potato taste). Home-use tests confirmed that the shift to thickness was positive, and focus group research was conducted to help develop meaningful, motivating ways of describing a thick potato chip. Crunchy, hearty, and more potato taste seemed to be most appealing.

From a market simulation test, the interest generating ability of the concept and the fit of the product with the concept, as well as the trial and repeat and volume potential of the brand, were determined. Only two sizes and a plain flavor were tested. The results were positive but indicated the product wouldn't surpass the corporate hurdle rate. So, an additional au gratin cheese flavor was developed and was selected via further home-use tests. At the same time, focus group copy development research led Frito-Lay to emphasize or embody simplicity, small-town values, implied wholesomeness, and heartiness. This commercial, opening with a potato plant, was found to be positively intrusive and memorable and to elicit positive consumer reactions with appropriate images being conveyed.

While in test market a full range of research was conducted to monitor O'Grady's performance. An awareness and trial study was conducted. A diary panel was set up to measure trial, repeat, and depth of repeat. An image study was set up to make sure the desired positioning was conveyed. And, finally, distribution checks helped monitor distribution and out-of-stock levels. These test market data allowed for fine tuning of the national program and also provided standards against which to measure O'Grady's performance during expansion.

Source: Keynote talk by Norman Heller, president and chief executive officer, PepsiCo Wines & Spirits International, at the Association of National Advertisers' New Product Marketing Workshop, October 16, 1984. Reprinted with permission of Norman Heller. See also "Spotting Competitive Edges Begets New Product Success," *Marketing News*, 18 (December 21, 1984), p. 4.

a Louis Harris poll were "fed up" with the current system because of how unfair it was. "But," as Kent Smith, who headed a study of taxpayer compliance for the American Bar Association, commented, "the polls don't explain precisely why people think the current system is unfair. We've been frustrated by the way the fairness questions have been asked . . . Is it tax enforcement that bothers people? Tax rates? The way laws are written? Tax avoidance by other people? Or is it because they believe their taxes are poorly spent by government?"[5] Exploratory research would play a particularly important role in clarifying a concept like this.

In sum, an exploratory study is used for any or all of the following purposes:[6]

- formulating a problem for more precise investigation or for developing hypotheses;
- establishing priorities for further research;
- gathering information about the practical problems of carrying out research on particular conjectural statements;
- increasing the analyst's familiarity with the problem;
- clarifying concepts.

In general, exploratory research is appropriate to any problem about which little is known. Exploratory research then becomes the foundation for a good study.

Because knowledge is lacking when an inquiry is begun, exploratory studies are characterized by *flexibility* with respect to the methods used for gaining insight and developing hypotheses. "Formal design is conspicuous by its absence in exploratory studies."[7] Exploratory studies rarely use detailed questionnaires or involve probability sampling plans. Rather, investigators frequently change the research procedure as the vaguely defined initial problem is transformed into one with more precise meaning. Investigators very much follow where their noses lead them in an exploratory study. Ingenuity, judgment, and good luck inevitably play a part in leading to the one or two key hypotheses that, it is hoped, will account for the phenomenon. Notwithstanding the flexibility, research experience has demonstrated that literature surveys, experience surveys, and the analysis of selected cases are particularly productive in exploratory research.[8]

Literature Search

One of the quickest and cheapest ways to discover hypotheses is in the work of others, through a **literature search.** The search may involve conceptual literature, trade literature, or, quite often, published statistics.

---

[5]Alan Murray, "To Revamp Tax Code, Reagan Will Tap Belief That System Is Unfair," *Wall Street Journal,* 65 (April 15, 1985), p. 21.

[6]Selltiz, Wrightsman, and Cook, *Research Methods,* p. 91.

[7]Harper W. Boyd, Ralph Westfall, and Stanley F. Stasch, *Marketing Research: Text and Cases,* 6th ed. (Homewood, Ill.: Irwin, 1985), p. 40.

[8]Selltiz, Wrightsman, and Cook, *Research Methods;* Chapter 4 has a particularly informative discussion of the types of research that are productive at the exploratory stages of an investigation. Our treatment follows theirs closely.

Stouffer's, for example, relied very heavily on the search of a variety of literature and published statistics when developing its highly successful Lean Cuisine low-calorie frozen entree line. "After studying medical and consumer literature for about seven years, Stouffer launched an intensive study of the entire diet food market . . . Consumer media were studied to determine what people were buying, reading and doing about their diet. Stouffer scrutinized trends such as jogging."[9]

The literature that is searched depends, naturally, on the problem being addressed. For example, a search of conceptual literature would be warranted for a firm that feels its field sales force is largely dissatisfied. The search would include works on psychology, sociology, and personnel, in addition to marketing journals. The focus would be on the factors determining employee satisfaction–dissatisfaction. The analyst would keep a keen eye out for those factors also found in the company's environment. The question of how to measure an employee's satisfaction would also be researched at the same time.

Suppose the problem was one that typically triggers much marketing research: "Sales are off; why?" Exploratory insights into this problem could easily and cheaply be gained by analyzing published data and trade literature. Such an analysis would quickly indicate whether the problem was an industry problem or a firm problem. Very different research is in order if the firm's sales are down, but (1) the company's market share is up, since industry sales are down further; (2) the company's market share has remained stable; or (3) the company's market share has declined. The last situation would trigger an investigation of the firm's marketing-mix variables, while the first condition would suggest an analysis to determine why industry sales are off. The great danger in omitting exploratory research is obvious from the above example; without the analysis of secondary data as a guide, there is a great danger of researching the wrong "why."

A company's own internal data should be included in the literature examined in exploratory research, as Mosinee Paper Company found to its pleasant surprise. The company was contemplating dropping one of its products because of its dismal sales performance. Before doing so, though, the company tallied sales of the product by salesperson and found that only a single salesperson was selling that specific grade of industrial paper. Upon further investigation, Mosinee discovered how the buyers "were using the paper—an application that had been known only to the one salesman and his customers. This information enabled management to educate its other salesmen as to the potential market for the paper and sales rose substantially."[10]

It is important to remember that in a literature search, as in any exploratory research, the major emphasis is on the discovery of ideas and tentative explanations of the phenomenon and not on demonstrating which explanation is *the* explanation. The demonstration is better left to descriptive and causal research. Thus, the analyst must be alert to the hypotheses that can be derived from available material, both published material and the company's internal records.

---

[9]Anna Sobczynski, "Reading the Consumer's Mind," *Advertising Age,* 55 (May 3, 1984), p. M16. See also Kevin Higgins, "Meticulous Planning Pays Dividends at Stouffer's," *Marketing News,* 17 (October 28, 1983), pp. 1 and 20.

[10]Jon G. Udell and Gene R. Laczniak, *Marketing in an Age of Change* (New York: John Wiley & Sons, 1981), p. 154.

Experience Survey

The **experience survey,** sometimes called the *key informant survey,* attempts to tap the knowledge and experience of those familiar with the general subject being investigated. In studies concerned with the marketing of a product, anyone who has any association with the marketing effort is a potential source of information. This would include the top executives of the company, sales manager, product manager, and sales representatives. It would also include wholesalers and retailers who handle the product as well as consumers who use the product. It might even include individuals who are not part of the chain of distribution but who might, nevertheless, possess some insight into the phenomenon. For example, a publisher of a children's book investigating a sales decrease gained valuable insights by talking with librarians and schoolteachers. These discussions indicated that an increased use of library facilities, both public and school, coincided with the product's sales decline. These increases were, in turn, attributed to a very sizable increase in library holdings of children's books resulting from federal legislation that provided money for this purpose.

Usually, a great many people know something about the general subject of any given problem. However, not all of them should be contacted.

Research economy dictates that the respondents in an experience survey be carefully selected. The aim of the experience survey is to obtain insight into the relationships between variables rather than to get an accurate picture of current practices or a simple consensus as to best practices. One is looking for provocative ideas and useful insights, not for the statistics of the profession. Thus the respondents must be chosen because of the likelihood that they will offer the contributions sought. In other words, a selected *sample of people working in the area is called for.*[11]

One *does not,* therefore, use a probability sample in an experience survey. It is a waste of time to interview those who have little competence or little relevant experience. It is also a waste of time to interview those who cannot articulate their experience and knowledge. It is important, though, to include people with differing points of view. The following were all interviewed with varying degrees of success when the children's books sales decline was being researched: company executives, key people in the product group, sales representatives, managers of retail outlets in which the books were sold, teachers, and librarians.

The interviews were all unstructured and informal. The emphasis in each interview among those immediately concerned with the distribution of the product was "How do you explain the sales decrease? In your opinion, what is needed to reverse the downward slide?"[12] Most of the time in each interview was then devoted to exploring in detail the various rationales and proposed solutions. A number of sometimes conflicting hypotheses emerged. This provided the researchers with an opportunity to "bounce" some

---

[11]Selltiz, Wrightsman, and Cook, *Research Methods,* p. 94.

[12]Selltiz, Wrightsman, and Cook suggest it is often useful in an exploratory study to orient questions towards "what works." That is, they recommend that questions be of the following form: "If (a given effect) is desired, what influences or what methods will, in your experience, be most likely to produce it?", p. 95.

of the hypotheses off groups with differing vantage points and, in the process, get a feel for which of the hypotheses would be most fruitful to research. The interviews with librarians and teachers were divorced from the immediate problem. Here the emphasis was on discovering changes in children's reading habits.

The respondents were given a great deal of freedom in choosing the factors to be discussed. This is consistent with the notion that the emphasis in exploratory research is on developing tentative explanations and not on demonstrating the viability of a given explanation.

This emphasis, as well as the conduct of the experience survey, is reflected in the experience of an industrial goods manufacturer who used this technique to gain insight into a declining sales situation.

After several years of declining revenues followed ten years of revenue and profit growth, the firm's board of directors questioned the advisability of continuing with one line of business. A review of internal sales records revealed that their market for the service line was limited to approximately thirty large packaged goods manufacturers. No significant external secondary data sources were located. Executives of the firm were then asked to identify the three most knowledgeable persons in the country with respect to the service line characteristics, its market, and the capabilities of competitive suppliers. All three persons nominated were executives of present or past customers of the firm. Appointments for personal interviews were made with each nominee by telephone, using the firm's president as a reference.

Each of the three personal interviews were conducted at the informant's place of business, and lasted from 1½ to 3½ hours. . . . The sessions ranged over a wide variety of topics. Informants were asked to assess the past, current, and probable future developments of the service line, the market, and the comparative strengths and weaknesses of the major suppliers of the service line, including the research sponsor.

The findings . . . revealed that there had been no decline in market activity during the past two years. There had been, however, a concerted effort by a number of packaged goods manufacturers to divert business to two new service suppliers during the period. This was done to assure additional sources of supply and capacity in order to handle a significant expansion of demand that was expected to occur within two years. As a result, established suppliers were allocated less business during the period but could expect a resumption of their previous growth in the near future. The manufacturers were reluctant to divulge these plans to the established suppliers for fear they would add excess capacity and act to limit the competitiveness of the new suppliers.[13]

---

[13]William E. Cox, Jr., *Industrial Marketing Research* (New York: John Wiley and Sons, 1979), pp. 25–26. For further discussion about the general conduct and uses of experience surveys, see Michael J. Houston, "The Key Informant Technique: Marketing Applications," in Thomas V. Greer, ed., *Conceptual and Methodological Foundations of Marketing* (Chicago: American Marketing Association, 1974), pp. 305–308; John Siedler, "On Using Informants: A Key Technique for Collecting Qualitative Data and Controlling Measurement Error in Organization Analysis," *American Sociological Review,* 39 (December 1974), pp. 816–831; Lynn W. Phillips, "Assessing Measurement Error in Key Informant Reports: A Methodological Note on Organizational Analysis in Marketing," *Journal of Marketing Research,* 18 (November 1981), pp. 395–415; George John and Torger Reve, "The Reliability and Validity of Key Informant Data from Dyadic Relationships in Marketing Channels" *Journal of Marketing Research,* 19 (November 1982), pp. 517–524.

The insight from these three interviews was used to focus further personal interviews investigating its general truth, and the notion of continued growth was indeed supported.

One very common type of experience survey is a focus group session among users or potential users of a product. Stouffer's, for example, used focus groups among panels of consumers to find out what dieters did not like about diet meals when developing their Lean Cuisine line. These very informal, loosely structured group discussions surfaced four common objections: the food did not look good, it did not taste good, it wasn't filling, and it was boring in variety and appearance.[14] The four objections served to stimulate the company's thinking with respect to the product's composition and positioning objectives.

Analysis of Selected Cases

The **analysis of selected cases** is sometimes referred to as the analysis of "insight-stimulating examples." By either label, the approach involves the *intensive study of selected cases* of the phenomenon under investigation. Examination of existing records, observation of the occurrence of the phenomenon, unstructured interviewing, or some other approach may be used. The focus may be on entities (individual people or institutions) or groups of entities (sales representatives or distributors in various regions).

The method is characterized by several features.[15] First, the attitude of the investigator is key. The proper attitude is one of alert receptivity, of seeking explanations rather than testing explanations. The investigator is likely to make frequent changes in direction as new information emerges. This may include the search for new cases. More often it will mean a change in the data collected in a given case. Second, the success of the method depends heavily on the investigator's integrative powers. The analyst must be able to assemble many diverse bits of information into a unified interpretation. Finally, the method is characterized by its intensity. The analyst attempts to obtain sufficient information to characterize and explain both the unique features of the case being studied and the features it has in common with other cases.

In one study to improve the productivity of the sales force of a particular company, the investigator studied intensively two or three of the best sales representatives and two or three of the worst. Data was collected on the background and experience of each representative and then several days were spent making sales calls with them. As a result, a hypothesis was developed. It was that checking the stock of retailers and suggesting items on which they were low were the most important differences between the successful and the poor sales representatives.[16]

In this example, the key insight good sales representatives had in common, and in which they differed from poor sales representatives, was that they checked retailer inventory.

---

[14]The purpose, design, and conduct of focus groups are discussed more fully in Chapter 6.

[15]These features are detailed further in Selltiz, Wrightsman, and Cook, *Research Methods*, pp. 98–99. See also Thomas V. Bonoma, "Case Research in Marketing: Opportunities, Problems, and a Process," *Journal of Marketing Research*, 22 (May 1985), pp. 199–208.

[16]Boyd, Westfall, and Stasch, *Marketing Research*, p. 51.

Some situations that are particularly productive of hypotheses are:

1. Cases reflecting changes and, in particular, abrupt changes. The adjustment of a market to the entrance of a new competitor can be quite revealing of the structure of an industry, for example.

2. Cases reflecting extremes of behavior. The example of the best and worst sales representatives was cited above. Similarly, if one wanted to gain some idea of what factors account for the variation in company territory performance, one would be well advised to compare the best and worst territories rather than looking at all territories.

3. Cases reflecting the order in which events occurred over time. For example, in the territory performance question, it may be that in one territory sales are handled by a branch office where they were formerly handled by a manufacturer's agent, whereas in another the sales branch office replaced an industrial distributor.

Which cases will be most valuable depends, of course, on the problem in question. It is generally true, though, that cases that display *sharp contrasts* or have *striking features* are most useful. This is because minute differences are usually difficult to discern. Thus, instead of trying to determine what distinguishes the average case from the slightly above-average case, we contrast the best and worst to magnify whatever differences may exist.

Descriptive Research

A great deal of marketing research can be considered descriptive research. Descriptive research is used when the purpose is:

1. To describe the characteristics of certain groups. For example, based on information gathered from known users of our particular product, we might attempt to develop a profile of the ''average user'' with respect to income, sex, age, educational level, and so on.

2. To estimate the proportion of people in a specified population who behave in a certain way. We might be interested, say, in estimating the proportion of people within a specified radius of a proposed shopping complex who would shop at the center.

3. To make specific predictions. We might be interested in predicting the level of sales for each of the next five years so that we could plan for the hiring and training of new sales representatives.

Descriptive research encompasses an array of research objectives. However, the fact that a study is a descriptive study does not mean it is simply a fact-gathering expedition.

Facts do not lead anywhere. Indeed, facts, as facts, are the commonest, cheapest, and most useless of all commodities. Anyone with a questionnaire can gather thousands of facts a day—and probably not find much real use for them. What makes facts practical and valuable is the glue of explanation and understanding, the framework of theory, the tie-rod of conjecture. Only when facts can be fleshed to a skeletal theory do they become meaningful in the solution of problems.[17]

The researcher should not fall prey to the temptation of beginning a descriptive research study with the vague thought that the data collected should be interesting. A good descriptive study presupposes much prior knowledge about the phenomenon studied. It rests on one or more specific hypotheses. These conjectural statements guide the research in specific directions. In this respect, a descriptive study design is very different from an exploratory study design. Whereas an exploratory study is characterized by its flexibility, descriptive studies can be considered rigid. Descriptive studies require a *clear specification* of the *who, what, when, where, why,* and *how* of the research.

Consider the chain of food convenience stores planning to open a new outlet. The company wants to determine how people come to patronize the new outlet. Consider some of the questions that would need to be answered before data collection for this descriptive study could begin. Who is to be considered a patron? Anyone who enters the store? What if they do not buy anything but just participate in the grand-opening prize giveaway? Perhaps a patron should be defined as anyone who purchases anything from the store. Should patrons be defined on the basis of the family unit or should they be defined as individuals, even though the individuals come from the same family? What characteristics of these patrons should be measured? Are we interested in their age and sex, or perhaps in where they live and how they came to know about our store? When shall we measure them, while they are shopping or later? Should the study take place during the first weeks of operation of the store or should the study be delayed until the situation has stabilized somewhat? Certainly if we are interested in word-of-mouth influence, we must wait at least until that influence has a chance to operate. Where shall we measure the patrons? Should it be in the store, immediately outside of the store, or should we attempt to contact them at home? Why do we want to measure them? Are we going to use these measurements to plan promotional strategy? In that case the emphasis might be on measuring how people become aware of the store. Or are we going to use them as a basis for locating other stores? In that case the emphasis might shift more to determining the trading area of the store. How shall we measure them? Shall we use a questionnaire or shall we observe their purchasing behavior? If we use a questionnaire, what form will it take? Will it be highly structured? Will it be in the form of a scale? How will it be administered? By telephone? By mail? Perhaps by personal interview?

These questions are not the only ones that would be or should be asked. Certainly, some of the answers will be implicit in the hypothesis or hypotheses that guide the descriptive research. Others, though, will not be obvious. The researcher will only be able to specify them after some labored thought or even after a small pilot or exploratory study. In either case, the researcher is well advised to delay collecting that first item of

---

[17]Robert Ferber, Donald F. Blankertz, and Sidney Hollander, Jr., *Marketing Research* (New York: The Ronald Press Co., copyright 1964), p. 153. See also, "Marketing Research Needs Validated Theories," *Marketing News,* 17 (January 21, 1983), p. 14. For an alternative view, see Raymond J. Lawrence, "To Hypothesize or Not to Hypothesize? The Correct 'Approach' to Survey Research," *Journal of the Market Research Society,* 24 (October 1982), pp. 335–343.

Table 3.1
Dummy Table: Store Preference by Age

Age	Prefer A	Prefer B	Prefer C
Less than 30			
30–39			
40 or more			

information with which to test the hypotheses until clear judgments of the who, what, when, where, why, and how of descriptive research have been made.

The researcher should also delay data collection until how the data are to be analyzed has been clearly determined. Ideally one would have a set of dummy tables developed before beginning the collection process. A **dummy table** is a table that is used to catalog the data collected. It is a statement of how the analysis will be structured and conducted. It is complete in all respects save for filling in the actual numbers, that is, it contains a title, headings, and specific categories for the variables making up the table. All that remains after collecting the data is to count the number of cases of each type. Table 3.1 illustrates a table that might be used by a women's specialty store investigating whether it is serving a particular age segment and whether this segment differs from that of its competitors.

Note that the table lists the particular age segments the proprietor wishes to compare. It is crucial that this specification of variables and categories be made before data collection begins. The statistical tests that will be used to uncover the relationship between age and store preference should also be specified before data collection begins. Inexperienced researchers often question the need for such hard, detailed decisions before collecting the data. They assume that delaying these decisions until after the data are collected will somehow make them easier. Just the opposite is true, as any experienced researcher will attest.

Most difficult for the beginning researcher to anticipate will be the analytical problems he may face after the data are gathered. He tends to believe that a wide variety of facts will be enough to solve anything. Only after struggling with sloppy, stubborn, and intractable facts, with data not adequate for the testing of hypotheses and with data that are interesting but incapable of supporting practical recommendations for action will he be fully aware that the big "mistakes" of research usually are made in the early stages. Each definition of a problem or problem variable will create different facts or findings, and a formulation once made serves to restrict the scope of analysis. No problem is definitively formulated until the researcher can specify how he will make his analysis and how the results will contribute to a practical solution.[18]

---

[18]Ferber, Blankertz, and Hollander, *Marketing Research*, p. 171.

Table 3.2

Output Planning Module for Several Questions in a Food Study

Question Number(s) and Variable Name(s)	Primary Analysis and Information Value
Questions #5.0 and 5.1 asking number of packages of hot dogs consumed per month by household and usual number of hot dogs per package plus number of loose links per month.	I. *Frequency Distribution:* Indicates number of dogs used per month for all respondents. These will be coded into three categories: *Light, Moderate, and Heavy Users.*

Information Content of Question(s)

Computer coding will multiply number of packages per month by dogs per package plus links to obtain the total household usage of hot dogs per month.

II. *Relation to Demographics:* Usage types will be cross-tabulated with size of household, age of household shopper, total income, sex, and education of shopper in order to identify the characteristics of the three user segments. Statistic—Chi square.

Reasons for Including Question(s)

These questions provide information needed in order to segment the population of hot dog users into submarkets based on usage level. Usage volume can serve as an excellent predictor of future purchase patterns, may be related to interest in proposed new hot dog product and may support media selection that will reach high-usage households at least cost.

III. *Relation to Price:* Usage will be systematically related to responses on purchase probability under different pricing conditions. This will tell us the importance of price for the user segments and help in estimating volume of sales at different price points.

Additional Analysis and Information Value

Relation to Importance of Product Features: User segments will be compared in terms of their mean responses to the 10-point importance-attribute scales including package, brand name, quality, contents, taste, texture, smell, shape, and color of the hot dogs. This will provide information on the relative importance of attributes and assist in formulating advertising approaches for the target segments.

Source: Benjamin D. Sackmary, "Data Analysis & Output Planning Improve Value of Marketing Research," *Marketing News,* 17 (January 21, 1983), p. 6. Published by the American Marketing Association.

Once the data have been collected and analysis is begun, it is too late to lament, "If only we had collected information on that variable" or "If only we had measured the Y variable using a finer scale." Rectifying such mistakes at this time is next to impossible. Rather, the analyst must account for such contingencies when planning the study. Structuring the tables used to analyze the data makes such planning easier.

An alternative way of ensuring that the information collected in a descriptive study will address the objectives motivating it is to specify in advance the objective each question addresses, the reason the question is included, and the analysis in which the question will be used, although not going as far as laying out all of the cross-classification tables. Table 3.2, for example, contains these specifications for several questions in a study for a meat packer investigating the market potential for a new sport-related hot dog. While output planning like this is extremely valuable, there is added merit in specifying all anticipated dummy tables in advance, as we have suggested previously. The dummy tables are particularly valuable in providing clues on how to phrase the individual questions and code the responses.

Figure 3.2
Classification of Descriptive Studies

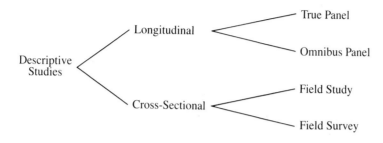

Figure 3.2 is an overview of the various types of descriptive studies. The basic division is between longitudinal and cross-sectional designs. The **cross-sectional study** is the most common and most familiar. It typically involves a sample of elements from the population of interest. A number of characteristics of the elements or sample members are measured once. **Longitudinal studies,** on the other hand, involve panels. A **panel** is a fixed sample of elements. The elements may be stores, dealers, individuals, or other entities. The panel or sample remains relatively constant through time, although there are periodic additions to replace dropouts or to keep it representative. The sample members in a panel are measured repeatedly, as contrasted to the one-time measurement in a cross-sectional study. Both cross-sectional and longitudinal studies have weaknesses and advantages. Since they are both common, let us briefly review the principal advantages and disadvantages of each.

Longitudinal Analysis

True longitudinal studies rely on panel data and panel methods. As mentioned, a panel is a fixed sample of subjects that is measured repeatedly. There are two types of panels. The older type relies on repeated measurements of the same variables. For example, National Purchase Diary Panel (NPD) maintains a consumer panel of 13,000 families.[19] Each family records its purchases of each of a number of products monthly. Similarly, the Nielsen Retail Store Audit involves a sample of 10,000 stores.[20] Each store is checked monthly for its sales of each of a number of products. While the operations of these panels will be detailed when discussing secondary sources of information in Chapter 5, the important point to note now is that each sample member is measured with respect to the same characteristics at each time, purchases in the NPD panel and sales in the Nielsen data.

---

[19]*We Make the Market Perfectly Clear* (New York: National Purchase Diary Panel, Inc., undated).

[20]*Management with the Nielsen Retail Index System* (Northbrook, Ill.: A. C. Nielsen Company, 1980).

In recent years, a new type of panel, called the **omnibus panel,** has sprung up. In an omnibus panel, a sample of elements is still selected and maintained, but the information collected from the members varies. At one time, it may be attitudes with respect to a new product. At another time, the panel members might be asked to evaluate alternative advertising copy. In each case, a sample might be selected from the larger group, which is in turn a sample of the population. The subsample might be drawn randomly. More than likely, though, participants with the desired characteristics will be chosen from a total panel. For example, the Parker Pen Company maintains a panel of 1,100 individuals, who were chosen because they expressed some interest in writing instruments and, of course, because of their willingness to participate. Parker Pen will often use selected members of this panel to evaluate new writing instruments. If the new instrument is a fountain pen, they will often choose individuals who prefer fountain pens to test the products. Those chosen and the information sought will vary from project to project.

R. J. Reynolds, on the other hand, uses ability criteria rather than interest criteria in selecting its panel members. The company maintains a panel of 350 of its employees whose job it is to provide information for quality control and new brand development.[21] Only those employees who can successfully pass a screening test in which they smoke three cigarettes and can then identify which two were alike are allowed in the panel. As members of the panel, the employees are called upon to smoke, sniff, feel, and draw on unlit cigarettes and then provide their sensory evaluations. While the information that is collected is fairly standardized, the cigarettes being evaluated vary from test to test.

The distinction between the traditional panel and the omnibus panel is important. True longitudinal analysis, also called time series analysis, can only be performed on the first type of data, repeated measurements of the same entities over time. We shall see why when we discuss the method of analysis unique to panel data—the turnover table. The turnover table can only be used when individuals and variables are held constant through time. This is not to deny the value of the newer types of panels. Rather, the purpose is simply to erect a caution flag, because in other respects (for example, sample design, information collection, and so forth) both types of panels have about the same advantages and disadvantages when compared to cross-sectional studies. Consequently, we shall treat both types together when discussing these general advantages.

Probably the single most important advantage of panel data is analytical. Suppose we are presently subscribing to the type of service that generates consumer purchase data from a panel of 1,000 families. Suppose further that we are interested in determining the impact of a recent package design for our Brand A and that our brand has two main competitors, B and C, and a number of other smaller competitors. Let us classify all these miscellaneous brands in the single category, Brand D, and let us consider the performance of our brand at time period t_0, before the change, and time period t_1, after the package change.

---

[21]Margaret Loeb, "Testers of Cigarettes Find On-Job Puffing Really Isn't a Drag," *Wall Street Journal*, 64 (August 22, 1984), pp. 1 and 15.

Table 3.3
Number of Families in Panel Purchasing Each Brand

Brand Purchased	At Time t_0	At Time t_1
A	200	250
B	300	270
C	350	330
D	150	150
Total	1,000	1,000

We could perform several types of analyses on these data.[22] We could look at the proportion of those in the panel who bought our brand in period t_0. We could also calculate the proportion of those who bought our brand in period t_1. Suppose these calculations generated the data shown in Table 3.3. Table 3.3. indicates that the package change was successful. Brand A's market share increased from 20 percent to 25 percent. Further, Brand A seemed to make its gains at the expense of its two major competitors, whose market shares decreased.

But that is not the whole story or even a completely accurate picture of the market changes that occurred. Look at what happens when, in assessing the impact of the package change, the identity of the sample members is maintained. Since we have repeated measures of the same individuals, we can count the number of families who bought Brand A in both periods, those who bought B or C or one of the miscellaneous brands in both periods, and those who switched brands between the two periods. Suppose Table 3.4 resulted from these tabulations. Table 3.4, which is a **turnover table** or a **brand-switching matrix,** contains the same basic information as Table 3.3. That is, we see that 20 percent of the families bought Brand A in period t_0, while 25 percent did so in period t_1. But Table 3.4 also shows that Brand A did not make its market share gains at the expense of Brands B and C as originally suggested, but rather captured some of the families who previously bought one of the miscellaneous brands; 75 families switched from Brand D in period t_0 to Brand A in period t_1. And, as a matter of fact, Brand A lost some of its previous users to Brand B during the period; 25 families switched from Brand A in period t_0 to Brand B in period t_1.

Table 3.4 also allows the calculation of brand loyalty. Consider Brand A, for example; 175 of the 200 or 87.5 percent of those who bought Brand A in period t_0 remained "loyal to it" (bought it again) in period t_1. By dividing each cell entry by the row or previous period totals, one can assess these brand loyalties and can also throw the basic changes that occurred in the market into bolder relief. Table 3.5 produced by such

---

[22]Hans Zeisel, *Say It With Figures,* 5th ed. (New York: Harper & Row, 1968), pp. 200–239, has a highly readable version of the analyses that can be performed with panel data. See also David Rogosa, "Comparisons of Some Procedures for Analyzing Longitudinal Panel Data," *Journal of Economics and Business,* 32 (Winter 1980), pp. 136–151, and Gregory B. Markus, *Analyzing Panel Data* (Beverly Hills, Calif.: Sage Publications, 1979).

Table 3.4

Number of Families in Panel Buying Each Brand in Each Period

		At Time t_1				
		Bought A	**Bought B**	**Bought C**	**Bought D**	**Total**
	Bought A	175	25	0	0	200
	Bought B	0	225	50	25	300
At Time t_0	Bought C	0	0	280	70	350
	Bought D	75	20	0	55	150
	Total	250	270	330	150	1,000

Table 3.5

Brand Loyalty and Brand Switching Probabilities among Families in Panel

		At Time t_1				
		Bought A	**Bought B**	**Bought C**	**Bought D**	**Total**
	Bought A	.875	.125	.000	.000	1.000
	Bought B	.000	.750	.167	.083	1.000
At Time t_0	Bought C	.000	.000	.800	.200	1.000
	Bought D	.500	.133	.000	.367	1.000

calculations suggests, for example, that among the three major brands, Brand A exhibited the greatest buying loyalty and Brand B the least. This is important to know because it indicates whether families like the brand when they do try it.[23]

Whether those who switched from one of the miscellaneous brands to Brand A were induced to do so by the package change is open to question for reasons that will be discussed in the next chapter. The point is that turnover or brand-switching analysis can only be performed when there are *repeated* measures over time for the same variables for the same subjects. It is *not* appropriate for omnibus panel data, in which the variables being measured are constantly changing, nor is it appropriate for cross-sectional studies, even if successive cross-sectional samples are taken.

The turnover table is the heart of panel analyses because the raw data it generates admit all sorts of elaborations. Any analysis that does not start with a turnover table is

[23]Table 3.5 can also be viewed as a transition matrix, since it depicts the brand buying changes occurring from period to period. Knowing the proportion switching allows early prediction of the ultimate success of some new product or some change in market strategy. See, for example, Seymour Sudman and Robert Ferber, *Consumer Panels* (Chicago: American Marketing Association, 1979), pp. 19–27, which also provides an excellent review of the literature on such facets of consumer panels as uses of, sampling and sampling biases, data collection methods, conditioning, data processing and file maintenance, costs of operating, and choosing a consumer panel service.

overlooking the unique contribution that panels can make to the study of change, and the use of sophisticated statistical algorithms cannot compensate for this shortcoming. From an economic point of view, when we analyze panel data without constructing and using a turnover table, the cost per bit of information conveyed to management will probably be excessive in comparison to the cost of trend or time series studies.[24]

Considering that information is available from panels for multiple periods, the unique advantage of longitudinal analysis becomes obvious. One can look at changes in individual entity behavior and attempt to relate them to a succession of marketing tactics, for example, advertising copy changes, package changes, price changes, and so on. Further, since the same subjects are measured before and after changes in marketing variables, small changes in the criterion variable are more easily identified than if separate studies were made using two or more independent samples. Variation of the criterion variable in the latter case may be due to changes in the composition of the sample.

Although the major advantage of a panel is analytical, panels also have some advantages with respect to the information collected in a study. This is particularly true with respect to classification information, such as income, education, age, and occupation. In many studies, there is a great deal of classification information we would like to secure, as this allows more sophisticated analysis of the results. Unfortunately, cross-sectional studies are limited in this respect. Respondents being contacted for the first and only time typically do not stand still for lengthy, time-consuming interviews. The situation is different in panels because panel members are usually compensated for their participation; thus, the interviews can be longer and more exacting, or there can be several interviews. Further, the sponsoring firm can afford to spend more time and effort securing accurate classification information, as this information can be used in a number of studies.

Panel data are also believed to be more accurate than cross-sectional data because panel data tend to be freer from the errors associated with reporting past behavior.[25] Errors arise in reporting past behavior because humans tend to forget, partly because time has elapsed but partly for other reasons. In particular, research has shown that

---

[24]Francesco M. Nicosia, "Panel Designs and Analyses in Marketing," in Peter D. Bennett, ed., *Marketing and Economic Development* (Chicago: American Marketing Association, 1965), pp. 222–243. For applications of brand switching or turnover analysis, see Alan R. Andreason, "Potential Marketing Applications of Longitudinal Methods," and Robert W. Pratt, Jr., "Understanding the Decision Process for Consumer Durable Goods: An Example of the Application of Longitudinal Analysis," both of which can also be found in Bennett on pp. 261–275 and pp. 244–260, respectively.

[25]The arguments as to why panel data are less susceptible to these problems are developed in detail in Granbois and Engel, "The Longitudinal Approach." The errors due to these sources are elaborated in the chapters on measurement and data collection. For some empirical evidence, see Seymour Sudman and Robert Ferber, "A Comparison of Alternative Procedures for Collecting Consumer Expenditure Data for Frequently Purchased Products," and Robert A. Wright, Richard H. Beisel, Julia D. Oliver, and Michele C. Gerzowski, "The Use of a Multiple Entry Diary in a Panel Study on Health Care Expenditure," both of which can be found in Robert Ferber, ed., *Readings in Survey Research* (Chicago: American Marketing Association, 1978), on pp. 487–502 and pp. 503–512, respectively; Yoram Wind and David Lerner, "On the Measurement of Purchase Data: Surveys Versus Purchase Diaries," *Journal of Marketing Research,* 16 (February 1979), pp. 39–47; and John McKenzie, "The Accuracy of Telephone Call Data Collected by Diary Methods," *Journal of Marketing Research,* 20 (November 1983), pp. 417–427.

events and experiences are forgotten more readily if they are inconsistent with attitudes or beliefs that are important to the person or threaten the person's self-esteem. Because behavior is recorded as it occurs in a panel, less reliance is placed on a respondent's memory. When diaries are used to record purchases, the problems should be virtually eliminated because the respondent is instructed to record the purchases immediately upon returning home. When other behaviors are of interest, respondents are asked to record those behaviors as they occur, thus minimizing the possibility that they will be forgotten or distorted when they are eventually asked about. Table 3.6 shows, for example, one of three diaries that participants in a study investigating children's requests for products and services were asked to keep. All 261 participating mothers were asked to fill out the product-request diary that is shown, as well as a product-purchase diary and a television-viewing log that are not shown, *each day*. The panel diary method was chosen because the reliability of much of the self-report data investigating parent–child interactions when purchasing products and services was suspect.

Errors also occur because the interviewer and the respondent represent distinct personalities and different social roles. Very often respondents say what they think the interviewers *want* to hear or what they feel the interviewers *should* hear. The panel design helps reduce this interaction bias. First, respondents come to trust the interviewer, to a greater degree because of repetitive contact. Second, more frequent contact creates rapport.

The main disadvantage of panels is that they are nonrepresentative. The agreement to participate involves a commitment on the part of the designated sample member. Some individuals refuse this commitment. They do not wish to be bothered with filling out consumer diaries or testing products or evaluating advertising copy or whatever else may be involved with the panel operation. Consumer panels that require households to keep a record of their purchases, for example, generally have cooperation rates of about 60 percent when contacted in person and lower participation rates if telephone or mail is used for the initial contact.[26]

The better ongoing panel operations select prospective participants very systematically. They attempt to generate and maintain panels that are representative of the total population of interest with respect to such characteristics as age, occupation, education, and so on. Quite often they will use quota samples to create a representative panel.[27] All the research organization can do, though, is designate the families or respondents that are to be included in the sample. They cannot force individuals to participate, nor can they require continued participation from those who initially choose to cooperate. They often encourage participation by offering some premium or by paying panel members for their cooperation. Nevertheless, a significant percentage of individuals designated for inclusion refuse to cooperate initially or quickly drop from the panel. Depending on the type of cooperation needed, the refusal and mortality rates might run over 50

[26]See also Sudman and Ferber, *Consumer Panels,* p. 31. For suggestions on recruiting and maintaining cooperation from panel members, see William H. Motes, ''How to Solve Common Problems in Longitudinal Studies,'' *Marketing News,* 18 (January 6, 1984), p. 3.

[27]Quota samples are explained in Chapter 9.

percent.[28] Of course, not all panel mortality is due to quitting. Some individuals move away and others die. In any case, the question arises as to whether the panel is then indeed representative of the population, since those designated to participate are not participating. Further, the payment of a reward for cooperation raises the question of whether particular types of people are attracted to such panels.

It seems, for example, that "panel cooperation appears to be best in households with more than two members, in households having wives in the younger age groups, and in households with more education."[29] Of course, this nonrepresentative quality may not be a problem in every study. It depends on the purpose of the study and the particular variables of interest. The trouble with such bias, of course, is that one never knows in advance whether it will affect the results, much less how.

Cross-Sectional Analysis

The cross-sectional study is the best known and most important descriptive design, as measured by the number of times it is used in comparison to other methods. It is distinguished by its use of a sample of elements from the population of interest where the elements are measured at a single point in time. This study provides a snapshot of the variables of interest at that point in time, as contrasted to the longitudinal study that provides a series of pictures which, when pieced together, provide a movie of the situation and the changes that are occurring.

Just as there are two types of panels, there are two types of cross-sectional studies: **field studies** and **sample surveys.** Although the distinction is not a fine one, there are practical differences between field studies and sample surveys that call for somewhat different techniques and skills. The basic difference is between the greater scope of the survey and the greater depth of the field study. The survey attempts to be representative of some known universe, both in terms of the number of cases included and in the manner of their selection. The field study is less concerned with the generation of large representative samples, and more concerned with the in-depth study of a few typical situations. The emphasis in a survey is on the generation of summary statistics such as averages and percentages and the relation of these summary statistics. The emphasis in a field study is on the interrelationship of a number of factors. The field study is particularly useful when a number of factors bear on a phenomenon and when it is difficult to understand the phenomenon without considering the interrelationships among the factors.

The main advantages of field studies lie in their realism, strength of variables, and heuristic quality.[30] They are realistic because they involve the investigation of phenom-

---

[28]Sudman and Ferber, *Consumer Panels,* p. 31. Winer demonstrates the biasing effects of attrition on the parameters of models fit to panel data. See Russell S. Winer, "Attrition Bias in Econometric Models Estimated With Panel Data," *Journal of Marketing Research,* 20 (May 1983), pp. 177–186.

[29]Sudman and Ferber, *Consumer Panels,* p. 32.

[30]See Charles B. McClintock, Diane Brannon, and Steven Maynard-Moody, "Applying the Logic of Sample Surveys to Qualitative Case Studies: The Case Cluster Method," *Administrative Science Quarterly,* 24 (December 1979), pp. 612–629 for discussion of how the logic and methods of survey research can improve qualitative case studies. See Kerlinger, *Foundations of Behavioral Research,* pp. 373–375, for a general discussion of the advantages and disadvantages of field studies.

Table 3.6
Product Request Diary

Date: / Product Type	1 Products — Brand Name (if child asks for a specific brand)	2 Where were you when your child asked? (check as many as apply)				3 How did your child try to get you to buy it? (check as many as apply)								4 If you said yes to child's request, did you: (check one and skip to column 8)			5 If you didn't say yes to child's request, did you (check one)					6 If you didn't say yes, how did your child react? (check one)			
		At home	On the way to the store	At the store	Other	Just asked, didn't nag about it	Really pleaded w/you over & over	Said he/she had seen product on TV	Said brother, sister, or friend has or likes it	Bargained (offered to do chores, pay for part, etc.)	Gave bunch of ways he or she would use product	Just put in shopping basket at store	Other	Didn't mind buying it—said yes right away	Didn't mind buying it, but discussed with child before saying yes	Say yes, but not to the brand the child wanted	Say no, and that was that	Say no and explain why	Say no, but agree to buy something else instead	Say maybe sometime, but not now	Seemed to take it okay	Disappointed, but didn't say anything more	Argued a little, then let it drop	Argued a lot, kept nagging	Got really angry with you

Source: Leslie Isler, Edward Popper, and Scott Ward, *Children's Purchase Requests and Parental Responses: Results from a Diary Study* (Cambridge, Mass.: Marketing Science Institute, 1979), pp. 26–27. Reprinted with permission.

ena in their natural setting. No attempt is made to manipulate a controlled variable. Because the variables are allowed to exert their influence in a natural setting, their effects are typically strong. The effects may or may not be pronounced, though, as there is often a great deal of noise from other variables confounding the interpretation. Field studies are also highly heuristic. The intensive study of a few cases is often productive of a great many additional hypotheses. The investigator must be continually on guard against being diverted from examining the basic hypotheses guiding the descriptive research. As this comment suggests, the field study is often used in exploratory research where the emphasis is on generating, rather than testing, hypotheses. When used for descriptive research, though, there should be a clear specification of the who, what, why, and so on questions, and the investigator must hold steadfast in this regard.

7 If child argued or got angry, how did you respond to the child's reaction? (check as many as apply)					8 Main reason(s) child asked for this (check as many as apply)						9 Has child asked for this product before?		10 If you said yes to #9: When was the last time child asked for it? (check one)							11 If you said yes to #9: How often does your child ask for this product? (check one)							12 Has your child asked for this specific brand before? (check one)			13 If you said yes to #12: How often does your child ask for this specific brand (check one)						
Ignored it	Repeated what you'd said before	Got angry with child	Made some compromise	Decided to buy what child asked for	Saw it in store	Saw TV commercial for it	Brother, sister, or friends have it	Saw other advertising for it (not TV)	Don't know	Other	Yes	No	Yesterday	Earlier this week	Last week	In last 2 weeks	In last month	Over a month ago	Don't know	3–4 times a week	1–2 times a week	Once every couple of weeks	About once a month	Once every few months	Once or twice a year	Don't know	Yes	No, child doesn't prefer any particular brands of this product	No	3–4 times a week	1–2 times a week	Once every couple of weeks	About once a month	Once every few months	Once or twice a year	Don't know
			'																																	

Field studies also have weaknesses. The most serious is their *ex post facto* character. They do not contain the control afforded field and laboratory experiments. A great many variables always affect the response of interest, and it is hard to separate their effects. Part of the difficulty lies in the precision with which variables can be measured in a field study. A questionnaire of some sort must often be used.

As mentioned, surveys attempt to be representative of some known universe. Therefore, a great deal of emphasis is placed on selecting sample members, usually with a probability sampling plan. This allows the sampling error associated with the statistics, generated from the sample but used to describe the universe, to be determined. The "large" number of cases usually resulting from a sample survey also allows for cross-classification of the variables.

The objective of cross-classification analysis is to establish categories such that classification in one category implies classification in one or more other categories. The method of cross-classification analysis will be detailed later, in the discussion of tabulation. For the moment, simply note that it involves counting the *simultaneous occurrence* of the variables of interest. For example, suppose management believes that occupation is an important factor in determining the consumption of its product. Further, suppose the proposition to be examined is that white-collar workers are more apt to use the product than blue-collar workers. This hypothesis could be examined in a cross-sectional study. Measurements would be taken from a representative sample of the population with respect to their occupation and use of the product. In cross tabulation, researchers would count the number of cases that fell in each of the following classes:

- white-collar and use the product
- blue-collar and use the product
- white-collar and do not use the product
- blue-collar and do not use the product.

That is, the emphasis would be on the relative frequency of occurrence of the joint phenomenon—white-collar occupation and user of the product. If the hypothesis is to be supported by the sample data, the proportion of white-collar workers using the product should exceed the proportion of blue-collar workers using the product.

As the chapters on analysis should illustrate, cross-classification analysis is a bread-and-butter technique that marketing researchers use to make sense out of survey data. One type of cross-classification analysis that is particularly effective for descriptive research arises when there is a series of "properly spaced" surveys, as this allows cohort analysis of the data. The **cohort,** which refers to the aggregate of individuals who experience the same event within the same time interval, serves as the basic unit of analysis in such studies. A very common analysis emphasis is on birth cohorts or groups of people born within the same time interval.[31] The potential usefulness of cohort analysis can be seen using the age-based per capita soft drink consumption data shown in Table 3.7. What do you think such data portend for the future of the soft drink industry? A typical interpretation would suggest dire consequences as the large but young cohorts age and are replaced by smaller cohorts because of declining birthrates in the United States. As a matter of fact, most people, upon seeing this data, might be inclined to agree with the *Business Week* article that stated, ". . . by 1985, there will be four million fewer persons in the thirteen-to-twenty-four age group. And these four million persons would have consumed some 3.3 billion cans of soft drinks annually."[32]

A birth cohort analysis of soft drink consumption data would focus on the changing consumption patterns of identifiable groups as they age—for example, all those born between 1940 and 1949. Table 3.8, for example, shows the percentage of people in each age cohort born between 1900 and 1969 who consume soft drinks on a typical

[31]Joseph O. Rentz, Fred D. Reynolds, and Roy G. Stout, "Analyzing Changing Consumption Patterns With Cohort Analysis," *Journal of Marketing Research,* 20 (February 1983), pp. 12–20.

[32]"The Graying of the Soft Drink Industry," *Business Week* (May 23, 1977), p. 68.

Table 3.7

Per Capita Consumption of Soft Drinks by Various Age Categories

Age	Per Capita Consumption, 1979
20–29	48 gallons
30–39	42 gallons
40–49	35 gallons
50+	24 gallons

Source: Joseph O. Rentz, Fred D. Reynolds, and Roy G. Stout, "Analyzing Changing Consumption Patterns with Cohort Analysis," *Journal of Marketing Research,* 20 (February 1983), p. 12. Published by the American Marketing Association.

Table 3.8

Consumption of Soft Drinks by Various Age Cohorts
(Percentage Consuming on a Typical Day)

Age	1950	1960	1969	1979	
8–19	52.9	62.6	73.2	81.0	
20–29	45.2	60.7	76.0	75.8	C8
30–39	33.9	46.6	67.7	71.4	C7
40–49	28.2	40.8	58.6	67.8	C6
50+	18.1	28.8	50.0	51.9	C5
		C1	C2	C3	C4

C1—cohort born prior to 1900	C5—cohort born 1931–1940
C2—cohort born 1901–1910	C6—cohort born 1940–1949
C3—cohort born 1911–1920	C7—cohort born 1950–1959
C4—cohort born 1921–1930	C8—cohort born 1960–1969

Source: Joseph O. Rentz, Fred D. Reynolds, and Roy G. Stout, "Analyzing Changing Consumption Patterns with Cohort Analysis," *Journal of Marketing Research,* 20 (February 1983), p. 12. Published by the American Marketing Association.

day. Note that Table 3.8 is constructed so that the interval between any two surveys or measurement periods corresponds approximately to the age class interval that is used to define the age cohorts used in the study, ten years in this case. Because of this, the consumption of the various age cohorts over time can be determined by reading down the diagonal. Consider Cohort C5, for example, which refers to all those born between 1931 and 1940. The C5 diagonal indicates that 52.9 percent of the people in this age group who were interviewed in 1950 consumed soft drinks on a typical day; by 1960 that percentage had increased to 60.7 percent, to 67.7 percent by 1969, and to 67.8 percent by 1979. A complete analysis of the cohort data in Table 3.7 that looks at the percentage consuming soft drinks and other data that show the amount consumed per capita suggests just the opposite conclusion of the *Business Week* article.

Specifically, each succeeding cohort has increased its consumption and once the level is established consumption will remain relatively stable over the life course. Thus consumption in the cohort aged 20–29 will not decrease as the cohort ages. Further, total soft drink consumption would increase as the larger and younger cohorts (whose per capita consumption is high) replace the smaller and older cohorts (whose per capita consumption is lower).[33]

Not only does cross-classification analysis serve, then, as a basic analytic technique in descriptive research studies, but when there are a series of properly spaced surveys, cohort analysis, or a special form of cross-classification analysis, can be used to advantage.

The sample survey has several disadvantages. These include superficial analysis of the phenomenon, cost, and the technical sophistication required to conduct survey research. Let us consider each disadvantage in turn.

One common criticism of survey data is that it typically does not penetrate very deeply below the surface, since breadth is often emphasized at the expense of depth. There is ordinarily an emphasis on the calculation of statistics that efficiently summarize the wide variety of data collected from the sometimes large cross section of subjects. Yet, the very process of generating summary statistics to describe the phenomenon suggests that the eventual "average" might not accurately describe any individual entity making up the aggregate. The situation is very much like "the guy who slept with his feet in the refrigerator and his head in the stove who on the average was comfortable."

Second, a survey is expensive in terms of both time and money. It will often be months before a single hypothesis can be tested because of the necessary preliminaries so vital to survey research. The entire research process, from problem definition through measuring instrument development, design of the sample, collecting the data, and editing, coding, and tabulating the data, must be executed before an analyst can begin to examine the hypotheses that guide the study. As parts of the remainder of this book will show, each of these tasks can be formidable in its own right. Each can require large investments of time, energy, and money.

Survey research also requires a good deal of technical skill. The research analyst must either have the skills required at each stage of the process or have access to such skills in, say, the form of technical consultants. It is the rare individual indeed who has the technical sophistication both to develop an attitude scale and to design a complex probability sample.

Summary

A research design is the blueprint for a study that guides the collection and analysis of data. Just as different blueprints reflect differing degrees of detail, research designs vary in their specificity. Some are very detailed and involve the investigation of specific "if–then" relationships, while others simply provide a picture of the overall situation.

Exploratory research is basically "general picture" research. It is quite useful in becoming familiar with a phenomenon, in clarifying concepts, in developing but not testing "if–then" statements, and in establishing priorities for further research. Exploratory studies are characterized by their flexibility. The investigator's imagination and

[33]Rentz, Reynolds, and Stout, "Analyzing Changing," p. 13. This article explains cohort analysis and uses it to analyze the effects of aging and cohort succession on consumption of a product class.

ingenuity will guide the pursuit, although literature searches, experience surveys, and selected cases have proven useful for gaining insight into a phenomenon.

Descriptive studies are anything but flexible. Rather, they are rigid in requiring a precise specification of the who, what, when, where, why, and how of the research. Descriptive studies rest on one or more specific hypotheses. They are used when the research is intended to describe the characteristics of certain groups, to estimate the proportion of people who behave in a certain way, or to make predictions.

Descriptive studies are of two types: longitudinal and cross-sectional. Longitudinal studies rely on panel data. A panel is simply a fixed sample of individuals or some other entities from whom repeated measurements are taken. There are two different kinds of panels—panels in which the same measurements are taken in each measurement period (true panels) and panels in which different measurements are taken in each measurement period (omnibus panels). The turnover table, a most informative method of analysis that is unique to panel data, is only applicable to panels in which the same variables are measured over time.

Cross-sectional studies rely on a sample of elements from the population of interest that are measured at a single point in time. There are also two basic kinds of cross-sectional studies. The field study is a detailed analysis of a select number of cases. It is a small sample approach, which is particularly useful when examining the interrelationships among a number of variables. The field study is very popular in exploratory research. It can also be used in descriptive research. Of course, this latter use assumes that specific hypotheses are being tested. The sample survey is a large-sample, cross-sectional study. A great deal of emphasis is placed on the scientific generation of the sample so that the members are representative of the population of interest. A typical sample survey involves summarizing and generalizing the data collected. The analysis of sample survey results rests heavily on the cross-classification table. The cross-classification table reports the joint occurrence of the variables of interest.

Cohort analysis is a special type of cross-classification analysis that can be used when there are a series of surveys and the spacing between them corresponds to a natural or cohort division of the population, where a cohort refers to the aggregate of individuals who experience the same event within the same time interval.

Questions

1. What is a research design? Is a research design necessary to conduct a study?
2. What are the different types of research designs? What is the basic purpose of each?
3. What is the crucial tenet of research?
4. What are the basic uses for exploratory research?
5. What is the key characteristic of exploratory research?
6. What are some of the more productive types of exploratory research? What are the characteristics of each type?
7. What are the basic uses of descriptive research?
8. What is the key characteristic of descriptive research?
9. What are the main types of descriptive studies, and what do their differences mean?
10. What are the basic types of panels, and what is the import of the differences that exist?

11. What is the turnover table? How is it read? What kinds of analyses does a turnover table allow that cannot be done with other types of studies?

12. What are the general advantages and disadvantages of panel data?

13. What are the basic types of cross-sectional studies? How do they compare in terms of advantages and disadvantages?

14. What is a cross-tabulation table? What is the objective of cross-classification analysis?

15. What is a cohort? What is cohort analysis?

Applications and Problems

1. The TelBel Company was a large supplier of residential telephones and related services in the southeast United States. The Department of Research and Development recently designed a prototype with a memory function that could store the number of calls and the contents of the calls for a period of 48 hours. A similar model, introduced by their competitors three months earlier, was marginally successful. However, both the models, their competitors' and their own, suffered from a technical flaw. It was found that a call lasting for over 20 minutes would result in a loss of the dial tone for 90 seconds. This was mainly attributable to the activation of the memory function. Notwithstanding the flaw, management was excited about the efforts of the research and development department. They decided to do a field survey to gauge consumer reaction to the memory capability. A random sample of 1,000 respondents was to be chosen from three major metropolitan centers in the Southeast. The questionnaires were designed to find out respondents' attitudes and opinions toward this new instrument.

   In this situation, is the research design appropriate? If yes, why? If no, why not?

2. The management of a national book club was convinced that the company's market segment consisted of individuals in the "25–35 years" age group, while their major competitors' market segment seemed more widely distributed with respect to age. They attributed this difference to the type of magazines in which the competitor advertised. Management decided to do a study to determine the socioeconomic characteristics of their market segment. They decided to form a panel of 800 heads of households who had previously shown a strong interest in reading. Mail questionnaires would be sent to all the panel members. One month after receiving all the questionnaires, the company would again send similar questionnaires to all the panel members.

   In this situation, is the research design appropriate? If yes, why? If no, why not?

3. A medium-sized manufacturer of high-speed copiers and duplicators was introducing a new desk top model. The vice-president of communications had to decide between two advertising programs for this product. He preferred advertising program gamma and was sure it would generate more sales than its counterpart, advertising program beta. The next day he was to meet with the senior vice-president of marketing and planning to decide on an appropriate research design for a study that would aid in the final decision as to which advertising program to implement.

   What research design would you recommend? Justify your choice.

4. A local mail-order firm was concerned with improving its service. In particular, management wanted to assess if customers were dissatisfied with current service and the nature of this dissatisfaction.

   What research design would you recommend? Justify your choice.

5. The Pen-Lite Company was a manufacturer of writing instruments such as fountain pens, ball-point pens, soft-top pens, and mechanical pencils. Typically, these products were retailed through small and large chains, drugstores, and grocery stores. The company had recently diversified into the manufacture of disposable cigarette lighters. The distribution of this product was to be restricted to drugstores and grocery stores. The reason was that management believed that its target market of low and middle-income classes would use these outlets. Your expertise is required in order to decide on an appropriate research design to determine if this would indeed be the case.

   What research design would you recommend? Justify your choice.

6. Airways Luggage is a producer of cloth-covered luggage, one of the primary advantages of which is its light weight. The company distributes its luggage through major department stores, mail-order houses, clothing retailers, and other retail outlets such as stationery stores, leather goods stores, and so on. The company advertises rather heavily, but it also supplements this promotional effort with a large field staff of sales representatives, numbering around 400. The numbers vary because one of the historical problems confronting Airways Luggage has been the large number of sales representatives' resignations. It is not unusual for 10 to 20 percent of the sales force to turn over every year. Since the cost of training a new person is estimated at $5,000 to $10,000, not including the lost sales that might result because of a personnel switch, Mr. Brooks, the sales manager, is rightly concerned. He has been concerned for some time and, therefore, has been conducting exit interviews with each departing sales representative. On the basis of these interviews, he has formulated the opinion that the major reason for this high turnover is general sales representatives' dissatisfaction with company policies, promotional opportunities, and pay. But top management has not been sympathetic to Mr. Brooks' pleas regarding the changes needed in these areas of corporate policy. Rather, it has tended to counter Mr. Brooks' pleas with arguments that too much of what he is suggesting is based on his gut reactions and little hard data. Top management desires more systematic evidence that job satisfaction, in general, and these dimensions of job satisfaction, in particular, are the real reasons for the high turnover before they would be willing to change things. Mr. Brooks has called on the Marketing Research Department in Airways Luggage to assist him in solving his problem.

   (a) As a member of this department, identify the general hypothesis that would guide your research efforts.
   (b) What type of research design would you recommend to Mr. Brooks? Justify your answer.

7. Mr. Faust, as the advertising manager for *Chemical Topics* magazine, is charged with the responsibility for selling advertising space in the magazine. The magazine deals primarily with chemical processing technology and is distributed solely by subscription. Major advertisers in the magazine are the producers of chemical processing equipment since the magazine is primarily directed at engineers and other technical people concerned with the design of chemical processing units.

   Since the size and composition of the target audience for *Chemical Topics* are key concerns for prospective advertisers, Mr. Faust is interested in collecting more detailed data on the readership. While he presently has total circulation figures, he feels that these understate the potential exposure of an advertisement in *Chemical Topics*. In particular, he feels that for every subscriber to *Chemical Topics,* there are several others in the firm to whom *Chemical Topics* is routed for their perusal. He wishes to determine how large this "secondary" audience is and also wishes to develop more detailed data on readers such as degree of technical training, level in the administrative hierarchy, and so on, since he feels that this detail would be quite helpful in influencing potential clients to commit their advertising dollars to *Chemical Topics*. Mr. Faust has requested you to assist him in solving his problems.

(a) Does Mr. Faust have a specific hypothesis? If yes, state the hypothesis.

(b) What type of research design would you recommend? Justify your answer.

8. Investment Services, Inc., was a real estate developer headquartered in Florida but operating throughout the southeastern United States. One of the military bases located in one of the cities within Investment Services' market area recently closed, and the forty housing units for military people located at the base were put up for public sale. The housing units, which were all duplexes, were somewhat run-down because the decision to phase out the base was made some time ago. Only minimum maintenance was conducted after the fateful decision.

Investment Services feels that these units will command only a very low price at the public sale because of their dilapidated condition. Investment Services feels that because of this low price, they could be repaired and sold at a nice profit.

Before bidding on the contract, though, Investment Services was interested in determining what kind of demand there might be for these units. Management has asked you to assist it in determining this reaction.

What kind of research design would you suggest? Why?

9. The Merlin Magic Company, a large manufacturer of women's beauty aids, conducted a study in 1986 in order to assess how its brand of hair dye was faring in the market. Questionnaires were mailed to a panel of 1,260 families. Merlin Magic (MM) brand of hair dye had three major competitors: Brand A, Brand B, and Brand C. A similar study conducted in 1985 had indicated the following market shares: Merlin Magic 31.75% (i.e., 400 families); Brand A 25% (315 families), Brand B 32.54% (410 families), Brand C 10.71% (135 families). The present study indicated that its market share had not changed during the one-year period. They noted that Brand B had increased its market share to 36.5% (460 families). However, this increase could be accounted for by a decrease in Brand A's and Brand C's market shares. (Brand A now had a market share of 22.23% or 280 families; Brand C now had a market share of 9.52% or 120 families). The management of MM Company decided it had little to worry about.

The study of 1986 also revealed some additional facts. Over the one-year period 70 families from Brand A and 30 families from Brand C had switched to MM Brand. Five families from Brand B and 30 families from Brand C had switched to Brand A while none of MM brand users had switched to Brand A. The above facts further led management to believe that it had little to worry about. Finally, 45 families switched from Brand B to Brand C while none of the families using MM Brand or Brand A had switched to Brand C. Brand C's loyalty was estimated to be .556.

(a) Do you think that management of Merlin Magic Company was accurate in analyzing the situation? Justify your answer.

(b) You are called upon to do some analysis. From the data given above construct the brand switching matrix (Hint: begin by filling in the row and column totals.)

(c) Indicate what this matrix reveals for each of the brands over the one-year period.

(d) Complete the table on page 101 and compute the brand loyalties.

	At Time t_1				
	Bought MM	**Bought A**	**Bought B**	**Bought C**	**Total**
At Time t_0: Bought MM					
Bought A					
Bought B					
Bought C					

(e)   What can be said about the degree of brand loyalty for each of the four products?

10. The LoCalor Company was a medium-sized manufacturer of highly nutritional food products. The products were marketed as diet foods with high nutritional content. Recently, the company was considering marketing these products as snack foods but was concerned about their present customers' reaction to the change in the products' images. The company decided to assess customers' reaction by conducting a study using one of the established consumer panels.

   What type of panel would you recommend in the above situation? Why?

11. The American Lung Association wanted to determine the socioeconomic and demographic characteristics of the adult population that supported the association. The association decided to conduct a study using cross-sectional analysis.

   In the above situation would you recommend a field study or a field survey? Why?

Chapter 4
Causal Designs

Many times the marketing manager has one or more specific X-causes-Y hypotheses that need to be examined: for example, a 5 percent increase in the price of the product will have no appreciable impact on the quantity demanded by customers; redesigning the cereal package so that it is shorter and less likely to tip over will improve consumer attitudes toward the product. When the research question can be framed this explicitly, the researcher is dealing with a situation ripe for causal analysis. Descriptive research can be used for testing hypotheses. However, descriptive designs are not as satisfactory as experiments for establishing causality. The reasons depend on an understanding of the notion of causality, the types of evidence that establish causality, and on an understanding of the effect of extraneous variables in a research setting. In addition to explaining experimental design, this chapter deals with these concepts.

Concept of Causality

The concept of causality is complex. A detailed discussion of it would take us too far afield. However, a few essentials will allow us to properly determine the role of the experiment in establishing the validity of an X-causes-Y statement.

The scientific notion of causality is very much different from the commonsense everyday notion.[1] First, the commonsense notion suggests there is a single cause of an event. The everyday interpretation of the statement X is the cause of Y implies that X is indeed *the* cause. The scientific notion holds that X would only be one of a number of determining conditions.

Another difference between the commonsense and scientific notions of causality is that while the everyday interpretation implies a completely deterministic relationship, the scientific notion implies a probabilistic relationship. That is, the commonsense notion suggests that for X to be a cause of Y, X must always lead to Y. The scientific notion, on the other hand, suggests that X can be a cause of Y if the occurrence of X makes the occurrence of Y more likely or more probable.

---

[1] See Claire Selltiz, *et al., Research Methods in Social Relations,* rev. ed. (New York: Holt, Rinehart and Winston, 1959), pp. 80–82, for a brief but lucid discussion of the differences between the commonsense and scientific notions of causality. See also David A. Kenny, *Correlation and Causality* (New York: John Wiley & Sons, 1979), especially Chapter 1.

Finally, the scientific notion implies that we can *never prove* that X is a cause of Y. Rather, we always *infer,* but never prove, that a relationship exists. The inference, of course, will be based on some observed data, perhaps acquired in a very controlled experimental setting. Nevertheless, the scientific notion recognizes the fallibility of such procedures. Thus, the scientific notion holds that causality is inferred; it is never demonstrated conclusively. This begs the question of what kinds of evidence can be used to support scientific inferences. There are three basic kinds of evidence: concomitant variation, time order of occurrence of variables, and elimination of other possible causal factors.[2]

Concomitant Variation

Consider the statement *"X is a cause of Y."* Evidence of concomitant variation as to the validity of this statement refers to the extent to which X and Y occur together or vary together in the way predicted by the hypothesis. Two cases can be distinguished— the qualitative and the quantitative.

Consider the qualitative case first. Suppose the causal factor X was "dealer quality" and the effect factor Y was the company's market share, and suppose that we were interested in examining the statement, "The success of our marketing efforts is highly dealer dependent. Where we have good dealers, we have good market penetration, and where we have poor dealers, we have unsatisfactory market penetration." Now, if X is to be considered a cause of Y, we should expect to find the following: In those territories where our good dealers are located, we would expect to have satisfactory market shares, while in those territories where our poor dealers are located, we would expect to have unsatisfactory market shares. On the other hand, if we found that the proportion of territories with unsatisfactory market shares was higher where the good dealers were located, we would conclude that the hypothesis was untenable.

Consider Table 4.1, in which the 100 dealers in each of the company's sales territories have been classified as good or poor. Suppose the research department has also investigated the firm's market penetration in each sales territory and has categorized these market shares using some criteria supplied by management as either satisfactory or unsatisfactory. This table provides evidence of concomitant variation. Where we find the presence of X, a good dealer, we also find the presence of Y, satisfactory market share, and where X is lacking, we are more likely to find a territory where our market share is unsatisfactory. Stating it another way, 67 percent of the good dealers are found in territories where our market share is satisfactory. However, only 25 percent of the poor dealers are located in territories where the market share is satisfactory.

Perfect evidence of concomitant variation would be provided, of course, if all good dealers were located in territories with satisfactory market shares and all poor dealers were located in territories with unsatisfactory market shares. The "pure" case will rarely be found in practice, as other causal factors will produce some deviation from a one-to-one correspondence between X and Y. So we search for the proportion of cases having X that also possess Y and compare that to the proportion of cases not having X that possess Y.

---

[2]*Ibid.*, pp. 83–88.

Table 4.1
Evidence of Concomitant Variation: Qualitative Case

Dealer Quality–X	Market Share–Y		Total
	Satisfactory	Unsatisfactory	
Good	40 (67%)	20 (33%)	60 (100%)
Poor	10 (25%)	30 (75%)	40 (100%)

When the cause and effect factors can logically be considered continuous variables, the approach is similar. Now, though, the evidence should be consistent with regard to the amount of X in comparison to the amount of Y. Consider the relationship between advertising effort and sales. The firm's dollar expenditure on advertising is logically considered the cause, X, and sales the effect, Y. Further, the hypothesis would probably state that the higher the level of advertising expenditure, the greater the sales. Quantitative evidence of concomitant variation would be provided by finding evidence consistent with this hypothesis in that X was higher in those territories or in those years where Y was also greater. Again, the relationship could not be expected to be perfect, since that would deny the existence of other sales determining factors. However, we would expect to find some positive relationship between the variables.

Suppose an analysis of the relationship between X and Y provided supporting evidence of concomitant variation. What can we say? All we can say is that *the association makes the hypothesis more tenable; it does not prove it.*[3] Similarly, the absence of an association between X and Y cannot be taken in and of itself as evidence that there is no causal relationship between X and Y, because we are always inferring, rather than proving, that a causal relationship exists.

Consider first the case in which positive evidence of concomitant variation was provided. Table 4.2, which might be of interest to a candy manufacturer, suggests that candy consumption is affected by marital status.[4] Single people are more likely than married people to eat candy regularly. Seventy-five percent of the single people in the sample ate candy regularly, while only 63 percent of the married people were regular consumers. Further, the evidence is not to be taken lightly because it was taken from a rather large sample of 3,009 cases. On the basis of this evidence, can we safely conclude that marriage causes a decrease in candy consumption? Or are there other possible explanations? What about the effects of age? Married people are usually older than

---

[3]Chapter 12 will discuss the various conditions that can arise when looking at evidence of concomitant variation. For the moment, we simply wish to emphasize through example that association between X and Y does not mean there is causality between X and Y, and that the absence of such association does not mean there is no causality.

[4]The example is adapted from Hans Zeisel, *Say It with Figures,* 5th ed., rev. (New York: Harper & Row, 1968), pp. 137–139. This classic book is recommended reading for all who are faced with the task of analyzing some data.

Table 4.2

Evidence of Concomitant Variation between
Marital Status and Candy Consumption

	Candy Consumption–Y		
Marital Status–X	Eat Candy Regularly	Do Not Eat Candy Regularly	Total
Single	750 (75%)	249 (25%)	999 (100%)
Married	1,265 (63%)	745 (37%)	2,010 (100%)

Source: Adapted from *Say It with Figures*, 5th ed., rev. by Hans Zeisel, after Table 9–8 (p. 138). Copyright © 1968 by Harper & Row, Publishers, Inc. By permission of Harper & Row, Publishers, Inc.

Table 4.3

Candy Consumption by Age and Marital Status

	Up to 25 Years			25 Years and Over		
	Eat Candy Regularly	Do Not Eat Candy Regularly	Total	Eat Candy Regularly	Do Not Eat Candy Regularly	Total
Single	632 (79%)	167 (21%)	799 (100%)	120 (60%)	80 (40%)	200 (100%)
Married	407 (81%)	96 (19%)	503 (100%)	873 (58%)	634 (42%)	1,507 (100%)

Source: Adapted from *Say It with Figures*, 5th ed., rev. by Hans Zeisel, after Table 9–6 (p. 138). Copyright © 1968 by Harper & Row, Publishers, Inc. By permission of Harper & Row, Publishers, Inc.

single people, and perhaps older people eat less candy. Table 4.3 shows the relationship between candy consumption and marital status for different age segments of the population, up to 25 years and 25 years and over. This is equivalent to holding the effects of age constant. As Table 4.3 suggests, there is little difference in the candy eating habits of married and single people; up to 25 years of age, 79 percent of the singles and 81 percent of the marrieds eat candy regularly, while for those over 25 years of age, 60 percent of the singles and 58 percent of the marrieds eat candy regularly. In effect, Table 4.3 suggests that a person's candy consumption is unaffected by the individual's marital state. The original association suggested by Table 4.2 was spurious.

Consider now the case of the absence of initial evidence of concomitant variation, and why that does not imply there is no causation between X and Y. Table 4.4 suggests that there is no relationship between a person's listening to classical music and the individual's age; in a sample of 1,279 cases, 64 percent of those under 40 and 64 percent of those over 40 listen to classical music.[5] For a record manufacturer interested in delineating market segments, this is a finding of considerable import. It is also somewhat unexpected. Consider what happens, though, when educational level is also introduced as an additional explanatory variable. As Table 4.5 reveals, there is an association

---

[5]The example is taken from *ibid.*, pp. 123–125.

Table 4.4

**Lack of Evidence of Concomitant Variation between
Age and Listening to Classical Music**

	Listening to Classical Music–Y		
Age–X	Listen	Do Not Listen	Total
Below 40	390 (64%)	213 (36%)	603 (100%)
40 and Over	433 (64%)	243 (36%)	676 (100%)

Source: Adapted from *Say It with Figures,* 5th ed., rev. by Hans Zeisel, after Table 8–7 (p. 123). Copyright © 1968 by Harper & Row, Publishers, Inc. By permission of Harper & Row, Publishers, Inc.

Table 4.5

Listening to Classical Music by Age and Education

	College			Below College		
Age	Listen	Do Not Listen	Total	Listen	Do Not Listen	Total
Below 40	162 (73%)	62 (27%)	224 (100%)	228 (61%)	151 (39%)	379 (100%)
40 and Over	195 (78%)	56 (22%)	251 (100%)	238 (56%)	187 (44%)	425 (100%)

Source: Adapted from *Say It with Figures,* 5th ed., rev. by Hans Zeisel, after Table 8–8 (p. 124). Copyright © by Harper & Row, Publishers, Inc. By permission of Harper & Row, Publishers, Inc.

between age and listening to classical music. Take college-educated people. As they get older, they display a higher propensity to listen to classical music; 78 percent of those 40 and over listen, while only 73 percent of the under-40 respondents listen. The reverse situation occurs among those who do not have a college education; whereas 61 percent of the under-40 age group listen to classical music, only 56 percent of the 40-and-over age group do so. The relationship between age and listening to classical music was originally obscured by the effect of education. When education was properly held constant, the relationship became visible.

The situations illustrated are not the only ones that can occur. A more complete picture will be presented in Chapter 12. For the moment, you should simply be aware that concomitant variation is one type of evidence that supports the existence of a causal relationship between X and Y. However, it is not the whole story. It may be that there is a causal relationship when there is no initial evidence of concomitant variation, or there is no causal relationship when there is initial evidence. Further evidence of the existence of a causal relationship can be provided by looking at the order of occurrence of variables and by eliminating other possible sources of explanation.

Time Order of Occurrence of Variables

The time order of occurrence of variables as evidence of a causal relationship between two variables is conceptually simple.

One event cannot be considered the "cause" of another if it occurs after the other event. The occurrence of a causal factor may precede or may be simultaneous with the occurrence of an event; by definition, an effect cannot be produced by an event that occurs only after the effect has taken place. However, it is possible for each term in the relationship to be both a "cause" and an "effect" of the other term.[6]

While conceptually simple, the application of this type of evidence to support causality requires an intimate understanding of the time sequence governing the phenomenon.

Consider the relationship between a firm's annual advertising expenditures and sales. This relationship is frequently used as evidence of the effect of advertising on sales for a given product. However, many companies follow a rule of thumb that uses past sales in allocating resources to advertising, for example, 10 percent of last year's sales. This practice begs the question of which way the relationship runs. Does advertising lead to higher sales or do higher sales lead to an increased ad budget? An intimate understanding of the way the company establishes the ad budget should resolve the dilemma in this situation.

Elimination of Other Possible Causal Factors

The elimination of other possible causal factors is very much like the Sherlock Holmes approach to analysis. Just as Sherlock Holmes holds that if you can eliminate all of the possible suspects but one, the remaining one is guilty, this type of evidence of causality focuses on the elimination of possible explanations other than the one being studied. This may mean physically holding other factors constant, or it may mean "adjusting" the results to remove the effects of factors that do vary.

Take the situation of the divisional manager of a chain of supermarkets investigating the effects of end displays on apple sales. Suppose that the manager found that per-store sales of apples increased during the past week and that a number of stores were using end displays for apples. To reasonably conclude that the end displays were responsible for the sales increase, the manager would need to eliminate such explanatory variables as price, size of store, and apple type and quality. This might involve looking at apple sales for stores of approximately the same size, checking to see if the prices were the same in stores having an increase in sales and stores with no increase, and checking to determine if the type and quality of apples were consistent with the previous week's.

An interesting example of eliminating other possible causal factors by adjusting the results occurred with the 1983 Nielsen television ratings. A study, commissioned by the National Association of Broadcasters and dealing with people's attitudes toward advertising, indicated that people were dissatisfied with the offerings on broadcast TV and were spending less time watching it. At the same time, Nielsen data suggested otherwise. In fact, the Nielsen ratings were so high for that season that many were questioning the numbers, particularly since 1983 marked the first year that Nielsen reported the ratings based on its larger metered sample of 1,420 households versus the 1,260 it had

---

[6]Selltiz *et al., Research Methods*, p. 85.

used previously. Were the Nielsen data wrong? If not, what could account for the dramatic increase in broadcast TV viewership? Several of the most promising explanations were an increase in the amount of special event programming, the weather, economic conditions, a change in the proportion of working women, and a change in the number of pay cable homes. Through systematic investigation of each of these factors, it was discovered that broadcast TV viewing was indeed up and the most likely explanation was the abnormal weather the country experienced in 1983, particularly in the East Central, Pacific, and Northeast states.[7]

Role of the Evidence

We shall see shortly that the controlled experiment provides strong evidence of all three types. It allows us to check for concomitant variation and time order of occurrence of variables, secure in the fact that if the experiment has been designed correctly, many of the other possible explanations will have been eliminated. However, even in an experiment not all other explanations will have *necessarily* been eliminated. There is also the possibility that in concluding that *X* caused *Y,* we may have neglected another factor that is associated with *X* and, in fact, caused *Y.* Alternatively, we may be wrong when we conclude that *X* did not cause *Y,* in that we have neglected some condition under which *X* is indeed a determiner of *Y.*

The correct posture towards these three types of evidence is that they provide a reasonable basis for believing that *X* is, or is not, a cause of *Y.* We can never be absolutely sure, though, that the relationship has been conclusively demonstrated. Study replication and knowledge of the problem are fundamental in increasing our confidence in the conclusion. The accumulation of studies pointing to a specific conclusion increases our confidence in its correctness. Similarly, an intimate knowledge of the phenomenon under investigation, in conjunction with a pattern of evidence, serves as a more reasonable basis for interpreting the results of research than does an examination of the evidence by one untrained in the subject matter of concern. Method knowledge is not a substitute for conceptual knowledge.

Experimentation

As mentioned, an experiment is capable of providing more convincing evidence of causal relationships than are exploratory or descriptive designs. This is why experiments are often called causal research. An experiment has greater ability to supply evidence of causality because of the *control* it affords investigators.

An experiment *is taken to mean a scientific investigation in which an investigator manipulates and controls one or more independent variables and observes the dependent variable or variables for variation concomitant to the manipulation of the independent*

---

[7]Kevin Burns, ''TV Viewing Up—Maybe,'' *Media Message: An Ogilvy & Mather Commentary on Media Issues* (October 1983), pp. 1–7.

variables. An experimental design, *then, is one in which the investigator* manipulates *at least one independent variable.*[8]

Because investigators are able to control at least some manipulations of the presumed causal factor, they can be more confident that the relationships discovered are "true" relationships.

Both exploratory and descriptive designs are distinguished from experimental designs in that they are examples of *ex post facto* research. *Ex post facto* literally means "from what is done afterward." In *ex post facto* research, the criterion variable Y is observed. The analyst then attempts to find one or more causal variables, X's, which afford plausible explanations as to why Y occurred. This kind of retrospective analysis affords little control of the X's and therefore contains great potential that the occurrence of Y is attributable to some other X's than the ones being investigated. One is limited to supplying evidence of concomitant variation in *ex post facto* research. The lack of evidence about the time order of occurrence of variables and the systematic exclusion of other possible explanations of the phenomenon make such designs suspect for establishing causality.

Laboratory and Field Experiments

Two types of experiments can be distinguished—the laboratory experiment and the field experiment. Since each has its own advantages and disadvantages, research analysts need to be familiar with both.

A **laboratory experiment** is one in which an investigator creates a situation with the desired conditions and then manipulates some while controlling other variables. The investigator is consequently able to observe and measure the effect of the manipulation of the independent variables on the dependent variable or variables in a situation in which the impact of other relevant factors is minimized. A **field experiment** is a research study in a realistic or natural situation, although it, too, involves the manipulation of one or more independent variables under as carefully controlled conditions as the situation will permit.

The laboratory experiment is distinguished from the field experiment, then, primarily in terms of environment. The analyst creates a setting for a laboratory experiment, while a field experiment is conducted in a natural setting. The distinction is not always a clear one, since it is one more of degree than of kind, as both involve control and manipulation of one or more presumed causal factors. The degree of control and precision afforded by each type varies, however.[9] A specially designed or artificial situation provides more control.

---

[8]Fred N. Kerlinger, *Foundations of Behavioral Research*, 3rd ed. (New York: Holt, Rinehart and Winston, 1986), p. 293. See also Geoffrey Keppel, *Design and Analysis: A Researcher's Handbook*, 2nd ed. (Englewood Cliffs, N.J.: Prentice-Hall, 1982), especially Chapter 1 for a description of the essential ingredients in experiments.

[9]Laboratory and field experiments typically play complementary roles in providing managerially useful marketing information. For a discussion of their respective roles, see Alan G. Sawyer, Parker M. Worthing, and Paul E. Sendak, "The Role of Laboratory Experiments to Test Marketing Strategies," *Journal of Marketing*, 43 (Summer 1979), pp. 60–67.

The distinction can perhaps best be made by seeing how each is used to investigate the effects of the same causal variable. Price is particularly interesting in this regard, as a number of laboratory and field experiments have investigated the impact of price on the quantity sold. The following investigation was designed to ascertain the closeness with which the price–demand estimates generated in a laboratory experiment correspond to the estimates generated in a field experiment.[10]

The laboratory experiment consisted of a set of simulated shopping trips. In each, subjects chose the brand they preferred to purchase from a full assortment of prepriced brands of cola and coffee. The relative prices of the different brands were changed for each of the eight simulated purchase trips for each subject. These price changes were communicated to each subject by index cards listing the available brands and their corresponding prices.[11] Each subject was free to switch brands to obtain the best product for the money. The trial purchase was not unlike an actual purchase in this respect. These simulated shopping trips were administered in the homes of a systematic sample of 135 homemakers in a small town in Illinois. The laboratory experiment followed a field experiment also designed to test the effect of price on the demand of different brands of cola and coffee.

The prices of the brands were also manipulated in the field experiment. The field experiment was conducted in two small towns in Illinois, ten miles apart. The manipulations here, though, involved actual changes in price for the respective brands. Four supermarkets were used in all, two from each town. Two units in one town were designated as control stores, where the price of each brand was maintained at its regular level throughout the experiment. In the experimental town, the prices were systematically varied in the two stores during the experiment. Prices were marked on the package of each brand so as to be clearly visible but not conspicuous. After each price change, a cooling-off period was introduced to offset any surplus accumulated by consumers. The impact of the price change was monitored by recording weekly sales for each brand. This allowed brand market shares for each price condition to be determined. No displays, special containers, or other devices were used to draw consumer attention to the fact that the relative prices of the brands had been altered. All other controllable factors were also held as constant as possible.

Note the distinction between the two studies. In the field experiment, no attempt was made to set up special conditions. The situation was accepted as found, and manipula-

[10]John R. Nevin, "Using Controlled Experiments to Estimate and Analyze Brand Demand," unpublished Ph.D. dissertation, University of Illinois, 1972. See also John R. Nevin, "Laboratory Experiments for Estimating Consumer Demand: A Validation Study," *Journal of Marketing Research,* 11 (August 1974), pp. 261–268. Another area in which laboratory and field experiments have been used to examine the same phenomenon is comparative advertising. See George E. Belch, "An Examination of Comparative and Noncomparative Television Commercials: The Effects of Claim Variation and Repetition on Cognitive Response and Message Acceptance," *Journal of Marketing Research,* 18 (August 1981), pp. 333–349; and William R. Swinyard, "The Interaction Between Comparative Advertising and Copy Claim Variation," *Journal of Marketing Research,* 18 (May 1981), pp. 175–186.

[11]The laboratory experiment also included a paired-preference experiment. The paired-preference experiment required each subject to make preference choices among all possible pairs of brands in a single-merchandise classification with each brand listed at its regular price. Subjects were also asked to indicate how much the price of the preferred brand would increase before they would switch to the original nonpreferred brand.

tion of the experimental variable—price—was imposed in this natural environment. The laboratory experiment, on the other hand, was contrived. Subjects were told to behave as if they were actively shopping for the product. The prices of the respective brands were varied for each of these simulated shopping trips. Whereas the simulated shopping trips generated reasonably valid estimates of consumers' reactions to "real life" (field experiment) price changes for brands of cola, they produced relatively invalid estimates for brands of coffee, in that they tended to overstate the effects of the price changes.[12]

Internal and External Validity

There are certain advantages and disadvantages that result from the difference in procedure in the two types of experiments. The laboratory experiment typically has the advantage of greater internal validity because of the greater control it affords. To the extent that we are successful in eliminating the effects of other factors that may obscure or confound the relationships under study, either by physically holding these other factors constant or by allowing for them statistically, we may conclude that the observed effect was due to the manipulation of the experimental variable. That is, we may conclude the experiment is internally valid. Thus, **internal validity** refers to our ability to attribute the effect that was observed to the experimental variable and not to other factors. In the pricing experiment, internal validity focused on the need to obtain data demonstrating that the variation in the criterion variable—brand demanded—was the result of exposure to the treatment or experimental variable—relative price of the brand—rather than other factors, such as advertising, display space, store traffic, and so on. These other factors were nonexistent in the simulated shopping trip.

Whereas the laboratory experiment is generally believed to be more internally valid, the field experiment is typically more externally valid.[13] **External validity** focuses on the problems of collecting data that will demonstrate that the changes in the criterion

---

[12]Nevin, "Laboratory Experiments," p. 266. In a related study, Stout compared the ability of three techniques to estimate price-quantity relationships for four different products: (1) a field or in-store experiment in which different prices were employed in different stores; (2) a laboratory experiment in which homemakers were asked to go through a trailer set up as a "store" and to select products as if they were on a regular shopping trip; and (3) personal interviews in which homemakers were interviewed on their way to the store and were shown different products at the different prices and were asked what purchases they would make if they saw the same items while on an actual shopping trip. Only the in-store experiment produced the expected negative relationship between price and quantity for all four products and relationships that were statistically significant. Neither the laboratory experiment nor the personal interviews produced results similar to the in-store test. Roy G. Stout, "Developing Data to Estimate Price-quantity Relationships," *Journal of Marketing,* 33 (April 1969), pp. 34–36. For a general review of the evidence regarding the investigation of the price–demand relationship see Vithala R. Rao, "Pricing Research in Marketing: The State of the Art," *Journal of Business,* 57 (January 1984), pp. 539–560.

[13]Cook and Campbell distinguish four types of validity: (1) statistical conclusion, (2) internal, (3) construct, and (4) external. Their definitions of internal and external validity parallel ours. Statistical conclusion validity addresses the extent and statistical significance of the covariation that exists in the data; construct validity examines the operations used in the experiment and attempts to assess whether they indeed capture the construct they were supposed to measure. We will have more to say on construct validity in the measurement chapters and statistical conclusion validity in the analysis chapters. Thomas D. Cook and Donald T. Campbell, *Quasi-Experimentation: Design and Analysis Issues for Field Settings* (Chicago: Rand McNally College Publishing Company, 1979), pp. 37–94.

variable observed in the experiment as a result of changes in the predictor variables can be expected to occur in other situations. Can the effect be generalized? Since laboratory experiments are more artificial than field experiments, it is questionable whether the results can be generalized to other populations and settings.[14] In the simulated shopping trip, no real purchase takes place. Further, we might suppose that the experimenter's calling attention to the price may induce people to be more price conscious than they would be in a supermarket.[15] They may attempt to act more ''rationally'' than they normally would. Further, those who agreed to participate in the laboratory experiment may not be representative of the larger population of shoppers, either because the location of the study was atypical or because those who willingly participate in such a study may be systematically different from those who decline to participate. This would seriously jeopardize the external validity of the findings.

The example in Research Realities 4.1 illustrates the difference between internal and external validity. Internal validity addresses the questions of whether the auto editor of the *Boston Globe* actually experienced a 25 percent increase in miles per gallon, and if he did, whether the improvement could be attributed to using Tufoil in the crankcase. External validity refers to whether that result could be generalized to other drivers, other cars, and other situations.

The distinction between internal validity and external validity is an important one, in that the controls needed for each often conflict. A control or procedure required to establish internal validity will often jeopardize representativeness, and vice versa for reasons that should become obvious from the discussion that follows of the various types of experimental designs and the account they take of extraneous influences. Both internal and external validity are matters of degree rather than all-or-nothing propositions.

Experimental Design

A common terminology will facilitate the discussion of the basic types of experimental designs.[16]

Let X *refer to the exposure of an individual or group to an experimental treatment; an* experimental treatment *is the alternative whose effects are to be measured and compared. The experimental variables may be alternative prices, package designs, advertising themes, or any of a number of other variables. Certainly, the possible experimental treatments in marketing would include all the elements of the marketing mix.*

---

[14]For a general discussion of how the usefulness of experimental results is affected by the researcher's treatment of unmanipulated background factors in the experiment, see John G. Lynch, Jr., ''On the External Validity of Experiments in Consumer Research,'' *Journal of Consumer Research,* 9 (December 1982), pp. 225–244.

[15]Mark I. Alpert, *Pricing Decisions* (Glenview, Ill.: Scott, Foresman, 1971), p. 104. Chapter 4 on ''Demand Curve Estimation'' discusses in more detail the use of the laboratory experiment and field experiment in estimating price-quantity relationships. See also Sidney J. Bennett and J. B. Wilkinson, ''Price-Quality Relationships and Price Elasticity Under In-Store Experimentation,'' *Journal of Business Research,* 2(1974), pp. 27–38 and Kent B. Monroe, *Pricing: Making Profitable Decisions* (New York: McGraw-Hill, 1979).

[16]The basic symbolism follows Donald T. Campbell and Julian C. Stanley, *Experimental and Quasi-Experimental Designs for Research* (Chicago: Rand McNally, 1966). It is also used by Seymour Banks, *Experimentation in Marketing* (New York: McGraw-Hill, 1965).

Research Realities 4.1

Illustration of Internal and External Validity

Some technical breakthroughs sound too good to be true. With so many new devices and gadgets on the market that purport to save fuel, for example, it can be difficult to tell an effective product from a fraud.

The case of Tufoil, a popular motor-oil additive that's supposed to improve a car's gasoline mileage an average 10% to 20%, shows how difficult making a judgment can be.

. . . Tufoil's basic technology is a suspension of tiny particles of Teflon-like materials that reduces friction. Dudley Fuller and Glenn Rightmire, engineering professors at Columbia University, say the technology "shows promise." At the request of the *Wall Street Journal*, they read Tufoil's patent description and other technical documents.

. . . Tufoil has had rave reviews in several newspapers. In May, the *New York Times* cited testimonials from police departments and race-car drivers, and concluded: "Tufoil apparently does just what it says it does." The *Boston Globe's* auto editor wrote about a test he did on his own car.

"It worked!" wrote the editor. "We have good records on the car. We have kept track of every dime spent and every drop of gas put into it." With Tufoil in the crankcase, he said, the car got 12.5 miles to the gallon, compared with 10 before. Said the editor, "That's a 25% increase."

So it is. But tests performed by consumers, even those who are as expert as racers and auto editors, generally prove little. "There's a placebo effect," says William Haynes, an attorney for the Federal Trade Commission. "If you put a product in your car that you think will improve gas mileage, you may subconsciously change your driving habits."

Changes in temperature and humidity can alter a car's mileage significantly, too. "There are just so many variables" in such tests, Mr. Haynes says, that the only way to be certain is to test a product in a laboratory on a number of cars hooked to a dynamometer, an apparatus that measures engine power. Other authorities say dynamometer tests should be supplemented by tests on whole fleets of cars on the road, in which none of the drivers knows if the car has the product.

. . . This summer, the Energy Department finally ran limited dynamometer tests on Tufoil and other products, including three special motor oils made by major oil companies. Fuel economy improved 2.8% to 5% for Tufoil, 4.1% for Arco Graphite and 3.6% for Mobile 1; Exxon Uniflo made no difference. Mr. Reick believes the results for Tufoil were low because the car was a small four-cylinder Pontiac. But an Energy Department engineer involved in the tests says a 5% improvement is impressive for a lubricant.

Double-digit savings from additives don't make sense, other experts say. Peter Hutchins, who tests energy-saving devices for the Environmental Protection Agency, says only about 25% to 30% of the energy in a typical automobile engine is lost to friction. Thus, he reasons, "even if you eliminate all the friction in an engine—which is impossible—the best you could hope for is about a 25% improvement in fuel economy."

That's true for most cars, concedes Mr. Reick. But he insists Tufoil can work wonders in engines with acute friction caused by sticking piston rings and other problems.

Meanwhile, the Federal Trade Commission is complaining about some of Tufoil's advertising claims. The agency questions such language in Tufoil brochures as "average 10% to 20% better mileage," and "fully guaranteed and insured."

Though Mr. Reick bristles at the FTC criticisms, he also concedes he has "reservations" about some of the techniques being used to promote Tufoil. Indeed, if he could have his way, he would avoid the business end of Tufoil's operation: "I'd just stay in my lab in my garage and invent things."

Source: Paul Blustein, "Fuel-Saver Additive Gets Raves, but Claims Are Tougher to Prove," *The Wall Street Journal*, 60 (August 29, 1980), p. 15. Reprinted by permission of *The Wall Street Journal*, © Dow Jones & Company, Inc. 1980. All Rights Reserved.

Let O *refer to the process of observation or measurement of the test units. The* test units *are the individuals or other entities whose response to the experimental treatments is being studied. The test units could be stores, dealers, sales representatives, consumers, or any of the many other entities that serve as objects for a firm's marketing efforts.*

Further, let movement through time be represented by a horizontal arrangement of X's and O's. Thus the symbolic arrangement

$$X \qquad O_1 \qquad O_2$$

would indicate that one or more test units were exposed to an experimental variable and that their response was then measured at two different points in time. Let a vertical arrangement of X's and O's reflect simultaneous exposure or measurement of different test units. The symbolic arrangement

$$X_1 \qquad O_1$$

$$X_2 \qquad O_2$$

would then indicate that there are two different groups of test units; that each group of test units was exposed to a different experimental treatment but at the same time; and that the response of the two groups was also simultaneously measured.

Extraneous Variables

We worry about experimental design because we want to be able to conclude that the observed response was due to our experimental manipulations. The key ingredient affecting our ability to do this is advance planning. In particular, we need to design the study so as to be able to rule out extraneous factors as possible causes. These extraneous factors fall into several categories.

History   **History** refers to the specific events, external to the experiment but occurring at the same time, that may affect the criterion or response variable. Suppose one of the major appliance manufacturers was interested in investigating the price sensitivity of consumers in regard to refrigerators. Suppose the company conceived the following experiment to take place in Gary, Indiana, a big steel-producing center.[17] Refrigerator sales at regular prices would be monitored for a four-week period. Then the price of all units would be cut 10 percent and these sales monitored for four weeks. The measure of price sensitivity would derive from comparing per-week sales at the lower price with per-week sales at the higher price. The experiment would be diagrammed as

$$O_1 \qquad X \qquad O_2$$

Now suppose that soon after the price reduction, the union contract with the steel industry expired, and there was a strike. What do you think would happen to refrigerator

---

[17]The experiment is admittedly bad. The issue was purposely presented this way so as to demonstrate more vividly the history effect.

sales? Since major appliance purchases are usually postponable, it could be expected that there would be fewer sales at the lower price than at the higher one. Would we therefore conclude that the demand curve for refrigerators is upward sloping in that the higher the price the greater the number of units that could be sold? Obviously not, for we know there were extenuating circumstances in the experiment that caused the observed aberration.

Unfortunately, the effects of history on a research conclusion are rarely so obvious. There are always a great many variables that can and do affect what we observe, and whose impact is subtle and hidden. What we need is some way of isolating the effects of history, since we are rarely in a position to physically control it. This is particularly true in the field experiment, since laboratory experiments often give us some control in this regard.[18]

Maturation   **Maturation** is similar to history, but specifically refers to changes occurring within the test units that are not due to the impact of the experimental variable but result from the passage of time. Thus, when the test units are people, maturation refers to the fact that people get older, become tired, and perhaps become hungry. Measured changes in attitude toward a product, for example, may occur simply because people have become older while using the product and not because of the reinforcement advertising to which they were exposed. Similarly, it may turn out that individuals who belong to a consumer panel changed their consumption of our brand over time not because of any changes in our marketing strategy but simply because of some change in them. They matured, so to speak, in that their tastes changed, or perhaps their marital status or family status changed.

Maturation effects are not limited to test units composed of people. Organizations also change. Dealers grow, become more successful, diversify, and so on. Stores change. Store traffic increases; its composition changes; the store's physical makeup decays; and then the store is perhaps renovated.

Of course, the type of maturation effect depends on the timing of the specific experiment in question. It would be hard to justify the argument that the people whose response was measured changed significantly due to, say, age maturation in an experiment that lasted a week. On the other hand, if the interview securing their responses lasted a couple of hours, they could very well have grown tired or have become hurried for some reason; for example, their spouses will be home from work in one-half hour and they have not even started preparing dinner yet. Thus, their responses to the later questions may differ from those to the former simply because their own personal situation has changed, and for no other reason.

Testing   The **testing effect,** which can be of two types, is concerned with the fact that the process of experimentation itself may affect the observed response. The **main test-**

---

[18]In one study designed to estimate the price elasticity of sugar using data related to the 1974 sugar shortage, the impact of the history factors—advertising, new products, competition, and industry growth trends—all had to be taken into account, since the study took place in a natural setting. See Scott A. Neslin and Robert W. Shoemaker. ''Using a Natural Experiment to Estimate Price Elasticity: The 1974 Sugar Shortage and the Ready-to-Eat Cereal Market,'' *Journal of Marketing,* 47 (Winter 1983), pp. 44–57.

ing effect is the effect of a prior observation on a later observation. For example, students taking achievement and intelligence tests for the second time usually do better than those taking the tests for the first time, even though the second one is given without any information about the scores or items missed in the first test.[19] The first administration in and of itself is responsible for the improvement. In many situations, this main testing effect will manifest itself in the respondents' desire to be consistent. Thus, in successive administrations of an attitude questionnaire, respondents reply in a consistent manner even though there has been some change in their attitudes. Alternatively, in a single administration, they answer later questions so that their replies parallel their replies to similar early questions as best they can recall them; that is, their responses to the latter part of the questionnaire are not made independently but are conditioned by their responses to the early questions.

The main testing effect may also be reactive, as there are very few things in social science that can be measured in which the process of measurement does not itself change what is being measured. The very fact that persons report their attitudes to someone else may change those attitudes. Similarly, the very fact that a person is a member of a consumer panel that reports purchasing behavior may change that person's purchasing behavior.

There is also an **interactive testing effect,** which means that a prior measurement affects the test unit's response to the experimental variable. People who are asked to indicate their attitudes toward Chevrolet may become very much more aware of the Chevrolet ads than those who are not queried. Yet if we are interested in the attitude impact of the ads, we are interested in their effect on the population as a whole and not simply on those individuals comprising our sample.

The results of the two testing effects are different. The main effect manifests itself in the relationship between observations or within an observation and can be depicted as

$$O_1 \quad X \quad O_2$$

That is, the process of measurement O_1 in turn affects the measurement O_1 or the later measurement O_2. The interactive testing effect, on the other hand, can be diagrammed as

$$O_1 \quad X \quad O_2$$

That is, the process of measurement O_1 results in some change in the test unit's reaction to the experimental stimulus. The distinction is an important one, since the main testing effect usually exerts its greatest impact on the internal validity of an experiment, while the interactive testing effect most typically affects the external validity of a conclusion.

---

[19]Campbell and Stanley, *Experimental and Quasi-Experimental Designs,* p. 9.

Instrument Variation   **Instrument variation** refers to any and all changes in the measuring instruments that might account for differences in measurements. The change may occur in the instrument itself, or it may result from variations in its administration. When there are many observers or interviewers, there can be significant instrument variations, as it is difficult indeed to ensure that all the interviewers will ask the same questions with the same voice inflections, with the same probes, with the same rapport, and so on. Thus, the recorded differences between the awareness level, say, of two respondents may not actually reflect a true difference in awareness but rather a difference that arose because each interviewer handled the interview slightly differently. Of course, the same thing can occur with interviews conducted by the same interviewer. It is highly unlikely that each situation will be handled in exactly the same way. Interviewers may become more adept at eliciting the desired responses, or they may become bored with the project and tired of interviewing. In either case, part of the difference in the reported scores will be due to the way each assignment is handled.

The measuring instrument may also undergo some modification during the course of an investigation. Modifications may be major or minor. If major (for example, a completely new set of attitude statements), the responses to each questionnaire would probably be analyzed separately. Sometimes, though, a minor modification is needed, such as a slight change in wording of a specific question that makes it more understandable without changing its meaning. Although slight, this kind of change could cause variations in the reported answers, and the analyst is well advised to be aware of this.

Statistical Regression   **Statistical regression** is the tendency of extreme cases of the phenomenon to move closer to the average during the course of experiment. The test units may be extreme by happenstance, or they may have been specifically selected because of their extreme positions. For example, people may be chosen for investigation because they exhibit extreme behavior, say, in their alcohol consumption. Suppose a consumer panel is formed of these test units. It is very likely that in subsequent monitoring, their reported alcohol intake would be closer to the average.

Alternatively, a cross-sectional study investigating the use of one brand of orange juice might reveal several families who used ten cans in a week. This may be due to the fact they had house guests, and thus it would not be surprising that in a subsequent observation their orange juice consumption would be more typical.

There is always some variation in behavior, attitudes, knowledge, and so on, and it stands to reason that the most extreme cases of the phenomenon have the most room in which to vary. Statistical regression is concerned with the occurrence of this phenomenon.

Selection Bias   **Selection bias** arises from the way in which test units are selected and assigned in an experiment. Selection bias is said to be in evidence when there is no way of certifying that groups of test units were equivalent prior to being tested.

The following example typifies the problem of selection bias. "Many say the President has at least convinced them that the energy crisis is real or that the problems are more serious than they thought. In an Associated Press–NBC poll last week, 60% of those who heard the President's speech agreed that there is a world-wide crisis, while

46% of those who didn't hear the speech believe the crisis is real.''[20] The fallacy in the argument is that there is no way of determining if those who saw the President's speech had similar attitudes, before viewing, to those who did not see it. What typically occurs is that exposure to some mass communication has been voluntary, and thus the exposed and unexposed groups inevitably possess a systematic difference on the factors determining the choice. Republicans listen to the speeches of Republican candidates; Democrats listen to those of Democratic candidates; those who have a favorable attitude toward a product pay more attention to the product's ads, and so on. If we are to conclude that exposure to the experimental stimulus (TV special, speech, ad, and so on) was responsible for the observed effect, we must somehow ensure that the comparison groups were equal before exposure.[21]

The prior equality of comparison groups is established in two main ways: matching and randomization. Suppose there are twenty stores in total, ten to be designated for an experimental group and ten for a control group, and suppose that an experiment is designed to examine the impact of a special aisle display on sales of, say, ketchup. Now certainly we would expect the sales of ketchup in any store to be associated with the store's traffic. We could therefore be far off in our conclusion if we somehow ended up with most of the large stores in one group and most of the small stores in the other group. To prevent this, we could consider matching the stores according to some external criterion, such as annual sales or square feet of floor space, and then assign one store from each matched pair to each group.

Alternatively, we could assign the twenty stores at random to each of the groups, using a table of random digits. In general, randomization is the preferred procedure in assuring the prior equality of the comparison groups.[22] First, it is hard to match test units on any but a few characteristics, so the test units may be equal in terms of the variables chosen but unequal in terms of others. In addition, if the matched characteristic is not an important determinant of the response, then the researcher has wasted time and money in matching the test units. The general principle is

Whenever it is possible to do so, randomly assign subjects to experimental groups and conditions and randomly assign conditions and other factors to experimental groups.[23]

Randomization does not play its usually productive role when the sample of test units is small, since randomization only produces groups that are ''equal on the average'' when the sample is large enough to allow the positive and negative deviations about the average to balance. With small samples, matching becomes a complement to, and not

---

[20]''For Most Americans Saving Energy Isn't a Patriotic Principle,'' *Wall Street Journal,* 59 (July 23, 1979), p. 1.

[21]For an interesting discussion of the controversy that surrounds the medical profession when attempting to make groups equal before a treatment is administered, see Jerry E. Bishop, ''Doctors Debate Use of Controlled Studies to Test Effectiveness of New Treatments,'' *Wall Street Journal,* 62 (August 12, 1982), p. 17.

[22]See Kerlinger, *Foundations,* pp. 288–289, for a general discussion of the pros and cons associated with matching.

[23]*Ibid.,* p. 288.

a substitute for, randomization, in that matched test units should then be randomly assigned to treatment conditions.[24]

Experimental Mortality   **Experimental mortality** refers to the loss of test units during the course of an experiment. Experimental mortality is a problem because there is no way of knowing if the test units that were lost would respond to the experimental stimulus in the same way as those that were retained.

Consider again the special aisle display and ketchup sales example. Suppose that during the course of the experiment, two managers of stores in the experimental group decided to use the display for another product. This would reduce the number of experimental stores to eight, and even though our major interest would be on average store sales in the experimental group in comparison to average store sales in the control group, we would have no way of knowing if this average would have been higher or lower if the two dropout stores had continued participating. We *cannot* simply *assume* that their sales would have been very much like those in the other experimental stores. They may have been, but again they might have been vastly different. The problem with experimental mortality, as with all of these other extraneous sources of variation, is not that they have indeed operated but rather that we *do not know whether or not they have operated* and whether or not they have affected the criterion variable. The key then becomes one of designing investigations so that this doubt can be eliminated.

Specific Designs

Three types of experimental designs are commonly distinguished: preexperimental designs, true experimental designs, and quasi-experimental designs.[25] True experimental designs are the most effective in eliminating the doubt that can arise in interpreting research results, as they provide the most control over the various extraneous factors. Unfortunately, not all marketing problems allow the use of true experimental designs. An understanding of their features, though, should allow a more scientific interpretation of the results, with due allowance for the necessary caveats when preexperimental or quasi-experimental designs are used.

Preexperimental Designs

A preexperimental design is distinguished by the fact that the researcher has very little control over both the *when* and *to whom* of exposure to experimental stimuli and over the *when* and *to whom* of measurement.

[24]Cook and Campbell suggest that "perhaps the best way of reducing the error due to differences between persons is to match *before* random assignment to treatments" with the best matching variables being those "that are most highly correlated with posttest scores." *Quasi-Experimental Designs*, p. 47.

[25]See Campbell and Stanley, *Experimental and Quasi-Experimental Designs*, for an extensive discussion of the three types.

The One-Shot Case Study   A useful point of departure for discussing experiments is the one-shot case study. The one-shot case study can be diagrammed

$$X \qquad O$$

A single group of test units is exposed to an experimental variable, and its response is observed once. There is no random allocation of test units in the group, but rather the group is self-selected or is selected arbitrarily by the experimenter. For example, we might interview a convenience sample of those who read a particular trade journal for their reaction to our product. The experimental stimulus here would be the ad.

The one-shot case study is of little value in establishing the validity of hypothesized causal relationships (the ad was responsible for creating a favorable attitude toward our product) because it provides too little control over the extraneous influences. It provides no basis for comparing what happened in the presence of X with what happened when X was absent. Yet the minimum demands of scientific inquiry require that such comparisons be made.

The one-shot case study is more appropriate for exploratory than conclusive research. It is appropriately used to suggest hypotheses; it is not appropriate for testing their validity.

The One-Group Pretest–Posttest Design   The one-group pretest–posttest design

$$O_1 \qquad X \qquad O_2$$

adds a pretest to the one-shot case study design. In effect, the convenience sample of designated respondents is interviewed for their attitudes toward our product before the ad is placed. They are also interviewed after the ad is run, and the effectiveness of the ad is taken as the difference in their attitudes before and after exposure to the ad:

$$d = O_2 - O_1.$$

Although widely used to argue the effectiveness of marketing strategies, the one-group pretest-posttest design's failure to control extraneous error nullifies its conclusions. Consider just some of the factors that might be responsible for the $O_2 - O_1$ difference aside from the experimental variable X. First, history is uncontrolled. There may have been other ads, trade journal articles, some firsthand experience with the product, or any of a host of other factors occurring simultaneously with the experiment that caused the attitude change observed in a particular respondent. The respondent's position may have changed. Because of a change in the individual's status, the respondent is more responsive to the product in question at O_2 than at O_1 (maturation). Both the interactive and main testing effects might be at work. Because respondents were interviewed to secure O_1, they pay more attention to the trade journal ad than the normal reader might (interactive testing effect), so that the $O_2 - O_1$ difference cannot be generalized to the population of interest. In addition, respondents attempt to appear consistent with their O_1 score (main testing effect). Perhaps the respondents' initial responses created an extreme attitude score in either a positive or negative direction; then statistical regression is likely to occur with the O_2 scores. Suppose there is some experimental mortality. Would the $O_2 - O_1$ difference be larger or smaller if the lost participants were included? We do not know. Further, the sample was a convenience sample, and the result probably cannot be generalized to the larger population. Even if the intial sample had been a probability sample, all of the other extraneous sources of error could still affect the results.

The Static-Group Comparison   The static-group comparison is a design in which there are two groups, one that has experienced X and another that has not. A key feature is that the groups have not been created by randomization. The static-group comparison is diagrammed

$$\text{EG:} \quad X \quad O_1$$

$$\text{CG:} \quad \quad O_2$$

To continue with our previous example of the effectiveness of a particular ad, the static-group comparison would be conducted as follows: After the ad is run, interviews would be conducted among a sample of readers. Those who remembered seeing the ad would be considered the "experimental group," EG. Those who did not recall seeing the ad would be considered the "control group," CG. The attitudes of each group toward the product would be measured, and the effectiveness of the ad would be taken to be

$$d = O_1 - O_2,$$

that is, the difference in attitudes among those seeing the ad and those not seeing it.

   There are two fundamental sources of extraneous error in the static-group comparison. First, there is no way of ensuring that the groups were equivalent prior to the comparison. Those who have favorable attitudes toward a product often pay more attention to ads for the product than those who have unfavorable attitudes. It may be that the $O_1 - O_2$ difference reflects the initial attitude of the two groups and is not in any way attributable to the ad.

   The second fundamental weakness of the static-group comparison also involves its representativeness. It may be that the two groups were indeed equal at some prior time. Now, though, all individuals contacted are not willing to supply their attitudes toward the product. The design suffers experimental mortality due to this nonresponse, since the question of what the O_2 and O_1 scores would have been if all those designated to participate had indeed cooperated is unanswered.

True Experimental Designs

Randomization is the factor that makes the data from true experimental designs more valid than data from any preexperimental design. The true experimental design is distinguished by the fact that the experimenter can randomly assign treatments to randomly selected test units. In effect, the experimenter can control the *when* and *to whom* of exposure. The experimenter can also control the *when* and *to whom* of measurement. So as to distinguish the true experiment, let us denote a random assignment of test units to treatments by (R).

Before–After with Control Group Design   The before–after with control group design was considered an experimental ideal for a number of years. The design can be diagrammed

$$EG: \quad (R) \quad O_1 \quad X \quad O_2$$

$$CG: \quad (R) \quad O_3 \quad \quad O_4$$

Although it diagrams quite simply, this design imposes a number of requirements on the researcher.[26] First, the division of the test units is under the researcher's control. The researcher alone is able to decide which test units will receive the experimental stimulus and which will not. It is *not* up to the test units to self-select whether they will be members of the control or experimental groups as they did in the preexperimental designs. Further, the experimenter cannot arbitrarily assign test units to the experimental and control groups. He or she must do this randomly. The experimenter may match the test units on some external criterion and then assign one member from each of the matched pairs to the experimental and control groups, but this final assignment is made randomly. Finally, each of the test units in both groups is measured before and after the introduction of the experimental stimulus.

Consider the problem faced by an in-house credit union in promoting the credit union idea among the company's workers. Suppose the company is considering the effectiveness of a rather expensive brochure, "Know Your Credit Union," in creating awareness and understanding of the functioning of the firm's credit union. Let the brochure be the experimental stimulus X. The use of the before–after with control group design to investigate the effectiveness of the brochure would proceed along the following lines. First, a sample of the firm's employees would be selected at random. Second, one-half of these employees would be randomly assigned to the experimental group receiving the brochure, while the other half would form the control group. Third, each of the respondents selected for the sample would be measured using some scale or questionnaire to ascertain the employee's knowledge of the credit union. Fourth, the brochure would be mailed to those respondents who were designated for the experimental group.[27] After the lapse of some appropriate time interval, say one to two weeks, the knowledge scale or questionnaire would again be administered to each of the sample respondents.

Now consider this design in terms of the various sources of extraneous error. The difference O_4 minus O_3 reflects the effects of the extraneous influences. For instance, consider the possibility that during the course of the experiment there was a change in the bank prime lending rate and credit became more expensive. This history effect would be partially responsible for any differences in O_4 and O_3. However, it would also

---

[26]The before–after control group design is commonly used. For examples of its use, see the study by Levine investigating the effectiveness of comparative commercials, or the study by Smith and Lusch on the effectiveness of advertising in positioning a brand. Philip Levine, "Commercials that Name Competing Brands," *Journal of Advertising Research,* 16 (1976), pp. 7–14; and Robert E. Smith and Robert F. Lusch, "How Advertising can Position A Brand," *Journal of Advertising Research,* 16 (1976), pp. 37–43.

[27]The brochure would be mailed if that were the normal way of distributing it. If some other method of distribution were commonly used, the experimental procedure would also follow this mode of distribution.

exert a similar influence on those belonging to the experimental group. Thus if we were to consider the effect of the experimental variable to be E and the effect of these extraneous or uncontrolled sources of variation to be U, the impact of the experimental stimulus X could be secured as follows:

$$
\begin{array}{rcl}
O_2 - O_1 & = & E + U \\
O_4 - O_3 & = & U \\
\hline
(O_2 - O_1) - (O_4 - O_3) & = & E
\end{array}
$$

But note that this calculation applies to the following sources of extraneous variation: history, maturation, main testing effect, statistical regression, and instrument variation. All these influences should affect both groups approximately equally. Selection bias, of course, was eliminated by the random assignment of individuals to groups. The design can suffer from experimental mortality, however, if some of the employees designated for the study refuse to participate.

Assuming proper procedures were employed to eliminate experimental mortality, one can readily appreciate why this design was long considered ideal. But this changed with the discovery that the design may not control for the interactive testing effect. The pretest can make the experimental subjects respond to X, wholly or partially, because they have been sensitized. Yet the key question for credit union management is how employees in general, not just those pretested, respond to the brochure.

The situation in calculating the impact of the experimental stimulus then becomes

$$
\begin{array}{rcl}
O_2 - O_1 & = & E + U + I \\
O_4 - O_3 & = & U \\
\hline
(O_2 - O_1) - (O_4 - O_3) & = & E + I
\end{array}
$$

where I measures the interactive effect of testing. The analyst is unable to determine the impact of the experimental stimulus when the interactive effect of testing is present in the before–after with control group design. His or her calculation of the net differences provides a result. But this result has two components—a component due to the experimental stimulus and a component due to the interactive testing effect.

A classic example of the interactive testing effect occurred in a United Nations education campaign.[28] The study employed a sample of 2,000 individuals split into two equivalent groups of 1,000 each. Each member of the first group was interviewed to determine his or her knowledge of and attitudes toward the United Nations. This was followed by a publicity campaign of several months' duration, in turn followed by interviews with the second sample. A comparison of the two sets of scores produced practically no results—the members of the second sample were no better informed and did not have any more favorable attitudes than the first sample. The second sample was not even generally aware that the publicity campaign had been going on. In terms of the population of interest, the campaign was indeed a failure. Yet when the first sample was reinterviewed, there was a decided change in the members' attitudes toward and

---

[28]S. A. Star and H. M. Hughes, "Report on an Educational Campaign: The Cincinnati Plan for the United Nations," *American Journal of Sociology*, 40 (1949–1950), p. 389.

information about the United Nations. They had been sensitized to watch for and pay more attention to United Nations publicity.[29] The same kind of testing effect can operate in a before–after with control group design.

Four-Group Six-Study Design   In many research problems, the prior measurement is of such a nature that the test units are not sensitized to the experiment. In cases such as these, the before–after with control group design provides an estimate of the effect of the experimental variable. When an interactive testing effect is likely to be present, the four-group six-study design is a good choice.

The four-group six-study design can be diagrammed as

$$EG \quad I: \quad (R) \quad O_1 \quad X \quad O_2$$

$$CG \quad I: \quad (R) \quad O_3 \qquad\quad O_4$$

$$EG \quad II: \quad (R) \qquad\quad X \quad O_5$$

$$CG \quad II: \quad (R) \qquad\qquad\quad O_6$$

Consider again the problem of measuring the impact of the "Know Your Credit Union" brochure. The four-group six-study design would impose the following requirements on the researcher. First, a sample of the firm's employees would be selected at random. Second, the sample would be randomly divided into four groups. Those designated for the first experimental and control groups would be measured, using some appropriate instrument, for their knowledge of the credit union. The brochure would then be mailed to those designated as belonging to the first and second experimental groups. Then all four groups would be measured on their knowledge of the credit union. There are thus six measurements in all, as suggested by the name of the design.

One can readily appreciate the control afforded by the four-group six-study design. Selection bias is handled by the random assignment of test units to groups. The other extraneous sources of error are handled much as they were in the before–after with control group design, that is, by making the logical assumption that factors such as history, maturation, and so on, should affect all groups. By thus looking at the "difference in differences," the impact of these extraneous factors should be netted out. Further, while there is a possible interactive testing effect with the first experimental group, there can be none with the second experimental group, since there is no prior measurement to sensitize the respondents. The lack of a prior measurement raises the question of how to calculate the effect of X in the second experimental and control groups. One thing that can be done is to estimate what the prior measurements would have been. The most logical estimate is one that takes account of the random assignment of the test units to groups, assuming that, except for sampling variations, the four groups were equal *a priori* in their knowledge of the credit union. Thus, the best estimate of the

---

[29]For a discussion of the procedures that can be used to minimize sensitization effects, see Anthony Greenwald, "Within-Subjects Designs: To Use or Not to Use?," *Psychological Bulletin,* 83 (No. 2) (1976), pp. 314–320.

"before measurement" for the second experimental and control groups is the average of the before measurements actually taken, that is $\frac{1}{2}(O_1 + O_3)$.

Upon substituting this estimate, the various differences between after and before measurements are as follows:

$$\text{EG} \quad \text{I:} \quad O_2 - O_1 \qquad\qquad = E + U + I$$

$$\text{CG} \quad \text{I:} \quad O_4 - O_3 \qquad\qquad = \qquad U$$

$$\text{EG} \quad \text{II:} \quad O_5 - \tfrac{1}{2}(O_1 + O_3) = E + U$$

$$\text{CG} \quad \text{II:} \quad O_6 - \tfrac{1}{2}(O_1 + O_3) = \qquad U$$

What is the impact of the experimental stimulus? Clearly, it is determined by comparing the second experimental and control groups and is given specifically by the calculation

$$[O_5 - \tfrac{1}{2}(O_1 + O_3)] - [O_6 - \tfrac{1}{2}(O_1 + O_3)] = [E + U] - [U] = E.$$

However, that is not the only estimated effect provided by the four-group six-study design. This design also allows the effect of the uncontrolled extraneous factors on the response to be estimated, and it provides for an estimate of the magnitude of the interactive testing effect. Two independent estimates of extraneous error are in fact provided, one by each of the control groups. An estimate of the size of the interactive testing effect is provided by comparing Experimental Groups I and II through the calculation

$$[O_2 - O_1] - [O_5 - \tfrac{1}{2}(O_1 + O_3)] = [E + U + I] - [E + U] = I.$$

One need only look at the estimates of the various effects to appreciate why the four-group six-study design has become a conceptual ideal. However, its practical application in marketing is somewhat limited because the design is expensive in terms of time and money.[30] Further, marketing samples are not always so large as to afford the luxury of dividing the samples of test units into four equal groups. If the group samples are small, it is unlikely they will, in fact, be equal even if assigned randomly. Rather, the equality-of-groups assumption depends on the operation of the statisticians' "law of large numbers." Nevertheless, the isolation of the various effects afforded by the four-group six-study design makes it a standard against which other designs may be compared.

After-Only with Control Group Design   The careful reader will have observed that the researcher can estimate the impact of the experimental stimulus in the four-group six-study design simply by comparing Experimental Group II to Control Group II, which raises the question of why Experimental Group I and Control Group I are included. They are certainly *not* needed to generate an estimate of a "before measurement" for Experimental Group II and Control Group II, because regardless of what this

---

[30]For an example of its use, see Richard W. Mizerski, Neil K. Allison, and Stephen Calvert, "A Controlled Field Study of Corrective Advertising Using Multiple Exposures and a Commercial Medium," *Journal of Marketing Research*, 17 (August 1980), pp. 341–348.

measurement is, it cancels in the basic calculation of the effect of the experimental variable, that is,

$$[O_5 - \tfrac{1}{2}(O_1 + O_3)] - [O_6 - \tfrac{1}{2}(O_1 + O_3)] = O_5 - O_6.$$

Thus, the before measurements are not needed to estimate the effect of the experimental stimulus. They do allow the researcher to study individual cases of change and to develop better methodology because they enable study of the experimental variable under different conditions. If the researcher's sole interest is estimating the impact of the experimental variable, though, as is often the case, this estimate can be provided by studying the last two groups of the four-group six-study design in an after-only with control group design.

The after-only with control group design can be diagrammed

$$\text{EG:} \quad (R) \quad X \quad O_5$$

$$\text{CG:} \quad (R) \quad \quad O_6$$

where the observations have been subscripted with a 5 and 6 to indicate that these groups are the unpretested groups in the four-group six-study design. To use this design to investigate the impact of the "Know Your Credit Union" brochure, the researcher would again select a random sample of employees. One-half would be randomly assigned to the experimental group, and the other half would form the control group. Neither group would be premeasured, and the brochure would be mailed to all those in the experimental group. After some appropriate time lapse, both groups would be measured for their knowledge, and the estimated impact of the brochure would be provided by the difference O_5 minus O_6.

One can readily appreciate how the extraneous sources of error are eliminated in this experiment. The main extraneous factors are assumed to affect both groups, and thus their impact is eliminated by calculating the difference between O_5 and O_6. There is no interactive testing effect since there is no pretest. The experimental test units should behave much like the larger population of employees, in that some might read the brochure carefully, some might read it casually, and some might simply throw it away without reading it. This is as it should be, and the results can therefore be generalized to the population of employees.

There are two very important caveats, though, with respect to the after-only with control group design. This design is very sensitive to problems of selection bias and experimental mortality. The prior equality of the groups is assumed because of the random assignment of test units to groups. Since there is no before measurement, the assumption cannot be checked. It must be taken on faith, and this faith demands that the assignment of test units to groups was indeed random. Further, the design is highly sensitive to experimental mortality. There is simply no way of determining whether those who refuse to cooperate or drop out of the experimental group are similar to those dropping out of the control group. Experimental mortality, if it exists, calls into question the foundation on which the after-only with control group design rests, namely, that the groups are equal save for the impact of the experimental stimulus.

Be aware that the after-only with control group design does not allow the investigation of individual cases of change. This can sometimes be of real concern. For example, the design would not allow credit union management to investigate the impact of the "Know Your Credit Union" brochure on those who already had a good working knowledge of the credit union versus those who had little awareness and knowledge. The design affords no way of determining an employee's prior knowledge. Both the before–after with control group design and the four-group six-study design are superior in this respect.[31] However, if the individual cases of change are not of interest, the after-only with control group design is a viable one. As a matter of fact, it is probably the most frequently used experimental design in marketing research, since it possesses a number of sample size, cost, and time advantages, involving as it does only two groups and two measurements.

Quasi-Experimental Designs

We have just seen that the true experimental design is distinguished by the control it affords the researcher. The researcher is able to determine who will be exposed to the experimental stimulus, when the exposure will occur, who will be measured, and when that measurement will take place. In some cases, the investigator simply will not have control of the when and whom of exposure. The researcher will not be able to schedule the experimental stimuli or randomly assign test units to groups. If the researcher does have control of the when and whom of measurement, though, a quasi-experimental design results.

There are a number of quasi-experimental designs, although we shall discuss only the time-series experiment.[32] The discussion should indicate the emphasis in quasi-experimental designs. The time-series experiment was selected because it is uniquely suited to some types of marketing data that are routinely generated.

Time-Series Experiment   The time-series experiment can be diagrammed as

$$O_1 \quad O_2 \quad O_3 \quad O_4 \quad X \quad O_5 \quad O_6 \quad O_7 \quad O_8$$

This diagram suggests that a group of test units is observed over some time, that an experimental stimulus is introduced, and that the test units are again observed for their reaction. A change in the previous pattern of observations is taken as the effect of the experimental stimulus.[33]

The time-series experiment demands that researchers have repeated access to the same test units. Further, while researchers cannot schedule the exposure of these test

---

[31]For a unified treatment of the types of information and interpretation insights provided by "before–after" and "after-only" designs and their combinations, see N. K. Namkoodiri, "A Statistical Exposition of the 'Before–After' and 'After-Only' Designs and Their Combinations," *American Journal of Sociology,* 76 (July 1970), pp. 83–102.

[32]Campbell and Stanley, *Experimental and Quasi-Experimental Designs,* pp. 36–64, and Banks, *Experimentation in Marketing,* pp. 37–45, both present a number of useful quasi-experimental designs.

[33]Lehmann, for example, reports a natural experiment in which knowledge, attitude, intention to buy, and confidence in judgment were measured at four different points in time prior to and after an advertising campaign for a new product. Donald R. Lehmann, "Responses to Advertising a New Car," *Journal of Advertising Research,* 17 (1977), pp. 23–27.

units to the experimental stimulus, they can control when the units will be measured. Panel data conform nicely, then, to the time-series experiment. Further, there are a number of panels supplying marketing data as a routine matter. This is why the time-series experiment is one of the most important quasi-experimental designs for the marketing researcher.

Of course, our interest when using the time-series experiment is in establishing that the observed effect is due to the experimental variable. This requires that we eliminate other plausible hypotheses for the occurrence of the phenomenon. Now the time-series experiment bears some resemblance to the preexperimental, one-group pretest–posttest design. The resemblance is superficial, since the series of observations affords additional control. Consider some of the possible patterns of responses that may result as illustrated in Figure 4.1.

Note first of all that the pattern of responses, rather than any single observation, is key in interpreting the data from a time-series experiment. Consider, say, the impact of a package change, *X*, on the firm's market share. On the basis of the plot of the data points in Figure 4.1, it would seem logical to conclude that the package change:

1.   exerted a positive impact in situation *A* (it raised the firm's market share),

2.   had a positive impact in situation *B* (it halted a decline in market share),

3.   had no long-run impact in situation *C* (sales in Period 5 seem to be borrowed from sales in Periods 6 and 7),

4.   had no impact in situation *D* (the firm's market share growth remained steady),

5.   had no impact in situation *E* (the observed fluctuation after the introduction of the experimental variable is no greater than what was previously observed).

Of course, we would be interested in testing for the statistical significance of any observed changes.

Consider now the additional control afforded by the time-series experiment versus the one-group pretest–posttest design in interpreting the after and before measurements. First, maturation can be partially ruled out as causing the difference in O_5 and O_4 because it is unlikely that it would only operate in this one instance. Rather, it would logically have an impact on a number of other observations. Instrument variation, statistical regression, and the main testing effect would be similarly avoided. Selection bias can be reduced by the random selection of test units. Experimental mortality can hopefully be controlled by paying some premium to maintain cooperation. Of course, we saw in Chapter 3 that the ability to solicit and maintain cooperation in panels presents some problems, and a panel may not completely control the problems of selection bias and experimental mortality. These are conditions that also occur in the one-group, pretest–posttest, preexperimental design.

The failure to control history is the most fundamental weakness of the time-series experiment. Despite this, a carefully executed time-series experiment can provide some useful insight. If the careful examination of, say, consumer panel data before, during, and after introducing the experimental variable fails to turn up any unusual competitive reaction and if researchers also record other environmental changes as they occur, the researchers are in a position to make a valid assessment of the impact of the experimental stimulus. Of course, researchers can never be as sure that the impact of history has been ruled out in a quasi-experimental design as they can in a true experimental design.

Figure 4.1

Some Possible Outcomes in a Time-Series Experiment When Introducing an Experimental Variable X

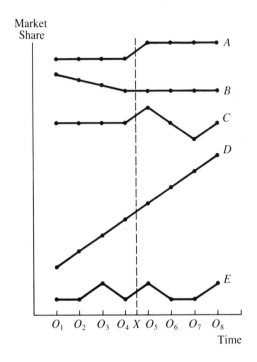

However, a repeatable stimulus, such as a cents-off coupon program, will afford greater certainty, since the effect of history will not be the same each time.

Another weakness of the time-series experiment is that it may be affected by the interactive testing effect. There may be some peculiarity in the experimental stimulus such that it affects only those sampling units subjected to repeated testing.

Experimental Versus Nonexperimental Designs

By now you should appreciate the fact that exploratory and descriptive designs are not particularly useful in establishing the existence of causal relationships. They simply do not provide the control necessary to infer that a causal relationship does indeed exist. Exploratory studies are less of a problem in this regard, since they are rarely used to make causal statements. Unfortunately, the same thing cannot be said about descriptive studies. Frequently, the evidence of a cross-sectional survey is employed to argue that X caused Y or the evidence from some time-series data is analyzed using, say, regression analysis to establish X as causing Y.

The error in such arguments can be appreciated by dissecting the typical descriptive study. A random sample of respondents is selected. The respondents are measured with respect to some effect or response variable Y. Next they are queried as to the hypothesized causal factor X. If it is then found that those who possess X also possess Y and those who lack X also lack Y, the truth of the assertion that *"X causes Y"* is established. The research is *ex post facto* in that the researcher is starting with the observation of a dependent or criterion variable and is retrospectively searching for plausible explanations.[34]

A problem arises in descriptive studies with respect to all three types of evidence used to support causality. Concomitant variation is observed. However, there is no way of knowing that those who did and did not possess Y were at some prior time equivalent with respect to both Y and X. In the experiment, the researcher is able to establish this equivalence by the random assignment of test units to groups. The researcher also knows quite accurately who was exposed to X and does not have to rely on a respondent's memory. The analyst is thus able to determine whether Y occurs more frequently among the subjects who have been exposed to X than it does among those who have not.

The researcher is also better able to establish the time order of occurrence of variables in an experiment. First, the experimental and control groups are set up in such a way that it is reasonable to assume they did not differ in terms of the response variable before exposure to the experimental stimulus. Second, with some experimental designs, the researcher actually measures the test units with respect to the criterion variable before exposing them to the experimental stimulus. In descriptive studies, the researcher simply has to assume that prior equality exists.

The descriptive study affords little control in eliminating other possible explanations. All the factors that affect experimental results also operate in descriptive research. In descriptive research, though, the analyst has no way of removing their effects. The analyst ends up in the awkward position of asserting it is this X and no other X that is causing Y. This assertion rests on a great deal of faith.

This is not to deny the very important role played by descriptive designs in marketing research. They are, after all, the dominant form. Rather, the reader must be aware of the dangers of using descriptive designs to establish causal linkages between variables.

Experimentation in Marketing Research

Experiments in marketing were rare before 1960, but their growth since then has been steady. One of the most significant growth areas has been in market testing or test marketing.[35] Although some writers make a distinction between the terms, the essential feature of the **market test** is that "it is a controlled experiment, done in a limited but carefully selected part of the marketplace, whose aim is to predict the sales or profit consequences, either in absolute or relative terms, of one or more proposed marketing

---

[34]Kerlinger, *Foundations*, pp. 347–360, has a particularly illuminating discussion of the problems of interpretation in *ex post facto* research.

[35]For recent assessments of what is happening in the test marketing arena, see *Sales and Marketing Management* magazines' annual coverage of the topic, which typically appears in the March issue. See also ''To Test or Not to Test Seldom the Question,'' *Advertising Age*, 55 (February 20, 1984), pp. M10–M11.

actions.''[36] Very often the action in question is the marketing of a new product or an improved version of an old product.

Notwithstanding previous tests of the product concept, the product package, the advertising copy, and so on, the test market is still the final gauge of consumer acceptance of the product. A. C. Nielsen data, for example, indicate that roughly three out of four products that have been test marketed succeed, while four out of five that have not been test marketed fail.[37] An example of the benefits to be gained from test marketing is provided by the experience of Green Giant in developing Oven Crock baked beans, which came already sweetened in the can. On the basis of blind taste tests, the executives at Green Giant thought they had a certain success.

"We did a series of blind taste tests and had a significant winner over bland pork and beans by a 3-to-1 or 4-to-1 preference margin," says John M. Stafford, now an executive vice-president at Pillsbury. But Oven Crock was a disaster in a test market. Surveys later showed that people who ate heavily flavored baked beans added their own fixings to the bland variety, and didn't want somebody to do it for them. "Our beans were terrific, but they were a solution to no known problem," Mr. Stafford says.[38]

Test marketing is not restricted to testing the sales potential of new products but has been used to examine the sales effectiveness of almost every element of the marketing mix. Market tests, for example, have been employed to measure the sales effectiveness of a new display, the responsiveness of food sales to supermarket shelf space changes, the impact of a change in retail price on the product's market share, the price elasticity of demand for a product, the effect of different commercials upon sales of a product, the sales effects of two different campaign themes, and the differential effects of price and advertising on demand, in addition to their use in determining the sales potential of new products.

Experimentation is not restricted to test marketing. Rather, it can be used whenever the manager has some specific mix alternatives to consider (for example, package design A versus B), and when the researcher can control the conditions sufficiently to allow an adequate test of the alternatives. Experiments are often used, therefore, when testing product or package concepts and advertising copy, although they have also been used to determine the optimal number of sales calls to be made upon industrial distributors.[39]

---

[36]Alvin R. Achenbaum, ''Market Testing: Using the Marketplace as a Laboratory,'' in Robert Ferber, ed., *Handbook of Marketing Research* (New York: McGraw-Hill, 1974), pp. 4–31 to 4–54.

[37]''Test Marketing: What's In Store,'' *Sales and Marketing Management,* 128 (March 15, 1982), pp. 57–85.

[38]Lawrence Ingrassia, ''A Matter of Taste: There's No Way to Tell If a New Food Product Will Please the Public,'' *Wall Street Journal,* 60 (February 26, 1980), pp. 1 and 23.

[39]There are several references that provide useful overviews of the use in marketing of experiments in general and test markets in particular. In addition to the Banks reference previously cited, one should also see Robert Holloway, ''Experimental Work in Marketing: Current Research and New Developments,'' in Frank Bass, Charles King, and Edgar Pessemier, eds., *Applications of the Sciences in Marketing Management* (New York: John Wiley, 1968), pp. 383–430; M. Venkatesen and R. J. Holloway, *An Introduction to Marketing Experimentation* (New York: Macmillan, 1970); and David M. Gardner and Russell W. Belk, *A Basic Bibliography on Experimental Design in Marketing* (Chicago: American Marketing Association, 1980).

Table 4.6

**Experience of National Geographic Society
in Marketing** *Journey Into China*

The Society had set aside $1.8 million to sell 380,000 copies of the new book to its members and subscribers. The offer included a separate wall map of China.

Before putting all $1.8 million into a mass mailing, the Society conducted a test mailing. One thing it wanted to find out was which of three prices to sell the book for: $19.95, $22.95, or $24.95. In addition, for the first time it offered the option of buying a more expensive deluxe edition for an extra $10.

The test also sought to determine which of the two brochure covers would work best. One displayed a photograph of a person carrying two baskets through a deep-green rice paddy, bannered with the caption "Take a spectacular tour of today's China." The other cover was red with a small color photograph of a pagoda and a waterfall; its caption read "Take a family tour of China for only (book's price)."

The brochure was accompanied by a perforated order card and a blue and black two-tone photograph of the Forbidden City in Peking. A four-page sales letter on National Geographic Society letterhead used the blue and black ink for alternating paragraphs. The package was completed with a half-page letter from the publisher folded inside a small map of China.

The version with the photograph of the rice paddy achieved the best response in the test, so it was chosen for the mass mailing. And the most profitable price turned out to be $19.95.

The results were stunning. It was the second most successful direct-mail campaign for a single book in the Society's history. The original mailing to Society members produced sales of more than 410,000 (a 4.28 percent response), well above the goal of 380,000. Moreover, 30 percent requested the deluxe edition. Since only 420,000 copies were printed in the first run, two additional press runs of 50,000 were required that year to fill later orders resulting from an insert card sent out with bills and from the Society's Christmas catalog.

Source: Courtland L. Bovee and William F. Arens, *Contemporary Advertising,* 2nd ed. (Homewood, Ill.: Richard D. Irwin, Inc., 1986), p. 468. Reprinted with permission.

An interesting example of the use of experimentation to examine the appeal of a new product while simultaneously fine tuning the other elements of the marketing mix can be found in the experience of the National Geographic Society in marketing *Journey into China,* a 518-page book with 400 full-color illustrations, which is reported in Table 4.6.

Future and Problems of Experimentation

Although it is probably true that marketing experiments will be used more frequently in the future, particularly when the research problem is one of determining which is the best of an available set of limited marketing alternatives, experimentation is not without its problems. Test marketing is a useful vehicle for illustrating these problems, since test marketing has been characterized as a double-edged sword, although to a greater or lesser extent they are present in other types of experiments. As Larry Gibson, director of corporate marketing research for General Mills, comments, "It costs a mint, tells the competition what you're doing, takes forever, and is not always accurate . . . For the moment, it's the only game in town."[40] Three of the more critical problems with experimentation in general and test marketing in particular are cost, time, and control.

[40]"To Test or Not to Test Seldom the Question," *Advertising Age,* 55 (February 20, 1984), pp. M10–M11.

Cost has always been a major consideration in test marketing. There are the costs of the experiment itself with which to contend. These costs include the normal research costs associated with designing the data-collection instruments and the sample and with the wages paid to the field staff that collects the data. While the direct research costs are often substantial, other costs must be borne as well. For instance, the test market should reflect the marketing strategy to be employed on the national scale if the results are to be useful. So the test also includes marketing costs for advertising, personal selling, displays, and so on. Philip Morris, for example, test marketed Like, its 99 percent caffeine-free cola, in eight cities. Its ad budget for those eight cities, which contain approximately five percent of the U.S. population, was $2.3 million. That amounts to $45 million on a national basis, which is more than Pepsi or Coke spend. The market test also included coupons, free samples, and other promotions, the cost of which was approximately equal to the ad budget.[41] With new product introductions, there are also the costs associated with producing the merchandise. To produce the product on a small scale is typically inefficient. Yet to gear up immediately for large-scale production can be tremendously wasteful if the test market indicates that the product is a failure. Given all of these various expenses, the fact that it typically costs $3.1 million to take a new product from research and development through test marketing in only 2 percent of the U.S. should not be too surprising.[42]

The time required for an adequate test market can be substantial. For example, it took Procter and Gamble nine years to go national with Pampers disposable diapers after they were first introduced in Peoria, Illinois.[43] One reason for extending the length of test markets is that the empirical evidence indicates their accuracy increases directly with time. According to A. C. Nielsen data, after two months, forecast accuracy is only one out of seven in the sense that when test market results were compared to national sales figures, the test market statistics only predicted national sales in 13 percent of the cases. The odds steadily increased, though, to five out of six after ten months.[44] Consequently, a year is often recommended as a minimum before any kind of go–no go decision is made to account for seasonal sales variations and repeat purchasing behavior. However, experiments continued over long periods are costly and raise additional problems of control and competitive reaction. while experiments conducted over short periods do not allow for the cumulative impact of the marketing actions.[45]

The problems associated with control manifest themselves in several ways. First, there are the control problems in the experiment itself. What specific test markets will

[41]"Seven-Up's No-Caffeine Cola," *Wall Street Journal*, 62 (March 25, 1982), p. 27.

[42]Eleanor Johnson Tracy, "Testing Time for Test Marketing," *Fortune*, 110 (October 29, 1984), pp. 75–76.

[43]Julie B. Solomon, "P&G Rolls Out New Items at Faster Pace, Turning Away from Long Marketing Testing," *Wall Street Journal*, 64 (May 11, 1984), p. 25.

[44]"How to Improve Your Chances for Test-Market Success," *Marketing News*, 18 (January 6, 1984), pp. 12–13.

[45]Some work has been done on early prediction of a new product's success, but these efforts still must have a sufficient time frame to allow assessment of repeat purchasing tendencies. See Chakravarthi Narasimhan and Subrata K. Sen, "New Product Models for Test Market Data," *Journal of Marketing*, 47 (Winter 1983), pp. 11–24 for a review of a number of these models. For an empirical comparison of the predictive power of five of them, see Vijay Mahajan, Eitan Muller, and Subhash Sharma, "An Empirical Comparison of Awareness Forecasting Models of New Product Introduction," *Marketing Science*, 3 (Summer 1984), pp. 179–197.

be used?[46] How will product distribution be organized in those markets? Can the firm elicit the necessary cooperation from wholesalers? From retailers? Can the test markets and control cities be matched sufficiently to rule out market characteristics as the primary determinant of the different sales results? Can the rest of the elements of the marketing strategy be controlled so as not to induce unwanted aberrations in the experimental setting? A common problem firms have to overcome when test marketing products is too much control. Precisely because the product is being test marketed, it receives more attention in the test market in the form of always-stocked shelves, extra effort from the sales force, and so on, than can ever be given to it on a national scale. One reason given for the failure of Pringles potato chips, which was very successful in test market but bombed nationally, is that quality slipped when the product was mass produced on the necessarily larger scale.[47] There are control problems associated with competitive reaction. While the firm might be able to coordinate its own marketing activities and even those of intermediaries in the distribution channel so as not to contaminate the experiment, it can exert little control over its competitors. Competitors can, and do, sabotage marketing experiments by cutting the prices of their own products, by gobbling up quantities of the test marketer's product and thereby creating a state of euphoria and false confidence on the part of the test marketer, and by other devious means. It has been called the most dangerous game in all of marketing because of the great opportunity it affords for misfires, as attested by the examples in Research Realities 4.2.

One could argue that the misfire reflected in Example 5 in Research Realities 4.2 represents one of the fundamental reasons why one test markets products. Indeed it seems better to find out about product performance problems like this in test market than after a product is introduced nationally. Consider, for example, the losses in company prestige that would have resulted if the following problems had not been discovered in test markets.

1. Because packages would not stack, the scouring pads fell off the shelf.
2. A dog food discolored on the store shelves.
3. In cold weather, baby food separated into a clear liquid and a sludge.
4. In hot weather, cigarettes in a new package dried out.
5. A pet food gave the test animals diarrhea.

---

[46]See, for example, Leonard Lodish and Dov Pekelman, "Increasing Precision of Marketing Experiments by Matching Sales Areas," *Journal of Marketing Research,* 15 (August 1978), pp. 449–455; Eileen Norris, "Product Hopes Tied to Cities with the 'Right Stuff,' " *Advertising Age,* 55 (February 20, 1984), pp. M10, M39, and M40; and Mitchell J. Shields, "Screening the Nation for the Four-Star Audience," *Advertising Age,* 54 (February 21, 1983), pp. M9, M31, and M32 for discussion of conceptual issues, and see "Test Marketing: For More Marketers No New Products Without Its Test," *Sales and Marketing Management,* 132 (March 12, 1984), pp. 81–110, for a list of frequently used test markets.

[47]Damon Darden, "Faced With More Competition, P&G Sees New Products as Crucial to Earnings Growth," *Wall Street Journal,* 63 (September 13, 1983), pp. 37 and 53. For discussion of the general problems of overcontrolling the marketing effort in test markets, see "How to Keep Well-Intentioned Research from Misleading New-Product Planners" and "How to Improve Your Chances for Test-Market Success," *Marketing News,* 18 (January 6, 1984), pp. 1 and 8, and pp. 12 and 13, respectively.

Research Realities 4.2

Examples of Test-Marketing Misfires

Example 1: When Campbell Soup first test-marketed Prego spaghetti sauce, Campbell marketers say they noticed a flurry of new Ragu ads and cents-off deals that they believe were designed to induce shoppers to load up on Ragu and to skew Prego's test results. They also claim that Ragu copied Prego when it developed Ragu Homestyle spaghetti sauce, which was thick, red, flecked with oregano and basil, and which Ragu moved into national distribution before Prego.

Example 2: Procter & Gamble claims that competitors stole its patented process for Duncan Hines chocolate chip cookies when they saw how successful the product was in test market.

Example 3: A health and beauty aids firm developed a deodorant containing baking soda. A competitor spotted the product in test market, rolled out its own version of the deodorant nationally before the first firm completed its testing, and later successfully sued the product originator for copyright infringement when it launched its deodorant nationally.

Example 4: When Procter & Gamble introduced its Always brand sanitary napkin in test market in Minnesota, Kimberly-Clark Corporation and Johnson & Johnson countered with free products, lots of coupons, and big dealer discounts, which caused Always to not do as well as expected.

Example 5: A few years ago, Snell (Booz, Allen, and Hamilton's design and development division, which does product development work under contract) developed a temporary hair coloring that consumers used by inserting a block of solid hair dye into a special comb. "It went to market and it was a bust," the company's Mr. Schoenholz recalls. On hot days when people perspired, any hair dye excessively applied ran down their necks and foreheads. "It just didn't occur to us to look at this under conditions where people perspire," he says.

Source: Example 1—Betty Morris, "New Campbell Entry Sets Off a Big Spaghetti Sauce Battle," *Wall Street Journal,* 63 (December 2, 1982), p. 25; Example 2—Eleanor Johnson Tracy, "Testing Time for Test Marketing," *Fortune,* 110 (October 29, 1984), pp. 75–76; Example 3—Kevin Wiggins, "Simulated Test Marketing Winning Acceptance," *Marketing News,* 19 (March 1, 1985), pp. 15 and 19; Example 4—Damon Darden, "Faced With More Competition, P&G Sees New Products as Crucial to Earning's Growth," *Wall Street Journal,* 63 (September 13, 1983), pp. 37 and 53; Example 5—Roger Recklefs, "Success Comes Hard in the Tricky Business of Creating Products," *Wall Street Journal,* 58 (August 23, 1978), pp. 1 and 27.

6. When it was combined with a price reduction, a product change in a liquid detergent was thought by consumers to be dilution with water.

7. Because of insufficient glue, over half of the packages came apart during transit.

8. Excessive settling in a box of paper tissues caused the box to be one-third empty at purchase.[48]

9. Sunlight dishwashing liquid was confused with Minute Maid lemon juice by at least 33 adults and 45 children, who became ill after drinking it.[49]

---

[48]Problems 1–8 are discussed in Jay E. Klompmaker, G. David Hughes, and Russell I. Haley, "Test Marketing in New Product Development," *Harvard Business Review,* 54 (May–June 1976), pp. 135–136.

[49]Lynn G. Reiling, "Consumer Misuse Mars Sampling for Sunlight Dishwashing Liquid," *Marketing News,* 16 (September 3, 1982), pp. 1 and 12.

Examples 1 through 4 in Research Realities 4.2, however, are of a different sort. By exposing the product to competitors through a test market, each of the firms lost much of its differential development advantage.

The simple point is that the marketing manager contemplating a market test must weigh the costs of such a test against its anticipated benefits. While it may serve as the final yardstick for consumer acceptance of the product, perhaps more careful early product testing in the form of need-satisfaction studies and in-home product performance tests would indicate that the market test is not warranted in particular instances.[50]

Table 4.7 lists in alphabetical order the most commonly used **standard test markets.** A standard market is one in which companies sell the product through their normal distribution channels. The results are typically monitored by one of the standard distribution services discussed in the next chapter. An increasingly popular variation of the standardized test market is the **controlled test market,** which is sometimes called the forced-distribution test market. In the controlled market, the entire test program is conducted by an outside service. The service pays retailers for shelf space and therefore can guarantee distribution to those stores that represent a predetermined percentage of the marketer's total food store sales volume. A number of research firms operate controlled test markets, including Audits & Surveys' Burgoyne, Inc., Nielsen, and Dancer, Fitzgerald, Sample.[51]

Another relatively recent variation when test marketing products is for firms to engage in **simulated test marketing (STM)** as a prelude to a full-scale market test. Most STM studies operate similarly. First, consumers are interviewed in shopping malls or sometimes in their homes. During the interview, they are exposed to the new product and are asked to rate its features. Then they are shown commercials for it and for competitors' products. In a simulated store environment, they are then given the opportunity to buy the product using seed money or cents-off coupons to make the purchase. Those not purchasing the test product are typically given free samples. After a use period, follow-up phone interviews are conducted with the participants to assess their reactions to the product and their repeat-purchase intentions. All the information is fed into a computer model, which has equations for the repeat purchase and market share likely to be achieved by the test model. The key to the simulation is the equations built into the computer model. Validation studies indicate that most STM models can come within 10% of actual sales in 80% of the cases.[52] A prime advantage of STM is the protection from competitors they provide. They are also faster and cheaper than full-scale tests and are particularly good for spotting weak products, which allows firms to

---

[50]On the basis of in-depth interviews with 31 marketing executives, Klompmaker, Hughes, and Haley "Test Marketing in New Product Developments," offer some specific suggestions regarding when a firm should conduct a test market, what can be learned from such a test, and how information from test markets should be used. See also "How to Improve Your Chances for Test Market Success."

[51]For a full list of the research firms operating controlled test markets and the cities that they use, see "Test Marketers on Target," *Sales and Marketing Management,* 134 (March 11, 1985), pp. 81–116.

[52]"Simulated Test Marketing Winning Acceptance," *Marketing News,* 19 (March 1, 1985), pp. 15 and 19. See also Henry P. Khost, "Pretesting to Avoid Product Postmortems," *Advertising Age,* 53 (February 22, 1982), pp. M10–M11; and " 'Magic Town' Doesn't Exist for Test Marketers," *Marketing News,* 19 (March 1, 1985), pp. 5 and 18, for other discussions of the operation, advantages, and disadvantages of STMs.

Table 4.7
Most Popular Standard Test Markets

Akron	Fort Wayne	Peoria
Albany–Schenectady–Troy	Fresno	Philadelphia
Albuquerque	Grand Rapids–Kalamazoo–	Phoenix
Ann Arbor	Battle Creek	Pittsburgh
Atlanta	Green Bay, WI	Portland, ME
Augusta, GA	Greensboro–Winston–Salem–	Portland, OR
Austin	High Point	Providence
Bakersfield	Greenville–Spartanburg–Asheville	Quad Cities: Rock Island &
Baltimore–Washington, DC	Harrisburg	Moline, IL, Davenport &
Bangor	Houston	Bettendorf, IA (Davenport–Rock
Baton Rouge	Huntsville	Island–Moline metro market)
Beaumont–Port Arthur–Orange, TX	Indianapolis	Raleigh–Durham
Binghamton, NY	Jacksonville, FL	Reading, PA
Birmingham–Anniston	Kansas City	Roanoke–Lynchburg
Boise	Knoxville	Rochester, NY
Boston	Lansing	Rockford
Buffalo	Las Vegas	Sacramento–Stockton
Cedar Rapids–Waterloo	Lexington, KY	Salt Lake City
Charleston, SC	Little Rock	St. Louis
Charleston, WV	Los Angeles	San Antonio
Charlotte	Louisville	San Diego
Chattanooga	Lubbock, TX	San Francisco–Oakland
Chicago	Macon, GA	Savannah
Cincinnati	Madison	Seattle–Tacoma
Cleveland	Manchester, NH	Shreveport
Colorado Springs	Memphis	South Bend–Elkhart
Columbus, GA	Miami–Fort Lauderdale	Spokane
Columbus, OH	Milwaukee	Springfield–Decatur–Champaign, IL
Corpus Christi	Minneapolis–St. Paul	Syracuse
Dallas–Fort Worth	Mobile	Tallahassee
Dayton	Modesto	Tampa–St. Petersburg
Denver	Montgomery	Toledo
Des Moines	Nashville	Topeka
Detroit	New Orleans	Tucson
Duluth	Newport News	Tulsa
El Paso	New York	West Palm Beach
Erie, PA	Oklahoma City	Wichita–Hutchinson
Eugene, OR	Omaha	Youngstown
Evansville	Orlando–Daytona Beach	
Fargo, ND	Pensacola	
Flint		

Source: "Test Marketers on Target," *Sales and Marketing Management,* 134 (March 11, 1985), pp. 110 and 112.

avoid full-scale testing of these products. The Achilles heel of STMs is that they do not provide any information about the firm's ability to secure trade support for the product or about what competitive reaction is likely to be. Thus, they are more suited for evaluating product extensions than for examining the likely success of radically different new products.

Summary

The emphasis in this chapter was on the third basic type of research design—causal design. The notion of causality was reviewed, and it was found that the scientific interpretation of the statement "X causes Y" was (1) that we could never prove that X caused Y, and (2) if the inference that it did was supported by the evidence, then X was one factor that made the occurrence of Y more probable, but it did not make it certain.

The three types of evidence that support the establishment of causal linkages were reviewed. Concomitant variation implies that X and Y must vary together in the way predicted by the hypothesis, while the time order of occurrence of variables suggests that X must precede Y in time if indeed it is to be considered a cause of Y. The elimination of other factors requires that the analyst design the investigation so that the results do not lend themselves to a number of conflicting interpretations.

The experiment was emphasized as providing the most convincing evidence of the three types. An experiment is simply a scientific investigation, in which an investigator manipulates and controls one or more predictor variables and observes the response of a criterion variable. There are two general types of experiments: the laboratory experiment, in which an investigator creates an artificial situation for the manipulation of the predictor variables, and the field experiment, which allows these manipulations to take place in a natural setting. The greater control afforded by a laboratory experiment allows the more precise determination of the impact of the experimental stimulus. There is also, though, a greater danger of generalizing the results of a laboratory experiment because of its artificial nature.

In either type of experiment, the investigator has to be on guard against extraneous sources of error that may confound interpretation: history, maturation, testing (both main and interactive), instrument variation, statistical regression, selection bias, and experimental mortality. The true experimental designs are particularly useful in controlling, or at least removing from the observed results, the impact of these errors. True experimental designs are distinguished from preexperimental and quasi-experimental designs by the fact that they allow the investigator to control who are to be exposed to the experimental stimulus and when they are to be exposed.

While experiments were rarely used in marketing before 1960, their growth since then has been steady. The market test to establish the sales potential of new products has become standard practice for some companies, and test marketing is being increasingly used to determine the effectiveness of contemplated changes of any elements of the marketing mix. Two increasingly popular variations when market testing new products are the use of a controlled test, in which the distribution of the product is guaranteed by the service provider, or a simulated test market (STM), in which reactions from users of the product are used in a series of equations to predict repeat purchase behavior and market share likely to be realized by the test product. Descriptive designs, though, are still the dominant form of marketing research investigations. This is partly due to tradition, but it also reflects the cost, time, and control problems associated with experimental research.

Questions

1. How do the scientific notions and commonsense notions of causality differ?
2. What types of evidence can be employed to support an inference of causality?
3. What is an experiment?
4. What is the distinction between laboratory and field experiments?
5. What is the difference between internal and external validity?
6. What are the basic extraneous variables that can affect the outcome of a research investigation?
7. What is the difference between the main testing effect and the interactive testing effect? Why is the distinction important?
8. What are the main ways of establishing the prior equality of groups? Which method is preferred, and why?
9. What are the distinctions between preexperimental, true experimental, and quasi-experimental designs?
10. What are the basic types of preexperimental designs?
11. What are the main types of true experimental designs? What are the key issues or problems associated with each of these designs?
12. How is the effect of the experimental stimulus determined in a before–after with control group design? In a four-group six-study design? In an after-only with control group design?
13. How does the true experimental, after-only with control group design differ from the preexperimental, static-group comparison research design?
14. When would one want to employ a four-group six-study design instead of a before–after with control group design and vice versa?
15. When would one want to employ a before–after with control group design or a four-group six-study design in lieu of an after-only with control group design and vice versa?
16. What is the basic nature of the time-series experiment? How does the time-series experiment differ from the preexperimental, one-group pretest–posttest design? What is the import of this difference?
17. Compare descriptive research and true experimental design with respect to the ability of each to control or allow for extraneous factors.
18. How would you explain marketing's infrequent use of experimental research before 1960 and its steadily increasing use since then?
19. What is a test market? For what kinds of investigations can test markets be used? What are the problems associated with test markets?
20. What is the primary difference between a standard test market and a controlled test market?
21. How does simulated test marketing (STM) work? What are its main advantages and disadvantages versus full market tests?

Applications and Problems

1. Consider the following statement: "The increase in sales is due to the new sales personnel that we recruited from the vocational school over the last several years. Sales of the new salespeople are up substantially while sales for longer term salespeople have not increased."

    Identify the causal factor X and the effect factor Y in the above statement.

2. The research department of the company in Question 1 investigated the change in sales for each of the company's salespeople. Using criteria supplied by management, the department categorized all territory sales changes as increased substantially, increased marginally, or no increase. Consider the following table, in which 260 sales personnel have been classified as old or new:

Salesperson Assigned	Territory Sales Change			
	Increased Substantially	Increased Marginally	No Increase	Total
New	75	30	5	110
Old	50	40	60	150

    (a) Does this table provide evidence of concomitant variation? Justify your answer.
    (b) What conclusions can be drawn about the relationship between X and Y on the basis of the above table?

3. Six months later, the research department in Question 2 investigated the situation once again. However, a new variable was considered in the analysis, namely, the type of territory to which the salesperson was assigned; more specifically, whether the salesperson was assigned to an essentially urban metropolitan or nonmetropolitan territory. The following table summarizes the research department's findings:

Salesperson Assigned	Metropolitan Territory			
	Territory Sales Change			
	Increased Substantially	Increased Marginally	No Increase	Total
New	70	20	—	90
Old	54	16	—	70

Salesperson Assigned	Nonmetropolitan Territory			
	Territory Sales Change			
	Increased Substantially	Increased Marginally	No Increase	Total
New	5	10	5	20
Old	20	40	20	80

    (a) If the type of territory to which the salesperson was assigned is ignored, does this table provide evidence of concomitant variation between change in sales and whether the salespeople are new or old? Justify your answer.
    (b) If type of territory is considered, does the table provide evidence of concomitant variation between sales changes and whether the salespeople are new or old? Justify your answer.

Several experimental designs are described in Questions 4 through 7. For each design answer the following questions:

(i) What type of design is being used? Explain.

(ii) Diagramatically represent the design.

(iii) Discuss the threats to internal and external validity for the design.

4. A leading manufacturer of frozen food products decided to test the effectiveness of an in-store display. Four large supermarkets, located near the company's main office, were selected for the experiment. The display was set up in two of the stores and sales were monitored for a period of two weeks. The sales of the other two stores were also recorded but no displays were used. Sales volume for the frozen food products increased 2 percent more in the stores that used the in-store displays than in the stores that did not use the displays.

5. A branch of Alcoholics Anonymous wanted to test consumer attitudes toward an anti-drinking advertisement. Two random samples of respondents in Piscataway, New Jersey, were selected for the experiment. Personal interviews, relating to consumer attitudes toward alcoholism, were conducted with both samples. One of the samples was shown the anti-drinking advertisement and following this, personal interviews were conducted with both samples in order to examine consumer attitudes toward alcoholism.

6. A manufacturer of a line of office equipment, based in Houston, Texas, marketed its products in the southwest United States. The region consisted of 30 geographic divisions, each headed by a divisional manager who had a staff of salespeople. The firm's management wanted to test the effectiveness of a new sales training program in which the sales personnel in five of the divisions typically participated. The divisional managers of these five divisions were instructed to monitor sales for each salesperson for each of the five months before and after the training program. The results were to be sent to the vice-president of sales in Houston, who planned to compare them against sales changes in the other divisions.

7. A new manufacturer of women's cosmetics was planning to retail the firm's products through mail-order. The firm's management was considering the use of direct mail advertisements to stimulate sales of their products. Prior to committing themselves to advertising through direct mail, management conducted an experiment. A random sample of 1,000 housewives was selected from Memphis, Tennessee. The sample was divided into two groups with each subject being randomly assigned to one of the two groups. Direct-mail advertisements were sent twice over a period of one month to respondents of one of the groups. Two weeks later, respondents of both the groups were mailed the company's catalog of cosmetics. Sales to each group were monitored.

Cases to Part 2

Case 2.1
Nostalgia, Inc.[1]

The Nostalgia Company was founded on March 23, 1950, in Corpus Christi, Texas, by Douglas J. Kennedy. The company, which employs 35 full-time workers, manufacturers and sells one basic product, a "datebook calendar." These calendars are distinguished by their large 5- by 8-inch size, one week of days to the page, and a picturesque scene on the facing page of each week. In addition, the calendar has a space for each day that provides considerable room for recording appointments and other important events. The calendar has consistently been one of the least expensive in its competitive market.

Industry Background

The calendar printing industry is by nature one of the most difficult to analyze. The industry comprises hundreds of companies both large and small, some dealing primarily with calendar printing but most doing it only as a sideline. For this reason there is very little published data on the calendar industry per se, except for a few trade statistics from the advertising specialty and printing industries.

The calendar business generates over $250 million in sales each year. It is divided into three main categories: custom produced, stock, and calendars for retail sales to customers. The first two categories are sometimes combined under the heading of advertising specialty calendars. These calendars are made up on special order for firms that wish to use them as promotional items to customers. Most of the calendars produced for this part of the industry are done by printing firms; however, there are nonprinting firms that have set up in-house print shops.

In the calendar printing for retail sales side of the industry, of which Nostalgia is part, the leading manufacturer is Hallmark Cards, Inc., of Kansas City, Missouri. Hallmark offers a number of different styles of calendars ranging from the traditional wall type to posters, address books, diaries, desk models, and towels. In the retail part of the industry 50 percent of the sales occur in November and December, with these months representing 20 percent and 30 percent of the total annual sales, respectively. It is estimated that 90 percent of all customers for this part of the industry are women, and that most calendars are priced between $6.95 and $8.95.[2]

The major types of calendars are art or wall calendars, which come in 12, 6, or 4 sheets per calendar; year-at-a-glance calendars, which are a one-sheet calendar; pin-up

[1]The contributions of Larry Foy to the development of this case are gratefully acknowledged.

[2]Supplied through the courtesy of Specialty Advertising Association, Chicago, Illinois. See also Marcia Newlands Fero, "Calendars—The Essential Sideline," *Publishers Weekly,* (April 22, 1983), p. 45.

Table 1
Nostalgia Calendar Sales Data

Calendar	No. Printed	Calendar Printing Cost	Unit Cost (cents)	Total Income	Gross Profit	Total Sold	Total Refunds
1975	226,982	221,288.28	195.36	415,615.74	194,327.46	226,026	17,280
1976	221,498	226,365.48	208.35	401,894.70	175,529.22	221,120	25,266
1977	261,682	286,356.00	219.72	453,781.98	167,425.98	259,902	33,732
1978	305,880	320,419.74	204.84	480,674.04	160,254.30	256,902	46,302
1979	285,800	314,126.70	221.46	503,784.06	189,657.36	278,140	NOT ALLOWED
1980	288,400	411,607.86	286.95	577,861.56	166,253.70	244,366	NOT ALLOWED
1981	254,530	358,936.50	286.92	554,561.52	195,625.02	242,470	NOT ALLOWED
1982	256,430	364,771.44	285.18	566,691.18	201,919.74	197,660	23,094
1983	209,202	316,435.86	302.61	534,322.08	217,886.22	190,246	43,032
1984	188,500	352,105.92	373.47	593,130.66	241,024.74	162,124	6,822

calendars, which are 12 and 6 sheet; commercial calendars that have one illustration with a calendar pad attached; desk calendars or calendar pads; diary calendars; and one-a-day calendars, which is a stack of sheets with one date per page. The Nostalgia calendar is considered a desk calendar.[3]

Company Background

Doug Kennedy began his business in 1950 after five moderately successful years as a commercial photographer. Mr. Kennedy believed that if he put his pictures together in a calendar, it would serve two major purposes. First, it would bring in additional revenues, which he needed to purchase more photography equipment. Second, it would increase the sales of the pictures printed in the calendar.

As it turned out, the calendar business became much more lucrative than he had imagined, and in 1958 he dropped the sale of individual photographs completely and concentrated all his efforts on the datebook calendar. Calendar sales data for the recent 10-year period 1975–1984 are presented in Table 1.

Nostalgia sells its calendar to a number of segments of the market, as indicated in Table 2. These segments are contacted through two primary channels of distribution: direct orders from consumers, and direct orders from retailers and resellers. To reach these segments Nostalgia does a small amount of advertising. Retailers are mailed a flyer three times a year, and all other segments are mailed a flyer once a year, in May. In addition, each calendar contains a blank for ordering more copies of the current year's calendar, and/or a copy of the following year's calendar. Table 3 traces the rate of retail price increases for 1979–1984 and includes the discount schedules at retail and resale for the calendars.

---

[3]For a description of the calendars available from each of 125 publishers and the prices for each, see "Calendars 1985," *Publishers Weekly* (April 27, 1984), pp. 32–64.

Table 2
Nostalgia Calendar Group Sales

	Total Calendars Sold				
Segments	1980	1981	1982	1983	1984
Individuals (over 12 copies)	14,396	13,106	11,868	10,244	7,206
Schools & libraries	39,426	42,208	24,954	27,508	8,846
Church groups	8,566	10,550	6,374	6,008	3,798
General organizations	34,980	33,078	23,938	14,282	15,130
Institutions	7,082	8,456	7,956	7,352	8,076
Professional	8,022	8,568	6,420	5,290	5,808
Manufacturing	2,180	3,020	2,968	1,808	1,890
Complimentary	1,810	2,276	3,874	3,164	3,428
Information desk	1,380	1,602	1,480	970	1,016
Staff	594	752	492	640	688
Retailers	55,744	55,092	47,776	57,076	49,782
Imprinters	57,334	48,990	45,990	45,410	38,500
Individuals (under 12 copies)	12,852	12,530	11,434	10,494	9,236

Table 3
Nostalgia Price Increases and Discount Structures

		Discount Structures			
Price Increases		Retail		Resale	
Year	Retail Price	Quantity	Discount	Quantity	Discount
1979	$3.00	48–96	35%	12–49	25%
1980	$3.00	97–144	40%	50–150	30%
1981	$3.75	145–288	45%	151–250	35%
1982	$3.75	289–432	45%	251–500	40%
1983	$4.50	433–616	47%	501–999	45%
1984	$6.00	617 +	50%	1,000 +	50%
1985	$7.50				

As an added feature for retailers, Nostalgia allows all customers who order directly to return unsold calendars by February 15 of the calendar year. This is done in the hope that retailers will be induced to order larger amounts. The retailer pays the postage for returns. The cost to mail calendars through the U.S. Postal Service was 72 cents each.

The Problem

As J. M. Evans, marketing manager for Nostalgia, reviewed the sales results from 1984, he was well aware of the problem the company faced. Calendar sales had reached a peak of 278,140 in 1979 but had declined steadily every year thereafter (see Table 1).

Evans had originally believed it to be a temporary decline due to general economic conditions, but, with a sales drop of 28,000 calendars for 1984, this decline had placed the company in a very weak position.

Evans began to ponder the possible sources of the problem. He was due in Kennedy's office at the end of the week with a full report of the company's dilemma.

Questions

1. What kind of research is in order to solve Mr. Evans' problem? Why?
2. Describe the procedure you would follow in determining the reason for the sales decrease. Be specific.

Case 2.2
Bonita Baking Company (B)[1]

As sales manager at Bonita Baking Company, Frank Fortunada, Jr., has elected to undertake a research project concerned with Bonita Health Breads. Bonita Health is a line of specialty breads competing with national brands (such as Roman Meal and Pepperidge Farms) and regional brands (such as Orowheat—the market leader). Although the specialty bread segment was rapidly growing, the Bonita Health line has not been performing well. Most specialty brands (including Bonita) are actively promoted through television, radio and newspaper advertising, coupons, and special price promotions.

Fortunada decided to undertake a research study to help him determine the source of the problem underlying the Bonita Health line's poor sales results. He was interested in ascertaining Bonita's relative position and image in the specialty bread market. Fortunada also needed to know more about the consumer profile of specialty bread users and how to reach them most effectively.

Fortunada solicited and received three separate proposals for the research study.

Proposal One—Consumer Research Analysts

The proposal from Consumer Research Analysts (CRA) suggested doing a two-stage mail survey to better understand the behavior of the speciality bread market. CRA had a reputation for doing sophisticated research for a number of consumer product areas. The proposal itself had been prepared by an associate of the firm who had recently completed an M.B.A. degree with an emphasis in consumer behavior. Excerpts from the proposal are shown on the following page.

---

[1]Source: From: *Cases in Marketing Research* by William G. Zikmund, William J. Lundstrom, and Donald Sciglimpaglia, pp. 61–64 (Chicago: Dryden). Copyright © 1982 by CBS College Publishing. Reprinted by permission of CBS College Publishing.

Statement of the Problem

Studies examining the process of adoption of products support the fact that consumers follow a general procedure that involves a series of stages:

Awareness Before a person can consider purchase, the first requirement is that he or she be aware of the product's existence.

Interest Often the level of interest is dictated by the need the consumer feels he or she has for a product. At other times, the mere awareness of the product stimulates interest.

Evaluation At this stage, the consumer will determine whether or not the product should be considered for purchase.

Trial In most cases the consumer will try the product—if possible—and form attitudes and further evaluations based on this trial.

Re-evaluation Attitudes toward the product are formed based on the trial.

Adoption At this stage the consumer continues to use the product on a continuous basis or abandons it in search of another.

The problem to be studied here includes the determination of how many consumers (or potential consumers) currently are at each stage of this process, why they are there, and how they might be moved toward adoption of Bonita Health Breads.

Objectives

To determine the above, the following objectives will be sought:

1. Determination of levels of awareness of the product;
2. Determination of attributes considered important in purchasing Bonita Health (or competitive lines);
3. Determination of number of individuals trying Bonita Health and evaluation of the same;
4. Analysis of those attributes considered as important in evaluating Bonita Health Bread (or competitive lines).

In addition, demographic and media-viewing characteristics of the users and non-users will be provided.

Method

Preliminary evaluation of existing data will constitute the initial phase of the research. This procedure will utilize any existing sources of information that may provide insight into the problem.

The second phase will involve a two-step mail survey of consumers. The initial sample will consist of approximately 4,000 households selected from a city directory. The first survey will be used to identify the market profile for specialty breads and for Bonita Health specifically. A second (follow-up) survey questionnaire will be sent to those households identified in the first survey as Bonita Health and other specialty brand consumers. Its purpose will be to assess the objectives noted above.

Results

The results of the research presented will include a report covering:

1. levels of awareness of Bonita Health, attitudes toward the same, and attributes considered salient in the determination of these attitudes;

2. positioning of Bonita Health relative to the competition and relative strengths and weaknesses; and

3. demographic and media-viewing characteristics of users and non-users.

A copy of the computer output generated will be included.

Costs

The total cost of this project would be $8,000.

Proposal Two—Lancaster Associates

Another proposal was received from James Lancaster, a local management and marketing consultant. Lancaster's proposal was in the form of a letter to Fortunada in which he suggested using focus groups to research the problem. The essence of the letter proposal is shown below.

Dear Frank,

Thank you for allowing me to propose my research approach for the Bonita Health study.

I think that we need to really do an in-depth study of consumer awareness, attitudes, and behavior regarding specialty breads in general and Bonita Health specifically. In this way we can get an understanding of the reasons behind the consumer purchase or nonpurhcase of your product. I strongly feel that the way to do this is by using a series of focus group studies.

I propose to conduct four focus groups of roughly twelve specialty bread buyers each. The consumers would be recruited by phone to meet certain criteria. The panelist screening criteria include:

1. Total household income—$20,000 plus
2. Female head of household who is the principal shopper
3. Fourteen (14) plus years of education
4. Specialty bread users of the following breads:
   a. Bonita Health
   b. Orowheat
   c. Northridge
   d. Fresh Horizons
   e. Pepperidge Farms
   f. Millbrook

g. Roman Meal

h. Specialty store brands

I will personally conduct the focus groups and provide a written summary report of the findings. The total cost, including recruiting and participant incentives, is $4,000.

Sincerely,
James Lancaster
Lancaster Associates

Proposal Three—Action Research

The third proposal came from Action Research. Dale Dash, the person that Fortunada spoke to on the phone, suggested that the most fruitful course of action would be to conduct what he termed an experience survey. He suggested that his firm would telephone roughly 20 bread department managers or store managers to determine their feelings about specialty breads and the Bonita line. In addition, Dash proposed that baking industry people in other parts of the country could be interviewed to get an understanding of what other regional marketers were doing to promote and market their brands of specialty breads. Dash thought that about ten baking industry marketing persons should be interviewed.

Dash told Fortunada that the total cost of the project would be between $1,500 and $3,000, although he could not say for sure. He indicated that he would be glad to give Fortunada a written proposal if he wished.

Questions

1. What are the strengths and weaknesses of each suggested approach?

2. Which (if any) proposal should Fortunada accept?

3. Write a short proposal that indicates how you would research this problem. You may want to refer to Part A of the Bonita Baking Company case for more information about the problem.

Case 2.3
Rumstad Decorating Centers (A)

In 1929, Joseph Rumstad opened a small paint and wallpaper supply store in downtown Rockford, Illinois. For the next 45 years the store enjoyed consistent, though not spectacular, success. Sales and profits increased steadily but slowly as, in order to keep pace with the competition, the original line of products was expanded to include unpainted furniture, mirrors, picture framing material, and other products. In 1974, due to a declining neighborhood environment, Jack Rumstad, who had taken over management of the store from his father in 1970, decided to close the downtown store and to open a new outlet on the far west side of the city. The west side was chosen because it was experiencing a boom in new home construction. In 1983, a second store was opened on the east side of the city and the name of the business was changed to Rumstad Decorating Centers. The east side store was staffed with sales clerks but was basically managed by Jack Rumstad himself from the west side location. All ordering, billing, inventory control, and even the physical storage of excess inventory was concentrated at the west side store.

In 1984, the east side store was made an independent profit center. Jack Rumstad personally took over the management of the outlet and hired a full-time manager for the west side store. With the change in accounting procedures occasioned by this organizational change, it became possible to examine the profitability of each outlet separately.

Jack Rumstad conducted such an examination early in 1986, using the profit and loss figures in Table 1, and became very concerned with what he discovered. Both stores

Table 1
Profit and Loss Statement for Rumstad Decorating Centers

	East Side Store		West Side Store	
	1985	1984	1985	1984
Total Sales	$114,461	$91,034	$ 87,703	$108,497
Cash sale discounts	4,347	2,971	4,165	2,930
Net sales	110,114	88,063	83,538	105,567
Beginning inventory	53,369	49,768	1,936	0
Purchases	64,654	56,528	163,740	59,366
Total	118,023	106,206	165,676	59,366
Ending inventory	51,955	53,369	115,554	1,936
Cost of sales	66,068	52,837	50,122	57,430
Gross profit or loss	44,046	35,226	33,416	48,137
Direct Costs				
Salaries	24,068	19,836	24,549	26,583
Payroll taxes	2,025	1,814	1,764	2,060
Depreciation—furniture and fixtures	92	92	92	92
Freight	6	43	511	800
Store supplies	694	828	607	4,153
Accounting and legal expenses	439	433	439	433
Advertising	2,977	4,890	4,820	5,252
Advertising—yellow pages	1,007	618	1,387	956
Convention and seminar expenses	0	33	83	216
Insurance	226	139	1,271	1,643
Office expense and supplies	4,466	4,393	5,327	5,010
Personal property tax	139	139	140	140
Rent	7,000	7,000	4,900	4,900
Utilities	2,246	1,651	2,746	2,359
Total direct costs	45,385	41,909	48,636	54,597
Profit or loss	(1,339)	(6,683)	(15,220)	(6,460)

had suffered losses for 1985, and, while he had anticipated incurring a loss during the first couple of years of operation of the east side store, he was not at all prepared for a second successive loss at the west side outlet. He blamed the 1984 loss on the disruptions caused by the change in organizational structure. Further, from 1984 to 1985, the east side had a 25 percent increase in net sales, a 25 percent increase in gross profits, an 8 percent increase in total direct costs, and, although the east side store still showed a net loss, it was 80 percent less than the previous year's loss. The west side store, on the other hand, had shown a 21 percent decrease in net sales, a 31 percent decrease in gross profit, an 11 percent decrease in direct costs, and a 136 percent increase in net loss. Mr. Rumstad is very concerned about the survival of the business and particularly concerned with what is happening to the west side store. He has called you in as a research consultant to help him pinpoint what is happening so that he might take corrective action.

West Side Store

The west side store is located in the heart of the census tract with the highest per capita income in the city. Most of the residents in the area are professional people or white-collar workers. The store is a freestanding unit located on a frontage road with the word "Rumstad" printed across the front. Since Jack Rumstad's transfer to the east side store, there has been a succession of managers at the west side store. The first one lasted six months, the second and third four months, while the current manager, previously a sales clerk at the store for four years, has held the job for ten months. While the products carried and the prices charged are the same in both stores, there is some difference in advertising emphasis. The west side store does all of its advertising in the *Shopper's World,* a weekly paper devoted exclusively to advertising, which is distributed free to all households in the community. Delivery is by and large door-to-door, although it is quite typical for a group of newspapers to be placed at the entrance to apartment buildings and for residents to pick up a copy if they so choose.

East Side Store

The east side store is located in a predominantly blue-collar area. Most of the residents in the immediate vicinity work for one of the various machine tool manufacturers that comprise one of the basic industries in Rockford. The store is located in a small shopping center. It has a large window display area with a readily visible "Rumstad Decorating Center" sign above the store. The east side store advertises periodically in the *Rockford Morning Star* in addition to its yellow pages advertising.

Question

1.   How would you proceed to answer Mr. Rumstad's problem?

Case 2.4
Gibbons College Library[1]

The library staff of Gibbons College in Iowa has been deeply committed to serving the needs of the college's undergraduate student body. The library offers its students an attractive atmosphere in which to conduct individual or group study and provides numerous workshops and seminars designed to improve student study, writing, and test taking skills. Of special significance has been the administration's commitment to meeting the information needs of library patrons. For example, during the past academic year the library received some 70,000 requests for information and reference referral, and it had more than 169,000 library items checked out to registered students.

Because of the diversity in student backgrounds, meeting patron information demands is a very difficult and challenging activity. The facilities and installations must be specific enough to serve individual student needs, yet targeted to reach as large an audience as possible. Careful staff consideration must be continually given, therefore, to the establishment of new library policies and procedures.

Recently, the library staff contemplated the installation of a computer data base of bibliographic references to replace the manual methods of searching indexes and abstracts for information on research topics. The need for a computer search facility at the library had become especially acute in the last several years because:

■ Library users had become more sophisticated in their awareness of the potential resources available to them;

■ Library users and staff had become increasingly cognizant of the use and application of computers in educational and library settings; and

■ Library staff had become aware of the ways in which reference questions and search strategy problems could be solved through on-line data bases.

By having computer search facilities available, students could—for a relatively small fee that was based on the amount of computer time used and the length of the computer printout—quickly access information and coordinate research activities.

Since well over 150 bibliographic data bases are on the market, the library staff decided to conduct a study that would provide information directly related to decisions on choosing a computer data base searching service. First, the staff wanted to learn more about who currently uses the library and to what extent, what are the characteristics of people using the library, and what differences exist between heavy and low-level users of library facilities. Second, the staff wanted to focus on preferred features of a data base searching service. For example, how large is the potential user population for the service, and what characteristics of the service will best meet the needs of an undergraduate student body?

[1]The contributions of David M. Szymanski to the development of this case are gratefully acknowledged.

Sampling Procedure

To obtain information necessary for making an informed judgment on the best data base to install, the library staff conducted a survey of library patrons. The population was defined to be all undergraduate users of the college's library.

Because a list of known sampling units was not available, a nonprobability convenience sample was used for the study. The staff decided to draw the sample from individual users of the library during one particular day. A sample of 300 subjects was projected as being (1) necessary to be representative of the user population, and (2) needed to do cross-tabulation analysis. Because a convenience sample is dependent on volunteer returns, it was considered important that researchers secure an adequate response by sampling morning, afternoon, and evening library patrons. A questionnaire (see Figure 1) was therefore distributed to students entering the building during three

Figure 1
Gibbons College Library Survey

The College Library needs information from you in order to improve library service. We would appreciate it if you could answer the following questions and place the completed survey in the questionnaire return box (located at all exits) when you leave the library.

1. *What one thing do you like most about the College Library?*
   _____

2. *What one thing do you like least about the College Library?*
   _____

3. *Approximately how many times per week have you used the College Library this semester?*
   _____ this is my first visit to the College Library
   _____ less than once a week
   _____ once a week
   _____ 2–4 times a week
   _____ 5 or more times a week

4. *For what purpose do you most often use the College Library?*
   _____ to study
   _____ to do homework (nonresearch-work homework)
   _____ to do research work
   _____ other: please specify _____

5. *Have you used the* Reader's Guide to Periodical Literature, The Magazine Index, Business Periodicals Index, *or any other index to find magazine and journal articles this semester?*
   _____ yes   _____ no
   If yes, how often during the current school year have you used such indexes?
   _____ 1–2 times   _____ 3–4 times   _____ 5 or more times

---

continued on next page

Figure 1
Gibbons College Library Survey *continued*

6. *A computer data base searching service finds references to magazine and journal articles as in a printed index but retrieves them from an on-line computer data base. Have you ever used such a service before?*

    _____ yes   _____ no

    If yes, how often have you used such a service before?

    _____ 1–2 times   _____ 3–4 times   _____ 5 or more times

    If yes, did you find these indexes:

    _____ very easy to use   _____ difficult to use
    _____ easy to use   _____ very difficult to use

7. *If a computer data base service was available at the College Library, would you use it?*

    _____ yes   _____ no   _____ don't know

    If yes, how often would you anticipate having a need for such a service?

    _____ 1–2 times a year   _____ 3–4 times a year
    _____ 5 or more times a year

8. *When using a computer data base service, the user must pay the library a fee based on the amount of computer time used and the length of the computer printout. How important would the cost of the service be in your decision to use a computer data base?*

    _____ not at all important
    _____ somewhat unimportant
    _____ neither important nor unimportant
    _____ somewhat important
    _____ very important

9. *One of the advantages of a computer data base is that it can provide many bibliographic references in a short period of time. How important is this factor in your decision to use a computer data base?*

    _____ not at all important
    _____ somewhat unimportant
    _____ neither important nor unimportant
    _____ somewhat important
    _____ very important

10. *Of the many types of data bases available to library users, which would you find most useful (check all relevant categories)?*

    _____ psychological abstracts
    _____ business & economic abstracts
    _____ science abstracts
    _____ engineering abstracts
    _____ health-related abstracts
    _____ general periodical indexes
    _____ Other: please specify _____

Figure 1
Gibbons College Library Survey *continued*

---

11. What is your current class standing?

_____ freshman   _____ junior
_____ sophomore   _____ senior
_____ special student
_____ other: please specify _____

12. What is your declared or intended major area of study?

_____ agriculture and life sciences
_____ allied health fields
_____ business
_____ education
_____ engineering
_____ family resources
_____ letters & sciences
_____ nursing
_____ other: please specify _____

13. What is your sex:

_____ male   _____ female

---

periods: 9 to 11 a.m., 2 to 4 p.m., and 7 to 9 p.m. A large sign was posted informing patrons about the survey, and a questionnaire return box was placed near the library exits to facilitate survey returns.

The number of questionnaires distributed and returned for each period is listed in Table 1. Questionnaires lacking responses to major questions and questionnaires appearing to be carelessly done (for example, all "4's" being checked) were eliminated

---

Table 1
Questionnaires Distributed and Returned During
Each of the Time Periods Surveyed

Time Period	Questionnaires Distributed	Questionnaires Returned	Response Rate
7–9 a.m.	855	317	.37
2–4 p.m.	600	217	.36
7–9 p.m.	790	237	.30
TOTAL	2,245	771	.34

from the analysis. For the final tabulations, 100 arbitrarily chosen responses from each of the three surveyed time frames were used, making the total number of subjects included in the analysis 300.

Questions

1. Using the research objectives as guidelines, construct dummy tables that can be used to help analyze the results obtained from the questionnaire.

2. Critique the research design. Will the research study as presented here lead to an ''ideal'' marketing research study of users' needs for a computer data base? Why or why not?

Case 2.5
Chestnut Ridge Country Club (A)[1]

The Chestnut Ridge Country Club has long maintained a distinguished reputation as one of the outstanding country clubs in the Elma, Tennessee, area. The club's golf facilities are said by some to be the finest in the state, and its dining and banquet facilities are highly regarded as well. This reputation is due in part to the commitment by the Board of Directors of Chestnut Ridge to offer the finest facilities of any club in the area. For example, several negative comments by club members regarding the dining facilities prompted the board to survey members to get their feelings and perceptions of the dining facilities and food offerings at the club. Based upon the survey findings, the Board of Directors established a quality control committee to oversee the dining room and a new club manager was hired.

Most recently, the board became concerned with the number of people seeking membership to Chestnut Ridge. Although no records are kept on the number of membership applications received each year, the board sensed that this figure was declining. They also believed that membership applications at the three competing country clubs in the area—namely, Alden, Chalet, and Lancaster—were not experiencing similar declines. Because Chestnut Ridge had other facilities, such as tennis courts and a pool, that were comparable to the facilities at these other clubs, the board was perplexed as to why membership applications would be falling at Chestnut Ridge.

To gain insight into the matter, the Board of Directors hired an outside research firm to conduct a study of the country clubs in Elma, Tennessee. The goals of the research were: (1) to outline areas where Chestnut Ridge fared poorly in relation to other clubs

---

[1]The contributions of David M. Szymanski to the development of this case are gratefully acknowledged.

in the area; (2) to determine people's overall perception of Chestnut Ridge; and (3) to provide recommendations for ways to increase membership applications at the club.

Research Method

The researchers met with the Board of Directors and key personnel at Chestnut Ridge to gain a better understanding of the goals of the research and the types of services and facilities offered at a country club. A literature search of published research relating to country clubs uncovered no studies. Based solely upon their contact with individuals at Chestnut Ridge, therefore, the research team developed the survey contained in Figure 1. Because personal information regarding demographics and attitudes would be asked of those contacted, the researchers decided to use a mail questionnaire.

The researchers thought it would be useful to survey members from Alden, Chalet, and Lancaster country clubs in addition to those from Chestnut Ridge for two reasons. One, members of these other clubs would be knowledgeable regarding the levels and types of services and facilities desired from a country club, and, two, they had at one time represented potential members of Chestnut Ridge. Hence, their perceptions of Chestnut Ridge might reveal why they chose to belong to a different country club.

No public documents were available that contained a listing of each club's members. Consequently, the researchers decided to contact each of the clubs personally to try to obtain a mailing list. Identifying themselves as an independent research firm conducting a study on country clubs in the Elma area, the researchers first spoke to the chairman of the board at Alden Country Club. The researchers told the chairman they could not reveal the organization sponsoring the study but that the results of their study would not be made public. The chairman was not willing to provide the researchers with the mailing list. The chairman cited an obligation to respect the privacy of the club's members as the primary reason for turning down the research team's request.

The researchers then made the following proposal to the board chairman: in return for the mailing list, the researchers would provide the chairman a report on Alden members' perceptions of Alden Country Club. In addition, the mailing list would be destroyed as soon as the surveys were sent. The proposal seemed to please the chairman, for he agreed to give the researchers a listing of the members and their addresses in return for the report. The researchers told the chairman they must check with their sponsoring organization for approval of this arrangement.

The research team made similar proposals to the chairmen of the board of directors of both the Chalet and Lancaster country clubs. In return for a mailing list of the club's members, they promised each chairman a report outlining their members' perceptions of their clubs, contingent upon their securing approval from their sponsoring organization. Both agreed to supply the requested list of members.

The researchers subsequently met with the Chestnut Ridge Board of Directors. In their meeting, the researchers outlined the situation and asked for the board's approval to provide each of the clubs with a report in return for the mailing lists. The researchers emphasized that the report would contain no information regarding Chestnut Ridge nor information by which each of the other clubs could compare itself to any of the other clubs in the area, in contrast to the information to be provided to the Chestnut Ridge Board of Directors. The report would only contain a small portion of the overall study's

Figure 1
Questionnaire Used to Survey Alden, Chalet, and
Lancaster Country Club Members

1. *In which club are you currently a member?* _____

2. *How long have you been a member of this club?* _____

3. *How familiar are you with each of the following country clubs?*

   Alden Country Club?

   _____ very familiar (I am a member or I have visited the club as a guest)
   _____ somewhat familiar (I have heard about the club from others)
   _____ unfamiliar

   Chalet Country Club

   _____ very familiar
   _____ somewhat familiar
   _____ unfamiliar

   Chestnut Ridge Country Club

   _____ very familiar
   _____ somewhat familiar
   _____ unfamiliar

   Lancaster Country Club

   _____ very familiar
   _____ somewhat familiar
   _____ unfamiliar

4. *The following is a list of factors that may be influential in the decision to join a country club. Please rate the factors according to their importance to you in joining your country club. Circle the appropriate response where 1 = not at all important and 5 = extremely important.*

Golf facilities	1	2	3	4	5
Tennis facilities	1	2	3	4	5
Pool facilities	1	2	3	4	5
Dining facilities	1	2	3	4	5
Social events	1	2	3	4	5
Family activities	1	2	3	4	5
Number of friends who are members	1	2	3	4	5
Cordiality of members	1	2	3	4	5
Prestige	1	2	3	4	5
Location	1	2	3	4	5

5. *The following is a list of phrases pertaining to Alden Country Club. Please place an X in the space that best describes your impressions of Alden. The ends represent extremes; the center position is neutral.* Do so even if you are only vaguely familiar with Alden.

Club landscape is attractive.	:___:___:___:___:___:___:	Club landscape is unattractive.
Clubhouse facilities are poor.	:___:___:___:___:___:___:	Clubhouse facilities are excellent.

Figure 1
**Questionnaire Used to Survey Alden, Chalet, and
Lancaster Country Club Members** *continued*

Question 5 continued

Locker room facilities are excellent.	:___:___:___:___:___:___:	Locker room facilities are poor.
Club management is ineffective.	:___:___:___:___:___:___:	Club management is effective.
Dining room atmosphere is pleasant.	:___:___:___:___:___:___:	Dining room atmosphere is unpleasant.
Food prices are unreasonable.	:___:___:___:___:___:___:	Food prices are reasonable.
Golf course is poorly maintained.	:___:___:___:___:___:___:	Golf course is well maintained.
Golf course is challenging.	:___:___:___:___:___:___:	Golf course is not challenging.
Membership rates are too high.	:___:___:___:___:___:___:	Membership rates are too low.

6. *The following is a list of phrases pertaining to Chalet Country Club. Please place an X in the space that best describes your impressions of Chalet.* Do so even if you are only vaguely familiar with Chalet.

Club landscape is attractive.	:___:___:___:___:___:___:	Club landscape is unattractive.
Clubhouse facilities are poor.	:___:___:___:___:___:___:	Clubhouse facilities are excellent.
Locker room facilities are excellent.	:___:___:___:___:___:___:	Locker room facilities are poor.
Club management is effective.	:___:___:___:___:___:___:	Club management is ineffective.
Dining room atmosphere is pleasant.	:___:___:___:___:___:___:	Dining room atmosphere is unpleasant.
Food prices are unreasonable.	:___:___:___:___:___:___:	Food prices are reasonable.
Food quality is excellent.	:___:___:___:___:___:___:	Food quality is poor.
Golf course is poorly maintained.	:___:___:___:___:___:___:	Golf course is well maintained.
Golf course is challenging.	:___:___:___:___:___:___:	Golf course is not challenging.
Tennis courts are in excellent condition.	:___:___:___:___:___:___:	Tennis courts are in poor condition.
There are too many tennis courts.	:___:___:___:___:___:___:	There are too few tennis courts.
Membership rates are too high.	:___:___:___:___:___:___:	Membership rates are too low.

continued on next page

Figure 1
Questionnaire Used to Survey Alden, Chalet, and
Lancaster Country Club Members *continued*

7. *The following is a list of phrases pertaining to Chestnut Ridge Country Club. Please place an X in the space that best describes your impressions of Chestnut Ridge. Do so even if you are only vaguely familiar with Chestnut Ridge.*

Club landscape is attractive.	:___:___:___:___:___:___:	Club landscape is unattractive.
Clubhouse facilities are poor.	:___:___:___:___:___:___:	Clubhouse facilities are excellent.
Locker room facilities are excellent.	:___:___:___:___:___:___:	Locker room facilities are poor.
Club management is ineffective.	:___:___:___:___:___:___:	Club management is effective.
Dining room atmosphere is pleasant.	:___:___:___:___:___:___:	Dining room atmosphere is unpleasant.
Food prices are unreasonable.	:___:___:___:___:___:___:	Food prices are reasonable.
Food quality is excellent.	:___:___:___:___:___:___:	Food quality is poor.
Golf course is poorly maintained.	:___:___:___:___:___:___:	Golf course is well maintained.
Tennis courts are in poor condition.	:___:___:___:___:___:___:	Tennis courts are in excellent condition.
There are too many tennis courts.	:___:___:___:___:___:___:	There are too few tennis courts.
Swimming pool is in poor condition.	:___:___:___:___:___:___:	Swimming pool is in excellent condition.
Membership rates are too high.	:___:___:___:___:___:___:	Membership rates are too low.

8. *The following is a list of phrases pertaining to Lancaster Country Club. Please place an X in the space that best describes your impression of Lancaster.* Do so even if you are only vaguely familiar with Lancaster.

Club landscape is attractive.	:___:___:___:___:___:___:	Club landscape is unattractive.
Clubhouse facilities are poor.	:___:___:___:___:___:___:	Clubhouse facilities are excellent.
Locker room facilities are excellent.	:___:___:___:___:___:___:	Locker room facilities are poor.
Club management is ineffective.	:___:___:___:___:___:___:	Club management is effective.
Dining room atmosphere is pleasant.	:___:___:___:___:___:___:	Dining room atmosphere is unpleasant.
Food prices are unreasonable.	:___:___:___:___:___:___:	Food prices are reasonable.
Food quality is excellent.	:___:___:___:___:___:___:	Food quality is poor.
Golf course is poorly maintained.	:___:___:___:___:___:___:	Golf course is well maintained.
Tennis courts are in poor condition.	:___:___:___:___:___:___:	Tennis courts are in excellent condition.

Figure 1
Questionnaire Used to Survey Alden, Chalet, and
Lancaster Country Club Members *continued*

Question 8 continued

There are too many tennis courts.	:___:___:___:___:___:___:	There are too few tennis courts.
Swimming pool is in poor condition.	:___:___:___:___:___:___:	Swimming pool is in excellent condition.
Membership rates are too high.	:___:___:___:___:___:___:	Membership rates are too low.

9. *Overall, how would you rate each of the country clubs? Circle the appropriate response where 1 = poor and 5 = excellent.*

Alden	1	2	3	4	5
Chalet	1	2	3	4	5
Chestnut Ridge	1	2	3	4	5
Lancaster	1	2	3	4	5

10. **The following questions are designed to give a better understanding of the members of country clubs.**

Have you ever been a member of another club in the Elma area?

_____ yes   _____ no

Approximately what is the distance of your residence from your club in miles?

_____ 0–2 miles   _____ 3–5 miles   _____ 6–10 miles

_____ 10+ miles

Age: _____ 21–30   _____ 31–40   _____ 41–50

_____ 51–60   _____ 61 or over

Sex: _____ male   _____ female

Marital status: _____ married   _____ single   _____ widowed

_____ divorced

Number of dependents including yourself?

_____ 2 or less   _____ 3–4   _____ 5 or more

Total family income:

___ Less than $20,000
___ $20,000–$29,999
___ $30,000–$49,999
___ $50,000–$99,999
___ $100,000 or more
___ Do not know/Refuse to answer

Thank you for your cooperation!

results. After carefully considering the research team's arguments, the Board of Directors agreed to the proposal.

Membership Surveys

A review of the lists subsequently provided by each club showed Alden had 114 members, Chalet had 98 members, and Lancaster had 132 members. The researchers believed that 69 to 70 responses from each membership group would be adequate. Anticipating a 70 to 75 percent response rate because of the unusually high involvement and

Table 1

Average Overall Ratings of Each Club by Club Membership of the Respondent

Club Rated	Club Membership			Composite Ratings Across All Members
	Alden	Chalet	Lancaster	
Alden	4.57	3.64	3.34	3.85
Chalet	2.87	3.63	2.67	3.07
Chestnut Ridge	4.40	4.44	4.20	4.35
Lancaster	3.60	3.91	4.36	3.95

Table 2

Average Ratings of the Respective Country Clubs Across Dimensions

Dimension	Country Club			
	Alden	Chalet	Chestnut Ridge	Lancaster
Club landscape	6.28	4.65	6.48	5.97
Clubhouse facilities	5.37	4.67	6.03	5.51
Locker room facilities	4.99	4.79	5.36	4.14
Club management	5.38	4.35	5.00	5.23
Dining room atmosphere	5.91	4.10	5.66	5.48
Food prices	5.42	4.78	4.46	4.79
Food quality	a	4.12	5.48	4.79
Golf course maintenance	6.17	5.01	6.43	5.89
Golf course challenge	5.14	5.01	a	4.77
Condition of tennis courts	b	5.10	4.52	5.08
Number of tennis courts	b	4.14	4.00	3.89
Swimming pool	b	b	4.66	5.35
Membership rates	4.49	3.97	5.00	4.91

[a]Question not asked.
[b]Not applicable.

Table 3
Attitudes Toward Chestnut Ridge by Members of the Other Country Clubs

Dimension	Alden	Chalet	Lancaster
Club landscape	6.54	6.54	6.36
Clubhouse facilities	6.08	6.03	5.98
Locker room facilities	5.66	5.35	5.07
Club management	4.97	5.15	4.78
Dining room atmosphere	5.86	5.70	5.41
Food prices	4.26	4.48	4.63
Food quality	5.52	5.75	5.18
Golf course maintenance	6.47	6.59	6.22
Condition of tennis courts	4.55	4.46	4.55
Number of tennis courts	4.00	4.02	3.98
Swimming pool	5.08	4.69	4.26
Membership rates	5.09	5.64	4.24

familiarity of each group with the subject matter, the research team decided to mail 85 to 90 surveys to each group and a simple random sample of members was chosen from each list. In all, 87 members from each country club were mailed a questionnaire (348 surveys in total). Sixty-three usable surveys were returned from each group (252 in total) for a response rate of 72 percent.

Summary results of the survey are presented in Tables 1–3. Table 1 gives people's overall ratings of the country clubs, while Table 2 shows people's ratings of the various clubs on an array of dimensions. Table 3 is a breakdown of attitudes toward Chestnut Ridge by the three different membership groups: Alden, Chalet, and Lancaster. The data are average ratings of respondents. Table 1 scores are based upon a five-point scale, where one is poor and five is excellent. Tables 2 and 3 are based upon seven-point scales in which one represents an extremely negative rating and seven an extremely positive rating.

Questions

1. What kind of research design is being used? Is it a good choice?

2. Do you think it was ethical for the researchers not to disclose the identity of the sponsoring organization? Do you think it was ethical for the board of directors to release the names of their members in return for a report that analyzes their members' perceptions toward their own club?

3. Overall, how does Chestnut Ridge compare to the three country clubs: Alden, Chalet, and Lancaster?

4. In what areas might Chestnut Ridge consider improvements to attract additional members?

Case 2.6
N–Rich Coffee Creamer

N–Rich is a powdered, nondairy coffee creamer produced by the Sanna Division of Beatrice Foods Company. N–Rich was originally introduced in 1965, but a series of events during the early 1980s led to a reconsideration of the product's marketing strategy. John Bendt, Marketing Manager of the Sanna Division, and Gregg Ostrander, the N–Rich Product Manager, while discussing this revised marketing strategy in early 1986, directed their attention to the results of a study regarding a new package for the product. They had definitely decided a new package was in order, and they had narrowed the choice to two alternatives. The only question that still remained was which alternative they should adopt.

N–Rich, like its competitors, had historically been packaged in glass jars with screw tops. Both of the new containers under consideration were cylinder-shaped cardboard canisters. The cardboard package was lighter, unbreakable, and most important, cheaper to make. The primary problem with the cardboard containers was to convince consumers of the benefits of cardboard containers and to persuade them to change their habit of using glass jars.

The two alternatives differed primarily in their tops. Alternative Y had an aluminum pull top with a resealable plastic lid, much like the top of a tennis ball can. Alternative X had a plastic twist top with two openings, much like the top of a parmesan cheese container. The small opening in Package X enabled the user to pour the creamer, while the larger opening in Package Y allowed the user to spoon out the creamer, the traditional way of serving with the glass jars.

To assist them in the package choice, Sanna had commissioned a marketing research study by an independent marketing research organization. The purposes of the study were to determine which alternative was preferred and to measure consumer reaction to the cardboard containers versus the glass containers. The study results, which Bendt and Ostrander were now reviewing, had been generated in an in-home product usage test in Fresno, California.

The Sample

Four large grocery stores were judgmentally chosen from the larger population of grocery stores in Fresno. Two of the stores had discount, lower price images and two of the stores had higher quality images. One store was chosen from each side of town so as to balance the study geographically.

As shoppers entered each store, they were asked in a screening interview if anyone in their household used powdered, nondairy creamer. If they answered yes, they were then asked how often they used creamers, what brand(s) and why. All those households that used creamer more than two to three times per week were then asked to participate in a marketing research study. Approximately 20 percent of those asked to participate declined to do so. Those who did agree to cooperate were given a free sample of each package and were asked to use the samples interchangeably until they received a questionnaire in two weeks' time. Fifty households were chosen in this fashion from each store for a total sample of 200 households.

The Use Test

The product samples that the participating households received were full-sized, 16-ounce creamer containers with a plain brown exterior and no graphic design. The only labeling was a sticker listing the manufacturer and the ingredients that the creamer contained. The only differences between the two packages were the tops and an "X" placed on the pour top and a "Y" placed on the pull top.

Each participating household was mailed a copy of the questionnaire in Figure 1 two weeks after the initial store contact. Each was then called three days after the questionnaires were mailed to ascertain whether they had received it and to remind them to send it back promptly. Those households that were not reached by telephone on the first try were called back at a different time or on a different day. Telephone contact was not made, though, with about one-quarter of the households. Some of these households, as well as some of those households that were contacted, did not return the questionnaire within the two-week cut-off period established for the study.

The results Bendt and Ostrander were reviewing were based on the 136 questionnaires that were received in time to be tabulated.

Figure 1
Coffee Creamer Questionnaire

Two weeks ago you were provided with coffee creamer samples "X" and "Y." Please provide us with your reactions to each of the samples by answering the following questions in the space provided.

1. *Has your household had a chance to try each of the two sample products given to you at the grocery store two weeks ago?*

   _____ Yes
   _____ No

2. *Please rate each product on the following attributes by circling the appropriate number.* (1 is poor, 2 is fair, 3 is o.k., 4 is good, 5 is excellent)

	Product X	Product Y	Your Brand
Taste	1 2 3 4 5	1 2 3 4 5	1 2 3 4 5
Whitening power	1 2 3 4 5	1 2 3 4 5	1 2 3 4 5
How the product dissolves	1 2 3 4 5	1 2 3 4 5	1 2 3 4 5
Creaminess	1 2 3 4 5	1 2 3 4 5	1 2 3 4 5

continued on next page

Figure 1
Coffee Creamer Questionnaire *continued*

3. *For each of the following, please check the space that best describes the packages X and Y.*

	Hard to Open	Moderately Hard to Open	Neutral	Moderately Easy to Open	Easy to Open
Package X	_____	_____	_____	_____	_____
Package Y	_____	_____	_____	_____	_____

	Inconvenient to Use	Moderately Inconvenient	Neutral	Moderately Convenient	Convenient to Use
Package X	_____	_____	_____	_____	_____
Package Y	_____	_____	_____	_____	_____

	Looks Unattractive	Looks Moderately Unattractive	Neutral	Looks Moderately Attractive	Looks Attractive
Package X	_____	_____	_____	_____	_____
Package Y	_____	_____	_____	_____	_____

	Messy to Use	Moderately Messy to Use	Neutral	Moderately Unmessy to Use	Not At All Messy to Use
Package X	_____	_____	_____	_____	_____
Package Y	_____	_____	_____	_____	_____

	Difficult to Get Product Out With Spoon	Moderately Difficult to Get Product Out With Spoon	Neutral	Moderately Easy to Get Product Out With Spoon	Easy to Get Product Out With Spoon
Package X	_____	_____	_____	_____	_____
Package Y	_____	_____	_____	_____	_____

	Product Gets Lumpy	Product Doesn't Get Lumpy
Package X	_____	_____
Package Y	_____	_____

4. *Please rate Packages X and Y according to how you feel they protect the quality of the product.*

	Poor	Fair	O.K.	Good	Excellent
Package X	_____	_____	_____	_____	_____
Package Y	_____	_____	_____	_____	_____

5. *Did you household prefer one of the sample packages?*

_____ Prefer Package X   _____ No Package Preference

_____ Prefer Package Y

Figure 1
Coffee Creamer Questionnaire *continued*

---

6. *If your household prefers one of the sample packages, why?*

7. *Does your household prefer one of the sample packages over the glass container of the brand you usually buy?*

_____ Prefer Package X   _____ Prefer the Glass Container
_____ Prefer Package Y   _____ No Package Preference

8. *What are the reasons for your answer to Question #7?*

9. *Does your household prefer one of the sample products over the brand of coffee creamer you usually buy?*

_____ Prefer Product X   _____ Prefer Usual Brand
_____ Prefer Product Y   _____ No Preference

10. *What are the reasons for your answer to Question #9?*

11. *Would you buy one of the sample products over the brand you usually buy?*

_____ Would Buy Product X   _____ Will Continue To Buy Usual
                                               Brand
_____ Would Buy Product Y

12. *What are the reasons for your answer to Question #11?*

Questions

1. What kind of research design is being used?

2. Evaluate the design with respect to each of the extraneous influences that can affect experiments.

Case 2.7
Bakhill Foods

Mike Gill, the marketing manager for Bakhill Foods, was discussing the future advertising strategy for Bakhill Coffee with the firm's advertising agency when the discussion turned to magazine ads and the copy for those ads.

Gill had recently been to a conference on psychological perception. At that conference it was pointed out that in spite of the old adage "you can't judge a book by its cover," we do just that in our interpersonal relations; an individual's initial perception of and reaction to another individual is affected by the physical attractiveness of the other person. Further, a fair summary statement of that research is "what is beautiful is good." The evidence cited at the conference supporting this proposition was impressive.

What particularly impressed Gill, though, was that the positive attributes one associates with a physically attractive person do not depend on actual contact with that person. They arise when the judge is simply shown photographs of physically attractive and unattractive individuals but is otherwise unaware of subjects' traits.

Gill thought that this knowledge could be used to advantage in the advertising copy for Bakhill Coffee. He proposed that the product be shown with a physically attractive female. The advertising agency countered with the argument that it would be better to employ physically unattractive people in the ads so as to make the ads more believable and effective by making them less "romantic," since coffee is not a romantic product. Further, the agency suggested it might be better to employ males in the ads rather than females. After considerable discussion, the advertising agency proposed and conducted the following research to answer the questions: Should physically attractive or unattractive individuals be used in the ads? Should male or female models be employed?

The Design

Four different advertisements were prepared. The copy was the same in each ad; only the person holding the coffee was changed. The four ads included an attractive male, an attractive female, an unattractive male, and an unattractive female. The attractiveness of each model was determined by having a convenience sample of subjects view photographs of twenty different models—ten of each sex—and rate each model on a seven-point scale where "1" was unattractive and "7" was attractive. The male and female models with the highest and the lowest mean scores were then selected as the stimulus persons for the experiment.

A color ad with each of the four models and the planned copy was then developed. A sample of subjects for the experiment was developed by random sampling from the New York City telephone book. Contacted subjects were asked to participate in a marketing research experiment. The subjects were paid for their participation, and they were also reimbursed for their travel to the agency's headquarters.

Upon their arrival at the ad agency, the 96 subjects who agreed to participate were randomly assigned to one of the advertisements. The 48 males and 48 females were first divided randomly into 12 groups of four persons each, and one member of each group was then assigned to one of the four ads. Each saw one, and only one, test ad. However, three other dummy ads were also used so as to disguise the particular ad of interest. The dummy ads were the same for each subject. Each subject was introduced to the experiment with the following instructions:

We are interested in obtaining your opinions concerning particular test advertisements. You will be shown four ads, one at a time, and after each showing, you will be asked several questions concerning your reaction to the ad and also the particular product depicted in the ad. You should note that this is not *a contest to see which ad is better, so please do* not *compare the four ads in making your evaluations. Each ad should be judged in and of itself, without references to the other ads.*

After answering any questions, the experimenter gave the first ad to the subject. After the subject had read the advertisement, it was taken away; and the experimenter then handed the subject a copy of the data collection sheet (Figure 1). Upon completion of this form, the experimenter handed the subject a copy of the second ad and the process

Figure 1

Sample Questionnaire for Bakhill Coffee Study

On each of the scales below, please check the space that you feel best describes the advertisement you just read.

Interesting :__:__:__:__:__:__:	Dull
Unappealing :__:__:__:__:__:__:	Appealing
Unbelievable :__:__:__:__:__:__:	Believable
Impressive :__:__:__:__:__:__:	Unimpressive
Attractive :__:__:__:__:__:__:	Unattractive
Uninformative :__:__:__:__:__:__:	Informative
Clear :__:__:__:__:__:__:	Confusing
Not eye catching :__:__:__:__:__:__:	Eye catching

What is your overall reaction to the above advertisement?

Unfavorable :__:__:__:__:__:__: Favorable

With regard to the product itself, how do you feel this product compares to similar products put out by other manufacturers?

Distinctive :__:__:__:__:__:__: Ordinary

Would you like to try this product?

No—Definitely not :__:__:__:__:__:__: Yes—Definitely

Would you buy this product if you happened to see it in a store?

Yes—Definitely :__:__:__:__:__:__: No—Definitely not

Would you actively seek out this product in a store in order to purchase it?

No—Definitely not :__:__:__:__:__:__: Yes—Definitely

was repeated. At no time were subjects allowed to look back at the advertisements once they had surrendered them to the researcher. So as to allow subjects to warm up to the task, the test ad was always placed third in the sequence of four.

The Scale

The items in the scale contained in Figure 1 were chosen so as to tap all three components (cognitive, affective, and conative) of attitude. *A priori,* it was thought that the cognitive component would be measured by the believable, informative, and clear items; that the affective or liking component would be effectively tapped by the items interesting, appealing, impressive, attractive, and eye catching; and that the conative component would be captured by the three behavioral intention items at the bottom of the questionnaire.

These *a priori* expectations were not strictly confirmed. A basic item analysis suggested the term ":interesting" was not related to any of the three components, and it was dropped from the analysis.[1] Responses to the remaining items in each component were summed to produce a total score for each component. The analysis of these scale scores indicated that:[2]

1. The attractive male model produced the highest cognition scores for the ad among females and males.

2. The attractive male model produced the highest affective scores among female subjects, while the attractive female model produced the highest affective scores among males.

3. The attractive male model produced the highest conative scores toward the product for female subjects, while the unattractive male model produced the highest conative scores among male subjects.

On the basis of these results the advertising agency suggested the attractive male model be employed in the advertisement.

Questions

1. What kind of design is being employed in this investigation?
2. Evaluate the design.

Case 2.8
Madison Gas and Electric Company (A)[3]

Madison Gas and Electric Company (MG&E) is a public utility that generates and distributes electric power and natural gas for the city of Madison, Wisconsin, and surrounding towns and villages. Providing service to approximately 200,000 customers over a 750-square-mile area, the company's load profile includes such diverse entities as government, manufacturers, wholesalers, retailers, agriculture, and private housing. Since government is the largest employer in the area, MG&E's loads are not seriously affected by fluctuations in the economy at large. As a consequence, load growth over the company's history has been stable and manageable.

In recent years MG&E's advertising has been largely educational. The company has tried in particular to provide its customers with information on how to conserve energy and how to use electricity and natural gas safely. One of the advertisements, for example, featured "free energy audits." Any customer in MG&E's service area could call a special number to schedule a free energy audit. The company would send two company

[1]The rationale for, and method of conducting, an item analysis is explored more fully in Chapter 8 and Appendix C to that chapter.

[2]The analysis of this kind of data is elaborated in the appendix to Chapter 14.

[3]The contributions of Thomas Noordewier to the development of this case are gratefully acknowledged.

representatives who would thoroughly examine the dwelling unit and would make specific recommendations for ways the household could save money on their energy costs. The recommendations would include approximate cost estimates for the recommended changes (e.g., more insulation in the attic, weatherstripping on the doors) as well as the savings likely to be realized and the payback period. MG&E's corporate executives believed that customers benefited directly from such information since it allowed them to better control their energy costs. The company also profited, since reduced energy demand permitted it to use its existing facilities, thereby deferring new plant construction until further in the future. Customer reaction to the advertising (which is primarily television, although it includes radio and print media) had thus far been very favorable.

In 1983, the state of Wisconsin passed legislation requiring that a public utility may not charge its ratepayers for any expenditure for advertising unless the advertising contains a disclaimer explaining that the expenditure is ultimately charged to the utility's ratepayers. According to the law, the disclaimer must be conspicuous in relation to how the advertisement is presented. More specifically, the law stated that the "written disclaimer shall be located in a conspicuous place in the advertising and shall appear in conspicuous and legible type in contrast by typography, layout or color with other printed matter in the advertising." While committed to its safety and conservation advertising, MG&E's management was concerned about possible adverse customer reactions to advertisements containing such disclaimers. It was felt that inclusion of a rider alerting customers to the fact that they were paying for the advertising might have a negative impact on viewers' evaluations of the presented message.

Research Study

To address this concern, the company commissioned a study to examine how customers' perceptions of advertisements would be affected by disclaimers. The basic design of the research to be used was straightforward. A sample of 450 adult MG&E customers from each of three research sites were to be selected. More particularly, 150 subjects were to be selected at each of the three major Madison-area shopping centers: East Towne, West Towne, and South Towne. Located at the outskirts of Madison, these three shopping centers attract shoppers from the city of Madison as well as surrounding towns and villages included in MG&E's service area. All three shopping centers were used because each caters to a somewhat different clientele. The West Towne center was located in the higher income area of the city and served mainly professionals and other white-collar workers. The East Towne center was located in the lower income area and served primarily blue-collar workers. The South Towne center served a mix of the two groups.

Three different treatment levels were then randomly assigned to the groups. The three treatment levels consisted of presenting subjects television advertising messages without any disclaimer, presenting them messages with disclaimers, or presenting them messages both with and without disclaimers. The objective of the research was to ascertain whether differences in evaluations of the advertisements existed between subjects assigned to each of the three treatment levels.

The following procedures were decided upon to select subjects. First, the interviewers were assigned specific spots in the corridors of each mall. They were instructed to stop adults going by the designated spots at irregular intervals. They were to ask each adult whether they had heard, seen, or read any utility advertising in the past few months and whether they were MG&E customers. If the adult said yes to both questions, the person was considered to be qualified to serve as a study subject. All others were thanked for their cooperation and dismissed.

Each qualified subject was then assigned to one of three treatment conditions. In each treatment condition, the subject was exposed to four ads and was asked to rate each commercial immediately after having seen it using a scale that ran from "highest rating" to "worst rating" with respect to how "helpful," "informative," "necessary," and "believable" the ad was. After viewing all four ads, each subject was asked to provide an overall (summary) evaluation of the commercials, using "excellent" to "poor" descriptors. In addition, each subject was asked to indicate which ad he or she liked the "best" and the "least" and why. Finally, each subject was asked to respond to a set of demographic and socioeconomic questions so that the representativeness of the sample could be checked. See Figure 1 for a copy of the questionnaire (in this case, the one used at South Towne).

Figure 1
Viewing Questionnaire (South Towne, Treatment A)

Subject is shown one commercial at a time and is asked after viewing each:

1. *How would you evaluate this commercial in terms of the following characteristics (1 = highest rating, 2 = next highest, 3 = average, 4 = below average, 5 = worst rating, 6 = not sure)*

Commercial #1
Home Energy Audit

	1	2	3	4	5	6
a. helpful	[ ]	[ ]	[ ]	[ ]	[ ]	[ ]
b. informative	[ ]	[ ]	[ ]	[ ]	[ ]	[ ]
c. necessary	[ ]	[ ]	[ ]	[ ]	[ ]	[ ]
d. believable	[ ]	[ ]	[ ]	[ ]	[ ]	[ ]

Commercial #2
Congratulations for Conserving Energy

	1	2	3	4	5	6
a. helpful	[ ]	[ ]	[ ]	[ ]	[ ]	[ ]
b. informative	[ ]	[ ]	[ ]	[ ]	[ ]	[ ]
c. necessary	[ ]	[ ]	[ ]	[ ]	[ ]	[ ]
d. believable	[ ]	[ ]	[ ]	[ ]	[ ]	[ ]

Commercial #3
Gas Safety

	1	2	3	4	5	6
a. helpful	[ ]	[ ]	[ ]	[ ]	[ ]	[ ]
b. informative	[ ]	[ ]	[ ]	[ ]	[ ]	[ ]
c. necessary	[ ]	[ ]	[ ]	[ ]	[ ]	[ ]
d. believable	[ ]	[ ]	[ ]	[ ]	[ ]	[ ]

Commercial #4
Commercial Energy Audit

Figure 1
Viewing Questionnaire (South Towne, Treatment A) *continued*

Question 1 continued

	1	2	3	4	5	6
a. helpful	[ ]	[ ]	[ ]	[ ]	[ ]	[ ]
b. informative	[ ]	[ ]	[ ]	[ ]	[ ]	[ ]
c. necessary	[ ]	[ ]	[ ]	[ ]	[ ]	[ ]
d. believable	[ ]	[ ]	[ ]	[ ]	[ ]	[ ]

Interviewer: Ask the following *after* showing all the commercials.

2. *Overall, how would you rate these MG&E television commercials?*

Excellent	[ ]
Very good	[ ]
Average	[ ]
Not very good	[ ]
Poor	[ ]
Not sure	[ ]

3. *Of the four commercials you saw, which one did you like the most?*

Commercial 1   [   ]
Commercial 2   [   ]
Commercial 3   [   ]
Commercial 4   [   ]

Why? _____
_____
_____
_____
_____
_____
_____
_____

4. *Of the four commercials you saw, which one did you like the least?*

Commercial 1   [   ]
Commercial 2   [   ]
Commercial 3   [   ]
Commercial 4   [   ]

*Why?*_____
_____
_____
_____
_____
_____
_____
_____

Now, we would like to ask you just a few more questions for classification purposes.

continued on next page

Figure 1
Viewing Questionnaire (South Towne, Treatment A) *continued*

5. *Which of the following categories includes your age?*

18–24	[ ]
25–34	[ ]
35–49	[ ]
50–64	[ ]
65 and over	[ ]

6. *What is your education level?*

Grade school or less	[ ]
High school graduate	[ ]
Some college	[ ]
College graduate	[ ]
Graduate degree	[ ]

7. *Are you male or female?*

Male [ ]   Female [ ]

8. *Are you presently a university student or not?*

Student [ ]   Not a student [ ]

9. *Do you own or rent your residence?*

Own	[ ]
Rent	[ ]
Live with parents/friends/relatives	[ ]
Other	[ ]

10. *Do you pay the electric and gas bill for the household, or is it paid for by someone else?*

I pay	[ ]
Landlord pays	[ ]
Another member of the household pays	[ ]
Someone else pays	[ ]
It depends	[ ]

11. *What is your main source of your home heating? Do you heat your residence with gas, oil, electricity, coal, or how?*

Gas	[ ]
Oil	[ ]
Electricity	[ ]
Coal	[ ]
Wood	[ ]
Other	[ ]
Not sure	[ ]

Figure 1
Viewing Questionnaire (South Towne, Treatment A) *continued*

12. *To the best of your knowledge, what was the approximate amount of your gas and electric bill last month?*

Under $10.00	[ ]	$51–$75	[ ]
$11–$20	[ ]	$76–$100	[ ]
$21–$30	[ ]	$101–$200	[ ]
$31–$40	[ ]	Over $200	[ ]
$41–$50	[ ]	Not sure	[ ]

13. *Which of the following categories includes your total family income for 1982,* before *taxes?*

$7,500 or less	[ ]
$7,501 to $15,000	[ ]
$15,001 to $25,000	[ ]
$25,001 to $35,000	[ ]
$35,001 to $50,000	[ ]
$50,001 and over	[ ]
Not sure	[ ]

14. *How would you describe the area in which you live?*

City	[ ]
Suburb	[ ]
Town/rural	[ ]

15. *The Public Service Commission now requires all utility advertising to carry a disclaimer saying that the cost of advertising is included in customers' rates. What's your reaction to having MG&E's advertising carry this disclaimer?*

16. *Is there anything you'd like to add regarding MG&E's overall performance?*

The treatment conditions differed with respect to the types of ads shown subjects. While the basic content of all four ads was the same for each treatment group (for example, one discussed the availability of a home energy audit, another a commercial energy audit, a third gas safety, and a fourth congratulations for conserving energy), the ads differed with respect to whether or not they contained the disclaimer. All those in Treatment Condition A were shown videotaped television commercials without any disclaimers. All those in Treatment Condition B were shown the same four ads with the disclaimer "the cost of this message is included in MG&E's rates" inserted at the end of the message. Those in Treatment Condition C saw two ads with the disclaimers attached and two ads without disclaimers. The ads to which the disclaimers were attached varied by shopping center, and the order in which the ads were seen also varied by shopping center. The complete design is displayed in Table 1.

Table 1
Summary of Treatment Conditions*

| | Shopping Center/Treatment Group | | | | | | | | |
| | South Towne | | | West Towne | | | East Towne | | |
Commercial Number	A	B	C	A	B	C	A	B	C
1	DW/0	DW	FW	EW/0	EW	FW/0	FW/0	FW	FW
2	EW/0	EW	DW/0	GW/0	GW	DW/0	DW/0	DW	DW
3	FW/0	FW	GW	DW/0	DW	GW	GW/0	GW	GW/0
4	GW/0	GW	EW/0	FW/0	FW	EW	EW/0	EW	EW/0

*The various symbols are:
  D: home energy audit ad;
  E: congratulations for conserving energy ad;
  F: gas safety ad;
  G: commercial energy audit ad;
  W: with the disclaimer;
W/0: without the disclaimer.

Questions

1. What kind of research design is being used?

2. Evaluate the design with respect to its control of the various extraneous factors that might affect the interpretation of the research results.

3. Are there any logical reasons for changing the order of the ads and mixing up which ads contain the disclaimer and which ones do not?

4. What do you think of the way the subjects were selected?

Part 3

Design Data Collection Method and Forms

	Formulate Problem
	Determine Research Design
	Design Data Collection Method and Forms
	Design Sample and Collect Data
	Analyze and Interpret Data
	Prepare the Research Report

Part 3 treats the third stage in the research process—design the methods of data collection and the data collection forms. Chapter 5 focuses on secondary data as an information resource, while in Chapter 6, observation and communication, the main methods of data collection, are discussed. Chapter 7 deals with the construction of questionnaires and observational data collection forms. Chapter 8 discusses the general topic of attitude measurement using scales and the many types of attitude scales.

Chapter 5
Data Collection:
Secondary Data

Once the research problem is defined and clearly specified, the research effort logically turns to data collection. The natural temptation among beginning researchers is to advocate some sort of survey among appropriate respondent groups. This should be a last rather than a first resort. "A good operating rule is to consider a survey akin to surgery—to be used only after other possibilities have been exhausted."[1] First attempts at data collection should logically focus on secondary data.

Secondary data are statistics not gathered for the immediate study at hand but for some other purpose. **Primary data,** on the other hand, are originated by the researcher for the purpose of the investigation at hand. The purpose, therefore, defines the distinction. If General Electric Company collected information on the demographic characteristics of refrigerator purchasers to determine who buys the various sizes of refrigerators, this would be primary data. If they secured this same information from internal records gathered for other purposes (for example, warranty information) or from published statistics, the information would be considered secondary data.

Using Secondary Data

Beginning researchers are apt to underestimate the amount of secondary data available. Table 5.1, for example, lists some of the information on people and households concerning very small geographic areas available in the published literature because of the census of population. Not searching for the secondary data that are available on a topic is unfortunate, as secondary data possess some significant advantages over primary data. Further, because of the recent "information explosion," such an oversight will be even more consequential in the future.

Advantages of Secondary Data

The most significant advantages of secondary data are the cost and time economies they offer the researcher. If the required information is available as secondary data, the researcher need simply go to the library, locate the appropriate source or sources, and

---

[1] Robert Ferber and P. J. Verdoorn, *Research Methods in Economics and Business* (New York: Macmillan, 1962), p. 208.

Table 5.1
Information Items Available from the 1980 Census of Population

Population	Housing
Items collected at every household ("complete-count items")	
Household relationship[1]	Number of units at address
Sex	Complete plumbing facilities[1]
Race	Number of rooms
Age	Tenure (whether the unit is owned or rented)
Marital status	Condominium identification[1]
Spanish/Hispanic origin or descent[1]	Value of home (for owner-occupied units and condominiums)
	Rent (for renter-occupied units)
	Vacant for rent, for sale, and so forth; and period of vacancy
Additional items collected at sample households*	
School enrollment	Type of unit
Educational attainment	Stories in building and presence of elevator
State or foreign country of birth	Year built
Citizenship and year of immigration	Year moved into this house[1]
Current language and English proficiency[2]	Acreage and crop sales
Ancestry[2]	Source of water
Place of residence 5 years ago	Sewage disposal
Activity 5 years ago	Heating equipment
Veteran status and period of service	Fuels used for house heating, water heating, and cooking
Presence of disability or handicap	Costs of utilities and fuels[1]
Children ever born	Complete kitchen facilities
Marital history	Number of bedrooms
Employment status last week	Number of bathrooms
Hours worked last week	Telephone
Place of work	Air-conditioning
Travel time to work[2]	Number of automobiles
Means of transportation to work[1]	Number of light trucks and vans[2]
Persons in carpool[2]	Homeowner shelter costs for mortgage, real-estate taxes, and hazard insurance[2]
Year last worked	
Industry	
Occupation	
Class of worker	
Work in 1979 and weeks looking for work in 1979[2]	
Amount of income by source[1] and total income in 1979	
Derived variables (illustrative examples)	
Families	Persons per room ("crowding")
Family type and size	Household size
Poverty status	Plumbing facilities
Population density	Institutions and other group quarters
Size of place	Gross rent
	Farm residence

[1]Changed relative to 1970.

[2]New items.

*For most areas of the country in 1980, one out of every six housing units or households received the sample form. Areas estimated to contain 2,500 or fewer persons in 1980 had a 3-out-of-every-6 sampling rate, which is required in order to obtain reliable statistics needed for participation in certain federal programs.

Source: Charles P. Kaplan and Thomas L. VanValey, *Census '80: Continuing the Factfinder Tradition* (Washington, D.C., U.S. Bureau of the Census, 1980), p. 173.

extract and record the information desired. This should take no more than a few days and would involve little cost. If the information were to be collected in a field survey, the following steps would have to be executed: data collection form designed and pre-tested; field interviewing staff selected and trained; sampling plan devised; data gathered and checked for accuracy and omissions; data coded and tabulated. As a conservative estimate, this process would take two to three months and could cost several thousand dollars, since it would include expenses and wages for a number of additional field and office personnel. With secondary data, these expenses have been incurred by the original source of the information and do not need to be borne by the user. Expenses are shared by the users of commercial sources of secondary data, but even here the user's costs will be much less than they would be if the firm collected the same information itself.

These time and cost economies prompt the general admonition: *Do not bypass secondary data. Begin with secondary data, and only when the secondary data are exhausted or show diminishing returns, proceed to primary data.* Sometimes secondary data may provide enough insight by themselves that there will be no need to collect primary data on the topic. This will be particularly true when all the analyst needs is a ballpark estimate, which is often the case. For example, a common question that confronts marketing research analysts is, "What is the market potential for the product or service?" Are enough people or organizations interested in it to justify providing it? Research Realities 5.1 illustrates how secondary data were used to advantage by a manufacturer of pet foods to assess the potential demand for a dog food that included both moist chunks and hard, dry chunks.

As the example indicates, when using secondary data it is often necessary to make some assumptions in order to use the data effectively (e.g., the number of owners who were good prospects). The key is to make reasonable assumptions and to vary these assumptions to determine how sensitive a particular conclusion is to variations in them. In the dog food example, ". . . altering the assumption regarding the number of owners who were good prospects for the new product to include as few as one-tenth of the original number did not alter the decision to proceed with the product. Under such circumstances, the value of additional information would be quite small."[2]

While it is rare when secondary data completely solve the particular problem under study, secondary data will typically (1) help to better state the problem under investigation, (2) suggest improved methods or data for better coming to grips with the problem, and/or (3) provide comparative data by which primary data can be more insightfully interpreted.

Disadvantages of Secondary Data

There are two problems that commonly arise when secondary data are used: (1) they do not completely fit the problem; and (2) there are problems with their accuracy.

---

[2]David W. Stewart, *Secondary Research: Information Sources and Methods* (Beverly Hills, Calif.: Sage Publications, 1984), p. 113. See also *Measuring Markets: A Guide to the Use of Federal and State Statistical Data* (Washington, D.C., U.S. Department of Commerce, 1979) for discussion of the marketing-related information that is available from the federal and state governments and how that information can be used for such marketing tasks as market potential estimation, establishing sales quotas, allocating advertising budgets, locating retail outlets, and so on.

Research Realities 5.1

Use of Secondary Data by a Manufacturer of Pet Foods to Assess the Potential Demand for a Dog Food That Included Both Moist Chunks and Hard, Dry Chunks

The question was, "Is there currently a significant number of persons who mix moist or canned dog food with dry dog food?" At this early stage in the exploration of this product concept, the firm did not want to expend funds for primary research. While an actual survey of pet owners would have yielded the best answer, such a survey would have required the expenditure of several thousand dollars. In addition, further development of the idea would have required a delay of several weeks to obtain the survey results. An effort to develop an acceptable first answer to the question of demand using secondary sources was initiated.

The firm identified the following information:

1. From published literature on veterinary medicine, the firm identified the amount (in ounces) of food required to feed a dog each day by type of food (dry, semimoist, moist), age, size, and type of dog.

2. From an existing survey conducted annually by the firm's advertising agency, the firm obtained information on

a. the percentage of U.S. households owning dogs;
b. the number, sizes, and types of dogs owned by each household in the survey;
c. the type(s) of dog food fed to the dogs; and
d. the frequency of use of various types of dog food.

It was assumed that dog owners who reported feeding their dogs two or more different types of dog food each day were good prospects for a product that provided premixed moist and dry food. Combining the information in the survey with the information from the literature on veterinary medicine and doing some simple multiplication produced a demand figure for the product concept. The demand exceeded 20 percent of the total volume of dog food sales, a figure sufficiently large to justify proceeding with product development and testing.

Source: David W. Stewart, *Secondary Research: Information Sources and Methods* (Beverly Hills, Calif.: Sage Publications, 1984), p. 112. Reprinted by permission of Sage Publications, Inc.

Problems of Fit   Since secondary data are collected for other purposes, it will be rare when they fit the problem as defined perfectly. In some cases, the fit will be so poor as to render them completely inappropriate. Secondary data are ill-suited to problems for three reasons: (1) units of measurement, (2) class definitions, or (3) publication currency.[3]

It is not uncommon for secondary data to be expressed in units different from those deemed most appropriate for the project. Size of retail establishment, for instance, can be expressed in terms of gross sales, profits, square feet, and number of employees. Consumer income can be expressed by individual, family, households, and spending unit. So it is with many variables, and a recurring source of frustration in using second-

---

[3]Jerry E. Drake and Frank J. Millar, *Marketing Research: Intelligence and Management* (Scranton, Pa.: International Textbook Co., 1969), p. 227.

ary data is that the source containing the basic information desired presents that information in units of measurement different from that needed.

Assuming the units are consistent, we find that the class boundaries presented are often different from those needed. If the problem demands income by individual in increments of $5,000 (0–$4,999, $5,000–$9,999, and so on), it does the researcher little good if the data source offers income by individual using boundaries $7,500 apart (0–$7,499, $7,500–$14,999, and so on).

Finally, secondary data quite often lack publication currency. The time from data collection to data publication is often long, sometimes as much as three years, for example, as with much government census data. While census data have great value while current, this value diminishes rapidly with time, as many marketing decisions require current, rather than historical, information.

Problems of Accuracy   The accuracy of much secondary data is also questionable. As this book should indicate, there are a number of sources of error possible in the collection, analysis, and presentation of marketing information. When the researcher collects the information, the individual's firsthand experience should allow the assessment of the accuracy of the information and its bounds of error. These bounds can be critical for marketing decisions based on the information. When using secondary data, the researcher is in no way relieved from assessing accuracy. It is still the researcher's responsibility, although the task is indeed more difficult.[4] The following criteria, though, should help the researcher judge the accuracy of any secondary data; they are the source, the purpose of publication, and general evidence regarding quality.[5]

Consider the source first. Secondary data can be secured from either a primary source or a secondary source. A **primary source** is the source that originated the data. A **secondary source** is a source that, in turn, secured the data from an original source. The *Statistical Abstract of the United States,* which is published each year, contains a great deal of useful information for many research projects. The researcher using the *Statistical Abstract* would be using a secondary source of secondary data, as none of what is published in the *Statistical Abstract* originates there. Rather, all of it is taken from other government and trade sources. The researcher who *terminated* the search for secondary data with the *Statistical Abstract* would violate the most fundamental rule in using secondary data—*always use the primary source of secondary data.*

There are two main reasons for this rule. First and foremost, the researcher will need to search for general evidence of quality, e.g., the methods of data collection and analysis. The primary source will typically be the only source that describes the process of collection and analysis, and thus it is the only source by which this judgment can be made. Second, a primary source is usually more accurate and complete than a secondary source. Secondary sources often fail ''to reproduce significant footnotes, or textual com-

---

[4]Jacob has a particularly helpful discussion on the various errors that are present in published data and what remedies are available to the analyst for treating these errors. See Herbert Jacob, *Using Published Data: Errors and Remedies* (Beverly Hills, Calif.: Sage Publications, 1984).

[5]For an alternative list of criteria, see Stewart, *Secondary Research,* pp. 23–33.

ments, by which the primary source had qualified the data or the definition of units.''[6] Errors in transcription can also occur in copying the data from a primary source. Once made, transcription errors seem to hold on tenaciously, as the following example illustrates. In 1901, Napoleon Lajoie produced the highest batting average ever attained in the American League when he batted .422 on 229 hits in 543 times at bat. In setting the type for the record book after that season, a printer correctly reported Lajoie's .422 average, but incorrectly reported his hits, giving him 220 instead of 229. A short time later, someone pointed out that 220 hits in 543 at bats yields a batting average of .405, and so Lajoie's reported average was changed. The error persisted for some 50 years until an energetic fan checked all the old box scores and discovered the facts.[7]

A second criterion by which the accuracy of secondary data can be assessed is the purpose of publication.

Sources published to promote sales, to advance the interests of an industrial or commercial or other group, to present the cause of a political party, or to carry on any sort of propaganda, are suspect. Data published anonymously, or by an organization which is on the defensive, or under conditions which suggest a controversy, or in a form which reveals a strained attempt at "frankness," or to controvert inferences from other data, are generally suspect.[8]

The above is not to say that such data cannot be used by the researcher. Rather, it is simply to suggest that such data should be viewed most critically by the research user. A source that has no ax to grind but, rather, publishes secondary data as its primary function deserves confidence. If data publication is a source's *raison d'être,* high quality must be maintained. Inaccurate data offer such a firm no competitive advantage, and their publication represents a potential loss of confidence and eventual demise. The success of any organization supplying data as its primary purpose depends on the long-run satisfaction of its users that the information supplied is indeed accurate.

The third criterion by which the accuracy of secondary data can be assessed is the general evidences of quality. One item of evidence here is the ability of the supplying organization to collect the data. The Internal Revenue Service, for example, has greater leverage in securing income data than an independent marketing research firm. Related to this issue, though, is the question of whether the additional leverage introduces bias. Would a respondent be more likely to hedge in estimating his or her income in completing a tax return or in responding to a consumer survey? In addition, the user needs to ascertain how the data were collected. A primary source should provide a detailed description of how the data were collected, including definitions, data collection forms,

---

[6]Erwin Esser Nemmers and John H. Myers, *Business Research: Text and Cases* (New York: McGraw-Hill, 1966), p. 38.

[7]*The Chicago Tribune,* September 19, 1960. If there had not been a cult of "baseball superfans whose passion is to dig up obscure facts about the erstwhile national pastime," the error might never have been discovered. See "You May Not Care But 'Nappie' Lajoie Batted .422 in 1901," *Wall Street Journal,* 54 (September 13, 1974), p. 1.

[8]Nemmers and Myers, *Business Research,* p. 43.

method of sampling, and so forth. If it does not, researcher beware! Such omissions are usually indicative of sloppy methods.

When the details of data collection are provided, the user of secondary data should examine them thoroughly. Was the sampling plan sound? Was this type of data best collected through questionnaire or by observational methods? What about the quality of the field force? What kind of training was provided? What kinds of checks of the field-work were employed? What was the extent of nonresponse, due to refusals, not at home, and by item? Are these statistics reported? Is the information presented in a well-organized manner? Are the tables properly labeled, and are the data within them internally consistent? Are the conclusions supported by the data? As these questions suggest, the user of secondary data must be familiar with the research process and the potential sources of error. The remainder of this book should provide much of the needed insight for evaluating secondary data. For the moment, though, let us examine some of the main sources of secondary data.

Types of Secondary Data

There are a number of ways by which secondary data can be classified. One of the most useful is by source, which immediately suggests the classification of internal and external data. **Internal data** are those found within the organization for whom the research is being done, while **external data** are those obtained from outside sources. The external sources can be further split into those that regularly publish statistics and make them available to the user at no charge, e.g., the United States government, and those organizations that sell their services to various users, e.g., A. C. Nielsen Company. In the remainder of this chapter, we will review some of the more important sources of commercialized statistics, while Appendix 5A treats some of the main sources of published statistics. Together they represent some of the most commonly used sources of secondary data, the ones with which the researcher would typically commence the search.

Internal Secondary Data

Data that originate within the firm for which the research is being conducted are internal data. If they were collected for some other purpose, they are internal secondary data. The sales and cost data compiled in the normal accounting cycle represent promising internal secondary data for many research problems. This is particularly true when the problem is one of evaluating past marketing strategy or of assessing the firm's competitive position in the industry. It is less helpful in future directed decisions, such as evaluating a new product or a new advertising campaign. Even here, though, sales and cost data can serve as a foundation for planning this research.

Two of the most significant advantages associated with internal secondary data are their ready availability and low cost. Internal secondary data are the least costly of any type of marketing research, and if maintained in an appropriate form, internal sales data can be used to analyze the company's sales performance by product, geographic location, customer, channel of distribution, and so on, while the cost data allow the further determination of the profitability of these segments of the business. We shall not go into the details of this type of analysis here because it is a somewhat specialized topic and is extensively reported elsewhere.[9] The aspiring researcher should not bypass this information, but rather should begin most studies with internal secondary data.

Published External Secondary Data

There is such a wealth of published external data that beginning researchers typically underestimate what is available. Furthermore, researchers who do have an inkling of how much valuable secondary data there is are typically unsure of how to go about searching for it. Table 5.2 provides some general guidelines that can be used to get started on a search of secondary data on a particular topic.[10] A couple key sources to keep in mind when conducting the search process are reference librarians, associations, on-line computer searches, and general guides to marketing information.

Reference librarians, who represent one of the single best guides to a library and its holdings, are specialists who have been trained to know the contents of many of the key information sources as well as how to search those sources most effectively. It is a rare problem indeed for which a reference librarian cannot uncover some relevant published information.

Associations are another good general source. Most associations gather and often publish detailed information on such things as industry shipments and sales, growth patterns, environmental factors affecting the industry, operating characteristics, and the like. Trade associations are often able to secure information from members that other research organizations cannot because of the working relationships that exist between the association and the firms who belong to it. Two useful sources for locating associations serving a particular industry are the *Directory of Directories* and the *Encyclopedia of Associations,* described in Appendix 5A.

On-line computer searches have become increasingly useful for locating published information and data in the last ten years, as computer-readable storage systems for data bases have come into their own.[11] Many public libraries, as well as college and university libraries, have invested in the equipment and personnel that are necessary to make data base searching available to their patrons. A key benefit of an on-line computer search is the user's ability to search through the data base and to retrieve selected items according to his or her own needs. On-line data bases can be used to search for journal articles, reports, speeches, marketing data, economic trends, legislation, and any of a

---

[9]See, for example, Charles H. Sevin, *Marketing Productivity Analysis* (New York: McGraw-Hill, 1965); or Sanford R. Simon, *Managing Marketing Profitability* (New York: American Management Association, Inc., 1969) for two of the best treatments of sales and profitability analysis.

[10]See also Jac L. Goldstucker, *Marketing Information: A Professional Reference Guide* (Atlanta: College of Business Administration, Georgia State University, 1982).

[11]It has been estimated that by 1982, for example, there were more than 200 on-line data bases containing almost 1,200 data files, and the number continues to grow daily. See R. N. Cuadra, D. M. Abels, and J. Wranger, eds., *Directory of Online Data Bases* (Fall 1982); W. Kiechel III, "Everything You Always Wanted to Know May Soon Be On-Line," *Fortune,* 101 (May 5, 1980), pp. 226–240. For discussion on how to go about using on-line data bases effectively, see Robert Donati, "Decision Analysis for Selecting Online Data Bases to Answer Business Questions," *Database,* (December 1981), pp. 49–63; and H. Webster Johnson, Anthony J. Faria, and Ernest L. Maier, *How to Use the Business Library: With Sources of Business Information,* 5th ed. (Cincinnati: South-Western Publishing, 1984), pp. 29–57.

Table 5.2

How to Get Started When Searching Published Sources of Secondary Data

Step 1: Identify what you wish to know and what you already know about your topic. This may include relevant facts, names of researchers or organizations associated with the topic, key papers and other publications with which you are already familiar, and any other information you may have.

Step 2: Develop a list of key terms and names. These terms and names will provide access to secondary sources. Unless you already have a very specific topic of interest, keep this initial list long and quite general.

Step 3: Now you are ready to use the library. Begin your search with several of the directories and guides listed in Appendix 5A. If you know of a particularly relevant paper or author, start with the *Social Science Citation Index* (or *Science Citation Index*) and try to identify papers by the same author, or papers citing the author or work. At this stage it is probably not worthwhile to attempt an exhaustive search. Only look at the previous two or three years of work in the area, using three or four general guides. Some directories and indices use a specialized list of key terms or descriptors. Such indices often have thesauri that identify these terms. A search of these directories requires that your list of terms and descriptors be consistent with the thesauri.

Step 4: Compile the literature you have found. Is it relevant to your needs? Perhaps you are overwhelmed by information. Perhaps you've found little that is relevant. Rework your list of key words and authors.

Step 5: Continue your search in the library. Expand your search to include a few more years and one or two more sources. Evaluate your findings.

Step 6: At this point you should have a clear idea of the nature of the information you are seeking and sufficient background to use more specialized resources.

Step 7: Consult the reference librarian. You may wish to consider a computer-assisted information search. The reference librarian can assist with such a search but will need your help in the form of a carefully constructed list of key words. Some librarians will prefer to produce their own lists of key words or descriptors, but it is a good idea to verify that such a list is reasonably complete. The librarian may be able to suggest specialized sources related to the topic. Remember, the reference librarian cannot be of much help until you can provide some rather specific information about what you want to know.

Step 8: If you have had little success or your topic is highly specialized, consult the *Directory of Directories, Directory Information Guide, Guide to American Directories, Statistics Sources, Statistical Reference Index, American Statistics Index,*

Encyclopedia of Geographic Information Sources, or one of the other guides to information listed in Appendix 5A. These are really directories of directories, which means that this level of search will be very general. You will first need to identify potentially useful primary directories, which will then lead you to other sources.

Step 9: If you are unhappy with what you have found or are otherwise having trouble, and the reference librarian has not been able to identify sources, use an authority. Identify some individual or organization that might know something about the topic. The various *Who's Who* publications, *Consultants and Consulting Organizations Directory, Encyclopedia of Associations, Industrial Research Laboratories in the United States,* or *Research Centers Directory* may help you identify sources. Don't forget faculty at universities, government officials, or business executives. Such individuals are often delighted to be of help.

Step 10: Once you have identified sources you wish to consult, you can determine whether they are readily available in your library. If they are not, ask for them through interlibrary loan. Interlibrary loan is a procedure whereby one library obtains materials from another. This is accomplished through a network of libraries that have agreed to provide access to their collections in return for the opportunity to obtain materials from other libraries in the network. Most libraries have an interlibrary loan form on which relevant information about requested materials is written. Interlibrary loans are generally made for some specific period (usually one to two weeks). Very specialized, or rare, publications may take some time to locate, but most materials requested are obtained within a couple of weeks. If you would like to purchase a particular work, consult *Ulrich's International Periodicals Directory, Irregular Serials and Annuals: An International Directory,* or *Books in Print* to determine whether a work is in print and where it may be obtained. Local bookstores often have computerized or microform inventories of book wholesalers and can provide rapid access to books and monographic items.

Step 11: Even after an exhaustive search of a library's resources, it is possible that little information will be found. In such cases, it may be necessary to identify experts or other authorities who might provide the information you are seeking or suggest sources you have not yet identified or consulted. Identifying authorities is often a trial-and-error process. One might begin by calling a university department, government agency, or other organization that employs persons in the field of interest. Reference librarians often can suggest individuals who might be helpful. However, a large number of such calls may be necessary before an appropriate expert is identified.

Source: David W. Stewart, *Secondary Research: Information Sources and Methods* (Beverly Hills, Calif.: Sage Publications, 1984), pp. 20–22. Reprinted by permission of Sage Publications, Inc.

Table 5.3
Sources of Data on the Hardware Industry

Trade Associations and Professional Societies

American Hardware Manufacturers Association. 117 East Palatine Road, Palatine, Illinois 60067.

Builders Hardware Manufacturers Association. c/o Trade Group Associates, Managers, 60 East 42nd Street, Room 1807, New York, New York 10017.

Door and Hardware Institute. 1815 North Fort Myer Drive, Suite 412, Arlington, Virginia 22209.

National Retail Hardware Association. 770 North High School Road, Indianapolis, Indiana 46224.

National Wholesale Hardware Association. 1900 Arch Street, Philadelphia, Pennsylvania 19103.

Periodicals

Blueprint. Door and Hardware Institute, 1815 North Fort Myer Drive, Arlington, Virginia 22209. Bimonthly. Membership.

Hardware Age. Chilton Book Company, Incorporated. Chilton Way, Radnor, Pennsylvania 19089. Monthly. $35.00 per year.

Hardware Retailing. National Retail Hardware Association, 770 North High School Road, Indianapolis, Indiana 46224. Monthly.

Housewares. Harcourt Brace Jovanovich Publications, 757 Third Avenue, New York, New York 10017. Order from Harcourt Brace and Jovanovich Publications, One East First Street, Duluth, Minnesota 55802. Eighteen times per year. $8.00 per year.

Periodicals continued

Housewares Promotions. Munroe Publications, Incorporated, Post Office Drawer Seven, Indian Rocks Beach, Florida 33535. Bimonthly. $7.50 per year.

Directories

Directory of Hardlines Distributers. Hardware Age, Chilton Book Company, Chilton Way, Radnor, Pennsylvania 19089. Biennial. $175.00. Also, **Hardware Age Buyer's Guide—Who Makes It Issue.** Annual. $15.00.

National Hardware Wholesalers Guide. Southern Hardware, 1760 Peachtree Road, Northwest, Atlanta, Georgia 30357. Annual. Price available on request.

Statistics Sources

Annual Survey of Manufactures. Bureau of the Census, U.S. Department of Commerce. Available from Subscriber Services Section, Bureau of the Census, Washington, D.C. 20233. Annual.

Monthly Retail Trade, Sales, Accounts Receivable and Inventories. Bureau of the Census, U.S. Department of Commerce. Available from U.S. Government Printing Office, Washington, D.C. 20402. Monthly. $25.00 per year (includes **Advance Monthly Retail Sales and Annual Retail Trade**).

Source: Excerpted from *Encyclopedia of Business Information Sources*, edited by Paul Wasserman (copyright © 1980,1983 by PaulWasserman; reprinted by permission of the publisher), fifth edition, Gale Research, 1983.

number of other types of information on a particular topic. Some especially useful guides to on-line data bases are described in Appendix 5A.

Other very useful sources for locating information on a particular topic are the general guides to secondary data described in Appendix 5A. Table 5.3, for example, lists what the *Encyclopedia of Business Information Sources* has to say about data sources on the hardware industry. Aspiring researchers are also well advised to acquaint themselves with the more important general sources of marketing information so that they know what statistics are available and where they can be found. Many of the most important of these are listed and briefly described in Appendix 5A.

Standardized Marketing Information Services

The many standardized marketing information services that are available are another important source of secondary data for the marketing researcher. These services are available at some cost to the user and in this respect are a more expensive source of

Price Sources

Producer Prices and Price Indexes. Bureau of Labor Statistics, U.S. Department of Labor. U.S. Government Printing Office, Washington, D.C. 20402. Monthly. $17.00 per year.

Financial Ratios

Annual Statement Studies. Robert Morris Associates, Credit Division, Philadelphia National Bank Building, Philadelphia, Pennsylvania 19107. Annual. $22.20.

Bottom Line. National Retail Hardware Association, 770 North High School Road, Indianapolis, Indiana 46224. Annual. $15.00.

Cost of Doing Business—Corporations. Dun and Bradstreet, Incorporated, 99 Church Street, New York, New York 10007. Irregular. Single copies free.

Cost of Doing Business—Proprietorships and Partnerships. Dun and Bradstreet, Incorporated, 99 Church Street, New York, New York 10007. Irregular. Single copies free.

Expenses in Retail Business. NCR Corporate Education—Learning Systems, Dayton, Ohio 45479. $1.25.

Key Business Ratios in 800 Lines. Dun and Bradstreet, Incorporated, 99 Church Street, New York, New York 10007. Annual. $40.00.

National Retail Hardware Association Management Report. 770 North High School Road, Indianapolis, Indiana 46224. Annual. $15.00.

Research Centers and Institutes

Human Resources Center. I.U. Willets Road, Albertson, New York 11507.

ICD Rehabilitation and Research Center. 340 East 24th Street, New York, New York 10010.

University Rehabilitation Center. University of Arizona, Second and Vine Streets, Tucson, Arizona 85721.

Vocational and Rehabilitation Research Institute. 3304 33rd Street, Northwest, Calgary, Alberta T2L 2A6, Canada.

On-line Data Bases

ABI/Inform. Data Courier, Incorporated, 620 South Fifth Street, Louisville, Kentucky 40202. General business literature, August 1971 to present inquire as to online cost and availability. Covers journal literature.

Labordoc. International Labor Organization, Washington Office, 1750 New York Avenue, Northwest, Washington, D.C. 20006. Citations and abstracts to literature on labor, 1965 to present. Inquire as to online cost and availability.

Management Contents. Management Contents, Incorporated, Box 1054, Skokie, Illinois 60076. General business journal literature, September 1974 to present. Inquire as to online cost and availability.

Pais International. Public Affairs Information Service, 11 West 40th Street, New York, New York 10018. Literature of social and political science, 1976 to present. Worldwide coverage. Inquire as to online cost and availability.

secondary data than published information. However, they are also typically much less expensive than primary data, because purchasers of these data share the costs incurred by the supplier in collecting, editing, coding, and tabulating them. Because it must be suitable for a number of users, though, what is collected and how the data are gathered must be uniform. Thus, the data may not always ideally fit the needs of the user, which is their main disadvantage over primary data.

This section reviews some of the main types and sources of standardized marketing information service data.

Industry Services

There are more information services available to the consumer goods manufacturer than to the industrial goods supplier. The consumer goods services are also much older than the industrial goods services. For instance, whereas the Nielsen Retail Index dates from 1934, the industry information services were born in the 1960s. This means that the

Figure 5.1
DMI Record

D-U-N-S NUMBER	NAME & ADDRESS (MAIL ADDR. BELOW LINE)		SEQ #
00-050-0108	Castle Corp.		5

Castle Corp.
549 Oldham St.
Outway, N. Y. 10498
P. O. Box 3537
Outway, N. Y. 10498

SIC CODES		JOB #
3559 3391		4321
3449 3369		STARTED ★
3589		1935

LINE OF BUSINESS	SALES VOLUME ★
Mfg. Ind. Mach.	2,000,000

EMPL HERE	TOT EMPLS	HQS	BR	MFG	SINGLE LOC	SUB	HQS D-U-N-S NO.
60	90	Yes	No	No	No	Yes	00-050-0108

NATL	STATE	CNTY	CITY	S.M.T.A.	PARENT D-U-N-S NO.
000	63	132	1913	406	00-050-2542

TELEPHONE NO.	CHIEF EXECUTIVE
317-435-0041	R. T. Drewery PR

★ Does not apply to branches   R indicates minimum of range   N/A not available

DUN'S MARKET IDENTIFIERS

© **Dun & Bradstreet, Inc.**   PRINTED IN USA

Source: Reprinted with permission from Dun's *Marketing Services* © Dun & Bradstreet, Inc.

industrial goods services are still evolving in terms of the type of information being collected and how it is made available to users. One of the more important suppliers of industry market data is Dun and Bradstreet.

Dun and Bradstreet "Market Identifiers"   Dun's "Market Identifiers" (DMI) is a special name given by Dun and Bradstreet to its marketing information service. DMI is a roster of over 4,300,000 establishments that is updated on a monthly basis so that the record on each company is accurate and current. Figure 5.1 is an example of a 3 × 5 card record. These detailed records on a company-by-company basis allow sales management to construct sales prospect files, define sales territories and measure territory potentials, and isolate potential new customers with particular characteristics. They allow advertising management to select prospects by size and location, to analyze market prospects and select the media to reach them, to build, maintain, and structure current mailing lists, to generate sales leads qualified by size, location, and quality, and to locate new markets for testing. Finally, they allow marketing research to assess market potential by territory, to measure market penetration in terms of numbers of prospects and numbers of customers, and to make comparative analyses of overall performance by districts and sales territories and in individual industries.

Distribution Services

In an increasingly competitive marketplace, it is critical that the marketing manager have accurate information about the productivity of any change in marketing decision variables. Sales volume (or market share) is a typical yardstick employed to assess the effectiveness of various marketing strategies. Unfortunately, sales volume itself is an elusive yardstick. Using factory shipments as the sales barometer neglects the filling or depleting of distribution pipelines that may be occurring. Yet the measurement of actual purchases by consumers raises a whole host of questions with respect to sampling and data gathering procedures. The distribution services have come to grips with this and now collect consumer sales data on a continuing basis through store audits or via scanners.

The basic concept of a store audit is very simple. The research firm sends field workers, called auditors, to a select group of retail stores at fixed intervals. On each visit the auditor takes a complete inventory of all products designated for the audit. The auditor also notes the merchandise moving into the store by checking wholesale invoices, warehouse withdrawal records, and direct shipments from manufacturers. Sales to consumers are then determined by the calculation

Beginning inventory + Net purchases (from wholesalers and manufacturers)

− Ending inventory = Sales.

Two of the best-known distribution information services are A. C. Nielsen's Retail Index and Audits and Surveys Product Audit.

Nielsen Retail Index   Nielsen's Retail Index Services are based on national samples of more than 7,500 supermarkets, 2,400 drug stores, 550 mass merchandisers, and 900 alcoholic beverage outlets, taken every two months. The auditors collect the basic product turnover data described previously, as well as information on retail prices, store displays, promotional activity, and local advertising.

Auditing records serve as the basic input to the Nielsen retail service. The company takes these records and in turn generates the following information for each of the brands of each of the products audited:

- sales to consumers,
- purchases by retailers,
- retail inventories,
- number of days' supply,
- out-of-stock stores,
- prices (wholesale and retail),
- special factory packs,
- dealer support (displays, local advertising, coupon redemption),
- total food store sales (all commodities), and
- major media advertising (from other sources).

Figure 5.2

Sample Structure for Nielsen Retail Index

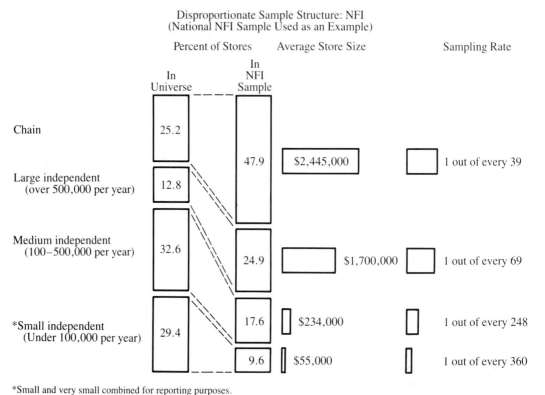

Disproportionate Sample Structure: NFI
(National NFI Sample Used as an Example)

*Small and very small combined for reporting purposes.

Source: *Management with the Nielsen Retail Index System* (Northbrook, Ill.: A. C. Nielsen Company, 1980), p. 11.

Subscribers to the Nielsen service can get this data broken down by competitor, geographic area, or store type. Nielsen will also provide special reports to clients on a fee basis. These special reports include such things as the effect of shelf facings on sales, the sales impact of different promotional strategies, premiums or prices, or the analysis of sales by client-specified geographic areas.

The stores included in all Nielsen Index samples (regular, test, major market, and so on) are determined by using a "disproportionate, stratified" sampling technique. Those stores expected to display greater variability in sales (that is, the largest stores) are sampled most heavily, while those expected to show little sales variation are sampled less than proportionately to their number. For reasons that will be explained in the chapters on sampling, this type of sampling plan is more efficient than other sampling methods in terms of information accuracy versus cost. Figure 5.2 depicts the composition of the Nielsen sample. The sample results are then adjusted using a complex weighting scheme to provide population estimates of the key statistics. The stores pinpointed for inclusion in the panel are contacted personally to secure their cooperation.

Further, the stores are compensated for their cooperation on a per-audit basis. The auditors collecting the data are full-time people with college educations who have all undergone an in-house six-month training program.

Since the late 1970s, Nielsen has been supplementing its Retail Index service with its Scantrack service. The Scantrack service emerged from the revolutionary development in the grocery industry brought about by the installation of scanning equipment in retail food stores to read Universal Product Codes. Universal Product Codes are 11-digit numbers imprinted on each product sold in a supermarket. The first digit, called the number system character, indicates the type of product it is (e.g., grocery or drug). The next five digits identify the manufacturer and the last five a particular product of the manufacturer, be it a different size, variety, or whatever. There is a unique 11-digit code for every product in the supermarket. As the product with its bar code is pulled across the **scanner,** the scanner identifies the 11-digit number, looks up the price in the attached computer, and immediately prints the description and price of the item on the cash register receipt. At the same time, the computer can keep track of the movement of every item that is scanned.[12] The Scantrack service provides weekly sales data from a nationwide sample of scanner-equipped stores. The data allow clients to evaluate the effectiveness of short-term promotions, to evaluate pricing changes, to follow new product introductions, and to monitor unexpected events, such as product recalls and shortages, among other things.

Audits and Surveys National Total-Market Index   The Audits and Surveys National Total-Market Index is similar to the Nielsen Retail Index except in three important respects: It is based on a product audit rather than a type-of-store audit; it uses part-time rather than full-time auditors; and the Audits and Surveys program is based on a calendar bimonthly schedule—January–February, and so on. Nielsen's schedule varies by type of outlet: drug is reported for December–January, food for January–February. Audits and Surveys employs a permanent staff of six regional supervisors to administer its field quality control program. The product audit is distinguished by its emphasis on the total retail market for a product in all the outlets in which the product is sold; a product audit requires that for a product like dentifrice, department stores, drug stores, grocery stores, general stores, variety stores, cigar stores, and other stores where dentifrice might be sold all be canvassed. The product audit can provide the firm subscribing to the service the following types of information:

1. Retail sales: How large is the total market? What is your brand's market share . . . and each of your competitors'? Is your position different by outlet type, by region, by size of city?

2. Retailer inventory: How much inventory is stocked by all retailers? How does your brand compare with competition in the struggle for store space? Does it vary by store type or geographically?

---

[12]For discussion of the trends in bar coding, see "Bar Codes are Black-and-White Stripes and Soon They Will Be Read All Over," *Wall Street Journal,* 65 (January 8, 1985), p. 37. For discussion of the trends in optical scanners, see Bob Gatty, "The Spreading Computer Revolution," *Nation's Business,* 71 (February 1983), pp. 72–73 and 76.

3. Distribution and out-of-stock: How many stores handle your brand? What volume of the product category's business do these stores represent? What is the prevalence of out-of-stock conditions on your brand? Your competition? What are the patterns by region, by outlet type?[13]

The bimonthly reports are made available 30 days after the close of each audit period. Since the notion of product audit defines the basic service, some of the products covered by Audits and Surveys are very much different from those covered by the Nielsen Retail Index and include such product categories as automotive products, electrical products, food products, tobacco products, photographic products, health and beauty aids, household products, and writing instruments.

Selling Areas Marketing, Inc.   Selling Areas Marketing, Inc. (SAMI) is also a distribution service.[14] However, SAMI reports are based on warehouse withdrawals rather than retail store sales. Only food operators participate, but since the SAMI sample includes warehouses of chains, wholesalers, rack jobbers, and frozen food warehousemen, the product movement figures include the volume retailed by chain supermarkets, "mom and pop" stores, independent supermarkets, and food discounters. SAMI reports the movement of all dry grocery and household supplies, frozen food, health and beauty aids, and certain warehoused refrigerated items. However, fresh meat, perishables, and store-delivered items such as milk, bread, and soft drinks do not appear in the SAMI reports.

The basic SAMI reports are generated from food distribution records. SAMI reports are available for each of 51 major markets, which together account for over 86 percent of national food sales. The basic SAMI reports are issued every twenty-eight days and are delivered to manufacturers purchasing the service three to four weeks following the end of the reporting period. A manufacturer may purchase any or all markets in a given category and any or all products. Since the reports detail each brand's share and volume movement every four weeks, they allow participating manufacturers to continuously assess the competitive conditions in each market. The manufacturer can therefore make appropriate changes in marketing strategy and can assess the impact of these changes rather quickly.

Consumer Services

A number of standardized marketing information services directly involve consumers and their behavior. Some are concerned with purchase or consumption behavior (for example, the National Purchase Diary Panel and BehaviorScan), some with viewing and reading habits (for example, the Nielsen Television Index, the Starch Advertisement Readership Service, and the Simmons Media/Marketing Services), while still others are

---

[13]Taken from "The National Total-Market Audit Index," A division of Audits & Surveys, Inc., 1 Park Avenue, New York, N.Y.

[14]Taken from *The Facts of Sami Saudi, and Market Segmentation* (Chicago: Selling Areas Marketing, Inc., 1984).

used for a variety of purposes (for example, National Family Opinion Panel and the Consumer Mail Panel).

National Purchase Diary Panel   The National Purchase Diary Panel (NPD) operates the largest diary panel in the United States[15]: over 13,000 families use a preprinted diary to record their monthly purchases in approximately 50 product categories. Figure 5.3 illustrates the sample diary for soup products. Note the diary asks for significant details regarding the brand and amount bought, the price paid, whether there were any deals involved (by type), the store where purchased, the flavor, and intended use.

The families comprising NPD are geographically dispersed while the panel is demographically balanced so it can be projected onto total U.S. purchasing. The total panel contains 29 miniature panels, each representative of a local market. Panel members are recruited quarterly and are added to the active panel only after they have maintained a training diary and satisfactorily met NPD's standards for accuracy. Families are recruited so that the composition of the panel mirrors the population of the United States with respect to a 288-cell matrix where the cells are determined on the basis of a combination of family size, age of housewife, income, whether in or out of SMSA, and census division. Panel members are compensated for their participation with gifts, and families are dropped from the panel at their request or if they fail to return three of their last five diaries.

The diaries are returned to NPD monthly, the purchase histories are aggregated, and reports prepared. Using these reports the subscribing company is able to assess, among other things,

- the size of the market, the proportion of families buying over time, and the amount purchased per buyer;
- brand share over time;
- brand loyalty and brand switching behavior;
- frequency of purchase and amount purchased per transaction;
- influence of price and special price deals as well as average price paid;
- characteristics of heavy buyers;
- impact of a new brand on the established brands; and
- impact of a change in advertising or distribution strategy.[16]

BehaviorScan   BehaviorScan also attempts to measure household consumption behavior. Instead of relying on diary panels, though, it makes use of scanners. Scanner data have an obvious advantage over panel data, since they reflect purchasing behavior that is not subject to the interview, recording, or expert biases that may be present with mail diaries. Mail diaries, on the other hand, have the advantage that the recorded purchase behavior can be linked to the demographic characteristics of those forming the panel.

[15]See *We Make the Market Perfectly Clear* (New York: NPD Research, Inc., undated).

[16]See *Insights: Issues 1–13* (New York: NPD Research, Inc., undated) for discussion of these and other analyses using diary panel data.

Figure 5.3
Sample Page from National Purchase Diary

PAGE EIGHT

NOTE: Extra space page 1. Free Gift and Samples, on Back cover.

Dairy Tip: Enter all kinds of soups in this section that come in cans, boxes, pouches, or other containers including dry packaged ingredients for making homemade soup.

Date Of Month pur-chase was made	Write in **BRAND NAME** as shown on label **SOUPS** Include Canned, Dry and Bouillon (Write in Brand and/or Company Name — Not Flavor)	HOW MANY of each kind did you buy? Write in number of packages, or other containers	TOTAL CASH PAID Don't include taxes		Check (✓) ONE — Did you redeem a coupon or was there a special price offer?										WHERE DID YOU PURCHASE?			WEIGHT (size) shown on label	FLAVOR	TYPE Check (✓) One						INTENDED USE Check (✓) One		MANUFACTURER CODE
																KIND OF STORE Check (✓) or Write In				CANNED		DRY MIX						
			$	¢	No Special Price	Price Off on Label	Mail-in Cash Refund	Redeemed Coupon from Newspaper	Redeemed Coupon from Magazine	Redeemed Coupon received in Mail	Redeemed Coupon from prior purchase of same item	Redeemed Coupon from Other Purchase	Other Special Price	TOTAL CENTS OFF IF ANY WRITE IN	NAME OF STORE (or company if purchased from door-to-door or home delivery salesperson)	GROCERY OR FOOD	Other — Describe	Write in weight (such as: ounces, pints, etc.) per item or can/or number of packets or cubes.	Describe Flavor Write in Such as: Tomato, Chicken Noodle, Beef Broth, etc.	Condensed	Ready to Serve	REGULAR — to be cooked	INSTANT — No cooking needed	Dry Packaged Ingredients for Homemade Soup	CUBE	Used as Soup	Used as Ingredient in another dish	On many cans or packages, you will find a 6 digit or 10 digit code number underneath a series of vertical lines or bars. Please fill in these code numbers below. If you can't find them, leave this question blank.

Information Resources Inc., has tried to get the advantages of both methods through their BehaviorScan system. BehaviorScan, which started in two test markets—Marion, Indiana, and Pittsfield, Massachusetts—in 1979, planned to operate in 24 sampling areas by the end of 1985.[17]

More than 2,500 households in each of the markets have been recruited by Information Resources to present an identification card at each of the grocery stores every time they make a purchase. Almost all the supermarkets in each area are provided scanners by Information Resources. Each household presents its identification card when checking out. The card is scanned along with the household's purchases, allowing Information Resources to relate a family's purchases by brand, size, and price to the family's demographic characteristics and the household's known exposure to coupons, newspaper ads, free samples, and point-of-purchase displays.

Information Resources also has the capability to direct different TV advertising spots to different households through the "black boxes" that have been attached to the television sets in each test household, in cooperation with the cable television systems serving the markets. This allows Information Resources the opportunity to monitor the buying reactions to different advertisements or to the same advertisement in different types of households (e.g., whether the buying reactions to a particular ad are the same or different among past users and nonusers of the product). This targetable TV capability allows Information Resources to balance the panel of members for each ad test within each market according to the criteria the sponsor chooses (e.g., past purchasers of the product), thereby minimizing the problem of having comparable experimental and control groups.

Nielsen Television Index The Nielsen Television Index is probably the most generally familiar commercial information service. The most casual television watcher has probably heard of the Nielsen ratings and their impact on which TV shows are canceled by the networks and which are allowed to continue. The index itself is designed to provide estimates of the size and nature of the audience for individual television programs. The basic data are gathered through the use of Audimeter® instruments, which are electronic devices attached to the television sets in approximately 1,200 cooperating households. Each Audimeter is connected to a central computer, which records when the set is on and to what channel it is tuned.

Through the data provided by these basic records, Nielsen develops estimates of the number and percentage of all TV households viewing a given TV show. The most popular report (the "Pocketpiece") is issued biweekly, forty-eight weeks a year, and is generally available to clients less than two weeks after a measurement period. For those requiring more frequent reports, Nielsen installs a special terminal in the client's office that permits receipt of national household ratings within 24 hours of a broadcast. Nielsen

---

[17]See *BehaviorScan Market Profiles* (Chicago: Information Resources, undated), and *The Marketing Fact Book* (Chicago: Information Resources, undated). For discussion of the tremendous impact such "test market" systems are having on marketing research, see "New Tools Revolutionize New Product Testing," *Marketing and Media Decisions* (November 1984), pp. 76–78 and 128–134; Richard Kreisman, "Buy the Numbers," *Inc.,* (March 1985), pp. 104–112; and "Big Brother Gets a Job in Market Research," *Business Week,* (April 8, 1985), pp. 96–97.

also breaks down these aggregate ratings by ten socioeconomic and demographic characteristics, including territory, education of head of house, county size, time zones, household income, age of woman of house, color TV ownership, occupation of head of house, presence of nonadults, and household size. Nielsen also collects data from a separate sample of 3,200 households with respect to who is viewing a particular program. These breakdowns assist the network, of course, in selling advertising on particular programs, while they assist the advertiser in choosing to sponsor programs which reach households with the desired characteristics.[18]

Starch Advertisement Readership Service   The Starch Readership Service measures the reading of advertisements in magazines and newspapers. Some 75,000 advertisements in 1,000 issues of consumer and farm magazines, business publications, and newspapers are assessed each year using over 100,000 personal interviews.

The Starch surveys employ the "recognition method" to assess a particular ad's effectiveness. With the magazine open, the respondent is asked to indicate whether he or she has read *each ad*. Four degrees of reading are recorded:

1. non-reader—a person who did not remember having previously seen the advertisement in the issue being studied;

2. noted—a person who remembered seeing the advertisement in that particular issue;

3. associated—a person who not only "noted" the advertisement but also saw or read some part of it that clearly indicates the brand or advertiser;

4. read most—a person who read 50 percent or more of the written material in the ad.[19]

During the course of the interview, data are also collected on the observation and reading of the component parts of each ad, such as the headlines, subheadings, pictures, copy blocks, and so forth.

Interviewing begins a short time after the issue of the magazine is placed on sale. For weekly and biweekly consumer magazines, interviewing begins three to six days after the on-sale date and continues for one to two weeks. For monthly magazines, interviewing begins two weeks after the on-sale date and continues for three weeks.

The interviews are conducted by a trained staff of field interviewers who have the responsibility of selecting those to be interviewed, since a quota sample is employed. Each interviewer must locate an assigned number of readers within a particular area who are 18 years of age and over, with various occupations, family sizes, and marital and economic statuses. The quotas are determined so that different characteristics will be represented in the sample in proportion to their representation in the population. Readers are included in the sample when they conform to the specified demographic characteristics and they reply in the affirmative when asked if they had read the particular magazine issue in question. The size of the sample varies by publication. Most Starch studies, though, are based on 100 to 150 interviews per sex.

---

[18]Greater detail regarding the Nielsen television rating can be found in *The Nielsen Ratings in Perspective* (Northbrook, Ill.: A. C. Nielsen Company, 1980).

[19]*Starch Readership Report: Scope, Method, and Use* (Mamaroneck, N.Y.: Starch INRA Hooper, undated).

Since newspaper and magazine space cost data are also available, a "readers per dollar" variable can be calculated. The final summary report from Starch shows each ad's (one-half page or larger) overall readership percentages, readers per dollar, and rank when grouped by product category. The summary sheet is attached to the labeled copy of the issue in which each ad is marked to show the readership results for the ad as a whole and for each component part. The data allow the magazine and newspaper advertiser to compare (with respect to readership) his or her ads with those of competitors, current ads with prior ads, and current ads against product averages. This process can be effective in assessing changes in theme, copy, layout, use of color, and so on.

Simmons Media/Marketing Service   The Simmons Media/Marketing Service uses a national probability sample of some 19,000 respondents and serves as a comprehensive data source allowing the cross referencing of product usage and media exposure. Four different interviews are conducted with each respondent so that magazine, television, newspaper, and radio can all be covered by the Simmons Service. Information is reported for total adults and for males and females separately.[20]

The service conducts two personal interviews, which obtain measures of respondent readership of individual magazines and newspapers. During the second personal interview, respondents are also asked about their radio listening behavior. A self-administered questionnaire is used to gather product purchase and use information for over 800 product categories, which remain relatively fixed from year to year. Finally, television viewing behavior is ascertained by means of a personal viewing diary, which each respondent is asked to keep for two weeks.

A disproportionate stratified sample is used in selecting respondents for the study. High-income households are sampled more than proportionately, while low-income households are sampled less than proportionately to their number. All households receive a premium for participating and a minimum of six calls are made in the attempt to interview previously unavailable respondents. A large number of demographic characteristics are gathered from each respondent included in the study.

Simmons determines magazine readership using the "through-the-book" or editorial interest method for 43 major magazines and by the "recent reading" method for 95 smaller monthly magazines. In the "through-the-book" method, respondents are screened to determine which magazines they might have read during the past six months. They are then shown actual issues of magazines stripped of confusing material (for identification purposes), such as advertising pages and recurring columns and features. Ten feature articles unique to the issue are exhibited, and an indirect approach, asking respondents to select the articles they personally find especially interesting, is employed. At the end, a qualifying question is asked: "Now that you have been through this magazine, could you tell me whether this is the first time you happened to look into this particular issue, or have you looked into it before?" Respondents must affirm prior exposure to the issue to qualify as readers. Expressions of doubt or uncertainty would disqualify them.

---

[20]*The 1984 Study of Media and Markets* (New York: Simmons Market Research Bureau, Inc., 1984). See also *Dependable Data for Advertising and Marketing Decisions* (New York: Simmons Market Research Bureau, Inc., undated).

The "recent reading" method operates by having respondents physically sort a deck of four-color magazine logo cards. First, respondents are asked to sort the cards into two piles, representing magazines read and not read in the past six months. For all the cards in the "read pile," respondents are asked to indicate which ones they have read in the past month. The following types of information are gathered from the more than 800 products included in the annual Simmons study:

- users of products, brands, or services
- ownership of products
- price paid for selected items
- brand used most often
- volume/frequency of use
- store at which purchased.

This product information can then be tabulated against such things as magazines read, television programs viewed, newspapers read, and radio listening behavior and simultaneously against a number of demographic characteristics that enable a client to identify target groups and to determine the combinations of media vehicles required to reach them most efficiently and with the desired frequency.

NFO Research, Inc.   NFO is an independent research firm specializing in custom-designed consumer surveys using mail panels and, in this sense, is not a true source of secondary data since the data collected are specifically designed to meet the client's needs.

NFO maintains representative panels drawn from a sampling frame of well over 250,000 U.S. families who have agreed to cooperate without compensation in completing self-administered questionnaires on a variety of subjects. The topics may include specific product usage, reaction to the product or advertising supporting it, reaction to a product package, attitude toward or awareness of some issue, product, service or ad, and so on.

The national panel is dissolved and rebuilt every two years so that it matches current family population characteristics with respect to income, population density, age of homemaker, and family size, for the continental United States and each of the nine geographic divisions in the census.

A current demographic profile is maintained for each family in the data bank. Included are such characteristics as size of family, education, age of family members, presence and number of children by sex, occupation of the principal wage earner, race, and so on. This information is used to generate highly refined population segments. If the user's needs require it, NFO can offer the client panels composed exclusively of mothers of infants, teenagers, elderly people, dog and cat owners, professional workers, mobile home residents, multiple car owners, or other specialized types. Each of these panels can be balanced to match specific quotas dictated by the client.[21]

---

[21]More detailed information regarding the mail panel can be found in the company's publication *NFO* (Toledo, Ohio: NFO Research, Inc., undated).

Consumer Mail Panel   The Consumer Mail Panel (CMP) is part of Market Facts, Inc. The panel is a sample of households that have agreed to respond to mail questionnaires and product tests. Samples of persons for each product test or use are drawn from the 120,000 persons in the CMP pool. The pool is representative of the geographical divisions in the United States and Canada and is broken down, within these divisions, according to census data on total household income, population density and degree of urbanization, and age of panel member.

According to CMP, their mail panel is ideally suited for experimental studies since the samples are matched. In particular, CMP is believed to be particularly valuable when

1. large samples are required at low cost because the size of the subgroups is large or there are many subgroups to be analyzed;

2. large numbers of households must be screened to find eligible respondents;

3. continuing records are to be kept by respondents to report such data as products purchased, how products are used, TV programs viewed, magazines read, and so on.

CMP has recorded a number of other characteristics with respect to each participating household that allow for cross tabulation of the client's criterion variable against such things as place of residence (state, county, and standard metropolitan area), marital status, occupation and employment status, household size, age, sex, home ownership, type of dwelling, and ownership of pets, dishwashers, washing machines, dryers, other selected appliances, and automobiles.[22]

Summary

When confronted by a new problem, the researcher's first attempts at data collection should logically focus on secondary data. Secondary data are statistics gathered for some other purpose, in contrast to primary data, which are collected for the purpose at hand. Secondary data possess significant cost and time advantages, and it is only when their pursuit shows diminishing returns and the problem is not yet resolved that the researcher should proceed to primary data. The problem will typically not be resolved completely with secondary data because secondary data rarely suit the problem perfectly. There are usually problems of appropriateness, and when the data are appropriate there still remain the problems of different units of measurement, class definitions, and publication currency from that required. Nevertheless, their diligent pursuit still typically offers the researcher a great deal of insight into the problem, information required to resolve it, and ways in which the information can be obtained. Sometimes, secondary data will eliminate completely any need to collect primary data.

Secondary data can be found in either primary or secondary sources. A primary source is the source that originated the data, while a secondary source is a source that

---

[22]More detail regarding the Market Facts mail panel can be found in *Why Consumer Mail Panel is the Superior Option* (Chicago: Market Facts, Inc., undated) or *Market Facts, Inc.: Data Collection and Analysis for Reducing Business Decision Risks* (Chicago: Market Facts, Inc., undated).

secured the data from an original source. The primary source should always be used. Further, the researcher should make some judgment about the quality and accuracy of secondary data by examining the purpose of publication, the ability of the organization to collect the data, and general evidence of careful work in their presentation and collection.

Secondary data include internal company data, published external secondary data, and data supplied by commercial marketing information services. Internal sales and cost data are a most inexpensive source of marketing control information and can also be used effectively to gain a perspective on research problems. There is such a wealth of published external secondary data available that it is easy to overlook them, and the researcher is well advised to follow the process listed in Table 5.2, or some variation of it, when locating secondary data. Further, aspiring researchers should personally examine the sources described in Appendix 5A so that their contents are familiar.

Standardized marketing information services can be an important adjunct to the researcher's data collection efforts. These services offer economies of scale because they serve a number of clients for a variety of purposes, and thus they are able to spread their costs of operation among clients. This means that if they are suitable for the clients' needs, they offer significant time and cost advantages in the collection of primary data. Not all of the information services reviewed provide what we have called secondary data, since some of them collect information of a specific nature for a specific client (primary data in the true sense of the word). Nonetheless, it was convenient to review some of the types of information services that are available in one place.

Questions

1. What is the difference between primary and secondary data?

2. What are the advantages and disadvantages of secondary data?

3. What criteria can be employed to judge the accuracy of secondary data?

4. What is the difference between a primary source and a secondary source of secondary data? Which is preferred? Why?

5. What distinguishes internal secondary data from external secondary data?

6. How would you go about searching for secondary data on a particular topic?

7. What is the basic operation of a store audit?

8. What is the difference between a product audit and a type-of-store audit? Give an example of each. If you were a producer of canned vegetables, which would you prefer? Which, if you were a producer of automotive replacement parts?

9. If you were a product manager for Brand X detergent and you needed up-to-date market share information by small geographical sectors, would you prefer National Purchase Diary Panel data or Nielsen data? Why?

10. For what types of studies would you prefer NPD consumer diary data versus BehaviorScan consumption data? Vice versa?

11. How are Starch scores determined?

12. What is the basis for the Nielsen television ratings?

13. How do the ''through-the-book'' and ''recent reading'' methods for assessing magazine readership differ?

14. For what types of studies would you use mail panels?

Applications and Problems

1. List some major secondary sources of information for the following situations.

   (a) The marketing research manager of a national soft-drink manufacturer has to prepare a comprehensive report on the soft-drink industry.

   (b) Mr. Baker has several ideas for instant cake mixes and is considering entering this industry. He needs to find the necessary background information to assess its potential.

   (c) The profit margins in the fur business are high! This is what Mr. Adams has heard. The fur industry has always intrigued him and he decides to do some research to determine if the claim is true.

   (d) A recent graduate hears that condominiums are the homes of the 80's. He decides to collect some information on the condominium market.

   (e) Owning a grocery store has been Mrs. Smith's dream. She finally decides to make this into a reality. The first step she wishes to take is to collect information on the grocery business in her hometown.

2. Assume you are interested in opening a fast-food Mexican restaurant in St. Louis, Missouri. You are unsure of its acceptance by consumers and are considering doing a marketing research study to evaluate their attitudes and opinions. In your search for information you find the following studies:

Study A was recently conducted by a research agency for a well-known fast food chain. In order to secure a copy of this study you would be required to pay the agency $225. The study evaluated consumers' attitudes toward fast food in general. The findings, based on a sample of 500 housewives for the cities of Springfield, Illinois, St. Louis and Kansas City, Missouri, and Topeka, Kansas, indicated that respondents did not view fast food favorably. The major reason for the unfavorable attitude was the low nutritional value of the food.

Study B was completed by a group of students as a requirement for an MBA marketing course. This study would not cost you anything as it is available in your university library. The study evaluated consumers' attitudes toward various ethnic fast foods. The respondents consisted of a convenience sample of 200 students from St. Louis. The findings indicated a favorable attitude toward two ethnic fast foods, Italian and Mexican. Based on these results, one of the students planned to open a pizza parlor in 1985 but instead, accepted a job as sales representative in General Foods Corporation.

   (a) Critically evaluate the two sources of data.

   (b) Which do you consider better? Why? ·

   (c) Assume you decide that it will be profitable to become a franchisee in fast food. Identify five specific secondary sources of data and evaluate the data.

3. Home Decorating Products for many years had been a leading producer of paint and painting-related equipment such as brushes, rollers, turpentine, and so on. The company is now considering adding wallpaper to its line. At least initially it did not intend to actually manufacture the wallpaper, but rather planned to subcontract the manufacturing. Home Decorating Products would assume the distribution and marketing functions.

Before adding wallpaper to its product line, however, Home Decorating secured some secondary data assessing the size of the wallpaper market. One mail survey made by a trade association showed that, on the average, families in the United States wallpapered two rooms in their homes each year. Among these families, 60 percent did the task themselves. Another survey, which had also been done by mail, but by one of the major home magazines, found that 70 percent of the subscribers answering the questionnaire had wallpapered one complete wall or more during the last twelve months. Among this 70 percent of the families, 80 percent had done the wallpapering themselves. Home Decorating Products thus has two sets of secondary data on the same problem, but the data are not consistent.

Discuss the data in terms of the criteria one would use to determine which set, if either, is correct. Assume that you are forced to make the determination on the basis of the information in front of you. Which would you choose?

Appendix 5A
Published External Secondary Data

There is so much published external secondary data that it is impossible to mention all of it in a single appendix. For this reason, only items of general interest are included.[1] The material is organized by the source of data.

Census Data

The Bureau of the Census of the United States Department of Commerce is the largest gatherer of statistical information in the country. The original census was the Census of Population, which was required by the Constitution to serve as a basis for apportioning representation in the House of Representatives. The first censuses were merely head counts. Not only has the Census of Population been expanded, but the whole census machinery has also been enlarged—at this point there are nine different censuses, all of which are of interest to the marketing researcher. Table 5.1, for example, listed some of the most useful data on population and housing that is available in the Census of Population. Table 5A.1 lists some of the most useful data that is collected in the various economic censuses described below.

Census data are of generally high quality. Further, they are quite often available on the detailed level that the researcher needs. When not available in this form, the researcher can purchase either computer tapes or flexible diskettes from the Bureau of the Census for a nominal fee to create one's own tabulations. Alternatively, the researcher

---

[1]For more detailed treatment, see H. Webster Johnson, Anthony J. Faria and Ernest L. Maier, *How to Use the Business Library: With Sources of Business Information,* 5th ed. (Cincinnati: South-Western Publishing, 1984); Eleanor G. May, *A Handbook for Business on the Use of Federal and State Statistical Data* (Washington, D.C.: Department of Commerce, 1979); and David W. Stewart, *Secondary Research: Information Sources and Methods* (Beverly Hills, Calif.: Sage Publications, 1984).

can contract with one of the private companies that market census-related products for information on a particular issue.[2] Not only does this allow getting the information tailored to one's own needs, but it is also one of the fastest ways to get census data. Further, many of the private providers update the census data at a detailed geographic level for the between-census years.

There are two major drawbacks to the use of census data: (1) censuses are not taken every year, and (2) the delay from time of collection to time of publication is quite substantial, often two years or more. This last weakness, however necessary because of the massive editing, coding, and tabulation tasks involved, renders the data obsolete for many research problems. The first difficulty requires that the researcher supplement the census data with current data. Unfortunately, current data are rarely available in the detail the researcher desires. This is particularly true with respect to detailed classifications by small geographic area, unless one takes advantage of the services of a private provider with update capability.

Census of Population

The *Census of Population* is taken every ten years, in the years ending with ''0''. The census reports the population by geographic region. It also provides detailed breakdowns on such characteristics as sex, marital status, age, education, race, national origin, family size, employment and unemployment, income, and other demographic characteristics. The *Current Population Reports,* which are published annually and make use of the latest information on migrations, birth and death rates, and so forth, update the information in the *Census of Population.*

Census of Housing   The *Census of Housing* is also published decennially for the years ending in ''0.'' It was first taken in 1940 in conjunction with the *Census of Population* and lists such things as type of structure, size, building condition, occupancy, water and sewage facilities, monthly rent, average value, and equipment including stoves, dishwashers, air conditioners, and so on. For large metropolitan areas, it provides detailed statistics by city block. The periods between publications of the *Census of Housing* are covered by the bureau's annual *American Housing Survey.*

Census of Retail Trade

The *Census of Retail Trade,* which is taken every five years in the years ending in ''2'' and ''7,'' contains detailed statistics on the retail trade. Retail stores are classified by type of business, and statistics are presented on such things as the number of stores, total sales, employment, and payroll. The statistics are broken down by small geographic areas such as counties, cities, and standard metropolitan statistical areas. Current data with respect to some of the information can be found in *Monthly Retail Trade.*

---

[2]Martha Farnsworth Riche, ''Choosing 1980 Census Data Products,'' *American Demographics,* 3 (December 1981), pp. 12–16. See also Martha Farnsworth Riche, ''Data Companies 1983,'' *American Demographics,* 5 (February 1983), pp. 28–39.

Table 5A.1

Information Available from Economic Censuses

Major Data Items	Retail Trade	Wholesale Trade	Service Industries	Construction Industries	Manufactures	Mineral Industries
Number of Establishments and Firms:						
All establishments	X			X		
Establishments with payroll	X	X	X	X	X	X
Establishments by legal form of organization	X	X	X	X	X	X
Firms	X	X	X		X	X
Single-unit and multi-unit firms	X	X	X		X	X
Concentration by major firms	X	X	X		X	
Employment:						
All employees	X	X	X	X	X	X
Production (construction) workers				X	X	X
Employment size of establishments	X	X	X	X	X	X
Employment size of firms	X	X	X			
Production (construction) worker hours				X	X	X
Payrolls:						
All employees, entire year	X	X	X	X	X	X
All employees, first quarter	X	X	X	X	X	
Production (construction) workers				X	X	X
Supplemental labor costs, legally required and voluntary	X	X	X	X	X	X
Sales Receipts, or Value of Shipments:						
All establishments	X			X	X	X
Establishments with payroll	X	X	X	X		
By product or line or type of construction	X	X	X	X	X	X
By class of customer	X	X				
By size of establishments	X	X	X	X	X	X
By size of firm	X	X	X			

Source: Adapted from *Guide to the 1982 Economic Censuses and Related Statistics* (Washington, D.C.: Bureau of the Census, U.S. Department of Commerce, 1984), p. 3.

Table 5A.1
Information Available from Economic Censuses *continued*

Major Data Items	Retail Trade	Wholesale Trade	Service Industries	Construction Industries	Manufactures	Mineral Industries
Operating Expenses:						
Total	X	X	X			
Cost of materials, etc.	X	X		X	X	X
Specific materials consumed (quantity and cost)	X	X			X	X
Cost of fuels	X	X	X	X	X	X
Electric energy consumed (quantity and cost)	X	X	X		X	X
Contract work		X		X	X	X
Products bought and sold					X	X
Advertising	X	X	X			
Rental payments, total	X	X	X	X	X	X
Buildings and structures	X	X	X	X	X	X
Machinery and equipment	X	X	X	X	X	X
Communications services	X	X	X	X	X	X
Purchased repairs	X	X	X	X	X	
Capital Expenditures:						
Total	X	X	X	X	X	X
New, total	X	X	X	X	X	X
Buildings/equipment	X	X	X	X	X	X
Used, total	X	X	X	X	X	X
Buildings/equipment				X		X
Depreciable Assets, Gross Value Buildings/Equipment:						
End of 1981	X	X	X	X	X	X
End of 1982	X	X	X	X	X	X
Depreciation (total and detail for buildings/equipment)	X	X	X	X	X	X
Retirements (total and detail for buildings/equipment)	X	X	X	X	X	X
Inventories:						
End of 1981	X	X		X	X	X
End of 1982	X	X		X	X	X
Other:						
Value added	X	X		X	X	X
Specialization by type of construction/manufacturing				X	X	
Central administrative offices and auxiliaries	X	X	X	X	X	X
Water use					X	X

Census of Service Industries

The *Census of Service Industries* is taken every five years in the years ending in "2" and "7." The service trade census provides data on receipts, employment, type of business (for example, hotel, laundry, and so on), and number of units by small geographic areas. Current data can be found in *Monthly Selected Services Receipts*.

Census of Wholesale Trade

The *Census of Wholesale Trade,* which is taken every five years in the years ending in "2" and "7," contains detailed statistics on the wholesale trade. For instance, it classifies wholesalers into over 150 business groups and contains statistics on the functions they perform, sales volume, warehouse space, expenses, and so forth. It presents these statistics for counties, cities, and standard metropolitan statistical areas. Current data can be found in *Monthly Wholesale Trade*.

Census of Manufacturers

The *Census of Manufacturers* has been taken somewhat irregularly in the past, but is now authorized for the years ending in "2" and "7." It categorizes manufacturing establishments by type using some 450 classes, and contains detailed industry and geographic statistics for such items as the number of establishments, quantity of output, value added in manufacture, capital expenditures, employment, wages, inventories, sales by customer class, and fuel, water, and energy consumption. The *Annual Survey of Manufacturers* covers the years between publications of the census, while *Current Industrial Reports* contains the monthly and annual production figures for some commodities.

Census of Mineral Industries

The *Census of Mineral Industries* is taken in the years ending in "2" and "7." The information here parallels that for the *Census of Manufacturers* but is for the mining industry. The census offers detailed geographic breakdowns with respect to some 50 mineral industries on such things as the number of establishments, production, value of shipments, capital expenditures, cost of supplies, employment, payroll, power equipment, and water use. The *Minerals Yearbook,* published by the Bureau of Mines of the Department of the Interior, supplements the *Census of Mineral Industries* by providing annual data, although the two are not completely comparable in that they employ different classifications—an industrial classification for the Census Bureau data and a product classification for the Bureau of Mines data.

Census of Transportation

The *Census of Transportation,* too, is taken in the years ending in "2" and "7." It covers three major areas: passenger travel, truck and bus inventory and use, and the transport of commodities by the various classes of carriers.

Census of Agriculture

The *Census of Agriculture* was formerly taken in the years ending in "4" and "9." Since 1982, it is taken in years ending in "2" and "7." This census offers detailed breakdowns by state and county on the number of farms, farm types, acreage, land-use practices, employment, livestock produced and products raised, and value of products. It is supplemented by the annual publications *Agriculture Statistics* and *Commodity Yearbook*. In addition, the Department of Agriculture issues a number of bulletins, which often contain data not otherwise published.

Census of Government

The *Census of Government* presents information on the general characteristics of state and local governments, including such things as employment, size of payroll, amount of indebtedness, and operating revenues and costs. The census is authorized in the years ending in "2" and "7."

Other Government Publications

The federal government also collects and publishes a great deal of statistical information in addition to the censuses. Some of this material is designed to supplement the various censuses and is gathered and published for this purpose (e.g., *Current Population Reports*), while other data is generated in the normal course of operations, such as collecting taxes, social security payments, claims for unemployment benefits, and so forth. Some publications also result from the desire to make the search for information more convenient. This section reviews some of the more important publications, chosen because they are of general interest in that they present a number of data series. Many of them also provide references to original sources, where more detailed data can be found. The sources are presented in alphabetical order.

Business Statistics

Published every two years by the Department of Commerce, this publication provides an historical record of the data series appearing monthly in the *Survey of Current Business* (see below).

County Business Patterns

This annual publication of the Department of Commerce contains statistics on the number of businesses by type and their employment and payroll broken down by county. These data are often quite useful in industrial market potential studies.

County and City Data Book

Published once every five years by the Bureau of the Census, it serves as a convenient source of statistics gathered in the various censuses and provides breakdowns on a city and county basis. Included are statistics on such things as population, education, employment, income, housing, banking, manufacturing output and capital expenditures, retail and wholesale sales, and mineral and agricultural output.

Economic Indicators

This monthly publication by the Council of Economic Advisors contains charts and tables of general economic data such as gross national product, personal consumption expenditures, and other series important in measuring general economic activity. An annual supplement presenting historical and descriptive material on the sources, uses, and limitations of the data is also issued.

Economic Report of the President

This publication results from the President's annual address to Congress regarding the general economic well-being of the country. The back portion of the report contains summary statistical tables using data collected elsewhere.

Federal Reserve Bulletin

Published monthly by the Board of Governors of the Federal Reserve System, this publication is an important source of financial data including statistics on banking activity, interest rates, savings, the index of industrial production, an index of department store sales, prices, and international trade and finance.

Federal Statistical Directory

This directory lists the names, office addresses, and telephone numbers of key people engaged in statistical programs and related activities, including agencies of the executive branch of the federal government. It is published by the Department of Commerce and is a useful source of who in Washington might be of some help in locating specific types of data.

Handbook of Cyclical Indicators

Published monthly by the Department of Commerce, it contains at least 70 indicators of business activity designed to serve as a key to general economic conditions.

Historical Statistics of the United States from Colonial Times to 1970

This volume was prepared by the Bureau of the Census to supplement the *Statistical Abstract*. The *Statistical Abstract* is one of the more important general sources for the marketing researcher, since it contains data on a number of social, economic, and political aspects of life in the United States. One problem a user of *Statistical Abstract* data faces is incomparability of figures at various points in time because of the changes in definitions and classifications occasioned by a dynamic economy. *Historical Statistics* contains annual data on some 12,500 different series using consistent definitions and going back to the inception of the series.

Monthly Labor Review

Published monthly by the Bureau of Labor Statistics, this publication contains statistics on employment and unemployment, labor turnover, earnings and hours worked, wholesale and retail prices, and work stoppages.

State and Metropolitan Area Data Book

This book is a statistical abstract supplement put out by the Department of Commerce. It contains information on population, housing, government, manufacturing, retail and wholesale trade, and selected services by state and standard metropolitan statistical areas.

Statistical Abstract of the United States

Published annually by the Bureau of the Census, this publication reproduces more than 1,500 tables originally published elsewhere that cover such areas as the economic, demographic, social, and political structure of the United States. The publication is intended to serve as a convenient statistical reference and as a guide to more detailed statistics. This latter function is fulfilled through reference to the original sources in the introductory comments to each section, the table footnotes, and a bibliography of sources. The *Statistical Abstract* is a source with which many researchers begin the search for external secondary data.

Statistics of Income

Published annually by the Internal Revenue Service of the Treasury Department, this publication is prepared from federal income tax returns of corporations and individuals. There are different publications for each type of tax report—one for corporations, one for sole proprietorships and partnerships, and one for individuals. The *Corporate Income Tax Return* volume, for example, contains balance sheet and income statement statistics compiled from corporate tax returns and broken down by major industry, asset size, and so on.

Survey of Current Business

Published monthly by the Bureau of Economic Analysis in the Department of Commerce, this publication provides a comprehensive statistical summary of the national income and product accounts of the United States. There are some 2,600 different statistical series reported, covering such topics as general business indicators, commodity prices, construction and real estate activity, personal consumption expenditures by major type, foreign transactions, income and employment by industry, transportation and communications activity, and so on. Most of the statistical series present data on the last four years.

U.S. Industrial Outlook

Produced annually by the Department of Commerce, this publication covers the recent trends and five-year outlook for over 350 manufacturing and service industries.

Privately Produced Publications and Marketing Guides

In addition to the censuses and other government publications, a number of private publications containing secondary data are of general interest to the marketing researcher. This section lists some of the more important ones in alphabetical order.

Almanac of Business and Industrial Financial Ratios

Published annually by Prentice-Hall, this publication contains number of establishments, sales, and selected operating ratios for a number of industries (e.g., food stores). The figures are derived from tax return data supplied by the Internal Revenue Service and are reported for twelve categories, based on assets, within each industry. The data thus allow the comparison of a particular company's financial ratios with competitors of similar size.

Commodity Yearbook

Published annually by the Commodity Research Bureau, this publication contains data on prices, production, exports, stocks, and so on, for approximately 100 individual commodities.

Editor and Publisher Market Guide

Published annually by *Editor and Publisher* magazine, this guide contains data on some 1,500 United States and Canadian cities, including location, population, number of households, principal industries, retail sales and outlets, and climate.

Fortune Directory

Published annually by the editors of *Fortune* magazine, this directory provides information on sales, assets, profits, invested capital, and employees for the 500 largest United States industrial corporations.

A Guide to Consumer Markets

Issued annually by The Conference Board, this publication contains data on the behavior of consumers in the marketplace. It includes statistics on population, employment, income, expenditures, and prices.

Handbook of Basic Economic Statistics

Published annually by the Economics Statistics Bureau, this handbook contains current and historical United States statistics on industry, commerce, labor, and agriculture.

Marketing Economics Guide

Published annually by the Marketing Economics Institute, this publication provides detailed operating information on 1,500 retailing centers throughout the country on a regional, state, county, and city basis. It contains information on population, percent of households by income class, disposable income, total retail sales, and retail sales by store group.

Million Dollar Directory

Published annually by Dun & Bradstreet, this reference source lists the offices, products, sales, and number of employees by company. Volume I contains this information for companies with a total worth of more than $1 million, while Volume II contains the same information for companies with assets of $500,000 to $999,999.

Moody's Manuals

Published annually, these manuals—*Banks and Finance, Industrials, Municipals and Governments, Public Utilities, Transportation*—contain balance sheet and income statements for individual companies and government units.

Poor's Register of Corporations, Directors and Executives

Published annually by Standard and Poor, this register lists officers, products, sales, addresses, telephone numbers, and employees for some 45,000 U.S. and Canadian corporations.

Rand McNally Zip Code Atlas and Marketing Guide

Published annually by Rand McNally Company, this atlas contains marketing data and maps for some 100,000 cities and towns in the United States. Included are such things as population, auto registrations, and retail trade.

Sales Management Survey of Buying Power

Published annually by *Sales Management* magazine, this survey contains market data for states, a number of counties, cities, and standard metropolitan statistical areas. Included are statistics on population, retail sales, and household income and a combined index of buying power for each reported geographic area.

Thomas Register of American Manufacturers

Published annually by Thomas Publishing Company, this 17-volume publication lists the specific manufacturers of individual products and provides information on their address, branch offices, and subsidiaries.

United Nations Statistical Yearbook

This annual United Nations publication contains statistics on a wide range of foreign and domestic activities including forestry, transportation, manufacturing, consumption, and education.

World Almanac and Book of Facts

Issued annually by the Newspaper Enterprise Association, this publication serves as a well-indexed handbook on a wide variety of subjects. Included are industrial, financial, religious, social, and political statistics.

Guides to Secondary Data

The previously listed sources are general. They contain information applicable to a wide number of research problems. They will typically provide a productive start through the search for secondary data. If this search results in a dead end, all is not lost by any means. The required secondary data may still be available in industry trade publications. The amount of data available on an industry-by-industry basis is extensive indeed, and researchers are well advised not to finish their search without reviewing the appropriate industry sources. Often the source of industry statistics will be the industry trade association, while in other cases it may be trade journals serving the industry. Researchers new to an area may not be aware of these sources and thus may feel they face a hopeless task in ferreting them out. Fortunately, a number of published guides should be of assistance. This section lists some of the main guides. It includes guides to government statistics as well as privately produced statistics.

American Statistics Index (Washington, D.C.: Congressional Information Service). Published annually and updated monthly, the publication is intended to serve as a comprehensive index of statistical data available to the public from any agency of the federal government.

Brownstone, David M., and Gorton Carruth, *Where to Find Business Information* (New York: John Wiley & Sons, 1979). This publication lists over 5,000 books, periodicals, or data bases of current interest and contains subject, title, and publisher indexes.

Consultants and Consulting Organizations Directory, 5th ed. (Detroit: Gale Research, 1982). This directory lists approximately 6,000 firms and individuals who are active in consulting and briefly describes their services and fields of interest.

Daniells, Lorna M., *Business Information Sources* (Berkeley, Calif.: University of California Press, 1982). A guide to the basic sources of business information organized by subject area.

Directory of Directories, 3rd. ed. (Detroit: Gale Research, 1985). This directory, which is arranged by subject, lists, among other things, commercial and manufacturing directories, directories of individual industries, trades, and professions, and rosters of professional and scientific societies.

Directory of Federal Statistics for Local Areas: A Guide to Sources (Washington, D.C.: U.S. Bureau of the Census, 1978). A guide to the sources of federal statistics for local areas on such topics as population, health, education, income, and finance.

Directory of Federal Statistics for States: A Guide to Sources (Washington, D.C.: U.S. Bureau of the Census, 1976). Similar to the guide for local sources, this guide outlines the sources of federal statistics for states on such topics as population, income, education, and so on.

Directory of Nonfederal Statistics for State and Local Areas: A Guide to Sources (Washington, D.C.: U.S. Bureau of the Census, 1970). Similar to the above census guides, this guide details the private, local, and state organizations collecting and publishing data on economic, political, and social subjects for state and local areas.

Encyclopedia of Associations (Detroit: Gale Research). Published annually, this encyclopedia lists the active trade, business, and professional associations and briefly describes each organization's activities and lists their publications.

Encyclopedia of Business Information Sources, 5th ed. (Detroit: Gale Research, 1983). A guide to the information available on various subjects, including basic statistical sources, associations, periodicals, directories, handbooks, and general literature.

Frank, Nathalie D., *Data Sources for Business and Market Analysis,* 3rd. ed. (Metuchen, N.J.: Scarecrow Press, 1983). An annotated guide to original statistical sources arranged by source of information rather than by topic.

Guide to American Directories, 10th ed. (Coral Springs, Fla.: B. Klein Publications, 1978). This guide provides information on directories published in the U.S., categorized under 300 technical, mercantile, industrial, scientific, and professional headings.

Guide to Foreign Trade Statistics (Washington, D.C.: U.S. Bureau of the Census, 1972). A guide to the published and unpublished sources of foreign trade statistics.

Guide to Industrial Statistics (Washington, D.C.: U.S. Bureau of the Census, 1977). A guide to the Census Bureau's programs relating to industry, including the type of statistics gathered and where these statistics are published.

Industrial Research Laboratories of the United States, 16th ed., (New York: Bowker, 1979). A guide to research and development capabilities of more than 6,000 industrial organizations in the United States. It contains an alphabetical listing of the organizations, address of facilities, sizes of staffs, and fields of research and development.

Jablonski, Donna M., ed., *How to Find Information About Companies* (Washington, D.C.: Washington Researchers, 1979). A useful guide to locating information about specific companies.

Nelson, Theodore A., *Measuring Markets: A Guide to the Use of Federal and State Statistical Data* (Washington, D.C.: Department of Commerce, 1979). This book serves as an excellent guide to both federal and state statistical data.

Social Sciences Citation Index (Philadelphia: Institute for Scientific Information). Published three times yearly, with annual cumulations, this publication indexes all articles in about 1,400 social science periodicals and selected articles in approximately 1,200 periodicals in other disciplines.

Statistics and Maps for National Market Analysis (Washington, D.C.: Small Business Administration, 1978). This small reference booklet (only eight pages) contains sources of interest to researchers needing statistics and maps for such market analysis projects as allocation of sales effort by area and appraisal of market opportunity by area.

Statistical Reference Index (Washington, D.C.: Congressional Information Service). Published annually, this publication is intended to serve as a selective guide to American Statistical publications from private organizations and state government sources.

Wasserman, Paul, *et al., Statistics Sources,* 7th ed. (Detroit: Gale Research, 1982). A guide to federal, state, and private sources of statistics on a wide variety of subjects.

Who's Who in Consulting (Detroit: Gale Research, 1982). This directory provides biographical information on consultants in a variety of fields including their subject area and geographical location.

Guides to Information Banks

As mentioned, the growth in computer-readable storage systems for data bases has been spectacular. Keeping up with the growth is difficult as new on-line search services are being created all the time. Fortunately, there are several good guides to the on-line data bases and search services that are available.

Directory of Online Databases (Santa Monica, Calif.: Cuadra Associates, Inc.). Published quarterly, this publication describes more than 275 bibliographic and nonbibliographic databases.

Garven, Andrew P., and Hubert Bermont, *How to Win with Information or Lose Without It* (New York: Find/SVP, 1984). This publication, written in nontechnical language especially for executives, discusses data banks and information retrieval services.

Hoover, Ryan E., *et al., The Library and Information Manager's Guide to Online Services* (White Plains, N.Y.: Knowledge Industry Publications, 1980). See also *Online Search Strategies* by the same author, which contains practical tips on the effective use of bibliographic data bases and search systems.

Kruzas, Anthony T., and Linda Varekamp Sullivan, eds., *Encyclopedia of Information Systems and Services,* 6th ed. (Detroit: Gale Research, 1985). This encyclopedia lists and describes over 2,500 organizations involved in data storage and retrieval. Included are data base producers and publishers, on-line vendors, information centers, research centers, banks, and data base producers and publishers.

Chapter 6
Data Collection:
Primary Data

In Chapter 5 the point was made and emphasized that secondary data represented fast and inexpensive research information and that the researcher who only gives secondary data a cursory look is being reckless. However, it was also mentioned that rarely will secondary data provide a complete solution to a research problem. The units of measurement or classes employed to report the data will be wrong; the data will be somewhat obsolete by the time of their publication; the data will not be sufficiently complete, and so on. When these conditions occur, the researcher logically turns to primary data.

This chapter is the first of three dealing with primary data. It is intended as an introduction and is divided into four parts. Part 1 discusses the types of primary data generally obtained from and about subjects. Part 2 discusses the two main means employed—communication and observation—and the suitability of each method for securing the different kinds of primary data. Part 3 elaborates communication methods. In particular, it discusses the many types of questionnaires and means of administration. Part 4 does the same for observational methods.

Types of Primary Data Generally Obtained

Demographic/Socioeconomic Characteristics

One type of primary data of great interest to marketers is the subject's demographic and socioeconomic characteristics, such as age, education, occupation, marital status, sex, income, or social class. These variables are used to cross-classify the collected data and in some way make sense of it. We might be interested, for instance, in determining whether people's attitudes toward ecology and pollution are related to their level of formal education. Alternatively, a common question asked by marketers is whether the consumption of a particular product is related in any way to a person's or family's age, education, income, and so on, and if so, in what way. These are questions of market segmentation. Demographic and socioeconomic characteristics are often used to delineate market segments.[1]

---

[1]See Yoram Wind, "Issues and Advances in Segmentation Research," *Journal of Marketing Research,* 15 (August 1978), pp. 317–337.

Demographic and socioeconomic characteristics are sometimes called states of being, in that they represent attributes of people. Some of these states of being, such as a respondent's age, sex, and level of formal education, can be readily verified. Some, such as social class, cannot be verified except very crudely, since they are relative and not absolute measures of a person's standing in society.[2] Income represents an intermediate degree of difficulty in verifiability. Although a person's income in any given year is some actual quantity, ascertaining the amount sometimes proves difficult.

Psychological/Life-Style Characteristics

Another type of primary data of interest to marketers is the subject's psychological and life-style characteristics in the form of personality traits, activities, interests, and values. **Personality** refers to the normal patterns of behavior exhibited by an individual. It represents the attributes, traits, and mannerisms that distinguish one individual from another. We often characterize people by the personality traits—aggressiveness, dominance, friendliness, sociability—they display. Marketers are interested in personality because the traits people possess would seem to be important in affecting the way consumers and others in the marketing process behave. The argument is often advanced, for example, that personality can affect a consumer's choice of stores or products or an individual's response to an advertisement or point-of-purchase display. Similarly, it is believed that certain characteristics like extroversion or empathy are more likely to be possessed by successful than by unsuccessful salespeople. While the empirical evidence regarding the ability of personality to predict consumption behavior or salesperson success is weak, personality remains a variable dear to the hearts of marketing researchers.[3] Personality is typically measured by one of the standard personality inventories that have been developed by psychologists.[4]

Life-style or psychographic analysis rests on the premise that the firm can plan more effective strategies to reach its target market if it knows more about its customers in

---

[2]See James H. Myers and William H. Reynolds, *Consumer Behavior in Marketing Management* (Boston: Houghton Mifflin, © 1967), pp. 206–216, for a useful discussion of social class, its role in marketing-related phenomena, and the various ways in which it is measured. See Charles M. Schaninger, "Social Class Versus Income Revisited: An Empirical Investigation," *Journal of Marketing Research,* 18 (May 1981), pp. 192–208, for a comparison of the ability of social class and income to predict consumption of a number of household products.

[3]For a review of the evidence regarding the relationship of personality to consumer behavior, see Harold H. Kassarjian, "Personality and Consumer Behavior: A Review," *Journal of Marketing Research,* 8 (November 1971), pp. 409–418; or Richard C. Becherer and Lawrence M. Richard, "Self-Monitoring as a Moderator Variable in Consumer Behavior," *Journal of Consumer Research,* 5 (December 1978), pp. 159–162. For a review of the evidence regarding the relationship between personality characteristics and salesperson success, see Gilbert A. Churchill, Jr., Neil M. Ford, Steven W. Hartley, and Orville C. Walker, Jr., "The Determinants of Salesperson Performance: A Meta Analysis," *Journal of Marketing Research,* 22 (May 1985), pp. 103–118.

[4]There are a number of guides to the various personality inventories. Three of the more extensive ones are C. M. Bonjean, R. J. Hill, and S. D. McLemore, *Sociological Measurement: An Inventory of Scales and Indices* (San Francisco: Chandler, 1967); Ki-Taek Chun, Sidney Cobb, and J. R. P. French, *Measures for Psychological Assessment* (Ann Arbor, Mich.: Institute for Social Research, University of Michigan, 1975); and D. G. Lake, M. B. Miles, and R. B. Earle, Jr., *Measuring Human Behavior: Tools for the Assessment of Social Functioning* (New York: Teachers College Press, Columbia University, 1973).

Table 6.1
Life-Style Dimensions

Activities	Interests	Opinions
Work	Family	Themselves
Hobbies	Home	Social issues
Social events	Job	Politics
Vacation	Community	Business
Entertainment	Recreation	Economics
Club membership	Fashion	Education
Community	Food	Products
Shopping	Media	Future
Sports	Achievements	Culture

Source: Adapted from Joseph T. Plummer, "The Concept and Application of Life Style Segmentation," *Journal of Marketing,* 38 (January 1974), p. 34. Published by the American Marketing Association.

terms of how they live, what interests them, and what they like. The general thrust in psychographic research has been to develop a number of statements that reflect a person's Activities, Interests, and Opinions (AIO) and consumption behavior. The statements might include such things as "I like to watch football games on television," "I like stamp collecting," "I am very interested in national politics." There would be a great many statements that would be administered to a large sample of respondents.[5] For example, Needham, Harper, and Steers, the advertising agency, annually conducts a life-style study that includes 3,500 respondents answering 700 questions.[6] Table 6.1 contains the list of characteristics that are usually assessed with AIO inventories. The attempt in the analysis is to identify groups of consumers who are likely to behave similarly toward the product and who have similar life-style profiles.

One problem that marketers experienced when using psychographics or AIO inventories was that the categories of users distinguished in one study focusing on one type of product would be very different from the categories of individuals identified in another study examining a different product. This meant that each product required a new data collection and analysis exercise. Because of the instability of profiles across products, it was also impossible to develop demographic descriptions of the various groups

---

[5]One of the more popular lists is the 300-question inventory that appears in William D. Wells and Douglas Tigert, "Activities, Interests, and Opinions," *Journal of Advertising Research,* 11 (August 1971), pp. 27–35. For a general review of the origins, development, and thrust of life-style and psychographic research, see William D. Wells, ed., *Life Style and Psychographics* (Chicago: American Marketing Association, 1974). For evidence regarding the reliability and validity of psychographic inventories, see Alvin C. Burns and Mary Carolyn Harrison, "A Test of the Reliability of Psychographics," *Journal of Marketing Research,* 16 (February 1979), pp. 32–38; John L. Lastovicka, "On the Validation of Lifestyle Traits: A Review and Illustration," *Journal of Marketing Research,* 19 (February 1982), pp. 126–138; and Ian Fenwick, D. A. Schellinck, and K. W. Kendall, "Assessing the Reliability of Psychographic Analyses," *Marketing Science,* 2 (Winter 1983), pp. 57–74.

[6]Cara S. Frazer, "Staying Afloat in Oceans of Data," *Advertising Age,* 54 (October 31, 1983), pp. m42–m43.

that would be useful when developing marketing strategies for new products or brands. The purpose of value and life-style research (VALS) is to avoid these problems by creating a standard psychographic framework that can be used for a variety of products. One particularly popular VALS classification scheme, for example, divides people into four main groups—need driven, outer directed, inner directed, and combined outer and inner directed—and nine subgroups.[7] Research Realities 6.1 describes these groups and their size.

Attitudes/Opinions

Some authors distinguish between attitudes and opinions, while others use the terms interchangeably. Most typically **attitude** is used to refer to an individual's ''preference, inclination, views or feelings toward some phenomenon,'' while **opinions** are ''verbal expressions of attitudes.'' Since attitudes are typically secured from respondents by questioning, we shall not make the distinction between the terms but will treat attitudes and opinions interchangeably as representing a person's ideas, convictions, or liking with respect to a specific object or idea.

Attitude is one of the more important notions in the marketing literature, since it is generally thought that attitudes are related to behavior.

Obviously, when an individual likes a product he will be more inclined to buy it than when he does not like it; when he likes one brand more than another, he will tend to buy the preferred brand. Attitudes may be said to be the forerunners of behavior.[8]

Thus, marketers are often interested in people's attitudes toward the product itself, their overall attitudes with respect to specific brands, and their attitudes toward specific aspects or features possessed by several brands. Attitude is such a pervasive notion in behavioral science, and particularly in marketing, that Chapter 8 is devoted to various types of instruments used to measure it.

Awareness/Knowledge

Awareness/knowledge as used in marketing research refers to what respondents do and do not know about some object or phenomenon. For instance, a problem of considerable importance is the effectiveness of magazine ads. One measure of effectiveness is the product awareness generated by the ad, using one of the three approaches described in Table 6.2. Although all three approaches are aimed at assessing the respondent's awareness of and knowledge about the ad, there is a definite increase in retention when knowledge is measured by recognition rather than by recall and by aided rather than unaided recall. This, of course, raises the question of which method is the ''most ac-

---

[7]Arnold Mitchell, *The Nine American Lifestyles* (New York: MacMillan, 1983).

[8]Fred L. Schreier, *Modern Marketing Research: A Behavioral Science Approach* (Belmont, Calif.: Wadsworth, 1963), p. 273. For a general review of the relationship between attitude and behavior, see Susan T. Fiske and Shelley E. Taylor, *Social Cognition* (Reading, Ma.: Addison-Wesley, 1984), pp. 369–399.

Research Realities 6.1

The Nine American Life-Styles

Need Driven Groups

Survivor

Old, intensely poor; fearful; despairing; far removed from the cultural mainstream; misfits
Number: 7 million
Age: Most over 65
Sex: 73% female
Income: most under $7,500
Education: Few have completed high school

Sustainer

Living on the edge of poverty; angry and resentful; streetwise; involved in the underground economy
Number: 12 million
Age: 67% under 35
Sex: 57% female
Income: Median, under $10,000
Education: More than half did not graduate from high school

Outer-Directed Groups

Belonger

Aging; traditional and conventional; contented; intensely patriotic; sentimental; deeply stable
Number: 64 million
Age: Median, 57
Sex: 58% female
Income: Median, $17,300
Education: Median, high school graduate

Emulator

Youthful and ambitious: macho; show-off; trying to break into the system, to make it big
Number: 17 million
Age: Median 28
Sex: 53% male
Income: Median, $18,000
Education: high school graduate plus

Achiever

Middle-aged and prosperous; able leaders; self-assured; materialistic; builders of the "American dream"
Number: 35 million
Age: Median 42
Sex: 58% male
Income: Median, over $40,000
Education: 25% college graduates

Inner-Directed Groups

I-Am-Me

Transition state; exhibitionist and narcissistic; young; impulsive; dramatic; experimental; active; inventive
Number: 5 million
Age: 94% under 25
Sex: 51% male
Income: Median, $8,800
Education: Some college

Experiential

Youthful; seek direct experience; person-centered; artistic; intensely oriented toward inner growth
Number: 8 million
Age: Median, 28
Sex: 55% female
Income: Median, over $30,000
Education: 38% college graduates or more

Societally Conscious

Mission-oriented; leaders of single-issue groups; mature; successful; some live lives of voluntary simplicity
Number: 20 million
Age: Median, 37
Sex: 51% male
Income: Median, over $35,000
Education: 70% college graduates, many have attended graduate school

Combined Outer- and Inner-Directed Group

Integrated

Psychologically mature; large field of vision; tolerant and understanding; sense of fittingness
Number: 3.2 million

Source: Adapted with permission of Macmillan Publishing Company from *The Nine American Lifestyles: Who We Are and Where We Are Going* by Arnold Mitchell, and the Values and Lifestyles (VALS™) Program, SRI International, Menlo Park, CA. Copyright © 1983 by Arnold Mitchell.

Table 6.2

Approaches Used to Measure Awareness

Unaided recall:	The consumer is given no cues at all, but is simply asked to recall what advertising he or she has seen recently. No prompting is used because, presumably, if prompting even in a general category were used (for example, cake mixes), the respondent would have a tendency to remember more advertisements in that product category.
Aided recall:	The consumer is given some prompting. Typically this prompting might be in the form of questions about advertisements in a specific product category. Alternatively, the respondent might be given a list showing the names or trademarks of advertisers which appeared in the particular magazine issue, along with names or trademarks that did not appear, and is asked to check those to which he or she was exposed.
Recognition:	The consumer is actually shown an advertisement and is asked whether or not he or she remembers seeing it.

Source: Adapted from James H. Myers and William H. Reynolds, *Consumer Behavior in Marketing Management* (New York: Houghton Mifflin, © 1967), pp. 65–67. Used by permission of the publisher.

curate.'' There are problems with each method.[9] The important thing to note is that when marketers speak of a person's awareness, they often mean the individual's knowledge of the advertisement. A person ''very much aware'' or possessing ''high awareness'' typically knows a great deal about the ad.

Awareness and knowledge are also used interchangeably when marketers speak of product awareness. Marketing researchers are often interested in determining whether the respondent is aware of[10]

- the product,
- its features,
- where it is available,
- its price,
- its manufacturer,
- where it is made,
- how it is used, and for what purpose, and
- its specific distinctive features.

Although framed in terms of awareness, these questions, to a greater or lesser degree, aim at determining the individual's knowledge of the product. For our purposes, then, knowledge and awareness will be used interchangeably to refer to what a respondent does indeed know about an advertisement, product, retail store, and so on.

---

[9]See Myers and Reynolds, *Consumer Behavior,* pp. 68–72, for a succinct discussion of the problems common to each.

[10]Schreier, *Modern Marketing Research,* pp. 269–273.

Intentions

A person's **intentions** refer to the individual's anticipated or planned future behavior. Marketers are interested in people's intentions primarily with regard to purchasing behavior. One of the better known studies regarding purchase intentions is that conducted by the Survey Research Center at the University of Michigan. The center regularly conducts surveys for the Federal Reserve Board to determine the general financial condition of consumers and their outlook with respect to the state of the economy in the near future. The center asks consumers about their buying intentions for big ticket items such as appliances, automobiles, and homes during the next few months. The responses are then analyzed, and the proportion of the sample that indicates each of the following is reported:

- definite intention to buy,
- probable intention to buy,
- undecided,
- definite intention not to buy.

Intentions receive less attention in marketing than do other types of primary data, largely because there is often a great disparity between what people say they are going to do and what they actually do. This is particularly true with respect to purchase behavior. Purchase intentions are most often used when studying the purchase of commodities requiring large outlays, such as an automobile for a family or plant and equipment for a business. The general assumption is that the larger the dollar expenditure, the more preplanning necessary and the greater the correlation between anticipated and actual behavior. Nevertheless, the evidence with regard to the predictive accuracy of intended purchasing behavior is still something less than encouraging.[11]

Motivation

The concept of motivation seems to contain more semantic confusion than most terms in the behavioral sciences.

Some writers insist that motives *are different from* drives *and use the latter term primarily to characterize the basic physiological "tissue" needs (e.g., hunger, thirst, shelter, sex). Others distinguish between* needs *and* wants, *stating that needs are the basic motivating forces which translate themselves into more immediate wants which satisfy these needs (e.g., hunger needs give rise to wanting a good steak dinner).*[12]

For our purposes a **motive** may refer to a need, a want, a drive, an urge, a wish, a desire, an impulse, or any inner state that directs or channels behavior toward goals.

---

[11]Manohar U. Kalwani and Alvin J. Silk, "On the Reliability and Predictive Validity of Purchase Intention Measures" *Marketing Science,* 1 (Summer 1982), pp. 243–286. Murphy A. Sewall, "Relative Information Contributions of Consumer Purchase Intentions and Management Judgment as Explanations of Sales," *Journal of Marketing Research,* 18 (May 1981), pp. 249–253; and Gary M. Mullett and Marvin J. Karson, "Analysis of Purchase Intent Scales Weighted by Probability of Actual Purchase," *Journal of Marketing Research,* 22 (February 1985), pp. 93–96.

[12]Myers and Reynolds, *Consumer Behavior,* p. 80.

A marketing researcher's interest in motives typically involves determining *why* people behave as they do. There are several reasons that explain this interest. In the first place, it is believed that a person's motives tend to be more stable than the individual's behavior, and, therefore, motives offer a better basis for predicting future behavior than does past behavior. Second, if we understand the motives behind a person's behavior, we better understand the behavior and, in turn, are in a better position to influence future behavior or at least have offerings consistent with that anticipated behavior.

Behavior

Behavior concerns what subjects have done or are doing. Most typically in marketing this means purchase and use behavior. Now, behavior is a physical activity. It takes place under specific circumstances, at a particular time, and involves one or more actors or participants. The focus on behavior, then, involves a description of the activity with respect to the various components, and the marketing researcher investigating behavior is well advised to use Table 6.3[13] as a checklist in designing data collection instruments so that the key behavioral dimensions of interest are secured. There are many subdimensions to each cell, and the researcher also has to make a conscious inclusion–omission decision with regard to each subdimension. Consider the *where,* for example. The "where of purchase" may be specified with respect to kind of store, the location of the store by broad geographic area or specific address, size of the store, or even the name of the store. So it is with each of the many cells. The study of behavior, then, involves the development of a description of the purchase or use activity, either past or current, with respect to some or all of the characteristics contained in Table 6.3.

Basic Means of Obtaining Primary Data

The researcher attempting to collect primary data has a number of choices to make among the means that will be used. Figure 6.1 presents an overview of these choices. The primary decision is whether to employ communication or observation. **Communication** involves questioning respondents to secure the desired information, using a data collection instrument called a questionnaire. The questions may be oral or in writing, and the responses may also be given in either form. **Observation** does not involve questioning. Rather, it means that the situation of interest is checked and the relevant facts, actions, or behaviors recorded. The "observer" may be a person or persons, or the data may be gathered using some mechanical device. For example, a researcher interested in the brands of canned vegetables the family buys might arrange a pantry audit in which the shelves are checked to see which brands the family has on hand.

Choosing a primary method of data collection implies a number of supplementary decisions. For example, should we administer questionnaires by mail, over the telephone, or in person? Should the purpose of the study be disguised or remain undisguised? Should the answers be open ended or should the respondent be asked to choose

---

[13]The checklist is adapted from Schreier, *Modern Marketing Research,* p. 251. Schreier also has a productive discussion of the many kinds of questions that need to be answered to complete the checklist.

Table 6.3
Behavior Checklist

	Purchase Behavior	Use Behavior
What		
How much		
How		
Where		
When		
In what situation		
Who		

Source: Adapted with permission from Fred L. Schreier, *Modern Marketing Research: A Behavioral Science Approach* (Belmont, Calif.: Wadsworth Publishing Company, 1963), p. 251.

from a limited set of alternatives? While Figure 6.1 implies that these decisions are independent, they are actually intimately related. A decision with respect to method of administration, say, has serious implications regarding the degree of structure that must be imposed on the questionnaire.

Communication and observation each has its own advantages and disadvantages, and this section will review these general pluses and minuses. The next section then amplifies the supplementary decisions associated with the communication method, and the final section does the same for observational methods.

The communication method of data collection has the general advantages of versatility, speed, and cost, while observational data are typically more objective and accurate.

Versatility

Versatility is the ability of a technique to collect information on the many types of primary data of interest to marketers. A respondent's demographic/socioeconomic characteristics and life-style, the individual's attitudes and opinions, awareness and knowledge, intentions, the motivation underlying the individual's actions, and even the person's behavior may all be ascertained by the communication method. All we need to do is ask, although there may be some problem with the accuracy of the replies.

Not so with observation. Observation is limited in scope to information about behavior and certain demographic/socioeconomic characteristics. But there are certain limitations to these observations. Our observations are limited to present behavior, for example. We cannot observe a person's past behavior. Nor can we observe the person's intentions as to future behavior. If we are interested in past behavior or intentions, we must ask.

Some demographic/socioeconomic characteristics can be readily observed. Sex is the most obvious example. Others can be observed but with less accuracy. A person's age and income, for example, might be inferred by closely examining the individual's mode of dress and purchasing behavior. Clearly, though, both of these observations may be in error, with income likely to be the farthest off. Still others, such as social class,

Figure 6.1
Basic Choices among Means for Collecting Primary Data

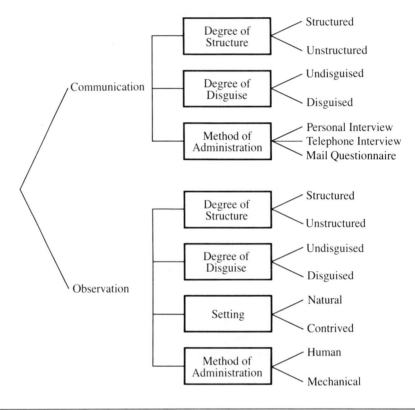

cannot be observed with any degree of confidence about the accuracy of the recorded data.

The other basic types of primary data cannot be measured by observation. We simply cannot observe an attitude or opinion, a person's awareness or knowledge, or motivation. Certainly we can attempt to make some inferences about these variables on the basis of the individual's observed behavior. For instance, if a person is observed purchasing a box of new XYZ detergent, we might infer that the person had a favorable attitude toward XYZ. There is a real question, though, as to the correctness of the inference. A great deal of controversy exists over whether attitudes precede behavior or behavior precedes attitude formation. Perhaps the latter explanation is correct, and the person, in fact, has no particular attitudes toward XYZ but just thought he or she would try it. The individual may not have even been aware of XYZ previously, but just saw it for the first time on the shelf. Generalizing from behavior to states of mind is clearly risky, and researchers need to recognize this. Questioning clearly encompasses a broader base of primary data.

Speed and Cost

The speed and cost advantages of the communication method are closely intertwined. Assuming the data lend themselves to either means, communication is a faster means of data collection than observation, because it provides a greater degree of control over data-gathering activities. The researcher is not forced to wait for events to occur with the communication method as she or he is with the observation method. In some cases, it is impossible to predict the occurrence of the event precisely enough to observe it. For still other behaviors, the time interval can be substantial. For instance, an observer checking for brand purchased most frequently in one of several appliance categories might have to wait a long time to make any observations at all. Much of the time the observer would be idle. Such idleness is expensive, as the worker will probably be compensated on an hourly rather than a per-contact basis. Events of long duration also cause difficulty. An observational approach to studying the relative influence of a husband and wife in the purchase of an automobile would be prohibitive in terms of both time and money.

Objectivity and Accuracy

Balanced against these disadvantages of limited scope, time, and cost are the objectivity and accuracy of the observational method. Data that can be secured by either method will typically be more accurately secured by observation. This is because the observational method is independent of the respondent's unwillingness or inability to provide the information desired. For example, respondents are often reluctant to cooperate whenever their replies would be embarrassing, humiliating, or would in some way place them in an unfavorable light.[14] Sometimes respondents conveniently forget embarrassing events, while in other cases the events are not of sufficient importance for them to remember what happened.[15] Since observation allows the recording of behavior as it occurs, it is not dependent on the respondent's memory or mood in reporting what occurred.

Observation typically produces more objective data than does communication. The interview represents a social interaction situation. Thus, the replies of the person being questioned are conditioned by the individual's perceptions of the interviewer. The same is true of the interviewer, although the interviewer's selection and training affords the researcher a greater degree of control over these perceptions than those of the interviewee.

With observation, though, the subject's perceptions play less of a role. Sometimes people are not even aware that they are being observed. This removes the opportunity

---

[14]Claire Selltiz, Lawrence S. Wrightsman, and Stuart W. Cook, *Research Methods in Social Relations,* 3rd ed. (New York: Holt, Rinehart and Winston, 1976), p. 293. See also Ed Blair, Seymour Sudman, Norman M. Bradburn, and Carol Stocking, "How to Ask Questions about Drinking and Sex: Response Effects in Measuring Consumer Behavior," *Journal of Marketing Research,* 14 (August 1977), pp. 316–321; and Norman M. Bradburn and Seymour Sudman, *Improving Interview Method and Questionnaire Design: Response Effects to Threatening Questions in Survey Research* (San Francisco: Jossey Bass, 1979).

[15]Charles F. Cannel, Lois Oksenberg, and Jean M. Converse, "Striving for Response Accuracy: Experiments in New Interviewing Techniques," *Journal of Marketing Research,* 14 (August 1977), pp. 306–315.

for them to tell the interviewer what they think the interviewer wants to hear or to give socially acceptable responses. The problems of objectivity are concentrated in the observer's methods, and this makes the task easier. The observer's selection, training, and control, and not the subject's perceptions of the field worker, become the crucial elements.

Communication Methods

As Figure 6.1 suggests, researchers must make a number of related decisions once they have chosen a method. Two of these involve structures and disguise, which we will discuss together.[16]

Structure is the degree of standardization imposed on the questionnaire. In a highly structured questionnaire, the questions to be asked and the responses permitted the subjects are completely predetermined. In a highly unstructured questionnaire, the questions to be asked are only loosely predetermined, and the respondents are free to respond in their own words. A questionnaire in which the questions are fixed but the responses are "open ended" would represent an intermediate degree of structure. **Disguise** is the amount of knowledge about the purpose of a study communicated to a respondent. An undisguised questionnaire makes the purpose of the research obvious by the questions posed, while a disguised questionnaire attempts to hide the purpose of the study.

Structured–Undisguised Questionnaires

Structured–undisguised questionnaires are most commonly used in marketing research. "Questions are presented with exactly the same wording, and in exactly the same order, to all respondents. The reason for standardization, of course, is to ensure that all respondents are replying to the same question."[17] If one interviewer asks, "Do you drink orange juice?" and another asks, "Does your family use frozen orange juice?" the replies would not be comparable.

In the typical structured–undisguised questionnaire, the responses as well as the questions are standardized. **Fixed-alternative questions** in which the responses are limited to the stated alternatives are used. Consider the following question regarding the subject's attitude toward pollution and the need for more government legislation controlling it.

Do you feel the United States needs more or less antipollution legislation?

☐   Needs more

☐   Needs less

☐   Neither more nor less

☐   No opinion

---

[16]The simultaneous treatment of structure and disguise was suggested by Donald T. Campbell, "The Indirect Assessment of Social Attitudes," *Psychological Bulletin,* 47 (January 1950), pp. 15–38. A similar treatment can be found in Harper W. Boyd, Jr., Ralph Westfall, and Stanley F. Stasch, *Marketing Research: Text and Cases,* 6th ed. (Homewood, Ill.: Richard D. Irwin, 1985), pp. 115–121.

[17]Selltiz, Wrightsman, and Cook, *Research Methods,* p. 309.

No claim is made that this is a good question or even one that would be used. Rather, it is an example of a structured–undisguised question. The question's purpose is clear. It deals with the subject's attitudes toward antipollution legislation. The question is structured in that respondents are limited to one of four stated replies.

Probably the greatest advantages of the structured–undisguised question are that it is simple to administer and easy to tabulate and analyze.[18] Respondents should have little difficulty replying. Their responses should be reliable in that if they were asked the question again, they would respond in a similar fashion (assuming, of course, their attitudes have not changed in the meantime).

The fixed-alternative question is reliable for several reasons. First, the frame of reference is often obvious from the alternatives. For example, consider the question, "How much do you watch television?" If no alternatives are supplied, one respondent might say "every day," another might say "regularly," and still another might respond with the number of hours per day. These responses would be more difficult to interpret than would an alternative form which included the response categories "every day," "at least three times a week," "at least once a week," "less than once a week."

Providing alternative responses also often helps to make the question clear. The question "What is your marital status?" is more confusing than is the question, "Are you married, single, widowed, or divorced?" Providing the dimensions in which to frame the reply helps assure the reliability of the question.

The reliability of fixed-alternative questions is sometimes associated with loss of validity in that the answers do not accurately reflect the true state of affairs. Fixed alternatives may force a response to a question on which the subject does not have an opinion. This is particularly true if the "no opinion" category is not provided as an alternative. Even when it is provided, there is often a tendency to keep the number of "no opinions" at a minimum. Thus the interviewer presses the respondent for a reply, which the person gives. Whether or not it accurately reflects the individual's attitude is another matter.

It may also be that the respondent has an opinion, but none of the response categories allows the accurate expression of that attitude. The example makes no allowance for distinguishing among those who feel we definitely need a great deal more antipollution legislation (the "true" environmentalists) versus those who feel, though not too strongly, that something more should be done to clean up our air and water, and more legislation prohibiting pollution may be one answer.

Fixed-alternative responses may also lower validity when the response categories themselves introduce bias. This is particularly acute when an "appropriate" response is omitted because of an oversight or insufficient prior research as to the response categories that are appropriate. The provision of an "other" category does not eliminate this bias either, since there is a general reluctance on the part of subjects to respond in the "other" category. In using a fixed-alternative question, one must be reasonably certain that the alternatives adequately cover the range of probable replies.

---

[18]This general discussion of advantages and disadvantages of the structured–undisguised question follows that of Selltiz, Wrightsman, and Cook, *Research Methods,* pp. 309–321.

The fixed-alternative question is thus most productive when possible replies are "well known, limited in number, and clear-cut. Thus they are appropriate for securing factual information (age, education, home ownership, amount of rent, and so on) and for eliciting expressions of opinion about issues on which people hold clear opinions."[19] They are therefore not very appropriate for securing primary data on motivations, but certainly could be used (at least sometimes) to collect data on attitudes, intentions, awareness, demographic/socioeconomic characteristics, and behavior.

Unstructured–Undisguised Questionnaires

The unstructured–undisguised questionnaire is distinguished by the fact that the purpose of the study is clear, but the response to the **question is open ended.** Consider the question, "How do you feel about pollution and the need for more antipollution legislation?" The initial stimulus (that is, question) here is constant. With it the interviewer attempts to get the subject to talk freely about his or her attitudes toward pollution. After presenting this initial stimulus, the interview becomes very unstructured. The respondent's initial reply, the interviewer's probes for elaboration, and the respondent's subsequent answers determine its direction. The interviewer may attempt to follow a rough outline. However, the order and the specific framing of the questions will vary from interview to interview. The specific content of each of these so-called **depth interviews** will therefore vary.

The freedom permitted the interviewer in conducting these depth interviews reveals the major advantages and disadvantages of the method. By not constraining the respondent to a fixed set of replies and by careful probing, an experienced interviewer should be able to derive a more accurate picture of the respondent's true position on some issue. This is particularly true with respect to sensitive issues in which there is social pressure to conform and to offer a "socially acceptable" response. Note the caveats— "experienced interviewer" and "careful probing"—contained in the above statement. The depth interview requires highly skilled interviewers. They are hard to find and are expensive when found. Further, the lack of structure allows the interviewer to influence the result. The interviewer's judgment as to when to probe and how to word the probes can affect the response. Good depth interviews often take a long time to complete. This makes it difficult to secure the cooperation of respondents. It also means that a study using depth interviews, as opposed to fixed-alternative questions, may take longer to complete, will involve fewer observations, or will require a greater number of interviewers. The more interviewers there are, the greater the likelihood that the variation in responses will be partly interviewer induced because of differences in administering the questionnaire.[20]

The depth interview also causes severe problems in analysis. The services of one or more skilled psychologists are typically required to interpret the responses. These people

[19]Selltiz, Wrightsman, and Cook, *Research Methods,* p. 316.

[20]Barbara Bailar, Leroy Bailey, and Joyce Stevens, "Measures of Interviewer Bias and Variance," *Journal of Marketing Research,* 14 (August 1977), pp. 337–343; and J. R. McKenzie, "An Investigation into Interviewing Effects in Market Research," *Journal of Marketing Research,* 14 (August 1977), pp. 330–331.

do not come cheaply. Further, the psychologist's own background and frame of reference will affect the interpretation. This subjectivity raises questions about both the reliability and validity of the results. It also causes difficulty in determining what the correct interpretation is and thus presents problems when tabulating the replies.[21]

Some of the problems with coding open-ended questions may be changing with new technology. Researchers are increasingly feeding respondents' answers into computers programmed to recognize a large vocabulary of words in their search for regularities in the replies. The computers are able to rank each word by the frequency of usage, and then can print out sentences containing the key words. The detailed analysis of these sentences allows researchers to pick up on recurring themes.[22] While these systems automate the coding of unstructured interviews, they leave interpretation to the individual analyst. Nevertheless, the systems can achieve in hours what a purely human review might take weeks to accomplish.

The depth interview is probably best suited to exploratory research, since it is productive with respect to just about all of the common purposes of exploratory research.

Focus Group A variation of the depth interview is the **focused group interview.** In the focused group interview, a small number of individuals are brought together, rather than being interviewed one at a time, as in the depth interview. The dynamics of the encounter are also different. In contrast to the individual interview in which the flow of information is one way, from the respondent to the interviewer, the focus group setting attempts to have the comments of each person considered in group discussion. Each individual is thereby exposed to the ideas of the others and submits his or her ideas to the group for consideration.

The interaction among the group members is only loosely directed by the group interviewer, called the moderator. Focus groups are currently one of the most frequently used techniques in marketing research; they have proven productive for:

1. generating hypotheses that can be further tested quantitatively;

2. generating information helpful in structuring consumer questionnaires;

3. providing overall background information on a product category;

4. securing impressions on new product concepts for which there is little information available;

5. stimulating new ideas about older products;

6. stimulating ideas for new creative concepts; and

7. interpreting previously obtained quantitative results.[23]

---

[21]Martin Collins and Graham Kalton, "Coding Verbatim Answers to Open Questions," *Journal of the Market Research Society,* 22 (October 1980), pp. 239–247.

[22]Jeffrey Zaslow, "A Maverick Pollster Promotes Verbosity That Others Disdain," *Wall Street Journal,* 65 (February 13, 1985), pp. 1 and 23.

[23]See Danny N. Bellenger, Kenneth L. Bernhardt, and Jac L. Goldstucker, *Qualitative Research in Marketing* (Chicago: American Marketing Association, 1976), pp. 7–28, for an elaboration of these uses with examples and for other insightful comments on the conduct of focus groups. Another useful general reference is James B. Higgenbotham and Keith K. Cox, eds., *Focus Group Interviews: A Reader* (Chicago: American Marketing Association, 1979).

Pillsbury, for example, held focus group discussions around the United States in early 1976 to find out what consumers did not like about frozen pizza. "The response was overwhelming; about 60% hated the crust, which many said tasted like cardboard."[24] This initial insight, which was further verified by other research, led to the development of Pillsbury's very successful Totino's Crisp Crust Frozen Pizza.

While groups do vary in size, most consist of eight to twelve members. Smaller groups are too easily dominated by one or two members, while frustration and boredom can set in with larger groups as individuals have to wait their turn to respond or get involved. Respondents for groups are generally selected so that they are relatively homogeneous, minimizing both conflicts among group members on issues not relevant to the study objectives and differences in perceptions, experiences, and verbal skills. Most firms conducting focus groups use screening interviews to determine the individuals that will compose a particular group. One type they try to avoid is the individual who has participated before in a focus group, since some of these people tend to behave as "experts." Their presence can cause the group to behave in dysfunctional ways, as they continually try to make their presence felt. As focus groups have become more popular, problems in recruiting rookies have intensified. There are documented cases of professional focus group participants that have created quite a controversy.[25] Firms also try to avoid groups in which some of the participants are friends and relatives, since this tends to inhibit spontaneity in the discussion as the acquaintances begin talking to each other.

The typical focus group session lasts from one and one-half to two hours. Groups can be arranged at a number of sites, including the client's home office, a neutral site, the office of the research agency, or even one of the respondents' homes. Each of these sites has its own advantages and disadvantages with respect to the ability to recruit respondents, the costs of the session, the rapport that can be induced, and the ability to record the interviews for later transcription and analysis.[26]

The moderator in the focus group has a key role. The moderator must not only lead the discussion so that all objectives of the study are met, but must do so in such a way that *interaction* among the group members is stimulated and promoted, rather than allowing the focus group session to dissolve into nothing more than a set of concurrent interviews where the participants each take their respective turns in responding to a

---

[24]Lawrence Ingrassia, "A Matter of Taste: There's No Way to Tell if a New Food Product Will Please the Public," *Wall Street Journal,* 60 (February 26, 1980), pp. 1 and 23. For similar experiences of Fisher-Price, Coke, and GE with focus groups, see, respectively, Ronald Alsop, "Fisher-Price Banks on Name, Design in Foray into Playwear," *Wall Street Journal,* 64 (August 2, 1984), p. 23; "In Soft-Drink Wars, Brand Loyalty Can Last as Long as a Few Minutes," *Wall Street Journal,* 65 (May 13, 1985), p. 21; and "Getting Consumers in Focus," *Dun's Business Month,* 119 (May 1982), pp. 78–80.

[25]See, for example, The Unknown Researcher, "Shoddy Recruiting Practices Lead to Focus Group Biases," *Marketing News,* 12 (May 18, 1979), p. 2, for a comment on the seriousness of the problem; and Joel Henkin, "Time to Stop Talking about Problems and Do Something, Such as 'Cold' Recruiting," *Marketing News,* 13 (September 21, 1979), p. 4, for a reply

[26]Wells discusses the pros and cons of the various sites as well as a number of other operational questions that arise with the conduct of focus groups. See William D. Wells, "Group Interviewing," in Robert Ferber, ed., *Handbook of Marketing Research* (New York: McGraw-Hill, 1974), pp. 2–133 to 2–146. See also *Focus Groups: Issues and Approaches,* prepared by the Qualitative Research Counsel of the Advertising Research Foundation, 1985.

Table 6.4
Claimed Advantages of Focused Group Interview
over Individual Depth Interviews

Respondent Interaction Advantages

1. Synergism: The combined effort of the group will produce a wider range of information, insight, and ideas than will the cumulation of the responses of a number of individuals when these replies are secured privately.

2. Snowballing: A bandwagon effect often operates in a group interview situation in that a comment by one individual often triggers a chain of responses from the other participants.

3. Stimulation: Usually after a brief introductory period the respondents get ''turned on'' in that they want to express their ideas and expose their feelings as the general level of excitement over the topic increases in the group.

4. Security: In an interviewer–interviewee situation, respondents may not be willing to expose their views for fear of having to defend these views or fear of appearing ''unconcerned'' or ''radical'' or whatever the case may be. In the well-structured group, on the other hand, ''the individual can usually find some comfort in the fact that his feelings are not greatly different from those of his peers, and that he can expose an idea without necessarily being forced to defend, follow through or elaborate on it. He's more likely to be candid because the focus is on the group rather than the individual; he soon realizes that the things he says are not necessarily being identified with him.''*

5. Spontaneity: Since no individual is required to answer any given question in a group interview, the individual's responses can be more spontaneous, less conventional, and should provide a more accurate picture of the person's position on some issue. In the group interview, people speak only when they have definite feelings about a subject and not because a question requires a response.

Sponsor Advantages

1. Serendipity: It is more often the case in a group rather than an individual interview that some idea will ''drop out of the blue.'' The group also affords the opportunity to develop it to its full significance.

2. Specialization: The group interview allows the use of a more highly trained, but more expensive, interviewer, since a number of individuals are being ''interviewed'' simultaneously.

3. Scientific scrutiny: The group interview allows closer scrutiny. First, the session itself can be observed by several observers. This affords some check on the consistency of the interpretations. Second, the session itself may be tape-recorded or even video-taped. Later detailed examination of the recorded session allows additional insight and also can help clear up points of disagreement among analysts.

4. Structure: The group interview affords more control than the individual interview with regard to the topics that are covered and the depth with which they are treated, since the ''interviewer'' in the role of moderator has the opportunity to reopen topics that received too shallow a discussion when initially presented.

5. Speed: Since a number of individuals are being interviewed at the same time, the group interview permits the securing of a given number of interviews more quickly than do individual interviews.

*John M. Hess, ''Group Interviewing,'' in R. L. King, ed., *New Science of Planning* (Chicago: American Marketing Association, 1968); p. 194. Reprinted by permission.

predetermined set of questions. This is an extremely delicate role. It requires someone who is intimately familiar with the purpose and objectives of the research and at the same time possesses good interpersonal communication skills.

Some of the key qualifications moderators must have are described in Research Realities 6.2.

Research Realities 6.2

Key Qualifications of Focus Group Moderators

1. Kind but firm—In order to elicit necessary interaction, the moderator must combine a disciplined detachment with understanding empathy. To achieve this, he must simultaneously display a kindly, permissive attitude toward the participants, encouraging them to feel at ease in the group interview environment, while insisting that the discussion remain germane to the problem at hand. Only with experience can the moderator achieve an appropriate blending of these two apparently antithetical roles.

   It is also the moderator's responsibility to encourage the emergence of leadership from within the group, while at the same time avoiding tendencies of domination of the group by a single member. The kindly but firm moderator must be sensitive to bids for attention and must maintain his leadership without threatening or destroying the interactional process.

2. Permissiveness—While an atmosphere of permissiveness is desirable, the moderator must be at all times alert to indications that the group atmosphere of cordiality is disintegrating. Before permissiveness leads to chaos, the moderator must reestablish the group purpose and maintain its orientation to the subject.

   The moderator must be ready and willing to pursue clues to information that may at first appear tangential to the subject for it may open new areas of exploration. He must also be prepared to cope with expressions of unusual opinions and eruptions of personality clashes within the group. The manner in which these are handled may well be the difference between a productive and an unproductive group session.

3. Involvement—Since a principal reason for the group interview is to expose feelings and to obtain reactions indicative of deeper feelings, the moderator must encourage and stimulate intensive personal involvement. If the moderator is unable to immerse himself completely in the topic being discussed, the group will sense his detachment, and the depth contribution of the interview will be lost.

4. Incomplete Understanding—A most useful skill of the group moderator is his ability to convey lack of complete understanding of the information being presented. Although he may understand what the participant is trying to express, by carefully inserting noncommittal remarks, phrased in questioning tones, the respondent is encouraged to delve more deeply into the sources of his opinion. He is, by this process, able to reveal and elaborate on the kinds of information for which the group interview is designed. The goal is to encourage respondents to be more specific about generalized comments made by group members.

   The usefulness of this technique can be endangered if its application is inappropriate. If the "in-

Source: Donald A. Chase, "The Intensive Group Interview in Marketing," *MRA Viewpoints* 1973 as adopted by Danny N. Bellenger, Kenneth L. Bernhardt, and Jac L. Goldstucker, *Qualitative Research in Marketing* (Chicago: American Marketing Association, 1976).

The claimed advantages of the focused group interview over an individual depth interview are several (Table 6.4).[27] While group interviews do offer certain benefits not obtainable with individual depth interviews, they also have their weaknesses. Although

---

[27]The list of advantages is taken from John M. Hess, "Group Interviewing," in *New Science of Planning,* ed. R. L. King (Chicago: American Marketing Association, 1968), pp. 193–196. See also Bobby J. Calder, "Focus Groups and the Nature of Qualitative Marketing Research," *Journal of Marketing Research,* 14 (August 1977), pp. 353–364, and *Focus Groups: Issues and Approaches* for a discussion of some philosophical and operational issues surrounding the use of focus groups.

complete understanding'' is a superficially assumed role, the group will soon detect this artificiality, and will feel that the moderator is playing some sort of cryptic game with the group. The group interview will then deteriorate into a sterile collection of mutual suspicions. Incomplete understanding on the part of the moderator must be a genuine curiosity about the deeper sources of the participant's understanding.

5. Encouragement—Although the dynamics of the group situation facilitate the participation of all members in the interaction, there may be individuals who resist contributing. The skillful moderator should be aware of unresponsive members and try to break down their reserve and encourage their involvement.

    The unresponsive member offers a real challenge to the group moderator. There are numerous ways in which a resistant or bashful member can be encouraged to participate, such as by assigning him a task to perform, or by providing an opening for his remarks. If this is inappropriately attempted, it may only reinforce a reluctance to participate in a verbal fashion. The ability to interpret nonverbal clues may provide a means of discovering a tactic to broaden the scope of the group's active participation.

6. Flexibility—The moderator should be equipped prior to the session with a topic outline of the subject matter to be covered. By committing the topics to memory before the interview, the moderator may use the outline only as a reminder of content areas omitted or covered incompletely.

    If a topic outline is followed minutely, the progress of the interview will be uneven and artificial, jumping from topic to topic without careful transitions. This procedure communicates a lack of concern to the participants, for its mechanical nature makes the moderator appear to lack genuine interest in their responses.

    At the same time, the interview cannot be allowed to wander aimlessly. Under such conditions, control of the situation soon passes from the moderator to a self-appointed group leader.

    The group interview should be conducted the way one walks across a rope bridge. The handrails are gripped firmly and the objective is kept in mind constantly. If the bottom foot rope should break, the walk is continued hand over hand until the destination is reached. This requires an ability to improvise and alter predetermined plans amid the distractions of the group process.

7. Sensitivity—The moderator must be able to identify, as the group interview progresses, the informational level on which it is being conducted, and determine if it is appropriate for the subject under discussion. Sensitive areas will frequently produce superficial rather than depth responses. Depth is achieved when there is a substantial amount of emotional responses, as opposed to intellectual information. Indications of depth are provided when participants begin to indicate how they feel about the subject, rather than what they think about it.

they are easy to set up, they are difficult to moderate and to interpret. It is easy to find evidence in one or more of the group discussions that supports almost any preconceived position. Because executives have the ability to observe the discussions through one-way mirrors or the opportunity to listen to the tape recordings of the sessions, focus groups seem more susceptible to executive and even researcher biases than do other data-collection techniques.[28] One has to constantly keep in mind that the discussion, and

---

[28]''Focus Groups Being Subverted by Clients,'' *Marketing News*, 18 (June 8, 1984), p. 7.

consequently the results, are greatly influenced by the moderator and the specific direction he or she provides. Moderators possessing all of the desired skills listed in Research Realities 6.2 are extremely rare. One also has to remember that the results are not representative of what would be found in the general population and thus are *not* projectable. Further, the unstructured nature of the responses makes coding, tabulation, and analysis difficult. Focus groups should *not* be used, therefore, to develop head counts of the proportion of people who feel a particular way. Consequently, the focused group interview, like the individual depth interview, is better suited to exploratory research than to descriptive or causal research. The method is better for generating ideas and insights than for systematically examining them.[29]

Unstructured–Disguised Questionnaires

Unstructured–disguised questionnaires lie at the heart of what has become known as motivation research.

A person needs only limited experience in questionnaire type surveys to realize that many areas of inquiry are not amenable to exploration by direct questions. Many important motives and reasons for choice are of a kind that the consumer will not *describe because a truthful description would be damaging to his ego. Others he* cannot *describe, either because he himself does not have the words to make his meaning clear or because his motive exists below the level of awareness. Very often such motives are of paramount importance in consumer behavior. If one tries to inquire into them with direct questions, especially categorical questions, one tends to get replies that are either useless or dangerously misleading.*[30]

Researchers have attacked the subjects' reluctance to discuss their feelings by developing techniques that are largely independent of the subjects' self awareness and willingness to reveal themselves. The main thrust in these projective methods has been that of concealing the subject of inquiry by using a disguised stimulus. Though the stimulus is typically standardized, subjects are allowed to respond to it in a very unstructured form, and thus the label disguised–unstructured questionnaires. The basic assumption in **projective methods** is that an individual's organization of a relatively unstructured stimulus is indicative of the person's basic perceptions of the phenomenon and reactions to it.

. . . the more unstructured and ambiguous a stimulus, the more a subject can and will project his emotions, needs, motives, attitudes, and values. The structure *of a stimulus . . . is the degree of choice available to the subject. A highly structured stimulus leaves very little choice: the subject has unambiguous choice among clear alternatives . . . .*

[29]For an empirical assessment of the relative ability of individual interviews versus focus groups of various sizes and composition to generate ideas, see Edward F. Fern, "The Use of Focus Groups for Idea Generation: The Effects of Group Size, Acquaintanceship, and Moderator on Response Quantity and Quality," *Journal of Marketing Research*, 19 (February 1982), pp. 1–13.

[30]F. P. Kilpatrick, "New Methods of Measuring Consumer Preferences and Motivation," *Journal of Farm Economics* (December 1957), p. 1314.

A stimulus of low structure has a wide range of alternative choices. It is ambiguous: the subject can "choose" his own interpretation.[31]

While almost any stimulus can serve, some of the most common types of projective methods are word association, sentence completion, and storytelling.

Word Association   With **word association** projective methods, subjects respond to a list of words read to them with the first word that comes to mind. The test words are dispersed throughout the list and are intermixed with some neutral words to conceal the purpose of the study. In the study of pollution, some of the key words might be

- Water ——————
- Air ——————
- Lakes ——————
- Industry ——————
- Smokestack ——————
- City ——————

The subject's responses to each of the key words are recorded verbatim and later analyzed for their meaning. The responses are usually judged in three ways: by the frequency with which any word is given as a response, by the amount of time that elapses before a response is given, and by the number of respondents who do not respond at all to a test word after a reasonable period of time.

Some common responses will often emerge. These common responses when classified and grouped are then used to reveal patterns of interest, underlying motivations, or stereotypes. It is often possible to categorize the associations as favorable–unfavorable, pleasant–unpleasant, modern–old-fashioned, and so forth, depending upon the problem.

The amount of time that elapses before a response is given to a test word is carefully determined. Sometimes a stopwatch is used, while in other cases the interviewer will count to himself while waiting for a reply. Respondents who hesitate (operationally defined as taking longer than three seconds to reply) are judged to be sufficiently emotionally involved in the word so as to provide not their immediate reaction but an acceptable response. If they do not respond at all, their emotional involvement is judged to be so high as to block a response. An individual's pattern of responses, along with the details of the response to each question, are then used to assess the person's attitudes or feelings on the subject.

Sentence Completion   The **sentence completion** method requires that the respondent complete a number of sentences similar to the following:

- Many people behave as if our natural resources were ——————.
- A person who does not use our lakes for recreation is ——————.

---

[31]Fred N. Kerlinger, *Foundations of Behavioral Research,* 3rd ed. (New York: Holt, Rinehart and Winston, 1986), p. 471. For an overview of projective tests from the standpoint of psychology, see W. G. Klopfer and E. S. Taulkie, "Projective Tests," in M. R. Rosenzweig and L. W. Porter, eds., *Annual Review of Psychology* (1976), pp. 543–567.

■   The number-one concern for our natural resources is _____.

■   When I think of living in a city, I _____.

Again respondents are instructed to reply with the first thoughts that come to mind. The responses are recorded verbatim and are later analyzed.

In one study, Kassarjian and Cohen asked 179 smokers who believed cigarettes to be a health hazard why they continued to smoke. The majority gave responses such as, "Pleasure is more important than health," Moderation is OK," "I like to smoke." One gets the impression that smokers are not dissatisfied with their lot. However, in a portion of the study involving sentence-completion tests, smokers responded to the question, "People who never smoke are _____" with comments such as "better off," "happier," "smarter," "wiser," "more informed." To the question, "Teenagers who smoke are _____," smokers responded with "foolish," "crazy," "uninformed," "stupid," "showing off," "immature," "wrong." Clearly, the impression one gets from the sentence completion test is that smokers are anxious, uncomfortable, dissonant, and dissatisfied with their habit. This is quite different from the results of a probed open-end question.[32]

One advantage of sentence completion over word association projective methods is that respondents can be provided with a more directed stimulus. There should be just enough direction to evoke some association with the concept of interest. The researcher needs to be careful not to convey the purpose of the study or provoke the "socially accepted" response. Obviously skill is needed to develop a good sentence completion or word association test.

Storytelling   The **storytelling** approach often relies on pictorial material such as cartoons, photographs, or drawings, although other stimuli are also used. These pictorial devices are descendants of the psychologists' **Thematic Apperception Test (TAT).** The TAT consists of a copyrighted series of pictures about which the subject is asked to tell stories. Some of the pictures are of ordinary events and some of unusual events; in some of the pictures the persons or objects are clearly represented, and in others they are relatively obscure. A respondent's interpretation of these events is employed to interpret the individual's personality; for example, whether the person is impulsive or shows intellectual control in interpreting the stimulus, whether the subject is creative or unimaginative, and so on.

When used in a marketing situation, the same pattern is followed. Respondents are shown a picture and asked to tell a story about the picture. The responses are used to assess attitudes toward the phenomenon, rather than to interpret the subject's personality. Continuing with the pollution example, the stimulus might be a picture of a city, and the respondent might be asked to describe what it would be like to live there. The analysis of the individual's response would then focus on the emphasis given to pollution in its various forms. If no mention were made of traffic congestion, dirty air, noise,

---

[32]Harold H. Kassarjian, "Projective Methods," in Robert Ferber, ed., *Handbook of Marketing Research* (New York: McGraw-Hill, 1974), p. 3—91.

Table 6.5
Reported Differences in Shopping List Study

Nescafé Shopper	Maxwell House Shopper
48% said lazy	4% said lazy
48% said failed to plan household purchases	12% said failed to plan household purchases
4% said thrifty	16% said thrifty
12% said spendthrift	0% said spendthrift
4% said good wife	16% said good wife

Source: Mason Haire, ''Projective Techniques in Marketing Research,'' *Journal of Marketing,* 14 (April 1950), pp.649–651. Published by the American Marketing Association.

and so on, the person would be classified as displaying little concern for pollution and its control.

One of the classic examples of the storytelling approach involves Nescafé instant coffee, one of the early instant food preparations.[33] When women who did not use instant coffee were asked directly, ''What do you dislike about it?'' most of them replied that they did not like the flavor. The investigators suspected that this might be a stereotyped answer, so they switched to a storytelling approach.

A new sample of homemakers was split into two groups of fifty homemakers each. One group was then shown the following shopping list:

- pound and a half of hamburger
- 2 loaves Wonder Bread
- bunch of carrots
- 1 can Rumford's baking powder
- Nescafé instant coffee
- 2 cans Del Monte peaches
- 5 lb potatoes

The other half of the sample was shown the same list except that ''1 lb Maxwell House coffee (drip ground)'' was substituted for the Nescafé instant coffee. Each homemaker was asked to read the shopping list and then describe the personality and character of the woman who made it out. Some of the reported differences were rather striking, as Table 6.5 indicates.

The evidence in Table 6.5 was interpreted as showing that the decision of whether or not to buy instant coffee was influenced as much by prevailing social ideas of what constitutes good housekeeping as it was by the flavor of instant coffee. Yet the direct approach failed to uncover this perhaps subconscious, but certainly important, posture. Interestingly enough, a 1968 replication of the Haire study produced no significant dif-

---

[33]Mason Haire, ''Projective Techniques in Marketing Research,'' *Journal of Marketing,* 14 (April 1950), pp. 649–652.

ferences in the description of the Maxwell House shopper versus the Nescafé shopper, although both were seen in a more negative light.[34]

Note that the various projective methods differ somewhat in their degree of structure of the stimulus. The word association and sentence completion methods involve presenting the stimuli to the respondent in the same sequence and in this sense are quite structured. They are unstructured as far as the response is concerned, as is the storytelling method. Respondents are free to interpret and respond to the stimuli in terms of their own perceptions and own words, and that is why these methods are typically categorized as disguised–unstructured techniques.

The unstructured nature of the projective methods produces many of the same difficulties encountered with the undisguised–unstructured methods of data collection. The greater standardization of the stimulus is a distinct advantage, but the problem with replies remains. The final interpretation of what was said often reflects the interpreter's frame of reference as much as it does the respondent's. Different interpreters often reach different conclusions about the same response. This raises havoc with the editing, coding, and tabulation of replies and suggests that projective methods are also more suited for exploratory research than for descriptive or causal research.

Structured–Disguised Questionnaires

Structured–disguised questionnaires are the least used in marketing research. They were developed in an attempt to secure the advantages of disguise in revealing subconscious motives and attitudes along with the advantages in coding and tabulation common to structured approaches. The arguments supporting the structured–disguised approach typically rest on some proposition regarding the role of attitude in the person's mental and psychological makeup.

One proposition holds, for example, that an individual's knowledge, perception, and memory are conditioned by the person's attitudes. Thus, in order to secure information about people's attitudes when a direct question would produce a biased answer, we can simply ask them what they know. Presumably greater knowledge reflects the strength and direction of an attitude. Democratic voters could be expected to know more about Democratic candidates and the Democratic platform than would those intending to vote Republican, for example. This argument is consistent with what we know about the operation of the selective processes—that individuals tend to selectively expose themselves, selectively perceive, and selectively retain ideas, arguments, events, and phenomena that are consistent with the individual's own beliefs. Conversely, people tend to avoid, see differently, and forget situations and items that are inconsistent with their preconceived beliefs.

---

[34]Frederick E. Webster, Jr., and Frederick Von Peckmann, "A Replication of the Shopping List Study," *Journal of Marketing,* 34 (April 1970), pp. 61–63. For similar shopping list studies involving beer brands and cat food, see, respectively, A. G. Woodside, "A Shopping List Experiment of Beer Brand Images," *Journal of Applied Psychology,* 56 (December 1972), pp. 512–513; and L. N. Reid and L. Buchanan, "A Shopping List Experiment of the Impact of Advertising on Brand Images," *Journal of Advertising,* 8 (Spring 1979), pp. 26–28.

This proposition would suggest that one way of avoiding the socially acceptable response in securing a respondent's attitude toward pollution and the need for antipollution legislation would be to ask the person what he or she knows rather than how he or she feels. Thus, the researcher might frame questions such as the following: What is the status of the antipollution legislation listed below? A number of bills would be listed, some actual and some hypothetical, and the respondent would be asked to check the box that best describes the current status of the legislation. Some of the descriptions might be: ''In committee,'' ''Passed by the House but not the Senate,'' ''Vetoed by the President,'' and so on. Respondents' attitudes toward the need for more legislation would then be assessed by the accuracy of their responses.

The main advantages of this approach emerge in analysis. Responses are easily coded and tabulated and an objective measure of knowledge quickly derived. Whether this measure of knowledge can also be interpreted as a measure of the person's attitude, though, is another matter. Is high legislative awareness indicative of a favorable or an unfavorable attitude toward the need for more antipollution legislation? While this example raises some questions, a more imaginative approach might eliminate the confusion in interpretation. There is evidence that suggests, for instance, that the results obtained with structured–disguised approaches can be quite comparable to those obtained with unstructured–disguised approaches.[35]

Questionnaires Classified by Method of Administration

Questionnaires can also be classified by the method that will be used to administer them. The main methods are mail, phone, and personal interview.

A **personal interview** implies a direct face-to-face conversation between the interviewer and the respondent or interviewee. The interviewer asks the questions and records the respondent's answers either while the interview is in progress or immediately afterward. The **telephone interview** means that this conversation occurs over the phone. The most normal administration of a **mail questionnaire** involves mailing the questionnaires to designated respondents with an accompanying cover letter. The respondents complete the questionnaire at their leisure and mail their replies back to the research organization.

The above descriptions suggest the most common or ''pure'' methods of administration. A number of variations are possible. Questionnaires for a ''mail'' administration may simply be attached to products or printed in magazines and newspapers. Similarly, questionnaires in a personal interview may be self-administered. When self-administered, respondents complete the questionnaire themselves. This might be done in the interviewer's presence, in which case there would be an opportunity for the respondents to seek clarification on points of confusion from the interviewer. Alternatively, the respondents might complete the questionnaire in private for later pickup by a representative of the research organization, in which case the interaction would less resemble a personal interview. Another possibility is for the interviewer to hand the designated

---

[35]Ralph Westfall, Harper Boyd, Jr., and Donald T. Campbell, ''The Use of Structured Techniques in Motivation Research,'' *Journal of Marketing*, 22 (October 1957), pp. 134–139.

respondent the questionnaire personally, but then have the respondent complete it in private and mail it directly to the research organization. In this case, the personal interview is indistinguishable from the mail questionnaire method.

Each of the methods of communication possesses some advantages and disadvantages. When discussing these pros and cons, the pure cases logically serve as a frame of reference. When a modified administration is used, the general advantages and disadvantages may no longer hold. They may also cease to hold in specific situations, in which case a general advantage may become a disadvantage and vice versa. The specific problem will actually dictate the benefits and weaknesses that are associated with each method. Nevertheless, a general discussion of advantages and disadvantages serves to highlight the various methods and criteria that need to be considered in deciding on the manner in which the data will be collected. **Sampling control, information control, and administrative control** are definite points to consider when comparing the methods.

Sampling Control

Sampling control concerns the researcher's ability to direct the inquiry to a designated respondent and to get the desired cooperation from that respondent.

Directing the Inquiry   The direction of the inquiry is guided by the **sampling frame,** that is, by the list of population elements from which the sample will be drawn. With the telephone method, for example, one or more phone books typically serve as the sampling frame. Respondents are selected by some random method from the phone books serving the areas in which the study is to be done. Phone book sampling frames are inadequate in at least two important respects: They do not include those who do not have telephones or those who have unlisted numbers.

Of course, a great percentage of the U.S. population has phones—90 percent of all households in 1983.[36] Yet there are some rather surprising variations by region, in urban and rural locations, and even within urban areas. The regional range was from a high of 92 percent in the Midwest to a low of 88 percent in the South, while in urban areas the percentage was 91 percent as compared to 88 percent in the rural areas.[37]

The census data also indicate that telephone penetration is higher for whites than blacks and lower for low-income households. The proportion of households with telephones increases each year, though, and thus the problem of bias due to the exclusion of nontelephone households should diminish in the future.

Studies that rely on phone book sampling frames also underrepresent transient households, whose numbers were assigned after the current directory was published, and the segment of the population that has requested an unlisted telephone number. The voluntary "nonpub" segment has been growing steadily and now represents approximately 20 percent of all residential phones.[38] The combination of voluntary unlisted numbers

---

[36]*Annual Housing Survey,* 1983 (Washington, U.S. Bureau of the Census, 1984).

[37]*Ibid.*

[38]Clyde L. Rich, "Is Random Digit Dialing Really Necessary," *Journal of Marketing Research,* 14 (August 1977), pp. 300–305.

and numbers that have been assigned since the directory was published account for almost 40 percent of the total telephone households in some metropolitan areas.

A comparison of unlisted versus listed households indicates that the following characteristics are associated with heads of unlisted households:

- younger;

- nonwhite;

- live in large cities;

- less likely to be a college graduate;

- more likely to be employed by someone else in an unskilled or semi-skilled job.[39]

One recent attempt at overcoming the sampling bias of unlisted numbers is **random digit dialing.** This approach simply entails the random generation of numbers to be called and often the automatic dialing of those calls as well. The calls are typically handled through one central interviewing facility employing the Wide Area Telephone Service (WATS).[40] This procedure allows geographically wide distribution or coverage. One problem with the random generation of phone numbers is that it can increase survey costs, since there are approximately 34,000 area-code prefix combinations in use in the continental United States. When the last four digits are generated randomly, there are approximately 340 million possible phone numbers that can be called. However, there are only about 80 million working residential telephone numbers in the United States. A simple comparison suggests that calling random telephone numbers will result in residential contacts only about one-fourth of the time.[41] An alternative scheme to random digit dialing is **Plus-One sampling,** where a probability sample of phone numbers is selected from the telephone directory and a single, randomly determined digit is added to each selected number.[42]

One or more mailing lists typically serve as the sampling frame in mail questionnaires. The quality of these lists determines the sampling biases. If the list is a reasonably good one, the bias can be small. For example, some firms have established panels,

---

[39]Tyzoon T. Tyebjee, "Telephone Survey Methods: The State of the Art," *Journal of Marketing,* 43 (Summer 1979), pp. 68–78; A. B. Blankenship, "Listed Versus Unlisted Numbers in Telephone-Survey Samples," *Journal of Advertising Research,* 17 (February 1977), pp. 39–42; and Patricia E. Moberg, "Biases in Unlisted Phone Numbers," *Journal of Advertising Research,* 22 (August–September 1982), pp. 51–55.

[40]G. J. Glasser and G. D. Metzger, "Random-Digit Dialing as a Method of Telephone Sampling," *Journal of Marketing Research,* 9 (February 1972), pp. 59–64; *The Use of Random Digit Dialing in Telephone Surveys: An Annotated Bibliography* (Monticello, Ill.: Vance Bibliographies, 1979); and *Telephone Interviewing Bibliography,* (Washington, D.C.: U.S. Bureau of the Census, 1981).

[41]Albert G. Swint and Terry E. Powell, "CLUSFONE Computer-Generated Telephone Sampling Offers Efficiency and Minimal Bias," *Marketing Today* (Elrick and Lavidge), 21 (1983). There is some evidence to suggest that certain sampling schemes can produce a higher proportion of working residential numbers without introducing any appreciable bias in the process. See, for example, Joseph Waksberg, "Sampling Methods for Random Digit Dialing," *Journal of the American Statistical Association,* 73 (March 1978), pp. 40–46; and Robert Groves and Robert L. Kahn, *Surveys by Telephone* (New York: Academic Press, 1979). More sophisticated sampling schemes have also been used with random digit dialing to locate relatively rare segments of the population. See Johnny Blair and Ronald Czaja, "Locating a Special Population Using Random Digit Dialing," *Public Opinion Quarterly,* 46 (Winter 1982), pp. 585–590.

[42]E. Laird Landon, Jr., and Sharon K. Banks, "Relative Efficiency and Bias of Plus-One Telephone Sampling," *Journal of Marketing Research,* 14 (August 1977), pp. 294–299.

which can be used to answer mail questionnaires and which are representative of the population in many important respects. Further, some mailing lists that may be ideally suited for certain types of studies can be purchased.

Say you run a direct-mail business that specializes in selling monogrammed baby bibs. For a fee at any given time you can obtain a mailing list containing the names and addresses of up to one million pregnant women. And if it should suit your purposes, it's easy enough to get the list limited to women whose babies are expected in a certain month or who are expecting their first child.[43]

The fact remains, though, that the mailing list determines the sampling control in a mail study. If there is an accurate, applicable, and readily available list of population elements, the mail questionnaire allows a wide and representative sample, since it costs no more to send a questionnaire across country than it does to send one across town. Even ignoring costs, it is sometimes the only way of contacting the relevant population, such as busy executives who will not sit still for an arranged personal or telephone interview but may respond to a mail questionnaire. It is estimated that the average consumer has his or her name on anywhere from 25 to 40 separate mailing lists and receives 80 pieces of unsolicited mail per year. All those who think unsolicited mail is a bother, however, can send one letter to the Direct Mail Marketing Association, a trade group of more than 2,600 direct mail marketers, and that organization will remove the name from every member's list. The statistics indicate, though, that for every person requesting to have his or her name removed, two more request that their names be added.[44]

Sampling control for the administration of questions via personal interview is conceptually difficult but practically possible. For some select populations (for example, doctors, architects, or firms), a list of population elements from which a sample can be drawn may be readily available in association or trade directories. For studies focused on consumer goods, however, there are few lists available and those available are typically badly out-of-date. What is often done here is to use area sampling procedures. The general approach is dealt with in a later chapter. For now, simply be aware that it involves the substitution of areas and dwelling units for people as the sampling units. The substitution offers the advantage of accurate, current lists of sampling units, in the form of maps, for the generally inaccurate, unavailable lists of people. There remains the problem of ensuring that the field interviewer contacted the right household and person, but the personal interview does afford some sampling control in directing the questionnaire to specific sample units.

---

[43]Mailing List Brokers Sell More than Names to Their Many Clients," *Wall Street Journal,* 54 (February 19, 1974), pp. 1 and 18. For other discussions of how firms go about developing mailing lists and their value, see Jeffrey H. Birnbaum, "Firms Try Shredders, Special Tasks to Protect Valuable Mailing Lists," *Wall Street Journal,* 61 (April 27, 1981), p. 27; "Lists Make Targeting Easy," *Advertising Age,* 55 (July 9, 1984), p. 20; and "Making a List, Selling It Twice," *Wall Street Journal,* 65 (May 20, 1985), pp. 64–65.

[44]Bruce Shawkey, "Mail Order Peddlers Pan Gold in Them Thar Lists," *Wisconsin State Journal* (July 31, 1983), pp. 1 and 4.

Table 6.6
Results of First Dialing Attempts

Result	Number of Dialings	Probability of Occurrence
No answer	89,829	.347
Busy	5,299	.020
Out-of-service	52,632	.203
No eligible person	75,285	.291
Business	10,578	.041
At home	25,465	.098
Refusal	3,707	.014 (.146)*
Completion	21,758	.084 (.854)
Total	259,088	1.000

*Probability of occurrence *given* eligible individual is at home.

Source: Roger A. Kerin and Robert A. Peterson, "Scheduling Telephone Interviews." Reprinted from the *Journal of Advertising Research,* 23 (April/May 1983), p. 44. Copyright 1983 by the Advertising Research Foundation.

Getting Cooperation   Directing the inquiry to a specific respondent is one thing; getting a response from that individual is quite another. In this respect, the personal interview affords the most sample control. With a personal interview, the respondent's identity is known, and thus there is little opportunity for anyone else to reply. The problem of nonresponse due to refusals to participate is also typically lower with personal interviews than with either telephone interviews or mail administered questionnaires. There is sometimes a problem with not-at-homes, but this can often be handled by calling back at more appropriate times.

Telephone methods also suffer from not-at-homes or no-answers. In one very large study involving more than 259,000 telephone calls, it was found, for example, that over 34 percent of the calls resulted in a no-answer.[45] What was even more disturbing was that the probability of making contact with an eligible respondent on the first call was less than one in ten (see Table 6.6). Fortunately, calling back is much simpler and more economical than it is with personal interviews. The relatively low expense of a telephone contact allows a number of follow-up calls to secure a needed response, while the high cost of field contact restricts the number of follow-ups that can be made in studies employing personal interviews. Making sure the intended respondent replies is somewhat more difficult with telephone interviews than with personal interviews. So is the problem of determining which person in the household should be interviewed.[46]

[45]Roger A. Kerin and Robert A. Peterson, "Scheduling Telephone Interviews," *Journal of Advertising Research,* 23 (April/May 1983), pp. 41–47.

[46]Ronald Czaja, Johnny Blair, and Jutta P. Sebestik, "Respondent Selection in a Telephone Survey: A Comparison of Three Techniques," *Journal of Marketing Research,* 19 (August 1982), pp. 381–385; Diane O'Rourke and Johnny Blair, "Improving Random Respondent Selection in Telephone Interviews," *Journal of Marketing Research,* 20 (November 1983), pp. 428–432; and Terry L. Childers and Steven J. Skinner, "Theoretical and Empirical Issues in the Identification of Survey Respondents," *Journal of the Market Research Society,* 27 (January 1985), pp. 39–53.

Mail questionnaires afford the researcher little control in securing a response from the intended respondent. The researcher can simply direct the questionnaire to the designated respondent and offer the individual some incentive for cooperating.[47] However, the researcher cannot control that cooperation. A great many subjects may refuse to respond. In many cases, only those most interested in the subject will respond. Some subjects will be incapable of responding because they are illiterate. For example, the International Reading Association estimates that some 20 million English-speaking, native-born American adults read or write so poorly that they have trouble holding jobs, while the author of *Illiterate America* suggests that 60 million adult Americans are illiterate.[48] Since many of these people have difficulty with everyday tasks like reading job notices, making change, or getting a driver's license, is it any wonder that they might not respond to a mail questionnaire that is at all complex! Whatever the reason, the nonresponse may cause a bias of indeterminate direction and magnitude. Also, it is not always clear who is responding in mail surveys, nor can the researcher exercise a great deal of control in this regard.

Information Control

The differing methods of data collection also permit a good deal of variation with respect to the type of questions that can be asked and the amount and accuracy of the information that can be obtained from respondents.

The personal interview can be conducted using almost any form of questionnaire, from structured–undisguised through structured–disguised. The personal interaction between interviewer and respondent allows the use of pictures or examples of advertisements, lists of words, scales, and so on, as stimuli. The use of the telephone rules out most aids, while the mail questionnaire allows the use of some of them. Figures 6.2 and 6.3, for instance, display an example that requires personal interviews. The study demands that respondents be allowed to see the lighting devices but that exposure to them be controlled by the interviewer. This precludes administration by other means. Note the detailed instructions to the interviewer that are part of the research design. Note also the open-ended questions and the difficulty one will likely encounter in tabulating the responses. (The numbers in parentheses indicate the computer card image columns that will be used for the coded answers.) Some of the open-ended questions require extensive probes. Mail questionnaires simply do not allow the use of questions requiring extensive probes for a complete response. Telephone interviews can incorpo-

---

[47]See Paul L. Erdos, *Professional Mail Surveys* (Malabar, Fla.: Robert E. Kreiger, 1983), for a discussion of the problem of sample control in mail surveys and what can be done to overcome respondent resistance. For general references on conducting telephone surveys, see A. B. Blankenship, *Professional Telephone Surveys* (New York: McGraw-Hill, 1977); or James H. Frey, *Survey Research by Telephone* (Beverly Hills, Calif.: Sage Publications, 1983).

[48]Daniel Machalaba, "Hidden Handicap: For Americans Unable to Read Well, Life is a Series of Small Crises," *Wall Street Journal*, 64 (January 17, 1984), pp. 1 and 12; and Chris Martell, "Illiteracy Hurts All, Author Says," *Wisconsin State Journal* (April 3, 1985), pp. 1–2. The illiteracy problem is also severe in England. See *Journal of the Market Research Society*, 26 (April 1984), for a number of articles on the subject and its consequences for survey research.

Figure 6.2
Interviewer Instructions for Portable Lighting Fixtures
Study (Courtesy Ray-O-Vac Corporation)

Background

Your city will be responsible for the completion of 100 interviews, half with males between the ages of 20 and 64, the other half with females in the same age category. Quota sheets have been enclosed to insure that about:

30% of the males are 20–29
25% of the males are 30–39
30% of the males are 40–54
15% of the males are 55–64

Female quota sheets have been enclosed so as to obtain the following approximate distribution:

30% of the females are 20–29
20% of the females are 30–39
35% of the females are 40–54
15% of the females are 55–64

Inventory

Please inventory for the following materials:

1 Rectangular lamp (#381 on back)
1 Round (brown) lamp (#492 on back)
Preprinted numbered ID stickers which will attach to front of display area directly above the respective lamps
One laminated concept statement which will attach to the wall under the rectangular #381 lamp
One laminated concept statement for use in Question 3
One laminated exhibit card for use in Question 4
One laminated price card for use in Question 11
Two laminated age/income cards fixed back to back

The Display

Both lamps will be attached to the wall approximately 5½′ from the floor with the string switches hanging straight down. The number 381 will be attached to the wall right under the rectangular lamp; the number 492 will be under the round brown fixture.

A laminated concept statement will be attached to the wall right under the number identifier for model 381.

A white towel will be used to cover the brown fixture, this can most easily be accomplished by tacking the towel to the wall several inches above the brown fixture and placing a second tack far to the right so that when the towel is removed it can be hung off to the right side (see drawing enclosed).

When a consumer first enters the display area, only lamp #381 will be visible to him/her.

continued on next page

Figure 6.2
Interviewer Instructions for Portable Lighting Fixtures
Study (Courtesy Ray-O-Vac Corporation) *continued*

The Interview

Approach adult shoppers who appear to be at least 20 years old or older and read the introduction. This interview should not take much more than 5 to 8 minutes, which is specified in the introduction.

Question 1: Terminate any adult consumer who has been in a research study within the last three months.

Question 2: Terminate any consumer who is affiliated with a marketing research firm, advertising agency or lighting appliance manufacturer.

Question 3: Hand a laminated copy of the concept statement to the consumer, then read aloud with him/her. Once you have finished reading, hand the exhibit card for Question 4 and allow the respondent to evaluate the concept/lamp.

DO NOT ALLOW THE RESPONDENT TO TOUCH THE LAMPS, IF THE RESPONDENT WANTS TO TURN THEM ON OR MENTIONS LIGHTING CAPABILITY, SAY . . . This is only a model and the batteries are not installed.

DO NOT ATTEMPT TO PULL THE ON/OFF STRING ON ANY OF THESE LAMPS.

If the respondent likes the idea (Question 4—One of the top 3 responses) you will ask Questions 5 and 6. If the respondent does not like the idea (Question 4—the last 2 responses) you will ask Questions 7 and 8.

Question 5/6: These are open-end questions which deal with the respondent's likes and dislikes. Probe and clarify fully, then skip to Question 9.

Question 7/8: These open ends are almost identical to those references above but they ask the respondent for dislikes first, then likes. Once again, probe and clarify fully, then skip to Question 9.

Question 9: Read the first paragraph of Question 9 slowly and pause so the respondent has time to think of the various places where he/she could use such a lamp. Then continue with the second paragraph. Put a number 1 next to the very first place the respondent mentions—and then ask why it would be used there? Then ask the third paragraph of Question 9 probing for additional places. Put a number 2 in the left hand blank provided for the second place mentioned and repeat the above probe. Continue placing 3's, 4's, 5's, 6's etc. next to the places where they would be used in the order mentioned until the respondent indicates no additional places of use.

Again, if the respondent would not use the light anywhere, merely circle the x at the bottom of the page and go on to Question 10.

Question 10: Encourage the respondent to best guess—without batteries.

Figure 6.2
Interviewer Instructions for Portable Lighting Fixtures
Study (Courtesy Ray-O-Vac Corporation) *continued*

The Interview continued

Question 11:   Be sure to use the exhibit card.

Question 12:   Remove the covering from Fixture 492—allow inspection—obtain overall preference.

Question 13:   Self-explanatory. Read slowly.

Question 14:   This question reveals the difference in price—be absolutely sure to point to the different models as you are reading the prices. Allow the respondent ample time to make up his/her mind and then record final choice.

Question 15, 15A: Self-explanatory.

Question 16, 17:   Self-explanatory. Use the exhibit card.

At the completion of the interview circle the quota cell group on the top of page one and the city.

Your city is responsible for the completion of 100 interviews, other cities are waiting for the use of the lights, so as soon as you have completed field work, ship the lights (well packed) and the exhibit cards:

> Milwaukee—ship to Livingston, New Jersey
> Houston—ship to Los Angeles, California

Ship via Federal Air Express—priority service and notify M. Maloney of the date and time of shipment.

---

rate them, but not nearly to the same extent. Note finally, the automatic sequencing of questions; for example, if the answer to question 4 is positive, ask questions 5 and 6, while if negative, ask questions 7 and 8. While automatic sequencing is also possible with telephone interviews, mail questionnaires permit much less of it.

The computer-controlled cathode-ray terminal (CRT) has had a significant impact on the conduct of telephone interviews and the amount of information control they allow, both with respect to the questions asked and the analysis of replies. After dialing the selected number, the computer leads the interviewer through the survey questionnaire. The computer displays the exact wording of the question to be asked the respondent on the CRT. The interviewer records the responses on a keyboard for direct entry into the computer. Only when an acceptable answer is provided will the computer display the next question. If a respondent says she or he bought a brand that is not in that particular locale, for example, the computer is programmed to reject the answer. This greatly simplifies skipping or branching procedures. The interviewer does not have to grapple with selecting the next question given the response to the current one; the computer

Figure 6.3
Questionnaire Used in Portable Lighting Fixtures
Study (Courtesy Ray-O-Vac Corporation)

(APPROACH SHOPPERS WHO APPEAR TO BE 20 YEARS OLD OR OVER AND SAY . . .)

Hi, I'm _____ from U.S. Testing Co. Many companies are asking consumers for their opinions in order to develop the kinds of products that you really want, and if you have about 5 minutes, I'd like to include your opinions in our market research study. (IF REFUSED, TERMINATE)

1. Have you participated in any consumer research studies in this center within the last three months? (IF YES, TALLY AND TERMINATE)   (07)

2. Do you, or any members of your family, or close friends, work for any marketing research firm, advertising agency, or lighting appliance manufacturer? (IF YES, TALLY AND TERMINATE)   (08)

3. Here is a brief description of this new type of area light.

"This is a battery operated light fixture . . . it operates on four regular flashlight batteries . . . designed to give you light in places where you don't have electricity available or in places where expensive wiring jobs can be avoided.

Both the non-glare globes and body are made of rugged high impact plastic which will not rust or corrode—ideal wherever you need wireless light; made by Ray-O-Vac, a United States manufacturer of quality lighting devices."

4. Which of the following phrases best describes your overall reaction to the product you have just read?

(09)—1 It's a great idea
     2 It's a pretty good idea   —(ASK Q. 5 AND 6)
     3 So-so
     4 It's not a very good idea   —(ASK Q. 7 AND 8)
     5 It's a poor idea

(IF RESPONSE WAS POSITIVE, ASK:)

5. What is it that you particularly like about this idea? (Probe and Clarify)

Likes
(10)
(11)
(12)
(13)
(14)

6. What, if anything, do you dislike about this idea? (Probe and Clarify)
(15)
(16)
(17)
(18)
(19)

Figure 6.3

**Questionnaire Used in Portable Lighting Fixtures
Study (Courtesy Ray-O-Vac Corporation)** *continued*

(SKIP TO Q. 9)

(IF RESPONSE WAS NEGATIVE, ASK:)

7. *What is it that you* dislike *about this idea?* (Probe and Clarify)

Dislikes
(20)
(21)
(22)
(23)
(24)
(25)
(26)
(27)
(28)
(29)

8. *Is there anything at all that you particularly* like *about this idea?*
(Probe and Clarify)

9. *Now, take a minute or two to think about all the places where you might use a product of this type.* (ALLOW TIME AND THEN CONTINUE BY SAYING . . .)

Where would you use a product of this type and why? (RECORD FIRST ITEM MENTIONED ON THE LINE PROVIDED IN THE LEFT HAND COLUMN, USE THE SPACE PROVIDED TO PROBE AND CLARIFY REASONS WHY, THEN CONTINUE BY SAYING . . .)

What other areas would you use it in? (RECORD SECOND MENTIONED, ETC., CONTINUE TO PROBE FOR OTHER AREAS UNTIL RESPONDENT INDICATES THERE ARE NO MORE)

continued on next page

Figure 6.3
Questionnaire Used in Portable Lighting Fixtures
Study (Courtesy Ray-O-Vac Corporation) *continued*

(30) _____ Tent	(40)
	(41)
(31) _____ Camper	(42)
	(43)
(32) _____ Boat	(44)
	(45)
(33) _____ Cottage/Cabin	(46)
	(47)
(34) _____ Home	(48)
	(49)
(35) _____ Garage	(50)
	(51)
(36) _____ Porch/Patio	(52)
	(53)
(37) _____ Car	(54)
	(55)
(38) _____ Other (SPECIFY)	(56)
	(57)
(39) _____ Other (SPECIFY)	(58)
	(59)

X   _____   Would not use anywhere

10. *About how much would you expect a light like this to cost, without batteries?*
(URGE A GUESS IF NECESSARY)

$\underset{\text{(60-61-62)}}{\$\underline{\hspace{2cm}}}$

11. *Assuming this light sold for $*_____ *in your local discount store, how likely would you be to buy it? Would you say you would . . .* **(SHOW CARD)**

(63)—1   I definitely would buy it
    2   I probably would buy it
    3   I might or might not buy it
    4   I probably would not buy it
    5   I definitely would not buy it

12. **(UNCOVER 492 LIGHT AND SAY . . .)**
Here is another light fixture that is basically the same as the first one, but its styling and design are somewhat different. Considering just the design of these two lights, which one do you prefer?

(64)– 1 381
      2 492

Figure 6.3

Questionnaire Used in Portable Lighting Fixtures Study (Courtesy Ray-O-Vac Corporation) *continued*

13. If you were going to buy a light fixture like either of these, would you be satisfied with the colors we've shown here, or would you prefer a wider variety of colors be available to coordinate with the decor in the places where you might use a light of this type?

    (65)—1 Satisfied with these colors
           2 Prefer a wider variety

14. While model 381 and 492 are basically the same type of light, they do differ in styling and quality. Model 492 sells for $3.00 without batteries, compared to model 381 which sells for $5.00 without batteries. Please take one last look at them and then considering their overall appearance, features, and prices, please tell me which one you'd be most likely to buy.

    (66)—1 381
           2 492

15. Just for classification purposes, do you live in a single family house or apartment?

    (67)—1 Single family house
           2 Apartment
           Other _____ (SPECIFY)

15a. Do you own or rent it?

    (68)—1 Own
           2 Rent

16. Please look at this card (HAND CARD) *and tell me which letter best represents your age group.*

(69)—1 A 18–20	6 F 40–44
2 B 21–24	7 G 45–49
3 C 25–29	8 H 50–54
4 D 30–34	9 I 55–59
5 E 35–39	0 J 60–64
	X K 65 and over

17. Which letter on the other side of that card best represents your total family income before taxes?

    (70)—1 A Up to $5,000 a year
           2 B $5,000–$7,499
           3 C $7,500–$9,999
           4 D $10,000–$12,499
           5 E $12,500–$14,999
           6 F $15,000–$19,999
           7 G $20,000–$24,999
           8 H $25,000 or more

does this automatically. This saves considerable time and confusion in administering the questionnaire and permits a more natural flow to the interview. It also assures that there will be no variation in the sequence with which the questions are asked, as can happen with personal interviews or mail questionnaires.[49]

Two other advantages of computer control of the questions are:

1. Personalization of questions by forward control. During the course of the interview, the computer is aware of all previous responses (e.g., name of wife, cars owned, supermarket patronized) and can customize the wording of future questions, for example, "When your wife, Ann, shops at the Acme, does she usually use the Fiat or the Buick?" Such personalized questions could enhance rapport and thus provide for higher-quality interviews.

2. Customized questionnaires. Key information elicited early in the interview is used to customize the questionnaire for each respondent. For example, only product attributes previously acknowledged by a respondent as determinants of his or her decision are used for measuring brand perception, rather than using an *a priori* list of attributes common to all respondents.[50]

Another advantage to CRT interviews is that preliminary tabulations of the answers are available at a moment's notice, since the replies are already stored in memory. One does not have the typical two-to-three week delay due to coding and data entry that happens when questionnaires are completed by hand. Partly because of the advantages that accrue with CRT administration of questionnaires, telephone interviews are currently the most popular and have also experienced the greatest increase in popularity over the last few years among members of the Council of American Survey Research Organization (CASRO). See Research Realities 6.3.

Note that the CRT can be used with personal interviews. This requires, however, that the interviews be conducted at central locations instead of door to door. Typically, this will mean shopping malls, in which case the previous comments on possible sampling control with personal interviews no longer apply.[51]

There is a greater danger of sequence bias with mail questionnaires. Respondents can see the whole questionnaire, and thus their replies to any single question may not be independently arrived at but, rather, are more likely to be conditioned by their responses

---

[49]The empirical evidence indicates that computer-assisted telephone interviewing indeed produces less interviewer variability and fewer skip problems than normal telephone interviews, although no time savings. See Robert A. Groves and Nancy Mathiowetz, "Computer Assisted Telephone Interviewing: Effects on Interviewers and Respondents," *Public Opinion Quarterly,* 48 (Spring 1984), pp. 356–359.

[50]Tyebjee, "Telephone Survey Methods," p. 76.

[51]For a discussion of desirable sampling procedures to use with mall intercept interviewing, see Seymour Sudman, "Improving the Quality of Shopping Center Sampling," *Journal of Marketing Research,* 17 (November 1980), pp. 423–431. See also Alan J. Bush and Joseph F. Hair, Jr., "An Assessment of the Mall Intercept as a Data Collection Method," *Journal of Marketing Research,* 22 (May 1985), pp. 158–167, for an empirical assessment of response quality and the extent of the nonresponse problem in mall intercept interviewing.

Research Realities 6.3

Popularity of Various Data Collection Techniques among CASRO Members

Technique	1983	1982	1981
WATS/centralized telephone	41%	38%	38%
Central location/mall	19	17	16
Personal interview/door-to-door	13	19	20
Non-WATS telephone (local)	7	8	7
Mail/diary	7	7	6
Focus group	6	5	6
All other	7	6	7

Source: Jack J. Honomichl, "Survey Results Positive," *Advertising Age,* 55 (November 1, 1984), p. 23.

to other questions than they would be if either personal interviews or telephone interviews were employed.

The mail questionnaire permits control of the bias caused by interviewer–interviewee interaction. With a mail questionnaire, respondents are also able to work at their own pace. This may produce better-thought-out responses than would be obtained in personal or telephone interviews, where there is a certain urgency associated with giving a response. A thought-out response, however, is no guarantee of an appropriate reply. If the question is ambiguous, the mail survey offers no opportunity for clarification. The question must succeed or fail on its own merits. Since researchers cannot decipher differences in interpretation among respondents, they cannot impose a consistent frame of reference on the replies. Thus the responses to an open-ended question in a mailed questionnaire may be excessive or inadequate. With structured questions, the answers may simply reflect differences in the frame of reference being employed, rather than any subject-to-subject variation in the particular characteristic being measured. The anonymity sometimes associated with a mailed questionnaire does afford people an opportunity to be more frank on certain sensitive issues (for example, sexual behavior).

As mentioned, both personal and telephone interviews can cause interviewer bias because of the respondent's perception of the interviewer or because different interviewers ask questions and probe in different ways. Both of these biases can be more easily controlled in telephone surveys. There are fewer interviewer actions to which the respondent can react, and a supervisor can be present during telephone interviews to ensure that they are being conducted consistently. It is typically more difficult, though, to establish rapport over the phone than in person. The respondent in a telephone interview often demands more information about the purposes of the study, the credentials of the interviewer and research organization, and so on.[52]

With regard to length of questionnaire or amount of information to be collected, the general rule of thumb is that long questionnaires can be handled best by personal interview and least well by telephone interview. So much, though, depends on the subject of inquiry, the form of the questionnaire, and the approach used to secure cooperation that a rigid interpretation of this advice would be unwarranted and hazardous.

Administrative Control

The telephone survey is one of the quickest ways of obtaining information. A number of calls can be made from a central exchange in a short period, perhaps 15 to 20 per hour per interviewer if the questionnaire is short. The personal interview affords no such time economies, since there is dead time between each interview in which the interviewer travels to the next respondent. If the researcher wishes to speed up the replies secured with personal interviews, the size of the field force must be increased. This raises problems of interviewer-induced variation in responses because of slight differences in approach. Some of these can be reduced through proper selection and training of interviewers, but the personal interview still presents more formidable problems of control than the telephone interview, including control of interviewer cheating. With the telephone method, the researcher can also increase the speed with which replies are secured by increasing the number of interviewers. Since the researcher can supervise interviewers directly when they are making their calls, problems of variation in administration and cheating should be much less acute.

While the mail questionnaire represents a standardized stimulus, and thus allows little variation in administration, it also affords little speed control. It often takes a couple of weeks to secure the bulk of the replies at which time a follow-up mailing is often begun. It, too, will involve a time lapse of several weeks for the questionnaires to reach the respondents, be completed, and find their way back. Depending on the number of follow-up mailings required, the total time needed to conduct a good mail study can often be substantial.[53] Of course, with a mail study the time required to secure a great many replies with a very large sample is little different from the time necessary for a small sample. This is not so with personal and telephone interviews, where there is a direct relationship between the number of interviews and the time required to complete them.

---

[52]Peter U. Miller and Charles F. Cannell, ''A Study of Experimental Techniques for Telephone Interviewing,'' *Public Opinion Quarterly,* 46 (Summer 1982), pp. 250–269; Charles F. Cannell, Peter U. Miller, and Lois Oksenberg, ''Research on Interviewing Techniques,'' in Samuel Leinhardt, ed., *Sociological Methodology 1981* (San Francisco: Jossey-Bass, 1981); and Pamela G. Guengel, Tracy R. Berchman, and Charles F. Cannell, *General Interviewing Techniques: A Self-Instructional Workbook for Telephone and Personal Interviewer Training* (Ann Arbor, Mich.: Survey Research Center, University of Michigan, 1983).

[53]Because of the need to send follow-up mailings to reduce the typically high incidence of nonresponse that occurs to any single mailing, researchers sometimes attempt to predict the ultimate response rate to a mailing based on the early returns. See Stephen J. Huxley, ''Predicting Response Speed in Mail Surveys,'' *Journal of Marketing Research,* 17 (February 1980), pp. 63–68; and Richard W. Hill, ''Using S-Shaped Curves to Predict Response Rates,'' *Journal of Marketing Research,* 18 (May 1981), pp. 240–242, for discussion of how this can be done.

Personal interviews tend to be the most expensive per completed contact and the mail questionnaire tends to be the cheapest, but the subject and procedures of the inquiry can change the relative cost picture dramatically.[54] For example, the per-contact cost of the mail questionnaire is generally low. However, if nonresponse is substantial, the cost per return may be quite high. For the most part, though, the mail, telephone, mall, and in-home personal interview methods require progressively larger field staffs, and the larger the field staff, the greater the problems of control. Good quality control costs money, and that is why the personal interview in the home is typically the most expensive data collection method.

Combining Methods

Each method of data collection thus has its uses, and none is superior in all situations. The problem as finally defined will often suggest one approach over the others, but the researcher should recognize that the approaches often can be used most productively in combination. In one home product use test, for example, interviewers were employed to place the product, self-administered questionnaires, and return envelopes with the respondents, while telephone interviews were used for follow-up. The combination of methods produced telephone cooperation from 97 percent of the testing families, while 82 percent of the mail questionnaires were returned.[55]

Another example demonstrating advantages that can accrue through the creative use of a combination of data collection techniques is the locked box approach recommended for industrial surveys.[56] Surveying the industrial market is a relatively expensive proposition. One has to contend with busy executives who have better things to do with their time than answer questionnaires, and with efficient secretaries and receptionists who prescreen executive mail, telephone calls, and personal visitors. Industrial surveys consequently produce very low response rates. The locked box has proven effective in getting through the prescreens and in generating executive cooperation. It is nothing more than a metal, shoe-sized box that is locked with a three-digit combination lock and that contains flash cards, interview exhibits, concept statements, or other survey materials. It is accompanied by a cover letter explaining the purpose of the survey and telling the respondent that an interviewer will be contacting him or her in a few days. The box becomes the gift for cooperating. However, it is of no use unless one knows the combination, information that is given the executive after he or she cooperates in the follow-up telephone interview. Thus, mail is used to deliver the box and the telephone to conduct the actual interview. At the same time, the box provides an opportu-

---

[54]The National Opinion Research Council, for one, has conducted a number of studies aimed at investigating the information quality–cost trade-offs associated with the various data collection methods. The results of some of these studies are contained in Seymour Sudman, *Reducing the Cost of Surveys* (Chicago: Aldine, 1967). See also R. M. Groves and R. L. Kahn, *Surveys by Telephone: A National Comparison with Personal Interviews* (New York: Academic Press, 1979).

[55]Stanley L. Payne, "Combination of Survey Methods," *Journal of Marketing Research,* 1 (May 1964), p. 62.

[56]David Schwartz, "Locked Box Combines Survey Methods, Helps End Some Woes of Probing Industrial Field," *Marketing News,* 11 (January 27, 1978), p. 18.

nity to use stimuli such as pictures, examples, lists of words, scales, and so on—stimuli that otherwise might be restricted to personal interviews.

Methods of Observation

Observation is a fact of everyday life. We are constantly observing other people and events as a means of securing information about the world around us. Admittedly, some people make more productive use of those observations than do others. One of the more interesting stories told about William Benton, one of the co-founders of the Benton and Boles advertising agency, concerned his walk along a street in Chicago during a hot day in 1929. Since it was hot, most of the windows were open, so he could hear the radios in the apartments he passed. What he mainly heard were the voices of the actors in *Amos and Andy,* one of the leading comedy programs at that time. Struck by this, Benton retraced his steps, this time counting the radios he could hear. He counted 23 of them in all, and found that 21 were tuned to *Amos and Andy*. Rushing back to his advertising firm, Benton suggested that they advertise one of their clients' products, Pepsodent toothpaste, on *Amos and Andy*. The sales of Pepsodent took off like a rocket, all because of Benton's first audience survey of radio listenership.[57]

Observation is also a tool of scientific inquiry. When used for that purpose, however, the observations are more systematically planned and recorded, so as to relate to the specific phenomenon of interest. While planned, they do not have to be sophisticated to be effective. They can be as basic as the retailer who color-coded the promotional flyers it was sending according to zip code so that it could identify the trading area the store was serving by counting the flyers of each color that were returned. This is a less sophisticated scheme than that used by many malls to determine their trading areas. A number of malls use enumerators, who walk the parking lot recording every unique license number they find, 2,500 different numbers on a typical day. The data is then fed into R. L. Polk, which matches the license plates to zip code areas or census tracts and returns a color-coded map showing customer density from the various areas. At a cost of $5,000 to $25,000, these studies are not only less expensive, but they are quicker and more reliable than store interviews or examinations of credit card records.[58]

Observation offers the researcher a number of possible approaches. Like communication methods, observational data may be gathered employing structured or unstructured methods that are either disguised or undisguised. Further, as Figure 6.1 shows, the observations may be made in a contrived or a natural setting, and may be secured by a human or mechanical observer.

---

[57]Edward Cornish, "Telecommunications: What's Coming," paper delivered at the American Marketing Association's 1981 Annual Conference held in San Francisco, California, June 14–17, 1981.

[58]See James G. Barnes, G. A. Pym, and A. C. Noonan, "Marketing Research: Some Basics for Small Business," *Journal of Small Business Management,* 20 (July 1982), pp. 62–66; Steve Raddock, "Follow That Car," *Marketing and Media Decisions,* 16 (January 1981), pp. 70–71, 103; and "I've Got Your Number," *Wall Street Journal,* 61 (February 5, 1981), p. 21.

Structured–Unstructured Observation

The distinction here parallels that for communication methods. Structured observation applies when the problem has been defined precisely enough to permit a clear *a priori* specification of the behaviors that will be observed and the categories that will be used to record and analyze the situation. Unstructured observation is used for studies in which the formulation of the problem is not specific, so that a great deal of flexibility is allowed the observers in terms of what they note and record.

Consider a study investigating the amount of deliberation and search that goes into a detergent purchase. On the one hand, the observers could be instructed to stand at one end of a supermarket aisle and record what they deem appropriate with respect to each sample customer's deliberation and search. This might produce the following record: "Purchaser first paused in front of ABC brand. He picked up a box of ABC, glanced at the price, and set it back down again. He then checked the label and price for DEF brand. He set that back down again, and after a slight pause, picked up a smaller box of ABC than originally looked at, placed it in his cart, and moved down the aisle." Alternatively, observers might simply be told to record the first detergent examined, the total number of boxes picked up by any customer, and the time in seconds that the customer spent in front of the detergent shelves by checking the appropriate boxes in the observation form. The last situation represents a good deal more structure than the first.

To use the more structured approach, it would have been necessary to previously decide precisely what is to be observed and the specific categories and units that would be used to record the observations. These decisions presuppose specific hypotheses, and the structured approach is again more appropriate for descriptive and causal studies. The unstructured approach would be useful in generating insights into the relevant dimensions of deliberation and search behavior; it would not be appropriate, though, for testing hypotheses about this kind of behavior, because of the many different kinds of behaviors that could be recorded and the difficulty of coding and quantifying the data in a consistent manner.

One way to develop consistency in coding is to use multiple coders who are extremely well trained. This technique was used, for example, in an observational study examining the patterns of interactions between parents and children in making selections of breakfast cereals. The observers here recorded verbatim the verbal exchanges between parent and child when making the choice. The coders then tried to assess:

1. which party initiated the selection episode.
2. how the other party responded.
3. the content and tone of the communication.
4. the occurrence of unpleasant consequences such as arguments or unhappiness.

The ultimate aim of the study was to determine if the child was unhappy with the resolution of the situation.[59]

---

[59]Charles K. Atkin, "Observation of Parent-Child Interaction in Supermarket Decision Making," *Journal of Marketing,* 42 (October 1978), pp. 41–45.

The advantages and disadvantages of structure in observation are very similar to those in communication. Structuring the observation reduces the potential for bias and increases the reliability of observations. However, the reduction in bias may be accompanied by a loss of validity, since the number of seconds spent in deliberation or the number of boxes of detergent picked up and examined may not represent the complete story of deliberation and search.[60] What about the effort spent simply looking at what is available but not picking them up, or the discussion between husband and wife as to which detergent to select? A well-trained, highly qualified observer might be able to interpret these kinds of behavior and relate them in a meaningful way to search and deliberation.

The major problem of behavioral observation is the observer himself. . . . In behavioral observation the observer is both a crucial strength and a crucial weakness. Why? The observer must digest the information derived from observations and then make inferences about constructs. . . . The strength and the weakness of the procedure is the observer's powers of inference. If it were not for inference, a machine observer would be better than a human observer. The strength is that the observer can relate the observed behavior to the constructs or variables of a study: he brings behavior and construct together.[61]

Disguised–Undisguised Observation

Disguise in observational methods refers to whether the subjects know they are being observed. In the search and deliberation study, observers may assume a position well out of the way so shoppers are not aware that their behavior is being observed. In some cases, the disguise is accomplished by observers becoming part of the situation with the other participants unaware of this role. One firm, for example, uses observers disguised as shoppers to assess package designs. The observers record such things as how long shoppers spend in the display area, whether they have difficulty finding the product, and whether the information on the package appeared hard to read.[62] Other retailers are increasingly turning to on-site cameras not only to assess package designs but also to make general improvements in counter space and floor displays and to study traffic flows.[63] Still others are using paid observers disguised as shoppers to evaluate sales service with respect to promptness of service and the attitudes and courtesy of the employees.[64]

---

[60]For a detailed account of the advantages and disadvantages associated with making direct observations of purchasing behavior, complete with examples of the kinds of interpretation problems that arise, see William D. Wells and Leonard A. Lo Scinto, "Direct Observation of Purchasing Behavior," *Journal of Marketing Research,* 3 (August 1966), pp. 227–233.

[61]Kerlinger, *Foundations,* p. 487.

[62]David A. Schwartz, "Research Can Help Solve Packaging Functional and Design Problems," *Marketing News,* 9 (January 16, 1976), p. 8.

[63]"On-Site's Cameras Focus on the Retail Marketplace," *Marketing News,* 18 (November 9, 1984), p. 46.

[64]Larry Gulledge, "Evaluation Services Pay Off in Bigger Bottom Lines," *Marketing News,* 18 (October 12, 1984), p. 30.

The reason the observer's presence is disguised, of course, is to control the tendency for people to behave differently when they know their actions are being watched. There are at least two practical questions that can be raised about the disguised observation, though. First, it is often very difficult to disguise an observation completely, and second, identifying oneself as a research worker often increases one's ability to secure other relevant information such as background data. There is also, though, an ethical question associated with disguised observation.

> . . . the investigator who proposes to enter a situation without revealing his research purpose has an obligation to ask himself whether there is any possibility that his disguised activities will harm any of the people in the situation and if so, whether the potential results of his research are valuable enough to justify their acquisition under these circumstances.[65]

Disguised observations may be made *directly* or *indirectly*. An observer stationed at the checkout counter counting the number of boxes of each brand of detergent being purchased would be engaged in direct observation. However, an observer who counted inventory on hand by brand at the end of each day and adjusted the results for additions to inventory would be engaged in indirect observation. The key is that instead of observing the behavior itself, the researcher is observing the *effects or results* of that behavior.

There are many types of indirect observation.[66] One could, for example, derive measures of share of market for the various brands of detergent by conducting pantry audits. In a pantry audit, respondents' homes would be visited and permission would be sought to examine the ''pantry inventory'' and determine the presence and amount of various brands of detergent. While one would typically not incur the expense of a pantry audit for a single product, the audit could be used to advantage to assess consumption of a prespecified set of products.

Over the years, a number of innovative, indirect measures of behavior have been developed. For example, a car dealer in Chicago checked the position of the radio dial of each car brought in for service. The dealer then used this as a proxy for share of listening audience in deciding upon the stations on which to advertise. Similarly, the number of different fingerprints on a page has been used to assess the readership of various ads in a magazine, and the age and condition of the cars in the parking lot has been used to gauge the affluence of the group patronizing the outlet.[67]

---

[65]Selltiz, Wrightsman, and Cook, *Research Methods,* p. 218.

[66]For insight into some of the many ingenious ways that have been developed to make indirect measurements by observation, see Eugene J. Webb, *et al., Unobtrusive Measures: Nonreactive Research in the Social Sciences* (Chicago: Rand McNally, 1966); Lee Sechrest, *New Directions for Methodology of Behavior Science: Unobtrusive Measurement Today* (San Francisco: Jossey-Bass, 1979); and Thomas J. Bouchard, Jr., ''Unobtrusive Measures: An Inventory of Uses,'' *Sociological Methods and Research* (February 1976), pp. 267–301.

[67]See Bouchard, ''Unobtrusive Measures,'' for a relatively detailed list of studies using indirect measures of behavior.

In an ongoing study, a group of professors and students at the University of Arizona are studying the behavior of consumers by sifting through the waste at the city dump.[68] In 1975, there were over 100 people spending at least three hours per week at the dump sifting garbage and systematically recording what they observed. Some of the more interesting findings to date are:

After four years of poking through the city's trash, the crews have found that the average family wastes about 10% of the food it buys . . . the middle class wastes more than either the rich or the poor . . . when the price of a product is rising, people tend to throw away more of it, not less.[69]

When asked directly, people tended to report much less waste than this. Observation is often more useful than surveys in sorting fact from fiction with respect to desirable behaviors. For example, a group of electric utilities secured permission from 150 households to put TV cameras into the homes when their projections of energy usage continually fell short of reality. The cameras, which were focused on the thermostat, revealed that what people said and what they did were vastly different. They said they set the thermostats at 68 degrees and left them there. It turned out that they fiddled with them all the time. "Older relatives and kids—especially teenagers—tended to turn them up, and so did cleaning ladies. Even visitors did it. In a lot of homes, it was guerrilla warfare over the thermostat between the person who paid the bill and everyone else."[70]

Natural Setting–Contrived Setting Observation

Observations may be obtained either in natural or contrived settings. The former may be "completely" natural, or there may be an induced experimental manipulation. In the search and deliberation study, for example, we may simply choose to study the amount of these activities that normally go into the purchase of detergents. Alternatively, we may have introduced some point-of-purchase display materials and might be interested in measuring their effectiveness. One measure of effectiveness might be the amount of search and deliberation they stimulate for the particular brand being promoted. Both of these studies could take place in a supermarket, which would be the natural setting. Alternatively, we could bring a group of people into a controlled environment, where they might engage in some simulated shopping behavior. We might have established a detergent display in this controlled environment and might study the degree of deliberation and search of each participant as he or she proceeds to make the purchase choices.

The advantage of the laboratory environment is that we are better able to control extraneous influences that might affect the interpretation of what happened; for example, shoppers in a natural setting pause to visit with their neighbors while deliberating over

---

[68]William L. Rathje, Wilson W. Hughes, and Sherry L. Jernigan, "The Science of Garbage: Following the Consumer through His Garbage Can," in William Locander, ed., *Marketing Looks Outward* (Chicago: American Marketing Association, 1977), pp. 56–64.

[69]In Tucson, Students Are Down in Dumps, But Most Are Happy," *Wall Street Journal,* 55 (December 5, 1975), pp. 1 and 25.

[70]Frederick C. Klein, "Researcher Probes Consumers Using 'Anthropological Skills,' " *Wall Street Journal,* 63 (July 7, 1983), p. 21.

which detergent to buy. If we were measuring the time spent in deliberation, this interruption could raise havoc with the accuracy of the measurement. The disadvantage of the laboratory setting is that the contrived setting itself may cause differences in behavior and thus raise real questions about the external validity of the findings.

A contrived setting, though, also has a tendency to speed the data collection process, result in lower-cost research, and allow the use of more objective measurements.[71] The researcher need not wait for events to occur, but rather instructs the participants to engage in the needed kind of behavior. This means that a great many observations may be made in a short period of time; perhaps an entire study can be completed in a couple of days or a week. This can substantially reduce costs. The laboratory also allows the greater use of electrical and/or mechanical equipment than does the natural setting and thereby frees the measurement from the observer's selective processes.

Human–Mechanical Observation

Much scientific observation is of the pencil-and-paper variety. One or more individuals are trained to systematically observe a phenomenon and to record on the observational form the specific events that took place.

DuPont, for example, relies on a human observer to deal with one of the most difficult problems it faces in its automotive paint division, color matching. It seems that no matter how much time and energy goes into the metal repair work after an accident, the slightest difference in color shading upsets the customer. There is no problem in matching colors for domestic cars, since new models are introduced each fall in an orderly fashion and factory color information is available well before the vehicles reach the showrooms. New models of imported cars reach dealer showrooms on a much more random basis throughout the year, though, and having paint shades available for their repair is a much greater problem. DuPont handles this problem via Charlie Smith, who operates out of a dockside laboratory at Jacksonville, Florida, the port of entry for thousands of imported cars each month. Smith not only has all the equipment that is necessary to mix colors to match the cars outside, but he also has a direct computer hook-up to DuPont's Troy, Michigan, laboratory, where the formulas for 17,000 different colors are stored.

DuPont has formulas to match almost any color I see coming ashore," reports Smith. "As each new color arrives, I spray out the DuPont formula on a test panel and compare it to the new car. If the spray-out matches the color, I report this to our Troy lab to verify the formula already in the computer. If it doesn't match, I go back to my lab and make adjustments in the formula.

This may take a few hours or a few days, but once satisfied with the match, Smith relays the new formula directly to the Troy computer. This information then is distributed to body shops through DuPont's Refinish sales network.[72]

---

[71]Roger D. Blackwell, James S. Hensel, Michael B. Phillips, and Brian Sternthal, *Laboratory Equipment for Marketing Research* (Dubuque, Iowa: Kendall/Hunt, 1970), pp. 7–8.

[72]"Mixing and Matching," *Special Report News from DuPont of Interest to the College Community,* 76 (November–December 1982), p. 18.

Electrical and/or mechanical observation also has its place in marketing research. In the last chapter, we saw, for example, that television ratings use data collected by an Audimeter®, an electronic device that is attached to a participant's TV set to indicate when the set is on and to which channel it is tuned. Several firms are experimenting with people meters, which attempt to measure not only the channels to which a set is tuned but who in the household is watching. Each member in the family has his or her own viewing number, which is entered when the set is first turned on if they are watching, when channels are changed, and in response to other prompts from the people meter. All of this information is transmitted immediately to the central computer for processing.[73]

The optical scanner, which has automated the checkout process at many stores and which was reviewed in the last chapter, is another electronic device having a tremendous impact on marketing research involving products sold in grocery stores. Since scanners can keep track of the item movement of every item that is scanned, they allow retailers and manufacturers to receive prompt sales feedback on ads, point-of-purchase displays, special promotions, special prices, and so on.[74]

Some other electrical/mechanical devices used in marketing research—the psycho-galvanometer, tachistoscope, and eye camera—are commonly used in copy research.[75]

The **galvanometer** is used to measure the emotional arousal induced by an exposure to specific advertising copy. It records changes in the electrical resistance of the skin associated with the minute degree of sweating that accompanies emotional arousal. The subject is fitted with small electrodes to monitor electrical resistance and is shown different advertising copy, for example. The strength of the current induced is then used to infer the subject's interest or attitude toward the copy.[76]

The **tachistoscope** is a device that provides the researcher timing control over a visual stimulus. The exposure interval may range from less than one hundredth of a second to several seconds. After each exposure, respondents are asked to describe everything they saw and what it meant. By systematically varying the exposure, the

---

[73]For discussions of the operation of the people meter and experiments testing its effectiveness, see Elizabeth Berry, "Nielsen May Face U.K. Rival in Researching TV Audiences," *Wall Street Journal,* 64 (February 2, 1984), p. 31; and Fred Gardner, "Acid Test for the People Meter," *Marketing and Media Decisions,* 19 (April 1984), pp. 74–75 and 115.

[74]For general discussions of the impact scanners are having on marketing research for frequently purchased items, see Edward Tauber, "Checkout Scanner Ultimately a Marketing Data Goldmine," *Marketing News,* 13 (May 18, 1979), pp. 1–13; Jack J. Honomichl, "Turning a Dream into a Reality," *Advertising Age,* 52 (February 9, 1981), pp. 54–59; "Checkout Scanners Soon Will Revolutionize Market Research Packaged Goods Marketing," *Marketing News,* 14 (December 12, 1980), p. 5; Derek Bloom, "Point of Sale Scanners and Their Implications for Market Research," *Journal of the Market Research Society,* 22 (October 1980), pp. 221–238; "Supermarket Scanners Get Smarter," *Business Week* (August 17, 1981), pp. 88, 91–92; Carol Posten, "Scanning the Market for Changes in Tempo," *Advertising Age,* 53 (February 22, 1982), pp. M19–M20; and Fern Schumer, "The New Magicians of Market Research," *Fortune,* 108 (July 25, 1983), pp. 72–74.

[75]A succinct overview of examples of this equipment, as well as many other types, and the problems encountered in their use can be found in Blackwell, Hensel, Phillips, and Sternthal, *Laboratory Equipment.*

[76]A review of 118 studies on involuntary responses to advertising found that pupil dilation, skin moisture, and heart rate are the most commonly used. See Paul J. Watson and Robert J. Gatchel, "Autonomic Measures of Advertising," *Journal of Advertising Research,* 19 (June 1979), pp. 15–26.

researcher is able to measure how quickly and accurately a particular stimulus (ad) can be perceived and interpreted. Note, though, that the use of a verbal reply implies that the tachistoscope is not a mechanical observer but rather a mechanical means of presenting stimuli.

The **eye camera** is employed to study eye movements while reading advertising copy. The original eye cameras utilized a light that was positioned to strike the cornea of the subject's eye, from which it was reflected to a moving film. The reflected light traced eye movements on the film. The researcher had to then project the film, frame-by-frame, while manually recording eye movements on a sheet of paper. Since the mid-1970s, though, computers have been developed that can automatically perform this analysis from videotape. There have also been significant advances in the cameras themselves. Some of the new videocameras are so small now, weighing only a few ounces, that they can be clipped to a respondent's eyeglasses. The visual record produced as an individual reads an advertisement, for example, allows the detailed study of the person's behavior. What points did the individual perceive first? How long did the person linger on a given item? Did the individual read all the copy or part of it? The small video cameras that follow the path of the eye have also been used to analyze package designs, billboards, and displays in the aisles of supermarkets.[77]

Two other "mechanical observers" that promise to provide useful supplementary information in telephone interviews–response latency and voice pitch analysis—owe their current popularity to mechanical/electronic recorders and the computer's ability to diagnose what is recorded. **Response latency** is the amount of time a respondent deliberates before answering a question. Since response time seems to be directly related to the respondent's uncertainty in the answer, it assists in assessing the individual's strength of preference when choosing among alternatives. It thus provides a very unobtrusive measure of brand preference, for example, or ambiguity experienced by a respondent in answering a particular question. The measure depends upon a voice-operated relay that triggers an electronic stopwatch. When an interviewer approaches the end of a question, he or she simply presses a pedal that sets the stopwatch to zero and alerts the electronic mechanism to listen for the offset (end of the question) of the interviewer's voice. The stopwatch is automatically triggered at the offset. The moment the respondent begins answering, the watch is stopped by the voice-operated relay system and a digital readout system indicates response latency to the interviewer, who can then record the deliberation time on the interview form. Note there are several advantages in such a system. First, the method provides an accurate response latency measure without respondents being aware that this dimension of behavior is being recorded. Second, since the time is measured by an automatic device, the technique does not make

---

[77]For discussions of the operation and use of eye camera technology to study the effectiveness of ads, packages, and displays, see J. E. Russo, "Eye Fixation Can Save the World," in H. K. Hunt, ed., *Advances in Consumer Research* (Ann Arbor, Mich.: Association for Consumer Research, 1978), pp. 561–570; J. Treistman and J. P. Gregg, "Visual, Verbal, and Sales Response to Print Ads," *Journal of Advertising Research,* 19 (August 1979), pp. 41–47; "Determining How Ads Are Seen," *Dun's Business Month,* 119 (February 1982), pp. 85–86; "Recall Scores Are Giving Short Shrift to Outdoor Ads, Study Finds," *Marketing News,* 18 (November 23, 1984), p. 16; and "Study Disputes Earlier Findings," *Marketing News,* 19 (May 24, 1985), pp. 1 and 38.

the interviewer's task any more difficult, nor does it appreciably lengthen the interview.[78]

For example, DuPont, with little additional effort in an otherwise routine research survey, used response latency to assess brand awareness and prospects' perception of quality of an industrial product in which there were many competitive brands.[79]

Voice pitch analysis relies on the same basic premise as the galvanometer: subjects experience a number of involuntary physiological reactions, such as changes in blood pressure, rate of perspiration, or heart rate, when emotionally aroused by external or internal stimuli. **Voice pitch analysis** examines changes in the relative vibration frequency of the human voice that accompanies emotional arousal. All individuals function at a certain physiological pace, called the baseline. The baseline in voice analysis is established by engaging the respondent in unemotional conversation that is recorded. Deviations from the baseline level indicate that the respondent has reacted to the stimulus question. These deviations can be assessed by special audioadapted computer equipment that can measure the abnormal frequencies in the voice caused by changes in the nervous system, changes that may not be discernable to the human ear. A net reaction score can be generated by comparing the abnormal frequency produced by the stimulus to the person's normal frequency. The greater the difference, the greater the emotional intensity of the subject's reaction is said to be. Voice pitch analysis has at least two advantages over other physiological reaction techniques. First, these techniques measure the intensity but not the direction of feeling. With voice pitch analysis, the "recording of the physical phenomenon (voice pitch) occurs simultaneously with the subject's conscious interpretation of the attitude (verbal response); the direction (positive or negative) of the attitude is ascertained from the subject's self-report, while the intensity of the emotion is measured at the same time by mechanical means."[80] Second, while the measurement of blood pressure, pulse rate, psychogalvanic response, or other physiological reactions requires subjects be connected to the equipment, voice pitch analysis allows a much more natural interaction between researcher and participant. This tends to make it less time-consuming and expensive to use.[81]

---

[78]For general discussions of the use of response latency measures in marketing research, see James MacLachlan, John Czepiel, and Priscilla LaBarbera, "Implementation of Response Latency Measures," *Journal of Marketing Research,* 16 (November 1979), pp. 573–577; James MacLachlan and Priscilla LaBarbera, "Response Latency in Telephone Interviews," *Journal of Advertising Research,* 19 (June 1979), pp. 49–56; Tyzoon T. Tyebjee, "Response Latency: A New Measure for Scaling Brand Preference," *Journal of Marketing Research,* 16 (February 1979), pp. 96–101; and David A. Aaker, Richard P. Bagozzi, James M. Carman, and James M. MacLachlan, "On Using Response Latency to Measure Preference," *Journal of Marketing Research,* 17 (May 1980), pp. 237–244.

[79]Robert C. Grass, Wallace H. Wallace, and Samuel Zuckerkandel, "Response Latency in Industrial Advertising Research," *Journal of Advertising Research,* 20 (December 1980), pp. 63–65.

[80]Nancy Nischwonger and Claude R. Martin, "On Using Voice Analysis in Marketing Research," *Journal of Marketing Research,* 18 (August 1981), pp. 350–355.

[81]For general discussions of the use of voice pitch analysis in marketing research, see *ibid.,* or see Ronald G. Nelson and David Schwartz, "Voice Pitch Analysis," *Journal of Advertising Research,* 19 (October 1979), pp. 55–59; Glen A. Buckman, "Uses of Voice-Pitch Analysis," *Journal of Advertising Research,* 20 (April 1980), pp. 69–73; and Linda Edwards, "Hearing What Consumers Really Feel," *Across the Board,* 17 (April 1980), pp. 62–67.

At the other extreme, **brain wave research,** which is in its infancy and which is surrounded by a good deal of controversy, requires a rather elaborate hookup of the subject to equipment. The purpose is to assess the stimuli that subjects find arousing or interesting. To do this, subjects are fitted with electrodes that monitor the electrical impulses emitted by the brain as the subject is exposed to various stimuli. While the two hemispheres of the brain seem to respond differently to specific stimuli, with the right hemisphere responding more to emotional stimuli, the full implications of this for the study of consumer behavior and for the practice of marketing research are less clear.[82]

As mentioned, electrical/mechanical equipment frees the observation from the observer's selective processes. This is both its major strength and major weakness. Certainly recording when a TV set is turned on and to what channel it is tuned, for example, can be accomplished much more accurately by the Audimeter® than it can by other means. The fact the set is tuned to a particular channel does not say anything, though, about whether anyone is watching, the number that might be watching, or their level of interest. A trained human observer's record might be more difficult to analyze, and it might be less objective, but his or her powers of integration could certainly produce a more valid assessment of what occurred. The essential point is that the marketing researcher needs to be aware of the electrical/mechanical equipment that is available so that he or she can make an informed choice as to whether a piece of equipment might make a better observer than a human in a given instance (or vice versa) or whether a combination approach might be most productive.

Summary

A researcher who cannot find the data needed in secondary sources resorts to primary data collection. The types of primary data of interest to marketing researchers include demographic/socioeconomic characteristics, psychological/life-style characteristics, attitudes/opinions, awareness/knowledge, intentions, motivation, and behavior of individuals and groups.

Communication and observation are the two basic means of obtaining primary data. Communication involves the direct questioning of respondents, while observation entails the systematic checking of appropriate facts or actions. Observation is the much more limited approach. It can be used to secure behavioral primary data and some demographic/socioeconomic and life-style characteristics, and has the advantage of accuracy over communication methods. Observation is not useful, though, for measuring attitudes, awareness, knowledge, intentions, or motivation. When these constructs are of interest, communication methods must be used, although mechanical devices are sometimes employed to assist in interpreting attitudes.

---

[82]For general discussions of the status of brain wave research, see F. Hansen, ''Hemispherical Lateralization: Implications for Understanding Consumer Behavior,'' *Journal of Consumer Research,* 8 (June 1981), pp. 23–36; and A. Weinstein, ''A Review of Brain Hemisphere Research,'' *Journal of Advertising Research,* 22 (June/July 1982), pp. 59–63.

Communication methods may be classified by their degree of structure, degree of disguise, and method of administration. A structured questionnaire has a well-defined sequence and standardized response categories. It is most productively used for testing specific hypotheses, as would occur in descriptive or causal research. When the research is exploratory, unstructured questionnaires can be used. In an unstructured questionnaire, the response categories are not predetermined; the respondents are allowed to answer in their own terms.

The disguised questionnaire attempts to hide the purpose of the research from the respondent. This is particularly important on sensitive issues where there may be a temptation to give the socially accepted response.

Questionnaires can be administered by personal interview, over the phone, or by mail. Each approach has some general advantages and disadvantages, which may or may not occur in a specific study. The methods were compared in terms of the control they offer the researcher with respect to sample, information, and administration. They should not be considered mutually exclusive data collection methods, but can often be used more productively in combination.

Observation methods can also be classified by several criteria including degree of structure and degree of disguise as well as by the "naturalness" of the setting and whether human or mechanical devices are employed to secure the data. The arguments for structure and disguise here parallel those for communication.

Most observations in marketing research are probably obtained in a completely natural setting, although certain types of observations are regularly obtained in contrived or laboratory settings using electrical/mechanical equipment. The laboratory setting allows greater control of extraneous influences and thus may be more internally valid, although less externally valid. Electrical/mechanical measuring instruments permit more objective, reliable measurements by eliminating the opportunity for a human observer's selective processes to operate. They also eliminate the human observer's integrative powers, though, and in this respect may be less valid.

Questions

1. What types of primary data are of most interest to marketing researchers? How are they distinguished?

2. What are the general advantages and disadvantages associated with obtaining information by questioning or by observation? Which method provides more control over the sample?

3. What is a disguised questionnaire? What is a structured questionnaire?

4. What are the advantages and disadvantages of structured–undisguised questionnaires? Of unstructured–undisguised questionnaires?

5. What is a focused group interview? For what type of research is it likely to be most productive?

6. What is the rationale for employing unstructured–disguised stimuli? What is a word association test? A sentence completion test? A storytelling test?

7. What operating principle or assumption underlies the use of structured–disguised questionnaires? What are the advantages and disadvantages associated with structured–disguised questionnaires?

8. How do mail, telephone, and personally administered questionnaires differ with respect to
   (a) sampling control
   (b) information control
   (c) administrative control?

9. How can observational methods be classified? What are the key distinctions among the various types?

10. What principle underlies the use of a galvanometer? What is a tachistocope? What is an eye camera? What is an optical scanner?

11. What does response latency assess? How is it measured?

12. What is voice pitch analysis? What does it measure?

Applications and Problems

Should the communication or observational method be used in the situations captured in Questions 1 and 2? (Justify your choice. Also specify the degree of structure and disguise that should be used.)

1. In 1985, the Metal Product Division of Geni Ltd. devised a special metal container to store plastic garbage bags. Plastic bags posed household problems, as they gave off unpleasant odors, looked disorderly, and provided a breeding place for insects. The container overcame these problems as it had a bag-support apparatus that held the bag open for filling and sealed the bag when the lid was closed. In addition, there was enough storage area for at least four full bags. The product was priced at $53.81 and was sold through hardware stores. The company had done little advertising and relied on in-store promotion and displays. The divisional manager was wondering about the effectiveness of these displays. She has called on you to do the necessary research.

2. Cardworth is a national manufacturer and distributor of greeting cards. The company recently began distributing a lower-priced line of cards that was made possible by using a lower-grade paper. Quality differences between the higher and lower-priced cards did not seem to be noticeable to laypeople. The company followed a policy of printing its name and the price on the back of each card. The initial acceptance of the new line of cards convinced the Vice-President of Production, Bill Murray, that they should use this lower grade paper for all their cards and increase their profit margin from 12.3% to 14.9%. The sales manager was strongly opposed to this move and commented, ''Bill, consumers are concerned about the quality of greeting cards, a price difference of 5 cents on a card does not matter.'' The vice-president has called upon you to undertake the study.

Which survey method (mail, telephone, personal) would you use for the situations captured in Questions 3 through 7? Justify your choice.

3. Administration of a questionnaire to determine the number of people who listened to the ''100 Top Country Tunes in 1986'' a program that aired on December 31, 1986?

4.   Administration of a questionnaire to determine the number of households having a mentally ill individual and a history of mental illness in the household.

5.   Administration of a questionnaire by a national manufacturer of microwave ovens in order to test people's attitudes and opinions toward a new model.

6.   Administration of a questionnaire by a local drycleaner who wants to determine customers' satisfaction with a recent discount scheme.

7.   Administration of a questionnaire by the management of a small hotel that wants to assess customers' opinions of their service.

Chapter 7
Data Collection
Forms

In the previous chapter the various types of questionnaires and observation forms and their methods of administration were discussed. The general advantages and disadvantages of using communication and observational methods, as well as the pros and cons associated with the many specific types of questionnaire or observational methods, were also dealt with. This chapter builds on that discussion. It reviews the procedures to follow in developing a questionnaire or observational data collection form.

Questionnaire Design

Although much progress has been made, designing questionnaires is still an art and not a science. Much of the progress has been in the form of admonitions, such as "Avoid leading questions" or "Avoid ambiguous questions." It is much easier to embrace the admonitions than it is to develop questions that are indeed not leading or ambiguous. Nevertheless, Figure 7.1 offers a method the beginning researcher can use to develop questionnaires. More experienced researchers would be expected to develop their own patterns, although the steps listed in Figure 7.1[1] would still be part of that pattern.

While the stages of development are presented here in sequence, researchers will rarely be so fortunate as to develop a questionnaire in step-by-step fashion. A more typical development will involve some iteration and looping. The researcher finds that the possible wordings of a response do not secure the content decided upon, or that the content is not completely consistent with the information desired. This discovery, of course, would require a loop back to an earlier stage to make the necessary changes. Researchers should not be surprised, then, if they find themselves working back and forth among some of the stages. That is natural.

Researchers should also be warned not to take the stages too literally. They are presented as a guide or a checklist. With questionnaires, the proof of the pudding is very much in the eating. Does the questionnaire produce accurate data of the kind needed? Blind adherence to procedure is no substitute for creativity in approach, nor is

---

[1]This procedure is adapted from one suggested by Arthur Kornhauser and Paul B. Sheatsley, "Questionnaire Construction and Interview Procedure," in Claire Selltiz, Lawrence S. Wrightsman, and Stuart W. Cook, *Research Methods in Social Relations,* 3rd ed. (New York: Holt, Rinehart and Winston, 1976), pp. 541–573.

Figure 7.1
Procedure for Developing a Questionnaire

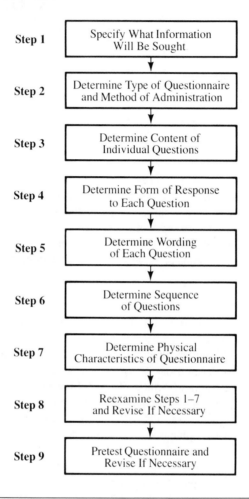

Step 1 — Specify What Information Will Be Sought

Step 2 — Determine Type of Questionnaire and Method of Administration

Step 3 — Determine Content of Individual Questions

Step 4 — Determine Form of Response to Each Question

Step 5 — Determine Wording of Each Question

Step 6 — Determine Sequence of Questions

Step 7 — Determine Physical Characteristics of Questionnaire

Step 8 — Reexamine Steps 1–7 and Revise If Necessary

Step 9 — Pretest Questionnaire and Revise If Necessary

it any substitute for a pretest (Step 9 of Figure 7.1) with which one can discover if the typical respondent indeed understands each question and is able and willing to supply the information sought.

Information Sought

Deciding what information will be sought is easy, to the extent that researchers have been meticulous and precise at earlier stages in the research process. By the same token, if researchers have been sloppy and careless, the decision will prove difficult. Both descriptive and causal research demand sufficient prior knowledge to allow the framing of some specific hypotheses for investigation, which then guide the research. The hypotheses also guide the questionnaire. They determine what information will be sought, and from whom, because they specify what relationships will be investigated. If researchers have heeded the earlier admonition to establish ''dummy tables'' to structure the data analysis, their job of determining what information is to be collected is essentially complete. Researchers must collect information on the variables specified in the dummy tables in order to investigate these hypotheses. Further, researchers must collect this information from the right people and in the right units. The hypotheses, then, will not only be a guide as to what information will be sought but in large part will also determine the type of question and form of response used to collect it.

This is not meant to deny that the preparation of the questionnaire itself may suggest further hypotheses and other relationships that might be investigated at slight additional effort and cost. A most important warning is in order here. If the new hypothesis is indeed vital to understanding the phenomenon, by all means include it and use it to advantage when designing the questionnaire. On the other hand, and we are repeating ourselves, if it simply represents one of those potentially ''interesting findings'' but is not vital to the research effort, forget it. The inclusion of ''interesting but not vital'' items simply lengthens the questionnaire, causes problems in administration and analysis, and often increases nonresponse.

The exploratory research effort is, of course, aimed at the discovery of ideas and insights and not at their systematic investigation. The questionnaire for an exploratory study is, therefore, loosely structured, with only a rough idea of the kind of information that might be sought. This is particularly true at the earliest stages of exploratory research. It is also true, but to a lesser extent, at the later stages of exploratory research, when the emphasis is on determining the priorities that should be given to various hypotheses in guiding future research.

Type of Questionnaire and Method of Administration

After specifying the basic information that will be sought, the researcher needs to specify how it will be gathered. The *how* requires decisions with respect to the structure and disguise to be used in the questionnaire and whether it will be administered by mail, telephone, or personal interviews. We saw in the last chapter that these decisions are not independent. If the researcher decides on a disguised–unstructured questionnaire using a picture stimulus storytelling format, this precludes straight telephone administration and raises serious questions about a mail administration of the instrument.[2] Similarly, mail administration is not recommended for unstructured–undisguised questionnaires with open-ended questions, particularly if they should have probes.

The type of data to be collected will have an important effect, of course, on these questions. A researcher investigating the relationship between some behavior and a series of demographic characteristics (for example, how is dishwasher ownership related to income, age, family size, and so on?) might use either mail, telephone, or personal interviews to gather the data. The methods would not be equally attractive because of cost and other considerations, but they all could be used. On the other hand, a researcher interested in measuring attitudes could not use all of the methods, although

---

[2]The two methods might possibly be used in combination through the locked-box approach.

which could or could not be used would depend largely on previous decisions regarding structure and disguise. A decision to use a lengthy attitude scale, for example, would preclude a telephone administration, although it would allow the collection of data by either mail or personal interview. On the other hand, an open-ended questionnaire on attitudes would raise serious questions about mail administration. Thus, the researcher must specify precisely what primary data are needed, how these data might be collected, what degree of structure and disguise will be used, and how the questionnaire will be administered.

Figure 7.2 on pages 275–278 offers an example. The primary data at issue are use of 6-volt batteries and attitudes and purchase intentions toward a 6-volt battery recharger. The questions are all very structured and undisguised. The questionnaire is to be administered by mail, using part of the NFO panel. Note the ease with which most of the responses could be tabulated, although the statements about likes and dislikes would prove difficult to code and tabulate.

Individual Question Content

The researcher's previous decisions regarding information needed, the structure and disguise to be imposed on its collection, and the method for administering the questionnaire will largely control the decisions regarding individual question content. But the researcher can and should ask some additional questions.[3]

Is the Question Necessary?   Suppose an issue is important. Then the researcher needs to ask whether the point has been adequately covered by other questions. If not, a new question is in order. The question should then be framed to secure an answer with the required detail, but not an answer with more detail than needed. Very often in marketing, for example, we employ the concept of stage in the life cycle to explore family consumption behavior. Stage in the life cycle is a composite variable in which the various stages are defined in terms of marital status, presence of children, and the ages of the children. The presence of children is important because it indicates a dependency relationship, particularly if the youngest child is under 6 and thus represents one type of responsibility or is over 6 but under 17, representing another type of responsibility for the parents. In a study using stage in the life cycle as a variable, there is no need to ask the age of each child. Rather, all that is needed is one question aimed at securing the age of the youngest child if there are any children. Once again the role of the hypotheses and dummy tables is obvious when designing the questionnaire.

---

[3]These questions were suggested by Kornhauser and Sheatsley, "Questionnaire Construction." For a systematic treatment of questionnaire construction, see the classic work by Stanley L. Payne, *The Art of Asking Questions* (Princeton, N.J.: Princeton University Press, 1951). Three other good general sources are A. N. Oppenheim, *Questionnaire Design and Attitude Measurement* (New York: Basic Books, 1966); Douglas R. Berdie and John F. Anderson, *Questionnaires: Design and Use* (Metuchen, N.J.: Scarecrow Press, 1974); and Seymour Sudman and Norman M. Bradburn, *Asking Questions: A Practical Guide to Questionnaire Design* (San Francisco: Jossey-Bass, 1982). For specific suggestions on the construction of mail and telephone questionnaires, see Paul L. Erdos, *Professional Mail Surveys* (Malabar, Fla.: Robert E. Krieger, 1983); and A. B. Blankenship, *Professional Telephone Surveys* (New York: McGraw-Hill, 1977). For a general bibliography on questionnaire construction, see Wayne G. Daniel, *Questionnaire Design: A Selected Bibliography for the Survey Researcher* (Monticello, Ill.: Vance Bibliographics, 1979).

Figure 7.2
Cover Letter and Mail Questionnaire for 6-Volt Battery Study

National Family Opinion, Inc.

CONSUMER MARKET RESEARCH SINCE 1946

444 N. MICHIGAN AVENUE

CHICAGO, ILLINOIS 60611

TELEPHONE | AREA CODE 312
467-5222

Dear Homemaker:

Today's questionnaire is about 6-VOLT LANTERN BATTERIES. Please give this questionnaire to the person in your family who is most responsible for purchasing 6-VOLT LANTERN BATTERIES.

TO THE PERSON WHO IS MOST RESPONSIBLE FOR PURCHASING 6-VOLT LANTERN-TYPE BATTERIES:

This questionnaire is about a new 6-Volt Lantern Battery with a recharger. I would like for you to read the descriptions, look at the pictures and then give me your opinions of the battery and recharger. Remember, it is just as important for me to know what you DO NOT like about the ideas as it is to know what you like about them.

After you have answered all my questions, please return this questionnaire in the enclosed postage-paid envelope.

Thank you so much for your help!

Sincerely,

Carol Adams

TOLEDO (HOME OFFICE): P.O. BOX 315 43691   NEW YORK: 630 THIRD AVENUE 10017
WEST COAST: 43 QUAIL COURT, WALNUT CREEK, CALIF. 94596

Source: Courtesy Ray-O-Vac Corporation.

continued on next page

1. *During the past 12 months, have you, or any member of your family (living at home) purchased a 6-VOLT LANTERN BATTERY?*

   ☐ Yes—Continue ⟶   ☐ NO—Stop here, return questionnaire!

2. a) *In Column "A", please write in the number of 6-Volt lantern batteries your family purchased during the past 12 months for each of the devices listed on the left.*

   b) *In Column "B" for each of the devices you bought 6-volt lantern batteries for, please write in the number of batteries that fit into that device at one time.*

	Number of 6-Volt Lantern Batteries purchased for this device in the past 12 months.	Number of 6-Volt Lantern Batteries that fit into this device at one time.
Toy	____	____
Lantern	____	____
Depth/Fish Finder	____	____
Lighting Device	____	____
Garden Tool	____	____
Alarm/Security Device	____	____
Other (Specify): ____	____	____
____	____	____

3. *Below are pictures of a new type of 6-Volt Lantern Battery and Recharger. This battery is the same size and works the same way as the 6-Volt lantern battery you usually purchase. However, this battery is* rechargeable. *When the battery wears down all you do is plug the charger into a regular household electrical outlet and put the battery upside down in the charger for an overnight recharge. This battery is made by a leading U.S. battery manufacturer and is guaranteed for three years or 150 charges (cycles), whichever comes first.*

THE PRODUCT   HOW TO RECHARGE BATTERY

4. *Which of the following phrases best describes your feelings about the type of battery described above?*

   ☐ It's a great idea
   ☐ It's a pretty good idea
   ☐ It's a "so-so" idea
   ☐ It's not a very good idea
   ☐ It's a poor idea

5. *About how much would you expect this lantern-type battery and recharger combination to cost at your local discount store?*

   $_____ for battery and recharger combination

6. *Is there anything that you particularly LIKE about this idea? Please be as specific as possible.*

_____

_____

_____

7. *Is there anything that you particularly DISLIKE about this idea? Please be as specific as possible.*

_____

_____

_____

8. *Let us assume this battery and recharger combination would sell for about $20. Extra rechargeable batteries would cost about $10.*

   Thinking only about the $20 battery and recharger combination, please indicate below how likely you would be to buy it at that price. Please check ONE box.

   ☐ I definitely would buy it ⎤
   ☐ I probably would buy it   ⎬ →Continue with Question 9
   ☐ I might or might not buy it ⎦

   ☐ I probably would not buy it ⎤ → Stop here, return
   ☐ I definitely would not buy it ⎦   questionnaire

9. a) *In Column "A" below, check the device(s) for which you would buy the combination lantern-type battery and recharger.*
   b) *In Column "B" below, check the devices for which you would purchase any* additional *rechargeable batteries mentioned above in Question 8.*
   c) *In Column "C" below, write in the number of additional rechargeable batteries you think you would purchase during the next year for each item you checked in column "B".*

	A Would buy combination lantern-type battery and recharger for this item(s).	B Would purchase *additional* rechargeable batteries for this item(s).	C For item(s) checked in "B", number of *additional* rechargeable batteries I would purchase in next year.
Toy	☐	☐	_____
Lantern.	☐	☐	_____
Depth/Fish Finder	☐	☐	_____
Non-Lantern Lighting Device.	☐	☐	_____
Garden Tool	☐	☐	_____
Alarm/Security Device	☐	☐	_____

continued on next page

Figure 7.2
Cover Letter and Mail Questionnaire for 6-Volt Battery Study *continued*

Other(s) (Specify)
☐ ☐ ___
☐ ☐ ___
_____ ☐ ☐ ___
_____

10. *Suppose that the battery/recharger combination were available just as described in Question 3, except that the charger would charge two batteries at the same time (See Picture B). Also, this new battery charger combination would cost $22 instead of $20.*

A

B

Battery and a charger that
would charge 2 batteries
at one time for $22

Battery and single unit charger for $20

| The Product | How To Recharge Battery | The Product | How To Recharge Battery |

Now, looking at the two different combinations, please indicate which one you would prefer:

☐ Prefer battery and single unit charger for $20 (Illustration "A")
☐ Prefer battery and a charger that would charge 2 batteries at one time for $22 (Illustration "B")

Are Several Questions Needed Instead of One? There will often be situations in which several questions are needed instead of one. Consider the question, "Why do you use Crest?" One respondent may reply, "To reduce cavities," while another may reply, "Because our dentist recommended it." Obviously two different frames of reference are being employed to answer this question. The first respondent is replying in terms of why he is using it now, while the second is replying in terms of how she started using it. It would be better to break this one question down into separate questions that reflect the possible frames of reference that could be used, for example:

☐ *How did you first happen to use Crest?*

☐ *What is your primary reason for using it?*

Do Respondents Have the Necessary Information? The researcher should carefully examine each issue to ascertain whether the typical respondent can be expected to have the information sought. Respondents will give answers. Whether the answers mean anything, though, is another matter. In one public opinion survey, the following question was asked:[4]

Which of the following statements most closely coincides with your opinion of the Metallic Metals Act?

☐ It would be a good move on the part of the United States.

☐ It would be a good thing, but should be left to the individual states.

☐ It is all right for foreign countries, but should not be required here.

☐ It is of no value at all.

☐ No opinion.

The proportion of respondents checking each alternative was, respectively, 21.4 percent, 58.6 percent, 15.7 percent, 4.3 percent, and 0.3 percent. The second alternative captures the prevailing sentiment. Right? Wrong! There was no Metallic Metals Act, and the point of the example is that *most questions will get answers, but the real concern is whether the answers mean anything.*[5] In order for the answers to mean anything, the questions need to mean something to the respondent. This means that, first, the respondent needs to be informed with respect to the issue addressed by the question, and, second, the respondent must remember the information.

Consider the question, "How much does your family spend on groceries in a typical week?" Unless the respondent does the grocery shopping or the family operates with a fairly strict budget, he or she is unlikely to know. In a situation like this, it might be helpful to ask "filter questions" before this question to determine if the individual is indeed likely to have this information. An example filter question might be "Who does the grocery shopping in your family?" It is not unusual, for example, to use filter questions of the sort, "Do you have an opinion on . . .?" before asking about the specific issue in question in opinion surveys. The empirical evidence indicates that providing a filter like this will typically increase the proportion responding "no opinion" by 20 to 25 percentage points.[6]

Not only should the individual have the information sought, but he or she should remember it. Our ability to remember various events is influenced by the event itself and its importance, the length of time since the event, and the presence or absence of

---

[4]Sam Gill, "How Do You Stand on Sin?" *Tide,* 21 (March 14, 1947), p. 72.

[5]There are a number of other examples in the literature that report findings of people having opinions about totally fictional issues like the Metallic Metals Act. See, for example, George F. Bishop, Robert W. Oldendick, Alfred J. Tuchfarber, and S. E. Bennett, "Pseudo-Opinions on Public Affairs," *Public Opinion Quarterly,* 44 (1980), pp. 198–209; Herbert Schuman and Stanley Presser, "Public Opinion and Public Ignorance: The Fine Line Between Attitudes and Nonattitudes," *American Journal of Sociology,* 85 (1980), pp. 1214–1225; and Del J. Hawkins and Kenneth A. Coney, "Uninformed Response Error in Survey Research," *Journal of Marketing Research,* 18 (August 1981), pp. 370–374. The phenomenon is not unique to opinions. It also applies when measuring brand awareness, where it has been observed that the more plausible sounding a brand name, the more likely consumers are to claim they are aware of it even though it does not exist. See " 'Spurious Awareness' Alters Brand Tests," *Wall Street Journal,* 64 (September 13, 1984), p. 29.

[6]Herbert Schuman and Stanley Presser, "The Assessment of 'No Opinions in Attitude Surveys,' " in Karl F. Schnessler, ed., *Sociological Methodology, 1979* (San Francisco: Jossey-Bass, 1979), pp. 241–275. See also George F. Bishop, Robert W. Oldendick, and Alfred J. Tuchfarber, "Effects on Filter Questions in Public Opinion Surveys," *Public Opinion Quarterly,* 47 (Winter 1983), pp. 528–546.

stimuli that assist in recalling it. Important events are more easily remembered than are unimportant events. While most people might be able to remember who shot President John F. Kennedy, the year in which the assassination occurred, or what happened to the assassin, or might be able to recall the first car they ever owned, many of them will be unable to recall the amount of television or the particular shows they watched last Wednesday evening, or the first brand of mouthwash they ever used, when they switched to their current brand, or why they switched. While the switching and use information might be very important to a *brand manager for mouthwashes,* it is unimportant to most individuals, a condition we have to continually keep in mind when designing questionnaires. We need to put outselves in the shoes of the respondent, not those of the product manager, when deciding whether the information is important enough for the individual to remember it.

We also need to recognize that an individual's ability to remember an event is influenced by how long ago it happened. While we might recall the television programs we watched last evening, we might have much greater difficulty remembering those we watched last week on the same evening and might find it all but impossible to recall our viewing pattern of a month ago. The moral of this is that if the event could be considered relatively unimportant to most individuals, we should ask about very recent occurrences of it. For more important events, there are two effects operating in opposite directions that affect a respondent's ability to provide accurate answers about things that happened in some specified time period (for example, how many times the person has seen a doctor in the last six months); these are telescoping error and recall loss. **Telescoping error** refers to the fact that most people remember an event as having occurred more recently than in fact is the case, while **recall loss** means they forget it happened at all. The extent of the two sources of error on the accuracy of the reported information depends on the length of the reference period. For long periods, the telescoping effect is smaller while the recall loss effect is larger. For short periods, the reverse is true. "Thus, for short reference periods, the telescoping error may outweigh the recall loss, while for long periods the reverse will apply; in between there will be a length of reference periods at which the two effects counterbalance each other."[7] Unfortunately, there is no single reference period that can be used to frame questions for all events, because what is optimal depends on the importance of the event to those involved.

A third factor that affects our ability to remember is the stimulus we are given. As we saw in the last chapter, there is a definite increase in retention when a respondent's memory is jogged using a recognition measure rather than an aided recall measure, and the aided recall measure, in turn, produces more "remembering" than an unaided recall measure.

Will Respondents Give the Information?   The situation sometimes arises in which respondents have the necessary information but they will not give it. Their willingness, in turn, seems to be a function of the amount of work involved in producing an answer, their ability to articulate an answer, and the sensitivity of the issue.

---

[7]Graham Kalton and Howard Schuman, "The Effect of the Question on Survey Responses: A Review," *Journal of the Royal Statistical Society, Series A,* 145 (Part 1, 1982), pp. 44–45.

While a purchasing agent may be able to determine to the penny how much the company spent on cleaning compound last year or the relative amount spent on each brand bought, the agent is unlikely to take the time to look up this data to reply to an unsolicited questionnaire. Questionnaire developers need to be constantly mindful of the amount of effort it might take respondents to give the information sought. When the effort is excessive, they may have to settle for approximate answers, or they may be better off omitting the issue completely, since these types of questions tend to irritate respondents and damage their cooperation with the rest of the survey.

When respondents are unable to articulate their answers on an issue, they are likely to ignore it and also refuse to cooperate with the other parts of the survey. Such issues should be avoided, or else the researcher should use a good deal of creative energy designing a mechanism that allows respondents to articulate their views. While they might not be able to express their preferences in car styling, for example, they should be able to indicate the style they like best when shown pictures of different body styles. General Motors used this picture scheme to determine preferences for grill designs when they found that respondents could not articulate their likes and dislikes.[8]

When an issue is embarrassing or otherwise threatening to respondents, they are likely to refuse to cooperate. Such issues should be avoided whenever possible. If that is impossible because the issue is very germane to the study, the researcher needs to pay close attention to how the issue is addressed, particularly with respect to question location and question phrasing. Income, for example, is often a sensitive issue. Respondents' willingness to cooperate depends on how and when the researcher asks for income data. One particularly interesting study investigated the four different versions of the income question shown in Table 7.1 as part of a larger study employing 1,000 telephone interviews. One-fourth of the total sample received each of the four versions. The "less than" and "split point" forms, Versions 3 and 2, produced better cooperation and better income estimation. The two "more than" versions, on the other hand, produced an early response tendency; that is, respondents answered quickly and thus tended to fall in the lower income categories. The general conclusion was that Versions 2 and 3 were less threatening to respondents, while the general admonition was that "researchers should try to design question forms considering both the direction of the expectation and the threat impact of the question."[9]

In general, it is better to address sensitive issues later, rather than earlier, in the survey.[10] Most surveys will produce some initial mistrust in respondents. One has to overcome this skepticism and establish rapport. This is made easier when respondents have the opportunity to warm to the task by answering nonthreatening questions early in the interview, particularly questions that establish the legitimacy of the project.

---

[8]Harper W. Boyd, Jr., Ralph Westfall, and Stanley F. Staasch, *Marketing Research: Text and Cases,* 6th ed. (Homewood, Ill.: Richard D. Irwin, 1985), p. 272.

[9]William B. Locander and John P. Burton, "The Effect of Question Form on Gathering Income Data by Telephone," *Journal of Marketing Research,* 13 (May 1976), p. 192.

[10]Question sequence will be discussed more fully later in the chapter.

Table 7.1
Four Versions of An Income Question

Form 1
What was the approximate annual income for all members of your family before taxes during 1974? Was it . . .
(REPEAT UNTIL "NO." THEN CIRCLE)

more than $5,000	no 1		more than $20,000	no 5
more than $7,500	no 2		more than $25,000	no 6
more than $10,000	no 3			yes 7
more than $15,000	no 4		Don't know/refused	X

Form 2
What was the approximate annual income for all members of your family before taxes during 1974 . . . would it be $15,000 or more or would it be less than that?

less than $15,000 .... **ASK:**
IF LESS would it be ....
Over $10,000 4
Under $10,000 .... **ASK:**
IF UNDER would it be ....
Over $7,500 3
Under $7,500 .... **ASK:**
IF UNDER would it be ....
Over $5,000 2
Under $5,000 1

$15,000 or more .... **ASK:**
IF MORE would it be ....·
Under $20,000 or 5
Over $20,000 .... **ASK:**
IF OVER would it be ....·
Under $25,000 6
Over $25,000 7

Form 3
What was the approximate annual income for all members of your family before taxes during 1974? Was it . . .
(REPEAT UNTIL "YES". THEN CIRCLE)

less than $5,000	yes 1		less than $20,000	yes 5
less than $7,500	yes 2		less than $25,000	yes 6
less than $10,000	yes 3			no 7
less than $15,000	yes 4		Refused/Don't Know	X

What was the approximate annual income for all members of your family before taxes during 1974? Was it . . .
(REPEAT UNTIL "YES." THEN CIRCLE)

more than $25,000	yes 7		more than $7,500	yes 3
more than $20,000	yes 6		more than $5,000	yes 2
more than $15,000	yes 5			no 1
more than $10,000	yes 4		Don't Know/Refused	X

Source: William B. Locander and John P. Burton, "The Effect of Question Form and Gathering Income Data by Telephone," *Journal of Marketing Research*, 13 (May 1976), pp. 189–192. Published by the American Marketing Association.

When sensitive questions must be asked, it helps to consider ways to make them less threatening. Some helpful techniques in this regard are:[11]

1. Hide the question in a group of other more innocuous questions.

2. State that the behavior or attitude is not unusual before asking the specific questions of the respondent, e.g., "Recent studies show that one of every four households has trouble meeting their monthly financial obligations." This technique, known as the use of counterbiasing statements, makes it easier for the respondent to admit the potentially embarrassing behavior.

3. Phrase the question in terms of others and how they might feel or act, e.g., "Do you think most people cheat on their income tax? Why?" While respondents might readily reveal their attitudes toward cheating when preparing income tax forms when asked these questions, they might be very reluctant to do so if they were asked outright if they ever cheat on their taxes and why.

4. State the response in terms of a number of categories that the respondent may simply check. Instead of asking women for their age, for example, one could simply hand them a card with the age categories

    A: 20–29   D: 50–59
    B: 30–39   E: 60 +
    C: 40–49

    and ask them to respond with the appropriate letter.

5. Use the **randomized response model.** The randomized response model has the respondent answer one of several paired questions. The particular question is selected at random—for example, by having the respondent draw colored balls from an urn. The respondent is instructed to answer Question A if the ball is, say, blue, and Question B if the ball is red. The interviewer is unaware of the question being answered by the respondent, because he or she never sees the color of the ball drawn. Under these conditions the respondent is less likely to refuse to answer or to distort the answer he or she provides. A study to investigate the incidence of shoplifting might pair the sensitive question, "Have you ever shoplifted?" with the innocuous question, "Is your birthday in January?" The incidence of shoplifting can still be estimated by using an appropriate statistical model, since the percentage of respondents answering each question is controlled by the proportion of red and blue balls in the urn. Suppose, for example, there are five red and five blue balls in the urn, and thus the probability that the respondent will answer Question A, "Have you ever shoplifted?" is one-half. Further, the proportion of people whose birthdays fall in January is also known to be .05 from census data. Suppose the proportion who answered "yes" to either Question A or B is .20. Using the stan-

---

[11]For more extensive treatments on how to handle sensitive questions, see Kent H. Marquis, *et al., Response Errors in Sensitive Topic Surveys: Estimates, Effects, and Correction Options* (Santa Monica, Calif.: Rand Corporation, 1981); and Thomas W. Mangione, Ralph Hingson, and Jane Barrett, "Collecting Sensitive Data: A Comparison of Three Survey Strategies," *Sociological Methods and Research,* 10 (February 1982), pp. 337–346.

dard laws of probability we could then estimate that the proportion of the people in the sample who were responding "yes" to the sensitive question from the formula

$$\lambda = p\pi_S + (1 - p)\pi_A,$$

where

λ = the total proportion of "yes" responses to both questions,
p = the probability that the sensitive question is selected,
$1 - p$ = the probability that the innocuous question is selected,
π_S = the proportion of "yes" responses to the sensitive question, and
π_A = the proportion of "yes" responses to the innocuous question.[12]

Substituting the appropriate quantities indicates that

$$.20 = .50\pi_S + .50(.05)$$

and $\pi_S = .35$,

or that 35 percent of the respondents had shoplifted. Note, though, that the researcher cannot use the randomized response technique to determine specifically which respondents had shoplifted. This would preclude any opportunity, for example, to determine if shoplifting behavior was associated with any particular demographic characteristics.

Form of Response

Once the content of the individual questions is determined, the researcher needs to decide on the particular form of the response. Will the question be open-ended or fixed-alternative? If fixed-alternative, will it be a dichotomy, a multichotomy, or perhaps a scale?

Open-Ended Questions   Respondents are free to reply to **open-ended questions** in their own words rather than being limited to choosing from a set of alternatives. The following are examples:

How old are you? ⎯⎯⎯⎯

Do you think laws limiting the amount of interest businesses can charge consumers are needed? ⎯⎯⎯⎯

---

[12]James E. Reinmuth and Michael D. Geurts, "The Collection of Sensitive Information Using a Two-Stage Randomized Response Model," *Journal of Marketing Research,* 12 (November 1975), pp. 402–407. For an elementary overview of the randomized response model, see Cathy Campbell and Brian L. Joiner, "How to Get the Answer Without Being Sure You've Asked the Question," *American Statistician,* 26 (December 1973), pp. 229–231. For reviews of its use, see D. G. Horvitz, B. G. Greenberg, and J. R. Abernathy, "Randomized Response: A Data Gathering Device for Sensitive Questions," *International Statistical Review* (August 1976), pp. 181–195; and Paul E. Tracy and James Alan Fox, "The Validity of Randomized Response for Sensitive Measurements," *American Sociological Review,* 46 (April 1981), pp. 187–200. For discussion of randomization devices and methodologies for self-administered and telephone interview applications of the randomized response method, see Donald E. Stem, Jr., and R. Kirk Steinhorst, "Telephone Interview and Mail Questionnaire Applications of the Randomized Response Model," *Journal of the American Statistical Association,* 79 (September 1984), pp. 555–564.

Who sponsors the Monday night football games? _____

Do you intend to purchase an automobile this year? _____

Why did you purchase a Zenith brand color TV? _____

Do you own a sewing machine? _____

These questions span the gamut of the types of primary data that could be collected from demographic characteristics and through attitudes, intentions, and behavior. The open-ended question is indeed a versatile device.

Open-ended questions are often used to begin a questionnaire. The general feeling is that it is best to proceed from the general to the specific in constructing questionnaires. So an opening question like, "When you think of television sets, which brands come to mind?" gives some insight into the respondent's frame of reference and could be most helpful in interpreting the individual's replies to later questions. The open-ended question is also often used to probe for additional information. The probes "Why? Why do you feel that way? Please explain" are often used to seek elaboration of a respondent's reply.

Multichotomous Questions   The **multichotomous question** is a fixed-alternative question; respondents are asked to choose the alternative that most closely corresponds to their position on the subject. Table 7.2, for example, presents some of the open-ended questions posed above as multichotomous questions. Respondents would be instructed to check the box or boxes that apply.

The examples in Table 7.2 illustrate some of the difficulties encountered in using multiple choice questions. None of the alternatives in the interest ceiling legislation question, for example, may correctly capture the respondent's true feeling on the issue. The individual's opinion may be more complex, for one thing. He or she may believe that interest ceiling legislation is needed, assuming that a number of provisos or contingent possibilities can be satisfied (for example, that business firms will not reduce the amount of credit available to customers nor will they shorten the length of the repayment period). If these conditions cannot be satisfied, the respondent may feel just the opposite. The multiple choice question does not permit individuals to elaborate their true position but requires them to condense their complex attitude into a single statement. Of course, a well-designed series of multiple choice questions could allow for such elaborations. An exhaustive coverage of the potential qualifiers would also substantially increase the length of the questionnaire.

The interest ceiling legislation question also illustrates a general problem in question design: Should respondents be provided with a "don't know" or "no opinion" option? There is no question that if a respondent truly does not know an answer or has no opinion on an issue that he or she should be allowed to state that when responding. However, the issue is whether that option should be *explicitly* provided the respondent in the form of a "don't know" or "no opinion" category by asking a filter question like "Do you have an opinion on . . . .?" The arguments regarding the provision of a neutral point or category revolve around data accuracy versus respondent cooperation. Those suggesting that a neutral point, or "no opinion," answer should not be provided argue that most respondents are not likely to be exactly neutral on an issue. Instead of providing them an easy way out, it is much better to have them think about the issue

Table 7.2
Examples of Multichotomous Questions

Age:

How old are you?
- ☐ Less than 20
- ☐ 20–29
- ☐ 30–39
- ☐ 40–49
- ☐ 50–59
- ☐ 60 or over

Interest-Ceiling Legislation:

Do you think laws limiting the amount of interest businesses can charge consumers are needed?
- ☐ Definitely needed
- ☐ Probably needed
- ☐ Probably not needed
- ☐ Definitely not needed
- ☐ No opinion

Television Purchase:

Why did you purchase a Zenith brand color TV?
- ☐ Price was lower than other alternatives
- ☐ Feel it represents the highest quality
- ☐ Availability of local service
- ☐ Availability of a service contract
- ☐ Picture is better
- ☐ Warranty was better
- ☐ Other

so that they can frame their preference, however slight it may be; further that is certainly better than allowing the researcher to infer the majority opinion using only the responses from those taking a stand on the issue. Those who argue for including a neutral or "no opinion" category among the responses are inclined to suggest that forcing a respondent to make a choice when his or her preference is fuzzy or non-existent simply introduces response error into the results. Further, it makes it harder for respondents to answer and may turn them off to the whole survey. The jury is still out with respect to which form better captures respondents' true position on an issue, although there is no question that the two alternatives can produce widely differing proportions regarding the number holding a neutral view, potentially in the range of 10 to 50 percent.[13] For example, in one fairly large study using four-point versus five-point purchase intention scales, which were the same except for the provision of the neutral category in the five-point scale, it was found that if one used only the extreme points (i.e., definitely will buy/definitely will not buy) for evaluating a new product or idea, *either* scale could be used. On the other hand, the researcher who wanted to use two categories as the percentage likely to buy the product (i.e., definitely will buy or probably will buy) would find a difference in the two scales, with the four-point scale providing more positive responses than the five-point scale.[14]

---

[13]Kalton and Schuman, "The Effect of the Question on Survey Responses: A Review," pp. 51–52.

[14]Gregory J. Spagna, "Questionnaires: Which Approach Do You Use?" *Journal of Advertising Research,* 24 (February/March 1984), pp. 67–70.

The TV-set-purchase question illustrates a number of problems associated with multiple choice questions. First, the list of reasons cited for purchasing a Zenith color TV may not exhaust the reasons that could have been used by the respondent. The person may have purchased a Zenith out of loyalty to a friend who owns the local Zenith distributorship or because she or he really practices the "buy locally" admonition advanced by many small town chambers of commerce. The "other" response category attempts to solve this problem. A great many respondents checking the "other" category, though, will render the study useless. Thus, the burden is on the researcher to make the list of alternatives in a multiple choice question exhaustive. This may entail a good deal of prior research into the phenomenon that is to serve as the subject of a multiple choice question.

Unless the respondent is instructed to check all alternatives that apply, or is to rank the alternatives in order of importance, the multiple choice question also demands that the alternatives be mutually exclusive. The income categories

- $5,000–$10,000
- $10,000–$15,000

violate this principle. A respondent with an income of $10,000 would not know which alternative to check. A legitimate response with respect to the color TV purchase question might include several of the alternatives listed. The respondent thought the picture, warranty, and price were all more attractive on the Zenith than they were on other makes. Thus, the instructions would necessarily have to be "Check the most important reason," "Check all those reasons that apply," or "Rank all the reasons that apply from most important to least important."

A third difficulty with the TV purchase question is its great number of alternative responses. The list should be exhaustive. Yet the alternative statements an individual can simultaneously process appears to be limited. In one early study, the researchers presented each respondent with a card with six alternative statements. After each respondent had made his or her choice, the card was immediately replaced with another. On the second card, two of the six statements had been changed, and one statement from the original list was omitted. Yet only one-half of the respondents "could identify the changes and a mere handful located the omission."[15] The meaning of all this is that in designing multiple choice questions, the researcher should remain cognizant of human beings' limited data-processing capabilities. Perhaps a series of questions is more appropriate than one question. If there are a great many alternatives to a single question, then they should be shown to respondents, using cards, and not simply read to them.

The fourth weakness of the TV purchase question is that it is susceptible to a potential order bias. Respondents have a tendency to check either the first or last statement on a list with a somewhat heavier concentration of replies on the first.[16] The recom-

---

[15]Hadley Cantril and Edreta Fried, *Gauging Public Opinion* (Princeton, N.J.: Princeton University Press, 1944), chap. 1, as reported in Payne, *The Art of Asking Questions*, p. 93. For a discussion of people's limited information-processing abilities, see Jacob Jacoby, "Perspectives on Information Overload," *Journal of Consumer Research*, 10 (March 1984), pp. 432–435.

[16]Payne, *The Art of Asking Questions*, p. 84. This tendency to reply at the extremes is reversed when numbers are attached to the alternatives. Then respondents tend to choose an alternative near the middle of the list.

mended procedure for combating this order bias is to prepare several forms of the questionnaire, or several cards, if cards are used to list the alternatives. The order in which the alternatives are listed is then altered from form to form. If each alternative appears once at the extremes of the list, once in the middle, and once somewhere in between, the researcher can feel reasonably comfortable that the possible effects of position bias have been neutralized.[17]

Dichotomous Questions   The **dichotomous question** is also a fixed-alternative question, but one in which there are only two alternatives listed; for example:

Do you think laws limiting the amount of interest businesses can charge consumers are needed?

☐   Yes

☐   No

Do you intend to purchase an automobile this year?

☐   Yes

☐   No

We have already seen how the first of these questions could also be handled as a multiple choice question. The second could also be given a multichotomous structure. Instead of simply presenting the yes–no alternatives, the list could be framed as "Definitely intend to buy," "Probably will buy," "Definitely intend not to buy," and "Undecided." Dichotomous questions can often be framed as multichotomous questions, and vice versa. (The two possess similar advantages and disadvantages, which were reviewed earlier when discussing structured questions. They will not be repeated here.) The dichotomous question offers the ultimate in ease of coding and tabulation, and this probably accounts for its being the most commonly used type of question in communication studies.

   One special problem with the dichotomous question is that the response can well depend on how the question is framed. This is true, of course, of all questions, but with the dichotomous question it represents a special problem. Consider two alternative questions:

Do you think that gasoline will be more expensive or less expensive next year than it is now?

☐   More expensive

☐   Less expensive

Do you think that gasoline will be less expensive or more expensive next year than it is now?

☐   Less expensive

☐   More expensive

---

[17]Although it is commonly done, Niels, J. Blunch, "Position Bias in Multiple-Choice Questions," *Journal of Marketing Research,* 21 (May 1984), pp. 216–220, argues to the contrary that position bias in multiple-choice questions cannot be eliminated by rotating the order of the alternatives.

Now, the questions appear identical, and certainly we might want to expand each to include categories for ''No opinion'' and ''About the same.'' The fact remains, though, that the two questions will elicit different responses.[18] The simple switching of the positions of ''More expensive'' or ''Less expensive'' can affect the response an individual gives. Which, then, is the correct wording?

One generally accepted procedure for combating this order bias is to employ a split ballot. One phrasing is used on one-half of the questionnaires, and the alternative phrasing is employed on the other one-half of the questionnaires. The averaged percentages from the two forms should then cancel out any biases.

Scales   Another type of fixed-alternative question is the question that employs a scale to capture the response. For instance, when inquiring about the various sewing machine features that home seamstresses use, the following question might be asked:

How often do you use the zigzag stitch on your machine?

☐   Never

☐   Occasionally

☐   Sometimes

☐   Often

In this form, the question is a multichotomous question. However, the responses also represent a scale of use. The scale nature of the question would be more obvious perhaps if the following form were used to secure the replies:

Never	Occasionally	Sometimes	Often

The advantage of this scheme is that the descriptors could be presented at the top of the page, and a number of possible features could be listed along the left margin (for example, decorative stitch, blind stitch, built-in buttonholer, and so on). The respondent would then be instructed to designate the frequency of use for each feature. The instruction would only need to be given once at the beginning, and thus a great deal of information could be secured from the respondent in a short period of time.

Decide on Question Wording

Step 5 in the questionnaire development process involves the phrasing of each question. This is a critical task, since poor phrasing of a question can cause respondents to refuse to answer it, even though they agreed to cooperate in the study, or to answer incorrectly, either on purpose or because of misunderstanding. The first condition, known as **item**

---

[18]Two of the best discussions of this are to be found in Payne, *The Art of Asking Questions,* and Howard Schuman and Stanley Presser, *Questions and Answers in Attitude Surveys* (Orlando: Academic Press, 1981), especially pp. 56–77.

Research Realities 7.1

Some Multi-Meaning Problem Words Researchers Should Use with Caution

about

Among other uses, "about" is sometimes intended to mean somewhere near in the sense that both 48% and 52% are "about" half. It is also used to mean nearly or almost, in the sense that 48% is "about" half while 52% is "over" half. This small difference in interpretation may make a slight difference in the way various respondents answer certain questions.

all

Here is the first mention of a "dead giveaway" word, a term you will see frequently from here on.

Your own experience with true-false tests has probably demonstrated to you that it is safe to count almost every all-inclusive statement as false. That is, you have learned in such tests that it is safe to follow the idea that "all statements containing 'all' are false, including this one." Some people have the same negative reaction to opinion questions which hinge upon all-inclusive or all-exclusive words. They may be generally in agreement with a proposition, but nevertheless hesitate to accept the extreme idea of *all, always, each, every, never, nobody, only, none,* or *sure.*
Would you say that all cats have four legs?
Is the mayor doing all he can for the city?

It is correct, of course, to use an all-inclusive word if it correctly states the alternative. But you will usually find that such a word produces an overstatement. Most people may go along with the idea, accepting it as a form of literary license, but the purists and quibblers may either refuse to give an opinion or may even choose the other side in protest.

always

This is another dead giveaway word.
Do you always observe traffic signs?
Is your boss always friendly?

and

This simple conjunction in some contexts may be taken either as separating two alternatives or as connecting two parts of a single alternative.
Is there much rivalry among the boys who sell soda pop and cracker jacks?

Some people will answer in terms of rivalry between two groups—those who sell pop and those who sell crackerjack. Others will take it as rivalry within the single group comprising both pop and crackerjack salesmen.

any

The trouble with this word is a bit difficult to explain. It's something like that optical illusion of the shifting stairsteps, which you sometimes seem to see from underneath and sometimes seem to see from above but which you aren't able to see both ways at the same time. The trouble with "any" is that it may mean "every," "some," or "one only" in the same sentence or question, depending on the way you look at it.

See whether you can get both the "every" and "only one" illusions from this question and notice the difference in meaning that results:
Do you think any word is better than the one we are discussing?

You could think, "Yes, I think just any old word (every word) is better." On the other hand, you might think, "Yes, I believe it would be possible to find a better word."

Another difficulty with "any" is that when used in either the "every" or the "not any" context it becomes as much a dead giveaway word as are "every" and "none."

bad

In itself the word "bad" is not at all bad for question wording. It conveys the meaning desired and is satisfactory as an alternative in a "good or bad" two-way question.

Experience seems to indicate, however, that people are generally less willing to criticize than they are to praise. Since it is difficult to get them to state their negative views, sometimes the critical side needs to be softened. For example, after asking, *What things are good about your job?,* it might seem perfectly natural to ask, *What things are bad about it?* But if we want to lean over backwards to get as many criticisms as we can, we may be wise not to apply the "bad" stigma but to ask, *What things are not so good about it?*

Source: Stanley L. Payne, *The Art of Asking Questions.* Copyright 1951, © 1979 renewed by Princeton University Press. Excerpts, pp. 158–176, reprinted with permission of Princeton University Press.

could

No fault is found with the word itself, but we are well advised to remember that it should not be confused with ''should'' or ''might.''

ever

This word tends to be a dead giveaway in a very special sense. ''Ever'' is such a long time and so inclusive that it makes it seem plausible that some unimpressive things may have happened.

Have you ever listened to the Song Plugger radio program?

   ''Yes—I suppose I must have at some time or other.''

go

''Go'' is given more space in the index of *The American Thesaurus of Slang* than any other word—a total of about 12½ columns.

When did you last go to town?

   If the respondent takes this literally, it is a good question, but the ''go to town'' phrase has more than a dozen different slang meanings, including a couple that might get your face slapped.

heard

Sometimes these words are used in a very general sense *(Have you heard of . . .?)* to include learning about not only through hearing but also through reading, seeing, etc. Unfortunately, however, some respondents apparently take such words literally. They don't say that they've heard when they've only seen, for instance. In one study, only half as many people said that they had ''heard or read'' anything about patents as reported having attended a patents exposition. Evidently, they considered whatever they learned from attendance as separate from hearing or reading.

less

This word is usually used as an alternative to ''more,'' where it may cause a minor problem. The phrase ''more or less'' has a special meaning all its own in which some respondents do not see an alternative. Thus, they may simply answer ''yes, more or less'' to a question like:

Compared with a year ago, are you more or less happy in your job?

The easy solution to this problem is to break up the ''more or less'' expression by introducing an extra word or so to reverse the two:

Compared with a year ago, are you more or less happy in your job?

Compared with a year ago, are you less or more happy in your job?

like

This word is on the problem list only because it is sometimes used to introduce an example. The problem with bringing an example into a question is that the respondent's attention may be directed toward the particular example and away from the general issue which it is meant only to illustrate. The use of examples may sometimes be necessary, but the possible hazard should always be kept in mind. The choice of an example can affect the answers to the question—in fact, it may materially change the question, as in these two examples:

Do you think that leafy vegetables like spinach should be in the daily diet?

Do you think that leafy vegetables like lettuce should be in the daily diet?

you

The dictionary distinguishes only two or three meanings of ''you''—the second person singular and plural and the substitution for the impersonal ''one''—''How do you get there?'' in place of ''How does one get there?'' In most questions ''you'' gives no trouble whatever, it being clear that we are asking the opinion of the second person singular. However, and here is the problem, the word sometimes may have a collective meaning as in a question asked of radio repairmen:

How many radio sets did you repair last month?

   This question seemed to work all right until one repairman in a large shop countered with, ''Who do you mean, me or the whole shop?''

   Much as we might want to, therefore, we can't give ''you'' an unqualified recommendation. Sometimes ''you'' needs the emphasis of ''you yourself'' and sometimes it just isn't the word to use, as in the above situation where the entire shop was meant.

nonresponse, can create a great many problems when analyzing the data. The second condition produces measurement error, in that the recorded or obtained score does not equal the respondent's true score on the issue.[19]

Experienced researchers know that the phrasing of a question can directly impact the responses to it. One humorous anecdote in this regard involves two priests, a Dominican and a Jesuit, who are discussing whether it is a sin to smoke and pray at the same time. "After failing to reach a conclusion, each goes off to consult his respective superior. The next week they meet again. The Dominican says, 'Well, what did your superior say?' The Jesuit responds, 'He said it was all right.' 'That's funny,' the Dominican replies, 'my superior said it was a sin.' Jesuit: 'What did you ask him?' Reply: 'I asked him if it was all right to smoke while praying.' 'Oh,' says the Jesuit, 'I asked my superior if it was all right to pray while smoking.' "[20]

While it is recognized, then, that question wording can affect the answers obtained, it is sometimes hard to develop good phrasings of questions, in that there are few basic principles researchers can rely upon when framing questions. Instead, the literature is replete with rules-of-thumb. While the rules-of-thumb are often easier to state than to practice, researchers need to be aware of the admonitions that surround the wording of questions.

Use Simple Words A "vocabulary problem" confronts most researchers. Because they are more highly educated than the typical questionnaire respondent, researchers are prone to use words familiar to them but not understood by many respondents. This is a difficult problem, because it is not easy to dismiss what one knows and put oneself instead in the respondent's shoes when trying to assess his or her vocabulary. A significant proportion of the population, for example, does not understand the word *Caucasian,* although most researchers do.[21] The researcher needs to be constantly aware that the average person in the United States has a high school, not a college, education and that many people have difficulty in coping with usual tasks, such as making change, reading job notices, or completing a driver's application blank. A basic admonition is to keep the words simple. When there is a choice between more difficult and simpler wording, it is best to choose simplicity. There is always great potential for respondents to misunderstand what they are being asked even when simple words are used. Research Realities 7.1, for example, lists some problem words identified by Payne more than 30 years ago and why these words can cause difficulty. Payne identified more than 80 such words, which is one very important reason, and there are many, that those charged with

---

[19]The notion of measurement error is defined more formally in Appendix 8C. For a review of the literature on the quality of questionnaire data, including item omission, see Robert A. Peterson and Roger A. Kerin, "The Quality of Self-Report Data: Review and Synthesis," in Ben Enis and Kenneth Roering, eds., *Annual Review of Marketing 1981* (Chicago: American Marketing Association, 1981), pp. 5–20.

[20]Sudman and Bradburn, *Asking Questions,* p. 1.

[21]Alan E. Bayer, "Construction of a Race Item for Survey Research," *Public Opinion Quarterly,* 36 (Winter 1972–1973), p. 596. Payne, *The Art of Asking Questions,* has a list of the recommended words, while John O'Brien, "How Do Market Researchers Ask Questions?" *Journal of the Market Research Society,* 26 (April 1984), pp. 93–107, reports on the relative frequency with which Payne's recommended words are used on a sample of British questionnaires.

the task of designing questionnaires would be well advised to read Payne's classic book.[22]

Avoid Ambiguous Words and Questions   Not only should the words used be simple, they should also be unambiguous. The same is true for the questions. Consider again the multichotomous question:

How often do you use the zigzag stitch on your machine?

☐   Never

☐   Occasionally

☐   Sometimes

☐   Often

For all practical purposes, the replies to this question would be worthless. The words *occasionally, sometimes,* and *often* are ambiguous. To one respondent, the word *often* might mean "every time I sew." To another it might mean, "yes, I use it when I have the specific need. This happens on about one of every four projects." The words *occasionally* and *sometimes* could also be interpreted differently by different respondents. Thus, while the question would get answers, it would generate little real understanding of the frequency of use of the zigzag stitch.

A much better strategy would be to provide concrete alternatives for the respondent, rather than the ambiguous options above. The alternatives might read, for example:

☐   Never use

☐   Use on approximately one of ten projects

☐   Use on approximately one of three projects

☐   Use on almost every project.

Whether these would be the appropriate categories depends on the purpose of the study. The important thing is that the researcher has provided a consistent frame of reference for each respondent. Respondents are no longer free to superimpose their own definitions on the response categories.

An alternative way to avoid ambiguity in response categories when asking about the frequency of some behavior is to ask about the most recent instance of the phenomenon. The above question might be framed in the following way, for example:

When you last sewed, did you use the zigzag stitch?

☐   Yes

☐   No

☐   Can't recall

---

[22]Payne, *The Art of Asking Questions.* For evidence regarding the words marketing research firms use most frequently in questionnaires, see Brien, "How Do Market Researchers Ask Questions?"

The proportion responding *yes* would then be used to infer the frequency with which the zigzag stitch was used, while the follow-up question among all those responding yes, "For what purpose?" would give insight as to how respondents are using it. While some respondents who normally use it might not have used the zigzag stitch the last time they sewed, the opposite would be true for others. The same would be true with respect to purposes for which it was used. There might be some variation in comparison to what individuals normally do. The variation, though, should cancel out if a large enough sample of respondents is used, and the aggregate sample should provide a good indication of the proportion of times the zigzag stich is used and the proportion of these occurrences it is used for each of several purposes. The researcher, in effect, relies on the sample to provide insight into the frequency of occurrence of the phenomenon, rather than a specific question that may contain ambiguous alternatives. It is important that the sample be large enough in this instance so that the proportions can be estimated with the appropriate degree of confidence.

Avoid Leading Questions   A **leading question** is one framed so as to give the respondent a clue as to how he or she should answer. Consider the question:

Do you feel that limiting taxes by law is an effective way to stop the government from picking your pocket every payday?

☐   Yes

☐   No

☐   Undecided

This was one of three questions in an unsolicited questionnaire that the author received as part of a study sponsored by the National Tax Limitation Committee. The committee intended to make the results of the poll available to Congress and to state legislators. Given the implied purpose, it is probably not surprising to see the leading words "picking your pocket" being used in this question, or the leading word "gauge" being used in another question. What is especially unfortunate is that it is unlikely the questions themselves accompanied the report to Congress. Rather, it is more likely that the report suggested that some high percentage, e.g., 90 percent of those surveyed, favored laws that limited taxes. Conclusion: Congress should pay attention to the wishes of the people and pass such laws.

One sees instances of this phenomenon everyday in the newspaper. While not seeing the questionnaire, the public is treated to a discussion of the results of this or that study with respect to how the American people feel on issues. One interesting report in this regard was published during New York City's financial crisis.

Question: What percentage of the American public favors federal aid for New York City? Choose one of the following: a. 69; b. 55; c. 42; d. 15; e. all of the above.
Answer: All of the above.
One apparent key to the different responses was whether the aid was described as a "bailout," "federal funds," or "the federal government guaranteeing loans." [23]

---

[23]"Why the Polls Get Differing Results on Aid to New York," *Capital Times* (November 8, 1975), p. 2.

The correct phrasing of this or almost any question could, of course, be argued. The important point for both researchers and managers to remember is that the phrasing finally chosen will impact the responses secured. If one truly wants an accurate picture of the situation, one needs to avoid leading the respondent as to how he or she should answer.

Avoid Implicit Alternatives   An **implicit alternative** is one that is not expressed in the options. Consider the following two questions, which were used in two random samples of nonworking housewives to investigate their attitudes toward having a job outside the home.[24]

☐   *Would you like to have a job, if this were possible?*

☐   *Would you prefer to have a job, or do you prefer to do just your housework?*

While the two questions appear very similar, they produced dramatically different responses. The first version indicated 19 percent would not like to have a job, while the second suggested 68 percent would not prefer to have one, over three and one-half times as many. The difference in the two questions is that Version two makes implicit the alternative implied in Version one.

As a general rule, one should avoid implicit alternatives unless there is a special reason for including them. Further, because the order in which the alternatives appear can affect the responses, one should rotate the order of the options in samples of questionnaires.

Avoid Implicit Assumptions   Questions are frequently framed so that there is an **implied assumption** as to what will happen as a consequence. The question "Are you in favor of placing price controls on crude oil?" will elicit different responses from individuals, depending upon their views as to what that might produce in the way of rationing, long lines at the pumps, and so forth. A better way to state the question is to make explicit the consequence(s). Thus, the question would be altered to ask "Are you in favor of placing price controls on crude oil if it would produce gas rationing?"

Avoid Generalizations and Estimates   Questions should always be asked in specific rather than general terms. Consider the question: "How many salespeople did you see last year?" which might be asked of a purchasing agent. To answer the question, the agent would probably estimate how many salespeople call in a typical week and would multiply this estimate by 52. This burden should not be placed on the agent. Rather, a more accurate estimate would be obtained if the purchasing agent were asked. "How many representatives called last week?" and the researcher multiplied the answer provided by 52.

---

[24]E. Noelle-Neumann, "Wanted: Rules for Wording Structured Questionnaires," *Public Opinion Quarterly,* 34 (Summer 1970), p. 200.

Avoid Double-Barreled Questions   A **double-barreled question** is one that calls for two responses and thereby creates confusion for the respondent. The question, "What is your evaluation of the price and convenience offered by catalog showrooms?" is asking respondents to react to two separate attributes by which such showrooms could be described. The respondent might feel the prices are attractive but the location is not, for example, and thereby is placed in a dilemma as to how to respond. The problem is particularly acute if the individual must choose an answer from a fixed set of alternatives. One can and should avoid double-barreled questions by splitting the initial question into two separate questions. A useful indicator that two questions might be needed is the use of the word *and* in the initial wording of the question.

Decide on Question Sequence

Once the form of response and specific wording for each question have been decided, the researcher is ready to begin putting them together into a questionnaire. The researcher needs to recognize immediately that the order in which the questions are presented can be crucial to the success of the research effort. Again, there are no hard-and-fast principles but only rules-of-thumb to guide the researcher in this activity.

Use Simple, Interesting Opening Questions   The first questions asked the respondent are crucial. If respondents cannot answer them easily, find them uninteresting, or find them suspicious or threatening in any way, they may refuse to complete the remainder of the questionnaire. Thus, it is essential that the first few questions be simple, interesting, and in no way threatening to respondents. Questions that ask respondents for their opinion on some issue are often good openers, as most people like to feel their opinion is important. Sometimes it is helpful to use such an opener even when responses to it will not be analyzed, since opinion questions are often productive in relaxing respondents and getting them to talk freely.

Use Funnel Approach   The **funnel approach** to question sequencing gets its name from its shape, starting with broad questions and progressively narrowing down the scope. If respondents are to be asked "What improvements are needed in the company's service policy?" and also "How do you like the quality of service?" the first question needs to be asked before the second. Otherwise, quality of service will be emphasized disproportionately in the responses simply because it is fresh in the respondents' minds.

There should also be some logical order to the questions. This means that sudden changes in topics and jumping around from topic to topic should be avoided. Transitional devices are sometimes necessary to smooth the flow when a change in subject matter occurs. Sometimes the simple insertion of appropriate filter questions will serve this purpose well, although the insertion of a brief explanation is the most commonly used bridge when a change in subject matter occurs.

Design Branching Questions With Care   **Branching questions** are used to direct respondents to different places in the questionnaire based on their response to the question at hand. Thus, for example, a respondent replying "yes" to the question of whether he or she bought a new car within the last six months would be directed to one place in the questionnaire where he or she might then be asked for specific details surrounding the purchase, while someone responding "no" to the same question would be directed elsewhere. Branching questions are used to reduce the number of alternatives that are needed in individual questions while simultaneously ensuring that the information needed is secured from those capable of supplying it. Those for whom a question is irrelevant are simply directed around it. Branching questions and directions are much easier to develop for surveys administered by telephone or in person than for those sent through the mail. With mail questionnaires, the number of branching questions needs to be kept to an absolute minimum so that respondents do not become confused when responding or refuse to cooperate because the task becomes too difficult. While they can be used more liberally with telephone and personal interview surveys, branching questions still need to be designed with care since evidence indicates that branching instructions increase the rate of item nonresponse for items immediately following the branch.[25] When using branching questions, it is generally good practice to (1) develop a flow chart of the logical possibilities and then prepare the branching questions and instructions to follow the flow chart; (2) place the question being branched to as close as possible to the question causing the branching so as to minimize the amount of page flipping that is necessary; and (3) order the branching questions so that respondents cannot anticipate what additional information is required.[26] This last point suggests that the questionnaire should first ask, for example, whether the respondent owns any of the following small appliances before beginning to ask for the brand name, the store where purchased, and so on, for each appliance to which the respondent replied "yes." Otherwise, respondents will quickly recognize that "yes" answers to the ownership question lead to a number of other questions and that is less taxing to say "no" in the first place.

Ask for Classification Information Last   The typical questionnaire contains two types of information—basic information and classification information. Basic information refers to the subject of the study (for example, intentions or attitudes of respondents). Classification information refers to the other data we collect to classify respondents so as to extract more information about the phenomenon of interest. For instance, we might be interested in determining if a respondent's attitudes toward the need for interest ceiling legislation are in any way affected by the person's income. Income here would be a classification variable. Demographic/socioeconomic characteristics of respondents are often used as classification variables for understanding the results.

The proper questionnaire sequence is to present questions securing basic information first and those seeking classification information last. There is a logical reason for this. The basic information is most critical. Without it, there is no study. Thus, the researcher should not risk alienating the respondent by asking a number of personal questions before getting to the heart of the study, since it is not unusual for personal characteristics

---

[25]Donald J. Messmer and Daniel J. Seymour, "The Effects of Branching on Item Nonresponse," *Public Opinion Quarterly,* 46 (Summer 1982), pp. 270–277.
[26]Sudman and Bradburn, *Asking Questions,* pp. 223–227.

to alienate respondents most. Respondents who readily offer their attitudes toward the energy crisis may balk when asked for their income. An early question aimed at determining their income may affect the whole tenor of the interview or other communication. It is best to avoid this possibility by placing the classification information at the end.

Place Difficult or Sensitive Questions Late in the Questionnaire   The basic information itself can also present some sequence problems. Some of the questions can be sensitive. Early questions should not be, for the reasons previously mentioned. If respondents feel threatened, they will turn off to the questionnaire. Thus, the sensitive questions should be relegated to the body of the questionnaire and intertwined and hidden among some not-so-sensitive ones. Once respondents have become involved in the study, they are less likely to react negatively or be turned off completely when delicate questions are posed. One study investigating the impact of time and memory factors on response in surveys found, for example, that response bias becomes smaller as the interview progresses and that aided recall has no effect at the start of an interview but has a large effect late in the interview.[27]

Determine Physical Characteristics

The physical characteristics of the questionnaire can affect the accuracy of the replies that are obtained. Figure 7.3 contains, for example, two versions of a question that was asked to determine which brands they were after it was determined that households had specific products. The letters are used instead of the actual brand names to protect the confidentiality of the data. The only fundamental difference in the questions was that a set of parentheses was provided in Form B for the "other brand" category, whereas Form A had a line where respondents wrote in the name of those brands not on the original list. The difference in results regarding the percentage of households owning Brands F and G among the 4,000 households surveyed was remarkable, as Table 7.3 indicates. Form B results were within a couple of percentage points of the results from the survey conducted one year earlier. It seems that respondents counted up from the bottom when checking the brand category, and the line on which the other brand was to be entered in Form A was too close to the ruled line separating this question from the next one.[28]

The physical characteristics of a questionnaire can also affect how respondents react to it and the ease with which the replies can be processed. In determining the physical format of the questionnaire, a researcher wants to do those things that help get the respondent to accept the questionnaire and that facilitate handling and control by the researcher.

---

[27]Seymour Sudman and Norman M. Bradburn, "Effects of Time and Memory Factors on Response in Surveys," *Journal of the American Statistical Association,* 68 (December 1973), pp. 805–815.

[28]Charles S. Mayer and Cindy Piper, "A Note on the Importance of Layout in Self-Administered Questionnaires," *Journal of Marketing Research,* 19 (August 1982), pp. 390–391.

Figure 7.3
Two Forms of a Brand-Owned Question

Form A

Important: For each type, *if* you have more than one, answer for the newest.
3a. What make or brand is it?

	Product X	**Product Y**	**Product Z**
Brand A	( ) 1	( ) 1	( ) 1
Brand B	( ) 2	( ) 2	( ) 2
Brand C	( ) 3	( ) 3	( ) 3
Brand D	( ) 4	( ) 4	( ) 4
Brand E	( ) 5	( ) 5	( ) 5
Brand F	( ) 6	( ) 6	( ) 6
Brand G	( ) 7	( ) 7	( ) 7
Other brand (Specify)	_____	_____	_____

Form B

3. What make or brand is the newest one?

	Product X	**Product Y**	**Product Z**
Brand A	( ) 1	( ) 1	( ) 1
Brand B	( ) 2	( ) 2	( ) 2
Brand C	( ) 3	( ) 3	( ) 3
Brand D	( ) 4	( ) 4	( ) 4
Brand E	( ) 5	( ) 5	( ) 5
Brand F	( ) 6	( ) 6	( ) 6
Brand G	( ) 7	( ) 7	( ) 7
Other brand	( ) 8	( ) 8	( ) 8

Source: Charles S. Mayer and Cindy Piper, "A Note on the Importance of Layout in Self-Administered Questionnaires," *Journal of Marketing Research,* 19 (August 1982), p. 390. Published by the American Marketing Association.

Securing Acceptance of the Questionnaire   The physical appearance of the questionnaire can influence respondents' cooperation. This is particularly true with mail questionnaires, but applies as well to questionnaires administered by personal interviews. If the questionnaire looks sloppy, for whatever reason, respondents are likely to feel the study is unimportant and refuse to cooperate, despite words to the contrary about its importance. If the study is important, and why conduct it if it is not, make the questionnaire reflect that importance. This means that good-quality paper should be used for the questionnaires. It also means that the questionnaires should be printed, not mimeographed or otherwise photocopied.

It is also a good idea to include the name of the sponsoring organization and the name of the project on the first page or on the cover if the questionnaire is in book form. Both of these lend credibility to the study. However, since awareness of the sponsoring firm can often induce bias in respondents' answers, many firms use fictitious

Table 7.3
Brand Share among Owners

	Percentage Owning Brand		
	Form A	Form B	Net Difference
Product X			
Brand F	30	3	27
Brand G	47	71	24
Product Y			
Brand F	18	2	16
Brand G	27	41	14
Product Z			
Brand F	27	3	24
Brand G	35	58	23

names for the sponsoring organization. This also helps eliminate phone calls or other inquiries from respondents asking for the results of the study.

Facilitate Handling and Control   Several things that facilitate handling and control by the researcher also contribute to acceptance of the questionnaire by respondents. These include such things as questionnaire size and layout and question sequencing.

Questionnaire size is important.[29] Smaller questionnaires are better than larger ones if (and this is a big if) they do not appear crowded. Smaller questionnaires seem easier to complete; they appear to take less time and are less likely to cause respondents to refuse to participate. They are easier to carry in the field and are easier to sort, count, and file in the office than are larger questionnaires. If, on the other hand, smaller size is gained at the expense of an open appearance, these advantages are lost. A crowded questionnaire has a bad appearance, leads to errors in data collection, and results in shorter and less informative replies. For both self-administered and interviewer-administered questionnaires, for example, researchers have found that the more lines or space left for recording the response to open-ended questions, the more extensive the reply. Similarly, it has been found that giving respondents more detailed information about the type of information sought through longer questions, improves reporting behavior.[30]

---

[29]A. Regula Herzog and Jerald G. Bachman, "Effects of Questionnaire Length on Response Quality," *Public Opinion Quarterly,* 45 (Winter 1981), pp. 549–559.

[30]Charles F. Cannell, Lois Oksenberg, and Jean M. Converse, "Striving for Response Accuracy: Experiments in New Interviewing Techniques," *Journal of Marketing Research,* 14 (August 1977), pp. 306–315; Ed Blair, Seymour Sudman, Norman M. Bradburn, and Carol Stocking, "How to Ask Questions About Drinking and Sex: Response Effects in Measuring Consumer Behavior," *Journal of Marketing Research,* 14 (August 1977), pp. 316–321; and Andre Laurent, "Effects of Question Length on Reporting Behavior in the Survey Interview," *Journal of the American Statistical Association,* 67 (June 1972), pp. 298–305.

Both of these techniques increase the physical size of the questionnaire needed for the study.

While post-card size probably represents the lower limit, letter size probably represents the upper limit to the size of an individual page in a questionnaire. When the questions will not all fit on the front and back of one sheet, multiple sheets need to be used. When this happens, the questionnaire should be made into a booklet rather than stapling or paper clipping the pages together. This not only facilitates handling but also reinforces an image of quality.

Another thing that facilitates handling and also promotes respondent cooperation is numbering the questions. While this is true in general, it is particularly true when branching questions are employed. Without numbered questions, instructions as to how to proceed (e.g., "If the answer to Question 2 is yes, please go to Question 5") cannot be used. Even with numbered questions, though, it is helpful if the respondent can be directed by arrows to the appropriate next question after a branching question. Another technique researchers have found useful with branch-type questions is the use of color-coding on the questionnaire, where the next question to which the respondent is directed matches the color of the space in which the answer to the branching or filter question was recorded.

Numbering the questions makes it easier to edit, code, and tabulate the responses.[31] It also helps if the questionnaires themselves are numbered. This makes it easier to keep track of the questionnaires and to determine which ones, if any, are lost. It also makes it easier to monitor interviewer performance and to detect interviewer biases, if any. The research director will be able to develop a log listing which questionnaires were assigned to which interviewers. Mail questionnaires are an exception to the principle that the questionnaires themselves should be numbered. Respondents often interpret an assigned number on a mail questionnaire as a mechanism by which their responses can be identified. The accompanying loss in anonymity is threatening to many of them, and they refuse to cooperate or otherwise distort their answers.

Reexamination and Revision of the Questionnaire

A researcher should not expect that the first draft will result in a usable questionnaire. Rather, reexamination and revision are the order of the day in questionnaire construction. Each question should be reviewed to ensure that the question is not confusing or ambiguous, potentially offensive to the respondent, leading or bias inducing, and that it is easy to answer. How can one tell? An extremely critical attitude and good common sense should help. The researcher should examine each word in each question. The literature on question phrasing is replete with examples of how some seemingly innoc-

---

[31]These elementary steps, which are involved in the processing of all questionnaires, are discussed in Chapter 12.

uous questions produce response problems.[32] When a potential problem is discovered, the question should be revised. After examining each question, and each word in each question, for its potential meanings and implications, the researcher might test the questionnaire in some role-playing situations, using others working on the project as subjects. This role playing should reveal some of the most serious shortcomings and should lead further revision of the instrument.

Pretesting the Questionnaire

The real test of a questionnaire is how it performs under actual conditions of data collection. For this assessment, the questionnaire **pretest** is vital. The questionnaire pretest serves the same role in questionnaire design that test marketing serves in new product development. While the product concept, different advertising appeals, alternative packages, and so on, may all have been tested previously in the product development process, test marketing is the first place where they all come together. Test marketing provides the real test of customer reactions to the product and the accompanying marketing program. Similarly, the pretest provides the real test of the questionnaire and the mode of administration.

Data collection should never begin without an adequate pretest of the instrument. The pretest can be used to assess both individual questions and their sequence.[33] It is best if there are two pretests. The first pretest should be done by personal interview, regardless of the actual mode of administration that will be used. An interviewer can watch to see if people actually remember data requested of them, or if some questions seem confusing, or if some questions produce respondent resistance or hesitancy for one reason or another. The pretest interviews should be conducted among respondents similar to those who will be used in the actual study, by the firm's most experienced interviewers.

The personal interview pretest should reveal some questions in which the wording could be improved or the sequence changed. If the changes are major, the revised questionnaire should again be pretested employing personal interviews. If the changes are minor, the questionnaire can be pretested a second time using mail, telephone, or personal interviews, whichever is going to be used for the full-scale study. This time though, less experienced interviewers should also be used in order to determine if typical interviewers will have any special problems with the questionnaire. The purpose of the second pretest is to uncover problems unique to the mode of administration.

---

[32]Payne's book is particularly good in this regard. Chapter 13, for example, is devoted to the development of a passable question. When one considers that an entire chapter can be devoted to the development of one passable question (not great question, mind you), one can appreciate the need for reexamining each question under a microscope for its potential implications. A condensed treatment of the things to be avoided in a question is to be found in Lyndon O. Brown and Leland L. Beik, *Marketing Research and Analysis,* 4th ed. (New York: Ronald, 1969), pp. 242–262. Sudman and Bradburn, *Asking Questions,* have recommendations specific to the type of question being asked (e.g., opinions versus demographic characteristics).

[33]An empirical examination of the usefulness of the pretest in uncovering various problems can be found in Shelby D. Hunt, Richard D. Sparkman, Jr., and James B. Wilcox, "The Pretest in Survey Research: Issues and Preliminary Findings," *Journal of Marketing Research,* 19 (May 1982), pp. 265–275.

Figure 7.4
Observation Form and Portion of Coding Form for "Garbage Project"

RECORD OF GARBAGE SAMPLES

NAME OF RECORDER _Kelly Allen_

DATE OF ANALYSIS _Oct. 30_

13

| 1/2 | 75 |

(FOR OFFICE USE ONLY)

MATERIAL COMPOSITION CODES
(LIST MOST PREVALENT MATERIAL FIRST)

CODE
A PAPER
B FERROUS (STEEL/TIN)
C ALUMINUM
D PLASTIC (CELLOPHANE)
E NON-RETURN GLASS

H RETURNABLE GLASS
J AEROSOL CANS
K WOOD
M CERAMICS
P LEATHER
Q RUBBER

R COPPER AND BRASS
S BIODEGRADABLE PLASTIC
T TEXTILE
V CORRUGATED CARDBOARD
X OTHER (SPECIFY ON BACK)

PACK NUMBERS TO RIGHT OF COLUMN, LETTERS TO LEFT (49-68)
WRITE NUMBERS CLEARLY AND USE CAPITAL LETTERS ONLY.

	CENSUS TRACT (16 17 18)	COLLECTION MO (19 20)	DAY (21 22)	ITEM CODE (23 24 25)	NO. OF ITEMS (26 27 28)	FLUID OUNCES (29 30 31 32 33)	SOLID OUNCES (34 35 36 37 38)	COST (39 40 41 42 43 44)	WASTE (GRAMS) (45 46 47 48)	SPOILAGE INDICATOR (SEE VEG LIST) (49)	BRAND (50 51 52 53 54 55 56 57)	TYPE (58 59 60 61 62 63 64 65)	MATERIAL COMPOSITION CODE (66 67 68)
1	019	10	30	041	003		16.0		70		MARSHBUR	CARROT	D
2	019	10	30	086	003	36.0		.87			SCHLITZ	MALT	C
3	019	10	30	079	002	27.0					SEVENUP		BC
4	019	10	30	027	001		16.0	.65	282		NORTHRID	HONEYEGG	D
5	019	10	30	011	001	32.0		.43			CIRCLER	WHOLE	A
6	019	10	30	086	002	27.0					LITE		C
7	019	10	30	051	001		32.0	1.19	40		WELCHS	JELLY	E
8	019	10	30	041	001				55	X		LETTUCE	
9	019	10	30	048	003				45	X	LONGHORN	CHEDDAR	D
10	019	10	30	187	001				260	X		BANANA	
11	019	10	30	044	001							CITIZEN	A
12	019	10	30	284	001	25.0		.15	95		ROYALOCC	VODKA	ED
13	019	10	30	027	001						HARVESTD	BUNS	D
14	019	10	30	096	001		10.7	.65			CAMPBELL	TURKEYNO	B
15	019	10	30	108	001		16.0	.23			WESTERN	HARDMARG	A
16	019	10	30	124	001			.40			MARLBORO	FILTER	A
17	019	10	30	069	001								
18	019	10	30	002	001		12.0	1.73			FOODGIAN	PORKCHOP	D
19	019	10	30	095	001						HARDEES	FRENCHFR	A
20	019	10	30	055	001		1.2	.15			REESES	CHOCOLAT	E
21	019	10	30	102	001		9.0				BAYER		A
22	019	10	30	037	001		20.0				CRISPIES	PRETZELS	S
23	019	10	30	001	001		18.0				FOODGIAN	GROUND	A
24	019	10	3	001	001				85	X	FOODGIAN	SIRLOIN	D
25													

Source: From William L. Rathje, Wilson W. Hughes, and Sherry L. Jernigan, "The Science of Garbage: Following the Consumer Through His Garbage Can," in William Locander, ed., _Marketing Looks Outward_ (Chicago: American Marketing Association, 1977), pp. 56–64. Used by permission.

Figure 7.4 *continued*

Garbage Item Code List (F-75)

*See Special Notes
(cf. Rathje and Hughes, 1975)

▲See Fruit and Vegetable Page
(cf. Rathje and Hughes, 1975)

Meat—beef only*	001
Meat—other*	002
Poultry—chicken only	003
Poultry—other	004
Fish (fresh, frozen, canned, dried)*	005
Crustaceans & Mollusks (shrimp, clams, etc.)	006
T.V.P.—Type foods*	007
Cheese (including cottage cheese)	010
Milk*	011
Ice Cream (also ice milk, sherbet, popsicles)*	012
Other Dairy (*not* butter)	013
Eggs (regular, powdered, liquid)*	014
Beans (*not* green beans)*	015
Nuts	016
Peanut Butter	017
Fats: Saturated*	018
Unsaturated*	019
Corn (also corn meal and masa)*	022
Flour (also pancake mix)*	023
Rice*	024
Other Grain (barley, wheat germ, etc.)	025
Noodles (pasta)	026
White Bread	027
Dark Bread	028
Tortillas*	029
Dry Cereals: Regular	030
High sugar (first or second ingredient)	031
Cooked Cereals (instant or regular)	032
Crackers	033
Chips (also pretzels)	034
Fresh Vegetables ▲	041
Canned Vegetables (dehydrated also) ▲	042
Frozen Vegetables ▲	043
Potato *Peel* ▲	044
Fresh Fruit ▲	045
Canned Fruit (dehydrated also) ▲	046
Frozen Fruit ▲	047
Fruit *Peel* ▲	048
Condiments (relish, pickles, olives, vinegar, etc.)	049

Syrup, Honey, Jellies, Molasses	051
Pastries (cookies, cakes and mix, pies, etc.)*	052
Sugar*	053
Artificial Sweeteners	054
Candy*	055
Salt*	056
Spices (solid or powdered)	057
Baking Additives (yeast, baking powder, etc.)*	058
Pudding	061
Gelatin	062
Instant Breakfast	063
Dips (for chips)	064
Nondairy Creamers & Whips	065
Health Foods*	066
Slop*	069
Regular Coffee (instant or ground)*	070
Decaf Coffee	071
Exotic Coffee*	072
Tea*	073
Chocolate Drink Mix or Topping	074
Fruit (or veg.) Juice (canned or bottled)	075
Fruit Juice Concentrate	076
Fruit Juice Powder (Tang, Koolaid)	077
Diet Soda	078
Regular Soda	079
Cocktail Mix (carbonated)	080
Cocktail Mix (noncarb. liquid)	081
Cocktail Mix (powdered)	082
Premixed Cocktails (alcoholic)	083
Spirits (booze)	084
Wine (still + sparkling)	085
Beer*	086
Baby Food + Juice*	087
Baby Cereal (pablum)	088
Baby Formula (liquid)*	089
Baby Formula (powdered)*	090
Pet Food (dry)	091
Pet Food (canned or moist)	092
TV Dinners (also pot pies)	094
Take-Out Meals	095
Soups*	096

Sauces*	097
Prepared Meals (canned or packaged)*	098
Vitamin Pills and Supplements (commercial)*	100
Prescribed Drugs (prescribed vitamins)	101
Commercial Drugs Aspirin (also acetaminophen)	102
Stimulants and Depressants*	103
Remedies (physical)*	104
Illicit Drugs*	105
Commercial Drug Paraphernalia	106
Illicit Drug Paraphernalia	107
Contraceptives: Male	108
Female	109
Baby Supplies (diapers, etc.)*	111
Injury Oriented (iodine, bandaids, etc.)	112
Personal Sanitation*	113
Cosmetics*	114
Cigarettes (pack)*	124
Cigarettes (carton)*	125
Cigars	126
Pipe, Chewing Tobacco, Loose Tobacco	127
Rolling Papers	128
Household Cleaners (also laundry)*	131
Household Cleaning *Tools* (not detergents)	132
Household Maint. Items (paint, wood, etc.)	133
Cooking & Serving Aids	134
Tissue Container	135
Toilet Paper Container	136
Napkin Container	137
Paper Towel Container	138
Plastic Wrap Container	139
Bags (paper *or* plastic)*	140
Bag Container	141
Aluminum Foil Sheets	142
Aluminum Foil Package	143
Wax Paper Package	144
Mechanical Appliance (tools)	147

From William L. Rathje, Wilson W. Hughes, and Sherry L. Jernigan, "The Science of Garbage: Following the Consumer Through His Garbage Can" in William Locander, ed., *Marketing Looks Outward* (Chicago: American Marketing Association, 1977): 56–64. Used by permission.

Finally, the responses that result from the pretest should be coded and tabulated. We have previously discussed the need for the preparation of dummy tables prior to the development of the questionnaire. The tabulation of pretest responses can check on our conceptualization of the problem and the data and method of analysis necessary to answer it.

. . . the tables will confirm the need for various sets of data. If we have no place to put the responses to a question, either the data are superfluous or we omitted some contemplated analysis. If some part of a table remains empty, we may have omitted a necessary question. Trial tabulations show us, as no previous method can, that all data collected will be put to use, and that we will obtain all necessary data.[34]

The researcher who avoids a questionnaire pretest and tabulation of replies is either naive or a fool. The pretest is the most inexpensive insurance the researcher can buy to assure the success of the questionnaire and the research project. A careful pretest, along with proper attention to the do's and don'ts presented in this chapter and summarized in Research Realities 7.2, see pages 306–307, should make the questionnaire development process successful.

Observational Forms

There are generally fewer problems in constructing observational forms than questionnaires, because the researcher is no longer concerned with the fact that the question and the way it is asked will affect the response. Through proper training of observers, the researcher can create the necessary expertise so that the data-collection instrument is handled consistently. Alternatively, the researcher may simply use a mechanical device to measure the behavior of interest and secure complete consistency in measurement. This is not to imply that observational forms offer no problems of construction. Rather, the researcher needs to make very explicit decisions about what is to be observed and the categories and units that will be used to record this behavior. Figure 7.4, pages 302–303, is the observational form and coding sheet used in the garbage project described in Chapter 6; it offers an example of how detailed these decisions can be.

The statement that "One needs to determine what is to be observed before one can make a scientific observation" seems trite indeed. Yet this is exactly the case. Almost any event can be described in a number of ways. When we watch someone making a cigarette purchase, we might report that: (1) the person purchased one package of cigarettes; (2) the woman purchased one package of cigarettes; (3) the woman purchased a package of Tareyton cigarettes; (4) the woman purchased a package of Tareyton 100's; (5) the woman, after asking for and finding that the store was out of Virginia Slims, purchased a package of Tareyton 100's, and so on.

A great many additional variations are possible (for example, the type, name, or location of the store where this behavior occurred). In order for this observation to be productive for scientific inquiry, we must predetermine which aspects of this behavior

---

[34]Brown and Beik, *Marketing Research and Analysis*, pp. 265–266.

Research Realities 7.2

Some Do's and Don'ts When Preparing Questionnaires

Step 1.   Specify What Information Will Be Sought

1. Make sure that you have a clear understanding of the issue and what it is that you want to know (expect to learn). Frame your research questions, but refrain from writing questions for the questionnaire at this time.

2. Make a list of your research questions. Review them periodically as you are working on the questionnaire.

3. Use the "dummy tables" that were set up to guide the data analysis to suggest questions for the questionnaire.

4. Conduct a search for existing questions on the issue.

5. Revise existing questions on the issue, and prepare new questions that address the issues you plan to research.

Step 2.   Determine Type of Questionnaire and Method of Administration

1. Use the type of data to be collected as a basis for deciding on the type of questionnaire.

2. Use degree of structure and disguise as well as cost factors to determine the method of administration.

3. Compare the special capabilities and limitations of each method of administration and the value of the data collected from each with the needs of the survey.

Step 3.   Determine Content of Individual Questions

1. For each research question ask yourself, "Why do I want to know this?" Answer it in terms of how it will help your research. "It would be interesting to know" is not an acceptable answer.

2. Make sure each question is specific and addresses only one important issue.

3. Ask yourself whether the question applies to all respondents; it should, or provision should be made for skipping it.

4. Split questions that can be answered from different frames of reference into multiple questions, one corresponding to each frame of reference.

5. Ask yourself whether respondents will be informed about and can remember the issue that the question is dealing with.

6. Make sure the time period of the question is related to the importance of the topic. Consider using aided-recall techniques like diaries, records, or bounded recall.

7. Avoid questions that require excessive effort, that have hard-to-articulate answers, and that deal with embarrassing or threatening issues.

8. If threatening questions are necessary,

   a. hide the questions among more innocuous ones.
   b. make use of a counterbiasing statement.
   c. phrase the question in terms of others and how the respondent might feel or act.
   d. ask respondents if they have ever engaged in the undesirable activity, and then ask if they are presently engaging in such an activity.
   e. use categories or ranges rather than specific numbers.
   f. use the randomized response model.

Step 4:   Determine Form of Response to Each Question

1. Determine which type of question—open-ended, dichotomous, or multichotomous—provides data that fits the information needs of the project.

2. Use structured questions whenever possible.

3. Use open-ended questions that require short answers to begin a questionnaire.

4. Try to convert open-ended questions to closed (fixed) response questions to reduce respondent work load and coding effort for descriptive and causal studies.

5. If open-ended question are necessary, make the question sufficiently directed to give respondents a frame of reference when answering.

6. When using dichotomous questions, state the negative or alternative side in detail.

7. Provide for "don't know," "no opinion," and "both" answers.

8. Be aware that there may be a middle ground.

9. Be sensitive to the mildness or harshness of the alternatives.

10. When using multichotomous questions, be sure the choices are exhaustive and mutually exclusive, and if combinations are possible, include them.

11. Be sure the range of alternatives is clear and that all reasonable alternative answers are included.

12. If the possible responses are very numerous, consider using more than one question to reduce the potential for information overload.

13. When using dichotomous or mutichotomous questions, consider the use of a split ballot procedure to reduce order bias.

14. Clearly indicate if items are to be ranked or if only one item on the list is to be chosen.

Step 5: Determine Wording of Each Question

1. Use simple words.

2. Avoid ambiguous words and questions.

3. Avoid leading questions.

4. Avoid implicit alternatives.

5. Avoid implicit assumptions.

6. Avoid generalizations and estimates.

7. Use simple sentences, and avoid compound sentences.

8. Change long, dependent clauses to words or short phrases.

9. Avoid double-barreled questions.

10. Make sure each question is as specific as possible.

Step 6: Determine Question Sequence

1. Use simple, interesting questions for openers.

2. Use the funnel-approach, first asking broad questions and then narrowing them down.

3. Ask difficult or sensitive questions late in the questionnaire when rapport is better.

4. Follow chronological order when collecting historical information.

5. Complete questions about one topic before moving on to the next.

6. Prepare a flow chart whenever filter questions are being considered.

7. Ask filter questions before asking detailed questions.

8. Ask demographic questions last so that if respondent refuses, the other data is still usable.

Step 7: Determine Physical Characteristics of Questionnaire

1. Make sure the questionnaire looks professional and is relatively easy to answer.

2. Use quality paper and print; do not photocopy the questionnaire.

3. Attempt to make the questionnaire as short as possible while avoiding a crowded appearance.

4. Use a booklet format for ease of analysis and to prevent lost pages.

5. List the name of the organization conducting the survey on the first page.

6. Number the questions to ease data processing.

7. If the respondent must skip more than one question, use a "go to."

8. If the respondent must skip an entire section, consider color coding the sections.

9. State how the responses are to be reported, such as a checkmark, number, circle, etc.

Step 8: Reexamine Steps 1–7 and Revise If Necessary

1. Examine each word of every question to ensure the question is not confusing, ambiguous, offensive, or leading.

2. Get peer evaluations of the draft questionnaire.

Step 9: Pretest Questionnaire and Revise If Necessary

1. Pretest the questionnaire first by personal interviews among respondents similar to those to be used in the actual study.

2. Obtain comments from the interviewers and respondents to discover any problems with the questionnaire, and revise it if necessary. When the revisions are substantial, repeat Steps 1 and 2.

3. Pretest the questionnaire by mail or telephone to uncover problems unique to the mode of administration.

4. Code and tabulate the pretest responses in dummy tables to determine if questions are providing adequate information.

5. Eliminate questions that do not provide adequate information, and revise questions that cause problems.

are relevant. The decision as to what to observe requires that the researcher specify the following:

- Who should be observed? Anyone entering the store? Anyone making a purchase? Anyone making a cigarette purchase?

- What aspects of the purchase should be reported? Which brand they purchased? Which brand they asked for first? Whether the purchase was of king size or regular cigarettes? What about the purchaser? Is the person's sex to be recorded? Is the individual's age to be estimated? Does it make any difference if the person was alone or in a group?

- When should the observation be made? On what day of the week? At what time of the day? Should day and time be reported? Should the observation be recorded only after a purchase occurs or should an approach by a customer to a salesclerk also be recorded even if it does not result in a sale?

- Where should the observation be made? In what kind of store? How should the store be selected? How should it be noted on the observational form—by type, by location, by name? Should vending-machine purchases also be noted?

The careful reader will note that these are the same kinds of who, what, when, and where decisions that need to be made in selecting the research design. The why and how are also implicit. The research problem should dictate the why of the observation, while the how involves choosing the observation device or form that will be used. A paper-and-pencil form should be very simple to use. It should parallel the logical sequence of the purchase act (for example, a male approaches the clerk, asks for a package of cigarettes, and so on, if these behaviors are relevant) and should permit the recording of observations by a simple check mark if possible. Again, careful attention to detail, exacting examination of the preliminary form, and an adequate pretest should return handsome dividends with respect to the quality of the observations made.

Summary

A researcher wishing to collect primary data will need to tackle the task of designing the data collection device sooner or later. Most typically this will mean designing a questionnaire, although it may mean framing an observational form.

Questionnaire design is still very much of an art rather than a science, and there are many admonitions of things to avoid when doing so. Nevertheless, a nine-step procedure was offered as a guide. This guide indicates that researchers need to ask and answer some specific questions when designing questionnaires, including ''What information will be sought? What type of questionnaire will be used? How will that questionnaire be administered? What will be the content of the individual questions? What will be the form of response—dichotomous, multichotomous, or open-ended—to each question? How will each question be phrased? How will the questions be sequenced? What will the questionnaire look like physically?'' Researchers should not be surprised to find themselves repeating the various steps when designing a questionnaire. Further, while the temptation is somtimes great, one should never omit a pretest of the questionnaire. Regardless of how well it looks in the abstract, the pretest provides the real test of the questionnaire and the mode of administration. Actually, at least two pretests should be conducted. The first should use personal interviews, and after all the troublesome spots have been smoothed over, a second pretest using the normal mode of administration should be conducted. The data collected in the pretest should then be subjected to the analyses planned for the full data set, as this will reveal serious omissions or other shortcomings while it is still possible to correct these deficiencies.

Observational forms generally present fewer problems of construction than do questionnaires, because the researcher no longer needs to be concerned with the fact that the question and the way it is asked will affect the response. Observational forms do, however, require a precise statement of who or what is to be observed, what actions or characteristics are relevant, and when and where the observations will be made.

Questions

1. What role do the research hypotheses play in determining the information that will be sought?

2. Suppose you were interested in determining the proportion of men in a geographic area who use hair sprays. How could the necessary information be obtained by open-ended question, by multiple choice question, and by dichotomous question? Which would be preferable?

3. How does the method of administration of a questionnaire affect the type of question to be employed?

4. What criteria can a researcher employ to determine whether a specific question should be included in a questionnaire?

5. What is telescoping error? What does it suggest about the period to be used when asking respondents to recall past events?

6. What are some recommended ways by which one can ask for sensitive information?

7. What is an open-ended question? A multichotomous question? A dichotomous question? What are some of the key things researchers must be careful to avoid in framing multichotomous and dichotomous questions?

8. What is a split ballot, and why is it employed?

9. What is an ambiguous question? A leading question? A question with implicit alternatives? A question with implied assumptions? A double-barreled question?

10. What is the proper sequence when asking for basic information and classification information?

11. What is the funnel approach to question sequencing?

12. What is a branching question? Why are they used?

13. Where should one ask for sensitive information in the questionnaire?

14. How can the physical features of a questionnaire affect its acceptance by respondents? Its handling and control by the researcher?

15. What is the overriding principle guiding questionnaire construction?

16. What decisions must the researcher make when developing an observational form for data collection?

Applications and Problems

1. Evaluate the following questions:

    (a) *Which of the following magazines do you read regularly?*
        _____ Time
        _____ Newsweek
        _____ Business Week

    (b) *Are you a frequent purchaser of Birds Eye Frozen vegetables?*
        _____ Yes   _____ No

    (c) *Do you agree that the government should impose import restrictions?*
        _____ Strongly agree
        _____ Agree
        _____ Neither agree or disagree
        _____ Disagree
        _____ Strongly disagree

    (d) *How often do you buy detergent?*
        _____ Once a week
        _____ Once in two weeks
        _____ Once in three weeks
        _____ Once a month

    (e) *Rank the following in order of preference:*
        _____ Kellogg's Corn Flakes
        _____ Quaker's Life
        _____ Post Bran Flakes
        _____ Kellogg's Bran Flakes
        _____ Instant Quaker Oat Meal
        _____ Post Rice Krinkles

    (f) *Where do you usually purchase your school supplies?*

    (g) *When you are watching television, do you also watch most of the advertisements?*

    (h) *Which of the following brands of tea are most similar?*
        _____ Liptons Orange Pekoe
        _____ Turnings Orange Pekoe
        _____ Bigelow Orange Pekoe
        _____ Salada Orange Pekoe

    (i) *Do you think that the present policy of cutting taxes and reducing government spending should be continued?*
        _____ Yes   _____ No

    (j) *In a seven-day week, how often do you eat breakfast?*
        _____ Every day of the week
        _____ 5–6 times a week
        _____ 2–4 times a week
        _____ Once a week
        _____ Never

2. Make the necessary corrections to the above questions.

3. Evaluate the following multichotomous questions. Would dichotomous or open-ended questions be more appropriate?

    (a) *Which one of the following reasons is most important in your choice of stereo equipment?*
        _____ Price
        _____ In-store service

     _____ Brand name
     _____ Level of distortion
     _____ Guarantee/warranty

(b) *Please indicate your education level.*
     _____ Less than high school
     _____ Some high school
     _____ High school graduate
     _____ Technical or vocational school
     _____ Some college
     _____ College graduate
     _____ Some graduate or professional school

(c) *Which of the following reflects your views toward the issues raised by ecologists?*
     _____ Have received attention
     _____ Have not received attention
     _____ Should receive more attention
     _____ Should receive less attention

(d) *Which of the following statements do you most strongly agree with?*
     _____ Eastern Airlines has better service than Republic Airlines
     _____ Republic Airlines has better service than United Airlines
     _____ United Airlines has better service than Eastern Airlines
     _____ United Airlines has better service than Republic Airlines
     _____ Republic Airlines has better service than Eastern Airlines
     _____ Eastern Airlines has better service than United Airlines

4. Evaluate the following open-ended questions. Rephrase them as multichotomous or dichotomous questions if you think it would be appropriate.

    (a) *Do you go to the movies often?*
    (b) *Approximately how much do you spend per week on groceries?*
    (c) *What brands of cheese did you purchase during the last week?*

5. A small brokerage firm was concerned with the declining number of customers and decided to do a quick survey. The major objective was to find out the reasons for patronizing a particular brokerage firm and to find out the importance of customer service. The following questionnaire was to be administered by telephone.

Good Afternoon Sir/Madam:

We are doing a survey on attitudes towards brokerage firms. Could you please answer the following questions? Thank you.

1. Have you invested any money in the stock market?

  ____ Yes   ____ No

If respondent replies *yes*, continue, otherwise terminate interview.

2. Do you manage your own investments or do you go to a brokerage firm?

  ____ Manage own investments   ____ Go to a brokerage firm

If respondent replies "go to a brokerage firm" continue, otherwise terminate interview.

---

continued on next page

Questionnaire *continued*

3. *How satisfied are you with your brokerage firm?*

Very Satisfied	Satisfied	Neither Satisfied or Dissatisfied	Dissatisfied	Very Dissatisfied
____	____	____	____	____

4. *How important is personal service to you?*

Very Important	Important	Not Particularly Important	Not at All Important
____	____	____	____

5. *Which of the following reasons is the most important in patronizing a particular firm?*
   ____ the commission charged by the firm
   ____ the personal service
   ____ the return on investment
   ____ the investment counselling

6. *Approximately how long have you been investing through the brokerage firm you are currently using?*
   ____ about 3 months   ____ about 9 months
   ____ about 6 months   ____ about 1 year or more

7. *How much capital do you have invested?*
   ____ $500–$750   ____ $1,000–$1,500
   ____ $750–$1,000   ____ $1,500 or more

Good-bye and thank you for your cooperation.

Evaluate the above questionnaire.

Chapter 8
Attitude
Measurement

Attitude is one of the most pervasive notions in all of marketing. It plays a pivotal role in the major models describing consumer behavior, as well as in many, if not most, investigations of consumer behavior that do not rely on a formal integrated model.[1] The main reason attitude plays this central role is because it is believed to strongly influence behavior. "Attitudes *directly affect* purchase decisions and these, in turn, *directly affect* attitudes through experience in using the product or service selected. In a broad sense, purchase decisions are based *almost solely* upon attitudes existing at the time of purchase, however these attitudes might have been formed"[2] (emphasis added). Academic researchers, therefore, use attitude as an important explanatory variable in creating models of behavior.

Practitioners have no less an interest. Sometimes an entire industry will sponsor a study of attitudes. Research Realities 8.1, for example, reports the findings of studies sponsored by the American Association of Advertising Agencies to assess whether people's attitudes toward advertising were changing as this could have important implications for the agency industry. Most typically though, individual firms will sponsor a study of attitudes, often for a variety of reasons. Consider, for example, the following: (1) The appliance manufacturer's interest in present dealer and prospective dealer attitudes toward the company's warranty policy. If the dealers embrace the policy, the company feels they are more likely to give adequate, courteous service and, in the process, produce more satisfied customers. (2) The cosmetic manufacturer's interest in the early assessment of the attitudes of consumers in the test market toward the company's new shampoo. If unfavorable, the company will consider changing the introductory marketing strategy. (3) The industrial marketer's interest in the general job satisfaction (an attitude) of its highly trained, highly skilled field staff of sales engineers. These few examples indicate some of the many groups of people in whose attitudes the marketer is typically interested: the company's employees, its intermediaries, and its

---

[1] See, for example, James F. Engel, Roger D. Blackwell, and Paul Miniard, *Consumer Behavior,* 5th ed. (Hinsdale, Ill.: Dryden Press, 1985).

[2] James H. Myers and William H. Reynolds, *Consumer Behavior and Marketing Management* (Boston: Houghton Mifflin, © 1967), p. 146. Used by permission of the publisher. For discussion of the role of attitudes and its impact on consumer behavior, see Robert B. Zajonc and Hazel Markus "Affective and Cognitive Factors in Preferences," *Journal of Consumer Research,* 9 (September, 1982), pp. 123–131.

Research Realities 8.1

Attitudes Toward Advertising: 1974–1985

	1974* % Agree	1985 % Agree		1974* % Agree	1985 % Agree
Consumer Benefits			**Credibility continued**		
Advertising is a good way to learn about new products.	92%	92%	Most advertising is in poor taste.	45	43
Advertising is a good way to learn about what products and services are available.	88	87	**Entertainment Value**		
Advertising is a good way to find out how products and services work.	77	76	A lot of advertising is funny or clever.	72	81
Without advertising there would be fewer enjoyable programs on free TV.	74	75	A lot of advertising is enjoyable.	56	56
Advertising results in better products for the public.	57	60	**Manipulation or Motivation?**		
Advertising gives you a good idea about products by showing the kinds of people who use them.	37	37	Advertising makes people want things they don't really need.	78	84
			Most ads try to work on people's emotions.	79	80
Credibility			It is really the manufacturers of products and not the advertising agencies who decide how truthful advertising is and what is said in ads.	60	63
Most ads don't tell facts, but just create a mood.	72%	73%	In general, advertisements present an honest picture of the products advertised.	41	30
Most advertising insults the intelligence of the average consumer.	60	72			
Products don't perform as well as the ads claim.	72	72	**Clutter or Intrusiveness**		
People really "tune out" ads and don't remember what they've seen or heard soon after.	57	65	There are too many commercials in a row on television.	87	92
			The same ads are constantly shown again and again.	87	90

Source: "Advertiser to Consumer: How 'm I Doin?" Ogilvy & Mather, *Listening Post*, 61 (April 1985), p. 2. Reprinted with permission.
*Findings from 4A's survey conducted in 1974.

customers. Their posture, stance, or predisposition to act can be important determinants of the company's success, and the marketer needs devices for measuring these postures. This chapter reviews some of the many techniques for assessing a person's posture on an issue.

Researchers and practitioners share some common problems as well as a common interest in attitude. For one thing, while it is one of the most widely used notions in all of social psychology, it is also one of the most inconsistently used concepts. There are a variety of interpretations, although there does seem to be substantial agreement about the following:

1. Attitude represents a predisposition to respond to an object, not actual behavior toward the object. Attitude thus possesses the quality of readiness.

2. Attitude is persistent over time. It can change, to be sure, but alteration of an attitude that is strongly held requires substantial pressure.

3. Attitude is a latent variable that produces consistency in behavior, either verbal or physical.

4. Attitude has a directional quality. It connotes a preference regarding the outcomes involving the object, evaluations of the object, or positive–neutral–negative feelings for the object.[3]

These consistencies led to our definition of attitude as representing a person's ideas, convictions, or liking with regard to a specific object or idea, presented in Chapter 6.

Scales of Measurement

To properly address the subject of attitude measurement, it is necessary to define measurement and to briefly review the types of scales that can be used in measurement.

Measurement consists of "rules for assigning numbers to objects in such a way as to represent quantities of attributes."[4] Note two things about the definition. First, it indicates that we measure the attributes of objects and not the objects themselves. We do not measure a person, for example, but may choose to measure the individual's income, social class, education, height, weight, attitudes, or whatever, all of which are attributes of this person. Second, the definition is broad in that it does not specify how the numbers are to be assigned. In this sense, the rule is too simplistic and conveys a false sense of security, because there is a great temptation to read more meaning into the numbers than they actually contain. We often incorrectly attribute all the properties of the scale of numbers to the assigned numerals.

Consider the properties of the scale of numbers for a minute. Take the numbers 1, 2, 3, and 4. Now let the number "1" stand for one object, "2" for two objects, and so on. The scale of numbers possesses a number of properties. For example, we can say that "2" is larger than "1" and "3" is larger than "2," and so on. Also, we can say that the interval between "1" and "2" is the same size as the interval between "3" and "4," which is the same as that between "2" and "3," and so on. We can say still further that "3" is three times greater than "1," while "4" is four times greater than "1" and two times greater than "2," and so on. However, when we assign numerals to attributes of objects, these relations do not necessarily hold. Rather, we

---

[3]Adapted from the introduction by Gene F. Summers, ed., *Attitude Measurement* (Chicago: Rand McNally, 1970), p. 370 See also Engel, Blackwell, and Miniard, *Consumer Behavior*. One of the reasons for the many definitions of attitude is the age-old scientific problem of going from construct to operational definition, a problem that is reviewed in Appendix 8C.

[4]Jum C. Nunnally, *Psychometric Theory,* 2nd ed. (New York: McGraw-Hill, 1978), p. 3.

have to determine which properties of the scale of numbers actually apply. "This problem has nothing to do with determining the properties of the number; rather, we must determine the *properties of the attribute itself,* and then be sure that the numerals are assigned so that the *numerals properly reflect the properties of the attribute*"[5] (emphasis added). Consider the different types of scales on which the attribute can be measured, namely, nominal, ordinal, interval, and ratio.[6] Table 8.1 summarizes some of the more important features of these scales, which are elaborated below.

Nominal Scale

One of the simplest properties of the scale of numbers is *identity*. A person's social security number is a **nominal scale,** as are the numbers on football jerseys, lockers, and so on. These numbers simply *identify* the individual assigned the number. Similarly, if in a given study males are coded "1" and females "2," we have again made use of a nominal scale. The individuals are uniquely identified as male or female. All we need to determine an individual's sex is to know whether the person is coded as a "1" or as a "2." Note further that there is nothing implied by the numerals other than identification of the sex of the person. Females, although they bear a higher number, are not necessarily "superior" to males, or "more" than males, or twice as many as males as the numbers 2 and 1 indicate, or vice versa. We could just as easily reverse our coding procedure so that each female is a "1" and each male a "2."

The reason we could reverse our codes is that the only property conveyed by the numbers is identity. With a nominal scale, the only permissible operation is counting. Thus, the mode is the only legitimate measure of central tendency. It does not make sense in a sample consisting of 60 men and 40 women to say that the average sex is 1.4, given males were coded "1" and females "2" [0.6(1) + 0.4(2)]. All we can say is that there were more males in the sample than females, or that 60 percent of the sample was male.

Ordinal Scale

A second property of the scale of numbers is that of *order*. Thus, we could say that the number "2" was greater than the number "1", and that "3" was greater than both "2" and "1," and that "4" was greater than all three of these numbers. The numbers 1, 2, 3, and 4 are ordered, and the larger the number the greater the property. Note that the **ordinal scale** implies identity, since the same number would be used for all objects that are the same. An example would be the assignment of the number "1" to denote

---

[5]Wendell R. Garner and C. D. Creelman, "Problems and Methods of Psychological Scaling," in Harry Helson and William Bevan, eds., *Contemporary Approaches to Psychology* (New York: Van Nostrand, 1967), p. 3. The following discussion relies heavily on this excellent article. See also Earl R. Babbie *The Practice of Social Research,* 2nd ed. (Belmont, Calif.: Wadsworth Publishing Company, 1979), especially pages 141–146.

[6]Our classification follows that of Stanley S. Stevens, "Mathematics, Measurement and Psychophysics," in Stanley S. Stevens, ed., *Handbook of Experimental Psychology* (New York: John Wiley, 1951) the most accepted classification in the social sciences.

Table 8.1
Scales of Measurement

Scale	Basic Comparisons[a]	Typical Examples	Measures of Average[b]
Nominal	Identity	Male–female User–nonuser Occupations Uniform numbers	Mode
Ordinal	Order	Preference for brands Social class Hardness of minerals Graded quality of lumber	Median
Interval	Comparison of intervals	Temperature scale Grade point average Attitude toward brands	Mean
Ratio	Comparison of absolute magnitudes	Units sold Number of purchasers Probability of purchase Weight	Geometric mean Harmonic mean

[a]All the comparisons applicable to a given scale are permissible with all scales below it in the table. For example, the ratio scale allows the comparison of intervals and the investigation of order and identity, in addition to the comparison of absolute magnitudes.

[b]The measures of average applicable to a given scale are also appropriate for all scales below it in the table; i.e., the mode is also a meaningful measure of the average when measurement is on an ordinal, interval, or ratio scale.

freshmen, "2" to denote sophomores, "3" juniors, and "4" seniors. Note that we could have just as well used the numbers "10" for freshmen, "20" for sophomores, "25" for juniors, and "30" for seniors. This assignment would still indicate the class level of each person and the *relative standing* of two persons when compared in terms of who is further along in the academic program. Note further that this is all that is conveyed by an ordinal scale. The difference in rank says nothing about the difference in academic achievement between two ranks. This is perhaps easier to see if we talk about the three top people in a graduating class. The fact that one person was ranked number one while the second was ranked number two tells us nothing about the difference in academic achievement between the two. Nor can we say that the difference in academic achievement between the first- and second-ranked people equals the difference between the second- and third-ranked people, even though the difference between "1" and "2" equals the difference between "2" and "3."

As suggested, we can transform an ordinal scale in any way we wish as long as we maintain the basic ordering of the objects. The ordinal scale is thus said to allow any monotonic positive transformation of the assigned numerals, since the differences in numerals are void of meaning other than order.

Again, whether we can use the ordinal scale to assign numerals to objects depends on the attribute in question. The attribute itself must possess the ordinal property to allow ordinal scaling that is meaningful.

With ordinal scales, both the median and mode are permissible or meaningful measures of average. Thus, if twenty people ranked Product A, say, first in comparison with Products B and C, while ten ranked it second and five ranked it third, we could say that (1) the average rank of Product A as judged by the median response was one (with thirty-five subjects, the median is given by the eighteenth reponse when ranked from lowest to highest) and that (2) the modal rank was also one.

Interval Scale

A third property of the scale of numbers is that the *intervals* between the numbers are meaningful in the sense that the numbers tell us how far apart the objects are with respect to the attribute. This means that the *differences* can be compared. The difference between ''1'' and ''2'' is equal to the difference between ''2'' and ''3.'' Further, the difference between ''2'' and ''4'' is twice the difference that exists between ''1'' and ''2.''

One classic example of an **interval scale** is the temperature scale, as it indicates what we can and cannot say when we have measured an attribute on an interval scale. Suppose the low temperature for the day was 40°F and the high was 80°F. Can we say that the high temperature was twice as hot (that is, represented twice the heat) as the low temperature? The answer is an unequivocal no. To see the folly in claiming 80°F is twice as warm as 40°F, one simply needs to convert these temperatures to their centigrade equivalents where $C = (5F - 160)/9$. Now we see that the low was 4.4°C and the high was 26.6°C, a much different ratio between low and high than was indicated by the Fahrenheit scale.

The example serves to illustrate that we cannot compare the absolute magnitude of numbers when measurement is made on the basis of an interval scale. The reason is that in an interval scale, the zero point is established arbitrarily.[7] This means that any positive linear transformation of the form $y = a + bx$, where b is positive, x is the original number, and y is the transformed number, will preserve the properties of the scale.

What, then, can we say when measurement is made on an interval scale? First, we can say that 80°F is warmer than 40°F. Second, given a third temperature, we *can compare the intervals;* that is, we can say the difference in ''heat'' between 80°F and 120°F is the *same* as the difference between 40°F and 80°F, and that the difference between 40°F and 120°F is *twice* the difference between 40°F and 80°F. To see that this conclusion is legitimate, we can simply resort to the centigrade equivalents; 120°F represents 48.8°C, and the difference between 4.4°C (40°F) and 26.6°C (80°F) is the same as that between 26.6°C (80°F) and 48.8°C (120°F), namely, 22.2°. Further, the difference of 44.4°C between 4.4°C and 48.8°C is twice as large as that between 4.4°C and 26.6°C, as it was when the Fahrenheit scale was used. The comparison of intervals is legitimate with an interval scale because the relationships among the differences hold regardless of the particular constants chosen for a and b when transforming an interval

---

[7]The zero point on the Fahrenheit scale was originally established by mixing equal weights of snow and salt.

set of numbers. With an interval scale, the mean, median, and mode are all meaningful measures of average.

Ratio Scale

The **ratio scale** differs from an interval scale in that it possesses a *natural* or *absolute* zero, one for which there is universal agreement as to its location. Height and weight are obvious examples.

With a ratio scale, the comparison of the *absolute magnitude* of the numbers is legitimate. Thus, a person weighing 200 pounds is said to be twice as heavy as one weighing 100 pounds, and a person weighing 300 pounds is three times as heavy. Further, we have already seen that the more powerful scales include the properties possessed by the less powerful ones. This means that with a ratio scale we can compare intervals, rank objects according to magnitude, or use the numbers to identify the objects.

Ratio scales only allow the proportionate transformation of the scale values and not the addition of an arbitrary constant as do interval scales. A proportionate transformation is of the form $y = bx,$ where x again represents the original values and y the transformed values and b is some positive constant. The conversion of feet to inches ($b = 12$) is an obvious example. All the relationships among the objects are preserved whether the comparison is made in feet or inches.

The geometric mean as well as the more usual arithmetic mean, median, and mode are meaningful measures of average when attributes are measured on a ratio scale.

Scaling of Psychological Attributes

The attribute determines the most powerful scale that can be used to measure the characteristic. That is always the way it is in measurement. The characteristic and its qualities set the upper limit for the assignment of numerals to objects. Because of the procedures used in generating the instrument, it is always possible to end up with what we might call a less powerful measure of the attribute (for example, a nominal rather than an ordinal scale). However, we can never exceed the basic nature of the attribute with our measure; for example, we can never generate an interval scale for an attribute that is only ordinal in nature. Thus, it is critical to know something about the attribute itself before we assign numbers to it using some measurement procedure.

Further, the procedure used in constructing the scale determines the type of scale actually generated. The more powerful scales allow stronger comparisons and conclusions to be made. Thus, we can make certain types of comparisons that allow particular conclusions when measurement is on a ratio scale, say, that we cannot make when measurement is on an interval, ordinal, or nominal scale. There is a great temptation to assume that our measures have the properties of the ratio or at least the interval scale. Whether they do in fact is another question, and the simple condition that the attributes of the objects have been assigned numbers should not delude us. Rather, we should critically ask: What is the basic nature of the attribute? Have we captured this basic nature by our measurement procedure?

There are few psychological constructs that can reasonably be assumed to have a natural or absolute zero.

For example, what would an absolute zero of intelligence be? Or what is the absolute zero of attitude toward the Republican Party? There can be neutrality of feeling, and neutral position is often used as the zero point on the scale, but it does not represent an absolute lack of the attitude.[8]

The problem is no less real in marketing. Many of our constructs, borrowed from psychology and sociology, possess no more than interval measurement and some even less. We have to be very careful in conceptualizing the construct or characteristic so as not to delude ourselves or mislead others with our measures and, more importantly, *with our interpretation of those measures.*

The second problem we must face squarely is the ability of our measures to capture the construct as conceptualized. Even if an absolute zero logically exists, for example, do our measures determine it? The procedures used to generate the measure in large part determine the answer. If all we require is that the respondent rank five objects in terms of their overall desirability, we need to recognize that we have only generated an ordinal scale in the absence of further assumptions.[9]

Attitude-Scaling Procedures

There are a number of ways in which attitudes have been measured, including self reports, observation of overt behavior, indirect techniques, performance of "objective" tasks, and physiological reactions.[10] By far the most common approach has been **self reports,** in which people are asked directly for their beliefs or feelings toward an object or class of objects. A number of scales and scaling methods have been devised to secure these feelings. The main types will be reviewed in the next section. For the moment we will consider very briefly the other approaches to attitude determination.

Observation of Behavior   The observation approach to attitude determination rests on the presumption that a subject's behavior is conditioned by his or her attitudes, and, thus, we can use the observed behavior to infer these attitudes. What is often done is to create an artificial situation and see how the individual behaves. For example, to assess a person's attitude toward antipollution legislation, the subject might be asked to sign a "strong" petition prohibiting pollution. The individual's attitude toward pollution would be inferred on the basis of whether or not he or she signed. Alternatively, subjects might be thrust into a group discussing the issue of pollution and their behavior observed. Did the persons oppose or support antipollution legislation in the discussion?

Indirect Techniques   The indirect techniques of attitude assessment use some unstructured or partially structured stimuli as discussed in Chapter 6, such as word association

---

[8]Garner and Creelman, "Problems and Methods," p. 4.

[9]We shall have more to say on this issue in Appendix 8A when discussing nonmetric multidimensional scaling.

[10]This classification of approaches is taken from Stuart W. Cook and Claire Selltiz, "A Multiple Indicator Approach to Attitude Measurement," *Psychological Bulletin,* 62 (1964), pp. 36–55.

tests, sentence completion tests, storytelling, and so on. Since the arguments concerning the use of these devices were detailed there, they will not be repreated here.

Performance of "Objective" Task   These approaches rest on the presumption that a subject's performance of a specific assigned task will depend upon the person's attitude. Thus, to assess a person's pollution posture, we might ask him or her to memorize a number of facts about the extent of pollution, the magnitude of the cleanup task, and pending antipollution legislation. This material would reflect both sides of the issue. The researcher would then attempt to determine what facts the person assimilated. The assumption is that subjects would be more apt to remember those arguments that are most consistent with their own position.

Physiological Reactions   The physiological reaction approach to attitude measurement was also detailed in Chapter 6. Here, through electrical or mechanical means, such as the galvanic skin response technique, the researcher monitors the subject's response to the controlled introduction of some stimuli. One problem that arises in using these measures to assess attitude is that the individual's physiological response only provides an indication of the intensity of the individual's feelings and not whether they are negative or positive.

Multiple Measures   Although self-report techniques for attitude assessment are the most widely used in marketing research studies because they are easy to administer, one should be aware of these other approaches, particularly when one is attempting to establish the validity of a self-report measure. They can provide useful insight into how the method of measurement, and not the differences in the basic attitudes of subjects, caused the scores to vary. This is consistent with the notion of using multiple indicators to establish the convergent and discriminant validity of a measure.[11]

Self-Report Attitude Scales

Given that attitude is one of the most pervasive concepts in all of sociopsychology, it should not prove surprising to find that there have been a number of methods advanced to measure it. While the self-report technique is common to many of the methods, they still differ in terms of the way the scales are constructed and used. In this section, we shall review some of these self-report scales, particularly those that have novel features or have been used extensively in marketing studies. The discusion should give you an appreciation of the main types and their construction and use. Incidentally, in following the arguments, you will find it helpful to distinguish between how a scale is constructed and how it is used.

---

[11]The arguments are elaborated in Cook and Selltiz, "A Multiple-Indicator Approach." The ideas of convergent and discriminant validity are discussed in Appendix 8C. Evidence of the convergent validity of a measure is provided by the extent to which it correlates highly with other measures designed to assess the same construct. Evidence of the discriminant validity of a measure is indicated by low correlations between the measure of interest and other measures that are supposedly not measuring the same variable or construct.

Equal-Appearing Intervals

Suppose one of the banks in town is interested in comparing its image to the images of its competitiors and has developed a list of statements that can be employed to describe each of the banks. Now suppose that, when presented with a list of characteristics, a respondent describes Bank A, the sponsor of the research, as having convenient hours and a convenient location but generally discourteous service and higher service charges on personal checking accounts. Does this respondent have a favorable or unfavorable attitude toward Bank A? Suppose the respondent decribes Bank B as just the opposite. To which bank is the individual more favorably disposed? We cannot say without knowing what the individual statements imply with respect to the person's overall attitude. It is the purpose of **equal-appearing interval** scaling to develop values for the statements (characteristics) so that we can assess a person's attitude toward Bank A or any other bank by analyzing the statements with which the individual describes each bank.[12]

Scale Construction   The general procedure for constructing a scale using equal-appearing intervals is first to generate a large number of statements concerning the psychological object of interest. The statements are then edited to remove obviously ambiguous, irrelevant, and awkward statements, as well as statements that are matters of fact rather than opinion. A relatively large sample of judges is then asked to sort the statements by their degree of favorableness, and a scale value is determined for each statement by the frequency with which the statement is placed in each of the piles. The statements are then screened on the basis of two criteria: the scale values and the dispersion in judgments exhibited by the subjects. A final scale is formed from those statements that span the range of scale values and that display relatively good interjudge reliability. Let us illustrate the procedure using our bank example.

The first task would be to generate a large number of statements. These statements could be generated from a search of the literature, discussions with knowledgeable people, personal experience, or in any of the other ways one uses to develop insight into a phenomenon. The important thing at this stage is that the statements be as exhaustive as possible; that is, they reflect all the attributes of the object that may lead to formation of attitudes about it. Thus, we would want to incorporate statements about a bank's level of service, convenience, interest paid on savings accounts, interest required on loans, and so on.[13] Further, it is often productive at this stage to include several statements that apply to the same attribute but are worded differently. The following would be examples.

---

[12]The equal-appearing interval technique was developed by L. L. Thurstone and E. J. Chave, *The Measurement of Attitude* (Chicago: University of Chicago Press, 1929). The procedure provided an alternative to the paired comparison method of determining statement scale values when the number of statements was large. The paired comparison method, which was also devised by Thurstone, was a forerunner of much modern-day psychological measurement. See L. L. Thurstone, "A Law of Comparative Judgement," *Psychological Review,* 34 (1927), pp. 273–286, and "Psychological Analysis," *American Journal of Psychology,* 38 (1927), pp. 368–389.

[13]See Neil M. Ford, *How to Measure Your Bank's Personality* (Chicago: Bank Marketing Association, 1973), p. 19, for a list of some of the attributes of a bank one might wish to inquire about. See also Sid C. Dudley, Gary F. Young, and Richard L. Powers, "A Study of Factors Affecting Individuals' Banking Preferences," *Journal of Professional Services Marketing,* 1 (1985), pp. 163–168.

Figure 8.1
Thurstone Equal-appearing Interval Continuum

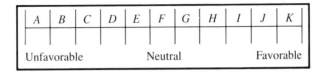

1. The bank offers courteous service.
2. The bank has a convenient location.
3. The bank has convenient hours.
4. The bank offers low-interest rates on loans.
5. The bank pays low interest on its savings accounts.

.

.

.

n.   The bank's service is friendly.

Ideally, *n* would be in the neighborhood of 100 to 200, and each statement would be presented on a separate card.

   After editing the statements, a large sample of subjects would be recruited as judges.[14] Each judge would be instructed to sort the statements into one of eleven piles based on the "degree of favorableness" of the statement. Note this. The judges are not asked whether they agree or disagree with a statement, but rather they are asked to evaluate the statement on its own merits. For example, they would be asked to place (1) those statements that seem to express the *most unfavorable* things one could say about the object in the *A* pile of Figure 8.1, (2) those statements that express the *most favorable* things one could say in the *K* pile, and (3) those statements that are neither positive nor negative in the *F* pile. Those statements that express some intermediate level of favorableness or unfavorableness would, of course, be placed in one of the other piles. The piles are most typically formed by arranging a set of cards with letters on them in front of the judge. Only the two end points and the middle position are anchored with word descriptions in addition to the letter. The presumption is that each judge will perceive the categories as representing equal increments of favorableness, and thus the name equal-appearing intervals.

---

[14]Thurstone and Chave used 300 judges. Edwards summarizes a number of studies, though, in which fewer judges have been used to produce reliable scales. See Allen L. Edwards, *Techniques of Attitude Scale Construction* (New York: Appleton-Century-Crofts, 1957), pp. 94–95. The serious student of attitude measurement would be well advised to read Edwards' good little book.

The researcher attempts to determine a scale value and measure of dispersion for each of the statements from the judgments of the total group of judges. These scale values and measures of dispersion are then employed to select a subset of statements to serve as the final instrument. In effect, these measures serve as "filters" for reducing the total stimuli to a more manageable number. To see how this is accomplished, suppose that Table 8.2 resulted from the reponses of 200 judges to the first four statements.

The first line for each statement, labeled f, indicates the frequency with which each statement is placed in each of the categories. Statement 1, for example, was placed in the slightly unfavorable E category by 60 of the judges, in the neutral F category by 60 judges, and so on. The second line, p, is the proportion of the judges who placed the statements in the category; the entries here were generated by dividing each frequency in Line 1 by 200. The third line, cp, indicates the cumulative proportion of all judges who placed the statement in that specific category or a category more unfavorable; thus, the entry 0.24 for the first statement reflects the fact that 24 percent of all the judges placed Statement 1 in Category D or below ($0.04 + 0.05 + 0.15 = 0.24$). With the cumulative proportions it is relatively easy to calculate the values of the median and interquartile range for each statement, the recommended statistics for scale value and measure of dispersion.

The median, that value above which one-half of the observations lie and below which the other one-half lie, is given, of course, by the fiftieth centile. With grouped data, any centile is calculated by the formula[15]

$$V_c = l + \left[\frac{C - \Sigma p_b}{p_w} \right] i,$$

where

$V_c =$ the value corresponding to the cth centile;

$l =$ the value of the lower boundary of the interval in which the centile falls;

$C =$ the centile in question (for example, 0.50 in the case of the median);

$\Sigma p_b =$ the sum of the proportions below the interval in which the centile falls;

$p_w =$ the proportion within the interval in which the centile falls;

$i =$ the width of the interval, which is assumed to be equal to 1.0.

The only term in the expression that perhaps needs a little elaboration is the value of the lower boundary l. Consider Category D, for example. Although 4 is assigned to the category, the category is assumed to reflect all those values from 3.5 to 4.5; 3.5 is assumed to be the value of the left or lower boundary and 4.5 the value of the right or upper boundary. This is in keeping with our standard notions of measurement, in which 11 inches represents all those measurements greater than 10.5 inches and less than 11.5 inches. The lower boundary in each instance is the category value less 0.5.

The calculation formula addresses the question: How far must one proceed into the interval to reach a particular centile, and what value corresponds to this centile? Take

[15]The formula is adapted from Edwards, *Techniques,* p. 87.

Table 8.2

Equal-Appearing Interval Sort of the Statements into Categories

					Sorting Categories								
	A	B	C	D	E	F	G	H	I	J	K	Scale	Q
Statement	1	2	3	4	5	6	7	8	9	10	11	Value	Value
f	0	8	10	30	60	60	14	12	6	0	0		
1 p	0.00	0.04	0.05	0.15	0.30	0.30	0.07	0.06	0.03	0.00	0.00	5.4	1.7
cp	0.00	0.04	0.09	0.24	0.54	0.84	0.91	0.97	1.00	1.00	1.00		
f	0	0	0	0	0	6	16	28	44	66	40		
2 p	0.00	0.00	0.00	0.00	0.00	0.03	0.08	0.14	0.22	0.33	0.20	9.6	1.8
cp	0.00	0.00	0.00	0.00	0.00	0.03	0.11	0.25	0.47	0.80	1.00		
f	0	0	0	0	10	10	14	32	84	34	16		
3 p	0.00	0.00	0.00	0.00	0.05	0.05	0.07	0.16	0.42	0.17	0.08	8.9	1.5
cp	0.00	0.00	0.00	0.00	0.05	0.10	0.17	0.33	0.75	0.92	1.00		
f	0	0	8	16	36	58	48	24	10	0	0		
4 p	0.00	0.00	0.04	0.08	0.18	0.29	0.24	0.12	0.05	0.00	0.00	6.2	2.0
cp	0.00	0.00	0.04	0.12	0.30	0.59	0.83	0.95	1.00	1.00	1.00		

Statement 1, for example, and consider the calculation of its scale value as given by the median. The fiftieth centile occurs in Category E. Further, we know that the fiftieth centile is somewhere near the upper limit of Category E, which has a value of 5.5 since the cumulative proportion corresponding to the right-hand boundary is 0.54. In particular, the value for the fiftieth centile is

$$V_{50} = 4.5 + \left[\frac{0.50 - 0.24}{0.30} \right] 1 = 5.4.$$

The scale values for the other three statements are computed similarly and are entered in the right-hand side of Table 8.2.

As mentioned, the interquartile range is generally used as the measure of dispersion with the method of equal-appearing intervals. The interquartile range is defined as the difference between the seventy-fifth centile and the twenty-fifth centile; that is, $Q = V_{75} - V_{25}$. All that is required, therefore, to compute it is to find the values corresponding to the seventy-fifth centile and the twenty-fifth centile following basically the same procedure used to calculate the median. For Statement 1 the interquartile range is thus found to be

$$V_{75} = 5.5 + \left[\frac{0.75 - 0.54}{0.30} \right] 1 = 6.2;$$

$$V_{25} = 4.5 + \left[\frac{0.25 - 0.24}{0.30} \right] 1 = 4.5;$$

$$Q = V_{75} - V_{25} = 1.7.$$

Both the scale values and the Q values are used in selecting the list of statements for the final scale. The researcher selects 20 to 22 statements that span the scale of favorableness; that is, some of the statements in the final list would have low scale values, some intermediate values, and some high values. Ideally, the scale values would be equally spaced. One can see from the limited example that several, if not many, of the initial statements will have approximately equal scale values. How does one then choose among them? This is where the interquartile range enters. We would like to have items in our final scale that are likely to be interpreted consistently by those responding. Thus, we do not want to include a statement that could be agreed to by both those with positive and negative attitudes toward the object. Large values of Q indicate that, at least in our judgment sample, there was wide disagreement among the judges as to the degree of favorableness expressed in the statement, and, therefore, the statement is ambiguous. Given that two statements have approximately equal values, we choose the one that has the smallest Q.

Scale Use   Assume that some 20 to 22 statements have been selected from the larger list of n statements using the procedure detailed above. The statements are randomly placed in the final instrument so that there is no order to the scale values. The instrument is then ready to be administered to one or more samples of subjects whose attitudes we are interested in assessing.

When the instrument is administered, subjects are asked to indicate those statements with which they agree or disagree. For example, subjects would be asked to select those statements from the total list that reflect their feelings toward Bank A. A subject's attitude score is considered to be the average of the scale scores for the statements with which the person agrees. Thus, if the subject agreed with three statements with the scale scores 8.2, 8.7, and 9.8, the person's attitude score would be 8.9.[16] Since the scale value 6 represents a neutral attitude, the conclusion would be that the subject had a favorable attitude toward Bank A.

Several criticisms have been leveled at the method of scoring. One centers on subjects' only being asked to select those statements with which they agree and not being asked to respond to each of the statements. This makes it possible for two subjects who respond quite differently to have the same attitude score. Thus, a subject agreeing with statements with scale scores 4, 6, and 8 would have the same attitude score as another person who only agreed with the statement having a scale score of 6. But do they, in fact, have the same attitude? There is still considerable controversy on this point.

Another frequent criticism is that the method does not allow subjects to express the intensity of their feelings. For example, a subject could feel quite strongly that the bank had very convenient hours or he might feel that while basically convenient, the hours could be improved. In either case, all that the subject would be able to do would be to

---

[16]There is a good deal of controversy over whether the mean or median should be used to calculate the average score. The argument centers on what one is willing to assume about the level of scaling. If the scale is assumed to be interval, then the mean is certainly an appropriate measure of central tendency. However, some critics contend that the procedure does not produce an interval scale but rather only an ordinal one, and that the median is therefore the more appropriate average.

Table 8.3
Example of Likert Summated Rating Form

	Strongly Disagree	Disagree	Neither Agree Nor Disagree	Agree	Strongly Agree
1. The bank offers courteous service.	_____	_____	_____	_____	_____
2. The bank has a convenient location.	_____	_____	_____	_____	_____
3. The bank has convenient hours.	_____	_____	_____	_____	_____
4. The bank offers low–interest-rate loans.	_____	_____	_____	_____	_____

indicate that he agrees with the statement. Yet, are not the two attitudes basically different?

As you might suspect from the above, the equal-appearing interval scale is relatively expensive and time consuming to construct. Once constructed, though, it is very easy to administer and is easy for respondents to complete. It can further be used to assess attitudes toward a variety of objects (for example, each bank in town). The technique can also be employed to scale other things besides attitude, such as the amount of perceived puffery in each of a series of advertising claims or the consistency in the favorableness of various adjectives across groups of people.[17] The effort involved in its construction and the limited diagnostic information it provides have tended to limit its use though in assessing attitudes. Research Realities 8.2 on page 328, indicates, for example, that it is used less than the other self-report techniques discussed below. Nonetheless, its other potential uses still make the equal-interval technique a valuable component in the marketing researcher's measurement arsenal.

Summated Ratings

The Likert method of **summated ratings** overcomes the previous criticisms about scoring and allowing an expression of intensity of feeling.[18] The method is both constructed and used in a slightly different way than that of equal-appearing intervals.

Scale Construction   The basic format of the scale for the summated ratings method is the same in both construction and use. Subjects are asked to indicate their degree of agreement or disagreement with each and every statement in a series by checking the appropriate cell. Table 8.3 serves as an example. Again the researcher attempts to de-

---

[17]Used in this way, the method is helpful in developing anchors for scales that are perceived by respondents to be equally spaced. See James H. Myers and W. Gregory Warner, ''Selected Properties of Selected Evaluation Adjectives,'' *Journal of Marketing Research,* 5 (November 1968), pp. 409–412.

[18]The scale was first proposed by Rensis Likert, ''A Technique for the Measurement of Attitudes,'' *Archives of Psychology,* No. 140 (1932).

Research Realities 8.2

Percentage of Firms Using Various Attitude Scaling Techniques

| Type | Type of Company | | Consumer & Industrial | Retailer-Wholesaler | Utilities |
	Consumer	Industrial			
Semantic Differential	52	9	47	9	44
Likert Scale	17	4	13	0	28
Q-sort Technique	21	0	13	0	6
Thurstone Scale	12	0	7	0	11
Total Number of Firms	(42)	(68)	(15)	(11)	(18)

Source: Adapted from Barnett A. Greenberg, Jac L. Goldstucker, and Danny N. Bellenger, "What Techniques are Used by Marketing Researchers in Business?," *Journal of Marketing*, 41 (April 1977), pp. 64–65.

velop a great many statements that should reflect qualities of things about the object that possibly influence a person's attitude toward it. In this respect, the procedure is no different from that used in the method of equal-appearing intervals. The method is quite different, though, in terms of the judgment sample and what is asked of the subjects.

It is often argued that those judging the statements need not represent the population on which an equal-appearing interval scale will be used because the judges are only asked to indicate the degree of favorableness of each statement.[19] With a Likert scale, there is no question that the screening sample should be representative of the larger group, both because of the different task assigned the subjects and the method by which the total set of statements is reduced to a smaller, more consistent subset. It must be pointed out that a screening sample has not always been used in the published marketing applications of the summated rating scale. This is unfortunate, since omitting refinement of a scale is likely to result in a more ambiguous, less reliable, less valid instrument.

Once again, assume that there are 200 subjects in the screening sample. First, each statement is classified *a priori* as favorable or unfavorable. Subjects are then asked to indicate their degree of agreement or disagreement with each statement.[20] The various degrees of agreement are assigned scale values, although the particular values differ from researcher to researcher. Sometimes the values -2, -1, 0, 1, 2 are employed, while other researchers prefer the values 1, 2, 3, 4, 5 for the respective response categories. It makes no difference in the conclusions we can draw, since the decision is completely arbitrary. Suppose we decide to use the values 1 through 5. Now, a subject

---

[19]There is some empirical evidence that tends to refute this argument. Even though the judges are supposed to evaluate each statement on its own merits, there does seem to be some tendency for a judge's own attitudes to influence his or her placement of the statements. Edwards, *Techniques*, pp. 106–116, summarizes these studies.

[20]Paul E. Spector, "Choosing Response Categories for Summated Rating Scales," *Journal of Applied Psychology*, 61 (June 1976), pp. 374–375, contains a list of typical category descriptors and their numerical values.

Communications	Market Research & Consulting	Finance & Insurance	Other Services	Others	Total Sample Using Technique
27	39	37	27	20	30
18	30	20	20	13	16
18	15	3	7	0	9
5	12	10	7	13	7
(22)	(33)	(30)	(15)	(15)	(269)

could be considered to feel positively about the bank if he or she either agreed with a favorable statement or disagreed with an unfavorable statement. It is, therefore, necessary to reverse the scaling with negative statements. Thus, a *strongly agree* response to a favorable statement and a *strongly disagree* response to an unfavorable statement would both receive scores of 5.

A total attitude score can be calculated for each subject using the same scoring procedure. The distribution of total scores is then used to refine the original list of n statements. The procedure, known as item analysis, rests on the proposition that there should be consistency in the response pattern of any individual. If the individual has a very favorable attitude toward the object, he or she should basically agree with the favorable statements and disagree with the unfavorable ones and vice versa. If we should happen to have a statement that generates a very mixed response, we would tend to question it on the grounds that it must be ambiguous or at the very least not discriminating of attitude. A parallel example would be the problem $2 + 2 = 4$ for a college math course. The problem tells us little about a person's math ability because both poor and good students could be expected to answer the problem correctly. Thus, the problem would be unsuitable for scaling the students on their math ability.

The same argument holds for attitude scales. We do not want to clutter up the scale with irrelevant statements but rather wish to include only those statements that discriminate among subjects with respect to their attitude. Although you embrace the premise, you may be wondering about the procedure. After all, did we not just say that those with a "very favorable" attitude could be expected to respond favorably to positive statements? How does one determine who has a favorable or unfavorable attitude, though? After all, aren't we developing the scale so that we are in a position to measure a person's attitude, and thus aren't we engaged in circular reasoning of "using a person's basic attitude to select statements by which that attitude can be measured"? You would be right, of course. There is a way out of the circle, though. The trick is to assume that the total score generated by the response to all n statements serves as a proxy for the person's true attitude. One can then relate each statement in turn to this total score to ascertain which statements are nondiscriminating.

One can relate individual statement scores to total scores by several methods. The most conceptually appealing approach calculates the product moment correlation of each item with the total score.[21] Those items that have the highest correlation with the total are the best. Those with correlations near zero are suspect and should be eliminated. By ranking the correlations, one can use this method to devise a final scale of any length desired. One simply selects those 25, 50, or however many statements having the highest correlations with the total score, although there usually is some attempt to include negative as well as positive statements.

An alternative way of performing an item analysis involves the division of subjects into some arbitrarily defined groups. For example, those subjects with the top 25 percent of all total scores would be considered to have the most favorable attitudes, while those with the lowest 25 percent of all total scores would be considered to have the least favorable attitudes. If the item is a good one, it would seem reasonable that after correcting for the scoring direction, the mean score for each statement for the favorable attitude group should exceed the mean score for the unfavorable attitude group. The statements can then be ranked according to their difference in mean scores. Those with mean differences near zero are poor statements and should be eliminated. Sometimes the researcher will go one step further and will test for the statistical significance of the difference in mean scores for the two groups, in which case only those statements that show a statistically significant difference would be retained.[22] Table 8.4 displays a comparison of means, without testing for the statistical significance of the difference, for a sample statement "The bank has a convenient location" and assumed responses for the 50 subjects with the most favorable and the 50 subjects with the least favorable attitudes. The calculation indicates that the statement is a discriminating one, since the difference in mean scores is indeed positive.

Scale Use   One advantage of the Likert scale of summated ratings is that directions for its use are the same as the directions employed to generate scores by which to screen statements. The statements remaining after purification of the original list are randomly ordered on the scale form so as to mix positive and negative ones, and subjects are asked to indicate their degree of agreement with each statement. Subjects generally find it easy to respond, because the response categories do allow the expression of the intensity of the feeling. The subject's total score is generated as the simple sum of the scores on each statement.[23]

A problem of interpretation arises with the summated rating scale that did not exist with the equal-appearing interval scale. With the latter, a score of 9.2 represented a favorable attitude toward Bank A, but what does a score of 78 on a 20-item Likert scale

---

[21]Nunnally, *Psychometric Theory,* Chaps. 6–8, has a rather compelling argument as to why correlation coefficients should be used to refine scales. The correlation coefficient is discussed in Chapter 15.

[22]The statistical test would be the *t* test for the difference in two means described in Chapter 14.

[23]For an example, see William C. Lundstrom and Lawrence M. Lamont, "The Development of a Scale to Measure Consumer Discontent," *Journal of Marketing Research,* 13 (November 1976), pp. 373–381, which reports the procedures used and the results obtained in the development of a Likert scale to measure consumer discontent. For a generalizable procedure on how to go about constructing scales, see Gilbert A. Churchill, Jr., "A Paradigm for Developing Better Measures of Marketing Constructs," *Journal of Marketing Research,* 16 (February 1979), pp. 64–73.

Table 8.4
Difference in Means for One Statement for the Two Groups with the
Most Favorable and the Least Favorable Attitudes

Response Category	Scale Value x	High Group f	High Group fx	Low Group f	Low Group fx
Strongly agree	5	28	140	2	10
Agree	4	14	56	6	24
Neither agree nor disagree	3	6	18	18	54
Disagree	2	2	4	20	40
Strongly disagree	1	0	0	4	4
Sums		50	218	50	132

$$\bar{x}_H \frac{218}{50} = 4.36, \qquad \bar{x}_L = \frac{132}{50} = 2.64, \qquad d = \bar{x}_H - \bar{x}_L = 4.36 - 2.64 = 1.72$$

indicate? Since the maximum is $20 \times 5 = 100$, can we assume that the person's attitude toward the bank is favorable? We cannot, since the raw scores only assume meaning when we compare them to some standard. This problem is not unique to psychological scaling, but arises every day of our lives in a variety of ways. We are always making judgments on the basis of comparisons with some standard. Most typically the standard is established via our experiences and rarely is rigorously defined. Thus, when we say "The man is sure tall," we are in effect saying that on the basis of the experience we have, the man is taller than average.

In psychological scaling, this is formalized somewhat by clearly specifying the standard. Very often the standard is taken as the average score for all subjects, although averages are also computed for certain predefined subgroups. The procedure is called developing norms. Comparisons can then be made against the norms to determine whether the person has a positive or negative attitude toward the object. Norms are not, of course, necessary for comparing subjects to determine which person has the more favorable attitude. Here one can simply compare the raw scores of the subjects. Nor are norms necessary when attempting to determine whether an individual's attitude has changed over time or whether a person likes one object better than another. One can simply compare the later and earlier scores or the difference in scores for the two objects.

Semantic Differential

The **semantic differential** scale grew out of some research at the University of Illinois designed to investigate the underlying structure of words.[24] The technique has been adapted, however, to measure attitudes.

[24] Charles E. Osgood, George J. Suci, and Percy H. Tannenbaum, *The Measurement of Meaning* (Champaign, Ill.: University of Illinois Press, 1957).

The original semantic differential scale consisted of a great many bipolar adjectives, which were employed to secure people's reactions to the objects of interest. It was found that the reactions to the bipolar scales tended to be correlated and that three basic uncorrelated dimensions could be found to account for most of the variation in ratings: an *evaluation* dimension represented by adjective pairs such as good–bad, sweet–sour, helpful–unhelpful; a *potency* dimension represented by bipolar items such as powerful–powerless, strong–weak, deep–shallow; and an *activity* dimension captured by adjective pairs such as fast–slow, alive–dead, noisy–quiet. The same three dimensions tended to emerge regardless of the object being evaluated.[25] Thus, the general thrust in using the semantic differential technique to form scales has been to select an appropriate sample of adjective pairs so that a score could be generated for the object for each of the evaluation, potency, and activity dimensions. The object could then be compared to other objects using these scores.[26]

The approach in marketing has been somewhat different from the general thrust. First, instead of applying the *basic* adjective pairs to the objects of interest, marketers have generated items of their own. These items have not always been antonyms, nor have they been single words. Rather, marketers have used phrases to anchor the ends of the scale, and some of these phrases have been attributes possessed by the product. Since a negative amount of the attribute is often a meaningless notion, lack of the attribute has been used as one end of the scale and a great deal of the attribute as the other.[27] Second, instead of attempting to generate evaluation, potency, and activity scores, marketers have been more interested in developing profiles for the brands, stores, companies, or whatever is being compared, and total scores by which the objects could be compared. In this respect, the use of the semantic differential approach in marketing studies has tended to follow the Likert approach to scale construction rather than the semantic differential tradition. Unfortunately, marketers have often failed to engage in the recommended scale purification procedures that should accompany this switch in emphasis, thus raising questions about the validity of the resulting semantic differential scales.[28]

---

[25]See David R. Heise, "The Semantic Differential and Attitude Research," in Summers, ed., *Attitude Measurement,* pp. 235–253, for an overview of the many studies in which the three dimensions were found. Factor analysis is the basic procedure employed to reduce a number of bipolar adjective pairs to basic dimensions. The rudiments of factor analysis are presented in Chapter 16.

[26]Several comparisons can be made: (1) The objects can be compared on the factor scores when the factors are considered one at a time; (2) the emotional value of the concept can be assessed by calculating the distance from the origin or neutral point to the object in three-space; and (3) the difference between objects or concepts in three-space can be assessed using Euclidean distance, since the three dimensions are independent of one another. For a discussion of these comparisons, see Heise, "*The Semantic Differential and Attitude Research,*" pp. 241–244.

[27]Much of the impetus for these practices seems to have been provided by W. A. Mindak, "Fitting the Semantic Differential to the Marketing Problem," *Journal of Marketing,* 25 (April 1961), pp. 28–33.

[28]After a sample of subjects uses the scale to evaluate an attitude object, the scale should be purified in the same manner as was the summated rating scale. The total score for each subject would be calculated and the ambiguous or nondiscriminating items eliminated by calculating item to total correlations or by looking at the mean scores by item of the high and low total scorers. While this is rarely done with semantic differential scales, it is an important step in ensuring that the scale is really measuring what it was designed to measure.

Figure 8.2
Example of Semantic Differential Scaling Form

Service is discourteous   :___:___:___:___:___:___: Service is courteous
Location is convenient   :___:___:___:___:___:___: Location is inconvenient
Hours are inconvenient   :___:___:___:___:___:___: Hours are convenient
Loan interest-rates are high :___:___:___:___:___:___: Loan interest-rates are low

Let us again use the bank attitude scaling problem to illustrate the semantic differential method. First, a researcher would generate a large list of bipolar adjectives or phrases.[29] Figure 8.2 parallels Table 8.4 in terms of the attributes used to describe the bank, but it is arranged in a semantic differential format. All we have done in Figure 8.2 is to try to express the things that could be used to describe a bank, and thus serve as a basis for attitude formation, in terms of positive and negative statements. Note that the negative phrase sometimes appears at the left side of the scale and other times at the right. This is to prevent a respondent with a positive attitude from simply checking either the right- or left-hand sides without even bothering to read the descriptions.

The scale would then be administered to a sample of subjects. Each respondent would be asked to read each set of bipolar phrases and to check the cell that best described his feelings toward the object. The end positions are usually defined for the respondent in the instructions as being very closely descriptive of the object, the center position as being neutral, and the intermediate positions as slightly descriptive and quite closely descriptive. Thus, for example, if the subject felt that Bank A's service was courteous, but only moderately so, he would check the sixth position reading from left to right.

The subject could be asked to evaluate two or more banks using the same scale.[30] When several banks are rated, the different profiles can be compared. Figure 8.3, for example (which is sometimes referred to as a **"snake" diagram** because of its shape), illustrates that Bank A is perceived as having more courteous service and a more convenient location and as offering lower interest rates on loans, but as having more inconvenient hours than Bank B. Note in constructing these profiles, the customary practice of placing all positive descriptors on the right, so as to facilitate communication, has been followed. The plotted values simply represent the average score of all subjects on each descriptor. While the mean is most often used, there is some controversy as to

---

[29]For a discussion of ways to go about this task, as well as other issues surrounding the construction of semantic differential scales, see John Dickson and Gerald Albaum, "A Method for Developing Tailormade Semantic Differentials for Specific Marketing Content Areas," *Journal of Marketing Research,* 14 (February 1977), pp. 87–91.

[30]The most popular form of the semantic differential scale places the objects being evaluated at the top and the descriptors used for the evaluation along the sides as the rows. One somewhat popular variation lists the descriptors at the top and the objects being evaluated along the side. For an empirical comparison of the two approaches, see Eugene D. Jaffe and Israel D. Nebenzahl, "Alternative Questionnaire Formats for Country Image Studies," *Journal of Marketing Research,* 21 (November 1984), pp. 463–471.

Figure 8.3
Contrasting Profiles of Banks A & B

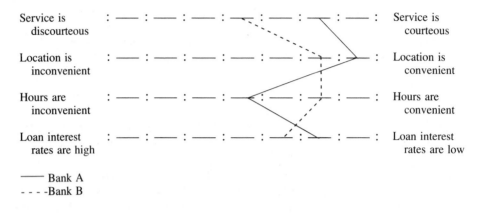

Service is discourteous : —— : —— : —— : —— : —— : —— : —— : Service is courteous

Location is inconvenient : —— : —— : —— : —— : —— : —— : —— : Location is convenient

Hours are inconvenient : —— : —— : —— : —— : —— : —— : —— : Hours are convenient

Loan interest rates are high : —— : —— : —— : —— : —— : —— : —— : Loan interest rates are low

—— Bank A
- - - -Bank B

whether the seven scale increments can be treated as an interval scale. If not, as critics contend, then the median scores should be used to develop the profiles. In either case, the plotted profiles communicate readily the perceived positions of Banks A and B by the sample respondents.

When a total score by which objects can be compared is desired (for example, which alternative package design is preferred by customers), the score is generated by summing the scores for the individual descriptors. The individual items may be scored -3, -2, -1, 0, 1, 2, 3, or 1, 2, 3, 4, 5, 6, 7. Again, while the decision is arbitrary because of the arbitrary nature of the zero point, these scores are simply summed in the same way as they were in the Likert procedure. It is unfortunate that few marketing studies employ a screening sample with semantic differential scales by which an original sample of items could be refined. While not extremely important in an item-by-item profile comparison, the lack of a rudimentary item analysis is critical when comparing total scores to determine which subject had the most favorable attitude or which object was evaluated most favorably by a given subject. The total scores may be meaningless if the items used in generating the scores are inappropriate, as they very well can be when simply made up but not analyzed for their internal consistency of meaning. The argument and the procedure for accomplishing an item analysis here parallel that for the Likert scale.

Perhaps it is the ease with which semantic differential scales can be developed, or the ease with which the findings can be communicated, or accumulated experience as to their value, that accounts for the semantic differential scale's great popularity in marketing.[31] The technique does allow subjects to express the intensity of their feelings

---

[31]Barnett A. Greenberg, Jac L. Goldstucker, and Danny N. Bellenger, "What Techniques Are Used by Marketing Researchers in Business," *Journal of Marketing*, 41 (April 1977), pp. 62–68. For an example of the use of the semantic differential, see Sunil Mehrotra, Stuart Van Auken, and Subhash C. Lonial, "Adjective Profiles in Television Copy Testing," *Journal of Advertising Research*, 21 (August 1981), pp. 21–25.

toward company, product, package, advertisement, or whatever. When combined with proper item analysis techniques, the semantic differential seems to offer the marketing researcher a most valuable research tool.

Stapel Scale

A modification of the semantic differential scale that has received some attention in marketing literature is the **Stapel scale.** It differs from the semantic differential scale in that (1) adjectives or descriptive phrases are tested separately instead of simultaneously as bipolar pairs; (2) points on the scale are identified by number; and (3) there are ten scale positions rather than seven. Respondents are told to rate how accurately each of a number of statements describes the object of interest, Bank A, for example. Instructions such as the following are given to respondents:

You would select a plus *number for words that you think describe (Bank A) accurately. The more accurately you think the word describes it, the larger the* plus *number you would choose. You would select a* minus *number for words you think do not describe it accurately. The less accurately you think a word describes it, the larger the* minus *number you would choose. Therefore, you can select any number from +5, for words that you think are very accurate, all the way to −5, for words that you think are very inaccurate.*[32]

The advantage claimed for the Stapel scale is that it frees the researcher from the need to develop bipolar adjectives for the many items affecting attitudes, which can indeed be a formidable task. Despite this advantage, the Stapel scale has not been as warmly embraced as the semantic differential form, judging by the number of published marketing studies using each.[33] One problem with using it is that many of the descriptors used to evaluate an object can be phrased one of three ways—positively, negatively, or neutrally—and the phrasing chosen seems to affect the results as well as subjects' ability to respond.[34] Nevertheless, it is a useful addition to the researcher's equipment arsenal. For one thing it lends itself to administration by telephone.[35]

It should be pointed out that a total score on both the semantic differential and Stapel scales is like a total score on a Likert scale. The score 48, for example, is meaningless by itself but takes on meaning when compared to some norm or other score. There is a good deal of controversy as to whether semantic differential, Stapel, or even Likert-generated total scores represent interval scaling or, in actuality, reflect ordinal scaling. While the controversy rages, marketers have been inclined to assume the posture of

---

[32]Irving Crespi, "Use of a Scaling Technique in Surveys," *Journal of Marketing,* 25 (July 1961), p. 71.

[33]One study that compared the performance of the Stapel scale to the semantic differential found basically no difference between the results produced by, nor respondents ability to use, each. See Del I. Hawkins, Gerald Albaum, and Roger Best, "Stapel Scale or Semantic Differential in Marketing Research," *Journal of Marketing Research,* 11 (August 1974), pp. 318–322.

[34]Michael J. Etzel, Terrell G. Williams, John C. Rogers, and Douglas J. Lincoln, "The Comparability of Three Stapel Scale Forms in a Marketing Setting," in Ronald F. Bush and Shelby D. Hunt, eds., *Marketing Theory: Philosophy of Science Perspectives* (Chicago: American Marketing Association, 1982), pp. 303–306.

[35]Gregory D. Upah and Steven C. Cosmas, "The Use of Telephone Dials as Attitude Scales," *Journal of the Academy of Marketing Science,* (Fall 1980), pp. 416–426.

many psychological scaling specialists, who assume interval scaling of their constructs not because they believe they have necessarily measured them on an interval scale but because interval scaling allows more powerful methods of analysis to be brought to bear. The persistence of this posture in psychological scaling attests to its general fruitfulness, and it seems reasonable that marketers have also found the assumption of interval scaling productive if not entirely correct. There is also a logical justification for this assumption.

By assuming interval measurement where only ordinal measurement exists, some measurement errors will occur. The result of errors generally is the attenuation of relations among variables. That is, one's apparent results will be more attenuated than they are in reality. Thus it is unlikely that the decision to assume interval measurement when it does not exist will lead to the spurious overestimation of results.[36]

Further, from a statistical point of view, the assumption of intervality often makes sense. Statistical tests of significance, for example, "do not care from where the numbers come" as long as the assumptions underlying the use of a particular statistical test are satisfied.[37] It is not necessary therefore to be *overly* concerned about the level of measurement from a *statistical* point of view. What we must be careful about, though, is the *interpretation* of the results (for example, arguing that a person with a score of 80 has twice as favorable an attitude toward an object as a person with a score of 40 unless the measurement scale is ratio).

Q *Sort*

The **Q-sort technique** is a general methodology for gathering data and processing the information collected. The task of the subjects in *Q*-sort analysis parallels that for the judgment sample in developing a Thurstone equal-appearing interval scale except (1) the subjects respond to each stimulus in terms of their attitudes toward it and not in terms of its degree of favorableness; (2) the subjects are instructed to place a specific number of statements in each category—that is, a distribution of responses is forced on the subject. Very often the specified distribution is normal or quasi-normal.

For the bank scaling example, the subject might be asked to sort the statements into "piles representing the degree of desirability of each characteristic for him specifically." Each subject would be asked to place the number of statements in each category indicated in Table 8.5. That is, each characteristic of interest would be printed on a separate card, and the subject would be told to place the four characteristics he finds

---

[36]George W. Bohrnstedt, "Reliability and Validity Assessment in Attitude Measurement," in Summers, ed., *Attitude Measurement,* pp. 81–82.

[37]There is evidence that demonstrates, for example, that there is little difference in results when ordinal data are analyzed by procedures appropriate to interval data. See Sanford Labovitz, "Some Observations on Measurement and Statistics," *Social Forces,* 46 (1967), pp. 151–160; Sanford Labovitz, "The Assignment of Numbers to Rank Order Categories," *American Sociological Review,* 35 (1970), pp. 515–524; and John Gaito, "Measurement Scales and Statistics: Resurgence of an Old Misconception," *Psychological Bulletin,* 87 (1980), pp. 564–567. We will have more to say on the relationship between scales of measurements and statistical techniques in Chapter 13.

Table 8.5
Forced Distribution of *Q*-Sort Items

Number of statements	4	8	16	24	28	40	28	24	16	8	4	
Least desirable	0	1	2	3	4	5	6	7	8	9	10	Most desirable

most desirable or preferable in the tenth pile, the four characteristics he finds least desirable in the zeroth pile, and so on. *Q*-sort scaling is then used to determine the relative ranking of stimuli by individuals and to derive clusters of individuals who display similar preferences, thus perhaps representing unique market segments. Factor analysis, detailed in a later chapter, is used to analyze the responses to identify these clusters of individuals. The objective of *Q*-sort analysis is, then, the intensive study of individuals, a task much different from the scaling of objects, such as banks.

Rating Scales

The previous discussion dealt with some of the main scaling methods that have been used to measure attitudes. The treatment was by no means exhaustive. Particularly conspicuous by its absence was a discussion of the importance of the various attributes to the individual. That is, in each scaling method discussed, we attempted to determine the individual's perceptions of Bank A. This may not be enough. Even though the individual believes the bank has convenient hours, the person may not value this attribute, and, therefore, it may not affect his attitude toward the bank. On the other hand, suppose the individual values location convenience; if he perceives the bank as being inconveniently located, this will have a negative, and perhaps a strong negative, impact on his feeling towards the bank. There is a good deal of controversy regarding how the importance of various attributes should be incorporated in determining a person's attitude toward an object.

We shall not delve into this controversy, since it involves some very complex arguments as to how one determines which attributes are salient (that is, used in forming an attitude) and how they should be measured.[38] Rather, we shall simply use importance

---

[38]This question is just one of the points of debate in attitude models. For an overview of the many points of controversy, as well as for an extensive bibliography of marketing studies, see William L. Wilkie and Edgar A. Pessemier, "Issues in Marketing's Use of Multiattribute Attitude Models," *Journal of Marketing Research*, 10 (November 1973), pp. 428–441. The empirical evidence suggests that incorporating importance weights seems to make very little difference in the predictive power of attitude models. See, for example, Neil E. Beckwith and Donald R. Lehmann, "The Importance of Differential Weights in Multiattribute Models of Consumer Attitude," *Journal of Marketing Research*, 10 (May 1973), pp. 141–145. Knowledge of the importance of various attributes can be important, though, in the design of marketing strategy. See, for instance, John A. Martella and John C. James, "Importance-Performance Analysis," *Journal of Marketing*, 41 (January 1977), pp. 77–79.

Table 8.6
Graphic Rating Scale

Please evaluate each attribute in terms of how important the attribute is to you personally by placing an "X" at the position on the horizontal line that most reflects your feelings.

Attribute	Not Important	Very Important
Courteous service		
Convenient location		
Convenient hours		
Low–interest-rate loans		

values to focus a discussion of general types of rating scales.[39] Some of these scales were employed previously, but now we wish to describe the basic rating scales in one place, using importance values as a vehicle to make the differences between them more vivid. Knowledge of the basic types should facilitate the development of special scales for particular purposes.

There is one feature that is common to all rating scales: "The rater places the person or object being rated at some point along a continuum or in one of an ordered series of categories; a numerical value is attached to the point or the category."[40] The scales differ, though, in the fineness of the distinctions they allow and in the procedures involved in assigning objects to positions. Three of the most common rating scales are the graphic, the itemized, and the comparative.[41]

Graphic

When using **graphic rating scales,** individuals indicate their rating by placing a check at the appropriate point on a line that runs from one extreme of the attribute to the other. Many variations are possible. The line may be vertical or horizontal; it may be unmarked or marked; if marked, the divisions may be few or many as in the case of a thermometer scale, so called because it looks like a thermometer. Table 8.6 is an example of a horizontal, end anchored only, graphic rating scale. Each individual would be instructed to indicate the importance of the attribute by checking the appropriate position on the scale. The importance value would then be inferred by measuring the length of the line from the left origin to the marked position.

---

[39]Self reports are just one of the ways attribute importance can be measured. Several other ways are using conjoint analysis, information display boards, or even deriving them statistically for groups of respondents. For examples of these approaches, see Roger M. Heeler, Chike Okechuku, and Stan Reid, "Attribute Importance: Contrasting Measurement," *Journal of Marketing Research,* 16 (February 1979), pp. 60–63; and Scott A. Neslin, "Linking Product Features to Perceptions: Self-Stated Versus Statistically Revealed Importance Weights," *Journal of Marketing Research,* 18 (February 1981), pp. 80–86.

[40]Claire Selltiz, Lawrence S. Wrightsman, and Stuart W. Cook, *Research Methods in Social Relations,* 3rd ed. (New York: Holt, Rinehart and Winston, 1976), pp. 403–404.

[41]*Ibid.,* pp. 404–406.

One of the great advantages of graphic rating scales is the ease with which they can be constructed and used. They provide an opportunity to make fine distinctions and are limited in this regard only by the discrimination abilities of the rater.[42] Yet, for their most effective use, the researcher is well advised to avoid end statements that are so extreme that they are unlikely to be used and to place descriptive statements as close as possible to their numerical points on the scale.[43]

Itemized

The **itemized rating scale** is similar to the graphic in that individuals make their judgments independently, that is, without the benefit of direct comparison. The itemized rating scale is distinguished by the fact that the rater must select from a limited number of categories. In general, five to nine categories work well, in that they permit fine distinctions and yet seem to be readily understood by respondents, although ten or more can be used.[44] There are a number of possible variations with itemized scales. Table 8.7, for example, depicts three different forms of itemized rating scales that have been used to measure customer satisfaction. Note that the categories are ordered in terms of their scale positions. Note further that while in some cases the categories have verbal descriptions attached, in other cases they do not. Category descriptions are not absolutely necessary in itemized rating scales, although their presence and nature does seem to affect the responses.[45] When they are used, it is important to ensure that the descriptors mean similar things to those responding.[46] When they are not used, it is tempting to conclude that a graphic rating scale is being used. That is an erroneous conclusion, however. The distinguishing feature of an itemized scale is that the possible response categories are limited in number. Thus, a set of faces varying systematically in terms of whether they are frowning or smiling used to capture a person's satisfaction or preference (appropriately called a faces scale) would be considered an itemized scale, even when no descriptions are attached to the face categories.[47]

---

[42]While easy to construct, there is some evidence that suggests graphic rating scales are not as reliable as itemized scales. See A. O. Gregg, "Some Problems Concerning the Use of Rating Scales for Visual Assessment," *Journal of the Market Research Society,* 8 (January 1980), pp. 29–43.

[43]Selltiz, Wrightsman, and Cook, *Research Methods,* p. 204.

[44]Eli P. Cox III, "The Optimal Number of Response Alternatives for a Scale: A Review," *Journal of Marketing Research,* 17 (November 1980), pp. 407–422.

[45]Albert R. Wildt and Michael B. Mazis, "Determinants of Scale Response: Label Versus Position," *Journal of Marketing Research,* 15 (May 1978), pp. 261–267; and H. H. Friedman and J. R. Liefer, "Label Versus Position in Rating Scales," *Journal of the Academy of Marketing Science,* (Spring 1981), pp. 88–92.

[46]For lists of category descriptors and their numerical values, see Myers and Warner, "Selected Properties of Selected Evaluation Adjectives"; Spector, "Choosing Categories for Summated Rating Scales"; and Robert A. Mittelstaedt, "Semantic Properties of Selected Adjectives: Other Evidence," *Journal of Marketing Research,* 8 (May 1971), pp. 236–237.

[47]Faces scales are often used to measure the reactions of children. See, for example, M. E. Goldbert, G. J. Gorn, and W. Gibson, "TV Messages for Snack and Breakfast Foods: Do They Influence Children's Preferences?" *Journal of Consumer Research,* 5 (September 1978), pp. 73–81. Because of the ease with which they can be understood, they are also used to depict such things as corporate performance; see, for example, Bill Abrams, "With Computer Help, Marketing Professor Faces Up to Corporations Financial Data," *Wall Street Journal,* 61 (July 22, 1981), p. 25.

Table 8.7
Three Different Forms of Itemized Rating Scales Used to Measure Satisfaction

Measure	Description
Delighted–Terrible Scale	*How do you feel about* _____ *?* *I feel:* 7 6 5 4 3 2 1 Delighted Pleased Mostly Satisfied Mixed (About Equally Satisfied and Dissatisfied) Mostly Dissatisfied Unhappy Terrible A = Neutral (neither satisfied nor dissatisfied) B = I never thought about it
Percentage Scale	*Overall, how satisfied have you been with this* _____ *?* 100% 90 80 70 60 50 40 30 20 10 0% Completely Satisfied Not at All Satisfied
Need Satisfaction–Dissatisfaction	*To what extent does this* _____ *meet your needs at this time?* Extremely Well: ___:___:___:___:___:___:___ : Extremely Poorly (7) (1)

Source: Adapted from Robert A. Westbrook, "A Rating Scale for Measuring Product/Service Satisfaction," *Journal of Marketing*, 44 (Fall 1980), p. 69. Published by the American Marketing Association.

Table 8.8
Itemizing Rating Scale

Please evaluate each attribute in terms of how important the attribute is to you personally by placing ''X'' in the appropriate box.

Attribute	Not Important	Somewhat Important	Fairly Important	Very Important
Courteous service	☐	☐	☐	☐
Convenient location	☐	☐	☐	☐
Convenient hours	☐	☐	☐	☐
Low–interest-rate loans	☐	☐	☐	☐

A Likert statement serves as an example of a five-point itemized rating scale, while a semantic differential adjective pair is an example of a seven-point scale. Table 8.8 is an itemized rating scale used to ascertain importance values; this four-point scale has the descriptor labels attached to the categories.

The itemized rating scale is also easy to construct and use, and although it does not permit the fine distinctions possible with the graphic rating scale, the clear definition of categories generally produces more reliable ratings.

Comparative

Unlike graphic and itemized scales, **comparative rating scales** involve relative judgments in that raters make their judgments of each attribute with direct reference to the other attributes being evaluated. The *Q*-sort method of scale construction is an example, since each attribute is compared to all other *n* attributes when making judgments.

An example of a comparative rating scale used for securing importance values is the constant sum scaling method. In the **constant sum** method, the individual is instructed to divide some given sum among two or more attributes on the basis of their importance to him or her. Thus, in Table 8.9, if the subject assigned 50 points to courteous service and 50 points to convenient location, the attributes would be judged to be equally important; if the individual assigned 80 to courteous service and 20 to convenient location, courteous service would be considered to be four times as important.[48] Note the difference in emphasis with this method. All judgments are now made in comparison to some other alternative, and all possible pairs of the *n* stimuli would be presented to the individual for rating.

Comparison of two attributes is not mandatory in the constant sum method, although it is the most common. The individual could also be asked to divide 100 points among

---

[48]By considering all possible pairs of attributes in combination, one is able to construct scale values to reflect the importance ratings of each attribute to each individual. See Joy P. Guilford, *Psychometric Methods,* 2nd ed. (New York: McGraw-Hill, 1954), pp. 214–220, or Warren S. Torgerson, *Theory and Methods of Scaling* (New York: John Wiley, 1958), pp. 104–116, for a discussion of the procedure.

Table 8.9
Comparative Rating Scale

> Please divide 100 points between the following two attributes in terms of the relative importance of each attribute to you.
>
> Courteous service   _____
>
> Convenient location   _____

---

three or more attributes; again all possible combinations would be presented to the individual for judgment.[49]

Although comparative scales require more judgments from the individual than either graphic or itemized scales, they do tend to eliminate **halo effects** that so often manifest themselves in scaling. Halo effects occur when there is carryover from one judgment to another.[50]

The great temptation in securing importance values by either the graphic or itemized scaling methods is for the individual to indicate that all, or nearly all, of the attributes are important. Yet empirical research indicates that when individuals are confronted by decisions that are complex because many alternatives or attributes are involved, they tend to simplify the decision by reducing the number of alternatives or attributes they actually consider.[51] This is consistent with the notion that only certain attributes are salient when forming attitudes. The comparative scaling methods do allow more insight into the relative ranking, if not the absolute importance, of the attributes to each individual.

The various rating methods do not take into account, though, the situation that an attribute may be important but not a **determinant attribute** because it is not used to differentiate one object from another.[52]

In the electrical appliance business, we have been impressed over and over by the way in which certain characteristics of products come to be taken for granted by consumers, especially those concerned with basic functional performance or with values like safety. If these values are missing in a product, the user is extremely offended. But if they are

---

[49]See Valentine Appel and Babette Jackson, ''Copy Testing in a Competitive Environment,'' *Journal of Marketing,* 39 (January 1975), pp. 84–86, and Clyde E. Harris, Jr., Richard R. Still, and Melvin R. Crask, ''Stability or Change in Marketing Methods,'' *Business Horizons,* 21 (October 1978), pp. 32–40, for empirical examples based on the use of constant sum scales.

[50]Comparative scales help to ensure that all respondents are approaching the rating task from the same perspective. See Richard R. Batsell and Yoram Wind, ''Product Development: Current Methods and Needed Developments,'' *Journal of the Market Research Society,* 8 (1980), pp. 122–126.

[51]Jerome S. Bruner, Jacqueline J. Goodnaw, and George R. Austin, *A Study of Thinking* (New York: John Wiley, 1956); James G. Miller, ''Sensory Overloading,'' in Bernard E. Flaherty, ed., *Psychopysiological Aspects of Space Flight* (New York: Columbia University Press, 1961), pp. 215–224; and Jacob Jacoby, ''Perspectives on Information Overload,'' *Journal of Consumer Research,* 10 (March 1984), pp. 432–435.

[52]The notion of determinant attribute was introduced by James H. Myers and Mark I. Alpert, ''Determinant Buying Attitudes: Meaning and Measurement,'' *Journal of Marketing,* 32 (October 1968), pp. 13–20.

present, the maker or seller gets no special credit or preference because, quite logically, every other maker or seller is assumed to be offering equivalent values. In other words, the values that are salient in decision making are the values that are problematic—that are important to be sure, but also those that differentiate one offering from another.[53]

One interesting approach to uncovering determinant attributes is **dual questioning.**[54] First, using one of the methods previously described, each individual is asked about the importance of each attribute. He or she is then asked for perceptions of the differences that exist among competing products with respect to each attribute. "Attributes judged high in combined performance and differences are selected as determinant."[55]

Which Scale to Use

For some readers, the discussion in this chapter might beg the question of which scale they should use when faced with a problem of measuring attitudes. When making the choice among scale types, number of scale points to use, whether or not to reverse some of the items, and so on, readers might find comfort in the findings of a very extensive study of the marketing measurement literature that examined these questions and more with respect to their impact on the reliability of measures. Reviewing the marketing literature over a 20-year period, the study examined measures for which at least two indicants of their quality were reported, and then quantitatively assessed the impact of a measure's features on its reliability.[56] **Reliability** assesses the issue of the similarity of results provided by independent but comparable measures of the same object, trait, or construct; it is an important indicator of a measure's quality because it determines the impact of inconsistencies in measurement on the results. Reliability is a necessary, but not a sufficient, condition for ensuring the validity of a measure.[57]

Table 8.10 reports the study's findings with respect to some of the major questions surrounding the construction of attitude scales. The general conclusion emerging from Table 8.10 is that many of the choices do not seem to materially affect the quality of the measure that results. The exceptions are the number of items and the number of scale points. For both of these characteristics, the reliability of the measure increases as

---

[53]Nelson N. Foote, *Consumer Behavior: Household Decision Making,* Vol. 4 (New York: New York University Press, 1961), p. 11.

[54]Dual questioning is just one of the methods that has been suggested for isolating determinant attributes. Some of the others are indirect questioning, the use of discriminant or regression analysis, observation, and experimentation. For a discussion of these approaches, see Myers and Alpert, "Determinant Buying Attitudes," and for an empirical assessment of the performance of the various methods, see Mark I. Alpert, "Identification of Determinant Attributes: A Comparison of Methods," *Journal of Marketing Research,* 8 (May 1971), pp. 184–191. See also W. Thomas Anderson, Jr., Eli P. Cox III, and David G. Fulcher, "Bank Selection Decisions and Market Segmentation," *Journal of Marketing,* 40 (January 1976), pp. 40–45.

[55]Alpert, "Identification of Determinant Attributes," p. 185.

[56]Gilbert A. Churchill, Jr., and J. Paul Peter, "Research Design Effects on the Reliability of Rating Scales: A Meta-Analysis," *Journal of Marketing Research,* 21 (November 1984), pp. 360–375.

[57]The issue of reliability and its relationship to the validity of a measure are discussed in Appendix 8C.

Table 8.10

Impact of Selected Measure Characteristics on Reliability Estimates

Measure Characteristic	Conclusion
Number of items in final scale	The hypothesis that there is a positive relationship between the number of items used in the scales and the reliability of the measure is supported.
Difficulty of items	The hypothesis that a negative relationship exists between the difficulty of the items and the reliability of the measure is not supported.
Reverse scoring	The hypothesis that scales with reverse-scored items will have lower reliability than scales without them is not supported.
Type of scale	No *a priori* prediction was made that one of the scale types is superior, and no relationship was found between scale types and the reliability of the measure.
Number of scale points	The hypothesis that a positive relationship exists between the number of scale points over the normal range and the reliability of the measure is supported.
Type of labels	No *a priori* prediction was made that numerical and verbal labels are superior to verbal labels only, or vice versa, and no relationship was found between type of labels and the reliability of the measure.
Extent of scale points description	The hypothesis that scales for which all points are labeled have higher reliability than scales for which only polar points are labeled is not supported.
Respondent uncertainty or ignorance	The hypothesis that scales with neutral points have higher reliability than forced-choice scales is not supported.

Source: Adapted from Gilbert A. Churchill, Jr., and J. Paul Peter, "Research Design Effects on the Reliability of Rating Scales: A Meta-Analysis," *Journal of Marketing Research,* 21 (November 1984), pp. 365–366. Published by the American Marketing Association.

they increase. For the other characteristics, though, there are no choices that are superior in all instances. Many of the choices are and will probably remain in the domain of researcher judgment, including the choice among semantic differential, Likert, or other rating scales. All the scales have proven useful at one time or another. All rightly belong in the researcher's measurement tool kit. The nature of the problem, the characteristics of the respondents, and the planned mode of administration of the questionnaire will and should all affect the final choice. So should expected respondent commitment to the task.[58]

---

[58]John R. Hauser and Steven M. Shugan, "Intensity Measures of Consumer Preference," *Operations Research,* 28 (March–April 1980), pp. 278–320.

Summary

This chapter sought to review the methods suggested for measuring attitudes, which were defined as representing the person's ideas of, or liking for, a specific object or idea. Typically, marketers are concerned with objects such as companies, brands, advertisements, packages, and the like.

Measurement was defined as the assignment of numbers to objects to represent quantities of attributes. Measurement can occur on either a nominal, ordinal, interval, or ratio scale. The properties of these scales were distinguished, and it was pointed out that a controversy exists over whether the measurement of attitudes has been accomplished with ordinal or interval scales. The scales have certainly not been ratio, since the origin is not natural, and they are definitely something more than nominal, because they possess more than the identity property. The debate focuses on whether the differences in scores convey meaning other than relative ranking of individuals. The prevailing posture in marketing seems to agree with that of the psychologists—that many of the scales are interval.

Historically, attitudes have been measured by observing behavior, by indirect questioning, by the performance of objective tasks, and by physiological reactions, although direct assessment via self-report devices has been the most common. The main self-report techniques were reviewed, including the methods of equal-appearing intervals, summated ratings, semantic differential, Stapel scale, and Q sort.

As typically constructed, these scales attempt to measure what individuals believe about specific objects. Many would argue that simply measuring beliefs about the attributes possessed by the object is not sufficient if we want to assess a person's attitude toward the object. Rather, we must somehow ascertain the importance of the various attributes to the individual. The methods for securing importance values—the graphic, itemized, or comparative rating scales—were thus reviewed. The itemized scale is most commonly used, but there is a good deal of controversy as to which rating scale can more accurately measure an individual's importance values and also how one isolates determinant attributes or those attributes that are decisive in affecting choice.

The empirical evidence indicates that none of the attitude scaling devices is superior in all instances. Each one has its place. Nor is there one single optimal number of scale positions or single optimal condition for other measure characteristics. The nature of the problem, the characteristics of the respondents, and the planned mode of administration will and should affect the choice as to which technique should be used in a particular instance and what features the scale should possess.

Questions

1. What is an attitude?
2. What is measurement? What are the scales of measurement and what information is provided by each?
3. How does one construct a Thurstone equal-appearing interval scale?
4. In a Thurstone equal-appearing interval scale, what is the scale value for a statement? What is the interquartile deviation, and what is the rationale for its use?
5. How are scale scores determined with a Thurstone equal-appearing interval scale?

6. How does one construct a Likert summated rating scale?

7. How are subjects scaled with a Likert scale? What must be done, in contrast to a Thurstone equal-appearing interval scale, to give meaning to the scores?

8. What is a semantic differential scale? How is a person's overall attitude assessed with a semantic differential scale?

9. How does a Stapel scale differ from a semantic differential scale? Which is more commonly used?

10. What is the task assigned subjects and what is the thrust or emphasis of Q-sort methodology?

11. What is a graphic rating scale? An itemized scale? A constant sum scale?

12. What is a determinant attribute?

Applications and Problems

1. Identify the type of scale (nominal, ordinal, interval, ratio) being used in each of the following questions. Justify your answer.

   (a) *During which season of the year were you born?*
       ____ Winter   ____ Spring   ____ Summer   ____ Fall

   (b) *What is your total household income?* _____

   (c) *Which are your three most preferred brands of cigarettes? Rank them from 1 to 3 according to your preference with 1 as most preferred.*
       ____ Marlboro   ____ Salem
       ____ Kent   ____ Kool
       ____ Benson and Hedges   ____ Vantage

   (d) *How much time do you spend on traveling to school every day?*
       ____ Under 5 minutes   ____ 16–20 minutes
       ____ 5–10 minutes   ____ 30 minutes and over
       ____ 11–15 minutes

   (e) *How satisfied are you with Newsweek magazine?*
       ____ very satisfied   ____ dissatisfied
       ____ satisfied   ____ very dissatisfied
       ____ neither satisfied or dissatisfied

   (f) *On an average, how many cigarettes do you smoke in a day?*
       ____ over 1 pack   ____ less than 1/2 pack
       ____ 1/2 to 1 pack

   (g) *Which one of the following courses have you taken?*
       ____ marketing research   ____ sales management
       ____ advertising management   ____ consumer behavior

   (h) *What is the level of education for the head of the household?*
       ____ some high school   ____ some college
       ____ high school graduate   ____ college graduate and/or graduate work

2. The analysis for each of the above questions is given below. Is the analysis appropriate for the scale used?

   (a) About 50% of the sample was born in the fall, while 25% of the sample was born in the spring and the remaining 25% was born in the winter. It can be concluded that the fall is twice as popular as the spring and the summer seasons.

(b) The average income is $25,000. There are twice as many individuals with an income of less than $9,999 than individuals with an income of $40,000 and over.

(c) Marlboro is the most preferred brand. The mean preference is 3.52.

(d) The median time spent on traveling to school is 8.5 minutes. There are three times as many respondents traveling less than 5 minutes than respondents traveling 16–20 minutes.

(e) The average satisfaction score is 4.5 which seems to indicate a high level of satisfaction with *Newsweek* magazine.

(f) Ten percent of the respondents smoke less than 1/2 pack of cigarettes a day, while three times as many respondents smoke over one pack of cigarettes a day.

(g) Sales management is the most frequently taken course since the median is 3.2.

(h) The responses indicate that 40% of the sample have some high school education, 25% of the sample are high school graduates, 20% have some college education, and 10% are college graduates. The mean education level is 2.6.

3. (a) Your assistance is required in the construction of a Thurstone Equal Appearing Interval Scale. The following table shows the frequencies for five statements. You are requested to complete the following table by computing the following:
   (i)   the proportions
   (ii) the cumulative proportions
   (iii) the median
   (iv) the interquartile range
   Show all your calculations.

Sorting Categories

Statement		A 1	B 2	C 3	D 4	E 5	F 6	G 7	H 8	I 9	J 10	K 11	Scale Value	Q Value
1	f	0	0	0	4	8	12	20	56	44	38	18		
	p													
	cp													
2	f	0	0	8	16	36	58	48	24	10	0	0		
	p													
	cp													
3	f	0	2	10	18	38	46	36	24	20	6	0		
	p													
	cp													
4	f	0	6	12	36	60	64	18	4	0	0	0		
	p													
	cp													
5	f	2	6	14	30	34	20	28	28	30	8	0		
	p													
	cp													

(b) You are required to choose three of the five statements in the above table. On the basis of your calculations, which would you choose? Why?

4. **(a)** Assume that a manufacturer of a line of packaged meat products wanted to evaluate customer attitudes towards the brand. A panel of 500 regular consumers of the brand responded to a questionnaire that was sent to them and that included several attitude scales that produced the following results:

(i) the average score for the sample on a 20-item Likert scale was 105.

(ii) the average score for the sample on a 20-item Semantic differential scale was 106.

(iii) the average score for the sample on a 15-item Stapel scale was 52.

The vice-president has requested you to indicate whether his customers have a favorable or unfavorable attitude towards the brand. What would you tell him? Please be specific.

(b) Following your initial report, the vice-president has provided you with some more information. The following memo is given to you: "The company has been using the same attitude measures over the past eight years. The results of the previous studies are given below:

	Likert	Semantic Differential	Stapel
1978	86	95	43
1979	93	95	48
1980	97	98	51
1981	104	101	55
1982	110	122	62
1983	106	112	57
1984	104	106	53
1985	105	106	52

We realize that there may not be any connection between attitude and behavior but it must be pointed out that sales peaked in 1982 and since then have been gradually declining." With this information, do your results change? Can anything more be said about customer attitudes?

Appendix 8A
Multidimensional Scaling

The discussion in the chapter emphasized the measurement of people's attitudes toward objects. A related issue to marketing managers is how people *perceive* various objects, be they products or brands. In its constant quest for a differential advantage, the firm needs to correctly position its products against competitive offerings. In order to do this, the product manager needs to identify:

1. the number of dimensions consumers use to distinguish products;

2. the names of these dimensions;

3. the positioning of existing products along these dimensions;
4. where consumers prefer a product to be on the dimensions.[1]

One way in which managers can grasp the positioning of their brand versus competing brands is through the study of perceptual maps. Research Realities 8A.1, for example, depicts the situation in the automobile industry.

There are several ways by which perceptual maps can be created. As Figure 8A.1 indicates, they can be created using nonattribute-based or attribute-based approaches. The attribute-based approaches use procedures similar to those discussed in the chapter, in that they rely on characteristic-by-characteristic assessments of the various objects using, for example, Likert-type or semantic differential scales. The ratings of the objects on each of the items are subsequently analyzed using typically either factor or discriminant analysis to identify the key dimensions consumers use to distinguish the objects.

The nonattribute-based approaches use different methods in determining how individuals perceive the relationships among objects. Instead of asking a subject to rate objects on designated attributes, they ask individuals to make some *summary* judgments about the objects and then attempt to infer which characteristics were used to form those judgments. Typically, subjects are asked for their *perceptions of the similarity* between various objects and their *preferences* among these objects. An attempt is then made to locate the objects in a multidimensional space where the number of dimensions corresponds to the number of characteristics the individual used in forming the judgments. **Multidimensional scaling** analysis is the label that is typically used to describe the similarity- and preference-based approaches.[2]

The preference-based approaches for perceptual mapping are not used nearly as much as the similarity-based approaches. The discussion, therefore, will concentrate on the similarity-based approaches and, in particular, on the essential steps that need to be completed in order to develop perceptual maps using them. The attribute-based approaches are discussed briefly at the end of this appendix, because a full appreciation of them requires understanding of the essential purposes and operation of factor and discriminant analyses, topics that are discussed in Chapter 16.

Example

The purpose and nature of multidimensional scaling are best illustrated by example. Consider, therefore, that our interest is in developing a multidimensional map to characterize the perceived relationships among a set of ten banks serving a particular area. Label the banks *A, B, C, D, E, F, G, H, I,* and *J.* One factor of critical interest in

---

[1]Glen L. Urban and John R. Hauser, *Design and Marketing of New Products* (Englewood Cliffs, N.J.: Prentice-Hall, 1980), p. 195.

[2]There are actually three basic types of techniques: fully metric, fully nonmetric, and nonmetric multidimensional scaling. They differ according to the kind of input data and output information used. *Fully metric* methods have metric input (interval or ratio-scaled data) and metric output, while *fully nonmetric* methods have ordinal input and generate ranked output. By far the most interesting from the marketing researcher's vantage point, at least as judged by the relative emphasis in the literature, are the *nonmetric methods,* which generate *metric output from ordinal input.* The nonmetric methods are emphasized here.

Research Realities 8A.1

Product Positioning in the Automobile Industry

Exasperated by the growing similarity of cars on the road, a former Detroit auto executive recently remarked that if all of today's models were lined up end to end, even the top officers of the Big Three car makers would have a hard time telling them apart at a respectable distance.

The comment addresses an increasing challenge for automotive stylists and marketers. As fuel-efficiency requirements have narrowed design and performance characteristics for cars, the auto companies have had to turn to more subtle ways of drawing distinctions between different models. An example of how that is done is the "brand image" map shown in the Figure.

According to Mr. R. N. Harper, Jr., manager of product marketing plans and research, Chrysler draws up a series of such maps about three times a year, using responses to customer surveys. The surveys ask owners of different makes to rank their autos on a scale of one to 10 for such qualities as "youthfulness," "luxury" and "practicality." The answers are then worked into a mathematical score for each model and plotted on a graph that shows broad criteria for evaluating customer appeal.

The illustration below uses the technique to measure the images of the major divisions of U.S. auto makers, plus a few import companies. Using it, Chrysler would conclude, for instance, that the position of its Plymouth division in the lower left-hand quadrant means that cars carrying the Plymouth name generally have a practical, though somewhat stodgy, image. The Chrysler nameplate, by contrast, is perceived as more luxurious—though not nearly as luxurious as its principal competitors—Cadillac and Lincoln.

The map has other strategic significance, as well. By plotting on the map strong areas of customer demand, an auto maker can calculate whether its cars are on target. It can also tell from the concentration of dots representing competing models how much opposition it is likely to get in a specific territory on the map. Presumably, cars higher up on the graph should also fetch a higher price than models ranked toward the bottom, where the stress is on economy and practicality.

After viewing the results for its divisions, Chrysler concluded that Plymouth, Dodge and Chrysler all needed to present a more youthful image. It also decided that Plymouth and Dodge needed to move up sharply on the luxury scale.

Similarly, General Motors Corp. might find after looking at the map that its Chevrolet division, traditionally for entry-level buyers, ought to move down in practicality and more to the right in youthfulness. Another problem for GM on the map: the close proximity of its Buick and Oldsmobile divisions, almost on top of each other in the upper left-hand quadrant. That would suggest the two divisions are waging a marketing war more against each other than the competition.

Chrysler also uses its marketing map to plot individual models—both those it sells currently and those it plans for the future. By trying to move a model into an unoccupied space on the map through changes in styling, price or advertising, the company believes it can better hope to carve out a distinctive niche in the market.

"The real advantage of the map," says Mr. Harper, "is that it looks at cars from a consumer perspective while also retaining some sort of tangible product orientation." He says, for example, that his bosses were delighted when, on a recent map, Chrysler's forthcoming Lancer and Commander models showed up on the map next to the Honda Accord. (The two new Chrysler compacts are due out this fall.) "That told us that consumers think of our two new cars exactly the way we hoped they would," says Mr. Harper. "It was tangible evidence of where the car would compete in the market. And frankly, that can be hard to get these days."[1]

[1]John Koten, "Car Makers Use 'Image' Map as Tool to Position Products," *The Wall Street Journal*, March 22, 1984, p. 31. Reprinted by permission of *The Wall Street Journal*, © Dow Jones & Company, Inc., 1984. All Rights Reserved.

multidimensional scaling is the perceived similarity of the objects of study. For example, are certain banks seen to be alike, while others are viewed as very dissimilar? Are they all alike? All dissimilar? Just how close are they perceived to be in psychological space? The notion of psychological proximity plays a central role in the technique of

Perceptual Map of Automobiles

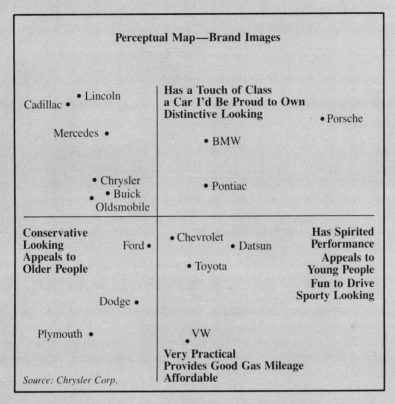

Perceptual Map—Brand Images

Source: Chrysler Corp.

Source: John Koten, "Car Makers Use 'Image' Map as Tool to Position Products," *The Wall Street Journal,* March 22, 1984, p. 31. Reprinted by permission of *The Wall Street Journal,* © Dow Jones & Company, Inc., 1984. All Rights Reserved.

multidimensional scaling, and the technique is sometimes referred to as the analysis of proximities data.[3]

---

[3]Psychological proximity may be defined on the basis of the psychological distance between the perceptions of two objects or between a person's preference and perception of an object, resulting in the scaling of similarities and preferences, respectively.

Figure 8A.1

Alternative Approaches to the Development of Perceptual Maps

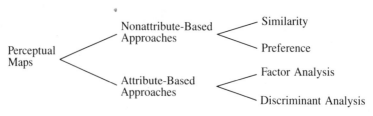

Suppose we were to ask a single respondent for that respondent's perceptions of the *similarities* among the ten banks in the area by asking for his or her judgments about all possible *pairs* of banks. For instance, we might form all possible pairs of the ten banks, 45 pairs in all. We could then place each pair of banks on a separate card and could ask the individual to rank the cards by increasing dissimilarity of the bank pairs using whatever criteria he or she normally employs to distinguish banks. Initially the individual could be instructed to sort the cards into four piles, for example, with the piles labeled extremely similar, somewhat similar, somewhat dissimilar, and extremely dissimilar. After placing each of the 45 cards in one of the piles, the individual would then be asked to order those within each pile from most similar to least similar. Suppose Table 8A.1 resulted from this process. Table 8A.1 indicates that the respondent perceived Banks *E* and *J* as the most similar, Banks *D* and *G* as the next most similar, and Banks *I* and *J* as the least similar.

Given the ranking contained in Table 8A.1, there are at least three questions of concern: (1) How many dimensions underlie this respondent's judgments about the similarity–dissimilarity of the ten banks? (2) What does the configuration look like—which banks are perceived as most similar and which are most dissimilar when all ten banks are considered simultaneously? (3) What attributes is the individual using in making his or her judgments?

Table 8A.1

Respondent Similarity Judgments

Bank	A	B	C	D	Bank E	F	G	H	I	J
A		24	6	17	28	8	27	26	14	29
B			9	38	11	7	42	36	40	13
C				32	18	4	37	35	21	19
D					23	22	2	3	39	20
E						10	33	16	44	1
F							34	25	30	12
G								5	41	31
H									43	15
I										45
J										

Multidimensional scaling can be used to generate answers to the first two questions, although the identification of the attributes underlying the judgments requires the collection of additional information or an intuitive assessment on the part of someone connected with the research. Note this: nonmetric multidimensional scaling can take this ordinal or rank order input data and can indicate the dimensionality and shape of the configuration needed to reflect the preceived relationships among the banks. How this is accomplished is a technical subject, to which we cannot do justice in a limited space, although we will try to develop a conceptual feel for the approach.

Conceptual Operation of Computer Program

There are many computer programs for performing a multidimensional scaling analysis, although they all owe their existence to the early work done by Shepard.[4] If we attempted to plot the ten points (banks) in one space, we would need ten coordinates, one for each bank. Similarly, with two axes (two-space) we would need twenty coordinates, one for each bank in each dimension; with five axes (five-space) we would need fifty coordinates; and in r space with n points we would need rn coordinates.

Now consider any three banks in Table 8A.1, for example, A, B, and C. The entries in Table 8A.1 represent an ordered metric scale; that is, the order relationships are on pairs of points. The similarity rankings of 24 for AB, 6 for AC, and 9 for BC mean that when plotting the three objects the distance from A to C must be less than that from B to C, and this in turn must be less than that from A to B if the plotted distances are to be in the same order as the perceived differences among the objects. Technically, this means we wish the plotted distances to be *monotonic* with the perceived distances. These ordered distance relationships can be captured by a number of arbitrary plots in two-dimensional space. Figure 8A.2 contains several such plots. Suppose we attempted to capture the relationships $\overline{AB} > \overline{BC} > \overline{AC}$ in a one-dimensional space. The points would all lie on one line, and while there are still variations possible, they are more limited; Points A and B must always lie at the ends of the line, and Point C must always be closer to A than to B if again the plotted distances are to match the judged distances among the objects. The Point C is *constrained* to lie between Points A and B if we plot the three points in one-space and still preserve the ordered relationships that exist in the data of Table 8A.1.

The same kind of logic prevails in multidimensional scaling analysis. The ten stimuli (banks) can be plotted rather arbitrarily in any nine-space just as any ordered n stimuli can be plotted somewhat arbitrarily in any $(n - 1)$-space. However, multidimensional scaling analysis seeks the *minimum dimensionality* necessary to capture the expressed order relationships. Further, with n stimuli there are $\frac{1}{2}n(n - 1)$ ranked relationships to be preserved. The number of relationships serves to restrict or constrain the movement of each point in a reduced space [less than $(n - 1)$ dimensions], because moving one point changes its distances from the remaining $(n - 1)$ points. This allows the determination of a unique configuration for all practical purposes in the reduced space. The objective, then, in multidimensional scaling analysis is to find a configuration of points

---

[4]Roger N. Shepard, ''The Analysis of Proximities: Multidimensional Scaling with an Unknown Distance Function, I,'' *Psychometrika,* 27 (June 1962), pp. 125–140, and ''The Analysis of Proximities: Multidimensional Scaling with an Unknown Distance Function, II,'' *Psychometrika,* 27 (September 1962), pp. 219–246.

Figure 8A.2
Arbitrary Plots of Three Points in Two-Space Satisfying the Constraints that
Distance *AB* > *BC* > *AC*

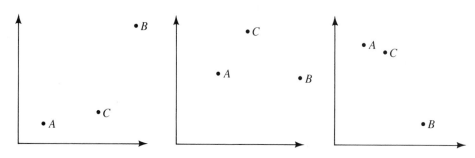

in each of the reduced spaces that most nearly matches the original order of judged distances among objects, that is, a geometrical configuration in which the physical distances between points are *monotone* with (in the same order as) the original similarity judgments.

Consider the banks *A, B, C, D,* and *E,* for example. The respondent's judgments in Table 8A.1 suggest that, when the computer locates these five objects in multidimensional space, the distances between the objects should be ordered in the following way,

$$AC < BC < BE < AD < CE < DE < AB < AE < CD < BD,$$

if the actual distances between the objects are to be in the same order as the respondent's judgments. In four-space this would be a relatively easy task, as the computer would have a good deal of latitude in locating the objects; however, in two dimensions or one dimension the computer would have much less latitude in locating the five banks while still satisfying all the inequalities.

The computer program operates iteratively. It starts with a given dimensionality, say four dimensions with five objects. It generates an initial solution. It then assesses how well the ordering of the actual distances between the objects matches the original rankings of similarity and determines whether the fit can be improved. If the answer is yes, it moves selected banks around in such a way as to improve the fit. It continues doing this until the fit in a given dimensionality can no longer be improved. It then moves to the next dimensionality, three in this instance, and repeats the process.

The number of dimensions "actually required" is then determined by looking at the "quality of fit" in each of the reduced spaces, with the basic aim of finding the lowest dimensionality for which the monotonicity constraint is "closely" met.[5] The analyst in effect trades off a perfect match between the rank order judgments and the plotted

---

[5]When the number of objects or stimuli is small (less than seven or eight), it is relatively easy to get a "good fit" in three dimensions or less. However, when the number of objects being compared gets beyond ten, one will not get a "good fit" in a few dimensions unless the model has validity.

Figure 8A.3
Multidimensional Scaling Map of Similarity Judgments of Table 8A.1

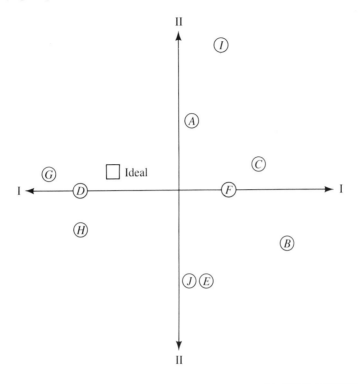

distances between the objects in $(n - 1)$ space for a lower space solution in which the distances between the points do not perfectly match the ordering of the judged similarities between objects but come "close," a notion that is elaborated below.

Example Solution

Figure 8A.3 displays the computer-determined two-space solution for the rank-order data of Table 8A.1. Disregard the small square for the moment. As Figure 8A.3 shows, the banks are seen to be relatively heterogeneous, although Banks *J* and *E* appear similar to the respondent, and Banks *G, D,* and *H* seem to form another cluster. One can immediately see how a picture like this could help a firm or product manager quickly identify the company's or product's major competitors and how it could be used to formulate a repositioning strategy.

Why two dimensions? As mentioned, the basic objective in multidimensional scaling (MDS) is to find the lowest space solution in which the monotonicity constraint is adequately met. The lower space solutions will rarely provide a perfect fit. Rather, it is to be expected that there will always be some differences between the rank orders of the plotted distances and the rank orders of the judged similarities. Thus, one can com-

Figure 8A.4
Stress Index for Bank Similarity Judgments

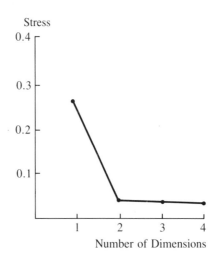

pute a measure of the lack of fit for each dimension. The lower the lack-of-fit index, the better the computer configuration matches the original configuration.

Different MDS programs, and there are a great many, employ different lack-of-fit indices. The particular configuration displayed in Figure 8A.3 was developed employing the TORSCA algorithm,[6] which uses Kruskal's stress for its lack-of-fit index.[7] Figure 8A.4 displays the plot of the stress value as a function of the number of dimensions employed to represent the solution. The fit in one dimension is poor using Kruskal's own verbal evaluations.[8]

Stress	Goodness of Fit
20%	poor
10%	fair
5%	good
2.5%	excellent
0%	perfect

The fit in two dimensions appears adequate enough, though, to conclude that the two-space solution is appropriate. The stress value of 0.06 is good, and there is an elbow in

---

[6]The great many multidimensional scaling programs are discussed and compared in A.P.M. Coxon, *The User's Guide to Multidimensional Scaling* (London: Heinemann Educational Books, 1982).

[7]Kruskal's stress is probably the most commonly used measure for lack of fit. See J. B. Kruskal, "Multidimensional Scaling by Optimizing Goodness of Fit to a Nonmetric Hypothesis," *Psychometrika,* 29 (March 1964), pp. 1–27.

[8]*Ibid.,* p. 3. These descriptions of what is "good" stress depend on the use of Formula 1 to calculate stress.

the stress function. The elbow indicates that there is substantial improvement in the goodness of fit with an increase in the number of dimensions from one to two, but only slight additional improvement in fit as the number of dimensions is increased to three or even to four. The two-space solution seems most consistent with the objective of minimum dimensionality, since it reproduces the original rankings just as efficiently as do the three-and four-space solutions.

Accepting the two-space solution as adequately capturing the individual's similarity judgments is one thing; naming the dimensions that serve as a basis for these judgments is quite another, and this output is not provided by the computer program. Rather, the names of the dimensions are supplied by someone associated with the research effort. There are several approaches that can be used. First, the individual can be asked to evaluate the objects (that is, banks), in terms of several defined attributes such as service, location convenience, and so on. The researcher then correlates the attribute scale scores for each object with the coordinates for each object in the plot. In this scheme, the size of the respective correlation coefficients between attributes and dimensions is used to attach labels. Another approach is to have the manager or researcher interpret the dimensions using his or her own experience and the visual configuration of points. Still a third approach is to attempt to relate the dimensions to physical characteristics of the banks, such as the interest rates required on loans or paid on savings deposits.

Suppose the dimensions were named using one of these schemes, that Dimension 1 turned out to be a "convenience" dimension while Dimension 2 turned out to be a "friendliness, courteous" dimension, and that you were the manager of Bank B. The perceptual map in Figure 8A.3 indicates that your bank is perceived as being the most convenient but also quite unfriendly by our single respondent. If a large enough number of respondents felt this way, and you are suffering market share problems, it might behoove you to change the internal environment so that your employees project a friendly, courteous image when interacting with customers. This finding might also call for some changes in your promotional strategy.

While the example demonstrates the placement of stimuli (that is, banks) only, it also is possible to locate preferences in the same geometric space. Figure 8A.3, for example, displays the position of the "ideal" bank of our sample respondent by a small square. An ideal bank is a hypothetical bank possessing just the perfect combination of the two attributes, convenience and friendliness. The individual's ideal point is located from the preference data that he supplies. Once again the objective is to locate the ideal so that the distance between the subject's ideal and each of the objects corresponds as closely as possible to the individual's preferences for the objects. If, when asked, the individual stated that he preferred, in order, banks D, G, H, A, F, J, E, C, I, and B, there would be perfect monotonicity between fitted preference and stated preference because this is the ascending order of the distances between the respondent's ideal and each of the ten banks in Figure 8A.3.

The previous paragraph should provide some appreciation for the keen interest displayed by marketing people in MDS analysis. Suppose our sample respondent is indeed banking at Bank D. Judging by the map, our respondent's banking choice may not represent a choice in which she is maximizing her satisfaction, but simply one in which Bank D is the best of a set of relatively undesirable alternatives. The individual would most decidedly switch her account if there were an alternative choice closer to her ideal. Suppose there were other individuals with the same perceptions as our sample respon-

Figure 8A.5
Key Decisions When Conducting a Multidimensional Scaling Analysis

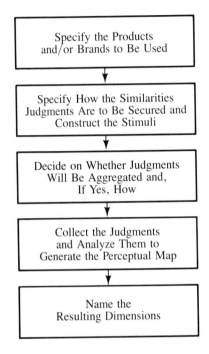

dent and with similar problems in satisfying their true preferences. The presence of market segments where the ideal points concentrate as well as potential marketing opportunities would then be obvious from the map.

Key Decisions

While the example provides some appreciation for the conceptual underpinnings of multidimensional scaling analysis, it does not capture the various decisions an analyst has to make in order to complete a multidimensional scaling analysis. Several of the more basic of these are pictured in Figure 8A.5.

The first decision an analyst has to make is to specify the products or brands at issue. While they will be partly determined by the purpose of the study, they will not be completely specified by it, and analysts will have some discretion in choosing products or brands to use. When exercising this discretion, analysts need to recognize that the dimensions that appear in the perceptual map will be a direct function of the stimulus set that was used to secure the judgments. Suppose the study was being conducted to determine respondents' perceptions of various soft drinks. If no unsweetened or low calorie soft drinks were included in the stimulus set, this very important dimension may not appear in the results. So as not to run such a risk, analysts may be tempted to include every conceivable product or brand in the stimulus set. This strategy, though, can place such a burden on respondents that their answers may be meaningless.

The burden on respondents is going to depend partly on the number of judgments each has to make and partly on the difficulty of each judgment. Both of these issues in turn depend upon how the similarity judgments are to be secured.[9] There are two main alternatives and a number of options under each alternative. The two major options are direct or indirect similarity judgments, two terms that are relatively self-explanatory. The direct methods rely on data collection mechanisms in which respondents compare stimuli using whatever criteria they desire and, on the basis of that comparison, state which of the stimuli are most similar, least similar, and so on. All possible pairs of the brands being evaluated could be formed, for example, and respondents could be asked to rank-order the various pairs from most similar to least similar. Alternatively, a brand could be singled out as a focal brand, and respondents could be asked to rank-order each of the other brands in terms of their similarity to the focal brand. Each brand could serve, in turn, as the focal brand. While there are a number of alternative ways of collecting these judgments, they all have one thing in common: the respondents are asked to judge directly how similar the various alternatives are using criteria that they choose. The indirect methods operate differently. Instead of respondents selecting the criteria on which to compare the alternatives, they are asked to evaluate each brand using prespecified criteria. Some kind of measure of similarity is then calculated for each pair of brands (for example, the correlation between the ratings of the brands).

The third decision analysts have to make is whether the judgments of individual respondents will be aggregated so that group perceptual maps can be developed or whether individual maps will be generated. The problem with individual maps is that they become very difficult for the marketing manager to use to develop marketing strategy. Managers typically look at marketing planning questions in terms of segments, not individuals. Yet, as soon as the segment issue is raised, the question becomes one of deciding how the individual judgments will be aggregated. Is it likely that individuals used the same number of criteria when evaluating the various brands? Even if they used the same number, are the criteria themselves likely to be the same? If they are not, what criteria should be used to group respondents? One of the most popular algorithms, INDSCAL, for example, assumes that all subjects use the same criteria to judge the similarity of objects but that they weight the dimensions differently when forming their judgments.[10]

---

[9]For discussion of some of the main ways by which similarity judgments can be secured, see M. L. Davison, *Multidimensional Scaling* (New York: Wiley-Interscience, 1983); T. Deutcher, "Issues in Data Collection and Reliability in Multidimensional Scaling Studies—Implication for Large Stimulus Sets," in R. G. Golledge and J. N. Rayner, eds., *Proximity and Preference: Problems in the Multidimensional Scaling Analysis of Large Data Sets* (Minneapolis: University of Minnesota Press, 1982); or S. S. Schiffman, M. L. Reynolds, and F. W. Young, *Introduction to Multidimensional Scaling: Theory, Methods, and Applications* (New York: Academic Press, 1981).

[10]For an overview of some marketing studies that have used various algorithms, see Lee G. Cooper, "A Review of Multidimensional Scaling in Marketing Research," *Applied Psychological Measurement*, 7 (Fall 1983), pp. 427–450.

Step 4 in Figure 8A.5 involves the actual collection of the judgments and their processing. The processing involves two steps. First, an initial configuration must be determined for each of the dimensions. Different programs use different routines to generate an initial solution. Second, the points must be moved around until the fit is the best it can be in that dimensionality, using the criterion under which the program operates. The output of this analysis is the **stress** or other goodness-of-fit diagram alluded to earlier, which analysts use to decide on the ''proper number'' of dimensions.

The last decision analysts have to make when conducting a nonmetric multidimensional scaling analysis involves what to call the dimensions. As suggested before, there are several procedures that are used to help name the dimensions. The practical fact, though, is that difficulty in naming the dimensions is one of management's major concerns with nonmetric multidimensional scaling analysis.

Attribute-Based Approaches

One of the advantages of the attribute-based approaches to the development of perceptual maps is that they do make the naming of dimensions easier. They also seem to be easier for respondents to use.[11] As mentioned earlier, the attribute-based approaches rely on having individuals rate various brands, typically using either semantic differential or Likert scales. These judgments are usually then input to either discriminant analysis or factor analysis.

The emphasis in discriminant analysis is upon determining the combinations of attributes that best discriminate between the objects or brands. The dependent measures are the ''products rated,'' and the predictor variables are the attribute ratings. The analysis is typically run across groups of respondents to find a common structure. The dimensions are named by examining the weightings of the attributes that make up a discriminant dimension or by computing the correlations between the attributes and each of the discriminant scores. The use of discriminant analysis to develop perceptual maps seems to work particularly well when one is concerned with product design attributes that can be clearly and unequivocally perceived by consumers.[12]

Factor analysis relies on the assumption that there are only a few basic dimensions that underlie the attribute ratings. It examines the correlations among the attributes to identify these basic dimensions. The correlations are typically computed across brands and groups of consumers. The dimensions usually are named by examining the factor loadings which represent the correlations between each attribute and each factor. The use of factor analysis in the development of perceptual maps seems to be particularly useful when the marketing emphasis is on the formulation of communications strategy in which the linguistic relations between the attributes are key.[13]

---

[11]John R. Hauser and Frank S. Koppelman, ''Alternative Perceptual Mapping Techniques: Relative Accuracy and Usefulness,'' *Journal of Marketing Research*, 16 (November 1979), pp. 495–506.

[12]Joel Huber and Morris B. Holbrook, ''Using Attribute Ratings for Product Positioning: Some Distinctions Among Compositional Approaches,'' *Journal of Marketing Research*, 16 (November 1979), pp. 507–516.

[13]*Ibid.*

Table 8A.2

Comparison of the Nonattribute- and Attribute-based
Approaches for Developing Perceptual Maps

Technique	Respondent Measures	Advantages	Disadvantages
Nonattribute-based similarity judgments	Judged similarity of various products and/or brands	Does not depend on a predefined attribute set. Allows respondents to use their normal criteria when judging objects. Allows for condition that perception of the ''whole'' may not be simply the sum of the perceptions of the parts.	Difficult to name dimensions. Difficult to determine if, and how, the judgments of individual respondents should be combined. Criteria respondents use depend on the stimuli being compared. Requires special programs. Provides oversimplified view of perceptions when few objects are used.
Attribute-based discriminant or factor analysis	Ratings on various products and/or brands on prespecified attributes	Facilitates naming the dimensions. Easier to cluster respondents into groups with similar perceptions. Easy and inexpensive to use. Computer programs are readily available.	Requires a relatively complete set of attributes. Rests on assumption that overall perception of a stimulus is made of the individual's reactions to the attributes making up the stimulus.

Comparison of Approaches

The advantages of the attribute-versus the nonattribute-based approaches to multidimensional scaling analysis are summarized in Table 8A.2.[14] Most of the nonattribute-based applications in marketing use similarity judgments. Similarity measurement has the advantage of not depending on a predefined attribute set. This is a two-edged sword. Although it allows respondents to use only those dimensions they normally use in making judgments among objects, it creates difficulties in naming the dimensions. Further, different consumers can use different dimensions and one then has to grapple with how best to combine consumers when forming maps. Constructing a separate map for each individual is prohibitively costly. Aggregating all the responses and then developing one map distorts reality in that it implies a homogeneity in perceptions that probably does not exist. The middle ground of grouping consumers into segments raises the whole

---

[14]For additional discussion of the advantages and the disadvantages of the nonattribute- and attribute-based approaches for the development of perceptual maps, see Hauser and Koppelman, ''Alternative Perceptual Mapping . . .''; Huber and Holbrook, ''Using Attribute Ratings . . .''; or Urban and Hauser, *Design and Marketing of New Products,* pages 185–234.

issue of how the aggregation should be effected. Even individual consumers have been known to vary the criteria they are using when making a series of judgments, indicating the criteria depend on the products or brands in the stimulus set. The fact that the criteria can change as a series of similarity judgments are made makes an already difficult problem of naming the dimensions even harder. One has to be especially careful when using the similarity-based programs if the number of objects being judged is less than eight, as it is then very easy to secure an oversimplified picture of the competitive environment.

As previously mentioned, the attribute-based approaches facilitate naming the dimensions, and they also make the task of clustering respondents into groups with similar perceptions easier to deal with. They presume, though, that the list of attributes used to secure the ratings are relatively accurate and complete. They contain the implicit assumption that a person's perception or evaluation of a stimulus is some combination of the individual's reactions to the attributes making up the stimulus. Yet, people may not perceive or evaluate objects in terms of underlying attributes, but may perceive them as some kind of whole that is not decomposable in terms of separate attributes. Further, the measures used to group people imply some assumptions about how consumers' reactions to the various attribute scales should be combined. The attribute-based approaches are easier to use than the similarity method, since the programs employed are more readily available and less expensive to run.

Regardless of the approach taken, the appeal of multidimensional scaling analysis lies in the maps produced by the technique. These maps can be used to provide insight into some very basic questions about markets, including, for product markets:

1. the salient product attributes perceived by buyers in the market;
2. the combination of attributes buyers most prefer;
3. the products that are viewed as substitutes and those that are differentiated from one another;
4. the viable segments that exist in a market;
5. those "holes" in a market that can support a new product venture.

Further, the technique also appears suited for product life cycle analysis, market segmentation, vendor evaluation, the evaluation of advertisements, test marketing, sales representative and store image research, brand switching research, and attitude scaling.[15]

Applications and Problems

1. XYZ Company, a medium-sized manufacturer of frozen food products, wanted to expand its line of concentrated fruit drinks by the introduction of a concentrated apple juice. Five major brands served the market. The market research department decided to use multidimensional scaling to determine the viable "holes" in the market. Perceptions of the similarities among the five brands resulted in the following similarity judgments.

---

[15]For a review of these applications, see Cooper, "A Review of Multidimensional Scaling in Marketing Research."

Table 1.
Respondent Similarity Judgments

Brand	A	B	C	D	E
A		5	9	10	8
B			1	2	7
C				6	4
D					3
E					

The computer determined two-space solution for the above rank order data is:

Figure 1.
Multidimensional Scaling Map of Similarity Judgments

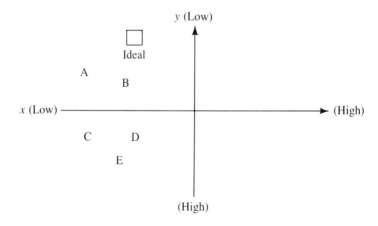

Figure 2 displays the plot of the stress value as a function of the number of dimensions employed:

Figure 2.
Stress Index for Brand Similarity Judgments

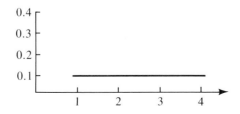

a. In Figure 1 the computer has located the five brands in two dimensional space. How are the distances between the objects ordered? _____ _____

b. Do you think that the similarity judgments between the brands can be captured by one dimension? Give three reasons to support your decision.

c. The market research department has identified the Y axis in Figure 1 as "price." How would you advise management to position their brand?

Appendix 8B
Conjoint Measurement

Like multidimensional scaling analysis, **conjoint analysis** relies on the ability of respondents to make judgments about stimuli. In multidimensional scaling analysis, the stimuli are products or brands, and respondents are asked to make judgments about their relative *similarity*. In conjoint analysis, the stimuli represent some *predetermined combinations of attributes*, and respondents are asked to make judgments about their *preference* for these various attribute combinations. The basic aim is to determine the features respondents most prefer. Respondents might use, for example, such attributes as miles per gallon, seating capacity, price, length of warranty, and so on in making judgments about which automobile they most prefer. Yet, if asked to do so directly, many respondents might find it very difficult to state which attributes they were using and how they were combining them to form overall judgments. Conjoint analysis attempts to handle this problem by estimating how much each of the attributes is valued on the basis of the choices respondents make along product concepts that are varied in systematic ways. In essence, respondents' value systems are inferred from their behaviors as reflected in their choices rather than from self reports as to how important, say, each of the various attributes are to them.

The word "conjoint" has to do with the notion that the relative values of things considered jointly can be measured when they might not be measurable if taken one at a time. Quite often respondents are asked to express the relative value to them of various alternatives by ordering the alternatives from most desirable to least desirable. The attempt in a conjoint analysis solution is, then, to assign values to the levels of each of the attributes so that the resulting values or utilities are as monotonic as possible with the input rank-order judgments.

Example

Suppose we were considering introducing a new drip coffee maker and wished to assess how consumers evaluated the following levels of each of these product attributes.

■ Capacity—4, 8, and 10 cups
■ Price—$18, $22, and $28
■ Brewing time—3, 6, 9, and 12 minutes

Table 8B.1
Respondent Ordering of Various Product Descriptions

Capacity	4 cup			8 cup			10 cup		
Price	$18	$22	$28	$18	$22	$28	$18	$22	$28
Brewing Time:									
3 minutes	17	15	6	30	26	24	36	34	28
6 minutes	16	12	5	29	25	22	35	33	27
9 minutes	9	8	3	21	20	8	32	31	23
12 minutes	4	2	1	14	13	7	19	18	11

All three of these attributes are "motherhood" attributes in the sense that, other things equal, most consumers would prefer either the most or least of each property, in this instance, the largest capacity maker with the shortest brewing time and the lowest price. Unfortunately, life is not that simple. The larger coffee maker will cost more; faster brewing means a larger heating element for the same pot capacity, which also raises the cost; a larger capacity maker with no change in the heating element will require increased brewing time. In sum, a consumer is going to have to trade off one property to secure more of another. What the manufacturer is interested in determining is how consumers value these specific attributes. Is low price most valued, or are consumers willing to pay a higher price to secure some of the other properties? What price? What properties? One thing we might do to answer these questions would be to form all possible combinations of these product attributes, 36 combinations in all, taking one feature from each set and placing that on an index card.

Suppose we then asked a respondent to order these product descriptions or cards from least desirable (rank = 1) to most desirable (rank = 36). The respondent could be instructed, for example, to sort the cards first into four categories labeled very undesirable, somewhat undesirable, somewhat desirable, and very desirable, and then, after completing the sorting task, to order the cards in each category from least to most desirable. Suppose the ordering contained in Table 8B.1 resulted from this process.

Note several things about these entries. First, the respondent least preferred the $28 maker with 4 cup capacity and 12 minutes brewing time (rank = 1) and most preferred the 10 cup maker with 3 minutes brewing time priced at $18 (rank = 36). Second, if the respondent cannot have her first choice, she is willing to "suffer" with a longer brewing time so that she could still get the 10-cup maker for $18 (rank = 35). She is not willing to suffer too much, though, as reflected by her third choice (rank = 34). Rather, she is willing to pay a little more to secure the faster 3-minute brewing time rather than having to endure an even slower 9-minute brewing time. In effect, she is willing to trade off price for brewing time.

The type of question that conjoint analysis attempts to answer is: What are the individual's utilities for price, brewing time, and pot capacity in determining her choices?

Procedure

The procedure for determining the individual's utilities for each of several product attributes followed in conjoint analysis is quite similar to that followed in multidimensional scaling analysis. Again the technique is quite dependent on the availability of a high-speed computer. Just as in multidimensional scaling, the computer program emphasis is on generating an initial solution and subsequently on modifying that solution through a series of iterations to improve the goodness-of-fit.[1] More specifically, given a set of input judgments, the computer program will:

1. assign arbitrary utilities to each level of each attribute;
2. calculate the utilities for each alternative by somehow combining, most typically adding, the individual utility values;
3. calculate the goodness-of-fit between the ranking of the alternatives using these derived utility values and the original ordering of the input judgments;
4. modify the utility values in a systematic way until the derived utilities produce evaluations that when ordered, correspond as closely as possible to the order of the input judgments.

For example, suppose at the first iteration, the computer assigned the following utilities to each level of each attribute:

Capacity		Price		Brewing Time	
4 cup	0.2	$18	0.6	3 minutes	0.5
8 cup	0.3	$22	0.3	6 minutes	0.3
10 cup	0.5	$28	0.1	9 minutes	0.1
				12 minutes	0.1

Suppose further that an additive function is being used so that the utility of any combination of features is given simply by the sum of the utilities of the attribute levels making up the combination. Thus, a 4-cup, 12-minute brewing time, $28 pot would have a utility of 0.4 (0.2 + 0.1 + 0.1). The utilities for each of the other alternatives are shown in Table 8B.2.

An easy way of finding whether the assigned utilities produce an ordering of the product alternatives that corresponds to the original order of the input judgments is by plotting one against the other. For example, the least preferred alternative (rank = 1) was the 4- cup, $28 maker that took 12 minutes. The estimated utility for this combination in Table 8B.2 is 0.4. These two numbers (0.4, 1) serve as coordinates for the

---

[1]There are several programs available. One of the most popular is MONANOVA. See J. B. Kruskal, "Analysis of Factorial Experiments by Estimating Monotone Transformations of the Data," *Journal of the Royal Statistical Society,* Series B, 27 (1965), pp. 251–263; and J. B. Kruskal and F. Carmone, "Use and Theory of MONANOVA, a Program to Analyze Factorial Experiments by Estimating Monotone Transformations of the Data," unpublished paper, Bell Laboratories, 1968. For an empirical comparison involving MONANOVA versus other prediction schemes, see Dick R. Wittink and Philippe Cattin "Alternative Estimation Methods for Conjoint Analysis: A Monte Carlo Study," *Journal of Marketing Research,* 18 (February 1981), pp. 101–106.

Table 8B.2
Utilities for the Feature Combinations Given the Assumed Values

Capacity	4 cup			8 cup			10 cup		
Price	$18	$22	$28	$18	$22	$28	$18	$22	$28
Brewing Time:									
3 minutes	1.3	1.0	0.8	1.4	1.1	0.9	1.6	1.3	1.1
6 minutes	1.1	0.3	0.6	1.2	0.9	0.7	1.4	1.1	0.9
9 minutes	0.9	0.6	0.4	1.0	0.7	0.5	1.2	0.9	0.7
12 minutes	0.9	0.6	0.4	1.0	0.7	0.5	1.2	0.9	0.7

point in the lower left-hand corner in Figure 8B.1. Figure 8B.1 shows the relationship that results when each of the derived cell values is plotted against the corresponding preference judgment. If there was a perfect ordering of the derived cell values, the curve would, of course, always increase, since the higher cell values would be associated with higher stated preference. Clearly, the function in Figure 8B.1 does not. The derived cell values are not monotonic with the original judgments. The computer program would recognize this by computing some measure of goodness-of-fit between the two orderings. The computer program would also take corrective action and would change the values assigned to the attribute levels in a systematic way so as to improve the correspondence between the two orders. The computer would continue this process of calculating the goodness-of-fit, changing the assigned values in a systematic way so as to improve the fit, until it was no longer possible to improve the fit between the two. The program would report the goodness-of-fit for the final iteration and would also report the utility values assigned to each level of each attribute at this final iteration.

The utilities or part-worth functions for our single subject that resulted from such a process are captured in Figure 8B.2. These utilities suggest several things about our subject. In the first place, they indicate that our subject's preferences for price and size are monotonic; other things equal, she prefers the least costly and largest coffee maker, and her utility function for each attribute declines with increasing price and decreasing size. Her preference function for brewing time is not monotonic, though: she has a higher utility for a 6-minute maker than for a faster or slower one.

Second, these utilities can be used to determine the relative *importance* of each of these attributes; these are provided by the *spread* in utilities between the highest- and lowest-rated levels of the attribute. The rationale is that, if all levels of an attribute have the same utility to an individual, the attribute is unimportant to the person. Conversely, if different levels of an attribute produce widely differing utilities, the individual is sensitive to the level, implying the attribute is important to her. In interpreting these importance values, one has to remain cognizant of the fact that they depend on the level of the attributes used to structure the stimuli. Thus, if price levels of $18, $28, and $38 were used instead of $18, $22, and $28, the differences in utilities for the various price levels would have been greater, suggesting that price was relatively more important to the individual than other attributes. Given the attribute levels used, capacity is most important and price least important to the subject.

Figure 8B.1
Input Ranks versus Derived Cell Values

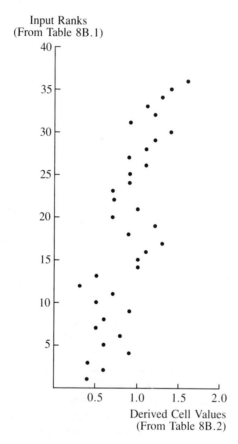

Input Ranks
(From Table 8B.1)

Derived Cell Values
(From Table 8B.2)

The real pay-off from the above analysis comes from the fact that one can use the results to identify the optimal levels and importance of each attribute in structuring a new product offering. Further, by aggregating consumers who have similar preferences or utility functions, products can be designed that come closer to satisfying particular market segments. Thus, conjoint analysis seems to have great promise at the concept evaluation stage of the product development process.[2]

---

[2]See Paul E. Green, J. Douglas Carroll, and Stephen M. Goldberg, "A General Approach to Product Design Optimization Via Conjoint Analysis," *Journal of Marketing*, 45 (Summer 1981), pp. 17–37, for a general procedure for optimizing product/service designs using input data based on conjoint analysis methods.

Figure 8B.2
Utilities for Various Coffee Maker Attributes

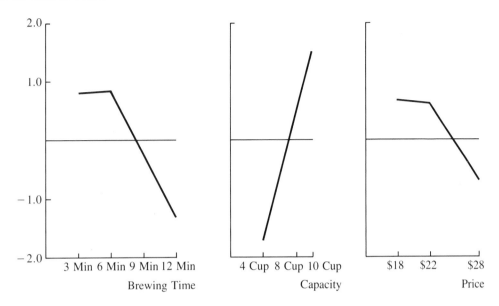

Key Decisions

While the example illustrates the essential thrust in a conjoint analysis study, it also provides somewhat of an oversimplified picture of the situation, in that it does not convey the proper appreciation for the many decisions analysts have to make in order to conduct such a study. Figure 8B.3 highlights the more critical decision points.[3]

The first step in the process involves deciding upon the attributes to be used when constructing the stimuli. These will stem primarily from the purpose of the investigation, but the analyst will have some discretion in this regard. When choosing, analysts should be guided by the principles that the attributes used should be both actionable and important to individuals. Actionable attributes are those that the company can do something about, in that the company has the technology or other resources to make the changes that might be indicated by consumer preferences. Important attributes are those that actually affect consumer choice. The attributes actually used can be determined by

---

[3]The article by Paul E. Green and V. Srinivasan, "Conjoint Analysis in Consumer Research: Issues and Outlook," *Journal of Consumer Research,* 5 (September 1978), pp. 103–123, discusses a number of issues in the implementation of conjoint analysis. The article by Philipe Catlin and Dick R. Wittink, "Commercial Use of Conjoint Analysis: A Survey," *Journal of Marketing,* 46 (Summer 1982), pp. 44–53, describes the more common practices among a sample of commercial firms who use conjoint analysis on a regular basis. The firm's surveyed completed almost 700 projects between 1971 and 1981. Much of the following discussion is developed from these two excellent sources.

Figure 8B.3
Key Decisions When Conducting a Conjoint Analysis

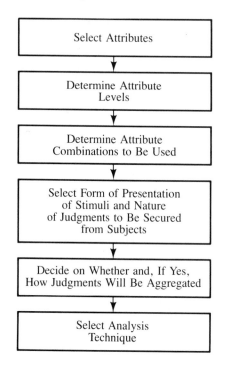

managerial judgment or by any of the other techniques that are typically productive at the exploratory research stage of an investigation, including depth interviews with individual subjects, focus groups, analysis of insight-stimulating examples, and so on. In any single conjoint analysis study, only a handful of all the attributes that could be used will be used, so it is important that they be selected with care. When the number of attributes that need to be varied exceed reasonable limits with respect to data collection problems, a series of conjoint analysis studies can be conducted. The number of attributes actually used in a typical conjoint analysis study averages six or seven.[4]

Step 2 in the process involves specifying the actual levels for each attribute. The number of levels for each attribute has a direct bearing on the number of stimuli respondents will be asked to judge and consequently on the burden placed upon each subject. In general, we would like to minimize that burden. At the same time, we would like to end up with good estimates of the utility of each attribute level. Our ability to generate good estimates requires that the number of stimuli be relatively large versus the number of parameters that need to be estimated, and the number of parameters in

---

[4]Cattin and Wittink, "Commercial Use of Conjoint Analysis," p. 47.

turn depends upon the preference model being embraced. Is the model linear in the sense that more or less of the attribute can be expected to be most desired, or is it nonlinear in a systematic way, or could there be a very nonsystematic relationship between preference and attribute levels? Most subjects might prefer the lowest price or the highest quality when choosing a ballpoint pen, suggesting a linear relationship between their utilities and the attribute levels. At the same time, many might prefer a medium point to a fine or broad point, suggesting a smooth nonlinear relationship might be appropriate. The nonlinear model requires the estimation of more parameters than does the linear model, and, other things being equal, we would like more stimuli when estimating it than when estimating the parameters of the linear model. A very irregular and nonsystematic relationship between utilities and attribute levels would require even more stimuli for good estimation.

Another factor that affects the choice of attribute levels is their impact on consumer choice. Using levels that are similar to those in existence increases respondents' believability in the task and the validity of their preference judgments. Using attribute levels that are outside the range normally encountered decreases the believability of the task for respondents but can increase the accuracy by which the parameters can be estimated statistically. Similarly, decreasing the intercorrelations among the attributes being varied (such as by combining a very low price with very high quality) decreases the believability of the options for respondents but also increases the accuracy with which the parameters can be estimated. The general recommendation seems to be to make the ranges for the various attributes somewhat larger than what is normally found but not so large as to make the options unbelievable.[5]

The third major decision analysts have to make to conduct a conjoint analysis involves deciding upon the specific combinations of attributes that will be used, that is, what the full set of stimuli will look like. In our example, there were only three attributes being considered, but the respondent was required to make 36 judgments. Since the number of possible combinations is given by the product of the number of levels of the attributes, one can readily appreciate what happens to the judgment task if the number of attributes or the number of levels for any attribute is increased. Can we reasonably expect the respondent, for example, to provide meaningful judgments if there are five attributes at three levels each (not an unusual case) requiring then $3 \times 3 \times 3 \times 3 \times 3 = 243$ rank order judgments? In such a situation, analysts might be tempted to reduce the number of attributes that are varied or the number of levels at which individual attributes are set. An alternative scheme is to use only select combinations of the attributes. For example, it is possible to use orthogonal designs to select only a very small subset of the total number of stimuli if the analyst is willing to assume that there are no interactions among the attributes.[6] This simply means that a person's utility for various width tips on a ballpoint pen, say, is independent of the person's utility for

---

[5]Green and Srinivasan, "Conjoint Analysis in Consumer Research," p. 109.

[6]The use of orthogonal designs and select combinations of the stimuli can produce significant economies in the number of stimuli respondents need to evaluate. See Sidney Addleman, "Orthogonal Main-Effect Plans for Asymetrical Factorial Experiments," *Technometrics*, 4 (February 1962), pp. 21–46, which is an excellent general source on orthogonal designs, or Paul E. Green, "On the Design of Choice Experiments Involving Multifactor Alternatives," *Journal of Consumer Research*, 1 (September 1974), pp. 61–68, which discusses the notions involved more from the perspective of designing choice experiments.

Figure 8B.4

Pairwise Approach to Data Collection in Conjoint Analysis

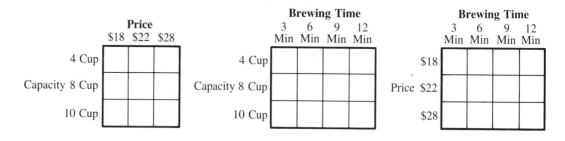

various prices. It is possible to augment the stimuli that are suggested by an orthogonal array with some particularly interesting combinations or ones that allow the estimation of certain select interactions suspected of affecting choice.[7]

The example used the **full profile** approach to collect the judgments; that is, each stimulus was made up of a combination of each of the attributes. One can simplify the judgment task by using the **pairwise procedure** to structure the stimuli instead of the full profile approach. The pairwise procedure treats two attributes at a time but considers all possible pairs. Thus, in the example, the subject would be asked to indicate her preference ordering for each combination of brewing time and price, brewing time and capacity, and price and capacity by completing independently each of the matrices contained in Figure 8B.4.

It is typically easier for subjects to supply pairwise judgments than full profile judgments. On the other hand, they typically need to make more judgments, and there is a danger of missing some important trade-offs among attributes when the pairwise approach to data collection is used. There can also be a potential loss in realism when only two attributes are considered at a time in that respondents are then forced to make some implicit assumptions about the levels of the other attributes not explicitly varied.[8] Not only is the full profile approach more popular than the pairwise approach, but its popularity is increasing. Panel A in Research Realities 8B.1, for example, indicates the full profile approach historically has been used on over half of all conjoint analysis projects and lately has been used on almost 70 percent of them.

Step 4 in the process involves selecting the form of presentation of the stimuli and the nature of the judgments to be secured from subjects. The full profile approach has used variations and combinations of three basic approaches—verbal description, paragraph description, and pictorial representation.[9] Verbal description relies on presenting

---

[7]See, for example, Frank J. Carmone and Paul E. Green, "Model Misspecification in Multiattribute Parameter Estimation," *Journal of Marketing Research,* 18 (February 1981), pp. 69–74.

[8]See, for example, Madhav N. Segal, "Reliability of Conjoint Analysis: Contrasting Data Collection Procedures," *Journal of Marketing Research,* 19 (February 1982), pp. 139–143, for an empirical assessment of the performance of the two approaches.

[9]Green and Srinivasan, "Conjoint Analysis in Consumer Research," p. 111.

Research Realities 8B.1

Relative Frequency of Usage of Various Techniques in Conjoint Analysis

	Percentage of Projects on Which Used	
	Since Company Started	During Most Recent 12 Months
A. Data Collection Methods		
Full profile (concept evaluation)	56	69
Two factors at a time (trade off matrices)	27	13
Combination of full profile and two factors at a time	14	15
Other	3	3
B. Methods of Presenting Stimuli		
Verbal descriptions	50	46
Paragraph descriptions	20	23
Pictorial descriptions	19	17
Actual products	7	9
Other including models or pseudoproducts	4	5
C. Nature of the Judgments		
Preference	33	44
Liking	10	8
Intention to buy	54	46
Other including actual purchase or order placement	3	2
D. Nature of Task		
Rank order	45	41
Paired comparison	11	5
Rating scale	34	39
Other including the grading of paired comparisons	10	15
Total number of projects	698 (100%)	160 (100%)

Source: Developed from the tables in Philipe Catlin and Dick R. Wittink, "Commercial Use of Conjoint Analysis: A Survey," *Journal of Marketing*, 56 (Summer 1982), pp. 44–53.

the cues in list form, typically one stimulus per card, much as was assumed in the example. Paragraph description operates just as the name implies; a paragraph is used to describe each stimulus. Pictorial description relies on some kind of visual prop or three-dimensional model. When visual aids are used, they are typically used in combination with verbal descriptions which are the most common. As Panel B of Research Realities 8B.1 indicates, verbal descriptions are the most popular.

Related to the issue of the form of presentation of the stimuli is the issue of the nature of the judgments that will be secured from respondents. The two most common approaches measure respondents' preferences for each alternative or their intention to buy each alternative. See Panel C in Research Realities 8B.1. Historically, this information has been secured most often by asking respondents to rank order the alternatives with respect to preference or intention to buy. Rating scales have recently become much more popular, though, when securing the needed judgments. Some of the main reasons advanced by those using rank order judgments are their ease of use of subjects, ease of administration, and a desire to keep the judgment task as close as possible to a consumer's behavior while actually shopping. Those using rating scales believe they are less time consuming, are more convenient for respondents to use, and are easier to analyze.[10] The nature of the task is different in the two schemes. When the rank-order method is used, subjects are asked to make relative judgments with respect to their preference for one alternative versus another. When the rating method is used, the judgments are typically made independently; that is, subjects are asked to indicate their degree of liking of each stimulus by checking the appropriate location along the preference or intention-to-buy scale as the alternative is presented. As Panel D of Research Realities 8B.1 indicates, rank order historically has been the preferred procedure, but the use of rating scales now almost matches it in popularity.

Step 5 in the process involves deciding if the responses from individual subjects will be aggregated and, if so, how? While it is possible to derive the utilities for each level of each attribute at the individual level, much as we did in the example, individual-level results are very difficult for marketing managers to use for developing marketing strategy. The other extreme is to pool the results across all respondents and then to estimate one overall utility function. This option fails to recognize any heterogeneity in preference that might exist among respondents, which in turn reduces the predictive power of the model. The middle ground is to form segments from groups of respondents in such a way that the models for the groups will have predictive power close to that found for the individual level models while having at the same time some clear marketing strategy implications for managers. This raises the question, of course, of how these groups should be formed.[11] Most typically it is done by forming segments that are homogeneous with respect to the benefits they want from the product or service. Operationally, this often translates into estimating utilities for the individual level models and then clustering respondents into groups that are homogeneous with respect to the utilities assigned to the various levels of the individual attributes.[12]

Step 6 in the execution of a conjoint analysis study involves selecting the technique by which the input data will be analyzed. The choice depends in part, but not exclu-

---

[10]Cattin and Wittink, "Commercial Use of Conjoint Analysis," pp. 48–49.

[11]For additional discussion and empirical assessment of the aggregation issue, see William L. Moore, "Levels of Aggregation in Conjoint Analysis: An Empirical Comparison," *Journal of Marketing Research,* 17 (November 1980), pp. 516–523.

[12]See, for example, Saul Sands and Kenneth Warwick, "What Product Benefits to Offer to Whom: An Application of Conjoint Segmentation," *California Management Review,* 24 (Fall 1981), pp. 69–74.

sively, on the type of preference model embraced and the method that was used to secure the input judgments. When linear or smooth nonlinear models are hypothesized to capture preference, one of the constrained parameter estimation models can be used to estimate the functions.[13] When an irregular model is assumed, utilities or **part-worth functions** need to be estimated for each level of each attribute. There are several methods used to estimate the individual part-worths. When rank order data has been secured from respondents, then the nonmetric MONANOVA model, the essential operation of which was described in the example, is most often used to estimate the utilities. Dummy variable regression can be, and is, increasingly being used for this purpose, however, because regression programs are much more readily available than is MONANOVA, and the results from the two approaches are highly correlated.[14] When dummy variable regression is used, the rank ordering of the alternatives is the dependent variable while each of the independent variables is coded into a series of 0–1 alternatives.[15] When the preference judgments are collected using rating scales, it is most typical to use either analysis-of-variance techniques or, again, dummy variable regression analysis to estimate the part-worth utilities.[16] In both of these instances, the ratings of each alternative serve as the criterion variable.

General Comments

It is only after the analyst has made decisions with respect to each of the steps listed in Figure 8B.3 that he or she is in a position to actually collect data for a conjoint analysis study. Unfortunately, there seems to be some propensity among beginning researchers to hurry into the data collection task. This can be a mistake, because there are a great many interrelationships among the many decisions that need to be made, as Figure 8B.3 and the surrounding discussion hopefully point out. Rushing into the data collection effort before the interrelated choices are all spelled out can only result in suboptimizing some of the choices. For example, one technique that has become popular in recent years is to obtain conjoint responses to a limited set (usually three to nine) of full profiles drawn for a larger master set and to combine that information with other information respondents directly provide as to the relative importance to them of each of the attributes and which levels of each attribute they prefer. Called hybrid models, the

---

[13]For discussion of the philosophy and some of the more popular techniques for constrained parameter estimation, see V. Srinivasan, Arun K. Jain, and Naresh K. Malhotra, "Improving Predictive Power of Conjoint Analysis by Constrained Parameter Estimation," *Journal of Marketing Research,* 20 (November 1983), pp. 433–438.

[14]For empirical comparisons of the *predictive* accuracy of several of the more popular estimation techniques, see Franklin Acito and Arun K. Jain, "Evaluation of Conjoint Analysis Results: A Comparison of Methods," *Journal of Marketing Research,* 17 (February 1980), pp. 106–112; Wittink and Cattin, "Alternative Estimation Methods for Conjoint Analysis: A Monte Carlo Study," and Ishmael Akaah and Pradeep K. Korgaonkar, "An Empirical Comparison of the Predictive Validity of Self-Explicated, Huber-Hybrid, Traditional Conjoint, and Hybrid-Conjoint Models," *Journal of Marketing Research,* 20 (May 1983), pp. 187–197.

[15]The essential notions underlying dummy variable regression are described in Chapter 15.

[16]Analysis of variance is described in Appendix 14A.

essential purpose is to combine the simplicity of the self-explicated approach to attribute measurement with the greater generality of conjoint models.[17]

One can see that vital marketing questions in product design are being addressed by conjoint analysis. Further, the technique is not restricted to product evaluations. It can be used whenever one is making a choice among multiattribute alternatives. With multiattribute alternatives one typically does not have the option of having more of everything that is desirable and less of everything that is not desirable. Instead, most decisions involve trading off part of something in order to get more of something else. Conjoint analysis attempts to mirror the trade-offs one is willing to make. Thus, while it has most often been used for product design issues, including concept evaluation, it is also used quite regularly as an aid in pricing decisions, market segmentation questions, or advertising decisions. It has been used less frequently for making distribution decisions, to evaluate vendors, to determine the rewards that salespeople value, and to determine consumer preferences for various attributes of health organizations, among other things.

Applications and Problems

1.   The management of XYZ company decided to introduce Apple-Down, a frozen concentrated apple juice. However, the management was uncertain as to the price and size of the product. The market research department decided to use conjoint analysis to determine the level of each attribute which would come closest to satisfying consumers. The following levels of each of the product attributes were used:

Price	$0.70	$1.10	$1.50
Size	4 fl. oz	8 fl. oz.	16 fl. oz.

A respondent's rank ordering of the various product descriptions are noted in Table 1:

Table 1.
Respondent Ordering of Various Product Descriptions

Price	Size		
	4 fl. oz.	8 fl. oz.	16 fl. oz.
$ .70	4	1	2
$1.10	6	5	3
$1.50	9	8	7

---

[17]For an exposition of hybrid models and a review of their comparative performance in cross-validation tests, see Paul E. Green, "Hybrid Models for Conjoint Analysis: An Expository Review," *Journal of Marketing Research,* 21 (May 1984), pp. 155–169. For an empirical comparison on how the reliability and validity of conjoint analysis compares with that of self-explicated weights, see Thomas W. Leigh, David B. MacKay, and John O. Summers, "Reliability and Validity of Conjoint Analysis and Self-Explicated Weights: A Comparison," *Journal of Marketing Research,* 21 (November 1984), pp. 456–462.

At the first iteration, the computer assigned the following utilities:

Price	Utility	Size	Utility
$0.70	0.7	4 fl. oz.	.6
$1.10	0.4	8 fl. oz.	.2
$1.50	0.1	16 fl. oz.	.1

(a) Using the linear additive rule and assigned utilities, calculate the utilities for each alternative. Enter these in Table 2.

Table 2.
Utilities for the Feature Combinations Given the Assumed Utilities

Price	4 fl. oz.	Size 8 fl. oz.	16 fl. oz.
$ .70			
$1.10			
$1.50			

(b) Plot the original order of the input judgments (Table 1) against the derived utilities for each alternative from Table 2. Discuss your findings.

Appendix 8C
Psychological Measurement

As suggested early in the chapter, part of the explanation for the many conceptualizations of attitude is the difficulties inherent in measuring psychological constructs. The problem is similar to that faced in other areas of scientific inquiry, save for the fact that we do not have a visual referent for many of the constructs. The essence of the measurement problem is captured in Figure 8C.1.[1] The basic researcher or scientist uses theories in an attempt to explain phenomena. These theories or models consist of constructs (denoted by the circles with C's in them), linkages among and between the constructs (single lines connecting the C's), and data that connect the constructs with the empirical world (double lines). The single lines represent **conceptual** or **constitutive definitions,** in that a given construct is defined in terms of other constructs in the set. The definition may take the form of an equation that precisely expresses the interrela-

---

[1]Figure 8C.1 and the discussion surrounding it are adapted from the classic book by Warren S. Torgerson, *Theory and Methods of Scaling* (New York: John Wiley, 1958), pp. 1–11.

Figure 8C.1

Schematic Diagram Illustrating the Structure of Science and the Problem of Measurement

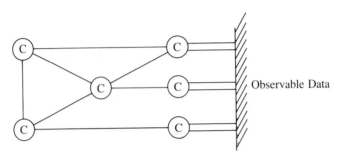

tionship of the construct to the other constructs, such as the equation in mechanics that suggests that force equals mass times acceleration. Alternatively, the relationship may be only imprecisely stated, which is typically the case in the social sciences. The double lines represent operational definitions. An **operational definition** describes how the construct is to be measured. It specifies the activities that the researcher must complete in order to assign a value to the construct (e.g., sum the scores on the ten Likert-type statements to generate a total score). Conceptual definitions logically precede operational definitions and guide their development, for we must specify what a construct is before we can develop rules for assessing its magnitude.

The role of scientific inquiry is to establish the relationships that exist among the constructs of the model. It is necessary that some of the constructs be related to observable data if scientists are to accomplish their task. Otherwise, the model will be circular, with given unobservable constructs being defined in terms of other unobservable constructs. Since a circular model cannot be supported or refuted by empirical data, it is not legitimately considered a theory. Rather, a theory or system of explanation rests upon the condition that at least some of the constructs can be operationalized sufficiently so as to allow their measurement. Recall that measurement is defined as ''rules for assigning numbers to objects to represent quantities of attributes.'' The rigor with which these rules are defined and the skill with which they are implemented determine whether the construct has been captured by the measure.

You would undoubtedly scoff at the following measurement procedure. John has blue eyes and Bill has brown eyes and, therefore, John is taller than Bill. You might reply that ''the color of a person's eyes has nothing to do with the person's height and, therefore, you have not in fact measured their height, if that is indeed your purpose. Further, if you wanted to see who was taller, the best procedure would be to measure them with a yardstick or to stand them side by side and compare their heights.'' You would be right on both counts. If I measured both John and Bill by asking them how tall they were, you would have probably voiced less objection to my procedure, unless

I concluded that John was taller whereas Bill was definitely the bigger man upon observation of the two together. Now the interesting thing about most psychological constructs is that we cannot rely on visual comparisons to either confirm or refute a measure. We cannot see an attitude, a personality characteristic, a person's knowledge about or awareness of a particular product, or other psychological characteristics such as intelligence, mental anxiety, or whatever. These characteristics are all part of the consumer's black box. Their magnitude must be inferred from our measurements. Since we cannot resort to a visual check on the accuracy of our measures, we must rely on assessing the procedures employed to derive the measure. Eye color is certainly not height, but have we captured the sales representatives' satisfaction with their job if we directly ask them how satisfied they are? Probably not, for reasons that will become obvious below.

Note that the problem of establishing operational definitions for constructs (measuring the constructs) is not unique to the researcher interested in scientific explanation. The practitioner shares this concern. Consider the examples in the introductory paragraphs of Chapter 8. The shampoo manufacturer needs to know that the company is in fact measuring consumer attitudes toward the new product and not the many other factors with which the research must contend. The appliance manufacturer must be sure that the full spectrum of dealer attitudes has been correctly tapped, and not a small segment of them. The industrial marketer must be certain that the research has not only assessed the sales representative's satisfaction with the obvious dimensions of the work itself, pay, and promotion opportunities, but has also correctly gauged the sales representative's attitudes toward the company, fellow workers, top management, sales supervisor, and customers. The ability to make these assessments relies heavily on an understanding of measurement, measurement error, and the notions of reliability and validity. Understanding these notions is the task to which we now turn.

Variations in Measured Scores

Recall that the definition of measurement states that it is the attributes of objects we measure and not the objects themselves. Now measurement, particularly psychological measurement, always takes place in a rather complex situation in which there are a great many factors that affect the attribute or characteristic being measured, including the process of measurement itself. Consider, for example, during the peak of the energy crisis, the oil companies' interest in measuring people's attitudes toward the energy crisis and, particularly, their feelings as to the role played by the oil companies in deliberately precipitating such a crisis. Suppose one of the procedures described in the chapter was used to develop an attitude scale to measure these feelings and that the scale was administered to a sample of respondents. A high score means that the respondent felt the oil companies had little to do with precipitating the crisis, while a low score indicates just the opposite and, therefore, reflects a poor attitude toward the petroleum producers. Suppose Mary had a score of 75 and Jane had a score of 40 on the instrument, while the minimum and maximum scores possible were 25 and 100. Conclusion: Mary has a much more favorable attitude toward the oil companies than does Jane. Ideally, yes; practically, maybe. It depends on the quality of the measurement.

Consider some of the potential sources of differences in these two scores of 75 and 40.[2]

1. True differences in the characteristic that one is attempting to measure: In the ideal situation, the difference in scores would reflect true differences in the attitudes of Mary and Jane and nothing else. This situation will rarely, if ever, occur. Rather, the difference will also reflect the factors listed below.

2. True differences in other relatively stable characteristics of the individual that affect the score: Not only does a person's position on an issue affect the score, but other characteristics can also be expected to have an effect. Perhaps the difference between Mary's and Jane's scores is simply due to the greater willingness of Jane to express her negative feelings. Mary, by contrast, follows the adage, "If you can't say something nice, don't say anything at all." Her cooperation in the study has been requested and so she responds, but not truthfully.

3. Differences due to transient personal factors: A person's mood, state of health, fatigue, and so on, may all affect the individual's responses. Yet these factors are temporary and can vary. Thus, if Jane had just returned from a long unsuccessful wait in line to get gas, her responses may be decidedly different than if she were interviewed after a successful trip for gas with no wait in line, or several days after she had made her last fill-up trip.

4. Differences due to situational factors: The situation surrounding the measurement also can affect the score. Mary's score might be different if her husband were there while the scale was being administered. Incidentally, this problem is the bane of researchers studying the decision-making process of married couples. When the husband is asked for the respective roles of husband and wife in purchasing a new automobile, for instance, one set of responses is secured; when the wife is asked, the responses are different; when the two are asked together, still a third set is obtained. Which is correct? It is hard to say, since the fact remains that the situation surrounding a measurement can affect the scores that are obtained.

5. Differences due to variations in administration: Much measurement in marketing involves the use of questionnaires administered by phone or in person. Since interviewers can vary in the way they ask questions, the responses also may vary as a function of the interviewer. The same interviewer may even handle two interviews differently enough to trigger a variance in recorded answers, although the respondents do not really differ on the characteristic.

6. Differences due to sampling of items: When we measure any construct, we tap only a sample of items relevant to the characteristic being measured. Thus, our attitude scale for the petroleum companies will contain only a sample of all the items or

---

[2]These differences are adapted from Claire Selltiz, Lawrence L. Wrightsman, and Stuart W. Cook, *Research Methods in Social Relations,* 3rd ed. (New York: Holt, Rinehart and Winston, 1976), pp. 164–168. See also Duane F. Alwin and David J. Jackson, "Measurement Models for Response Errors in Surveys: Issues and Applications," in Karl F. Schuessler, ed., *Sociological Methodology 1980* (San Francisco: Jossey-Bass, 1979), pp. 69–119; and Frank E. Saal, Ronald G. Downey, and Mary Anne Lakey, "Rating the Ratings: Assessing the Psychometric Quality of Ratings Data," *Psychological Bulletin,* 88 (September 1980), pp. 413–428.

statements we could possibly have included. If we added, deleted, or changed the wording of some items, we would undoubtedly change the absolute score achieved by Mary and Jane and could conceivably even change their relative scores so that Jane came out with the more positive attitude. Thus, we must be constantly aware that our measurement represents a narrow conception of the construct and that the resulting score will vary as a function of the items included to capture the construct. A man's height can serve as an indicator of his "size," but so can his weight, the size of his waistline, chest size, and so on. We certainly could expect to have a better measure of a man's size if we included all these items. So it is with psychological measurements. Other things being equal, a one-item scale is a less adequate sample of the universe of items relevant to a characteristic than is a twenty-five-item scale.

7. Differences due to lack of clarity of the measuring instrument: Sometimes a difference in response to a questionnaire or an item on a scale may represent differences in interpretation of an ambiguous or complex question rather than any fundamental differences in the characteristic one is attempting to measure. One of the researcher's main tasks is to generate items or questions that mean the same thing to all respondents, so that the observed differences in scores are not caused by differences in interpretation.

8. Differences due to mechanical factors: "Circumstances such as broken pencils, check marks in the wrong box, poorly printed instructions, and lack of space to record responses fully, play their role in preventing the most effective functioning of a measuring instrument."[3]

Classification and Assessment of Error

As mentioned, the ideal in measurement is to generate a score that reflects true differences in the characteristic one is attempting to measure and nothing else. What we in fact obtain, though, is something else. A measurement, call it X_0, for what is observed can be written as a function of several components:

$$X_0 = X_T + X_S + X_R,$$

where

X_T represents the "true" score of the characteristic being measured;

X_S represents systematic error; and

X_R represents random error.

The total error of a measurement is given, of course, by the sum of X_S and X_R; it is important to note that it has two components. **Systematic error** is also known as constant error, since it affects the measurement in a constant way. An example would be

---

[3]Selltiz, Wrightsman, and Cook, *Research Methods.,* p. 168.

the measurement of a man's height with a poorly calibrated wooden yardstick. Differences in other stable characteristics of the individual, which affect the person's score, are a source of systematic error. **Random error** is not constant error, but rather is due to transient aspects of the person or measurement situation. A random error manifests itself in the lack of consistency of repeated or equivalent measurements when the measurements are made on the same object or person. An example would be the use of an elastic ruler to measure a man's height. It is unlikely that on two successive measurements the observer would stretch the elastic ruler to the same degree of tautness, and, therefore, the two measures would not agree although the man's height had not changed. Differences due to transient personal factors are an example of this type of error in psychological measurement.

The distinction between systematic error and random error is critical because of the way the validity of a measure is assessed. **Validity** is synonymous with accuracy or correctness. The validity of a measuring instrument is defined as "the extent to which differences in scores on it reflect true differences among individuals on the characteristic we seek to measure, rather than constant or random errors."[4] When a measurement is valid, $X_0 = X_T$, since there is no error. The problem is to develop measures in which the score we observe and record actually represents the true score of the object on the characteristic we are attempting to measure. This is much harder to do than to say. It is not accomplished by simply making up a set of questions or statements to measure (for example, a person's attitude toward the petroleum companies' precipitation of the energy crisis). Rather, the burden is on the researcher to establish that the measure accurately captures the characteristic of interest. This relationship between measured score and true score is never established unequivocally but is always inferred. The bases for the inference are two: (1) direct assessment employing validity and (2) indirect assessment via reliability.[5] Let us consider each of these sources of evidence in turn.

Direct Assessment   As mentioned, a measuring instrument is valid to the extent that differences in scores among objects reflect true differences of the objects on the characteristic that the instrument tries to measure. We normally do not know the true score of an object with respect to a given characteristic. If we did know it, there would be no need to measure the object on that characteristic. What we do, therefore, is infer the validity of the measure by looking for evidence of its pragmatic, content, and construct validity.

Pragmatic Validity   The pragmatic approach to validation focuses on the usefulness of the measuring instrument as a predictor of some other characteristic or behavior of the individual, and is thus sometimes called predictive validity or criterion-related validity. **Pragmatic validity** is ascertained by how well the measure predicts the criterion, be it another characteristic or a specific behavior. An example would be the Graduate Man-

---

[4]Selltiz, Wrightsman, and Cook, *Research Methods,* p. 169.

[5]For detailed discussion of the conceptual relationships that should exist among the various indicants of reliability and validity and an empirical assessment of the evidence, see J. Paul Peter and Gilbert A. Churchill, Jr., "The Relationship Among Research Design Choices and Psychometric Properties of Rating Scales: A Meta-Analysis," *Journal of Marketing Research,* 23 (February 1986), pp. 1–10.

agement Admissions Test. The fact that this test is required by most of the major schools of business attests to its pragmatic validity; it has proved useful in predicting how well a student with a particular score on the exam will do in an accredited MBA program. The test score is used to predict the criterion of performance. An attitude scale example might be using scores sales representatives achieved on an instrument designed to assess their job satisfaction to predict who might quit. The attitude score would again be used to predict a behavior—the likelihood of quitting. Both of these examples illustrate predictive validity in the true sense of the word, that is, use of the score to predict some future occurrence. However, there is another type of pragmatic validity—concurrent validity. **Concurrent validity** is concerned with the relationship between the predictor variable and the criterion variable when both are assessed at the same point in time. For example, the "frog test," administered to women to ascertain whether they are pregnant, provides an example of concurrent validity. The interest here is not in forecasting whether the woman will become pregnant in the future, but in determining if she is pregnant now.

Pragmatic validity is determined strictly by the correlation between the two measures—if the correlation is high, the measure is said to have pragmatic validity.

Thus if it were found that accuracy in horseshoe pitching correlated highly with success in college, horseshoe pitching would be a valid measure for predicting success in college. This is not meant to imply that sound theory and common sense are not useful in selecting predictor instruments for investigation, but after the investigations are done, the entire proof of the pudding is in the correlations.[6]

Pragmatic validity is relatively easy to assess. It requires, to be sure, a reasonably valid measure of the criterion with which the scores on the measuring instrument are to be compared. Given that such scores are available, though (for example, the grades the student actually achieves in a MBA program, the sales representative's quitting or not), all that the researcher needs to do is to establish the degree of relationship, usually in the form of some kind of correlation coefficient, between the scores on the measuring instrument and the criterion variable. While easy to assess, pragmatic validity is rarely the most important kind of validity. We are often concerned with "what the measure in fact measures" rather than simply whether it predicts accurately or not.

Content Validity   **Content validity** focuses on the adequacy with which the domain of the characteristic is captured by the measure. Consider, for example, the characteristic "spelling ability" and suppose that the following list of words was used to assess an individual's spelling ability: puck, stick, goalie, linesman, assist, penalty, faceoff, blue line, offside, forecheck. Now, you would probably take issue with this spelling test. Further, the basis for your objection probably would be the fact that all the words relate to the sport of hockey. Therefore, you could argue that an individual who is basically a very poor speller could do well on this test simply because he or she is a hockey enthusiast. You would be right, of course. A person with a basic capacity for spelling but with little interest in hockey might, in fact, do worse on this spelling test than one

---

[6]Jum C. Nunnally, *Psychometric Theory,* 2nd ed. (New York: McGraw-Hill, 1978), p. 88.

with less native ability but a good deal more interest in hockey. The test could be said to lack content validity, since it does not properly sample the domain of all possible words that could be used but is very selective in its emphasis.

The above example illustrates how content validity is assessed, although not how it is established. Content validity is sometimes known as "face validity" because it is assessed by examining the measure with an eye toward ascertaining the domain being sampled. If the included domain is decidedly different from the domain of the variable as conceived, the measure is said to lack content validity. Theoretically, to capture a person's spelling ability, we should administer all words in the English language. The person who spelled the greatest number of these words correctly would be said to have the most spelling ability. This is a completely unrealistic procedure. It would take several lifetimes to complete. We, therefore, resort to sampling the domain of the characteristic by constructing spelling tests that consist of samples of all the possible words that could be used. Different samplings of items can produce different comparative performances by individuals. We need to recognize that whether we have assessed the true characteristic depends on how well we have sampled the domain of the characteristic. This is not only true for spelling ability, but also holds for psychological characteristics in which we have an interest.

How can we ensure that our measure will possess content validity? We can never guarantee it because it is partly a matter of judgment. We may feel quite comfortable with the items included in a measure, for example, while a critic may argue that we have failed to sample from some relevant domain of the characteristic. While we can never guarantee the content validity of a measure, we can severely diminish the objections of the critics. The key to content validity lies in the *procedures* that are used to develop the instrument.

One of the most critical elements in generating a content valid instrument is conceptually defining the domain of the characteristic. The researcher has to specify what the variable is and what it is not. The task of definition is expedited by examining the literature to determine how the variable has been defined and used. Since it is unlikely that all the definitions will agree, the researcher must specify which elements in the definition underlie his or her use of the term. The researcher's next step is to formulate a large collection of items that broadly represent the variable as defined. The researcher needs to be quite careful to include items from all the relevant dimensions of the variable. Again, a literature search may be quite productive in indicating the various dimensions or strata of a variable. At this stage, the researcher may wish to include items with slightly different shades of meaning, since the original list of items will be refined to produce the final measure.

The collection of items must be large, so that after refinement the measure still contains enough items to adequately sample each of the domains of the variable. In the example cited previously, a measure of a sales representative's job satisfaction would need to include items about each of the components of the job (duties, fellow workers, top management, sales supervisor, customers, pay, and promotion opportunities) if it is to be content valid. The process of refinement, the essence of which is the internal consistency exhibited by the items within the test, is statistical in nature.

Construct Validity   **Construct validity** is most directly concerned with the question of what the instrument is, in fact, measuring. What construct, concept, or trait underlies the performance or score achieved on that test? Does the measure of attitude measure attitude or some other underlying characteristic of the individual that affects his or her score? Construct validity lies at the very heart of scientific progress. Scientists need constructs with which to communicate. So do you and I. Thus, in marketing we speak of people's socioeconomic class, their personality, their attitudes, and so on. These are all constructs that we use as we try to explain marketing behavior. And while vital, they also are unobservable. We can observe behavior related to these constructs, but we cannot observe the constructs themselves. Rather, we operationally define the constructs in terms of a set of observables. When we agree on the operational definitions, precision in communication is advanced. Instead of saying that what is measured by these 75 items is the person's brand loyalty, we can speak of the notion of brand loyalty.

While the measurement of constructs is vital to scientific progress, construct is the most difficult type of validity to establish.[7] We need to ensure, through the plans and procedures used in constructing the instrument, that we have adequately sampled the domain of the construct and that there is internal consistency among the items of the domain. The assumption regarding internal consistency of a set of items is that "if a set of items is really measuring some underlying trait or attitude, then the underlying trait causes the covariation among the items. The higher the correlations, the better the items are measuring the same underlying construct."[8] We saw that internal consistency was also at issue in determining content validity, and as a matter of fact, negative evidence of the content validity of a measure also provides negative evidence about its construct validity. A measure possessing construct validity must be internally consistent insofar as the construct is internally consistent. On the other hand, it is not true that a consistent measure is a construct-valid measure. "To the extent that the elements of . . . a domain show . . . consistency, it can be said that *some* construct may be employed to account for the data, but it is by no means sure that it is legitimate to employ the construct name which motivated the research. In other words, consistency is a *necessary* but not *sufficient* condition for construct validity."[9]

Given that the domain of the construct has been specified, a set of items relevant to the breadth of the domain has been generated, the items have been refined, and the remaining items have been shown to be internally consistent, the remaining step is to see how well the measure relates to measures of other constructs to which the construct is theoretically related. Does it behave as expected? Does it fit the theory or model relating this construct to other constructs? For example, consider Figure 8C.1 again, and suppose two of the constructs stand for the concepts job satisfaction and job turnover, and suppose we had developed a measure to assess a sales representative's job

---

[7]See Gilbert A. Churchill, Jr., "A Paradigm for Developing Better Measures of Marketing Constructs," *Journal of Marketing Research,* 16 (February 1979), pp. 64–73, for a procedure that can be used to construct scales having construct validity. See J. Paul Peter, "Construct Validity: A Review of Basic Issues and Marketing Practices," *Journal of Marketing Research,* 18 (May 1981), pp. 133–145, for an in-depth discussion of the notion of construct validity.

[8]George W. Bohrnstedt, "Reliability and Validity Assessment in Attitude Measurement," in Gene F. Summers, ed., *Attitude Measurement* (Chicago: Rand McNally, 1970), p. 93. See also George W. Bohrnstedt, "Measurement," in Peter H. Rossi, James D. Wright, and Andy B. Anderson, eds, *Handbook of Survey Research* (Orlando: Academic Press Inc., 1983), pp. 69–121.

[9]Nunnally, *Psychometric Theory,* p. 103.

satisfaction. Now, the construct validity of the measure could be assessed by ascertaining the relationship between job satisfaction scores and company turnover. Those companies in which the scores are low, indicating less job satisfaction, should experience more turnover than those with high scores. If they do not, one would question the construct validity of the job satisfaction measure. In other words, the construct validity of a measure is assessed by whether the measure confirms or denies the hypotheses predicted from the theory based on the constructs. Is the evidence consistent with the hypothesized linkages among the constructs as captured in a model like Figure 8C.1? The fallacy, of course, is that the failure of the hypothesized relationship to obtain among the observables may be due to a lack of construct validity or incorrect theory. We often try to establish the construct validity of a measure, therefore, by relating it to a number of other constructs rather than simply one, and we also try to use those theories and hypotheses that are sufficiently well founded to inspire confidence in their probable correctness.

If the trait or construct exists, it is also true that it should be measurable by several different methods. These methods should be independent insofar as possible. If they are all measuring the same construct, though, the measures should have a high level of correlation. This provides evidence of **convergent validity,** which is defined as "the confirmation of a relationship by independent measurement procedures." Discriminant validity is also required to establish the construct validity of a measure. **Discriminant validity** requires that a measure not correlate too highly with measures from which it is supposed to differ.[10] If the correlations are too high, this suggests that the measure is not actually capturing an isolated trait, or is simply reflecting method variance. **Method variance** is the variation in scores attributable to the method of data collection. "The assumption is generally made . . . that what the test measures is determined by the content of the items. Yet the final score . . . is a composite of effects resulting from the content of the item and effects resulting *from the form of the items used*"[11] (emphasis added).

Indirect Assessment via Reliability

Reliability means the similarity of results provided by independent but comparable measures of the same object, trait, or construct. It is distinguished from validity in that whereas validity is represented in the agreement between two attempts to measure the same trait through *maximally different* methods, reliability is the agreement between two efforts to measure the same trait through *maximally similar* methods.[12] If a measure

---

[10]One convenient way of establishing the convergent and discriminant validity of a measure is through the multitrait–multimethod matrix of Campbell and Fiske. See Donald T. Campbell and Donald W. Fiske, "Convergent and Discriminant Validation by the Multitrait–Multimethod Matrix," *Psychological Bulletin,* 56 (1959), pp. 81–105. See also Neal Schmitt, Bryan W. Coyle, and Bruce B. Saari, "A Review and Critique of Analyses of Multitrait–Multimethod Matrices," *Multivariate Behavioral Research,* 12 (October 1977), pp. 447–478 and Donald P. Schwab, "Construct Validity in Organizational Behavior," in B. Staw and L. L. Cummings, eds., *Research in Organizational Behavior,* Vol. 2 (Greenwich, Ct.: JAI Press, 1980), pp. 3–43.

[11]L. J. Cronbach, "Response Sets and Test Validity," *Educational and Psychological Measurement,* 6 (1946), p. 475.

[12]Campbell and Fiske, "Convergent and Discriminant Validation," p. 83.

were valid, there would be little need to worry about its reliability. If a measure is valid, it reflects the characteristic it is supposed to measure and is not distorted by other factors, either systematic or transitory.

Evaluating the reliability of any measuring instrument consists of determining how much of the variation in scores is due to inconsistencies in measurement.[13] The reliability of the instrument should be established before it is used for a substantive study and not after.

Before discussing how this evidence is generated, one point needs emphasis. Reliability involves determining the consistency of independent or comparable measures of the same object, group, or situation. To the extent that a measure is reliable, it is not influenced by transitory factors. In other words, the more reliable the measure, the lower is X_R in the equation for observed scores. Note, though, what this implies. A measure could be reliable and still not be valid, since even if X_R equals zero, $X_0 = X_T + X_S$. The converse is, of course, not true. If the measure is valid, $X_0 = X_T$, since the measure is simply reflecting true scores without error. Thus, it is often said that (1) if a measure is valid, it is reliable; (2) if it is not reliable, it cannot be valid, since at a very minimum $X_0 = X_T + X_R$; and (3) if it is reliable, then it may or may not be valid, since reliability does not account for systematic error. In other words, while lack of reliability provides negative evidence of the validity of a measure, the mere presence of reliability does not mean the measure is valid. Reliability is a necessary, but not a sufficient, condition for validity. Reliability is more easily measured than validity, though, and this accounts for the emphasis on it over the years. Research Reality 8C.1 indicates, for example, that even among studies in which a major thrust is the assessment of the psychometric quality of the measures, reliability is the most frequently investigated property.

Stability   One of the more popular ways of establishing the reliability of a measure is to measure the same objects or individuals at two different points in time and to correlate the obtained scores. Assuming that the objects or individuals have not changed in the interim, the two scores should correlate perfectly. To the extent that they do not, random disturbances were operating in either one or both of the test situations to produce random error in the measurement. The procedure is known as test–retest reliability assessment.

One of the critical decisions the researcher must face in determining the **stability** of a measure is how long to wait between successive administrations of the instrument. Suppose the researcher's instrument is an attitude scale. If the researcher waits too long, the person's attitude may change, thus producing a low correlation between the two scores. On the other hand, a short wait will likely produce test bias—people may remember how they responded the first time and be more consistent in their responses than is warranted by their attitudes. To handle this problem, many researchers will use alternate forms for the two administrations. Instead of putting all the items in one form,

---

[13]See J. Paul Peter, ''Reliability: A Review of Psychometric Basics and Recent Marketing Practices,'' *Journal of Marketing Research,* 16 (February 1979), pp. 6–17, for a detailed treatment of the issue of reliability in measurement. See Gilbert A. Churchill, Jr., and J. Paul Peter, ''Research Design Effects on the Reliability of Rating Scales: A Meta-Analysis,'' *Journal of Marketing Research,* 21 (February 1984), pp. 360–375, for an empirical assessment of the factors that seem to affect the reliability of rating scales.

Research Realities 8C.1

Relative Frequency with Which Various Psychometric Properties of Measures Are Investigated

Reliability	95%
Convergent validity	25
Discriminant validity	17
Construct validity	83

Source: Developed from the information in J. Paul Peter and Gilbert A. Churchill, Jr., "The Relationship Among Research Design Choices and Psychometric Properties of Rating Scales: A Meta-Analysis," *Journal of Marketing Research,* 23 (February 1986), pp. 1–10.

the researcher generates two instruments that are as identical as possible in content. That is, each form should contain items from the same domains, and each domain of content should receive approximately the same emphasis in each form. Ideally, there would be a one-to-one correspondence between items on each of the two forms so that the means and standard deviations of the two forms would be identical and the intercorrelations among the items would be the same in both versions.[14] While it is next to impossible to achieve the ideal, it is possible to construct forms that are roughly parallel, and the parallel forms are correlated across time as the measure of test–retest reliability. The recommended time interval between administrations is two weeks.[15]

Equivalence   The basic assumption in constructing an attitude scale is that when several items are summed into a single attitude score, the items are measuring the same underlying attitude. Each item can, in one sense, be considered a measure of the attitude, and the items should be consistent (or equivalent) in what they indicate about the attitude. Within a given scale, then, the **equivalence** measure of reliability focuses on the internal consistency or internal homogeneity of the set of items forming the scale.

The earliest measure of the internal consistency of a set of items was the split-half reliability of the scale. In assessing split-half reliability, the total set of items is divided into two equivalent halves; the total scores for the two halves are correlated; and this is taken as the measure of reliability of the instrument. Sometimes the division of items is made randomly, while at other times the even items are assumed to form one-half and the odd the other half of the instrument. The total score on the even items is then correlated with the total score obtained from the odd items.

---

[14]Bohrnstedt, "Reliability and Validity," p. 85.

[15]Nunnally, *Psychometric Theory,* p. 234, presents a rather scathing argument against test–retest reliability when alternative forms of the instrument are not available. See pages 232–236 in particular.

Pointed criticism is increasingly being directed at split-half reliability as the measure of the internal consistency of a scale. The criticism focuses on the necessarily arbitrary division of the items into equivalent halves. Each of the many possible divisions can produce different correlations between the two forms or different reliabilities. Which division is correct or, alternatively, what is then the reliability of the instrument? For example, a ten-item scale has 126 possible splits or 126 possible reliability coefficients.[16]

An increasingly popular approach for assessing the internal homogeneity existing among the items on a scale looks at *all* the items simultaneously. While the rationale and calculation formulas would take us too far afield, the basic emphasis is on a search for the covariation that exists among the items. If the items are, in fact, reflecting the same trait, there should be substantial correlation among them. Lack of correlation of an item with other items in the scale is evidence that the item does not belong and should be deleted. Thus, measures of internal consistency are used when developing instruments and in establishing the internal consistency of the items in the final form. The two most popular measures are the KR20 coefficient for dichotomous items, and coefficient α for multichotomous items.[17]

The above discussion dealt with the equivalence of reliability when applied to a *single* instrument. An alternate equivalence measure is used when different observers or different instruments measure the same individuals or objects at the same point in time. Do these methods produce consistent results? Are they equivalent as measured by the correlations among the total scores? An example would be a beauty contest. Do the judges, using the established criteria of beauty, talent, poise, and so on, rank the girls in the same order in terms of winner, first runner-up, second runner-up, and so on? The reliability of the measure is greater to the extent that the judges agree. This type of equivalence is the basis of convergent validation when the measures are independent.

Applications and Problems

1.   Discuss the notion that a particular measure could be reliable and still not be valid. In your discussion, distinguish between reliability and validity.

2.   Briefly discuss the importance of reliability and validity in the measurement of attitudes.

---

[16]In general, for a scale with $2n$ items, the total number of possible splits of the items into two halves is $(2n!)/2(n!)(n!)$. See Bohrnstedt, "Reliability and Validity," p. 86.

[17]See Nunnally, *Psychometric Theory*, Chaps. 6 and 7, pp. 190–255, for the rationale behind these coefficients and formulas for computing them.

Cases to Part 3

Case 3.1
Generic Drugs (A)

The state of Wisconsin passed a law in 1977 that permitted generic drugs to be substituted for brand name drugs when prescriptions were being filled. Consumers simply had to request the substitution and the pharmacist was legally bound to make it. The legislation was designed to save customers money on their prescriptions. Thus, it proved disconcerting to the Department of Health and Social Services when, some eight years after its passage, few customers were taking advantage of the law by asking for the substitution.

The experience in Wisconsin was not unusual. By 1985 almost every state and every province in Canada had passed legislation enabling pharmacists to substitute interchangeable generic drugs for the brand prescribed. Yet the empirical evidence suggested that less than 15 percent of all the prescriptions written were filled with generic drugs.[1]

One speculation held that use of the law was low because awareness of the law was low. *American Druggist,* for example, conducted an informal survey among pharmacists regarding generic drug substitution. The pharmacists indicated that approximately 12 percent of chain drug store customers and 9 percent of independently owned drug store customers asked outright for substitutions on prescriptions.

Another speculation held that requests for drug substitutions were lower than expected because customers had unfavorable attitudes toward the quality and the actual price differential of generic drugs.

Still a third speculation was that requests for generic drug substitutions were affected by a number of personal and situational factors. Whether customers paid for their own medication or were part of a third-party pay plan, the number of prescriptions filled per year, and the amount spent per year on prescriptions would all appear to be factors affecting the use of the substitution rule. Given two consumers who were both favorably inclined toward generics, for example, it was expected that the customer who spent relatively more on prescriptions would be more likely to buy generic drugs than the one who spent less. Since the elderly spend a greater percentage of their incomes on prescription drugs than any other age group, they might be more likely to purchase generic drugs. There also might be some correlation between family size and generic drug purchase behavior, the expectation being that larger families had more expenses and, therefore, also had a greater need to search for bargains. Family income also might be related to use of the law, with lower income families likely to have a greater need to take advantage of the lower generic prices. Finally, it was believed that educational level

[1]M. Stratman and T. T. Tyebjee, "Strategic Responses to Changes in Public Policy: The Case of the Pharmaceutical Industry and Drug Substitution Laws," *Journal of Public Policy and Marketing,* 3 (1984), pp. 99–112.

might be influencing generic drug purchasing behavior. People with more formal education might be expected to be more aware of current social trends, especially consumer-oriented trends, and would, therefore, be more likely to purchase a generic drug.

Questions

1. Develop specific hypotheses as to why generic drug purchasing behavior has not been greater.

2. Should observation or communication methods of data collection be used in gathering the information that addresses these hypotheses? Why?

3. Design a data collection instrument and methods for using it so as to secure information bearing on each of the hypotheses.

Case 3.2
Suchomel Chemical Company

Suchomel Chemical Company was an old-line chemical company that was still managed and directed by its founder, Jeff Suchomel, and his wife Carol. Jeff served as president and Carol as chief research chemist. The company, which was located in Savannah, Georgia, manufactured a number of products that were used by consumers in and around their homes. The products included waxes, polishes, tile grout, tile cement, spray cleaners for both windows and other surfaces, aerosol room sprays, and insecticides. The company distributed its products regionally. It had a particularly strong consumer following in the northern Florida and southern Georgia areas.

The company had not only managed to maintain but had increased its market share in several of its key lines in the past half dozen years in spite of increased competition from the national brands. Suchomel Chemical had done this largely through product innovation, particularly innovation that emphasized modest product alterations rather than new technologies or dramatically new products. Jeff and Carol both believed that the company should stick to the things it knew best rather than trying to be all things to all people and in the process getting the company's resources spread too thin, particularly given its regional nature. One innovation the company was now considering was a new scent for its insect spray that was rubbed or sprayed on a person's body. The new scent had undergone extensive testing in both the laboratory and in the field. The tests indicated it repelled insects, particularly mosquitos, as well as, or even better than, the two leading national brands. One of the things that the company was particularly concerned about as it considered the introduction of the new brand was what to call it.

The Insecticide Market

The insecticide market had become a somewhat tricky one to figure out over the past several years. While there had been growth in the purchase of insecticides in general, much of this growth had occurred in the tank liquid market. The household spray market had decreased slightly over the same time span. Suchomel Chemical had not suffered from the general sales decline, though, but had managed to increase its sales of spray insecticides slightly over the past three years. The company was hoping that the new scent formulation might allow it to make even greater market share gains.

The company's past experience in the industry led it to believe that the name that was given to the new product would be a very important element in the product's success, because there seemed to be some very complex interactions between purchase and usage characteristics among repellent users. Most purchases are made by women for their families. Yet repeat purchase is dependent on support by the husband that the product works well. Therefore, the name must appeal to both the buyer and the end user, but the two people are not typically together at the time of purchase. To complicate matters further, past research had indicated that a product with a name that appeals to both purchaser and end user will be rejected if the product's name and scent do not match. In sum, naming a product like this that is used on a person's body is a complex task.

Research Alternatives

The company followed its typical procedures in developing possible names for the new product. First, it asked those who had been involved in the product's development to suggest names. It also scheduled some informal brainstorming sessions among potential customers. Subjects in the brainstorming sessions were simply asked to throw out all the names they could possibly think of with respect to what a spray insecticide could or should be called. A panel of executives, mostly those from the product group but a few from corporate management as well, then went through the names and reduced the large list down to a more manageable subset based on their personal reactions to the names and subsequent discussion as to what the names connoted to them. The subset of names was then submitted to the corporate legal staff, who checked them for possible copyright infringement. Those that survived this check were then discussed again by the panel, and a list of 20 possibles was generated. Those in the product group were charged with the responsibility of developing a research design by which the final name could be chosen.

The people in the product group charged with the name test were considering two different alternatives for finding out which name was preferred. Both alternatives involved personal interviews at shopping malls. More specifically, the group was planning to conduct a set of interviews at one randomly determined mall in Atlanta, Savannah, Tallahasee, and Orlando. Each set of interviews would involve 100 respondents. The target respondents were married females, ages 21 to 54, who purchased the product category during the past year. Likely looking respondents were to be approached at random and were to be asked if they used any insect spray at all over the past year and asked their age. Those that qualified would be asked to complete the insecticide-naming exercise using one of the two alternatives being considered.

Alternative 1 involved a sort of the 20 tentative names by the respondents. The sort would be conducted in the following way. First, respondents would be asked to sort the 20 names into two groups based on their appropriateness for an insect repellent. Group 1 was to consist of the ten best names and Group 2 the ten worst. Next, respondents would be asked to select the four best from Group 1 and the four worst from Group 2.

Then they would be asked to pick the one best from the subset of the four best and the one worst from the subset of the four worst. Finally, all respondents would be asked why they picked the specific names they did as the best and the worst.

Alternative 2 also had several stages. All respondents would first be asked to rate each of the 20 names on a seven-point semantic differential scale with end anchors "Extremely inappropriate name for an insect repellent" and "Extremely appropriate name for an insect repellent." After completing this rating task, they would be asked to spray the back of their hands or arm with the product and would then be asked to repeat the rating task using a similar scale, but this time one in which the polar descriptors referred to the appropriateness of the name with respect to the specific scent. Next they would be asked to indicate their interest in buying the product by again checking one of the seven positions on a scale that ranged from "Definitely would not buy it" to "Definitely would buy it." Finally, each respondent would be asked why she selected each of the names she did as being most appropriate for insect repellents in general and the specific scent in particular.

Questions

1. Evaluate each of the two methods being considered for collecting the data. Which would you recommend and why?

2. How would you use the data from each method to decide what the brand name should be?

3. Do you think personal interviews in shopping malls are a useful way to collect this data? If not, what would you recommend as an alternative?

Case 3.3
Suncoast National Bank[1]

Suncoast National Bank maintains its headquarters and 23 branch offices in the San Diego metropolitan area. As such, Suncoast National is one of the largest locally head-quartered banks in the region. Most of the other major financial institutions located in the San Diego area (such as Bank of America and Security Pacific Bank) are headquartered in either Los Angeles or San Francisco.

The San Diego metropolitan area presently has a population of about 1.8 million persons. It is the second largest city in California and is the eighth largest metropolitan area in the United States. Figures from the U.S. Census show that the San Diego area grew roughly 35 percent in population between 1970 and 1979. Estimates indicate further growth of about 20 percent by 1985.

[1]From: Cases in Marketing Research by William G. Zikmund, William Lunstrom, and Donald Sciglimpaglia (Hinsdale, Ill.: Dryden), p. 45–52. Copyright © 1982 by CBS College Publishing. Reprinted by permission of CBS College Publishing.

Exhibit 1

Suncoast National Bank—Interdepartmental Communication

> TO: Robert R. Redmund, Vice President, Marketing
> FROM: Steven R. Bennett, Marketing Research Analyst
> DATE: July 21, 1981
> SUBJECT: NEWCOMER RESEARCH PROPOSAL
>
> *Purpose and Background.* That we live in a highly mobile society is reflected by the fact that approximately one out of five U.S. citizens changes residence every year.
>
> As people relocate, their life-styles are temporarily disrupted and certain "needs" become self-evident at their new locale. Among those needs are services provided by financial institutions.
>
> The match between newcomers and financial institutions seems to be a natural one; however, many feel that the difficulty in reaching prospective newcomers outweighs the advantages of designing a newcomer program. Contrary to this belief, the newcomer is one of the best retail markets available to the bank. Rather than expend an entire marketing effort to redistribute the existing market, we should develop a program to tap this newcomer segment with the advantage being that we would have little or no competition from other institutions.
>
> The newcomer program will have to be based upon information. In order for us to identify, locate, and capture this market segment, we must understand the key issues of the newcomer segment, their needs as newcomers to San Diego, and what it will take to attract them to our bank. We must understand how newcomers learn about banks (and savings and loans), who in a family will make the banking decision, at what point do they decide on a bank, and what their profile is.
>
> Research must be undertaken to provide us with the necessary information to design and effectively market a newcomer program.
>
> *Methodology:* A survey instrument will be designed to gather the above information via mail questionnaire of prospective San Diego residents and newcomers to San Diego. Address lists will be generated by the San Diego Chamber of Commerce and from San Diego Hospitality Hostess. The survey will be conducted among those persons most responsible in a household for the banking activities, and it will be designed to gather the necessary attitudinal and demographic information in order to maximize the success of a future newcomer program.
>
> *Focus Groups:* To better understand the problems that newcomers experience, we need to conduct some focus group research. This research will result in our being better able to design a survey instrument which relates to the needs of this segment. I think that two or three group sessions should be sufficient.

Time Schedule:	Completed By:
Focus groups	August 21
Questionnaire design	September 7
Pre-test questionnaire	September 12
Survey	September 29
Data analysis	October 5

Newcomer Project

Steven Bennett, the marketing research analyst for Suncoast National, was impressed with these population growth figures. In recent years Suncoast had been losing market share to other banks, and its management was looking to the marketing area to help retain its place in the market. Bennett's direct superior, Bob Redmund, had asked him to give some thought to any research that could be conducted to help him formulate Suncoast National's marketing strategy.

Bennett was aware of programs used by banks in other cities that targeted new people moving into the area. In particular, he was familiar with one such "newcomer" program conducted by a bank in Atlanta that was so successful that it had earned the bank an award from the Bank Marketing Association. No doubt, Bennett thought, it probably also earned its originator a substantial raise in salary.

As he understood it, the Atlanta program worked this way. The bank accumulated the names of persons about to move to Atlanta from elsewhere and names of persons who had moved there within a very short time. The names were obtained through Atlanta employers, the Chamber of Commerce, realtors, and welcoming services such as Welcome Wagon and Hospitality Hostess. The bank offered each person a complete kit to help make his or her transition a little easier. Included in the kit were such things as maps, city guides, guides to services, bus schedules, and discount coupons. Each person contacted was sent an engraved invitation that entitled him or her to receive a newcomer kit at one of the bank's branch offices. Reportedly, the Atlanta bank had been successful in converting into new customers many of those who accepted the invitiation.

Since San Diego is a high-growth and highly mobile community, Bennett thought that such a program should be investigated by Suncoast National. Accordingly, he wrote the memo seen in Exhibit 1 to Redmund.

Newcomer Focus Group Studies

Bennett received approval to proceed with the project. He knew that, in addition to information that would be available from industry sources, he needed to know more about the feelings and experiences of newcomers. This would assist him in designing a

---

Exhibit 2

Newcomers Study Focus Group Outline

General Purpose: (1) To determine problems and inconveniences experienced in moving to San Diego or shortly after arrival; (2) to understand how initial banks were selected, and (3) to determine problems associated with banking transactions.

Topics

1. Reasons for moving to San Diego

2. Problems in *planning* the move

3. Problems *during* the move

4. Problems *after* the move

5. How problems could have been corrected

6. Problems related to banking

7. How participants learned about various banks available in the city

8. How they selected initial bank

9. What banks could to to make move less inconvenient

10. What other groups or organizations could do to make the move easier

better survey questionnaire for the mail study. Bennett was especially interested in knowing about the problems that were encountered in moving, how newcomers selected a new bank, and what kinds of information newcomers thought would be useful to them. All of this would be thoroughly evaluated in the survey.

Bennett selected Professional Interviewing to conduct two focus groups to help find out more about problems experienced by newcomers. That firm, a local field interviewing company, was instructed to recruit 12 persons who had moved into San Diego within the last month for each of two group interview sessions. Bennett prepared the outline seen in Exhibit 2 for the interviews.

Paula Jackson, the owner of Professional Interviewing, was to be the group moderator. For the first group session, seven participants, six women and one man, attended. The transcript of that session is seen in Exhibit 3.

Exhibit 3
Newcomers Study Focus Group

Moderator I'm Paula from Professional Interviewing and I really appreciate your participation in this group session. As you can see, we are taping this session because after the end of this it would be impossible to remember what has transpired. First of all, we are here tonight to talk about your reasons for moving to San Diego. Let's start out by having each of you introduce yourself and state how you came about coming to San Diego . . . how you got here and where you're from.

Mary My name is Mary—and we came to San Diego because my husband works here, and I came from New York.

Brenda Brenda Cole from Maine—was headed for Arizona but came to San Diego by chance. Came west because of the weather.

Marian Marian from Kansas City—came here because my husband took a job here.

Lisa Lisa, Pacific Northwest, read in a magazine that San Diego had the most perfect climate and wanted to get away from Redlands where it was all smog. Came alone by bus.

Anna I'm Anna, from Sacramento area, and I came to go to San Diego State, pre-med student.

Carolyn Carolyn, from Virginia. My husband took a job in San Diego.

Roger Roger from Los Angeles, came because of a transfer in the company and liked a smaller city.

Moderator Undoubtedly, some of you had situations that arose when you got ready to come here, inconveniences that happened to you. They may have been major things or minor things, but no matter what, they were still problems that came about when you got ready to move. I'd like to talk about the problems and inconveniences you had in getting ready to come to San Diego.

Brenda What do you mean by inconveniences?

Marian Like changes of addresses in banks or your subscriptions?

Moderator Things that disrupted your living the way you were living.

Marian Taking my daughter, who is a senior in high school, away and leaving all her friends. She dispises it. That is an inconvenience. The move itself. The movers were late naturally. The furniture was broken. The claim is still not settled.

Moderator You mentioned banking, was that a problem?

Marian I've changed banks since I've been here. I don't like the banking hours here. In Kansas City, the banks were open just like department stores, day and night. So the banking was very easy. Here I started with Bank of America, but they were never open so I switched real quick.

Moderator What do you mean they were never open?

Marian They didn't open early, the one near me didn't open until 10:00 in the morning and is only open until 3:00 and we're used to 7:00 to 7:00 hours. I'm surprised by the banks. In such a big place, why not open longer and on Saturdays. I found a bank that is open Saturdays for my checking account. I've never seen such long lines in my whole life. With so many working in such a large population you would think they would accommodate more. You could wait an hour just to get a check cashed. I'm trying to get my account going, just to add a name.

Exhibit 3

Newcomers Study Focus Group *continued*

The drive-up is open, but they can't pass the card. I have to go inside and stand in the hour-long lines to do that, and I'm not willing to do that. I learned a long time ago that anything you open up, use the word *or* not *and*. Like Marty *or* Marian—not *and*. Then you don't have any trouble.

Moderator Brenda, how about you?

Brenda Trying to weed out what to bring or throw away. We brought only what we could take in the car. We have a few things in storage but not much. Like everyone, I feel the banks out here are the most horrendous situations I've ever seen. I've never found it so hard to get a check cashed. My husband, in his own bank, has to show his drivers license, and if you don't have a picture ID, you're out of luck. They are too untrusting, it's outrageous. I've been in many cities in many states and have never run into anything so outrageous in my entire life.

Moderator Then your difficulty in cashing a check is your main difficulty in banking?

Brenda Just everything . . . people's attitudes. Out here it's like everyone is for themselves, no one wants to help anyone else. Everybody is on their own. The last place I lived was a small town and the people were more willing to help you out. Most people I've run into out here are not willing to be helpful, especially the banks. I haven't been here long enough for firsthand evidence, but from what I've heard, even the residents have trouble. The lady I'm staying near has had to change banks three times in the last year.

Moderator Lisa, what problems have you encountered?

Lisa Well, not really very much. I take life as it comes, living day-to-day. I don't have any money in banks. I would never put money in a bank. Why? Because I don't like the way they do business. I don't like what they do with the money while it's in there. I don't like the interest they give you and I don't like the waiting in lines. I don't like anything about it. The banks aren't interested in us, they just want the money so they can use it.

Moderator Carolyn?

Carolyn The moving van gave us the most problems. Many of our things were damaged and many stolen. I don't know how to claim these items. We were delayed one day because the vans won't move less than five tons and we only had two. We paid for five. Also the banks . . . cashing out-of-state checks in your own bank. My husband applied for a Visa card here. Our credit is fantastic but we were denied the credit because they say they have no record of our credit rating. We could not transfer it out here, so fine, they won't use our money, we'll just keep sending it back to Virginia. The service charge out here is outrageous. I had a totally free checking account. No service charge, no minimum balance, everything was free. The checks were free. We figured it will cost about $40 a year to maintain a checking account.

Lisa So she has the right idea not to put money in the bank, put everything in cash. Also your records are not closed. The government can get your records. They can come in and construct a whole life-style by your transactions, so if you want the whole world to know about you, where you bank, where you buy, where you borrow, what church you donate or go to, then just use a bank!

Carolyn Another thing that surprised me is that when you buy a money order, even in the city, the banks won't cash it. That's wrong. This is just like cash. It was bought and paid for. Where can you cash them? You have to open an account and leave them there for so many days . . . in the city a couple of days, out of the city probably two weeks, and out of state up to eighteen to twenty days. A cashier's check is the same. Nobody trusts nobody. It took a friend about thirty days to cash a cashier's check. It was for $1,000 from Las Vegas so they couldn't cash it. The money is there so why can't they cash it? Travelers checks are not acceptable everywhere. Some stores and gas stations will not accept them.

Moderator Anna, tell us about your problems.

Anna You wouldn't believe it. Being a student, I have no credit cards, no credit. I have a driver's license and a military ID and it's impossible to cash a check without a credit card. Also, trying to find a place to live. I'm not twenty-one so they won't let you rent an apartment. They would not take my signature. I had to call my Dad and have him fly down, which is $50 one-way, and sign for me to get the apartment, and then fly back home. My parents send me money each month in a cashier's check, but I go through the problem all the time to cash it. I could get my parents to put me on their Visa card as a signer.

Roger Couldn't you go to a bank and get a check guarantee card?

Anna I've heard of it, but I don't have one. I have a military ID and a driver's license. I feel those two should be sufficient.

continued on next page

Exhibit 3

Newcomers Study Focus Group *continued*

Moderator Did you experience any other problems as you were planning the move?

Anna Yes, getting into school. They sent my application to San Jose instead of San Diego State, so by the time I got it back it was too late to register and I had to go contract register and it cost me $40 more per unit. At the time I was taking fifteen units, so I dropped all but ten units. I paid $400 instead of $100 and after moving down here and everything, I couldn't move back home.

Moderator Roger, how about you? When you were planning to move from Los Angeles?

Roger I had no problems moving down as I moved all my own stuff so if anything was broken, it was no one's fault but my own. As far as banking, you just go down and open an account and hope the bank has interest in other personal accounts in California. Most banks don't. I don't feel San Diego is any different than Los Angeles. In transferring down here, Bank of America would not give me a check guarantee card here, even though my account was with them in L.A., because they say I have not established my record with them. I closed my account with them. I switched. Of course, I had the same problem, but I'd rather give them the chance and build my record than a bank that didn't consider my past twelve-year record where I held two existing loans. I think it's like a franchise, you should get the same service here that you did in the other place if it's the same bank.

Moderator What bank do you bank with now?

Roger Security Pacific Bank.

Moderator Do you notice any difference?

Roger No. No difference. They all have the same policy. Their cause is not for you. You put a large sum of money into their savings account, you don't ask them their life history, they just take your money and put it in there. Just try to borrow money or try to get your own money out . . . it seems to be a different story. The interest they pay you is nothing. They're using that to invest at a much higher rate. You're donating to their cause when you have money in the bank, but yet they're a necessary evil, I wouldn't feel safe with that money at home. I think you need a bank. It's a must! They need some of the starch taken out of them. There are exceptions, some managers are nice but they're very few. Most are VIPs and we are the peons.

Lisa If we could figure some other way to handle our money that would put them down to size and then they wouldn't be VIPs anymore. They would be human beings and maybe they would treat us better.

Roger Credit unions are an alternative to banks if you have one; they are good.

Lisa Why do you feel credit unions are better than banks?

Roger I think they are more concerned with the people that are in that organization. They make loans to people in their organizations. They come first, not just someone who comes in off the street. If you're not a member, you don't get a loan. They deal more with people who are willing to invest some of their savings with them. They in turn give priority to that person. When you borrow money from a bank, they decide whether it's a good investment or not. What is a good investment to one person may not be to another. If he has a past record of paying back money, they should give him the same responsibility. The money is there to lend. And money should be there to lend when they hold "X" amount of money in savings accounts. When they have money to build new branches and furnish them quite lavishly, then I think they've got money. The bank manager shouldn't feel like the money is coming out of his own personal checking account. Their business is making loans. They don't make it on checking accounts. Even if checking accounts aren't free, that $2 or $3 a month isn't paying the salaries, it's the loans. As an example, we took out a loan for $125,000 for constructing apartments in L.A. through a savings and loan. We were putting $25,000 of our own money into the S & L when they OK'd the loan. We then sold the land prior to construction, never used one penny out of the account, but it cost us for that loan . . . $10,000—it was never used. Not only the cost for the loan but there was the prepayment penalty on the construction loan. Now in personal loans, if I was to borrow that amount of money from someone here, they would not be allowed to do that.

Lisa What makes a bank an exception? I don't understand, but there is nothing you can do. It's in the fine print, they are above the law.

Moderator Let's talk about immediately after you all moved here . . . what situations you came up against and what inconveniences.

Marian Finding the shopping areas and schools. It's pretty hard to find out which schools are for which districts . . . and which ones are good. We have found that the schools here are a little behind in their teaching. Get-

continued on next page

Exhibit 3
Newcomers Study Focus Group *continued*

ting your children to feel as though they belong in the new school . . . everyone is in their little cliques and no one wants new people.

Carolyn I find the people here very unfriendly. It seems that it's each to themselves. The drivers here are wild. I need to get a new driver's license and, I think, California plates. I'm not sure.

Moderator Brenda, how about you?

Brenda Finding an apartment was hard. Knowing what area is good or not. Getting the apartment is hard. They need your life history even though you have the first month's rent and the deposit. They expect you to take a motel for awhile. They feel their apartments are worth gold and you are going to destroy them or something.

Carolyn They don't want to rent to people with children. I have only an infant but they don't want to rent to me. I think the best thing going on now are the people that are trying to stop these apartment owners from not renting to families.

Brenda Oh yea . . . and I'd bet that some of you had trouble finding out where to pay your utility deposits for gas and electricity and for the telephone. I had to go to four separate places. We had to wait two weeks for our phone to be installed.

Moderator If you had it to do over again, can you come up with any suggestions or other ways you may have handled the move to prevent some of these problems?

Brenda I don't think I would move here. The weather is great, but that's about it. I've lived in a lot of big and little cities, all over, and the people around here are the hardest to get to know of anyplace I've lived. There is a housing shortage here for renting and buying.

Roger There is no way to solve the problems of housing since it is a bureaucracy. If you could get the bureaucracy out of it, then private enterprises would take over and meet the demands of the people, but it can't be done.

Moderator Well, thanks very much for coming in to participate. You've been very helpful.

Questions

1. What kind of information should Bennett attempt to get from banking industry sources about newcomer programs?

2. Do you think it was wise to have a group with both men and women included and with participants of various ages?

3. Did the moderator do an adequate job of getting at the information needed by Bennett?

4. Analyze the focus group transcript very thoroughly. Make a list of problems generated and ideas for the proposed newcomer kit.

Case 3.4
Rumstad Decorating Centers (B)

Rumstad Decorating Centers was an old-line Rockford, Illinois, business. The company was originally founded as a small paint and wallpaper supply store in 1929 by Mr. Joseph Rumstad, who managed the store until his retirement in 1970, at which time Jack Rumstad, his son, took over. In 1974, the original downtown store was closed and a new outlet was opened on the city's rapidly expanding west side. In 1983, a second store was opened on the east side of the city, and the name of the business was changed to Rumstad Decorating Centers.

Jack Rumstad's review of 1985 operations proved disconcerting. Both stores had suffered losses for the year (see Rumstad Decorating Centers (A)). The picture was far more dismal at the west side store. Losses at the east side store were 80 percent less than the previous year's, which was partially due to some major organizational changes. Further, the east side store had experienced a 25 percent increase in net sales and a 25 percent increase in gross profits over 1984. The west side store, in contrast, had shown a 21 percent decrease in net sales and a 31 percent decrease in gross profit.

Some preliminary research by Mr. Rumstad suggested the problem at the west side store might be traced to the store's location and/or its advertising. Was the location perceived as convenient? Were potential customers aware of Rumstad Decorating Centers, the products they carried, and where they were located? Did people have favorable impressions of Rumstad? How did attitudes towards Rumstad compare with those towards Rumstad's major competitors?

Mr. Rumstad realized he did not have the expertise to answer these questions. Consequently, he called in Mrs. Sandra Parrett, who owned and managed her own marketing research service in the Rockford area. Mrs. Parrett handled all liaison work with the client and assisted in the research design. In addition to Mrs. Parrett, Lisa Parrett, her daughter, supervised the field staff of four, analyzed data, and prepared research reports. Although the company was small, it had an excellent reputation within the business community.

Research Design

Rumstad agreed with Mrs. Parrett's suggestion that the best way to investigate Rumstad's concerns would be to use a structured, somewhat disguised questionnaire (see Figure 1). The sponsor of the research was to be hidden from the respondents so as to prevent them from answering "correctly" instead of honestly, and so questions about two of Rumstad's main competitors, the Nina Emerson Decorating Center and the Wallpaper Shop, were introduced. Both of these stores offered products and services similar to those carried by Rumstad, and they were located in the same area as Rumstad's west side store. The study was to be confined to the west side store because of cost; loss of profits for the last several years had severely constrained Rumstad's ability to engage in research of this sort. However, the west side store was so critical to the very survival of Rumstad Decorating Centers that Jack Rumstad was willing to commit funds to this investigation, although he repeatedly stressed to Mrs. Parrett the need to keep the cost as low as possible.

Even though the Emerson Decorating Center and the Wallpaper Shop were similar to Rumstad, there were differences in their marketing strategies. Both stores seemed to advertise more than did Rumstad, for example, although the exact amounts of their advertising budgets were not available. Emerson advertised in the *Shopper's World* (a weekly paper devoted exclusively to advertising that is distributed free), ran ads four times a year in the *Rockford Morning Star,* and did a small amount of radio and outdoor advertising. The Wallpaper Shop also advertised regularly in the *Shopper's World* but ran small ads daily in the *Morning Star* and daily radio commercials as well. Rumstad

Figure 1

Sample Questionnaire—Rumstad Decorating Centers

Section I

For Questions 1–8, please indicate your opinion as to the importance of the following factors in choosing a decorating center. Place an X in the appropriate blank.

	Not Important	Slightly Important	Fairly Important	Very Important
1. Saw or heard an advertisement	___	___	___	___
2. Special sale	___	___	___	___
3. Convenient location	___	___	___	___
4. Convenient hours	___	___	___	___
5. Knowledgeable sales personnel	___	___	___	___
6. Good quality products	___	___	___	___
7. Additional services (e.g. matching paints, decorator services, etc.)	___	___	___	___
8. Reasonable prices in relation to quality	___	___	___	___

Below is a list of abbreviations for the three west side stores which will be referred to throughout the questionnaire:

Emerson Decorating Center—''Emerson''
Rumstad Decorating Center—''Rumstad''
Wallpaper Shop—''Wallpaper Shop''

Please indicate your response with an X in the appropriate blank.

9. Do you know where any of the following west side stores are located? (i.e., could you find any of these stores without referring to another source?)

	Yes	No
Emerson	___	___
Rumstad	___	___
Wallpaper Shop	___	___

10. When was the last time you heard or saw any advertisements for the following stores?

	Never	Within the Last Month	1–6 months	More than 6 Months
Emerson	___	___	___	___
Rumstad	___	___	___	___
Wallpaper Shop	___	___	___	___

11. Please indicate the source(s) of any advertisements you have seen or heard.

	Have Not Seen/Heard	Shopper's World	Rockford Morning Star	Radio	TV	Other	Don't Recall
Emerson	___	___	___	___	___	___	___
Rumstad	___	___	___	___	___	___	___
Wallpaper Shop	___	___	___	___	___	___	___

12. Do you know which of the following items are available in these stores? If so, check the item(s) that apply.

	Don't Know	Paint	Paneling	Carpeting	Draperies	Other
Emerson	___	___	___	___	___	___
Rumstad	___	___	___	___	___	___
Wallpaper Shop	___	___	___	___	___	___

13. Which name brands of paint, if any, do you associate with the following stores?

	Benjamin Moore	Dutch Boy	Glidden	Pittsburgh	Do not associate any listed
Emerson	___	___	___	___	___
Rumstad	___	___	___	___	___
Wallpaper Shop	___	___	___	___	___

continued on next page

Figure 1

Sample Questionnaire—Rumstad Decorating Centers *continued*

14. *Have you ever visited any of these west side stores?*

	Never	Within Last Year	1–5 yrs. Ago	More than 5 Yrs. Ago
Emerson	_____	_____	_____	_____
Rumstad	_____	_____	_____	_____
Wallpaper Shop	_____	_____	_____	_____

Section II

If you have visited or have knowledge of *one or more* of the stores listed below, please indicate your opinion as to the extent to which you agree or disagree with the following statements for each store(s). For instance, if you have knowledge of only one store, please answer each question for that particular store. If you have not visited or have no knowledge of any of these stores, omit this section and proceed to Section III.

	Strongly Agree	Agree	Neither Agree Nor Disagree	Disagree	Strongly Disagree

15. *The location of the store is convenient.*

Emerson	_____	_____	_____	_____	_____
Rumstad	_____	_____	_____	_____	_____
Wallpaper Store	_____	_____	_____	_____	_____

16. *The sales personnel are knowledgeable.*

Emerson	_____	_____	_____	_____	_____
Rumstad	_____	_____	_____	_____	_____
Wallpaper Store	_____	_____	_____	_____	_____

17. *The store lacks additional services* (e.g., matching paint, decorator services, etc.).

Emerson	_____	_____	_____	_____	_____
Rumstad	_____	_____	_____	_____	_____
Wallpaper Store	_____	_____	_____	_____	_____

18. *The store carries good quality products.*

Emerson	_____	_____	_____	_____	_____
Rumstad	_____	_____	_____	_____	_____
Wallpaper Store	_____	_____	_____	_____	_____

19. *The prices are reasonable in relation to the quality of the products.*

Emerson	_____	_____	_____	_____	_____
Rumstad	_____	_____	_____	_____	_____
Wallpaper Store	_____	_____	_____	_____	_____

20. *The store hours are inconvenient.*

Emerson	_____	_____	_____	_____	_____
Rumstad	_____	_____	_____	_____	_____
Wallpaper Store	_____	_____	_____	_____	_____

Figure 1
Sample Questionnaire—Rumstad Decorating Centers *continued*

Section III

1. Your sex: _____ Male   _____ Female

2. Your age: _____ Under 25 _____ 25–29 years _____ 30–39 years _____ 40–54 years
_____ 55 or over

3. How long have you lived in Rockford?
_____ Less than 1 year   _____ 1–3 years   _____ 4 or more years

4. Do you: _____ Own a home or condominium _____ Rent a house
_____ Rent an apartment _____ Other

5. When was the last time you painted or remodeled your residence?
_____ Never   _____ Within past year   _____ 1–5 years ago
_____ More than 5 years ago

6. Approximately how many times have you received the weekly Shopper's World *in the past 3 months?*
_____ Never   _____ 1–5 times   _____ 6–12 times

7. Do you read or page through the Shopper's World?
_____ Do not receive it   _____ Never   _____ Less than ½ the time
_____ About ½ the time   _____ More than ½ the time

---

had formerly advertised in the *Morning Star* but now relied exclusively on the *Shopper's World*.

Sample

Because of the financial constraints imposed on the study by Jack Rumstad, it was decided to limit the study to households within a two-mile radius of Rumstad, Emerson, and the Wallpaper Shop. Aldermanic districts within the two-mile radius were identified; there were four in all, and the wards within each district were listed. Two of the 12 wards were then excluded because they were outside of the specified area. Blocks within each of the remaining 10 wards were enumerated, and 5 blocks were randomly selected from each ward. An initial starting point for each block was determined, and then the questionnaires were administered by the Parrett field staff at every sixth house on the block. All interviews were conducted on Saturday and Sunday. If there was no one at home or if the respondent refused to cooperate, the next house on the block was substituted; there was no one at home at 39 households, and 18 others refused to participate. The field work was completed within one weekend and produced a total sample of 123 responses.

Questions

1. Evaluate the questionnaire. Do you think the questionnaire adequately addresses the concerns raised by Rumstad?

2. How would you suggest the data collected be analyzed so as to best solve Rumstad's problem?

3. Do you think personal administration of the questionnaires was called for in this study, or would you suggest an alternative scheme? Why or why not?

Case 3.5
Borchert Mulching Mowers[1]

Since the late 1950s David M. Borchert had been the chief designer and engineer for the Zerbe Corporation—a manufacturer of lawn and garden appliances located in Ekert, Nebraska. Mr. Borchert was responsible for the development of almost all of the company's current line of lawn mowers and had played a major role in transforming the Zerbe Corporation from a small tool and die company to the successful firm it was today.

Recently, the Zerbe Corporation began contemplating phasing out its lawn and garden division in order to concentrate its efforts in other higher profit margin items involving the logging and wood cutting industry. Company experts believed that the growth rate in the sale of log splitters, chain saws, telescoping buckets for trimming the upper branches of trees, and so on experienced during the past five years would continue the next two decades and would greatly exceed the expected growth rate of lawn and garden appliance sales for this same time period. However, in order for the Zerbe Corporation to be competitive in the logging industry, it would have to allocate all its resources to the production of wood cutting and handling machinery. This would necessitate the elimination of all lawn and garden equipment from the company's current line of products.

Faced with the possibility of reassignment to the logging equipment division, or at worst termination, Mr. Borchert decided it would be best to resign from the company and use his expertise in the lawn mower area to form his own firm—the Borchert Power Mower Company. Obtaining the necessary financial resources from friends and business associates, Mr. Borchert, along with his wife Brenda, established operations in Depew, Kansas. It was Mr. Borchert's intent to manufacture a complete line of walking and riding power lawn mowers to be positioned as medium-priced, fuel-efficient, easy-to-operate, and dependable products. The lawn mowers were an immediate success. Within three years of its inception, the Borchert Power Mower Company had captured a 15 percent share of the regional lawn mower market—a remarkable accomplishment considering the competitiveness of the industry and the short time the firm had been in operation.

[1]The contributions of David M. Szymanski to the development of this case are gratefully acknowledged.

Encouraged by the company's sales performance, Mr. Borchert decided to expand the product line by offering a new mower: the Borchert Mulching Mower. This product differed from the company's other lawn mowers in that a mulching mower essentially cuts the grass twice before releasing the grass clippings. More traditional lawn mowers only cut the grass once before the clippings are released. The advantage of the mulching feature is that grass clippings put nutrients back into the lawn. However, clippings that are too big smother the lawn at the same time when there is a build-up of mulch. Finally, cut clippings avoid thatch build-up.

Borchert was not the first company to introduce a mulching mower. Other corporations such as Ariens, Bolens, and John Deere had been manufacturing mulching mowers for several years. However, the Borchert Mulching Mower was to be priced considerably below that of the competitors', and the Borchert mower was engineered to be superior in performance to any mulching mower on the market. These features, along with the fine reputation the company had established for itself, were thought to be strong attributes that would help ensure the product's success in the marketplace.

Introduced in the early spring, company sales of mulching mowers were disappointing. The number of units sold for the first three months was 18 percent below initial company projections, despite the fact that sales of Borchert's other mowers had exceeded prior expectations and the sales of mulching mowers by all other companies combined had experienced a 10 percent growth in the number of units sold. Mr. Borchert turned to the company's marketing department for help. Gus Kondilis, Vice President of Marketing for the Borchert Company, suggested that the company poll customers to assess their satisfaction with the Borchert Mulching Mower. He believed that the results of such a survey might reveal areas where product features needed improvement, as well as people's level of satisfaction with distributors and the firm's pricing and promotional policies. Slight changes in any of these product and marketing mix factors might result in increased sales of the company's mulching mowers. Mr. Borchert agreed with Mr. Kondilis's recommendation and gave the marketing department the go-ahead to conduct the survey.

Customer Satisfaction

When purchasing a product, consumers typically form expectations regarding the performance of the good. As the product is demonstrated or used, people compare the product's actual performance to their initial expectations. Should the actual level of performance be the same as, or above, prior expectations, the consumer is said to be satisfied. If the product performs worse than expected, consumers are normally dissatisfied. Furthermore, it is believed that consumers only judge products on a limited set of factors. The product's other attributes are deemed less important but become critical if performance on the important characteristics fall short of expectations. Therefore, unsatisfactory performance with respect to any product characteristic could lead to (1) no initial sale of the item, (2) no repeat purchase of the product, and/or (3) negative word of mouth that could adversely affect sales.

Research Method

The task of assessing customer satisfaction was assigned to a team of researchers from Borchert's marketing department. The researchers conducted a preliminary search of the literature to see if any studies on customer satisfaction with lawn and garden appliances had been published; no studies were found. This forced the researchers to develop their own scale items to assess customer satisfaction. However, the team was not sure which scale, Likert or semantic differential, would be more appropriate. Yet the research team thought the proper choice of scale could be critical to the proper assessment of customer satisfaction and to the future success of the Borchert Mulching Mower. Because the marketing team had no empirical evidence on which to base a decision, the researchers decided to construct both a Likert and a semantic differential scale. The two scales would be pretested to determine which one better measured customer satisfaction. The scale that yielded the more accurate assessment would then be used to investigate people's perception of the Borchert Mulching Mower.

Sampling Plan

A completely random sample of purchasers of the Borchert Mulching Mower was used to pretest the scales. The sample was chosen from the warranty card file of people who had purchased the mower from the time it was first introduced onto the market to the present. Because of the geographical dispersion in customer residency and the fact that that warranty cards do not contain the customer's phone number, a mail survey was used in lieu of personal or telephone interviews.

A total of 800 owners of Borchert Mulching Mowers were sent questionnaires. Four hundred households received the Likert scale survey shown in Figure 1, and 400 different households received the semantic differential scale survey presented in Figure 2. Of

---

Figure 1
Likert Scale Questionnaire

The following statements refer only to the Borchert Mulching Mower that you purchased.

Please respond to each statement by putting an "X" in the column that most closely approximates your level of agreement. For example, if you strongly disagree with the statement, then put an "X" in the *strongly disagree* column for that statement.

Please do not skip any statements and do not put more than one "X" in response to any statement.

	Strongly Disagree	Disagree	Neither Agree nor Disagree	Agree	Strongly Agree
1. Adjusting the blade height on the mower is a lot of trouble.	⎯	⎯	⎯	⎯	⎯
2. Borchert has a good reputation as a manufacturer of lawn mowers.	⎯	⎯	⎯	⎯	⎯
3. Parts for the mower are not readily available.	⎯	⎯	⎯	⎯	⎯

Figure 1
Likert Scale Questionnaire *continued*

	Strongly Disagree	Disagree	Neither Agree nor Disagree	Agree	Strongly Agree
4. The thoughtful design features on the mower make it worth the price.	___	___	___	___	___
5. The Borchert mower requires frequent repair.	___	___	___	___	___
6. Borchert is the leader in the manufacture of mulching mowers.	___	___	___	___	___
7. Borchert advertisements about its lawn mowers do not exaggerate their good features.	___	___	___	___	___
8. The mower has adequate safety features.	___	___	___	___	___
9. The Borchert mower means less work when cutting the lawn.	___	___	___	___	___
10. The mower cuts grass evenly.	___	___	___	___	___
11. The mower is very durable.	___	___	___	___	___
12. Borchert supplies little useful information in its owner's manual.	___	___	___	___	___
13. Borchert dealers are honest.	___	___	___	___	___
14. The mower starts easily.	___	___	___	___	___
15. Borchert is responsive to customer complaints.	___	___	___	___	___
16. The handle controls on the mower are difficult to use.	___	___	___	___	___
17. The mower requires too much care.	___	___	___	___	___
18. The mower is safe to use.	___	___	___	___	___
19. The Borchert dealer clearly demonstrated the various features of the mower.	___	___	___	___	___
20. Borchert dealers are not conveniently located.	___	___	___	___	___
21. Borchert salespeople are not very helpful.	___	___	___	___	___
22. Borchert salespeople are familiar with the features of the mulching mower.	___	___	___	___	___
23. The Borchert mower is difficult to maneuver.	___	___	___	___	___

continued on next page

Figure 1
Likert Scale Questionnaire *continued*

	Strongly Disagree	Disagree	Neither Agree nor Disagree	Agree	Strongly Agree
24. The optional features (i.e., bag adaptor) on the mower are too expensive.	——	——	——	——	——
25. The mower engine needs frequent adjustment.	——	——	——	——	——
26. The controls on the mower are hard to get at.	——	——	——	——	——
27. The mower warranty excludes too many things.	——	——	——	——	——
28. Borchert dealers have inconvenient hours.	——	——	——	——	——
29. The Borchert mower is too heavy.	——	——	——	——	——
30. The mower is too expensive.	——	——	——	——	——
31. The self-propelled feature of the Borchert mower is very good.	——	——	——	——	——
32. The mower is hard to use in tight spots.	——	——	——	——	——
33. Borchert retail stores have capable repair people.	——	——	——	——	——
34. The automatic choke on the mower works well.	——	——	——	——	——
35. Salespeople for Borchert products are friendly.	——	——	——	——	——
36. The mower does a good job with tall grass.	——	——	——	——	——
37. It is difficult to get the mower to start.	——	——	——	——	——
38. Borchert has a fair warranty policy.	——	——	——	——	——
39. Oil leakage is not a problem with the mower.	——	——	——	——	——
40. The mower is quiet.	——	——	——	——	——
41. The mower is powerful enough to do the job.	——	——	——	——	——
42. Mechanical parts vibrate loose on a Borchert mower.	——	——	——	——	——
43. The mower is well built.	——	——	——	——	——
44. The lawn is better nourished and greener from using a Borchert Mulching Mower.	——	——	——	——	——

Figure 1
Likert Scale Questionnaire *continued*

	Strongly Disagree	Disagree	Neither Agree nor Disagree	Agree	Strongly Agree
45. The mower is easy to store.	____	____	____	____	____
46. Repair service on the mower takes a long time.	____	____	____	____	____
47. The Borchert Mulching Mower does not cause thatch buildup on my lawn.	____	____	____	____	____
48. The Borchert Mulching Mower uses a lot of gas.	____	____	____	____	____
49. The Borchert Mulching Mower keeps lawn clippings out of garden beds and off of sidewalks.	____	____	____	____	____
50. When using the Borchert Mulching Mower, you have to cut more frequently for it to work properly.	____	____	____	____	____
51. The Borchert Mulching Mower does not leave excessive tire tracks in my lawn.	____	____	____	____	____
52. The Borchert Mulching Mower power drive moves the mower at just the right pace.	____	____	____	____	____

53. *Please place a mark to indicate your overall satisfaction with the Borchert Mulching Mower.*

Extremely Dissatisfied _____ **Extremely Satisfied**

54. *Would you recommend a Borchert Mulching Mower to a friend? (Check one)*
_____ Extremely likely
_____ Likely
_____ Maybe
_____ Unlikely
_____ Extremely unlikely

55. *If you had to make the decision again today, would you buy a Borchert Mulching Mower?*
_____ Extremely likely
_____ Likely
_____ Maybe
_____ Unlikely
_____ Extremely unlikely

continued on next page

Figure 1
Likert Scale Questionnaire *continued*

Instructions

Listed below are a number of statements that relate to the Borchert Mulching Mower you have purchased. Please read through the list carefully and then:

(1) Circle the ten items from the list that most distinguish your Borchert Mower from other mulching or rotary lawn mowers you are familiar with (in comparison with a Toro, Sears, Lawn-Boy, etc.).

(2) Next, in the space provided to the right of each statement, rank those ten items you have just circled from 1 to 10 in terms of *their importance to you*, with 1 being the most important.

56. Evenness of lawn after cutting _____
57. Price of mower _____
58. Ease of installing bag adaptor _____
59. Amount of work when cutting the grass _____
60. Convenience of handle controls _____
61. Ease in trimming small areas _____
62. Safety of mower _____
63. Ease of adjusting cutting height _____
64. Convenience of dealer location _____
65. Ease of handling height adjustment _____
66. Noise of mower _____
67. Adequacy of mower warranty _____
68. Ease of starting mower _____
69. Sturdy construction of mower _____
70. Speed of repair service _____
71. Lawn is better nourished _____
72. Motor of the mower is trouble free _____
73. Ease of storing mower _____

Finally we would like some information from you by which we can analyze the responses. Please circle the appropriate answer in each of the following questions.

74. *What is the size of your lot?* _____ *ft.* × _____ *ft. or;*

1. Less than ¼ acre
2. ¼ to less than ½ acre
3. ½ to less than ¾ acre
4. ¾ to less than 1 acre
5. 1 to less than 1¼ acres

6. 1¼ to less than 1½ acres
7. 1½ to less than 1¾ acres
8. 1¾ to less than 2 acres
9. 2 acres or more

75. *Where do you live?* _____
    (Town)

76. *What is the approximate current market value of your home and property?*

1. Under $15,000
2. $15,000–$34,999
3. $35,000–$49,999

4. $50,000–$74,999
5. $75,000–$99,999
6. $100,000 and over

Figure 1
Likert Scale Questionnaire *continued*

77. *What is the age of the household head?*
   1. Under 25 years
   2. 25–29 years
   3. 30–34 years
   4. 35–39 years
   5. 40–44 years
   6. 45–49 years
   7. 50–54 years
   8. 55–64 years
   9. 65 years and over

78. *What is the approximate total BEFORE TAX family yearly income?*
   1. Under $5,000
   2. $5,000–$9,999
   3. $10,000–$14,999
   4. $15,000–$19,999
   5. $20,000–$24,999
   6. $25,000–$29,999
   7. $30,000–$34,999
   8. $35,000 and over

79. *What is the occupation of the household head?*
   1. Clerical
   2. Craftsman, foreman
   3. Farmer
   4. Laborer, factory worker
   5. Proprietor, manager
   6. Professional
   7. Sales
   8. Retired
   9. Other (specify)

80. *In what year did you buy your Borchert mower?* _____

Thank you. Please return in the envelope provided.

Figure 2
Semantic Differential Scale

The Borchert people would appreciate you taking about 15 minutes of your time to complete the following questionnaire. For each of the items below, please place a check in the space that bests corresponds to your opinion of the Borchert Mulching Mower. If you feel the mower performed much better than you expected, you would check the right-hand box. If you feel the mower performed much worse than you expected, you would check the left-hand box. If you feel the mower merely met your expectations, you would check the middle box. For intermediate degrees of satisfaction or dissatisfaction you would check something between the neutral and extreme positions. We need your opinion on each of the items, so please do not skip any question. Thank you very much.

continued on next page

Figure 2
Semantic Differential Scale *continued*

1. *The ability of the mulching mower to hide grass clippings in the lawn so that raking is never necessary*

   Much worse than I expected :___:___:___:___:___:___: Much better than I expected

2. *The capability of the mulching mower to eliminate the need for bagging grass clippings*

   Much worse than I expected :___:___:___:___:___:___: Much better than I expected

3. *The mulching mower's contribution to making the lawn look greener and healthier*

   Much less than I expected :___:___:___:___:___:___: Much more than I expected

4. *The amount of time it takes to cut the lawn with the mulching mower.*

   Much less than I expected :___:___:___:___:___:___: Much more than I expected

5. *The capability of the mulching mower to trim in small and hard-to-get-at areas*

   Much worse than I expected :___:___:___:___:___:___: Much better than I expected

6. *The amount of effort that must be expended in operating the mulching mower*

   Much less than I expected :___:___:___:___:___:___: Much more than I expected

7. *The capability of the mulching mower to withstand punishment*

   Much worse than I expected :___:___:___:___:___:___: Much better than I expected

8. *The amount of time it takes the mulching mower to burn up a tank of gas*

   Much less than I expected :___:___:___:___:___:___: Much more than I expected

9. *The proficiency of the mulching mower at keeping lawn clippings out of garden beds and off sidewalks*

   Much less than I expected :___:___:___:___:___:___: Much more than I expected

10. *The ability of the mulching mower to start fast and easily even when the engine is cold*

    Much worse than I expected :___:___:___:___:___:___: Much better than I expected

11. *How often the cutting blade must be sharpened to enable the mulching feature to operate properly*

    Much less than I expected :___:___:___:___:___:___: Much more than I expected

12. *The ability to easily set the mulching mower to any cutting height desired*

    Much worse than I expected :___:___:___:___:___:___: Much better than I expected

13. *The capability of the mulching mower to cut the whole lawn evenly*

    Much worse than I expected :___:___:___:___:___:___: Much better than I expected

14. *How the mulching mower can eliminate the worry that children or others nearby will be hit by twigs or stones scattered by the motor*

    Much worse than I expected :___:___:___:___:___:___: Much better than I expected

15. *The average number of times a month the lawn must be cut when using the mulching mower*

    Much less than I expected :___:___:___:___:___:___: Much more than I expected

Figure 2
Semantic Differential Scale *continued*

16. *The amount of noise made by the mulching mower*

    Much less than I expected :___:___:___:___:___:___: Much more than I expected

17. *The efficiency with which the mulching mower can be stored out of the way after use*

    Much less than I expected :___:___:___:___:___:___: Much more than I expected

18. *How easy it is for other members of the household besides the husband to cut the lawn using the mulching mower*

    Much less than I expected :___:___:___:___:___:___: Much more than I expected

19. *The noticeability of tire tracks left in the lawn by the mulching mower*

    Much less than I expected :___:___:___:___:___:___: Much more than I expected

20. *The ability of the mulching mower's power drive to move the mower at just the right pace*

    Much worse than I expected :___:___:___:___:___:___: Much better than I expected

21. *The number of times cleaning the mower is necessary because clippings stick in the cutting chamber*

    Much less than I expected :___:___:___:___:___:___: Much more than I expected

22. *The difficulty with pushing or pulling the mulching mower when the self-propelling power drive is not engaged*

    Much less than I expected :___:___:___:___:___:___: Much more than I expected

23. *The capability of the mulching mower to virtually eliminate scalping*

    Much worse than I expected :___:___:___:___:___:___: Much better than I expected

24. *The amount of danger the operator of the mulching mower is exposed to*

    Much less than I expected :___:___:___:___:___:___: Much more than I expected

25. *The ability of the mulching mower to cut through thick and wet grass without clogging*

    Much worse than I expected :___:___:___:___:___:___: Much better than I expected

26. *How convenient it is to fill the gas tank on the mulching mower*

    Much less than I expected :___:___:___:___:___:___: Much more than I expected

27. *How convenient is it to get prompt service on the mulching mower*

    Much less than I expected :___:___:___:___:___:___: Much more than I expected

28. *The amount of time it takes for the grass clippings to decompose*

    Much less than I expected :___:___:___:___:___:___: Much more than I expected

29. *The efficiency of the built-in hose attachment in cleaning the mulching mower easily and thoroughly*

    Much less than I expected :___:___:___:___:___:___: Much more than I expected

continued on next page

Figure 2
Semantic Differential Scale *continued*

Instructions

Listed below are a number of statements that relate to the Borchert Mulching Mower you have purchased. Please read through the list carefully and then:

(1) Circle the ten items from the list that most distinguish your Borchert Mower from other mulching or rotary lawn mowers you are familiar with (in comparison with a Toro, Sears, Lawn-Boy, etc.).

(2) Next, in the space provided to the right of each statement, rank those ten items you have just circled from 1 to 10 in terms of *their importance to you* with 1 being the most important.

31. Evenness of lawn after cutting   _____
32. Price of mower   _____
33. Ease of installing bag adaptor   _____
34. Amount of work when cutting the grass   _____
35. Convenience of handle controls   _____
36. Ease in trimming small areas   _____
37. Safety of mower   _____
38. Ease of adjusting cutting height   _____
39. Convenience of dealer location   _____
40. Ease of handle height adjustment   _____
41. Noise of mower   _____
42. Adequacy of mower warranty   _____
43. Ease of starting mower   _____
44. Sturdy construction of mower   _____
45. Speed of repair service   _____
46. Lawn is better nourished   _____
47. Motor of the mower is trouble free   _____
48. Ease of storing mower   _____

Finally, we would like some information from you by which we can analyze the responses. Please circle the appropriate answer in each of the following questions.

49. *What is the size of your lot? ____ ft. × ____ ft. or:*

1. Less than ¼ acre   6. 1¼ to less than 1½ acres
2. ¼ to less than ½ acre   7. 1½ to less than 1¾ acres
3. ½ to less than ¾ acre   8. 1¾ to less than 2 acres
4. ¾ to less than 1 acre   9. 2 acres or more
5. 1 to less than 1¼ acres

50. *Where do you live? _____*
                                      (Town)

51. *What is the approximate current market value of your home and property?*

1. Under $15,000   4. $50,000–$74,999
2. $15,000–$34,999   5. $75,000–$99,999
3. $35,000–$49,999   6. $100,000 and over

Figure 2
Semantic Differential Scale *continued*

52. *What is the age of the household head?*

    1. Under 25 years
    2. 25–29 years
    3. 30–34 years
    4. 35–39 years
    5. 40–44 years
    6. 45–49 years
    7. 50–54 years
    8. 55–64 years
    9. 65 years and over

53. *What is the approximate total BEFORE TAX family yearly income?*

    1. Under $5,000
    2. $5,000–$9,999
    3. $10,000–$14,999
    4. $15,000–$19,999
    5. $20,000–$24,999
    6. $25,000–$29,999
    7. $30,000–$34,999
    8. $35,000 and over

54. *What is the occupation of the household head?*

    1. Clerical
    2. Craftsman, foreman
    3. Farmer
    4. Laborer, factory worker
    5. Proprietor, manager
    6. Professional
    7. Sales
    8. Retired
    9. Other (specify)

55. *In what year did you buy your Borchert mower?* _____

Thank you. Please return in the envelope provided.

the surveys mailed, 330 Likert scale and 297 semantic differential scale questionnaires were returned. The respective response rates were 83 percent and 74 percent. A listing of the data that was collected in the case is available from your instructor.

Questions

1. How might the sampling plan affect the research results?

2. In your opinion, which scale, Likert or semantic differential, better assesses customer satisfaction with the Borchert Mulching Mower.

Case 3.6
Calamity-Casualty Insurance Company[1]

Calamity-Casualty is an insurance company located in Dallas, Texas, that deals exclusively with automobile coverage. Their policy offerings include the standard features
offered by most insurers, such as collision, comprehensive, emergency road service,
medical, and uninsured motorist. The unique aspect of Calamity-Casualty Insurance is
that all policies are sold through the mail. Agents do not make personal calls on clients,
and the company does not operate district offices. As a result, Calamity-Casualty's
capital–labor requirements are greatly reduced at a substantial cost savings to the company. A great portion of these savings are passed on to the consumer in the form of
lower prices. The data indicate that Calamity-Casualty offers its policies at 20 to 25
percent below the average market rate.

The company's strategy of selling automobile insurance by mail at low prices has
been very successful. Calamity-Casualty has traditionally been the third largest seller of
automobile insurance in the Southwest. During the past five years, the company has
consistently achieved an average market share of some 14 percent in the four states it
serves—Arizona, New Mexico, Nevada, and Texas. This compares favorably to the 19
percent and 17 percent market shares realized by the two leading firms in the region.
However, Calamity-Casualty has never been highly successful in Arizona. The largest
market share gained by Calamity-Casuality in Arizona for any one year was 4 percent,
which placed the company seventh among firms competing in that state.

The company's poor performance in Arizona greatly concerns Calamity-Casualty's
board of executives. Demographic experts estimate that during the next six to ten years,
the population in Arizona will increase some 10 to 15 percent, the largest projected
growth rate of any state in the Southwest. Thus, for Calamity-Casualty to remain a
major market force in the area, the company needs to improve its sales performance in
Arizona.

In response to this matter, Calamity-Casualty sponsored a study that was conducted
by the Automobile Insurance Association of American (AIAA), the national association
of automobile insurance executives, to determine Arizona residents' attitudes toward and
perception of the various insurance companies selling policies in that state. The results
of the AIAA research showed that Calamity-Casualty was favorably perceived across
most categories measured. Calamity-Casualty received the highest ratings with respect
to service, pricing, policy offering, and image. While these findings were well received
by the company's board of executives, they provided little strategic insight into how
Calamity-Casualty might increase sales in Arizona.

Since the company was committed to obtaining information useful for developing a
more effective Arizona sales campaign, the executive board sought the services of
Aminbane, Pedrone, and Associates, a marketing research firm specializing in insurance

[1]The contributions of David M. Szymanski to the development of this case are gratefully acknowledged.

consulting, to help with the matter. After many discussions between members of the research team and executives at Calamity-Casualty, it was decided that the most beneficial approach toward designing a more appropriate sales campaign would be to ascertain the psychographic profiles of nonpurchasers and direct mail purchasers of Calamity-Casualty insurance. This would help the company better understand the personal factors influencing people's decision to respond or not to respond to direct mail solicitation.

Table 1
Calamity-Casualty Marketing Research Questionnaire Items

Risk Aversion

1. It is always better to buy a used car from a dealer than from an individual.
2. Generally speaking, I avoid buying generic drugs at the drugstore.
3. It would be a disaster to be stranded on the road due to a breakdown.
4. It would be important to me to plan a long road trip very carefully and in great detail.
5. I would like to try parachute jumping sometime.
6. Before buying a new product, I would first discuss it with someone who had already used it.
7. Before deciding to see a new movie in a threater, it is important to read the critical reviews.
8. If my car needed even a minor repair, I would first get cost estimates from several garages.

Powerlessness

1. Persons like myself have little chance of protecting our personal interests when they conflict with those of strong pressure groups.
2. A lasting world peace can be achieved by those of us who work toward it.
3. I think each of us can do a great deal to improve world opinion of the United States.
4. This world is run by the few people in power, and there is not much the little guy can do about it.
5. People like me can change the course of world events if we make ourselves heard.
6. More and more, I feel helpless in the face of what's happening in the world today.

Convenience Orientation

1. I like to buy things by mail or catalog because it saves time.
2. I feel it is not worth the extra effort to clip coupons for groceries.
3. I would rather wash my own car than pay to have it washed at a car wash.
4. I would prefer to have an automatic transmission rather than a stick shift in my car.
5. When choosing a bank, I feel that location is the most important factor.
6. When shopping for groceries, I would be willing to drive a longer distance in order to buy at lower prices.

Note: Each item requires one of the following responses:

Responses	Code
S.A.—Strongly Agree	5
A.—Agree	4
N.—Neither Agree Nor Disagree	3
D.—Disagree	2
S.D.—Strongly Disagree	1

Research Design

To gain insight as to which psychographic factors are important in describing purchasers of automobile insurance, some exploratory research was undertaken. In-depth interviews were held with two insurance salespersons who offered various insights on the subject. These experience interviews were followed by a focus group meeting with Arizona residents who had received a direct mail offer from Calamity-Casualty. Finally, the research team consulted university professors in both psychology and mass communications to uncover other determinants of buyer behavior. Output from these procedures revealed three primary factors that could be used to describe purchasers of insurance by mail—namely, risk aversion, powerlessness, and convenience orientation. It was believed that people who were risk averse, had a low sense of powerlessness, and were convenience oriented would be more favorably disposed toward direct mail marketing efforts and thus would be more likely to purchase Calamity-Casualty automobile insurance.

Method of Data Collection

Given these factors of interest, the list of the items contained in Table 1 was generated to form the basis of a questionnaire to be administered to Arizona residents. Two samples of subjects were to be used—one of direct mail buyers and one of nonbuyers. The research team estimated that 175 subjects would be required from both samples to adequately assess the three constructs. Because a mail questionnaire dealing with psychographic subject matter might have a very low response rate, and because attitude toward direct mail was one of the attributes being measured, a telephone interview was believed to be best suited to the needs at hand.

Questions

1. Conceptually, what are the constructs risk aversion, convenience, and powerlessness?

2. Do you think the sample of items adequately assesses each construct? Can you think of any additional items that could or should be used?

Case 3.7
Consumer Medical Attitudes[1]

In planning and designing this research project, a number of practical concerns—such as implications and strategies for which the data might be used and methodological concerns for achieving the highest validity and reliability consistent with the resources available for the study—were considered.

Objectives of the Study

The purpose of this study is to assess attitudes and behavior of consumers concerning health care and physician services, with special attention to consumer support for possible solutions to the medical malpractice problem. More specifically, the objectives of this study are:

1. to describe criteria used by patients to select and evaluate health care by physicians,

2. to identify persons likely to bring a malpractice suit in specified situations, and

3. to determine levels of support for alternative approaches for dealing with the malpractice study.

Research Methodology

Telephone Sample

This study was conducted using a telephone questionnaire administered to a random sample of 1,500 adult residents in Ohio. The telephone format was selected after consideration of both mail and personal interviews, which it was felt would provide less reliable data in this particular study than would telephone interviews. The sample was drawn with the assistance of the Chicago-based Reuben Donnelly Company, which maintains telephone directories from all cities of the United States. It provided a computer-generated random sample of telephone numbers in Ohio cities and rural areas.

A sample of 1,500 is reliable and provides a reasonable base for making inferences about the Ohio adult population. However, all samples have some limitations. For example, persons who were not at home when calls were made or who do not have telephones could be underrepresented in this study. To minimize these problems, three callbacks were attempted at various time periods.

The interviewing for this study was completed by Dwight Spencer Associates from WATS line facilities in Columbus, Ohio, using skilled and continuously monitored interviewers.

---

[1]Source: *Contemporary Cases in Marketing*, Third Edition, by W. Wayne Talarzyk, pp. 116–128. Copyright © 1983 by CBS College Publishing. Reprinted by permission of CBS College Publishing. This case has been adapted from Roger D. Blackwell and W. Wayne Talarzyk, *Consumer Attitudes toward Health Care and Medical Malpractice* (Columbus, Ohio: Grid, Inc., 1977). The adaptation was made with the permission of Grid, Inc. The research reported in the case was conducted under a grant from the Malpractice Research Fund of the Ohio State Medical Association. Results from the research are presented in Consumer Medical Attitudes (B).

Figure 1
Medical Practices Survey Form* *continued*

(24–25)   8. Other MD (specify _____)   _____

(26–27)   9. Other non-MD (specify _____)   _____

(28–29)   Total number of treatments   _____

(30)   4. *Thinking about your primary doctor or family doctor, can you think back and tell me how you happened to choose that doctor? (Record all reasons mentioned.) Were there any other reasons? (Check all reasons mentioned.)*

           1. Recommended by friend or relative   _____

           2. Recommended by another physician   _____

           3. Looked in yellow pages of directory   _____

           4. Recommended by hospital   _____

           5. Met the doctor socially or heard of him as civic leader _____

           6. Treated as member of hospital staff (emergency, etc.) _____

           7. Required physician (clinics, insurance, etc.)   _____

           8. Can't remember, always been our doctor, etc. _____

           9. Other (specify) _____   _____

(31)   5. *Of those reasons, which one would be the most important for your choice?* _____ *(1–9)*

      6. *Here's an imaginary question. Suppose your present doctor were to move away suddenly and you had to choose a new one. I have a list of characteristics of doctors that people sometimes use to evaluate a doctor. I would like for you to rate each characteristic on a scale of 1 to 5 according to its importance to you personally. If something is very important to you, you should rate it as a 1; if it is somewhat important, you should rate it a 2; if it is neutral in importance, rate it 3; if it is somewhat unimportant, rate it a 4; and if it is very unimportant, rate it a 5.*

(32)   1. The doctor's office is near you.   1 2 3 4 5

(33)   2. The doctor has access to the hospital you want. 1 2 3 4 5

(34)   3. The doctor has a good personality and appearance. 1 2 3 4 5

(35)   4. How much the doctor charges   1 2 3 4 5

(36)   5. The doctor is willing to talk with you about your illness.   1 2 3 4 5

(37)   6. The doctor has many years of experience.   1 2 3 4 5

(38)   7. The doctor has never been sued for malpractice. 1 2 3 4 5

(39)   8. The doctor is recommended by other doctors. 1 2 3 4 5

(40)   9. The doctor has evening or weekend office hours. 1 2 3 4 5

(41)   10. The doctor is recommended by your friends. 1 2 3 4 5

(42)   11. How long it takes to get an appointment   1 2 3 4 5

(43)   7. *What is your feeling about the quality of health care given by your doctor? Would you describe it as:*

           1. Excellent _____ 2. Good _____

           3. Average _____ 4. Poor _____ or 5. Very poor _____

continued on next page

Figure 1
Medical Practices Survey Form* *continued*

(44) 8. *What is your feeling about the quality of health care given by doctors in general?*
   1. Excellent _____ 2. Good _____
   3. Average _____ 4. Poor _____ or 5. Very poor _____

(45) 9. *What is your feeling about the charges you pay your doctor? Are they:*
   1. Entirely too high for the services provided you?   _____
   2. Too high for the services provided you?   _____
   3. Reasonable for the services provided you?   _____
   4. Low considering the services provided you?   _____

(46) 10. *In recent years, the amount that doctors pay for malpractice insurance has increased drastically. In a few words, what do you personally believe is the cause of increased costs of malpractice insurance?*

   _____

   _____

   _____

   1. Doctors are at fault.   _____
   2. Lawyers are at fault.   _____
   3. Insurance companies are at fault.   _____
   4. The government or laws are at fault.   _____
   5. Juries and/or judges are giving too much.   _____

   11. *Several ways of handling the malpractice problem have been proposed. We would like to describe some of these methods and ask you to rate your support for them on a 1 to 5 scale. If you would be strongly for this method, rate it 1. If you would be somewhat for the method, rate it a 2. If you are neutral, a 3; somewhat against it, a 4; and strongly against it, a 5.*

(47) 1. A law that lowered the proportion of the settlement that lawyers could receive for malpractice suits   1 2 3 4 5

(48) 2. A requirement that patients agree to arbitration of malpractice claims (the patient and the doctor would appoint skilled arbitrators to settle malpractice claims).   1 2 3 4 5

(49) 3. A state agency, something like the workmen's compensation bureau, which would collect malpractice insurance premiums from all physicians and decide what benefits would be given all patients with malpractice claims.   1 2 3 4 5

(50) 4. A state law which limited the amounts that could be collected by patients with malpractice claims.   1 2 3 4 5

(51) 5. A peer group review system in which a group of physicians reviewed malpractice claims and decided which ones should be taken to trial.   1 2 3 4 5

(52) 6. A release signed before a person is accepted as a patient agreeing not to sue for malpractice.   1 2 3 4 5

Figure 1
Medical Practices Survey Form* *continued*

(53)   7. More time spent by your physician in explaining the risks or potential problems of your operation or medicine even though the charge for the doctor's services would be higher than now.   1   2   3   4   5

(54)   8. A state law which requires insurance companies to reduce malpractice rates to doctors in return for correspondingly higher rates on health insurance to the general public.   1   2   3   4   5

(55)   9. Countersuits by physicians against patients and their attorneys who sue for malpractice with no basis for the malpractice suit.   1   2   3   4   5

(56–58)   *12. Of the malpractice suits that are brought against physicians, what percentage would you say are instances in which the doctor was negligent?* ☐ ☐ ☐ %

(59–61)   *13. Of the malpractice settlement, what percentage of the money do you believe goes to the lawyer?* ☐ ☐ ☐ %

(62)   *14. Let's assume that your doctor was unable to determine a cure for you, and you thought your doctor might be at fault. Would you be very likely to bring a malpractice suit, somewhat likely, undecided, somewhat unlikely, or very unlikely to bring a malpractice suit?*

    1. Very likely _____   4. Somewhat unlikely _____
    2. Somewhat likely _____   5. Very unlikely _____
    3. Undecided _____

(63)   *15. Let's assume that you developed a serious medical problem in which you thought your physician might be at fault. Would you be very likely to bring a malpractice suit, somewhat likely, undecided, somewhat unlikely, or very unlikely to bring a malpractice suit.*

    1. Very likely _____   4. Somewhat unlikely _____
    2. Somewhat likely _____   5. Very unlikely _____
    3. Undecided _____

(64)   *16. Let's assume that your spouse or your parent died and you thought your physician might be at fault. Would you be very likely to bring a malpractice suit, somewhat likely, undecided, somewhat unlikely, or very unlikely to bring a malpractice suit?*

    1. Very likely _____   4. Somewhat unlikely _____
    2. Somewhat likely _____   5. Very unlikely _____
    3. Undecided _____

(65)   *17. Have you ever personally brought a malpractice suit against a physician?*

    1. Yes _____ (please continue)
    2. No _____ (skip to Question 24)

continued on next page

Figure 1
Medical Practices Survey Form* *continued*

(66)   18. *What happened to your suit? What is the current status?*

1. Dismissed with a settlement to you _____
2. Dismissed without a settlement to you _____
3. Brought to trial with a judgment to you _____
4. Brought to trial with no judgment to you _____
5. Case currently pending _____

(67)   19. *What was the specialty of the physician who was sued?*

1. Family practice _____
2. Surgeon _____
3. OB-Gyn _____
4. Ophthalmologist _____
5. Pediatrician _____
6. Other (specify _____) _____

(68)   20. *In a few words, can you tell me what caused you to decide to pursue a malpractice suit against the physician?*

_____
_____
_____

1. Self influences _____
2. Family influences _____
3. Physician influences _____
4. Other medical personnel (nurses, etc.) _____
5. Attorney influences _____
6. Other influences _____
7. Other reasons _____

(69–71)   21. *Of the amount that was paid to you, what percentage went to the attorney?* □ □ □

(72)   22. *If you had to decide again to pursue the malpractice suit, would you be very likely to do it again, somewhat likely, undecided, somewhat unlikely, or very unlikely to bring the malpractice suit if you were able to do it over?*

1. Very likely _____   4. Somewhat unlikely _____
2. Somewhat likely _____   5. Very unlikely _____
3. Undecided _____

(73)   23. *If you were to need medical treatment again, would you be very likely to go to the same physician, somewhat likely, undecided, somewhat unlikely, or very unlikely to go to the same physician again?*

1. Very likely _____   4. Somewhat unlikely _____
2. Somewhat likely _____   5. Very unlikely _____
3. Undecided _____

Figure 1
Medical Practices Survey Form* *continued*

> 24. *Now, I would like to read some statements that some people agree with and some do not agree with. We would like to know if you strongly agree, somewhat agree, are neutral, somewhat disagree, or strongly disagree with each statement. There are no right or wrong answers. We are simply interested in your opinion about each statement.*

(CC)(1–4)
Same as
Card 1

		SA	A	N	D	SD
(5)	1. I generally have a physical checkup at least once a year.	1	2	3	4	5
(6)	2. I generally approve of abortion if a woman wants one.	1	2	3	4	5
(7)	3. I have a great deal of confidence in my doctor.	1	2	3	4	5
(8)	4. About half of the physicians in Ohio are not really competent to practice medicine.	1	2	3	4	5
(9)	5. If I had a terminal illness, I would not want my physician to tell me.	1	2	3	4	5
(10)	6. Most doctors are overpaid.	1	2	3	4	5
(11)	7. I wish there were brochures which explained things to me when a doctor treats me.	1	2	3	4	5
(12)	8. I often watch TV programs that discuss health problems.	1	2	3	4	5
(13)	9. In most malpractice suits, the physician is actually negligent or in the wrong.	1	2	3	4	5
(14)	10. My physician adequately explains my medical problems to me.	1	2	3	4	5
(15)	11. Most physicians are ethical and responsible persons.	1	2	3	4	5
(16)	12. Most physicians are more concerned about making money than the welfare of their patients.	1	2	3	4	5
(17)	13. Most physicians in Ohio are not very competent.	1	2	3	4	5
(18)	14. It is wrong for a doctor to go on strike for any reason.	1	2	3	4	5
(19)	15. I usually read the nutrition information on food packages.	1	2	3	4	5
(20)	16. In most malpractice suits, the physician is not really to blame.	1	2	3	4	5

continued on next page

Figure 1
Medical Practices Survey Form* *continued*

(CC)(1–4) Same as Card 1		SA	A	N	D	SD
(21)	17. I believe that a very ill person should be allowed to die when there is no chance of recovering again.	1	2	3	4	5
(22)	18. I generally do exercises (like push-ups or sit-ups or jogging) at least twice a week.	1	2	3	4	5
(23)	19. I am careful about what I eat.	1	2	3	4	5
(24)	20. I usually have a good tan every year.	1	2	3	4	5
(25)	21. I frequently play tennis or other sports where I can get a lot of exercise.	1	2	3	4	5
(26)	22. I weigh about what my doctor says I should.	1	2	3	4	5
(27)	23. I usually go on a weight control diet at least twice a year.	1	2	3	4	5
(28)	24. It seems that I am sick a lot more than my friends are.	1	2	3	4	5

Finally, we have just a few questions to make sure we have all types of opinions represented in our survey.

(29) 25. *With what religion or denomination, if any, do you identify?*

1. Catholic _____   6. Other Protestant
2. Baptist _____   (specify   ) _____
3. Methodist _____   7. Jewish _____
4. Lutheran _____   8. Other (specify   ) _____
5. Presbyterian _____   9. None _____

(30) 26. *Would you consider your political views to be:*

1. Very liberal _____
2. Somewhat liberal _____
3. Middle of the road _____
4. Somewhat conservative _____
5. Very conservative _____

(31) 27. *Please stop me when I come to the category that describes your age.*

1. Under 25 _____   4. 45 to 54 _____
2. 25 to 34 _____   5. 55 to 64 _____
3. 35 to 44 _____   6. 65 & older _____

(32) 28. *What is the last year of school you have completed? (check appropriate category below)*

1. Did not attend _____
2. Elementary or grammar school _____

Figure 1
Medical Practices Survey Form* *continued*

(CC)(1–4)
Same as
Card 1

    3. Went to high school or trade school for less than 4 years   _____
    4. Graduated from high school or trade school   _____
    5. Some college, junior college, or technical school   _____
    6. Graduated from college   _____
    7. Some postgraduate work   _____
    8. Have postgraduate degree   _____

(33)   29. *Is your residence in: (check appropriate category below)*
    1. A rural area   _____
    2. A small town   _____
    3. An urban area   _____
    4. A suburban area   _____

(34)   30. *Counting your spouse and children as well as yourself, how many persons in your family are living at home now?*
    _____ 1, _____ 2, _____ 3, _____ 4, _____ 5, _____ 6,
    _____ 7, _____ 8, _____ 9 or more

(35)   31. *Finally, as I read a number of income categories, please stop me when I come to the one that describes your household's total income last year (before taxes).*
    1. Less than $3,000 _____   6. $20,000 to $24,999 _____
    2. $3,000 to $7,999 _____   7. $25,000 to $34,999 _____
    3. $8,000 to $9,999 _____   8. $35,000 to $49,999 _____
    4. $10,000 to $14,999 _____   9. $50,000 or more _____
    5. $15,000 to $19,999 _____

(36)   32. *Record sex of respondent:*
    1. Male _____   2. Female _____

Questions

1. In what ways do you believe the questionnaire in the research project could have been improved?

2. Evaluate the research methodology used in this study. What changes would you recommend in sample design, pretesting, and ways of gathering the data?

3. What methods of analysis would you recommend for evaluating the data acquired via this questionnaire?

Part 4

Sample Design and Data Collection

	Formulate Problem
	Determine Research Design
	Design Data Collection Method and Forms
⊞	Design Sample and Collect Data
	Analyze and Interpret Data
	Prepare the Research Report

Part 4 is concerned with the actual collection of data needed to answer a problem. Chapter 9 discusses the various types of sampling plans that can be employed to determine the population elements from which the data should be collected; Chapter 10 treats the question of how many of these elements are needed to answer the problem with precision and confidence in the results; and Chapter 11 discusses the many errors that can arise in completing this data collection task.

Chapter 9
Sampling Procedures

Once the researcher has clearly specified the problem and developed an appropriate research design and data collection instruments, the next step in the research process is to select those elements from which the information will be collected. One way to do this would be to collect information from each member of the population of interest by completely canvassing this population. A complete canvass of a population is called a **census.** Another way would be to collect information from a portion of the population by taking a **sample** of elements from the larger group, and, on the basis of the information collected from the subset, to infer something about the larger group. One's ability to make this inference from subset to larger group depends on the method by which the sample of elements was chosen. A major part of this chapter is devoted to the "why" and "how" of taking a sample.

Incidentally, *population* here refers not only to people but also to manufacturing firms, retail or wholesale institutions, or even inanimate objects such as parts produced in a manufacturing plant. **Population** is defined as the totality of cases that conform to some designated specifications. The specifications define the elements that belong to the target group and those that are to be excluded. A study aimed at establishing a demographic profile of vodka drinkers requires specifying who is to be considered a vodka drinker. Anyone who has ever had a drink of vodka? Those who have at least one drink a month? A week? Those who drink a certain minimum amount per month? Researchers need to be very explicit in defining the target group of interest and most careful that they have actually sampled the target population and not some other population because an inappropriate or incomplete sampling frame was used.

One might choose a sample to infer something about a population rather than canvassing the population itself for several reasons. First, complete counts on populations of moderate size are very costly. Few marketing research studies warrant complete counts, also, because the information will often be obsolete by the time the census is completed and the information processed. Further, sometimes a census is impossible, such as when testing the life of electric light bulbs. A 100 percent inspection using the bulbs until they burned out would reveal the average bulb life but would leave no product to sell. Finally, and to novice researchers surprisingly, one might choose a sample over a census for purposes of accuracy. Censuses involve larger field staffs, which, in turn, introduce greater potential for nonsampling error. This is one of the reasons the Bureau of the Census uses sample surveys to check the accuracy of various censuses. That is correct; samples are used to infer the accuracy of the census.[1]

Required Steps

Figure 9.1 outlines a useful six-step procedure that researchers can follow when drawing a sample of a population. Note that it is first necessary to define the population or the collection of elements about which the researcher wishes to make an inference. Relevant elements thus are the objects on which measurements are taken. Does the relevant population consist of individuals, households, business firms, other institutions, credit-card transactions, or what? In making this specification, the researcher also has to be careful to specify what units are to be excluded. This means specifying at a minimum both the geographic boundaries and the time period for the study, although additional restrictions are often placed on the elements. When the elements are individuals, for example, the relevant population may be defined as all those over 18, or females only, or those with a high school education only. A combination of age, sex, education, race, and other restrictions could also be used. In general though, the simpler the definition of the target population, the easier and less costly it is to find the sample.[2] The most important thing is that the researcher is precise in specifying exactly what elements are of interest and what elements are to be excluded. A clear statement of research purpose helps immeasurably in determining the appropriate elements of interest.

The second step in the sample selection process is identifying the **sampling frame,** which is the listing of the elements from which the actual sample will be drawn. A telephone book is an obvious example of a sampling frame, which also illustrates the condition that there is rarely a perfect correspondence between the sampling frame and the target population of interest. While the target population may be all households living in a particular metropolitan area, the telephone directory provides an inaccurate listing of these households, omitting some without phones and unlisted numbers and double counting others that have multiple listings. One of the researcher's more creative tasks in sampling is developing an appropriate sampling frame when the list of population elements is not readily available. Sometimes this means sampling geographic areas or institutions and then subsampling within these units when, say, the target population is individuals, but a current, accurate list of appropriate individuals is not available.

The third step in selecting a sample procedure is inextricably intertwined with the identification of the sampling frame in that the choice of sampling method depends largely on what the researcher can develop for a sampling frame. A simple random sample, for example, requires that a complete, accurate list of population elements by name or other identification code be available. The rest of this chapter reviews the main types of nonprobability and probability samples employed in marketing research. The

[1]See "Census Bureau, Cities Skirmish Over Count; Money, Power at Stake," *Wall Street Journal,* 60 (September 30, 1980) pp. 1–27, and "Census is Still Assailed, But Many Say Count Is Most Accurate Yet," *Wall Street Journal,* 60 (December 9, 1980), pp. 1 and 24, for discussion of the controversy that surrounds the accuracy of the 1980 Census.

[2]Seymour Sudman, "Applied Sampling," in Peter H. Rossi, James D. Wright, and Andy B. Anderson, eds., *Handbook of Survey Research* (Orlando: Academic Press, 1983), pp. 145–194.

Figure 9.1
Six-Step Procedure for Drawing a Sample

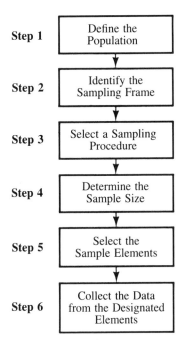

Step 1	Define the Population
Step 2	Identify the Sampling Frame
Step 3	Select a Sampling Procedure
Step 4	Determine the Sample Size
Step 5	Select the Sample Elements
Step 6	Collect the Data from the Designated Elements

connection between sampling frame and sampling method should become obvious from this discussion.

Step 4 in the sample selection process requires that sample size be determined. Chapter 10 discusses this question. Step 5 indicates that the researcher needs to actually pick the elements that will be included in the study. How this is done depends upon the type of sample being used, and consequently the discussion of sample selection is woven into the discussion of sampling methods. Finally, the researcher needs to actually collect data from the designated respondents. A great many things can go wrong with this task. These problems are reviewed, and some methods for handling them are discussed in Chapter 11.

Types of Sampling Plans

Sampling techniques can be divided into the two broad categories of probability and nonprobability samples. **Probability samples** are distinguished by the fact that each population element has a *known, nonzero* chance of being included in the sample. It is not necessary that the probabilities of selection be equal, but only that one can specify the probability with which each element of the population will be included in the sample. With **nonprobability samples,** on the other hand, there is no way of estimating the probability that any population element will be included in the sample, and thus there

Figure 9.2

Classification of Sampling Techniques

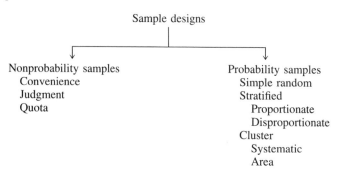

is no way of ensuring that the sample is representative of the population. All nonprobability samples rely on personal judgment somewhere in the process, and while these judgment samples may indeed yield good estimates of a population characteristic, they do not permit an objective evaluation of the adequacy of the sample. It is only when the elements have been selected with known probabilities that one is able to evaluate the precision of a sample result.

Samples can also be distinguished by whether they are fixed or sequential. **Fixed samples** imply an *a priori* determination of sample size and the collection of needed information from the designated elements. The question of sample size is discussed in the next chapter for fixed samples. Fixed samples are the most commonly employed types in marketing research and the kind we shall emphasize. Nevertheless, you should be aware that sequential samples can also be taken. Further, they can be employed with each of the basic sampling plans to be discussed. **Sequential samples** are distinguished by the successive decisions they imply. They aim at answering the research question on the basis of accumulated evidence. If the evidence is not conclusive after a small sample is taken, more observations are made; if still inconclusive, still more population elements are designated for inclusion in the sample, and so on. At each stage a decision is made as to whether more information should be collected or whether the evidence is now sufficient to permit a conclusion. The sequential sample allows trends in the data to be evaluated as the data are being collected, and this affords an opportunity to reduce costs when additional observations show diminishing usefulness.[3]

Both probability and nonprobability sampling plans can be further divided by type. Nonprobability samples, for instance, can be classified as convenience, judgment, or quota, while probability samples can be simple random, stratified, or cluster, and some of these can be further divided. Figure 9.2 shows the types of samples we shall discuss

---

[3]For a good exposition of the principles and advantages of sequential sampling, see E. J. Anderton, R. Tudor, and K. Gorton, "Sequential Analysis: A Reappraisal for Market Research," *Journal of the Market Research Society,* 18 (October 1976), pp. 166–179; and/or E. J. Anderton, K. Gorton, and R. Tudor, "The Application of Sequential Analysis in Market Research," *Journal of Marketing Research,* 17 (February 1980), pp. 97–105.

in this chapter, and except for convenience samples, Research Realities 9.1 shows the relative frequency with which they are used by industry. These basic sample types can be combined into more complex sampling plans. If you understand the basic types, though, you should well appreciate the more complex designs.

Nonprobability Samples

Nonprobability samples involve personal judgment somewhere in the selection process. Sometimes this judgment is imposed by the researcher, while in other cases the selection of population elements to be included is left to individual field workers. The fact that the elements are not selected probabilistically precludes an assessment of "sampling error." Without some knowledge of the error that can be attributed to sampling procedures, we cannot place bounds on the precision of our estimates.

Convenience Samples

Convenience samples are sometimes called *accidental samples* because those composing the sample enter by "accident"—they just happen to be where the information for the study is being collected. Examples of convenience samples abound in our everyday lives. We talk to a few friends, and on the basis of their reactions, we infer the political sentiment of the country; our local radio station asks people to call in and express their reactions to some controversial issue, and the opinions expressed are interpreted as prevailing sentiment; we ask for volunteers in a research study and use those who come forward.

The problem with convenience samples, of course, is that we have no way of knowing if those included are representative of the target population. And while we might be hesitant to infer that the reactions of a few friends indicate prevailing political sentiment, there does seem to be some temptation to conclude that large samples, even though selected conveniently, are representative. The fallacy of this assumption is illustrated by a personal incident.

One of the local television stations in the city where the author resides conducted a daily public opinion poll several years ago on topics of interest to the local community. The polls were labeled the "Pulse of Madison" and were conducted in the following way. During the six o'clock news every evening, the station would ask a question about some controversial issue to which people could reply with a yes or no. Persons in favor would call one number; persons opposed would call another. The number of viewers calling each number was recorded electronically. Percentages of those in favor and opposed would then be reported on the 10:00 p.m. news. With some 500 to 1,000 people calling in their opinions each night, the local TV commentator seemed to interpret these results as reflecting the true state of opinion in the community.

On one 6:00 p.m. broadcast, the following question was posed: "Do you think the drinking age in Madison should be lowered to 18?" The existing legal limit was 21. Would you believe that almost 4,000 people called in that night and that 78 percent were in favor of lowering the age requirement! Clearly, 4,000 responses in a community of 180,000 people "must be representative!" Wrong. As you may have suspected, certain segments of the population were more vitally interested in the issue than others. Thus, it was no surprise, when discussing the issue in class a few weeks later, to find

Research Realities 9.1

Relative Frequency with Which Various Sampling Techniques Are Used by Industry

	Type of Company		Consumer & Industrial	Retailer-Wholesaler	Utilities
	Consumer	Industrial			
Nonprobability Sampling Techniques					
Judgmental sampling	52%	29%	40%	36%	39%
Quota sampling	60	18	33	36	56
Probability Sampling Techniques					
Simple random sampling	76	41	53	36	89
Stratified sampling	69	31	67	27	78
Cluster sampling	43	15	53	27	50
Total number of firms	(42)	(68)	(15)	(11)	(18)

Source: Adapted from Barnett A. Greenberg, Jac L. Goldstucker, and Danny N. Bellenger, "What Techniques are Used by Marketing Researchers in Business?" *Journal of Marketing*, 41 (April 1977), pp. 64–65. Published by the American Marketing Association.

that students took one-half hour phone shifts on an arranged basis. Each person would call the yes number, hang up, call again, hang up, and so on, until it was the next person's turn. Thus neither the size of the sample nor the proportion favoring the age change was surprising. The sample was simply not representative. Further, increasing its size would not make it so. The representativeness of a sample must be insured by the sampling procedure. When participation is voluntary or sample elements are selected because they are convenient, the sampling plan provides no assurance that the sample is representative. Empirical evidence, as a matter of fact, is much to the contrary. Rarely do samples selected on a convenience basis, regardless of size, prove representative. Convenience samples are not recommended, therefore, for descriptive or causal research. They may be used with exploratory designs in which the emphasis is on generating ideas and insights, but even here the judgment sample seems superior.

Judgment Samples

Judgment samples are often called *purposive samples;* the sample elements are handpicked because it is expected that they can serve the research purpose. Most typically, the sample elements are selected because it is believed that they are representative of the population of interest. One example of a judgment sample is seen every four years at presidential election time, when television viewers are treated to indepth analyses of the swing communities. These communities are handpicked because they are "represen-

Communications	Market Research & Consulting	Finance & Insurance	Other Services	Others	Total Sample Using Technique
23%	46%	27%	27%	27%	35%
32	39	43	53	20	37
59	73	87	67	53	63
32	61	73	60	53	53
23	49	53	27	13	34
(22)	(33)	(30)	(15)	(15)	(269)

tative'' in that historically the winner there has been the next president. Thus, by monitoring these pivotal communities, election analysts are able to offer an early prediction of the eventual winner, and while election analysis and prediction have become much more sophisticated in recent years, the judgment sample of representative communities is still used.

As mentioned, the key feature of judgment sampling is that population elements are purposively selected. This selection may not be made on the basis that they are representative, but rather because they can offer the contributions sought. When the courts rely on expert testimony, they are in a sense using judgment samples, and the same kind of philosophy prevails in creating exploratory designs. When searching for ideas and insights, the researcher is not interested in sampling a cross section of opinion but rather in sampling those who can offer some perspective on the research question.

The **snowball sample** is a judgment sample that is sometimes used to sample special populations.[4] This sample relies on the researcher's ability to locate an initial set of respondents with the desired characteristics. These individuals are then used as informants to identify others with the desired characteristics. Thus, if one were doing a study

---

[4]The technique was originally suggested by Leo A. Goodman, ''Snowball Sampling,'' *Annals of Mathematical Statistics,* 32 (1961), pp. 148–170.

among the deaf investigating the desirability of various product configurations that would allow deaf people to communicate over telephone lines, one might attempt to initially identify some key people in the deaf community and then ask them for names of other deaf people who might be used in the study. Those initially asked to participate would also be asked for names of others whose cooperation would be solicited.[5] Thus, the sample "snowballs" by getting larger as participants identify still other possible respondents.

As long as the researcher is at the early stages of research where ideas or insights are being sought or when the researcher realizes its limitations, the judgment sample can be used productively. It becomes dangerous, though, when it is employed in descriptive or causal studies and its weaknesses are conveniently forgotten.[6] The Consumer Price Index (CPI) provides a classic example of this. As Sudman points out, "the CPI is in only 56 cities and metropolitan areas selected judgmentally and to some extent on the basis of political pressure. In reality, these cities *represent only themselves* although the index is called the *Consumer Price Index for Urban Wage Earners and Clerical Workers,* and most people believe the index reflects prices everywhere in the United States. Within cities, the selection of retail outlets is done judgmentally, so that the *possible size of sample bias is unkown* (emphasis added)."[7]

Quota Samples

A third type of nonprobability sample is the quota sample. **Quota samples** attempt to ensure that the sample is representative by selecting sample elements in such a way that the proportion of the sample elements possessing a certain characteristic is approximately the same as the proportion of the elements with the characteristic in the population. Consider, for example, an attempt to select a representative sample of undergraduate students on a college campus. If the eventual sample of 500 contained no seniors, one would have serious reservations about the representativeness of the sample and the generalizability of the conclusions beyond the immediate sample group. With a quota sample, the researcher could ensure that seniors would be included and in the same proportion as they occur in the entire undergraduate student body.

Consider that a researcher was interested in sampling the undergraduate student body in such a way that the sample would reflect the composition of the student body by class and sex. Suppose further that there were 10,000 undergraduate students in total

---

[5]AT&T used such a process for this communications problem, according to Robert Whitelaw, Division Manager for Market Research, in a speech "Research Solutions and New High Technology Service Concepts," which was delivered at the American Marketing Association's 1981 Annual Conference held in San Francisco, California, June 14–17, 1981.

[6]When certain very strict procedures are followed when listing members of the rare population, the snowball sample can be treated as a probability sample. For discussion of the requirements, see Martin R. Frankel and Lester R. Frankel, "Some Recent Developments in Sample Survey Design," *Journal of Marketing Research,* 14 (August 1977), pp. 280–293; or Patrick Biernacki and Dan Waldorf, "Snowball Sampling: Problems and Techniques of Chain Referred Sampling," *Sociological Methods and Research,* 10 (November 1981), pp. 141–163. For an example, see George S. Rothbart, Michelle Fine, and Seymour Sudman, "On Finding and Interviewing the Needles in the Haystack: The Use of Multiplicity Sampling," *Public Opinion Quarterly,* 46 (Fall 1982), pp. 408–421.

[7]Seymour Sudman, *Applied Sampling* (San Francisco: Academic Press, 1976), p. 10.

and that 3,200 were freshmen, 2,600 sophomores, 2,200 juniors, and 2,000 seniors, and further that 7,000 were males and 3,000 females. In a sample of 1,000, the quota sampling plan would require that 320 sample elements be freshmen, 260 sophomores, 220 juniors, and 200 seniors, and further that 700 of the sample elements be male and 300 be female. The researcher would accomplish this by giving each field worker a quota—thus the name *quota sample*—specifying the types of undergraduates he or she is to contact. Thus, one field worker assigned 20 interviews might be instructed to find and collect data from

- 6 freshmen—5 male and 1 female
- 6 sophomores—4 male and 2 female
- 4 juniors—3 male and 1 female
- 4 seniors—2 male and 2 female

Note that the specific sample elements to be used would not be specified by the research plan but would be left to the discretion of the individual field worker. The field worker's personal judgment would govern the choice of specific students to be interviewed. The only requirement would be that the interviewer diligently follow the established quota and interview five male freshmen, one female freshman, and so on.

Note further that the quota for this field worker accurately reflects the sex composition of the student population, but does not completely parallel the class composition; 70 percent (14 of 20) of the field worker's interviews are with males but only 30 percent (6 of 20) are with freshmen, whereas freshmen represent 32 percent of the undergraduate student body. It is not necessary or even usual with a quota sample that the quotas per field worker accurately mirror the distribution of the control characteristics in the population; usually only the total sample has the same proportions as the population.

Note finally that quota samples still rely on personal, subjective judgment rather than objective procedures for the selection of sample elements. Here the personal judgment is that of the field worker rather than the designer of the research, as it might be in the case of a judgment sample. This raises the question of whether quota samples can indeed be considered ''representative'' even though they accurately reflect the population with respect to the proportion of the sample possessing each control characteristic. Three points need to be made in this regard.

First, the sample could be very far off with respect to some other important characteristic likely to influence the result. Thus, if the campus study is concerned with racial prejudice existing on campus, it may very well make a difference whether field workers interview students from urban or rural areas. Since a quota for the urban–rural characteristic was not specified, it is unlikely that those participating will accurately reflect this characteristic. The alternative, of course, is to specify quotas for all potentially important characteristics. The problem is that increasing the number of control characteristics makes specifications more complex and makes the location of sample elements more difficult (perhaps even impossible) and certainly more expensive. It is a much more difficult task, assuming geographic origin and socioeconomic status are important characteristics, for a field worker to locate an upper middle-class male freshman from an urban area than to locate a male freshman.

Second, it is difficult to verify whether a quota sample is indeed representative. Certainly one can check the distribution of characteristics in the sample not used as controls to ascertain whether the distribution parallels that of the population. However, this type of comparison only provides negative evidence. It can indicate that the sample does not reflect the population if the distributions on some characteristics are different. If the sample and population distributions are similar for each of these characteristics, it is still possible for the sample to be vastly different from the population on some characteristic not explicitly compared.

Finally, interviewers left to their own devices are prone to follow certain practices.[8] They tend to interview their friends in excessive proportion. Since their friends are often similar to themselves, this can introduce bias. Interviewers who fill their quotas by stopping passers-by are likely to concentrate on areas where there are large numbers of potential respondents, such as business districts, railway and airline terminals, and the entrances to large department stores. This practice tends to overrepresent the particular kinds of people that frequent these areas. When home visits are used, interviewers display a propensity for convenience and appearance, concentrating their interviews at certain times of the day so that working people are underrepresented; avoiding upper stories of buildings without elevator service; and selecting corner buildings and avoiding dilapidated ones.

Depending on the subject of the study, all of these tendencies have the potential for bias. They may or may not in fact actually bias the result, but it is difficult to correct them when analyzing the data. When the sample elements are selected objectively, on the other hand, researchers have certain tools they can rely on to make the question of whether a particular sample is representative less difficult. In these probability samples, one relies on the sampling procedure and not the composition of the specific sample to solve the problem of representation.

Probability Samples

One can calculate the likelihood that any given population element will be included in a probability sample because the final sample elements are selected objectively by a specific process and not according to the whims of the researcher or field worker. The objective selection of elements in turn allows the objective assessment of the reliability of the sample results, something not possible with nonprobability samples regardless of the careful judgment exercised in selecting individuals.

This is not to say that probability samples will always be more representative than nonprobability samples. Far from it. A nonprobability sample may indeed be more representative. What probability samples allow, though, is an assessment of the amount of "sampling error" likely to occur because a sample rather than a census was employed when gathering the data. Nonprobability samples allow the investigator no objective method for evaluating the adequacy of the sample.

---

[8]Isidor Chein, "An Introduction to Sampling," in Claire Selltiz, Lawrence S. Wrightsman, and Stuart W. Cook, *Research Methods in Social Relations,* 3rd ed. (New York: Holt, Rinehart and Winston, 1976), pp. 520–521.

Simple Random Sampling

Simple random samples are by far the best known probability samples to beginning researchers since they are used to frame the concepts and arguments in beginning statistics courses. Simple random samples are distinguished by the fact that each population element has not only a known but an equal chance of being selected, and, further, that every combination of n population elements is a sample possibility and is just as likely to occur as any other combination of n units.

Parent Population   In discussing the various probability sampling plans and the objective assessment of sampling error they allow, it will prove useful to explore the notion of sampling distribution in some detail.[9] Consider the hypothetical population of 20 individuals shown in Table 9.1. This population can be described by certain parameters. A **parameter** is simply a characteristic or measure of a parent or target population; it is a fixed quantity that distinguishes one population from another. We can calculate a number of parameters to describe this hypothetical population. We could calculate the average income, the dispersion in educational levels, the proportion of the population subscribing to each newspaper, and so on. Note that these quantities are fixed in value. Given a census of this population, we can readily calculate them. Rather than relying on a census, we usually select a sample and use the values calculated from the sample observations to estimate the required population values.

Suppose our task was one of estimating the average income in this population from a sample of two elements selected randomly. Let μ denote the mean population income and σ^2 the variance of incomes. Both μ and σ are population parameters, one measuring central tendency and the other spread; that is, μ and σ^2 are defined as

$$\mu = \frac{\sum_{i=1}^{N} X_i}{N} = \frac{5,600 + 6,000 + \ldots + 13,200}{20} = 9,400.$$

$$\sigma^2 = \frac{\sum_{i=1}^{N} (X_i - \mu)^2}{N}$$

$$= \frac{(5,600 - 9,400)^2 + (6,000 - 9,400)^2 + \ldots + (13,200 - 9,400)^2}{20}$$

$$= 5,320,000,$$

where X_i is the value of the ith observation and N is the number of population elements. Thus, to compute the population mean, we divide the sum of all the values by the number of values making up the sum. To compute the population variance, we calculate

---

[9]The notion of a sampling distribution is treated in detail in most introductory statistics texts. The reader who understands the notion of sampling distribution should consider these next few pages an elementary review that will return dividends when discussing the more complex sample designs.

Table 9.1
Hypothetical Population

Element	Income (Dollars)	Education (Years)	Newspaper Subscription
1 A	5,600	8	X
2 B	6,000	9	Y
3 C	6,400	11	X
4 D	6,800	11	Y
5 E	7,200	11	X
6 F	7,600	12	Y
7 G	8,000	12	X
8 H	8,400	12	Y
9 I	8,800	12	X
10 J	9,200	12	Y
11 K	9,600	13	X
12 L	10,000	13	Y
13 M	10,400	14	X
14 N	10,800	14	Y
15 O	11,200	15	X
16 P	11,600	16	Y
17 Q	12,000	16	X
18 R	12,400	17	Y
19 S	12,800	18	X
20 T	13,200	18	Y

the deviation of each value from the mean, square these deviations, sum them, and divide by the number of values making up the sum.

Derived Population   It seems logical that our estimates of these population parameters would rest on similar calculations. A **statistic** is a characteristic or measure of a sample. While we typically use the similarly calculated statistic to estimate the parameter, we need to recognize that the value of the statistic depends on the particular sample selected from the parent population under the specified sampling plan. Different samples yield different statistics and different estimates.

Consider the **derived population** of *all* possible distinguishable samples that can be drawn from this parent population under a given sampling plan which specifies that a sample of Size $n = 2$ is to be drawn by simple random sampling without replacement.[10] Assume, for example, that the information for each element, including its identity, is to be placed on a disk and that these elements are to be placed in an urn and mixed thoroughly. The investigator will reach in the urn, pull out one disk, record the identity

[10]The term ''sample space'' is also used for the notion of derived population. See Martin Frankel, ''Sampling Theory,'' in Peter H. Rossi, James D. Wright, and Andy B. Anderson, eds., *Handbook of Survey Research* (Orlando: Academic Press, 1983), pp. 21–67.

and the income of the person and then, without replacing the first disk, will draw a second disk from the urn and record the identity and income. Table 9.2 displays the derived population of all possible samples from following this procedure. There are 190 combinations of the 20 disks possible. For each combination, one can calculate the sample mean income. Thus, for the sample AB, the sample mean income $\bar{x}_1 = (5,600 + 6,000)/2 = 5,800$, and, in general,

$$\bar{x}_k = \sum_{i=1}^{n} \frac{X_i}{n},$$

where k refers to the sample number, $\bar{x}$ to the sample average, and n to the sample size.

Before discussing the relationship between the sample mean income (a statistic) and population mean income (the parameter to be estimated), a few words are in order regarding the notion of derived population. First, note that in practice, we do not actually generate the derived population. This would be extremely wasteful of time and data. Rather, all that the practitioner will do is to generate one sample of the needed size. But the researcher will make use of the *concept* "derived population" and the associated notion of sampling distribution in making inferences. We shall see how in just a moment. Second, note that the derived population is defined as the population of all possible distinguishable samples that can be drawn under a *given sampling plan*. Change any part of the sampling plan, and the derived population will also change. Thus, when selecting disks, if the researcher is to replace the first disk drawn, the derived population will include the sample possibilities AA, BB, and so on. With samples of Size 3 instead of 2, drawn without replacement, ABC is a sample possibility, and there are a number of additional possibilities as well—1,140 versus the 190 with samples of Size 2. Change the method of selecting elements by using something other than simple random sampling and the derived population will also change. Finally, note that picking a sample of a given size from a parent population is equivalent to picking a single element (one of the 190 disks) out of the derived population. This fact is basic in making statistical inferences.

Sample Mean versus Population Mean   Now consider the relationship between the sample means and the population mean. We wish to make three points. First, suppose we add up all the sample means in Table 9.2 and divide by the number of samples, that is, average the averages. By sheer doing, this yields

$$\frac{5,800 + 6,000 \cdots + 13,000}{190} = 9,400,$$

which is the mean of the population. This is what is meant by an unbiased statistic. A statistic is **unbiased** when its average value equals the population parameter it is supposed to estimate. Note that the fact it is unbiased says nothing about any particular value of the statistic. Even though unbiased, a particular estimate may be very far from the true population value, for example, if either sample AB or sample ST were selected. In some cases, the true population value may even be *impossible* to achieve with any possible sample even though the statistic is unbiased; this is not true in the example, though, since a number of sample possibilities, for example, AT, yield a sample mean that equals the population average.

Table 9.2
Derived Population of All Possible Samples of Size
$n = 2$ **with Simple Random Selection**

k	Sample Identity	Mean	k	Sample Identity	Mean	k	Sample Identity	Mean	k	Sample Identity	Mean
1	AB	5,800	26	BI	7,400	51	CQ	9,200	76	EK	8,400
2	AC	6,000	27	BJ	7,600	52	CR	9,400	77	EL	8,600
3	AD	6,200	28	BK	7,800	53	CS	9,600	78	EM	8,800
4	AE	6,400	29	BL	8,000	54	CT	9,800	79	EN	9,000
5	AF	6,600	30	BM	8,200	55	DE	7,000	80	EO	9,200
6	AG	6,800	31	BN	8,400	56	DF	7,200	81	EP	9,400
7	AH	7,000	32	BO	8,600	57	DG	7,400	82	EQ	9,600
8	AI	7,200	33	BP	8,800	58	DH	7,600	83	ER	9,800
9	AJ	7,400	34	BQ	9,000	59	DI	7,800	84	ES	10,000
10	AK	7,600	35	BR	9,200	60	DJ	8,000	85	ET	10,200
11	AL	7,800	36	BS	9,400	61	DK	8,200	86	FG	7,800
12	AM	8,000	37	BT	9,600	62	DL	8,400	87	FH	8,000
13	AN	8,200	38	CD	6,600	63	DM	8,600	88	FI	8,200
14	AO	8,400	39	CE	6,800	64	DN	8,800	89	FJ	8,400
15	AP	8,600	40	CF	7,000	65	DO	9,000	90	FK	8,600
16	AQ	8,800	41	CG	7,200	66	DP	9,200	91	FL	8,800
17	AR	9,000	42	CH	7,400	67	DQ	9,400	92	FM	9,000
18	AS	9,200	43	CI	7,600	68	DR	9,600	93	FN	9,200
19	AT	9,400	44	CJ	7,800	69	DS	9,800	94	FO	9,400
20	BC	6,200	45	CK	8,000	70	DT	10,000	95	FP	9,600
21	BD	6,400	46	CL	8,200	71	EF	7,400	96	FQ	9,800
22	BE	6,600	47	CM	8,400	72	EG	7,600	97	FR	10,000
23	BF	6,800	48	CN	8,600	73	EH	7,800	98	FS	10,200
24	BG	7,000	49	CO	8,800	74	EI	8,000	99	FT	10,400
25	BH	7,200	50	CP	9,000	75	EJ	8,200	100	GH	8,200

Second, consider the spread of these sample estimates and particularly the relationship between this spread of estimates and the dispersion of incomes in the population. We saw previously that $\sigma^2 = 5,320,000$. We can calculate the *variance of mean incomes* similarly, that is, by taking the deviation of each mean around its overall mean, squaring and summing these deviations, and then dividing by the number of cases.

$$\frac{(5,800 - 9,400)^2 + (6,000 - 9,400)^2 + \cdots + (13,000 - 9,400)^2}{190} = 2,520,000.$$

Now note the relationship between σ^2—the spread of the variable in the original population—and the spread of the estimates in the derived population—call it $\sigma_{\bar{x}}^2$ to denote the variance of means. Instead of direct calculations using the 190 sample estimates, $\sigma_{\bar{x}}^2$ could have also been calculated by the following expression:

$$\sigma_{\bar{x}}^2 = \frac{\sigma^2}{n} \frac{N - n}{N - 1} = \frac{5,320,000}{2} \frac{20 - 2}{20 - 1} = 2,520,000.$$

Table 9.2
Derived Population of All Possible Samples of Size
$n = 2$ **with Simple Random Selection** *continued*

k	Sample Identity	Mean	k	Sample Identity	Mean	k	Sample Identity	Mean	k	Sample Identity	Mean
101	GI	8,400	126	IK	9,200	151	KQ	10,800	176	OP	11,400
102	GJ	8,600	127	IL	9,400	152	KR	11,000	177	OQ	11,600
103	GK	8,800	128	IM	9,600	153	KS	11,200	178	OR	11,800
104	GL	9,000	129	IN	9,800	154	KT	11,400	179	OS	12,000
105	GM	9,200	130	IO	10,000	155	LM	10,200	180	OT	12,200
106	GN	9,400	131	IP	10,200	156	LN	10,400	181	PQ	11,800
107	GO	9,600	132	IQ	10,400	157	LO	10,600	182	PR	12,000
108	GP	9,800	133	IR	10,600	158	LP	10,800	183	PS	12,200
109	GQ	10,000	134	IS	10,800	159	LQ	11,000	184	PT	12,400
110	GR	10,200	135	IT	11,000	160	LR	11,200	185	QR	12,200
111	GS	10,400	136	JK	9,400	161	LS	11,400	186	QS	12,400
112	GT	10,600	137	JL	9,600	162	LT	11,600	187	QT	12,600
113	HI	8,600	138	JM	9,800	163	MN	10,600	188	RS	12,600
114	HJ	8,800	139	JN	10,000	164	MO	10,800	189	RT	12,800
115	HK	9,000	140	JO	10,200	165	MP	11,000	190	ST	13,000
116	HL	9,200	141	JP	10,400	166	MQ	11,200			
117	HM	9,400	142	JQ	10,600	167	MR	11,400			
118	HN	9,600	143	JR	10,800	168	MS	11,600			
119	HO	9,800	144	JS	11,000	169	MT	11,800			
120	HP	10,000	145	JT	11,200	170	NO	11,000			
121	HQ	10,200	146	KL	9,800	171	NP	11,200			
122	HR	10,400	147	KM	10,000	172	NQ	11,400			
123	HS	10,600	148	KN	10,200	173	NR	11,600			
124	HT	10,800	149	KO	10,400	174	NS	11,800			
125	IJ	9,000	150	KP	10,600	175	NT	12,000			

This result is not unique but is true in general, although the expression relating the two spreads is typically modified slightly when the sample size is only a small proportion of the population.[11]

Third, consider the distribution of the estimates in contrast to the distribution of the variable in the parent population. Figure 9.3 indicates that the parent population distribution depicted by Panel A is spiked—each of the 20 values occurs once—and is symmetrical about the population mean value of 9,400. The distribution of estimates displayed in Panel B was constructed by placing each of the estimates in categories according to size and then counting the number contained in each category (Table 9.3).

---

[11]The expression $(N - n)/(N - 1)$ is known as the finite population correction factor. Whenever the sample size is less than 10 percent of the population size, the finite population correction factor is ignored, since $(N - n)/(N - 1)$ is very close to 1 and the more complex form $\sigma_{\bar{x}}^2 = (\sigma^2/n)(N - n)/(N - 1)$ reduces to $\sigma_{\bar{x}}^2 = \sigma^2/n$.

Figure 9.3
Distribution of Variable in Parent Population and
Distribution of Estimates in Derived Population

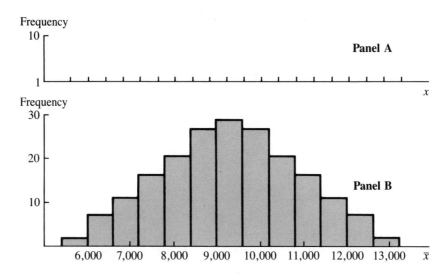

Panel B is the traditional histogram discussed in beginning statistics courses and represents the *sampling distribution of the statistic*. Note this: The notion of **sampling distribution** is the single most important notion in statistics; it is the cornerstone of statistical inference procedures. If one knows the sampling distribution for the statistic in question, one is in a position to make an inference about the corresponding population parameter. If, on the other hand, one knows only that a particular sample estimate will vary with repeated sampling and has no information as to *how* it will vary, then it will be impossible to devise a measure of the sampling error associated with that estimate. Since the sampling distribution of an estimate describes how that estimate will vary with repeated sampling, it provides a basis for determining the reliability of the sample estimate. This is why probability sampling plans are so important to statistical inference. With known probabilities of inclusion of any population element in the sample, statisticians are able to derive the sampling distribution of various statistics. Researchers then rely on these distributions—be they for a sample mean, sample proportion, sample variance, or some other statistic—in making their inferences from single samples to population values. Note that the distribution of sample means is mound shaped and symmetrical about the population mean with samples of size 2.

Recapitulating, we have shown that

1. the mean of all possible sample means is equal to the population mean;
2. the variance of sample means is related to the population variance by the expression

$$\sigma_{\bar{x}}^2 = \frac{\sigma^2}{n} \frac{N-n}{N-1};$$

Table 9.3
Classification of Estimates by Size

Sample Mean	Number of Samples
$6,000 or less	2
$6,100 to 6,600	7
$6,700 to 7,200	11
$7,300 to 7,800	16
$7,900 to 8,400	20
$8,500 to 9,000	25
$9,100 to 9,600	28
$9,700 to 10,200	25
$10,300 to 10,800	20
$10,900 to 11,400	16
$11,500 to 12,000	11
$12,100 to 12,600	7
$12,700 or more	2

3. The distribution of sample means is mound shaped, whereas the population distribution is spiked.

This first result is true in general for simple random sampling. The mean of the sample means is equal to the population mean if sampling is with or without replacement of the elements and whether sampling is from a finite or infinite parent population. The second result is true only when sampling from a finite population without replacement. If sampling from an infinite population or when sampling from a finite population with replacement, then the simpler expression $\sigma_{\bar{x}}^2 = \sigma^2/n$ holds.

The simpler expression derives from the fact that when the size of the sample is small in *comparison* to the size of the population, the term on the far right in the exact equation for the variance of sample means is approximately equal to one and can be ignored. For many, if not most, problems in marketing, the simpler expression is used to relate the variance of sample means to the variance of the variable.

Central-Limit Theorem   The third result of a mound-shaped distribution of estimates provides preliminary evidence of the operation of the Central-Limit Theorem. The **Central-Limit Theorem** holds that if simple random samples of Size n are drawn from a parent population with mean μ and variance σ^2, then when n is large, the sample mean $\bar{x}$ will be approximately normally distributed with mean equal to μ and variance equal to σ^2/n. The approximation will become more and more accurate as n becomes larger. Note the impact of this. It means that *regardless* of the shape of the parent population, the distribution of sample means *will be normal* if the sample is large enough. How large is large enough? If the distribution of the variable in the parent population is normal, then the means of samples of Size $n = 1$ will be normally distributed. If the distribution of the variable is symmetrical but not normal, then samples of very small size will produce a distribution in which the means are normally distributed. If the distribution of the variable is highly skewed in the parent population, then samples of a larger size will be needed. The fact remains, though, that the distribution of the statistic, sample mean, can be assumed normal if only we work with a sample of sufficient size. We do not need to rely on the assumption that the variable is normally distributed in the parent population in order to make inferences using the normal curve. Rather, we rely on the Central-Limit Theorem and adjust the sample size according to the population distribution so that the normal curve can be assumed to hold. Fortunately, the normal distribution of the statistic obtains with samples of relatively small size, as Figure 9.4 indicates.

Confidence Interval Estimates   How does all of the above help us in making inferences about the parent population mean? After all, in practice we do not draw all possible samples of a given size, but only one, and we use the results obtained in it to infer something about the target group. It all ties together in the following way.

It is known that with any normal distribution, a specific percentage of all observations is within a certain number of standard deviations of the mean, for example, 95 percent of the values are within ± 1.96 standard deviations of the mean. The distribution of sample means is normal if the Central-Limit Theorem holds and thus is no exception. Now, the mean of this sampling distribution is the population mean μ, and its standard deviation is given by the standard error of the mean $\sigma_{\bar{x}} = \sigma/\sqrt{n}$. Therefore, it is true that

- 68.26 percent of the sample means will be within ± 1 $\sigma_{\bar{x}}$ of the population mean,
- 95.45 percent of the sample means will be within ± 2 $\sigma_{\bar{x}}$ of the population mean, and
- 99.73 percent of the sample means will be within ± 3$\sigma_{\bar{x}}$ of the population mean,

and, in general, that $\mu \pm z\sigma_{\bar{x}}$ will contain some certain proportion of all sample means depending on the selected value of z. This expression can be rewritten as an inequality relation that

$$\mu - z\sigma_{\bar{x}} \le \bar{x} \le \mu + z\sigma_{\bar{x}}, \tag{9.1}$$

which is held to be true a certain percentage of the time and which implies that the sample mean will be in the interval formed by adding and subtracting a certain number of standard deviations to the mean value of the distribution. This inequality can be transferred to the equivalent inequality

$$\bar{x} - z\sigma_{\bar{x}} \le \mu \le \bar{x} + z\sigma_{\bar{x}}, \tag{9.2}$$

and if Equation 9.1 was true, say, 95 percent of the time ($z = 1.96$), then Equation 9.2 is also true 95 percent of the time. *When we make an inference on the basis of a single sample mean, we make use of Equation 9.2.*

It is important to note that Equation 9.2 says *nothing about the interval constructed from a particular sample as including the population mean.* Rather, the interval addresses the *sampling procedure.* The interval around a single sample mean may or may not contain the true population mean. Our confidence in our inference rests on the property that 95 percent of all the intervals we could construct under that sampling plan

Figure 9.4

**Distribution of Sample Means for Samples of
Various Sizes and Different Population Distributions**

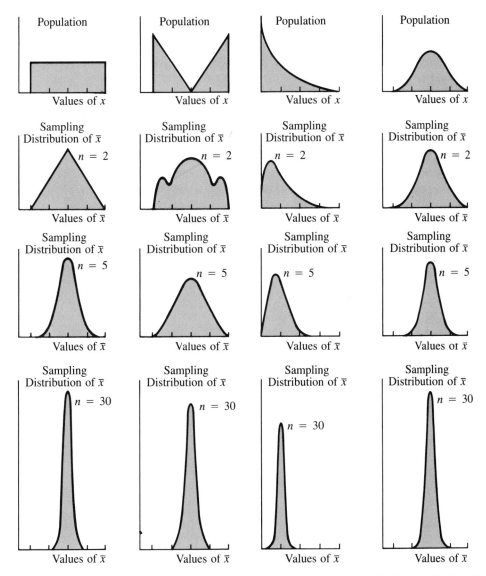

Source: Reproduced with permission from Ernest Kurnow, Gerald J. Glasser, and Frederick R. Ottman, *Statistics for Business Decisions* (Homewood, Ill.: Richard D. Irwin, Inc., © 1959), pp. 182–183.

would contain the true value. We trust or hope that our sample is one of those 95 out of 100 that does (when we are 95 percent confident) include the true value.[12]

To illustrate this important point, suppose for the moment that the distribution of sample means of Size $n = 2$ for our hypothetical example was normal. Suppose further that by chance the sampling process yielded sample AB, in which the mean income was 5,800. The 95 percent confidence interval ($z = 1.96$) using Equation 9.2 would then be ($\sigma_{\bar{x}} = \sqrt{\sigma_{\bar{x}}^2} = \sqrt{2,520,000} = 1,587$):

$$5,800 - 1.96(1,587) \leq \mu \leq 5,800 + 1.96(1,587) = 2,689 \leq \mu \leq 8,911,$$

and the confidence interval would not include the true, in this case known, population value, and an inferential error would have been made. The example illustrates that after the sample has been drawn, it is a matter of fact whether or not the particular interval estimate covers the universe mean. Table 9.4 illustrates the outcome pictorially for the first 10 out of the possible 190 samples that could be drawn under the specified sampling plan. Note that only 7 of the 10 intervals contain the true population mean. Confidence in the estimate arises because of the *procedure,* therefore, and not because of a particular estimate. The procedure suggests that with, say, a 95 percent confidence interval, if 100 samples were to be drawn and the sample mean and the confidence interval computed for each, 95 of the constructed intervals would include the true population value. The accuracy of a specific sample is evaluated only by reference to the procedure by which the sample was obtained. A sampling plan that is representative does not guarantee that a particular sample is representative. Statistical inference procedures rest on the representativeness of the sampling plan, and this is why probability samples are so critical to those procedures. Probability samples allow an estimate of the **precision** of the results in terms of how closely the estimates will tend to cluster around the true value. The greater the standard error of the statistic, the more variable the estimates and the less precise the procedure.

If it disturbs you that the confidence level applies to the procedure and not a particular sample result, you can take refuge in the fact that you can control the level of confidence with which the population value is estimated. Thus, if you do not wish to take the risk that you might have 1 of the 5 sample intervals in 100 that does not contain the population value, you might employ a 99 percent confidence interval, in which the risk is that only 1 in 100 sample intervals will not contain the population mean. Further, if you are willing to increase the size of the sample, you can increase your confidence

---

[12]The argument expressed here on the interpretation of a confidence interval is the traditional or classical statistics argument, which holds that the parameter being estimated is fixed in value. Thus, it is meaningless to interpret the statement probabilistically, since a given interval will or will not contain the population parameter. Bayesian analysts, though, adopt a different perspective. Bayesians hold that it is legitimate to assign personal probabilities to the states of nature, values of the unknown parameter in this case. One can then combine these judgments with sample information to produce posterior probabilities regarding the value of the unknown parameter. The confidence interval formed for a population mean is the same under the two approaches if one adopts the Bayesian assumption that the initial probabilities for each of the possible values of the unknown parameter are equal. The difference in perspectives, though, allows Bayesian analysts to interpret the resulting interval as a probability statement; that is, there is a 95 percent probability that the interval $\bar{x} \pm z\sigma_{\bar{x}}$ contains the true population mean. This interpretation tends to be much more satisfying to decision makers. For a discussion of the difference in the two perspectives, see Frankel, "Sampling Theory."

Table 9.4
Confidence Intervals for First Ten Samples Assuming the
Distribution of Sample Means was Normal

Sample Number	Sample Identity	Mean	Confidence Interval Lower Limit	Confidence Interval Upper Limit	Pictorial True $\mu = 9,400$
1	AB	5,800	2,689	8,911	
2	AC	6,000	2,889	9,111	
3	AD	6,200	3,089	9,311	
4	AE	6,400	3,289	9,511	
5	AF	6,600	3,489	9,711	
6	AG	6,800	3,689	9,911	
7	AH	7,000	3,889	10,111	
8	AI	7,200	4,089	10,311	
9	AJ	7,400	4,289	10,511	
10	AK	7,600	4,489	10,711	

and at the same time maintain the precision with which the population value is estimated. This will be explored more fully in the next chapter.

Population Variance Unknown   There is one other perhaps disturbing ingredient in our procedure. The confidence interval estimate made use of three values: $\bar{x}$, z, and $\sigma_{\bar{x}}$. Now $\bar{x}$ is computed from the selected sample, and z is specified to produce the desired level of confidence. But what about $\sigma_{\bar{x}}$? It is equal to $\sigma_{\bar{x}} = \sigma/\sqrt{n}$, and thus in order to calculate it, we need to know the standard deviation of the variable in the population. What do we do if σ is unknown? There is no problem for two reasons. First, variation typically changes much more slowly than level for most variables of interest in marketing. Thus, if the study is a repeat, we can use the previously discovered value for σ. Second, once the sample is selected and the information gathered, we can calculate the sample variance to estimate the population variance. The unbiased sample variance $\hat{s}^2$ is calculated as

$$\hat{s}^2 = \frac{\sum_{i=1}^{n} (X_i - \bar{x})^2}{n - 1},$$

where $\bar{x}$ is the sample mean and n the sample size.[13] To compute the sample variance, then, we first calculate the sample mean. We then calculate the differences between

---

[13]Division by n, the sample size, is more intuitive since it produces the normal conception of average, which here is the average of the deviations squared. However, the sample variance, when defined as

$$s^2 = \frac{\sum_{i=1}^{n} (X_i - \bar{x})^2}{n}$$

produces a biased estimate of the population variance. Thus it is customary to use either the unbiased definition of the sample variance or to generate an estimate of σ^2, denoted by $\hat{\sigma}^2$, by the formula $\hat{\sigma}^2 = [n/(n - 1)]s^2$.

each of our sample values and the sample mean, square them, sum them, and divide the sum by one less than the number of sample observations. The sample variance not only provides an estimate of the population variance, but it can also be used to secure an estimate of the standard error of the mean. When the population variance, σ^2 is known, the standard error of the mean, $\sigma_{\bar{x}}$, is also known since $\sigma_{\bar{x}} = \dfrac{\sigma}{\sqrt{n}}$. When the population variance is unknown, the standard error of the mean can only be estimated. The estimate is given by $s_{\bar{x}}$, which equals $\hat{s}/\sqrt{n}$. The estimate calculation parallels that for the true value, with the sample standard deviation substituted for the population standard deviation. Thus if we draw sample AB, with mean of 5,800,

$$\hat{s}^2 = \frac{(5,600 - 5,800)^2 + (6,000 - 5,800)^2}{1} = 80,000,$$

and thus $\hat{s} = 283$ and $s_{\bar{x}} = \hat{s}/\sqrt{n} = 283/\sqrt{2} = 200$ and the 95 percent confidence interval is now

$$5,800 - 1.96(200) \leq \mu \leq 5,800 + 1.96(200) = 5,408 \leq \mu \leq 6,192,$$

which is somewhat smaller than before.[14]

Drawing the Simple Random Sample Although it was useful for illustrating the concepts "derived population" and "sampling distribution," the selection of sample elements from an urn containing all the population elements is not particularly recommended because of its great potential for bias. It is unlikely that the disks would be exactly uniform in size or feel, and slight differences here could affect the likelihood that any single element would be drawn. The national draft during the Vietnam war using a lottery serves as an example. Draft priorities were determined by drawing disks with birth dates stamped on them from a large container in full view of a TV audience. Unfortunately, the dates of the year had initially been poured into the bowl systematically, January first and December last. Although the bowl was then stirred vigorously, December dates tended to be chosen first and January dates last. The procedure was later revised to produce a more random selection process.

The preferred way of drawing a simple random sample is through the use of a table of random numbers. Using a random number table involves the following sequence of steps. First, the elements of parent population would be numbered serially from 1 to N; for the hypothetical population, the element A would be numbered 1, B as 2, and so on. Next, the numbers in the table would be treated so as to have the same number of digits as N. With $N = 20$, two-digit numbers would be used; if N was between 100 and 999, three-digit numbers would be required, and so on. Third, a starting point would be determined randomly. We might simply open the tables to some arbitrary place and point to a position on the page with our eyes closed. Since the numbers in a random number table are in fact random, that is, without order, it makes little difference

---

[14]The t distribution would strictly be used when σ was unknown. We shall say more about this in Chapter 14.

where we begin.[15] Finally, we would proceed in some arbitrary direction, for example, up, down, or across, and would select those elements for the sample for which there is a match of serial number and random number.

To illustrate, consider the partial list of random numbers contained in Table 9.5. Since $N = 20$, we need work with only two digits, and therefore we can use the entries in Table 9.5 as is, instead of having to combine columns to produce numbers covering the range of serial numbers. Suppose we had previously decided to read down and that our arbitrary start indicated the eleventh row, fourth column, specifically the number 77. This number is too high and would be discarded. The next two numbers would also be discarded, but the fourth entry 02 would be used, since 2 corresponds to one of the serial numbers in the list, Element B. The next five numbers would also be passed over as too large, whereas the number 05 would designate the inclusion of Element E. Elements B and E would thus represent the sample of two from whom we would seek information on income.

You should note that a simple random sample requires a serial numbered list of population elements. This means that the identity of each member of the population must be known. For some populations this is no problem, for example, if the study is to be conducted among *Fortune* magazine's list of the 500 largest corporations in the United States. The list is readily available, and a simple random sample of these firms could be easily selected. For many other populations of interest, the list of universe elements is much harder to come by (for example, all families living in a particular city), and applied researchers often resort to other sampling schemes.

Stratified Sampling

A **stratified sample** is a probability sample that is distinguished by the following two-step procedure:

1. The parent population is divided into mutually exclusive and exhaustive subsets.
2. A simple random sample of elements is chosen independently from each group or subset.

Note these features. The defining characteristics say nothing about the criterion or criteria that may be used to separate the universe elements into subsets. Admittedly, they will make a difference with respect to the advantages obtained in stratified sampling, but the criteria do not determine whether or not a stratified sample has been drawn. As long as the sample reflects the two-stage process, it is a stratified sample. This argument will be of assistance later when distinguishing cluster samples from stratified samples.

The subsets into which the universe elements are divided are called *strata* or *sub-populations*. Note that the division is mutually exclusive and exhaustive. This means that every population element must be assigned to one and only one stratum and that no

---

[15]There are two major errors to avoid when using random number tables: (1) starting at a given place because one knows the distribution of numbers at that place; and (2) discarding a sample because it does not "look right" in some sense and to continue using random numbers until a "likely looking" sample is selected. Sudman, "Applied Sampling," p. 165.

Table 9.5

Abridged List of Random Numbers

10 09 73 25 33	76 52 01 35 86	34 67 35 48 76	80 95 90 91 17	39 29 27 49 45
37 54 20 48 05	64 89 47 42 96	24 80 52 40 37	20 63 61 04 02	00 82 29 16 65
08 42 26 89 53	19 64 50 93 03	23 20 90 25 60	15 95 33 47 64	35 08 03 36 06
99 01 90 25 29	09 37 67 07 15	38 31 13 11 65	88 67 67 43 97	04 43 62 76 59
12 80 79 99 70	80 15 73 61 47	64 03 23 66 53	98 95 11 68 77	12 17 17 68 33
66 06 57 47 17	34 07 27 68 50	36 69 73 61 70	65 81 33 98 85	11 19 92 91 70
31 06 01 08 05	45 57 18 24 06	35 30 34 26 14	86 79 90 74 39	23 40 30 97 32
85 26 97 76 02	02 05 16 56 92	68 66 57 48 18	73 05 38 52 47	18 62 38 85 79
63 57 33 21 35	05 32 54 70 48	90 55 35 75 48	28 46 82 87 09	83 49 12 56 24
73 79 64 57 53	03 52 96 47 78	35 80 83 42 82	60 93 52 03 44	35 27 38 84 35
98 52 01 77 67	14 90 56 86 07	22 10 94 05 58	60 97 09 34 33	50 50 07 39 98
11 80 50 54 31	39 80 82 77 32	50 72 56 82 48	29 40 52 42 01	52 77 56 78 51
83 45 29 96 34	06 28 89 80 83	13 74 67 00 78	18 47 54 06 10	68 71 17 78 17
88 68 54 02 00	86 50 75 84 01	36 76 66 79 51	90 36 47 64 93	29 60 91 10 62
99 59 46 73 48	87 51 76 49 69	91 82 60 89 28	93 78 56 13 68	23 47 83 41 13
65 48 11 76 74	17 46 85 09 50	58 04 77 69 74	73 03 95 71 86	40 21 81 65 44
80 12 43 56 35	17 72 70 80 15	45 31 82 23 74	21 11 57 82 53	14 38 55 37 63
74 35 09 98 17	77 40 27 72 14	43 23 60 02 10	45 52 16 42 37	96 28 60 26 55
69 91 62 68 03	66 25 22 91 48	36 93 68 72 03	76 62 11 39 90	94 40 05 64 18
09 89 32 05 05	14 22 56 85 14	46 42 75 67 88	96 29 77 88 22	54 38 21 45 98
91 49 91 45 23	68 47 92 76 86	46 16 28 35 54	94 75 08 99 23	37 08 92 00 48
80 33 69 45 98	26 94 03 68 58	70 29 73 41 35	53 14 03 33 40	42 05 08 23 41
44 10 48 19 49	85 15 74 79 54	32 97 92 65 75	57 60 04 08 81	22 22 20 64 13
12 55 07 37 42	11 10 00 20 40	12 86 07 46 97	96 64 48 94 39	28 70 72 58 15

Source: This table is reproduced from page 1 of The Rand Corporation, *A Million Random Digits with 100,000 Normal Deviates* (New York: The Free Press, 1955). Copyright © 1955 and 1983 by The Rand Corporation. Used by permission.

population elements are omitted in the assignment procedure. To illustrate the process, suppose we were to divide our hypothetical population of Table 9.1 into two strata on the basis of educational level. In particular, suppose all those with a high school education or less were to be considered as forming one stratum and those with more than a high school education as forming another. Table 9.6 displays the results of this stratification procedure; Elements A through J form what is labeled the *first stratum* and Elements K through T form the *second stratum*. There is no magic in the choice of two strata. The parent population can be divided into any number of strata. Two were chosen for purposes of convenience in illustrating the technique.

Stage 2 in the process then requires that a simple random sample be drawn independently from *each* stratum. Suppose we again work with samples of Size 2, formed this time by selecting one element from each stratum. The number of elements from each stratum do not have to be equal, but again the assumption is made simply for exposition purposes. The procedure that would be used to select two elements for the stratified sample would now parallel that for the simple random sample. Within each stratum, the population elements would be serially numbered from 1 to 10. A table of random numbers would be consulted. The first number encountered between 1 and 10 would desig-

Table 9.5

Abridged List of Random Numbers *continued*

63 60 64 93 29	16 50 53 44 84	40 21 95 25 63	43 65 17 70 82	07 20 73 17 90
61 19 69 04 46	26 45 74 77 74	51 92 43 37 29	65 39 45 95 93	42 58 26 05 27
15 47 44 52 66	95 27 07 99 53	59 36 78 38 48	82 39 61 01 18	33 21 15 94 66
94 55 72 85 73	67 89 75 43 87	54 62 24 44 31	91 19 04 25 92	92 92 74 59 73
42 48 11 62 13	97 34 40 87 21	16 86 84 87 67	03 07 11 20 59	25 70 14 66 70
23 52 37 83 17	73 20 88 98 37	68 93 59 14 16	26 25 22 96 63	05 52 28 25 62
04 49 35 24 94	75 24 63 38 24	45 86 25 10 25	61 96 27 93 35	65 33 71 24 72
00 54 99 76 54	64 05 18 81 59	96 11 96 38 96	54 69 28 23 91	23 28 72 95 29
35 96 31 53 07	26 89 80 93 54	33 35 13 54 62	77 97 45 00 24	90 10 33 93 33
59 80 80 83 91	45 42 72 68 42	83 60 94 97 00	13 02 12 48 92	78 56 52 01 06
46 05 88 52 36	01 39 09 22 86	77 28 14 40 77	93 91 08 36 47	70 61 74 29 41
32 17 90 05 97	87 37 92 52 41	05 56 70 70 07	86 74 31 71 57	85 39 41 18 38
69 23 46 14 06	20 11 74 52 04	15 95 66 00 00	18 74 39 24 23	97 11 89 63 38
19 56 54 14 30	01 75 87 53 79	40 41 92 15 85	66 67 43 68 06	84 96 28 52 07
45 15 51 49 38	19 47 60 72 46	43 66 79 45 43	59 04 79 00 33	20 82 66 95 41
94 86 43 19 94	36 16 81 08 51	34 88 88 15 53	01 54 03 54 56	05 01 45 11 76
98 08 62 48 26	45 24 02 84 04	44 99 90 88 96	39 09 47 34 07	35 44 13 18 80
33 18 51 62 32	41 94 15 09 49	89 43 54 85 81	88 69 54 19 94	37 54 87 30 43
80 95 10 04 06	96 38 27 07 74	20 15 12 33 87	25 01 62 52 98	94 62 46 11 71
79 75 24 91 40	71 96 12 82 96	69 86 10 25 91	74 85 22 05 39	00 38 75 95 79
18 63 33 25 37	98 14 50 65 71	31 01 02 46 74	05 45 56 14 27	77 93 89 19 36
74 02 94 39 02	77 55 73 22 70	97 79 01 71 19	52 52 75 80 21	80 81 45 17 48
54 17 84 56 11	80 99 33 71 43	05 33 51 29 69	56 12 71 92 55	36 04 09 03 24
11 66 44 98 83	52 07 98 48 27	59 38 17 15 39	09 97 33 34 40	88 46 12 33 56
48 32 47 79 28	31 24 96 47 10	02 29 53 68 70	32 30 75 75 46	15 02 00 99 94
69 07 49 41 38	87 63 79 19 76	35 58 40 44 01	10 51 82 16 15	01 84 87 69 38

Table 9.6

Stratification of Hypothetical Population by Education

Stratum I Elements	Stratum II Elements
A	K
B	L
C	M
D	N
E	O
F	P
G	Q
H	R
I	S
J	T

Table 9.7
Derived Population of All Possible Samples of Size 2 with Stratified Sampling

k	Sample Identity	Mean	k	Sample Identity	Mean	k	Sample Identity	Mean	k	Sample Identity	Mean
1	AK	7,600	26	CP	9,000	51	FK	8,600	76	HP	10,000
2	AL	7,800	27	CQ	9,200	52	FL	8,800	77	HQ	10,200
3	AM	8,000	28	CR	9,400	53	FM	9,000	78	HR	10,400
4	AN	8,200	29	CS	9,600	54	FN	9,200	79	HS	10,600
5	AO	8,400	30	CT	9,800	55	FO	9,400	80	HT	10,800
6	AP	8,600	31	DK	8,200	56	FP	9,600	81	IK	9,200
7	AQ	8,800	32	DL	8,400	57	FQ	9,800	82	IL	9,400
8	AR	9,000	33	DM	8,600	58	FR	10,000	83	IM	9,600
9	AS	9,200	34	DN	8,800	59	FS	10,200	84	IN	9,800
10	AT	9,400	35	DO	9,000	60	FT	10,400	85	IO	10,000
11	BK	7,800	36	DP	9,200	61	GK	8,800	86	IP	10,200
12	BL	8,000	37	DQ	9,400	62	GL	9,000	87	IQ	10,400
13	BM	8,200	38	DR	9,600	63	GM	9,200	88	IR	10,600
14	BN	8,400	39	DS	9,800	64	GN	9,400	89	IS	10,800
15	BO	8,600	40	DT	10,000	65	GO	9,600	90	IT	11,000
16	BP	8,800	41	EK	8,400	66	GP	9,800	91	JK	9,400
17	BQ	9,000	42	EL	8,600	67	GQ	10,000	92	JL	9,600
18	BR	9,200	43	EM	8,800	68	GR	10,200	93	JM	9,800
19	BS	9,400	44	EN	9,000	69	GS	10,400	94	JN	10,000
20	BT	9,600	45	EO	9,200	70	GT	10,600	95	JO	10,200
21	CK	8,000	46	EP	9,400	71	HK	9,000	96	JP	10,400
22	CL	8,200	47	EQ	9,600	72	HL	9,200	97	JQ	10,600
23	CM	8,400	48	ER	9,800	73	HM	9,400	98	JR	10,800
24	CN	8,600	49	ES	10,000	74	HN	9,600	99	JS	11,000
25	CO	8,800	50	ET	10,200	75	HO	9,800	100	JT	11,200

nate the element from the first stratum. The element from the second stratum could be selected after another independent start or by continuing from the first randomly determined start. In either case it would again be designated by the first encounter with a number between 1 and 10.

Derived Population   Although only one sample of Size 2 will in fact be selected, let us look briefly at the derived population of all possible samples of Size 2 that could be selected under this sampling plan. This derived population, along with the mean of each sample, is displayed in Table 9.7.

Note first that every possible combination of sample elements is no longer a possibility, since every combination of two elements from the same stratum is precluded. There are now only 100 possible sample combinations of elements, whereas with simple random sampling there were 190 possible combinations. In this sense, stratified sam-

Table 9.8
Classification of Sample Means by Size with Stratified Sampling

Sample Mean	Number of Samples
7,300 to 7,800	3
7,900 to 8,400	12
8,500 to 9,000	21
9,100 to 9,600	28
9,700 to 10,200	21
10,300 to 10,800	12
10,900 to 11,400	3

pling is always more restrictive than simple random sampling. Note further that every element has an equal chance of being included in the sample—1 in 10—since each can be the single element selected from the stratum. This explains why we specified an additional requirement to define a simple random sample. Although simple random samples provide each element an equal chance of selection, other techniques can also. Thus equal probability of selection is a necessary but not a sufficient condition for simple random sampling; in addition, each combination of n elements must be a sample possibility and as likely to occur as any other combination of n elements.

Sampling Distribution   Table 9.8 contains the classification of sample means by size, and Figure 9.5 displays the plot of this sample statistic. Note that in relation to Figure 9.3 for simple random sampling, stratified sampling can produce a more concentrated distribution of estimates. This suggests one reason why we might choose a stratified sample; stratified samples can produce sample statistics that are more precise or that have smaller error due to sampling than simple random samples. With education as a stratification variable, there is a marked reduction in the number of sample means that deviate widely from the population mean.

A second reason for drawing a stratified sample is that stratification allows the investigation of the characteristic of interest for particular subgroups. Thus, by stratifying, one is able to guarantee representation of those with a high school education or less and those with more than a high school education. This can be extremely important when sampling from populations with rare segments. If a manufacturer of diamond rings is conducting a study of sales of the product by social class, for example, it is likely that unless special precautions are taken, the upper class will not be represented at all or will be represented by so few cases as to defy conclusion, since it is estimated to represent only 3 percent of the total population. Yet this can be an extremely important segment to the ring manufacturer. It is often true of many populations of interest in marketing that a small subset will account for a large proportion of the behavior of interest, for example, consumption of the product. It then becomes imperative that this subgroup be adequately represented in the sample. Stratified sampling is one way of ensuring adequate representation from each subgroup of interest.

Figure 9.5
Distribution of Sample Means with Stratified Sampling

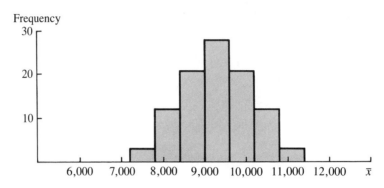

Confidence Interval Estimate   In establishing a confidence interval with a simple random sample, we saw that we needed three things to complete the confidence interval
specifications given by $\bar{x} - zs_{\bar{x}} \le \mu \le \bar{x} + zs_{\bar{x}}$:

1.   the degree of confidence desired so that a z value can be selected;
2.   a point estimate of the population mean given by the sample mean $\bar{x}$;
3.   an estimate of the amount of sampling error associated with the sample mean,
      which was given by $s_{\bar{x}} = \hat{s}/\sqrt{n}$ when the population variance was unknown.

    The same three quantities are required for making inferences with a stratified sample.
The only difference in the procedure occurs in the way Items 2 and 3 are generated.
With stratified sampling, the sample estimate of the population mean and the standard
error of estimate associated with this statistic are determined by "appropriately weighting" the individual strata results.
    What are the appropriate weights? They are related to the stratum population size in
comparison to the total population size. Consider, for example, because of the need to
make one specific point that a sample of Size 2 was to be selected from each stratum,
producing a total sample of Size 4. In particular, suppose that Elements B and E were
randomly selected from the first stratum and Elements N and S from the second stratum.
Figure 9.6 contains the sample means, sample variances, and estimated standard errors
of estimates for each stratum. *These quantities are calculated for each stratum in exactly
the same way as they were calculated for the sample as a whole with simple random
sampling.*
    Consider first the combination of strata sample means to produce a point estimate of
the population mean. The weights here are the relative proportions of the population in
each of the strata, that is,

Figure 9.6
Sample Means, Sample Variances, and Estimated Standard Errors of Estimate
for Each Stratum

	Stratum I			*Stratum II*	
	Element	*Income*		*Element*	*Income*
	B	6,000		N	10,800
	E	7,200		S	12,800

Mean:

$$\bar{x}_1 = \frac{\sum_{i=1}^{n_1} X_i}{n_1} = \frac{6,000 + 7,200}{2} \qquad\qquad \bar{x}_2 = \frac{\sum_{i=1}^{n_2} X_i}{n_2} = \frac{10,800 + 12,800}{2}$$

$$= 6,600 \qquad\qquad\qquad\qquad\qquad = 11,800$$

Variance:

$$\hat{s}_1^2 = \frac{\sum_{i=1}^{n_1} (X_i - \bar{x}_1)^2}{n_1 - 1} \qquad\qquad \hat{s}_2^2 = \frac{\sum_{i=1}^{n_2} (X_i - \bar{x}_2)^2}{n_2 - 1}$$

$$= \frac{(6,000 - 6,600)^2 + (7,200 - 6,600)^2}{2 - 1} \qquad = \frac{(10,800 - 11,800)^2 + (12,800 - 11,800)^2}{2 - 1}$$

$$= 720,000 \qquad\qquad\qquad\qquad = 2,000,000$$

Standard error of estimate:

$$s_{\bar{x}_1} = \frac{\hat{s}_1}{\sqrt{n_1}} = \frac{\sqrt{720,000}}{\sqrt{2}} \qquad\qquad s_{\bar{x}_2} = \frac{\hat{s}_2}{\sqrt{n_2}} = \frac{\sqrt{2,000,000}}{\sqrt{2}}$$

$$= 600 \qquad\qquad\qquad\qquad\qquad = 1,000$$

Variance of estimate:

$$s_{\bar{x}_1}^2 = 360,000 \qquad\qquad\qquad s_{\bar{x}_2}^2 = 1,000,000$$

$$\bar{x}_{st} = \sum_{h=1}^{L} \frac{N_h}{N} \bar{x}_h \qquad\qquad\qquad (9.3)$$

where

N_h is the number of elements in the population in stratum h,

N is the total size of the population,

$\bar{x}_h$ is the sample mean for stratum h,

$\bar{x}_{st}$ is the sample mean for a stratified sample,

and where summation is across all L strata. In the example of Figure 9.6, $L = 2$, there are 10 elements in each stratum, 20 in all, and the overall point estimate of the population mean is

$$\bar{x}_{st} = \frac{N_1}{N}\bar{x}_1 + \frac{N_2}{N}\bar{x}_2 = \frac{10}{20}(6,600) + \frac{10}{20}(11,800) = 9,200.$$

The combined standard error of estimate also employs the relative sizes of the strata in the population; however, it is calculated using the relative proportions squared because the linear combination holds with respect to *variances* and *not* standard deviations. That is, one must compute the variance of the overall estimate and take the square root. The formula for the variance of the estimate is

$$s_{\bar{x}_{st}}^2 = \sum_{h=1}^{L} \left(\frac{N_h}{N}\right)^2 s_{\bar{x}_h}^2, \tag{9.4}$$

and for the example

$$s_{\bar{x}_{st}}^2 = \left(\frac{N_1}{N}\right)^2 s_{\bar{x}_1}^2 + \left(\frac{N_2}{N}\right)^2 s_{\bar{x}_2}^2 = \left(\frac{10}{20}\right)^2 (360,000) + \left(\frac{10}{20}\right)^2 (1,000,000)$$

$$= 90,000 + 250,000 = 340,000,$$

so that

$$s_{\bar{x}_{st}} = \sqrt{340,000} = 583.$$

The 95 percent confidence interval for this sample would then be

$$\bar{x}_{st} - z s_{\bar{x}_{st}} \leq \mu \leq \bar{x}_{st} + z s_{\bar{x}_{st}}$$

$$9,200 - 1.96(583) \leq \mu \leq 9,200 + 1.96(583)$$

$$8,057 \leq \mu \leq 10,343.$$

This interval is interpreted as before. The true mean may or may not be in the interval, but since 95 of 100 intervals constructed by this process will contain the true mean, we are 95 percent confident that the true population mean income is between $8,057 and $10,343.[16]

Increased Precision of Stratified Samples   We mentioned previously that one of the reasons one might choose a stratified sample is that such samples offer an opportunity for reducing sampling error or increasing precision. When estimating a mean, sampling

---

[16]Note that we are again assuming the normal distribution applies in making this inference. While this assumption is not strictly correct in this instance because of the size of the sample taken from each stratum, we are making it to allow more direct comparison with the interval constructed using simple random sampling. In most situations the normal distribution would hold because the Central-Limit Theorem also applies to the individual strata means, and the linear combination of these means produces a normally distributed $\bar{x}_{st}$.

error is given by the size of $s_{\bar{x}}$; the smaller $s_{\bar{x}}$, the less the sampling error and the more precise the estimate as indicated by the narrower confidence interval associated with a specified degree of confidence.

Consider Equation 9.4 again. The total size of the population and the population within each stratum are fixed. The only way, therefore, for total sampling error to be reduced is for the variance of the estimate within each stratum to be made smaller. Now, the variance of the estimate by strata, in turn, depends on the variability of the characteristic within the strata since $s^2_{\bar{x}_h} = \hat{s}_h^2/n_h$, where $\hat{s}_h^2$ is the sample variance within the hth stratum and n_h is the size of the sample selected from the hth stratum. Thus, the estimate of the mean can be made more precise to the extent that the population can be partitioned so that there is little variability within each stratum, that is, to the extent the strata can be made internally homogeneous.

A characteristic of interest will display a certain amount of variation in the population. The investigator can do nothing about this total variation because it is a fixed characteristic of the population. But he or she can do something when dividing the elements of the population into strata so as to increase the precision with which the average value of the characteristic can be estimated. Specifically, the investigator should divide the population into strata so that the elements within any given stratum are as similar in value as possible and the values between any two strata are as disparate as possible. In the limit, if the investigator is successful in partitioning the population so that the elements in each stratum are exactly equal, there will be no error associated with the estimate of the population mean. That is right! The population mean could then be estimated without error because the *variability that exists between strata does not enter into the calculation of the standard error of estimate with stratified sampling.*

One can see this readily in a simple case with a limited number of values. Suppose that in a population of 1,000 elements, 200 had the value 5, 300 had the value 10, and 500 had the value 20. Now, the mean of this population $\mu = 14$ and the variance $\sigma^2 = 39$. If a simple random sample of Size $n = 3$ was to be employed to estimate this mean, then the standard error of estimate is

$$\sigma_{\bar{x}} = \frac{\sigma}{\sqrt{n}} = \frac{\sqrt{39}}{\sqrt{3}} = 3.61,$$

and the width of confidence interval would be $\pm z$ times this value 3.61. Suppose, on the other hand, a researcher employed a stratified sample and was successful in partitioning the total population so that all the elements with a value of 5 on the characteristic were in one stratum, those with the value of 10 in the second stratum, and those with the value 20 in the third stratum. To generate a completely precise description of the mean of each stratum, the researcher would then only need to take a sample of one from each stratum. Further, when the investigator combined these individual results into a global estimate of the overall mean, the standard error of the estimate would be zero, since each stratum standard error of estimate is zero. The population mean value would be determined exactly.

Bases for Stratification The fact that variation among strata does not enter into the calculation of the standard error of estimate suggests two things. First, it indicates the kinds of criteria that should be used to partition the population. The values assumed by the characteristic will be unknown, for if they were known, there would be no need to take a sample to estimate their mean level. What the investigator attempts to do, therefore, is to partition the population according to one or more criteria that are expected to be related to the characteristic of interest. Thus it was no accident that in the hypothetical example, education was employed to divide the population elements into strata. As Table 9.1 indicates, there is a relationship between education level and income level: the more years of school, the higher the income. Newspaper subscriptions, on the other hand, would have made a poor variable for partitioning the population into segments since there is almost no relation between the paper to which a person subscribes and the individual's income. Whether one selects a ''good'' or a ''bad'' variable for partitioning the population does not affect whether a stratified sample is selected or not. It is significant in determining whether a good or poor sample is selected, but the two features defining a stratified sample are still (1) the partitioning of the population into subgroups and (2) the random selection of elements from each subgroup.

Second, the calculation of the standard error of estimate provides some clue as to the number of strata that should be employed. Since the standard error of estimate only depends on variability within strata, the various strata should be made as homogeneous as possible. One way of doing this is to employ a great many very small strata. There are practical limits, though, to the number of strata that should be and are used in actual research studies. First, the creation of additional strata is often expensive in terms of sample design, data collection, and analysis. Second, there is an upper limit to the amount of variation that can be accounted for by any practical stratification. Regardless of the criteria by which the population is partitioned, a certain amount of variation is likely to remain unaccounted for, and thus the additional strata will serve no productive purpose.

Proportionate and Disproportionate Stratified Sampling   Whether one chooses a stratified sample over a simple random sample depends in part on the trade-off between cost and precision. Although stratified samples typically produce more precise estimates, they also usually cost more than simple random samples. If the decision is made in favor of a stratified sample, the researcher must still decide whether to select a proportionate stratified sample or a disproportionate stratified sample.

With a **proportionate stratified sample,** the number of observations in the total sample is allocated among the strata in proportion to the *relative* number of elements in each stratum in the population. A stratum containing one-fifth of all the population elements would account for one-fifth of the total sample observations and so on. Proportionate sampling was employed in the example since each stratum contained one-half of the population, and thus they were sampled equally.

One advantage of proportionate allocation is that the investigator only needs to know the relative sizes of each stratum in order to determine the number of sample observations to select from each stratum with a given sample size.

There is an alternative allocation scheme, however, that can produce still more efficient estimates—disproportionate stratified sampling. **Disproportionate stratified sampling** involves balancing the two criteria of strata size and strata variability. With a fixed sample size, strata exhibiting more variability are sampled more than proportionately to their relative size. Conversely, those strata that are very homogeneous are sampled less than proportionately.

While a full discussion of how the sample size for each stratum should be determined would take us too far afield and would be much too technical for our purpose, some feel for the rationale behind disproportionate sampling is useful. Consider at the extreme a stratum with zero variability. Since all the elements are indentical in value, a single observation tells all. On the other hand, a stratum that is characterized by great variability will require a large number of observations to produce a precise estimate of the stratum mean (recall $s_{\bar{x}_h}^2 = \hat{s}_h^2/n_h$). One can expect greater precision when the various strata are sampled proportionate to the relative variability of the characteristic under study rather than proportionate to their relative size in the population.

A disproportionate stratified sample requires more knowledge about the population of interest than does a proportionate stratified sample. To sample the strata in relation to their variability, one needs knowledge of relative variability. Sampling theory is a peculiar phenomenon in that knowledge begets more knowledge. Disproportionate sampling can produce more efficient estimates than proportionate sampling, but the former method also requires that some estimate of the relative variation within strata be known. One can sometimes anticipate the relative homogeneity likely to exist within a stratum on the basis of past studies and experience. Sometimes the investigator may have to rely on logic and intuition in establishing sample sizes for each stratum. For example, it might reasonably be expected that large retail stores would show greater variation in sales of some product than would small stores. In a disproportionate sample, the large stores would be sampled more heavily as, for instance, they are in the Nielsen Retail Index.

Stratified versus Quota Samples   Stratified samples are sometimes confused with quota samples by the inexperienced researcher. There are similarities. Both involve the division of the population into segments and the selection of elements from each segment. There is one key difference, though. <u>Sample elements are selected probabilistically with stratified samples, whereas they are selected judgmentally in quota samples.</u> This has important implications. Because the sample elements are selected probabilistically, stratified samples allow the establishment of the sampling distribution of the statistic in question, which in turn allows confidence interval judgments. Quota samples allow no objective assessment of the degree of sampling error and thus preclude confidence interval estimates and statistical tests of significance.

Cluster Sampling

Cluster sampling involves the following steps. First, the parent population is divided into mutually exclusive and exhaustive subsets. Second, a random sample of the subsets is selected. If the investigator then uses all of the population elements in the selected subsets for the sample, the procedure is one-stage cluster sampling. If, on the other hand, a sample of elements is selected probabilistically from the selected subsets, the procedure is known as two-stage cluster sampling.

Note the similarities and differences between cluster sampling and stratified sampling. Both involve the division of the population into mutually exclusive and exhaustive subgroups, though the criteria used are different. The criteria for dividing the population are not the key in differentiating the techniques. The key ingredient that distinguishes the procedures is that with stratified sampling, a sample of elements is selected *from each subgroup*. With cluster sampling, one chooses a *sample of subgroups*.

Because one chooses a sample of subgroups with cluster sampling, it is desirable that each subgroup be a small scale model of the population. At the extreme, if the distribution of the characteristic in each subgroup exactly parallels that for the population, then one subgroup can tell all. Thus in cluster sampling, the subgroups ideally should be formed to be as heterogeneous as possible. In the hypothetical example, newspaper subscription would be a good basis for forming subgroups for a cluster sample. If all those subscribing to Paper X were considered to form one subgroup and all those subscribing to Paper Y a second subgroup, then one could be relatively safe in randomly selecting either subgroup to estimate the mean income in the population. While the distribution of incomes within each subgroup is not exactly the same as it is in the population, the range of incomes is such that there would be only a slight error if one were to estimate the mean income and variance of incomes of the population with the elements from either subset.

Admittedly, in practice clusters are not always formed to be as heterogeneous as possible. Because of the way cluster samples are often drawn, the defined clusters are homogeneous rather than heterogeneous in regard to the characteristic of interest. Beginning researchers display a proclivity for then calling the procedure stratified sampling, since it involves the construction of homogeneous subgroups of population elements. As long as subgroups are selected for investigation randomly, the procedure is cluster sampling, regardless of how the subgroups are formed. Admittedly, homogeneous subgroups produce less ideal cluster samples from a statistical efficiency viewpoint than do heterogeneous subgroups.

Statistical efficiency is a relative notion by which sampling plans can be compared. One sampling plan is said to be more statistically efficient than another if, for the same size sample, it produces a smaller standard error of estimate. When the characteristic of interest is the mean, for example, the sampling plan that produces the smallest value of $s_{\bar{x}}$ for a given size sample is most statistically efficient. Cluster samples are typically much less statistically efficient than comparable stratified samples or even simple random samples, because the probable margin of error with a fixed size sample is often greatest with cluster sampling.

Even with its typically lower statistical efficiency, cluster sampling is probably the most used sampling procedure in large-scale field surveys. Why? Simply because it is often more *economically efficient* in that the cost per observation is less. The economies permit the selection of a larger sample at a smaller cost. Often, so many more observations can be secured for a given cost with cluster sampling that the margin of error associated with the estimate is smaller for cluster sampling than it is for stratified sampling with the smaller number of observations. That is, cluster sampling is often more *overall efficient* than the other forms of sampling in that although it requires a large sample for the same degree of precision and is thus less statistically efficient, the smaller cost per observation allows samples so much larger that estimates with a smaller standard error can be produced for the same cost.

Systematic Sampling The **systematic sample** offers one of the easiest ways of sampling many populations of interest. A systematic sample involves selecting every *k*th element after a random start.

Consider again the hypothetical population of 20 individuals, and suppose a sample of 5 is to be selected from this population. Number the elements from 1 to 20. With 20 population elements and a sample size of 5, the sampling fraction is $f = n/N = 5/20 = 1/4$, meaning that one element in four will be selected. The sampling interval $i = 1/f$ will be 4. This means that after a random start, every fourth element will be chosen. The random start, which must be some number between 1 and 4, 1 and i in general, is determined from a random number table. Thus, if the random start were 1, the first, fifth, ninth, thirteenth, and seventeenth items would be the sample, if it were 2, the second, sixth, tenth, fourteenth, and eighteenth items would be the sample, and so on.

Systematic sampling is one-stage cluster sampling, since the subgroups are not sampled but rather all of the elements in the selected clusters are used. The subgroups or clusters in this case are

Cluster I	A, E, I, M, Q
Cluster II	B, F, J, N, R
Cluster III	C, G, K, O, S
Cluster IV	D, H, L, P, T

and one of these clusters is selected randomly for investigation. The random start, of course, determines the cluster that is to be used.

One can readily see the ease with which a systematic sample can be drawn. It is much easier to draw a systematic sample than it is to select a simple random sample of the same size, for example. With a systematic sample one needs to enter the random number table only once. The problem of checking for the duplication of elements, which is cumbersome with simple random samples, does not occur with systematic samples. All the elements are uniquely determined by the selection of the random start.[17]

A systematic sample can often be made more representative than a simple random sample. With our hypothetical population, for example, we are guaranteed representation from the low income segment and the high income segment. Regardless of which of the four clusters is chosen, one element must have an income of $6,800 or less; another must have an income of $12,000 or more; and the remaining three elements must have incomes between these two values. A simple random sample of Size 5 might or might not include low-income or high-income people.

The same is true when sampling from other populations. Thus, if we are sampling retail stores, we can guarantee representation of both small and large stores by employing a systematic sample, if the stores can be arrayed from smallest to largest according to some criteria such as annual sales or square footage. The ability to guarantee representation from each size segment depends on the availability of knowledge about the size of each store so that they can be arrayed from smallest to largest and numbered serially. A simple random sample of stores will likely contain inadequate representation from the large stores, since there are fewer large stores than small stores. Yet the fewer large stores account for a great proportion of all sales.

---

[17]For an example of the use of systematic sampling, see Mark E. Slama and Armen Tashchian, "Selected Socioeconomic and Demographic Characteristics Associated with Purchasing Involvement," *Journal of Marketing,* 49 (Winter 1985), pp. 72–82.

The degree to which the systematic sample will be more representative than a simple random sample thus depends on the clustering of objects within the list from which the sample will be drawn. The ideal list for a systematic sample will have elements similar in value on the characteristic close together and elements diverse in value spread apart.

There is at least one danger with systematic samples. If there is a natural periodicity in the list of elements, the systematic sample can produce estimates seriously in error. For example, suppose we have the annual ticket sales of an airline by day and suppose that we wish to analyze these sales in terms of length of trip. To analyze all 365 days may be prohibitively costly, but suppose the research budget does allow the investigation of 52 days of sales. A systematic sample of days using a sampling interval of 7 (365 ÷ 52) would obviously produce some misleading conclusions, since the day's sales will reflect all Monday trips, Friday trips, or Sunday trips, for example.[18] Of course, any other sampling interval will be acceptable, and in general, an enlightened choice of the sampling interval can do much to eliminate the problems associated with natural periodicities in the data. The enlightened choice of sampling interval, of course, depends on knowledge of the phenomenon and nature of the periodicity.

Area Sampling In every probability sampling plan discussed so far, the investigator needed a list of population elements in order to draw the sample. A list identifying each population element was a necessary requirement for simple random samples, stratified samples, and systematic samples. The latter two procedures also required knowledge about some other characteristic of the population if they were to be designed optimally. For many populations of interest, these detailed lists will be unavailable. Further, it will often prove prohibitively costly to construct them. When this condition arises, the cluster sample offers the researcher another distinct benefit—he or she only needs the list of population elements for the selected clusters.

Suppose, for example, that an investigator wished to measure certain characteristics of industrial sales representatives such as their earnings, attitudes toward the job, hours worked, and so on. It would be extremely difficult, if not impossible, and certainly costly to develop an up-to-date roster listing each industrial sales representative. Yet such a list would be required for a simple random sample. A stratified sample would further require that the investigator possess knowledge about some additional characteristics of each sales representative, for example, education or employer, so that the population could be divided into mutually exclusive and exhaustive subsets. With a cluster sample, on the other hand, one could use the companies as sampling units. The investigator would generate a sample of business firms from the population of firms of interest. The business firms would be *primary sampling units* where a **sampling unit** is defined as "that element or set of elements considered for selection in some stage of

---

[18]Sudman suggests that when the "sampling interval *i* is not a whole number, the easiest solution is to use as the interval the whole number just below or above *i*. Usually, this will result in a selected sample that is only slightly larger or smaller than the initial sample required, and this new sample size will have no noticeable effect on either the accuracy of the results or the budget. For samples in which the interval *i* is small (generally for *i* less than 10), so that the rounding has too great an effect on the sample size, it is possible to add or delete the extra cases . . . it is usually easier to round down in computing *i* so that the sample is larger, and then to delete systematically." Sudman, *Applied Sampling*, p. 54.

sampling.''[19] The investigator could then get a list of sales representatives working for each of the selected firms, a much more plausible assignment. If the investigator then studied each of the sales representatives in each of the selected firms, it would be one-stage cluster sampling. If the researcher subsampled sales representatives from each company's list, it would be two-stage cluster sampling.

The same principle underlies **area sampling.** Current, accurate lists of population elements are rarely available. Directories of all those living in a city at a particular moment simply do not exist for many cities, and when they do exist, they are obsolete when published: people move, others die, new households are constantly being formed.[20] While lists of families are nonexistent, relatively accurate lists of primary sampling units are available in the form of city maps, if the areal divisions of the city serve as the primary sampling units. While the details of area sampling are much too complex for our purposes, some appreciation for the rationale underlying the various approaches can be gathered by considering some of the basic types of area sampling.

One-Stage Area Sampling   Suppose the investigator is interested in estimating the amount of wine consumed per household in the city of Chicago and how consumption is related to family income. An accurate listing of all households is unavailable for the Chicago area. A phone book when published is already somewhat obsolete, in addition to the other inadequacies previously mentioned. One approach to this problem would be to

1. choose a simple random sample of n city blocks from the population of N blocks;
2. determine wine consumption and income for all households in the selected blocks and generalize the sample relationships to the larger population.

The probability of any household being included in the sample can be calculated. It is given simply as n/N, since it equals the probability that the block on which it is located will be selected. Since the probabilities are known, the procedure is indeed probability sampling. Here, though, blocks have been substituted for households when selecting primary sampling units. The substitution is made because the list of blocks in the Chicago area can be developed from city maps. Each block can be identified, and the existence of this universe of blocks permits the calculation of the necessary probabilities.

Since each household on the selected blocks is included in the sample, the procedure is one-stage area sampling. Note that the blocks serve to divide the parent population into mutually exclusive and exhaustive subsets. Note further that the blocks do not serve very well as ideal subsets statistically for cluster samples; households on a given block

---

[19]Earl R. Babbie, *The Practice of Social Research,* 2nd ed. (Belmont, Calif.: Wadsworth Publishing, 1979), p. 167.

[20]R. L. Polk and Company in Taylor, Michigan, publishes some 1,400 directories for most medium-sized cities in the range of 50,000–800,000 people. The directories contain both an alphabetical list of names and businesses and a street address directory of households. While the alphabetic list can contain a reasonably large percentage of inaccurate listings at any one time, the address directory is reasonably accurate since it only omits new construction after the directory is published and the directories are revised every two or three years.

can be expected to be somewhat similar with respect to their income and wine consumption rather than heterogeneous as desired.[21] On the other hand, the data collection costs will be very low because of the concentration of households within each block.

Two-Stage Area Sampling   The distinguishing feature of the one-stage area sample is that all of the households in the selected blocks (or other areas) are enumerated and studied. It is not necessary to employ all items in a selected cluster; the selected areas themselves can be subsampled, and it is often quite advantageous to do so. Two types of two-stage sampling need to be distinguished:

1.   simple, two-stage area sampling;

2.   probability-proportional-to-size area sampling.

With simple, two-stage area sampling, a certain proportion of second-stage sampling units (for example, households) is selected from each first-stage unit (for example, blocks). Consider a universe of 100 blocks; suppose there are 20 households per block; assume that a sample of 80 households is required from this total population of 2,000 households. The overall sampling fraction is thus $80/2,000 = 1/25$. There are a number of ways by which the sample can be completed: by (1) selecting 10 blocks and 8 households per block; (2) selecting 8 blocks and 10 households per block; (3) selecting 20 blocks and 4 households per block; or (4) selecting 4 blocks and 20 households per block. The last alternative would, of course, be one-stage area sampling, while the first three would all be two-stage area sampling.

The probability with which the blocks are selected is called the block or first-stage sampling fraction and is given as the ratio of n_B/N_B, where n_B and N_B are the number of blocks in the sample and in the population, respectively. For the first three schemes illustrated above, the first-stage sampling fractions would be, in order, 1 in 10, 1 in 12.5, and in 1 in 5. The probability with which the households are selected is the household or second-stage sampling fraction. Since there must be a total of 80 households in the sample, the second-stage sampling fraction differs for each alternative. The second-stage sampling fraction is given as $n_{H/B}/N_{H/B}$, where $n_{H/B}$ and $N_{H/B}$ are the number of households per block in the sample and in the population. For Sampling Scheme 1, the household sampling fraction is calculated to be $8/20 = 2/5$, while for Scheme 2 it is $10/20 = 1/2$, and for Scheme 3 $4/20 = 1/5$. Note that the product of the first-stage and second-stage sampling fractions in each case equals the overall sampling fraction of $1/25$.

Which scheme would be preferable? Although we do not wish to get into the detailed calculation of what would be optimal, we would like to illustrate the general principle. Economies of data collection would dictate that the second-stage sampling fraction be high. This means that a great many households would be selected from each designated block, as with Scheme 2. Statistical efficiency would dictate a small second-stage sampling fraction, since it can be expected that the blocks would be relatively homoge-

---

[21]When geographic clustering of rare populations occurs, it can be used to advantage when designing the sample. See, for example, Seymour Sudman, ''Efficient Screening Methods for the Sampling of Geographically Clustered Special Populations,'' *Journal of Marketing Research*, 22 (February 1985), pp. 20–29.

Table 9.9
Illustration of Probability-Proportional-to-Size Sampling

Block	Households	Cumulative Number of Households
1	800	800
2	400	1,200
3	200	1,400
4	200	1,600
5	100	1,700
6	100	1,800
7	100	1,900
8	50	1,950
9	25	1,975
10	25	2,000

neous, and thus it would be desirable to have a very few households from any one block. Scheme 3 would be preferred on statistical grounds. Statistical sampling theory would suggest the balancing of these two criteria. There are formulas for this purpose that reflect essentially the cost of data collection and the variability of the characteristic within and between clusters, although a useful rule of thumb is that clusters of three to eight households per block or segment are near optimum for most social science variables.[22]

Simple two-stage area sampling is quite effective when there is approximately the same number of second-stage units per first-stage unit. When the second-stage units are decidedly unequal, simple two-stage area sampling can cause bias in the estimate. Sometimes the number of second-stage units per first-stage unit can be made approximately equal by combining areas. When this option is not available or is cumbersome to implement, probability-proportional-to-size sampling can be employed.

Consider, for example, the data of Table 9.9, and suppose a sample of 20 elements is to be selected from this population of 2,000 households. With **probability-proportional-to-size sampling**, a *fixed* number of second-stage units is selected from each first-stage unit.[23] Suppose after balancing economic and statistical considerations that the number of second-stage units per first-stage unit is determined to be ten. Two first-stage units must be selected to produce a total sample of 20. The procedure gets its name from the way these first-stage units are selected. The probability of selection is variable in that it depends on the size of the first-stage unit. In particular, a table of four-digit random numbers would be consulted. The first two numbers encountered between 1 and 2,000 will be employed to indicate the blocks that will be used. All numbers between

---

[22]Sudman, *Applied Sampling,* p. 81.

[23]For an empirical example that uses probability-proportionate-to-size cluster sampling, see Johnny Blair and Ronald Czaja, "Locating a Special Population Using Random Digit Dialing," *Public Opinion Quarterly,* 46 (Winter 1982), pp. 585–590.

1 and 800 will indicate the inclusion of Block 1, those from 801 to 1,200 Block 2, from 1,201 to 1,400 Block 3, and so on.

The probability that any particular household is included in the sample is equal, since the unequal first-stage selection probabilities are balanced by unequal second-stage selection probabilities. Consider, for example, Blocks 1 and 10, the two extremes. The first-stage selection probability for Block 1 is $800/2,000 = 1/2.5$, since 800 of the permissible 2,000 random numbers correspond to Block 1. On the other hand, only 25 of the permissible random numbers (1,976 to 2,000) correspond to Block 10, and thus the first-stage sampling fraction for Block 10 is $25/2,000 = 1/80$. Since ten households are to be selected from each block, the second-stage sampling fraction for Block 1 is $10/800 = 1/80$, while for Block 10 it is $10/25 = 1/2.5$. The products of the first- and second-stage sampling thus compensate, since

$$\frac{800}{2,000} \times \frac{10}{800} = \frac{25}{2,000} \times \frac{10}{25},$$

which is also true for the remaining blocks.

Probability-proportional-to-size sampling is another illustration of how information begets information with applied sampling problems. One can avoid the bias of simple two-stage area sampling and can also produce estimates that are more precise when there is great variation in the number of second-stage units per first-stage unit. The price one pays, of course, is that probability-proportional-to-size sampling requires that one have detailed knowledge about the size of each first-stage unit. This is not quite as high a price as it might be, since the Census Bureau has reported the number of households per block for all cities of over 50,000 in population as well as for a number of other urbanized areas.[24] Maps are included in each report. While somewhat obsolete when published, these map and block statistics can be updated. The local electrical utility will have records of connections current to the day, and so will the telephone company. In many cases, these statistics will be broken down by blocks.

Summary Comments on Probability Sampling

As you can probably begin to appreciate, sample design is a very detailed subject. Our discussion has concentrated on only a few of the fundamentals and, in particular, the basic types of probability samples. You should be aware, though, that the basic types can be, and are, combined in large-scale field studies to produce some very complex designs.

The Gallup poll, for example, is probably one of the best known of all the polls. The sample for the Gallup poll for each survey "consists of 1,500 adults selected from 320 locations, using area sampling methods. At each location the interviewer is given a map with an indicated starting point and is required to follow a specified direction. At each occupied dwelling unit, the interviewer must attempt to meet sex quotas."[25] In

[24]*U.S. Census of Housing: 1980, Vol. III City Blocks,* HC(3)—No. (city number).

[25]Sudman, *Applied Sampling,* p. 71.

sum, the Gallup poll uses a combination of area and quota sampling. Further, it is not uncommon to have several levels of stratification, such as by geographic area and density of population, precede several stages of cluster sampling. Thus, you cannot expect to be a sampling expert with the brief exposure to the subject contained here.[26] But you should be able to communicate effectively about sample design, and while you may not understand completely, say, why n_1 observations were taken from one stratum and n_2 from another, you should appreciate the basic considerations determining the choice.

Summary

This chapter reviewed the basic types of samples that might be used to infer something about a population. A sample might be preferred to a census on grounds of cost or impossibility of taking a census, or because of its greater accuracy.

A useful six-step procedure to follow when drawing a sample includes:

1. define the population,
2. identify the sampling frame,
3. select a sampling procedure,
4. determine the sample size,
5. select the sample elements, and
6. collect the data from the designated elements.

Probability samples are distinguished by the fact that every population element has a known, nonzero chance of being included in the sample. With nonprobability samples, the chance of inclusion is noncalculable since personal judgment is involved somewhere in the actual selection process, and thus nonprobability samples do not allow the construction of the sampling distribution of the statistic in question. This, in turn, means that the traditional tools of statistical inference are not legitimately employed with nonprobability samples.

The basic types of nonprobability samples are convenience, judgment, and quota. Convenience samples are also known as accidental samples, because those elements

---

[26]Those interested in pursuing the subject further should see one of the excellent books on the subject, such as William G. Cochran, *Sampling Techniques,* 3rd ed. (New York: John Wiley, 1977); Morris H. Hansen, William N. Hurwitz, and William G. Madow, *Sample Survey Methods and Theory, Vol. 1, Methods and Applications* (New York: John Wiley, 1953); R. L. Jensen, *Statistical Survey Techniques* (New York: John Wiley, 1978); Graham Kalton, *Introduction to Survey Sampling,* (Beverly Hills, Calif.: Sage Publications, 1982); Leslie Kish, *Survey Sampling* (New York: John Wiley, 1965); Richard L. Schaeffer, William Mendenhall, and Lyman Ott, *Elementary Survey Sampling,* 2nd ed. (North Scituate, Mass.: Duxbury Press, 1979); or Bill Williams, *A Sampler on Sampling* (New York: John Wiley, 1978). The little book by John Monroe and A. L. Finkner, *Handbook of Area Sampling* (Philadelphia: Chilton, 1959), provides an easy-to-read discussion of the design of an area sample. The books by Sudman, *Applied Sampling,* and A. C. Rosander, *Case Studies in Sample Design* (New York: Marcel Dekker, Inc., 1977), illustrate ways these sampling principles were applied to actual problems, while the articles by Seymour Sudman, "Improving the Quality of Shopping Center Sampling," *Journal of Marketing Research,* 17 (November 1980), pp. 423–431, and Edward Blair, "Sampling Issues in Trade Area Maps Drawn from Shopper Surveys," *Journal of Marketing,* 47 (Winter 1983), pp. 98–106, illustrate how the principles of sampling can be applied to improve sampling in shopping center studies.

included just happen to be at the study site at the right time. Population elements are handpicked to serve a specific purpose with judgment samples, while with quota samples, the interviewers personally select subjects with specified characteristics so as to fulfill their quota.

Simple random samples are probability samples in which each population element has an equal chance of being included and every combination of sample elements is just as likely as any other combination of n sample elements. Simple random samples were used to illustrate the basis of statistical inference in which a parameter (a fixed characteristic of the population) is estimated from a statistic (a characteristic of a sample). The value of the statistic depends on the sample actually selected since it varies from sample to sample. The derived population is the set of all possible distinguishable samples that could be drawn from a parent population under a given sampling plan, and the distribution of the values of some sample statistic is the sampling distribution of the statistic. The concept of the sampling distribution is the cornerstone of statistical inference, since statistical inferential procedures rely on the sampling distribution of the specific statistic in question. The sampling distributions of a number of statistics of interest to the applied researcher are known from the work of theoretical statisticians.

A stratified sample is a probability sample in which the parent population is divided into mutually exclusive and exhaustive subsets and a sample of elements is drawn from each subset. Stratified samples are typically the most statistically efficient, that is, have the smallest standard error of estimate for a given size; they also allow the investigation of the characteristic of interest for particular subgroups within the population. The most statistically efficient stratified samples result when the strata are made as homogeneous as possible. Thus, variables expected to be correlated to the characteristic of interest, and whose values are known, are often employed when establishing the strata. In proportionate stratified sampling, the size of the sample taken from each stratum only depends on the relative size of the stratum in the population, whereas with disproportionate stratified sampling, sample size depends on the variability within the stratum as well.

A cluster sample is a probability sample in which the parent population is divided into mutually exclusive and exhaustive subsets and then a random sample of subsets is selected. If each of the elements within the selected subsets is studied, it is one-stage cluster sampling, while if the selected subsets are also subsampled, the procedure is two-stage cluster sampling. Since only a sample of subsets is selected for analysis, statistical efficiency considerations suggest that the subsets be established to be as heterogeneous as possible. A systematic sample is a form of cluster sample in which every kth element is selected after a randomly determined start.

An area sample is one of the most important types of cluster samples, or any kind of probability sample for that matter, in applied, large-scale studies. Area samples make use of one very desirable feature of cluster samples—one only needs the list of population elements for the selected clusters. By defining areas as clusters, then randomly selecting areas, the investigator only needs to develop lists of population elements for the selected areas. Even here the researcher can use dwelling units and select them systematically. Thus, area samples permit probability samples to be drawn when current lists of population elements are unavailable. In drawing area samples, the researcher typically attempts to balance statistical and economic considerations. Since small areas are basically homogeneous, statistical considerations suggest a great many areas be used, while the economies of data collection dictate few areas be used and a great many observations be collected within each area.

Many applied sample designs represent combinations of the basic types reviewed here.

Questions

1. What is a census? What is a sample?

2. Is a sample ever preferred to a census? Why?

3. What distinguishes a probability sample from a nonprobability sample?

4. What is a convenience sample?

5. What is a judgment sample?

6. Explain the operation of a quota sample. Why is a quota sample a nonprobability sample? What kinds of comparisons should one make with the data from quota samples to check their representativeness, and what kinds of conclusions can one legitimately draw?

7. What are the distinguishing features of a simple random sample?

8. What is a derived population? How is it distinguished from a parent population?

9. Consider the estimation of a population mean. What is the relationship between the mean of the parent population and the mean of the derived population? Between the variance of the parent population and the variance of the derived population?

10. What is the Central-Limit Theorem? What role does it play in making inferences about a population mean?

11. What procedure is followed in constructing a confidence interval for a population mean when the population variance is known? When the population variance is unknown? What does such an interval mean?

12. How should a simple random sample be selected? Describe the procedure.

13. What is a stratified sample? How is a stratified sample selected?

14. Is a stratified sample a probability or nonprobability sample? Why?

15. What principle should be followed in establishing the strata for a stratified sample? Why? How can this principle be implemented in practice?

16. Describe the procedure that is followed in developing a confidence interval estimate for a population mean with a stratified sample. Be specific.

17. Which sampling method typically produces more precise estimates of a population mean—simple random sampling or stratified sampling? Why?

18. What is a proportionate stratified sample? What is a disproportionate stratified sample? What must be known about the parent population to select each?

19. What is a cluster sample? How is a cluster sample selected?

20. What are the similarities and differences between a cluster sample and a stratified sample?

21. What is statistical efficiency? What is economic efficiency? What is overall efficiency?

22. Which sampling method is typically most statistically efficient? Which method is typically most economically efficient? Which method is typically most overall efficient? Why?

23. What is a systematic sample? How are the random start and sampling interval determined with a systematic sample?

24. What are the advantages and disadvantages associated with systematic samples?

25. What is an area sample? Why are area samples used?

26. How does a two-stage area sample differ from a one-stage area sample?

27. Illustrate the selection of a simple, two-stage area sample using hypothetical data of your own choosing.

28. Illustrate probability-proportional-to-size two-stage area sampling using an example of your own choosing.

29. What information is needed to draw effectively

    (a) a simple, two-stage area sample?
    (b) a probability-proportional-to-size area sample?

Applications and Problems

1. For each of the following situations identify the appropriate target population and sampling frame.

    (a) A local chapter of the American Lung Association wants to test the effectiveness of a brochure titled "12 Reasons For Not Smoking" in the city of St. Paul, Minnesota.

    (b) A medium-sized manufacturer of cat food wants to conduct an in-home usage test of a new type of cat food in Sacramento, California.

    (c) A large wholesaler dealing in household appliances in the city of New York wants to evaluate dealer reaction to a new discount policy.

    (d) A local department store wants to assess the satisfaction with a new credit policy offered to charge account customers.

    (e) A national manufacturer wants to assess whether adequate inventories are being held by wholesalers in order to prevent shortages by retailers.

    (f) Your school cafeteria wants to test a new soft drink manufactured and sold by the staff of the cafeteria.

    (g) A manufacturer of cake mixes selling primarily in the Midwest wants to test market a new brand of cake mixes.

2. The management of a popular tourist resort on the west coast had noticed a decline in the number of tourists and length of stay over the past three years. An overview of industry trends indicated that the overall tourist trade was expanding and growing rapidly. Management decided to conduct a study to determine people's attitudes towards the particular activities that were available. They wanted to cause the minimum amount of inconvenience to their customers and hence adopted the following plan. A request was deposited in each hotel room of the two major hotels indicating the nature of the study and encouraging customers to participate. The customers were requested to report to a separate desk located in the lobby of the hotels. Personal interviews, lasting 20 minutes, were conducted at this desk.

    (i) What type of sampling method was used?
    (ii) Critically evaluate the method used.

3. A national manufacturer of baby food was planning to enter the Canadian market. The initial thrust was to be in the provinces of Ontario and Quebec. Prior to the final decision

of launching their product, management decided to test market the products in two cities. After reviewing the various cities in terms of external criteria such as demographics, shopping characteristics and so on, the research department settled on the cities of Hamilton, Ontario, and Sherbrooke, Quebec.

(i) What type of sampling method was used?

(ii) Critically evaluate the method used.

4. The My-Size Company, a manufacturer of clothing for large-sized consumers, was in the process of evaluating their product and advertising strategy. Initial efforts consisted of a number of focus group interviews. The focus groups consisted of 10 to 12 large men and women of different demographic characteristics who were selected by the company's research department using on-the-street observations of physical characteristics.

(i) What type of sampling method was used?

(ii) Critically evaluate the method used.

5. The Hair-Fair Company was a chain of beauty salons located in San Diego, California. During the past five years the company had witnessed a sharp increase in the number of outlets they operated and the company's gross sales and net profit margin. The owner plans to offer a free service of hair analysis and consultation, a service for which other competing salons charge a substantial price. In order to offset the increase in operating expenses, the owner plans to raise the rates on other services by 5 percent. Prior to introducing this new service and increasing rates, the owner decides to do a survey using her customers as a sample and employing the method of quota sampling. Your assistance is required in planning the study.

(a) On what variables would you suggest the quotas be based? Why? List the variables with their respective levels.

(b) The owner has kept close track of the demographic characteristics of her customers over a five-year period and decides that these would be most relevant in identifying the sample elements to be used.

Variable	Level	Percent of Customers
Age	0–15 years	5%
	16–30 years	30%
	31–45 years	30%
	46–60 years	15%
	61–75 years	15%
	Over 76 years	5%
Sex	Male	24%
	Female	76%
Income	$0–$9,999	10%
	$10,000–$19,999	20%
	$20,000–$29,999	30%
	$30,000–$39,999	20%
	Over $40,000	20%

Based on these three quota variables, indicate the characteristics of a sample of 200 subjects.

(c) Discuss the possible sources of bias with the sampling method.

6. The Wisconsin National Bank, headquartered in Milwaukee, Wisconsin, has some 400,000 users of its credit card scattered throughout the state of Wisconsin. The appli-

cation forms for the credit card asked for the usual information on name, address, phone, income, education, and so on, that is so typical of such applications. The bank is now very much interested in determining if there is any relationship between the uses to which the card is put and the socioeconomic characteristics of the using party; for example, is there a difference in the characteristics of those people who use the credit card for major purchases only, for example, appliances, and those who use it for minor as well as major purchases.

(a) Identify the population and sampling frame that would be used by Wisconsin National Bank.
(b) Indicate how you would draw a simple random sample from the above sampling frame.
(c) Indicate how you would draw a stratified sample from the above sampling frame.
(d) Indicate how you would draw a cluster sample from the above sampling frame.
(e) Which method would be preferred? Why?

7. Fine Supermarkets is considering entering the New Orleans market. Before doing so though, management wishes to estimate the average square feet of selling space among potential competitors so as to plan better the size of the proposed new outlet. A stratified sample of supermarkets in New Orleans produced the following results.

Size	Total Number in City	Number of This Size in Sample	Mean Size of Stores in Sample	Standard Deviation of Stores in Sample
Small supermarkets	1,000	20	4,000 sq. ft.	2,000 sq. ft.
Medium supermarkets	600	12	10,000 sq. ft.	1,000 sq. ft.
Large supermarkets	400	8	60,000 sq. ft.	3,000 sq. ft.

(a) Estimate the average-size supermarket in New Orleans. Show your calculations.
(b) Develop a 95 percent confidence interval around this estimate. Show your calculations.
(c) Was a proportionate or an optimal stratified sample design used in determining the number of sample observations for each stratum? Explain.

Chapter 10
Sample Size

Thus far, our discussion of sampling has concentrated on sample type. Another important consideration is sample size. Unless the researcher is going to use a sequential sample, he or she needs some means of determining the necessary size of the sample before collecting data.

The question of sample size is complex since it depends on, among other things, the type of sample, the statistic in question, the homogeneity of the population, and the time, money, and personnel available for the study. There is no way we can do all of these issues justice in one chapter. Rather, our objective will be to illustrate the statistical principles determining sample size, using only simple random samples and a few of the more popular statistics. The reader interested in the determination of sample size for stratified or cluster samples should consult one of the standard references on sampling theory, while the reader using a simple random sample to estimate a population variance, for example, should consult an intermediate level statistics text to determine the proper sample size. The principles will remain the same in each case, but the formulas differ, since they depend on the sampling plan and the statistic in question.

Basic Considerations

It should not be surprising to find that the sampling distribution of the statistic underlies the determination of sample size. Recall that the sampling distribution of the statistic indicates how the sample estimates vary as a function of the particular sample selected. The spread of the sampling distribution thus indicates the error that can be associated with any estimate. For instance, the error associated with the estimation of a population mean by a sample mean was given by the standard error of the mean $\sigma_{\bar{x}} = \sigma/\sqrt{n}$, when the population variance was known, and $s_{\bar{x}} = \hat{s}/\sqrt{n}$, when the population variance was unknown. The first factor one must consider in estimating sample size, then, is the standard error of the estimate obtained from the known sampling distribution of the statistic.

A second consideration is the precision desired from the estimate. Precision is the size of the estimating interval when the problem is one of estimating a population parameter. For example, a researcher investigating mean income might want the sample estimate to be within $\pm \$100$ of the true population value. This is a more precise estimate than one required to be within $\pm \$500$ of the true value.

A third factor that must be considered is the desired degree of confidence associated with the estimate. There is a trade-off between degree of confidence and degree of precision with a sample of fixed size; one can specify either the degree of confidence or the degree of precision but not both. It is only when sample size is allowed to vary that one can achieve both a specified precision and a specified degree of confidence in the result, and, as a matter of fact, the determination of sample size involves balancing the two considerations against each other.[1]

To illustrate the distinction between confidence and precision, consider a point estimate of a population parameter, say, mean income. A point estimate is a precise estimate in that there are no associated bounds of error; for example, the sample mean indicates that the population mean income is $19,243. This point estimate is also most assuredly wrong, and thus we can have no confidence in it. On the other hand, we can have complete confidence in the statement: The population mean income is between zero and $1 million. While completely confident about the accuracy of the statement, we must admit that the statement is not particularly helpful since it tells us next to nothing about mean income. The statement is simply too imprecise to be of value.

Sample Size Determination When Estimating Means

The interrelationship of the basic factors affecting the determination of sample size is best illustrated through example. Consider a simple random sample to estimate the mean annual expenditures of licensed fishermen on food and lodging while on fishing trips within a given state.[2] Now, the Central-Limit Theorem suggests that the distribution of sample means will be normal for samples of reasonable size regardless of the distribution of expenditures in the population of fishermen. Consider, then, the sampling distribution of sample means in Figure 10.1 and distinguish two cases: Case I, in which the population variance is known, and Case II, in which the population variance is unknown.

Case I: Population Variance Known   The population variance might be known from past studies, even though the average expenditures for food and lodging might be unknown, since variation typically changes much more slowly than level.[3] This means that the spread of the distribution given by $\sigma_{\bar{x}}$, as shown in Figure 10.1, is also known up to a proportionality constant, the square root of the sample size, since $\sigma_{\bar{x}} = \sigma/\sqrt{n}$. Thus, we have some idea of the first ingredient in sample size determination, the standard error of estimate.

[1]Bayesian analysts also consider the cost of wrong decisions when determining sample size. See, for example, Robert Schlaifer, *Probability and Statistics for Business Decisions* (New York: McGraw-Hill, 1959), pp. 536–552. For a comparison of classical and Bayesian procedures for determining sample size, see Seymour Sudman, *Applied Sampling* (New York: Academic Press, 1976), pp. 85–105.

[2]The problem would be of interest to the tourist industry, and it also could be of interest to the division of state government concerned with economic development. The problem was chosen because the availability of a list of population elements allows a simple random sample to be selected.

[3]Morris H. Hansen, William N. Hurwitz, and William G. Madow, *Sample Survey Methods and Theory: Vol. 1: Methods and Applications* (New York: John Wiley, 1953). One of the best treatments on securing variance estimates from past data is to be found in pages 450–455.

Figure 10.1
Sampling Distribution of Sample Means

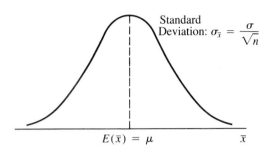

Suppose the decision maker desired the estimate to be within $\pm\$25$ of the true population value. Total precision is thus $50, and half precision, call it H, is $25. The reason we work with H instead of the full length of the interval is that the normal curve is symmetrical about the true population mean, and it simplifies the calculations to work with only one-half of the curve.

The remaining item that needs to be specified is the degree of confidence desired in the result. Suppose the decision maker further wishes to be 95 percent confident that the interval the researcher constructs will contain the true population mean. This implies that z is approximately equal to 2.[4]

Now we have all we need for determining sample size, since it is known that a number of standard deviations on each side of the mean will include a certain proportion of all observations with a normal curve and, in particular, that two standard deviations will include 95 percent of all observations. In Figure 10.1, each observation is a sample mean; the distribution of these sample means is centered about the population mean, and two standard deviations are $2\sigma_{\bar{x}}$, or $z\sigma_{\bar{x}}$ in the general case. Since we want our estimate to be no more than $25 removed from the true population value, we can simply equate the size of the specified half interval with the number of standard deviations to yield

$$H = z\sigma_{\bar{x}} \tag{10.1}$$

$$= z\,\frac{\sigma}{\sqrt{n}}.$$

This equation can be solved for n, since H and z have been specified and σ is known from past studies. Specifically, n can be shown to be equal to

$$n = \frac{z^2}{H^2}\,\sigma^2. \tag{10.2}$$

---

[4] z more correctly equals 1.96 for a 95 percent confidence interval. The approximation $z = 2$ is used since it simplifies the calculations.

To illustrate, suppose the historic variation in expenditures on food and lodging as measured by σ was $100. Then

$$n = \frac{(2)^2}{(25)^2} (100)^2$$

and $n = 64$. Thus, only a relatively small sample needs to be taken to estimate the mean expenditure level when the population standard deviation is $100 and the allowed precision is $50.

Note what happens, though, if the estimate must be twice as precise, i.e., $25 is the total width of the desired interval and $H = 12.5$. Substituting in Equation 10.2,

$$n = \frac{(2)^2}{(12.5)^2} (100)^2$$

and $n = 256$; doubling the precision (halving the total width of the interval) increased the required sample size by a factor of four. This is the basic trade-off between precision and sample size. Whenever precision is increased by a factor c, sample size is increased by a factor c^2. Thus, if the desired precision were $10 instead of $50 — the estimate must be five times more precise ($c = 5$) — the sample size would be 1,600 instead of 64 ($c^2 = 25$).

One also pays dearly for increases in the degree of confidence. Suppose, for example, that one wished to be 99 percent confident in one's estimate rather than 95 percent confident. Using the integer approximations for z means that $z = 3$ instead of 2 as before. Suppose $H = 25$ and σ = 100 as originally. Then

$$n = \frac{(3)^2}{(25)^2} (100)^2$$

and $n = 144$, whereas $n = 64$ when $z = 2$. When z was increased by a factor of $d(d = \frac{3}{2}$ in the example), sample size increased by a factor of $d^2(d^2 = \frac{9}{4}$ in the example).

The upshot of all these gyrations is that you should be well aware of the price that must be paid for increased precision and confidence. Although we might constantly strive for very precise estimates in which we can have a great deal of confidence, one can see why applied researchers often learn to live with risky, somewhat imprecise estimates. The degree of precision and lack of confidence that can be tolerated is, of course, a function of the consequences of the decision associated with the result. The more dire the consequences, the more precise and confident must be the results.

Case II: Population Variance Unknown   The previous examples were all framed employing a known population variance. What happens in the more typical case when the population variance is unknown? The procedure in estimating the sample size is the same except that an estimated value of σ is used in place of the previously known value of σ. Once the sample is selected, though, the variance calculated from the sample is used in place of the originally estimated variance when establishing confidence intervals.

Suppose, for example, that there were no past studies on which to base an estimate of σ. How does one then generate an estimate of the population standard deviation?

One could do a pilot study. An alternative is to take into account the fact that for a normally distributed variable, the range of the variable is approximately equal to plus or minus three standard deviations. Thus, if one can estimate the range of variation, one can estimate the standard deviation by dividing by six. A little *a priori* knowledge of the phenomenon is often enough to estimate the range. If the estimate is in error, the consequence is a confidence interval more or less precise than desired. Let us illustrate.

Certainly there would be some licensed fisherman who would spend zero dollars on food and lodging while on fishing trips since they would only be making one-day trips. Some might also be expected to go on several one-week trips a year. Suppose that 15 days a year were considered typical of the upper limit, and food and lodging expenses were calculated at $30 per day; the total dollar upper limit would be $450. The range would also be 450, and the estimated standard deviation would then be $450/6 = 75$.

With desired precision of $\pm\$25$ and a 95 percent confidence interval, the calculation of sample size is now

$$n = \frac{z^2}{H^2}\,(\text{est. }\sigma)^2$$

$$= \frac{(2)^2}{(25)^2}\,(75)^2$$

and $n = 36$.

A sample of Size 36 would then be selected and the information collected. Suppose these observations generated a sample mean, $\bar{x} = 35$, and a sample standard deviation, $\hat{s} = 60$. The confidence interval is then, as before,[5]

$$\bar{x} \pm zs_{\bar{x}}$$

or

$$35 \pm 2\,\frac{\hat{s}}{\sqrt{n}} = 35 \pm 2\,\frac{60}{\sqrt{36}} = 35 \pm 20$$

or

$$15 \le \mu \le 55.$$

Note what has happened. The desired precision was $\pm\$25$; the obtained precision is $\pm\$20$. The interval is narrower than planned (a bonus) because we overestimated the population standard deviation as judged by the sample standard deviation. If we had underestimated the standard deviation, the situation would have been reversed, and we would have ended up with a wider confidence interval than desired.

---

[5]One would more strictly use the *t* distribution to establish the interval, since the population variance was unknown. The example was framed using the approximate $z = 2$ value for a 95 percent confidence interval so as to better illustrate the consequences of a poor initial estimate of σ.

Relative Precision

The above examples were all framed employing **absolute precision.** The estimates were to be within plus or minus so many units (dollars). It is also possible, though, to frame the calculations of sample size employing relative precision. **Relative precision** means that precision is expressed relative to level. When level is measured by the mean, relative precision would suggest that the estimate be within plus or minus so many percentage points of the mean regardless of its value. Thus, it may be that an estimate within $\pm$ 10 percent of the mean is required; if the mean is 50, the interval will be from 45 to 55, while if the mean is 100, the interval will be from 90 to 110.

Relative precision presents few new problems for the calculation of sample size. The measure of absolute precision H is simply replaced by the measure of relative precision in Equation 10.1. That is,

$$H = z \frac{\sigma}{\sqrt{n}}$$

is changed to

$$r\mu = z \frac{\sigma}{\sqrt{n}},$$

where r is the measure of relative precision and μ is the unknown parent population mean. This formula can be transformed so that sample size can be read directly. Simply divide both sides of the equation by $r\mu$ and multiply both sides by n^2 to yield

$$n = \frac{z^2}{r^2} \left(\frac{\sigma}{\mu} \right)^2. \tag{10.3}$$

Recall from your beginning statistics course that σ/μ is the coefficient of variation C, and thus the formula for sample size reduces to

$$n = \frac{z^2}{r^2} C^2.$$

Here z^2 would be known since z is determined by the desired level of confidence, and r^2 would also be known because r is determined by the expressed level of precision. C would have to be estimated. This would entail making a judgment as to the size of the population standard deviation relative to the size of the population mean. Again, there might be past studies to guide the judgment. If prior studies are unavailable or prove to be in error, the interval will be wider or narrower to the extent that the estimate of C is larger or smaller than that actually produced by the ratio of the sample standard deviation to the sample mean.

Multiple Objectives

A study is rarely conducted to estimate a single parameter. It is much more typical for a study to involve multiple objectives. Let us assume more realistically, therefore, that the researcher is also interested in estimating the annual mean level of expenditures on

Table 10.1

Sample Size Needed to Estimate Each of Three Means

Variable	Expenditures on Food and Lodging	Expenditures on Tackle and Equipment	Miles Traveled
Confidence level	95 percent ($z = 2$)	95 percent ($z = 2$)	95 percent ($z = 2$)
Desired precision	± $25	± $10	± 100 miles
Estimated standard deviation	± $75	± $20	± 500 miles
Required sample size	36	16	100

tackle and equipment by licensed fishermen and the number of miles traveled in a year on fishing trips. There are now three means to be estimated. Suppose each is to be estimated with 95 percent confidence and that the desired absolute precision and estimated standard deviation are as given in Table 10.1. Table 10.1 also contains the sample sizes (which were calculated using Equation 10.2) needed to estimate each variable.

The three requirements produce conflicting sample sizes; n should equal 36, 16, or 100 depending on the variable being estimated. The researcher must somehow reconcile these values to come up with a sample size suitable for the study as a whole. The most conservative approach would be to choose $n = 100$, the largest value. This would ensure that each variable is estimated with the required precision, assuming that the estimates of the standard deviations are accurate.

If the estimate of miles traveled were less critical than the others, however, the use of a sample of Size 100 would be wasteful of resources. A preferred approach would be to focus on those variables that are most critical and to select a sample sufficient in size to estimate them with the required precision and confidence. Those variables that indicated a larger sample needed to be taken would then be estimated with either a lower degree of confidence or less precision than planned. Suppose in this case that the expenditure data were most critical and that the analyst, therefore, decided on a sample size of 36. Suppose also that the information from this sample of 36 fishermen produced a sample mean of $\bar{x} = 300$ and a sample standard deviation of $s = 500$ miles traveled. The estimate of the population standard deviation is thus seen to agree with the sample result, so the confidence interval estimate will not be affected by inaccuracies here.

The confidence interval for miles traveled is then calculated as

$$\bar{x} \pm z s_{\bar{x}} = \bar{x} + z \frac{\hat{s}}{\sqrt{n}} = 300 \pm 2 \frac{500}{\sqrt{36}},$$

or $133.3 \leq \mu \leq 466.7$. Whereas the desired precision was ± 100 miles, the obtained precision is ± 166.7 miles. In order to produce an estimate with the desired precision, the degree of confidence would have to be lowered from its present 95 percent level.

Sample Size Determination When Estimating Proportions

Absolute Precision

The examples considered above all concern determining sample size to estimate mean values. The population proportion π is often another parameter of interest in marketing. Thus, the researcher might be interested in determining the proportion of licensed fishermen who are from out of state, or from rural areas, or who took at least one overnight trip. This section focuses on the determination of sample size necessary to estimate a population proportion.

At the beginning of this chapter we suggested three things were needed to determine sample size: a specified degree of confidence, specified precision, and knowledge of the sampling distribution of the statistic. The first two items are specified to reflect the requirements of the research problem. Precision can again be expressed absolutely or relatively. With percentages, absolute precision means that the estimate will be within plus or minus so many percentage points of the true value, as, for example, within $\pm$ 5 percentage points of the true value.

The remaining consideration is then the sampling distribution of the sample proportion. If the sample elements are selected independently, as can reasonably be assumed if the sample size is small relative to the population size, then the *theoretically correct distribution of the sample proportion is the binomial*. But the binomial becomes indistinguishable from the normal with large-size samples or when the population proportion is close to one-half.[6] It is *convenient* to use the normal approximation when estimating sample size. After the sample is drawn and the sample proportion determined, the researcher can always fall back on the binomial distribution to determine the confidence interval if the normal approximation proves to be in error.

The distribution of sample proportions is centered about the population proportion (Figure 10.2). The sample proportion is an unbiased estimate of the population proportion. The standard deviation of the normal distribution of sample proportions, that is, the standard error of the proportion, denoted by σ_p, is equal to $\sqrt{\pi(1 - \pi)/n}$. Since we are working again with the normal curve, the level of precision is again equated to the number of standard deviations the estimate can be removed from the mean value. But now the mean value is the population proportion, while the standard deviation is the standard error of the proportion; that is,

$$H = z\sigma_p. \tag{10.4}$$

Substituting $\sqrt{\pi(1 - \pi)/n}$ for σ_p and solving for n yields,

$$n = \frac{z^2}{H^2} \pi(1 - \pi). \tag{10.5}$$

Suppose the researcher is interested in estimating the proportion of all fishermen who took at least one overnight fishing trip in the past year. The researcher wanted this

---

[6]The strict requirement is that $n\pi$ must be above a certain level if the normal curve is to provide a good approximation to the binomial. Some books hold that $n\pi$ must be greater than 5, while others suggest that the product must be greater than 10.

Figure 10.2

Approximate Sampling Distribution of the Sample Proportion

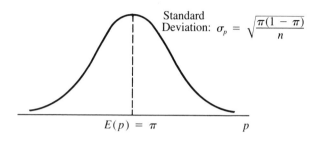

estimate within $\pm$ 2 percentage points and he or she wished to be 95 percent confident in the result. Substitution in Equation 10.5 yields

$$n = \frac{(2)^2}{(.02)^2} \, \pi(1 \, - \, \pi).$$

This equation contains two unknowns, the population proportion being estimated and the sample size, and is thus not solvable as it stands. In order to determine sample size, the researcher needs to estimate the population proportion. That is right! *The researcher must estimate the very quantity the study is being designed to get at in order to determine sample size.*

This fact is often bewildering and certainly disconcerting to decision makers and beginning researchers alike. Nevertheless, it is true that with proportions one is forced to make some judgment about the approximate value of the parameter in order to determine sample size. This is another example of how information begets information in sample design. One might use past studies or published data to generate an initial estimate. Alternately, one might conduct a pilot study. In the absence of both of these options, one might simply use informed judgment as to the approximate likely value of the parameter.

A poor estimate will make the confidence interval more or less precise than desired. Suppose, for example, that the best considered judgment was that 20 percent of all licensed fishermen could be expected to take an overnight fishing trip during the year. Sample size is then calculated to be

$$n = \frac{(2)^2}{(.02)^2} \, (.20)(1 \, - \, .20)$$

and $n = 1,600$. Upon receipt of the information from the designated 1,600 fishermen, suppose that the sample proportion p actually turned out to be equal to 0.40. The confidence interval is then established, employing s_p to estimate the unknown σ_p where $s_p = \sqrt{p(1 \, - \, p)/n}$; that is,

$$s_p = \sqrt{\frac{0.40(0.60)}{1,600}} = \sqrt{\frac{0.24}{1,600}} = 0.012.$$

The confidence interval is then

$$p \pm zs_p = 0.40 \pm 2(0.012)$$

or

$$0.376 \leq \pi \leq 0.424.$$

The interval is wider than desired, since the sample proportion was larger than the estimated population proportion.

Suppose a wider interval than planned was unacceptable. One way of preventing it is to choose the sample size so as to reflect the "worst of worlds." Note from the formula that the largest sample size will be obtained when the product $\pi(1 - \pi)$ is greatest, since sample size is directly proportional to this quantity. This product is in turn greatest when $\pi = 0.5$, as might be intuitively expected, since if one-half of the population behaves one way and the other half the other way, one would require more evidence for a valid inference than if the situation were more clear-cut and a substantial proportion all behaved in the same way.

In the absence of any other information about the population proportion, then, one can always conservatively assume that π is equal to 0.5. The established confidence interval will simply be more precise to the extent that the sample estimate deviates from the assumed 0.5 value.

Relative Precision

The sample size necessary to estimate a population proportion also can be based on a specification of the relative precision to be provided by the estimate. Relative precision means that the size of the interval will be a function of the value, that is, within a certain percent of the value regardless of its level. Thus, if the relative precision were to be specified to be within $\pm$ 10 percent, this would mean that if the sample proportion were 0.20, the interval would be from 0.18 to 0.22, while if the sample proportion were 0.30, the interval would be from 0.27 to 0.33.

When the interval is specified employing relative precision, the following differences in the calculation of sample size result from the basic formula contained in Equation 10.4. Whereas before

$$H = z\sigma_p,$$

now

$$r\pi = z\sigma_p$$

where r is the specified relative precision. The formula can be manipulated to express sample size directly, since

$$r\pi = z \sqrt{\frac{\pi(1 - \pi)}{n}}$$

upon substituting the value of σ_p. Simplifying,

$$n = \frac{z^2}{r^2}\frac{(1 - \pi)}{\pi}.$$ (10.6)

Once again some initial estimate of the population proportion is needed to determine the size of sample necessary to estimate that proportion.

To illustrate the calculation, suppose the population proportion were estimated to be 0.2; the level of confidence was specified at 95 percent ($z = 2$); and the desired level of relative precision $r = 0.10$. Then

$$n = \frac{(2)^2}{(0.10)^2}\frac{(0.8)}{(0.2)} = 1{,}600.$$

After the information is collected from the sample respondents,

$$s_p = \sqrt{p\,(1 - p)/n}$$

would again be used in calculating the confidence interval.

Population Size and Sample Size

Although you may not have noticed it before, note it now: *The size of the population did not enter into the calculation of the size of sample.* That is right! Except for one slight modification to be discussed shortly, the size of the population has *no direct effect* on the size of the sample.

Although perhaps contrary to your expectations at first, consider this statement for a minute. When estimating a mean, if all population elements have exactly the same value of the characteristic, then a sample of one is all that is needed to determine the mean. This is true whether there are 1,000, 10,000, or 100,000 elements in the population. The thing that directly affects the size of the sample is the variability of the characteristic in the population. The more variable the characteristic, the larger the sample needed to estimate it with some specified level of precision. This not only makes intuitive sense, but it can be seen directly in the formulas for determining sample size to estimate a population mean; for example, $n = z^2\,\sigma^2/H^2$ with absolute precision and $n = (z^2/r^2)C^2$ with relative precision. Thus, population size only affects sample size indirectly via its impact on variability. The larger the population, the greater the potential for variation of the characteristic.

It is perhaps less startling to find that population size does not affect sample size when estimating a proportion than when estimating a mean. With a proportion, the determining factor, as we have seen, is the estimated proportion of the population possessing the characteristic; the closer the proportion is to 0.5, the larger the sample that will be needed, regardless of the size of the population. A value of 0.5 signifies greatest variability, because one-half of the population possesses the characteristic and one-half does not.

The slight modification alluded to earlier arises through the finite population correction. We saw previously that many of our results hold when the sample elements are drawn independently of one another. When the sample is small relative to the population, the independence assumption is justified. However, when the sample represents a large portion of the population, the independence assumption is no longer warranted, and the formulas derived under this assumption must be altered accordingly. Thus, for example, we saw in Chapter 9 that the formula for the standard error of the mean was $\sigma_x = \sigma/\sqrt{n}$ under the independence assumption, whereas it was

$$\sigma_{\bar{x}} = \frac{\sigma}{\sqrt{n}} \sqrt{\frac{N-n}{N-1}}$$

when the sample elements were not independent of one another. The factor $(N-n)/(N-1)$ is the finite population correction factor.

When the estimated sample represents more than 5 percent of the population, the calculated size should be reduced by the finite population correction factor.[7] Thus, for example, if the population contained 100 elements and the calculation of sample size indicated a sample of 20 needed to be taken, less than 20 observations would, in fact, be taken to reflect the dependency that existed among the observations. The required sample would be given as $n' = nN/(N + n - 1)$, where n was the originally determined size and n' was the revised size. Thus, with $N = 100$ and $n = 20$, only 17 sample elements would, in fact, be employed.

Other Probability Sampling Plans

So far, the discussions of sample size were based on simple random samples. You should be aware, though, that there are also formulas for determining sample size when other probability sampling plans are used. The formulas are more complex, to be sure, but the same underlying principles still apply. One still needs a knowledge of the sampling distribution of the statistic in addition to the research specifications regarding level of precision and degree of confidence.

The issue of sample size is compounded, though, by the fact that one now has a number of strata or a number of clusters with which to work. This means that one has to deal with within-strata variability and within- and between-cluster variability in calculating sample size, whereas with simple random sampling only total population variability entered the picture. As before, the more variable the strata or cluster, the larger the sample that needs to be taken from it, other things being equal. This is precisely the basis for disproportionate stratified sampling discussed in Chapter 9. One of the other things that must be equal, though, is cost. Cost did not enter directly into the calculation of sample size with simple random sampling, although it does affect sample size. Perhaps the costs of data collection with a sample of the calculated size would simply

---

[7]The 5 percent correction factor is not a hard-and-fast rule. Some books contend that the finite population correction factor should be ignored if the sample includes no more than 10 percent of the population. Cochran suggests that the finite population correction can be ignored whenever the "sampling fraction does not exceed 5 percent and for many purposes even if it is as high as 10 percent." William G. Cochran, *Sampling Techniques*, 3rd ed. (New York: John Wiley, 1977), p. 25. Ignoring the finite population correction will result in overestimating the standard error of estimate.

exceed the research budget, in which case cost would act to constrain sample size below that indicated by the formulas. Of course, with a simple random sample one could also base the calculation of sample size directly on cost per observation and the size of the data collection budget. The fact remains, though, that cost per observation did not enter into the formulas for calculating sample size with simple random samples.

With stratified or cluster samples, cost exerts a direct impact. In calculating sample size, one has to allow for unequal costs per observation by strata or by cluster, and in implementing the sample size calculation, one has to have some initial estimate of these costs. The task then becomes one of balancing variability against costs and assessing the trade-off function relating the two. With a stratified sample, for example, one would want to sample most heavily that stratum which was most variable if cost was the same by strata, or which had the lowest cost per observation if the variability was the same within strata. Since the cost per observation or variability will not likely be the same for each stratum, the challenge becomes one of determining sample size by considering the precision likely to result from sampling each stratum at a given rate. Formulas are available for this purpose, as for cluster samples. We shall not go into these formulas here, as they are readily available in the standard works on sampling theory and fall largely in the domain of the sampling specialist.[8] You should be aware, though, that when dealing with stratified or cluster samples, cost per observation by subgroup directly enters the calculation of sample size.

You should also be aware that there are formulas for determining sample size when the problem is one of hypothesis testing and not confidence interval estimation. Once again, the principles are the same, although there are some additional considerations such as the levels of Type I and Type II errors to be tolerated and the issue of whether it is necessary to detect subtle differences or only obvious differences. We shall not deal with these formulas, since they are readily available in standard statistical works and their discussion would take us too far afield.

Using Anticipated Cross Classifications to Determine Sample Size

The discussion thus far has focused on the determination of sample size using only statistical principles, particularly the trade-off between degree of confidence and degree of precision while considering only sampling error. The arguments were framed this way to cast them into bold relief. In applied problems, the size of the sample is also going to be affected by certain practical considerations, such as the total size of the budget for the study and the anticipated cost per observation, the size of the sample that may be needed to convince skeptical executives who do not understand statistical notions that they indeed can have confidence in the results, and so on. One of the more

---

[8]See, for example, Cochran, *Sampling Techniques;* Hansen, Hurwitz, and Madow, *Sample Survey Methods;* Leslie Kish, *Survey Sampling* (New York: John Wiley, 1965); R. L. Jensen, *Statistical Survey Techniques* (New York: John Wiley, 1978); Richard L. Schaeffer, William Mendenhall, and Lyman Ott, *Elementary Survey Sampling,* 2nd ed. (North Scituate, Mass.: Duxbury Press, 1979); Bill Williams, *A Sampler on Sampling* (New York: John Wiley, 1978); or Richard M. Jaeger, *Sampling in Education and the Social Sciences* (New York: Longman, 1984).

important practical bases for determining the size of sample that will be needed is the anticipated cross classifications to which the data will be subjected.

Suppose, for example, that in our problem of estimating the proportion of all fishermen who took at least one overnight fishing trip in the past year we were also interested in assessing whether the likelihood of engaging in this behavior is somehow related to an individual's age and income. Suppose further that the age categories of interest were less than 20, 20–29, 30–39, 40–49, and 50 and over, while the income categories of interest were less than $10,000, $10,000–$19,999, $20,000–$29,999, $30,000–$39,999, and over $40,000. There are thus five age categories and five income categories for which the proportion of fishermen taking an overnight trip would be estimated. While we might reasonably estimate these proportions for each variable considered separately, we should also recognize that the two variables are interrelated in that increases in incomes are typically related to increases in age. To allow for this interdependence, we need to consider the impact of the two variables simultaneously. The way to do this is through a cross-classification table in which age and income jointly define the cells.[9]

Table 10.2, for instance, is a cross-classification table that could be used for the example at hand. Note that this dummy table is complete in all respects except for the numbers that actually go in each of the cells.[10] These would, of course, be determined by the data actually collected on the number and proportion of all those sampled who actually made at least one overnight trip. In the table there are 25 cells that need estimation. It is unlikely that the decision maker is going to be very comfortable with an estimate of the proportion staying overnight that is based on only a few cases of the phenomenon. Yet even with a sample of, say, 500 fishermen, there is only a potential of 20 cases per cell if the sample is evenly divided with respect to the age and income levels considered. Further, it is very unlikely that the sample would split this way, which would put the researcher in the awkward position of estimating the proportion in a cell engaging in this behavior on the basis of less than 20 cases.

One can reverse this argument to estimate how large a sample should be taken. One simply computes the number of cells in the intended cross classifications. It is given by the *product* of the number of levels of the characteristics forming the cross classification. One then allows for the likely distribution of the variables and estimates the sample size so that the important cells can be estimated with a sufficient number of cases to inspire confidence in the results. One general rule of thumb is that "the sample should be large enough so that there are 100 or more units in each category of the major breakdowns and a minimum of 20 to 50 in the minor breakdowns."[11] Major breakdown refers here to the cells in the most critical cross tabulations for the study and minor breakdown to the cells in the less important cross classifications. Through all of this one has to make due allowance for nonresponses, because some individuals designated for

---

[9] In Chapter 12 the procedures for setting up and analyzing cross-classification tables so that the proper inferences can be drawn are discussed.

[10] Refer again to Chapter 3 for a discussion of the notion of dummy tables and how they should be set up so that they are most productive.

[11] Sudman, *Applied Sampling*, p. 30.

Table 10.2
Number and Proportion of Fishermen Staying
Overnight as a Function of Age and Income

Income	\multicolumn{5}{c}{Age}
	Less than 20	20–29	30–39	40–49	50 and over
Less than $10,000					
$10,000–$19,999					
$20,000–$29,999					
$30,000–$39,999					
$40,000 and over					

inclusion in the sample will be unavailable and others will refuse to participate.[12] The researcher ''builds up'' the sample, so to speak, from the size of the cross-classification table with due allowance for these considerations.

Perhaps cross classification will not be the basic method used to analyze the data. Perhaps, instead, the main technique will be regression or discriminant analysis or one of the other statistical methods discussed in Part 5. If so, the same arguments for determining sample size apply. That is, one needs a sufficient number of cases to satisfy the requirements of the technique, so as to inspire confidence in the results. Different techniques have different sample size requirements, often expressed by the degrees of freedom required for the analysis. Some of these requirements should become obvious when the techniques are discussed. For now, we merely wish to reiterate the important point made earlier when introducing the research process—that the stages are very much related and a decision with respect to one stage can affect all of the other stages. Here a decision with respect to Stage 5 regarding the method of analysis can have an important impact on Stage 4, which precedes it, with respect to the size of the sample that should be selected. Thus, the researcher needs to think through the entire research problem, including how the data will be analyzed, before commencing the data collection process.

Using Historic Evidence to Determine Sample Size

A final method by which an analyst can determine the size of sample to employ is simply to use what others have used for similar studies in the past. While this may be different from the optimal size in a given problem, the fact that the contemplated sample size is in line with that used for other similar studies is psychologically comforting, particularly to inexperienced researchers. Research Realities 10.1 summarizes the evidence. It provides a crude yardstick for evaluating the size of sample determined by other means. Note that national studies typically involve larger samples than regional or

[12]Nonresponse and other nonsampling errors and what can be done about them are discussed in Chapter 11.

Research Realities 10.1

Typical Sample Sizes for Studies of Human and Institutional Populations

Number of Subgroup Analyses	People or Households		Institutions	
	National	Regional or Special	National	Regional or Special
None or few	1,000–1,500	200–500	200–500	50–200
Average	1,500–2,500	500–1,000	500–1,000	200–500
Many	2,500+	1,000+	1,000+	500+

Source: Seymour Sudman, *Applied Sampling* (New York: Academic Press, 1976), p. 87.

special studies. Note further that the number of subgroup analyses has a direct impact on sample size.

Summary

In this chapter we reviewed the basic statistical principles involved in determining the size of a sample. The principles were used to develop confidence interval estimates for either a population mean or a population proportion using simple random samples. The examples demonstrated the influence of the sampling distribution of the statistic, the degree of confidence, and the level of precision on sample size. Both absolute and relative precision were discussed. The general conclusion was that sample size must be increased whenever population variability, degree of confidence, or the precision required of the estimate were increased. The size of the parent population did not affect the size of the sample except indirectly, through its impact on variability or through the finite population correction. Sample size can also be determined using the anticipated cross classifications. One simply multiplies the number of cells by the number of observations required in each cell to inspire confidence in the conclusions. A similar argument applies when other data analysis techniques are to be used; the size of the sample must be large enough to satisfy the requirements of the technique.

Questions

1. In determining sample size, what factors must an analyst consider?
2. When estimating a population mean, what is meant by absolute precision? What is meant by relative precision?
3. What is the difference between degree of confidence and degree of precision?
4. Suppose the population variance is known. How does one then determine the sample size necessary to estimate a population mean with some desired degree of precision and

confidence? Given that the sample has been selected, how does one generate the desired confidence interval?

5. How does the procedure in Question 4 differ when the population variance is unknown?

6. What effect would doubling the absolute precision with which a population mean is estimated have on sample size? Increasing the degree of confidence from 95 percent to 99 percent?

7. Suppose one wanted to estimate a population mean within ± 10 percent at the 95 percent level of confidence. How would one proceed and what quantities would one need to estimate?

8. What is the difference between absolute precision and relative precision in the estimation of a population proportion?

9. Suppose one wanted to estimate a population proportion within ± 2 percentage points at the 95 percent level of confidence. How would one proceed and what quantities would one need to estimate?

10. Suppose in Question 9 that the researcher wanted the estimate to be within ± 2 percent of the population value. What would be the procedure now and what quantities would she or he need to estimate?

11. What happens if the sample proportion is larger than the estimated population proportion used to determine sample size? If it is smaller? What value of the population proportion should be assumed if one wishes to take no chance that the generated interval will be larger than the desired interval?

12. What is the correct procedure for treating multiple study objectives when calculating sample size?

13. How does one determine sample size based on anticipated cross-classifications of the data?

Applications and Problems

1. A survey was being designed by the market research department of a medium-sized manufacturer of household appliances. The general aim was to assess customer satisfaction with the company's refrigerators. As part of this general objective, management wished to measure the average maintenance expenditure per year per household, the average number of malfunctions or breakdowns per year, and the number of times a refrigerator is cleaned within a year. Management wished to be 95 percent confident in the results. Further, the magnitude of the error was not to exceed plus or minus $4 for maintenance expenditures, plus or minus 1 malfunction, and plus or minus 4 cleanings. The research department noted that while some households would spend nothing on maintenance expenditures per year, others might spend as much as $120. Also, while some refrigerators would experience no breakdowns within a year, the maximum expected would be no more than three. Finally, while some refrigerators might not be cleaned at all during the year, others might be cleaned as frequently as once a month.

   (a) How large a sample would you recommend if each of the three variables is considered separately? Show all your calculations.
   (b) What size sample would you recommend *overall* given that management felt that the expenditure on repairs was most important and the number of cleanings least important to know accurately?

(c) The survey indicated that the average maintenance expenditure is $30 and the standard deviation is $15. Estimate the confidence interval for the population parameter μ. What can you say about the degree of precision?

2. The management of a major brewery wanted to determine the average ounces of beer consumed per resident in the state of Washington. Past trends indicated that the variation in beer consumption (σ) was 4 ounces. A 95 percent confidence level is required and the error is not to exceed plus or minus $\frac{1}{2}$ an ounce.

(a) What sample size would you recommend? Show your calculations.
(b) Management wanted to double the level of precision and increase the level of confidence to 99 percent. What sample size would you recommend? Show your calculations. Comment on your results.

3. The manager of a local recreational center wanted to determine the average amount each customer spent on travelling to and from the center. On the basis of the findings, the manager was planning on raising the entrance fee. The manager noted that customers living near the center would spend nothing on travelling. On the other hand, customers living at the other side of town had to travel about 15 miles and spent about 20 cents per mile. The manager wanted to be 95 percent confident of the findings and did not want the error to exceed plus or minus 10 cents.

(a) What sample size should the manager use to determine the average travel expenditure? Show your calculations.
(b) After the survey was conducted, the manager found the average expenditure to be $1.00 and the standard deviation was $0.60. Construct a 95 percent confidence interval. What can you say about the level of precision?

4. A large manufacturer of chemicals recently came under severe criticism from various environmentalists for its disposal of industrial effluent and waste. In response, management launched a campaign to counter the bad publicity it was receiving. A study of the effectiveness of the campaign indicated that about 20 percent of the residents of the city were aware of the campaign and the company's position. In conducting the study, a sample of 400 was used and a 95 percent confidence interval was specified. Three months later, it was believed that 30 percent of the residents were aware of the campaign. However, management decided to do another survey and specified a 99 percent confidence level and a margin of error of plus or minus 2 percentage points.

(a) What sample size would you recommend for this study? Show all your calculations.
(b) After doing the survey it was found that 50 percent of the population was aware of the campaign. Construct a 99 percent confidence interval for the population parameter.

5. Pac-Trac, Inc., is a large manufacturer of video games. The market research department is designing a survey in order to determine attitudes towards the products. Additionally, the percentage of households owning video games and the average usage rate per week is to be determined. The department wants to be 95 percent confident of the results and does not want the error to exceed plus or minus 3 percentage points for video game ownership and plus or minus one hour for average usage rate. Previous reports indicate that about 20 percent of the households own video games and the average usage rate is 15 hours with a standard deviation of 5 hours.

(a) What sample size would you recommend assuming only the percentage of households owning video games is to be determined? Show all your calculations.
(b) What sample size would you recommend assuming only the average usage rate per week is to be determined? Show all your calculations.

(c) What sample size would you recommend assuming both the above variables are to be determined? Why?

After the survey was conducted, the results indicated that 30 percent of the households owned video games and the average usage rate was 13 hours with a standard deviation of 4.

(d) Compute the 95 percent confidence interval for the percentage of individuals owning video games. Comment on the degree of precision.

(e) Compute the 95 percent confidence interval for the average usage rate. Comment on the degree of precision.

6. The local gas and electric company in a city in the northeast United States recently started a campaign to encourage people to reduce unnecessary use of gas and electricity. To assess the effectiveness of the campaign, management wanted to do a survey to determine the proportion of people that had adopted the recommended energy saving measures.

(a) What sample size would you recommend if the error is not to exceed plus or minus .025 percentage points and the confidence level is to be 90 percent? Show your calculations.

(b) The survey indicated that the proportion adopting the measures was 40 percent. Estimate the 90 percent confidence interval. Comment on the level of precision. Show your calculations.

7. Worldly Travels was a large travel agency located in Indianapolis, Indiana. Management was concerned about its declining leisure travel-tour business. It believed that the profile of those engaging in leisure travel had changed in the past few years. To determine if that was indeed the case, management decided to conduct a survey to determine the profile of the current leisure travel-tour customer. Three variables were identified that required particular attention. Prior to conducting the survey, the following three dummy tables were developed.

	Age			
Income	18–24	25–34	35–54	55+
0–$9,999				
$10,000–$19,999				
$20,000–$29,999				
$30,000–$39,999				
Over $40,000				

	Education			
Age	Some High School	High School Graduate	Some College	College Graduate
18–24				
25–34				
35–54				
55+				

| Income | Education | | | |
	Some High School	High School Graduate	Some College	College Graduate
0–$9,999				
$10,000–$19,999				
$20,000–$29,999				
$30,000–$39,999				
Over $40,000				

(a) How large a sample would you recommend be taken? Justify your answer.

(b) The survey produced the following incomplete table for the variables of age and education. Complete the table on the basis of the assumption that the two characteristics are independent (even though that assumption is wrong). On the basis of the completed table, do you think an appropriate sample size was used? If yes, why? If not, why not?

| Age | Education | | | | Total |
	Some High School	High School Graduate	Some College	College Graduate	
18–24					100
25–34					200
35–54					350
55+					350
Total	200	400	300	100	1,000

Chapter **11**
Collecting the Data: Field Procedures and Nonsampling Error

The step after sample design in the research process is that of data collection. Data collection entails the use of some kind of field force, operating either in the field or from an office, as in a phone or mail survey. This, in turn, raises the questions of selection, training, and control of the field staff. This chapter investigates these issues from the perspective of what can go wrong in conducting a field study. The emphasis will be on those sources of error not previously dealt with. An understanding of the various sources of error in data collection should give much insight into the selection, training, and control questions and should also assist in evaluating the research information upon which decisions must be based.

Impact and Importance of Nonsampling Errors

Two basic types of errors arise in research studies: sampling errors and nonsampling errors. The concept of sampling error underlay much of the discussion in Chapters 9 and 10. Basic to that discussion was the concept of the sampling distribution of some statistic, be it the sample mean, sample proportion, or whatever. The sampling distribution arises because of sampling error. The sampling distribution reflects the fact that the different possible samples that could be drawn under the sampling plan will produce different estimates of the parameter. The statistic simply varies from sample to sample because we are only sampling part of the population in each case. **Sampling error,** then, is "the difference between the observed values of a variable and the long-run average of the observed values in repetitions of the measurement."[1] As we saw, sampling errors can be reduced by increasing sample size. The distribution of the sample statistic becomes more and more concentrated about the long-run average value, as the sample statistic is more equal from sample to sample when it is based on a larger number of observations.

Nonsampling errors reflect the many other kinds of error that arise in research, even when the survey is not based on a sample. They can be random or nonrandom. Nonran-

---

[1]Frederick Mosteller, "Nonsampling Errors," *Encyclopedia of Social Sciences* (New York: Macmillan, 1968), p. 113. See also Charles F. Turner and Elizabeth Martin, eds. *Surveying Subjective Phenomena, Vol. I* (New York: Russell Sage Foundations, 1985)

dom nonsampling errors are the more troublesome of the two. Random errors produce estimates that vary from the true value; sometimes these estimates are above and sometimes below the true value but on a random basis. The result is that, in the absence of sampling errors, the sample estimate will equal the population value. Nonrandom nonsampling errors, on the other hand, tend to produce mistakes only in one direction. They tend to bias the sample value away from the population parameter. Nonsampling errors can occur because of errors in conception, logic, misinterpretation of replies, statistics, arithmetic, errors in tabulation or coding, or errors in reporting the results. They are so pervasive that they have caused one writer to lament:

The roster of possible troubles seems only to grow with increasing knowledge. By participating in the work of a specific field, one can, in a few years, work up considerable methodological expertise, much of which has not been and is not likely to be written down. To attempt to discuss every way a study can go wrong would be a hopeless venture.[2] *(emphasis added)*

Not only are nonsampling errors pervasive, but they are not as well behaved as are sampling errors. Sampling errors decrease with increases in sample size. Nonsampling errors do not necessarily decrease with increases in sample size. They may, in fact, increase. Sampling errors can be estimated if probability sampling procedures are used. The direction, much less the magnitude, of nonsampling errors is often unknown. True, they bias the sample value away from the population parameter, but in many studies it is hard to see whether they cause underestimation or overestimation of the parameter. Nonsampling errors also distort the reliability of sample estimates; the bias due to them serves to increase the standard error of estimates of particular statistics to such an extent that the confidence interval estimates turn out to be faulty. Some of the most striking evidence in this regard was gathered in the Consumer Savings Project conducted at the University of Illinois, which specifically investigated the reliability of consumer reports of financial assets and debts by contrasting these reports with known data.

The empirical studies presented . . . indicate in striking fashion that nonsampling errors are not simply a matter of theory, but do in fact exist and are mainly responsible for the pronounced tendency of survey data to understate aggregates. . . . Not only was this bias present in the survey data, but in many instances the contribution of nonsampling errors to the total variance in the data was so large as to render meaningless confidence intervals computed by the usual statistical formulas . . . *the magnitude of this type of error tends, if anything, to increase with sample size.*[3] *(emphasis added)*

Further, more sophisticated samples are not the answer to eliminating nonsampling errors.

If the findings of this project are any indication, increasing attention must be given to the detection and correction of nonsampling errors. Such attention will be needed par-

---

[2]Mosteller, ''Nonsampling Errors'' p. 113.

[3]Robert Ferber, *The Reliability of Consumer Reports of Financial Assets and Debts* (Urbana, Ill.: Bureau of Economic and Business Research, University of Illinois, 1966), p. 261. There was a series of studies with respect to the single objective. Ferber's monograph provides an overview of the studies and results, although there are six monographs in all.

ticularly in the conduct of large-scale, well-designed probability samples, for as the efficiency of a sample design increases and the size of sampling variances decreases, the effect of nonsampling errors becomes progressively more important. Since nonsampling variances are virtually unaffected by sample size, we are faced with the paradoxical situation that the more efficient is the sample design, the more important are nonsampling errors likely to be and the more meaningless are confidence interval computations based on the usual error formulas.[4]

Nonsampling errors are frequently the most important errors that arise in research. In special Census Bureau investigations of their size, for example, nonsampling errors were found to be ten times the magnitude of sampling errors.[5] This is not an unusual finding. Rather, a consistent finding is that nonsampling error is the major contributor to total survey error, while random sampling error has minimal impact.[6] Nonsampling errors can be reduced, but their reduction depends on improving method rather than increasing sample size. By understanding the sources of nonsampling errors, the analyst is in a better position to reduce them.

Types of Nonsampling Errors

Figure 11.1 offers a general overview of nonsampling errors.[7] They are of two basic types—errors due to nonobservation or to observation. Nonobservation errors result from a failure to obtain data from parts of the survey population. **Nonobservation errors** can happen because part of the population of interest was not included or because some elements designated for inclusion in the sample did not respond. **Observation errors** occur because inaccurate information is secured from the sample elements or because errors are introduced in the processing of the data or in reporting the findings. In many ways, they are more troublesome than nonobservation errors. With nonobservation errors, we at least know we have a problem because of noncoverage or nonresponse. With observation errors, we may not even be aware that a problem exists. The very notion of an observation error rests on the presumption that there is indeed some "true" value for the variable or variables. An observational error, then, is simply the difference between the reported value and the "true" value. You can readily see that detection of an observational error places the researcher in the awkward position of knowing the very quantity the study is designed to estimate.

---

[4]*Ibid.*, p. 266. Wiseman and McDonald make a similar point with the comment, "The use of very sophisticated sampling schemes when other aspects of the data collection effort are much less sophisticated may result in higher costs than are justified for the resultant data quality." See Frederick Wiseman and Philip McDonald, "Noncontact and Refusal Rates in Consumer Telephone Surveys," *Journal of Marketing Research,* 16 (November 1979), p. 483.

[5]W. H. Williams, "How Bad Can 'Good' Data Really Be?," *The American Statistician,* 32 (May 1978), p. 61.

[6]See, for example, Ronald Andersen, Judith Kasper, Martin R. Frankel and Associates, *Total Survey Error* (San Francisco: Jossey Bass, 1979), or Henry Assael and John Keon, "Nonsampling vs. Sampling Errors in Survey Research," *Journal of Marketing,* 46 (Spring 1982), pp. 114–123.

[7]Figure 11.1 is adapted from Leslie Kish, *Survey Sampling* (New York: John Wiley, © 1965), p. 519, and is reprinted by permission of John Wiley & Sons, Inc. Kish's Chapter 13, "Biases and Nonsampling Errors," is particularly recommended for discussion of the biases arising from nonobservation.

Figure 11.1
Overview of Nonsampling Errors

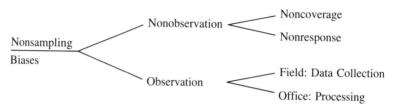

Source: Leslie Kish, *Survey Sampling* (New York: John Wiley & Sons, Inc., © 1965), p. 519. Reprinted by permission of John Wiley & Sons, Inc.

Studies have been specifically designed to estimate the direction and magnitude of data collection errors. Generally, they have:

1. relied on the actual availability of bias-free information, which then served as a validity check;
2. used split-run comparisons where the respondent received different forms of the same questions, say, so that the person's consistency in responding could be measured; or
3. measured the consistency of replies over time from the same respondent.[8]

These methods, while useful, cannot always be applied in substantive as opposed to method studies, and it becomes difficult to adjust the obtained information for response error. Instead this information is taken at face value. Thus, it is vital that researchers understand the sources of response bias so that they can better anticipate and prevent it.

Noncoverage Errors

Noncoverage denotes failure to include some units, or entire sections, of the defined survey population in the actual operational sampling frame. Because of the actual (though unplanned and usually unknown) zero probability of selection for these units, they are in effect excluded from the survey result. We do not refer here to any deliberate and explicit exclusion of sections of a larger population from the survey population. Survey objectives and practical difficulties determine such deliberate exclusions. For example, many surveys of attitudes are confined to adults, deliberately excluding persons under 21 years; residents of institutions are often excluded because of practical survey difficulties. These explicit exclusions differ both in intent and result from non-

---

[8]For discussion of the nonsampling error research being conducted at the Bureau of the Census, see Barbara A. Bailor, "Nonsampling Error Research At the Bureau of the Census," in Frederick Wiseman, ed., *Improving Data Quality in Sample Surveys* (Cambridge, Mass.: Marketing Science Institute, 1983), pp. 44–50. For discussion of the sampling techniques being considered for the 1990 Census, see Eugene Carlson, "New Head-Count Techniques Are Tested for 1990 Census," *Wall Street Journal*, 64 (April 24, 1984), p. 31.

coverage caused by failures in the procedures. When computing noncoverage rates, members of the deliberately and explicitly excluded sections should not be counted either in the survey population or in the noncoverage. Defining the survey population should be part of the stated essential survey conditions.[9]

Noncoverage error is essentially a sampling frame problem. Researchers realize that the telephone directory, for instance, does not provide a complete sampling frame for most general surveys. Not every family has a phone. Further, there is some variation between those having and not having phones in terms of some important demographic characteristics, and not all those people who have telephones have them listed in the directory.[10]

Noncoverage is also a problem in mail surveys. The mailing list here dictates the sampling frame. If the mailing list inadequately represents segments of the population, the survey will also suffer from the bias of noncoverage, and rare is the mailing list that exactly captures the population that the researcher wishes to study.

When the data are to be collected by personal interview, some form of area sample is typically used to pinpoint respondents. The sampling frame is one of areas and blocks and dwelling units rather than a list of respondents. This does not eliminate the incomplete frame problem, though. Maps of the city may not be totally current, so the newest areas may not have a proper chance of being included in the sample. The instructions to the interviewer may not be sufficiently rigorous. Thus, the direction ''Start at the northwest corner of the selected blocks, generate a random start, and take every fifth dwelling unit thereafter'' would not be sufficiently precise to handle those blocks, say, with a number of apartment units. The evidence indicates, for example, that lower income households are avoided when the selection of households is made by the field staff rather than in the home office. Further, interviewers typically select the most accessible individuals within the household, contrary to instructions for random selection. This again means that a portion of the intended population is underrepresented in the study, while the accessible segment is overrepresented.

Nor is noncoverage bias eliminated in quota samples. The interviewers' flexibility in choosing respondents can introduce substantial noncoverage bias. Interviewers typically underselect in both the high and low income classes. This bias is not always discovered since there is also a tendency for interviewers to falsify characteristics so that the appropriate number of cases per cell is achieved. Further, the more elaborate and complex the quota sample, the more critical this ''forcing'' problem becomes. With three or four variables defining the individual cells, the interviewer finds it difficult to locate respondents who have all the prescribed characteristics.

Overcoverage error can also be a source of bias. It can arise because of duplication in the list of sampling units. Units with multiple entries in the sampling frame (for example, families with several phone listings) have a higher probability of being in-

---

[9]Kish, *Survey Sampling*, p. 528.

[10]Randolph M. Grossman and Douglas K. Weiland, ''The Use of Telephone Directories as a Sample Frame: Patterns of Bias Revisited,'' *Journal of Advertising*, 7 (Summer 1978), pp. 31–35; Patricia E. Moberg, ''Biases in Unlisted Phone Numbers,'' *Journal of Advertising Research*, 22 (August-September 1982), pp. 51–55.

cluded in the sample than do sampling units with one listing. For most surveys, though, noncoverage is much more common and troublesome.

Noncoverage bias is not a problem in every survey. For some studies, clear, convenient, and complete sampling frames exist. Thus the department store wishing to conduct a study among its charge account customers should have little trouble with frame bias. The sampling frame is simply those with charge accounts. There might be some difficulty in distinguishing active accounts from inactive accounts, but this is essentially a definitional problem that should be dictated by the purpose of the study. Similarly, the credit union in a firm should experience little noncoverage bias in conducting a study among its potential clientele. The population of interest here would be the firm's employees, and it could be expected that the list of employees would be current and accurate since it is needed to generate the payroll.

Noncoverage bias raises two questions for the researcher: (1) How pervasive is it likely to be? (2) What can be done to reduce it? One difficulty is that its magnitude can only be estimated by comparing the sample survey results with some outside criterion.[11] The outside criterion can, in turn, be established through an auxiliary quality check of a portion of the results, or it may be available from another reliable and current study, such as the population census. Comparison with the census or another large sample, though, means that the basic sampling units must be similar in terms of operational definitions. The choice of a base, then (for example, dwellings or persons), becomes crucial in effecting such comparisons.

Given that noncoverage bias is likely, what can the researcher do to lessen its effect? The most obvious thing, of course, is to improve the quality of the sampling frame. This may mean taking the time to bring available city maps up to date, or it may mean taking a sample to check the quality and representativeness of a mailing list with respect to a target population. The unlisted number problem common to telephone surveys can be handled by random digit or plus-one dialing,[12] although this will not provide adequate sample representation for those without phones.

There are usually limits to the degree to which an imperfect sampling frame can be improved. Once they are encountered, the researcher's main opportunities for reducing noncoverage bias are through the selection of sampling units and the adjustment of the results, often through weighting subsample results, to account for the remaining imperfections in the frame and sampling procedure. When sampling from lists, for example, three problems are commonly encountered: both ineligibles and duplicates are included on the list, while some members of the target population are excluded. The first thing an analyst would want to do would be to update the list, using supplementary sources if possible. While this would help reduce the third problem, it might do little to correct the problems of ineligibles and duplicates. These problems can be corrected, though, when the sample is drawn and the data are collected. When the sample is drawn, all

[11]Kish, *Survey Sampling,* p. 529.

[12]E. Laird Landon, Jr., and Sharon K. Banks, "Relative Efficiency and Bias of Plus-One Telephone Sampling," *Journal of Marketing Research,* 14 (August 1977), pp. 294–299; and Frederick J. Kriz, "Random Digit Dialing and Sample Bias," *Public Opinion Quarterly,* 42 (Winter 1978), pp. 544–546; Albert G. Swint and Terry E. Powell, "CLUSFONE Computer–Generated Telephone Sampling Offers Efficiency and Minimal Bias," *Marketing Today,* 21 (Chicago; Elrick and Lavidge, 1983).

ineligibles are ignored. There is a great temptation when doing so to substitute the next name on the list. This is incorrect procedure, which introduces a bias in that the probability of selection is higher for those elements that follow ineligible listings. Rather, the correct procedure is to draw another element randomly if simple random selection procedures are being used. If systematic sampling procedures are being used, the sampling interval should be adjusted before the fact to allow for the percentage of ineligibles.[13] The problem of duplicates is then handled by adjustment. Specifically, the results are weighted by the inverse of the probability of selection. In a study using a list of car registrations, for example, each contacted respondent would be asked, ''How many cars do you own?'' The response of someone who said two would be weighted ½, while that of someone who said three would be weighted ⅓.[14]

The appropriate sampling and adjustment procedures to account for inadequate sampling frames can become quite technical in complex sample designs and fall largely in the domain of the sampling specialist. We shall consequently not delve into these processes but shall simply note that

1. noncoverage bias is a nonsampling error and is therefore not dealt with in our standard error formulas;

2. noncoverage bias is not likely to be eliminated by increasing the sample size;

3. it can be of considerable magnitude; and

4. it can be reduced, but not necessarily eliminated, by recognizing its existence, working to improve the sampling frame, and employing a sampling specialist to help reduce, through the sampling procedure, and adjust, through analysis, the remaining frame imperfections.[15]

Nonresponse Errors

Another source of nonobservation bias is **nonresponse error,** which represents a failure to obtain information from some elements of the population that were selected and designated for the sample. One problem in dealing with nonresponse error is simply appreciating all of the many things that can go wrong with an attempt to contact a designated respondent. Figure 11.2, for example, depicts the various outcomes of an attempted telephone contact. There is such a bewildering array of alternatives that even the calculation of a measure of the extent of the nonresponse problem becomes difficult.

Spurred by the concern that the absence of standard, industry-wide definitions and methods of calculation for rates of response and nonresponse had prevented an accurate

---

[13]The correct sampling interval is $i = Np/n$ where N is the total size of the list, p is the estimated percentage ineligible, and n is the desired sample size. Seymour Sudman, *Applied Sampling* (New York: Academic Press, 1976), p. 60.

[14]The general adjustment procedure for dealing with the problem of duplicates on a list is to weight sample elements discovered to have been listed k times by $1/k$. Sudman, *Applied Sampling,* p. 63. Most of the standard computer packages for statistically analyzing the data contain mechanisms by which the analyst can specify the weight to be applied to each sample observation.

[15]Kish, *Survey Sampling,* pp. 530–531, offers a number of suggestions as to what can be done to decrease the effect of noncoverage, as well as some general comments regarding the extent of noncoverage bias.

Figure 11.2
Possible Outcomes When Attempting to Contact Respondents for Telephone Surveys

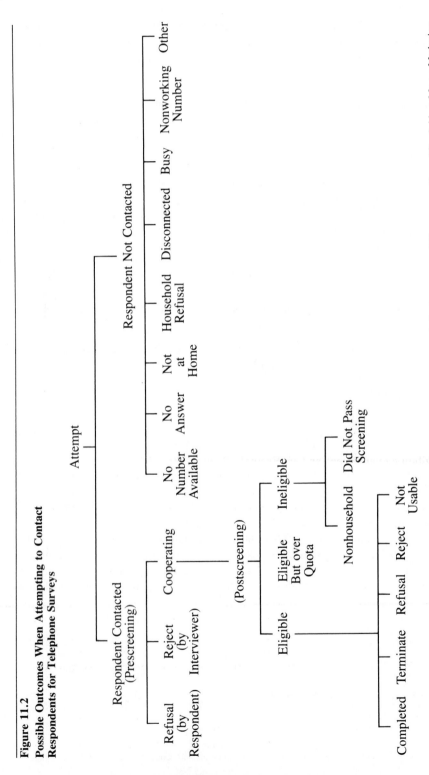

Source: Frederick Wiseman and Philip McDonald, *Toward the Development of Industry Standards for Response and Nonresponse Rates* (Cambridge, Mass.: Marketing Science Institute, 1980), p. 29.

assessment of the potential magnitude of the nonresponse problem, a study was conducted among a sample of members of the Council of American Survey Research Organizations (CASRO) and leading user companies. The study involved mailing questionnaires that displayed actual contact and response data from three different telephone surveys, a telephone directory sample, a random digit sample, and a list sample. Respondents were asked to calculate the response, contact, completion, and refusal rates for each of the three surveys.[16] The difference in results was rather startling. The upper part of Table 11.1, for example, displays the raw data from the telephone directory sample. Using the very same data, one responding organization reported the response rate as 12 percent while another suggested it was 90 percent. Further, there was little agreement among the other firms. No more than three firms out of forty agreed on any single definition of the response rate, and that occurred with respect to three different definitions. The lower part of Table 11.1 displays the three most frequently used definitions as well as the definitions producing the minimum and maximum response rates.

Not only does the variation in definitions cause confusion when nonresponse rates are reported for a survey, it also makes the treatment of the nonresponse error problem more difficult. It becomes hard to discern, for instance, whether a particular method proved effective or whether a different definition was responsible for a lower nonresponse error in a particular study. Because of the need to generalize findings so as to improve the practice of survey research, a special CASRO task force developed a definition of response rate that the industry is being encouraged to embrace as the standard definition, namely that[17]

$$\text{Response rate} = \frac{\text{Number of completed interviews with responding units}}{\text{Number of eligible responding units in the sample}}.$$

The key requirement in accurately calculating the response rate is properly handling eligibles. Table 11.2 displays in Example 1 the proper calculation when there is not an eligibility requirement and in Example 2 when there is an eligibility requirement for inclusion in the sample.

Nonresponse is a problem in any survey in which it occurs because it raises the question of whether those who did respond are different in some important way from those who did not respond. This is, of course, something we do not know, although study after study has indicated that the assumption that those who did not respond were in fact equal to those who did is risky.[18]

The two main sources of nonresponse bias are not-at-homes and refusals. Nonresponse bias can arise with studies using personal interviews or telephone or mail surveys to secure the data. With mail surveys, though, the not-at-home problem becomes one of nonreceipt of the questionnaire. The questionnaire may simply have been lost in the mail, in which case the nonsampling error could be considered random and nonbiasing,

[16]Fredrick Wiseman and Philip McDonald, *Toward the Development of Industry Standards for Response and Nonresponse Rates* (Cambridge, Mass.: Marketing Science Institute, 1980).

[17]"On the Definition of Response Rates," *CASRO Special Report* (Port Jefferson, N.Y.: The Council of American Survey Research Organizations, 1982).

[18]Wiseman and McDonald, "Toward the Development of Industry Standards."

Table 11.1
Response Rate Calculations for Telephone Directory Sample

Panel A: Outcome of Telephone Call

Disconnected/nonworking telephone number	426
Household refusal	153
No answer, busy, not at home	1,757
Interviewer reject (language barrier, hard of hearing, . . .)	187
Respondent refusal	711
Ineligible respondent	366
Termination by respondent	74
Completed interview	501
Total	4,175

Panel B: Most Frequent, Minimum, and Maximum Response Rates

Most frequent

$$\frac{\text{Household refusals + Rejects + Refusals + Ineligibles + Terminations + Completed interviews}}{\text{All}} = \qquad (1)$$

$$\frac{153 + 187 + 711 + 366 + 74 + 501}{\text{All}} = 48\%$$

$$\frac{\text{Rejects + Refusals + Ineligibles + Terminations + Completed interviews}}{\text{All}} = \qquad (2)$$

$$\frac{187 + 711 + 366 + 74 + 501}{4,175} = 44\%$$

$$\frac{\text{Completed interviews}}{\text{All}} = \frac{501}{4,175} = 12\% \qquad (3)$$

Minimum

$$\frac{\text{Completed interviews}}{\text{All}} = \frac{501}{4,175} = 12\%$$

Maximum

$$\frac{\text{Refusals + Ineligibles + Termination + Completed Interviews}}{\text{Rejects + Refusals + Ineligibles + Termination + Completed interviews}} =$$

$$\frac{711 + 366 + 74 + 501}{187 + 711 + 366 + 74 + 501} = 90\%$$

Source: Frederick Wiseman and Philip McDonald, *Toward the Development of Industry Standards for Response and Nonresponse Rates* (Cambridge, Mass.: Marketing Science Institute, 1980), pp. 12 and 19. Reprinted with permission.

Table 11.2

The Impact of an Eligibility Requirement on the Calculation of the Response Rate

Example 1. Single-stage Sample, No Eligibility Requirement

Suppose a survey is conducted to obtain 1,000 interviews with subscribers of a particular magazine. A random sample of $n = 1,000$ is selected, and the initial data collection effort produces the following results.

Completed interviews   = 660
Refusals   = 115
Respondents not contacted = 225

For each of the 340 nonrespondents, substitute subscribers are selected until a completed interview is obtained. Assume that in this follow-up data collection effort 600 substitute names are required to secure the 340 interviews. The recommended response rate is:

$$660/1,000 = 66.0\%$$

and not

$$1,000/1,600 = 62.5\%$$

Example 2. Single-stage Sampling, Eligibility Requirement

From a list of registered voters, a sample of $n = 900$ names is selected. Eligible respondents are defined as those planning to vote in an upcoming election. Assume the data collection effort produces the following results.

Completed interviews   = 300
Not contacted   = 250
Refused, eligibility not determined = 150
Ineligible   = 200

The recommended response rate is:

$$\frac{300}{300 + \left[\dfrac{300}{300 + 200}\right](250 + 150)} = \frac{300}{300 + 240} = 55.5\%.$$

As indicated, when using an eligibility requirement one first must estimate the number of eligibles among the nonrespondents. This is done by using the eligibility percentage, $(300/500) = 60\%$, obtained among persons successfully screened and applying this percentage to the nonrespondents. Thus, of the 400 nonrespondents, 60% (240) are estimated to have been eligible and the estimated response rate becomes (300/540) or 55.5%.

Source: Frederick Wiseman and Maryann Billington, "Comment on a Standard Definition of Response Rates," *Journal of Marketing Research,* 21 (August 1984), p. 337. Published by the American Marketing Association.

or there may be more fundamental reasons for nonreceipt: the addressee may have moved or died. These latter conditions would be a source of systematic nonsampling error.

Not-at-Homes   Replies will not be secured from some designated sampling units because the respondent will not be at home when the interviewer calls. The empirical evidence indicates there is a long upward trend in the **not-at-homes.**[19] The percentage of not-at-homes depends upon the nature of the designated respondent and the time of the call. Married women with young children are more apt to be at home during the day on weekdays than are men, married women without children, or single women. The probability of finding someone at home is also greater for low income families and for rural families. Seasonal variations, particularly during the holidays, do occur, as do weekday-to-weekend variations.[20] Further, it is much easier to find a "responsible adult" at home than a specified respondent, and thus the choice of the elementary sampling unit is key in the not-at-home problem.

Several things can be done to reduce the incidence of not-at-homes. For example, in some studies the interviewer might make an appointment in advance by telephone with the respondent. While this approach is particularly valuable in surveys of busy executives, it may not be justifiable in an ordinary consumer survey.[21] A commonly used technique in the latter instance is the callback, which is particularly effective if the callback (preferably callbacks) is made at a different time than the original call. As a matter of fact, the nonresponse problem due to not-at-homes is so acute and so important to the accuracy of most surveys that one leading expert has suggested that small samples with four to six callbacks are more efficient than large samples without callbacks, unless the percentage of initial response can be increased considerably above normal levels.[22] There is data that indicate, for example, that four to five

[19]Charlotte G. Steeh, "Trends in Nonresponse Rates," *Public Opinion Quarterly*, 45 (Spring 1981), pp. 40–57.

[20]The publication by the Bureau of the Census, *Who's Home When* (Washington: U.S. Government Printing Office, 1973), which contains data on the time of day when individuals with given socioeconomic characteristics may be expected to be home, is useful for planning personal or telephone interviews. See also M. F. Weeks, B. L. Jones, R. E. Folsum, Jr., and C. H. Benrud, "Optimal Times to Contact Sample Households," *Public Opinion Quarterly*, 44 (Spring 1980), pp. 101–114, while the report "Identifying Monthly Response Rates Aids in Mail Planning," *Specialty Advertising Report*, 15 (4th Quarter, 1979), contains a useful table for scheduling mail studies to coincide with the months in which people are most likely to respond.

[21]Urban B. Ozanne and Gilbert A. Churchill, Jr., "Five Dimensions of the Industrial Adoption Process," *Journal of Marketing Research*, 8 (August 1971), pp. 322–328; and Jane Williams Bergsten, Michael F. Weeks, and Fred A. Bryan, "Effects of an Advance Telephone Call in a Personal Interview Survey," *Public Opinion Quarterly*, 48 (Fall 1984), pp. 650–657.

[22]W. Edwards Deming, "On a Probability Mechanism to Attain an Economic Balance between the Resultant Error of Response and the Bias of Nonresponse," *Journal of the American Statistical Association*, 48 (December 1953), pp. 766–767. See also Benjamin Lipstein, "In Defense of Small Samples," *Journal of Advertising Research*, 15 (February 1975), pp. 33–40; and William C. Dunkelburg and George S. Day, "Nonresponse Bias and Callbacks in Sample Surveys," *Journal of Marketing Research*, 10 (May 1973), pp. 160–168, a study that provides "evidence on the rate at which sample values converge on their population distribution as the number of callbacks increases."

Research Realities 11.1

Percentage of Sample Homes Reached with Each Call in Personal Interview and Telephone Surveys

	Personal Interview		Telephone	
Call	Percent	Cumulative Percent	Percent	Cumulative Percent
1	25	25	24	24
2	25	50	18	42
3	18	68	14	56
4	11	79	11	67
5	7	86	8	75
6	5	91	6	81
7	3	94	5	86
8	6	100	3	89*

*It took 17 calls to reach all the homes in the telephone survey.

Source: Robert M. Groves and Robert L. Kahn, *Surveys by Telephone* (New York: Academic Press, 1979), pp. 56 and 58.

calls are often needed to reach three-fourths of the sample of households (see Research Realities 11.1).

An alternative to the "straight" callback is the "modified" callback. If the initial contact attempt and first few callbacks were made by an interviewer and a contact was not established, the interviewer might simply leave a self-administered questionnaire with a stamped, self-addressed envelope behind. If the not-at-home is simply a "designated-respondent-absent" rather than a "nobody-at-home," the interviewer can use the opportunity to inquire about the respondent's hours of availability.

One technique that is sometimes naively suggested for handling the not-at-homes is the substitution of the neighboring dwelling unit, while in a telephone survey it might mean calling the next name on the list. This is a very poor way of handling the not-at-home condition. All it does is substitute more at-homes (who may be different from the not-at-homes in a number of important characteristics) for the population segment we are in fact trying to reach. This increases the proportion of at-homes in the sample and, in effect, aggravates the problem instead of solving it.

The proportion of reported not-at-homes is likely to depend on the interviewer and the judgment used in scheduling initial contacts and callbacks. This suggests that one way of reducing not-at-home nonresponse bias is by better interviewer training, particularly with respect to how to schedule callbacks more efficiently.

The fact that interviewer effectiveness affects the number of not-at-homes also suggests one measure by which interviewers can be compared and evaluated, the **contact**

rate (K),[23] defined as the percentage of eligible assignments in which the interviewer makes contact with the designated respondent; that is,

$$K = \frac{\text{Number of sample units contacted}}{\text{Total number of sample units approached}}.$$

The contact rate measures the interviewer's persistence. Interviewers can be compared with respect to their contact rate, and corrective measures can often be taken. Those with low contact rates can be checked as to why. Perhaps these interviewers are operating in traditionally high not-at-home areas, such as high income sections of an urban area. Alternatively, by examining the call reports for time of each call, the trouble may be traced to poor follow-up procedures. This condition would suggest additional training is necessary, which might then be provided by the field supervisor while the study is still in progress. The contact rate can also be used to evaluate an entire study with respect to the potential nonresponse caused by not-at-homes.

Refusals   In almost every study, some respondents will refuse to participate. The rate of **refusals** will depend, among other things, on the nature of the respondent, the auspices of the research, the circumstances surrounding the contact, the nature of the subject, and the interviewer.

The method used to collect the data also makes a difference. The empirical evidence indicates, for example, that personal interviews are most effective and mail questionnaires least effective in generating response. Telephone interviews are somewhat less successful on average (about 10 percent) than personal interviews in getting target respondents to cooperate.[24]

While it is hard to generalize across data collection techniques regarding the types of people likely to cooperate in a survey, there does seem to be some tendency for females, nonwhites, those who are less well-educated, who have lower incomes, and who are older to be more likely to refuse to participate.[25] The auspices of the research can also make a difference in the number of refusals. People not only report differently to different sponsors, but the sponsor can also affect whether or not they report at all.[26] Sometimes the condition surrounding the contact can cause a refusal. A respondent may be too busy, or tired or may be sick when contacted and thus refuse to participate. The subject of the research also affects refusal rate. Those who typically respond are those

[23]Mathew Hauck and Stanley Steinkamp, *Survey Reliability and Interviewer Competence* (Urbana, Ill: Bureau of Economic and Business Research, University of Illinois, 1964), p. 13. There was far less variability in the calculation of the contact rate than in the calculation of the response rate in the survey of CASRO members. The most frequently used definition included household refusals, rejects, refusals, ineligibles, terminations, and completed interviews in the numerator and all contact attempts in the denominator. See Wiseman and McDonald, *Toward the Development of Industry Standards,* pp. 20 and 21.

[24]Julie Yu and Harris Cooper, "A Quantitative Review of Research Design Effects on Response Rates to Questionnaires," *Journal of Marketing Research,* 20 (February 1983), pp. 36–44.

[25]T. De Maio, "Refusals: Who, Where, and Why," *Public Opinion Quarterly,* 44 (Summer 1980), pp. 223–233.

[26]Tom W. Smith, "In Search of House Effects: A Comparison of Responses to Various Questions by Different Survey Organizations," *Public Opinion Quarterly,* 42 (Winter 1978), pp. 443–463; Wesley H. Jones, "Generalizing Mail Survey Inducement Methods: Population Interactions With Anonymity and Sponsorship," *Public Opinion Quarterly,* 43 (Spring 1979), pp. 102–111.

who are most interested in the subject.[27] On the other hand, nonresponse errors tend to increase with the sensitivity of the information being sought. Finally, interviewers themselves can have a significant impact on the number of refusals they obtain. Their approach, manner, and even their own demographic characteristics can affect a respondent's willingness to participate.[28]

What can be done to correct the nonresponse bias introduced when designated respondents refuse their participation? There seem to be three available strategies. One, the initial response rate can be increased. Two, the impact of refusals can be reduced through follow-up. Three, the obtained information can be extrapolated to allow for nonresponse.

Increasing Initial Response Rate It would appear that the nature of the respondent is beyond the researcher's control. The problem dictates the target population, and this population is likely to contain households with different educational levels, income levels, cultural and occupational backgrounds, and so forth. The task is not as hopeless as it might seem, though. A model for interviewer–interviewee interaction will be offered when discussing errors of observation. Granted that the nature of the respondent can affect the refusal rate, the interviewee's cooperation can be encouraged by an "appropriate choice" of interviewer. But more on this later.

There are also some more traditional things that can be done to assure respondents' participation. One thing, of course, is to sell respondents on the value of the research and the importance of their participation. Advance notice may help. Interviewers can be trained in useful approaches. The evidence suggests, for example, that the more information interviewers provide about the content and purpose of the survey, the higher the response rate in both personal and telephone interviews.[29] Some individuals refuse to participate because they do not wish to be identified with their responses. A guarantee that the replies will be held in confidence (if they truly will be) is often effective in calming such fears.[30] Sometimes money or some other incentive is offered. The research

[27]See, for example, T. A. Heberlein and R. A. Baumgartner, "Factors Affecting Response Rates to Mailed Questionnaires: A Quantitative Analysis of the Published Literature," *American Sociological Review,* 43 (August 1978), pp. 447–462; Leslie Kanuk and Conrad Berenson, "Mail Surveys and Response Rates: A Literature Review," *Journal of Marketing Research,* 12 (November 1975), pp. 440–453; and Michael J. Houston and Neil M. Ford, "Broadening the Scope of Methodological Research on Mail Surveys," *Journal of Marketing Research,* 13 (November 1976), pp. 397–403 for reviews of the literature on mail survey response rates.

[28]Robert L. Kahn and Charles L. Cannell, *The Dynamics of Interviewing* (New York: John Wiley, © 1957), pp. 193–196. For an overview of a number of studies investigating the impact of interviewers on gathering some sensitive health statistics, see *A Summary of Studies of Interviewing Methodology* (Washington: U.S. Department of Health, Education, and Welfare, 1977) while for a general overview see Charles F. Cannell, Peter H. Miller, and Louis Oksenberg, *Research on Interviewing Techniques* (Ann Arbor: Institute for Social Research, University of Michigan, 1981).

[29]Eleanor Singer, "Informed Consent: Consequences for Response Rate and Response Quality in Social Surveys," *American Sociological Review,* 43 (April 1978), pp. 144–162; and Eleanor Singer and Martin R. Frankel, "Informed Consent Procedures in Telephone Interviews," *American Sociological Review,* 47 (June 1982), pp. 416–427.

[30]Steven W. McDaniel and C. P. Rao, "An Investigation of Respondent Anonymity's Effect on Mailed Questionnaires Response Rate and Quality," *Journal of the Market Research Society,* 23 (July 1981), pp. 150–160.

suggests that monetary incentives are effective in increasing response rates in mail surveys[31] but that they are not effective when personal interviews are employed except when mall intercept surveys are being used.[32]

Nonresponse attributable to identification of the sponsor can be overcome by hiding this fact, by hiring a professional research organization to conduct the field study.[33] This is one reason why companies with established, sophisticated research departments do, in fact, employ research firms to collect data.

The ability to generalize what might happen if a particular inducement technique is used to increase the cooperation rate in a survey is clouded by the fact that the effects are different from survey to survey. The data in Table 11.3 are interesting in this regard. They reflect the results of a study that involved the quantitative analysis of the published literature from 1965–1981 that addressed response rates.[34] The basic criterion for including a study in the quantitative analysis was that it had to report at least one response rate that was associated with one of the survey techniques of interest. Some studies reported response rates for several different survey techniques. Each response rate was treated as one observation when this occurred. In the review, the "experimental response rate" was defined as the average response rate across those studies in which the technique was explicitly manipulated. The "control response rate" was the average response rate for these same studies in which the technique was absent. Since some studies had more than one technique variation (for example, they used several different levels of a monetary reward), the number of experimental and control response rates differed in many cases. Table 11.3 looks at the average net difference in response rates when the technique was used versus when it was absent. The table suggests that, on average, the three most effective ways to increase the response rate in a given study are (1) to get a foot-in-the-door by having respondents comply with some small request before presenting them with the larger survey; (2) to follow-up the initial request for cooperation with a letter to those who did not respond to the initial request; and (3) to offer a monetary incentive. Unfortunately, the study did not investigate whether the effectiveness of certain inducement techniques depended upon the method of data collection being used.

Follow-up   Since many of the circumstances surrounding a contact are temporary and changeable, this source of bias introduced through refusals can often be reduced. If a respondent declined participation because he or she was busy or sick, a callback at a

---

[31]James R. Chromy and Daniel G. Horowitz, "The Use of Monetary Incentives in National Assessment Household Surveys," *Journal of the American Statistical Association,* 73 (September 1978), pp. 473–478; J. Duncan, "Mail Questionnaires in Survey Research: A Review of Response Inducement Techniques," *Journal of Management,* 5 (September 1979), pp. 39–55; and *The Use of Monetary and Other Gift Incentives in Mail Surveys: An Annotated Bibliography* (Monticello, Ill.: Vance Bibliographies, 1979).

[32]Frederick Wiseman, Marianne Schafer, and Richard Schafer, "An Experimental Test of the Effects of a Monetary Incentive on Cooperation Rates and Data Collection Costs in Central Location Interviewing," *Journal of Marketing Research,* 20 (November 1983), pp. 439–442.

[33]Wesley H. Jones and James R. Lang, "Sample Composition Bias and Response Bias in a Mail Survey: A Comparison of Inducement Methods," *Journal of Marketing Research,* 17 (February 1980), pp. 69–76; and Wesley H. Jones and James R. Lang, "Reliability and Validity Effects Under Mail Survey Conditions," *Journal of Business Research,* 10 (September 1982), pp. 339–353.

[34]Yu and Cooper, "A Quantitative Review of Research Design Effects on Response Rates to Questionnaires."

Table 11.3
Impact of Selected Techniques on Response Rates

Techniques	Number of Response Rates Included in the Averages	Average Net Difference in Response Rates
Monetary Incentives		
Use/no use	49/30	15.3
Prepaid/not used	33/22	15.6
Promised/not used	13/7	5.8
Nonmonetary Incentives		
Premium/no premium	5/5	9.2
Offer of survey results/no offer	12/12	−2.6*
Response Facilitators		
Prior notification of survey/no prior notification	10/9	8.1
Foot-in-the-door/no prior request for respondent to do an initial task	34/12	18.3
Personalized cover letter/cover letter not personalized	35/32	6.6
Respondent promised anonymity/anonymity not promised	8/7	−0.4*
Deadline for responding specified/deadline not specified	7/7	−0.7*
Return postage provided/return postage not provided	6/5	1.3*
Follow-up letter sent/follow-up letter not sent	16/14	17.9

*Not a statistically significant difference.
Source: Developed from the data in Julie Yu and Harris Cooper, ''A Quantitative Review of Research Design Effects on Response Rates to Questionnaires,'' *Journal of Marketing Research,* 20 (February 1983), pp. 36–44.

different time or employing a different approach may be sufficient to secure cooperation. In a mail survey, this may mean a follow-up mailing at a more convenient time. One means of reducing this source of bias thus seems to be the training and control of the field staff.

It would seem that very little can be done with the subject of the research as a source of nonresponse bias, since it is dictated by the problem to be solved. A sensitive research subject or one of little interest to the respondents is likely to elicit a high rate of refusals. The researcher should not overlook the opportunity of making the study as interesting as possible, though. This often means that ''questions that are interesting but not vital'' should be avoided. The development of the measuring instrument thus becomes essential in reducing this source of refusals.

Generally, other than for refusals because of circumstances, callbacks will be less successful in personal interviews and telephone surveys for reducing the incidents of refusals than they are for treating the not-at-home condition. This is not so with mail surveys. Frequently responses are obtained with the second and third mailings from those who did not respond to earlier mailings. Of course, follow-up in a mail survey requires identification of those not responding earlier. This means that those who did respond need to be identified. However, as we have already seen, respondents who know that they can be identified may refuse to participate. Thus, identification of the respondents, which may serve to decrease one source of nonresponse, may actually increase another. The alternative of sending each mailing to each designated sample member, without screening those who have responded previously, can be expensive for the research organization and frustrating for the respondent.

Adjusting the Results   A third strategy for correcting nonresponse bias involves estimating its effects and then adjusting the results.[35] Suppose, for instance, that the problem was one of estimating the mean income for some population and that responses were secured from only a portion (p_r) of some designated sample. The proportion not responding could then be denoted p_{nr}. If $\bar{x}_r$ is the mean income of those responding and $\bar{x}_{nr}$ the mean income of those not responding, then the overall mean would be

$$\bar{x} = p_r\bar{x}_r + p_{nr}\bar{x}_{nr}.$$

This computation, of course, assumes that $\bar{x}_{nr}$ is known or at least can be estimated. An intensive follow-up of a *sample* of the *nonrespondents* is sometimes used to generate this estimate. The follow-up may be a modified callback. While this rarely generates a response from each nonrespondent designated for the follow-up, it does allow a crude adjustment of the initial results. Ignoring the initial nonresponse is equivalent to assuming that $\bar{x}_{nr}$ is equal to $\bar{x}_r$, which is usually incorrect.

A second way by which the adjustment is sometimes made involves keeping track of those responding to the initial contact, the first follow-up, the second follow-up, and so on. The mean of the variable (or other appropriate statistic) is then calculated, and each subgroup is compared to determine whether any statistically significant differences emerge as a function of the difficulty experienced in making contact. If not, the variable mean for the nonrespondents is assumed equal to the mean for those responding. If a discernible trend is evident, the trend is extrapolated to allow for nonrespondents. This method is particularly valuable in mail surveys, where it is an easy task to identify those responding to the first mailing, the second mailing, and so on.

A third way by which the results from personal interviews can be adjusted is to use the scheme developed by Politz and Simmons, which does not involve callbacks at all.[36] Rather, it relies on a single attempted contact with each sample member at a randomly determined time. During this contact, the respondent is asked if he or she was home at

---

[35]*Statistical Adjustment for Nonresponse in Sample Surveys: A Selected Bibliography with Annotations* (Monticello, Ill.: Vance Bibliographies, 1979); J. Scott Armstrong and Terry S. Overton, "Estimating Nonresponse Bias in Mail Surveys," *Journal of Marketing Research*, 14 (August 1977), pp. 396–402; Michael J. O'Neil, "Estimating the Nonresponse Bias Due to Refusals in Telephone Surveys," *Public Opinion Quarterly*, 40 (Summer 1976), pp. 218–232; and David Elliott and Roger Thomas, "Further Thoughts on Weighting Survey Results to Compensate for Nonresponse," *Survey Methodology Bulletin*, 15 (February 1983), pp. 2–11.

[36]While the technique also could possibly be used with telephone interviews, it was designed for personal interviews because of the tremendous expense of personal interview callbacks. Further, probing on the phone as to when a respondent was home during the last five days can cause mistrust. See Alfred Politz and Willard Simmons, "An Attempt to Get the Not-at-Homes into the Sample Without Callbacks," *Journal of the American Statistical Association*, 49 (March 1949), pp. 9–32, for explanation of the technique. For an empirical investigation of the impact of weighting on bias, see James Ward, Bertram Russick, and William Rudelius, "A Test of Reducing Callbacks and Not-At-Home Bias in Personal Interviews by Weighting At-Home Respondents," *Journal of Marketing Research*, 22 (February 1985), pp. 66–73.

the time of the interview for the preceding five days. These five answers and the time of the interview provide information on the time the respondent was at home for six different days. The responses from each informant are then weighted by the reciprocal of their self-reported probability of being at home; for example, the answers of a respondent who was home one out of six times would receive a weight of six. The basic rationale is that people who are usually not at home are more difficult to catch for an interview and therefore will tend to be underrepresented in the survey. Consequently, the less a subject reports being at home, the more that subject's responses should be weighted.

Evidence accumulated in past surveys also sometimes serves as the basis of the adjustment for nonresponse. This approach is particularly well suited to organizations that frequently conduct surveys involving similar sampling procedures. While no method of adjustment is perfect, the assumption that nonrespondents are similar to respondents on the characteristic of interest is risky. Yet this is the very assumption we make if no attempt is made to correct for nonresponse.

The above discussions all deal with total nonresponse. Item nonresponse, which can also be a problem, occurs when the respondent agrees to the total interview but refuses, or is unable, to answer some specific questions because of the content or form of the questions, or the amount of work required to produce the requested information. The primary mechanisms for treating these problems lie in the development of the questionnaire and methods for administering it, issues discussed earlier. Suppose that item nonresponses occur in spite of our best efforts on these tasks, though. Whether anything can then be done about item nonresponse depends on its magnitude. Here we must distinguish between flagrant item nonresponse and isolated or sporadic nonresponse. If too many questions are left unanswered, the reply becomes unusable and the treatment, or at least adjustment, is the same as that for a complete nonresponse. On the other hand, if only a few items are left unanswered on any questionnaire, the reply can often be made usable. At the very minimum, the "don't know" and "no answers" can be treated as separate categories when reporting the results. In many ways this is the best strategy, because the little evidence that is available on item nonresponse suggests that the problem is extensive and nonrandom.[37] Alternatively, the information from the missing item or items can sometimes be inferred from other information in the questionnaire.[38] This works if there are other questions on the questionnaire that relate to the same issue. The other questions are checked, and a consistent answer is formulated for the unanswered item. In the absence of such consistency checks, regression analysis is sometimes used. The missing item is treated as the criterion variable, and the functional

[37]J. Frances and L. Busch, "What We Know About 'I Don't Knows'," *Public Opinion Quarterly,* 39 (Summer 1975), pp. 207–218; Herbert Schuman and Stanley Presser, "The Assessment of 'No Opinion' in Attitude Surveys," in Karl F. Schuessler, ed., *Sociological Methodology 1979* (San Francisco: Jossey-Bass 1979), pp. 241–275; C. Coombs and L. Coombs, " 'Don't Know': Item Ambiguity or Respondent Uncertainty," *Public Opinion Quarterly,* 40 (Winter 1976), pp. 497–514; Glenn S. Omura, "Correlates of Item Nonresponse," *Journal of the Market Research Society,* 25 (October 1983), pp. 321–330; and Richard M. Durand, Hugh J. Guffey, Jr., and John M. Planchon, "An Examination of the Random Versus Nonrandom Nature of Item Omissions," *Journal of Marketing Research,* 20 (August 1983), pp. 305–313.

[38]Graham Kalton, *Compensating for Missing Survey Data* (Ann Arbor: Institute for Social Research, University of Michigan, 1983).

relationship is established between it and *a priori* related questions through regression analysis for those cases for which the item was answered. The equation is then used to estimate a response for the remaining questionnaires given the information they contain on the predictor variables. Finally, a third way by which item nonresponse is handled is by substituting the average response for the item of those who did respond. This technique, of course, carries the assumption that those who did not respond to the item are similar to those who did. As we have suggested many times, this assumption may be risky and, therefore, substituting the average should be done with caution.

Just as the contact rate can be used to compare and evaluate interviewers with respect to not-at-homes, at least two ratios have been suggested for comparing interviewers with respect to refusals: the **response rate *R*** and the **completeness rate *C*.** The response rate was discussed previously. It equals the ratio of the number of completed interviews with responding units divided by the number of eligible responding units in the sample. The response rate reflects the interviewer's effectiveness at the door or on the phone.

The completeness rate applies to the individual items in the study. Most typically it will be used to evaluate interviewers with respect to the crucial questions involved in the study (for example, a respondent's income, debt, or asset position), although it can also be used to evaluate the whole contact. The completeness rate simply determines whether the response is complete or not, either with respect to the crucial questions or the whole questionnaire.

Field Errors

Field errors are by far the most prevalent type of observation error. **Field errors** arise after the individual has agreed to participate in a study. Instead of cooperating fully, though, the individual refuses to answer specific questions or provides a response that somehow differs from what is actually true or correct. These errors have been referred to, respectively, as errors of omission and errors of commission.[39] It was convenient to discuss errors of omission or item nonresponse in the last section. Now we wish to turn our attention to errors of commission, which are most typically referred to as response errors.

When considering response errors, it is useful to keep in mind what needs to occur for respondents to answer questions put to them.[40] First, the respondent needs to understand what is being asked. Second, the individual needs to engage in some cognitive processing to arrive at an answer. That cognitive processing will typically include an assessment of the information needed for an accurate answer, retrieval of the pertinent attitudes, facts, or experiences, and the organization of the retrieved cognitions and the

---

[39]Robert A. Peterson and Roger A. Kerin, "The Quality of Self-Report Data: Review and Synthesis," in Ben Enis and Kenneth Roering, eds., *Annual Review of Marketing 1981* (Chicago: American Marketing Association, 1981), pp. 5–20. See also, C. A. Muircheartaigh, "Response Errors," in C. A. Muircheartaigh and Clive Payne, eds., *The Analysis of Survey Data: Model Fitting* (London: John Wiley and Sons, 1977), pp. 193–239; and Duane F. Alvin and David J. Jackson, "Measurement Models for Response Errors in Surveys: Issues and Applications" in Karl F. Schuessler, *Sociological Methodology 1980* (San Francisco: Jossey-Bass, 1980), pp. 68–119.

[40]Cannell, Miller, and Oksenberg, *Research on Interviewing Techniques.*

formulation of the response on this basis. Third, the person needs to evaluate the response in terms of its accuracy. Fourth, the subject needs to evaluate the response in terms of other goals he or she might have, such as preserving one's self image or attempting to please the interviewer. Finally, the subject needs to give the response that results from all this mental processing. Reaching the final step is the object of the survey process. Breakdowns can occur, though, at any of the preceding steps, resulting in an inaccurate answer or a response error.

The number of factors that can cause response errors is so large that the factors almost defy categorization. One seemingly useful scheme for dealing with data collection errors, though, is the interviewer–interviewee interaction model, proposed by Kahn and Cannell and shown in Figure 11.3.[41]

The model suggests several things. First, each person brings certain background characteristics and psychological predispositions to the interview. While some of the background characteristics are readily observable, others are not, nor can the psychological state of the other person be seen. Yet both interviewer and interviewee will form some attitudes toward and expectations of the other person on the basis of their initial perceptions. Second, the interview is an interactive process and both interviewer and interviewee are important determinants of the process. Each party perceives and reacts to the specific behaviors of the other. Note, though, that there is no direct link between the boxes labeled behavior. Rather, the linkage is more complicated, "involving a behavior on the part of the interviewer or respondent, the perception of this behavior by the other principal in the interview, a cognitive or attitudinal development from that perception, and finally a resultant motivation to behave in a certain way. Only at this point is a behavioral act carried out, which in turn may be perceived by and reacted to by the other participant in the interview."[42] The perceptions of this behavior may not be correct, just as the initial perceptions of each party may be in error. Nevertheless, such inferences will inevitably be made as both interviewer and respondent search for cues to help them understand each other and carry out the requirements imposed by the interview situation. In sum, not only do the specific behaviors of each party to the interaction affect the outcome, but so do the background characteristics and psychological predispositions of both interviewer and respondent.

The interviewer–interviewee interaction model is appealing for several reasons. One, it is consistent with the empirical evidence. Two, it offers some valuable insight on how response errors (as well as nonresponse errors due to refusals) can be potentially reduced. The model partly applies to telephone and mail surveys, thereby further increasing its value. For example, the respondents' perceptions of the background characteristics and behavior of a telephone interviewer will likely affect the answers he or she provides. The respondent's background is certainly going to affect the person's reported responses. So will the person's suspicions regarding the true purpose of the study, or the individual's assumption of how confidential his or her responses will truly be. These factors can distort the respondent's answers regardless of the manner used to collect the

---

[41]Kahn and Cannell, *The Dynamics of Interviewing,* p. 193. The figure is used by permission of John Wiley & Sons, Inc.

[42]*Ibid.,* p. 194.

Figure 11.3
A Model of Bias in the Interview

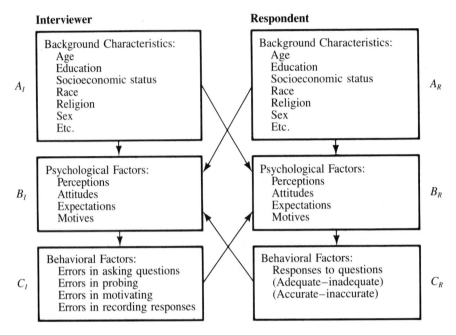

Source: Robert L. Kahn and Charles L. Cannell, *The Dynamics of Interviewing* (New York: John Wiley & Sons, Inc., © 1957), p. 193. Reprinted by permission of John Wiley & Sons, Inc.

data, and it is unlikely these distortions would be random. At any rate, the model suggests certain things that the researcher can do to generate accurate information.

Background Factors The empirical evidence is consistent with the supposition that background factors affect reported responses. More particularly, the evidence suggests that better cooperation and more information are obtained when the backgrounds of the interviewer and respondent are similar than when they are different. This is particularly true for readily observable characteristics, such as race, age, and sex, but applies as well to more unobservable characteristics, such as social class and income.[43] This suggests that it is productive to match the background characteristics of the interviewer and

---

[43]See, for example, the studies of Barbara Bailor, Leroy Bailey, and Joyce Stevens, "Measures of Interviewer Bias and Variance," *Journal of Marketing Research*, 14 (August 1977), pp. 337–343; Shirley Hatchett and Howard Schuman, "White Respondents and Race-of-Interviewer Effects," *Public Opinion Quarterly*, 39 (Winter 1975), pp. 523–528; and Patrick R. Cotter, Jeffrey Cohen, and Philip B. Coulter, "Race of Interviewer Effects on Telephone Interviews," *Public Opinion Quarterly*, 46 (Summer 1982), pp. 278–284.

respondent as closely as possible, as the more characteristics the two have in common, the greater the probability of a successful interview.[44]

Unfortunately, the research is somewhat constrained in this regard. Most interviewers are housewives who use interviewing as a mechanism to supplement their family income. Although the profession also attracts some part-time workers such as students or school teachers, interviewing by no means attracts a balanced demographic cross section of people. Nevertheless, the researcher needs to recognize that the interviewer's background can affect the results, and thus investigators should do what they can to minimize such biases. This may simply mean computing a measure of interviewer variability while analyzing the results. Alternatively, a slight modification of interviewer schedules may be made in a specific project to improve background matches. It certainly seems that recruiting should be aimed at securing interviewers with diverse socioeconomic backgrounds, if other things are equal.

Psychological Factors The evidence regarding the impact of psychological factors on responses tend to support the notion that interviewers' opinions, perceptions, expectations, and attitudes affect the responses they receive.[45] Now certainly these attitudes, opinions, expectations, and so on, are going to be conditioned by the interviewers' backgrounds, and since that is something we cannot control, how are we to control for these psychological factors? The primary way is through training. The fact that interviewers will have psychological predispositions is not critical, since these psychological factors are not observed by the respondent. What is critical, though, is that these factors not be allowed to affect interviewers' behavior during the interview and thereby contaminate the response.

Most surveys, therefore, are conducted using a rather rigid set of procedures that interviewers must follow. The instructions should be clear and should be written. Further, they should state the purpose of the study clearly. They should describe the materials to be used, such as questionnaires, maps, time forms, and so on. They should describe how each question should be asked, the kinds of answers that are acceptable, and the kinds and timing of probes that are to be used, if any. The instructions should also specify the number and identity of respondents that interviewers need to contact and the time constraints under which they will be operating. It is also important that the instructions be well organized and unambiguous.

The instructions must be clearly articulated; however, it is even more important that interviewers understand and can follow them. This suggests that practice training sessions will be necessary. It might also be necessary to actually examine the interviewers with respect to study purposes and procedures. Figure 11.4, for example, shows some

---

[44]Kahn and Cannell, *The Dynamics of Interviewing,* pp. 197–199.

[45]Seymour Sudman, Norman Bradburn, Ed Blair, and Carol Stocking, ''Modest Expectations: The Effects of Interviewers' Prior Expectations and Response,'' *Sociological Methods and Research,* 6 (November 1977), pp. 177–182; Eleanor Singer and Luanne Kohnke-Aguirre, ''Interviewer Expectation Effects: A Replication and Extension,'' *Public Opinion Quarterly,* 43 (Summer 1979), pp. 245–260; and Eleanor Singer, Martin R. Frankel, and Marc B. Glassman, ''The Effect of Interviewer Characteristics and Expectations on Response,'' *Public Opinion Quarterly,* 47 (Spring 1983), pp. 68–83.

Figure 11.4

**Some of the Questions Asked During Interviewer Qualifying
Examination Study of Farm Family Finances**

---

1. *In your own words, please explain the objective(s) of this study, i.e., what we hope to gain from it.*

2. *Suppose a farmer does not believe it is necessary for him to be interviewed. Which of the following explanations would be appropriate?*

   _____ a. The selection was done in a purely random manner.
   _____ b. The refusal of even one respondent lowers the amount of information we have available.
   _____ c. We cannot substitute names.
   _____ d. None of the above.

3. *Currently there are several reliable sources of family savings data, and this project aims to develop another source to be used as a check.*   T   F

4. *In each of the following situations, briefly explain how you would overcome the objections.*

   a. A small acreage farmer cannot understand why his name was chosen and not the people down the road.

   b. A wealthy farmer cannot understand why his name was chosen. Besides, he is too busy.

   c. A sample member states he does not have much savings and therefore does not have to be interviewed.

   d. The farm operator and his wife are both at home. They refuse to be interviewed because there have been several "surveyors" around recently who have turned out to be salesmen.

   e. The farm house is run down and poor looking. The farmer refuses to be interviewed because he never did like universities and refuses to have anything to do with them.

Source: Mathew Hauck and Stanley Steinkamp, *Survey Reliability and Interviewer Competence* (Urbana, Ill.: Bureau of Economic and Business Research, University of Illinois, 1964), pp. 91–102. Reprinted by permission.

Figure 11.4

**Some of the Questions Asked During Interviewer Qualifying
Examination Study of Farm Family Finances** *continued*

---

    f. A middle-aged farmer refuses because he believes that the interviewer is just check-
       ing on his income tax report.

    g. A sample member, while being interviewed, refuses to go any further because the
       questions are too personal.

    h. A harried-looking housewife says, "I'm busy."

5. *Which, if any, of the following is the recommended approach in contacting the
   farmer?*
   _____ a. Go to the respondent's house and attempt either to get an immediate interview
          or a firm appointment.
   _____ b. Telephone the respondent and make an appointment to see him.
   _____ c. Go to the respondent's home, fill in the classification data and make an ap-
          pointment to go back when all the adult family members can be present.
   _____ d. Go to the respondent's house and interview them if the entire adult family is
          present; otherwise, make an appointment to return when they are all present.
   _____ e. None of the above.

6. *(True or False) The Inter-University Committee for Research on Consumer Behavior is a branch of the Ford Foundation and was organized to conduct this study.*
   T   F

7. *In your own words explain why the farm study is being done.*

8. *During the interview the respondent digresses and goes into a long description of
   last year's poor production. You should:*
   _____ a. Change the subject quickly back to the interview.
   _____ b. Say, "Yes, that's very interesting, but I know your time is precious so to get
          back to the interview. . ."
   _____ c. Listen attentively and then ask whatever financial questions may be pertinent
          to the subject.
   _____ d. None of the above.

9. *Briefly explain why records are important and why every attempt should be made to
   get the farmer to refer to them at all times.*

continued on next page

Figure 11.4

Some of the Questions Asked During Interviewer Qualifying Examination Study of Farm Family Finances *continued*

---

10. *If a respondent tries to avoid being interviewed, which of the following, if any, is (are) the wrong method(s) of proceeding?*

_____ a. Put on a "hard sell."

_____ b. Say you will call again in two weeks.

_____ c. Make it clear that you are willing to come at any time that is convenient.

_____ d. Always try to forestall an outright refusal.

_____ e. None of the above.

11. *Two different experiments are being used on the first wave. List three experiments and briefly tell what you must know before attempting to conduct an interview.*

12. *What would you say to a farmer if he said this is his busy time and he has no time to stop and talk?*

13. *If a farmer does not comprehend the importance of the study, which of the following, if any, is (are) the correct way(s) to continue?*

_____ a. Explain the fact that this study will bring to light important figures on the savings of the farm population.

_____ b. Restate the fact that their name will not be used.

_____ c. Stress the importance of each farmer in the sample and how he cannot be replaced.

_____ d. Ignore the questions of the farmer and go on with the interview.

_____ e. None of the above.

14. *The respondent says he doesn't know how much money he has in his checking account, and it develops that he doesn't know offhand, but his checkbook is lying on top of the dresser upstairs. You should:*

_____ a. Ask him to give you an estimate.

_____ b. Tell him that you will call back later for the information.

_____ c. Chide him for not being more cooperative, and try to shame him into looking at his records.

_____ d. Re-emphasize that the study is of nationwide importance, and that we are seeking complete and accurate information.

_____ e. None of the above

15. *(True or False) Under no circumstances should the panel nature of the study be mentioned until the interview is completed.*   T   F

16. *Within a given savings unit we want to interview:*

_____ a. The oldest person in the savings unit.

_____ b. The person in the savings unit who has the most money.

_____ c. The person who makes the decisions on saving and borrowing.

_____ d. The person who keeps the records on spending and saving.

_____ e. The person who spends the most money.

_____ f. None of the above

Figure 11.4

**Some of the Questions Asked During Interviewer Qualifying
Examination Study of Farm Family Finances** *continued*

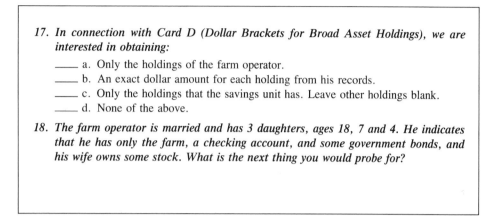

17. *In connection with Card D (Dollar Brackets for Broad Asset Holdings), we are interested in obtaining:*

_____ a. Only the holdings of the farm operator.

_____ b. An exact dollar amount for each holding from his records.

_____ c. Only the holdings that the savings unit has. Leave other holdings blank.

_____ d. None of the above.

18. *The farm operator is married and has 3 daughters, ages 18, 7 and 4. He indicates that he has only the farm, a checking account, and some government bonds, and his wife owns some stock. What is the next thing you would probe for?*

of the questions used to evaluate interviewers in the Study of Farm Family Finances conducted by the University of Illinois.[46] Finally, interviewers might also be required to complete the questionnaire so that, if there is a pattern between the interviewers' answers and the answers they get when administering the questionnaire, it can be determined.[47]

Behavioral Factors The respondents' background, attitudes, motives, expectations, and so on are also potentially biasing. Whether they actually do introduce bias depends on how the interviewer and respondent interact. In other words, the predispositions to bias only become operative in behavior.

Unfortunately the evidence indicates that even when the rules are rigid and the questionnaires relatively simple and structured, interviewers do not follow the rules. They thereby introduce bias. In one classic study, 15 college-educated interviewers interviewed the same respondent, who had previously been instructed to give identical answers to all 15.[48] All the interviews were recorded and were later analyzed for the incidence of errors by type and frequency. One of the most startling findings of the study was the sheer number of errors. For example, there were 66 failures to ask supplementary questions when inadequate responses were given, and the number of errors per interviewer varied from 12 to 36. In another study, it was found that ". . . one-third of the . . . interviewers deviated frequently and markedly from their instructions,

---

[46]The complete questionnaire is contained in Hauck and Steinkamp, *Survey Reliability,* pp. 91–102.

[47]Donald S. Tull and Larry E. Richards, "What Can Be Done About Interviewer Bias," in Jagdish Sheth, ed., *Research in Marketing* (Greenwich, Conn.: JAI Press, 1980), pp. 143–162.

[48]L. L. Guest, "A Study of Interviewer Competence," *International Journal of Opinion and Attitude Research,* 1 (March 1947), pp. 17–30.

sometimes failing to explain the key terms or to repeat them as required, sometimes leaving them out altogether, shortening questions, or failing to follow up certain ambiguous answers in the manner required."[49]

At least three interviewer behaviors lead to response bias: (1) errors in asking questions and in probing when additional information is required, (2) errors in recording the answer, and (3) errors due to cheating.

While errors in asking questions can arise with any of the basic question types, the problem is particularly acute with open-ended questions where probing follows the initial response. No two interviewers are likely to employ the same probes. The content as well as the timing of the probes may differ. This raises the possibility that the differences in answers may be due to the probes that are used rather than any "true" differences in the position of the respondents.

The manner in which the initial question is phrased can also introduce error. Two of the more common errors here are for interviewers to reword the question to fit their perceptions of what the respondent is capable of understanding or in a way that incorporates their own opinions of what constitutes an appropriate answer. Surprisingly, questions that include alternative answers possess great potential for interviewer bias. This bias occurs because the interviewer places undue emphasis on one of the alternatives in stating the question. Slight changes in tone can change the meaning of the entire question. In one of the most comprehensive studies that investigated interviewer error in asking questions, it was found, for example, that the *average number of errors per question by type* was:[50]

Reading error	0.293
Speech variations	0.116
Probes	0.140
Feedbacks to respondents	0.161

One of an interviewer's main tasks is keeping the respondent interested and motivated. At the same time, the interviewer tries to record what the respondent is saying by dutifully writing down the person's answers to open-ended questions or checking the appropriate box with closed questions. These dual, sometimes incompatible, responsibilities can also be a source of error. Interviewers may not correctly "hear" what the respondent is actually saying. This may be because the respondent is inarticulate and the response is garbled or because an interviewer's selective processes are operating. Interviewers may hear what they want to hear and retain what they want to retain. This is a common failing with all of us and, in spite of interviewer training, recording errors in the interview are all too common.[51]

---

[49]W. A. Belson, "Increasing the Power of Research to Guide Advertising Decisions," *Journal of Marketing*, 29 (April 1965), p. 38. See also Martin Collins and Bob Butcher, "Interviewer and Clustering Effects in an Attitude Survey," *Journal of the Market Research Society,* 25 (January 1983), pp. 39–58.

[50]Norman M. Bradburn and Seymour Sudman, *Improving Interview Method and Questionnaire Design* (San Francisco: Jossey-Bass, 1979), p. 29.

[51]Martin Collins, "Interviewing Variability: A Review of the Problem," *Journal of the Market Research Society,* 22 (April 1980), pp. 77–95. For ways of investigating interviewer errors, see Jean Morton-Williams and Wendy Sykes, "The Use of Interaction Coding and Follow-up Interviews to Investigate Comprehension of Survey Questions," *Journal of the Market Research Society,* 26 (April 1984), pp. 109–127.

Lest we be too hard on interviewers, we need to recognize that their job is a difficult one. It demands a good deal of ingenuity, creativity, and dogged determination. Research Realities 11.2 highlights, for example, what an interviewer for the Census Bureau must do to complete the work assigned.

Interviewer cheating can also be a source of response error. Cheating may range from the fabrication of a whole interview to the fabrication of one or two answers to make the response complete. The Advertising Research Foundation (ARF), for example, conducts validation studies for its members upon request by reinterviewing a sample of those who were reported to have been interviewed previously, to verify that the interview actually took place and the designated questions were asked. For the years 1972 and 1973, ARF found that 5.4 percent of the interviews across 33 separate studies could not be verified, and that an additional 7.9 percent contained at least two performance errors.[52] What was especially disturbing about these results is that it is generally believed that the surveys submitted for verification are among the best executed in the advertising area.

Most commercial research firms validate 10 to 20 percent of the completed interviews through follow-up telephone calls or by sending postcards to a sample of ''respondents'' to verify they have in fact been contacted. Generally, these follow-ups are most productive in detecting the flagrant cheating that occurs when a field worker fabricates the entire interview. They are much less effective in detecting more subtle forms of cheating in which (1) the interviewer asks only the key questions and fills in the remaining information later; (2) the interviewer interviews respondents in groups rather than separately as instructed; (3) the interviewer interviews the ''wrong'' respondent because the designated respondent is inaccessible or difficult to contact; and (4) the interviewer employs one contact for information for two separate studies and thereby introduces contamination through respondent fatigue.

Another form of cheating, which is not exactly response error but which has a strong effect on all nonsampling errors, is padding bills. The interviewer may falsify the number of hours worked or the number of miles traveled. The problem is widespread because of the nature of the interviewing situation. The interviewer works without direct supervision in a basically low-paying job. Further, the supervisor's pay is normally geared to the interviewer's charges, so that the higher the interviewer's bills, the higher the supervisor's compensation. Bill padding drains resources from other parts of the study and thereby decreases the efficiency (value) of the information because it is obtained at higher cost.

As suggested previously, it is much more difficult to adjust for response errors than for nonresponse errors. Their direction, much less their magnitude, is unknown, because in order to estimate their effects, the true value must be known. The researcher's main hope lies in prevention rather than subsequent adjustment of the results.[53] The various sources of errors themselves suggest preventives. For example, training can help reduce

---

[52]Lipstein, ''In Defense of Small Samples.''

[53]Another problem in addition to the fact that the true state is typically unknown is that response errors are not well behaved. See, for example, Lawrence C. Hamilton, ''Self-Reports of Academic Performance: Response Errors Are Not Well Behaved,'' *Sociological Methods and Research,* 10 (November 1981), pp. 165–185.

Research Realities 11.2

Adventures of a Census Interviewer

She is probably a middle-aged housewife who races down city streets and country lanes armed with No. 2 U.S. government lead pencils, a stack of questionnaires, a ponderous manual of instructions, and her wits. She finds that her wits are the most important equipment for the job.

"Field Interviewer" is the official title of this federal employee who gathers the information that ultimately is translated into all those vital statistics pouring out of the United States Census Bureau daily — statistics that influence major decisions in the private and public sectors. On her ability hangs the accuracy of the statistics. She is paid four dollars and change an hour and eighteen-and-a-half cents a mile.

Most field interviewers operating in the New York metropolitan area tend to be mothers of children in or past their teens, although an occasional mature man or young person turns up. Their education credentials range from high school diplomas to advanced degrees. Some once worked in professions; others never worked before. But they all share an indefinable mental sharpness. They have to. They couldn't survive without it.

Field interviewers are not thrown out to function in the world without training, of course. They attend classroom sessions and study at home. Supervisors observe their work when they begin, and then annually as they become more experienced. For the most part, however, they operate on their own, keeping in contact with their home office by mail or, in a crisis, by phone.

The information collected by the field interviewer is staggering. Not for her is the simple nose-counting of the decennial census. The Census Bureau, part of the Commerce Department, is the interviewing arm of the entire Federal government and collects data as requested for Health, Education and Welfare, Justice, and any other agency wanting facts from the field. Depending on the survey to which the field interviewer is assigned, she may be asking workers about their employment, teenagers about their health, prisoners about their visitors, or homeowners about their mortgages. For example, just the other week such questioning disclosed that college enrollment had grown by one third in the '70s, largely because of women seeking degrees. She must ask these questions of the exact household or individual scientifically selected as the target. And she is operating under an interesting handicap; unlike the decennial nose-count

in which participation is compulsory, those questioned do not have to answer.

One of the major Census Bureau continuing programs has an added difficulty — a strict time limit. This is the Current Population Survey, on which the national unemployment figures are based. This survey is taken every month all over the nation during the week in which the 19th falls, collecting employment information for the previous week. All work must be completed by the Saturday of that week, with an occasional exception for an out-of-town family expected back by the following Monday.

In this particular survey, selected households, names unknown, are warned the field interviewer is coming by a form letter mailed from the home office, if they have an adequate mailing address obtained from the 1970 census or from a Census Bureau listing. Unfortunately, in many rural areas home listings may read: "White colonial, black shutters, chimney center, garage left, Heatherwilde Drive," so no "occupant" letter can be sent and the interviewer arrives as a complete surprise.

Just *arriving* can be an accomplishment. The largest, most detailed map available is the interviewer's most cherished possession. Except in major cities, her assignment can be spread out over a wide area, and she quickly becomes expert in finding the shortest, quickest routes to the most obscure locations. As soon as this becomes known to her family and friends, she finds she has a side occupation — giving directions to remote destinations.

Ordinary houses or apartments with street numbers are no challenge, although vandalized street signs often produce momentary confusion and urban renewal areas can completely obliterate the target address. The fun begins in more remote sections where homes are listed by descriptions. A summer lake colony with unmarked roads, private roads, and long drives that look like roads can make the interviewer feel like a frantic rat in an endless maze. The frustration here is doubled in winter, with unplowed roads, and only a handful of year-round residents to turn to for help.

The greatest test of the interviewer's ingenuity is finding a house selected from a listing of building permits. She has the number of the permit (often taken out several years previously), the name of the person who took it out, and a description of the site's location (450 feet from the intersection of Matawan and Ivanhoe Roads), a

Source: Flora Gee, "Adventures of a Census Interviewer," *Across the Board,* 17 (February 1980), pp. 2–4 and 73. Reprinted with permission of Flora Gee and The Conference Board.

location that is frequently inaccurate. Did you ever meet a homeowner who knew the number of the permit under which his house was built? How nice it is when the current owner is the person who took out the permit and there is the name on a mailbox! How rare it is this happens! When it doesn't, the interviewer must locate the town hall and the assessor and building inspector. In most areas they know everything and everybody and are always happy to help this poor, tired, frustrated female locate her quarry.

While coping with these specific problems, the interviewer also encounters general, unchanging hazards. In big cities interviewers learn to operate with a minimum of personal possessions and cash, so the mugger or purse snatcher gets little loot. They develop a sixth sense for bottles and bricks thrown from rooftops, and harden their stomachs against the smells of squalid halls and the crunch of cockroaches under their shoes. They develop techniques for dealing with aloof doormen of luxury apartments and for getting past maids, butlers, and answering services.

In the country dogs top the list of dangers. For the sake of her shins an interviewer must be adept at evaluating what that growl really means and whether the length of the chain is sufficient to keep the dog from getting her before she reaches the doorbell. Weather is a continuing challenge. Heat wave, hurricane or blizzard, the survey must be completed that week. The ultimate in anxiety is seeing lights on in the target house and having no place to park because snowbanks have reduced the road to a lane and a half and the family cars are occupying the only shoveled area in the driveway.

When she finally rings the bell of the designated household the first time, the field interviewer has absolutely no notion of what to expect. After her first few months she knows the interview will probably not proceed in the neat and trouble-free manner of the scripts enacted in training sessions, but aside from that she is certain of nothing. The longer she works the job, the more that certainty grows.

In the first place, she is lucky if somebody answers the door. Some days it appears that only mothers of infants are home. All the other women are at work or playing tennis or volunteering in worthy causes. Retired couples are at senior citizen centers or touring the country in "golden age" buses. The men are at business. An unanswered knock means the interviewer must canvass the building or neighborhood, properly identifying herself,

until she can find a neighbor to tell her when someone might be at home. She cannot say what she wishes to see the family for, as this would violate their privacy. It has not been unknown for me to knock on eight doors before finding one person in. When you do get an answer it will probably be the discouraging information that the family is only home in the evening. Discouraging, because suitable evening hours are short and you're operating under that strict time limit.

When the door *is* answered, the reception can be as diverse as the people being interviewed. Reactions range from enthusiasm (rare) to friendly cooperation to tolerance to outright hostility. One family is proud of being a sample family for the United States government. Another shouts through an upstairs window: "Go away and never come back!" On the same street, one family may slam the door in your face the moment you've identified yourself, while another may snatch you in out of the snowstorm, sit you in front of the fire, and insist on putting a Scotch in your hand before answering a single question. One man may refuse admission to his house and insist the interview take place on the front steps in the rain. Another ushers the interviewer inside and serves tea. One woman may reluctantly talk through a locked screen door, while her neighbor offers the loan of a swimsuit and the use of her pool to escape from the heat wave.

Neighborhood events can influence the target's attitude alarmingly. In city sections with rising crime rates, or in rural areas where robbery-murders have occurred, getting the door open requires perseverance on the interviewer's part. Credentials must be held up to a window or peephole for examination, while communication is through an intercom system. Sometimes the resident makes excuses and delays admission. The reason becomes apparent when the police arrive to check the interviewer's ID.

No matter what the reception, the interviewer must do her best to get the information because she is helping to compile a sample survey and each household is important for the accuracy of the data. Some no-shows are inescapable — the family is away for the summer, or on winter vacation in the Caribbean, or on sabbatical in Israel. But if the family is in residence, it's up to the interviewer to get the members to participate in the voluntary survey. Refusals are frowned on, and rumor has it that an occasional thoroughly frustrated interviewer has

continued on next page

Adventures of a Census Interviewer *continued*

found a temporary way out by ''curbstoning'' — sitting down on the curb and making up information for the unreachable or refusing household. This does not solve the problem for long, though, as the deception is uncovered sooner or later by a reinterviewer checkup, performed at undisclosed intervals by the home office.

Getting inside is usually a sign the family is willing to play along, and the interviewer finds that the CPS questionnaire ordinarily proves inoffensive. Basic labor force information is sought, with the questions designed to show who is working, where and at what, and who is not working and why. Wives are sometimes embarrassed by their inability to describe their husbands' most important duties at work, and a musician may dig out his datebook to determine how many hours he worked the week before, but otherwise hitches are few. The real crisis comes at the end when the request for the family's phone number makes the interviewer explain what few have noticed in the introductory letter — that this is the first of eight interviews, two personal and six by telephone,

spread over two years. At this point, those unenthusiastic in the first place often balk, and considerable tact is required to persuade them to cooperate.

Many families find in the end that they enjoy the continued contact. Retired couples and spritely senior citizens living alone are particularly pleased to talk to someone new. Wives with problems find the interviewer a sort of unpaid psychiatrist and, trusting in the confidentiality they have been guaranteed, pour out their troubles. Over the two years the interviewer shares the sorrow of the lingering death of a beloved husband or the accident that kills the promising child. She experiences the excitement of a daughter's wedding and the joy of the birth of a grandchild. She hears of promotions, of college acceptances, of disputes with Social Security, and worries over unemployment. The strangers whose doors she knocked on become her friends. Then, suddenly, the final month of the two-year cycle is over and the interviewer's new friends vanish from her life.

errors in asking questions and recording answers. Similarly, the way interviewers are selected, paid, and controlled could reduce cheating. Overall interviewer performance can be assessed by rating the quality of the work with respect to appropriate characteristics such as costs, types of errors, ability to follow instructions, and so on. We shall not detail the established procedures in this regard, since that would be a book in its own right.[54] For our part we need to recognize the existence of response errors, their sources, and their potentially devastating impact. The interviewer–interviewee interaction model is helpful in visualizing these sources and in indicating some methods of prevention.

---

[54]Some useful general sources are: Ronald Anderson, Judith Kasper, Martin R. Frankel *et al.*, *Total Survey Error* (San Francisco: Jossey-Bass, 1979); Bradburn and Sudman, *Improving Interview Method and Questionnaire Design;* Donald Dillman, *Mail and Telephone Surveys* (New York: John Wiley and Sons, 1978); Paul L. Erdos, *Professional Mail Surveys* (Malabar, Fla.: Robert E. Kreiger, 1983); Robert Ferber, ed., *Handbook of Marketing Research* (New York: McGraw-Hill, 1974), particularly Section II-B; Robert M. Groves and Robert L. Kahn, *Surveys by Telephone* (New York: Academic Press, 1979); and J. Rothman, ''Acceptance Checks for Ensuring Quality in Research,'' *Journal of the Market Research Society,* 22 (July 1980), pp. 192–204.

Office Errors

Our problems with nonsampling errors do not end with data collection. Errors can and do arise in the editing, coding, tabulation, and analysis of the data.[55] For the most part, these errors can be reduced, if not eliminated, through the exercise of proper controls in data processing. These questions are discussed in the chapter dealing with analysis.

Total Error Is Key

By this time we would hope that the reader understands the admonition that total error, rather than any single type of error, is the key in designing a research investigation. The admonition particularly applies to sampling error, because there is a general tendency for beginning students of research method to argue for the "largest possible sample," since training in statistical method suggests that a large sample is much more likely to produce a statistic close to the population parameter being estimated than a small sample. What the student fails to appreciate, though, is that the argument only applies to sampling error. Increasing the sample size does, in fact, decrease sampling error. However, it may also increase nonsampling error, because the larger sample requires more interviewers, for instance, and this creates additional burdens in selection, training, and control. Further, nonsampling error is a much more insidious and troublesome error than sampling error. Sampling error can be estimated. Many forms of nonsampling error cannot. Sampling error can be reduced through more sophisticated sample design or by using a larger sample. The path is clear and relatively well-traveled, so the researcher should have little difficulty constraining sampling error within desired bounds. Not so with nonsampling errors. The path is not paved. New sources of nonsampling error are being discovered all the time, and even though known, many of these sources defy reduction by any automatic procedure. "Improved method" is critical, but what these methods should be is sometimes unknown, although the chapter has attempted to highlight some of the better known sources of nonsampling error and ways of dealing with them.

Research Realities 11.3 attempts to summarize what we have been saying about nonsampling errors and how they can be reduced or controlled. The table can be used as a sort of checklist for marketing managers and other users of research to evaluate the quality of the research before making substantive decisions on the basis of the research results. While not all of the methods for handling nonsampling errors will be applicable in every study, a systematic analysis of the research effort using the suggested approaches should provide the proper appreciation for the quality of research information that is obtained.

---

[55]The reader who believes that analysis errors should be no problem should see Mosteller, "Nonsampling Errors," in which he devotes 9 of 19 pages to the discussion of potential errors in analysis. For an empirical example illustrating the potential extent of the problem, see David Elliot, "A Study of Variation in Occupation and Social Class Coding—Summary of Results," *Survey Methodology Bulletin,* 14 (May 1982), pp. 48–49.

Research Realities 11.3

**Overview of Nonsampling Errors and
Some Methods for Handling Them**

Type	Definition	Methods for Handling
Noncoverage	Failure to include some units or entire sections of the defined survey population in the sampling frame.	1. Improve basic sampling frame using other sources. 2. Select sample in such a way as to reduce incidence, such as by ignoring ineligibles on a list. 3. Adjust the results by appropriately weighting the subsample results.
Nonresponse	Failure to obtain information from some elements of the population that were selected for the sample.	
Not at homes:	Designated respondent is not home when the interviewer calls.	1. Have interviewers make advance appointments. 2. Call back at another time, preferably at a different time of day. 3. Attempt to contact the designated respondent using another approach (i.e. use a modified callback).
Refusals:	Respondent refuses to cooperate in the survey.	1. Attempt to convince the respondent of the value of the research and the importance of his or her participation. 2. Provide advance notice that the survey is coming. 3. Guarantee anonymity. 4. Provide an incentive for participating. 5. Hide the identification of the sponsor by using an independent research organization. 6. Try to get a foot-in-the-door by getting the respondent to comply with some small task before getting the survey. 7. Use personalized cover letters. 8. Use a follow-up contact at a more convenient time. 9. Avoid interesting but not vital questions. 10. Adjust the results to account for the nonresponse.

*The things that can be done to reduce the incidence of office errors are discussed in more detail in the analysis chapters.

Type	Definition	Methods for Handling
Field	While the individual participates in the study, he or she refuses to answer specific questions or provides incorrect answers to them.	1. Match the background characteristics of the interviewer and respondent as closely as possible. 2. Make sure interviewer instructions are clear and written down. 3. Conduct practice training sessions with interviewers. 4. Examine the interviewers' understanding of the study's purposes and procedures. 5. Have interviewers complete the questionnaire and examine the replies they secure to see if there is any relationship between these answers and their own answers. 6. Verify a sample of each interviewer's interviews.
Office*	Errors that arise when coding, tabulating, or analyzing the data.	1. Use field edit to detect the most glaring omissions and inaccuracies in the data. 2. Use a second edit in the office to decide how data collection instruments containing incomplete answers, obviously wrong answers, and answers that reflect a lack of interest are to be handled. 3. Use closed questions to simplify the coding, but when open-ended questions need to be used, specify the appropriate codes that will be allowed before collecting the data. 4. When open-ended questions are being coded and multiple coders are being used, divide the task by questions and not by data collection forms. 5. Have each coder code a sample of the other's work to ensure a consistent set of coding criteria is being employed. 6. Follow established conventions; e.g., use numeric codes and not letters of the alphabet when coding the data for computer analysis. 7. Prepare a codebook that lists the codes for each variable and the categories included in each code. 8. Use appropriate methods to analyze the data.

Summary

This chapter concentrated on the data collection phase of the research process. The emphasis was on sources of error because it was thought that an understanding of sources is more fundamental than a how-to-do-it approach. Practitioners need to be aware of the many potential sources of error so that they can better evaluate research proposals and can place research results in a proper perspective. Researchers need an understanding of error sources so that they can design studies with proper controls and allowances.

The main distinction in errors is that between sampling error and nonsampling error. Sampling error represents the difference between the observed values of a variable and the long-run average of the observed values in repetitions of the measurement. Nonsampling errors include everything else. They may arise because of errors in conception, logic, analysis, data gathering, and so forth and are divided into the two major categories of errors of nonobservation and errors of observation. Errors of nonobservation can, in turn, be divided into errors of noncoverage and errors of nonresponse. Errors of observation can arise while collecting the data or while processing the information collected.

Noncoverage errors are essentially sampling frame problems. The list of population elements is rarely complete. Nonresponse errors reflect a failure to obtain information from certain elements of the population that were designated for inclusion in the sample. They can arise because the designated respondent was not at home or refused to participate. Empirical evidence indicates that the not-at-homes and the refusals are often different from respondents, and thus a systematic bias is introduced when they are excluded.

The interviewer–interviewee interaction model was offered as a useful vehicle for conceptualizing the errors that can arise while collecting the data. This model presents the interview as an interactive process between interviewer and respondent. Each principal brings different background and psychological factors to the interview. These affect each person's behavior and the way he or she perceives the other principal's behavior. Office errors occur because of weaknesses in the procedures for editing, coding, tabulating, and analyzing the collected data.

The research objective of minimization of total error was reiterated. Total error in conjunction with cost determines the value of any research effort.

Questions

1. Distinguish between sampling error and nonsampling error. Why is the distinction important?

2. What are noncoverage errors? Are they a problem with telephone surveys? How? With mail surveys? How? With personal interview studies? How?

3. How can noncoverage bias be assessed? What can be done to reduce it?

4. What is nonresponse error?

5. What are the basic types of nonresponse error? Are they equally serious for mail, telephone, or personal interview studies? Explain.

6. What can be done to reduce the incidence of not-at-homes in the final sample?

7. What is the contact rate? What role does it play in evaluating the results?

8. What are the typical reasons why designated respondents refuse to participate in a study? What can be done to reduce the incidence of refusals? Do refusals generally introduce random error or systematic biases into studies?

9. What is item nonresponse? What alternatives are available to the researcher for treating item nonresponse?

10. What is the response rate? What is the completeness rate? Is there any relation between the two?

11. What are observation errors? What are the basic types of observation errors?

12. Are observation errors likely to be a more serious or less serious problem than nonobservation errors? Explain.

13. Describe the interviewer–interviewee interaction model, including its basic propositions.

14. What does the interviewer–interviewee interaction model suggest with respect to the background characteristics of interviewers? With respect to their psychological characteristics?

15. What basic types of interviewer behavior can lead to response bias?

16. Explain the statement, "Total error is key."

Applications and Problems

1. Mrs. K. Smith was the owner of a medium-sized supermarket located in Portland, Oregon. She was considering altering the layout of the store so that, for example, the frozen food section would be near the section with fresh fruit and vegetables. These changes were designed to better accommodate customer shopping patterns and thereby increase customer patronage. Prior to making the alterations, she decided to administer a short questionnaire in the store to a random sample of customers. For a period of two weeks, three of the store cashiers were instructed to stand at the end of selected aisles and conduct personal interviews with every fifth customer. Mrs. Smith gave specific instructions that on no account were customers to be harassed or offended. Identify the major sources of noncoverage and nonresponse errors. Explain.

2. Deal-A-Wheel was a large manufacturer of radial tires located in Pittsburgh, Pennsylvania, that was experiencing a problem common to tire manufacturers. The poor performance of the auto industry was having a severe negative impact on the tire industry. To try and maintain sales and competitive positions, the various manufacturers were offering wholesalers additional credit and discount opportunities. Deal-A-Wheel's management was particularly concerned about wholesaler reaction to a new discount policy they were considering. The first survey the company conducted to explore these reactions was unsatisfactory to top management. Management felt it was conducted in a haphazard manner and contained numerous nonsampling errors. Deal-A-Wheel's management decided to conduct another study containing the following changes:

   ■ the sampling frame was defined as a list of 1,000 of the largest wholesalers that stocked Deal-A-Wheel tires and the sample elements were to be randomly selected from this list.

   ■ a callback technique was to be employed with the callbacks being made at different times than the original attempted contact.

■   the sample size was to be doubled, from 200 to 400 respondents.

■   the sample elements that were ineligible or refused to cooperate were to be substituted for by the next element from the list.

■   an incentive of $1.00 was to be offered to respondents.

Critically evaluate the steps that were being considered to prevent the occurrence of nonsampling errors. Do you think they are appropriate? Be specific.

3.   A major publisher of a diverse set of magazines was interested in determining customer satisfaction with three of the company's leading publications: *TrendSetter, BusWhizz,* and *CompuTech.* The three magazines dealt respectively with women's fashions, business trends, and computer technology developments. Three sampling frames, consisting of lists of subscribers residing in New York, were formulated. Three random samples were to be chosen from these lists. Personal interviews using an unstructured-undisguised questionnaire were to be conducted. The publishing company had a regular pool of interviewers that it called upon whenever interviews were to be conducted. The interviewers had varying educational backgrounds, though 95 percent were high school graduates and the remaining 5 percent had some college education. In terms of age and sex, the range varied from 18 years to 45 years with 70 percent females and 30 percent males. The majority of interviewers were housewives and students. Prior to conducting a survey the company sent the necessary information in the mail and requested interviewers to indicate whether they were interested. The questionnaires, addresses and other detailed information were then sent to those interviewers replying affirmatively. After the interviewer completed his or her quota of interviews, the replies were sent back to the company. The company then mailed the interviewer's remuneration.

(a)   Using the guidelines in Research Realities 11.3, critically evaluate the selection, training, and instructions given to the field interviewers.

(b)   Using Kahn and Cannell's model, identify the major sources of bias that would affect the interviews.

Cases to Part 4

Case 4.1
Local Government Pooled Investment Fund

The Local Government Pooled Investment Fund, created by law on February 19, 1976, enables local governments in the state of Wisconsin to invest any idle local funds, including state aid payments, in the State Investment Pool. The local funds are pooled with the state funds and invested by the State Investment Board to earn the same return as those in the State Investment Pool.

The operation of the Local Government Pooled Investment Fund is quite simple. The local governing body designates the Investment Fund as a public depository. An officer is designated as the local office authorized to transfer funds to the State Treasurer for deposit in the fund. The official then communicates to the State Treasurer's office in writing the local government's desire to participate.

Local governments participating in the fund earn interest at the same rate as the State Board does on short-term investments. All participants in the State Investment Fund share equally in interest earnings, computed on the average yield for a quarter-term investment and based on the average daily balance of each participant's share of the fund. Each participant in the fund therefore earns interest computed at the average rate for the quarter, regardless of the amount of money deposited in the fund or the term of deposit. Funds may be deposited by check or wire transfer and are returned in the same manner when they are withdrawn. Requests for withdrawals, if received before 10:00 a.m., are honored the same day.

Unless specifically requested, a receipt for amounts deposited is not sent. Instead, each local government receives a monthly statement of deposits and withdrawals that indicates the daily balances on which earnings were based.

The officers of the State Investment Fund have a great deal of investment expertise since that is their full-time job. They are in daily communication with banks, securities dealers, and other investors to achieve the highest competitive rate. With millions of dollars pooled in the fund, the board is able to purchase securities in large blocks, at high yields, and for long periods of time. All of these advantages result in much higher average returns for members of the pool than a local government would be able to earn on its own.

Because of the high rates of interest earned by the fund's investments and the fact that local governments can participate in the program, when only five percent of all eligible local units of government had decided to participate by the first anniversary of the enabling legislation, it proved disconcerting. Consequently, the State Budget Office, under the direction of Tom Landgraf, Director of Budget Operations, commissioned a study to determine why additional support had not materialized and to make recommendations of how participation in the pool could be increased.

Study Design

Some exploratory study of participants and nonparticipants suggested that nonparticipation might be traced to: lack of awareness of the fund and its potential value; concern about involvement in the investment of local funds; pressure to keep the funds locally; and mistrust among nonparticipants. The study team subsequently decided to survey participants and nonparticipants to determine how pervasive these characteristics were.

A mail questionnaire with fixed-alternative questions was to be used. The questionnaire was to be sent to both participants and nonparticipants in the fund. Participants were defined to include those local units of government that had passed resolutions to invest in the fund even if they were not currently doing so. There were 100 such local units, including 37 cities, 17 counties, and 46 towns and villages, and it was decided to send all 100 the questionnaire.

The nonparticipants were to be sampled in the following way. First, the total set of eligible local government units was to be divided into three subgroups of cities, counties, and towns and villages, of which there were, respectively, 172, 55, and 1,508 units. Second, a simple random sample was to be chosen from each subgroup using a random digit table to determine which elements would be included. More specifically, questionnaires were to be sent to 49 cities so designated, 46 counties, and 100 towns and villages. The mailing was to be addressed to the treasurer, and all those treasurers who did not return the questionnaire within a three-week cut-off period were to be contacted by phone to encourage their participation.

Questions

1. Is the study design adequate given the problem posed?

2. What kind of sample is being suggested here? Is this sample appropriate, or would you recommend changes in the sampling procedure?

Case 4.2
Rent Control Referendum

The arrival of spring, 1986, in Flint, Michigan, was accompanied by an upsurge of interest in the community's rent controversy. For several years, a small but highly vocal group of people, most of them living in the downtown area, had contended that apartment rents in the city were too high and that landlords were gouging the public. There had been a number of claims and counterclaims by both parties over the years, and while most of these had found their way into the local news, the issue remained at the level of an exchange of views until early 1986.

At this time, the downtown residents initiated a campaign for rent control. They petitioned the city council to pass legislation fixing rents at the previous year's level. The council refused to do so, but through a concerted campaign the residents succeeded in getting enough signatures to have the issue of rent control placed on the ballot as a public referendum in the fall elections.

This turn of events alarmed a group of realtors in the city and they commissioned a study to investigate rents in the Flint area. The purpose of the study was to provide some hard data regarding the legitimacy of the claims of the two feuding parties—the residents who claimed they were being gouged and the landlords who claimed that, although rents had risen, they had risen no faster than the price of many other things. The study was not intended to explore the perceived advantages and disadvantages of rent control. Its specific objective was to determine whether recent changes in apartment rents were greater or smaller than the changes in other consumer costs, as measured by the Consumer Price Index.

The original intention was to determine the percentage changes in rents for the last ten years. However, some initial exploratory research suggested that data for the last six years were sufficient. Also, since Census of Housing data were available for 1980, that year was picked as the base year for establishing rent changes.

The May Research Company, headed by Carol and Michelle May, was hired to conduct the investigation when it became apparent to the realty group that the information they were seeking was not available through any city agencies or as published data. Consequently, it was decided to generate a pseudo "rent index" by tracking the rents over the six-year period for apartment units selected at random. Insofar as possible, the study was to investigate whether the rates for different sized units had changed disproportionately.

Research Plan

The Flint area was arbitrarily divided into four sections of north, south, east, and west. The east side was chosen as an experimental district within which to test methodology, procedures, definitions, and data collection methods, since it had a good mix of apartments in terms of age of buildings and number of rooms.

An apartment was defined as a unit with a refrigerator, stove, and bathroom, that was unfurnished but included utilities. A room was defined as any unit of space in an apartment that was surrounded by four walls and a doorway. Bathrooms and kitchenettes were to be counted as half rooms, while porches, unfinished basements and attics, balconies, patios, hallways, and entryways were not to be counted when determining the size of the unit.

The sample was to be drawn using the Flint Block Statistics portion of the Census of Housing. A census block was sometimes more than one physical block. The census blocks within the east district were listed and a simple random sample of 64 blocks was selected using a table of random numbers. A field worker was sent to each selected block and was instructed to use the random number assigned to select a building within the block. Specifically, the worker was told to start at the northwest corner of the block, to count buildings proceeding counterclockwise, and to use the building that corresponded to the assigned random number. If the designated building had no rental units, the next building was to be used. The apartments within the building were to be counted, and the table of random numbers was to be used to select the specific apartment that was to be included.

A very short, structured questionnaire was to be administered to an adult occupant of the apartment. Four basic items of information were requested: (1) whether the unit qualified as an apartment under the definition that was being used; (2) whether utilities were paid and whether the apartment was furnished; (3) current and previous rent; and (4) the name of the landlord. The name of the landlord was requested to allow a double check of the accuracy of the rent information provided. Both landlords and occupants could have reasons for inflating or understating rents, and some tenants had not lived in their apartments continuously since 1980, the base year being used for the study.

While all occupant interviews were done in person, all landlord interviews were done by telephone. The landlord questionnaire was structured, and it was even shorter than the occupant questionnaire. All it asked for was the square footage of the unit and the monthly rent as of January 1 for 1980 through 1986.

Questions

1. What type of research design is being used? Is this design appropriate given the problem?

2. What type of sampling plan is being employed? Is this plan appropriate? Are there any changes in it you would recommend?

Case 4.3
Hart Machine Company[1]

Hart Machine Company of Newberry, South Carolina, is one of five major manufacturers of textile equipment in the country. It is also the only firm that *specializes* in the design and production of textile machinery rollers. Confining its distribution to the three state area of Georgia, North Carolina, and South Carolina, company sales have been lucrative, averaging some $50 million annually. Part of Hart's success is due to the company being the only roller manufacturer headquartered in the Southeast, an area where 40 percent of the nation's textile mills are located. This location advantage allows Hart to offer customers both prompt shipment and service at low prices (due to lower transportation costs), factors that have helped catapult Hart Machine Company to the number three position in the textile equipment industry during the relatively short seven-year period since Dean Hart founded it.

In an effort to determine how to best allocate sales personnel and to appraise the performance of current members of the selling team, Thomas Stein, the sales manager, decided to develop estimates of the sales potential for each state served by (1) measuring the inventory of rollers currently used by textile mills and (2) obtaining estimates of manufacturers' future needs. He hoped to develop a feel for new product demand by first time users and potential entrants into the textile mill industry as well as an indication of the replacement demand for Hart rollers by current users of the firm's product.

A search of the Standard Industrial Classification (SIC) codes identified nine 3-digit textile mill industries that were candidates for Hart rollers. Fortunately, there was a

[1]The contributions of David M. Szymanski to the development of this case are gratefully acknowledged.

Table 1

Total Number of Textile Mills by SIC Code Located in Georgia, North Carolina, and South Carolina

		State			
SIC Code	Type of Textile Mill	Georgia	North Carolina	South Carolina	Total
221	Weaving mills, cotton	45	48	44	137
222	Weaving mills, synthetics	34	76	108	218
223	Weaving & finishing	6	4	5	15
224	Narrow fabric mills	6	45	11	62
225	Knitting mills	45	597	47	689
226	Textile finishing	41	91	47	179
227	Floor covering mills	261	30	17	308
228	Yarn & thread mills	89	231	49	369
229	Miscellaneous textile goods	58	97	53	208
	Total	585	1,219	381	2,185

Source: U.S. Bureau of the Census, *County Business Patterns 1982*, for each of the states of Georgia, North Carolina, and South Carolina. U.S. Government Printing Office, Washington, D.C., 1984.

good deal of published data available on these industries, and much of the data was broken down by geographic region, state, and county. Stein also had access to data on individual textile mills that employed 20 or more individuals. Stein thought this information was especially useful because only the larger mills possessed the scale of operations necessary to have textile machinery requiring Hart rollers. The published data (see Tables 1 and 2) also indicated that most of the mills (74 percent) in Georgia, North Carolina, and South Carolina qualified as likely prospects for Hart equipment, in that they employed more than 20 people.

Because of limited research funds, the Hart Company decided to survey only a sample of textile plants in Georgia, North Carolina, and South Carolina. For each firm surveyed, Hart would attempt to ascertain the number of milling machines owned and operated, their age, and the number and brand of rollers used in each piece of equipment. The researchers also hoped to gain information on each mill's performance— including plans for expansion or curtailment of different operations—and brand preferences for roller supplies. From this information it would be possible to estimate the number of machines per textile mill type as well as the new and replacement demand for Hart rollers in the three-state market area. This data would aid Stein in the allocation of sales personnel to different sectors and industries in relation to the demand for rollers. Currently, Hart's sales force is assigned to seven geographic districts: the northern and southern sections of Georgia; the northeast, southeast, and western sections of North Carolina; and the eastern and western sections of South Carolina (see Table 3), according to the overall number of textile mills in each sector.

Industry figures indicate that the number of mills in each of the three states is declining across most industry types (see Table 2). Therefore, estimating the demand for rollers by each textile industry in each state could be crucial to optimal allocation of current sales personnel and to the determination of Hart's future sales force needs.

Table 2
Number of Textile Mills Employing 20 or More Persons by SIC Code for Georgia, North Carolina, and South Carolina between 1980 and 1982

	Year = 1980			
Type of Textile Mill	Georgia	North Carolina	South Carolina	Total
Weaving mills, cotton	45	47	51	143
Weaving mills, synthetics	26	68	98	192
Weaving & finishing mills, wool	5	4	4	13
Narrow fabric mills	3	34	12	49
Knitting mills	35	432	46	513
Textile finishing	36	69	34	139
Floor covering mills	153	10	14	177
Yarn & thread mills	89	223	50	362
Miscellaneous textile goods	32	56	34	122
Total	424	943	343	1,710

Having obtained a detailed listing of the addresses of the textile mills located in Georgia, North Carolina, and South Carolina by industry type, company officials tried to decide on the sampling plan that would best enable them to calculate the sales for Hart rollers quickly and inexpensively. Three plans were being considered for determining the mills at which production personnel were to be interviewed:

■ Plan A, in which textile mills in each of the seven sales regions would be sampled in proportion to the district's size. For example, given that the northeast sales region in the North Carolina district accounts for approximately 19 percent

Table 3
Total Number of Textile Mills Employing More Than 20 Persons in Each of Hart Machine Company's Seven Sales Regions, 1982

Georgia

North sales region	324	
South sales region	59	
Total		383*

North Carolina

Northeast sales region	306	
Southeast sales region	111	
Western sales region	486	
Total		903

South Carolina

East sales region	74	
West sales region	255	
Total		329*

*Due to differences in methods of reporting, totals differ slightly from those in Table 2.

Year = 1981				Year = 1982			
Georgia	North Carolina	South Carolina	Total	Georgia	North Carolina	South Carolina	Total
43	44	48	135	37	40	43	120
25	70	97	192	29	67	106	202
4	4	4	12	4	2	4	10
4	34	10	48	4	35	11	50
34	427	39	500	33	414	37	484
32	71	35	138	30	64	37	131
144	9	13	166	136	12	12	160
85	211	52	348	79	204	46	329
39	56	33	128	33	65	34	132
410	926	331	1,667	385	903	330	1,618

(306/1,615 × 100) of the textile mills in the three-state area, 19 percent of the sample would come from the northeast sales region. Interviewers would be allowed to pick the mills in which the interviews would be conducted.

- Plan B, in which after the total number of textile mills of each type in each sales region was determined, each of the 63 groups (9 SIC types × 7 regions) would be sampled in proportion to its size, and the plants at which the interviews would take place would be determined randomly.

- Plan C, in which two of the regions would be randomly selected, and production personnel at all of the plants in each of the two randomly selected regions would be interviewed.

Questions

1. What type of sampling plan is being proposed in each case?

2. What are the strengths and weaknesses of each plan? Which of the three plans would you recommend and why?

3. What other plans might the company consider?

Case 4.4
First Federal Bank of Bakersfield

The Equal Credit Opportunity Act, which was passed in 1974, was partially designed to protect women from discriminatory banking practices. It forbade, for example, the use of credit evaluations based on sex or marital status. While adherence to the law has changed the way many bankers do business, women's perception that there is a bias against them by a particular financial institution often remains unless some specific steps are taken by the institution to counter that perception.

Close to a dozen "women's banks," that is, banks owned and operated by and for women, opened their doors during the 1970s with the specific purpose of targeting and promoting their services to this otherwise underdeveloped market. Today, while "women's banks" are evolving into full service banks serving a wide range of clients, a number of traditional banks are moving in the other direction by attempting to develop services that are targeted specifically toward women. Many of these forward-looking institutions see such a strategy as a viable way to attract valuable customers and to increase their market share in the short term while gaining a competitive advantage by which they can compete in the long term as the roles of women in the labor force gain in importance. One can find, with even the most cursory examination of the trade press, examples of credit card advertising that depicts single, affluent, and head-of-the-family female card holders, financial seminar programs for affluent wives of professional men, informational literature that details how newly divorced and separated women can obtain credit, and entire packages of counseling, educational opportunities, and special services for women.

The First Federal Bank of Bakersfield was interested in developing its own program of this kind. The executives were curious about a number of issues. Were women's financial needs being adequately met in the Bakersfield area? What additional financial services would women especially like to have? How do Bakersfield's women feel about banks and bankers? Was First Federal in a good position to take advantage of the needs of women? What channels of communication might be best to reach women who may be interested in the services that First Federal had to offer?

The executives believed that First Federal might have some special advantages if it did try to appeal to women. For one thing, the Bakersfield community seemed to be quite sensitive to the issues being raised by the feminist movement. For another, First Federal was a small, personal bank. The executives thought that women might be more comfortable in dealing with a smaller, more personalized institution and that the bank might not have the traditional "image problem" among women that larger banks might have.

Research Objectives

One program the bank executives were considering that they believed might be particularly attractive to women was a series of financial seminars. The seminars could cover a number of topics including money management, wills, trusts, estate planning, taxes, insurance, investments, financial services, and establishing a credit rating. The executives were interested in determining women's reactions to each of these potential topics. They were also interested to know what the best format might be in terms of location, frequency, length of each program, and so on if there were a high level of interest. Consequently, they decided that the bank should conduct a research study that had the assessment of the financial seminar series as its main objective but that also shed some light on the other issues they had been debating. More specifically, the objectives of the research were:

1. to determine the interest that exists among women in the Bakersfield area for seminars on financial matters;

2. to identify the reasons why Bakersfield women would change, or have changed, their banking affiliations;

3. to examine the attitudes of Bakersfield women toward financial institutions and the people who run them;

4. to determine if there was any correlation between the demographic characteristics of women in the Bakersfield area and the services they might like to have; and

5. to analyze the media usage habits of Bakersfield-area women.

Method

The assignment to develop a research strategy by which these objectives could be assessed was given to the bank's internal marketing research department. The department consisted of only five members—Beth Anchurch, the research director, and four project analysts. As Beth pondered the assignment, she was concerned about the best way to proceed. She was particularly concerned with the relatively short time horizon she was given for the project. Top executives thought there was promise in the seminar idea. If they were right, they wanted to get on with designing and offering the seminars before any of their competitors came up with a similar idea. Thus, they specified that they would like the results of the research department's investigation to be available within 45 to 50 days.

As Ms. Anchurch began to contemplate the data collection, she became particularly concerned with whether the study should use mail questionnaires or telephone interviews. She had tentatively ruled out personal interviews because of the short deadline that had been imposed. After several days of contemplating the alternatives, she finally decided that it would be best to collect the information by telephone. Further, she decided that it would be better to hire out the telephone interviewing than to use her four project analysts to make the calls.

Ms. Anchurch believed that the multiple objectives of the project required a reasonably large sample of women so that the various characteristics of interest would be sufficiently represented to enable some conclusions to be drawn about the population of Bakersfield as a whole. After pondering the various cross tabulations in which the bank executives would be interested, she finally decided that a sample of 500 to 600 adult women would be sufficient. The sample was to be drawn from the white pages of the Bakersfield's telephone directory by the Bakersfield Interviewing Service, the firm that First Federal had hired to complete the interviews.

The sample was to be drawn using a scheme in which two names were selected from each page of the directory first by selecting two of the four columns on the page at random and then by selecting the fifteenth name in each of the selected columns. The decision to sample names from each page was made so that each interviewer could operate with certain designated pages of the directory, since each was operating independently out of her home.

The decision to sample every fifteenth name in the selected columns was determined in the following way. First, there were 328 pages in the directory with four columns of

Table 1

**Selected Demographic Comparison of Survey
Respondents with Bureau of Census Data**

	Percentage of Women	
Characteristic/Category	Survey	Census
Marital Status		
Married	53	42
Single	30	40
Separated	1	2
Widowed	9	9
Divorced	7	7
Age		
18–24	23	23
25–34	30	28
35–44	16	14
45–64	18	21
65+	13	14
Income		
Less than $10,000	9	29
$10,000–$19,999	19	29
$20,000–$50,000	58	36
More than $50,000	2	6
Refused	12	

names per page. There were 80 entries per column on average, or approximately 26,240 listings. Using Bureau of the Census data on household composition, it was estimated that 20 percent of all households would be ineligible for the study because they did not contain an adult female resident. This meant that only 20,992 (.80 × 26,240) of the listings would probably qualify. Since 500 to 600 names were needed, it seemed easiest to select two columns on each page at random and to take the same numbered entry from each column. The interviewer could then simply count or measure down from the top of the column. The number 15 was determined randomly; thus, the fifteenth listing in the randomly selected columns on each page was called. If the household did not answer or if the women of the house refused to participate, the interviewers were instructed to select another number from that column through the use of an abbreviated table of random numbers that each was supplied. They were to use a similar procedure if the household that was called did not have an adult woman living there.

First Federal decided to operate without callbacks because the interviewing service charged heavily for them. Ms. Anchurch did think it would be useful to follow up with a sample of those interviewed to make sure they indeed had been called, since the interviewers for Bakersfield Interviewing Service operated out of their own homes and it was impossible to supervise them more directly. She did this by selecting at random a handful of the surveys completed by each interviewer. She then had one of her project

Table 2
Results of Calls by Interviewer

| Interviewer | Number of Nonresponses | | | Number of Refusals | | Number of Completions |
	Line Busy	No Answer	Ineligibles*	Initial	After Partial Completion	
1	7	101	36	15	0	30
2	2	45	13	16	0	30
3	11	71	23	17	7	30
4	14	56	47	35	6	39
5	9	93	10	23	13	30
6	5	102	28	63	14	35
7	6	36	17	16	0	18
8	7	107	23	13	0	30
9	11	106	36	47	0	30
10	10	55	6	35	9	30
11	38	83	48	92	0	30
12	5	22	3	8	0	9
13	23	453	102	65	7	99
14	12	102	27	31	0	19
15	7	173	29	66	0	34
16	2	65	9	33	0	22
Total	169	1,670	457	575	56	515
		1,839			631	

*No adult female resident.

assistants call that respondent, verify the interview had taken place, and check the accuracy of the responses of a few of the most important questions. This audit revealed absolutely no instances of interviewer cheating.

The completed interview forms were turned over to First Federal for its own internal analysis. As part of this analysis, the project analyst compared the demographic characteristics of those contacted to the demographic characteristics of the population in the Bakersfield area as reported in the 1980 Census. The comparison is shown in Table 1. The analyst also prepared a summary of the nonresponses and refusals by interviewer. This comparison is shown in Table 2.

Questions

1. Compare the advantages and disadvantages of using telephone interviews versus personal interviews or mail questionnaires to collect the needed data.

2. Compare the advantages and disadvantages of using in-house staff versus a professional interviewing service to collect the data.

3. Do you think the telephone directory provided a good sampling frame given the purposes of the study, or would you recommend an alternative sampling frame?

4. What type of sample is being used here? Still using the white pages of the telephone directory as the sampling frame, would you recommend some other sampling scheme? Why or why not?

5. If you were Ms. Anchurch, would you be happy with the performance of the Bakersfield Interviewing Service? Why or why not?

Case 4.5
Holzem Business Systems

Holzem Business Systems serviced a number of small business accounts in the immediate area surrounding its Madison, Wisconsin, location. The company, which was headed by Mr. Claude Holzem, a certified public accountant, specialized in the preparation of financial statements, tax forms, and other reports required by various governmental units. Since its founding in 1962, the company had experienced steady, and sometimes spectacular, growth. Holzem, whose policy was high quality service at competitive rates, was so successful in Dane County that it was far and away the dominant firm serving small businesses in the area. Further growth seemed to depend more on expansion into new areas than on further penetration of the Madison market.

Faced with such a prospect, Holzem conceived a plan that would capitalize on the substantial talent at the company's main office. What he envisioned was an operation in which area field representatives would secure raw data from clients. At the end of each day, they would transmit this information to headquarters using microcomputers with modems. There it would be coded and processed and the necessary forms prepared. These income statements, balance sheets, or tax forms would then be returned to the area representative. The field person would go over them with the client and would answer any question that clients might have.

In Holzem's mind, the system had a number of advantages. First, it allowed Holzem Business Systems to capitalize on the substantial expertise it had in its Madison office. The quality control for which the company had become noted could be maintained, as could the company's record of quick service. Second, the company would not need to hire CPA's as field representatives, because these area managers would not actually be preparing financial statements. This was believed to be particularly crucial because, as a result of recent heavy demand, there was a current shortage of available CPA's. They were commanding premium salaries. The prospect of using business college graduates who understood financial statements and could explain their significance to clients thus had significant cost advantages.

The big question confronting Holzem was whether there would be a demand for such a service. There was no question in his mind there was a need for accounting services among small businesses. His Madison experience had demonstrated this. But he was concerned that the physical distance between the client and the office might prove to be a psychological barrier for clients. If it proved necessary to establish full service branches in each area, then geographic expansion was less attractive to him.

In order to help him decide whether to go ahead, he commissioned a research study that had as its objectives identifying the perceived problems and the need for CPA services in general, and, in particular, potential client attitudes toward the type of service arrangement he envisioned.

Hathaway Research Associates, headed by James and Nancy Hathaway, was retained to do the study. It was to be conducted using personal interviews among a representative sample of small businesses within the state. For purposes of the study, a small business was defined as one employing fewer than 50 people. The study was to be confined to small businesses in the industries designated contract construction, manufacturing, wholesale trade, retail trade, and commercial services. These categories represented approximately 95 percent of all Holzem accounts, 85 percent of the total small businesses, and 81 percent of all businesses in the state.

Sampling Plan

The businesses serving as the sample were to be selected in the following way. First, the state was to be divided into the three regions depicted in Figure 1 on page 550. Next, five counties were to be selected from each region by the following scheme.

1. The cumulative number of businesses was to be calculated from Table 1. The accumulation for the first ten counties in Region 1, for example, is:

County	Number of Businesses	Cumulative Number of Businesses
Douglas	668	668
Burnett	147	815
Polk	488	1,303
Washburn	282	1,585
Barron	565	2,150
Bayfield	178	2,328
Sawyer	324	2,652
Rusk	229	2,881
Ashland	307	3,188
Iron	122	3,310

2. A table of random numbers would be employed to determine which five counties would be selected. For example, if a number between 816 and 1,303 came up, Polk county would be used.

Hathaway Research associates then planned to contact the state Department of Industry, Labor, and Human Relations (DILHR) for a list of individual firms within each county. DILHR used the unemployment computer tape to prepare such lists. This tape was compiled each year and reflected payments by firms into the state's unemployment compensation system. The records within the tape were maintained county-by-county, by SIC (Standard Industrial Classification) code within county, and in alphabetical order within the SIC code. Since the number of employees of each firm was indicated, DILHR could screen the master list and print out only those firms that satisfied the location, industry, and geographic criteria Hathaway Research Associates specified. DILHR would sell these lists of firms to interested clients, but they would only provide the name, address, and phone number of the selected businesses.

Table 1

Number of Small Businesses by Major Industry Category

County	Contract Construction	Manufacturing	Wholesale Trade	Retail Trade	Commercial Services	Total
Adams	14	10	3	49	27	103
Ashland	26	37	26	127	91	307
Barron	88	52	82	295	48	565
Bayfield	20	25	8	85	40	178
Brown	387	187	330	871	804	2,579
Buffalo	23	14	22	92	47	198
Burnett	22	12	7	82	24	147
Calumet	62	47	48	162	128	447
Chippewa	105	67	94	300	216	782
Clark	60	76	82	203	101	522
Columbia	98	55	84	360	208	805
Crawford	33	25	32	119	64	273
Dane	638	314	493	1,800	1,705	4,950
Dodge	143	98	119	370	258	988
Door	76	27	27	206	168	504
Douglas	49	30	43	339	207	668
Dunn	37	21	55	187	110	410
Eau Claire	122	39	113	415	331	1,020
Florence	4	6	1	29	6	46
Fond du Lac	178	94	131	546	374	1,323
Forrest	9	25	8	116	27	185
Grant	88	60	125	341	200	814
Green	71	49	82	234	122	558
Green Lake	60	28	28	150	84	350
Iowa	41	23	55	135	65	319
Iron	11	15	10	60	26	122
Jackson	27	14	29	120	49	239
Jefferson	120	88	111	400	283	1,002
Juneau	38	28	27	172	79	344
Kenosha	159	75	105	624	167	1,130
Kewaunee	44	35	32	112	76	299
La Crosse	167	91	159	573	450	1,440
Lafayette	31	29	50	106	58	274
Langlade	29	53	59	135	92	368
Lincoln	50	43	38	184	109	424
Manitowoc	161	102	119	464	338	1,184

Source: County Business Patterns

Table 1

Number of Small Businesses by Major Industry Category *continued*

County	Contract Construction	Manufacturing	Wholesale Trade	Retail Trade	Commercial Services	Total
Marathon	244	148	196	520	432	1,540
Marinette	63	75	56	253	153	600
Marquette	27	11	9	68	34	149
Menominee	1	5	2	4	6	18
Milwaukee	1,200	1,238	1,711	4,914	5,708	14,771
Monroe	49	37	67	235	115	503
Oconto	49	43	50	143	97	382
Oneida	101	40	45	305	180	671
Outagamie	273	117	227	697	568	1,882
Ozaukee	151	109	95	313	245	915
Pepin	12	7	18	61	31	129
Pierce	50	27	29	206	104	416
Polk	59	44	51	234	100	488
Portage	83	42	71	280	171	647
Price	19	44	32	92	59	246
Racine	292	285	178	853	738	2,346
Richland	29	20	35	108	67	259
Rock	236	118	148	811	570	1,883
Rusk	24	34	34	95	42	229
St. Croix	80	44	61	225	144	554
Sauk	104	58	91	376	223	852
Sawyer	36	25	16	128	119	324
Shawano	65	58	61	232	110	526
Sheboygan	204	151	118	523	433	1,429
Taylor	29	28	36	93	57	243
Trempeleau	51	43	60	192	98	444
Vernon	37	39	52	154	85	367
Vilas	72	30	17	175	113	407
Walworth	144	106	90	522	345	1,207
Washburn	41	27	18	136	60	282
Washington	173	110	97	369	262	1,011
Waukesha	694	506	501	1,147	1,097	3,945
Waupaca	81	70	72	328	201	752
Waushara	26	22	30	114	71	263
Winnebago	244	157	151	759	632	1,943
Wood	141	83	104	427	303	1,058
Totals	8,475	5,995	7,466	26,655	20,957	69,548

Figure 1
Regional Breakdown of Counties

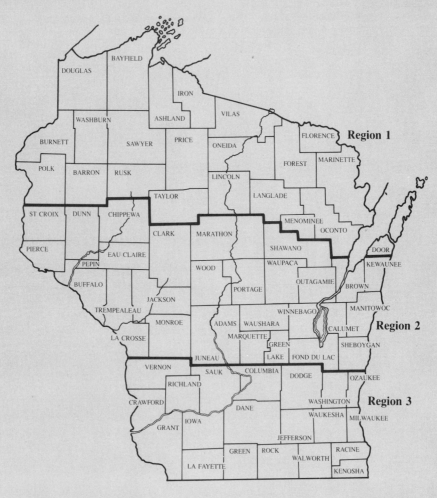

Hathaway Research Associates proposed to select 40 businesses from each county by the following procedure:

1. The total number of businesses within the county was to be divided by 40 to get a sampling interval. The sampling interval would be different, of course, for each county.

2. A random start was to be generated for each county, using a table of random numbers. The random number was to be some number between one and the sampling interval, and this number was to be used to designate the first business to be included in the sample.

3. The sampling interval was to be added repeatedly to the random start, and every number generated in this manner was to designate a business to be included in the sample.

The above procedure was to be followed for all counties except Milwaukee and Dane. Holzem believed that if he were to expand into the Milwaukee market at all, he wanted to do it with a completely self-sufficient branch and not with a satellite office tied to the Madison headquarters. He consequently instructed Hathaway Research Associates to exclude Milwaukee County from this part of the research investigation. Dane County was to be excluded because of the company's already successful penetration of this market.

Once the total sample of 600 businesses had been specified, Hathaway Research Associates would contact each firm by phone to set up an appointment for a personal interview with one of its highly trained field interviewers.

Questions

1. What kind of sample is being proposed by Hathaway Research Associates? Is this a good choice?

2. Is the sample a true probability sample (i.e., does every small business in Wisconsin have a known chance of selection)?

3. What is the probability that a small business in Menominee County (the county with the fewest small businesses) will be included in the sample? What is the probability that a small business in Waukesha County (of those counties eligible, the one with the most small businesses) will be included in the sample? Will this discrepancy cause any problems in analysis?

Case 4.6
WIAA Tournaments

The Wisconsin Interscholastic Athletic Association (WIAA) annually sponsors a number of state tournaments, all of which are held in the state capital of Madison. The tournaments include football, girls' tennis, girls' swimming, wrestling, boys' swimming, hockey, girls' basketball, boys' basketball, track, and boys' tennis, and the tournaments are held in the order listed. The first is usually held in late October and the last around the first week of June.

There were periodic discussions about the benefits and costs of these tournaments, in general and with respect to Madison in particular. In order to better assess the impact on Madison, the WIAA, in conjunction with the Greater Madison Chamber of Commerce, commissioned a study to determine the expenditures made in Madison that would not have been made if the tournaments had not been held there.

From the beginning, priorities were set concerning the importance of the various tournaments. The boys' basketball tournament was deemed most important because of

Figure 1

Questionnaire for WIAA Tournaments

Dear athletic fan:

Welcome to the WIAA tournaments! You are one of the selected few specially chosen to answer this questionnaire. Your past participation has made the WIAA tournaments a fun and exciting experience. Your cooperation in this survey will help us know you better. Due to the small size of the survey sample, please be sure to take this questionnaire home with you, and return it completed at your earliest convenience.

Thank you for giving us the help we need. Good luck in the competitions and have lots of fun!

Cordially,

Wisconsin Interscholastic Athletic Association

Greater Madison Chamber of Commerce

For official use only   ☐☐☐

Please check the most appropriate response for each of the questions:

1. *Are you from the Madison Area (*including City & Town of Madison, Fitchburg, Middleton, Shorewood, Monona, Town of Burke, Maple Bluff)?*
   1 ☐ Yes   2 ☐ No

2. *If you answered "no" to Question 1, was the WIAA tournament your main reason for visiting Madison?*
   1 ☐ Yes   2 ☐ No

Residents of the Madison area* please omit Questions 3, 4 & 5.

3. *How many days and nights did you spend in the Madison area? Please round-off parts of a day to a whole day.*
   A. DAYS—1 ☐ One   2 ☐ Two   3 ☐ Three   4 ☐ Four   5 ☐ Five or more
   B. NIGHTS—☐ None   2 ☐ One   3 ☐ Two   4 ☐ Three   5 ☐ Four   6 ☐ Five or more

the number of people it attracted. Further, it was decided to concentrate the study on the first three months of the calendar year, so football, girls' tennis, girls' swimming, track, and boys' tennis were not to be measured directly. Rather, total attendance at these events was known, and it was believed that if the attendance figures were multiplied by the per capita expenditure figures determined from the other events surveyed, a reasonable estimate could be obtained.

Data Collection

A self-administered questionnaire was used to collect the information (see Figure 1). The questionnaires were taped to predetermined seats at designated events. They were bright orange and had the words "PLEASE READ ME" stamped in green across the top so as to increase their visibility. The questionnaire instructed the respondent to complete it only after leaving the Madison area. It was hoped this would provide a more

Figure 1

Questionnaire for WIAA Tournaments *continued*

---

4. How many days did you actually view the tournament games?

1 ☐ One   2 ☐ Two   3 ☐ Three

5. How many people came to the Madison area with you but did not attend the games?

1 ☐ None   2 ☐ One   3 ☐ Two   4 ☐ Three   5 ☐ Four   6 ☐ Five or more

6. Please give your best estimate of how much you spent in the following categories while you were in the Madison area:

A. Eating and drinking .... $_____

B. Lodging (hotel, motel, tourist home, etc.) .... $_____

C. Transportation companies (railroad, airline, bus—only if
ticket was purchased locally, city or University bus, etc.) ... $_____

D. Service stations (repair, parts, gasoline, etc.) .... $_____

E. Auto dealers (car purchase only) .... $_____

F. Apparel store (clothing, shoes, accessories, etc.) .... $_____

G. Retail store (record, gift, drug, hardware, sporting goods,
etc.) .... $_____

H. Department, variety, discount or catalog stores .... $_____

I.   Entertainment places (theatre, bowling alley, concert,
amusement arcade, discotheque, etc.). .... $_____

J. Personal or business service (barber, beauty shop, dry
cleaner, doctor, etc.) .... $_____

K. Furniture and appliance store .... $_____

L. City government (parking fee and traffic ticket) .... $_____

M. Local households (babysitter, private parking, etc.) .... $_____

TOTAL VISIT EXPENDITURE = $_____

---

accurate picture of the person's total expenditures while in Madison. Hopefully, the individual would record expenditures as they were accruing and would complete the questionnaire soon after arriving home. Coding on the questionnaire denoted the tournament and the session in which it was distributed.

The target population was defined to include all ticket holders, contestants, and coaches attending the five individual WIAA tournaments surveyed. However, the most important segment with respect to economic impact were those people who were not from the Madison area but came to Madison expressly for the WIAA tournaments. Expenditure formulations did not include money spent by Madisonians except for the price of their tickets. It was believed that they would have spent approximately the same amount of money for other activities whether or not the tournaments were in Madison.

The seats to which the questionnaires were affixed were determined in the following way. First, the seats assigned various segments of the public were divided into groups by section number. Figure 2, for example, shows the seating arrangement for the bas-

Figure 2
Seat Assignments for Basketball Tournament

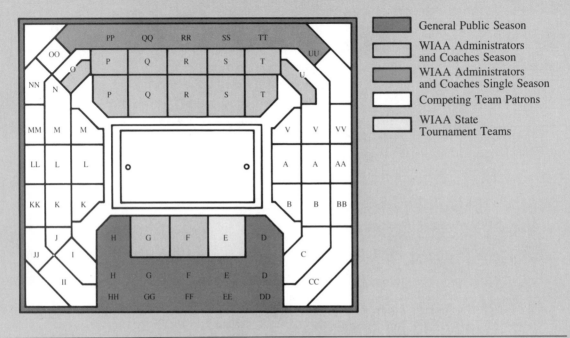

ketball tournament. All those seats assigned to the general public made up one group, those assigned to competing team patrons another group, and so on. Second, sections within each group were determined randomly. Finally, seats within each section were determined so that the five major groups were sampled in the same proportion. This was done by dividing the total number of seats assigned each group by 20, since the overall sampling fraction was one in twenty. A random start between one and the result of the division was determined from a random number table, and a questionnaire was affixed to that seat and every kth seat thereafter.

Both the sections sampled and the starting point were altered for each session of any tournament so as to lessen the likelihood of sampling people who held the same seat for more than one session. Further, the specific sampling pattern itself was altered for each tournament to reflect the forecast attendance and facility configuration.

The percentages of all questionnaires returned, by tournament, were: wrestling—12 percent; swimming—12 percent; hockey—9 percent; girls' basketball—15 percent; and boys' basketball—20 percent. Per capita expenditures of those responding were then multiplied by the total number of people attending the event to determine total direct expenditures attributed to the event. These expenditures were then multiplied by an economic multiplier to reflect the fact that every dollar brought into the community has secondary effects because of the additional spending it triggers.

Questions

1. Evaluate the study design and method of data collection.

2. What kind of sample is being used? What is the rationale for sampling each group at the same rate?

Case 4.7
Generic Drugs (B)

The State of Wisconsin passed a law in 1977 that permitted generic drugs to be substituted for brand name drugs when prescriptions were being filled. Consumers simply had to request the substitution and the pharmacist was legally bound to make it. The legislation was designed to save customers money on their prescriptions. Thus, it proved disconcerting to the Department of Health and Social Services when, some eight years after its passage, few customers were taking advantage of the law by asking for the substitution.

Several hypotheses were advanced as to why this was happening, including the suggestions that the law had not been well publicized, consumers were not aware of its existence, consumers had unfavorable attitudes toward generic drugs, and there were a number of personal and situational factors, such as age, income, household size, and education that were affecting customers' use of the law (see Generic Drugs [A]). It was decided that the best way to collect the needed information was through the use of self-administered questionnaires. Because of the difficulty of obtaining an accurate mailing list, the questionnaires were to be hand delivered but returned by mail. Further, it was decided that the feasibility of the data collection and sampling plans were to be determined by originally confining the study to Madison, the state capital and also the main campus location of the University of Wisconsin. By restricting the original investigation thusly, it was recognized there would probably be some bias in the results because of a number of demographic differences between Madison and the remainder of the state.

Being the state capital and also home to the University of Wisconsin-Madison, the city of Madison was home to numerous professional people. Because of the number of doctors, lawyers, accountants, professors, and other professionals living there, the city had both a higher average education level and a higher average income than the state average or any other city within the state. Most of the professional people lived on the city's west side, typically in more spacious, more expensive housing.

Much of the industry in the city was government related, although there were some very important exceptions, manufacturers like Oscar Mayer and Ray-o-Vac and a number of insurance companies. Most of the manufacturing was concentrated on the city's east side, and consequently most of the city's blue-collar workers lived there. Homes on the east side were typically smaller and less expensive than those on the west side, so there were more of them in the same size area.

Sampling Plan

The 1,000 households to be surveyed were selected in the following manner. First, the city was divided into aldermanic districts using detailed maps. To ensure geographic representation of the city, samples were drawn from each aldermanic district. This was done by randomly choosing city blocks within each aldermanic district and then randomly selecting ten households in each of the selected blocks that would receive questionnaires.

Consider Aldermanic District 11, for example, which was located on the city's west side. The study was to be limited to residents of Madison over 18. The total adult population in District 11 was 5,115, while the total adult population in the city was 122,016. The proportion of the total sample that was to come from Aldermanic District 11 was thus 5,115/122,016 = .0419. This meant that 42 households [1,000 (.0419) = 42] were to be included in the sample.

The 42 households were selected from five blocks within the district by first numbering all the blocks within the district. Then five blocks were randomly selected from this larger set of blocks. Ten households were interviewed on each of the first four blocks that were selected, and two households were interviewed in the fifth block. The households were selected by going around the block to count the number of dwelling units, then beginning at the southwest corner following the detailed instructions for the count of dwelling units that were provided each field worker. Suppose, for example, there were 50 dwelling units in a selected block. The field worker was then instructed to generate a random start between one and five, using the table of random numbers each was provided. Suppose the number was two; the field worker was then to drop off questionnaires at the second, seventh, twelfth, and so on households in the initial numbering scheme.

Questions

1. What type of sample is being used to distribute questionnaires?
2. Is this a good choice?

Case 4.8
The Dryden Press

The Dryden Press is a division of the publishing arm of CBS, Inc. The Dryden Press was established in the mid-1960s by Holt, Rinehart and Winston, which had traditionally been a strong social science publisher, as a response to the growth in enrollments that business schools were experiencing and the explosion in enrollments that was predicted they would experience in the future. The venture represented one of the first forays by a traditional nonbusiness text publisher into the college business market. The experiment turned out to be very successful, and by the mid-1980s The Dryden Press was one of the top six publishers in the business area in sales. Company executives believed that one of the key reasons for Dryden's success was its ability to target books for specific market segments. The company was one of the first to recognize the potential growth in courses in consumer behavior and managerial economics, for example, and introduced the very successful texts by Engel, Kollat, and Blackwell in consumer behavior and by Brigham and Pappas in managerial economics in response. Through careful management of the revisions, these books still maintained strong market positions more than 15 years after they had been introduced.

The Dryden Press editorial staff tried to maintain a posture of extreme sensitivity to changing market conditions brought about by the publication of new research findings or the changing demands placed on students due to changes in the environment and the needs of businesses. The editors made it a point to keep up with these changes so that the company would be prepared with new product when the situation demanded it. This was no small task, because the lead time on a book typically ran from three to four years from the time the author was first signed to a contract to when the book was actually published. It seemed to take most authors almost two years to develop a first draft of a book manuscript. The typical manuscript was then reviewed by a sample of experts in the field. Based on their reactions, most manuscripts would undergo some revision before being placed in production. The production process, which included such things as copy editing the manuscript, setting type, drawing all figures, preparing promotional materials, proofreading, and so on usually took about a year.

Research Questions and Objectives

So as not to be caught short if the needs and desires of the market in consumer behavior texts changed, the editorial staff decided to find out the current level of use of the various texts in consumer behavior and the directions in which the market was moving. What were the market shares of the respective texts? What features of the various books were liked and disliked? Did the use of the various texts and the preference for the certain features vary by class of school? Did four-year colleges have different requirements in consumer behavior texts than two-year schools? After a good deal of discussion among the members of the editorial staff, these general concerns were translated into specific research objectives. More specifically, the staff decided to conduct a research investigation that attempted to determine:

1. the importance of various topical areas in the teaching of consumer behavior within the next two to five years;

2. the importance and treatment of managerial applications in consumer behavior courses;

3. the level of satisfaction with the textbooks currently in use;

4. the relative market shares of the major consumer behavior textbooks;

5. the degree of switching of texts that goes on in consumer behavior courses from year to year;

6. the importance of various pedagogical aids such as glossaries, cases, learning objectives, and so on in the textbook selection decision; and

7. the importance of supplementary teaching tools such as student study guides, overhead transparency masters, or an instructor's manual, among others, in the consumer textbook selection decision.

The editorial staff thought it was important that the needed information be obtained from those who were actively involved in teaching consumer behavior courses. The staff also thought it imperative that only one respondent be used from any given school, even though the editors realized that some schools had multiple sections of the consumer behavior course and that different books might be used in different sections. For the most part, however, the editors believed that the same book would be used across sections, though not across courses, in the sense that the introductory courses at the undergraduate and graduate levels would use different books. The editors decided it would be better to target the questionnaires to one individual at each of the selected institutions and to simply have that person indicate on the questionnaire whether he or she normally taught a graduate or undergraduate course. Dryden could then analyze the responses to determine if there were any differences in them that could be attributed to the level at which the course was taught.

Method

There were several reasons why the editorial staff decided to use a mail questionnaire to collect the data. For one thing, the target population was geographically dispersed. Even though it was decided to limit the study only to those actively involved in teaching consumer behavior domestically, that still meant respondents could come from all over the United States, which in turn meant it could be prohibitive to collect this information by personal interview. At the same time, professors had no standard working schedule. Some might teach in the morning and some in the evening. When they were not teaching, some might work in their offices while others might work elsewhere. This variety of schedules and work conditions required that the questionnaires be available when the professors might be inclined to fill them out. Also, the objectives finally decided upon allowed the use of a relatively structured and undisguised questionnaire.

The big question facing the Dryden staff was how to draw a sample from the target population of those actively teaching the consumer behavior course, either at the undergraduate or graduate levels. For purposes of the study, "actively teaching" was operationally defined as having taught a consumer behavior course at least once in the last two years or being scheduled to teach one within the next year.

The company was considering drawing the sample from one of two lists it had at its disposal. One of the lists was an internal list consisting of all those professors whom the salespeople's reports indicated were interested in teaching specific courses such as financial planning, introductory accounting, marketing management, or consumer behavior. This meant that the salesperson had indicated on his or her reports that the professor was to receive sample copies of all those books in, say, consumer behavior that the Dryden Press publishes. Most of the entries on the list were developed from salespeople's calls, although some of them arose at the national association meetings at which Dryden displayed its list of titles. Professors would often request sample copies of selected titles at the meetings so that they could review them before making an adoption decision. All requests for complimentary copies were sent for authorization to the salesperson serving the school. By approving the request, the salesperson was aware of the professor's interest and could follow it up in an attempt to get the adoption. Because of how it was developed and used, the internal list paralleled the salesperson territory structure.

While most salespeople operated within one state and often within only part of a state, some operated across several states. Each salesperson was responsible for all the schools in his or her territory, including the universities with graduate programs, four-year colleges without graduate programs, and two-year institutions. The schools were listed alphabetically by salesperson, and each school had a computer code associated with it, designating its type. Each professor on the list had a set of computer codes associated with the name that identified his or her interest areas.

The alternate list The Dryden Press considered using was the printed membership directory of the Association for Consumer Research (ACR). ACR is an organization formed in the late 1960s that was designed for the pursuit of knowledge in the area of consumer behavior. Its membership is dominated by marketing professors (almost 80 percent of the total), although it also includes interested members from business and government as well as members representing other academic disciplines, such as sociology and psychology. The ACR directory was organized alphabetically by name of the member. Along with each member's name, the directory provided either the office or home address, depending on which the individual preferred to use, and both the office and home phone numbers. While about one-half of the addresses listed only the college at which the individual worked, the other 50 percent also listed the department. There were 64 pages in the directory, and all pages except the last one had 16 names. A small percentage of the addresses were international.

Questions

1. Given the purposes of the study, how would you recommend a sample be drawn from:
    (a) Dryden's internal computer list?
    (b) The ACR printed membership directory?
2. Which approach would you recommend and why?

Part 5

Analysis and Interpretation of Data

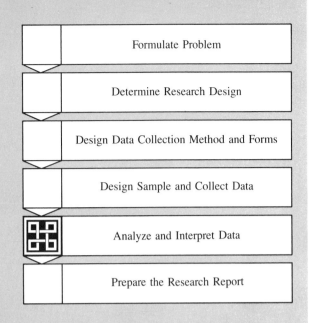

	Formulate Problem
	Determine Research Design
	Design Data Collection Method and Forms
	Design Sample and Collect Data
	Analyze and Interpret Data
	Prepare the Research Report

Once data have been collected, emphasis in the research process logically turns to analysis, which amounts to the search for meaning in the collected information. This search involves many questions and several steps. Chapter 12 is a review of the preliminary steps of editing, coding, and tabulating the data. Chapter 13 is a discussion of the main questions that need to be resolved before statistical examination of the data can begin. Chapters 14, 15, and 16 review the statistical techniques that are most useful in the analysis of marketing data. Chapter 14 is a discussion of the procedures appropriate for examining group differences, Chapter 15 the assessment of association, and Chapter 16 the multivariate techniques of discriminant, factor, and cluster analysis.

Chapter 12
Data Analysis:
Preliminary Steps

The purpose of analysis is to obtain meaning from the collected data. All previous steps in the research process have been undertaken to support the search for meaning. The specific analytical procedures to be used are closely related to the preceding steps, and the careful analyst will remember this when designing the other steps. Hopefully, the analyst will go so far as to develop dummy tables, indicating how each item of information will be used, before beginning data collection. Thorough preparatory work should reveal undesirable data gaps and should also pinpoint items that are "interesting" but which do not relate to the problem being examined.

The search for meaning can take many forms. However, the preliminary analytical steps of editing, coding, and tabulation are common to most studies, and a review of what they are and how they are used is desirable.

Editing

The basic purpose of editing is to impose some minimum quality standards on the raw data. Editing involves the inspection and, if necessary, correction of each questionnaire or observation form. Inspection and correction are often done in two stages: the field edit and the central-office edit.

Field Edit

The **field edit** is a preliminary edit, designed to detect the most glaring omissions and inaccuracies in the data. It is also useful in helping to control the field force and to clear up their misunderstandings about directions, procedures, specific questions, and so on.

Ideally, the field edit is done as soon as possible after the questionnaire or other data collection form has been administered, so that problems can be corrected before the interviewing or observation staff is disbanded, and while the particular contacts that were the source of trouble are still fresh in the interviewer's or observer's mind. The preliminary edit will more than likely be conducted by a field supervisor. Some of the things that will be checked are described in Research Realities 12.1.[1]

---

[1]The classification of items to be checked in the field edit is taken from Claire Selltiz, Lawrence S. Wrightsman, and Stuart W. Cook, *Research Methods in Social Relations,* 3rd ed. (New York: Holt, Rinehart and Winston, 1976), pp. 475–476. Reprinted by permission of Holt, Rinehart and Winston.

Research Realities 12.1

Items Checked in the Field Edit

1. **Completeness:** This check for completeness involves scrutinizing the data form to ensure that no sections or pages were omitted, and it also involves checking individual items. A blank for a specific question could mean that the respondent refused to answer; alternatively, it may simply reflect an oversight on the respondent's part or that he did not know the answer. It may be very important for the purposes of the study to know which reason is correct. Hopefully, by contacting the field worker while the interview is fresh in his mind, the needed clarification will be provided.

2. **Legibility:** It is impossible to code a questionnaire that cannot be deciphered because the interviewer's handwriting is unintelligible or because he used abbreviations not understood by others. It is a simple matter to correct this now, whereas it is often extremely time consuming later.

3. **Comprehensibility:** Sometimes a recorded response is incomprehensible to all but the field interviewer. By detecting this now, the necessary clarification can be easily provided.

4. **Consistency:** Marked inconsistencies within an interview or observation schedule typically indicate errors in collecting or recording the data and may indicate ambiguity in the instrument or carelessness in its administration. For instance, if a respondent indicated that he saw a particular commercial on TV last night on one part of the questionnaire, and later indicated that he did not watch TV last night, the analyst would indeed be in a dilemma. Hopefully, such inconsistencies would be detected and corrected in the field edit.

5. **Uniformity:** It is very important that the responses be recorded in uniform units. For instance, if the study is aimed at determining the number of magazines read per week per individual, and the respondent indicates the number of magazines for which he has monthly subscriptions, the response base is not uniform, and the result could cause no small amount of confusion in the later stages of analysis. If detected now, perhaps the interviewer can recontact the respondent and get the correct answer.

Central Office Edit

The field edit is typically followed by a **central office edit.** This involves more complete and exacting scrutiny and correction of the completed returns. The work calls for the keen eye of a person well versed in the objectives and procedures of the study. To ensure consistency of treatment, it is best if one individual handles all completed instruments. If this is impossible because of length and time considerations, the work can be divided. However, the division should be by parts of the data collection instruments rather than by respondents. That is, one editor would be concerned with editing Part A of all questionnaires, while the other would edit Part B.

Unlike the field edit, the central office edit depends less on follow-up procedures and more on deciding just what to do with the data. Accurate follow-up is now more difficult because of the time that has elapsed. In deciding what to do with the data, the editor will usually have to decide how data collection instruments containing incomplete answers, obviously wrong answers, and answers that reflect a lack of interest will be handled. Since such problems are more prevalent with questionnaires than observational forms, we will discuss these difficulties from that perspective, although the discussion applies generally to all types of data collection forms.

The study in which all the returned questionnaires are completely filled out is rare. Some will have complete sections omitted. Others will reflect sporadic item nonresponse. The editor's decision on how to handle these incomplete questionnaires depends on the severity of the problem. Questionnaires that omit complete sections are obviously suspect. Yet they should not automatically be thrown out. It might be, for example, that the omitted section refers to the influence of the spouse in some major durable purchase and the respondent is not married. This type of reply is certainly usable in spite of the incomplete section. Alternatively, there might not be a logical justification for the large number of questions that were not answered. In this case, the total reply would probably be thrown out, increasing the nonresponse rate for the study. Questionnaires containing only isolated instances of item nonresponse would be retained, although they might undergo some data cleaning after coding, a subject discussed later in this chapter.

Careful editing of the questionnaire will sometimes show that an answer to a question is obviously incorrect. For example, respondents might be asked for the type of store in which they purchased a camera in one part of the questionnaire and the name of the store in another. If the person responded "department store" while the name of the store indicated a catalog showroom, one of the answers is incorrect. The editor may be able to determine which from other information in the questionnaire. Alternatively, the editor may need to establish policies as to which answer will be treated as correct, if either, when these inconsistencies or other types of inaccuracies arise. These policies will reflect the purposes of the study.

Indications that the completed questionnaire reflects a lack of interest on the part of the subject are sometimes subtle and sometimes obvious. For example, a subject who checked the "5" position on a five-point scale for each of the 40 items in an attitude questionnaire where some items were expressed negatively and some positively is obviously not taking the study very seriously. An editor would probably throw out such a response. A discerning editor might also be able to pick up more subtle indications of disinterest, such as check marks that are not within the boxes provided, scribbles, spills on the questionnaire, and so on. An editor may not want to throw out these responses, but they should be coded so that it is later possible to run separate tabulations for both questionable instruments and obviously good questionnaires, to see if that makes any difference in the results and conclusions.

Coding

"**Coding** is the technical procedure by which data are categorized. Through coding, the raw data are transformed into symbols—usually numerals—that may be tabulated and counted. The transformation is not automatic, however; it involves judgment on the part of the coder."[2]

The first step in coding is specifying the categories or classes into which the responses are to be placed.[3] There is no magic number of categories. Rather, the number

---

[2] Selltiz, Wrightsman, and Cook, *Research Methods,* p. 473.

[3] Some writers would make the specification of categories part of the editing rather than the coding function. Its placement in one or the other function is not nearly as important as the recognition that it is an extremely critical step with significant ramifications for the whole research effort.

will depend on the research problem being investigated and the specific items used to generate the information. Nevertheless, several rules for specifying the classes can be stated. First, the classes should be mutually exclusive and exhaustive. Every response should logically fall into one and only one category. Multiple responses are legitimate, of course, if the question is "For what purposes do you use JELL-O?" and the responses include such things as "a dessert item," "an evening snack," "an afternoon snack," and so on. If the question focuses on the person's age, then only one age category is, of course, acceptable and the code should indicate unequivocally which category.

Coding closed questions and most scaling devices is simple because the coding is established, for all practical purposes, when the data collection instrument is designed. Respondents then code themselves with their responses, or the interviewer effectively codes them when he or she records the response on the checklist provided.

Coding open-ended questions can be very difficult. The coder has to determine appropriate categories on the basis of answers that are not always anticipated.[4] Consider the following question, which was used in a study of the fast-food franchise system of distribution:[5] "Please specify the product or service around which your franchise system is organized (for example, pancakes)." The expectation was that the respondents would reply with "hamburgers," or "chicken," or "pizza," and so on. Some did. Others responded with "hamburgers, hot dogs, and beverages." How should such a reply be treated? The decision, after much agonizing, was to establish the category "multiple fast foods."[6] If you were the coder, would you classify an A & W stand as a beverage franchise or a hamburger franchise?

The coding of open-ended questions can create an additional problem when the number of questionnaires necessitates the use of several coders: inconsistent treatment. To assure consistency of treatment, the work should again be divided by task and not by apportioning the questionnaires equally among the coders. The result of allowing coders to concentrate their energies on one or a few questions is that a consistent set of standards is applied to each question. This approach is also more efficient because coders can learn the codes and do not have to consult the code book for each instrument. When several persons do, in fact, code the same question on different batches of questionnaires, it is important that they also code a sample of the other's work to ensure that a consistent set of coding criteria is being employed.[7]

---

[4]In one study that explicitly compared the responses to open and closed questions, marked differences were found in the response distributions to the two types of questions. The authors concluded that the responses to closed questions were the more valid, because the responses to open questions are often so vague that they are misclassified by coders. See H. Scheman and S. Presser, "The Open and Closed Question," *American Sociological Review,* 44 (1979), pp. 692–712. To improve the consistency with which similar answers are coded, some researchers have attempted to develop systems by which computers can code open-ended responses. For an illustration, see Colin McDonald, "Coding Open-Ended Answers With the Help of a Computer," *Journal of the Market Research Society,* 24 (January 1982), pp. 9–27.

[5]Urban B. Ozanne and Shelby D. Hunt, *The Economic Effects of Franchising* (Madison, Wis.: Graduate School of Business, The University of Wisconsin, 1971).

[6]*Ibid.,* p. 34.

[7]For discussion of a set of indices that can be used to investigate coder reliability as well as to determine which questions might be proving particularly troublesome, see Martin Collins and Graham Kalton, "Coding Verbatim Answers to Open Questions," *Journal of the Market Research Society,* 22 (October 1980), pp. 239–247.

The second step in coding involves assigning code numbers to the classes. For example, sex might be assigned the letters M for male and F for female. Alternatively, the classes could be denoted by 1 for male and 2 for female. Generally, it is better to use numbers than letters to denote the classes. It also is better to treat numerical data in their reported form at this stage, rather than collapsing interval or ratio scale data into categories. For example, it is not advisable to code age in years as 1 = under 20, 2 = 20 to 29, 3 = 30 to 39, and so on. This would entail some unnecessary sacrifice of information in the original measurement and can just as easily be done at later stages in the analysis.

When the analysis of data is to be done by computer, it is necessary to code the data so that it can be readily input to the machine. Regardless of how that input will be effected, whether by punched cards or mark-sense forms or directly through a keyboard on a terminal, it is helpful to visualize the input in terms of an 80-column punched card or card image. Further, it is advisable to follow certain conventions when coding the data:

1. Use only one punch per column. Most computer programs cannot read multiple-punched cards. When the question allows multiple responses, spread or spray the answers by allowing separate columns in the coding for each answer. Thus, the question on JELL-O usage would dictate a separate column be provided in the coding form for indicating whether the respondent used it as a dessert item, another column for evening snack, and so on.

2. Use only numeric codes and not letters of the alphabet, special characters like @, or blanks. Most computer statistical programs have severe difficulty in manipulating anything but numbers.

3. The field or portion of the card assigned to a variable should consist of as many columns as are necessary to capture the variable. Thus, if the variable is such that the ten codes from 0 to 9 are not sufficient to exhaust the categories, then one should use two columns in the card, which provides 100 codes from 00 through 99. Moreover, no more than one variable should be assigned to any field.

4. Use standard codes for "No information." Thus, all "Don't know" responses might be coded "8," "No answers" as "9," and "Does not apply" as "0." It is best if the same code is used throughout the study for each of these types of "No information."

5. Code in a respondent identification number on each record. This number need not, and typically will not, identify the respondent by name. Rather, the number simply ties the questionnaire to the coded data. This is often useful information in data cleaning. If the questionnaire requires more than 80 columns of code, it will not fit on one card. Each card then should be coded with the respondent identification number and a card sequence number. Column 10 in Card 1 might then indicate how the respondent answered Question 2, while Column 10 in Card 2 might indicate whether the person is male or female.[8]

---

[8]Philip S. Siedl, "Coding," in Robert Ferber, ed., *Handbook of Marketing Research* (New York: McGraw-Hill, 1974), pp. 2–178 to 2–199. This article provides an excellent overview of the issues that arise in coding data and how they can be handled.

The final step in the coding process is to prepare a codebook. The codebook contains the general instructions indicating how each item of data was coded. It lists the codes for each variable and the categories included in each code. It further indicates where on the computer record the variable is located, and how the variable should be read, for example, with a decimal point or as a whole number. The latter information is provided by the format specifications.

Tabulation

Tabulation consists simply of counting the number of cases that fall into the various categories. The tabulation may take the form of a simple tabulation or a cross tabulation. **Simple tabulation** involves counting a single variable. It may be repeated for each of the variables in the study, but the tabulation for each variable is independent of the tabulation for the other variables. In **cross tabulation,** two or more of the variables are treated simultaneously; the number of cases that have the joint characteristics are counted (for example, the number of people who bought Campbell's soup at a Kroger store). The tabulations may be done entirely by hand, entirely by machine, or some by machine and some by hand. Which is more efficient depends partly on the number of tabulations necessary and partly on the number of cases in each tabulation. The number of tabulations is a direct function of the number of variables, while the number of cases is a direct function of the size of the sample. The fewer the number of tabulations required and the smaller the sample, the more attractive hand methods become. However, the attractiveness of either alternative is also highly dependent on the complexity of the tabulations. Complexity increases as the number of variables receiving simultaneous treatment in a cross tabulation increases. Complexity also increases as the number of categories per variable increases.

For hand tabulation a tally sheet is typically used. Consider the question, ''How many trips did you make to the grocery store this past week?'' The tally for a sample of Size 40 might look like this:

0	⊥⊥⊤	1		6
1	⊥⊥⊤	⊥⊥⊤	11	12
2	⊥⊥⊤	⊥⊥⊤		10
3	⊥⊥⊤	111		8
4 or more	1111			4

The hand tally also can be used to create cross-classification tables. Suppose one of the study questions was the relationship between shopping behavior and family size. The following table shows the cross tabulation that might then be constructed. The cross tabulation indicates, for instance, that of the six families that made zero trips to the grocery store, four were composed of only one member, one family had two members, and one family had four members. The cross tabulation thus provides information on the *joint occurrence* of shopping trips and family size.

Note that the right-hand totals (sometimes referred to as the marginal totals) are identical to the results for the straight tabulation. This shows that it is unnecessary to

Number of Trips	Number of Members					
	1	2	3	4	5 or more	Total
0	1111	1		1		6
1	111	1111	111	11		12
2	1	111	1111	11		10
3		1	̶1̶1̶1̶1̶	1	1	8
4 or more				1	111	4
Totals	8	9	12	7	4	40

make straight tabulations for individual variables that will be included in two-way tables.

While the hand tabulation might be useful in very simple studies involving a few questions and a limited number of responses, most studies rely on computer tabulation using packaged programs. A great many such programs are available.[9] Some will calculate summary statistics and will plot a histogram of the values in addition to reporting the number of cases in each category. The basic input to these statistical analyses will be the data array. The data array lists the value of each variable for each sample unit. Each variable occupies a specific place in the record for a sample unit, thereby making it easy to pick off the values for it from all of the cases. The location of each variable is given in the codebook. Table 12A.2 in the appendix to this chapter provides an example of a data array, and Table 12A.1 describes what is contained in each column. Note that only one line had to be devoted to each sample unit or observation. If the amount of information sought from each sample unit were greater, so that it would not fit as an 80-column card record, additional lines would have been devoted to each observation. The codebook would still indicate where the information for any particular variable was located.

There are a number of important questions concerning the analysis of data that can be illustrated, using one-way tabulations and cross tabulations as vehicles. Consider, therefore, the data in Table 12.1. Suppose that the data were collected for a study focusing on car ownership. Suppose, in particular, that the following questions were of research interest:

■ What characteristics distinguish families owning two or more cars from families owning one car?

■ What are the distinguishing characteristics of those who buy station wagons? Foreign economy cars? Vans?

■ Are there differences in the characteristics of families who financed their automobile purchase and those who did not?

---

[9]For a review of the features contained in the most popular statistical packages, see I. Francis, *Statistical Software: A Comparative Review* (Amsterdam: North Holland, 1981).

Table 12.1

Raw Data for Car Ownership Study

Family Ident. No.	(1) Income in Dollars	(2) Number of Members in Family	(3) Education of Household Head in Yrs.	(4) Region Where Live N = North S = South	(5) Life-style Orientation L = Liberal C = Conservative	(6) Number of Cars Family Owns	(7) Did Family Finance the Car Purchase?	(8) Does Family Own Station Wagon?	(9) Does Family Own Foreign Economy Car?	(10) Does Family Own Van?	(11) Does Family Own Some Other Kind of Car?
1001	16,800	3	12	N	L	1	N	N	N	Y	N
1002	17,400	4	12	N	L	1	N	N	N	N	Y
1003	14,300	2	10	N	L	1	N	N	N	N	Y
1004	15,400	4	9	N	L	1	N	N	N	N	Y
1005	14,000	3	8	N	L	1	N	N	N	N	Y
1006	17,200	2	12	N	L	1	N	N	Y	N	N
1007	17,000	4	12	N	L	1	N	N	N	N	Y
1008	16,900	3	10	N	L	1	N	N	N	N	Y
1009	16,700	2	12	N	L	1	N	N	N	N	Y
1010	13,800	4	6	N	C	1	Y	N	N	N	Y
1011	14,100	3	8	N	C	1	N	N	N	N	Y
1012	16,300	3	11	N	C	1	N	N	N	N	Y
1013	14,700	2	12	N	C	1	N	N	N	N	Y
1014	15,400	4	12	N	C	1	N	N	N	N	Y
1015	15,400	4	12	N	C	1	Y	N	N	N	Y
1016	15,900	3	11	N	C	1	Y	N	N	N	Y
1017	16,300	3	12	N	C	1	N	N	N	N	Y
1018	17,400	2	12	N	C	2	N	N	N	N	Y
1019	17,300	2	12	N	C	1	N	N	N	N	Y
1020	13,700	3	8	N	C	1	N	N	Y	N	Y
1021	16,100	2	12	N	C	1	Y	N	N	N	Y
1022	16,300	4	12	N	C	1	Y	N	N	N	Y
1023	13,800	3	6	N	C	1	N	N	N	N	Y
1024	14,400	4	8	N	C	1	N	N	N	N	Y
1025	15,300	2	9	N	C	1	Y	N	N	N	Y
1026	15,900	3	12	N	C	1	N	N	N	N	Y
1027	15,100	4	12	S	L	1	N	N	Y	Y	Y
1028	17,200	2	12	S	L	1	Y	N	N	N	Y
1029	15,400	4	10	S	L	1	N	N	N	N	Y
1030	15,600	3	12	S	L	1	N	N	Y	N	Y
1031	14,900	3	12	S	L	1	N	N	N	Y	Y
1032	14,800	4	11	S	C	1	N	N	N	N	Y
1033	14,600	4	12	S	C	1	N	N	N	Y	N
1034	13,100	3	9	S	C	1	N	N	N	N	Y
1035	15,900	3	12	S	C	1	N	N	N	Y	N
1036	16,700	4	12	S	C	1	N	N	N	Y	N
1037	17,300	4	12	S	C	1	N	N	Y	Y	Y
1038	17,100	3	12	S	C	1	N	N	N	Y	Y
1039	14,000	3	10	S	C	1	N	N	N	N	N
1040	13,600	3	10	S	C	1	N	N	N	N	Y
1041	16,200	3	12	S	C	1	N	N	N	Y	Y
1042	14,100	4	10	S	C	1	N	N	N	Y	Y
1043	12,700	2	8	S	C	1	N	Y	N	N	N
1044	15,400	4	13	N	L	1	N	Y	Y	N	N
1045	15,400	3	16	N	L	2	N	Y	Y	N	N
1046	16,900	4	16	N	L	1	N	N	N	N	Y

Z	Z	Z	Y	Y	1	C	S	10	6	13,800	1047
Y	Z	Y	Z	Y	2	L	N	16	8	17,100	1048
Y	Z	Z	Z	Y	2	C	S	15	5	16,800	1049
Z	Z	Z	Y	Z	1	L	N	8	5	12,900	1050
Z	Z	Z	Y	Y	1	L	S	8	6	13,700	1051
Y	Z	Z	Y	Y	2	C	N	12	8	16,800	1052
Y	Z	Z	Y	Z	2	L	N	12	8	16,100	1053
Y	Z	Z	Z	Z	1	C	N	12	6	15,700	1054
Y	Z	Z	Z	Z	1	L	N	12	2	18,200	1055
Y	Z	Z	Z	Y	1	L	N	12	3	19,800	1056
Y	Z	Z	Z	Y	1	L	N	12	4	20,400	1057
Y	Z	Z	Z	Z	1	L	N	12	2	19,000	1058
Y	Z	Z	Z	Y	1	L	N	12	4	17,600	1059
Z	Z	Z	Z	Z	1	L	N	12	3	32,000	1060
Z	Z	Z	Z	Z	1	L	N	12	3	28,600	1061
Y	Z	Y	Z	Y	1	L	N	12	4	46,400	1062
Y	Y	Z	Z	Z	1	L	N	12	2	21,200	1063
Y	Z	Z	Z	Z	1	C	N	10	4	19,300	1064
Y	Z	Y	Z	Y	1	C	N	12	4	17,700	1065
Z	Z	Z	Z	Y	2	C	N	12	3	32,400	1066
Y	Z	Z	Z	Y	1	L	S	12	3	38,700	1067
Y	Y	Y	Z	Y	1	L	S	12	2	24,200	1068
Y	Z	Z	Z	Z	2	L	S	12	3	25,100	1069
Z	Z	Z	Z	Z	1	L	S	12	4	23,300	1070
Y	Y	Z	Y	Y	2	C	S	12	2	20,200	1071
Y	Z	Z	Z	Z	1	C	S	10	3	19,300	1072
Z	Y	Z	Z	Z	1	C	N	12	4	18,200	1073
Y	Y	Z	Z	Z	1	L	N	12	2	17,800	1074
Y	Z	Z	Z	Y	1	L	N	10	3	18,000	1075
Y	Y	Z	Z	Z	1	C	N	16	4	31,300	1076
Z	Z	Z	Z	Z	2	L	S	16	4	26,900	1077
Y	Z	Z	Z	Y	1	L	S	14	3	24,700	1078
Y	Z	Z	Z	Y	1	L	S	17	2	27,300	1079
Y	Z	Z	Z	Y	2	L	S	13	2	18,100	1080
Y	Y	Z	Z	Z	1	L	N	14	3	104,200	1081
Z	Z	Z	Z	Z	1	L	N	16	4	26,100	1082
Y	Z	Z	Z	Z	9	L	N	13	4	19,300	1083
Y	Z	Z	Z	Z	1	L	N	16	4	20,800	1084
Y	Y	Z	Y	Y	1	L	N	16	2	28,100	1085
Z	Z	Z	Y	Z	2	L	S	14	6	26,400	1086
Z	Z	Z	Y	Z	2	C	S	10	5	18,300	1087
Y	Z	Z	Z	Z	2	L	S	10	7	17,800	1088
Z	Z	Z	Y	Z	2	L	S	8	9	18,000	1089
Z	Z	Z	Z	Z	2	L	N	12	11	19,600	1090
Y	Y	Z	Y	Y	2	L	S	10	6	24,200	1091
Y	Z	Z	Z	Y	3	L	S	12	5	22,100	1092
Z	Z	Y	Y	Y	2	L	S	10	6	49,000	1093
Z	Y	Z	Y	Y	2	L	N	12	9	23,300	1094
Z	Z	Z	Y	Z	2	C	N	10	7	22,200	1095
Y	Y	Z	Y	Y	2	L	N	12	6	24,700	1096
Z	Z	Y	Z	Y	2	L	S	16	6	27,300	1097
Z	Z	Y	Z	Z	3	L	S	18	10	26,900	1098
Z	Y	Z	Z	Z	1	L	S	15	7	21,200	1099
Z	Z	Y	Y	Y	2	C	S	16	5	23,800	1100

Table 12.2
Cars per Family

Number of Cars Per Family	Number of Families
1	74
2	23
3	2
9	1

Suppose that the data were collected from a probability sample of respondents using mailed questionnaires, and that the 100 people to whom the questionnaire was sent all replied. Thus, there are no problems of nonresponse with which to contend.

One-Way Tabulation

The one-way tabulation, in addition to communicating the results of a study, can be used for several other purposes: (1) to determine the degree of item nonresponse, (2) to locate blunders, (3) to locate outliers, (4) to determine the empirical distribution of the variable in question, and (5) to calculate summary statistics. The first three of these are often referred to as "data cleaning."

Item nonresponse and what to do about it are aggravating problems in most surveys. It seems that some percentage of the survey instruments invariably suffer from this problem. As a matter of fact, the degree of item nonresponse often serves as a useful indicator of the quality of the research. When it is excessive, it calls the whole research effort into question and suggests a critical examination of the research objectives and procedures be undertaken. When it is in bounds, it still demands that decisions be made with respect to what to do about the missing items before analyzing the data. There are several possible strategies:

1. Leave the items blank and report the number as a separate category. While this procedure works well for simple one-way and cross tabulations, it does not work very well at all for a number of statistical techniques.

2. Eliminate the case with the missing item in analyses using the variable. When using this approach, the analyst must continually report the number of cases on which the analysis is based, since the sample size is not constant across analyses. It also ignores the fact that a significant amount of no information on any item might in itself be insightful; respondents do not care very deeply about the issue being addressed by the question.

3. Substitute values for the missing items. Typically, the substitution will involve some measure of central tendency such as the mean, median, or mode. Alternatively, sometimes the analyst attempts to estimate the answer using other information contained in the questionnaire. The substitution of values makes maximum use of the data, since all the reasonably good cases are used. At the same time, it is

more work and it does contain some potential for bias. It also raises the question of which statistical technique should be used to generate the estimate.[10]

There is no "right" or single answer as to how missing items should be handled. It all depends on the purposes of the study, the incidence of missing items, and the methods that will be used to analyze the data.

A **blunder** is simply an error. It can happen during editing, coding, or when entering the data on the computer. Consider the one-way tabulation of the number of cars owned per family in Table 12.2. A check of the original questionnaire indicates the family having nine cars had, in fact, one car. The nine is a blunder. The simple one-way tabulation has revealed the error, and it can now be corrected at a very early stage in the analysis with a minimum of difficulty and expense.

The number of cases serving as a base for the one-way tabulation is 100, and thus the number entries are readily converted to percentages. Conversion will rarely be this easy, but it is good practice to indicate percentages in the table. Percentages facilitate communication, and a more typical presentation of the above result, corrected for blunders, is found in Table 12.3. Note that the *percentages are presented to zero decimal places*. Though in this case it is because the sample size was 100, in most cases it would be done deliberately. The sample is small, and with small samples one has to be particularly careful not to convey a greater accuracy than the figures can support. They also are easier to read when rounded off. On some occasions the analyst might wish to report percentages to one decimal place.[11] Rarely, if ever, would they be reported to two decimal places, since this will typically introduce a spurious sense of accuracy and might seriously impair the analysis by lulling the reader into assuming the data is more accurate than it actually is. The general rule in reporting percentages is: *Unless decimals serve a special purpose, they should be omitted*.

Sometimes the percentages also are presented in parentheses (see Table 12.4) immediately to the right or below the actual count entry in the table. Sometimes only the percentages are presented. In this case it is imperative that the total number of cases on which the percentages are based be provided.

The third use of the one-way tabulation is to locate **outliers.** An outlier is not an error. Rather, it is an observation so different in magnitude from the rest of the observations that the analyst chooses to treat it as a special case. This may mean eliminating

---

[10]David W. Stewart, "Filling the Gap: A Review of the Missing Data Problem," unpublished manuscript, provides an excellent review of the literature on the missing data problem, including various methods for eliminating cases and estimating answers. On the basis of this review, he concludes several things: missing data points should be estimated regardless of whether the data are missing randomly or nonrandomly; for very small amounts of missing data, almost any of the estimation procedures work reasonably well; when larger amounts of data are missing and the average intercorrelation of variables is .20 or less, the substitution of the mean seems to work best; and when the average intercorrelation of the variables exceeds .20, a regression or principal components procedure is the preferred choice when linearity among the variables may be assumed. See also Jae-On Kim and James Curry, "The Treatment of Missing Data in Multivariate Analysis," *Sociological Methods and Research,* 6 (November 1977), pp. 215–240. For a study that empirically examines the question of whether or not missing items are random, see Richard M. Durand, Hugh J. Guffey, Jr., and John M. Planchon, "An Examination of the Random Versus Nonrandom Nature of Item Omissions," *Journal of Marketing Research,* 20 (August 1983), pp. 305–313.

[11]See the classic book by Hans Zeisel, *Say It with Figures,* 5th ed. (New York: Harper & Row, 1968), pp. 16–17, for conditions that would support reporting percentages with decimal-place accuracy.

Table 12.3
Cars per Family

Number of Cars Per Family	Number of Families	Percent of Families
1	75	75
2	23	23
3	2	2
	100	100

Table 12.4
Income Distribution of Respondents in Car Ownership Study

Income	Number of Families		Cumulative Number of Families	
Less than $13,500	3	(3.0)	3	(3.0)
$13,500 to 15,400	23	(23.0)	26	(26.0)
$15,500 to 17,400	28	(28.0)	54	(54.0)
$17,500 to 19,400	14	(14.0)	68	(68.0)
$19,500 to 21,400	7	(7.0)	75	(75.0)
$21,500 to 23,400	4	(4.0)	79	(79.0)
$23,500 to 25,400	6	(6.0)	85	(85.0)
$25,500 to 27,400	6	(6.0)	91	(91.0)
$27,500 to 29,400	2	(2.0)	93	(93.0)
$29,500 to 55,400	6	(6.0)	99	(99.0)
More than $55,400	1	(1.0)	100	(100.0)
Total number of families	100	(100.0)		

the observation from the analysis or determining the specific factors that generate this unique observation. Consider, for example, the tabulation of incomes contained in Table 12.4, but ignore the right-hand column for the moment.

The tabulation indicates there is only one family with an income greater than $55,400. Table 12.1 indicates that this family (Number 1081) had an annual income of $104,200. This is clearly out of line with the rest of the sample and is properly considered an outlier. What the analyst chooses to do with this observation depends on the objectives of the study. In this case, it is not unreasonable for a family to have such an income, so the observation will be retained in the analysis.

The fourth use of the one-way frequency tabulation is to determine the *empirical distribution* of the characteristic in question. The distribution often is best visualized through a histogram. A **histogram** is a form of bar chart in which the values of the variable are placed along the abscissa, or X axis, and the absolute frequency or relative frequency of occurrence of the values is indicated along the Y axis, or ordinate. The

Figure 12.1
**Histogram and Frequency Polygon of Incomes of
Families in Car Ownership Study**

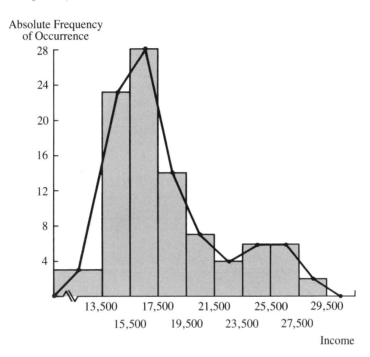

histogram for the income data in Table 12.4 appears as Figure 12.1, with the incomes over $29,500 omitted because their inclusion would have required an undue extension of the income axis. It is readily apparent that the distribution of incomes is skewed to the right. The actual distribution can be compared to some theoretical distribution to determine whether the data are consistent with some *a priori* model. Further insight into the empirical distribution of income can be obtained by constructing the **frequency polygon.** The frequency polygon is obtained from the histogram by connecting the midpoints of the bars with straight lines. The frequency polygon for incomes is superimposed on the histogram in Figure 12.1.

An alternative way of gaining insight into empirical distribution is through the empirical **cumulative distribution function.** The one-way tabulation is again the source. In this case, though, the number of observations with a value less than or equal to a specified quantity is determined; that is, the cumulative frequencies are generated. Thus, in the right-hand column of Table 12.4, we see that there are three families with incomes less than $13,500, whereas there are 26 families (3 + 23) with incomes of $15,400 or less and 54 families (3 + 23 + 28) with incomes of $17,400 or less. These cumulative frequencies are denoted along the ordinate in Figure 12.2, while the abscissa again contains incomes. The empirical cumulative distribution function is generated by

Figure 12.2
Cumulative Distribution of Incomes of Families in Car Ownership Study

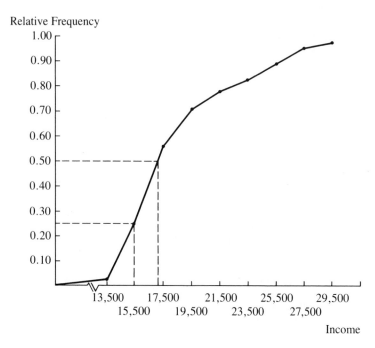

connecting the points representing the given combinations of Xs (values) and Ys (cumulative frequencies) with straight lines.

The cumulative distribution function can also be used to determine whether the distribution of observed incomes is consistent with some theoretical or assumed distribution. In addition, it can be used to calculate some of the commonly used measures of location such as the median, quartiles, and percentiles. These can simply be read from the plot once the cumulative relative frequencies are entered. In our case, the cumulative relative frequencies are equal to the cumulative absolute frequencies divided by 100, since there are 100 cases.

By definition, the sample median is that value for which 50 percent of the values lie below it and 50 percent are above it. To read the sample median from the plot of the cumulative distribution, simply extend a horizontal line from 0.50 on the relative frequency ordinate until it intersects the graph, and then drop a vertical line from the point of intersection to the X axis. The point of intersection with the X axis is the approximate sample median. In the case at hand, the sample median equals $17,300. The quality of the approximation could be checked by actually determining the median using the detailed data.

Sample quartiles could be determined in similar fashion. The first sample quartile (also known as the twenty-fifth percentile) is that value for which 25 percent of the observations are below it. This first sample quartile is determined by drawing a horizontal line from 0.25 on the relative frequency ordinate until it intersects the graph, dropping a vertical line from the point of intersection to the horizontal axis, and reading off the value of the first quartile at the point of intersection with the X axis. The first quartile is thus found to be \$15,300. The procedure for the third quartile (seventy-fifth percentile) or any other percentile would be the same as that for the median or first quartile. The only change would be where the horizontal line commenced.

The one-way tabulation is also useful in calculating other summary measures, like the mode, mean, and standard deviation. The mode, or the most frequently occurring item, can be read directly from the one-way tabulation. Thus, Table 12.3 suggests that most families own one car. The mean, or "average" response, can be calculated from a one-way tabulation by weighting each value by its frequency of occurrence, summing these products, and dividing by the number of cases. The average number of cars per family given the data in Table 12.3 would thus be estimated to be:

Value	Frequency	Value × Frequency
1	75	75
2	23	46
3	2	6
	100	127

or

$$\frac{127}{100} = 1.27 \text{ cars per family.}$$

The standard deviation provides a measure of spread in the data. It is calculated from the one-way tabulation by taking the deviation of each value from the mean, and squaring these deviations. The squared deviations are then multiplied by the frequency with which each occurs, these products are summed, and the sum is divided by one less than the number of cases to yield the sample variance. The square root of the sample variance then yields the sample standard deviation. The calculation of the standard deviation is thus very similar to that for ungrouped data, except for the fact that each value is weighted by the frequency with which it occurs. The standard deviation for the data in Table 12.3 is thus calculated to be:

Value	Value-Mean	(Value-Mean)^2	Frequency	Frequency Times Difference Squared
1	− .27	.0729	75	5.4675
2	.73	.5329	23	12.2567
3	1.73	2.9929	2	5.9858
				23.7100

yielding a variance of

$$\frac{23.7100}{99} = .2395$$

and a standard deviation of $\sqrt{.2395} = .4894$.

The one-way tabulation as a communication vehicle for the results has not been discussed. The reader only needs to look at Table 12.1 to see how much insight can be gathered about the variable income and then compare that with the insight generated in the one-way tabulation contained in Table 12.4. When one realizes they also serve as a basic input to the histogram, frequency polygon, and empirical cumulative distribution function, as well as in calculating summary statistics, it is an unwise analyst indeed who does not take the time to develop the one-way tabulations of the variables in the study.

Cross Tabulation

While the one-way tabulation is useful for examining the variables of the study separately, **cross tabulation** is a most important mechanism for studying the relationships among and between variables. In cross tabulation the sample is divided into subgroups, so as to learn how the dependent variable varies from subgroup to subgroup. It is clearly the most used data analysis technique in marketing research. Some would call it the bread-and-butter of applied research. Most marketing research studies go no further than cross tabulation, while many of the studies that do use more sophisticated analytical methods still contain cross tabulation as a significant component. Thus, the analyst and decision maker both need to understand how cross tabulations are developed and interpreted.

Consider, for example, the question of the relationship, if any, between the number of cars that the family owns and family income. To keep the example simple, suppose the analyst was simply interested in determining if a family above average in income was more likely to own two or more cars than a family below average in income. Suppose further that $17,500 was the median income in the population and that this figure was to be used to split the families in the sample into two groups, those with below average and those with above average incomes.

Table 12.5 presents the two-way classification of the sample families by income and number of cars. Looking at the marginal totals, we see that 75 families have one car or less, while 25 families have two cars or more. We also see that the sample is not unrepresentative of the population, at least as far as income is concerned; 54 families fall into the lower-than-average income group using the $17,500 cutoff.

Does the number of cars depend on income? It certainly seems so on the basis of Table 12.5, since 19 of the families owning two or more cars are in the upper income group. Is there anything that can be done to shed additional light on the relationship? The answer is *yes*. Compute percentages. Tables 12.6 and 12.7 are mathematically equivalent to Table 12.5, but are based on percentages calculated in different directions: horizontally in Table 12.6 and vertically in Table 12.7. The tables contain quite different messages. Table 12.6 suggests that multiple car ownership is affected by family income; 41 percent of the families with above-average incomes had two or more automobiles, while only 11 percent of the below-average-income families did so. This is a clear, interesting finding. Table 12.7, on the other hand, conveys a different story. It suggests that 64 percent of those who owned one car had below average incomes, while only 24 percent of those who owned two or more cars were below average in income. Does this mean that multiple car ownership paves the way to higher incomes? Definitely not. Rather, it simply illustrates a fundamental rule of percentage calculations: Always

Table 12.5
Family Income and Number of Cars Family Owns

Income	Number of Cars		
	1 or Less	2 or More	Total
Less than $17,500	48	6	54
More than $17,500	27	19	46
Total	75	25	100

Table 12.6
Number of Cars by Family Income

Income	Number of Cars			Number of Cases
	1 or Less	2 or More	Total	
Less than $17,500	89%	11%	100%	54
More than $17,500	59%	41%	100%	46

Table 12.7
Family Income by Number of Cars

Income	1 or less	2 or More
Less than $17,500	64%	24%
More than $17,500	36%	76%
Total	100%	100%
(Number of cases)	(75)	(25)

calculate percentages in the direction of the causal factor, or across the effect factor.[12] In this case, income is logically considered the cause or independent variable, and multiple car ownership the effect or dependent variable. The percentages are correctly calculated, therefore, in the direction of income as in Table 12.6.[13]

One very useful way to think about the direction in which to calculate percentages is to conceptualize the problem in terms of **conditional probability** or the probability of one event occurring given that another event has occurred or will occur. Thus, the notion of the probability that the family has two or more cars *given* they are high income

---

[12]See Zeisel, *Say It with Figures*, p. 28, for a slightly modified statement of the percentage-direction-calculation rule that takes into account the representativeness of the sample.

[13]At times the direction of causation will not be straightforward, and the calculation of percentages can logically proceed in either direction. *Ibid.*, pp. 30–32.

Table 12.8
Number of Cars and Size of Family

| | Number of Cars | | |
Size of Family	1 or Less	2 or More	Total
4 or less	70	8	78
5 or more	5	17	22
Total	75	25	100

Table 12.9
Number of Cars by Size of Family

| | Number of Cars | | | |
Size of Family	1 or Less	2 or More	Total	Number of Cases
4 or less	90%	10%	100%	(78)
5 or more	23%	77%	100%	(22)

makes sense, while the notion that the family is high income *given* they have two or more cars does not.

The two-way cross tabulation, although it provides some insight into a dependency relationship, is not the final answer. Rather, it represents a start. Consider now, for example, the relationship between multiple car ownership and size of family. Table 12.8 indicates the number of small and large (five or more members) families that possess two or more cars. Now, size of family is logically considered a cause of multiple car ownership and not vice versa. Thus, the percentages would be properly computed in the *direction of size of family* or *across number of cars*. Table 12.9 presents these percentages and suggests that the number of cars a family owns is affected by the size of the family—77 percent of the large families have two or more cars, while only 10 percent of the small families do.

This result raises the question: Does multiple car ownership depend on family size or, as previously suggested, on family income? The proper way to answer this question is through the *simultaneous* treatment of income and family size. In effect, the two-way cross-classification table needs to be partitioned and a three-way table of income, family size, and multiple car ownership formed. One way of doing this is illustrated in Table 12.10. This table is, in one sense, two cross-classification tables of multiple car ownership versus income—one for small families of four or fewer members and one for large families of five or more members.

Once again we would want to compute percentages in the direction of income within each table. Table 12.11 contains these percentages, which indicate that multiple car ownership depends both on income and on family size. For small families of four or less, 19 percent of those with above-average incomes have two or more cars, while only 4 percent of those with below-average incomes have more than one automobile. For

Table 12.10
Number of Cars by Income and Size of Family

Income	Four Members or Less: Number of Cars			Five Members or More: Number of Cars			Total Number of Cars		
	1 or Less	2 or More	Total	1 or Less	2 or More	Total	1 or Less	2 or More	Total
Less than $17,500	44	2	46	4	4	8	48	6	54
More than $17,500	26	6	32	1	13	14	27	19	46
Total	70	8	78	5	17	22	75	25	100

Table 12.11
Number of Cars by Income and Size of Family

Income	Four Members or Less: Number of Cars			Five Members or More: Number of Cars			Total Number of Cars		
	1 or Less	2 or More	Total	1 or Less	2 or More	Total	1 or Less	2 or More	Total
Less than $17,500	96%	4%	100% (46)	50%	50%	100% (8)	89%	11%	100% (54)
More than $17,500	81%	19%	100% (32)	7%	93%	100% (14)	59%	41%	100% (46)

large families, 93 percent of the above-average-income and 50 percent of the below-average-income families have more than one vehicle.

The above comparisons highlight the effect of income on multiple car ownership, holding family size constant. We could also compare the effect of family size on multiple car ownership, holding income constant. We would still find that each provides a partial explanation for multiple car ownership. Now, you may have felt a bit uncomfortable with the presentation of the data in Tables 12.10 and 12.11. The information is there to be mined, but perhaps you may have wondered whether it could not be presented in a more revealing manner. It can, if you are willing to accept a couple of refinements in the manner of presentation. Look specifically at the first row of the first section of Table 12.11, reproducing it as Table 12.12. All of the information contained in this table can be condensed into one figure, 4 percent. This is the percentage of small, below-average-income families that have two or more cars. It follows that the complementary percentage, 96 percent, represents those that have one automobile or none.

Table 12.13 shows the rest of the data in Table 12.11 treated in the same way. The entry in each case is the percentage of families in that category that own two or more automobiles. Table 12.13 conveys the same information as Table 12.11, but it delivers the message with much greater clarity. The separate effect of income on multiple car ownership, holding family size constant, can be determined by reading down the columns, while the effect of family size, holding income constant, can be determined by reading across the rows. Omitting the complementary percentages has helped reveal the

Table 12.12

Car Ownership for Small, Below-average-income Families

	Number of Cars		
Income	1 or Less	2 or More	Total
Less than $17,500	96%	4%	100% (46)

Table 12.13

Percentage of Families Owning Two or More Cars by Income and Size of Family

	Size of Family		
Income	4 or Less	5 or More	Total
Less than $17,500	4%	50%	11%
More than $17,500	19%	93%	41%

structure of the data. Therefore, let us agree to use this form of presentation whenever we attempt to determine the effect of several explanatory variables, considered simultaneously, in the pages that follow.

The original association between number of cars and family income reflected in Table 12.6 is called the **total (or zero order) association** between the variables. Table 12.13, which depicts the association between the two variables within categories of family size, is called a *conditional table* that reveals the **conditional association** between the variables. Family size here is a *control variable*. Conditional tables that are developed on the basis of one control variable are called *first-order* conditional tables, while those developed using two control variables are called *second-order* conditional tables, and so on.

Which variable has the greater effect on multiple car ownership—income or family size? A useful method for addressing this question is to calculate the difference in proportions as a function of the level of the variable.[14] This can be done for the zero order tables as well as the conditional tables of higher order. Consider again Table 12.6 and concentrate on the impact of income on the probability of the family having multiple cars. The proportion of low-income families that have two or more cars is 0.11, while the proportion of high-income families is 0.41. The probability of having multiple cars is clearly different depending on the family's income; specifically, high income increases the probability of having two or more cars by 0.30 (0.41–0.11) over low income. A similar analysis applied to Table 12.9 suggests the probability of multiple car ownership is clearly different depending on family size. While 0.10 of the small families

---

[14]See Ottar Hellevik, *Introduction to Causal Analysis: Exploring Survey Data by Crosstabulation* (London: George Allen & Unwin, 1984).

have multiple cars, 0.77 of the large families do. Thus, being a large family increases the probability of having two or more cars by 0.67 (0.77 − 0.10) over small families.

To determine whether income or family size has the greater impact, it is necessary to consider them simultaneously using a similar analysis. Table 12.13 contains the data that is necessary for this analysis. Let us first consider the impact of income. The proper way to determine the effect of income is to hold family size constant, which means in essence that we must investigate the relationship between income and multiple car ownership for small families and then again for large families. Among small families, having high income increases the probability of having multiple cars by 0.15 (0.19 − 0.04). Among large families, having high income increases the probability of having multiple cars by 0.43 (0.93 − 0.50) compared to small families. The size of the associations between income and multiple car ownership are different for different family sizes. This means there is a statistical interaction between the independent variables, and in order to generate a single estimate of the effect of income on car ownership, some kind of average of the separate effects needs to be computed. The appropriate average is a weighted average that takes account of the sizes of the groups on which the individual effects were calculated. There were 78 small families in the sample of 100 cases and 22 large families; the weight for small families is thus 0.78 and for large families 0.22. The weighted average is

$$0.15(0.78) + 0.43(0.22) = 0.21,$$

which suggests that on average high versus low income increases the probability of owning multiple cars by .21.

To investigate the impact of family size, it is necessary to hold income constant or, alternatively, to investigate the impact of family size on multiple car ownership for low-income families, then for high-income families, and then to generate a weighted average of the two results if they are not the same. Among low-income families, being large increases the probability of having multiple cars by 0.46 (0.50 − 0.04) compared to small families. Among high-income families, large size increases the probability by 0.74 (0.93 − 0.19) versus small size. Since there were 54 low-income families and 46 high-income families, the appropriate weights for weighting the two effects are 0.54 and 0.46, respectively. The calculation yields

$$0.46(0.54) + 0.74(0.46) = 0.59$$

as the estimate of the impact of family size on multiple car ownership.

Family size has a more pronounced effect on multiple car ownership than does income. It increases the probability of having two or more cars by 0.59, whereas income increases it by 0.21.

The previous example highlighted an important application of cross tabulation—the use of an additional variable to refine an initial cross tabulation. In this case, family size was used to refine the relationship between multiple car ownership and income. This is only one of the many applications of successive cross tabulation of variables, and, in fact, a number of conditions can occur when additional variables are introduced into a cross tabulation, as shown in the various panels of Table 12.14. The two-way tabulation may initially indicate the existence or nonexistence of a relationship between the variables. The introduction of a third variable may occasion no change in the initial

Table 12.14
Conditions That Can Arise with the Introduction of an
Additional Variable into a Cross Tabulation

Initial Conclusion	With the Additional Variable	
	Change Conclusion	Retain Conclusion
Some relationship	A. Refine explanation B. Reveal spurious explanation C. Provide limiting conditions I	II
No relationship	III	IV

conclusion, or it may indicate that a substantial change is in order. We have considered Panel 1–A. Let us now turn to an analysis of examples of these alternative conditions.

Panel I: An Initial Relationship Is Modified by the Introduction of a Third Variable

Case I–B: Initial Relationship Is Spurious   One of the purposes of the automobile purchase study was to determine the kinds of families that purchase specific kinds of automobiles. Consider vans. It was expected that van ownership would be related to life-style and, in particular, that those with a liberal orientation (''swingers'') would be more likely to own vans than would those who are conservative by nature. Table 12.15 was constructed, employing the raw data on car ownership in Table 12.1, to test this hypothesis. Contrary to expectation, conservatives are more apt than liberals to own vans; 24 percent of the conservatives, but only 16 percent of the liberals, in the sample owned vans.

Is there some logical explanation for this unexpected happening? Consider the addition of a third variable, region of the country in which the family resides, to the analysis. A clear picture of the relationship among the three variables considered simultaneously can be developed employing our previously agreed-upon convention; that is, simply report the percentage in each category. The complement, 100 minus the percentage, then indicates the proportion not owning vans.

As Table 12.16 indicates, van ownership is not related to life-style. Rather, it depends on the region of the country in which the family resides. When region is held constant, there is no difference in van ownership between liberals and conservatives. Families living in the South are much more likely to own a van than are families who live in the northern states. It just so happens that people in the South are more conservative with regard to their life-style than people in the North. The original relationship is therefore said to be spurious.

While it seems counterproductive to calculate the difference in proportions to determine the impact of each variable for each of the potential conditions in Table 12.14, it does seem useful to do it for this case to demonstrate what is meant by a main effect without a statistical interaction. The example is also useful in reinforcing how the dif-

Table 12.15
Van Ownership by Life-style

	Own Van?		
Life-style	Yes	No	Total
Liberal	9(16%)	46(84%)	55(100%)
Conservative	11(24%)	34(76%)	45(100%)

Table 12.16
Van Ownership by Life-style and Region of Country

	Region of Country		
Life-style	North	South	Total
Liberal	5%	41%	16%
Conservative	5%	43%	24%

ference-in-proportions calculation can be used to isolate the causal relationships that exist in cross-tabulation data. Consider first the zero order association between van ownership and life-style contained in Table 12.15. Being a conservative increases the probability of van ownership by 0.08 (0.24 − 0.16) compared to being liberal. Yet Table 12.16 shows that this is a spurious effect that is due to region of the country, since it disappears when region is held constant. Among those living in the North, the partial association between van ownership and life-style is 0.00 (0.05 − 0.05). Among those living in the South, there is a slightly higher probability of van ownership among conservatives, namely 0.02 (0.43 − 0.41). This effect is so small that it can be attributed to rounding error, particularly since the proportions were only carried to two decimal places and the number of cases is so small. Regardless of the region of the country in which the family resides, its liberal/conservative orientation has no effect on whether or not it owns a van.

Note to the contrary that the effect of region is pronounced and consistent. Among liberal families, living in the South increases the probability of van ownership by 0.36 (0.41 − 0.05) compared to living in the North. Among conservative families, living in the South increases the probability by 0.38 (0.43 − 0.05). Within rounding error, the effect is the same for families with both philosophical orientations, which means there is no interaction among the two predictor variables. Rather, there is only a main effect of region on van ownership, and the best estimate of its size is given by either of these estimates or their average.

The current public debate about the rising incidence of cancer that can be attributed to the use of pesticides, pollution, and so on provides an interesting example of a "spurious relationship that is revealed with the introduction of a third variable." Harry

Schwartz, a researcher affiliated with the Department of Surgery at Columbia University, made the following observation:

The official data suggest cancer death rates have risen much more slowly and for different reasons than the current public debate would suggest. The most important reason for the observed increase in cancer deaths and death rates the past decade, the Center for Health Statistics data show, is simply the aging of the American population. The American people have been getting older on the average for many years now, both because the number surviving beyond 65 or 70 is increasing rapidly and because the birth rate has trended downward for years.

What the center statisticians have done is to age-adjust the mortality data. They have taken the death rates for each decade of human life in years and applied them to a fixed population, that of 1940 with the age distribution of that year. Doing this makes it possible to compare the death rates of different years without the complications and misleading influence of changing age structure. When this is done, the cancer death rate is shown to have increased only about 2.5% between 1968 and 1978. Before age adjustment, the 1968–1978 cancer death rate seems to have jumped over 12%, or much more than when age is taken into account.

When one considers we must all die from something, and that typical Americans are now significantly less likely than they were a decade ago to die of a heart attack, stroke, or related ailments, Mr. Schwartz argues that "the 2.5% increase in age-adjusted cancer death rates between 1968 and 1978 is remarkably modest." This is particularly so since the only adjusted rate that "has gone up very sharply since 1968 is lung cancer," and that the "most effective anti-cancer action Americans can take is to stop smoking."[15]

Case I–C: Limiting Conditions Are Revealed   Consider now the question of ownership of foreign economy cars. Does it depend on the size of the family? Table 12.17 suggests it does. *Smaller* families are *less* likely to own a foreign economy car than are larger families! Only 8 percent of the small families, but 27 percent of the large families, have such automobiles. Can this counter-intuitive finding be accounted for?

Consider the expansion of this cross classification by adding a variable for the number of cars the family owns. Table 12.18 presents the percentage data, which indicate that it is only when large families have two or more cars that they own a foreign economy car. No large families with one car own such an automobile. The introduction of the third variable has revealed a condition that limits foreign economy car ownership—multiple car ownership where large families are concerned.

The recent study investigating the effectiveness of aspirin in treating blood clotting after surgery provides an interesting, important application of how the addition of a third variable to the analysis revealed a limiting condition. The two-way tabulation of those treated with aspirin or a placebo versus the presence or absence of blood clots revealed aspirin was effective in reducing the incidents of clots. When the sample was

[15]See Harry Schwartz, "A Look at the Cancer Figures," *The Wall Street Journal,* 15 November 1979, p. 20. Reprinted by permission of *The Wall Street Journal,* © Dow Jones & Company, Inc., 1979. All Rights Reserved.

Table 12.17
Foreign Economy Car Ownership by Family Size

	Own Foreign Economy Car?		
Size of Family	Yes	No	Total
4 or less	6 (8%)	72(92%)	78(100%)
More than 4	6(27%)	16(73%)	22(100%)

Table 12.18
Foreign Economy Car Ownership by Family Size and Number of Cars

	Number of Cars		
Size of Family	1 or Less	2 or More	Total
4 or less	6%	25%	8%
More than 4	0%	35%	27%

Table 12.19
Station Wagon Ownership by Family Size

	Own Station Wagon		
Size of Family	Yes	No	Total
Less than 4	3(4%)	75(96%)	78(100%)
More than 4	15(68%)	7(32%)	22(100%)

broken down by sex of the patient, though, it was found that aspirin was very useful in preventing blood clotting in men but not at all useful in treating women.[16]

Panel II: Initial Conclusion of a Relationship Is Retained

Consider now the analysis of station wagon ownership based on the data in Table 12.1. *A priori,* it would seem to be related to family size. A case could be made that larger families have a greater need for station wagons than have smaller families.

The cross tabulation of these two variables in Table 12.19 suggests that larger families do display a higher propensity to own station wagons; 68 percent of the large families and only 4 percent of the small families own wagons.

---

[16]See Joann S. Lublin, ''Aspirin Found to Cut Blood Clotting Risks in Men, Not Women,'' *Wall Street Journal,* 57 (December 8, 1977), p. 26.

Table 12.20
Station Wagon Ownership by Family Size and Income

	Income		
Size of Family	Less Than $17,500	More Than $17,500	Total
Less than 4	4%	3%	4%
More than 4	63%	71%	68%

Consider, though, whether income might also affect station wagon ownership. As Table 12.20 indicates, income has an effect over and above family size. As one goes from a small to a large family, there is a substantial increase in the propensity to own a station wagon. With larger families, though, the increase is larger. Alternatively, if one focuses solely on large families, there is an increase in station wagon ownership from below-average-income to above-average-income families. The initial conclusion, though, is retained: large families do display a greater tendency to purchase station wagons. Further, the effect of family size on station wagon ownership is much larger than the effect of income.

Panel III: A Relationship Is Established with the Introduction of a Third Variable

Suppose one of the purposes of the study was to determine the characteristics of families who financed the purchase of their automobile. Consider the cross tabulation of installment debt versus education of the household head. Table 12.21 results when the families included in Table 12.1 are classified into one of two educational categories—those with a high school education or less and those with some college training. As is evident, there is no relationship between education and installment debt; the percentage of families with outstanding car debt is 30 percent in each case.

Table 12.22 illustrates the situation when income is also considered in the analysis. For below-average-income families, the presence of installment debt increases with education. For above-average-income families, installment debt decreases with education. The effect of education was obscured in the original analysis because the effects canceled each other. When income is also considered, the relationship of installment debt to education is quite pronounced.

Panel IV: The Conclusion of No Relationship Is Retained with the Addition of a Third Variable

Consider once again the question of station wagon ownership. We have seen previously that it is related to family size. Let us forget this result for a minute and begin the analysis with the question: Is station wagon ownership affected by region of the country in which the family lives? Table 12.23 provides an initial answer. Station wagon ownership does not depend on region; 18 percent of the sample families living in both the North and in the South own wagons.

Table 12.21
Financed Car Purchase by Education of Household Head

| Education of Household Head | Financed Car Purchase | | Total |
	Yes	No	
High school or less	24(30%)	56(70%)	80(100%)
Some college	6(30%)	14(70%)	20(100%)

Table 12.22
Financed Car Purchase by Education of Household Head and Income

| Education of Household Head | Income | | Total |
	Less Than $17,500	More Than $17,500	
High school or less	12%	58%	30%
Some college	40%	27%	30%

Table 12.23
Station Wagon Ownership by Region

| Region | Own Station Wagon | | Total |
	Yes	No	
North	11(18%)	49(82%)	60(100%)
South	7(18%)	33(82%)	40(100%)

Table 12.24
Station Wagon Ownership by Region and Family Size

| Region | Size of Family | | Total |
	4 or Less	More Than 4	
North	4%	69%	18%
South	3%	67%	18%

Let us now consider the relationship when family size is again taken into account. Table 12.24 presents the data. Once again the percentages are constant across regions. There is minor variation, but this is due to round-off accuracy. Small families display a low propensity to purchase station wagons, regardless of whether they live in the North or the South. Large families have a high propensity, and this, too, is independent of where they live. The original lack of relationship between station wagon ownership and region of residence is confirmed with the addition of the third variable, family size.

Summary Comments on Cross Tabulation

The previous examples should certainly highlight the tremendous usefulness of cross tabulation as a tool in analysis. We have seen an application in which a third variable helped to uncover a relationship not immediately discernible, as well as applications in which a third variable triggered the modification of conclusions drawn on the basis of a two-variable classification. You may have paused to ask yourself: Why stop with three variables? Would the conclusion change with the addition of a fourth variable? A fifth? Indeed it might. The problem is that one never knows for sure when to stop introducing variables. The conclusion is always susceptible to change with the introduction of the "right" variable or variables. For example, there is currently great concern among a large segment of marketers about the disappearance of the middle class. Yet there is also the issue of whether the middle class is in fact disappearing. Research Realities 12.2 overviews the concern and highlights what happens when other factors are taken into account, i.e., other variables are introduced into the analysis. Thus, the analyst is always in the position of "inferring" that a relationship exists. Later research may demonstrate that the inference was incorrect. This is why the accumulation of studies, rather than a single study, supporting a particular relationship is so vital to the advancement of knowledge.

Table 12.25 is an overview of the dilemma that the researcher faces. The true situation is always unknown. If it were known, there would be no need to research it. Instead, the researcher is always in the position of making statements about an unknown true situation. The analyst may conclude that there is no relationship, or that there is some relationship between two or more variables when in fact there is none or there is some. Only one of these four possibilities in Table 12.25 *necessarily* corresponds to a correct conclusion—when the analyst concludes there is no relationship and in fact there is no relationship. Two of the other possibilities are necessarily incorrect, while one contains the possibility for error. That is, suppose the true situation is one of some relationship between or among the variables. The analyst has reached a correct conclusion only if he or she concludes that there is some relationship and has discovered its correct form.

Spurious noncorrelation results whenever the analyst concludes there is no relationship when, in fact, there is. Spurious correlation occurs when the true state of affairs is one of no relationship among the variables, and the analyst concludes that a relationship exists.

Thus, the opportunities for error are great. This necessarily gives rise to a temptation to continue adding variables to the analysis *ad infinitum*. Fortunately, the analyst will be constrained in this regard by theory and by data. Theory will constrain him or her, because certain tabulations simply will not make any sense.

The analyst will be constrained by the data in several ways. First, note that he or she will wish to successively add variables to the analysis in the form of higher dimensional cross-classification tables. This can be accomplished only if the analyst has correctly anticipated the tabulations that would be desirable. This is most important. It is too late to say, "If only we had collected information on Variable *X*!" once the analysis has

Research Realities 12.2

Controversy Surrounding the Disappearance of the Middle Class

Over the last few years, the news media, economic pundits, and academicians have held funerals for America's Great Middle Class.

They say President Reagan's economic policies are making the rich richer, driving middle-class workers into the lower class, and "polarizing" the job market—killing off middle-income jobs while increasing low-paid service jobs and high-paid professional/managerial jobs.

Late last year, *Fortune* magazine warned its readers: "Economic forces are propelling one family after another toward the high or low end of the income spectrum. For many marketers, particularly those positioned to sell to the well-to-do, this presages good times. For others used to selling millions of units of their products to middle-income folks, the prospects are altogether darker."

A few months ago, Lester C. Thurow, professor of economics and management at the Massachusetts Institute of Technology, Cambridge, told *Wall Street Journal* readers that the middle class is "disappearing." He blamed job polarization and said the trend "is a cause of concern for the American political democracy." The middle-class market is being eroded by a decrease in well-paid manufacturing jobs, particularly in the auto and steel industries, Thurow said.

The "Vanishing Middle-Class" scenario can be very compelling. Indeed, the census data in Table 1 seem to lend credence to the argument. From 1970 to 1982, the middle-income households dropped and the lower and upper brackets increased.

Looking only at those percentages, a marketer of luxury products would jump for joy while a seller of more modest goods and services would jump out of the window. The marketing implications of such a trend, if true, would be so staggering that they couldn't even be covered in a newspaper article.

But, as is usually the case, there is another side to the "disappearing middle-class" story. As marketing researchers know, raw data often are misleading. They must be analyzed, explained, and put into context and perspective before they can be acted upon.

"The middle-class isn't disappearing. It's alive and doing well," insists Fabian Linden, executive director of The Conference Board's Consumer Research Center, New York. "The problem is that the people making that claim have misinterpreted the data."

Table 1
Annual Household Income (Constant Dollars)

Bracket	1970	1982
Under $15,000	33.5%	37.4%
	21,775,000	31,416,000
$15–$35,000	48%	40.5%
	31,200,000	34,020,000
Over $35,000	18.5%	22.1%
	12,025,000	18,564,000
Household base	65 million	84 million

"The changes we've seen in the distribution of income are the result of demographic and social trends, and those trends are self-correcting. You have to look at census data over a continuum. You never get two extremes occurring simultaneously with the middle falling apart. The income shifts in the 1970s were caused by a passing demographic aberration."

That "aberration," he said, is the post-World War II baby boom—the 70 million born between 1946 and 1965. "The first baby boomers started flooding our colleges in the mid-1960s, and by the early 1970s millions of them were entering the labor market," Linden explains.

"So what we had in the 1970s was a huge infusion of households being started by people in their 20s, a time of life when incomes are modest. Households headed by people under age 35 increased 50% during that time, and that group accounts for a large percentage of the under-$15,000 bracket."

While the baby boomers were setting up house in the 1970s, another large age group, those over 65, was continuing to expand, putting even more downward pressure on the lower-income levels. About 60% of the households in the below-$15,000 bracket are headed by people under age 35 and over 65, Linden said.

The baby boomers' march up the population pyramid was the major cause of income-distribution changes in the 1970s and early 1980s, but not the only one he adds. Social and lifestyle trends also were important factors.

Source: Bernie Whelan, "The 'Vanishing' Middle Class: A Passing Demographic Aberration," *Marketing News*, 18 (May 25, 1984), pp. 1 and 6–7. Published by the American Marketing Association. Reprinted with permission.

continued on next page

Controversy Surrounding the Disappearance of the Middle Class *continued*

Households headed by individuals—divorced or separated women with children as well as singles—increased dramatically during the last decade, 67% and 25% respectively. Today, 16% of families are headed by women and 23% of households consist of individuals living alone, Linden points out. These household types have relatively lower incomes.

"Virtually all of the 'crowding' in the low-income bracket during the 1970s was caused by the sharp increases in the number of households headed by people under 35, divorced or separated women with children, and singles," Linden said.

(Census statistics show that households headed by women have a medium annual income of $11,000 while married-couple households' average income is $26,000.)

Demographers have offered a variety of explanations for the household increase in the $35,000+ bracket. But the most important factor, and the one virtually all agree on, is the impact of working women.

Only a hermit could be unaware of the tremendous influx of women into the labor force during the 1970s (more than 50% of women now have jobs outside the home). Many of them were college-educated baby boomers who commanded good incomes. And, while many younger women have tended to delay marriage and motherhood, census data show that 90% of women eventually marry.

In households where the wife does not work, the median income is $21,000; when the wife works part-time, it's $28,000. In the 50 million households in which both husband and wife work full-time, the median income is $32,000—meaning in 25 million households it's *more than* $32,000.

As Bryant Robey, editor of *American Demographics* magazine, observes: "Women's incomes . . . largely explain why poverty and affluence can be rising at the same time."

Indeed, census data show that, between 1970 and 1982, the $25,000–$35,000 income bracket recorded the largest percentage increase—from 16.9% of households to 23.4%. The $35,000+ households increased nearly 4%.

"I think it's also important to look at the absolute numbers of households by income level," Linden said. "The upper and lower brackets have increased; there's no question about that. But so has the middle class. There are about 10% more middle-income households today than there were in 1970."

Could it be that the income brackets used by demographers are hiding the real erosion of the middle class? For example, can a family with a $15,001 income really be considered middle class? Does a $35,001 income qualify one for upper-class status?

Statisticians will probably never agree on the answers to those questions because the brackets themselves can hide significant differences in household size, dwelling type, etc. For example, a childfree couple with a $25,000 annual income may be able to enjoy a comfortable middle-class life. A couple with a $25,000 income, five children, and a big mortgage may have trouble making ends meet.

The brackets are largely determined by the format and reporting practices of the census bureau. The bureau has a $12,000–$15,000 bracket, but the next one is $15,000–$20,000. It would be hard to argue that most households in the latter bracket are in the low economic class.

Table 12.25
The Researcher's Dilemma

Researcher's Conclusion	True Situation	
	No Relationship	Some Relationship
No relationship	Correct decision	Spurious noncorrelation
Some relationship	Spurious correlation	Correct decision if concluded relationship is of proper form

Similarly, the bureau brackets incomes from $20,000–$25,000; $25,000–$35,000; $35,000–$50,000; and over $50,000. Thus, data users typically bracket upper-income households at $35,000 ± .

In addition, the census bureau uses the $35,000 figure as the starting point to figure discretionary income for a family of four. Families with significant discretionary income are typically considered "high-income" households. (The bureau's "poverty" income level for a family of four is $9,862, and that level, as well as the others, are periodically revised to reflect changes in the Consumer Price Index.)

However, in the marketing community, $35,000 usually doesn't qualify as "high-income." Monroe-Mendelsohn Research and other research and consulting firms that offer customized data on the "affluent" consumer market, usually start at $40,000 or $50,000.

If a researcher used the census bureau's "poverty" cutoff and the marketing community's definition of upper-income as $50,000 + , he would end up with Table 2, which shows very little change from 1970–1982. (The data probably can be collapsed to prove or disprove just about any income-trend theory.)

Table 2
Household Income: Poverty, Middle, Affluent

Bracket	'70	'82
$10,000 –	21.8%	23.9%
$10–$50,000	70.4	67.2
$50,000 +	7.8	8.9

Linden prefers to cite census data showing the proportion of total income by fifths of the population. As Table 3 shows, the third or middle-income level has gone virtually unchanged. He points out that if wages were being "polarized," there would be evidence of "pull" at both ends of the distribution. There isn't.

Table 3
Income Distribution

Earnings Level	1972	1982
Lowest	4.2	3.9%
Second	10.5	10.0
Third	16.8	16.5
Fourth	24.6	24.6
Fifth	43.9	45.0

Source: U.S. Census Bureau

"The demographers and statisticians at the census bureau are pretty smart cookies," Linden said. "If the brackets needed changes, based on living costs or some other factor, they would have been changed.

"I'll admit that we're all slaves to the government's data-reporting policies. But it's nonsense to argue about where to bracket the income levels. There just wasn't that much change during the 1970s in the pattern of *real* income. The brackets may need to be changed in the future, but not right now."

begun. The relationships to be investigated, and thus the cross tabulations that should be appropriate, must be specified before the data are collected. Ideally, the analyst would construct dummy tables before beginning to collect the data. The dummy tables would be complete in all respects except for the number of observations falling in each cell. As a practical matter, it is usually impossible to anticipate all the cross tabulations one will want to develop. Nevertheless, careful specification of these tables at problem definition time can return substantial benefits.

The analyst also is going to be limited by the size of the sample. In the example, since we started with 100 observations, the two-way tables were not particularly troublesome. Yet as soon as we introduced the third variable, cell sizes became extremely small. This occurred even though we treated all variables as dichotomies. Families were either below average or above average in income; they were either small or large; they lived either in the North or in the South, and so on. This was done purposely so as to simplify the presentation. Yet even here the three-way tabulation offers 8 cells (2 × 2 × 2) into which the observations may be placed. Assuming an even allocation of the cases to the cells, this only allows 12.5 cases per cell. This is clearly a small number upon which to base any kind of conclusion. The problem, of course, would have been compounded if a greater number of levels had been used for any of the variables—for example, if families had been divided into four income groups rather than two, since the number of cells is the product of the number of levels for the variables being considered. For example, four income levels, three educational levels, and four family size levels would generate a cross-tabulation table with 48 separate cells (4 × 3 × 4). One would need a much larger sample than 100 to have any confidence in the suggested relationships.

Summary

This chapter reviewed the common analysis functions of editing, coding, and tabulation. Editing involves the inspection and correction, if necessary, of each questionnaire or observation form. The field edit, a preliminary edit most often conducted by the field supervisor, is aimed at correcting the most glaring omissions and inaccuracies while the field staff is still intact. The central office edit follows and involves a more careful scrutiny and correction of the completed data collection instruments. In the central office edit, particular attention is given to such things as incomplete answers, obviously wrong answers, and answers that reflect a lack of interest.

Coding is the procedure by which data are categorized. It involves the three step process of (1) specifying the categories or classes into which the responses are to be placed, (2) assigning code numbers to the classes, and (3) preparing a codebook. If the data are to be analyzed by computer, a number of conventions should be followed in assigning the code numbers, including:

1. use only one punch per column;
2. use only numeric codes;
3. assign as many columns as are necessary to capture the variable;
4. use the same standard codes throughout for ''No information''; and
5. code in a respondent identification number on each record.

Tabulation consists of counting the number of cases that fall into the various categories. The simple, or one-way, tabulation involves the count for a single variable, while cross tabulation involves counting the number of cases that have the characteristics described by two or more variables considered simultaneously. The one-way tabulation is useful in communicating the results of a study, and it can also be employed to locate blunders or errors, to determine the degree of item nonresponse, to locate outliers (observations very much different in value from the rest), and to determine the empirical distribution of the variable in question. It also serves as basic input to the calculation of measures such as the mean, median, and standard deviation that provide a summary picture of the distribution of the variable. Cross tabulation is one of the more useful devices for studying the relationships among and between variables since the results are easily communicated; further, cross tabulation can provide insight into the nature of a relationship, since the addition of one or more variables to a two-way cross-classification analysis is equivalent to holding each of the variables constant.

A useful method for determining the impact that one variable has on another variable in a cross-tabulation table is to compute the difference in proportions with which the dependent variable occurs as a function of the levels of the independent variable. This can be done for the zero order tables as well as the conditional tables of higher order. The higher order tables are used to remove the effects of other variables that might be affecting the dependent variable.

Questions

1. Distinguish among the preliminary data analysis steps of editing, coding, and tabulation.

2. What are the differences in emphasis between a field edit and a central office edit?

3. What should an editor do with incomplete answers? Obviously wrong answers? Answers that reflect a lack of interest?

4. What are the principles that underlie the establishment of categories so that collected data may be properly coded?

5. Suppose you have a large number of very long questionnaires, making it impossible for one person to handle the entire coding task. How should the work be divided?

6. What is the difference between a one-way tabulation and a cross tabulation? Illustrate through an example.

7. When should you use machine tabulation? Manual tabulation?

8. What are the possible ways for treating item nonresponse? Which strategy would you recommend?

9. What is a blunder?

10. What is an outlier?

11. With how many digits should percentages be reported?

12. What is a histogram? A frequency polygon? What information do they provide?

13. What is the cumulative distribution function? Of what value is it?

14. How is the mean calculated from the one-way tabulation? The standard deviation?

15. What is the proper procedure for investigating the following hypothesis using cross-tabulation analysis?
    (a) Consumption of Product X depends upon a person's income.
    (b) Consumption of Product X depends upon a person's education.
    (c) Consumption of Product X depends upon both.

16. How would you determine whether income or education had the greater impact on the consumption of Product X?

17. Illustrate the procedure from Questions 15 and 16 with data of your own choosing; that is, develop the tables, fill in the assumed numbers, and indicate the conclusions to be drawn from each table.

18. What is meant by the statement: the introduction of an additional variable
    (a) refined the original explanation,
    (b) revealed spurious explanation,
    (c) provided limiting conditions?

19. How do you explain the condition in which a two-way cross tabulation of Variables X and Y revealed no relationship between X and Y but the introduction of Z revealed a definite relationship between X and Y?

20. What is the researcher's dilemma with respect to cross-tabulation analysis?

21. What constraints operate on researchers that prevent them from adding variables to cross-classification tables *ad infinitum?*

Applications and Problems

1. The WITT TV station was conducting research in order to help develop programs that would be well received by the viewing audience and would be considered a dependable source of information. A two-part questionnaire was administered by personal interviews to a panel of 3,000 respondents residing in the city of Chicago. The field and office edits were simultaneously done, so that the deadline of May 1st could be met. A senior supervisor, Mr. Z, was placed in charge of the editing tasks and was assisted by two junior supervisors and two field workers. The two field workers were instructed to discard instruments that were illegible or incomplete. Both the junior supervisors were instructed to scrutinize 1,500 of the instruments each for incomplete answers, wrong answers and responses that indicated a lack of interest. They were instructed to discard instruments that had greater than five incomplete or wrong answers (the questionnaire contained 30 questions). In addition, they were asked to use their judgment in assessing whether the respondent showed a lack of interest in which case they should also discard the questionnaire.
   (a) Critically evaluate the above editing tasks. Please be specific.
   (b) Make specific recommendations to Mr. D. Witt, the owner of the WITT TV station, as to how the editing should be done.

2. (a) Establish response categories and codes for the question, "What do you like about this new brand of cereal?"
   (b) Code the following responses using your categories and codes.
      1. "$1.50 is a reasonable price to pay for the cereal."
      2. "The raisins and nuts add a nice flavor."
      3. "The sizes of the packages are convenient."
      4. "I like the sugar coating on the cereal."
      5. "The container does not tear and fall apart easily."
      6. "My kids like the cartoons on the back of the packet."
      7. "It is reasonably priced compared to other brands."
      8. "The packet is attractive and easy to spot in the store."
      9. "I like the price, it is not so low that I doubt the quality and at the same time it is not so high to be unaffordable."
      10. "The crispness and lightness of the cereal improve the taste."

3. (a) Establish response categories and codes for the following question that was asked to a sample of business executives. "In your opinion, which types of companies have not been affected by the present economic climate?"

(**b**) Code the following responses using your categories and codes.
1. Washington Post
2. Colgate Palmolive
3. Gillette
4. Hilton Hotels
5. Chase Manhattan
6. Prentice-Hall
7. Hoover
8. Fabergé
9. Marine Midlands Banks
10. Zenith Radio
11. Holiday Inns
12. Dryden Press
13. Singer
14. Saga
15. Bank America

4. A large manufacturer of electronic components for automobiles recently conducted a study to determine the average value of electronic components per automobile. Personal interviews were conducted with a random sample of 400 respondents. The following information was secured with respect to each subject's "main" vehicle when they had more than one.

Average Dollar Value of Electronic Equipment Per Automobile

Dollar Value of Electronic Equipment	Number of Automobiles
Less than $50	35
$ 51 to $100	40
$101 to $150	55
$151 to $200	65
$201 to $250	65
$251 to $300	75
$301 to $350	40
$351 to $400	20
More than $401	5
Total number of automobiles	400

(**a**) Convert the above information into percentages.
(**b**) Compute the cumulative absolute frequencies.
(**c**) Compute the cumulative relative frequencies.
(**d**) Prepare a histogram and frequency polygon with the average value of electronic equipment on the x-axis and the absolute frequency on the y-axis.
(**e**) Graph the empirical cumulative distribution function with the average value on the x-axis and the relative frequency on the y-axis.
(**f**) Locate the median, first sample quartile and third sample quartile on the above cumulative distribution function.
(**g**) Calculate the mean and standard deviation and variance for the frequency distribution. (Hint: Use the midpoint of each class interval and multiply that by the appropriate frequency. For the interval starting at $401, assume the midpoint is 425.5.)

5. A social organization was interested in determining if there were various demographic characteristics that might be related to people's propensity to contribute to charities. The organization was particularly interested in determining if individuals above 40 were more likely to contribute larger amounts than individuals below 40. The average contribution in the population was $1,500 and this figure was used to divide the individuals in the sample into two groups, those that contributed large amounts or more than average versus those that contributed less than average. The following table presents a two-way classification of the sample of individuals by contributions and age.

Table 1
Personal Contributions and Age

Personal Contribution	Age		Total
	39 or less	40 or more	
Less than or equal to $1,500	79	50	129
More than $1,500	11	60	71
Total	90	110	200

In addition, the social organization wanted to determine if contributions depended on income and/or age. The following table presents the simultaneous treatment of age and income. The median income in the population was $18,200 and this figure was used to split the sample into two groups.

Table 2
Personal Contributions by Age and Income

	Income					
	Less than or equal to $18,200		More than $18,200		Total	
	Age		Age		Age	
Personal Contributions	39 or Less	40 or More	39 or Less	40 or More	39 or Less	40 or More
Less than or equal to $1,500	63	22	16	28	79	50
More than $1,500	7	18	4	42	11	60
Total	70	40	20	70	90	110

(a) Does the amount of personal contributions depend on age? Generate the necessary tables to justify your answer.

    (b) Does the amount of personal contributions depend on age alone? Generate the necessary tables to justify your answer.

    (c) Present the percentage of contributions more than $1,500 by age and income in tabular form. Interpret the table.

Appendix 12A
Avery Sporting Goods

To provide some hands-on experience to the coding, tabulating, and analysis functions, this appendix and some of the remaining appendices discuss the results of a study on catalog buying. A portion of the data set is included as part of this appendix, so that those who are interested can duplicate the analyses to check the results and thereby increase their understanding of the various analysis techniques. The data are also rich enough to allow interested parties to investigate other questions not addressed in these appendices.

Study Background

The primary purpose of the study was to gain insight into people who are likely to buy from catalogs. Avery's management was stimulated to conduct the study by published research investigating the characteristics of in-home (mail order or catalog) shoppers versus store shoppers. This research had indicated that there were differences in the demographic characteristics of those likely to buy in-home from those likely to buy in a store.[1] These studies had also indicated that those who shop in-home are motivated by convenience. Further, the product "is not necessarily the most important determinant of the success or failure of an in-home sale; prior shopping experience, the quality of the product description, its price, delivery, and guarantee policies also interact to influence the degree of perceived shopping risk."[2] Finally, the evidence also indicated that the perceived risk in buying in-home was higher than it was with in-store buying. Those who purchased in-home had higher tolerances for perceived risk. Also important, though, was the fact that the degree of risk varied by product. It was highest for high-priced and personalized items.

Background Information

Through the years, Avery Sporting Goods had been one of the leading catalog sellers of sporting equipment in the country. Known for its wide assortment and colorful print displays, the company's catalogs had been very popular with customers and employees,

---

[1]See Peter L. Gillet, "In Home Shoppers—An Overview," *Journal of Marketing,* 40 (October 1976), pp. 81–88, for a review of the evidence on in-home shopping behavior.

[2]*Ibid.,* p. 85.

and workers had prided themselves on the high number of orders correctly filled. Still, management was considering expanding company operations by opening retail sporting goods stores. The three stores the company recently had opened on the east side of Buffalo, New York, had met with tremendous sales success, far surpassing company expectations. Filled with growing optimism, management had developed plans to open three other stores during the next six to eight months in other areas of western New York. However, executives were not sure what to do with the company's catalog sales division.

Although catalog sales had been substantial, the level of growth had begun to taper off. This appeared to be an industry trend, as other sporting equipment enterprises (as well as major department stores) offering catalog sales and services had experienced similar low rates of growth in sales revenues. While current income from catalog sales was adequate to financially support Avery's plan to develop retail stores, company management had no desire to de-emphasize its catalog operation. In fact, given the catalog's ability to reach a national market at relatively low costs, Avery believed that a large portion of its future success resided in catalog customers. Hence, the company was extremely interested in revitalizing this market segment. As a first step toward the formulation of a long-term strategy for ensuring the continued viability of catalog sales, Avery management decided to have its marketing research department survey a sample of past, present, and potential catalog customers, operationally defined as all those who had been sent catalogs in the past three years, to get a better feel for the catalog market. The issues that were to be addressed included:

- customer perceptions of buying merchandise, in particular sporting equipment, through catalogs;
- people's evaluation of Avery's offerings and services; and
- characteristics of Avery customers.

Randomly sampling individuals from company records and geographic areas served, the questionnaire shown in Figure 12A.1 was mailed to 225 subjects after it was found to work well when pretested on a sample of 25 customers. A three-dollar coupon toward the next item purchased through Avery's catalog was enclosed with each questionnaire; 124 usable surveys were returned, for a 55 percent response rate. The responses to the individual questions were converted to the codes indicated in Table 12A.1. Unanswered questions were coded with a "0" (except for Questions 24, in which blue-collar was coded as "0," and 25 in which a "0" is a valid partial response for the subject's age). The first three columns of the data listed in Table 12A.2 contain the customer's survey identification number.

One-Way Tabulation

As pointed out in the chapter, one-way tabulation is useful for locating blunders and outliers, for determining the empirical distribution of the variable, and for communicating results. Thus, an analyst would normally construct the one-way tabulations for each variable in the study. This is not done here because of space limitations. Rather, only the one-way tabulation of the percentage of sporting goods purchased from a catalog

Figure 12A.1

Questionnaire for Avery Sporting Goods Case

The following questions are designed to give the Avery Sporting Goods Company a better idea of people's perceptions of buying sporting goods and other general merchandise through catalogs. Please read each question carefully and indicate your response by putting an X next to the appropriate statement. (Answer each question with a single response.) Thank you for your cooperation in completing the questionnaire.

1. *During the past year, what percentage of the sporting goods you purchased was ordered through a catalog?*

   _____   0 percent
   _____   1–10 percent
   _____   11–15 percent
   _____   16–20 percent
   _____   21+ percent

2. *How willing are you to purchase merchandise offered through the Avery Sporting Goods catalog?*

   _____ Not at all willing
   _____ Somewhat willing
   _____ Very willing

3. *Have you ever ordered any merchandise from the Avery Sporting Goods catalog?*

   _____ Never
   _____ Ordered before, but not within the last year
   _____ Ordered within the last year

	Not at All Confident	Slightly Confident	Somewhat Confident	Confident	Very Confident
4. *How confident are you that the following sporting goods purchased through a catalog would be of high quality?*					
a. Athletic clothing (shirts, warm-up suits, etc.)	_____	_____	_____	_____	_____
b. Athletic shoes	_____	_____	_____	_____	_____
c. Fishing equipment	_____	_____	_____	_____	_____
d. Balls (basketballs, footballs, etc.)	_____	_____	_____	_____	_____
e. Skiing equipment	_____	_____	_____	_____	_____
5. *How confident are you that the following sporting goods would be of high quality if purchased in a retail sporting goods store?*					
a. Athletic clothing (shirts, warm-up suits, etc.)	_____	_____	_____	_____	_____
b. Athletic shoes	_____	_____	_____	_____	_____

continued on next page

Figure 12A.1
Questionnaire for Avery Sporting Goods Case *continued*

c. Fishing equipment	____	____	____	____	____
d. Balls (basketballs, footballs, etc.)	____	____	____	____	____
e. Skiing equipment	____	____	____	____	____

6. *Approximately how many items of sporting equipment did you purchase during the past year?*

   ____ 0–1
   ____ 2–3
   ____ 4–5
   ____ 6–7
   ____ 8 or more

	Strongly Disagree	Disagree	Neither Agree nor Disagree	Agree	Strongly Agree
7. *In general, Avery Sporting Goods sells a high-quality line of merchandise.*	____	____	____	____	____
8. *Avery Sporting Goods carries all of the most popular name brands of sporting equipment.*	____	____	____	____	____
9. *Avery Sporting Goods has a very high-quality catalog.*	____	____	____	____	____
10. *The descriptions of the products shown in the Avery catalog are very accurate.*	____	____	____	____	____
11. *The selection of sporting goods available through the Avery catalog is very broad.*	____	____	____	____	____
12. *When buying from a catalog, there is a low probability that the merchandise will get lost in the mail.*	____	____	____	____	____
13. *Before purchasing merchandise through a catalog, people do not need to discuss the product with someone who has already purchased it.*	____	____	____	____	____
14. *Most catalog merchandising companies can be trusted to deliver the product pictured in the catalog.*	____	____	____	____	____

Figure 12A.1

Questionnaire for Avery Sporting Goods Case *continued*

15. *I enjoy purchasing merchandise through a catalog because it saves time.*
    ——   ——   ——   ——   ——

16. *When buying from a catalog, it is not difficult to negotiate the price.*
    ——   ——   ——   ——   ——

17. *If given a choice, I would purchase merchandise from the catalog company that has the easiest form to fill out.*
    ——   ——   ——   ——   ——

18. *Merchandise purchased from a catalog is less expensive than merchandise purchased in a retail store.*
    ——   ——   ——   ——   ——

19. *I prefer ordering merchandise from a catalog because they deliver the product to your door.*
    ——   ——   ——   ——   ——

20. *Catalogs have lower prices because they do not have to pay salespeople.*
    ——   ——   ——   ——   ——

	Very Unimportant	Unimportant	Neither Important nor Unimportant	Important	Very Important
21. *How important are the following factors in your decision to purchase sporting goods through a catalog?*					
a. Availability of a toll-free number for placing orders	——	——	——	——	——
b. Availability of quantity discounts	——	——	——	——	——
c. Shipping time	——	——	——	——	——
d. The company's policy on returning merchandise	——	——	——	——	——
e. The provision of a trial period	——	——	——	——	——
f. Number of years the company has been in business	——	——	——	——	——
g. Reputation of the company	——	——	——	——	——
h. Guarantees	——	——	——	——	——
i. Company endorsements by celebrities, sports teams, etc.	——	——	——	——	——

continued on next page

Figure 12A.1
Questionnaire for Avery Sporting Goods Case *continued*

---

22. *In general, do you prefer to do your shopping:*

    ___ in a retail store
    ___ in a discount outlet store
    ___ through a catalog
    ___ over the phone
    ___ by having salespeople call on you at home

23. *What was your approximate before-tax family income during the past year?*

    ___ $ 0–$14,999   ___ $25,000–$34,999
    ___ $15,000–$24,999   ___ $35,000–$44,999
                              ___ $45,000 or more

24. *Can your current occupation best be described as blue-collar?* ___ *white-collar?* ___

25. *What is your age (in actual years)?* ___

26. *What is your current marital status?*

    ___ single   ___ separated
    ___ married   ___ divorced
                      ___ widowed

27. *Are you male?* ___ *female?* ___

Table 12A.1
Coding Format for Avery Sporting Goods Questionnaire

Column(s)	Question Number	Variable (Variable Number)	Coding Specification
1–3	—	Questionnaire identification number (V1)	—
4	1	Percentage of products purchased through a catalog (V2)	1 = 0 percent 2 = 1–10 percent 3 = 11–15 percent 4 = 16–20 percent 5 = 21+ percent
5	2	Willingness to purchase merchandise from the Avery Sporting Goods catalog (V3)	1 = Unwilling 2 = Somewhat willing 3 = Very willing

Note: Except for variables V1, V41, and V42, zeroes represent nonresponses.

Table 12A.1

Coding Format for Avery Sporting Goods Questionnaire *continued*

Column(s)	Question Number	Variable (Variable Number)	Coding Specification
6	3	Ever ordered from the Avery Sporting Goods catalog (V4)	1 = Never ordered 2 = Ordered before, but not within the last year 3 = Ordered within the last year
			Coding Specifications 4a–5e 1 = Not at all confident 2 = Slightly confident 3 = Somewhat confident 4 = Confident 5 = Very confident
7	4a	Confidence in buying athletic clothing through a catalog (V5)	
8	4b	Confidence in buying athletic shoes through a catalog (V6)	
9	4c	Confidence in buying fishing equipment through a catalog (V7)	
10	4d	Confidence in buying balls through a catalog (V8)	
11	4e	Confidence in buying skiing equipment through a catalog (V9)	
12	5a	Confidence in buying athletic clothing in a retail store (V10)	
13	5b	Confidence in buying athletic shoes in a retail store (V11)	
14	5c	Confidence in buying fishing equipment in a retail store (V12)	
15	5d	Confidence in buying balls in a retail store (V13)	
16	5e	Confidence in buying skiing equipment in a retail store (V14)	
17	6	Number of sporting equipment items purchased (V15)	1 = 0–1 2 = 2–3 3 = 4–5 4 = 6–7 5 = 8 or more
			Coding Specifications 7–20 1 = Strongly disagree 2 = Disagree 3 = Neither agree nor disagree 4 = Agree 5 = Strongly agree
18	7	Avery sells a high-quality line of merchandise (V16)	

continued on next page

Table 12A.1

Coding Format for Avery Sporting Goods Questionnaire *continued*

Column(s)	Question Number	Variable (Variable Number)	Coding Specification
19	8	Avery carries the most popular name brands of sporting equipment (V17)	
20	9	Avery has a high-quality catalog (V18)	
21	10	Descriptions of products in the Avery catalog are accurate (V19)	
22	11	Selection of goods available through Avery is very broad (V20)	
23	12	Low probability that merchandise will get lost in the mail (V21)	
24	13	No need to discuss product with someone who has purchased it before buying through a catalog (V22)	
25	14	Can be trusted to deliver product that's pictured in the catalog (V23)	
26	15	Catalog purchasing saves time (V24)	
27	16	Not difficult to negotiate the price (V25)	
28	17	Purchase from catalog with easiest form to fill out (V26)	
29	18	Catalog merchandise is less expensive (V27)	
30	19	Catalogs deliver the product to door (V28)	
31	20	Catalogs have lower prices because they do not have to pay salespeople (V29)	

Coding Specification 21a–21i

1 = Very unimportant
2 = Unimportant
3 = Neither important nor unimportant
4 = Important
5 = Very Important

Column(s)	Question Number	Variable (Variable Number)	Coding Specification
32	21a	Availability of a toll-free number for placing orders (V30)	
33	21b	Availability of quantity discounts (V31)	
34	21c	Shipping time (V32)	
35	21d	Company policy on returning merchandise (V33)	
36	21e	Provision of a trial period (V34)	
37	21f	Number of years company has been in business (V35)	

Table 12A.1

Coding Format for Avery Sporting Goods Questionnaire *continued*

Column(s)	Question Number	Variable (Variable Number)	Coding Specification
38	21g	Reputation of the company (V36)	
39	21h	Guarantees (V37)	
40	21i	Company endorsements (V38)	
			Coding Specifications
41	22	Prefer to do shopping (V39)	1 = in a retail store
			2 = in a discount outlet store
			3 = through a catalog
			4 = over the phone
			5 = by having salespeople call at home
42	23	Before-tax family income during the past year (V40)	1 = \$ 0–\$14,999
			2 = \$15,000–\$24,999
			3 = \$25,000–\$34,999
			4 = \$35,000–\$44,999
			5 = \$45,000 or more
43	24	Current occupation (V41)	0 = blue-collar
			1 = white-collar
44–45	25	Age (V42)	Actual years recorded
46	26	Current marital status (V43)	5 = single
			4 = married
			3 = separated
			2 = divorced
			1 = widowed
47	27	Sex (V44)	1 = male
			2 = female

Table 12A.2

Listing of Raw Data

```
00111155543444343444555445454554455444453112551
00212144555454534544445454544532425443142125514
00341355442453214555545554555550303050423214051
00432255435543245435454111555555242423243321 2551
00521135554535424544455555545053455555503412551
00613355435424354555534434425342444444402313651
00713144535453545444453443243214444453415112451
00852355435354454355545552513355555355145 13651
00931235555235555445544535555542435522423213651
01013244515534233454444342454242224343331 1412551
01113355535245553525454534544423333343421512351
01223154445335554345453342555455243444353 1515641
01323355555444445555534334225243444243321 414051
```

```
01441153555414555344454335555542444233332212341
01513344442554442555544555555553254553532214051
01632255515335545444353225553525544544313212341
01751344453555454535442343414344334444331 12551
01822253545354544444444444435323420404004 112451
01931155544355554543552432554424040505033412551
02033244454325555444444545353533344534325412451
02112353545542455555533444554455454544355 14041
02213152434555553255453234545223345451435312421
02313354354321544355541225422554525352535213651
02413154535351245554445555533552545553525413651
02511354555321235544454335252522254523253541 2541
02622153255214535344453315554545343525113211541
```

continued on next page

Table 12A.2

Listing of Raw Data *continued*

```
0272115244443541244545434253535244555554412313641
0282135555533333535554444153325342434342221361
0292125435523544544455343454555503050501311251
0301214554354241555544244555352242444341113951
0311125412355455335545345442433334433141251
0325225545324531544444323252424243424343421251
0331115354421453444454343434355453444453511251
0343222545435455255444353445151403050400415413651
0352122455455333455435444555454344443535341251
0362231321254154144553244555444343323342321542
0371113212354324244445345453523344533344412432
0381321234354354254555454455554252525251121372
0391231242354354253555555242525523052301140362
0401121242355555235545444555353434343431412742
0413312412354354444555544555454455543313300922
0424332131154354255555221444455252524143314052
0432231111154354311232154455555553445354131012
0441111222154354111111455335533344555525500412
0451322222223545221212124355552523555513524400812
0461333111145435122222331542525243434143540122
0471232122223545112313555322515335555542320092
0482332311154555121222322525524355545313300922
0491111221335423123112222535455405050401220092
0502233332245325321111444354534353515252210051
0511122222255555521113244345544533443333325008122
0521221411254333111112145554545344445354144005122
0531112423152244551135552334455255555525341009
0541231232154555112224231425334444243335200922
0551132222254355211111445422334433244532400412
0561223111225445122232030055055500050501430123
0571112131153334122133455554543344434324401232
0582311111244441111325455555555533554555155008
0592231232154354121222355554525433555553233009
0602122222555555522221222254443433242223235009
0614314535512455411111424545342332444423122004
0621325554545321521111332444233331433223411051
0631114444454351312313454342424444554442510112
0641234553324531312222355555515442433331330142
0653314555524513532122455545544444444403401231
0662115555415453544452443554354454043434212551
0674123545515432435551215442521414444143410255
0682235552554123535555555555555555555555543510275
0695124444425431355334454434444443455432111244
0701325435525413544544444332532444444443551255
0711133455555453555325554244141414444444415511531
0721314444545353445444235454543525351433412551
0731124535554354435544455545454004555240551255
0741334544435444444542353555252433453534131125
0751315555552355553555533355555555555455451111365
```

```
0762134454423545544444555555555555454555411112431
0772315435523555515554345545254423344521311245
0782335554423545555555534455553344334444433314051
0792114445532455435455444555454444444444141421253
0805224445435555555554444424241332444341521385
0811315545325143535545425535353543144252533112551
0821125432521545245455435455444323434432111365
0831235435454321353555433244545524243425311136511
0843223545524513544444544252515535343440211244
0852115555454321533554000545154403050400221244
0862325554354123544445434255454243335243222124411
0874134444412221434355434435251525553544353213253
0881335433535412344455323554345443335443313212551
0891125555552153553355553335555524343434343342124411
0901215342145123245555344454545452545453421365
0913121121254325235544424545555353535545255125422
0922233122222555415555555334433323355233331511255
0931132211134445111121444233424344442441310051
0941213221135445123111045545454544004353142009
0952111522135555222223543535353342334444250240123
0963121351214553211711444555454545454414340051
0972232222223555222222534424353335354333551123
0985121111455445131112222335342554454551450093
0991312211135554112322334555545454333343132012
1001132311154433121222000332222453245253230092
1015122322225435211111455452525454444444212004
1025221112125555121223342515115554445152200922
1032222221154354222223000504455202020201320123
1043113211235453212321111152515154535255133012
1054112112344444221214000331133000000000044008
1061235111235543232115000223355000000000005400932
1073231111124444112222555553535355555555515500927
1085123321115545323111314525151353534343540103
1092122123354555211111222554252242424233440041
1104311112355444123111143445152530303030231009
1111232221123455122224000515100535555551130123
1121313111145545122113212535353434354431220082
1135122112232555521121121035152444544554512200522
1143211111145454112453545555454545455555122018
1151112222255555124113332435454342424231310123
1162333222245355232111545545444304050500423300922
1174231212145544122221444352515305050502350123
1181122311153155235114324555534232224311245014
1192322243115555532142342455445454344442415501432
1204332132135435221233433443545444444441155001232
1211112451135453421424333525152434452541440133
1222213331154545211111534415154445535453320041
1234132131235555122221434212524434333433150123
1243122131145354135555344444524234353035255136522
```

Table 12A.3

**One-Way Tabulation Showing Percentage of Sporting Goods
Purchased from a Catalog during the Past Year**

Percent Category Label	Code	Absolute Frequency	Relative Frequency (Percent)	Adjusted Frequency (Percent)	Cumulative Frequency (Percent)
0%	1	56	45.2	45.2	45.2
1–10%	2	33	26.6	26.6	71.8
11–15%	3	14	11.3	11.3	83.1
16–20%	4	11	8.9	8.9	91.9
21+%	5	10	8.1	8.1	100.0
Missing Values	0	0	0.0	0.0	
Total		124	100.0	100.0	
Valid cases 124	Missing cases 0				

during the past year is shown in Table 12A.3. This, incidentally, will be a general strategy followed throughout the appendices investigating catalog buying behavior. While a number of relationships might be analyzed using a particular technique, only one is used in each case to illustrate the technique.

Table 12A.3 was constructed using the SPSS frequencies program. *SPSS (Statistical Package for the Social Sciences)* is a widely distributed system of computer programs for data management and statistical analysis. It is used whenever possible in the appendices that follow, which analyze the catalog buying data, because of its general availability.[3] The program that produced Table 12A.3 is itself listed in Table 12A.4.

SPSS control cards must follow a specified structure and must use SPSS control words. The control words for each run must *always* begin in the first column and *cannot extend* beyond the fifteenth column. Columns 16–80 on the SPSS control cards are used for operating instructions. The operating instructions also need to follow the particular format specified in the SPSS system. The control words used in the frequencies program are explained in the lower part of Table 12A.4. The use of statistical and data management packages to analyze marketing research data is very efficient. Once the control language for a package is learned, almost all of the most popular statistical analyses can be conducted using it, typically using no more than 20 to 30 control cards per program.[4]

Table 12A.3 indicates that most people receiving Avery catalogs buy only a small portion of their sporting goods through catalogs; 56, or 45 percent, of the respondents bought no sporting goods at all from catalogs in the previous year. Further, more than

---

[3]SPSS is really a family of compatible systems depending on whether the data is to be analyzed in a batch mode, an interactive mode, or on a microcomputer. See, for example, *SPSS^X User's Guide* (Chicago: SPSS, 1983); and Marija J. Norusis, *SPSS^X Advanced Statistics Guide* (Chicago: SPSS, 1985).

[4]Other powerful and very popular systems are BMDP and SAS. See W. J. Dixon *et al.*, eds., *BMDP Statistical Software* (Berkeley: University of California Press, 1983); and *SAS Introductory Guide, 3rd ed.* (Cary, N.C.: SAS Institute, 1985).

Table 12A.4

SPSS Program Structure for the Frequencies Program Used to Generate Table 12A.3 and Explanation of the Control Words

A. Program Structure

```
RUN NAME        FREQUENCY PROGRAM FOR AVERY DATA
VARIABLE LIST   V1 TO V44
INPUT MEDIUM    UNIVACNAME='AVERY*DAT.'
INPUT FORMAT    FIXED(F3.0,40F1.0,F2.0,2F1.0)
N OF CASES      124
MISSING VALUES  V2TO V40(0)/V43,V44(0)/
FREQUENCIES     GENERAL=V2
STATISTICS      ALL
FINISH
```

B. Explanation of Control Words

RUN NAME

The RUN NAME card identifies the current computer run, and the user-supplied label that follows is printed at the top of each page of output. The label may be up to 64 characters in length. This card is optional.

VARIABLE LIST

The VARIABLE.LIST card causes the designated variable names to be entered into the system and associated with the proper variables on the cases. For example, V1 is associated with the case label, V2 is associated with Question 1, and so on. By using the TO command, each input variable is sequentially defined as V1, V2, and so on.

INPUT MEDIUM

The INPUT MEDIUM card informs the SPSS system of the type of input medium from which the raw data will be entered into the system, in this case from a UNIVAC computer file named AVERY*DAT.

INPUT FORMAT

Three types of data information are contained on this card: how the data cases are organized, whether the variables are numeric or alphanumeric, and the column location of the variables. The FIXED command indicates that the values for each variable are located in the same column(s) for every case; the F's indicate that the variables are numeric; F3.0 indicates, for example, that the first variable is in Columns 1–3, while 40 F1.0 indicates that the next 40 Variables 2–41 are each one-column wide and are located in Columns 4–43, respectively.

N OF CASES

The N OF CASES informs the system of the number of cases in the user's file.

MISSING VALUES

Because some cases in a file do not have complete information for each variable, the MISSING VALUES command is used to specify missing values for each variable so that files containing cases with incomplete data may be processed. For instance, zeros are the missing value code for variables V2 to V40, V43, and V44.

FREQUENCIES

This card activates the FREQUENCIES subprogram of the SPSS system. The keyword GENERAL causes the FREQUENCY program to process any type of variable: alphanumeric, integer, or decimal. The variable(s) for which frequency tables are to be formed follow the equal sign.

STATISTICS

The STATISTICS card enables the user to select among a number of available statistics to accompany the calculations and to be reported on the output. ALL causes all available statistics for a given subprogram to be reported.

FINISH

The FINISH card terminates the processing of the current run. It must be the last card in the control-card deck.

83 percent of the catalog recipients satisfied 15 percent or less of their sporting goods purchases through catalogs. Only 8 percent purchased more than 20 percent of their sporting goods through catalogs.

Cross Tabulation

Table 12A.5 is offered as an illustration of the makeup of the two-way tabulation output by SPSS. It depicts the relationship between willingness to purchase merchandise offered through the Avery sporting goods catalog and whether respondents have previously ordered from the catalog. The cross tabulation can be used to assess the extent to

Table 12A.5
Cross Tabulation of Willingness to Purchase from Avery's Catalog (V3) with Whether Respondent Has Purchased from It Before (V4)

Count Row Percent Column Percent Total Percent	V4	Never Ordered 1	Ordered Before But Not Within Past Year 2	Ordered Within Past Year 3	Row Total
V3					
Unwilling	1	20	20	10	50
		40.0	40.0	20.0	40.3
		46.5	51.3	23.8	
		16.1	16.1	8.1	
Somewhat Willing	2	7	11	17	35
		20.0	31.4	48.6	28.2
		16.3	28.2	40.5	
		5.6	8.9	13.7	
Very Willing	3	16	8	15	39
		41.0	20.5	38.5	31.5
		37.2	20.5	35.7	
		12.9	6.5	12.1	
Column Total		43	39	42	124
		34.7	31.5	33.9	100.0

A Raw chi square = 10.997 with 4 degrees of freedom.
   Significance = .027, Cramer's V = .211.
B Contingency coefficient = .285.
C Lambda (asymmetric) = .095 with V3 dependent = .123 with V4 dependent Lambda symmetric = .110.
   Uncertainty coefficient (asymmetric) = .043 with V3 dependent = .043 with V4 dependent.
   Uncertainty coefficient (asymmetric) = .043.
   Kendall's Tau B = .103. Significance = .101.
   Kendall's Tau C = .102. Significance = .101.
   Gamma = .151.
   Somer's D (asymmetric) = .102 with V3 dependent = .103 with V4 dependent.
   Somer's D (symmetric) = .102.
   Eta = .205 with V3 dependent = .239 with V4 dependent.
   Pearson's r = .103. Significance = .127.

which catalog customers are satisfied and are likely to be repeat buyers in the sense that they have ordered before and are willing to order again. The cross tabulation also provides some insight into the size of an untapped market, defined as those who have received Avery catalogs in the past and have not purchased from them but are willing to.

Note that percentages based on row totals, column totals, and overall totals are reported in the table in addition to the raw frequencies. Willingness to buy through the Avery Sporting Goods catalog is the dependent variable we are interested in explaining. The percentages we should logically focus on, then, are those based on the column totals. These percentages suggest that the "most willing" group of catalog recipients are those who ordered from Avery within the past year. Over three-fourths of these people (40.5 + 35.7 percent) are somewhat willing or very willing to order from Avery again. At the same time, almost one-fourth of those who bought within the last year are not willing to place another order. This relatively large proportion of potentially dissatisfied customers would certainly deserve further investigation by Avery management.

The column percentages also suggest that there may be a sizeable untapped segment of people receiving Avery catalogs who might become customers if the right inducement can be found. Over 50 percent (16.3 + 37.2) of the people who have never placed an order with Avery said they were willing to place an order.

Note finally the statistics located at the bottom of Table 12.5 that are output by the SPSS cross-tabulation program. Most of these assess the degree of association between the two variables. Three of the more important for our purposes are the chi-squared statistic, the contingency coefficient, and the index of predictive association, which are labeled A, B, and C, respectively, on the output and which are described in Appendix 15A. Their interpretations, which you will appreciate after reading that appendix, are as follows:

A The chi-square value of $\chi^2 = 10.997$ with 4 degrees of freedom is significant at the .027 level. This indicates that the null hypothesis of independence between the two variables should be rejected in favor of the alternative that willingness to purchase from Avery's catalog is a function of having purchased from it before.

B The contingency coefficient value of $C = .285$ suggests that there is only moderate association between the variables, given the maximum value for C in a table with three rows and three columns is .816.

C The index of predictive association $\lambda_{3.4} = .095$ indicates that errors in predicting Variable 3, willingness to purchase through Avery's catalog, are only reduced by 9.5 percent by taking account of Variable 4, whether the respondent has ordered before from the Avery catalog. This again suggests that, while statistically significant, the strength of the relationship between the two variables is low.

Chapter 13
Data Analysis:
Basic Questions

Chapter 12 discussed the preliminary data analysis steps of editing, coding, and tabulation. The chapter was intended to convey the importance and potential value of these preliminary procedures, which are common to almost all research studies. Some studies stop with tabulation and cross tabulation. Many involve additional analyses, though, particularly the search for statistical significance. A recurring problem in this search is the determination of the appropriate statistical procedure. This chapter will highlight the basic considerations that dictate a choice of method.

Choice of Analysis Technique: An Example

The considerations that underlie a choice of analysis method and the interpretation of the results are best demonstrated through example. Assume that the following hypothetical study was completed by a consumer products firm that manufactures the dishwashing liquid Sheen. The study was designed to determine homemakers' perceptions of the gentleness of Sheen and its nearest competitor, Glitter. Assume that the study used a scientifically determined probability sample and that the data were collected by administering a rating scale to each respondent. The respondents were specifically asked to locate each brand on a five-point mildness scale with the descriptors

- very rough (VR)
- rough (R)
- neither rough nor gentle (N)
- mild (M)
- very mild (VM)

according to how they thought the brand affected their hands. The basic considerations underlying the choice of method can be easily illustrated using a small sample, so assume that the analysis was to be based on the ten responses contained in Table 13.1, which also contains some alternative ways of analyzing the data. Not all of these methods are correct, nor are all the conclusions that can be drawn from the data. As a matter of fact, it is the purpose of this section to demonstrate how the conclusion depends on the method. There is no problem in most studies in deciding, "What ways *can* the analysis be done?" There is an acute problem in deciding, "What way *should* the analysis be conducted?"

Table 13.1
Homemakers' Perceptions of Dishwashing Liquids

				Respondent Scores for Each Brand under Method							
	Perception of VR R N M VM		A −2 −1 0 1 2		B 1 2 3 4 5		C 5 4 3 2 1		D −1 0 1		E Higher-rated
Respondent	S	G	S	G	S	G	S	G	S	G	Alternative*
1	VM	VM	2	2	5	5	1	1	1	1	T
2	M	VM	1	2	4	5	2	1	1	1	G
3	N	VM	0	2	3	5	3	1	0	1	G
4	M	VM	1	2	4	5	2	1	1	1	G
5	M	VM	1	2	4	5	2	1	1	1	G
6	M	VM	1	2	4	5	2	1	1	1	G
7	M	M	1	1	4	4	2	2	1	1	T
8	M	R	1	−1	4	2	2	4	1	−1	S
9	N	R	0	−1	3	2	3	4	0	−1	S
10	N	M	0	1	3	4	3	2	0	1	G
Sums			8	12	38	42	22	18	7	6	
Averages			0.8	1.2	3.8	4.2	2.2	1.8	0.7	0.6	

*A "T" indicates a tie, in that both brands received the same rating.

The methods reported in Table 13.1 vary according to how values (numbers) were assigned to each of the scale locations. Consider Method A, for instance. Underlying Method A is the assumption that mildness is desirable and roughness undesirable in dishwashing liquids. Thus, if the respondent believed that the dishwashing soap was very mild on one's hands, that response received a positive score of +2. A response of "very rough" received a negative score of −2, a response of "rough" a score of −1, and so on. The scores are totaled and averaged at the bottom of Table 13.1.

Look at the average scores for Method A; Sheen had an average score of 0.8, while Glitter had an average score of 1.2. Both soaps are thus "mild." Now let us search for the milder product, looking at the average score differences between the products and converting them to a percentage mildness difference. With Sheen as the comparative yardstick, we find that

$$\frac{\bar{x}_G - \bar{x}_S}{\bar{x}_S} (100) = \frac{1.2 - 0.8}{0.8} (100) = 50 \text{ percent,}$$

and the conclusion is that Glitter is 50 percent milder on the hands.

With Glitter as the basis of comparison, the result is

$$\frac{\bar{x}_G - \bar{x}_S}{\bar{x}_G} (100) = \frac{1.2 - 0.8}{1.2} (100) = 33 \text{ percent,}$$

and the conclusion is that Glitter is 33 percent milder on your hands. Similar calculations underlie each of the comparisons reflected in Table 13.1 except for Method E, the conclusions for which are summarized in Table 13.2. Methods B and C, for example, employ assignments of numbers to response categories similar to those used in Method A, except Method B uses all positive numbers, with "very mild" receiving a score of

Table 13.2
Comparison of Dishwashing Liquids

Method	Base in Comparison	Calculation	Conclusion
A	Sheen	$\dfrac{\bar{x}_G - \bar{x}_S}{\bar{x}_S}(100) = \dfrac{1.2 - 0.8}{0.8}(100) = 50.0\%$	Glitter is 50% milder on the hands.
	Glitter	$\dfrac{\bar{x}_G - \bar{x}_S}{\bar{x}_G}(100) = \dfrac{1.2 - 0.8}{1.2}(100) = 33.3\%$	Glitter is 33% milder on the hands.
B	Sheen	$\dfrac{\bar{x}_G - \bar{x}_S}{\bar{x}_S}(100) = \dfrac{4.2 - 3.8}{3.8}(100) = 10.5\%$	Glitter is 11% milder on the hands.
	Glitter	$\dfrac{\bar{x}_G - \bar{x}_S}{\bar{x}_G}(100) = \dfrac{4.2 - 3.8}{4.2}(100) = 9.5\%$	Glitter is 10% milder on the hands.
C	Sheen	$\dfrac{\bar{x}_S - \bar{x}_G}{\bar{x}_S}(100) = \dfrac{2.2 - 1.8}{2.2}(100) = 18.2\%$	Glitter is 18% milder on the hands.
	Glitter	$\dfrac{\bar{x}_S - \bar{x}_G}{\bar{x}_G}(100) = \dfrac{2.2 - 1.8}{1.8}(100) = 22.2\%$	Glitter is 22% milder on the hands.
D	Sheen	$\dfrac{\bar{x}_S - \bar{x}_G}{\bar{x}_S}(100) = \dfrac{0.7 - 0.6}{0.7}(100) = 14.3\%$	Sheen is 14% milder on the hands.
	Glitter	$\dfrac{\bar{x}_S - \bar{x}_G}{\bar{x}_G}(100) = \dfrac{0.7 - 0.6}{0.6}(100) = 16.7\%$	Sheen is 17% milder on the hands.
E	....		60% of the respondents thought Glitter was milder on the hands, while 20% thought Sheen was milder.

5; Method C reverses the scoring in that a score of 5 represents a "very rough" evaluation. Method D assigns negative values to "rough" evaluations and positive values to "mild" evaluations, but the "rough" and "very rough" evaluations receive the same score, as do the "mild" and "very mild" evaluations. Method E, on the other hand, does not rely upon average scores for all respondents but focuses on the alternative rated higher by each respondent. In particular, the conclusions in Method E reflect the facts that Respondents 1 and 7 perceived Glitter and Sheen to be of equal mildness, while six of the ten respondents perceived Glitter as milder and two perceived Sheen as milder.

The right-hand column of Table 13.2 suggests a number of conclusions about which is the preferred detergent. Which of these conflicting statements is correct and why? The answer is the last one, corresponding to Method E, and the reasons are intimately associated with the considerations that dictate the choice of analysis method. These considerations include the type of data, the research design, and the assumptions underlying the test statistic.

Before discussing these considerations, let us indicate why the last statement is correct and, in the process, reveal some of the caveats associated with these data. First, some analysts would hold that the response categories reflect ordinal measurements, in that the difference between ''very rough'' and ''rough'' is not the same as the difference between ''rough'' and ''neither rough nor gentle.'' Further, we saw previously that the assignment of scale values is completely arbitrary with order data as long as the order relationships are preserved, but that the calculation of means is inappropriate. Thus, these analysts would argue that Methods A to D are inappropriate, *not because of the values that were assigned to the categories but rather because the values were averaged*.

Second, even if the data had interval properties, Methods A to D would still be incorrect. The evaluations of Sheen and Glitter are not independent and cannot be treated as such statistically. Instead, they represent multiple responses from the same individual. They are related or dependent samples, and the appropriate procedure involves an analysis of the differences in the evaluation per individual. Method E is the only procedure that correctly deals with these differences.

Third, the conclusion was that ''60 percent of the people thought Glitter was milder on the hands.'' The question has not been raised as to whether this is a statistically significant result. The question of statistical significance involves the size of the sample employed to generate the percentage. In this case, the result is not significant. Yet if 60 out of 100 people felt Glitter was milder on the hands than Sheen, the result would be statistically significant, although the percentage ''preferring'' Glitter remained the same. Sample size is an important barometer in determining whether a research finding is due to chance or represents an underlying condition in the population.

Basic Considerations

The example has highlighted some of the considerations involved in the choice of analysis method. One useful classification of these considerations is that the appropriate technique depends upon the type of data, the research design, and the assumptions underlying the test statistic and its related consideration, the power of the test. Research Realities 13.1, which overviews the legal arguments between Vidal Sassoon and Bristol-Myers regarding some comparative ad claims, highlights the importance careful specification and interpretation of these features can make.

Type of Data

The level at which attributes can be measured was discussed earlier. At that time it was pointed out that a useful classification is that of nominal, ordinal, interval, and ratio scales of measurement. Consider again some of the main differences in the application of these scales. The nominal scale is used when categorizing objects. A letter or numeral is assigned to each category so that each number represents a distinct category. For instance, if individuals are to be classified by sex, the numbers 1 and 2 serve equally as well as the letters M and F for denoting males and females. The nominal scale remains undistorted under a one-to-one substitution of the numerals. Thus, the number 2 could be used to denote males and the number 1 to denote females without a loss of information. It is important to recognize that the normal arithmetic operations are not

Research Realities 13.1

Comparative Ad Legal Battle in Which Type of Data and Research Design Were Central Issues

The latest wrinkle in the continuing battle over comparative advertising claims is to attack the validity of statements about the market research on the product, rather than complaining about statements directed at the product itself.

Philip Morris and R. J. Reynolds pioneered this line of attack in 1980 when they separately challenged references to consumer surveys in a Triumph cigarette ad campaign. One ad claimed ''an amazing 60%'' said Triumph tasted as good or better than Merit. The court ruled this ad was misleading because it failed to disclose that, on the same basis, Merit had obtained a score of 64% compared to Triumph.

Another lawsuit in 1980 now has been decided by the influential federal court of appeals in New York City. Vidal Sassoon Inc. took legal action against Bristol-Myers over a series of TV commercials and print ads for a shampoo named Body on Tap because of its beer content. The prototype commercial featured a well-known high fashion model saying ''In shampoo tests with over 900 women like me, Body on Tap got higher ratings than Prell for body. Higher than Flex, for conditioning. Higher than Sassoon for strong, healthy looking hair.''

The evidence showed that several groups of approximately 200 women each tested just one shampoo. They rated it on a six-step qualitative scale, from ''outstanding'' to ''poor,'' for 27 separate attributes, such as body and conditioning. It became clear 900 women did not, after trying both shampoos, make product-to-product comparisons between Body on Tap and Sassoon or between Body on Tap and any of the other brands mentioned. In fact, no woman in the tests tried more than one shampoo.

The basis for the claim that the women preferred Body on Tap to Sassoon for ''strong, healthy looking hair'' was to combine the data for the ''outstanding'' and ''excellent'' ratings and discard the lower four ratings on the scale. The figures then were 36% for Body on Tap and 24% (of a separate group of women) for Sassoon. When the ''very good'' and ''good'' ratings were combined with the ''outstanding'' and ''excellent'' ratings, however, there was only a statistically insignificant difference of 1% between the two products in the category of ''strong, healthy looking hair.''

The research was conducted for Bristol-Myers by Marketing Information Systems Inc. (MISI), using a technique known as blind monadic testing. The president

of MISI testified that this method typically is employed when what is wanted is an absolute response to a product ''without reference to another specific product.'' Although he testified that blind monadic testing was used in connection with comparative advertising, that was not the purpose for which Bristol-Myers retained MISI. Rather, they wished to determine consumer reaction to the introduction of Body on Tap. And Sassoon's in-house research expert stated flatly that blind monadic testing cannot support comparative advertising claims.

Sassoon also found some other things wrong with the tests and the way they were represented in the Bristol-Myers advertisements. The fashion model said 900 woman ''like me'' tried the shampoos. Actually, one-third of the women were aged 13 to 18. This was significant because Body on Tap appealed disproportionately to teenagers, and the advertising executive who created the campaign for Bristol-Myers testified that its purpose was to attract a larger portion of the adult women's shampoo market. A study by Bristol-Myers, shortly after the campaign was launched, showed that for women in the 18 to 34 age group, awareness and purchases of Body on Tap did increase.

Finally, Sassoon charged that the methodology of the tests was flawed. There was evidence the women who tested Sassoon shampoo were told to use it contrary to Sassoon's own instructions. Also, these women were allowed to use other brands while they were testing Sassoon. As a result, their responses might not have reflected accurately their reaction to Sassoon as distinct from other shampoo products.

Sassoon obtained an order for a preliminary injunction from the federal district court. This means that the campaign must stop, but that a full-scale trial (which might conceivably change the final result) has not yet taken place. The preliminary injunction order then was affirmed by the three-judge court of appeals.

The court of appeals was careful to point out that not every misrepresentation concerning consumer tests results will result automatically in legal liability. But a lawsuit like the one Sassoon filed is appropriate, in the words of the published opinion, ''where depictions of consumer test results or methodology are so significantly misleading that the reasonably intelligent consumer would be deceived about the product's inherent quality or characteristics.''

Source: Sidney A. Diamond, ''Market Research Latest Target in Ad Claims,'' *Advertising Age*, 53 (January 25, 1982), p. 52.

meaningful for nominally scaled variables. The mean and median are not appropriate measures of central tendency. The appropriate measure of central tendency is the mode. Only it remains unchanged under a one-to-one substitution of the numerals. Thus, if there are more females than males, the mode describes the category ''female'' regardless of whether we choose to call it 1, 2, or F.

The ordinal scale represents a higher level of measurement than the nominal because the numerals assigned reflect order as well as serving to identify the objects. For example, we might wish to classify students into three categories, such as good, average, and poor. We might simply choose to call the categories A, B, and C. Alternatively, we might use the numbers 1 = good, 2 = average, and 3 = poor, or perhaps the reverse, where good = 3 and poor = 1. The schemes are equally fruitful as long as the numeral assignment is understood by all. The structure of an ordinal scale is undistorted by any one-to-one substitution that preserves the order since only order is implied by the assignment of numerals. The median and the mode are now both legitimate measures of central tendency.

The assignment of numerals to objects using an interval scale conveys information about the magnitude of the differences between the objects. We can determine how much more one category is than another. We cannot, however, compare the ratio of absolute magnitudes of the objects; for example, A is five times larger than B. All comparisons must be made using differences between objects. The reason is that the interval scale contains an arbitrary zero. An interval scale is undistorted under linear transformations, that is, transformations of the form $y = b + cx$. The effect of this transformation is to shift the origin b units and multiply the unit of measurement by c, as in going from a Fahrenheit scale to a centigrade scale. The normal arithmetic operations are meaningful with an interval scale. The mean, the median, and mode are all appropriate measures of central tendency.

The ratio scale is similar to the interval scale except that it has a natural zero point. Thus, it makes sense to say A is twice as heavy or twice as tall as B, since both of the scales possess a natural zero. The ratio scale is undistorted under proportionate or scalar transformations, that is, transformations of the form $y = cx$. The effect of such a transformation is to change the scale of measurement by the factor c. The conversion of feet to inches is an example; c in this case would equal 12. All statistics appropriate for the interval scale are also appropriate for a ratio scale.

The analyst has to be very careful in interpreting numerical relationships so as to properly reflect the properties of the measurement scale. The user of information has to be equally cautious. Consider the following hypothetical ad claim, which is not too different from what one sees on television and in magazines.

New Lustre gets your clothes 20 percent brighter and you need 50 percent less detergent compared to old Lustre. Furthermore, even for linens you can use water temperatures 30 percent lower than that required for old Lustre.

Probably, the ''brighter'' claim in this ad is based on homemakers' reactions to clothes washed with old Lustre. It is also likely that these perceptions were determined by having the respondents complete ''dingy'' to ''bright'' rating scales. Suppose, indeed, that a seven-point scale was employed and that old Lustre received an average score of five and new Lustre an average score of six; thus, the 20 percent brighter claim results from the calculation

$$\frac{\bar{x}_{new} - \bar{x}_{old}}{\bar{x}_{old}} (100) = \frac{6 - 5}{5} = 20 \text{ percent}.$$

The use of adjective scales like this highlights the disagreement between those who insist that most marketing measurements reflect ordinal measurement and those who argue that such scales can be treated as interval measures. There is some evidence to support each position. Myers and Warner, for example, demonstrate empirically, using Thurstone equal-appearing interval scale construction techniques, that descriptors that might appear to the scale developer to reflect equal increments of the characteristic are not interpreted that way by those responding.[1] They go on to point out that it is possible to develop questions in which the descriptors do reflect equal increments of the characteristic by the proper choice of descriptors, that is, by carefully choosing descriptors on the basis of their scale positions. The descriptors "remarkably good," "good," "neutral," "reasonably poor," and "extremely poor" could be used, for example, to approximate a five-point interval scale. While the debate rages, a reasonably balanced argument suggests that:

1. it is very safe, and certainly productive, to treat the total score summed over a number of items as an interval scale;

2. it is sometimes safe to treat individual items as interval scales, such as when specific steps have been taken to assure the intervality of the response categories; and

3. it is always legitimate to treat the scale as ordinal when neither Condition 1 nor 2 is satisfied. Suppose Condition 3 applied to the "dingy" to "bright" rating scale so that the descriptors anchoring the categories did not reflect equal increments of "brightness." Then the calculation and comparison of the difference in means would be suspect.

Suppose, on the other hand, that appropriate procedures were employed, that the evaluation scale did reflect interval measurement, and that the calculation of means was appropriate. The "brighter" claim would still be in error, and for the same reason that the temperature claim is also probably erroneous. More likely than not, the temperature claim would be based on the fact that whereas old Lustre required 200° F water to be effective, a new Lustre requires only 140° F water; that is, new Lustre can operate effectively with temperatures

$$\frac{200 - 140}{200} (100) = 30 \text{ percent}$$

lower. We have previously seen, however, that the Fahrenheit scale is an interval scale in that it possesses an arbitrary zero and that the calculation of ratios with such scales is meaningless. To see the folly in this exercise, simply convert the 200° F and 140° F

[1]James H. Myers and W. Gregory Warner, "Semantic Properties of Selected Evaluation Adjectives," *Journal of Marketing Research,* 5 (November 1968), pp. 409–412. See also Paul E. Spector "Choosing Response Categories for Summated Rating Scales," *Journal of Applied Psychology,* 61 (September 1976), pp. 374–375.

temperatures to their centigrade equivalents of 93.3°C and 60.0°C, respectively. Now you can use 36 percent lower temperatures with new Lustre. The same argument applies to the "brightness" comparison. Unless the "dingy" to "bright" scale were ratio, it would be incorrect to divide the difference in mean ratings for the two formulations by the original rating.

Thus, only one of the three ad claims is probably legitimate—the claim that 50 percent less detergent is needed with new Lustre. The scale here is of the ratio variety, and if one uses, say, ½ cup of new Lustre whereas one used 1 cup of old Lustre, then indeed one needs 50 percent less detergent. This is not to say that the claims could not be supported with data. For instance, the temperature claim follows if all measurements were made on a Kelvin scale, which possesses an absolute zero. Similarly, the brightness claim would follow if measurements were made using the integrating sphere.[2] The brightness claim does not follow, though, from the aggregation of consumer perceptions.

An understanding of the level of measurement underlying data is crucial to proper interpretation. Incidentally, this comment is equally valid for day-to-day living. For instance, the other night on the news, a meteorologist reported that the month of December was 38 percent colder than normal. The statement was based on the fact that, although the average mean temperature in December is 40°F, this past December it was 25°F or 38 percent colder. In fact, using the proper Kelvin scale, it was only 3 percent colder than normal. Fortunately the meteorologist did not translate this into a 38 percent increase in fuel consumption.

Research Design

A second consideration that affects the choice of analysis technique is the research design used to generate the data. Some of the more important questions the analyst has to face involve the dependency of observations, the number of observations per object, the number of groups being analyzed, and the control exercised over the variables of interest. Consider several hypothetical cases.

Sample Independence   Consider first the question of dependent or independent samples. Without worrying at this point about the details of the research design (and whether it was good or poor), suppose you were interested in determining the effectiveness of a mailed brochure. Suppose, too, that the measure of effectiveness was attitudes toward a product, that the scale used to measure attitudes was interval, and in particular that the research design was

$$X \quad O_1$$

$$O_2$$

---

[2]The integrating sphere measures the amount of light reflected from an object placed in the sphere. Black objects do not reflect any of the light directed at them, while white objects reflect 100 percent of the light directed into the sphere. See, for instance, K. S. Gibson, *Spectrophotometry*, National Bureau of Standards, Circular Number 484, 1949.

where O_1 represents the attitudes of those who received the brochure and O_2 the attitudes of those who did not receive the brochure. In this case, the samples are independent. The O_2 measures do not depend on the O_1 measures. An appropriate test of significance would allow for the independence of the samples. In this case, the t test for the difference in two means would be appropriate.[3]

Consider another research design that could be diagrammed thus:

$$O_1 \quad X \quad O_2$$

There are again two sets of observations, O_1 and O_2. Now, however, they are made on the same individuals, before and after receiving the brochure. The measurements are not independent, and a t test of the difference between two means is inappropriate. The observations must be analyzed in pairs. The focus is on differences in attitudes per individual before and after exposure to the brochure. A paired difference test for statistical significance should be used in this case.[4]

Number of Groups   Consider next the question of number of groups being compared. Suppose you were interested in the relative effectiveness of two different brochures and you decided to explore the question through a controlled experiment. In the experiment, some respondents receive X_1, others X_2, and a third group receive neither. The design can be diagrammed:

$$X_1 \quad O_1$$
$$X_2 \quad O_2$$
$$O_3$$

This design parallels that for the single brochure, except for the addition of the alternative brochure X_2. Now, though, there are three groups, two experimental and one control, whereas previously there were two, one experimental and one control. The t test for the difference in two means is no longer applicable; the problem is best handled through analysis-of-variance procedures.[5]

Number of Variables   Let us return to the one brochure design to illustrate how the number of measurements per object affects the analysis procedure. Previously we have used attitudes toward the advertised product as the measure of effectiveness of the brochure; specifically, we contrasted the attitudes of the "receivers" with those of the "nonreceivers." Suppose we believe that attitude is indeed a legitimate measure of effectiveness but that the sales impact of the brochure must also be considered. That is, we now wish to contrast the "exposed" and "unexposed" groups not only with respect

[3]The t test for the difference in means is discussed in Chapter 14.
[4]The paired difference statistical test is discussed in Chapter 14.
[5]Analysis of variance is discussed in the appendix to Chapter 14.

to their differences in attitude but also with respect to the sales of the product to each group. The design has not changed. It is still diagrammed

$$X \quad O_1$$

$$O_2$$

only now O_1 and O_2 represent measures of both sales and attitudes.

Of course, one way to proceed would be to test separately for the differences in attitudes and the differences in sales to the two groups. What happens, though, if the two groups differ only slightly on each criterion, so that neither of the univariate tests detects a significant difference? Would we conclude that the brochure had no impact even though the average attitude score and average sales were higher for the experimental group? Or do we conclude that the small, nonsignificant differences, taken together, indicate a real difference? On the other hand, suppose that the individual tests are statistically significant but inconsistent; that is, one result is more favorable to the control group and the other to the experimental group. Do we take the favorable and unfavorable results at their face value, or do we take the position that one of them represents a Type I error and in reality is attributable to chance?[6] To answer this question, and it becomes much more conceptually difficult as the number of measurements per object increases, we need to have some means of looking at the differences among groups when a number of characteristics are considered simultaneously. This type of problem is handled using multivariate statistical procedures.

Variable Control   Another important question in analysis involves the control of variables that can affect the result. Return to the one brochure design

$$X \quad O_1$$

$$O_2$$

in which the emphasis is on the differences in attitudes between the two groups. One variable that would certainly seem to determine attitudes is previous usage of the product. If so, in the experimental design, the analyst would like to control for prior usage so as to minimize its impact. A good way of doing this would be to make the experimental and control groups equal with respect to prior usage by matching, by randomization, or by some combination of these approaches. If this control procedure is followed, the t test for analyzing the difference in two means can legitimately be employed. If the control is not effected but attitudes do depend on prior use of the product, the conclusions produced using the t test will be in error to the extent that the two groups differ in their previous use of the product. One way to adjust for these differences is by allowing prior use to be a covariate, that is, by regressing attitudes on use and adjusting the attitude scores represented by O_1 and O_2 by the resulting regres-

---

[6]Type I error is discussed in the appendix to this chapter.

sion equation.[7] The adjusted scores for the experimental and control groups would then be compared.

Assumptions Underlying Test Statistic

Also underlying the choice of a statistical method of analysis is a consideration of the assumptions supporting the various test statistics. Examine once again (you will be glad to know for the last time) the test for the differences in attitudes toward the product of those who received the brochure and those who did not. The *t* test for the difference in two means was deemed appropriate for this analysis. Let us, therefore, look at the assumptions implicit in the choice of this statistical test.

The samples are assumed to have been drawn independently of each other. Further, it is assumed that the individuals composing the experimental group come from a population with unknown mean μ_1 and unknown variance σ_1^2, that those in the control group come from a population with unknown mean μ_2 and unknown variance σ_2^2, and that attitudes toward the product are *normally distributed* in each of these populations. It is also assumed that the variances of the two populations are equal, that is, $\sigma_1^2 = \sigma_2^2$; thus, a pooled estimator for the overall variance is warranted.[8] In sum, the assumptions are

1.   independent samples;

2.   normal distribution of the characteristic of interest in each population; and

3.   equal variances in the two populations.

The *t* test is more sensitive to certain violations of these assumptions than others. For example, it still works well with respect to violations of the normality assumption but is quite sensitive to violations of the equal variance assumption. When the violation is "too severe," the conclusions drawn are inappropriate. Yet it is surprising how little attention is paid to these underlying conditions in published research. At least little mention is made of the tests used to verify that the assumptions were satisfied. This is surprising in view of the availability of such checks. For instance, the independent samples assumption can be checked by analyzing the sampling plan employed. The normality assumption can be investigated through a χ^2 goodness-of-fit test or Kolmogorov–Smirnov test, while the equality of the variances can be examined through an *F* test for homogeneity of variances.[9]

---

[7]See Paul E. Green and Donald S. Tull, "Covariance Analysis in Marketing Experimentation," *Journal of Advertising Research,* 6 (June 1966), pp. 45–53, for a discussion of some of the uncontrolled but measurable influences common to marketing experiments as well as a discussion of some other useful outputs of covariance analysis. See Geoffrey Keppel, *Design and Analyses: A Researcher's Handbook,* 2nd ed. (Englewood Cliffs, N.J.: Prentice-Hall, Inc., 1982), pp. 481–515 for a general discussion of the method of covariance analysis.

[8]The assumption of equality of variances is not mandatory. When the variances cannot be assumed to be equal, though, the "proper procedure" is shrouded in controversy. There is a vast statistical literature on this condition, which is known as the Behrens–Fisher problem.

[9]The chi-square goodness-of-fit test and the Kolmogorov–Smirnov test are discussed in Chapter 14, while most introductory statistics books discuss the *F* test for the equality of variances.

This is not the time or the place to discuss how such analyses would be conducted, nor to criticize the *t* test for differences in two means. Our purpose is simply to illustrate the basic fact that statistical tests depend on certain assumptions for their validity. If the assumptions are not met, there are several things the analyst can do. Perhaps the assumptions can be satisfied through some transformation (for example, change from actual units to log units). If not, analysts can perhaps choose a different test statistic that employs different assumptions. Perhaps they might even employ a distribution-free statistical test.[10] In any case, careful analysts will not neglect the assumptions that underlie the technique nor will they blindly assume that all the conditions for a valid test are satisfied. Analysts will be too concerned about the correctness of the results to neglect a check of assumptions.

Overview of Statistical Procedures

In the previous section some of the more important considerations in the choice of analysis technique were highlighted. Perhaps the section raised more questions than answers. This section will introduce some of the answers by overviewing the statistical techniques discussed in Chapters 14 to 16. Such an overview must necessarily be brief. However, it should serve to direct you to the section or sections that discuss the techniques appropriate for a given problem. Figures 13.1 and 13.2 and Table 13.3 and 13.4 should assist in this regard. The figures illustrate the sequence of questions an analyst needs to ask and answer in order to determine the appropriate statistical technique, while the tables classify the techniques by the factors dictating their use.

The most important question that needs to be answered in preparing to run the maze of statistical methods is to decide whether the problem is of a univariate or multivariate nature. The problem is **univariate** if there is a single measurement of each of the *n* sample objects, or if there are several measurements of each of the *n* observations but each variable is to be analyzed in isolation. In a **multivariate** problem, there are two or more measures of each observation (e.g., number of new accounts generated and total sales by salesmen), and the variables are to be analyzed simultaneously. Given that there are multiple measures per sample observation, we find ourselves dealing with two distinct emphases: the search for differences and the investigation of association. The search for group differences is the multivariate extension of much univariate analysis. These techniques are not discussed in this book,[11] although techniques for investigating association are.

---

[10]A *distribution-free statistical test* is one that involves minimal assumptions. The somewhat misleading nomenclature **nonparametric test** is often used interchangeably to distinguish such techniques from the **parametric tests.** The parametric tests include such tests as the *t, z,* or *F* and typically involve a greater number of and more rigorous assumptions. The nonparametric label is inappropriate for distribution-free tests because the researcher does, in fact, try to generate statements about population parameters with these tests. The emphasis is still on parameters, although the specific parameter in question may change; for example, the median rather than the mean is used as the measure of central tendency.

[11]See P. J. Rulon and W. D. Brooks, "On Statistical Tests of Group Differences," in Dean K. Whittla, ed., *Handbook of Measurement and Assessment in Behavioral Sciences* (Reading, Mass.: Addison-Wesley, 1968), pp. 60–99 for a succinct overview of the issues and procedures.

Figure 13.1
Flow Diagram for Choosing a Univariate Statistical Test

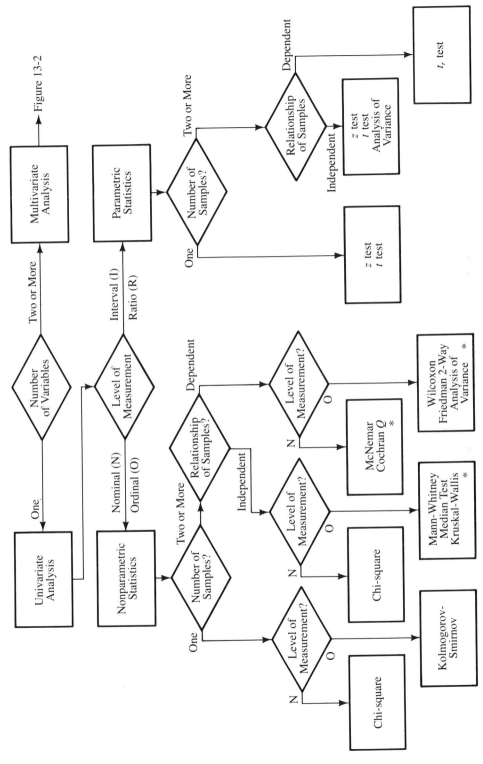

*These tests are not discussed in this book, although they are useful for some problems in marketing research.

Figure 13.2
Flow Diagram for Choosing a Multivariate Statistical Test

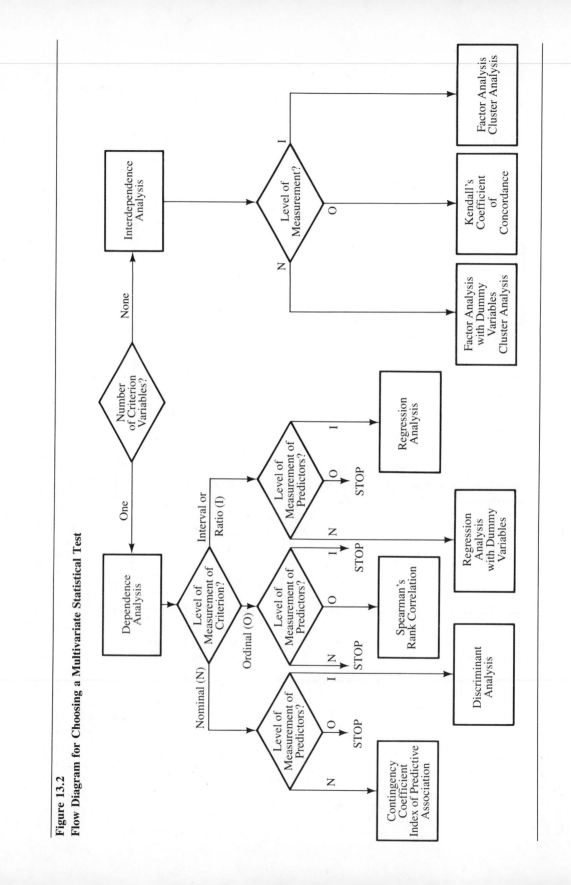

Table 13.3
Univariate Statistical Tests

Type of Data	Type of Test	Single Sample	Multiple Samples *(K)*	
			Independent	Dependent
Nominal	Nonparametric	chi-square	chi-square	McNemar (for $K = 2$)* Cochran Q (for $K > 2$)*
Ordinal	Nonparametric	Kolmogorov–Smirnov	Mann–Whitney (for $K = 2$) median test* Kruskal–Wallis one-way analysis of variance*	Wilcoxon (for $K = 2$)* Friedman two-way analysis of variance (for $K > 2$)*
Interval or Ratio	Parametric	z test t test	z test ($K = 2$) t test ($K = 2$) analysis of variance (for $K > 2$)	t_r test (for $K = 2$)

*These tests are not discussed here because of space limitations.

Univariate Analysis

Table 13.3 contains a classification of some important univariate procedures and Figure 13.1 overviews the subsequent decisions that must be made given that the problem is univariate. Let us review the several questions an analyst can ask in deciding among the procedures.

A useful first question involves the level of measurement of the data. Is the variable nominal, ordinal, interval, or ratio scaled? If it is nominal or ordinal, distribution-free (nonparametric) statistical procedures are appropriate. If the data are either interval or ratio scaled, the variable is metric, and parametric procedures apply. Actually, from a *statistical theory perspective,* the level of measurement is *not* important when selecting among techniques. As Lord said so elegantly thirty years ago, "the numbers do not know where they come from"[12]—meaning that statistical techniques do not "know" what the level of measurement of the input data is. Rather, it is the *assumptions* that are *key* in determining whether a particular statistical technique is appropriate for analyzing a particular set of data. If the assumptions are satisfied, or if the statistical technique is robust (works well anyway) to violations of the assumptions, the technique can be used. While scale of measurement may not be important from a statistical theory

---

[12]F. M. Lord, "On the Statistical Treatment of Football Numbers," *American Psychologist,* 8 (1953), p. 751. While Lord was one of the first to contradict Stevens' assertion that his four levels of measurement had important implications for choosing statistical techniques, a number of authors later made the same point. Gaito points out, for example, that "Scale properties do not enter into any of the mathematical requirements for the various statistical procedures. I have not known of any mathematical statistician who agreed with the Stevens' misconception. A number have indicated in print that this suggestion is erroneous." John Gaito, "Measurement Scales and Statistics: Resurgence of an Old Misconception," *Psychological Bulletin,* 87 (1980), p. 564.

Table 13.4

Classification of Statistical Techniques of Association According to the Role, Scale Type, and Number of Variables Involved

Type and Number of Independent or Predictor Variables

		Interval		Ordinal		Nominal	
		One	Two or More	One	Two or More	One	Two or More
Interval	None		Factor analysis Cluster analysis				Factor analysis with dummy variables Cluster analysis
	One	Regression analysis	Multiple regression analysis				Multiple regression analysis with dummy variables
Ordinal	None				Kendall's coefficient of concordance (W)		
	One			Spearman's rank correlation (r_s)			
Nominal	One		Discriminant analysis			Contingency coefficient Index of predictive association	Contingency coefficient Index of predictive association

Type and Number of a priori Dependent or Criterion Variables

Source: Excerpted from Maurice M. Tatsuoka and David V. Tiedeman, "Statistics as an Aspect of Scientific Method in Research on Teaching," in N. L. Gage, ed., *Handbook of Research on Teaching* (Chicago: Rand McNally, 1963), pp. 154–155. Copyright 1963, American Educational Research Association, Washington, D.C. Reprinted by permission.

perspective, it is important from a *measurement theory perspective*. In this sense, it is important that the numbers assigned be meaningful given the attributes of concern, that we are careful in interpreting what the numbers imply with respect to the "amount of the attribute" possessed by the object, and how we manipulate the numbers when generating meaning from the data. Further, it is difficult even to address the topic of how to choose a statistical test without considering the level of measurement. Level of measurement provides a useful heuristic or map for getting an analyst in the right ball park. Consequently, the heuristic is employed to organize the discussion on choosing a statistical test although one needs to be conscious of the fact that it may be perfectly appropriate to apply a parametric test, say, to data that is only ordinal.[13]

The analyst must then determine whether a single sample or multiple samples are involved. An hypothesis about the mean income of residents of Chicago is a single-sample analysis. If we were interested in determining how the mean income of Chicago compares with that of New York, two independent samples are involved, that is, the population of Chicago and the population of New York. Suppose we were interested in comparing the mean income in Chicago now with the mean income five years ago; again, two samples are involved. Whether the samples are dependent or independent depends on the specifics of the sampling procedure employed. Suppose the recent sample was selected without considering the sample five years ago. The samples are then independent. Suppose, instead, the study's emphasis was one of determining the income changes that occurred among the families comprising the first sample. The samples are then dependent; the latest income measurements are related to the earlier incomes, and those statistical methods that treat dependent samples should be used.

Suppose we were interested in how average income and average educational levels compare in Chicago and New York. Now there are two (multiple) measures—income and education—for two independent samples—residents of Chicago and New York. One of the multivariate tests for group differences could be used.

Multivariate Analysis

As was previously stated, multivariate procedures are distinguished by the fact that each of n sample observations bears the value of p different variates. The p variate condition means that additional considerations must be dealt with in choosing from among avail-

---

[13]The product moment correlation coefficient, for example, has been found to be quite robust to violations of the "continuous variable" assumption on which it is based. Thus, it can be used to assess the degree of association between two variables when the data are intervally scaled, ordinally scaled, or even when one or both of the variables are dichotomies. See, for example, Donald G. Morrison, "Regression with Discrete Random Variables: The Effect on R^2," *Journal of Marketing Research,* 9 (August 1972), pp. 338–340; or Jum Nunnally, *Psychometric Theory,* 2nd ed. (New York: McGraw-Hill, 1978), especially pp. 117–150. A number of other parametric techniques using the t and F distributions have also been found to be quite robust to violations of their assumptions, and work particularly well with ordinal data. See, for example, Sanford Lobovitz, "Some Observations on Measurement and Statistics," *Social Forces,* 46 (1967), pp. 151–160; Sanford Lobovitz, "The Assignment of Numbers to Rank Order Categories," *American Sociological Review,* 35 (1970), pp. 515–524; B. O. Baker, C. D. Hardyck, and L. F. Petrinovich, "Weak Measurement vs. Strong Statistics: An Empirical Critique of S. S. Stevens' Proscriptions on Statistics," *Educational and Psychological Measurement,* 26 (1966), pp. 291–309; John Gaito, "Scale Classification and Statistics," *Psychological Review,* 67 (1960), pp. 277–278; and Mark Traylor "Ordinal and Interval Scaling," *Journal of the Market Research Society,* 25 (October 1983), pp. 297–303.

able procedures. One of these considerations, previously mentioned, was the investigation of association and the determination of group differences, and this latter condition was categorized with univariate techniques. The following discussion will, therefore, emphasize association.

Two considerations dictate a choice of technique here: the type of scale used in making the measurements and the role the individual variables will play in the specific model being discussed. The most common distinction is that between independent (antecedent or predictor) variables and dependent (consequent or criterion) variables. The distinction suggests a division of the subject into two parts: dependence and interdependence.

In dependence, *one (or more) of the variates is selected for us by the conditions of the problem and we require to investigate the way in which it depends on the other variates. . . . In* interdependence *we are concerned with the relationship of a set of variates among themselves, no one being selected as special in the sense of the dependent variable.*[14]

Unfortunately, these dual considerations of scale and role of each variable interact to generate a somewhat complex classification scheme. The problem is particularly acute because there may be a great many variables involved, and they may represent different levels of measurement. One has to simultaneously entertain the following questions in order to determine the appropriate method:

1. Are one or more of the variables to be singled out for separate treatment as dependent or criterion variables? If so, how many and what level of measurement do they reflect?

2. How many independent variables are there? What level of measurement does each of these variables reflect?

Table 13.4 offers a classification of the multivariate statistical techniques for analyzing associations that are discussed in the remainder of this book. Figure 13.2 illustrates the sequence of decisions involved in the choice of a technique. The techniques were chosen because they represent the most useful procedures for the marketing research analyst, although all cases to which they are applicable are not shown in the table. For instance, one could convert nominal or ordinal variables to dummy variables and then run a multivariate regression analysis.[15] The table and figure are designed to clearly indicate the types of problems for which multivariate techniques of association are appropriate. The chapters on analysis should place some flesh on the skeleton so that you will be able to picture some of the modifications that are possible.

Note in the table that technique is highly dependent on the number and scaling of the variables. Change either of these and the technique typically changes. For instance, consider factor analysis and multiple regression analysis. In multiple regression analysis,

---

[14]M. G. Kendall, *A Course in Multivariate Analysis* (London: Charles Griffin, 1968), p. 6.

[15]Dummy variables are discussed in Chapter 15.

one of the variables is singled out for special treatment as a criterion variable, and the relationship between the single criterion variable and the predictor variables is investigated. If the emphasis was on determining the relationships that exist among all the variables considered at once, the problem would be dealt with using factor analysis procedures.

Similarly, suppose the variable singled out as the criterion variable reflected a nominal scale of measurement involving two categories (for example, purchase of Product A or B). It would then be appropriate to use linear discriminant analysis rather than multivariate regression.

Note also in the table the seeming void associated with ordinal data. Ordinal data are difficult to handle. Either the analyst must use methods uniquely suited to ordinal data, or else he or she must sacrifice some information by converting the order data to nominal data in the form of dummy variables. While dummy variables will be treated in later chapters, the methods uniquely suited to order data will generally not be covered. Only those methods indicated in Table 13.4 that are suited for ordinal criterion and predictor variables will be discussed.

Summary

The basic considerations involved in choosing a statistical method with which to analyze the collected data were discussed in this chapter. Scale of measurement, the research design, and the assumptions underlying the test statistic all affect this choice.

When considering the scale of measurement, an analyst must be careful to distinguish between ideas of measurement theory and statistical theory. The origin of the numbers is important from the standpoint of the interpretation of the results. That is, from a measurement theory perspective it makes a difference whether the level of measurement is nominal, ordinal, interval, or ratio. The level of measurement does not make a difference, however, from a statistical theory perspective. Rather, the key here in dictating a choice of technique is the assumptions underlying the technique. The assumptions should be satisfied or the technique should be robust to the violations of the assumptions at issue if the technique is to be used to analyze the data. Even here, though, scale of measurement provides a useful heuristic for identifying statistical techniques for which the assumptions are likely to be satisfied.

Several questions in the research design affect choice of method, including the independence of the sample observations, the number of groups, the number of variables, and the control exercised over those variables likely to affect the results.

In choosing from among the many available tests, the analyst needs to ask a number of questions, the first of which is whether the problem is univariate or multivariate. If univariate, the next questions are whether the variable reflects nonmetric or metric measurement, whether a single sample or multiple samples are involved, and if multiple, whether the samples are dependent or independent.

Multivariate analysis is distinguished by the fact that there are two or more variables to be analyzed simultaneously. If one (or more) of these variables is considered a criterion variable that is to be related to some other variables, the problem is one of dependence analysis. If we are solely concerned with the relationships among the set of variables considered together, the problem is one of interdependence analysis. The role of each variable in the analysis and the level of measurement reflected by each variable interact to produce a complex classification scheme of multivariate techniques.

Questions

1. What basic considerations underlie the choice of a statistical test? Explain.

2. What are the basic levels of measurement? How does the type of data affect the choice of a statistical test?

3. Discuss the difference between independent and dependent samples and indicate how sample independence/dependence affects the choice of a statistical test.

4. Discuss the difference between one-, two-, and three-group analyses and indicate how the number of groups affects the choice of a statistical test.

5. Discuss the difference between a univariate analysis and a multivariate analysis. What are the problems inherent in treating a multivariate problem as a number of univariate problems?

6. What is the distinction between a multivariate test of group differences and a multivariate test of the association among the variables?

7. Discuss the difference between dependence and interdependence analysis.

Applications and Problems

1. Evaluate the following two hypothetical advertising claims. Do you think the claims are legitimate?
   (a) "Con-Air gives you twice as much satisfaction while traveling and at a price 50% lower than other major airlines."
   (b) "In blind taste tests, the majority of people preferred our beer twice as much as any other major brand of beer. Is it any wonder we sell one and one-half times more beer than our nearest competitor?"

2. Discuss whether the use of adjective scales reflects ordinal or interval measurement.

3. Discuss the importance of the level of measurement from a statistical theory perspective and measurement theory perspective.

4. The Tobacco Institute wanted to test the effectiveness of two booklets that discuss the issue of whether advertising caused children to start smoking. A random sample of 1,200 is selected from a mailing list of 10,000 people. The sample is randomly divided into three groups of size 400 each; one group received one version of the booklet; the second the other version, and the third group received neither booklet. One week later the attitudes of all three groups as to whether advertising causes children to smoke was measured on an interval scale.
   (a) Present the experimental design in diagrammatic form.
   (b) What analysis technique would you recommend? Why?

5. A large national chain of department stores wanted to test the effectiveness of a promotional display for a new brand of household appliances. Fifty stores were randomly selected from a total of 263 stores. The sample of 50 stores was randomly divided into

two groups of 25 stores each. Only one group used the promotional display. For three weeks, sales of the new brand of appliances were monitored for both groups.

(a) Present the experimental design in diagrammatic form.

(b) What analysis technique would you recommend? Why?

6. A medium-sized life insurance company was concerned about its poor public image that resulted from a major lawsuit. The public relations department designed a 20-page bulletin that was to be mailed to all existing and prospective clients and shareholders in order to allay any negative feelings that might have resulted from the bad publicity. Prior to incurring the expenses of the complete mailing, the department randomly selected 300 clients and shareholders and mailed the 20-page bulletin to them. Attitudes toward the company were measured on an interval scale before and after sending the bulletin. However, top management was dissatisfied with this experiment and requested that another random sample of 500 clients and shareholders be generated. This sample was to be randomly divided into two groups of 250 respondents each. The bulletin was to be mailed to one group of respondents. Attitudes towards the company were to be measured for both groups on an interval scale two weeks after mailing the bulletin.

(a) Present the experimental designs in diagrammatic form.

(b) What analysis technique would you recommend for each? Why?

7. A large national automobile manufacturer wants to relate sales of their latest models by area to the demographic composition of each area as measured by such variables as average income, average size of household, average age of head of household, and so on.

(a) Is this dependence or interdependence analysis? Why?

(b) Are there any criterion or predictor variables? If so, what are they? Identify the level of measurement of each.

(c) On the basis of the above, what multivariate procedure would you recommend?

8. A medium-sized department store wanted to determine its customers' attitudes, opinions, interests, and so on using a five-point Likert scale.

(a) Is this dependence or interdependence analysis? Why?

(b) Are there any criterion or predictor variables? If so, what are they? Identify the level of measurement of each.

(c) On the basis of the above, what multivariate procedure would you recommend?

9. A large soft-drink manufacturer conducted a survey to determine customers' likes and dislikes about a new diet soft drink. The "lightness" of the soft drink was perceived as being one of the three most important soft drink attributes. The "low calorie" attribute was not ranked as high as "lightness." The company was wondering if most consumers believed that low calorie content of the soft drink was associated with lightness.

(a) Is this dependence or interdependence analysis? Why?

(b) Are there any criterion or predictor variables? If so, what are they? Identify the level of measurement of each.

(c) On the basis of the above, what multivariate procedure would you recommend?

Appendix 13A
Hypothesis Testing

Many procedures discussed in the next few chapters are used to test specific hypotheses. It therefore seems useful to review some basic concepts that underlie hypothesis testing, in classical statistical theory, such as framing the null hypothesis, setting the risk of error in making a wrong decision, and the general steps involved in testing the hypothesis.[1]

Null Hypothesis

One simple fact underlies the statistical test of an hypothesis: A null hypothesis may be rejected but can never be accepted except tentatively, since further evidence may prove it wrong. In other words, one "rejects" the null hypothesis (and accepts the alternate hypothesis) or "does not reject" the null hypothesis on the basis of the evidence at hand. It it wrong to conclude, though, that since the null hypothesis was not rejected, it can be accepted as valid.

A naive qualitative example should illustrate the issue.[2] Suppose we are testing the hypothesis that "John Doe is a poor man." We observe that Doe dines in cheap restaurants, lives in the slum area of the city in a run-down building, wears worn and tattered clothes, and so on. Although his behavior is certainly consistent with that of a poor man, we cannot "accept" the null hypothesis that he is poor. It is possible that Doe may, in fact, be rich but frugal or extremely tight in his spending. We can continue gathering information about him, but for the moment we must decide "not to reject the null hypothesis." One single observation, for example, that indicates he has a six-figure bank account or that he owns 100,000 shares of AT&T stock would allow the immediate rejection of the null hypothesis and "acceptance" of the alternate hypothesis that "John Doe is rich."

The upshot of this discussion is that the researcher needs to frame the null hypothesis in such a way that its rejection leads to the acceptance of the desired conclusion, that is, the statement or condition he or she wishes to verify. For example, suppose a firm was considering introducing a new product if it could be expected to secure more than 10 percent of the market. The proper way to frame the hypotheses then would be

$$H_0: \pi \leq 0.10,$$

$$H_a: \pi > 0.10.$$

If the evidence leads to the rejection of H_0, the researcher would then be able to accept the alternative, that the product could be expected to secure more than 10 percent of the

---

[1]Bayesian statistical theory assumes a different posture with respect to hypothesis testing than does classical statistics. Because classical statistical significance testing procedures are much more commonly used in marketing research though, only the basic elements underlying classical statistical theory are presented here.

[2]The author expresses his appreciation to Dr. B. Venkatesh of Burke Marketing Services, Inc., for suggesting this example to illustrate the rationale behind the framing of null hypotheses.

market and the product would be introduced. If H_0 cannot be rejected, though, the product should not be introduced unless more evidence to the contrary becomes available. The example as framed involves the use of a "one-tailed" statistical test in that the alternate hypothesis is expressed directionally, that is, as being greater than 0.10. The one-tailed test is most commonly used in marketing research, although there are research problems that warrant a "two-tailed" test; for example, the market share achieved by the new formulation of Product X is no different from that achieved by the old formulation, which was 10 percent. A two-tailed test would be expressed as

$$H_0 : \pi = 0.10,$$

$$H_a : \pi \neq 0.10.$$

There is no direction implied with the alternate hypothesis; the proportion is simply expressed as not being equal to 0.10.

The one-tailed test is more commonly used than the two-tailed test in marketing research for two reasons. First, there is typically some preferred direction to the outcome—for example, the greater the market share, the higher the product quality, the lower the expenses, the better. The two-tailed alternative is used when there is no preferred direction in the outcome or when the research is meant to demonstrate the existence of a difference but not its direction. Second, the one-tailed test, when it is appropriate, is more powerful statistically than the two-tailed alternative.

Most students seem to experience some difficulty in framing one-tailed statistical tests and commonly reverse the inequalities in the null and alternate hypotheses. Suppose the two hypotheses are incorrectly framed as

$$H_0 : \pi \geq 0.10,$$

$$H_a : \pi < 0.10,$$

and the sample results are $p = 0.15$. Even though the evidence is consistent with the results desired, the researcher cannot reasonably suggest that avenue because the null hypothesis can never be accepted, only rejected. The researcher could recommend the product introduction, though, if the two hypotheses were reversed in sign and the null hypothesis was rejected.

Types of Errors

Since the result of statistically testing a null hypothesis would be to reject it or not reject it, two types of errors may occur. First, the null hypothesis may be rejected when it is true. Second, it may not be rejected when it is false and, therefore, should be rejected. These two errors are, respectively, termed **Type I error** and **Type II error** or **α error** and **β error,** which are the probabilities associated with their occurrence. The two types of errors are not complementary in that $\alpha + \beta \neq 1$.

To illustrate each type of error and to demonstrate that they are not complementary, consider a judicial analogy.[3] Since under U.S. criminal law, a person is innocent until

---

[3] R. W. Jastram, *Elements of Statistical Inference* (Berkeley, Calif.: Book Company, 1947), p. 44.

Table 13A.1
Judicial Analogy Illustrating Decision Error

	True Situation: Defendant Is	
Verdict	Innocent	Guilty
Innocent	Correct decision: probability $= 1 - \alpha$	Error: probability $= \beta$
Guilty	Error: probability $= \alpha$	Correct decision: probability $= 1 - \beta$

Table 13A.2
Types of Errors in Hypothesis Testing

	True Situation: Null Hypothesis is	
Research Conclusion	True	False
Do not reject H_0	Correct decision Confidence level Probability $= 1 - \alpha$	Error: Type II Probability $= \beta$
Reject H_0	Error: Type I Significance level Probability $= \alpha$	Correct decision Power of test Probability $= 1 - \beta$

proven guilty, the judge and jury are always testing the hypothesis of innocence. The defendant may, in fact, be either innocent or guilty, but based on the evidence the court may reach either verdict regardless of the true situation. Table 13A.1 displays the possibilities. If the defendant is innocent and the jury finds him innocent, or if the defendant is guilty and the jury finds him guilty, the jury has made a correct decision. If, however, the defendant truly is innocent and the jury finds the person guilty, they have made an error, and similarly if the defendant is guilty and they find him innocent. The jury must find one way or the other, and thus the probabilities of the jury's decision must sum vertically to 1. Thus, if we let α represent the probability of incorrectly finding the person guilty when he is innocent, then $1 - \alpha$ must be the probability of correctly finding him innocent. Similarly, β and $1 - \beta$ represent the probabilities of findings of innocence and guilt when he is guilty. It is intuitively obvious that $\alpha + \beta$ is not equal to 1, although later discussion will indicate that β must increase when α is reduced if other things remain the same. Since our society generally holds that finding an innocent person guilty is more serious than finding a guilty person innocent, α error is reduced as much as possible in our legal system by requiring proof of guilt ''beyond any reasonable doubt.''

Table 13A.2 contains the analogous research situation. Just as the defendant's true status is unknown to the jury, the true situation regarding the null hypothesis is unknown to the researcher. The researcher's dilemma parallels that of the jury in that he or she has limited information with which to work. Suppose the null hypothesis is true. If the researcher concludes it is false, he or she has made an error, commonly referred to as a Type I error. The significance level associated with a statistical test indicates the probability with which this error may be made. Since sample information will always be somewhat incomplete, there will always be some α error. The only way it can be avoided is by never rejecting the null hypothesis (never finding anyone guilty, in the judicial analogy). The *confidence level* of a statistical test is $1 - \alpha$, and the more confident we want to be in a statistical result, the lower we must set α error. The **power** associated with a statistical test is the probability of correctly rejecting a false null hypothesis. One-tailed tests are more powerful than two-tailed tests because, for the same α error, they are simply more likely to lead to a rejection of a false null hypothesis. β error represents the probability of not rejecting a false null hypothesis. There is no unique value associated with β error.

Procedure

The relationship between the two types of errors is best illustrated through example, and the example would be most productive if developed following the general format of hypothesis testing. Research Realities 13A.1 overviews the typical sequence of steps that is followed. Suppose the problem was indeed one of investigating the potential for a new product and the research involved the preferences of consumers. Suppose that, in the judgment of management, the product should not be introduced unless at least 20 percent of the population could be expected to prefer it and that the research calls for 625 respondents to be interviewed for their preferences.

Step 1 The null and alternate hypotheses would be

$$H_0 : \pi \leq 0.20,$$

$$H_a : \pi > 0.20.$$

The hypotheses are framed so that if the null hypothesis is rejected, the product should be introduced.

Step 2 The appropriate sample statistic is the sample proportion. Although the sample proportion is theoretically binomially distributed, the large sample size permits the use of the normal approximation.[4] The z test therefore applies. The z statistic in this case equals

$$z = \frac{p - \pi}{\sigma_p},$$

---

[4]The binomial distribution tends toward the normal distribution for a fixed π as sample size increases. The tendency is most rapid when $\pi = 0.5$. With sufficiently large samples, normal probabilities may be used to approximate binomial probabilities with π's in this range. As π departs from 0.5 in either direction, the normal approximation becomes less adequate, although it is generally held that the normal approximation may be used safely if the smaller of $n\pi$ or $n(1 - \pi)$ is 10 or more. If this condition is not satisfied, binomial probabilities can either be calculated directly or found in tables that are readily available. In the example, $n\pi = 625(0.2) = 125$, and $n(1 - \pi) = 500$, and thus there is little question about the adequacy of the normal approximation to binomial probabilities.

Research Realities 13A.1

Typical Hypothesis Testing Procedure

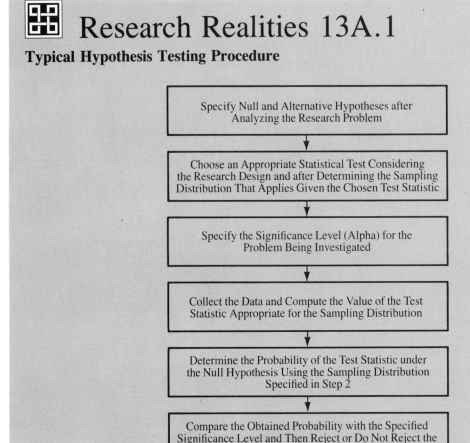

where p is the sample proportion preferring the product and σ_p is the standard error of the proportion or the standard deviation of the distribution of sample p's. σ_p in turn equals

$$\sqrt{\frac{\pi(1-\pi)}{n}} = \sqrt{\frac{0.20(0.80)}{625}} = 0.0160,$$

where n is the sample size. Note this peculiarity of proportions. As soon as we have hypothesized a population value, we have said something about the standard error of the estimate. The proportion is the most clear-cut case of "known variance" since the variance is specified automatically with an assumed π. The researcher thus knows all of the values for calculating z except p before ever taking the sample and further knows *a priori* the distribution to which the calculated statistic will be related. This is true in general, and the researcher should have these conditions clearly in mind before taking the sample.

Step 3   The researcher selects a significance level (α) using the following reasoning. In this situation α error is the probability of rejecting H_0 and concluding that $\pi > 0.2$, when in reality $\pi \leq 0.2$. This conclusion will lead the company to market the new product. However, since the venture will only be profitable if $\pi > 0.2$, a wrong decision to market would be financially unprofitable, possibly disastrous. The probability of Type I error should, therefore, be minimized as much as possible. The researcher recognizes, though, that the probability of a Type II error increases as α is decreased, other things being equal. Type II error in this case implies concluding $\pi \leq 0.2$ when in fact $\pi > 0.2$, which in turn suggests that the company would table the decision to introduce the product when it could be profitable. The opportunity loss from making such an error could be quite serious. Although, as explained later, the researcher does not know what β would be, he or she knows that α and β are interrelated and that an extremely low value of α, say $\alpha = 0.01$ or 0.001, would produce intolerable β errors. The researcher decides, therefore, on an α level of 0.05 as an acceptable compromise.[5]

Step 4   Since Step 4 involves the computation of the test statistic, it can only be completed after the sample is drawn and the information collected. Suppose 140 of the 625 sample respondents preferred the product. The sample proportion is thus $p = 140/625 = 0.224$. The basic question that needs to be answered is conceptually simple. "Is this value of p too large to have occurred by chance from a population with $\pi = 0.2$?" or, in other words, "What is the probability of getting $p = 0.224$ when $\pi = 0.2$?"

$$z = \frac{p - \pi}{\sigma_p} = \frac{0.224 - 0.20}{0.0160} = 1.500.$$

Step 5   The probability of occurrence of a z value of 1.500 can be found from standard tabled values of areas under the normal curve. (See Table 1 at the end of the book.) Figure 13A.1 shows the procedure. The shaded area between $-\infty$ and 1.500 equals 0.9332; this means the area to the right of $z = 1.500$ is $1.000 - 0.9332$, or 0.0668. This is the probability of securing a z value of 1.500 under a true situation of $\pi = 0.2$.

Step 6   Since the calculated probability of occurrence is higher than the specified significance level of $\alpha = 0.05$, the null hypothesis is not rejected. The product would not be introduced because, while the evidence is in the right direction, it is not sufficient to conclude beyond "any reasonable doubt" that $\pi > 0.2$. If the decision maker had been able to tolerate a 10 percent chance of committing a Type I error, the null hypothesis would have been rejected and the product marketed, since the probability of getting a sample $p = 0.224$ when the true $\pi = 0.20$ is, as we have seen, 0.0668.

---

[5] We shall have more to say about the choice of $\alpha = 0.05$ and its interpretation after we have introduced the notion of power.

Figure 13A.1
Probability of $z = 1.500$ with a One-Tailed Test

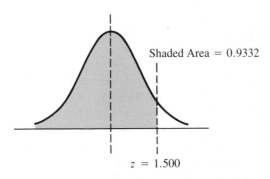

Shaded Area = 0.9332

$z = 1.500$

Power

The example illustrates the importance of correctly specifying the risk of error. If a 10 percent chance of an α error were tolerable and the researcher specified $\alpha = 0.05$, a potentially profitable opportunity would have been bypassed. The choice of the proper significance level involves weighing the costs associated with the two types of error, unfortunately a procedure that most researchers ignore, choosing out of habit $\alpha = 0.10$ or 0.05. Perhaps this lapse is due to the difficulty encountered in specifying β error or Type II error.

The difficulty arises because β error is not a constant. Recall that it is the probability of not rejecting a false null hypothesis. Other things being equal, we would prefer a test that minimized such errors. Alternatively, since the power of a test equals $1 - \beta$, we would prefer the test with the greatest power so that we would have the best chance of rejecting a false null hypothesis.[6] Now clearly our ability to do this depends on "how false H_0 truly is." It could be "just a little bit false" or "way off the mark," and the probability of an incorrect conclusion would certainly be higher in the first case.

Consider again the hypotheses

$$H_0 : \pi \le 0.2,$$

$$H_a : \pi > 0.2,$$

where $\sigma_p = 0.0160$ and $\alpha = 0.05$, as before. Any calculated z value greater than 1.645 will cause us to reject this hypothesis, since this is the z value that cuts off 5 percent of

---

[6]See Alan G. Sawyer and A. Dwayne Ball, "Statistical Power and Effect Size in Marketing Research," *Journal of Marketing Research,* 18(August 1981), pp. 275–290, for a persuasive argument as to why marketing researchers need to pay more attention to power in their research designs. The article also offers a number of suggestions on how to improve statistical power.

the normal curve. The z value can be equated to the *critical* sample proportion through the formula

$$z = \frac{p - \pi}{\sigma_p},$$

$$1.645 = \frac{p - 0.20}{0.0160},$$

or $p = 0.2263$. Thus, any sample proportion greater than $p = 0.2263$ will lead to the rejection of the null hypothesis that $\pi \leq 0.2$. This means that if 142 or more [$0.2263(625) = 141.4$] of the sample respondents prefer the new product, the null hypothesis will be rejected and the product introduced, while if 141 or less of the sample respondents prefer it, the null hypothesis will not be rejected and the new product will not be introduced.

The likelihood of a sample proportion of $p = 0.2263$ is much greater for certain values of π than for others. Suppose, for instance, that the true but unknown value of π was 0.22. The sampling distribution of the sample proportion is again normal, but now it is centered about 0.22. The probability of obtaining the critical sample proportion $p = 0.2263$ under this condition is found again from the normal curve table, where now[7]

$$z = \frac{p - \pi}{\sigma_p} = \frac{0.2263 - 0.22}{0.0166} = 0.380.$$

The shaded area between $-\infty$ and $z = 0.380$ is given in Table 1 at the end of the book as 0.6480, and thus the area to the right of $z = 0.380$ is equal to $1.000 - 0.6480 = 0.3520$ (see Panel B in Figure 13A.2). This is the probability that a value as large or larger than $p = 0.2263$ would be obtained if the true population proportion was $\pi = 0.22$. It is also the power of the test in that, if π is truly equal to 0.22, the null hypothesis is false and 0.3520 is the probability that the null will be rejected. Conversely, the probability that $p < 0.2263$ equals $1 - 0.3520 = 0.6480$, which is β error. The null hypothesis is false and yet the false null hypothesis is not rejected for any sample proportions $p < 0.2263$.

Suppose that the true population condition was $\pi = 0.21$ instead of $\pi = 0.22$, and the null hypothesis was again $H_0: \pi \leq 0.20$. Since the null hypothesis is less false in this second case, we would expect power to be lower and the risk of β error to be higher because the null hypothesis is less likely to be rejected. Let us see if that is indeed the case. The z value corresponding to the critical $p = 0.2263$ is 1.000. Power given by the area to the right of $z = 1.000$ is 0.1587 (the β error is 0.8413), and the expected result does obtain. (See Figure 13A.2, Panel C.)

---

[7]Note that σ_p is now $\sqrt{0.22(0.78)/625} = 0.0166$, since a different specification of π implies a different standard error of estimate.

Figure 13A.2

Computation of β Error and Power for Several Assumed True Population Proportions for the Hypothesis $\pi \leq 0.2$

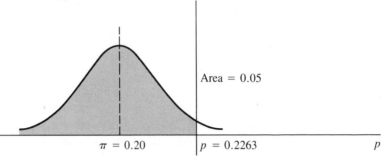

Area = 0.05

$\pi = 0.20$ $p = 0.2263$ p

Panel A: Critical Proportion under Null Hypothesis

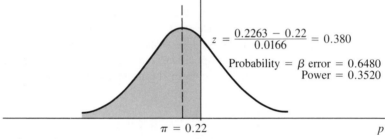

$$z = \frac{0.2263 - 0.22}{0.0166} = 0.380$$

Probability = β error = 0.6480
Power = 0.3520

$\pi = 0.22$ p

Panel B: Probability of Realizing Critical Proportion When $\pi = 0.22$, Which Means Null Hypothesis Is False

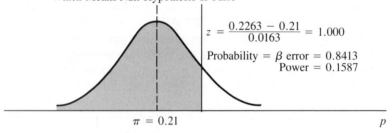

$$z = \frac{0.2263 - 0.21}{0.0163} = 1.000$$

Probability = β error = 0.8413
Power = 0.1587

$\pi = 0.21$ p

Panel C: Probability of Realizing Critical Proportion When $\pi = 0.21$, Which Means Null Hypothesis Is False

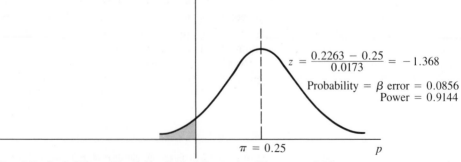

$$z = \frac{0.2263 - 0.25}{0.0173} = -1.368$$

Probability = β error = 0.0856
Power = 0.9144

$\pi = 0.25$ p

Panel D: Probability of Realizing Critical Proportion When $\pi = 0.25$, Which Means Null Hypothesis Is False

Table 13A.3

**β Error and Power for Different Assumed True Values of π
and the Hypotheses $H_0 : \pi \leq 0.20$ and $H_a : \pi > 0.20$**

Value of π	Probability of Type II or β Error	Power of the Test: $1 - \beta$
0.20	$(0.950) = 1 - \alpha$	$(0.05) = \alpha$
0.21	0.8413	0.1587
0.22	0.6480	0.3520
0.23	0.4133	0.5867
0.24	0.2133	0.7867
0.25	0.0856	0.9144
0.26	0.0273	0.9727
0.27	0.0069	0.9931
0.28	0.0014	0.9986
0.29	0.0005	0.9995
0.30	0.0000	1.0000

Consider one final value, true $\pi = 0.25$. The null hypothesis of $\pi = 0.20$ would be "way off the mark" in this case, and we would expect there would only be a small chance that it would not be rejected and a Type II error would be committed. The calculations are displayed in Figure 13A.2, Panel D; $z = -1.368$, and the area to the right of $z = -1.368$ is 0.9144. The probability of β error is 0.0856 and the *a priori* expectation is confirmed.

Table 13A.3 contains the power of the test for other selected population states, and Figure 13A.3 shows these values graphically.

Figure 13A.3 is essentially the power curve for the hypothesis

$$H_0 : \pi \leq 0.20,$$

$$H_a : \pi > 0.20,$$

and it confirms that the farther away the true π from the hypothesized value in the direction indicated by the alternate hypothesis, the higher the power. Note that power is not defined for the hypothesized value because if the true value in fact equals the hypothesized value, a β error cannot be committed.

Note that since power is a function rather than a single value, the researcher attempting to balance Type I and Type II errors logically needs to ask how false the null hypothesis is likely to be and to establish the decision rule accordingly. This requirement possibly explains why so many researchers content themselves with the specification of Type I or α error and allow β error to fall where it may.

The failure to even worry about, much less explicitly take into account, the power of the statistical test represents one of the fundamental problems with the classical statistics hypothesis testing approach as it is commonly practiced in marketing research.

Figure 13A.3
Power Function for Data of Table 13A.3

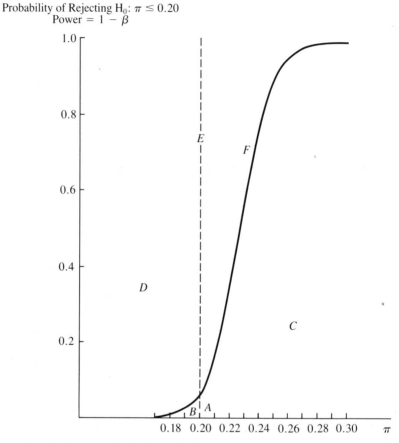

Probability of Rejecting H_0: $\pi \leq 0.20$
Power $= 1 - \beta$

A—Type I error; true null hypothesis is rejected; significance level.
B—Type I error; true null hypothesis is rejected.
C—No error; false null hypothesis is rejected.
D—No error; true null hypothesis is not rejected.
E—No error; true null hypothesis is not rejected; confidence level.
F—Type II error; false null hypothesis is not rejected.

Another common problem is the misinterpretation of what a "statistically significant result" really means. There are several common misinterpretations.[8]

One of the most frequent misinterpretations is to view a p value as representing the probability that the results occurred because of sampling error. Thus, the commonly

---

[8]For an excellent discussion of some of the most common misinterpretations of classical significance tests and some recommendations on how to surmount the problems, see Alan G. Sawyer and J. Paul Peter, "The Significance of Statistical Significance Tests in Marketing Research," *Journal of Marketing Research,* 20 (May 1983), pp. 122–133.

used $p = 0.05$ is taken to mean that there is a probability of only 0.05 that the results were caused by chance and thus there must be something fundamental causing them. In actuality, a p value of 0.05 means that *if,* and this is a big if, the null hypothesis is true, the odds are only 1 in 20 of getting a sample result of the magnitude that was observed. Unfortunately, there is no way in classical statistical significance testing to determine whether the null hypothesis is true.

A p *value reached by classical methods is not a summary of the data. Nor does the* p *value attached to a result tell how strong or dependable the particular result is . . . Writers and readers are all too likely to read .05 as* p(H/E) *"the probability that the Hypothesis is true, given the Evidence." As textbooks on statistics reiterate almost in vain,* p *is* p(E/H), *the probability that this Evidence would arise if the (null) hypothesis is true.*[9]

A second very frequent misinterpretation is to hold that the α or p level chosen is in some way related to the probability that the research hypothesis captured in the alternative hypothesis is true. Most typically, this probability is taken as the complement of the α level. Thus, a p value of 0.05 is interpreted to mean that its complement, $1 - 0.05 = 0.95$, is the probability that the research hypothesis is true. "Related to this misinterpretation is the practice of interpreting p values as a measure or the degree of validity of research results, i.e., a p value such as $p < .0001$ is "highly statistically significant" or "highly significant" and therefore much more valid than a p value of, say, 0.05."[10] Both of these related interpretations are wrong.

The only logical conclusion that can be drawn when a null hypothesis is rejected at some predetermined p level is that sampling error is an unlikely explanation of the results given the null hypothesis is true. In many ways that is not saying very much, because, as was argued previously, the null hypothesis is a weak straw man in that it is set up to be false. The null, as typically stated, holds that there is no relationship between a certain two variables, say, or that the groups are equal with respect to some particular variable. Yet, we do not really believe that. Rather, we investigate the relationship between variables because we believe there is some association between them, and we contrast the groups because we believe they are different with respect to the variable. Further, we can control our ability to reject the null hypothesis simply by the power we build into the statistical test, primarily through the size of the sample used to test it. "Given sufficiently high statistical power, one would expect virtually *always* to conclude the exact null hypothesis is false."[11]

Marketing researchers then need to be wary when interpreting the results of their hypothesis testing procedures so that they do not mislead themselves and others. They need constantly to keep in mind both types of errors that are possible to make. Further,

[9]Lee J. Cronbach and R. E. Snow, *Aptitudes and Instructional Methods: A Handbook for Research on Interactions* (New York: Irvington, 1977), p. 52.

[10]Sawyer and Peter, "The Significance . . .," p. 123. For other useful discussions of what statistical tests of significance mean, see Mick Alt and Malcolm Brighton, "Analyzing Data or Telling Stories?" *Journal of the Market Research Society,* 23 (October 1981), pp. 209–219 and Norval D. Glenn, "Replications, Significance Tests and Confidence in Findings in Survey Research," *Public Opinion Quarterly,* 47 (Summer 1983), pp. 261–269.

[11]*Ibid.,* p. 125.

they need to make certain they do not misinterpret what a test of significance reveals. It represents no more than a test against the null hypothesis. One useful way of avoiding misinterpretation is to calculate confidence intervals when possible because this gives decision makers a much better feel for how much faith they can have in the results. A test of significance is very much a yes–no situation: either the sample result is statistically significant or it is not. On the other hand, "the confidence interval not only gives a yes or no answer, but also, by its width, gives an indication of whether the answer should be whispered or shouted."[12] Although not every test of significance can be put in the form of a confidence interval estimate, many of them can, and it is advisable to do so when the opportunity arises.[13]

Questions

1. Comment on the statement: "An hypothesis can never be accepted, only rejected." Is the statement true? Why or why not?

2. What is the basic scientific proposition that guides the framing of hypotheses? Illustrate the principle with a research question of your own choosing.

3. When is a two-tailed test preferred to a one-tailed test and vice versa?

4. What is a Type I error? What is a Type II error? What is the relationship between these two types of error?

5. What is meant by the statistical notion of power?

6. Illustrate the steps involved in the statistical testing of hypotheses with your own example.

7. Explain the comment: "The farther away the true population parameter is from the hypothesized population value in the direction indicated by the alternate hypothesis, the higher the power." Is power not a constant? Why?

8. Using your own example, construct the power function.

9. What does it mean when the null hypotheses is rejected at the $\alpha = .10$ level?

Applications and Problems

1. Assume that the brand manager of a medium-sized manufacturer of consumer products decides to introduce a new brand of breakfast cereal if the company can initially acquire 1.5% of the market. The following hypotheses are to be tested:
    $H_0 : \pi \leq 0.015$
    $H_a : \pi > 0.015$
    Explain and discuss the Type I and Type II errors that could occur while testing these hypotheses. What are the implications for the company?

2. Discuss the danger of specifying Type I or α error and allowing β error to fall where it may.

---

[12]Mary G. Natrella, "The Relation Between Confidence Intervals and Tests of Significance," *American Statistician*, 14 (1960), p. 22.

[13]For an excellent discussion of the relationship between tests of significance and confidence interval estimates, see *Ibid.*, pp. 20–22, 33.

Chapter 14
Data Analysis: Examination of Differences

A question that arises regularly in the analysis of research data is, "Are the research results statistically significant? Could the result have occurred by chance due to the fact that only a sample of the population was contacted, or does it indicate an underlying condition in the population?" To answer, we use some kind of test of statistical significance.

This chapter reviews some of the more important tests for examining the statistical significance of differences. The difference at issue might be the difference between some sample result and some expected population value, or the difference between two or more sample results. The intent is to indicate the types of tests that are available and the types of problems to which they apply. The first part of the chapter reviews the χ^2 goodness-of-fit test, which is especially useful with nominal data, and the second part reviews the Kilmogorov–Smirnov test, which is useful with ordinal data. The latter sections focus on the parametric tests that are applicable when examining differences in means or proportions.

Goodness of Fit

In a number of marketing situations it is necessary to determine whether some observed pattern of frequencies corresponds to an "expected" pattern. Consider a breakfast food manufacturer who has recently developed a new cereal called Score. The cereal will be packaged in the three standard sizes: small, large, and family size. The manufacturer's past experience suggests that for every one small package, three of the large and two of the family size are also sold. The manufacturer wishes to see if this same tendency would hold with this new cereal, since a change in consumption patterns could have significant production implications. The manufacturer, therefore, decides to conduct a market test to determine the relative frequencies with which the various sizes would be purchased.

Suppose that, in an appropriate test market over a one-week period, 1,200 boxes of the new cereal were sold and that the distribution of sales by size was

Number Buying			
Small	Large	Family	Total
240	575	385	1,200

Does this preliminary evidence indicate that the firm should expect a change in the purchase patterns of the various sized packages with Score?

This is the type of problem for which the **chi-square goodness-of-fit test** is ideally suited. The variable of interest has been broken into k mutually exclusive categories ($k = 3$ in the example), and each observation logically falls into one of the k classes or cells. The trials (purchases) are independent, and the sample size is large.

All that is necessary to employ the test is to calculate the *expected* number of cases that would fall in each category and to compare that with the *observed* number actually falling in the category using the statistic

$$\chi^2 = \sum_{i=1}^{k} \frac{[O_i - E_i]^2}{E_i},$$

where

O_i is the observed number of cases falling in the ith category;

E_i is the expected number of cases falling in the ith category; and

k is the number of categories.

The expected number falling into a category is generated from the null hypothesis that the composition of sales of Score by package size would follow the manufacturer's normal sales; that is, for every small package, three large and two family sizes would be sold. In terms of proportions, $\pi_1 = 1/(1 + 3 + 2) = \frac{1}{6}$, $\pi_2 = \frac{3}{6}$, and $\pi_3 = \frac{2}{6}$. Thus the expected sales would be $E_1 = n\pi_1 = 1,200(\frac{1}{6}) = 200$ of the small size, $E_2 = n\pi_2 = 1,200(\frac{3}{6}) = 600$ of the large size, and $E_3 = n\pi_3 = 1,200(\frac{2}{6}) = 400$ of the family size. The appropriate χ^2 statistic is computed as

$$\chi^2 = \frac{(240 - 200)^2}{200} + \frac{(575 - 600)^2}{600} + \frac{(385 - 400)^2}{400} = 9.60.$$

The chi-square distribution is one of the statistical distributions that is completely determined by its degrees of freedom v. The mean of the chi-square distribution is equal to the number of degrees of freedom v, and its variance is equal to $2v$. For large values of v, the chi-square distribution is approximately normally distributed.

In the example, the number of degrees of freedom is one less than the number of categories k; that is, $v = k - 1 = 2$. This is because the sum of the differences between the observed and expected frequencies is zero. Both the expected and observed frequencies must sum to the total number of cases. Given any $k - 1$ differences, the remaining difference is thus fixed, and this results in the loss of one degree of freedom.

Suppose the researcher has chosen a significance level of $\alpha = 0.05$ for this test. The tabled value of χ^2 for two degrees of freedom and $\alpha = 0.05$ is 5.99 (see Table 2 in the appendix at the end of the book). Since the calculated value ($\chi^2 = 9.60$) is larger, the conclusion is that the sample result would be unlikely to occur by chance alone. Rather, the preliminary market test results suggest that sales of Score will follow a different pattern than is typical. The null hypothesis of sales in the ratio of $1:3:2$ is rejected.

The chi-square test outlined above is an approximate test.[1] The approximation is relatively good if, as a rule of thumb, the *expected* number of cases in each category is five or more, although this value can be as low as one for some situations.[2]

The previous example illustrated the use of the chi-square distribution to test a null hypothesis regarding k population proportions, $\pi_1, \pi_2, \ldots, \pi_k$. The proportions were needed to generate the expected number of cases in each of the k categories. Viewed in this light, the test of a single proportion discussed when reviewing the logic of hypothesis testing in the appendix to Chapter 13 is a special case; in the goodness-of-fit test, the single parameter π is replaced by the k parameters $\pi_1, \pi_2, \ldots, \pi_k$.

Another use of the chi-square goodness-of-fit test is in determining whether a population distribution has a particular form. For instance, we might be interested in finding out whether a sample distribution of scores might have arisen from a normal distribution of scores.[3] To investigate, we could construct the sample frequency histogram. The intervals would correspond to the k cells of the goodness-of-fit test. The observed cell frequencies would be the number of observations falling in each interval. The expected cell frequencies would be the number falling in each interval, if indeed the sample came from a normal distribution with mean μ and variance σ^2. If the population mean and variance were unknown, the sample mean and variance could be used as estimates. This would result in the loss of two additional degrees of freedom, but the basic test procedure would remain unchanged.

Kolmogorov–Smirnov Test

The **Kolmogorov–Smirnov test** is similar to the chi-square goodness-of-fit test in that it uses a comparison between observed and expected frequencies to determine whether observed results are in accord with a stated null hypothesis. But the Kolmogorov–Smirnov test takes advantage of the ordinal nature of the data.

Consider, for example, a manufacturer of cosmetics who is testing four different shades of a foundation compound—very light, light, medium, and dark. The company has hired a marketing research firm to determine whether any distinct preference exists toward either extreme. If so, the company would manufacture only the preferred shades. Otherwise, it was planning on marketing all shades. Suppose that in a sample of 100, 50 persons preferred the "very light" shade, 30 the "light" shade, 15 the "medium" shade, and 5 the "dark" shade. Do these results indicate some kind of preference?

Since shade represents a natural ordering, the Kolmogorov–Smirnov test can be used to test the preference hypothesis. The test involves specifying the cumulative distribu-

---

[1] The correct distribution to test the hypothesis is the hypergeometric. The hypergeometric distribution, however, is unwieldy for anything but very small samples. The chi-square distribution approximates the hypergeometric for large sample sizes. For a discussion of this point, as well as the other conditions surrounding a goodness-of-fit test, see Leonard A. Marascuilo and Maryellen McSweeney, *Nonparametric and Distribution Free Methods for the Social Sciences* (Belmont, Calif.: Brooks/Cole, 1977), pp. 243–248.

[2] W. G. Cochran, "The χ^2 Test of Goodness of Fit," *Annuals of Mathematical Statistics,* 23 (1952), pp. 315–345.

[3] The reader interested in the details of such a test should see Samuel Richmond, *Statistical Analysis,* 2nd ed. (New York: Ronald, 1964), pp. 291–295.

Table 14.1
Observed and Theoretical Cumulative Distributions
of Foundation Compound Preference

Shade	Observed Number	Observed Proportion	Observed Cumulative Proportion	Theoretical Proportion	Theoretical Cumulative Proportion
Very light	50	0.50	0.50	0.25	0.25
Light	30	0.30	0.80	0.25	0.50
Medium	15	0.15	0.95	0.25	0.75
Dark	5	0.05	1.00	0.25	1.00

tion function that would occur under the null hypothesis and comparing that with the observed cumulative distribution function. The point at which the two functions show the maximum deviation is determined, and the value of this deviation is the test statistic.

The null hypothesis for the cosmetic manufacturer would be that there is no preference for the various shades. Thus, it would be expected that 25 percent of the sample would prefer each shade. The cumulative distribution function resulting from this assumption is presented as the last column of Table 14.1.

Kolmogorov–Smirnov D, which is equal to the *absolute value of the maximum deviation* between the observed cumulative proportion and the theoretical cumulative proportion, is $0.80 - 0.50 = 0.30$. If the researcher chooses an $\alpha = 0.05$, the critical value of D for large samples is given by $1.36/\sqrt{n}$, where n is the sample size. In our case, the critical value is 0.136. Calculated D exceeds the critical value, and thus the null hypothesis of no preference among shades is rejected. The data indicate a statistically significant preference for the lighter shades.

The careful reader will have noticed that the hypothesis of no preference could also have been tested with the chi-square goodness-of-fit test. When the data are ordinal, though, the Kolmogorov–Smirnov test is the preferred procedure. It is more powerful than chi-square in almost all cases, is easier to compute, and does not require a certain minimum expected frequency in each cell as does the chi-square test.

The Kolmogorov–Smirnov test can also be used to determine whether two independent samples have been drawn from the same population or from populations with the same distribution. An example would be a manufacturer interested in determining whether consumer preference among sizes for a new brand of laundry detergent was the same as for the old brand. To apply the test, we would simply need to create a cumulative frequency distribution for each sample of observations using the same intervals. The test statistic would be the value of the maximum deviation between the two observed cumulative frequencies.[4]

---

[4]See Marascuilo and McSweeny, *Nonparametric and Distribution Free Methods*, pp. 250–251. See also Jean Dickinson Gibbons, *Nonparametric Statistical Inference*, 2nd ed. (New York: Marell Dekker, Inc., 1985).

Hypotheses about One Mean

A recurring problem in marketing research studies is the need to make some statement about the parent population mean. Recall that the distribution of sample means is normal, with the mean of the sample means equal to the population mean and the variance of the sample means, $\sigma_{\bar{x}}^2$, equal to the population variance divided by the sample size, that is, $\sigma_{\bar{x}}^2 = \sigma^2/n$. Thus, it should not prove surprising to find that the appropriate statistic for testing a hypothesis about a mean when the population variance is known is

$$z = \frac{\bar{x} - \mu}{\sigma_{\bar{x}}}$$

where

$\bar{x}$ is the sample mean;

μ is the population mean; and

$\sigma_{\bar{x}}$ is the standard error of the mean, which is equal to $\sigma/\sqrt{n}$ where n is the sample size.

The z statistic is appropriate if the sample comes from a normal population, or if the variable is not normally distributed in the population but the sample is large enough for the Central-Limit Theorem to be operative. What happens, though, in the more realistic case in which the population variance is unknown?

When the parent population variance is unknown, then, of course, the standard error of the mean, $\sigma_{\bar{x}}$, is unknown since it is equal to $\sigma/\sqrt{n}$. The standard error of the mean must then be estimated from the sample data. The estimate is $s_{\bar{x}} = \hat{s}/\sqrt{n}$, where $\hat{s}$ is the unbiased sample standard deviation; that is,

$$\hat{s} = \sqrt{\frac{\sum_{i=1}^{n} (X_i - \bar{x})^2}{n - 1}}$$

The test statistic now becomes $(\bar{x} - \mu)/s_{\bar{x}}$, which is t distributed with $n - 1$ degrees of freedom if the conditions for the t test are satisfied.

To use the t statistic appropriately for making inferences about the mean, two basic questions need to be answered:

■ Is the distribution of the variable in the parent population normal or is it asymmetrical?

■ Is the sample size large or small?

If the variable of interest is normally distributed in the parent population, then the test statistic $(\bar{x} - \mu)/s_{\bar{x}}$ is t distributed with $n - 1$ degrees of freedom. This is true whether the sample size is large or small. For small samples, we actually use t with $n - 1$ degrees of freedom when making an inference. Although t with $n - 1$ degrees of freedom is also the theoretically correct distribution for large n, the distribution approaches and becomes indistinguishable from the normal distribution for samples of 30 or more observations. The test statistic $(\bar{x} - \mu)/s_{\bar{x}}$ is therefore referred to a table of normal deviates when making inferences with large samples. Note, though, that this is

Research Realities 14.1

Summary Table of Inferences about a Single Mean

	σ Known	σ Unknown
Distribution of variable in parent population is normal or symmetrical.	Small *n:* Use $z = \dfrac{\bar{x} - \mu}{\sigma_{\bar{x}}} \sim N(0,1)$ Large *n:* Use $z = \dfrac{\bar{x} - \mu}{\sigma_{\bar{x}}} \sim N(0,1)$	Small *n:* Use $t = \dfrac{\bar{x} - \mu}{s_{\bar{x}}}$ where $s_{\bar{x}} = \hat{s}/\sqrt{n}$ and $\hat{s} = \sqrt{\dfrac{\displaystyle\sum_{i=1}^{n} (X_i - \bar{x})^2}{n - 1}}$ and refer to *t* table for $n - 1$ degrees of freedom. Large *n:* Since the *t* distribution approaches the normal as *n* increases, use $z = \dfrac{\bar{x} - \mu}{s_{\bar{x}}}$ for $n > 30$.
Distribution of variable in parent population is asymmetrical.	Small *n:* There is no theory to support the parametric test. One must either transform the variate so that it is normally distributed and then use the *z* test, or one must use a distribution-free statistical test. Large *n:* If the sample is large enough so that the Central-Limit Theorem is operative, use $z = \dfrac{\bar{x} - \mu}{\sigma_{\bar{x}}} \sim N(0,1)$	Small *n:* There is no theory to support the parametric test. One must either transform the variate so that it is normally distributed and then use the *t* test, or one must use a distribution-free statistical test. Large *n:* If sample is large enough so that 1. the Central-Limit Theorem is operative, 2. $\hat{s}$ is a close estimate of σ, use $z = \dfrac{\bar{x} - \mu}{s_{\bar{x}}} \sim N(0,1)$

because the theoretically correct *t* distribution (since σ is unknown) has become indistinguishable from the normal curve, which is somewhat easier to use.

   What happens if the variable is not normally distributed in the parent population when σ is unknown? If the distribution of the variable is symmetrical or displays only moderate skew, there is no problem. The *t* test is quite robust to departures from normality. However, if the variable is highly skewed in the parent population, the appropriate procedure depends upon the sample size. If the sample is small, the *t* test is

Table 14.2
Store Sales of Trial Product per Week

Store i	Sales X_i	Store i	Sales X_i
1	86	6	93
2	97	7	132
3	114	8	116
4	108	9	105
5	123	10	120

inappropriate. Either the variable has to be transformed so that it is normally distributed, or one of the distribution-free statistical tests must be used. If the sample is large, the normal curve could be used for making the inference, provided the following two assumptions are satisfied:

1. The sample size is large enough so that the sample mean $\bar{x}$ is normally distributed because of the operation of the Central-Limit Theorem. The greater the degree of asymmetry in the distribution of the variable, the larger the sample size needed to satisfy this assumption.

2. The sample standard deviation $\hat{s}$ is a close estimate of the parent population standard deviation σ. The higher the degree of variability in the parent population, the larger the size of the sample that is needed to justify this assumption.

Research Realities 14.1 summarizes the situation for making inferences about a mean for known and unknown σ and normally distributed and asymmetrical parent population distributions.

To illustrate the application of the t test, consider the supermarket chain investigating the desirability of adding a new product to the shelves of its associated stores. Suppose that 100 units must be sold per week in each store for the item to be sufficiently profitable to warrant handling it in lieu of the many products competing for the limited shelf space. Suppose that the research department decides to investigate the item's turnover by putting it in a random sample of ten stores for a limited period of time. Suppose further that the average sales per store per week were as shown in Table 14.2.

Since the variance of sales per store is unknown and has to be estimated, the t test is the correct parametric test if the distribution of sales is normal. The normality assumption seems reasonable and could be checked using one of the goodness-of-fit tests. The little sales evidence that is available does not indicate any real asymmetry, and therefore let us assume that the normality assumption is satisfied.

A one-tailed test is appropriate, since it is only when the sales per store per week are at least 100 that the product will be introduced on a national scale. The null and alternate hypotheses are

$$H_0 : \mu \leq 100,$$

$$H_a : \mu > 100.$$

Suppose the significance level is to be $\alpha = 0.05$. From the data in Table 14.2,

$$\bar{x} = \frac{\sum\limits_{i=1}^{n} X_i}{n} = 109.4,$$

and

$$\hat{s} = \sqrt{\frac{\sum\limits_{i=1}^{n} (X_i - \bar{x})^2}{(n-1)}} = 14.40.$$

Therefore, the standard error of the mean $s_x = \hat{s}/\sqrt{n} = 4.55$. Calculations yield

$$t = \frac{\bar{x} - \mu}{s_{\bar{x}}} = \frac{109.4 - 100}{4.55} = 2.07.$$

Critical t as read from the t table with $\nu = n - 1 = 9$ degrees of freedom is 1.833 ($\alpha = .05$). (See Table 3 in the appendix at the end of the book.) It is unlikely that the calculated value would have occurred by chance if the sales per store in the population were indeed less than or equal to 100 units per week.

Some insight into the sales per store per week that might be expected if the product was introduced on a national scale can be achieved by calculating the confidence interval. The appropriate formula is $\bar{x} \pm t s_{\bar{x}}$. For a 95 percent confidence interval and 9 degrees of freedom, $t = 1.833$, as we have already seen. The 95 percent confidence interval is thus $109.4 \pm (1.833)(4.55)$, or 109.4 ± 8.3, or, alternatively, $101.1 \le \mu \le 117.7$.

Suppose the product was placed in 50 stores and that the sample mean and standard deviation were the same; that is, $\bar{x} = 109.4$, $\hat{s} = 14.40$. The test statistic would now be $z = 4.62$, which would be referred to a normal table since the t is indistinguishable from the normal for samples of this size. Calculated z is greater than critical $z = 1.645$ for $\alpha = 0.05$, and, as expected, the same conclusion is warranted. The evidence is stronger now because of the larger sample of stores; the product could be expected to sell at a rate greater than 100 units per store per week.

The impact of the larger sample and the opportunity it provides to use the normal curve can also be seen in the smaller confidence interval the larger sample produces. When the normal curve rather than t distribution applies, the formula $\bar{x} \pm t s_{\bar{x}}$ for calculating the confidence interval changes to $\bar{x} \pm z s_{\bar{x}}$, where the appropriate z value is read from the normal curve table. Since for a 95 percent confidence interval $z = 1.645$, the interval is $109.4 \pm (1.645)(4.55)$, or 109.4 ± 7.5, which yields the estimate $101.9 \le \mu \le 108.6$, a slightly narrower interval than that produced when 10 stores rather than 50 were in the sample.

Hypotheses about Two Means

Consider testing an hypothesis about the difference between two population means. Assuming the samples are independent, there are three cases to consider:

■   The two parent population variances are known.

■   The parent population variances are unknown but can be assumed equal.

■   The parent population variances are unknown and cannot be assumed equal.

Variances Are Known   Experience has shown that the population variance usually changes much more slowly than does the population mean. This means that the "old" variance can often be used as the "known" population variance for studies that are being repeated. For example, we may have annually checked the per capita soft-drink consumption of people living in different regions of the United States. If we were now to test an hypothesis about the differences in per capita consumption of a new soft drink, we could use the previously determined variances as "known" variances for our new soft drink. Consider that our problem is indeed one of determining whether there are any differences between Northerners and Southerners in their consumption of a new soft drink our company has recently introduced, called Spark. Further, past data indicate that per capita variation in the consumption of soft drinks is 10 ounces per day for Northerners and 14 ounces per day for Southerners as measured by the standard deviation; that is, $\sigma_N = 10$ and $\sigma_S = 14$.

The null hypothesis is that there is no difference between Northerners and Southerners in their consumption of Spark ($H_0{:}\mu_N = \mu_S$), while the alternate hypothesis is that there is a difference ($H_a{:}\mu_N \neq \mu_S$). It so happens that if $\bar{x}_N$ and $\bar{x}_S$, the sample means, are normally distributed random variables, then their sum or difference is also normally distributed. The two sample means could be normally distributed because per capita consumption is normally distributed in each region or because the two samples are large enough so that the Central-Limit Theorem is operative. In either case, the test statistic is

$$z = \frac{(\bar{x}_1 - \bar{x}_2) - (\mu_1 - \mu_2)}{\sigma_{\bar{x}_1 - \bar{x}_2}}$$

where

$\bar{x}_1$ is the sample mean for the first (northern) sample;

$\bar{x}_2$ is the sample mean for the second (southern) sample;

μ_1 and μ_2 are the unknown population means for the northern and southern samples; and

$\sigma_{\bar{x}_1 - \bar{x}_2}$ is the standard error of estimate for the difference in means and is equal to $\sqrt{\sigma_{\bar{x}_1}^2 + \sigma_{\bar{x}_2}^2}$, where, in turn, $\sigma_{\bar{x}_1}^2 = \sigma_1^2/n_1$ and $\sigma_{\bar{x}_2}^2 = \sigma_2^2/n_2$. Now σ_1^2 and σ_2^2 are the "known" population variances of $\sigma_1^2 = (10)^2 = 100$ and $\sigma_2^2 = (14)^2 = 196$. Suppose that a random sample of 100 people from the North and South, respectively, was taken and that $\bar{x}_1 = 20$ ounces per day and $\bar{x}_2 = 25$ ounces per day. Does this result indicate a real difference in consumption rates? The standard error of estimate is

$$\sigma_{\bar{x}_1 - \bar{x}_2} = \sqrt{\frac{100}{100} + \frac{196}{100}} = \sqrt{2.96} = 1.720,$$

and the calculated z is

$$z = \frac{(20 - 25) - (\mu_N - \mu_S)}{1.720} = \frac{-5 - 0}{1.720} = -2.906.$$

Calculated z exceeds the critical tabled value of -1.96 for $\alpha = 0.05$, and the null hypothesis is rejected. There is a statistically significant difference in the per capita consumption of Spark by Northerners and Southerners.

The confidence interval for the difference in the two means is given by the formula

$$(\bar{x}_1 - \bar{x}_2) \pm z\sigma_{\bar{x}_1 - \bar{x}_2}.$$

For a 95 percent confidence interval $z = 1.96$ and the interval estimate of the difference in consumption of Spark by the two groups is $-5 \pm (1.96)(1.720) = -5 \pm 3.4$. Southerners on average are estimated to drink 1.6 to 8.4 ounces of Spark less per day than Northerners.

Variances Are Unknown   When the two parent population variances are unknown, the standard error of the test statistic $\sigma_{\bar{x}_1 - \bar{x}_2}$ is also unknown, since $\sigma_{\bar{x}_1}$ and $\sigma_{\bar{x}_2}$ are unknown and have to be estimated. As was true with one sample, the sample standard deviations are used to estimate the population standard deviations;

$$\hat{s}_1^2 = \frac{\sum\limits_{i=1}^{n_1} (X_{i1} - \bar{x}_1)^2}{(n_1 - 1)}$$

is used to estimate σ_1^2 and

$$\hat{s}_2^2 = \frac{\sum\limits_{i=1}^{n_2} (X_{i2} - \bar{x}_2)^2}{(n_2 - 1)}$$

is used to estimate σ_2^2, and the estimates of the standard error of the means become $s_{\bar{x}_1} = \hat{s}_1 / \sqrt{n_1}$ and $s_{\bar{x}_2} = \hat{s}_2 / \sqrt{n_2}$. The general estimate of $\sigma_{\bar{x}_1 - \bar{x}_2}$ is then

$$s_{\bar{x}_1 - \bar{x}_2} = \sqrt{s_{\bar{x}_1}^2 + s_{\bar{x}_2}^2} = \sqrt{\frac{\hat{s}_1^2}{n_1} + \frac{\hat{s}_2^2}{n_2}}.$$

Although unknown, if the two parent population variances *can be assumed equal,* a better estimate of the common population variance can be generated by *pooling* the samples to calculate

$$\hat{s}^2 = \frac{\sum\limits_{i=1}^{n_1} (X_{i1} - \bar{x}_1)^2 + \sum\limits_{i=1}^{n_2} (X_{i2} - \bar{x}_2)^2}{n_1 + n_2 - 2},$$

where $\hat{s}^2$ is the pooled sample variance used to estimate the common population variance. In this case the estimated standard error of the test statistic $s_{\bar{x}_1 - \bar{x}_2}$ reduces to

Table 14.3
Store Sales of Floor Wax in Units

Store	Plastic Container	Metal Container	Store	Plastic Container	Metal Container
1	432	365	6	380	372
2	360	405	7	422	378
3	397	396	8	406	410
4	408	390	9	400	383
5	417	404	10	408	400

$$s_{\bar{x}_1 - \bar{x}_2} = \sqrt{\frac{\hat{s}_1^{\,2}}{n_1} + \frac{\hat{s}_2^{\,2}}{n_2}} = \sqrt{\frac{\hat{s}^2}{n_1} + \frac{\hat{s}^2}{n_2}} = \sqrt{\hat{s}^2\left(\frac{1}{n_1} + \frac{1}{n_2}\right)}.$$

If the distribution of the variable in each population can further be assumed to be normal, the appropriate test statistic is

$$t = \frac{(\bar{x}_1 - \bar{x}_2) - (\mu_1 - \mu_2)}{s_{\bar{x}_1 - \bar{x}_2}},$$

which is t distributed with $\nu = n_1 + n_2 - 2$ degrees of freedom.

Suppose, for example, that a manufacturer of floor waxes has recently developed a new wax. The company is considering two different container designs for the wax, one plastic and one metal. The company decides to make the final determination on the basis of a limited sales test in which the plastic containers are introduced in a random sample of ten stores and the metal containers are introduced in an *independent* random sample of ten stores. The test results are contained in Table 14.3.

$$\text{Calculated } t = \frac{(\bar{x}_1 - \bar{x}_2) - (\mu_1 - \mu_2)}{s_{\bar{x}_1 - \bar{x}_2}} = \frac{(403.0 - 390.3) - (0)}{8.15} = 1.56.$$

This value is referred to a t table for $\nu = n_1 + n_2 - 2 = 18$ degrees of freedom. The test is two-tailed because the null hypothesis is that they were unequal; there was no *a priori* statement that one was expected to sell better than the other. For $\alpha = 0.05$, say, and 18 degrees of freedom, critical $t = 2.101$. (One needs to look in the column headed $1 - \alpha = .975$ rather than .95 in Table 3 in the appendix, since this is a two-tailed test.) Since calculated t is less than critical t, the null hypothesis of no difference would not be rejected. The sample data do *not* indicate that the plastic container could be expected to outsell the metal container in the total population, even though it did so in this limited experiment.

The example again demonstrates the importance of explicitly determining the statistical significance level by appropriately balancing Type I and Type II errors. Here α error was arbitrarily set equal to 0.05. This led to nonrejection of the null hypothesis and the conclusion that the plastic container would not be expected to outsell the metal container in the total population. Yet if the decision maker had been able to tolerate an

α error of, say, 0.20, just the opposite conclusion would have been warranted, since interpolating in Table 3 in the appendix for 18 degrees of freedom indicates that the probability of getting calculated $t = 1.56$ under an assumption of no difference in the population means is approximately 15 percent. Assuming the production and other costs associated with each container were the same, it would clearly seem that the final packaging decision should favor the plastic container. If the production and other costs were not the same, then these costs should clearly be reflected in the statistical decision rule.[5]

One of the assumptions underlying the above procedure was that the variances in sales of the plastic and metal containers were equal in the population. The assumption could be checked using an F test for the equality of variances, and indeed, the sample evidence does not contradict the assumption.[6] Suppose, though, that the assumption was not justified. Then the pooling of the variances is also no longer warranted, and the estimated standard error of the test statistic becomes

$$s_{\bar{x}_1 - \bar{x}_2} = \sqrt{\frac{\hat{s}_1^{\,2}}{n_1} + \frac{\hat{s}_2^{\,2}}{n_2}}$$

instead of

$$s_{\bar{x}_1 - \bar{x}_2} = \sqrt{\hat{s}^2 \left(\frac{1}{n_1} + \frac{1}{n_2} \right)}.$$

A real question now arises as to the appropriate degrees of freedom for the test statistic. A large amount of controversial literature deals with this condition known as the Behrens–Fisher problem. One suggested approach is the Aspin–Welch test, in which the degrees of freedom is a kind of weighted average of the degrees of freedom in each of the independent samples.[7] If the samples are both large so that $\hat{s}_1^{\,2}$ and $\hat{s}_2^{\,2}$ provide good estimates of their respective population variances $\sigma_1^{\,2}$ and $\sigma_2^{\,2}$, then the problem becomes less acute, as the normal z statistic can be used to examine the hypothesis.

The above discussion assumed that the samples are independent and that the variable of interest is normally distributed in each of the parent populations. The normality assumption was again necessary to justify the use of the t distribution. What happens, though, if the variable is not normally distributed or the samples are not independent? The lower half of Research Realities 14.2 summarizes the approach for nonnormal parent distributions for known and unknown σ, while the next section treats the case of dependent samples.

---

[5]The Bayesian posture would be to introduce the plastic container even with the obtained sample results if the opportunity costs associated with each alternative were the same. If they were not the same, then the Bayesian approach would incorporate these costs directly into the decision rule regarding which container should be produced.

[6]Most introductory statistics books detail the procedure for testing the equality of two parent population variances. See, for example, Donald L. Harnett and James L. Murphy, *Introductory Statistical Analysis,* 2nd ed. (Reading, Mass.: Addison-Wesley, 1980), pp. 366–371.

[7]See Acheson J. Duncan, *Quality Control and Industrial Statistics,* rev. ed. (Homewood, Ill.: Richard D. Irwin, 1959), pp. 476–478, for one of the better discussions of the Aspin–Welch test.

Research Realities 14.2

Summary Table of Inferences about the Difference in Two Means

	σ's Known	σ's Unknown
Distribution of variables in parent populations is normal or symmetrical.	Small n: Use $z = \dfrac{(\bar{x}_1 - \bar{x}_2) - (\mu_1 - \mu_2)}{\sigma_{\bar{x}_1 - \bar{x}_2}} \sim N(0,1)$ where $\sigma_{\bar{x}_1 - \bar{x}_2} = \sqrt{\dfrac{\sigma_1^2}{n_1} + \dfrac{\sigma_2^2}{n_2}}$ Large n: Use $z = \dfrac{(\bar{x}_1 - \bar{x}_2) - (\mu_1 - \mu_2)}{\sigma_{\bar{x}_1 - \bar{x}_2}} \sim N(0,1)$	Small n: Can you assume $\sigma_1 = \sigma_2$? 1. Yes: Use pooled variance t test where $t = \dfrac{(\bar{x}_1 - \bar{x}_2) - (\mu_1 - \mu_2)}{s_{\bar{x}_1 - \bar{x}_2}}$ and $s_{\bar{x}_1 - \bar{x}_2} =$ $\sqrt{\dfrac{\displaystyle\sum_{i=1}^{n_1} (X_{i1} - \bar{x}_1)^2 + \sum_{i=1}^{n_2} (X_{i2} - \bar{x}_2)^2}{n_1 + n_2 - 2} \left(\dfrac{1}{n_1} + \dfrac{1}{n_2}\right)}$ with $(n_1 + n_2 - 2)$ degrees of freedom. 2. No: Approach is shrouded in controversy. Might use Aspin–Welch test. Large n: Use $z = \dfrac{(\bar{x}_1 - \bar{x}_2) - (\mu_1 - \mu_2)}{s_{\bar{x}_1 - \bar{x}_2}}$ and use pooled variance if variances can be assumed equal and unpooled variance if equality assumption is not warranted.
Distribution of variables in parent populations is asymmetrical.	Small n: There is no theory to support the parametric test. One must either transform the variates so that they are normally distributed and then use the z test, or one must use a distribution-free statistical test. Large n: If the individual samples are large enough so that the Central-Limit Theorem is operative for them separately, it will also apply to their sum or difference. Use $z = \dfrac{(\bar{x}_1 - \bar{x}_2) - (\mu_1 - \mu_2)}{\sigma_{\bar{x}_1 - \bar{x}_2}} \sim N(0,1)$	Small n: There is no theory to support the parametric test. One must either transform the variates so that they are normally distributed and then use the t test, or one must use a distribution-free statistical test. Large n: One must assumpe that n_1 and n_2 are large enough so that the Central-Limit Theorem applies to the individual sample means. Then it can also be assumed to apply to their sum or difference. Use $z = \dfrac{(\bar{x}_1 - \bar{x}_2) - (\mu_1 - \mu_2)}{s_{\bar{x}_1 - \bar{x}_2}}$ employing a pooled variance if the unknown parent population variances can be assumed equal and unpooled variance if the equality assumption is not warranted.

Samples Are Related   A manufacturer of camping equipment wished to study consumer color preferences for a sleeping bag it had recently developed. The bag was of medium quality and price. Traditionally, the high-quality, high-priced sleeping bags used by serious campers and backpackers came in the earth colors, such as green and brown. Previous research indicated that the low-quality, low-priced sleeping bags were frequently purchased for children, to be used at slumber parties. The vivid colors were preferred by this market segment, with bright reds and oranges leading the way. Production capacity restrictions would not allow the company to produce both sets of colors. To make the comparison, it selected a random sample of five stores into which it introduced bags of both types. The sales per store are indicated in Table 14.4. Do the data present sufficient evidence to indicate a difference in the average sales for the different colored bags?

An analysis of the data indicates a difference in the two means of $(\bar{x}_1 - \bar{x}_2) = (50.2 - 45.2) = 5.0$. This is a rather small difference, considering the variability in sales that exists across the five stores. Further, application of the procedures of the last section suggests that the difference is not statistically significant. The pooled estimate of the common variance is

$$s^2 = \frac{\sum_{i=1}^{n_1} (X_{i1} - \bar{x}_1)^2 + \sum_{i=1}^{n_2} (X_{i2} - \bar{x}_2)^2}{n_1 + n_2 - 2} = \frac{1,512.8 + 1,222.8}{8} = 341.95,$$

and

$$s_{\bar{x}_1 - \bar{x}_2} = \sqrt{s^2\left(\frac{1}{n_1} + \frac{1}{n_2}\right)} = \sqrt{341.95\left(\frac{1}{5} + \frac{1}{5}\right)} = 11.70.$$

Calculated t is thus

$$t = \frac{(\bar{x}_1 - \bar{x}_2) - (\mu_1 - \mu_2)}{s_{\bar{x}_1 - \bar{x}_2}} = \frac{(50.2 - 45.2) - 0}{11.70} = 0.427,$$

which is less than the critical value $t = 2.306$ found in the table for $\alpha = 0.05$ and $v = n_1 + n_2 - 2 = 8$ degrees of freedom. The null hypothesis of no difference in sales of the two types of colors cannot be rejected on the basis of the sample data.

But wait a minute! A closer look at the data indicates a marked inconsistency with this conclusion. The bright-colored sleeping bags outsold the earth-colored ones in each store, and indeed an analysis of the per-store differences (the procedure is detailed below) indicates that there is a statistically significant difference in the sales of the two bags. The reason for the seeming difference in conclusions (the difference is not significant versus it is significant) arises because the t test for the difference in two means is *not appropriate* for the problem. The difference in means test assumes that the samples are independent. These samples are not. Sales of bright-colored and earth-colored bags are definitely related, since they are both found in the same stores. Note how this example differs from the floor wax example, in which the metal containers were placed in one sample of stores and the plastic containers were located in an independent sample of stores. We need a procedure that takes into account the fact that the observations are related.

Table 14.4
Per-store Sales of Sleeping Bags

Store	Bright Colors	Earth Colors
1	64	56
2	72	66
3	43	39
4	22	20
5	50	45

The appropriate procedure is the t test for related samples. The procedure is as follows. Define a new variable d_i, where d_i is the difference between sales of the bright-colored bags and the earth-colored bags for the ith store. Thus,

$$d_1 = 64 - 56 = 8$$

$$d_2 = 72 - 66 = 6$$

$$d_3 = 43 - 39 = 4$$

$$d_4 = 22 - 20 = 2$$

$$d_5 = 50 - 45 = 5.$$

Now calculate the mean difference

$$\bar{d} = \frac{\sum_{i=1}^{n} d_i}{n} = \frac{8 + 6 + 4 + 2 + 5}{5} = 5.0,$$

and the standard error of the difference

$$s_d = \sqrt{\frac{\sum_{i=1}^{n} (d_i - \bar{d})^2}{n - 1}} = \sqrt{\frac{20}{4}} = 2.24.$$

The test statistic is

$$t = \frac{\bar{d} - D}{s_d / \sqrt{n}},$$

where D is the difference that is expected under the null hypothesis. Since there is no *a priori* reason why one color would be expected to sell better than the other, the appropriate null hypothesis is that there is no difference, while the alternate hypothesis is that there is; that is,

$$H_0 : D = 0,$$

$$H_a : D \neq 0.$$

Calculated t is thus

$$t = \frac{5.0 - 0}{2.24/\sqrt{5}} = 5.0.$$

This value is referred to a t table for $v =$ (number of differences -1) degrees of freedom; in this case, there are five paired differences and thus $v = 4$. Critical t for $v = 4$ and $\alpha = 0.05$ is 2.776, and thus the hypothesis of no difference is rejected. The sample evidence indicates that the bright-colored sleeping bags are likely to outsell the earth-colored ones.

An estimate of how much sales per store of the vivid-colored sleeping bags would exceed those of the earth-colored bags can be calculated from the confidence interval formula $\bar{d} \pm t(s_d/\sqrt{n})$. The 95 percent confidence interval is $5.0 \pm (2.776)$ $(2.24/\sqrt{5}) = 5.0 \pm 2.8$, suggesting that sales of the vivid-colored bags would be in the range of 2.2 to 7.8 bags greater per store on average.

Hypotheses about Two Proportions

The appendix to Chapter 13 reviewed the essential nature of hypothesis testing, employing as an example the testing of an hypothesis about a single population proportion. In this section, we want to illustrate the procedure for testing for the difference between two population proportions.[8]

The test for the difference between two population proportions is basically a large sample problem. The samples from each population must be large enough so that the normal approximation to the exact binomial distribution of sample proportions can be used. As a practical matter, this means that np and nq should be greater than 10 for each sample, where p is the proportion of "successes" and q is the proportion of "failures" in the sample and n is the sample size.

To illustrate, suppose a cosmetics manufacturer was interested in comparing male college students and nonstudents in terms of their use of hair spray. Suppose random samples of 100 male students and 100 male nonstudents in Austin, Texas, were selected and their use of hair spray in the last three months was determined. Suppose further that 30 students and 20 nonstudents had used hair spray within this period. Does this evidence indicate that a significantly higher precentage of college students than nonstudents use hair spray?

---

[8]The tests for population proportions are logically considered with nominal data because they apply in situations in which the variable being studied can be divided into those cases *possessing* the characteristic and those cases lacking it, and the emphasis is on the number or proportion of cases falling into each category. Marketing examples abound: "prefer A" versus "do not prefer A"; "buy" versus "do not buy"; "brand loyal" versus "not brand loyal"; "sales representatives meeting quota" versus "sales representatives not meeting quota." The test for the significance of the difference between two proportions is treated here because the hypothesis is examined using the z test, and the procedure relies on an "automatic pooled sample variance" estimate. It was thought that these notions would be better appreciated after the discussion of the test of means rather than before.

Since we are interested in determining whether the two parent population proportions are different, the null hypothesis is that they are the same, that is,

$$H_0 : \pi_1 = \pi_2,$$

$$H_a : \pi_1 \neq \pi_2,$$

where Population 1 is the population of college students, and Population 2 is the population of nonstudents. The sample proportions are $p_1 = 0.30$ and $p_2 = 0.20$ and, therefore, $n_1 p_1 = 30$, $n_1 q_1 = 70$, $n_2 p_2 = 20$, $n_2 q_2 = 80$, and the normal approximation to the binomial distribution can be used. The test statistic is

$$z = \frac{(p_1 - p_2) - (\pi_1 - \pi_2)}{\sigma_{p_1 - p_2}},$$

where $\sigma_{p_1 - p_2}$ is the standard error of the difference in the two sample proportions. The one question that still remains in the calculation of z is what does $\sigma_{p_1 - p_2}$ equal.

A general statistical result that is useful for understanding the calculation of $\sigma_{p_1 - p_2}$ is that the *variance of the sum or difference of two independent random variables is equal to the sum of the individual variances.* For a single proportion, the variance is $\pi(1 - \pi)/n$, and thus the variance of the difference is

$$\sigma^2_{p_1 - p_2} = \sigma^2_{p_1} + \sigma^2_{p_2} = \frac{\pi_1 (1 - \pi_1)}{n_1} + \frac{\pi_2 (1 - \pi_2)}{n_2}.$$

Note that the variance of the difference is given in terms of the two unknown population proportions π_1 and π_2. Although unknown, the two population proportions have been assumed equal, and thus we have a "natural" case of a *pooled variance* estimate; $s^2_{p_1 - p_2}$ is logically used to estimate $\sigma^2_{p_1 - p_2}$, where

$$s^2_{p_1 - p_2} = pq \left(\frac{1}{n_1} + \frac{1}{n_2} \right)$$

and

$$p = \frac{\text{Total number of successes in the two samples}}{\text{Total number of observations in the two samples}},$$

$$q = 1 - p.$$

For the example

$$p = \frac{30 + 20}{100 + 100} = \frac{50}{200} = 0.25,$$

$$s^2_{p_1 - p_2} = (0.25)(0.75) \left(\frac{1}{100} + \frac{1}{100} \right) = 0.00375,$$

and

$$s_{p_1 - p_2} = 0.061.$$

Calculated z is found as follows:

$$z = \frac{(0.30 - 0.20) - (0)}{0.061} = \frac{0.10}{0.061} = 1.64,$$

while critical $z = 1.96$ for $\alpha = 0.05$. The sample evidence does not indicate that there is a difference in the proportion of college students and nonstudents using hair spray.

The 95 percent confidence interval calculated by the formula $(p_1 - p_2) \pm zs_{p_1 - p_2}$, which is $(.30 - .20) \pm 1.96 \, (0.061) = .10 \pm .12$ yields a similar conclusion. The interval includes zero, suggesting there is no difference in the proportions using hair spray in the two groups.

Summary

Several statistical tests that are useful to marketing researchers for examining differences were discussed in this chapter. The difference at issue might be the difference between some sample result and some expected population value or the difference between two sample results.

The chi-square goodness-of-fit test is appropriate when a nominally scaled variable falls naturally into two or more categories and the analyst wishes to determine whether the observed number of cases in each cell corresponds to the "expected" number.

The Kolmogorov–Smirnov test is the ordinal counterpart to the chi-square goodness-of-fit test in that it focuses on the comparison of observed and expected frequencies. It can be employed to test whether a set of observations could have come from some theoretical population distribution, such as a normal distribution, or whether two independent samples could have come from the same population distribution.

In testing an hypothesis about a single mean, the z test is appropriate if the variance is known, while the t test applies with unknown variance. A similar situation arises in the analysis of two means from independent samples. If the variances are known, the z test is used. If the variances are unknown but assumed equal, a t test using a pooled sample variance estimate applies. If unknown and likely unequal, there is controversy surrounding the correct procedure. If the samples are related rather than independent, then the t test for paired differences is appropriate.

The test of the equality of proportions from two independent samples involves a "natural" pooling of the sample variances. The z test applies.

Questions

1. What is the basic use of a chi-square goodness-of-fit test? How is the value of the test statistic calculated? How are the expected frequencies determined?

2. Suppose the data are ordinal and the analyst wishes to determine whether the observed frequencies correspond to some expected pattern. What statistical test is appropriate? What is the basic procedure to follow in implementing this test?

3. What is the appropriate test statistic for making inferences about a population mean when the population variance is known? When the population variance is unknown? Suppose the population variance is unknown, but the sample is large. What is the appropriate procedure then?

4. Suppose one is testing for the statistical significance of the observed difference between the sample means from two independent samples? What is the appropriate procedure when

(a) the two parent population variances are known;
(b) unknown but can be assumed equal;
(c) unknown and cannot be assumed equal?

What conditions must occur in each case regarding the distribution of the variable?

5. Would your response to Question 4 change if the samples were related? Explain.

6. How do you test whether two parent population proportions differ?

Applications and Problems

1. A large publishing house recently conducted a survey to assess the reading habits of teenagers. The company published four magazines specifically tailored to suit the needs of teenagers. Management hypothesized that there were no differences in the preferences for the magazines. A sample of 1,600 teenagers interviewed in the city of Buffalo, New York, indicated the following preferences for the four magazines.

Publication	Frequency of Preference
1. Rock-Town	350
2. Dis-Co	500
3. Teen-Tips	450
4. P.S.-Punk Sound	300
Total	1,600

Management needs your expertise to determine whether there are differences in teenager preferences for the magazines.

(a) State the null and alternate hypotheses
(b) How many degrees of freedom are there?
(c) What is the chi-square critical table value at the 5 percent significance level?
(d) What is the calculated χ^2 value? Show all your calculations.
(e) Should the null hypothesis be rejected or not? Explain.

2. Moon Shine Company is a medium-sized manufacturer of shampoo. During the past years the company has increased the number of product variations of Moon-Shine shampoo that are available from three to five to increase their market share. Management conducted a survey to compare sales of Moon Shine shampoo with sales of Sun Shine and Star Shine, their two major competitors. A sample of 1,800 housewives indicated the following frequencies with respect to most recent shampoo purchased.

Shampoo	Number Buying
1. Moon Shine	425
2. Sun Shine	1,175
3. Star Shine	200
Total	1,800

Past experience had indicated that three times as many households preferred Sun Shine to Moon Shine and that in turn twice as many households preferred Moon Shine to Star

Shine. Management wants to determine if the historic tendency still holds, given Moon Shine Company has increased the range of shampoos available.

(a) State the null and alternate hypothesis.
(b) How many degrees of freedom are there?
(c) What is the chi-square critical table value at the 5 percent level?
(d) What is the calculated χ^2 value? Show all your calculations.
(e) Should the null hypothesis be rejected or not? Explain.

3. A manufacturer of music cassettes wants to test four different cassettes varying in tape length: 30 minutes, 60 minutes, 90 minutes, and 120 minutes. The company has hired you to determine whether customers show any distinct preference toward either extreme. If there is a preference toward any extreme, the company would manufacture only cassettes of the preferred length; otherwise the company is planning to market cassettes of all four lengths. A sample of 1,000 customers indicated the following preferences.

Tape Length	Frequency of Preference
30 minutes	150
60 minutes	250
90 minutes	425
120 minutes	175
Total	1,000

(a) State the null and alternate hypotheses.
(b) Compute Kolmogorov-Smirnov D by completing the following table.

Tape Length	Observed Number	Observed Proportion	Observed Cumulative Proportion	Theoretical Proportion	Theoretical Cumulative Proportion
30 min.					
60 min.					
90 min.					
120 min.					

(c) Compute the critical value of D at $\alpha = 0.05$. Show your calculations.
(d) Would you reject the null hypothesis? Explain.
(e) What are the implications for management?
(f) Explain why the Kolmogorov-Smirnov test would be used in this situation.

4. A medium-sized manufacturer of paper products was planning to introduce a new line of tissues, hand towels, and toilet paper. However, management had stipulated that the new products should be introduced only if average monthly purchases per household were $2.50 or more. The product was market tested and the diaries of the 100 panel households living in the test market area were checked. They indicated that average monthly purchases were $3.10 per household with a standard deviation of $0.50. Management is wondering what decision they should make and has asked for your recommendation.

(a) State the null and alternate hypotheses.
(b) Is the sample size considered large or small?
(c) Which test should be used? Why?
(d) At the 5 percent level of significance would you reject the null hypothesis? Support your answer with the necessary calculations.

5. The president of a chain of department stores had promised the managers of the various stores a bonus of 8 percent if the average monthly sales per store increased $300,000 or more. A random sample of 12 stores yielded the following sales increases:

Store	Sales	Store	Sales
1	$320,000	7	$380,000
2	$230,000	8	$280,000
3	$400,000	9	$420,000
4	$450,000	10	$360,000
5	$280,000	11	$440,000
6	$320,000	12	$320,000

The president is wondering whether this random sample of stores indicates that the population of stores have reached the goal. (Assume the distribution of the variable in the parent population is normal.)

   (a) State the null and alternate hypotheses.
   (b) Is the sample size considered small or large?
   (c) Which test should be used? Why?
   (d) Would you reject the null hypothesis at the 5 percent level of significance? Support your conclusion with the necessary calculations.

6. Ruby Gem is the owner of two jewelry stores located in Los Angeles and San Francisco. During the past year the San Francisco store had spent a considerable amount on in-store displays as compared to the Los Angeles stores. Ruby Gem wants to determine if the in-store displays resulted in increased sales. The average sales for a sample of 100 days for the San Francisco and Los Angeles stores were $21.8 million and $15.3 million. (Past experience has shown that $\sigma_{SF} = 8$ and $\sigma_{LA} = 9$ where σ_{SF} is the standard deviation in sales for the San Francisco store and σ_{LA} is the standard deviation for the Los Angeles store.)

   (a) State the null and alternate hypotheses.
   (b) What test would you use? Why?
   (c) What is the calculated value of the test statistic? Show your calculations.
   (d) What is the critical tabled value at 5 percent significance level?
   (e) Would you reject the null hypothesis? Explain.
   (f) What can Ruby Gem conclude?

7. Travel Time Company, a large travel agency located in Baltimore, Maryland, wanted to study consumer preferences for their package tours to the East. For the past five years Travel Time had offered two similarly priced packaged tours to the East that only differed in the places included in the tour. A random sample of five months' purchases from the past five years was selected. The number of consumers that purchased the tours during these five months is listed below.

Month	Packaged Tour I	Packaged Tour II
1	90	100
2	70	60
3	120	80
4	110	90
5	60	80

The management of Travel Time needs your assistance to determine whether there is a difference in preferences for the two tours.

(a) State the null and alternate hypotheses.
(b) What test would you use? Why?
(c) What is the calculated value of the test statistic? Show your calculations.
(d) What is the critical tabled value at the 5 percent significance level?
(e) Would you reject the null hypothesis? Explain.
(f) What can the management of Travel Time Company conclude about preferences for the two tours?

Appendix 14A
Analysis of Variance

In Chapter 14 we used the example of packaging floor wax in plastic and metal containers to examine that statistical test of the difference in two population means. Let us now reconsider the data of Table 14.4 to demonstrate an alternate approach to the problem. Known as the **analysis of variance (ANOVA),** it has the distinct advantage of being applicable when there are more than two means being compared. ANOVA is a moderately popular analysis technique among practitioners. As Research Realities 14A.1 indicates, it is used most by consumer goods manufacturers and finance and insurance companies. Its use by 26 percent of the total firms surveyed ranks it sixth out of the 12 statistical analysis techniques studied. While ANOVA would not normally be applied when there are only two means, it is best illustrated using a familiar example.

Although not necessary for this simple example, a little additional notation at this time will pay dividends when more complex examples are introduced. Therefore, let

x_{ij} be the ith observation on the jth treatment or group. There are two treatments in the example: $j = 1$ refers to plastic containers and $j = 2$ to metal containers. For each treatment there are ten stores. Thus, for the first treatment $X_{11} = 432$, $X_{21} = 360$, ... , $X_{10,1} = 408$ and for the second treatment $X_{12} = 365$, $X_{22} = 405$, and $X_{10,2} = 400$.

n_j be the number of observations on the jth treatment; $n_1 = 10$ and $n_2 = 10$.

n be the total number of observations in all treatments combined: $n = n_1 + n_2 = 20$.

$\bar{x}_{.j}$ be the mean of the jth treatment:

$$\bar{x}_{.j} = \frac{\sum_{i=1}^{n_j} X_{ij}}{n_j}.$$

Thus,

$$\bar{x}_{.1} = \frac{432 + 360 + \cdots + 408}{10} = 403.0$$

and

$$\bar{x}_{.2} = \frac{365 + 405 + \cdots + 400}{10} = 390.3.$$

Research Realities 14A.1
Use of Analysis of Variance by Various Types of Companies

Type of Company	Percent Using
Consumer goods manufacturers	41
Industrial goods manufacturers	12
Retails and wholesalers	9
Utilities	39
Communications	18
Marketing research and consulting	24
Finance and insurance	40
Other services	27
Others	20
Total sample	26

Source: Barnett A. Greenberg, Jac L. Goldstucker, and Danny N. Bellenger, "What Techniques are Used by Marketing Researchers in Business?" *Journal of Marketing*, 41 (April 1977), pp. 64–65.

- $\bar{x}_{..}$ be the grand mean of all n observations:

$$\bar{x}_{..} = \frac{\sum_{j=1}^{2} \sum_{i=1}^{n_j} X_{ij}}{n}$$

$$= \frac{432 + \cdots + 408 + 365 + \cdots + 400}{20} = 396.7.$$

The basic idea underlying the analysis of variance is that the parent population variance can be estimated from the sample in several ways, and comparisons among these estimates can tell us a great deal about the population. Recall that the null hypothesis was that the two parent population means were equal, that is, $\mu_1 = \mu_2$. If the null hypothesis is true, then except for sampling error, the following three estimates of the population variance should be equal:

1. the *total variation,* computed by comparing each of the 20 sales figures with the grand mean;

2. the *between group variation,* computed by comparing each of the two treatment means with the grand mean; and

3. the *within group variation,* computed by comparing each of the individual sales figures with the mean of its own group.

If, however, the hypothesis is not true and there is a difference in the means, then the between group variation should produce a higher estimate than the within group variation, which only considers the variation within groups and is independent of differences between groups.

These three separate estimates of the population variation are computed in the following way when there are k treatments or groups.

1.   Total variation—sum of squares total SS_T:

$$SS_T = \sum_{j=1}^{k} \sum_{i=1}^{nj} (X_{ij} - \bar{x}_{..})^2$$

$$= (432 - 396.7)^2 + \cdots + (408 - 396.7)^2$$

$$+ (365 - 396.7)^2 + \cdots + (400 - 396.7)^2.$$

The difference between *each observation* and the *grand mean* is determined; the differences are squared and then summed.

2.   Between group variation—sum of squares between groups SS_B:

$$SS_B = \sum_{j=1}^{k} n_j(\bar{x}_{.j} - \bar{x}_{..})^2$$

$$= 10(403.0 - 396.7)^2 + 10(390.3 - 396.7)^2$$

The difference between each *group mean* and the *overall mean* is determined; the difference is squared; each squared difference is weighted by the number of observations making up the group; and the results are summed.

3.   Within group variation—sum of squares within groups SS_W:

$$SS_W = \sum_{j=1}^{k} \sum_{i=1}^{nj} (X_{ij} - \bar{x}_{.j})^2$$

$$= (432 - 403.0)^2 + \cdots + (408 - 403.0)^2$$

$$+ (365 - 390.3)^2 + \cdots + (400 - 390.3)^2$$

The difference between *each observation* and its *group mean* is determined; the differences are squared and then summed.

Let us take a closer look at the behavior of these three sources of variation. First, SS_T measures the overall variation of the n observations. The more variable the n observations, the larger SS_T becomes. Second, SS_B reflects the total variability of the means. The more nearly alike the k means are, the smaller SS_B becomes. If they differ greatly, SS_B will be large. Third, SS_W measures the amount of variation within each column or treatment. If there is little variation among the observations making up a group, SS_W is small. When there is great variability, SS_W is large.

It can be shown that $SS_T = SS_B + SS_W$ and that each of these sums of squares, when divided by the *appropriate number of degrees of freedom*, generates a mean square, which is essentially an unbiased estimate of the population variance.[1] Further, if the null hypothesis of no difference among population means is true, they are all estimates of the same variance and should not differ more than would be expected because of chance. If the variance between groups is significantly greater than the variance within groups, the hypothesis of equality of population means will be rejected.

In other words, we can view the variance within groups as a measure of the amount of variation in sales of containers that may be expected on the basis of chance. It is the *error variance* or *chance variance*. The between group variance reflects error variance *plus* any group-to-group differences occasioned by differences in popularity of the two containers. Therefore, if it is found to be significantly larger than the within group variance, this difference may be attributed to group-to-group variation, and the hypothesis of equality of means is discredited.

But what are these degrees of freedom? The total number of degrees of freedom is equal to $n - 1$, since there is only a single constraint $\bar{x}_{..}$ in the computation of SS_T. For the within group sum of squares, there are n observations and k constraints, one constraint for each treatment mean. Hence, the degrees of freedom for the within group sum of squares equals $n - k$. There are k values, one corresponding to each treatment mean, in the calculation of SS_B, and there is one constraint imposed by $\bar{x}_{..}$; hence the degrees of freedom for the between group sum of squares is $k - 1$.

The separate estimates of the population variance or the associated mean squares are

$$MS_T = \frac{SS_T}{df_T} = \frac{SS_T}{n - 1},$$

$$MS_B = \frac{SS_B}{df_B} = \frac{SS_B}{k - 1},$$

$$MS_W = \frac{SS_W}{df_W} = \frac{SS_W}{n - k}.$$

The mean squares computed from the sample data are estimates of the true mean squares. The true mean squares are in turn given by the expected values of the corresponding sample mean squares. Given that the samples are independent, the population variances are equal, and the variable is normally distributed in the parent population, it can be shown that these expected values are

$$E(MS_W) = \sigma^2 = \text{Error variance or chance variance,}$$

and

$$E(MS_B) = \sigma^2 + \text{Treatment effect.}$$

---

[1]See Geoffrey Keppel, *Design and Analysis: A Researcher's Handbook,* 2nd ed. (Englewood Cliffs, N.J.: Prentice Hall, 1982), pp. 24–64, for the derivation.

The ratio $E(MS_B)/E(MS_W)$ will equal 1 if there is no treatment effect. It will be greater than 1 if there is a difference in the sample means. Since the two expected values are not known, the sample mean squares are used instead to yield the ratio

$$\frac{MS_B}{MS_W} = F,$$

which follows the F distribution. Unlike the t or χ^2 distributions, the F distribution depends on two degrees of freedom, one corresponding to the mean square in the numerator and one corresponding to the mean square in the denominator. Since MS_B and MS_W are only sample estimates of the true variances, one should not expect the ratio MS_B/MS_W to be exactly 1 when the treatment effect is zero, and one should not immediately conclude that there is a difference among the group means when the ratio is greater than 1. Rather, given a significance level and the respective degrees of freedom for the numerator and denominator, a critical value of F may be read from standard tables. The critical value indicates the magnitude of the ratio that can occur because of random sampling fluctuations, even when there is no difference in the group means; that is, $E(MS_B)/E(MS_W) = 1$. The entire analysis is conveniently handled in an analysis of variance table.

Table 14A.1 is the analysis-of-variance table for the plastic and metal container sales data. The calculated F value is referred to an F table for 1 and 18 degrees of freedom (see Table 4 in the appendix at the end of the book). Using the same α as before, $\alpha = 0.05$, critical F is found to be 4.41, and again the sample evidence is not sufficient to reject the hypothesis of the equality of the two means. This should not be surprising, since it can be shown that when the comparison is between two means (the degrees of freedom in the numerator of the F ratio are then $v_1 = k - 1 = 1$), $F = t^2 = (1.56)^2 = 2.43.$[2] Both tests are identical in this special case, and if one test does not indicate a significant difference between the two means, neither will the other.

The plastic and metal container sales example is the simplest type of what is known as a **completely randomized design,** since there were only two treatments. The distinguishing feature of the completely randomized design is that experimental treatments are assigned to the stores on a random basis. In this case, the container types were assigned to the stores at random. There was no attempt to match stores or make the test units equal in any way.

An alternative statement of the hypothesis of equality of means can be generated from the model of a completely randomized design. The model statement has the added advantage of facilitating discussion when more complex models are introduced. The model for a completely randomized design is

$$X_{ij} = \mu + \tau_j + \epsilon_{ij}.$$

This means an observation, X_{ij}, is conceived of as being made up of three components: the overall mean μ; the effect of the jth treatment, τ_j; and the random error associated

---

[2]It can be shown mathematically that if a random variable is t distributed with v degrees of freedom, then t^2 is F distributed with $v_1 = 1$, $v_2 = v$ degrees of freedom; that is, if $t \sim t_v$, then $t^2 \sim F_{1,v}$.

Table 14A.1
Analysis of Variance of Sales of Plastic versus Metal Containers

Source of Variation	Sum of Squares	Degrees of Freedom	Mean Square	*F* Ratio
Between group	806.5	1	806.5	2.43
Within group	5,978.1	18	332.1	
Total	6,784.6	19		

with the ith observation on the jth treatment, ϵ_{ij}. The null hypothesis of equality of population means is equivalent to the hypothesis that the treatment effects are all zero, since $\mu_1 = \mu_2$ implies that $\tau_1 = \mu_1 - \mu_2 = 0$. The alternate hypothesis, when there are k treatments, is that at least one of the treatment effects is not zero; this is equivalent to the statement that at least one mean differs from the others. The symbolic statement of the hypotheses is[3]

$$H_0: \tau_j = 0 \quad \text{for all } j = 1, \ldots, k,$$

$$H_a: \tau_j \neq 0 \quad \text{for at least one } j \text{ where } j = 1, \ldots, k.$$

The assumptions underlying the model and the test are that the samples are independent, the variable is normally distributed, and the variance is the same for each treatment. The last assumption is necessary to justify the pooling of variances and, in this respect, is similar to the t test for two means.

Randomized Blocks

The reader can readily appreciate the difficulty that can arise in the above situation if, by chance, the stores selected to handle one type of container were, say, systematically larger than the stores chosen to distribute the other type. If a significant difference had been observed, it could have been due to the fact that the plastic container was sold in the large stores, which have greater sales potential because they have more traffic.

When, in fact, there is one source of extraneous variation distorting the results of an experiment, a **randomized-block design** can be employed. This design involves the grouping of "similar" test units into blocks and the random assignment of treatments to test units in each block. Similarity is determined by matching the test units on the expected extraneous source of variation (for example, store size in the container example). The hope is that the units within each block will be more alike than will units selected completely at random. Since the differences between blocks can be taken into account in the variance analysis, for the same number of observations the error mean

---

[3]For an insightful discussion of how one should set up hypotheses for analysis of variance, see Richard K. Burdick, "Statement of Hypotheses in the Analysis of Variance," *Journal of Marketing Research,* 20 (August 1983), pp. 320–324.

Table 14A.2

Sales Generated by Various Call Plans in Thousands of Dollars

	Plan				Plan		
Block	A	B	C	Block	A	B	C
1	42	51	43	6	29	35	30
2	36	35	36	7	52	50	54
3	40	52	44	8	46	49	44
4	38	47	42	9	40	44	40
5	32	38	36	10	38	36	35

square should be smaller than it would be if a completely randomized design had been used. The test should therefore be more efficient.

Consider, for example, an investigation of the effectiveness of alternative sales representatives' call frequency plans made by a manufacturer that sells primarily to industrial distributors. Suppose there are three plans: A, B, and C. The plans differ in the frequency with which the various sized accounts are called on, and the manufacturer is interested in determining which of the three would produce the most sales. The firm employs some 500 sales representatives. Rather than choose one of the schemes arbitrarily, it believed that it would be worthwhile to employ each on a trial basis before making a decision. The firm selected a sample of 30 sales representatives who were to try the new call plans. The company was concerned that differences in sales ability might affect the results of the test. Consequently, it decided to match the sales representatives in terms of their ability, employing their past sales as the matching criterion. The company thus formed ten blocks of three relatively equal sales representatives within a block, resulting in a randomized-block design.

Suppose the sales that resulted were as given in Table 14A.2. Now the model that underlies the randomized-block experiment is given by[4]

$$X_{ij} = \mu + \tau_j + \beta_i + \epsilon_{ij},$$

where

X_{ij} is the ith observation (ith block) on the jth treatment;

μ is the overall mean;

τ_j is the effect attributable to the jth treatment or call plan, $j = 1, 2, \ldots, k$;

β_i is the effect attributable to the ith block, $i = 1, 2, \ldots, r$;

ϵ_{ij} is the random error associated with the ith observation on the jth treatment.

---

[4]The example is an illustration of a mixed model. The treatments are fixed; only the three call plans being investigated are of interest. The test units are a random sample from the population of sales representatives, and thus a random-effects model would apply. The combination of fixed treatments and the random sample of test units creates the conditions for a mixed model.

The assumptions are that a random sample of Size 1 is drawn from each of the kr (k treatments times r blocks) populations; X is normally distributed in each of the kr populations; the variance of each is the same; and the block and treatment effects are additive. Except for the last assumption, these are the same assumptions that were made in the completely randomized design. But now there are kr populations, whereas there were k populations with the completely randomized design.

Let $j = 1$ be Call Plan A, $j = 2$ Call Plan B, and $j = 3$ Call Plan C. The average sales under each call plan are

$$\bar{x}_{.1} = \frac{\sum\limits_{i=1}^{r} X_{i1}}{r} = \frac{42 + 36 + \cdots + 38}{10} = 39.3,$$

$$\bar{x}_{.2} = \frac{\sum\limits_{i=1}^{r} X_{i2}}{r} = \frac{51 + 35 + \cdots + 36}{10} = 43.7,$$

$$\bar{x}_{.3} = \frac{\sum\limits_{i=1}^{r} X_{i3}}{r} = \frac{43 + 36 + \cdots + 35}{10} = 40.4,$$

while the overall mean is

$$\bar{x}_{..} = \sum_{j=1}^{k} \sum_{i=1}^{r} \frac{X_{ij}}{n}$$

$$= \frac{(42 + \cdots + 38) + (51 + \cdots + 36) + (43 + \cdots + 35)}{30} = 41.1$$

In addition to the total, treatment, and error sum of squares, the sum of squares corresponding to blocks must now be computed. The block means are helpful in determining this sum of squares. They are given by the formula

$$\bar{x}_{i.} = \frac{\sum\limits_{j=1}^{k} X_{ij}}{k},$$

where $\bar{x}_{i.}$ refers to the mean of the ith block. Thus for the first block, $i = 1$,

$$\bar{x}_{1.} = \frac{\sum\limits_{j=1}^{k} X_{1j}}{k} = \frac{(42 + 51 + 43)}{3} = 45.3.$$

The remaining block means, which are calculated similarly, are

$$\bar{x}_{2.} = 35.7 \qquad \bar{x}_{5.} = 35.3 \qquad \bar{x}_{8.} = 46.3$$

$$\bar{x}_{3.} = 45.3 \qquad \bar{x}_{6.} = 31.3 \qquad \bar{x}_{9.} = 41.3$$

$$\bar{x}_{4.} = 42.3 \qquad \bar{x}_{7.} = 52.0 \qquad \bar{x}_{10.} = 36.3.$$

The sums of squares are

$$SS_T = \sum_{j=1}^{k} \sum_{i=1}^{r} (X_{ij} - \bar{x}_{..})^2$$

$$= (42 - 41.1)^2 + (36 - 41.1)^2 + \cdots + (35 - 41.1)^2 = 1{,}333.5.$$

$$SS_{TR} = \sum_{j=1}^{k} r(\bar{x}_{.j} - \bar{x}_{..})^2$$

$$= 10 (39.3 - 41.1)^2 + 10(43.7 - 41.1)^2 + 10(40.4 - 41.1)^2$$

$$= 104.9.$$

$$SS_B = \sum_{i=1}^{r} k(\bar{x}_{i.} - \bar{x}_{..})^2$$

$$= 3(45.3 - 41.1)^2 + 3(35.7 - 41.1)^2 + \cdots + 3(36.3 - 41.1)^2$$

$$= 1{,}093.5.$$

$$SS_E = SS_T - SS_{TR} - SS_B = 1{,}333.5 - 104.9 - 1{,}093.5 = 135.1.$$

As mentioned, the model underlying the randomized-block design suggests that any sample response can be written as the sum of four additive factors: the overall mean, the effect of the jth treatment, effect of the ith block, and the error term. It may happen that the effect of an individual treatment will vary according to the type of test unit to which it is applied; for example, Call Plan A works best for the better sales representatives, while Call Plan B works better for the average sales representatives. Interaction between the treatment and the blocks is said to be present when this condition occurs, and the additive model is no longer applicable. The reasonableness of the additivity assumption can be checked with Tukey's test for nonadditivity.[5] If the additivity assumption is rejected, the interpretation of the results becomes difficult, since it is then hard to say which call plan is best.

The additivity assumption is not rejected in the sample at hand. Table 14A.3 is the analysis-of-variance table for the applicable linear model. There are now two F ratios of interest—one corresponding to blocks and one corresponding to treatments. Calculated F for the treatment mean square is 6.98; critical F for $\alpha = 0.05$ and $v_1 = 2$ and $v_2 = 18$ is 3.55. Calculated F exceeds critical F, and the null hypothesis of equal means is rejected. There is a difference in the effectiveness of at least one of the call plans. Call Plan B, in particular, produces significantly better sales.[6]

Calculated F for the block effect is 16.18. Critical F for $\alpha = 0.05$ and $v_1 = 9$ and $v_2 = 18$ is 2.46. Since calculated F exceeds critical F, the block variation is statistically significant. This means that the grouping of sales representatives according to ability

---

[5]See Keppel, *Design and Analysis*, pp. 155–156, for a discussion and calculation formulas for Tukey's test of nonadditivity.

[6]If the null hypothesis of equality of means is rejected, then it is reasonable to look for the means or other possible linear contrasts that are responsible. For discussion of the tests for determining which means are statistically significantly different, see *Ibid.*, pp. 144–156.

Table 14A.3
Analysis of Variance of Randomized-Block Design Investigating Sales Call Plans

Source of Variation	Sum of Squares	Degrees of Freedom	Mean Square	F Ratio
Blocks	1,093.5	$(r - 1) = 9$	121.50	16.18
Treatments	104.9	$(k - 1) = 2$	52.45	6.98
Error	135.1	$(r - 1)(k - 1) = 18$	7.51	
Total	1,333.5	$rk - 1 = 29$		

before assigning the call plans has eliminated a source of variation in the results. The blocking was indeed worthwhile. The randomized-block design was more efficient than a completely randomized design would have been.

Latin Square

The **Latin-square design** is appropriate when there are two extraneous factors that can cause serious distortion in the results. Suppose in the previous example that we wanted to conduct the investigation not only with sales representatives of different ability but also among sales representatives having different sized territories. Suppose, in fact, we had divided the sales representatives into three classes on the basis of ability—outstanding, good, and average—and the territories into the three classes—large, average, and small. There are thus nine different conditions with which to cope. One way of proceeding would be to use randomized blocks and test each of the three call plans under each of the nine conditions. This would require a sample of 27 sales representatives. An alternative approach would be to try each call plan only once with each size territory and each level of ability. This would require a sample of only nine test units or sales representatives. The primary gain in this case would be administrative control. In other cases, there may be cost advantages associated with the use of fewer test units. The interesting point is that if differences in territory size do indeed have an effect, the Latin-square design with nine test units could be as efficient as the randomized-block design with many more test units.

The Latin-square design requires that the number of categories for each of the extraneous variables we wish to control be equal to the number of treatments. With three call plans to investigate, it was no accident that we divided the sales representatives into three ability levels and the territories into three size categories. The Latin-square design also requires that the treatments be randomly assigned to the resulting categories. This is typically accomplished by selecting one of the published squares at random and then randomizing the rows, columns, and treatments using this square.[7]

---

[7]See R. A. Fisher and F. Yates, *Statistical Tables* (Edinburgh: Oliver and Boyd, 1948) for Latin squares from 4 × 4 to 12 × 12.

As an example of the analysis of a Latin square, consider the supermarket chain interested in the effect of an in-store promotion on sales of their private label cola. Suppose that the three promotional plans being considered were

■   A—no promotion

■   B—free samples with demonstrator

■   C—special end display

and the company decided to run a controlled experiment to test the effectiveness of the choices. The company was concerned that the timing of the experiment could affect the results because of changes in weather and that the size of the store might also influence the outcome. Since there are two potentially serious distorting factors, a Latin-square design is appropriate. Further, since there are three treatments, there also must be three categories for each extraneous variable. Let the stores therefore be divided into three size classes: 1, 2, and 3; and suppose one had been selected at random from each class. Let the time for the experiment also be broken into three segments, and suppose randomization of rows, columns, and treatments yielded the 3×3 design reported in Table 14A.4.

The underlying model for a Latin-square design is

$$X_{ijk} = \mu + \alpha_i + \beta_j + \tau_k + \epsilon_{ijk},$$

where

X_{ijk} is the result when the kth treatment is applied to cell ij;

μ is the overall mean;

α is the effect attributable to the ith block, say, time period, $i = 1, 2, \ldots, r$;

β_j is the effect attributable to the jth block, say, store size, $j = 1, 2, \ldots, r$;

τ_k is the effect attributable to the kth treatment (promotional plan), $k = 1, \ldots, r$;

ϵ_{ijk} is the random error associated with the ijk observation.

We have already remarked that the number of categories for each of the extraneous variables must equal the number of treatments in a Latin-square experiment. Thus, the ranges of i, j, and k are all the same, 1 to r in the general case and 1 to 3 in the example at hand. There are now r^2 populations—r populations for each blocking factor or $r \times r$ populations in all. The assumptions of the Latin-square experiment are that a random sample of Size 1 is drawn from each of the r^2 populations; X is normally distributed in each of the r^2 populations; the variance of each of the r^2 populations is the same; and the row, column, and treatment effects are additive. These are the same assumptions made in the randomized-block design, with two minor modifications: (1) There are r^2 populations, whereas there are rk populations in the randomized-block design; (2) There is an additional additive effect, that due to the second blocking factor.

The null hypothesis in a Latin-square experiment is that the means are equal or that sales are the same under the three treatments. This is equivalent to testing the hypothesis

$$H_0: \tau_k = 0 \text{ for } k = 1, 2, 3,$$

$$H_a: \text{not all the } \tau_k \text{ are zero.}$$

Table 14A.4

**Latin-Square Design and Results for Experiment
on Effect of Promotion on Cola Sales**

Time Period	Design Store: 1 2 3	Sales Store: 1 2 3
1	B C A	69 63 72
2	C A B	63 63 72
3	A B C	48 66 51

Time Period (rows) **Mean Sales**

1
$$\bar{x}_{1..} = \sum_{j,k=1}^{3} \frac{X_{1jk}}{3} = \frac{69 + 63 + 72}{3} = 68.0$$

2
$$\bar{x}_{2..} = \sum_{j,k=1}^{3} \frac{X_{2jk}}{3} = \frac{63 + 63 + 72}{3} = 66.0$$

3
$$\bar{x}_{3..} = \sum_{j,k=1}^{3} \frac{X_{3jk}}{3} = \frac{48 + 66 + 51}{3} = 55.0$$

Store (columns)

1
$$\bar{x}_{.1.} = \sum_{i,k=1}^{3} \frac{X_{i1k}}{3} = \frac{69 + 63 + 48}{3} = 60.0$$

2
$$\bar{x}_{.2.} = \sum_{i,k=1}^{3} \frac{X_{i2k}}{3} = \frac{63 + 63 + 66}{3} = 64.0$$

3
$$\bar{x}_{.3.} = \sum_{i,k=1}^{3} \frac{X_{i3k}}{3} = \frac{72 + 72 + 51}{3} = 65.0$$

Treatment

A
$$\bar{x}_{..1} = \sum_{i,j=1}^{3} \frac{X_{ij1}}{3} = \frac{48 + 63 + 72}{3} = 61.0$$

B
$$\bar{x}_{..2} = \sum_{i,j=1}^{3} \frac{X_{ij2}}{3} = \frac{69 + 72 + 66}{3} = 69.0$$

C
$$\bar{x}_{..3} = \sum_{i,j=1}^{3} \frac{X_{ij3}}{3} = \frac{63 + 63 + 51}{3} = 59.0$$

Overall
$$\bar{x}_{...} = \sum_{i,j,k=1}^{3} \frac{X_{ijk}}{9} = \frac{(69 + 63 + \ldots + 51)}{9} = 63.0$$

Suppose the sales reported in Table 14A.4 resulted from the experiment. The overall mean and the mean sales for each time period, store, and treatment must be determined so that the sums of the squares can be calculated. These means are presented in the lower portion of Table 14A.4, where it is understood that i, j, k are summed over the proper values. The various sums of squares are

$$SS_T = \sum_{i=1}^{r} \sum_{j=1}^{r} (X_{ijk} - \bar{x}_{...})^2$$

$$= (69 - 63)^2 + (63 - 63)^2 + \cdots + (51 - 63)^2 = 576.$$

$$SS_R = r \sum_{i=1}^{r} (\bar{x}_{i..} - \bar{x}_{...})^2$$

$$= 3 [(68 - 63)^2 + (66 - 63)^2 + (55 - 63)^2] = 294.$$

$$SS_C = r \sum_{j=1}^{r} (\bar{x}_{.j.} - \bar{x}_{...})^2$$

$$= 3 [(60 - 63)^2 + (64 - 63)^2 + (65 - 63)^2] = 42.$$

$$SS_{TR} = r \sum_{k=1}^{r} (\bar{x}_{..k} - \bar{x}_{...})^2$$

$$= 3 [(61 - 63)^2 + (69 - 63)^2 + (59 - 63)^2] = 168.$$

$$SS_E = SS_T - SS_R - SS_C - SS_{TR}$$

$$= 576 - 294 - 42 - 168 = 72.$$

Table 14A.5 contains the resulting mean squares and F ratios. Assuming $\alpha = 0.05$, critical F for $v_1 = 2$ and $v_2 = 2$ is 19.0. None of the calculated F ratios is statistically significant. The hypothesis of equal means is not rejected. The sample evidence does not indicate that the promotions significantly affected sales nor that stores or time periods significantly affected the results.

Factorial Designs

So far we have considered designs that involve only one experimental variable, although it may have had multiple levels (for example, three different call plans). It is often desirable to investigate the effects of two or more factors in the same experiment. For instance, it might be desirable to investigate the sales impact of the shape as well as the construction material of containers for floor wax. Suppose that in addition to packaging a new floor wax in metal or plastic containers, two shapes, A and B, were being considered for the containers. Package shape and package type would both be called factors. There would be two different levels of each factor, four different treatments in all since they can be used in combination, and a factorial design would be used. A **factorial design** is one in which the effects of two or more independent treatment variables are considered simultaneously.

There are three very good reasons why one might want to use a factorial design.[8] First, it allows the interaction of the factors to be studied. The plastic container might sell better in Shape A, while the metal container sells better in Shape B. This type of effect can only be investigated if the factors are considered simultaneously. Second, a factorial design allows a saving of time and effort, since all the observations are employed to study the effects of each of the factors. Suppose separate experiments were

---

[8]The following argument is basically that of William C. Guenther, *Analysis of Variance* (Englewood Cliffs, N.J.: Prentice-Hall, 1964), pp. 99–100.

Table 14A.5
Analysis of Variance Table for Latin-Square Experiment
on Effect of Promotion of Cola Sales

Source of Variation	Sum of Squares	Degrees of Freedom	Mean Square	F Ratio
Rows (time periods)	294	$r - 1 = 2$	147	4.083
Columns (stores)	42	$r - 1 = 2$	21	0.583
Treatments	168	$r - 1 = 2$	84	2.333
Error	72	$(r - 1)(r - 2) = 2$	36	
Total	576	$r^2 - 1 = 8$		

conducted, one to study the effect of container type and another to study the effect of container shape. Then some of the observations would yield information about type and some about shape. By combining the two factors in one experiment, all the observations bear on both factors. "Hence one two-factor experiment is more economical than two one-factor experiments."[9] Third, the conclusions reached have broader application, since each factor is studied with varying combinations of the other factors.[10] This result is much more useful than it would be if everything else had been held constant.

The factorial design may be used with any of the single-factor designs previously discussed—completely randomized, randomized block, and Latin square. The underlying model changes, as does the analysis of variance table, but the principle remains the same. Consequently, let us illustrate the method with the simplest case, a completely randomized design.

Consider again the sales representatives' call plan example. Suppose that the company was thinking of revising both the method and frequency of customer contact by supplementing sales representatives' personal contacts with office telephone contacts. Two phone contact plans, which differed in the frequency with which customers were contacted, were being considered. Call the telephone contact Plan A and the personal contact Plan B, and consider the 2 × 3 factorial experiment where each of the two levels of A occurs with each of the three levels of B to yield six treatments. Suppose that the treatments were randomly assigned to each of five sales representatives. Thus, there would be five replications for each treatment.

Telephone Call Plan	Personal Call Plan		
	B_1	B_2	B_3
A_1	A_1B_1	A_1B_2	A_1B_3
A_2	A_2B_1	A_2B_2	A_2B_3

---

[9]Guenther, *Analysis of Variance*, p. 100. For an example of the insight that can be gained from a factorial experiment, see J. B. Wilkinson, J. Barry Mason, and Christie H. Paksoy, "Assessing the Impact of Short-Term Supermarket Strategy Variables," *Journal of Marketing Research,* 19 (February 1982), pp. 72–86.

[10]One can often use select combinations of factor levels rather than every possible combination, which greatly simplifies the experiment. See Charles W. Holland and David W. Cravens, "Fractional Factorial Experimental Designs in Marketing Research," *Journal of Marketing Research,* 10 (August 1973), pp. 270–276.

Suppose the results were as contained in Table 14A.6. Let

α_i be the effect of the ith level of the A factor (telephone call plan), $i = 1, \ldots, a$;

β_j be the effect of the jth level of the B factor (personal call plan), $j = 1, \ldots, b$;

$(\alpha\beta)_{ij}$ be the effect of the ith level of the A factor and jth level of the B factor;

X_{ijk} be the kth observation on the ith level of the A factor and the jth level of the B factor;

μ be the grand mean; and

ϵ_{ijk} be the error associated with the kth observation on the ith level of A and jth level of B.

The underlying model for this completely randomized design suggests that any observation X_{ijk} can be written as the sum of the grand mean, treatment effects, and an error term; that is,

$$X_{ijk} = \mu + \alpha_i + \beta_j + (\alpha\beta)_{ij} + \epsilon_{ijk}.$$

The assumptions are the same as for a completely randomized design except there are now $r = ab$ populations, whereas in the completely randomized design there were k populations—one for each treatment. Otherwise, though, it is still assumed that the distribution of the variable in each of the populations is normal and that the populations have the same variance.

There are three main hypotheses, all of which essentially state that the treatment effects are zero (the cell means are equal). The alternate hypotheses are that at least some of the cell means differ. The hypotheses can be written:

$$H_0^{(1)}: \alpha_i = 0 \quad i = 1, \ldots, a,$$

$$H_a^{(1)}: \text{not all } \alpha_i \text{ are zero.}$$

$$H_0^{(2)}: \beta_j = 0 \quad j = 1, \ldots, b,$$

$$H_a^{(2)}: \text{not all } \beta_j \text{ are zero.}$$

$$H_0^{(3)}: (\alpha\beta)_{ij} = 0 \quad i = 1, \ldots, a \quad j = 1, \ldots, b,$$

$$H_a^{(3)}: \text{not all } (\alpha\beta)_{ij} \text{ are zero.}$$

The first two hypotheses state that there are no differences due, respectively, to the levels of the A and B factors, while the third says that the effects due to Factors A and B are additive. To test these hypotheses, the following sums of squares are needed ($n = 5$ replications):

$$SS_T = \sum_{i=1}^{a} \sum_{j=1}^{b} \sum_{k=1}^{n} (X_{ijk} - \bar{x}_{...})^2$$

$$= (42 - 41.1)^2 + (40 - 41.1)^2 + \cdots + (35 - 41.1)^2 = 1{,}333.5.$$

Table 14A.6

Sales Generated by Various Personal and Telephone Call Plans

Telephone Call Plan	Personal Call Plan			Total	Mean
	B_1	B_2	B_3		
A_1	42	51	43	691	46.1
	40	52	44		
	52	50	54		
	46	49	44		
	40	44	40		
A_2	36	35	36	543	36.2
	38	47	42		
	32	38	36		
	29	35	30		
	38	36	35		
Total	393	437	404	1,234	41.1
Mean	39.3	43.7	40.4		

Cell	A_1B_1	A_1B_2	A_1B_3	A_2B_1	A_2B_2	A_2B_3
Total	220	246	225	173	191	179
Mean	44.0	49.2	45.0	34.6	38.2	35.8

$$SS_{TR} = n \sum_{i=1}^{a} \sum_{j=1}^{b} (\bar{x}_{ij.} - \bar{x}_{...})^2$$

$$= 5\,[(44.0 - 41.1)^2 + (49.2 - 41.1)^2 + (45.0 - 41.1)^2$$

$$+ (34.6 - 41.1)^2 + (38.2 - 41.1)^2 + (35.8 - 41.1)^2] = 839.9.$$

$$SS_A = bn \sum_{i=1}^{a} (\bar{x}_{i..} - \bar{x}_{...})^2$$

$$= 3\,(5)\,[(46.1 - 41.1)^2 + (36.2 - 41.1)^2] = 735.1.$$

$$SS_B = an \sum_{j=1}^{b} (\bar{x}_{.j.} - \bar{x}_{...})^2$$

$$= 2\,(5)\,[(39.3 - 41.1)^2 + (43.7 - 41.1)^2 + (40.4 - 41.1)^2]$$

$$= 104.8.$$

$$SS_{AB} = SS_{TR} - SS_A - SS_B$$

$$= 839.9 - 735.1 - 104.8 = 0.0.$$

$$SS_E = SS_T - SS_{TR}$$

$$= 1.333.5 - 839.9 = 493.6.$$

Table 14A.7

Analysis-of-Variance Table for 2 × 3 Factorial Experiment of Telephone and Personal Call Plans

Source of Variation	Sum of Squares	Degrees of Freedom	Mean Square	F Ratio
A (telephone)	735.1	$(a - 1) = 1$	735.1	35.86
B (personal)	104.8	$(b - 1) = 2$	52.4	2.56
AB (interaction)	0.0	$(a - 1)(b - 1) = 2$	0.0	0.00
Error	493.6	$ab(n - 1) = 24$	20.5	
Total	1,333.5	$abn - 1 = 29$		

Table 14A.7 contains the various mean squares and F ratios. Consider the interaction term first. Calculated F is zero. Critical F for $\alpha = 0.05$ and $v_1 = 2$, $v_2 = 24$ is 3.40. Calculated F is less than critical F, and the null hypothesis is not rejected. The effects are additive. The effectiveness of the telephone call plan is not dependent on the personal sales call plan and vice versa. Consider next the effectiveness of the sales representative personal call plan. Calculated F is again less than critical F, and the null hypothesis of equality of means is not rejected. The data do not indicate that there is any difference in the effectiveness of the three personal call plans. Consider finally the telephone call plan. Calculated F is 35.86. Critical F for $v_1 = 1$, $v_2 = 24$ and $\alpha = 0.05$ is 4.26. Since calculated F exceeds critical F, the null hypothesis is rejected. There is a difference in effectiveness of the two telephone call plans. An examination of the cell means in Table 14A.6 indicates telephone call Plan A_1 is much better than Plan A_2. If the company were to make a change, this would be the plan they would adopt.

Suppose the interaction term had tested significantly. We would not have bothered to check for the significance of the A and B factors by themselves. Rather, we would have looked for the best combination of a telephone call plan with a personal call plan, because a significant interaction term would have indicated that the effects were not additive; a significant interaction term would have implied that the effects of A were different for some levels of B or vice versa.

Questions

1. What is the basic idea underlying the analysis-of-variance procedure? In general, how are these sources of variation computed? What is the basic statistic used to test for the differences among means in analysis of variance?

2. When is a randomized-block design preferred to a completely randomized design? How does the underlying model change? How do the calculations change?

3. When is a Latin square the preferred experimental design? What is its basic nature? What is the underlying model for a Latin-square design? What is the basic test procedure?

4. When is a factorial design appropriate? What is the basic model of a completely randomized factorial design? What sums of squares are calculated? What are the basic comparisons among the various mean squares?

Applications and Problems

1. Mr. Z, the advertising manager of a medium-sized manufacturer of rug and room deodorizers, has developed three preliminary advertising campaigns for the company's line of deodorizers. The three campaigns are tested in an independent sample of 24 cities across the United States and the sales in each city are monitored. (Note: (1) cities are randomly assigned to each treatment or campaign, and (2) the 24 cities are comparable in terms of various socioeconomic and demographic variables.) The results of this test market are shown below.

Sales (in thousands of dollars)

City	Advertising Campaign 1	City	Advertising Campaign 2	City	Advertising Campaign 3
1	10	9	9	17	12
2	6	10	7	18	10
3	8	11	6	19	8
4	12	12	10	20	13
5	6	13	6	21	11
6	8	14	4	22	10
7	9	15	5	23	9
8	7	16	5	24	7

Mr. Z wants to determine if there is a difference in sales as a result of the three advertising campaigns. Mr. Z requires your assistance in analyzing the above information.

(a) State the null and alternate hypotheses.
(b) What statistical test is appropriate in this situation? Identify the assumptions underlying the test of the above hypotheses.
(c) Compute the grand mean and the mean of the jth treatment ($j = 1, 2, 3$). Show your calculations.
(d) Compute the total variation (the sum of squares total). Show your calculations.
(e) Compute the between-group variation (sum of squares between groups). Show your calculations.
(f) Compute the within group variation (sum of squares within groups). Show your calculations.
(g) What are the degrees of freedom associated with each of these sums of squares?
(h) Compute the mean squares associated with each of the above sums of squares. Show your calculations.
(i) Complete the following analysis of variance table.

Source of Variation	Sum of Squares	Degrees of Freedom	Mean Square	F Ratio
Between-group				
Within-group				
Total				

(j) Discuss your findings on the basis of the above calculations. (Note: Assume α = .05 to find the critical *F* value.)

Appendix 14B
Analysis of Catalog Buying Data

Differences in Means

One question of major interest in the catalog buying study is the amount of confidence people have when purchasing products from a catalog. The CATCON "catalog confidence" index was formed to address this question. The CATCON index is the summed score for the responses to Questions 4a through 4e.

Table 14B.1 investigates whether the CATCON index depends on the person's sex. The table indicates the mean score for males is higher than that for females. The difference is also statistically significant indicating that males are more confident when buying from catalogs than females. Note that the variance in CATCON scores is the same for males and females, suggesting it is better to use the pooled sample variance when checking the statistical significance of the difference in the two means.

Paired Difference Test

To investigate whether there was a difference in confidence when purchasing sporting goods from retail stores rather than from catalogs, a second index was formed to go along with the CATCON index described above. Called RETCON for "retail store confidence," this index was formed by summing the numerical responses to Questions 5a through 5e. Note that each of these questions involving retail stores has an exact parallel for purchases made through a catalog. Thus, it makes sense to look at the difference in the two summed scores for each person, a comparison contained in Table 14B.2. The comparison indicates that there is indeed a statistically significant difference in the two summed scores. Subjects are more confident when buying sporting goods from retailers versus catalogs, at least with respect to the five items contained in the questionnaire.

Analysis of Variance

Table 14B.3 contains the analysis investigating whether the CATCON index varies as a function of the number of sporting goods items purchased in the past year. The analysis of variance portion of the table (the top portion) indicates the differences among the cell means are statistically significant; there is less than 1 chance in 1,000 that the difference in mean squares would have been as large as they were under the null hypothesis of no differences in the CATCON index as a function of the number of sporting good items purchased in the past year. The cell means in the lower portion of the table (the cell means are expressed as deviations from the grand mean) suggest that as the number of items purchased goes up, so does the CATCON index.

Table 14B.1
Difference in Means for CATCON Index Between Males and Females

					Pooled Variance Estimate			Separate Variance Estimate		
Variable/Group	Number of Cases	Mean	Standard Deviation	Standard Error	t Value	Degrees of Freedom	2-Tail Probability	t Value	Degrees of Freedom	2-Tail Probability
CATCON										
1. Males	65	21.462	2.001	.248	33.87	121	.000	33.87	119.42	.000
2. Females	58	9.224	2.000	.263						

Table 14B.2
Paired Difference Test for the CATCON and RETCON Indices

Variable/Group	Number of Cases	Mean	Standard Deviation	Standard Error	(Difference) Mean	Standard Deviation	Standard Error	t Value	Degrees of Freedom	2-Tail Probability
CATCON	124	15.605	6.494	.583	-3.790	8.402	.755	-5.02	123	.000
RETCON		19.395	3.154	.283						

Table 14B.3

Analysis of Variance of CATCON Index as a Function of Number of Sporting Good Items (V15) Purchased in this Past Year

Source of Variation	Sum of Squares	DF	Mean Square	F	Significance of F
Main effects (V15)	4320.278	4	1080.069	148.184	.000
Explained	4320.278	4	1080.069	148.184	.000
Residual	867.358	119	7.289		
Total	5187.635	123	42.176		

124 cases were processed
   0 cases were missing

Grand Mean = 15.60
Variable + Category

V15	N	Unadjusted Deviation	Eta	Adjusted for Independents Deviation	Eta
1	29	−7.85		−7.85	
2	27	−4.35		−4.35	
3	18	1.84		1.84	
4	15	5.26		5.26	
5	35	6.65		6.65	
			.91		.91

Multiple R squared   .833
Multiple R .913

Chapter 15
Data Analysis: Investigation of Association

In the discussion of data analysis so far, we have been primarily concerned with testing for the significance of *differences* obtained under various research conditions. It may have been a difference between a sample result and an assumed population condition, or between two or more sample results. Quite often, however, the researcher has the different assignment of determining whether there is any association between two or more variables and, if so, the strength and functional form of the relationship.

Typically, we try to predict the value of one variable (for example, consumption of a specific product by a family) on the basis of one or more other variables (for example, income and number of family members). The variable being predicted is called the dependent or, more aptly, the criterion variable. The variables that form the basis of the prediction are called the independent, or predictor, variables.

Simple Regression and Correlation Analysis

Regression and correlation analysis are terms referring to techniques for studying the relationship between two or more variables. Although the two terms are often used interchangeably, there is a difference in purpose. **Correlation analysis** involves measuring the *closeness* of the relationship between two or more variables; it considers the joint variation of two measures, neither of which is restricted by the experimenter. **Regression** analysis refers to the techniques used to derive an *equation* that relates the criterion variable to one or more predictor variables; it considers the frequency distribution of the criterion variable, when one or more predictor variables are held fixed at various levels.[1] It is perfectly legitimate to measure the closeness of the relationship between variables without deriving an estimating equation. Similarly, one can perform a regression analysis without investigating the closeness of the relationship between the variables. But, since it is common to do both, the body of techniques is usually referred to as either regression or correlation analysis.

---

[1]Although the regression model theoretically applies to fixed levels of the predictor variables (X's), it can also be shown to apply when the X's themselves are random variables, assuming certain conditions are satisfied. See John Neter, William Wasserman, and Michael H. Kutner, *Applied Linear Regression Models* (Homewood, Ill.: Richard D. Irwin, 1983), pp. 83–84; or Thomas H. Wonnacott and Ronald J. Wonnacott, *Regression: A Second Course in Statistics* (New York: John Wiley, 1981), pp. 49–50.

Before introducing simple correlation analysis, a comment on the distinction between correlation and causation is in order. The use of the terms dependent (criterion) and independent (predictor) variables to describe the measures in correlation analysis stems from the mathematical functional relationship between the variates and is in no way related to dependence of one variable on another in a *causal* sense. There is nothing in correlation analysis, or any other mathematical procedure, that can be used to establish causality. All these procedures can do is measure the nature and degree of *association* or *covariation* between variables. Statements of causality must spring from underlying knowledge and theories about the phenomena under investigation. They categorically do *not* spring from the mathematics.[2] Research Realities 15.1, for example, highlights what Lawrence Gibson, former director of marketing research at General Mills, has to say about the important role of theory in directing marketing inquiry.

The subject of regression and correlation analysis is best discussed through example. Consider, therefore, the national manufacturer of a ball point pen, Click, who is interested in investigating the effectiveness of the firm's marketing efforts.[3] The company uses regional wholesalers to distribute Click and supplements their efforts with company sales representatives and spot TV advertising. The company intends to use annual territory sales as its measure of effectiveness. These data and information on the number of sales representatives serving a territory are readily available in company records. The other characteristics to which they desire to relate sales—TV spot advertising and wholesaler efficiency—are more difficult to determine. Obtaining information on TV spot advertising in a territory requires analysis of advertising schedules and a study of area coverage by channel to determine what areas each broadcast could be considered to be reaching. Wholesaler efficiency requires rating the wholesalers on a number of criteria and aggregating the ratings into an overall measure of wholesaler efficiency, where 4 = outstanding, 3 = good, 2 = average, and 1 = poor. Because of the time and expense required to generate these advertising and distribution characteristics, the company has decided to carry out its analysis employing only a sample of sales territories. The data for a simple random sample of 40 territories are contained in Table 15.1.

The effect of each of the marketing mix variables on sales can be investigated in several ways. One very obvious way is simply to plot sales as a function of each of the variables. Figure 15.1 contains these plots, which are called scatter diagrams. Panel A suggests that sales increase as the number of TV spots per month increases. Panel B suggests that sales increase as the number of sales representatives serving the territory increases. Finally, Panel C suggests that there is little relationship between sales in a territory and the efficiency of the wholesaler serving the territory. Panels A and B further suggest that the relationship between sales and each of the predictor variables could be adequately captured with a straight line. One way to generate the relationship between sales and either TV spots or number of sales representatives would be to "eye-

---

[2]See Darrell Huff, *How to Lie with Statistics* (New York: Norton, 1954), pp. 87–99, for a discussion of this point using some rather humorous anecdotes.

[3]Many of the results contained in the discussion were determined by computer and thus may differ slightly from those generated using hand calculations because of the rounding errors associated with the latter method.

Research Realities 15.1
Role of Theory in Directing Marketing Inquiry

If marketing researchers want to acquire true marketing "knowledge" they should devote more time and effort to developing and validating marketing theories, according to Lawrence D. Gibson, director of marketing research, General Mills Inc., Minneapolis.

"There's a funny notion around that theories are vague, ephemeral, and useless, and data are nice, hard, real things. And that somehow knowledge is associated with facts and data. This is nonsense.

"Knowledge is an interrelated set of validated theories and established facts, not just facts. In marketing, we are profoundly ignorant of what we're doing because we're woefully short on theory while we're drowning in data."

Deploring the lack of validated marketing theories and overabundance of marketing "facts," Gibson quoted the scientist R. B. Braithwaite. "The world is not made up of empirical facts with the addition of the laws of nature. What we call the laws of nature are simply theories, the conceptual devices by which we organize our empirical knowledge and predict the future."

And he quoted Albert Einstein: "The grand aim of all science is to cover the maximum number of empirical facts, by logical deduction, into the smallest number of axioms, axioms which represent that remainder which is not comprehended."

In other words, Gibson said, "the axioms and theories are not our knowledge, they are our ignorance. They're part of the problem, we assume away." A theory, he said, is how "scientists choose to organize their knowledge and perceptions of the world. Theories are pretty well laid out, simplistic, general, have predicted usefulness, and fit the facts.

"Theory is basic to what data you choose to collect," he said, "You can't observe all the veins of all the leaves of all the branches of all the trees of all the forests in the world. You've got to choose what facts you choose to observe, and you're going to be guided in some sense by some kind of theory.

"And when you turn around to use the data, you're also going to be guided by theory. It will have a profound effect on what you do."

This shows up in the way researchers go about analyzing different kinds of data. For example, when working with observational data people simply don't realize the weak theoretical ground on which they stand. They wander around the data, happily and merrily, trying to find out what makes sense.

"Perhaps you've seen some fairly typical versions of this. The creative analyst looks at the data and the survey and they don't make sense. 'Make sense' means the findings are congenial to his prior judgment. But the world isn't working the way he thought it was supposed to be working."

"So he cross-tabs by big cities vs. little cities. Still doesn't make sense. But he is very creative, and observes there are more outer-directed people in big cities than in little cities, so he now cross-tabs by inner-directed vs. outer-directed by city size, and—lo and behold—he finds out he was right all along!"

"Now, obviously, as long as you keep analyzing and don't like what you see, and stop analyzing when you do like what you see, the world always will look to you the way it's supposed to look. You'll never learn anything."

Source: "Marketing Research Needs Validated Theories," *Marketing News*, 17 (January 21, 1983), p. 14. Published by the American Marketing Association.

ball" it; that is, one could draw a straight line through the points in the graphs. Such a line would represent the line of "average" relationship. It would indicate the average value of the criterion variable, sales, for given values of either of the predictor variables, TV spots or number of sales representatives. One could then enter the graph with, say, the number of TV spots in a territory and could read off the average level of sales expected in the territory. The difficulty with the graphic approach is that two analysts

Table 15.1

Territory Data for Click Ball Point Pens

Territory	Sales (In Thousands) Y	Advertising (TV Spots Per Month) X_1	Number of Sales Representatives X_2	Wholesaler Efficiency Index X_3
005	260.3	5	3	4
019	286.1	7	5	2
033	279.4	6	3	3
039	410.8	9	4	4
061	438.2	12	6	1
082	315.3	8	3	4
091	565.1	11	7	3
101	570.0	16	8	2
115	426.1	13	4	3
118	315.0	7	3	4
133	403.6	10	6	1
149	220.5	4	4	1
162	343.6	9	4	3
164	644.6	17	8	4
178	520.4	19	7	2
187	329.5	9	3	2
189	426.0	11	6	4
205	343.2	8	3	3
222	450.4	13	5	4
237	421.8	14	5	2
242	245.6	7	4	4
251	503.3	16	6	3
260	375.7	9	5	3
266	265.5	5	3	3
279	620.6	18	6	4
298	450.5	18	5	3
306	270.1	5	3	2
332	368.0	7	6	2
347	556.1	12	7	1
358	570.0	13	6	4
362	318.5	8	4	3
370	260.2	6	3	2
391	667.0	16	8	2
408	618.3	19	8	2
412	525.3	17	7	4
430	332.2	10	4	3
442	393.2	12	5	3
467	283.5	8	3	3
471	376.2	10	5	4
488	481.8	12	5	2

Figure 15.1
Scatter Diagrams of Sales versus Marketing Mix Variables

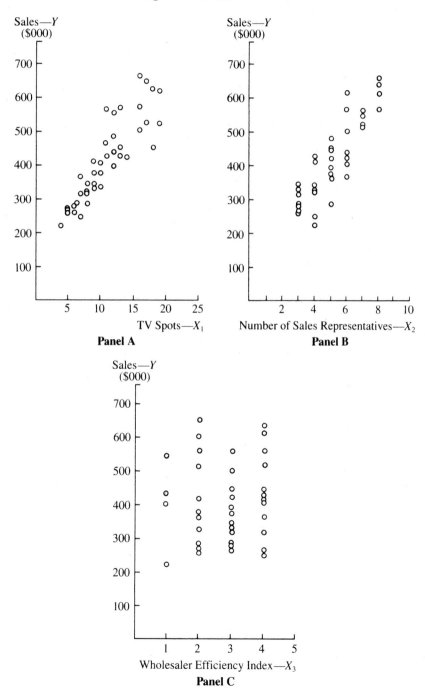

Panel A

Panel B

Panel C

might generate different lines to describe the relationship. This simply raises the question of which line is more correct or fits the data better.

An alternative approach is to mathematically fit a line to the data. The general equation of a straight line is $Y = \alpha + \beta X$, where α is the Y intercept and β is the slope coefficient. In the case of sales Y and TV spots X_1, the equation could be written as $Y = \alpha_1 + \beta_1 X_1$, while for the relationship between sales Y and number of sales representatives X_2, it could be written as $Y = \alpha_2 + \beta_2 X_2$, where the subscripts indicate the predictor variable being considered. As written, each of these models is a *deterministic* model. When a value of the predictor variable is substituted in the equation with specified α and β, a unique value for Y is determined and no allowance is made for error.

When investigating social phenomena, there is rarely, if ever, zero error. Thus in place of the deterministic model, we might substitute a *probabilistic model* and make some assumptions about the error. For example, let us work with the relationship between sales and the number of TV spots and consider the model

$$Y_i = \alpha_1 + \beta_1 X_{i1} + \epsilon_i,$$

where Y_i is the level of sales in the ith territory, X_{i1} is the level of advertising in the ith territory, and ϵ_i is the error associated with the ith observation. This is the form of the model that is used for regression analysis. The error term is part and parcel of the model. It represents a failure to include all factors in the model, the fact that there is an unpredictable element in human behavior, and the condition that there are errors of measurement.[4] The probabilistic model allows for the fact that the Y value is not uniquely determined for a given X_i value. Rather, all that is determined for a given X_i value is the "average value" of Y. Individual values can be expected to fluctuate above and below this average.

The mathematical solution for finding the line of "best fit" for the probabilistic model requires that some assumptions be made about the distribution of the error term. The line of best fit could be defined in a number of ways. The typical way is in terms of the line that minimizes the sum of the deviations squared about the line (the least-squares solution). Consider Figure 15.2 and suppose that the line drawn in the figure is the estimated equation. Employing a caret to indicate an estimated value, the error for the ith observation is the difference between the actual Y value, Y_i, and the estimated Y value, $\hat{Y}_i$; that is, $e_i = Y_i - \hat{Y}_i$. The least-squares solution is based on the principle that the sum of these squared errors should be made as small as possible; that is, $\sum_{i=1}^{n} e_i^2$ should be minimized. The sample estimates $\hat{\alpha}_1$ and $\hat{\beta}_1$ of the true population parameters α_1 and β_1 are determined so that this condition is satisfied.

There are three simplifying assumptions made about the error term in the least-squares solution:

1.   The mean or average value of the disturbance term is zero.

---

[4]Strictly speaking, the regression model requires that errors of measurement be associated only with the criterion variable and that the predictor variables be measured without error. See Wonnacott and Wonnacott, *Regression*, pp. 293–299, for a discussion of the problems and solutions when the predictor variables also have an error component.

Figure 15.2
Relationship between Y and X_1 in the Probabilistic Model

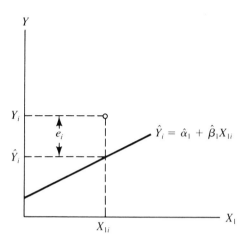

2. The variance of the disturbance term is constant and is independent of the values of the predictor variable.

3. The values of the error term are independent of one another.

Given these assumptions, the sample estimates of the intercept and slope population parameters, α and β in the general case, can be shown to be[5]

$$\hat{\alpha} = \bar{y} - \hat{\beta}\bar{x},$$

$$\hat{\beta} = \frac{n \sum\limits_{i=1}^{n} X_i Y_i - \left(\sum\limits_{i=1}^{n} X_i\right)\left(\sum\limits_{i=1}^{n} Y_i\right)}{n\sum\limits_{i=1}^{n} X_i^2 - \left(\sum\limits_{i=1}^{n} X_i\right)^2}$$

where

$$\bar{y} = \sum\limits_{i=1}^{n} \frac{Y_i}{n} \quad \text{and} \quad \bar{x} = \sum\limits_{i=1}^{n} \frac{X_i}{n}.$$

Thus, one needs various sums, sums of squares, and sums of cross products to generate the least-squares estimates.

---

[5]See Neter, Wasserman, and Kutner, *Applied Linear Regression Models*, pp. 23–40, for the derivation.

Consider only the sales Y and TV spots per month X_1 data provided in Table 15.1. It turns out that

$$\sum_{i=1}^{40} Y_i = (260.3 + 286.1 + \cdots + 481.8) = 16{,}451.5,$$

$$\sum_{i=1}^{40} X_{i1} = (5 + 7 + \cdots + 12) = 436.0,$$

$$\sum_{i=1}^{40} X_{i1} Y_i = 5(260.3) + 7(286.1) + \cdots + 12(481.8) = 197{,}634,$$

$$\sum_{i=1}^{40} X_{i1}^2 = (5)^2 + (7)^2 + \cdots + (12)^2 = 5{,}476,$$

$$\bar{y} = \frac{\sum_{i=1}^{40} Y_i}{n} = \frac{16{,}451.5}{40} = 411.3,$$

$$\bar{x}_1 = \frac{\sum_{i=1}^{40} X_{i1}}{n} = \frac{436}{40} = 10.9.$$

Therefore,

$$\hat{\beta}_1 = \frac{n \sum_{i=1}^{n} X_{i1} Y_i - \left(\sum_{i=1}^{n} X_{i1} \right) \left(\sum_{i=1}^{n} Y_i \right)}{n \sum_{i=1}^{n} X_{i1}^2 - \left(\sum_{i=1}^{n} X_i \right)^2}$$

$$= \frac{40(197{,}634) - (436)(16{,}451.5)}{40(5{,}476) - (436)^2} = 25.3,$$

$$\hat{\alpha} = \bar{y} - \hat{\beta}_1 \bar{x}_1 = 411.3 - (25.3)(10.9) = 135.4.$$

The equation is plotted in Figure 15.3. The slope of the line is given by $\hat{\beta}_1$. The value 25.3 of β_1 suggests that sales increase by $25,300 for every unit increase in TV spots. As mentioned previously, this is an estimate of the true population condition based on our particular sample of 40 observations. A different sample would most assuredly generate a different estimate. Further, we have not yet asked whether this is a statistically significant result or whether it could have occurred by chance. Nevertheless, it is a most vital item of information that helps in determining whether advertising expense is worth the estimated return. The estimate of the intercept parameter is $\hat{\alpha}_1 = 135.4$; this indicates where the line crosses the Y axis since it represents the estimated value of Y when the predictor variable equals zero.

Standard Error of Estimate

An examination of Figure 15.3 shows that, while the line seems to fit the points fairly well, there is still some deviation in the points about the line. The size of these deviations measures the goodness of the fit, and a numerical measure of the variation of the points about the line may be computed in much the same way as we compute the standard deviation of a frequency distribution.

Figure 15.3
Plot of Equation Relating Sales to TV Spots

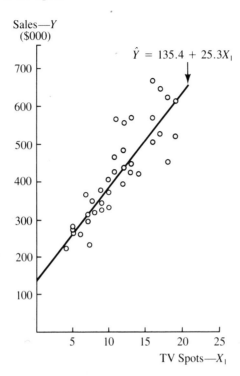

Just as the sample mean is an estimate of the true parent population mean, the line given by $Y_i = \hat{\alpha}_1 + \hat{\beta}_1 X_{i1} + e_i$ is an estimate of the true regression line $Y_i = \alpha_1 + \beta_1 X_{i1} + \epsilon_i$. Consider the variance of the random error ϵ around the true line of regression, that is, σ_ϵ^2 or $\sigma_{Y/X}^2$. When the population variance σ^2 is unknown, an unbiased estimate is given by

$$\hat{s}^2 = \frac{\sum\limits_{i=1}^{n} (X_i - \bar{x})^2}{(n-1)}.$$

Similarly, let $s_{Y/X}^2$ be an unbiased estimate of $\sigma_{Y/X}^2$. Now it can be shown that

$$s_{Y/X}^2 = \frac{\sum\limits_{i=1}^{n} e_i^2}{(n-2)} = \frac{\sum\limits_{i=1}^{n} (Y_i - \hat{Y}_i)^2}{(n-2)}$$

is an unbiased estimator of $\sigma_{Y/X}^2$, where Y_i and $\hat{Y}_i$ are, respectively, the observed and estimated values of Y for the ith observation. The square root of the above quantity $s_{Y/X}$

Figure 15.4
Rectangular Distribution of Error Term

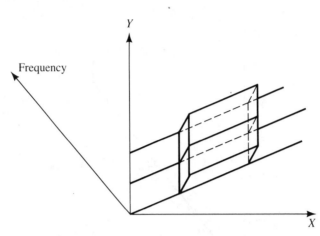

is often called the **standard error of estimate,** although the term standard deviation from regression is more meaningful.

The interpretation of the standard error of estimate parallels that for the standard deviation. Consider any X_{i1} value. What the standard error of estimate means is that for any such value of TV spots X_{i1}, Y_i (sales) tends to be distributed about the corresponding $\hat{Y}_i$ value—the point on the line—with a standard deviation equal to the standard error of estimate. Further, the variation about the line is the same throughout the entire length of the line. The point on the line, the arithmetic mean, changes as X_{i1} changes, but the distribution of Y_i values around the line does not change with changes in the number of TV spots. Figure 15.4 depicts the situation under the assumption that the error term is rectangularly distributed, for example.[6] Note that the assumption of constant $s_{Y/X}$, irrespective of the value of X_{i1}, produces parallel bands around the regression line.

The smaller the standard error of estimate, the better the line fits the data. For the line relating sales to TV spots it is $s_{Y/X} = 59.6$.

Inferences about the Slope Coefficient

The value of the slope coefficient, $\hat{\beta}_1 = 25.3$, was previously calculated, although at that time the question of whether the result could have been due to chance was not raised. To deal with that question requires an additional assumption, namely, that the errors are normally distributed rather than rectangularly distributed as previously as-

---

[6]This assumption will be modified shortly to that of normally distributed errors. It is made this way now in order to make more vivid the fact that the assumption of normally distributed errors is only necessary if statistical inferences are to be made about the coefficients.

sumed. Before proceeding, though, let us emphasize that the least-squares estimators of the parent population parameters are BLUE; that is, they are the _b_est, _l_inear, _u_nbiased _e_stimators of the true population parameters regardless of the shape of the distribution of the error term. All that is necessary is that the previous assumptions be satisfied. This is the remarkable result of the Gauss–Markov theorem. It is only if we wish to make statistical inferences about the regression coefficients that the assumption of normally distributed errors is required.

It can be shown that if the ϵ_i are normally distributed random variables, then $\hat{\beta}_1$ is also normally distributed. That is, if we were to take repeated samples from our population of sales territories and calculate a $\hat{\beta}_1$ for each sample, the distribution of these estimates would be normal and *centered* around the *true population* parameter β_1. Further, the variance of the distribution of $\hat{\beta}_1$'s can be shown to be equal to

$$\sigma_{\hat{\beta}_1}{}^2 = \frac{\sigma^2_{Y/X_1}}{\sum_{i=1}^{n} (X_{i1} - \bar{x}_1)^2}.$$

Since the population $\sigma_{Y/X}{}^2$ is unknown, $\sigma_{\hat{\beta}_1}{}^2$ is also unknown and has to be estimated. The estimate is generated by substituting the standard error of estimate $s_{Y/X}$ for $\sigma_{Y/X}$:

$$s_{\hat{\beta}_1}{}^2 = \frac{s^2_{Y/X_1}}{\sum_{i=1}^{n} (X_{i1} - \bar{x}_1)^2}.$$

The situation so far is as follows: Given the assumption of normally distributed errors, $\hat{\beta}_1$ is also normally distributed with a mean of β_1 and unknown variance $\sigma_{\hat{\beta}1}{}^2$. The situation thus parallels that of making an inference about the mean when the population variance is unknown. That set of conditions requires a t test to examine statistical significance, and the test for the significance of β_1 has a similar requirement.

The null hypothesis is that there is no linear relationship between the variables, while the alternate hypothesis is that a linear relationship does exist; that is,

$$H_0 : \beta_1 = 0,$$

$$H_a : \beta_1 \neq 0.$$

The test statistic is $t = (\hat{\beta}_1 - \beta_1)/s_{\hat{\beta}_1}$, which is t distributed with $n - 2$ degrees of freedom. In the example,

$$s_{\hat{\beta}_1}{}^2 = \frac{s^2_{Y/X_1}}{\sum_{i=1}^{n} (X_{i1} - \bar{x}_1)^2} = \frac{(59.6)^2}{723.6} = 4.91,$$

$$s_{\hat{\beta}_1} = \sqrt{4.91} = 2.22,$$

$$t = \frac{\hat{\beta}_1 - \beta_1}{s_{\hat{\beta}_1}} = \frac{25.3 - 0}{2.22} = 11.4.$$

For a 0.05 level of significance, the tabled t value for $\nu = n - 2 = 38$ degrees of freedom is 2.02. Since calculated t exceeds critical t, the null hypothesis is rejected; $\hat{\beta}_1$

is sufficiently different from zero to warrant the assumption of a linear relationship between sales and TV spots. Now, this does not mean that the true relationship between sales and TV spots is *necessarily* linear, only that the evidence indicates that Y (sales) changes as X_1 (TV spots) changes and that we may obtain a better prediction of Y using X_1 and the linear equation than if we simply ignored X_1.

What if the null hypothesis is not rejected? As we have noted, β_1 is the slope of the assumed line over the region of observation and indicates the linear change in Y for a one-unit change in X_1. If we do not reject the null hypothesis that β_1 equals zero, it *does not mean* that Y and X_1 are unrelated. There are two possibilities. First, we may simply be committing a Type II error by not rejecting a false null hypothesis. Second, it is possible that Y and X_1 might be perfectly related in some curvilinear manner, and we have simply chosen the wrong model to describe the physical situation.

Prediction of Y

Having established that the regression is not attributable to chance, let us use it to predict sales from given values of TV spots. There are two cases to consider:

1.   predicting the average value of Y for a given X_1,

2.   predicting an individual value of Y for a given X_1.

Let us consider these cases in order.

For a given X_1 value, say X_{01}, the Y value predicted by the regression equation is the *average* value of Y given X_1. Thus, in a territory with ten TV spots per month, the expected sales $\hat{Y}_0$ are

$$\hat{Y}_0 = \hat{\alpha}_1 + \hat{\beta}_1 X_{01} = 135.4 + 25.3\,(10) = 388.4.$$

This is an unbiased estimate of the true *average* value of sales to be expected when there are indeed ten TV spots per month in a territory. Individual territories may, of course, exhibit sales above or below the average, just as there are observations above and below a true population mean. Further, just as a sample mean may not exactly equal the population mean it is estimating, $\hat{Y}_0$ may not exactly equal Y_0, the population mean it is estimating for the given X_1 value. It would, therefore, seem useful to place bounds of error on the estimate.

To determine the bounds of error, it is necessary to know the variance of the distribution of Y_0 given X_{01}. This variance can be estimated, and in particular it is given by

$$s^2_{\hat{Y}_0/X_{01}} = s^2_{Y/X_1}\left[\frac{1}{n} + \frac{(X_{01} - \bar{x}_1)^2}{\sum\limits_{i=1}^{n}(X_{i1} - \bar{x}_1)^2}\right].$$

Note that this variance depends on the particular X_1 value in question. When X_1 equals the mean of the X_1's, the variance is smallest, since $(X_{01} - \bar{x}_1)$ is then equal to zero. As X_1 moves away from the mean, the variance increases. For ten TV spots per day

$$s^2_{\hat{Y}_0/X_{01}} = (59.6)^2\left[\frac{1}{40} + \frac{(10 - 10.9)^2}{723.6}\right] = 92.8.$$

The confidence interval for the estimate is given by

$$\hat{Y}_0 \pm t s_{\hat{Y}_0 / X_{01}},$$

where t is the tabled t value for the assumed level of significance and $v = n - 2$ degrees of freedom. We have already mentioned that for a 0.05 level of significance and $v = 38$, $t = 2.02$. Thus, the confidence interval for the average value of sales when there are ten TV spots per month is

$$\hat{Y}_0 \pm t s_{\hat{Y}_0 / X_{01}} = 388.4 \pm (2.02)(\sqrt{92.8}) = 388.4 \pm 19.5.$$

While the above enables us to predict the average level of sales for all sales territories with ten TV spots per month, we might wish to predict the sales that could be expected in some particular territory. This prediction contains an additional element of error, the amount by which the particular territory could be expected to deviate from the average. Thus, the error in predicting a specific value is larger than that for predicting the average value. Specifically, it equals

$$s^2_{Y_0 / X_{01}} = s^2_{Y / X_1} \left[1 + \frac{1}{n} + \frac{(X_{01} - \bar{x}_1)^2}{\displaystyle\sum_{i=1}^{n} (X_{i1} - x_1)^2} \right],$$

where the caret is removed from Y_0 to indicate that we are now talking about a specific value of Y_0 rather than an average value. Note that $s^2_{Y_0 / X_{01}}$ also equals $s^2_{\hat{Y}_0 / X_{01}} + s^2_{Y / X_1}$. This alternate expression shows why the confidence interval is wider when the prediction involves a specific value of Y_0 rather than the average value. The second term in this expression, s^2_{Y / X_1}, represents the estimated amount by which the particular value deviates from the average value. For ten TV spots per month

$$s^2_{Y_0 / X_{01}} = (59.6)^2 \left[1 + \frac{1}{40} + \frac{(10 - 10.9)^2}{723.6} \right] = 3,645,$$

and the confidence interval is

$$Y_0 \pm t s_{Y_0 / X_{01}} = 388.4 \pm (2.02)(\sqrt{3,645}) = 388.4 \pm 122.0.$$

Note that the bounds of error are much wider when a particular Y value is being predicted.

Correlation Coefficient

So far we have been concerned with the functional relationship of Y to X. Suppose we were also concerned with the *strength of the linear relationship* between Y and X. This leads to the notion of the correlation coefficient.

Two additional assumptions are made when discussing the correlation model. First, X_i is also assumed to be a random variable. A sample observation yields both an X_i and Y_i value. Second, it is assumed that the observations come from a bivariate normal distribution, that is, one in which the X variable is normally distributed and the Y variable is also normally distributed.

Figure 15.5

Scatter of Points for Sample of *n* Observations

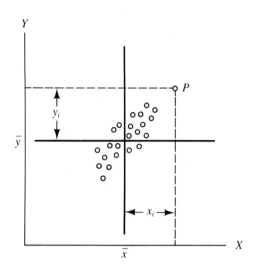

Now consider the drawing of a sample of *n* observations from a bivariate normal distribution. Let ρ represent the strength of the linear association between the two variables in the parent population. Let *r* represent the sample estimate of ρ. Suppose the sample of *n* observations yielded the scatter of points down in Figure 15.5, and consider the division of the figure into the four quadrants formed by erecting perpendiculars to the two axes at $\bar{x}$ and $\bar{y}$.

Consider the deviations from these bisectors. Take any point *P* with coordinates (X_i, Y_i) and define the deviations

$$x_i = X_i - \bar{x},$$

$$y_i = Y_i - \bar{y},$$

where the small letters indicate deviations around a mean. It is clear from an inspection of Figure 15.5 that the product $x_i y_i$ is

■ positive for all points in Quadrant I,

■ negative for all points in Quadrant II,

■ positive for all points in Quadrant III,

■ negative for all points in Quadrant IV.

Hence, it would seem that the quantity $\Sigma_{i=1}^{n} x_i y_i$ could be used as a measure of the linear association between *X* and *Y*,

■ for if the association is positive so that most points lie in the Quadrants I and III, $\Sigma_{i=1}^{n} x_i y_i$ tends to be positive,

- while if the association is negative so that most points lie in the Quadrants II and IV, $\sum_{i=1}^{n} x_i y_i$ tends to be negative, and

- while if no relation exists between X and Y, the points will be scattered over all four quadrants and $\sum_{i=1}^{n} x_i y_i$ will tend to be very small.

The quantity $\sum_{i=1}^{n} x_i y_i$ has two defects, however, as a measure of linear association between X and Y. First, it can be increased arbitrarily by adding further observations, that is, by increasing the sample size. Second, it can also be arbitrarily influenced by changing the units of measurement for either X or Y or both (for example, by changing feet to inches). These defects can be removed by making the measure of the strength of linear association a dimensionless quantity and dividing by n. The result is the Pearsonian, or product-moment, coefficient of correlation; that is,

$$r = \frac{\sum_{i=1}^{n} x_i y_i}{n s_X s_Y},$$

where s_X is the standard deviation of the X variable and s_Y is the standard deviation of the Y variable.

The correlation coefficient computed from the sample data is an estimate of the parent population parameter ρ, and part of the job of the researcher is to use r to test hypotheses about ρ. It is unnecessary to do so for the example at hand because the test of the null hypothesis H_0: $\rho = 0$ is equivalent to the test of the null hypothesis H_0: $\beta_1 = 0$. Since we have already performed the latter test, we know that the sample evidence leads to the rejection of the hypothesis that there is no linear relationship between sales and TV spots; that is, it leads to the rejection of H_0: $\rho = 0$.

The product-moment coefficient of correlation may vary from -1 to $+1$. Perfect positive correlation, where an increase in X determines exactly an increase in Y, yields a coefficient of $+1$. Perfect negative correlation, where an increase in X determines exactly a decrease in Y, yields a coefficient of -1. Figure 15.6 depicts these situations and several other scatter diagrams and their resulting correlation coefficients. An examination of these diagrams will provide some appreciation of the size of the correlation coefficient associated with a particular degree of scatter. The square of the correlation coefficient is the **coefficient of determination.** By some algebraic manipulation, it can be shown to be equal to

$$r^2 = 1 - \frac{s_{Y/X}^2}{s_Y^2}.$$

In the absence of the predictor variable, our best estimate of the criterion variable would be the sample mean. If there was low variability in sales from territory to territory, the sample mean would be a good estimate of the expected sales in any territory. However, high variability would render it a poor estimate. Thus, the variance in sales s_Y^2 is a measure of the "badness" of such an estimating procedure. The introduction of the covariate X might produce an improvement in the territory sales estimates. It depends on how well the equation fits the data. Since $s_{Y/X}^2$ measures the scatter of the points about the regression line, $s_{Y/X}^2$ can be considered a measure of the "badness" of an estimating procedure that takes account of the covariate. Now, if $s_{Y/X}^2$ is small in relation

Figure 15.6
Sample Scatter Diagrams and Associated Correlation Coefficients

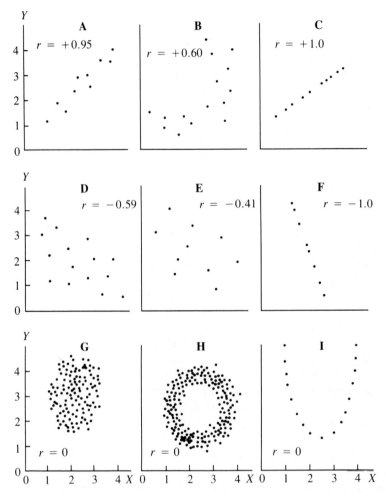

Source: Ronald E. Frank, Alfred A. Kuehn, and William F. Massy, *Quantitative Techniques in Marketing Analysis* (Homewood, Ill.: Richard D. Irwin, Inc., 1962), p. 71. Used with permission.

to s_Y^2, the introduction of the covariate via the regression equation can be said to have substantially improved the predictions of the criterion variable, sales. Conversely, if $s_{Y/X}^2$ is approximately equal to s_Y^2, the introduction of the covariate X can be considered not to have helped in improving the predictions of Y. Thus, the ratio $s_{Y/X}^2/s_Y^2$ can be considered to be the ratio of variation left unexplained by the regression line divided by the total variation; that is,

$$r^2 = 1 - \frac{\text{Unexplained variation}}{\text{Total variation}}.$$

The right side of the equation can be combined in a single fraction to yield

$$r^2 = \frac{\text{Total variation} - \text{Unexplained variation}}{\text{Total variation}}.$$

Total variation minus unexplained variation leaves "explained variation," that is, the variation in Y that is accounted for or explained by the introduction of X. Thus, the coefficient of determination can be considered to be equal to

$$r^2 = \frac{\text{Explained variation}}{\text{Total variation}},$$

where it is understood that total variation is measured by the variance in Y. For the sales and TV spot example, $r^2 = 0.77$. This means that 77 percent of the variation in sales from territory to territory is accounted for, or can be explained, by the variation in TV spot advertising across territories. Thus, we can do a better job of estimating sales in a territory if we take account of TV spots than if we neglect this advertising effort.

Multiple-Regression Analysis

So far we have considered only two variables in our analysis, sales and TV spot advertising. We now want to deal with the introduction of additional variables by considering multiple-regression analysis. The purposes will remain the same. We still want to construct an equation that will enable us to estimate values of the criterion variable, but now from given values of *several* predictor variables. And we still wish to measure the closeness of the estimated relationship. Our objective in introducing additional variables is basic—to improve our predictions of the criterion variable.

Revised Nomenclature

A more formal, revised notational framework is valuable for discussing multiple-regression analysis. Consider the general regression model with three predictor variables. The regression equation is

$$Y = \alpha + \beta_1 X_1 + \beta_2 X_2 + \beta_3 X_3 + \epsilon,$$

which is a simplified statement of the more elaborate and precise equation

$$Y_{(123)} = \alpha_{(123)} + \beta_{Y1.23}\, X_1 + \beta_{Y2.13}\, X_2 + \beta_{Y3.12}\, X_3 + \epsilon_{(123)}.$$

In this more precise system:

$Y_{(123)}$ is the value of Y that is estimated from the regression equation, in which Y is the criterion variable and X_1, X_2, and X_3 are the predictor variables.

$\alpha_{(123)}$ is the intercept parameter in the multiple-regression equation, in which Y is the criterion variable and X_1, X_2, and X_3 are the predictor variables.

$\beta_{Y1.23}$ is the coefficient of X_1 in the regression equation, in which Y is the criterion variable and X_1, X_2, and X_3 are the predictor variables. It is called the **coefficient of partial (or net) regression.** Note the subscripts. The two subscripts to the left of the decimal point are called primary subscripts. The first identifies the criterion variable, and the second identifies the predictor variable of which this β value is the coefficient. There are always two primary subscripts. The two subscripts to the right of the decimal point are called secondary subscripts. They indicate which other predictor variables are in the regression equation. The number of secondary subscripts varies from zero for simple regression to any number $k - 1$, where there are k predictor variables in the problem. In this case, the model contains three predictor variables, $k = 3$, and there are two secondary subscripts throughout.

$\epsilon_{(123)}$ is the error associated with the prediction of Y when X_1, X_2, and X_3 are the predictor variables.

When the identity of the variables is clear, it is common practice to use the simplified statement of the model. The more elaborate statement is helpful, though, in interpreting the solution to the regression problem.

Multicollinearity Assumption

The assumptions that we made about the error term for the simple regression model also apply to the multiple-regression equation. The multiple-regression model also requires the additional assumption that the predictor variables are not correlated among themselves. When the levels of the predictor variables can be set by the researcher, the assumption is easily satisfied. When the observations result from a survey rather than an experiment, the assumption is often violated because many variables of interest in marketing vary together. For instance, higher incomes are typically associated with higher education levels. Thus, the prediction of purchase behavior employing both income and education would violate the assumption that the predictor variables are independent of one another. **Multicollinearity** is said to be present in a multiple-regression problem when the predictor variables are correlated among themselves.

Coefficients of Partial Regression

Consider the introduction of a number of sales representatives into our problem of predicting territory sales. We could investigate the two-variable relationship between sales and the number of sales representatives. This would involve, of course, the calculation of the simple-regression equation relating sales to number of sales representatives. The calculations would parallel those for the sales and TV spot relationship. Alternatively, we could consider the simultaneous influence of TV spots and number of sales representatives on sales using multiple-regression analysis. Assuming that is indeed the research problem, the regression model would be written

$$Y_{(12)} = \alpha_{(12)} + \beta_{Y1.2} X_1 + \beta_{Y2.1} X_2 + \epsilon_{(12)},$$

indicating that the criterion variable, sales in a territory, is to be predicted employing two predictor variables, X_1 (TV spots per month) and X_2 (number of sales representatives).

Once again the parameters of the model could be estimated from sample data employing least-squares procedures. Let us again distinguish the sample estimates from the true, but unknown, population values by using a caret to denote an estimated value. Let us not worry about the formulas for calculating the regression coefficients. They typically will be calculated on a computer anyway and can be found in almost any introductory statistics book. The marketing analyst's need is how to interpret the results provided by the computer.

For this problem, the equation turns out to be

$$\hat{Y} = \hat{\alpha}_{(12)} + \hat{\beta}_{Y1.2} X_1 + \hat{\beta}_{Y2.1} X_2 = 69.3 + 14.2X_1 + 37.5X_2.$$

This regression equation may be used to estimate the level of sales to be expected in a territory, given the number of TV spots and the number of sales representatives serving the territory. Like any other least-squares equation, the line (a plane in this case since three dimensions are involved) fits the points in such a way that the sum of the deviations about the line is zero. That is, if sales for each of the 40 sales territories were to be estimated from this equation, the positive and negative deviations about the line would exactly balance.

The level at which the plane intercepts the Y axis is given by $\hat{\alpha}_{(12)} = 69.3$. Consider now the **coefficients of partial regression,** $\hat{\beta}_{Y1.2}$ and $\hat{\beta}_{Y2.1}$. *Assuming the multicollinearity assumption is satisfied,* these coefficients of partial regression can be interpreted as the *average change* in the criterion variable associated with a *unit change* in the appropriate predictor variable while holding the other predictor variable constant. Thus, assuming there is no multicollinearity, $\hat{\beta}_{Y1.2} = 14.2$ indicates that on the average, an increase of \$14,200 in sales can be expected with each additional TV spot in the territory if the number of sales representatives is not changed. Similarly, $\hat{\beta}_{Y2.1} = 37.5$ suggests that each additional sales representative in a territory can be expected to produce \$37,500 in sales, on the average, if the number of TV spots is held constant.

In simple-regression analysis, we tested the significance of the regression equation by examining the significance of the slope coefficient employing the t test. Calculated t was 11.4 for the sales and TV spot relationship. The significance of the regression could also have been checked with an F test. In the case of a two-variable regression, calculated F is equal to calculated t squared; that is, $F = t^2 = (11.4)^2 = 130.6$, while in general calculated F is equal to the ratio of the mean square due to regression to the mean square due to residuals. In simple regression, the calculated F value would be referred to an F table for $v_1 = n - 2$ degrees of freedom. The conclusion would be exactly equivalent to that derived by testing the significance of the slope coefficient employing the t test.

In the multiple-regression case, it is *mandatory that the significance of the overall regression* be examined using an F test. The appropriate degrees of freedom are $v_1 = k$ and $v_2 = n - k - 1$, where there are k predictor variables. Critical F for $v_1 = 2$ and $v_2 = 40 - 2 - 1 = 37$ degrees of freedom and a 0.05 level of significance is 3.25. Calculated F for the regression relating sales to TV spots and the number of sales representatives is 128.1. Since calculated F exceeds critical F, the null hypothesis of no relationship is rejected. There is a statistically significant linear relationship between sales and the predictor variables, number of TV spots and number of sales representatives.

The slope coefficients can also be tested individually for their statistical significance in a multiple-regression problem, given the overall function is significant. The t test is again used, although the validity of the procedure is highly dependent on multicollinearity that exists within the data. If the data are highly multicollinear, there will be a tendency to commit Type II errors; that is, many of the predictor variables will be judged as not being related to the criterion variable when in fact they are; it is even possible to have a high R^2 value and to conclude that the overall regression is statistically significant but that none of the coefficients are significant. The difficulty with the t tests for the significance of the individual slope coefficients arises because the standard error of estimate of the least-squares coefficients, s_{β_i}, increases as the dependence among the predictor variables increases. And, of course, as the denominator of calculated t gets larger, t itself decreases, occasioning the conclusion of no relationship between the criterion variable and the predictor variable in question.

Is multicollinearity a problem in our example? Consider again the simple regression of sales on TV spots; $\hat{\beta}_1$ ($\hat{\beta}_{Y1}$ in our more formal notational system) was equal to 25.3. Thus, when the number of sales representatives in a territory was not considered, the average change in sales associated with an additional TV spot was \$25,300. Yet when the number of sales representatives is considered, the average change in sales associated with an additional TV spot was \$14,200 $\hat{\beta}_{Y1.2} = 14.2$. Part of the sales effect that we were attributing to TV spots was in fact due to the number of sales representatives in the territory. We were thus overstating the impact of the TV spot advertising because of the way decisions have historically been made in the company. Specifically, those territories with the greater number of sales representatives have received more TV advertising support (or vice versa). Perhaps this was logical as they contained a larger proportion of the consuming public. Nevertheless, the fact that the two predictor variables are not independent (the coefficient of simple correlation between TV spots and number of sales representatives is 0.78) has caused a violation of the assumption of independent predictors. Multicollinearity is present within this data set.

A multicollinear condition within a data set *reduces the efficiency* of the estimates for the regression parameters. This is because the amount of information about the effect of each predictor variable on the criterion variable declines as the correlation among the predictor variables increases. The reduction in efficiency can be easily seen in the limiting case as the correlation between the predictor variables approaches 1 for a two-predictor model. Such a situation is depicted in Figure 15.7, where it is assumed that there is a perfect linear relationship between the two predictor variables, TV spots and number of sales representatives, and also that there is a strong linear relationship between the criterion variable sales and TV spots. Consider the change in sales from \$75,000 to \$100,000. This change is associated with a change in the number of TV spots, from three to four. This change in TV spots is also associated with a change in the number of sales representatives, from four to five. What is the effect of a TV spot on sales? Can we say it is $100 - 75 = 25$, or \$25,000? Most assuredly not, for historically a sales representative has been added to a territory whenever the number of TV spots have been increased by one (or vice versa). The number of TV spots and of sales representatives varies in perfect proportion, and it is impossible to distinguish their separate influences on sales, that is, their influence when the other predictor variable is held constant.

Very little meaning can be attached to the coefficients of partial regression when multicollinearity is present, as it is in our example. The "normal" interpretation of the coefficients of partial regression as "the average change in the criterion variable associated with a unit change in the appropriate predictor variable while holding the other

Figure 15.7

Hypothetical Relationship between Sales and TV Spots and between TV Spots and Number of Sales Representatives

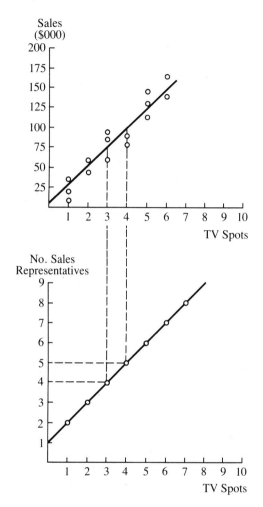

predictor variables constant'' simply does not hold.[7] The equation may still be quite useful for prediction, assuming conditions are stable. That is, it may be used to predict sales in the various territories for given levels of TV spots and number of sales representatives *if* the historical relationship between sales and each of the predictor variables,

[7]M. G. Kendall, *A Course in Multivariate Analysis* (London: Charles Griffin, 1957), p. 74.

and between or among the predictor variables themselves, can be expected to continue.[8] The partial-regression coefficients should not be used, though, as the basis for making marketing strategy decisions when significant multicollinearity is present.[9]

Coefficients of Multiple Correlation and Determination

One item of considerable importance in simple-regression analysis was the measure of the *closeness* of the relationship between the criterion and predictor variables. The coefficient of correlation and its square, the coefficient of multiple determination, were used for this purpose. In multiple regression, there are similar coefficients for the identical purpose.

The coefficient of multiple correlation is formally denoted by $R_{Y.123}$, where the primary subscript identifies the criterion variable and the secondary subscripts identify the predictor variables. When the variables entering into the relationship are obvious, the abbreviated form, R, is used. The **coefficient of multiple determination** is denoted formally by $R_{Y.123}^2$ and informally by R^2. It represents the proportion of variation in the criterion variable that is accounted for by the covariation in the predictor variables. In the investigation of the relationship between sales and TV spots and number of sales representatives, $R_{Y.12}^2 = 0.874$. This means that 87.4 percent of the variation in sales is associated with variation in TV spots and number of sales representatives. The introduction of the number of sales representatives has improved the fit of the regression line; 87.4 percent of the variation in sales is accounted for by the two-predictor variable model, whereas only 77.5 percent was accounted for by the one-predictor model. The square root of this quantity, $R_{Y.12} = 0.935$, is the **coefficient of multiple correlation.** It is always expressed as a positive number.

Coefficients of Partial Correlation

There are two additional quantities to consider when interpreting the results of a multiple-regression analysis that were not present in simple-regression analysis: The coefficient of partial correlation and its square, the coefficient of partial determination.

Recall that in the simple-regression analysis relating sales Y to TV spots X_1, the coefficient of simple determination could be written

---

[8]There are some things that the analyst faced with multicollinear data can do. See R. R. Hocking, "Developments in Linear Regression Methodology: 1959–1982," *Technometrics,* 25 (August 1983), pp. 219–230, and Ronald D. Snee, "Discussion," *Technometrics,* 25 (August 1983), pp. 230–237, for a discussion of the problem and some alternative ways for handling it.

[9]There is another interpretation danger in the example that was not discussed. It is not unreasonable to assume that both the number of sales representatives serving a territory and the number of TV spots per month were both determined on the basis of territorial potential. If this is the case, the implied causality is reversed or at least confused; instead of the number of sales representatives and number of TV spots determining sales, sales in a sense (potential sales anyway) determine the former quantities, and they in turn could be expected to affect realized sales. If this is actually the case, the coefficient estimating procedure needs to take into account the two-way "causation" among the variables. See Wonnacott and Wonnacott, *Regression,* pp. 284–292, for a discussion of the problems and the logic underlying the estimation of simultaneous-equation systems.

$$r_{Y.1}^2 = 1 - \frac{\text{Unexplained variation}}{\text{Total variation}},$$

and recall also that the unexplained variation was given by the square of standard error of estimate, $s_{Y.1}^2$, since the standard error of estimate measures the variation in the criterion variable that was unaccounted for by the predictor variable X_1. Total variation, of course, was given by the variance in the criterion variable s_Y^2. Thus,

$$r_{Y.1}^2 = 1 - \frac{s_{Y.1}^2}{s_Y^2}.$$

The last term in this formula is the ratio of the variation *remaining* in the criterion variable, after taking account of the predictor variable X_1, to the total variation in the criterion variable. It measures the *relative degree* to which the association between the two variables can be used to provide information about the criterion variable.

Now consider the multiple-regression case with two predictor variables, X_1 and X_2. Denote the standard error of estimate by $s_{Y.12}$ and its square by $s_{Y.12}^2$. The standard error of estimate measures the variation *still remaining* in the criterion variable Y after the two predictor variables X_1 and X_2 have been taken into account. Since $s_{Y.1}^2$ measures the variation in the criterion variable that remains after the first predictor variable has been taken into account, the ratio $s_{Y.12}^2/s_{Y.1}^2$ can be interpreted as measuring the relative degree to which the association among the three variables Y, X_1, and X_2 provides information about Y over and above that provided by the association between the criterion variable and the first predictor variable alone. In other words, the ratio $s_{Y.12}^2/s_{Y.1}^2$ measures the *relative degree* to which X_2 adds to the knowledge about Y after X_1 has already been fully utilized. The ratio is the basis for the **coefficient of partial determination,** which in the sales (Y) versus TV spots (X_1) and number of sales representatives (X_2) example is

$$r_{Y2.1}^2 = 1 - \frac{s_{Y.12}^2}{s_{Y.1}^2} = 1 - \frac{(45.2)^2}{(59.6)^2} = 1 - 0.576 = 0.424.$$

This means that 42.4 percent of the variation in sales that is not associated with TV spots is incrementally associated with the number of sales representatives. Alternatively, the errors made in estimating sales from TV spots are, as measured by the variance, reduced by 42.4 percent when the number of sales representatives X_2 is added to X_1 as an additional predictor variable. The square root of the coefficient of partial determination is the **coefficient of partial correlation.**

In our example there were two predictors. Thus, we defined the coefficient of partial determination for the number of sales representatives X_2 as $r_{Y2.1}^2$. We could have similarly defined a coefficient of partial determination for TV spots. It would be denoted as $r_{Y1.2}^2$ and it would represent the percentage of the variation in sales not associated with X_2 that is incrementally associated with X_1; this latter coefficient would show the incremental contribution of X_1 after the association between Y and X_2 had already been considered.

When there are more than two predictors, we could define many more coefficients of partial determination. Each would have two primary subscripts indicating the criterion variable and the newly added predictor variable. There could be a great many secondary subscripts, as they always indicate which predictor variables have already been considered. Thus, if we had three predictor variables, we could calculate $r_{Y2.1}$, $r_{Y3.1}$, $r_{Y1.2}$, $r_{Y3.2}$, $r_{Y1.3}$ and $r_{Y2.3}$. These would all be *first-order* partial correlation coefficients, since they have one secondary subscript indicating that one other predictor variable is taken into account. We could also calculate $r_{Y1.23}$, $r_{Y2.13}$, and $r_{Y3.12}$. These are all *second-order* partial correlation coefficients. Each has two secondary subscripts indicating that the incremental contribution of the variable is being considered after two other predictor variables have already been taken into account. Simple correlation coefficients, of course, have no secondary coefficients; they are, therefore, often referred to as *zero-order* partial correlation coefficients.

Dummy Variables

The analysis of the sales data of Table 15.1 is still not complete. No attention has yet been given to the effect of distribution on sales, particularly as measured by the wholesaler efficiency index. One way of considering the effect of wholesaler efficiency on sales would be to introduce the index directly; that is, the X_3 value for each observation would simply be the value recorded in the last column of Table 15.1. Letting X_3 represent the wholesaler efficiency index, the multiple-regression equation, using the informal notational scheme, would be

$$Y = \alpha + \beta_1 X_1 + \beta_2 X_2 + \beta_3 X_3 + \epsilon.$$

The least-squares estimate of β_3 in this equation turns out to be $\hat{\beta}_3 = 11.5$. Note what this number implies if the predictor variables are independent. It means that the estimated average change in sales is \$11,500 for each unit change in the wholesaler efficiency index. This means that a fair distributor could be expected to sell \$11,500 more on the average than a poor one; a good one could be expected to average \$11,500 more than a fair one; and an excellent one could be expected to sell \$11,500 more on the average than a good one. The sales increments are assumed constant for each change in wholesaler rating. The implication is that the wholesaler efficiency index is an interval scaled variable and that the difference between a poor and a fair wholesaler is the same as the difference between a fair one and a good one. This is a questionable assumption with an index that reflects ratings.

   An alternative way of proceeding would be to convert the index into a set of **dummy variables** or, more appropriately, *binary variables*. A binary variable is one which takes on one of two values, 0 or 1. Thus, it can be represented by a single binary digit. Binary variables are used mainly because of the flexibility one has in defining them. They can provide a numerical representation for attributes or characteristics that are not essentially quantitative. For example, one could introduce sex into a regression equation using the dummy variable X_i, where

$$X_i = 0 \quad \text{if the person is a female,}$$

$$X_i = 1 \quad \text{if the person is a male.}$$

The technique is readily extended to handle multichotomous as well as dichotomous classifications. For instance, suppose one wanted to introduce the variable social class into a regression equation, and there were three distinct class levels: upper class, middle class, and lower class. This could be handled using two dummy variables, say X_1 and X_2, where

	X_1	X_2
■ if a person belongs to the upper class	1	0
■ if a person belongs to the middle class	0	1
■ if a person belongs to the lower class	0	0

There are several other logically equivalent coding schemes; for example,

	X_1	X_2
■ if a person belongs to the upper class	0	0
■ if a person belongs to the middle class	1	0
■ if a person belongs to the lower class	0	1

It is therefore most important that the analyst interpreting the output from a regression run employing dummy variables pay close attention to the coding of the variables. It should be clear that an m category classification is capable of unambiguous representation by a set of $m - 1$ binary variables and that an mth binary would be entirely superfluous. As a matter of fact, the use of m variables to code an m-way classification variable would render most regression programs inoperative.

Suppose that we were to employ three dummy variables to represent the four-category wholesaler efficiency index in the Click ball-point pen example and that

	X_3	X_4	X_5
■ if a wholesaler is poor	0	0	0
■ if a wholesaler is fair	1	0	0
■ if a wholesaler is good	0	1	0
■ if a wholesaler is excellent	0	0	1

The regression model is

$$Y = \alpha + \beta_1 X_1 + \beta_2 X_2 + \beta_3 X_3 + \beta_4 X_4 + \beta_5 X_5 + \epsilon.$$

The least-squares estimates of the wholesaler efficiency parameters are[10]

$$\hat{\beta}_3 = 9.2,$$

$$\hat{\beta}_4 = 20.3,$$

$$\hat{\beta}_5 = 33.3.$$

These coefficients indicate that on the average a fair wholesaler could be expected to

---

[10]The data were artificially created employing specified parameter values and a random error term in a linear equation. The parameters were actually $\beta_3 = 2.0$, $\beta_4 = 22.0$, and $\beta_5 = 32.0$.

sell $9,200 more than a poor one, a good wholesaler could be expected to sell $20,300 more than a poor one, and an excellent wholesaler $33,300 more than a poor one. Note that all of these coefficients are interpreted with respect to the "null" state, that is, with respect to the classification "poor" in this case.[11]

The analyst wishing to determine the difference in sales effectiveness between other classifications must look at coefficient differences. Thus, if the researcher wanted to calculate the estimated difference in expected sales from a good wholesaler and a fair wholesaler, the appropriate difference would be $\hat{\beta}_4 - \hat{\beta}_3 = 20.3 - 9.2 = 11.1$ thousand dollars ($11,100). Similarly, an excellent wholesaler could be expected on the average to sell $\hat{\beta}_5 - \hat{\beta}_4 = 33.3 - 20.3 = 13.0$ thousand dollars ($13,000) more than a good one.

The use of dummy variables indicates that the relationship between sales and the wholesaler efficiency index is not linear as was assumed when the index was introduced as an interval scaled variable. Instead of an across-the-board increase of $11,500 with each rating change, the respective increases are 9.2 ($9,200) from poor to fair, 11.1 ($11,100) from fair to good, and 13.0 ($13,000) from good to excellent.

Variable Transformations

The use of dummy variables greatly expands the scope of the regression model. Dummy variables allow the introduction of classificatory and rank-order variables in regression problems. As we have seen, they also allow nonlinear criterion variable/predictor variable relationships to be dealt with. Another technique that expands the obvious scope of the regression model is that of variable transformations.

A **variable transformation** is simply a change in the scale in which the given variable is expressed. Consider the model

$$Y = \alpha X_1^{\beta_1} X_2^{\beta_2} X_3^{\beta_3} \epsilon$$

in which the relationship among the predictors and between the predictors and the error is assumed to be multiplicative. At first glance, it would seem that it would be impossible to estimate the parameters α, β_1, β_2, and β_3 using our normal least-squares procedures. Now consider the model

$$W = \alpha' + \beta_1 Z_1 + \beta_2 Z_2 + \beta_3 Z_3 + \epsilon'.$$

This is a linear model, and so it can be fitted by the standard least-squares procedures. But consider the fact that it is exactly equivalent to our multiplicative model if we simply let

---

[11]For a useful discussion of some alternative ways to code dummy variables and the different insights that can be provided by the various alternatives, see Jacob Cohen and Patricia Cohen, *Applied Multiple Regression/Correlation Analysis for the Behavioral Sciences*, 2nd ed. (Hillsdale, N.J.: Lawrence Erlbaum Associates, 1983), pp. 181–222.

$$W = \ln Y \qquad Z_2 = \ln X_2$$

$$\alpha' = \ln \alpha \qquad Z_3 = \ln X_3$$

$$Z_1 = \ln X_1 \qquad \epsilon' = \ln \epsilon$$

Thus, we have converted a nonlinear model to a linear model using variable transformations. To solve for the parameters of our multiplicative model we simply (1) take the natural log of Y and each of the X's; (2) solve the resulting equation by the normal least-squares procedures; (3) take the antilog of α' to derive an estimate of α; and (4) read the values of the $\hat{\beta}_i$, since they are the same in both models.

The transformation to natural logarithms involved the transformation of both the criterion and predictor variables. It is also possible to change the scale of either the criterion or predictor variables. Transformations to the exponential and logarithmic are some of the most useful, since they serve to relax the constraints imposed by the assumptions that[12]

- the relationship between the criterion variable and the predictor variables is additive,

- the relationship between the criterion variable and the predictor variables is linear, and

- the errors are homoscedastic (equal a constant for all values of the predictors).

Dummy variables are one form of transformation, and we have already seen how they allow the treatment of nonlinear relationships.

Summary

This chapter sought to examine the question of association or covariation between (among) variables when one of the variables is in some sense considered a criterion variable. Simple regression and correlation analysis is the primary statistical device for analyzing the association between a single predictor and a single criterion variable. This model allows the estimation of a functional equation relating the variables as well as an estimate of the strength of the association between them. Some of the more useful outputs from a simple regression analysis are:

1. the functional equation, which allows the prediction of the criterion variable for assumed values of the predictor variable,

2. the standard error of estimate, which provides an absolute measure of the lack of fit of the equation to the data,

---

[12]See Ronald E. Frank, "Use of Transformations," *Journal of Marketing Research,* 3 (August 1966), pp. 247–253, for a discussion of these conditions and how the proper transformation can serve to fulfill them. See Leonard Jon Parsons and Piet Vanden Abeele, "Analysis of Sales Call Effectiveness," *Journal of Marketing Research,* 18 (February 1981), pp. 107–113, for an example that uses the log transformation.

3. the coefficient of determination, which provides a relative assessment of the goodness of fit of the equation, and

4. the slope coefficient, which indicates how much the criterion variable changes, on the average, per unit of change in the predictor variable.

The regression model is readily extended to incorporate multiple predictor variables to estimate a single criterion variable. If the predictor variables are not correlated among themselves, each partial regression coefficient indicates the average change in the criterion variable per unit change in the predictor variable in question, holding the other predictor variables constant. If the predictor variables are correlated among themselves, little substantive meaning can be attached to the slope coefficients, although the regression equation often can still be used successfully to predict values of the criterion variable for assumed values of the predictor variables. The coefficient of multiple determination measures the proportion of the variation in the criterion variable accounted for or "explained" by all the predictor variables. The coefficient of partial determination measures the relative degree to which a given variable adds to our knowledge of the criterion variable over and above that provided by other predictor variables. Dummy or binary variables allow the introduction of classificatory or nominally scaled variables in the regression equation, while variable transformations considerably increase the scope of the regression model, since they allow certain nonlinear relationships to be considered.

Questions

1. What is the basic nature of the distinction between tests for group differences and tests to investigate association?

2. What is the difference between regression analysis and correlation analysis?

3. What is the difference between a deterministic model and a probabilistic model? Which type of model underlies regression analysis? Explain.

4. What assumptions are made about the error term in the least-squares solution to the regression problem? What is their effect; that is, what is the Gauss–Markov theorem? When the analyst wishes to make an inference about a regression population parameter, what additional assumption is necessary?

5. What is the standard error of estimate?

6. Suppose an analyst wished to make an inference about the slope coefficient in a regression model. What is the appropriate procedure? What does it mean if the null hypothesis is rejected? If it is not rejected?

7. What is the difference in procedure when one is predicting an individual value of Y for a given X_i and when one is predicting an average value of Y for a given X_i?

8. What is the correlation coefficient and what does it measure? What is the coefficient of determination and what does it measure?

9. What is a coefficient of partial or net regression and what does it measure? What condition must occur for the usual interpretation to apply? What happens if this condition is not satisfied?

10. What is the coefficient of multiple determination?

11. What is a coefficient of partial determination? What does it measure?

12. What is a dummy variable? When is it used? How is it interpreted?

13. What is a variable transformation? Why is it employed?

Applications and Problems

1. The Brite-Lite Bottling Company, which provides glass bottles to various soft-drink manufacturers, has the following information pertaining to the number of cases per shipment and the corresponding transportation cost:

Number of Cases per Shipment in 00's	Transportation Costs in $'s
15	200
22	260
35	310
43	360
58	420
65	480
73	540
82	630
85	710
98	730

The marketing manager is interested in studying the relationship between the number of cases per shipment and the transportation costs. Your assistance is required in performing a simple regression analysis.

(a) Plot the transportation costs as a function of the number of cases per shipment.

(b) Interpret the scatter diagram.

(c) Calculate the coefficients $\hat{\alpha}$ and $\hat{\beta}$ and develop the regression equation.

(d) What is the interpretation of the coefficient $\hat{\alpha}$ and $\hat{\beta}$?

(e) Calculate the standard error of estimate.

(f) What is the interpretation of the standard error of estimate you calculated?

(g) Compute the t value with $n - 2$ degrees of freedom with the use of the following formula for the square root of the variance of the distribution of β's

$$s_{\hat{\beta}} = \sqrt{\frac{s_{Y/X}^2}{\sum_{i=1}^{10} (X_i - \bar{x})^2}}$$

$$t = \frac{\hat{\beta}_1 - \beta_1}{s_{\hat{\beta}_1}}$$

where β is assumed to be zero under the null hypothesis of no relationship, that is:

$$H_0 : \beta_1 = 0$$

$$H_a : \beta_1 \neq 0$$

(h) What is the tabled t value at a 0.05 significance level?

(i)   What can you conclude about the relationship between transportation costs and number of cases shipped?

(j)   The marketing manager wants to estimate the transportation costs for 18 cases.

(i) Use the regression model to derive the average value of Y_0.

(ii) Provide a confidence interval for the estimate.

$$s_{\hat{Y}_0/X_{01}}{}^2 = s_{Y/X_1}{}^2 \left[\frac{1}{n} + \frac{(X_{01} - \bar{x})^2}{\sum\limits_{i=1}^{10} (X_{i1} - \bar{x})^2} \right]$$

$$\hat{Y}_0 \pm t\, s_{\hat{Y}_0/X_{01}} =$$

2.   The marketing manager of Brite-Lite Company wanted to determine if there was an association between the size of carton and the transportation cost per shipment. (The company followed a policy of including the same sized cartons for any particular shipment.) The information pertaining to size of carton is given below. Refer to the previous question for information on the transportation costs per shipment.

(a)   Calculate the correlation coefficient.

(b)   Interpret the correlation coefficient.

(c)   Determine the coefficient of determination.

(d)   Interpret the coefficient of determination.

3.   The marketing manager of Brite-Lite Company is considering multiple regression analysis with number of cartons per shipment and size of cartons as predictor variables and transportation costs as the criterion variable (refer to the previous problem). He has devised the following regression equation.

$$\hat{Y} = \hat{\alpha}_{(12)} + \hat{\beta}_{Y1.2}\, X_1 + \hat{\beta}_{Y2.1}\, X_2 = -41.44 - 3.95\, X_1 + 24.44\, X_2$$

where X_1 is the number of cartons per shipment and X_2 is the size of the carton.

(a)   Interpret $\hat{\alpha}_{(12)}$, $\hat{\beta}_{Y1.2}$, and $\hat{\beta}_{Y2.1}$

(b)   Is multiple regression appropriate in this situation? If yes, why? If no, why not?

4.   An analyst for a large shoe manufacturer had developed a formal linear regression model to predict sales of its 122 retail stores located in different SMSA's in the United States. The model is:

$$Y_{(123)} = \alpha_{(123)} + \beta_{1.23}X_1 + \beta_{2.13}X_2 + \beta_{3.12}X_3$$

where

X_1 = population in surrounding area in thousands

X_2 = marginal propensity to consume

X_3 = median personal income in surrounding area in thousands of dollars

Y = sales in thousands of dollars.

Some empirical results were:

Variable	Regression Coefficient	Coefficient Standard Errors ($s_{\hat{\beta}_i}$)
X_1	$\hat{\beta}_{1.23} =$ 0.49	0.24
X_2	$\hat{\beta}_{2.13} = -0.40$	95
X_3	$\hat{\beta}_{3.12} =$ 225	105
$R^2 = 0.47$	$\hat{\alpha}\ \ =\ -40$	225

(a) Interpret each of the regression coefficients.
(b) Are X_1, X_2, and X_3 significant at the 0.05 level? Show your calculations.
(c) Which independent variable seems to be the most significant predictor?
(d) Provide an interpretation of the R^2 value.
(e) The marketing research department of the shoe manufacturer wants to include an index which indicates whether the service in each store is poor, fair, or good. The coding scheme is as follows:

1 = poor service
2 = fair service
3 = good service

    (i) Indicate how you would transform this index so that it could be included in the model. Be specific.
    (ii) Write out the regression model including the above transformation.
    (iii) Suppose two of the parameters for the index are 4.6 and 10.3. Interpret these values in light of the scheme you adopted.

Appendix 15A
Nonparametric Measures of Association

Chapter 15 focuses on the product-moment correlation as the measure of association. While the product-moment correlation coefficient was originally developed to deal with continuous variables, it has proven quite robust to scale type and can handle variables that are ordinal or dichotomous as well as those that are interval.[1] While it is therefore a rather general measure of association, it is not universally applicable. This appendix therefore treats some alternate measures of association, namely, the contingency table and coefficient and the index of predictive association, which are appropriate for nominal data, and Spearman's rank-order correlation coefficient and the coefficient of concordance, which are suited to the analysis of rank-order data.

Contingency Table

A problem frequently encountered in the analysis of nominal data is the independence of variables of classification. In Chapter 12, for example, a number of research questions involving the relationship between auto purchase and family characteristics were dealt with. No statistical tests of significance were computed at that time. The question of whether the results reflected sample aberrations or represented true population conditions was thus avoided. If statistical tests had been run at that time, they would have been primarily of the chi-square **contingency table** type, which is ideally suited for investigating the independence of variables in cross classifications.

---

[1] Jum Nunnally, *Psychometric Theory*, 2nd ed. (New York: McGraw-Hill, 1978), especially pp. 117–150.

Consider, for example, a consumer study involving the preferences of families for different sizes of washing machines. *A priori,* it would seem that larger families would be more likely to buy the larger units and that smaller families would tend to buy smaller washing machines. To investigate this question, suppose the manufacturer checked a random sample of those purchasers who returned their warranty cards. Included on the warranty cards was a question on the size of the family. Although not a perfect population for analysis, the manufacturer believed it was good enough for this purpose, since some 85 percent of all warranty cards are returned. Furthermore, it was a relatively economical way to proceed, since the data were internal. The study could be carried out by checking a random sample of warranty cards for family size and machine purchased.

A random sample of 300 of these cards provided the data in Table 15A.1. The assignment is to determine if family size affects the size of the machine that is purchased. The null hypothesis is that the variables are independent; the alternate is that they are not. Suppose a significance level of $\alpha = 0.10$ was chosen for the test. To calculate a χ^2 statistic, one needs to generate the expected number of cases likely to fall into each category. *The expected number is generated by assuming that the null hypothesis is indeed true,* that is, that there is no relationship between size of machine purchased and family size. Suppose size of machine purchased is denoted by the variable A and size of family by the variable B and that

- A_1—purchase of an 8-lb load washing machine,
- A_2—purchase of a 10-lb load washing machine,
- A_3—purchase of a 12-lb load washing machine,
- B_1—family of one to two members,
- B_2—family of three to four members,
- B_3—family of five or more members.

If variables A and B are indeed independent, then the probability of occurrence of the event A_1B_1 (a family of one to two members purchased an 8-lb load machine) is given as the product of the separate probabilities for A_1 and B_1; that is

$$P(A_1B_1) = P(A_1)P(B_1)$$

by the multiplication law of probabilities for independent events. Now $P(A)$ is given by the number of cases possessing the characteristic A_1, n_{A_1}, over the total number of cases n. $P(A_1)$ is thus

$$\frac{n_{A_1}}{n} = \frac{70}{300} = \frac{7}{30}.$$

Similarly, $P(B_1)$ is given by the number of cases having the characteristic B_1, n_{B_1}, over the total number of cases, or $P(B_1) = n_{B_1}/n = 40/300 = 2/15$. The joint probability $P(A_1B_1)$ is

$$P(A_1B_1) = P(A_1)P(B_1) = \left(\frac{7}{30}\right)\left(\frac{2}{15}\right) = \frac{7}{225}.$$

Given a total of 300 cases, the number expected to fall in the cell A_1B_1, E_{11}, is given

Table 15A.1

Size of Washing Machine versus Size of Family

Size of Washing Machine Purchased	Size of Family in Members			Total
	1 to 2	3 to 4	5 or more	
8-lb load	25	37	8	70
10-lb load	10	62	53	125
12-lb load	5	41	59	105
Total	40	140	120	300

as the product of the total number of cases and the probability of any one of these cases falling into the A_1B_1 cell; that is,

$$E_{11} = nP(A_1B_1) = 300(7/225) = 9.33.$$

Although this is the underlying rationale for generating the expected frequencies, there is an easier computational form. Recall that $P(A_1) = n_{A_1}/n$, that $P(B) = n_{B_1}/n$, and that $P(A_1B_1) = P(A_1)P(B_1)$. The formula for E_{11} upon substitution then reduces to

$$E_{11} = nP(A_1B_1) = nP(A_1)P(B_1)$$

$$= n\frac{n_{A_1}}{n}\frac{n_{B_1}}{n} = \frac{n_{A_1}n_{B_1}}{n}$$

$$= \frac{70 \times 40}{300} = 9.33.$$

Thus, to generate the expected frequencies for each cell, one needs merely to multiply the marginal frequencies and divide by the total. The remaining expected frequencies, which are calculated in like manner, are entered below the cell diagonals in Table 15A.2. The calculated χ^2 value is thus

$$\chi^2 = \sum_{i=1}^{3}\sum_{j=1}^{3}\frac{[O_{ij} - E_{ij}]^2}{E_{ij}}$$

$$= \frac{(25 - 9.33)^2}{9.33} + \frac{(37 - 32.67)^2}{32.67} + \frac{(8 - 28.00)^2}{28.00}$$

$$+ \frac{(10 - 16.67)^2}{16.67} + \frac{(62 - 58.33)^2}{58.33} + \frac{(53 - 50.00)^2}{50.00}$$

$$+ \frac{(5 - 14.00)^2}{14.00} + \frac{(41 - 49.00)^2}{49.00} + \frac{(59 - 42.00)^2}{42.00}$$

$$= 26.318 + 0.574 + 14.286 + 2.669 + 0.231 + 0.180 + 5.786 + 1.306$$

$$+ 6.881$$

$$= 58.231$$

Table 15A.2

**Size of Washing Machine versus Size of Family:
Observed and Expected Frequencies**

Size of Washing Machine Purchased	Size of Family in Members			Total
	B_1 1 to 2	B_2 3 to 4	B_3 5 or more	
A_1—8-lb load	25 9.33	37 32.67	8 28.00	70
A_2—10-lb load	10 16.67	62 58.33	53 50.00	125
A_3—12-lb load	5 14.00	41 49.00	59 42.00	105
Total	40	140	120	300

where O_{ij} and E_{ij}, respectively, denote the actual number and expected number of observations that fall in the ij cell. Now, the expected frequencies in any row add to the marginal total. This must be true because of the way the expected frequencies were calculated. Thus, as soon as we know any two expected frequencies in a row, say 9.33 and 32.67 in Row A_1, for example, the third expected frequency is fixed because the three must add to the marginal total. This means that there are only $(c - 1)$ degrees of freedom in a row, where c is the number of columns. A similar argument applies to the columns; that is, there are $(r - 1)$ degrees of freedom per column, where r is the number of rows. The degrees of freedom in total in a two-way contingency table are thus given by

$$v = (r - 1)(c - 1).$$

In our problem $v = (3 - 1)(3 - 1) = 4$. Using our assumed $\alpha = 0.10$, the tabled critical value of χ^2 for four degrees of freedom is 7.78 (see Table 2 in the appendix at the back of the book). Computed $\chi^2 = 58.231$ thus falls in the critical region. The null hypothesis of independence is rejected. Family size is a factor in determining size of washing machine purchased.

In one form or another, the chi-square test is probably the most widely used test in marketing research, and the serious student is well advised to become familiar with its requirements. Research Realities 15A.1 summarizes them.

Contingency Coefficient

While the χ^2 contingency table test indicates whether two variables are independent, it does not measure the strength of association when they are dependent. The **contingency coefficient** can be used for this latter purpose. Since the contingency coefficient is di-

Research Realities 15A.1

Requirements for the Chi-Square Test

1. The test deals with frequencies. Percentage values need to be converted to counts of the number of cases in each cell.[1]

2. The chi-square distribution, although continuous, is being used to approximate the distribution of a discrete variable. This results in the computed value being proportionately inflated if too many of the expected frequencies are small. It is generally agreed that only a few cells (less than 20 percent) should be permitted to have expected frequencies less than 5, and none should have expected frequencies less than 1.[2] Categories may be meaningfully combined to conform to this rule.

3. Multiple answers per respondent should not be analyzed with chi-square contingency table analysis in that the normal tabled critical values of the chi-square statistic for a specified alpha error no longer apply when more than one cross-tabulation analysis is conducted with the same data. If multiple answers per respondent are to be analyzed, special tables should be used for testing the statistical significance of the results.[3]

4. Each observation should be independent of the others. The chi-square test would not be appropriate, for example, for analyzing observations on the same individuals in a pretest-posttest experiment.[4]

[1]The test can also be used with proportions, but this type of application is much rarer. For an example, see George W. Snedecor and William G. Cochran, *Statistical Methods*, 6th ed. (Ames, Iowa: Iowa State University Press, 1967), pp. 240–242.

[2]Snedecor and Cochran, *Statistical Methods*, p. 235, suggest the χ^2 test is accurate enough if only the latter condition is satisfied, and they recommend combining classes only to ensure cell sizes of at least one. When there is only one degree of freedom, Yates' correction for continuity can be applied, which improves the test and removes cell size requirements. See F. Yates, "Contingency Tables Involving Small Numbers and the χ^2 Test," *Journal of the Royal Statistical Society*, 1, pp. 217–235.

[3]See C. Mitchell Dayton and William D. Schafer, "Extended Tables of *t* and Chi Square for Bonferroni Tests with Unequal Error Allocation," *Journal of the American Statistical Association*, 68 (March 1973), pp. 78–83.

[4]When the observations are related, rather than being independent, the McNemar or Cochran Q tests can be employed when the data are nominal. These tests are discussed in a number of nonparametric statistics books. See, for example, Leonard A. Marascuilo and Maryellen McSweeney, *Nonparametric and Distribution-Free Methods for the Social Sciences* (Belmont, Calif.: Brooks/Cole, 1977); or Wayne W. Daniel, *Applied Nonparametric Statistics* (Boston: Houghton Mifflin, 1978).

rectly related to the χ^2 test, it can be generated by the researcher with relatively little additional computational effort. The formula for the contingency coefficient, call it C, is

$$C = \sqrt{\frac{\chi^2}{n + \chi^2}},$$

when n is the sample size and χ^2 is calculated in the normal way.

Recall that calculated χ^2 for the data in Table 15A.1 was 58.23, and that since the calculated value was larger than the critical tabled value, the null hypothesis of independence was rejected. While the conclusion that naturally follows, that family size affects the size of washing machine purchased, is an interesting finding, it is only part of the story. Although the variables are dependent, what is the strength of the association between them? The contingency coefficient helps answer this question. The contingency coefficient is

$$C = \sqrt{\frac{58.23}{300 + 58.23}} = 0.403.$$

Does this value indicate strong or weak association between the variables? We cannot say without comparing the calculated value against its limits. When there is no association between the variables, the contingency coefficient will be zero. Unfortunately, though, the contingency coefficient does not possess the other attractive property of the Pearsonian product-moment correlation coefficient of being equal to one when the variables are completely dependent or perfectly correlated. Rather, its upper limit is a function of the number of categories. When the number of categories is the same for each variable, that is, when the number of rows r equals the number of columns c, the upper limit on the contingency coefficient for two perfectly correlated variables is

$$\sqrt{(r-1)/r}.$$

In the example at hand, $r = c = 3$, and thus the upper limit for the contingency coefficient is

$$\sqrt{\frac{2}{3}} = 0.816$$

The calculated value is approximately halfway between the limits of zero for no association and 0.816 for perfect association, suggesting there is moderate association between size of family and size of washing machine purchased.

Index of Predictive Association

One of the difficulties associated with the contingency coefficient is interpreting the strength of the association between the variables as judged by the calculated value. For instance, while we were able to say that there was moderate association between the variables of cross classification, the interpretation was not as straightforward as it would have been if the Pearsonian r had been calculated. Recall that the square of r is the coefficient of determination, which indicates the proportion of the variance in one variable that is accounted for by covariation in the other. This is a clear measure of the strength of the association between the variables. The contingency coefficient has no such standard to assist the analyst in interpreting the results. The index of predictive association is "more directly interpretable" in this regard.[2]

The **index of predictive association** is appropriate for nominally scaled variables. Consider for a moment a hypothetical example with the following conditions. First, there is one criterion and one predictor variable and both are divisible into three classes: A_1, A_2, and A_3 and B_1, B_2, and B_3, respectively. Second, the 100 observations are as arrayed in Table 15A.3. Third, the purpose is to predict the A classification of an object chosen at random, that is, should it be predicted as falling into category A_1, A_2, or A_3.

---

[2]The index was originally proposed by Leo A. Goodman and William H. Kruskal, "Measures of Association for Cross-Classifications," *Journal of the American Statistical Association,* 49 (December 1954), pp. 732–764. See also Lawrence J. Feick, "Analyzing Marketing Research Data with Association Models," *Journal of Marketing Research,* 21 (November 1984), pp. 376–386, for a discussion of a number of other association coefficients that can be used with categorical or nominal data.

Table 15A.3

Hypothetical Data: Some Relationship—$\lambda_{A.B}$ = 0.400

	A_1	A_2	A_3	Total
B_1	10	5	0	15
B_2	10	35	5	50
B_3	0	10	25	35
Total	20	50	30	100

Assume initially that we have no knowledge of the B classification. The best estimate for the randomly chosen object is classification A_2, since one-half of all the observations of the A variate fall in this category. Proceeding on this basis, we would make 50 percent of all assignments correctly, since we would assign them all to A_2. Conversely, we would be wrong half of the time. Suppose now we know the B classification of the object chosen at random. If the B classification is B_1, the best guess is A_1, since two-thirds of all cases possessing B_1 fall in the A_1 classification. Similarly, if it is B_2, the best guess is A_2, and if it is B_3, the best guess is A_3.

The **index of predictive association,** $\lambda_{A.B,}$ measures the relative decrease in the probability of error by taking account of the B classification in predicting the A classification, over the error of prediction when the B classification is unknown. In the example, $\lambda_{A.B}$ = 0.400. The errors in predicting the A classification are reduced by 40 percent by taking account of the B classification. The original classification error rate is 50 percent; these errors are decreased by 20 percent (50 percent times 0.400 equals 20 percent). In effect, one should now make 70 percent of the A classification predictions correctly (the original 50 percent plus the additional 20 percent) by taking account of B.

The index of predictive association varies from 0 to 1. It is zero if the B classification is of no help in predicting the A classification. In Table 15A.4, without any knowledge of the B classification, the logical guess for the A classification is A_2. Given that the randomly drawn element is in any of the three B classifications, B_1, B_2, or B_3, the best assignment for the element on the criterion variable is still A_2. The B classification is of no assistance in predicting the A classification.

Table 15A.5 illustrates the case in which B is a perfect predictor of A. Given no information about B, A_2 is the best classification estimate; 50 percent of the time this assignment is in error. Given the knowledge that the element drawn at random possesses characteristic B_1, the proper prediction of the criterion variable is classification A_1. For B_2, it is A_2, and for B_3, it is A_3. The B classification allows the A classification estimates to be made without error. That is, the errors in estimating A have been reduced 100 percent by taking account of B. The index of predictive association, $\lambda_{A.B.}$, equals 1.0.

The index of predictive association is calculated as follows. Assume we are indeed predicting the A classification from the B classification. Let

$n_{.m}$ be the *largest* marginal frequency among the A classes, and

n_{bm} be the *largest* frequency in the bth row (or column) of the table.

Table 15A.4

Hypothetical Data: No Relationship—$\lambda_{A.B} = 0$

	A_1	A_2	A_3	Total
B_1	5	10	0	15
B_2	15	20	15	50
B_3	0	20	15	35
Total	20	50	30	100

Table 15A.5

Hypothetical Data: Perfect Relationship—$\lambda_{A.B} = 1.0$

	A_1	A_2	A_3	Total
B_1	20	0	0	20
B_2	0	50	0	50
B_3	0	0	30	30
Total	20	50	30	100

Then

$$\lambda_{A.B} = \frac{\sum_b n_{bm} - n_{.m}}{n - n_{.m}},$$

where $\Sigma_b n_{bm}$ is taken across all the B classes. Now, for the washing machine and family size example, $n = 300$. Considering that size of machine purchased is to be predicted from family size, the largest marginal frequency among the A classes, $n_{.m}$, is 125, corresponding to the 10-lb load machines. Given that the family is one to two members, the largest frequency in the first column of the cross-classification table, n_{1m}, is 25; similarly, $n_{2m} = 62$ and $n_{3m} = 59$. Thus, the index of predictive association is

$$\lambda_{A.B} = \frac{n_{1m} + n_{2m} + n_{3m} - n_{.m}}{n - n_{.m}} = \frac{25 + 62 + 59 - 125}{300 - 125} = 0.12.$$

Given no information about family size, the best estimate of the size of the washing machine that would be purchased by a family chosen at random would be the 10-lb load machine. Some 41.7 percent, or 125 out of 300 families, purchased these machines. In 41.7 percent of the cases we would be right, and in 58.3 percent we would be wrong, if we predicted that a family chosen at random would purchase a 10-lb load washing machine. This error is reduced by 12 percent by taking account of family size. Since 12 percent of 58.3 is 7.0, this means that $41.7 + 7.0 = 48.7$ percent of the predictions would be made correctly if family size is considered.

The improvement in predictive accuracy is slight even though using the contingency-table test for independence of the variables of classification convincingly rejected the notion of independence between the variables. This demonstrates the two important questions in association analysis. First, is there association between the criterion and predictor variables, or are they independent? Second, if they are dependent, by how much are predictions about the criterion variable improved by taking into account the important predictor variables? The index of predictive association, as well as the other measures of association, is used to answer the latter question. The tests of their statistical significance answer the former.[3]

Spearman's Rank Correlation Coefficient

Spearman's rank correlation coefficient, denoted r_s, is one of the best known coefficients of association for rank-order data. The coefficient is appropriate when there are two variables per object, both of which are measured on an ordinal scale so that the objects may be ranked in two ordered series.[4]

Suppose, for instance, that a company wished to determine whether there was any association between the overall performance of a distributor and the distributor's level of service. Again, there are many measures of overall performance: sales, market share, sales growth, profit, and so on. The company thought that no single measure adequately defined distributor performance but that overall performance was a composite of all of these measures. Thus, the marketing research department was assigned the task of developing an index of performance that effectively incorporated all of these characteristics. The department was also assigned the responsibility of evaluating each distributor in terms of the service provided. This evaluation was to be based on customer complaints, customer compliments, service turnaround records, and so on. The research department believed that the indices it developed to measure these characteristics could be employed to rank-order the distributors with respect to overall performance and service.

Table 15A.6 contains the ranks of the company's 15 distributors with respect to each of the performance criteria. One way to determine whether there is any association between service and overall performance would be to look at the differences in ranks based on each of the two variables. Let X_i be the rank of the ith distributor with respect to service and Y_i be the rank of the ith distributor with regard to overall performance. Further, let $d_i = X_i - Y_i$ be the difference in rankings for the ith distributor. Now, if the rankings on the two variables are exactly the same, each d_i will be zero. If there is some discrepancy in ranks, some of the d_i's will not be zero. Further, the greater the discrepancy, the larger would be some of the d_i's. Thus, one way of looking at the association between the variables would be to examine the sum of the d_i's. The diffi-

---

[3]It is also possible to attempt to isolate the *sources of dependence* in a cross-classification table. See David L. Rados, "Two-Way Analysis of Tables in Marketing Research," *Journal of the Market Research Society,* 22 (October 1980), pp. 248–262, and Ottar Hellevik, *Introduction to Causal Analysis* (London: George Allen & Unwin, 1984), for discussion of techniques for doing so.

[4]The Spearman rank correlation coefficient is a shortcut version of the product moment correlation coefficient, in that both coefficients produce the same estimates of the strength of association between two sets of ranks. The rank correlation coefficient is easy to conceptualize and calculate, so it is often used when the data are ranked. See Nunnally, *Psychometric Theory,* pp. 134–135.

Table 15A.6
Distributor Performance

Distributor	Service Ranking X_i	Overall Performance Ranking Y_i	Ranking Difference $d_i = X_i - Y_i$	Difference Squared d_i^2
1	6	8	−2	4
2	2	4	+2	4
3	13	12	+1	1
4	1	2	−1	1
5	7	10	−3	9
6	4	5	−1	1
7	11	9	+2	4
8	15	13	+2	4
9	3	1	+2	4
10	9	6	+3	9
11	12	14	−2	4
12	5	3	+2	4
13	14	15	−1	1
14	8	7	+1	1
15	10	11	−1	1

$$\sum_{i=1}^{15} d_i^2 = 52$$

culty with this measure is that some of the negative d_i's would cancel some of the positive ones. To circumvent this difficulty, the differences are squared in calculating the Spearman rank-order correlation coefficient. The calculation formula is[5]

$$r_s = 1 - \frac{6\sum_{i=1}^{n} d_i^2}{n(n^2 - 1)}.$$

In the example at hand

$$\sum_{i=1}^{15} d_i^2 = 52$$

and

$$r_s = 1 - \frac{6(52)}{15(15^2 - 1)} = 1 - \frac{312}{3,360} = 0.907.$$

---

[5]See Marascuilo and McSweeney, *Nonparametric and Distribution-Free Methods*, pp. 429–439, for the development of the logic underlying the computational formula. An alternate measure of rank correlation is provided by Kendall's tau coefficient. See M. G. Kendall, *Rank Correlation Methods* (London: Griffin, 1948), pp. 47–48, for a discussion of the rationale behind the tau coefficient; and Edgar Pessemier and Moshe Handelsman, "Temporal Variety in Consumer Behavior," *Journal of Marketing Research*, 21 (November 1984), pp. 435–444, for a marketing example that uses it.

Now the null hypothesis for the example would be that there is no association between service level and overall distributor performance, while the alternate hypothesis would suggest there is a relationship. The null hypothesis that $r_s = 0$ can be tested by referring directly to tables of critical values of r_s or, when the number of sample objects is greater than ten, by calculating the t statistic,

$$t = r_s \sqrt{\frac{n - 2}{1 - r_s^2}},$$

which is referred to a t table for $\nu = n - 2$ degrees of freedom. Calculated t is

$$t = 0.907 \sqrt{\frac{15 - 2}{1 - (0.907)^2}} = 7.77,$$

while critical t for $\alpha = 0.05$ and $\nu = 13$ degrees of freedom is 2.16. Calculated t exceeds critical t, and the null hypothesis of no relationship is rejected. Overall distributor performance is related to service level. The upper limit for the Spearman rank correlation coefficient is one, since if there were perfect agreement in the ranks, $\Sigma_{i=1}^n d_i^2$ would be zero. Thus, the relationship is significant and relatively strong.

Coefficient of Concordance

So far we have been concerned with the correlation between *two* sets of rankings of n objects. There has been an X and Y measure in the form of ranks for each object. There will be cases in which we wish to analyze the association among three or more rankings of n objects or individuals. When there are k sets of rankings, Kendall's coefficient of concordance (W) can be employed to examine the association among the k variables.

One particularly important use of the coefficient of concordance is in examining interjudge reliability. Consider the computer equipment manufacturer interested in evaluating its domestic sales branch managers. Many criteria could be used: sales of the branch office, sales in relation to the branch's potential, sales growth, and sales representative turnover are just a few. It was believed that different executives in the company would place different emphasis on the various criteria and that a consensus with respect to how the criteria should be weighted would be hard to achieve. The company, therefore, decided that the vice-president in charge of marketing, the general sales manager, and the marketing research department should all attempt to rank the ten branch managers from best to worst. Table 15A.7 contains these rankings. The company wished to determine whether there was agreement among these rankings.

The right-hand column of Table 15A.7 contains the sum of ranks assigned to each branch manager. Now, if there was *perfect agreement* among the three rankings, the sum of ranks, R_i, for the top-rated branch manager would be $1 + 1 + 1 = k$, where $k = 3$. The second-rated branch manager would have sum of ranks $2 + 2 + 2 = 2k$, and the nth-rated branch manager would have sum of ranks $n + n + n = nk$. Thus, when there is perfect agreement among the k sets of rankings, the R_i would be k, $2k$, $3k$, . . . , nk. If there is little agreement among the k rankings, the R_i would be approximately equal. Thus, the degree of agreement among the k rankings could be measured by the variance of the n sums of ranks; the greater the agreement, the larger would be the variance in the n sums.

Table 15A.7

Branch Manager Rankings

Branch Manager	Rank Advocated by			Sum of Ranks R_i
	Vice-President Marketing	General Sales Manager	Marketing Research Department	
A	4	4	5	13
B	3	2	2	7
C	9	10	10	29
D	10	9	9	28
E	2	3	3	8
F	1	1	1	3
G	6	5	4	15
H	8	7	7	22
I	5	6	6	17
J	7	8	8	23

The **coefficient of concordance** (W) is a function of the variance in the sums of ranks. It is calculated in the following way. First, the sum of the R_i for each of the n rows is determined. Second, the average R_i, $\overline{R}$, is calculated by dividing the sum of the R_i by the number of objects. Third, the sum of the squared deviations is determined; call this quantity s, where

$$s = \sum_{i=1}^{n} (R_i - \overline{R})^2.$$

The coefficient of concordance is then computed as

$$W = \frac{s}{\frac{1}{12} k^2(n^3 - n)}.$$

The denominator of the coefficient represents the maximum possible variation in sums of ranks if there was perfect agreement in the rankings. The numerator, of course, reflects the actual variation in ranks. The larger the ratio, the greater the agreement among the evaluations.

$$\overline{R} = \frac{\sum_{i=1}^{n} R_i}{n} = \frac{13 + 7 + \ldots + 23}{10} = \frac{165}{10} = 16.5,$$

$$s = (13 - 16.5)^2 + (7 - 16.5)^2 + \ldots + (23 - 16.5)^2 = 720.5,$$

and

$$\frac{1}{12} k^2(n^3 - n) = \frac{1}{12} (3)^2(10^3 - 10) = 742.5.$$

Thus,

$$W = \frac{720.5}{742.5} = 0.970.$$

The significance of W can be examined by using special tables when the number of objects being ranked is small, in particular when $n \leq 7$. When there are more than seven objects, the coefficient of concordance is approximately chi-square distributed where $\chi^2 = k(n - 1) W$ with $\nu = n - 1$ degrees of freedom. The null hypothesis is that there is no agreement among the rankings, while the alternate hypothesis is that there is some agreement. For an assumed $\alpha = 0.05$, critical χ^2 for $\nu = n - 1 = 9$ degrees of freedom is 16.92, while calculated χ^2 is

$$\chi^2 = k(n - 1) W = 3 \ (9)(0.970) = 26.2.$$

Calculated χ^2 exceeds critical χ^2, and the null hypothesis of no agreement is rejected. There is agreement. Further, the agreement is good, as is evidenced by the calculated coefficient of concordance. The limits of W are zero with no agreement and one with perfect agreement among the ranks. The calculated value of W of 0.967 suggests that while the agreement in the ranks is not perfect, it is certainly good. The marketing vice-president, the general sales manager, and the marketing research department are applying essentially the same standards in ranking the branch managers.

Kendall has suggested that the best estimate of the true ranking of n objects is provided by the order of the various sums of ranks, R_i, when W is significant.[6] Thus the best estimate of the true ranking of the sales managers is that F is doing the best job and B the next best job, and that C is doing the poorest job.

Questions

1. What is the basic question at issue in a contingency-table test? What is the null hypothesis for this test? How are the expected frequencies determined?

2. What is the contingency coefficient and to what types of situations does it apply? How does one determine whether the association between the variables indicated by the calculated value of the contingency coefficient is "strong" or "weak"?

3. What is the index of predictive association? When is it properly used? What is meant by an index of predictive association of $\lambda_{A.B} = 0.750$?

4. What is the Spearman rank correlation coefficient? To what types of situations does it apply? How is it calculated and interpreted?

5. What is the coefficient of concordance? When is it used? What is the rationale underlying its computation?

---

[6]Kendall, *Rank Correlation Methods*, p. 87.

Applications and Problems

1. A large publishing house wants to determine if there is an association between news-paper–publication choice and the education level of the customer. A random sample of 400 customers provided the data in Table 1:

Table 1
Education Level versus Newspaper Choice: Observed Frequencies

Newspaper Publication	Level of Education			Total
	High School Degree	Undergraduate Degree	Graduate Degree	
A	75	45	5	125
B	35	10	30	75
C	50	35	10	95
D	65	35	5	105
Total	225	125	50	400

(a) State the null and alternate hypotheses.
(b) Generate the expected frequencies for each cell of Table 1. Enter the expected frequencies in the lower right-hand corner and the observed frequencies in the upper left-hand corner of Table 2.

Table 2
Education Level versus Newspaper Choice: Observed and Expected Frequencies

Newspaper Publication	Level of Education			Total
	High School Degree	Undergraduate Degree	Graduate Degree	
A				
B				
C				
D				
Total				

(c) Is there an association between newspaper-publication choice and level of educa-tion at $\alpha = 0.05$? Show all your calculations.
(d) What is the strength of association, as measured by the contingency coefficient between education level and newspaper choice? Show your calculations.

2. A marketing researcher from the publishing company in Problem 1 states that the best estimate of newspaper choice by a customer chosen at random would be the 'A' publi-

cation since 31.25 percent (or 125 out of 400) customers purchased this publication. The researcher further states that 68.75 percent of the time the company would be wrong and decides to discard the previous study.

(a) How could the predictive accuracy be improved? Show your calculations.
(b) The index of predictive association is "more directly interpretable" than the contingency coefficient. Discuss.

Appendix 15B
Analysis of Catalog Buying Data

Simple Regression

One of the questions of concern was the attitude of catalog recipients to buying from Avery and whether that attitude was related in any way to the person's demographic characteristics. To address this issue, an "attitude toward Avery" index, called ATTAVRY, was formed from the responses to Questions 7 through 11. ATTAVRY was formed in such a way that higher scores implied more favorable attitudes about buying from Avery. The responses to the five questions were summed to produce the ATTAVRY score for each subject.

Table 15B.1 investigates whether the ATTAVRY index varies as a function of the person's occupation. Recall that blue-collar workers were coded as 0 and white-collar workers as 1. Instead of the t value discussed in the text, the statistical significance of the equation is assessed in the program using analysis of variance techniques discussed in Appendix 14A. The calculated F value of 374.512 is statistically significant at the .01 level since the tabled F value for 1 and 122 degrees of freedom is approximately

Table 15B.1
Simple Regression Analysis of ATTAVRY Index versus Occupation

Dependent Variable . . . ATTAVRY
Variable(s) Entered on Step Number 1. V41

		Analysis of Variance	DF	Sum of Squares	Mean Square	F
Multiple R	.869	Regression	1	4071.174	4071.174	374.512
R square	.754	Residual	122	1326.213	10.871	
Adjusted R square	.752					
Standard error	3.297					

	Variables in the Equation			
Variable	B	Beta	Standard Error B	F
V41	11.534	.869	.596	374.512
(Constant)	9.727			

2.75. The relationship is also practically significant. The adjusted R square value of .752 indicates that approximately 75 percent of the variation in the ATTAVRY index can be accounted for or explained by the variation in occupation. There is a positive relationship between the two variables ($B = 11.534$); white-collar workers have more favorable attitudes toward Avery than blue-collar workers.

Multiple Regression

In an attempt to determine if the ATTAVRY index was related to other demographic characteristics, a multiple regression analysis was conducted in which the ATTAVRY index was regressed on the catalog recipient's age and marital status in addition to the person's occupation. Since marital status was categorical, it was necessary to convert it to a series of dummy variables before proceeding. More specifically, the five marital status categories were converted to four dummy variables with the following equivalences using SPSS's recode ability.

V43 =	Implying	D2	D3	D4	D5
1	Single	0	0	0	0
2	Married	1	0	0	0
3	Separated	0	1	0	0
4	Divorced	0	0	1	0
5	Widowed	0	0	0	1

Table 15B.2 contains the output. Note first that the overall regression equation is statistically significant; the calculated F value of 277.036 compares with a tabled F value of approximately 1.82 for 6 and 117 degrees of freedom for $\alpha = .01$. Further, the variables as a set account for 93 percent of the variation in the ATTAVRY index as witnessed by the adjusted R square value of .931.

The results also provide an interesting opportunity to interpret a dummy variable coding. Note that the respective values for the dummy variables D2 through D5 referring to the marital status categories are:

$$D2 = 2.851$$

$$D3 = 4.387$$

$$D4 = 7.006$$

$$D5 = 7.577$$

The four positive values all indicate that in comparison to the null state (defined as single), married, separated, divorced, and widowed people all have more favorable attitudes toward Avery. The D2 value indicates there is an increase in the ATTAVRY index of 2.85 on average if the person is married rather than single. The differential due to comparisons with other than single people is found by looking at appropriate differences in the dummy variable values. Thus, for example, divorced people have an ATTAVRY index approximately 2.62 higher on average than separated people, since $D4 - D3 = 2.619$.

Table 15B.2

**Multiple Regression Analysis of ATTAVRY Index
versus Several Demographic Characteristics**

Dependent Variable . . . ATTAVRY
Variable(s) Entered on Step Number 1 . .D2
V41
V42
D5
D4
D3

		Analysis of Variance	DF	Sum of Squares	Mean Square	F
Multiple R	.967	Regression	6	5042.459	840.410	277.036
R square	.934	Residual	117	354.928	3.034	
Adjusted R square	.931					
Standard error	1.742					

	Variables in the Equation			
Variable	**B**	**Beta**	**Standard Error B**	**F**
D2	2.851	.165	.627	20.668
V41	3.753	.283	.600	39.081
V42	.213	.368	.029	55.626
D5	7.577	.550	.935	65.625
D4	7.006	.391	.948	54.618
D3	4.387	.267	.646	46.076
(Constant)	4.491			

Chapter **16**
Data Analysis:
Discriminant, Factor,
and Cluster Analysis

The best known and most commonly used multivariate data-analysis technique is multiple-regression analysis. In Chapter 15 multiple regression's purpose and key interpretive quantities were discussed. In this chapter three multivariate techniques that have historically been used less often in the analysis of marketing problems—discriminant analysis, factor analysis, and cluster analysis—are discussed. Discriminant analysis is similar to multiple-regression analysis in that it involves the investigation of a criterion variable/predictor variable relationship. Only now the criterion variable is a dichotomy or multichotomy, whereas with regression analysis it is interval scaled. Factor analysis and cluster analysis are both methods of interdependence analysis in that no variable is singled out for special treatment as a criterion variable. While factor analysis is the most frequently used technique of the three, popularity varies by industry, and the magnitude of the usage differences are not great, either in total or within specific industries. See Research Realities 16.1.

Discriminant Analysis

Many marketing problems naturally involve the investigation of group differences. Two or more groups may be compared, but the problem is essentially determining whether they differ from one another and understanding the nature of these differences. For example, we might be interested in determining the characteristics that differentiate between (among):

- light and heavy users of the product;
- purchasers of our brand and those of competing brands;
- brand loyal and nonloyal customers;
- customers who patronize one type of retail outlet and those who patronize others;
- good, mediocre, and poor sales representatives.

Suppose the comparisons for any of the these problems were to be made along demographic-socioeconomic lines. One way to proceed would be simply to calculate the mean income, age, education level, and so on, for the comparison groups to determine which group is higher.

Research Realities 16.1

Relative Frequency of Use of Factor, Cluster, and Discriminant Analysis

Type of Company	Percent Using		
	Factor Analysis	Cluster Analysis	Discriminant Analysis
Consumer goods manufacturer	36	21	31
Industrial goods manufacturer	15	9	6
Retailers and wholesalers	9	18	9
Utilities	28	33	22
Communications	27	14	5
Marketing research and consulting	27	33	18
Finance and insurance	17	10	10
Other services	20	20	0
Others	13	0	7
Total sample	23	18	14

Source: Barnett A. Greenberg, Jac L. Goldstucker, and Danny N. Bellenger, "What Techniques Are Used by Marketing Researchers in Business?" *Journal of Marketing*, 41 (April 1977), pp. 64–65.

While such an approach might be interesting with respect to the individual variables, it would tell us little about their respective impacts when used in combination in that, it is unlikely that all the variables will have independent effects. Suppose, for example, that we were investigating the characteristics that distinguish light users from heavy users of our product. If the groups showed a difference with respect to mean income levels, it is also likely that they would show a difference with respect to mean educational levels because these two variables are fairly highly correlated. Yet if we were interested in segmenting the market using income and educational level as segmentation variables, we would be interested in the total effect of the two variables in combination, not their separate effects. Further, we would be interested in determining which of the variables was more important or had the greater impact. In essence, we need a mechanism that allows us to consider the variables *simultaneously* so as to take into account their interrelationship and partially overlapping information.

One alternative is to construct a *linear combination* of the variables—that is, a weighted sum—in such a way that the linear combination will *best discriminate* among the groups in some sense. We can then assess how the groups differ with respect to this new linear combination score and can also look at the relative weights assigned to each of the variables when forming the linear combination to get some idea as to their relative importance.

Discriminant analysis is the method by which such linear combinations are determined. It was first proposed by R. A. Fisher for the analysis of two-group situations.[1] When two groups are being compared, one linear combination or discriminant function results. The technique was later extended to the analysis of three or more groups (for example, light, medium, and heavy users), in which case several discriminant functions can result.[2]

Two-Group Case

The essential purpose and key interpretive output of discriminant analysis are best illustrated by example. Consider, in particular, the experience of the manufacturing firm that conducted a "new account world series" sales contest among its salespeople in an attempt to increase the number of distributors handling the firm's products. The contest ran for three months. Each salesperson was assigned a quota with respect to the number of new accounts he or she was expected to generate in that period. The quotas were determined by the sales analysis department and were based on a detailed examination of the segments the company served as defined by SIC codes. More specifically, the sales analysis department based the quotas on the historic penetration of the various segments and the number of accounts of each type that were not current customers in each salesperson's territory. All salespeople who had 15 or more new accounts place an order in the contest period received an all-expense-paid vacation to Hawaii for two. Those who had at least five new accounts place an order received a lesser prize of the choice of a new color TV set or VCR. Those converting less than five new accounts received nothing. As it turned out, 15 salespeople won the grand prize and another 15 the consolation prize, while a third of the salespeople won nothing.[3] The sales analysis department was interested in determining what salesperson activities made a difference with respect to whether a salesperson was a prizewinner or not.

Now, there are a number of ways to proceed with the analysis. The sales department could compare those who were grand prize winners against the others. Alternatively, it might compare those who won any kind of prize against those who won nothing. Still further, it might compare each group against each of the other two. For the moment, let us just consider the two prizewinning groups so as to throw the basic thrust of

[1]R. A. Fisher, "The Use of Multiple Measurements in Taxonomic Problems," *Annuals of Eugenics,* 8 (1936), pp. 376–386.

[2]The extension is customarily attributed to Rao, although it seems to have been accomplished by several researchers working independently. See J. G. Bryan, "A Method for the Exact Determination of the Characteristic Equation and Latent Vectors of a Matrix with Applications to the Discriminant Function for More than Two Groups," unpublished doctoral dissertation, Harvard University, 1950; C. R. Rao, "The Utilization of Multiple Measurements in Problems of Biological Classification, *Journal of the Royal Statistical Society, Series B,* 10 (1948), pp. 159–193; and J. W. Tukey, "Dyadic Anova, An Analysis of Variance for Vectors," *Human Biology,* 21 (1949), pp. 65–110.

[3]The contest had a number of the ingredients that are generally recommended for sales contests, including a specific objective, a theme, and a reasonable percentage of contest winners. See Gilbert A. Churchill, Jr., Neil M. Ford, and Orville C. Walker, Jr., *Sales Force Management,* 2nd ed. (Homewood, Ill.: Richard D. Irwin, 1985), pages 477–480, for a general discussion of the purposes and structure of sales contests.

discriminant analysis into bold relief. Specifically, let us see if we can determine what activities tended to have the greatest impact on whether a salesperson won a grand prize or only a consolation prize. We will take up the question of what activities tend to discriminate among all three groups below.

Table 16.1 contains the data the sales analysis department collected on each salesperson's new account activities. One way to proceed would be to plot the salespeople with respect to their activities while maintaining the identity of the group to which each salesperson belongs. Figure 16.1 contains several such plots comparing the grand prize and consolation prize winners. Consider Panel A, which displays the plot of the percentage of calls for which the salesperson had advance appointments against the total number of calls the salesperson made on new accounts. Panel A indicates that in general both of these variables were positively related to success, in that the more calls on new accounts the saleperson made and the greater the percentage of these calls for which the representative had advance appointments, the more likely the salesperson was to be a grand prize winner than a consolation prize winner. There were exceptions, though. Some consolation prize winners made more calls on new accounts than did grand prize winners. Similarly, some grand prize winners made a smaller percentage of advance appointments than did consolation prize winners. Overall, however, the mean number of calls on new accounts and the mean percentage with advance appointments are higher for grand prize winners versus consolation prize winners. A similar type of analysis,

Table 16.1
Salespeople's New Account Activities

	Number of Calls on New Accounts X_1	Percentage of Calls with Advance Appointments X_2	Telephone Calls Made to Prospects X_3	Number of New Accounts Visited X_4
Grand Prize Winner (W)				
1 RMB	130	62	148	42
2 ALB	122	70	186	44
3 BCC	89	68	171	32
4 JJC	104	58	135	40
5 EDC	116	40	160	36
6 WPD	100	65	151	30
7 RHH	85	66	183	42
8 BEK	113	59	130	25
9 DAK	108	52	163	41
10 JJN	116	48	154	48
11 MYS	99	57	188	32
12 PJS	78	70	190	40
13 CET	106	61	157	38
14 LLV	94	58	173	29
15 LMW	98	64	137	36
Mean	103.9	59.9	161.7	37.0

Table 16.1

Salespeople's New Account Activities *continued*

	Number of Calls on New Accounts X_1	Percentage of Calls with Advance Appointments X_2	Telephone Calls Made to Prospects X_3	Number of New Accounts Visited X_4
Consolation Prize Winner (C)				
1 JGB	105	39	155	45
2 RAB	86	60	140	33
3 HAF	64	48	132	36
4 PPD	104	36	119	29
5 BCE	102	53	143	41
6 ASG	73	62	128	30
7 WLH	94	51	152	36
8 LHL	59	64	130	28
9 RJL	84	31	102	32
10 WFM	91	47	96	35
11 JRP	83	40	87	30
12 EJS	95	42	114	28
13 VES	68	52	123	26
14 HMT	101	51	98	24
15 BMT	89	39	117	33
Mean	86.5	47.7	122.4	32.4
Unsuccessful Salespeople (U)				
1 RBB	80	23	69	32
2 GEB	47	42	74	33
3 ADC	26	37	132	20
4 JFC	94	24	68	26
5 LDE	57	32	94	23
6 JFH	38	41	83	28
7 JCH	29	52	96	22
8 RPF	48	24	73	26
9 APL	57	36	82	28
10 HAL	39	37	98	21
11 ERM	51	38	117	24
12 WRR	40	42	112	22
13 JTS	64	21	67	29
14 JMV	35	32	78	25
15 HEY	51	29	81	26
Mean	50.4	34.0	88.3	25.7
Overall				
Mean	80.3	47.2	124.1	31.7
Standard Deviation	15.91	8.97	19.99	5.37

Figure 16.1
Scatter Plots of Selected Two-variable Combinations

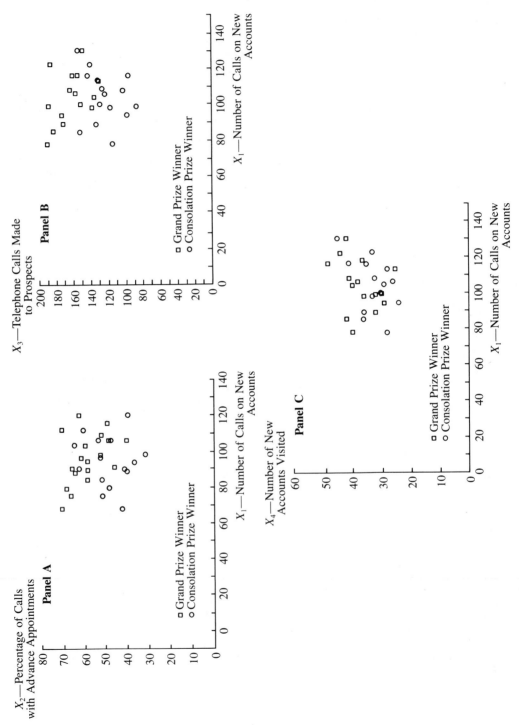

conducted with respect to Panels B and C of Figure 16.1, indicates that grand prize winners made more telephone calls to prospects and called on more new accounts on average than did consolation prize winners.

While the graphical approach for determining which activities seemed to make the most difference with respect to whether a salesperson was a grand prize or consolation prize winner is intuitively insightful, it has its problems. In the first place, it is difficult and time consuming to anticipate and then construct all the graphs that might be useful in a given situation. Even for our four-variable example, Figure 16.1 contains only three of the six possible combinations of the variables from which separate graphs could be constructed when the variables are taken two at a time.[4] While we might consider more variables at one time to reduce the number of potential graphs, higher dimensional graphs become exceedingly difficult to interpret. At the same time, two-dimensional graphs are limited in the amount of information they convey, since they allow us to consider only two independent variables at once. What is needed is a mechanism that allows us to assess the impact of each factor, taking into account their partially overlapping information.

One effective way to determine which variables discriminate between the two types of contest winners is to build an index that separates the two groups on the basis of their values on the measured characteristics. That is, consider when forming the index an arbitrary linear combination of number of calls of new accounts X_1, percentage of calls with advance appointments X_2, telephone calls made to prospects X_3, and number of new accounts visited X_4,

$$Y = v_1X_1 + v_2X_2 + v_3X_3 + v_4X_4,$$

where v_1, v_2, v_3, and v_4 are the arbitrary weights. Given values for v_1 through v_4, we can readily calculate a Y or index score for each of the 30 prize winners. The question at issue, though, is what criterion should be satisfied in deriving values for v_1 through v_4, or how should the Y scores behave?

In discriminant analysis, the weights are derived so that the *variation in Y scores between the two groups is as large as possible, while the variation in Y scores within the groups is a small as possible*. That is, the weights are derived so that the ratio

$$\frac{\text{Between-group variation}}{\text{Within-group variation}}$$

is maximized. This makes the groups as distinct as possible with respect to the new index scores.

Since the operation of the index score is seen most easily in the two-variable case, consider for the moment only the two predictors number of calls on new accounts X_1 and percentage of calls with advance appointments X_2. Given values for v_1 and v_2, we

---

[4]The number of possible two-way graphs is given by the standard combinatorial formula

$$C_2^m = \frac{m!}{(m - 2)!2!}$$

where m is the number of variables.

can readily calculate an index score for each of the 30 prize winners using the linear combination

$$Y = v_1 X_1 + v_2 X_2.$$

It turns out that the values for v_1 and v_2 that maximize the ratio of the between-group to within-group variation with respect to the new index scores are $v_1 = .064$ and $v_2 = .106$, that is, the linear combination

$$Y = .064X_1 + .106X_2.$$

Not only can we calculate each salesperson's score on the new index but we can graphically visualize what is happening, since a linear combination of variables essentially produces a new axis on which the scores in the original plot can be projected. The axis is constructed so that the perpendicular from each point to the Y axis meets the axis at the scale value equal to the appropriate Y score. Figure 16.2 displays the plot. Figure 16.2 is equivalent to Panel A of Figure 16.1 except for the inclusion of the new axis representing the linear combination.[5] Using the index score, we can now classify each of the salespeople as a grand prize winner or a consolation prize winner. If the salesperson's index score is closer to the mean of the index scores of the grand prize winners, we would classify him or her as a grand prize winner, and vice versa.

The basic approach in discriminant analysis is therefore similar to that employed in regression analysis. In each case, the analyst uses a weighted linear combination of independent variables to predict a dependent variable. In regression analysis, the dependent variable is continuous. In discriminant analysis, the dependent variable is group membership. As a matter of fact, one can transform a two-group discriminant analysis problem into a regression problem by using a dummy code for the dependent variable (for example, $Y = 0$ if consolation prize winner and $Y = 1$ if grand prize winner). The resulting regression coefficients will be proportional to those obtained using standard discriminant analysis procedures.

For the original four-variable problem, the discriminant weights are $v_1 = .059$, $v_2 = .063$, $v_3 = .034$, and $v_4 = -.032$, so that the linear combination that maximally differentiates between the groups is[6]

$$Y = .059X_1 + .063X_2 + .034X_3 - .032X_4.$$

---

[5]The linear combination is easily located, since the weights assigned each of the variables, when divided by the square root of the sum of the squared weights, equals the cosine of the angle between each of the variables and the new axis. That is, $(.064)^2 + (.106)^2 = .015$, and $\sqrt{.015} = .122$. Since $.064/.122 = .525$, the angle θ between the X_1 and the new discriminant axis is given by $\text{Cos } \theta = .525$ or $\theta = 58°$. The axis can also be located by first plotting the point that corresponds to the coefficients or some mutiple of the coefficients in the function, that is, .064 and .106 or some fixed multiple of these values. Next, a line is drawn from the origin through this point.

[6]The weights themselves are given by the eigenvector in the solution of the eigenvalue equation

$$(\mathbf{W}^{-1}\mathbf{B} - \lambda \mathbf{l})\mathbf{v} = \mathbf{0},$$

where $\mathbf{W}$ is the pooled sample variance-covariance matrix and $\mathbf{B}$ is the between-group sum-of-squares cross products matrix.

Figure 16.2
Scatter Plot Containing New Axis

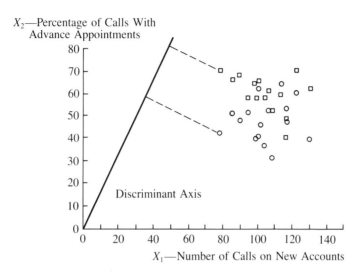

The function presents the weights to be applied to X_1 through X_4 so that the distribution of Y scores will show the largest separation between grand prize and consolation prize winners among all possible linear combinations we could have formed. These Y scores, which are known as discriminant scores, are presented for each sample member in Table 16.2. Note that the discriminant scores of grand prize winners are similar in magnitude, as are those of consolation prize winners, and that the two sets of scores are very different from each other. As a matter of fact, the members within the groups are as much alike as possible on these generated scores consistent with the fact that the groups themselves are as different as possible on these generated scores.

Note what we have done. We have taken a four-variable problem—the groups could be compared with respect to each of the salespeople's new account activities—and have reduced it to a univariate problem by forming a linear combination of X_1 through X_4, simplifying it in the process. We now need only to compare the discriminant scores of the groups rather than comparing the groups on all four variables. Further, we are secure in the knowledge that the groups are as different as possible with respect to these discriminant scores. Yes, but how does that help us in determining how grand prize winners differ from consolation prize winners with respect to their new account activities? Further, how does that help the sales analysis department isolate those factors that were most critical to salespeople's success? In effect, what can we do with this discriminant function now that we have it? These questions are answered by

- looking at the interpretation of the discriminant function, and
- employing the discriminant function to classify individuals in groups.

Table 16.2

**Calculated Discriminant Scores for Grand Prize and Consolation Prize Winners
Using the Discriminant Function** $Y = .058X_1 + .063X_2 + .034X_3 - .032X_4$

	X_1	X_2	X_3	X_4	Y
Grand Prize Winners					
1 RMB	130	62	148	42	15.2
2 ALB	122	70	186	44	16.5
3 BCC	89	68	171	32	14.3
4 JJC	104	58	135	40	13.0
5 EDC	116	40	160	36	13.6
6 WPD	100	65	151	30	14.1
7 RHH	85	66	183	42	14.0
8 BEK	113	59	130	25	13.9
9 DAK	108	52	163	41	13.8
10 JJN	116	48	154	48	13.5
11 MYS	99	57	188	32	14.8
12 PJS	78	70	190	40	14.2
13 CET	106	61	157	38	14.2
14 LLV	94	58	173	29	14.1
15 LMW	98	64	137	36	13.3
Mean	103.9	59.9	161.7	37.0	
Consolation Prize Winners					
1 JGB	105	39	155	45	12.4
2 RAB	86	60	140	33	12.5
3 HAF	64	48	132	36	10.1
4 PPD	104	36	119	29	11.4
5 BCE	102	53	143	41	12.8
6 ASG	73	62	128	30	11.6
7 WLH	94	51	152	36	12.7
8 LHL	59	64	130	28	11.0
9 RJL	84	31	102	32	9.3
10 WFM	91	47	96	35	10.4
11 JRP	83	40	87	30	9.4
12 EJS	95	42	114	28	11.2
13 VES	68	52	123	26	10.6
14 HMT	101	51	98	24	11.7
15 BMT	89	39	117	33	10.6
Mean	86.5	47.7	122.4	32.4	

Interpreting the Discriminant Function   Before attempting to interpret the discriminant function, the careful analyst will check on its statistical significance. A statistically significant function means that there is a meaningful differentiation of the groups on the discriminant scores. This implies that the investigation of the discriminant function can be worthwhile. The investigation is typically carried out by checking the statistical significance of Mahalanobis' D^2 statistic, which is a squared distance measure that is similar to the standard Euclidian distance measure. More particularly, it measures the distance from each case to the group mean while allowing for correlated axes and different measurement units for the variables. Fortunately, the F statistic for testing the significance of the D^2 statistic is routinely printed out by most canned computer programs.[7] It turns out that the discriminant function is statistically significant, and the interpretation of the function can proceed.

Discriminant coefficients are interpreted in much the same way as regression coefficients, in that each coefficient reflects the relative contribution of a unit change of each of the independent variables on the discriminant function. A small coefficient means that a one-unit change in that particular variable produces a small change in the discriminant function score, and vice versa. Like regression coefficients, discriminant coefficients are affected by the scale of the independent variables. That is, the original function $Y = .058X_1 + .063X_2 + .034X_3 - .032X_4$ contains the weights to be applied to the variables in raw-score scales. The problem with this is that if the unit of measurement for one or more variables were to be changed—for example, variable X_2 reflecting calls with advance appointments was measured as a proportion (a decimal) rather than as a percentage (a whole number)—the discriminant function would also change. To remove scale-of-measurement effects that are arbitrary, the discriminant weights that would be applied to the predictors in *standardized form* are employed when comparing the contributions of the individual variables. The relative magnitudes of these standardized weights are determined by multiplying each raw score weight by the *pooled standard deviation* of the corresponding variable. Define v_k^* as the standardized weight; v_k^* is related to the raw score weight v_k by the formula

$$v_k^* = v_k s_k,$$

where s_k is the pooled sample standard deviation of the kth variable. Considering only the grand and consolation prize winners, the pooled sample standard deviations are $s_1 = 16.76$, $s_2 = 10.89$, $s_3 = 28.16$, and $s_4 = 6.33$. Therefore

$$v_1^* = v_1 s_1 = .058(16.76) = .972,$$

$$v_2^* = v_2 s_2 = .063(10.89) = .686,$$

$$v_3^* = v_3 s_3 = .034(28.16) = .957,$$

$$v_4^* = v_4 s_4 = -.032(6.33) = -.203.$$

The absolute size of the standardized weights can be compared to determine the relative contribution of the variables. They indicate that the variable number of calls on new accounts (X_1) and telephone calls made to prospects (X_3) are the most important and number of new accounts visited (X_4) is the least important in differentiating grand prize from correlation prize winners. Further, variables X_1 through X_3 exert a positive

---

[7]See William R. Dillon and Matthew Goldstein, *Multivariate Analysis: Methods and Applications* (New York: John Wiley & Sons, 1984), pp. 366–369, for the details of how the significance of a discriminant function can be tested.

impact in that the greater the number of calls, the higher the percentage of calls with advance appointments, and the greater the number of telephone calls made to prospects, the more likely it is the salesperson was a grand prize versus a consolation prize winner. On the other hand, the number of new accounts the salesperson visited had a negative impact on the likelihood that the representative was a grand prize winner.

The standardized weights agree with what intuition might suggest regarding the importance of the variables when there is relatively little correlation among the predictors. For example, one very common intuitive assessment of the relative importance of the various variables in distinguishing between the groups is a comparison of their means. Large differences in the means on a particular variable suggest that the variable is an important discriminator between the groups, and vice versa. When there is little correlation among the predictors, the relative size of the coefficients in the discriminant function will yield the same ranking of importance of each variable in discriminating between the groups as ranking the size of their mean differences. When there is a high degree of correlation among the predictors, the ordering is not necessarily the same, and, as a matter of fact, the coefficients in the discriminant function need to be interpreted with a good deal more caution. Just as in regression analysis, a small standardized weight may then mean either that the variable is irrelevant in discriminating between the groups or, alternatively, that its impact has been partialed out of the relationship because of the high degree of multicollinearity in the data.

Discriminant *loadings* are also used to assess the importance of the variables in discriminating between groups. A discriminant loading gives the simple pairwise correlation between the variable and the discriminant score.[8] We can easily calculate, for example, the simple correlations between the discriminant scores Y and each of the predictors X_1 through X_4 in Table 16.2. It turns out that these correlations or loadings are

$$\text{Between } Y \text{ and } X_1: 0.627,$$

$$\text{Between } Y \text{ and } X_2: 0.679,$$

$$\text{Between } Y \text{ and } X_3: 0.847,$$

$$\text{Between } Y \text{ and } X_4: 0.441.$$

The loadings suggest that variable X_3 reflecting the telephone calls made to prospects is now the most important while variable X_4 reflecting the number of new accounts visited is still the least important in discriminating between grand prize and consolation prize winners. The difference in the ordering of the variables in comparison to the standardized weights is due to the correlations among the predictors. Like any correlation coefficient, the discriminant loadings can be squared, and the interpretation is similar to r^2 when they are. That is, the squared value for any loading indicates the amount of variance the discriminant score shares with the variable.

---

[8] We will have more to say about the notion of a loading later in this chapter when discussing factor analysis.

In sum, there are three quantities that are typically used to assess the relative importance of variables in discriminating between groups: the mean differences of the groups on each variable, the standardized coefficients, and the discriminant loadings. All three will produce similar conclusions as to the relative importance of the variables in discriminating between the groups when there is little intercorrelation among the predictors. When multicollinearity is a problem, their conclusions will differ, and the same caveats that apply when interpreting the coefficients in a regression analysis when the predictors are correlated apply here. The best posture is to display a good deal of caution.

Classifying Individuals Using the Discriminant Function   To assist in interpretation, we could also calculate the mean discriminant score for each group. To do this it is simply necessary to substitute the mean values of the variables for each group into the calculated discriminant function. For the grand prize winners, $\bar{x}_1 = 103.9$, $\bar{x}_2 = 59.9$, $\bar{x}_3 = 161.7$, and $\bar{x}_4 = 37.0$, and thus the mean discriminant score for grand prize winners, $\bar{Y}_W$, is

$$\bar{Y}_W = v_1\bar{x}_1 + v_2\bar{x}_2 + v_3\bar{x}_3 + v_4\bar{x}_4$$

$$= .059(103.9) + .063(59.9) + .034(161.7) - .032(37.0) = 14.2.$$

For consolation prize winners, $\bar{x}_1 = 86.5$, $\bar{x}_2 = 47.7$, $\bar{x}_3 = 122.4$, and $\bar{x}_4 = 32.4$, and the mean discriminant score, $\bar{Y}_C$, is similarly calculated as

$$\bar{Y}_C = .059(86.5) + .063(47.7) + .034(122.4) - .032(32.4) = 11.2.$$

This calculation indicates that grand prize winners on the average have higher discriminant scores than consolation prize winners. (The same result would be obtained if the discriminant scores in Table 16.2 had been averaged.)

To determine whether the discriminant function provides meaningful practical differentiation (versus statistical differentiation) between the two groups, it is possible to apply the discriminant function to each individual to predict the person's score and, on the basis of the generated score, to classify the salesperson as a grand prize or consolation prize winner. We could then compare this prediction with the individual's known actual classification to determine whether the function provides meaningful discrimination. Since we have already calculated the discriminant scores, let us create a predicted classification for each sample member using the very simple decision rule: *If a salesperson's discriminant score is closer to the mean score for grand prize winners than for consolidation prize winners, classify the salesperson as a grand prize winner; otherwise classify him or her as a consolation prize winner.* An alternative, but equivalent, procedure is to compute the score that divides the mean discriminant scores. This "cutting score" is then used to assign objects to groups in the following way: *If the individual's score is above the cutting score, classify the salesperson as a grand prize winner; if it is below, classify the salesperson as a consolation prize winner.* When the groups are equal in size, the **cutting score,** Y_{cs}, is given as the simple average of the mean discriminant scores for the groups, that is, by the calculation

$$Y_{cs} = (\bar{Y}_W + \bar{Y}_C)/2 = (14.2 + 11.2)/2 = 12.7.$$

When the groups are not equal, the formula needs to be modified to take the size of each group into account. The appropriate formula is then

$$Y_{cs} = \frac{n_2\overline{Y}_1 + n_1\overline{Y}_2}{n_1 + n_2},$$

where $\overline{Y}_1$ and $\overline{Y}_2$ are the mean discriminant scores and n_1 and n_2 the sizes of Groups 1 and 2, respectively.[9]

Either decision rule essentially defines the group to which the individual is most similar. Their application suggests the predicted classifications contained in the right-hand column of Table 16.3. Table 16.4, which is commonly referred to as a **confusion matrix,** summarizes the accuracy of this predictive classification decision rule.

The entries on the diagonal of Table 16.4 represent the **"hit rate"** or the proportion correctly classified, P_{cc}. This proportion is

$$P_{cc} = \frac{28}{30} = .933.$$

Approximately 93 percent of the salespeople are correctly classified as grand prize or consolation prize winners on the basis of their new account activities.

Assessing Classification Accuracy   A question that logically arises with any "hit rate" is assessing how good it is. One would probably argue for the example at hand that an approximate 93 percent hit rate is very good, given that one would only expect a 50 percent hit rate by chance alone, since there were as many consolation as grand prize winners in the sample of salespeople. How would you assess the hit rate, though, if the two groups were not equal in size. Suppose that in a sample of 100, 20 won grand prizes while 80 won consolation prizes, which could easily be the case if the quota requirements for the grand prize were changed. What is then a good hit rate? At least two criteria can be used: the maximum chance criterion, and the proportional chance criterion.[10]

The **maximum chance criterion** holds that any object chosen at random should be classified as belonging to the larger group, as that will maximize the proportion of cases correctly classified. In the sample of 100, we would thus classify anyone chosen at random as a consolation prize winner because that would make 80 percent of all the classifications correct.

The maximum chance classification rule is not very helpful from a marketing viewpoint, though. Rather, from a marketing perspective we wish to identify the two types

---

[9]See Joseph F. Hair, Jr., Ralph E. Anderson, Ronald L. Tatham, and Bernie J. Grablowsky, *Multivariate Data Analysis with Readings* (Tulsa: PPC Books, 1979), especially pp. 97–100, for a graphic portrayal of what happens to the optimal cutting score when the groups are not equal in size.

[10]Donald G. Morrison, "On the Interpretation of Discriminant Analysis," *Journal of Marketing Research,* 6 (May 1969), pp. 156–163. For a general discussion of the issues surrounding linear discriminant analysis and linear classification analysis, as well as an extensive bibliography, see Carl J. Huberty, "Issues in the Use and Interpretation of Discriminant Analysis," *Psychological Bulletin,* 95 (1984), pp. 156–171.

Table 16.3
Predicted Group Membership Using the Simple Classification Rule

Discriminant Score Y_i	Differences from Mean of		Predicted Group Membership
	First Group $Y_i - \overline{Y}_W = Y_i - 14.2$	Second Group $Y_i - \overline{Y}_C = Y_i - 11.2$	
Grand Prize Winners (W)			
1 15.2	1.0	4.0	W
2 16.5	2.3	5.3	W
3 14.3	0.1	3.1	W
4 13.0	−1.2	1.8	W
5 13.6	−0.6	2.4	W
6 14.1	−0.1	2.9	W
7 14.0	−0.2	2.8	W
8 13.9	−0.3	2.7	W
9 13.8	−0.4	2.6	W
10 13.5	−0.7	2.3	W
11 14.8	0.6	3.6	W
12 14.2	0.0	3.0	W
13 14.2	0.0	3.0	W
14 14.1	−0.1	2.9	W
15 13.3	−0.9	2.1	W
Consolation Prize Winners (C)			
1 12.4	−1.8	1.2	C
2 12.5	−1.7	1.3	C
3 10.1	−4.1	−1.1	C
4 11.4	−2.8	0.2	C
5 12.8	−1.4	1.6	W
6 11.6	−2.6	0.4	C
7 12.7	−1.5	1.5	W*
8 11.0	−3.2	−0.2	C
9 9.3	−4.9	−1.9	C
10 10.4	−3.8	−0.8	C
11 9.4	−4.8	−1.8	C
12 11.2	−3.0	0.0	C
13 10.6	−3.6	−0.6	C
14 11.7	−2.5	0.5	C
15 10.6	−3.6	−0.6	C

*The assignments were actually carried out using more significant digits in the calculations of discriminant scores. While the calculations to one decimal place suggest this case is equidistant from the two group means, it actually is slightly closer to the mean for the grand prize winners.

of winners. We would thus like to classify some salespeople chosen at random as grand prize winners and thereby defy the *a priori* odds. In such instances, the **proportional chance criterion,** C_{pro}, applies as the standard of evaluation, in which

$$C_{pro} = \alpha^2 + (1 - \alpha)^2,$$

Table 16.4

Confusion Matrix of Actual versus Predicted Group Membership

	Predicted Classification		
Actual Classification	Grand Prize Winner	Consolation Prize Winner	Total
Grand prize winner	15	0	15
Consolation prize winner	2	13	15

where

α = the proportion of individuals in Group 1

$1 - \alpha$ = the proportion of individuals in Group 2.

Suppose in the sample of 100 with unequal size groups that Group 1 was grand prize and Group 2 was consolation prize winners. The proportional chance criterion would then equal $C_{pro} = (0.20)^2 + (0.80)^2 = 0.68$. Thus, a classification accuracy of 85 percent, say, through the use of the discriminant function would represent a good improvement over chance alone, whereas 85 percent classification accuracy would not look very impressive against the maximum chance criterion. When the two groups are equal in size, as they are in the original example, the proportional chance criterion equals the maximum chance criterion.

There are a couple of comments that must be made in regard to the original classification procedure summarized in Table 16.4. First, there is an upward bias in the procedure because the proportion of correct hits is somewhat overstated.[11] This upward bias results because the data that were used to develop the discriminant model are also used to test the model. Since the criterion used to fit the model generates an equation that provides an optimal fit to the data at hand, the actual predictive accuracy of the model should be tested on a new sample of data. In many problems, this means that the original sample of observations is split into two subsamples. The one subsample, called the *analysis sample,* is used to develop the equation, while the other, called the *holdout sample,* is employed to examine how well the equation predicts group membership.[12]

---

[11]See R. E. Frank, W. F. Massy, and D. G. Morrison, "Bias in Multiple Discriminant Analysis," *Journal of Marketing Research,* 2 (August 1965), pp. 250–258, for the development of the bias argument. See also Robert A. Eisenbeis, "Pitfalls in the Application of Discriminant Analysis in Business, Finance, and Economics," *Journal of Finance,* 23 (June 1977), pp. 875–900, for a general discussion of the problems encountered in applying discriminant analysis to business problems.

[12]With small samples one often cannot afford the luxury of setting aside some of the observations for later use but rather needs all of them to develop the equation. In such instances, one can systematically delete one case in turn from a sample of size n and fit the equation to each of the remaining $n - 1$ observations. The process, which is repeated n times with each observation left out in turn, provides useful estimates of the coefficients and prediction accuracy of the equation. See Melvin R. Crask and William D. Perreault, Jr., "Validation of Discriminant Analysis in Marketing Research," *Journal of Marketing Research,* 14 (February 1977), pp. 60–68, which is technically called "jackknifing the estimates," for details of the procedure.

Second, the particular decision rule we used to classify grand prize and consolation prize winners will minimize the costs of misclassification (that is, will be optimal) when: (1) the costs of misclassifying a grand prize winner as a consolation prize winner, and vice versa, are equal; (2) the *a priori* probabilities of winning each prize are equal; and (3) the distribution of the variables in the two populations is multinormal with equal and known convariance matrices. When these conditions are not satisfied, the decision rule for classifying objects must be revised.[13]

Three-Group Case

We now want to entertain the question of $k \geq 3$ groups. The biggest change that occurs when we move beyond two groups is that there can be more than one discriminant function.[14] As a matter of fact, when there are k groups and p variables, the maximum number of discriminant functions will be given by the following rules:

- If there are more variables p than groups k (the typical case), there will be at most $k - 1$ discriminant functions.

- If the number of variables p is less than the number of groups k, there will be no more than p discriminant functions.

Regardless of which case results, the number of statistically significant discriminant functions can be less than the maximum number possible. It depends on whether the extracted functions provide "meaningful differentiation" among the objects forming the groups.

Consider again the sample of salespeople and their success in securing new accounts. This time, though, consider all three groups. Since the number of groups is less than the number of variables, the number of groups will determine the maximum number of discriminant functions that can be derived, $k - 1 = 2$ in this case.

The two discriminant functions turn out to be

$$Y_1 = .064X_1 + .079X_2 + .027X_3 - .002X_4;$$

$$Y_2 = -.036X_1 - .037X_2 + .041X_3 - .003X_4.$$

---

[13]For general discussions regarding the accuracy of the classification rules under various conditions, see Dillon and Goldstein, *Multivariate Analysis,* pp. 392–393; B. Efron, "Estimating the Error Rate of a Prediction Rule: Improvement and Cross-Validation," *Journal of the American Statistical Association,* 78 (1983), pp. 316–331; or William R. Dillon and Stuart Westin, "The Performance of the Linear Discriminant Function in Nonoptimal Situations and the Estimation of Classification Error Rates: A Review of Recent Findings," *Journal of Marketing Research,* 16 (August 1979), pp. 370–381.

[14]There are two variations in discriminant analysis when there are more than two groups: the classical and simultaneous approaches. The classical approach emphasizes the generation of classification functions, one for each group, that maximize the likelihood of correct classifications of the members of the group. The classical approach produces $g(g - 1)/2$ discriminant functions (where g is the number of groups) that separate each pair of groups; the coefficients for each variable in each discriminant function turn out to be equal to the differences in the coefficients for the variable in the respective classification functions. The coefficients for the discriminant function separating Groups 1 and 3, for example, would be equal to the differences in coefficients for the classification functions for Groups 1 and 3. The simultaneous approach, which is also known as the canonical approach, is the one emphasized here. For a very readable discussion of the differences in the two approaches, see Donald R. Lehman, *Market Research and Analysis,* 2nd ed. (Homewood, Ill.: Richard D. Irwin, 1985), pp. 691–697.

The functions have the following interpretation. Of all the linear combinations of the four variables that could be developed, the linear combination given by the first function provides maximum separation. Maximum separation is understood, of course, to be defined on the discriminant scores; the salespeople within a group are very similar with respect to their Y_1 scores, while the salespeople in different groups have very dissimilar Y_1 scores. Given the first linear combination, the second function provides maximum separation among all linear combinations that could be developed that were uncorrelated with the first set of scores. Thus, the second function provides maximum separation on a contingent set of scores, provided that they are uncorrelated with the first set of scores; that is, $r_{Y_1Y_2} = 0$.

Classifying Respondents   The statistical significance of these functions should be checked before they are employed to classify salespeople.[15] It turns out that only the first function is statistically significant. Thus, we can develop a classification rule that depends only on it. Let that rule simply be an extension of that previously employed; that is, let us simply assign salespeople to the group to which their discriminant score is closest. This rule requires that the mean discriminant scores be known for each group. They can be generated by substituting the means of the variables—number of calls on new accounts, percentage of calls with advance appointments, telephone calls made to prospects, and number of new accounts visited—for each group in the discriminant function.

Grand prize winner: $\bar{Y}_W = .064(103.9) + .079(59.9) + .027(161.7) - .002(37.0)$

$$= 15.67.$$

Consolation prize winner: $\bar{Y}_C = .064(86.5) + .079(47.7) + .027(122.4) - .002(32.4)$

$$= 12.54.$$

Unsuccessful salesperson: $\bar{Y}_U = .064(50.4) + .079(34.0) + .027(88.3) - .002(25.7)$

$$= 9.58.$$

The cutting scores $(15.67 + 12.54)/2 = 14.11$ and $(12.54 + 9.58)/2 = 11.06$ bisect the difference in mean scores between grand prize and consolation prize winners, and between consolation prize winners and unsuccessful salespeople, respectively. Thus, any salesperson with a score less than 11.06 would be considered an unsuccessful contest competitor, while all those with discriminant scores greater than 14.11 would be considered grand prize winners. Those with scores between 11.06 and 14.11 would be considered consolation prize winners. The scores and predicted classification of each of the 45 salespeople are contained in Table 16.5. Table 16.6 is the confusion matrix that

---

[15]See Dillon and Goldstein, *Multivariate Analysis*, pp. 400–406, for a discussion of how to test the statistical significance of each of the discriminant functions that can be generated where there are more than two groups.

Table 16.5
Discriminant Scores for Each Salesperson and Group to Which Salesperson
Would Be Predicted to Belong Employing the Function
$Y = .064X_1 + .079X_2 + .027X_3 - .002X_4$

Grand Prize Winners (W)			Consolation Prize Winners (C)			Unsuccessful Salespeople (U)		
1	RMB	17.25 W	1	JGB	14.00 C	1	RBB	8.80 U
2	ALB	18.40 W	2	RAB	14.06 C	2	GEB	8.32 U
3	BCC	15.73 W	3	HAF	11.47 C	3	ADC	8.18 U
4	JJC	14.91 W	4	PPD	12.74 C	4	JFC	9.76 U
5	EDC	14.94 W	5	BCE	14.60 W	5	LDE	8.73 U
6	WPD	15.66 W	6	ASG	13.06 C	6	JFH	7.92 U
7	RHH	15.63 W	7	WLH	14.18 W	7	JCH	8.58 U
8	BEK	15.45 W	8	LHL	12.38 C	8	RPF	6.94 U
9	DAK	15.45 W	9	RJL	10.59 U	9	APL	8.71 U
10	JJN	15.39 W	10	WFM	12.14 C	10	HAL	8.08 U
11	MYS	15.97 W	11	JRP	10.83 U	11	ERM	9.45 U
12	PJS	15.69 W	12	EJS	12.50 C	12	WRR	8.93 U
13	CET	15.88 W	13	VES	11.81 C	13	JTS	7.56 U
14	LLV	15.32 W	14	HMT	13.17 C	14	JMV	6.88 U
15	LMW	15.06 W	15	BMT	11.95 C	15	HEY	7.75 U

Table 16.6
Confusion Matrix for Salespeople

	Predicted Classification			
Actual Classification	Grand Prize Winner	Consolation Prize Winner	Unsuccessful Salesperson	Total
Grand Prize Winner	15	0	0	15
Consolation Prize Winner	2	11	2	15
Unsuccessful Salesperson	0	0	15	15

results from these predicted classifications. The performance of this procedure is quite good; the classification of 91.1 percent of the salespeople is predicted correctly against the chance criterion of 33 percent. All the incorrect predictions involve consolation prize winners, two of whom are predicted to be grand prize winners and two of whom are predicted to be unsuccessful in the sales contest. The function is particularly effective, then, in discriminating between grand prize winners and those who did not win anything in the sales contest. Of course, there is upward bias in the prediction because the data employed to generate the function are also being used to check its predictive validity. A different sample of salespeople who also participated in the sales contest but who are not used to fit the function would be preferred to truly assess predictive accuracy.

Key Variables   Disregarding the fact that the accuracy of the estimating procedure is biased, the sales analysis department would be interested in determining the key new account activities that differentiated salespeople's performance. We cannot use the raw-score coefficients for this purpose, but must generate the standardized coefficients to negate the effect of the units with which we measure the variables. The standardized weights, which are derived by multiplying the raw-score weights by the pooled standard deviations of the respective variables, are

$$v_1{}^* = v_1 s_1 = .064(15.91) = 1.018,$$

$$v_2{}^* = v_2 s_2 = .079(8.97) = .709,$$

$$v_3{}^* = v_3 s_3 = .027(19.99) = .540,$$

$$v_4{}^* = v_4 s_4 = -.002(5.37) = -.011.$$

Number of calls on new accounts, X_1, is the most important variable in differentiating among the levels of success in the sales contest, while the number of new accounts visited, X_4, is the least important. However, the relative importance of each predictor should be interpreted with a degree of caution because there is some intercorrelation among the predictors.

Marketing Applications

Although discriminant analysis has not been applied as often as regression analysis to marketing problems, it has been used for a variety of problems. Some of these uses include attempts to determine those characteristics that distinguish the listening audiences of various radio stations, to discriminate Ford buyers from Chevrolet buyers, to predict adopters and nonadopters of new products, to relate purchase behavior to advertising exposure, to determine the relationship between personality variables and the consumer decision process, to discriminate between those who choose to save at commercial banks and those who choose savings and loan institutions, to develop perceptual maps depicting the relationships among products so as to determine segmentation opportunities, to identify factors associated with aggressive price behavior, to assess the differences in importance of various attributes where the same products are being purchased in different countries, to assist in retail positioning, and to determine the factors supermarket buyers use in deciding whether to stock a new product.[16]

Factor Analysis

Factor analysis is one of the more popular "analysis of interdependence" techniques. In studies of interdependence, all the variables have equal footing, and the analyst is concerned with the whole set of relationships among the variables that characterize the

---

[16]For lists of references and some examples summarizing the use of discriminant analysis in marketing, see Dillon and Goldstein, *Multivariate Analysis;* Hair, Anderson, Tatham, and Grablowsky, *Multivariate Data Analysis;* and David A. Aaker, ed., *Multivariate Analysis in Marketing* (Palo Alto, Calif.: Scientific Press, 1980).

Table 16.7

Two Hypothetical Sets of Correlations Among Nine Variables

Panel A Variable	Variable								
	1	2	3	4	5	6	7	8	9
1	1.00								
2	.96	1.00							
3	.94	.88	1.00						
4	.91	.95	.89	1.00					
5	.05	.09	.08	.10	1.00				
6	.12	.04	.03	.11	.92	1.00			
7	.07	.14	.06	.03	.86	.91	1.00		
8	.10	.12	.08	.04	.94	.95	.88	1.00	
9	.08	.11	.06	.13	.97	.87	.91	.90	1.00

Panel B Variable	Variable								
	1	2	3	4	5	6	7	8	9
1	1.00								
2	.92	1.00							
3	.95	.98	1.00						
4	.07	.13	.02	1.00					
5	.09	.05	.11	.95	1.00				
6	.06	.09	.07	.90	.89	1.00			
7	.10	.08	.10	.08	.14	.10	1.00		
8	.05	.07	.09	.09	.06	.12	.94	1.00	
9	.13	.04	.08	.13	.09	.06	.91	.92	1.00

objects. Table 16.7, for example, shows two hypothetical sets of correlations among nine variables. A **factor analysis** would focus on the whole set of interrelationships displayed by the nine variables in that it would not treat one or more of the variables as dependent variables to be predicted by the others, as would, say, regression or discriminant analysis. The focus on the full set of relationships can be looked at in one of two ways, conceptually or mathematically. At the mathematical level, a **factor** is simply a linear combination of variables. The linear combination is not chosen arbitrarily, however, but is selected so as to capture the "essence" of the data. There are a variety of ways by which linear combinations of variables can be formed: consequently, the term "factor analysis" applies to a *body* of techniques. The various methods of factor analysis are differentiated in terms of how the weights used in forming the linear combinations are determined.

An alternative way of looking at factor analysis is conceptual. In this sense, a factor is a qualitative dimension of the data that attempts to depict the "way in which entities differ, much as the length of an object or the flavor of a product defines a qualitative dimension on which objects may or may not differ. A factor does not indicate how much different various entities are, just as knowing that length is an important physical

Table 16.8
Sales Performance Data for Sample of Sales Representatives
from Imaginative Development Company

Sales Representative	Sales Growth X_1	Sales Profitability X_2	New Account Sales X_3
1	93.0	96.0	97.8
2	88.8	91.8	96.8
3	95.0	100.3	99.0
4	101.3	103.8	106.8
5	102.0	107.8	103.0
6	95.8	97.5	99.3
7	95.5	99.5	99.0
8	110.8	122.0	115.3
9	102.8	108.3	103.8
10	106.8	120.5	102.0
11	103.3	109.8	104.0
12	99.5	111.8	100.3
13	103.5	112.5	107.0
14	99.5	105.5	102.3
15	100.0	107.0	102.8
16	81.5	93.5	95.0
17	101.3	105.3	102.8
18	103.3	110.8	103.5
19	95.3	104.3	103.0
20	99.5	105.3	106.3
21	88.5	95.3	95.8
22	99.3	115.0	104.3
23	87.5	92.5	95.8
24	105.3	114.0	105.3
25	107.0	121.0	109.0

dimension does not indicate how much longer one object is than another.''[17] The correlations among the nine variables depicted in Panel A of Table 16.7 suggest, for example, that the objects differ along two dimensions and, in particular, that Variables 1 through 4 seem to go together and Variables 5 through 9 also seem to covary in that the pairwise correlations between the variables in each set are uniformly high. Note that the two sets of variables seem to behave very differently, though, as the correlations between any two variables in different sets are very low. Panel B of Table 16.7, on the other hand, suggests there are three dimensions underlying the interrelationships among the nine variables. More particularly, it seems here that Variables 1 through 3, 4 through 6, and 7 through 9 covary or behave similarly.

The purposes of factor analysis are actually two: data reduction and substantive inter-

---

[17]David W. Stewart, "The Application and Misapplication of Factor Analysis in Marketing Research," *Journal of Marketing Research,* 18 (February 1981), pp. 51–52.

Table 16.8
Sales Performance Data for Sample of Sales Representatives
from Imaginative Development Company *continued*

Sales Representative	Sales Growth X_1	Sales Profitability X_2	New Account Sales X_3
26	93.3	102.0	97.8
27	106.8	118.0	107.3
28	106.8	120.0	104.8
29	92.3	90.8	99.8
30	106.3	121.0	104.5
31	106.0	119.5	110.5
32	88.3	92.8	96.8
33	96.0	103.3	100.5
34	94.3	94.5	99.0
35	106.5	121.5	110.5
36	106.5	115.5	107.0
37	92.0	99.5	103.5
38	102.0	99.8	103.3
39	108.3	122.3	108.5
40	106.8	119.0	106.8
41	102.5	109.3	103.8
42	92.5	102.5	99.3
43	102.8	113.8	106.8
44	83.3	87.3	96.3
45	94.8	101.8	99.8
46	103.5	112.0	110.8
47	89.5	96.0	97.3
48	84.3	89.8	94.3
49	104.3	109.5	106.5
50	106.0	118.5	105.0

pretation. The first purpose emphasizes summarizing the important information in a set of observed variables by a new, smaller set of variables expressing that which is common among the original variables. The second purpose is concerned with the identification of the constructs or dimensions that underlie the observed variables.

Consider the Imaginative Development Company. The company produces a line of highly sophisticated measuring devices, which it primarily sells to research laboratories. Many of the company's products are custom designed to meet particular measurement needs faced by the customer. Suppose the company was interested in isolating those personality traits that are likely to lead to success in this type of selling situation. Suppose further that no single measure of performance seemed adequate and that the company decided to employ several measures, namely, sales growth, profitability of sales, and new account sales. Further, to compensate for potential differences caused by differences in sales territory, the company converted each sales representative's performance on each of these variables to index form, employing an index of 100 to indicate "average" performance. Table 16.8 contains the data for a sample of 50 sales representatives.

Table 16.9
Simple Pairwise Correlations among the Performance Measures

	X_1	X_2	X_3
X_1	1.000		
X_2	0.926	1.000	
X_3	0.884	0.843	1.000

Table 16.10
Variable-Factor Correlations

	Factor		
Variable	1	2	3
1	0.976	0.083	−0.203
2	0.961	0.232	0.151
3	0.945	−0.321	0.056
	2.769	0.164	0.067

Summarizing Data

Consider the first purpose of factor analysis—summarizing the "important information" contained in the data by a fewer number of factors. This raises the question of what is "important information." Two quantities are typically highlighted: the variance of each variable, which is the measure of the variability of the variable across objects, and the correlation between variables, which is a measure of the covariation of the variables across objects.[18] Most factor analyses are implemented using standardized variables because in many problems the raw variables reflect widely differing units of measurement. By standardizing the variables to mean zero and unit standard deviation, the effect of units of measurement on the final solution is removed. In our case, standardization would not be necessary. The variables are measured in the same units. Since standardization is common, though, let us discuss the variability recovery and covariability recovery questions with standardized data.

Table 16.9 contains the simple pairwise correlations among the variables, while Table 16.10 is the factor-loading matrix that results from performing a principal components analysis on the data of Table 16.9.[19] The factor-loading matrix is one of the key outputs of a factor-analytic solution. Let us, therefore, closely examine the entries in Table 16.10.

---

[18]A factor analysis can be based on other measures of covariation. Correlations are most commonly used, though, and the exposition is most easily understood when the correlations between variables are used.

[19]Some would argue that the principal components procedure is not part and parcel of factor analysis. The point is controversial, and it would be confusing to illustrate the argument at this time. The argument centers on the communality question, which is discussed later in the chapter.

Consider first the individual row–column entries. These are the *correlations* between the *variables* and the *factors*. For example, 0.976, the entry in the first row and first column, represents the simple correlation between the first variable and the first factor, while 0.083 is the correlation between the first variable and the second factor. Similarly, 0.961 is the correlation between the second variable and first factor, and so on. These correlations are called **factor loadings.** When we examine the table of loadings, we find that all three variables load heavily on (correlate highly with) Factor F_1.

Since the entries are variable–factor correlations, their square indicates the proportion of variation in the variable that is accounted for by the factor. Thus,

$$(0.976)^2 = 0.952,$$

$$(0.961)^2 = 0.924, \text{ and}$$

$$(0.945)^2 = 0.894$$

are the proportions of variance in Variables 1, 2, and 3, respectively, accounted for by the first factor.[20]

Covariability recovery focuses on how closely the original pairwise correlations between the variables can be estimated. Consider the sum of the products of the respective

---

[20]The interpretation of these quantities as the proportion of the total variation in each variable accounted for by the factors parallels that for regression analysis. Recall that in regression analysis, the problem is one of predicting the value of a criterion variable, given one or more predictor variables. When the variables are standardized, the parallel problem in factor analysis becomes one of estimating a z score, a standardized criterion variable, from the factor scores, the predictor variables. There are potentially three factor scores for each sales representative, one corresponding to each of the three linear combinations that can be formed from the original variables. In a one-factor model, the question being addressed is how well the original variables can be estimated using only the first of the factor scores. The coefficient of determination employed in assessing the goodness of fit in a regression model provides a useful frame of reference.

The coefficient of determination is expressed as

$$R^2 = \frac{\text{Explained variation}}{\text{Total variation}} = 1 - \frac{\text{Unexplained variation}}{\text{Total variation}}.$$

Total variation, of course, is measured by the variance of the variable. Unexplained variation is conceptualized in the following way. Suppose the criterion variable was to be estimated for each object. The difference between the estimated value and the actual value could then be determined. If each of these residuals were then squared and the squared results were summed, the calculation would produce a measure of unexplained variation.

The factor-analytic case suggests a similar calculation. The difference between the standardized scores and the scores estimated using the first-factor scores (which do not have to be actually calculated to assess the fit) could be calculated for, say, variable z_1. If these differences were then squared and summed, the result could be considered a measure of the variation in z_1 left unexplained by the one-factor estimating procedure. If this unexplained variation were then to be divided by a measure of the total variation in z_1, and subtracted from 1, a measure of goodness of fit would be obtained. But what is the total variation in z_1? Since the variables are all standardized to unit variance, it is simply 1. Thus, the sum of the residuals squared when subtracted from 1 provides the needed summary measure. It turns out that

■ 95.2 percent of the variation in z_1,

■ 92.4 percent of the variation in z_2, and

■ 89.4 percent of the variation in z_3

is accounted for by the first factor, F_1.

column entries of any two rows of Table 16.10. Take Rows 1 and 2, for example. The sum of the products is

$$(0.976)(0.961) + (0.083)(0.232) + (-0.203)(0.151) = 0.926,$$

which is the original correlation, r_{12}, between Variables 1 and 2 displayed in Table 16.9. Any of the correlations in Table 16.9 can be *regenerated exactly* if all three factors extracted by the principal components procedure are used. The general calculation formula is

$$r_{jl} = \sum_{k=1}^{3} a_{jk}a_{lk},$$

where j and l denote the original variables and also the respective rows of Table 16.10, and k denotes the factor or column in the table.

What happens when fewer factors are used? The pairwise correlations are not regenerated but only *estimated*. The estimate is given by the same formula, but now the summation is from 1 to m, where m denotes the number of factors being considered. For a one ($m = 1$) factor estimating procedure, the estimated correlation between Variables 1 and 2 ($j = 1$, $\ell = 2$) is

$$\hat{r}_{12} = \sum_{k=1}^{1} a_{1k}a_{2k} = (0.976)(0.961) = 0.937,$$

an estimate that is quite close to the true value of 0.926. The other estimates are

$$\hat{r}_{13} = (0.976)(0.945) = 0.922 \text{ and}$$

$$\hat{r}_{23} = (0.961)(0.945) = 0.908$$

versus actual values of 0.884 and 0.843, respectively. These estimates are quite good.

Is one factor sufficient or is more than one factor needed to summarize the data adequately? To answer this question, it is helpful to realize that in a principal components solution, the m factors are uncorrelated. This means that the proportion of variance accounted for by m factors is simply the sum of the proportions accounted for by each factor. Take two factors, for example. The proportion of the variation in each variable accounted for by a two-factor solution is

$$\text{Variable 1: } (0.976)^2 + (0.083)^2 = 0.959;$$

$$\text{Variable 2: } (0.961)^2 + (0.232)^2 = 0.977;$$

$$\text{Variable 3: } (0.945)^2 + (-0.321)^2 = 0.997.$$

These values, which express the proportion of the variance of the variables extracted by m factors, are called the achieved **communalities** of the variables and are typically denoted as h_j^2, where j refers to the variable number. Thus, we see that two factors account for 95.9 ($=h_1^2$) percent of the variation in X_1, 97.7 ($=h_2^2$) percent of the variation in X_2, and 99.7 ($=h_3^2$) percent of the variation in X_3. The two-factor model does a remarkable job in accounting for the variability within the data. Variable 1 is most poorly captured, but even here 95.9 percent of the total variability in Variable 1 is captured by the first two factors in the principal components solution. This result raises the question of whether it would be wise to retain two factors as the "proper" factor-analytic solution.

There is no definitive answer. The column totals in Table 16.10 can assist the analyst, though, in making a decision. As mentioned, the row–column entries represent the correlations between the variables and the factors, and their squares, the proportions of variation in each variable explained by the factor. Thus, the sum of the squares in a column will provide a measure of the amount of variation accounted for by the factor representing the column. Take Column 1, for example,

$$(0.976)^2 + (0.961)^2 + (0.945)^2 = 2.769,$$

the column total. Now, since the three variables are all standardized to unit variance, total variance equals 3. The proportion of total variance that is accounted for by the first factor is $2.769/3 = 92.3$ percent. The first two factors, on the other hand, account for

$$\frac{2.769 + 0.164}{3} = 0.978$$

or 97.8 percent of the total variance. The second factor accounts for 5.5 percent of the total variance in the three variables. It seems that in the interest of scientific parsimony, a one-factor solution would suffice; there is only a small gain in explained variation with the addition of the second factor.[21]

Conceptual Basis of Principal Components Analysis   Unlike some of the less structured factor-analytic techniques, principal components analysis leads to unique results. The objective of a principal components analysis is to transform a set of interrelated variables into a set of unrelated linear combinations of these variables. The set of linear combinations is chosen so that each of the linear combinations (factors or components) accounts for a *decreasing proportion* of the variance in the original variables, subject to the condition that each linear combination is uncorrelated (geometrically at right angles) to all previous linear combinations.

The physical analogy of a watermelon should help in understanding the conceptual basis of principal components analysis. The watermelon could be considered to have three basic dimensions; call them length, width, and height and conceive of them as being at right angles to one another. Further, let length always refer to the longest dimension, width to the next longest dimension that is perpendicular to the length axis, and height to the axis perpendicular to the length and width axes. Now, the total size of the watermelon can be indicated by specifying its length, width, and height. Would fewer dimensions provide a reasonably accurate estimate of its size? It all depends on the shape of the watermelon. Suppose the watermelon was very long and narrow, much like a cigar. Then clearly its size would be closely indicated by simply specifying its length. If the melon was long and wide but rather flat, then two dimensions would be needed to accurately portray its size. Finally, if it was long, wide, and high, three dimensions would be needed to describe its size.

---

[21]One of the points of controversy surrounding factor analysis is when to stop factoring; that is, how many factors should be retained in the final solution. There is no "correct" answer, although a number of rules of thumb have been advanced. We discuss two of the more popular rules later in the chapter. All of the criteria suggest that one factor is adequate for the example.

The principal components correspond to the axes of the watermelon in this three-dimensional problem. Consider the sales performance data. Each sales representative has three scores, one for each of the performance criteria. The scores could thus be plotted in three space according to the reported values for X_1, X_2, and X_3. Now, the task in principal components analysis is to produce a set of uncorrelated composite scores that measure what the variables have in common and yet account for decreasing proportions of the total variance in the variables. The first component corresponds to the principal axis of the ellipsoid in three space (the length of the watermelon). Of all the linear combinations that could be formed, it possesses maximum variation. Whether it adequately captures the important information contained in the data depends upon the shape of the concentration of the swarm of points. If the plot of the data results in a cigar-shaped figure, then one factor is enough. If not, more than one factor is needed to summarize the data. The second principal component would be chosen so that it accounts for the maximum variation left unexplained, consistent with the condition that it is uncorrelated with the first component. (The second component would correspond to the width of the watermelon.) Thus, a principal components analysis reveals how several measures of a domain can be combined in a single measure, the first component, to produce maximum discrimination among objects along this single dimension. The variation accounted for by each component also indicates when several independent dimensions or components are needed to adequately define the domain under investigation.

Substantive Interpretation

While principal components analysis provides a useful tool from the standpoint of data reduction, it generally does not provide the optimal solution from an interpretive point of view. Interpretation of a factor solution focuses on the identification of the construct or constructs that underlie the observed variables. The problem is captured in Figure 16.3. There it is assumed that measures have been obtained for five variables across a set of objects. The question is: Do these variables have something in common? Do they reflect some underlying, unobserved construct or constructs? How many? What are they? Figure 16.3 suggests that the observed variables are really the result of two underlying factors or dimensions, and substantive interpretation in factor analysis would focus on isolating and identifying these factors.

The sales performance data pose little problem for substantive interpretation. One factor effectively summarizes the important information in the data. It could be considered a general performance factor. A factor score could be calculated for each sales representative using this first factor, and the sales representatives could then be ranked according to these factor scores. The "best" performing sales representative would have the highest score and the "worst" sales representative the lowest score.

Rarely is a factor solution so tidy. In more complex situations, it is useful to rotate the initial principal components solution to facilitate substantive interpretation. Since rotation would be fruitless in the sales performance example, we need another example to illustrate its use, particularly how it can be of assistance in interpreting factors. Consider, for this purpose, a study that was conducted to compare the images of various department stores in a particular city. The data were collected using a semantic differential scale. Figure 16.4 contains a portion of the items that were used. While the

Figure 16.3
Search for Substantive Interpretation in a Factor Analysis Solution

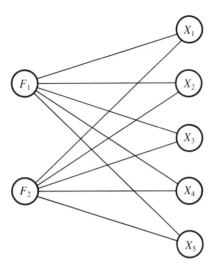

negative or undesirable descriptor sometimes appears on the left and sometimes on the right, the scoring was reversed for those variables where the negative descriptor appeared on the right, so that higher scores always reflect more desirable amounts of the property. Table 16.11 shows the correlations among the responses to these specific items.

One of the first issues that needs to be addressed is to determine the number of factors that are necessary to account for the variation in the data. As was the case

Figure 16.4
Portion of Items Used to Measure Department Store Image

1. Convenient place to shop	:___:___:___:___:___:___: Inconvenient place to shop
2. Fast checkout	:___:___:___:___:___:___: Slow checkout
3. Store is clean	:___:___:___:___:___:___: Store is dirty
4. Store is not well organized	:___:___:___:___:___:___: Store is well organized
5. Store is messy, cluttered	:___:___:___:___:___:___: Store is neat, uncluttered
6. Convenient store hours	:___:___:___:___:___:___: Inconvenient store hours
7. Store is far from home, school, or work	Store is close to home, school, :___:___:___:___:___:___: or work
8. Store has bad atmosphere	:___:___:___:___:___:___: Store has good atmosphere
9. Attractive decor inside	:___:___:___:___:___:___: Unattractive decor inside
10. Store is spacious	:___:___:___:___:___:___: Store is crowded

Table 16.11

Pairwise Correlations among the Items Used to Measure Department Store Image

	Question or Variable									
Variable	X_1	X_2	X_3	X_4	X_5	X_6	X_7	X_8	X_9	X_{10}
X_1	1.00	.79	.41	.26	.12	.89	.87	.37	.32	.18
X_2	.79	1.00	.32	.21	.20	.90	.83	.31	.35	.23
X_3	.41	.32	1.00	.80	.76	.34	.40	.82	.78	.72
X_4	.26	.21	.80	1.00	.75	.30	.28	.78	.81	.80
X_5	.12	.20	.76	.75	1.00	.11	.23	.74	.77	.83
X_6	.89	.90	.34	.30	.11	1.00	.78	.30	.39	.16
X_7	.87	.83	.40	.28	.23	.78	1.00	.29	.26	.17
X_8	.37	.31	.82	.78	.74	.30	.29	1.00	.82	.78
X_9	.32	.35	.78	.81	.77	.39	.26	.82	1.00	.77
X_{10}	.18	.23	.72	.80	.83	.16	.17	.78	.77	1.00

previously, we can look at the amount of variation accounted for by each factor in making the decision. That information is contained in Table 16.12. A number of decision rules have been advanced for making the decision as to how many factors to retain for the solution. Two of the most popular are (1) the latent roots criterion, and (2) the scree test.[22]

The latent roots criterion holds that the amount of variation explained by each factor or latent root must be greater than one.[23] The rationale is that the variation in each variable is one after the variable has been standardized. Thus, each factor should account for the variation in at least one variable if the factor is to be considered useful from a data summarization perspective. Since there are two factors with latent roots greater than one, the latent roots criterion would suggest a two-factor solution for the department store image data.

The scree test employs a plot of the size of the latent roots against the number of factors in their order of extraction. Figure 16.5 contains the plot for the department store image data. Note how the curve drops sharply at first and then levels off as it approaches the horizontal axis. This is often the case in such plots, and the method actually gets its name because of the resemblance of the plot to a side view of a mountain. Typically such a view will show a sharp drop representing the mountain face. At the foot of the mountain, there will be a straight line or two or even three at a much lesser angle to the horizontal where rocks that have fallen off the mountain have piled

---

[22]For a discussion of these criteria, plus several others that have been advanced for determining the number of factors, see Stewart, "The Application and Missapplication of Factor Analysis."

[23]The technique actually gets its name from the type of problem in matrix algebra that is solved in generating a factor analytic solution, namely a latent root or eigenvalue problem. Each eigenvalue equals the amount of variation explained by that factor or latent root.

Table 16.12
Variance Explained by Each Factor

Factor (Latent Root)	Variance Explained
1	5.725
2	2.761
3	0.366
4	0.357
5	0.243
6	0.212
7	0.132
8	0.123
9	0.079
10	0.001

Figure 16.5
Variance Explained by Each Factor or Latent Root

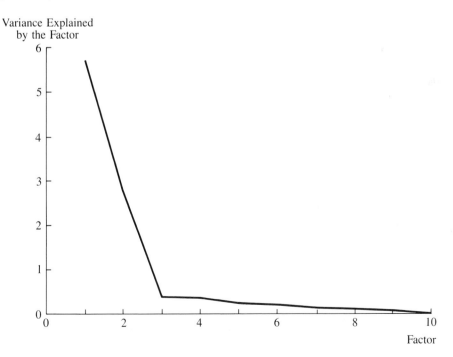

Table 16.13

Unrotated Factor Loading Matrix for Department Store Image Data Using Two Principal Components

	Factor		Achieved
Variable	1	2	Communality
1	0.633	0.707	0.900
2	0.621	0.695	0.869
3	0.872	−0.241	0.819
4	0.833	−0.366	0.828
5	0.774	−0.469	0.818
6	0.626	0.719	0.908
7	0.619	0.683	0.850
8	0.859	−0.303	0.829
9	0.865	−0.293	0.835
10	0.790	−0.454	0.831
Eigenvalue or latent root	5.725	2.761	

up. These various piles of stable rocks are called screes. The last real factor is considered to be that point *before the first scree begins*.[24] In the example, the first scree or straight line connects Factors 3 through 6. The scree plot criterion also suggests, therefore, that a two-factor solution is necessary to capture the store image data.

How much of the total variation in the data is explained by the two-factor solution? The total variance of the ten variables when standardized is 10. The first component accounts for $5.725/10 = 57.3$ percent, and the second component accounts for $2.761/10 = 27.6$ percent. The two components together account for 84.9 percent of the total variation in the ten variables.

What about the achieved communalities of each of the variables considered separately? How much of the variation in each variable is accounted for by the two-factor solution? This information can be obtained from the factor-loading matrix contained in Table 16.13. The achieved communalities shown in the right hand column are again secured by squaring each factor loading and adding the results across factors. Thus, for Variable 1, the achieved communality is

$$(.633)^2 + (.707)^2 = .900,$$

---

[24]Cattell and Vogelmann offer very specific instructions for determining the number of factors from a scree plot. See Raymond B. Cattell and S. Vogelmann, "A Comprehensive Trial of the Scree and KG Criteria for Determining the Number of Factors," *The Journal of Multivariate Behavioral Research*, 12 (1977), pp. 289–325.

Figure 16.6
Scatter Diagram Using Correlations between
Variables and Factors as Coordinates

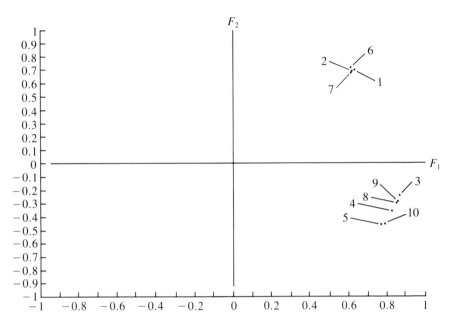

and it is similarly derived for the other variables. All the variables are captured rather nicely by the two-factor solution. Variable 5 is most poorly captured, but even here 81.8 percent of the variation in Variable 5 is reflected by the first two factors.

What are these factors? Their interpretation is obscure. All ten variables correlate highly with or load heavily on the first factor. Variables 1, 2, 6, and 7 also have high positive loadings on the second factor. Figure 16.6, which employs the correlations between the variables and the two factors as coordinates, suggests that the variables do cluster somewhat in two space. Variables 1, 2, 6, and 7 occupy the same general location, and Variables 3, 4, 5, 8, 9, and 10 also occupy the same general two-space location. The fact that some variables do share a common location raises the question of whether the original factor axes can be rotated to still new orientations so as to facilitate interpretation of the factors. There is no question of whether the axes can be rotated. They can be, since an axis rotation simply amounts to forming linear combinations of the factors. The key question is: *How* should these new linear combinations be selected so as to best facilitate interpretation?

A number of alternatives have been proposed by which the new linear combinations should be formed. Just about all of these methods attempt to produce loadings that are close to either 0 or 1, since such loadings show more clearly what things go together and in this sense are more interpretable. The methods differ in the criterion that is satisfied when these modified loadings are produced.[25] For example, both orthogonal and oblique rotations have been proposed. Orthogonal rotations are also called rigid or angle-preserving rotations, since they preserve the right angles that exist among the factor axes. Oblique rotations do not, which means that the factors themselves can be correlated.

Figure 16.7 displays the **varimax** rotation of the original axes. Varimax attempts to ''clean up'' the factors in the factor loading table, that is, force the entries in the columns to be near 0 or 1. The main alternative to varimax is quartimax, which attempts to clean up variables or rows in the factor loading table while maintaining the right angles between the factors. The empirical evidence indicates that varimax tends to produce loadings that are more interpretable except when there is a general factor present in the data, in which case quartimax is the preferred orthogonal rotation scheme. Varimax is consequently the most popular orthogonal rotation scheme.[26] Whereas the original axes are labeled F_1 and F_2, the rotated axes are labeled F_1' and F_2'.

Note in Figure 16.7 that each of the new axes seems to be ''purer'' than the original axes. That is, whereas the variables had high loadings—as represented by the *magnitude* of the *vertical projections*—on both of the original factor axes, they seem to have high loadings on either one *or* the other of the new axes, but not both. Table 16.14 presents the magnitudes of these vertical projections, loadings, or correlations of variables with factors.

What are these factors? In order to name them, it is useful to see what variables go with each factor and to name the factors accordingly. The following process is useful in this regard.

1. Begin with the first variable and first factor and move horizontally from left to right looking for the highest loading. Circle that loading. Repeat this procedure for each of the other variables in turn.

2. Examine each of the circled loadings and assess its significance. The significance of any loading can be judged using either statistical or practical criteria. Statistical criteria mean that the loading is statistically significant at some specified alpha

---

[25]The earliest axes rotations in factor analysis were done graphically by hand and were aimed at satisfying the five criteria of ''simple structure'' that Thurstone proposed. While the criteria of simple structure are intuitively appealing, they are mathematically unmanageable. Thus, two analysts working on a rotation of factor axes typically produced two distinct configurations even though both relied on Thurstone's qualitative rules of simple structure, setting off a controversy as to which configuration was more correct. Since the advent of large capacity, high-speed computers, ''objective'' rotations employing some analytic criteria have been used to transform the initial factor solution so that the variables may be more readily named and understood. One advantage of the objective methods is that two analysts working on the same data set and using the same rotation method should produce similar conclusions. See L. L. Thurstone, *Multiple Factor Analysis* (Chicago: University of Chicago Press, 1947), for the rationale for and the criteria of simple structure.

[26]Whereas the empirical evidence favors varimax when an orthogonal rotation is planned, the evidence as to which scheme to use is not as clear when an oblique rotation is contemplated. Oblique rotations tend to pass the axes through clusters of points without regard to the angles separating the axes. For a brief discussion of the criteria the major oblique rotations attempt to satisfy, see Dillon and Goldstein, *Multivariate Analysis*, pp. 91–95.

Figure 16.7
Scatter Diagram after Orthogonal Rotation of Axes

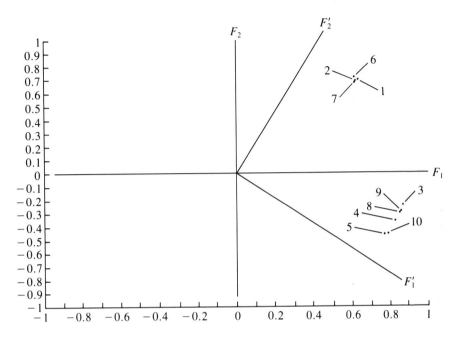

Table 16.14
Factor Loading Matrix for Department Store Image Data after Orthogonal Rotation of Two Principal Components Using Varimax

Variable	Factor 1	Factor 2	Achieved Communality
1	0.150	0.937	0.900
2	0.147	0.920	0.869
3	0.864	0.269	0.819
4	0.899	0.142	0.828
5	0.904	0.024	0.818
6	0.138	0.943	0.908
7	0.151	0.909	0.850
8	0.886	0.209	0.829
9	0.887	0.221	0.835
10	0.910	0.045	0.831
Eigenvalue or latent root	4.859	3.628	

level, typically .05. This means that for samples of less than 100, the loading would have to be greater than .30 to be considered statistically significant. The practical significance criterion means that the factor must account for a certain percentage of the variation in the variable. Note in this regard that a loading of .30 means that the factor accounts for 9 percent of the variation in the variable. Typically, the cutoff for saying that the loading is significant is somewhere in the neighborhood of .30 or .35 therefore.

3.   Underline the other significant loadings using the criteria decided upon in Step 2.

4.   Examine the loading matrix and identify all those variables that do not have significant loadings on any factor. It is hoped there is none, but if there are, the analyst has two options: ''(1) interpret the solution as it is and simply ignore those variables without a significant loading, or (2) critically evaluate each of the variables that do not load significantly on any factor. This evaluation would be in terms of the variable's overall contribution to the research as well as its communality index. If the variable(s) is of minor importance to the study's objective and/or has a low communality index, the analyst may decide to eliminate the variable or variables and derive a new factor solution with the 'non-loading' variables eliminated.''[27]

5.   Focus on the significant loadings, and attempt to name the factors on the bases of what the variables loading on a given factor seem to have in common. Variables having significant loadings on more than one factor complicate the naming task and are candidates for elimination, depending upon the purpose of the study and whether the mixed pattern of loadings makes sense or indicates there are fundamental problems with the variable or item.[28]

It turns out that when these steps are applied to the loadings in Table 16.13, each variable loads significantly on one and only one factor. Specifically, Variables 3, 4, 5, 8, 9, and 10 only load on Factor 1 while Variables 1, 2, 6, and 7 only load on Factor 2. An examination of the wording of the individual items suggests that Factor 1 is a ''store atmosphere'' factor in that it addresses the issue of whether the store is clean, organized, spacious, and has a nice atmosphere in general. Factor 2, on the other hand, reflects whether the store is a convenient place to shop because of the hours it is open, where it is located, and the speed of the checkouts. Therefore, we would probably want to call it a ''convenience'' factor. Instead of describing differences in department stores using the original ten variables, there is significant economy in describing these differences in terms of the two derived factors.

---

[27]Hair, Anderson, Tatham, and Grablowsky, *Multivariate Data Analysis,* p. 236.

[28]While we cannot go into a discussion of the criteria that are used to judge whether an item is a bad or garbage item because that would take us too far afield, readers should be aware that the criteria are intimately bound up in the psychometric processes one uses to develop measures of constructs. For a discussion of these processes, see Gilbert A. Churchill, Jr., ''A Paradigm for Developing Better Measures of Marketing Constructs,'' *Journal of Marketing Research,* 16 (February 1979), pp. 64–73.

Note that the rotation of a factor solution is contemplated for one reason and one reason only—to facilitate the isolation and identification of the factors underlying a set of observed variables. No additional variation in the observed variables is explained by the factors after an analytic rotation is done. If two factors were originally needed to capture the important information in the data, two factors will also be needed after the rotation, if information is not to be discarded. To see this, one simply has to compare Tables 16.13 and 16.14. First, note that the achieved communality for each variable is the same after rotation as it was before. The contribution of each factor in accounting for the variation in the respective variables has changed, but the total explained variation has not. For Variable 1, the achieved communality before rotation was $(.633)^2 + (.707)^2 = .900$, while after rotation it is $(.150)^2 + (.937)^2 = .900$, or still the same. However, whereas before rotation the second factor accounted for 50.0 percent of the total variation in Variable 1, after rotation it accounts for 87.8 percent of this variation. The contributions of the factors have simply been altered, although no additional variation has been accounted for. The same holds true for the contribution of factors to total explained variation. The total remains constant, although the contribution of each factor in explaining this total variation changes. Initially the contribution of the first factor was $5.725/10 = 57.3$ and the second was $2.761/10 = 27.6$, for a total of 84.9 percent. After rotation the contribution of the first factor is $4.859/10 = 48.6$ and the second is $3.628/10 = 36.3$ percent, so the total remains the same. Once again, rotation is undertaken for the sole purpose of naming the underlying factors. No additional variance is accounted for in any variable, nor in the variables as a set.

The Key Decisions

As one might suspect by now, factor analysis represents a *body of techniques* for studying the interrelationships among a set of variables. The method employed to analyze the sales performance data was based on a rather specific assumed underlying model, in particular, the principal components model which suggests

$$z_j = W_{j1}F_1 + W_{j2}F_2 + \ldots + W_{jm}F_m \qquad j = 1, 2, \ldots, p.$$

That is, it was assumed that any of the p performance variables could be perfectly described by a set of m common factors. Many would argue that this is inaccurate for several reasons.[29] First, if the measures were repeated, it is unlikely that the "new" variables would correlate perfectly with the "old." There would be errors of measurement, and it is unrealistic to expect the underlying model to account for these measurement aberrations. Second, and more important, it is unreasonable to expect all the variance of a variable to be summarized by common factors only; a fraction would certainly seem to be unique. Thus, although income and assets are both manifestations of the underlying trait of "being rich," they are not one and the same.

---

[29]The argument is technically known as the communality problem.

When these conditions are expected to arise, an alternative model is often suggested:

$$z_1 = W_{11}F_1 + W_{12}F_2 + \ldots + W_{1m}F_m + d_1V_1$$

$$z_2 = W_{21}F_1 + W_{22}F_2 + \ldots + W_{2m}F_m + \qquad d_2V_2$$

$$\vdots$$

$$z_p = W_{p1}F_1 + W_{p2}F_2 + \ldots + W_{pm}F_m + \qquad d_pV_p.$$

Each variable is described linearly in terms of m common factors and a factor unique to the particular observed variable. This is the *classical model* for factor analysis, and it involves a different approach for its solution. The distinction between the classical model and the principal components model can be best appreciated by again referring to the sales performance data. If we had used all three principal components and the factor loadings displayed in Table 16.10, we would have been able to reproduce *exactly* the value of *each variable* for each of the 50 observations contained in Table 16.8; alternatively, we would have been able to account for all the variation in each variable. Viewed from the vantage point of the variable-by-variable correlation matrix, we would have been able to generate the ones in the diagonal of the correlation matrix of Table 16.9. Under the assumption of the classical factor model, the correlations between variables are reproduced by means of the common factor coefficients alone. Thus, if the estimated correlations are to provide a good fit to the observed correlations, the diagonal elements in the correlation matrix must also be reproduced from the common factor portion of the classical model. If unities are placed on the diagonal of the correlation matrix, then the classical factor model could not possibly apply. There is simply no way in which a variable could be considered to have a unique portion and yet have it reproduced exactly by common factors only. Now, if numbers approximating communalities (measuring what the variable has in common with other variables) are placed in the diagonal of the matrix of observed correlations, the factor solution will involve both common and unique factors. Of course, this raises the question of how these communalities are to be secured.

There are at least three popular approaches for securing communality estimates. One approach uses the results from an initial principal component analysis. That is, the correlation matrix with 1's in the diagonal is factor analyzed using the principal components model. The communalities for each variable for a given m-factor solution are entered into the diagonal of the correlation matrix, and this matrix is then factor analyzed. A second alternative makes use of the multiple regression model. Each variable is regressed on each of the other variables in the analysis and the resulting R^2s are determined. The diagonal of the correlation matrix is replaced by these squared multiple correlations before the correlation matrix is factor analyzed. A third alternative is to determine the largest absolute value of the correlation of the variable with any other variable in the analysis by examining the off-diagonal elements in the correlation matrix. This correlation is then placed on the diagonal before the correlation matrix is factor

Figure 16.8
Key Decisions When Factor Analyzing Data

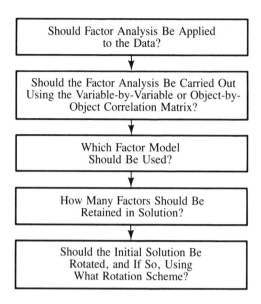

analyzed. Note that all three of these schemes attempt to assess what the variable in question has in common with the other variables in the analysis, and while the initial communality estimates are different depending on which alternative is used, that does not seem to make much difference in the results. That is, all three schemes tend to produce similar solutions in the typical situation of large numbers of observations and variables.

Not only must analysts make decisions with respect to what values to enter into the diagonal of the correlation matrix, but they also need to make decisions with respect to a number of other issues in order to conduct a factor analysis. Figure 16.8 outlines the sequence of decisions that need to be made. While we have already discussed the content of some of these decisions, let us briefly review the essential questions that need to be addressed at each stage in the process.[30]

1. Should factor analysis be applied to the data? While we just went ahead and applied factor analysis to the two examples in this section, analysts would typically want to ask whether it is wise to do so before proceeding. There are several useful methods for deciding whether a factor analysis should be applied to a set of data. Two of

---

[30]For a more detailed discussion of these questions, and the main options and empirical evidence addressing them, see Stewart, ''The Application and Misapplication of Factor Analysis.''

the simplest procedures are to examine the correlation matrix and to plot the latent roots. Factor analysis is concerned with the homogeneity of items. This means that some of the items in the correlation matrix should be large, indicating that they go together. A pattern of low correlations throughout the matrix indicates a heterogeneous set of items and suggests the matrix may be inappropriate for factoring. The plot of the latent roots or eigenvalues should indicate a sharp break. If the plot of the original, unrotated roots results in a continuous, unbroken line, factoring may be inappropriate.

2.   Should the factor analysis be carried out using the variable-by-variable or object-by-object correlation matrix? Typically, the variable-by-variable correlation matrix is analyzed because most studies aim at determining which variables go together. That is not the only alternative. The object-by-object matrix can also be analyzed, and there are other options as well.

3.   Which factor model would be used? We have already discussed whether to use the principal components model or the factor model, in which communalities are placed in the diagonal of the correlation matrix before it is factor analyzed. Suppose the analyst decides on the factor model to allow for the unique components in the variables. The question then becomes one of deciding which of the many factor models to use, as there are a number of choices. Most of the popular statistical packages have a default option that selects one of the more robust alternatives when a choice is not specified.

4.   How many factors should be retained in solution? We have already discussed some of the main criteria that can be used to decide on the proper number of factors. The latent roots and scree criteria generally work well, though not always perfectly, and analysts may be uncertain as to how many factors they should retain. When too few are retained and carried into rotation, the factor output can be very difficult to interpret. Recall that no additional variation can be accounted for by rotation. The amount of variance in each variable accounted for is exactly the same after rotation as it was before. The only thing that changes is how the variance accounted for is distributed among the factors. When too few factors are carried into rotation, the variance in each variable is forced upon too few factors, resulting in a number of mid-size loadings rather than loadings near zero and one. This, of course, makes interpretation much more difficult. When too many factors are carried into rotation, some factors come out capturing the variance of a single variable or, at most, two variables. This is counter to the whole notion underlying factor analysis, which suggests a factor is a latent variable that reflects what a number of observed variables have in common. In general, though, the empirical evidence suggests that over-factoring by one or two factors has less severe consequences for the final solution than does taking too few factors into rotation.[31]

5.   Should the initial solution be rotated, and if so, using what rotation scheme? In some ways, ''rotation is something like staining a microscope slide. Just as different stains reveal different structures in the tissue, different rotations reveal different

---

[31]*Ibid.*, p. 59.

structures in the data, even though in both cases all the structures are always actually there.''[32] It is possible that different rotations will yield results that appear to be entirely different. Rather than being bothered by this, it is useful to keep in mind the fact that all rotations are equivalent from a statistical point of view. They differ only in how they apportion the variation accounted for, which, of course, is what is used to name the factors. Thus, performing a number of rotations and examining the results to see which rotation produced the "most interpretable" structure is often a very productive analysis strategy. The "right rotation," just like the "right stain" on a microscope slide, can be very revealing of the underlying structure in the data or organism.

Marketing Applications

In marketing, factor analysis historically has been employed to "purify" original sets of scale items by isolating and then eliminating those items that do not seem to belong with the rest of the items, as well as to name the dimensions captured by a measure.[33] It has also been used in life-style and psychographic research problems to develop consumer profiles reflecting people's attitudes, activities, interests, opinions, perceptions, and preferences, so as to better predict their consumption and purchase behavior.[34] Factor analysis has also been used in marketing to determine the key attributes determining customer preferences for particular products or institutions, to assess a company's image, to isolate those dimensions of printed advertisements that most affect readership, to develop a measure by which the job satisfaction of industrial sales representatives can be assessed, to group objects, typically people, on the basis of their similarities in behavior, and to screen variables prior to performing a regression analysis to eliminate or at least reduce the problems of correlated predictors.[35]

Cluster Analysis

In marketing there is keen interest in developing useful ways of classifying objects. Very often the objects to be classified are customers. Consider a firm that is interested in segmenting its market. The objective is to group potential customers into homogeneous groups that are large enough to be profitably cultivated. The segmentation base

---

[32]William D. Wells and Jagdish N. Sheth, "Factor Analysis," in Robert Ferber, ed., *Handbook of Marketing Research* (New York: McGraw-Hill, 1974), p. 2-462.

[33]The emphasis on factor analysis in scale development is particularly evident in the semantic differential scales. See the original book describing the development of the semantic differential technique by Charles E. Osgood, George J. Suci, and Percy H. Tannenbaum, *The Measurement of Meaning* (Urbana, Ill.: University of Illinois Press, 1957). See also Roger M. Heeler, Thomas W. Whipple, and Thomas P. Hustad, "Maximum Likelihood Factor Analysis of Attitude Data," *Journal of Marketing Research*, 14 (February 1977), pp. 42–51.

[34]For a general review of the origins, development, and thrust of life-style and psychographic research, see William D. Wells, ed., *Life Style and Psychographics* (Chicago: American Marketing Association, 1974).

[35]For bibliographies listing some of the major studies in marketing that used factor analysis, see Dillon and Goldstein, *Multivariate Analysis;* Hair, Anderson, Tatham, and Grablowsky, *Multivariate Data Analysis;* or Stewart, "The Application and Misapplication of Factor Analysis."

could involve any number of characteristics, ranging from the commonly used socioeconomic bases to the more recently advocated buyer behavior and psychological bases. One thing is sure, it would be based on a number of factors and not simply one or two factors. This, of course, raises a problem for the researcher: how to identify natural groupings of the objects given the multivariate nature of the data. To base the classification on a single factor would be an oversimplification. Yet some means of combining variables must be found if more than one factor is to be used. **Cluster analysis** offers the researcher a way out of the dilemma. It specifically deals with how objects should be assigned to groups so that there will be as much similarity within and difference among groups as possible.

As an example, consider the problem faced by firms that wish to test market products, prices, promotional campaigns, and so on. The problem is to select "like" cities so that the results obtained are not attributable to differences in market areas. But how does one determine when cities are "alike"? Consider the situation when similarity is assessed on the basis of two city characteristics—population and median income. Now, this represents an oversimplification of the actual situation, but nevertheless it can be used to illustrate the purposes and procedures of cluster analysis. Since the variables possess vastly different measurement scales, it is advisable to effect the grouping using standardized scores. Otherwise, the grouping would change when the unit in which a variable was measured was altered; for example, population was specified as a number of thousands of people instead of simply number of people. Table 16.15 contains the standardized income and population scores for 15 test cities that a firm is considering grouping into like categories.

One way of effecting the grouping is simply to plot the results and make a visual assignment. Figure 16.9, which employs income and population as axes, suggests there are three distinct clusters in the data:

■ Cluster 1 consisting of Cities A, C, D, and G;
■ Cluster 2 consisting of Cities E, I, J, K, N, and O; and
■ Cluster 3 consisting of Cities B, F, H, L, and M.

The visual assignment procedure worked in this example because there were only two dimensions on which the grouping was to be based. There are potentially many characteristics on which the cities might be grouped, though, and graphic display becomes more difficult as the number of dimensions is increased. Thus, it would appear useful to have some objective measure of "similarity" or "likeness" with which to form the "natural groupings" of the objects in higher space.

Euclidean Distance to Measure Similarity

A rather obvious measure is the Euclidean distance between the points. In the two-dimensional figure, the distance between Cities A and C, say, would be calculated

$$d_{A,C} = \sqrt{(X_{C1} - X_{A1})^2 + (X_{C2} - X_{A2})^2},$$

where X_{C1}, for example, represents the coordinate of City C on the first dimension, median income. This distance turns out to be

$$D_{A,C} = \sqrt{(1.14 - 1.62)^2 + (1.72 - 0.89)^2} = 0.959.$$

Table 16.15
Key Characteristics of Cities to be Grouped Expressed in Standardized Units

City	Income X_1	Population X_2
A	1.14	1.72
B	−1.25	−1.17
C	1.62	0.89
D	1.64	1.35
E	0.55	0.10
F	−0.94	−1.25
G	0.89	1.32
H	−0.87	−0.63
I	−0.44	−0.07
J	0.08	−0.55
K	−0.18	0.62
L	−1.29	−0.86
M	−1.07	−1.38
N	−0.09	0.02
O	0.21	−0.11

Figure 16.9
Two-dimensional Plot of City Characteristics

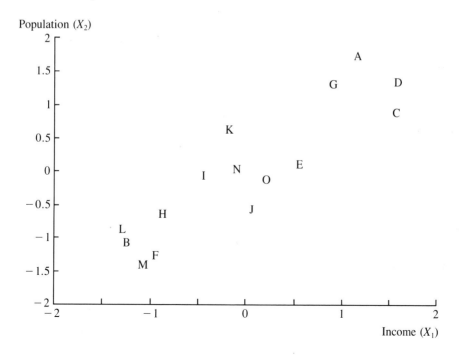

Table 16.16

Distance between Cities i and j in Two Space

	1	2	3	4	5	6	7	8	9	10	11	12	13	14	15
$i =$	A	B	C	D	E	F	G	H	I	J	K	L	M	N	O
1. (A)	0.000														
2. (B)	3.750	0.000													
3. (C)	0.959	3.533	0.000												
4. (D)	0.622	3.834	0.460	0.000											
5. (E)	1.724	2.203	1.330	1.658	0.000										
6. (F)	3.626	0.320	3.337	3.663	2.011	0.000									
7. (G)	0.472	3.283	0.847	0.751	1.266	3.155	0.000								
8. (H)	3.092	0.660	2.917	3.197	1.597	0.624	2.627	0.000							
9. (I)	2.388	1.366	2.273	2.518	1.004	1.282	1.924	0.706	0.000						
10. (J)	2.505	1.467	2.108	2.458	0.802	1.237	2.038	0.953	0.708	0.000					
11. (K)	1.718	2.085	1.820	1.961	0.896	2.019	1.279	1.428	0.737	1.199	0.000				
12. (L)	3.544	0.313	3.396	3.670	2.075	0.524	3.083	0.479	1.160	1.405	1.850	0.000			
13. (M)	3.807	0.277	3.520	3.847	2.194	0.184	3.336	0.776	1.454	1.418	2.189	0.565	0.000		
14. (N)	2.098	1.662	1.919	2.182	0.645	1.528	1.628	1.015	0.361	0.595	0.607	1.488	1.709	0.000	
15. (O)	2.053	1.804	1.729	2.044	0.400	1.619	1.583	1.199	0.651	0.459	0.828	1.677	1.803	0.327	0.000

In three dimensions, the expression for distance between A and C would be

$$d_{A,C} = \sqrt{(X_{C1} - X_{A1})^2 + (X_{C2} - X_{A2})^2 + (X_{C3} - X_{A3})^2},$$

while for any two objects, i and j, it would be

$$d_{ij} = \left\{ \sum_{k=1}^{3} (X_{ik} - X_{jk})^2 \right\}^{1/2}.$$

The generalization to n dimensions to account for n characteristics is obvious; the summation is simply taken from k equals 1 to n.

The distance between all 15 cities is presented in Table 16.16. An examination of Table 16.16 prompts several comments. First, distance is an inverse measure of similarity in that the larger the distance, the further apart are the objects. Second, one can readily appreciate why cluster analysis is highly dependent on computers.[36] In this simplified example involving 15 objects, there were $15(14)/2 = 105$ distances that needed computing. In the general case of n objects, there would be $n(n - 1)/2$ separate dis-

---

[36]The growth in popularity of cluster analysis paralleled the early growth in computer installations. The major stimulus was the classic book by R. Sokal and P. Sneath, *Principles of Numerical Taxonomy* (San Francisco: W. H. Freeman, 1963). The literature on cluster analysis virtually exploded after its publication in that the number of published applications of cluster analysis in all scientific fields approximately doubled once every three years for the next decade.

tances. Third, the specification of the clusters is not as readily apparent as it was when the data were presented graphically. As a matter of fact, without the two-dimensional figure to help us, there is a real question whether we could even specify some appropriate clusters. Clearly we need some alternate way of proceeding.

Clustering Methods

A number of methods have been suggested for forming "natural groupings" of objects employing variables. One of the most popular classifications includes:[37]

1. linkage procedures,

2. nodal procedures, and

3. factor procedures.

There are also variations within each method. Keep in mind, though, that the objective underlying each method is the same—to assign objects to groups so there will be as much similarity within groups and as much difference among groups as possible. Unfortunately, the different methods can produce some widely divergent results with the same data set, and none of the methods is as yet accepted as the "best." The research analyst must, therefore, be familiar with the various methods so that he or she can exercise the proper degree of caution in choosing the method that is most compatible with the desired nature of the classification.

Linkage Methods   A number of linkage methods have been advanced.[38] We shall discuss the single linkage method in some detail, because an understanding of this method is the key to understanding the other linkage procedures, such as complete linkage and average linkage.

Single Linkage   Single linkage computer programs operate in the following way. First the similarity values are arrayed from most to least similar. Then, those objects with the highest similarity (lowest distance) coefficients are clustered together. The similarity coefficient is then systematically lowered, and the union of objects at each similarity value is recorded. The union of two objects, the admission of an object into a cluster, or the union of two clusters is by the criterion of single linkage. This means that if the similarity level (distance level) in question is, say, 0.20, a *single linkage* of an object at that level with *any member* of a cluster would allow the object to join the cluster. Similarly, *any pair of objects* (one in each of two clusters) related at the criterion level *will make their clusters join.*

Consider, for example, all those similarity values less than 1.000 in Table 16.16. When arrayed from most similar to least similar, the tabulation in Table 16.17 results.

---

[37]For an alternative seven-category classification, see Mark S. Aldenderfer and Roger K. Blashfield, *Cluster Analysis* (Beverly Hills, Calif.: Sage Publications, 1984).

[38]The linkage methods are sometimes called hierarchical agglomerative methods. For useful introductions to the subject, see Aldenderfer and Blashfield, *Cluster Analysis,* or M. Lorr, *Cluster Analysis for Social Sciences* (San Francisco: Jossey-Bass, 1983).

Table 16.17

All Distances Less Than 1.000 Arrayed in Increasing Order of Dissimilarity

Distance Level	City Pairs	Distance Level	City Pairs	Distance Level	City Pairs
0.184	FM	0.524	FL	0.737	IK
0.277	BM	0.565	LM	0.751	DG
0.313	BL	0.595	JN	0.776	HM
0.320	BF	0.607	KN	0.802	EJ
0.327	NO	0.622	AD	0.828	KO
0.361	IN	0.624	FH	0.847	CG
0.400	EO	0.645	EN	0.896	EK
0.459	JO	0.651	IO	0.953	HJ
0.460	CD	0.660	BH	0.959	AC
0.472	AG	0.706	HI		
0.479	HL	0.708	IJ		

The highest reported similarity value is 0.184, the distance between F and M. Starting at a distance of zero, the first computer iteration would be to this value, and objects F and M would be joined to form a cluster. The next table entry is 0.277, the distance between objects B and M. Consider what happens at this second computer iteration value.

Since M has already been joined to F at the first iteration, the situation can be diagrammed:

Will B be allowed to join the cluster consisting of the elements F and M? The answer is yes under the criterion of single linkage. Even though the distance from B to F is 0.320, that does not matter under the criterion of single linkage. Rather, the one link between B and M that satisfies the criterion value is sufficient to allow B to join F and M to form the larger group BFM. The next iteration would be to the similarity value 0.313, representing the distance between B and L. Would L be allowed to join the group BFM at this iteration value? Again, the answer would be yes under the criterion of single linkage; even though the distance from F to L, which is 0.524, and the distance from L to M, which is 0.565, are both greater than the criterion value, that would not matter under the criterion of single linkage. Since BFL and M are already joined, nothing further happens at the similarity value 0.320. At the value 0.327, though, N joins O, and I joins this new pair at the iteration value 0.361 to form the larger group INO. E and J are subsequently admitted to this cluster of objects at the iteration values 0.400 and 0.459, respectively. The process would proceed similarly with objects joining to form pairs of objects or objects being admitted to previously formed groups until, after the fifteenth iteration corresponding to a distance of 0.607, the situation would look like this:

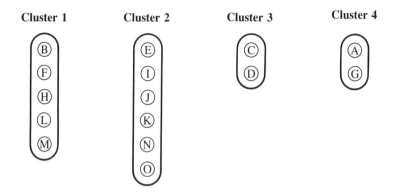

Cluster 1   **Cluster 2**   **Cluster 3**   **Cluster 4**

Thus, none of the variables would still be in clusters by themselves. When will the clusters themselves join to form larger groupings? According to the criterion of single linkage, the clusters will join when the distance between *any pair* of *objects* in the distinct clusters equals the iteration distance value. Consider, for example, the situation between Clusters 3 and 4, which can be diagrammed:

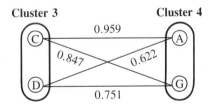

Cluster 3   **Cluster 4**

At an iteration value of 0.622, Cluster 3 will be joined with Cluster 4, because the single bond between A and D satisfies the criterion. Note that while the clusters are joined because of the single bond between two members of the respective clusters, some of the members within the newly formed cluster are much further removed from one another; e.g., the distance from A to C is 0.959 and the distance from C to G is 0.847, approximately 1½ times larger than the merging distance. Single linkage can thus produce "long, straggling" groups.

Before turning to alternate linkage methods, let us introduce the notion of the **dendrogram** as a way of presenting the results of cluster analysis. A dendrogram is simply a "tree" that indicates the groups of objects forming at various similarity (distance) levels. The dendrogram for the test city data employing the single linkage method is shown in Figure 16.10.

Objects A through O are shown at the top. As we saw, the class FM forms first ($d_{FM} = 0.184$); B is admitted to this cluster at a distance iteration value of 0.277, and so on. These unions and the values at which they occur are shown by the horizontal lines connecting the objects in Figure 16.10. The levels at which groups join to form even larger groups are depicted similarly in the figure. Question: what are the "natural

Figure 16.10
Dendrogram of City Data Using Single Linkage

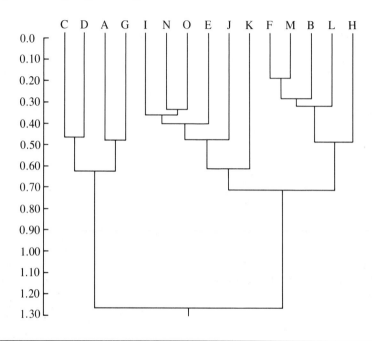

groupings" in the data? It all depends on what similarity level one is using. At a distance level of 0.50, there are five separate classes, reading from left to right:

■ Group 1—CD
■ Group 2—AG
■ Group 3—INOEJ
■ Group 4—K
■ Group 5—FMBLH

If, on the other hand, a distance level of 0.65 is to be used, then there are three classes:

■ Group 1—CDAG
■ Group 2—INOEJK
■ Group 3—FMBLH

Finally, if one selects a distance level of 0.80 there are only two classes:

■ Group 1—CDAG
■ Group 2—INOEJKFMBLH

Many would probably select a cutoff distance of 0.65 because the two-dimensional portrayal of the data suggests that there are three natural groupings. With p variables,

Figure 16.11
Plot of Number of Clusters versus Fusion Coefficient

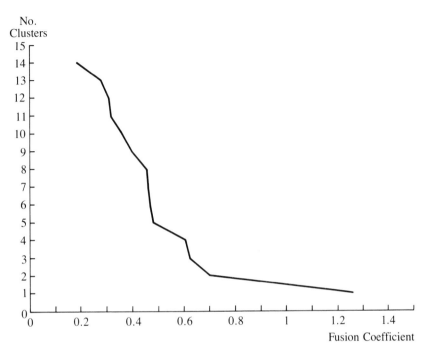

the decision as to the proper cutoff value must be made without such a visual referent, making the decision much more difficult. The purpose of the analysis would assist the analyst in making the choice. If the researcher simply needed two cities that were very much alike, he or she might use a more stringent criterion level, such as 0.35. The researcher would then have two groups with quite homogeneous cities, one group consisting of the pair of cities N and O and the other group consisting of the four cities F, M, B, and L. If, alternatively, the analyst needed a large number of similar test cities, he or she would use a more relaxed similarity coefficient, such as 0.65, which would produce three groups of four, six, and five members.

An alternative way of deciding the number of clusters is to plot the number of clusters against the **fusion coefficients,** which represent the numerical values at which various cases merge to form clusters. The fusion (or, as they are sometimes called, amalgamation) coefficients can be read directly from the dendogram. Note, for example, that at a value of 0.184 in the dendogram of Figure 16.10, where Objects F and M join, there are 14 groups. At the value of 0.277, where objects F, M, and B join, there are 13 groups, and so on. These fusion values and number of groups serve as the coordinates for the two points farthest to the left in Figure 16.11.

Figure 16.11 can be used in much the same way as the plot of the eigenvalues versus the number of factors was used in factor analysis. One can look for "significant" jumps in the fusion coefficient, indicating that two relatively dissimilar clusters have been merged. This suggests that the number of clusters prior to the merger is the most probable solution. Alternatively, one can use a scree-like test by searching where the curve flattens out. The flattening of the graph suggests no new information is portrayed by the subsequent mergers of the clusters. Note that in Figure 16.11 the curve flattens at two points, once when going from five to four clusters and once when going from two clusters to one, implying that there are five or two clusters in the data. The incremental change in the fusion coefficient also suggests there are either five or two clusters in the data, since there is a substantial jump in the value of the coefficient between five and four and between two and one clusters. As the example indicates, while these rules of thumb for determining the number of clusters can be helpful, they sometimes produce ambiguous results.

Complete Linkage   In the complete linkage method, an object joining a cluster at a certain similarity coefficient must have relations at that level or above with *every member* of the cluster. Thus, single bonds with just one member of the cluster would not be sufficient to effect the juncture. In practice, this is a fierce condition, with larger groups only forming when the criterion level is lowered considerably. Complete linkage has a tendency to produce very tight, compact clusters.

Consider again the Group ADGC. This group will eventually form under the complete linkage criterion, but consider how. The respective distances are

	A	C	D	G
A	0.000			
C	0.959	0.000		
D	0.622	0.460	0.000	
G	0.472	0.847	0.751	0.000

At a value of 0.460, Objects C and D join. Similarly, Objects A and G join at the value 0.472. When will the two groups join? Under the criterion of complete linkage, they will only come together when *all* the linkages among the objects in the two groups satisfy the criterion level. In other words, the largest distance among the objects in the groups controls the union. This means that the two groups will not join to form the larger group consisting of the elements ACDG until the iteration distance value 0.959 is reached, as that is the distance between Object A in the one group and Object C in the other.

Average Linkage   The average linkage method is an attempt to walk a middle ground between the single linkage and complete linkage methods. As the name implies, the *average* of all similarities between an object and a class of objects or between the members of two classes has to be above the given level for linkage to occur. The average linkage method involves a great deal more calculation than either single linkage or complete linkage methods. Both of the latter methods involve using a table look-up procedure. One simply calculates the distance between objects once. Subsequently, one checks the table of distances to see whether the criterion is satisfied. With average linkage, union is established when the average similarity between objects in distinct groups satisfies the criterion. As the composition of the groups changes, these average distances or similarities must be calculated anew. Thus, while perhaps intuitively compelling, the greater number of calculations this method involves has restricted its application, particularly when there are a large number of objects to be grouped.

Nodal Methods   The linkage methods are all considered hierarchical clustering methods. That is, a hierarchy of groupings is formed as the criterion similarity value is altered. The dendrogram captures the resulting hierarchy.

Another main type of clustering method is one of selecting an object or objects that will serve as focal objects or nodes for clusters. The remaining objects are then allocated to each cluster on the basis of their similarity to the focal objects. The basic operation of the nodal methods can be illustrated by the following scheme:

- Choose as nodes those objects that have the least similarity or greatest distance.

- Consider these two objects as polar nodes and allocate all remaining objects to one or the other cluster based on their similarity to the polar nodes.

- Split the two resulting clusters in the same way. Continue the process until the collection of objects is split into its original members.

In the test city example, Cities D and M are most dissimilar ($d_{DM} = 3.847$), and thus they would be considered as the nodes for the two clusters. Each of the remaining objects would then be allocated to each cluster on the basis of the shortest distance to either D or M. Thus, the original clusters would be:

- Group 1—DACEGK

- Group 2—MBFHIJLNO

In Group 1, the least similar cities are D and K ($d_{DK} = 1.961$). They would thus be considered new nodes, and the items in Group 1 would be allocated to each of the new clusters on the basis of their distances to these new nodes. Thus, the new groups would be

- Group 1A—DACG

- Group 1B—KE

Similarly, Group 2 would be divided (using B and J as new nodes) to yield

- Group 2A—BFHLM

- Group 2B—JINO

At each stage one could check to see if the resulting subgroups should be combined based on, say, some average measure of similarity between the objects within and among subgroups.

An alternative nodal clustering method is that employing a "prime" node. The prime node is the most "typical" object, that is, the object that has characteristics closest to the average characteristics for all the objects. Since the data has been standardized, the average median income and average population for the 15 cities are zero. City N is most typical, and it would be considered the prime node, and a cluster would be formed around it. Cities would be added to this cluster one at a time. After each addition, a measure of the resulting homogeneity of the cluster would be determined. When the measure of homogeneity—average-within-cluster distance in our case—took a large jump in value, the "natural" limits of the cluster would be considered to have been exceeded, and the last object added to the cluster would be removed.

After the primary clump was determined, it would be removed from the analysis. A new typical object would be determined from the remaining objects, and the process would be repeated. The procedure would continue until all the objects had joined clusters or until only a few residual objects remained. The residual objects could then be attached to those clusters that they seemed to fit best.

The nodal methods are also known as iterative partitioning methods because of the way they work; that is, they begin with some initial partition of the data and subsequently change these assignments. The use of polar nodes or a prime node represent just two of the many alternatives that have been proposed for effecting an initial partition of the objects. Two other alternatives are to specify "seed points" by picking certain objects to serve as group centroids or by randomly assigning objects to one of a prespecified number of clusters (for example, three).[39] Regardless of how the initial assignment of objects to groups is determined, the next step is to calculate the centroids or group means of each cluster and then to reallocate each data point to the cluster that has the nearest centroid. After all reassignments are made, the centroids of the new clusters are computed and the process is repeated until no reassignments occur. Thus, iterative partitioning methods make more than one pass through the data, which allows them to recover from a poor initial partition.

Factor Analysis   A third major way of attacking the clustering problem is through factor analysis. Previously we searched for the latent dimensions of the *variables* by determining which variables go together or measure common characteristics. We could just as easily attempt to determine which *objects* logically belong together. Object-by-object factor analysis is often called Q analysis or inverse factor analysis.[40]

Consider again the distance matrix contained in Table 16.16. It has been demonstrated that a distance matrix can be factored and, in particular, that factoring it is equivalent to factoring the raw score cross-products matrix.[41] The starting point for this sort of analysis is then the cross-products matrix computed across objects, which is presented as Table 16.18.[42]

---

[39]For a very readable discussion of some of the main options when using iterative partitioning methods, see Aldenderfer and Blashfield, *Cluster Analysis,* especially pp. 45–49.

[40]Variable-by-variable and object-by-object are just two types of factor analysis. See R. B. Cattell, "The Three Basic Factor Analytic Research Designs—Their Interrelationships and Derivatives," *Psychological Bulletin,* 49 (1952), pp. 449–520, for an extensive discussion of the basic types.

[41]Jum C. Nunnally, "The Analysis of Profile Data," *Psychological Bulletin,* 59 (1962), pp. 313–319.

[42]The entries in Table 16.18 were obtained in the following way. Consider the scores of Table 16.15 as defining the raw score matrix $X = (X_{ik})$, where X_{ik} represents the score of the ith city on the kth variable and where $i = 1, 2, \ldots, 15$ and $k = 1, 2$. Form the matrix sums of cross-products $S = (S_{ij})$ where

$$S_{ij} = \sum_{k=1}^{2} X_{ik}X_{jk}.$$

Thus, for $i = 1$ (City A) and $j = 2$ (City B),

$$S_{12} = \sum_{k=1}^{2} X_{1k}X_{2k} = X_{11}X_{21} + X_{12}X_{22} = (1.14)(-1.25) + (1.72)(-1.17) = -3.434$$

The remaining entries in the object-by-object cross-product matrix reported in Table 16.18 were computed in similar fashion.

Table 16.18
Object-by-Object Raw Scores Cross-product Matrix

$i =$	$j =$ 1 A	2 B	3 C	4 D	5 E	6 F	7 G	8 H	9 I	10 J	11 K	12 L	13 M	14 N	15 O
1. (A)	4.252														
2. (B)	−3.434	2.932													
3. (C)	3.371	−3.065	3.413												
4. (D)	4.186	−3.626	3.849	4.500											
5. (E)	0.809	−0.813	0.987	1.044	0.316										
6. (F)	−3.218	2.634	−2.626	−3.221	−0.647	2.443									
7. (G)	3.284	−2.654	2.608	3.236	0.626	−2.487	2.537								
8. (H)	−2.083	1.832	−1.976	−2.283	−0.548	1.609	−1.611	1.163							
9. (I)	−0.626	0.636	−0.777	−0.818	−0.250	0.502	−0.485	0.430	0.199						
10. (J)	−0.848	0.538	−0.355	−0.607	−0.013	0.610	−0.653	0.276	0.005	0.305					
11. (K)	0.861	−0.501	0.262	0.546	−0.033	−0.609	0.663	−0.237	0.033	−0.352	0.413				
12. (L)	−2.950	2.621	−2.856	−3.274	−0.803	2.285	−2.281	1.672	0.630	0.367	−0.304	2.407			
13. (M)	−3.595	2.952	−2.956	−3.615	−0.733	2.732	−2.778	1.807	0.570	0.672	−0.668	2.568	3.056		
14. (N)	−0.064	0.087	−0.127	−0.117	−0.048	0.056	−0.050	0.065	0.038	−0.020	0.030	0.098	0.065	0.009	
15. (O)	0.056	−0.139	0.247	0.200	0.105	−0.063	0.044	−0.116	−0.085	0.076	−0.104	−0.180	−0.076	−0.022	0.056

This cross-products matrix can be factored using any of the usual methods. Let us determine what happens when the principal components procedure is used. The sum of the diagonal elements in Table 16.18 yields the total variance in the data, which is 28.0. By again comparing the variance extracted by each factor with this total variance, we are in a position to estimate the number of factors that are needed to satisfactorily recover the data. It turns out that two factors are needed to summarize all of the variance in the data; 95 percent of the variance (26.5 in absolute magnitude) is accounted for by the first factor, while 5 percent (1.5 in absolute magnitude) is accounted for by the second factor. Thus, it would seem that the objects could be clustered along a single dimension. This should not prove surprising when you recall the conceptual basis of principal components analysis and apply it to the two-dimensional plot of the data contained in Figure 16.5. The first component is simply the major axis of the ellipse generated by this scatter of points extending from the southwest to the northeast quadrant of the graph.

The resulting factor loadings on this one factor are presented in Table 16.19. There seem to be three levels of magnitude: high positive values, near-zero values, and high negative values. The use of these criteria would generate three clusters:

- Cluster 1—ACDG
- Cluster 2—EIJKNO
- Cluster 3—BFHLM

These are the clusters that we visually distinguished from the scatter of cities in Figure 16.9. This tidy result is not generally to be expected but is simply due to the fact that the objects were aligned rather nicely along the southwest–northeast diagonal of the figure.

If more than one factor were necessary to "summarize" the basic variation in the data, the original factor solution could be rotated to simple structure. Then the objects that formed "natural groupings" would be determined by examining the rotated loadings matrix. The objects that loaded "similarly" on the same factors would be considered to form clusters.

When factor analysis is used to cluster objects, it is important to note that the number of clusters is *not* given by the number of factors. Only two factors are necessary to account for *all* the variation in the sum-of-squares-and-cross-products matrix, and the first factor accounts for the bulk of it. Yet, there are three clusters in the data even when only the first factor is used. Rather than using the number of factors to indicate the number of clusters, analysts need to examine the loading matrix. The *pattern* of loadings determines both the number of clusters and which objects belong to which cluster.

Key Decisions

The discussion so far may suggest that in order to use cluster analysis, the analyst must make one key decision: which clustering method to use. This is not the case. The topic has simply been presented this way to bring the basic objective of cluster analysis into bold relief. It is time to introduce additional complications.

Table 16.19
Factor Loadings on First Factor

Object	Loading	Object	Loading
A	2.02	I	−0.36
B	−1.71	J	−0.33
C	1.77	K	0.31
D	2.11	L	−1.52
E	0.46	M	−1.73
F	−1.55	N	−0.05
G	1.56	O	0.07
H	−1.06	λ	26.5

In order to perform a cluster analysis, it is actually necessary to make decisions with respect to each of the four stages depicted in Figure 16.12. The discussion so far has concentrated on Stage 3 in that process. Let us now look at each of the other stages in turn.

Select and Code Attributes   Stage 1 focuses on the related questions "Which attributes are to be employed to generate the natural groupings?" and "How are these attributes to be coded?" The example assumed that income and population were the characteristics of importance in defining similar test cities. Further, these are both ratio-scaled variables. No additional coding other than standardization was necessary before generating Euclidean distances to assess similarity. The example was artificial in these respects. The selection of attributes is key in its own right; a change in the characteristics used to define similarity will often change the "natural groupings" that exist among the objects.

There is not a great deal of guidance in the literature with regard to selecting attributes. Yet the choice of variables used to cluster the objects is one of the most critical decisions analysts make. The best advice seems to be to choose those variables that make sense conceptually, rather than using any and all variables simply because they are convenient or accessible.

When coding the attributes, it is necessary to keep their basic nature in mind. Some of them may be continuous in nature (for example, income), while others may be categorical (for example, geography). If categorical, they may be dichotomous or multichotomous. In the city example, we could classify the various cities by whether they were located in the southern half of the United States or the northern half. Alternatively, we could use finer geographical divisions. The important thing to note is that the coding decision depends fundamentally on the type of variables that are considered and, again, on what theory suggests with respect to how the variables should impact the natural grouping of objects.

The basic problem is to find that set of variables that best represents the concept of similarity under which the study operates. Ideally, variables should be chosen within

Figure 16.12
Key Decisions When Cluster Analyzing Data

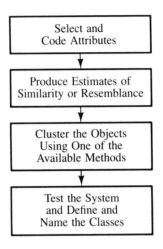

the context of an explicitly stated theory that is used to support the classification. The theory is the basis for the rational choice of the variables to be used in the study . . .

The importance of using theory to guide the choice of variables should not be underestimated. The temptation to succumb to a naive empiricism in the use of cluster analysis is very strong, since the technique is ostensibly designed to produce ''objective'' groupings of entities. By ''naive empiricism'' we mean the collection and subsequent analysis of as many variables as possible in hope that the ''structure'' will emerge if only enough data are obtained.[43]

Not only is the choice of attributes sometimes difficult to decide, but the weights that are to be given to each attribute when producing estimates of similarity can also prove troublesome. Again, theory should be used to guide the choice. When theory has little to say on the subject, the prevailing sentiment seems to be to consider all the attributes to be of equal importance and to weight them equally when producing estimates of resemblance.

Produce Estimates of Similarity or Resemblance   The estimates of resemblance that are used to specify how similar the objects are also depend on the level of measurement used to capture the attributes. There was little question in our example about the measures. Both income and population were ratio scaled, and it was natural to define similarity employing Euclidean distance. Consider now a situation in which the analyst's interest is in grouping people into similar groups, as in a market segmentation study.

---

[43]Aldenderfer and Blaskfield, *Cluster Analysis,* pp. 19–20.

Here a number of variables of interest would be nominally scaled, or ordinally scaled at best (for example, marital status, ethnic background, religious preference, stage in the life cycle). Such variables raise the question of what kind of estimate of resemblance is to be used as input to the cluster algorithm. Are they to be 0–1 (absence–presence of an attribute) matching coefficients (for example, a family is black or not), or are the coefficients to reflect the individual categories (for example, a family is black, white, yellow), and so on?

Given the input measures, the analyst has a number of decisions to make in order to produce estimates of resemblance. The decisions are in large part dictated by the scale quality of the measures. However, they are not completely dictated, and the analyst has some latitude. If the input measures reflect cardinal measurement, the analyst's most basic decision is whether to use a distance function or a correlation coefficient to capture resemblance. Further, if the researcher chooses a distance function, should the distance function be Euclidean distance as in the example, or should it be city-block distance or even perhaps Mahalanobis distance?[44] Euclidean distance is clearly the most popular. Yet one of the problems with it is that it is not scale invariant. This means that the relative ordering of the objects with respect to their similarity can be affected by a simple change in scale by which one or more of the variables are measured. For example, we could have measured income in thousands of dollars rather than in dollars in attempting to determine which cities were most similar and that could possibly have affected the ordering of the similarity coefficients if the data had not first been standardized to mean zero and standard deviation one. In general, we prefer that the similarity coefficients not be sensitive to the units in which we choose to measure variables. While standardization is one way to remove that sensitivity, standardization carries its own costs, in that it can reduce the differences between groups on those variables that may very well be the best discriminators of group differences. Ideally, we would like to standardize varibles within groups rather than across all cases.[45] Obviously this cannot be done until the cases have been placed into groups. In sum, the standardization issue is far from settled. The best advice is to decide the standardization issue on a case-by-case basis. If the units in which the variables are measured are roughly of the same magnitude, then it might be best not to standardize them. If the variables are measured on widely differing units, standardization is needed to prevent the variables measured in larger units from dominating the cluster solution.

Suppose the data are dichotomous or multichotomous rather than reflecting cardinal measurement. Some procedure other than using distance or product-moment correlations is then needed to measure resemblance. Some kind of matching coefficient is called for. The idea of a matching coefficient as a measure of similarity is simple—a matching

---

[44]Morrison suggests Mahalanobis distance is best, since it allows for intercorrelations among the variables and also provides for variable weighting by the investigator that is explicit rather than implicit. Implicit weighting occurs, for example, when correlated variables are used to compute a measure of similarity. If four highly correlated variables are used, the effect is the same as using only one variable that has a weight four times greater than any other variable. Donald G. Morrison, "Measurement Problems in Cluster Analysis," *Management Science,* 13 (August 1967), pp. 755–780.

[45]For a discussion of the issues involved in standardization, see B. Everett, *Cluster Analysis* (New York: Halsted Press, 1980).

coefficient should represent the number of characteristics on which two objects match in relation to the number of comparisons made. However, this simple notion begs the question of what kind of matches should count: positive matches? negative matches? both kinds?

To illustrate the fundamental dilemma with respect to what types of matches to emphasize, consider the hypothetical data for three objects contained in Panel A of Table 16.20. Each object has been measured on ten attributes; a one indicates the object possesses the attribute while a zero indicates it does not. The attributes could represent any of a number of features of the objects. Suppose for example, the attributes indicate which of ten magazines these three people read. A 1–1 indicates both people read the same magazine and represents a positive match; a 0–0 indicates neither person reads that particular magazine and represents a negative match; a 1–0 means the first person reads it but the second does not, while a 0–1 indicates the opposite, implying there is a mismatch in reading habits in both cases. Panel B of Table 16.20 summarizes the information contained in Panel A regarding the number of positive matches, negative matches, and mismatches for each of the three possible pairs of the three objects.

Panel C of Table 16.20 illustrates the computation of several possible coefficients that could be used to describe the similarity of the three pairs of objects.[46] Formula C1 expresses similarity as a function of the ratio of the number of positive matches versus the number of attributes on which the objects were measured. Formula C2 also emphasizes positive matches, but it is based on the ratio of the number of positive matches to the number of total matches, both positive and negative. Mismatches do not explicitly count in C2. Formula C3 compares the number of positive matches to the number of positive matches plus the number of mismatches; it explicitly deemphasizes negative matches while considering mismatches. Formula C4 also explicitly considers mismatches; it compares the number of positive matches plus the number of mismatches to the total number of comparisons that are made between the objects. Formula C5 looks at the number of features on which the objects are different versus the number on which they are the same.

As suggested, the essential difference among the formulas is how they handle the three types of comparisons. A case could be made for any one of them when deciding which people have more similar reading habits. We could argue that it is the magazines that two people *both* read that determines whether they have similar reading habits and thereby choose a coefficient that emphasized positive matches. Alternatively, we could argue that it is important to note that *neither* one reads, say, *Sports Illustrated* when determining whether they have similar reading habits and could thereby choose to emphasize negative matches as well. Still further, we could argue that the fact that one of the respondents reads *Sports Illustrated* while the other does not indicates something important about the similarity of their reading habits, and we would therefore want to give some weight to mismatches, although perhaps not as much as to positive or negative matches. The five sample coefficients reflect these type of considerations. The im-

---

[46]A great many coefficients have been proposed for assessing the similarity of objects. One of the most detailed discussions can be found in Sokal and Sneath, *Numerical Taxonomy*, who devote 74 pages to the discussion of the topic and provide formulas for most of the coefficients they discuss. See also H. Clifford and W. Stephenson, *An Introduction to Numerical Taxonomy* (New York: Academic Press, 1975).

Table 16.20
Some Alternative Similarity Coefficients

A. Attributes Possessed by Each Object

Object	\multicolumn{10}{c}{Attributes}

Object	1	2	3	4	5	6	7	8	9	10
A	1	0	0	0	1	0	0	1	1	1
B	0	1	0	0	1	0	0	1	0	0
C	0	0	1	0	0	1	0	1	1	0

B. Summary of the Number of Positive Matches, Negative Matches, and Mismatches

	AB	AC	BC
	\multicolumn{3}{c}{Object Pairs}
Number of positive matches (a)	2	2	1
Number of negative matches (b)	4	3	4
Number of mismatches (c)	4	5	5

C. Similarity of the Various Pairs Using Alternative Similarity Coefficients

Coefficient	Object Pair	Value
1. $\dfrac{a}{a + b + c}$	AB	.200
	AC	.200
	BC	.100
2. $\dfrac{a}{a + b}$	AB	.333
	AC	.400
	BC	.250
3. $\dfrac{a}{a + c}$	AB	.333
	AC	.286
	BC	.167
4. $\dfrac{a + c}{a + b + c}$	AB	.600
	AC	.700
	BC	.600
5. $\dfrac{c}{a + b}$	AB	.667
	AC	1.000
	BC	1.000

portant thing to note about these coefficients is that they produce different orderings with respect to the similarity of the three objects. Coefficient Cl indicates Object Pairs AB and AC are the most similar. Coefficient C2 suggests that Object Pair AC is more similar than Object Pair AB and that, in turn, is more similar than Object Pair BC. A different ordering of similarity is produced by Coefficient C3. Whereas for the first three coefficients Object Pair BC is always less similar than either of the other two pairs, that is not the case with Coefficients C4 and C5; with Coefficient C4 it is tied with Pair AB for being the least similar, while with Coefficient C5 it is tied with Pair AC for being the most similar. In sum, with as few as three objects, the ordering of the pairs with respect to their similarity is affected by the emphasis that is given to positive and negative matches and mismatches. The situation is simply exaggerated when more objects are being grouped. Further, there is no answer as to which emphasis is inherently correct. It all depends on the objectives of the study.

The most popular of the five coefficients highlighted in Table 16.20 are coefficients C1 and C3. Coefficient C1 is known as the simple matching coefficient, while Coefficient C3 is known as Jaccards' coefficient. Both coefficients emphasize the importance of positive matches.

Another problem can arise when determining the estimates of resemblance when the attributes reflect different levels of measurement. If they are all interval or ratio scaled variables, then the correlation coefficient or a distance measure can be, and is typically, used. If they are all categorical, then some sort of matching coefficient can be calculated to describe how similar they are. When some are cardinal and the others are categorical, the situation is more difficult. Should the continuous variables be converted to categorical variables so that a matching coefficient can be calculated, or should they be left as is? If they are left as is, how are the two types of measures to be combined?

One coefficient that is particularly attractive for this purpose is Gower's coefficient of similarity, which is capable of handling two state (e.g., sex), multistate (e.g., religious preference), and quantitative (e.g., age) characteristics. The coefficient is calculated by the formula

$$S_{ij} = \frac{\sum_{k=1}^{m} w_{ijk} s_{ijk}}{\sum_{k=1}^{m} w_{ijk}},$$

where

S_{ij} is the overall similarity of Objects i and j.

s_{ijk} is the similarity of Objects i and j on the kth characteristic and there are m characteristics in all. s_{ijk} must be greater than or equal to zero and less than or equal to one. With qualitative characters it is one when there is a match and zero with a mismatch. With quantitative characters $s_{ijk} = (|X_{ik} - X_{jk}|/R_k)$, where X_{ik} and X_{jk} are the values of Character k for the ith and j^{th} objects, respectively, and R_k is the range of Character k in the sample.

w_{ijk} is the weight attached to the kth character.

Note that the coefficient allows the analyst to specify which of the two types of matches to count with respect to any attribute. The analyst simply sets w_{ijk} at one if the comparison is to count and at zero if it is not. Further, the coefficient allows the analyst to weight certain attributes more than others. Consider, for example, the first two rows of Panel A of Table 16.20, and suppose the first five attributes refer to business magazines while the last five refer to general interest magazines like *Time* and *Newsweek*. Suppose further that the emphasis in the cluster analysis is on determining the similarity of reading habits of executives, particularly with respect to business literature, and that we therefore want to weight matches, *both* positive and negative, twice as much for the first five attributes as for the last five. The situation can be diagrammed

	Attribute									
Object	1	2	3	4	5	6	7	8	9	10
A	1	0	0	0	1	0	0	1	1	1
B	0	1	0	0	1	0	0	1	0	0
s_{ijk}	0	0	1	1	1	1	1	1	0	0
w_{ijk}	2	2	2	2	2	1	1	1	1	1

which suggests the overall similarity of Persons 1 and 2 is

$$s_{ij} = \frac{2(0) + 2(0) + 2(1) + 2(1) + 2(1) + 1(1) + 1(1) + 1(1) + 1(0) + 1(0)}{2 + 2 + 2 + 2 + 2 + 1 + 1 + 1 + 1 + 1}$$

$$= \frac{9}{15}$$

$$= 0.600.$$

To illustrate the computation of Gower's coefficient for quantitative characteristics, consider again the city data. For City A, income has a value of 1.14 and population a value of 1.72. For City E, income has a value of 0.55 and population a value of 0.10. The range of population values across all cases is greater than the range of income values; specifically, it is 3.10 for the former versus 2.93 for the latter. The similarity of Objects A($i = 1$) and E($j = 5$) with respect to income ($k = 1$) would be $s_{151} = (|1.14 - 0.55|/2.93) = .201$ while with respect to population ($k = 2$) it would be $s_{152} = (|1.72 - 0.10|/3.10) = .526$. Assuming we wanted to weight income and population equally, the overall similarity of Objects A and E is

$$S_{15} = \frac{1(.201) + 1(.526)}{1 + 1} = .364.$$

As can be seen, Gower's coefficient offers the analyst a great deal of flexibility in generating similarity values, which is one of the primary reasons for its popularity.

Cluster the Objects Using One of the Available Methods   We have already discussed the issue of clustering methods at some length and have only a few comments to add. One thing that should be pointed out is that all of the methods are heuristical in nature. While the heuristics that they use seem logical on their face, they are still heuristics and there is very little statistical theory in the normal sense of the term to back them up.[47] Thus, analysts need to display the proper caution when interpreting the out-

---

[47]For an empirical examination of some of the things that can affect the reliability of a clustering method, see G. Ray Funkhouser, "A Note on the Reliability of Certain Clustering Algorithms," *Journal of Marketing Research,* 20 (February 1983), pp. 99–102. For a summary of some of the main attempts to generate statistical criteria by which the results of a cluster analysis can be assessed, see Dillon and Goldstein, *Multivariate Analysis,* pp. 202–205. For a demonstration of how one can test whether given clusters differ significantly from clusters that are randomly determined, see T. D. Klastorin, "Assessing Cluster Analysis Results," *Journal of Marketing Research,* 20 (February 1983), pp. 92–98.

put produced by one of the clustering procedures. Equally important, all of the methods have the same aim. They should not be considered mutually exclusive alternatives but complementary procedures to get at the same objective. Sometimes they can be productively used in combination. One of the problems we discussed with the nodal methods, for example, is how the initial partition should be generated, as that can affect the outcome of the analysis. One relatively useful way is to use the output from the hierarchical analysis for the initial solution in the nodal procedure, as the combination allows the reassignment of objects to clusters, whereas the linkage procedures only make use of one pass through the data.

Test the System and Define and Name the Clusters   Given decisions with respect to the first three steps, a set of clusters will be obtained. The analyst then has the dual tasks of testing the system and naming the clusters. The system test focuses on whether the results offer a reasonable summary of the similarity, correlation, or distance matrix. First, are the individual clusters sufficiently homogeneous? Some measure of average similarity is typically useful in this regard.[48] Second, is the system as a whole consistent with the input similarities? Suppose one of the linkage methods was used to generate object groupings. A dendrogram would result. Now, for each pair of objects, the *cophenetic value* or amalgamation coefficient could be read from the dendrogram. The **cophenetic value** is the level at which the objects or classes are actually linked. If the dendrogram contained all of the information in the similarity matrix, the cophenetic value for each pair of objects would exactly equal the input similarity value. They will not be equal in practice, of course, because the union of any two objects is affected by their links with the other objects.

Consider again, for example, the application of the single linkage method to the city data. A comparison of the actual distances between Objects F, M, and H as read from the distance matrix in Table 16.16 and the distances where the objects joined as read from the dendrogram indicates the following differences:

Object Pair	Actual Distance	Distance When Joined
FM	0.184	0.184
FH	0.624	0.479
MH	0.776	0.479

A similar comparison could be made for each of the other 225 pairs of objects, and then some summary measure of the goodness of fit of the actual values with the obtained values could be calculated (for example, the product moment correlation between the two sets of distances).

One problem with the use of the cophenetic correlation is that it can only be used with hierarchical clustering methods. An alternative procedure that can be used with any of the clustering methods is to test whether the variables used to determine the clusters

---

[48]Milligan compared the performance of 30 measures that have been proposed for assessing the internal consistency of clusters. He found six of them that generally outperformed the others. See G. W. Milligan, "A Monte Carlo Study of Thirty Internal Measures for Cluster Analysis," *Psychometrika,* 46 (1981), pp. 187–199.

have statistically significant differences across the groups. This is typically done by comparing the mean levels across the groups. While this scheme is intuitively plausible, it turns out that the results are invariably statistically significant, regardless of whether clusters exist in the data or not, which led one pair of authors to conclude that "the performance of these tests is useless at best and misleading at worst."[49]

While both of these schemes for testing cluster solutions are commonly found in the literature, neither is particularly recommended by methodologists working in the area. Rather, their general recommendation is to estimate the reliability of a cluster solution across data sets. This typically involves splitting the data into multiple subsets and assessing whether the same sets of objects are produced when the various subsets are analyzed.

Another alternative that is less often used but that has much to recommend it is to perform significance tests comparing the clusters on variables that were not used to generate the cluster solution. We could, for example, compare our 15 test cities with respect to the average age of the population. Those within the same subgroup should be approximately equal with respect to average age, while those cities in different subgroups should be different.

If the resulting clusters are acceptable, the analyst must then describe and name them. The researcher's description will typically center on those variables that determine membership in a given class rather than membership in other classes. The example produced a large-size, high-income cluster, a medium-size, middle-income cluster, and a small-size, low-income cluster of cities. In most cases, the names will not be so obvious. The analyst has to be particularly careful that the names do not mislead others.

Marketing Applications

The example of forming homogeneous groups of cities that was employed to develop the purpose and logic of cluster analysis reflects a pervasive marketing problem. The problem of determining homogeneous groupings of objects is a real one in accurately assessing the impact of marketing manipulations. For many kinds of experimental manipulations, we must be sure that the groups of objects being manipulated were equal at some prior time.[50] Thus, when market-testing products or advertisements or packages, it is important that the test cities used be similar, so that the results cannot be attributed to idiosyncratic differences in the cities.

Although cluster analysis has not been as widely employed in marketing as factor analysis has, the number of applications continues to increase.[51] It has been used, for

---

[49]Aldenderfer and Blashfield, *Cluster Analysis,* p. 65. Pages 62–74 of this book have an excellent discussion of the various alternatives that are used to test the quality of a cluster solution.

[50]See George S. Day and Richard M. Heeler, "Using Cluster Analysis to Improve Marketing Experiments," *Journal of Marketing Research,* 8 (August 1971), pp. 340–347, for an example of how cluster analysis can be used to choose samples of stores for test marketing.

[51]For an excellent review of the applications of cluster analysis in marketing, see Girish Punj and David W. Stewart, "Cluster Analysis in Marketing Research: Review and Suggestions for Application," *Journal of Marketing Research,* 20 (May 1983), pp. 134–148. For reviews of the various programs for performing cluster analysis, see R. K. Blashfield and L. Morey, "Cluster Analysis Software," in P. Krishnaiah and L. Kanal, eds., *Handbook of Statistics,* Vol. 2 (Amsterdam: New Holland, 1982), pp. 245–266.

example, to sort householders' demand patterns for electricity into similar shapes, to group customers according to the product benefits they seek or according to their life-style, to group TV programs into similar types on the basis of viewers' reported listening tendencies, to group other kinds of media with respect to the similarity of audiences to which they appeal, to develop homogeneous configurations of census tracts, to construct market segments, to group personality profiles, to group brands and products on the basis of how similar to competitors they are perceived to be and also how they serve as substitutes in use, to determine spheres of opinion leadership, and to assess the similarity of world markets.

Summary

Three analysis techniques increasingly being advocated in the marketing literature for the solution of marketing research problems were reviewed in this chapter. The techniques are all multivariate in that they involve the analysis of p measures. Discriminant analysis treats the p measures in a dependency relationship, while factor analysis and cluster analysis involve the examination of interdependencies among the variables.

Discriminant analysis shows the relationship between a dichotomous or multichotomous criterion variable and a set of p predictor variables. The emphasis is on determining the variables that are most important in discriminating among the objects falling into the various classes of the criterion variable. With a number of predictor variables and a multichotomous criterion variable, several discriminant functions may be derived. Not all of these functions, though, will necessarily be statistically significant. The discriminant function or functions can also be used to predict the classification of new objects.

Factor analysis gives all p variables equal status. The emphasis is on isolating the factors that are common to the interrelated manifest variables so as to summarize the important information in the data and assist in interpreting the data. The initial factor solution and the choice of the number of factors to be retained are key in answering the first question, while the rotation of the initial solution is important for answering the latter. A number of options are open to the researcher in both regards.

Cluster analysis searches for the natural groupings among objects described by the p variables. The emphasis is on placing together those objects that are similar with respect to the p variables. Their similarity is properly captured with a coefficient reflecting the scale of measurement that underlies the variables. The analyst has a number of choices in this regard, as well as with respect to the clustering algorithm that will be used to generate the groupings.

Questions

1. How does the purpose of discriminant analysis differ from that of regression analysis?

2. What basic criterion is satisfied in determining the weights for a discriminant function?

3. Just as in regression analysis, there are two basic purposes of discriminant analysis: prediction or classification and structural interpretation. How are both of these purposes achieved with the discriminant model?

4. Suppose there are more than two groups to be discriminated. How many discriminant functions will there be?

5. Describe the basic purpose of factor analysis. What is meant by variability recovery and covariability recovery?

6. What is a factor-loading table? What do the individual entries measure? How does the table help to determine the ''appropriate'' number of factors?

7. What is the basic principle that underlies the principal components procedure?

8. What is the ''substantive interpretation'' question in factor analysis? How is such interpretation typically facilitated?

9. What is the essence of the communality question in factor analysis? What is the effect of the communality issue?

10. What is the basic purpose of cluster analysis?

11. Explain the differences among the linkage procedures, nodal procedures, and factor procedures in cluster analysis.

12. What is the difference between single and complete linkage cluster analysis?

13. What is a dendrogram? For what is it used?

14. Discuss what is at issue in each of the cluster analysis decision areas of
    (a) selecting and coding attributes;
    (b) producing estimates of resemblance;
    (c) clustering technique; and
    (d) testing the system and defining and naming the clusters.

Applications and Problems

1. The management of a large chain of grocery stores wanted to determine the characteristics that differentiated national brand name shoppers and private label shoppers. In particular, the management wanted to determine how these groups differed with respect to income and the size of household. Personal interviews with a random sample of national brand name shoppers and private label shoppers generated the following data.

	Annual Income (Thousands of Dollars) X_1	Household Size (Number of Persons) X_2
National Brand Shoppers		
1	16.8	3.0
2	21.4	2.0
3	17.3	4.0
4	18.4	1.0
5	23.2	2.0
6	21.1	5.0
7	14.5	4.0
8	18.9	1.0
9	17.8	2.0
10	19.3	1.0

continued on next page

	Annual Income (Thousands of Dollars) X_1	Household Size (Number of Persons) X_2
Private Label Shoppers		
1	17.3	4.0
2	15.4	3.0
3	14.3	4.0
4	14.5	5.0
5	17.4	2.0
6	16.7	6.0
7	13.9	7.0
8	12.4	7.0
9	15.3	6.0
10	13.3	4.0

A discriminant analysis of the data resulted in the following discriminant function: $Y = 0.333X_1 - .315X_2$.

(a) Identify the criterion that was satisfied in deriving these weights.

(b) On the basis of the above function, derive the discriminant scores for the two groups by completing the following table.

National Brand Shoppers	X_1	X_2	Y	Private Brand Shoppers	X_1	X_2	Y
1							
2							
3							
4							
5							
6							
7							
8							
9							
10							

(c) What do the discriminant scores indicate?

(d) Compute the pooled standard deviation for X_1 and X_2: (Hint: Refer to Chapter 14 of the text for the formula of the pooled standard deviation.)

(e) Convert the original weights of the discriminant function to standardized weights.

(f) Interpret the discriminant function by evaluating the standardized weights.

(g) Compute the mean values of the variables for each group.

(h) Compute the mean discriminant scores for each group.

(i) Interpret the mean discriminant scores for each group.

(j) Compute the cutting score.

(k) Predict the group membership for the entire sample and complete the following table.

Simple Decision Rule

	Discriminant Score Y_i	Difference from Mean of		Predicted Group Membership
		First Group $Y_i - \bar{Y}_1$	Second Group $Y_i - \bar{Y}_2$	
National Brand Shoppers				
1				
2				
3				
4				
5				
6				
7				
8				
9				
10				
Private Label Shoppers				
1				
2				
3				
4				
5				
6				
7				
8				
9				
10				

(l)   On the basis of the above, develop the confusion matrix.

(m) Compute the hit rate or the proportion correctly classified.

(n) Assess the goodness of the hit rate by computing the proportional chance criterion. Interpret your results.

(o) Suppose that the management wanted to classify two individuals as to whether they were national brand shoppers or private brand shoppers. The characteristics are:

Individual I
X_1—annual income-$18,300
X_2—household size-4 persons

Individual II
X_1—annual income-$21,000
X_2—household size-7 persons

How should management classify these individuals? Show your calculations.

(p) There is an upward bias in the proportion of correct hits. Why? What can be done to overcome this upward bias?

2.   Prefertronics, Inc., is a medium-sized manufacturer of electronic toys. The vice-president of sales has requested Mr. Smith, a product manager, to conduct a marketing re-

search study to determine the key attributes that result in consumer preferences for their products. Mr. Smith employed interviewers to conduct personal interviews with a random sample of 100 customers. The respondents were requested to rate Prefertronics' toys on four attributes (expensive–inexpensive, safe–unsafe, educational–uneducational, good quality–poor quality) using a seven-point semantic differential scale. Mr. Smith conducted a principal component analysis with the standardized scores which resulted in the following factor-loading matrix. Mr. Smith needs your help in analyzing this information.

The factor-loading matrix:

	Factors			
Variable	1	2	3	4
X_1	.812	.567	.121	.070
X_2	.532	−.743	.321	.249
X_3	.708	−.640	.205	.217
X_4	.773	.630	.018	.078

where

$$X_1 = \text{expensive-inexpensive}$$
$$X_2 = \text{safe-unsafe}$$
$$X_3 = \text{educational-uneducational}$$
$$X_4 = \text{good quality-poor quality}$$

(a) What are the individual row-column entries called and what do they indicate?
(b) What does the entry in the second row and first column indicate?
(c) What is the proportion of variation in each of the four variables that is accounted for by Factor 1? Show your calculations.
(d) What is the proportion of variation in each of the four variables that is accounted for by Factor 2? Show your calculations.
(e) The table below is a partially completed correlation matrix derived from the above factor-loading matrix. Complete the original correlation matrix using all the *four* factors. (Hint: Use the formula

$$r_{X_j X_l} = \sum_{k=1}^{4} a_{jk}\, a_{lk}$$

Simple Pairwise Correlations among the Attributes (computed from four factors)

	X_1	X_2	X_3	X_4
X_1	1.000			
X_2	0.067	1.000		
X_3			1.000	
X_4			0.165	1.000

(f) Complete the following correlation matrix using only the *first* and *second* factors to estimate the correlations. Comment on your results.

Simple Pairwise Correlations among the Attributes (Computed from two factors)

	X_1	X_2	X_3	X_4
X_1	1.000			
X_2		1.000		
X_3			1.000	
X_4				1.000

(g) Compute the achieved communalities of the four variables using the *first* and *second* factors. Show your calculations. Comment on your results.

(h) Compute the proportion of the total variation in the data that is accounted for by each of the four factors. Show your calculations. Comment on your results.

(i) On the basis of the above, discuss the variability and covariability recovery of two factors versus four factors.

(j) Construct a scatter diagram using the correlations between the variables and the *first* and *second* factors as coordinates of the points.

(k) On the basis of the above, would you recommend that the factors be rotated? If yes, why? If no, why not?

(l) Assume that the factors were rotated. Provide an interpretation of the factors.

(m) Assume that the original factor solution was rotated. Explain the following statement. The contribution of each factor in accounting for the variation in the respective variables has changed; however, the total variation accounted for by the factors has remained constant.

3. Adstar, Inc., is a large-sized advertising agency located in New York City. The market research manager wants to identify the market segments for one of their clients, a manufacturer of caffeine-free soft drinks, so that an effective advertising campaign could be developed. The manufacturer believes that the product would appeal to high income families with large households. The market research manager has collected this information from a probability sample of 500 regular purchasers of the caffeine-free soft drink. The manager has decided to use cluster analysis but is not familiar with the technique. Information pertaining to a sample of ten regular-purchasers is given to you. The following table contains the standardized scores for income and household size for the sample of 10 respondents.

Respondents	Average Ratings on Attributes Expressed in Standardized Units	
	Income X_1	Household Size X_2
1	−2.75	−2.50
2	3.00	3.00
3	2.50	2.75
4	−1.75	−2.25
5	4.00	3.50
6	−3.50	−2.75
7	2.75	3.25
8	−2.25	−2.50
9	3.50	2.50
10	−3.00	−3.25

(a) Plot the individual scores in two dimensions using the two attributes as axes. What does the plot suggest?

(b) Determine the similarity of each pair of respondents by computing the Euclidean distance between them.

(c) The single linkage clustering method is to be used in developing the clusters. Consider the similarity values less than 1.00 in part (b) and array the distances from most similar to least similar.

(d) What clusters exist after the fourth iteration (distance levels of approximately 0.70)?

(e) What clusters exist after the eighth iteration (distance levels of approximately 1.12)?

(f) Construct a dendrogram for similarity values up to approximately .56. Interpret the dendrogram.

(g) Suppose that the complete linkage method of clustering is used; indicate at what distance level the results will be the same as part (e) above.

Appendix 16A
Analysis of Catalog Buying Data

Discriminant Analysis

Another question of interest in the Avery study was catalog recipients' feelings toward the breadth of the Avery line. To address this question, two groups were formed from Question 11, "The selection of sporting goods available through the Avery catalog is very broad." Those agreeing or strongly agreeing with this statement were placed in one group, labeled as those perceiving Avery as having a broad product line. Those strongly disagreeing, disagreeing, or neither agreeing nor disagreeing with the statement were placed in the other group, labeled as those perceiving Avery as having a narrow product line.

Table 16A.1 contains the results of the discriminant analysis that relates group membership to the same demographic characteristics that were used in the multiple regression

Table 16A.1

Discriminant Analysis of Those Believing Avery's Product Line Is Narrow or Broad as a Function of Demographic Characteristics

Number of Cases by Group

	Number of Cases	
V20	Unweighted	Weighted
1	53	53.0
2	71	71.0
Total	124	124.0

Canonical Discriminant Function

Minimum number of functions . . . 1
Minimum cumulative percent of variance . . . 100.0
Maximum significance of Wilks' lambda . . . 1.0000
Prior probability for each group is .500

Classification Function Coefficients
(Fisher's Linear Discriminant Functions)

V20 =	1	2
V41	1.525	6.077
V42	.153	.184
V44	2.244	2.065
D5	6.168	13.186
D4	6.283	12.418
D3	7.967	11.394
D2	8.056	9.224
(Constant)	−5.625	−12.471

Canonical Discriminant Functions

Function	Eigenvalue	Percent of Variance	Cumulative Percent	Canonical Correlation
1	2.084	100.0	100.0	.822

After Function	Wilks' Lambda	Chi-squared	DF	Significance
0	.324	133.46	7	.000

Standardized Canonical Discriminant Function Coefficients

	Function 1
V41	.502
V42	.085
V44	−.042
D5	.959
D4	.752
D3	.468
D2	.139

Canonical Discriminant Functions Evaluated at Groups Means (Group Centroids)

Group	Function 1
1	−1.657
2	1.237

Table 16A.2
Confusion Matrix

| | | Classification Results | |
| | | Predicted Group Membership | |
Actual Group	Number of Cases	1	2
Group 1	53	48 (90.6%)	5 (9.4%)
Group 2	71	6 (8.5%)	65 (91.5%)

Percent of 'Grouped' Cases Correctly Classified: 91.13%

analysis with the ATTAVRY index, namely the individual's occupation, age, and marital status. In addition, the sex of the respondent (V44) is included as an additional predictor variable, with females recoded, using the SPSS RECODE command, to 1 and males to 0.

Note the calculated chi-square value of 133.46 is significant at the .001 level, suggesting these demographic variables can discriminate between those who think Avery has a broad product line and those who think Avery's line is narrow. Note further the discriminant function that states:

$$Y = \quad .502 \times \text{V41 (if white collar)}$$
$$.085 \times \text{V42 (age)}$$
$$-.042 \times \text{V44 (if female)}$$
$$.959 \times \text{D5 (if widowed)}$$
$$.752 \times \text{D4 (if divorced)}$$
$$.468 \times \text{D3 (if separated)}$$
$$.139 \times \text{D2 (if single)}$$

where Y is the discriminant score.

This function, of course, is constructed in such a way that it maximally discriminates between the two groups. The group centroid for those that think Avery has a broad product line is 1.237, while the group centroid for those who believe that Avery has a narrow product line is -1.657.

Note from the confusion matrix in Table 16A.2 that there were actually 53 people in Group 1 and 71 in Group 2. Using the discriminant function, 48 of the 53 belonging to Group 1 would be predicted to belong there and 65 of the 71 belonging to Group 2 would be predicted to belong there. The overall classification accuracy is approximately 91 percent. Since the proportional chance or C_{pro} criterion is

$$C_{pro} = \alpha^2 + (1 - \alpha)^2$$

$$= (71/124)^2 + (53/124)^2 = .328 + .182 = .511,$$

there is approximately a 40 percent $(91 - 51)$ improvement in prediction accuracy through the use of the discriminant function.

Factor Analysis

Another question of interest in the Avery study is the exploration of the issue of whether people's attitudes toward buying from catalogs is a unidimensional trait, or whether it has dimensions to it just like a person's arithmetic ability is a composite of the individual's addition, subtraction, multiplication, and division abilities. To explore this issue, the responses to Questions 12 through 20, which all deal with what might happen when ordering from catalogs, were factor analyzed.

Table 16A.3 contains the results. The principal factor method was used to generate the initial solution. The eigenvalues suggested a three-factor solution was appropriate. Consequently, three factors were rotated using the varimax criterion. Note that the achieved communality for each of the variables is high. Further, close to 72 percent of the total variation in the data is explained by the three-factor solution. The factors are, of course, named by looking at the variation in the variables accounted for by each factor. Panel C of Table 16A.3 suggests, for example, that Factor 1 does a particularly good job of accounting for the variation in Variables 24, 26, and 28, Factor 2 for the variation in Variables 21, 22, and 23, and Factor 3 for the variation in Variables 25, 27, and 29. Variables 24, 26, and 28 all address the convenience of ordering through catalogs, and thus Factor 1 might be called a convenience factor or dimension. Similarly, Factor 2 might be labeled a riskiness factor and Factor 3 an economy factor.

Cluster Analysis

Because of local availability, the BMDP package was used to cluster the responses to Question 21 concerning the importance of the various services and/or features when purchasing through catalogs. The purpose was to determine if various features go together in the sense that there are such things as convenience features, risk-reducing features, and so on. The single linkage method was used.

Note that the printout in Table 16A.4 contains an explanation of how the cluster diagram is read. Note also that the program operates by first converting input similarities, here in the form of correlations, to scale values between 0 and 100. These scale values are then employed in the analysis and are what are shown in the cluster diagram. The easiest way to interpret this output is to construct the dendrogram from the description of what is happening and the boundary specifications provided. In the dendrogram, for example, Variables 30 and 36 would be joined at the value 67. Variable 32 would be joined to this group of two variables at the similarity value 62, since the single linkage method is being used.

Table 16A.3
Factor Analysis of Attitude Statements Regarding Buying from Catalogs

Panel A. Initial Factor Analysis Solution

Variable	Estimated Communality	Factor	Eigenvalue	Percent of Variance	Cumulative Percent
V21	1.000	1	2.917	32.4	32.4
V22	1.000	2	1.935	21.5	53.9
V23	1.000	3	1.608	17.9	71.8
V24	1.000	4	.621	6.9	78.7
V25	1.000	5	.537	6.0	84.6
V26	1.000	6	.478	5.3	89.9
V27	1.000	7	.388	4.3	94.2
V28	1.000	8	.298	3.3	97.6
V29	1.000	9	.220	2.4	100.0

Panel B. Factor Loadings Before Rotation

Variable	Factor 1	Factor 2	Factor 3	Communality
V21	.612	.289	−.550	.760
V22	.594	.412	−.355	.648
V23	.605	.356	−.517	.760
V24	−.502	.615	.104	.641
V25	.364	.433	.609	.691
V26	−.520	.713	−.048	.781
V27	.705	.156	.491	.762
V28	−.575	.632	−.011	.731
V29	.584	.237	.536	.684

Panel C. Varimax Rotated Factor Matrix

Variable	Factor 1	Factor 2	Factor 3	Communality
V21	−.115	.864	.023	.760
V22	.001	.779	.204	.648
V23	−.055	.867	.068	.760
V24	.793	−.110	.018	.641
V25	.169	.016	.814	.691
V26	.881	.020	−.073	.781
V27	−.254	.184	.815	.762
V28	.846	−.073	−.103	.731
V29	−.119	.114	.811	.684

The values in this tree have been scaled 0 to 100 according to the following table:

Table 16A.4
Cluster Analysis of Importance Features

Panel A. Cluster Analysis

Name	Variable Number	Other Boundary of Cluster	Number of Items in Cluster	Distance or Similarity When Cluster Forms
V30	30	6	9	20.65
V36	36	1	2	67.41
V32	32	1	3	62.39
V34	34	1	4	55.08
V38	38	1	5	41.20
V31	31	6	4	35.74
V37	37	2	2	57.27
V33	33	2	3	42.38
V35	35	1	9	20.65

Panel B. Tree Printed Over Absolute Correlation Matrix Clustering by Minimum Distance Method

Name	Variable Number								
V30	(30)	67	43	42	38	11	8	0	4
V36	(36)	62	55	41	0	6	6	0	
V32	(32)	45	19	0	15	20	6		
V34	(34)	32	1	1	1	2			
V38	(38)	17	10	7	12				
V31	(31)	57	42	23					
V37	(37)	42	35						
V33	(33)	25							
V35	(35)								

continued on next page

Table 16A.4
Cluster Analysis of Importance Features *continued*

Value Above	Correlation	Value Above	Correlation
0	0.000	50	0.500
5	0.050	55	0.550
10	0.100	60	0.600
15	0.150	65	0.650
20	0.200	70	0.700
25	0.250	75	0.750
30	0.300	80	0.800
35	0.350	85	0.850
40	0.400	90	0.900
45	0.450	95	0.950

An explanation of the variable cluster tree printed above: One cluster consists of variable V30(30), the 1st variable listed in the tree. This cluster joins with the cluster below it consisting of the variable V36(36). The new cluster is indicated on the tree by the intersection of the dashes beginning above variable V30(30) with the slashes starting next to variable V36(36). This cluster joins with the cluster below it consisting of the variable V32(32). The new cluster is indicated on the tree by the intersection of the dashes beginning above variable V30(30) with the slashes starting next to variable V32(32), and so on.

Cases to Part 5

Case 5.1
University of Wisconsin-Extension:
Engineering Management Program[1]

Introduction

The University of Wisconsin-Extension is the outreach campus of the University of Wisconsin System. It is responsible for offering high-quality continuing education to adults in a variety of professions from around the country.

The Management Institute is one of the many specialized departments within the UW-Extension. It conducts programs aimed at providing education and training in at least a dozen areas of business management and not-for-profit management. Extension Engineering is another of the specialized departments. Since 1901, it has grown from its summer school origins into one of the finest organizations of its kind. Extension Engineering has offered institutes and short courses annually since 1949. It has a dedicated full-time faculty of engineering and science professors, most of whom have extensive business and industrial experience.

Opportunity for an Engineering Management Program

In the spring of 1984, William Nitzke, the director of Extension Engineering client services, set out to explore the possibility of establishing a certificate program in engineering management. He recognized this opportunity after speaking with attendees of Extension Engineering seminars and reading several articles that made reference to the need for management training for engineers. Mr. Nitzke believed it would be feasible to develop a coordinated curriculum in engineering management by combining the strengths of the Management Institute and Extension Engineering. This new program would include a comprehensive series of management courses specifically created to provide engineers with skills to better meet the challenges of management positions.

Background

More than half of the chief executives in major U.S. companies are engineers, and most of the middle management positions are filled by engineers.[2] Moreover, the American Association of Engineering Societies reports that about two-thirds of all engineers spend

[1]The contributions of Maria Papas Heide to the development of this case are gratefully acknowledged.

[2]*Management for Engineers*, University of Kentucky and University of Missouri Rolle joint sponsorship, October 5, 1983.

813

two-thirds of their careers in supervisory or management positions.[3] Yet, the crowded engineering curricula at major colleges and universities allow little room for courses that prepare engineers for the types of problems they will have to face as managers. Thus, many engineers, as they evolve in their careers, find themselves promoted into management positions without formal training and unprepared to deal with a quite different set of challenges. One estimate suggests that nearly a million engineering supervisors and managers are currently not well prepared for their positions.[4]

Major corporations throughout the U.S. are becoming aware that their technically capable engineers are inadequately trained to handle the management-related problems they confront. As a result, the efficiencies of the corporations are affected and the full potential of the engineers as managers is not realized.

The Management Institute of the UW-Extension does provide programs for the non-management manager. However, neither Extension Engineering nor the Management Institute offers a coordinated or comprehensive series of programs specifically designed for engineers or similar professions. Further, according to secondary data and direct client inquiry, few continuing education opportunities presently exist on a national level for engineers to gain specialized management training. The Extension Engineering department consequently decided it would attempt to establish itself and the Management Institute as a leading-edge provider of professional development programs in engineering management by being one of the first continuing education institutes to offer a certificate program in Engineering Management.

The original conceptualization of the certificate program held that:

Engineers would be granted a certificate only after successful completion of 10–12 seminars from the total set available. Each seminar would run 3–5 days. About 5–6 of these seminars would be required and the other 5–6 would be electives.

A study was undertaken to discover the degree of interest in this type of specialized management training among engineers who had previously attended Extension Engineering seminars. The thought was that the original conceptualization described above could be modified easily enough depending on the findings from the study.

More specifically, the research was to address the following specific issues:

1. The overall general interest in an engineering management program offered by the UW-Extension.

2. The appeal of earning a certificate in contrast to taking selected seminars on an ''as needed'' basis.

3. The preferred design of a certificate engineering management program with respect to schedules of attendance, availability of correspondence seminars, and years to complete the certificate requirements.

---

[3]Merrit A. Williamson, ''Engineering Schools Should Teach Management Skills,'' *Professional Engineer,* 53 (Summer 1983), pp. 11–14.
[4]*Ibid.*

4. The type of seminar topics that should comprise the certificate engineering management curriculum.

Research Method

The study had several stages. In the first preliminary stage, letters were sent to 212 recent attendees of UW-Extension engineering seminars, requesting them to participate in a telephone interview regarding the proposed engineering management program. Reply postcards were received from 100 of the attendees, providing a response rate of 47 percent. The respondents fit into the following categories:

Percentage	
38	agreed to participate in telephone interview.
49	did not wish to participate in the telephone interview but were willing to complete a written questionnaire and/or were interested in receiving information on the program when it was developed.
13	were not interested in an Engineering Management program.
100	

The respondents contacted for the telephone interviews were very helpful in designing the written questionnaire, which was subsequently pretested on attendees of a current Extension Engineering seminar. After incorporating the changes suggested from the pretest, a final version of the written questionnaire was mailed to 2,000 randomly selected participants of Extension Engineering seminars within the past two years. A second mailing of the questionnaire to the same 2,000 respondents followed two weeks after the first mailing. The questionnaires for 123 of the names on the mailing list were returned as undeliverable. A total of 502 usable surveys, providing a response rate of 27 percent, were returned from the first and second mailings.

In the second mailing, a reply postcard was included along with the questionnaire. The postcard was provided as an inducement for those contacted who were unwilling to complete an entire questionnaire to at least return a postcard answering the critical question regarding their interest in an Engineering Management program. One hundred ninety-one (191) usable postcards were returned. Including both the surveys and the postcards in which the single critical question regarding interest was answered, the response rate was 35 percent. It was found that 69 percent of all the respondents were interested in a program offering management seminars specifically designed for engineers.

One of the open-ended questions that was asked stated:

What are the three most important management-related problems you (or the engineers you supervise) face at work?

1. _____

2. _____

3. _____

Table 1

**Sample of Verbatim Responses Regarding the Most Important
Management-Related Problems Engineers Face**

1. Increasing productivity
2. Management/union relationships
3. Management does not relate to employees
4. Quality of job performed
5. Dealing with changing priorities
6. Human relations
7. Client/public interactions and manipulation
8. Quality control of projects
9. Getting bogged down on minor items and losing sight of the big picture
10. Keeping employees happy
11. Communicating technical items to nontechnical persons
12. Utilization of time
13. The lack of ability of some to see the big picture
14. Motivation of subordinates to achieve consistent level of performance
15. Quality of workmanship
16. Obtaining appropriate information on a timely basis
17. Contract administration
18. Communications between scattered segments of company
19. Contractor performance
20. Designing job to be motivating
21. Effective sharing of information
22. Managing employees for maximum productivity
23. More efficient use of time
24. Management of information related to many projects in progress simultaneously
25. Personnel management
26. Communicating with other divisions of the company
27. Peer communications
28. Motivating those I supervise
29. Lack of defined career plan
30. Ability to communicate in nonengineering terms
31. Handling below-standard employees with union ties
32. Long-term motivation
33. Data exchange
34. Time constraints
35. Motivation of subordinates
36. Getting the most productivity out of subordinates
37. Information exchange with other departments
38. Cope with upcoming computers
39. Salary management
40. Understanding of contract management
41. Sometimes lack of enthusiasm
42. Correspondence
43. Determining accurate fee estimates
44. Evaluation/selection of "best" applicant for position
45. Satisfying the client
46. Problem identification and solving
47. Bureaucracy
48. Building confidence
49. Market entry/penetration
50. Timely responses from other departments
51. Bolstering morale
52. Lack of salary increases
53. Learning computer management tools
54. Holding effective meetings
55. Results tracking
56. Contract compliance
57. Interface with other project groups
58. Understanding and setting goals
59. Making sales contacts
60. Gaining recognition and promotion for qualified people
61. Conveying engineering problems to nontechnical management
62. Effective technical writing
63. Cost reduction
64. Follow-through on projects
65. Personal development with respect to career
66. Priority rank of assignments
67. Keeping good relationship with employees
68. Improving work habits
69. Figuring of project costs
70. Researching and compiling information to generate realistic cost proposal
71. Interdepartmental coordination of work efforts
72. Low productivity
73. Seeing the forest through the trees
74. Getting time to do my own work while supervising other workers
75. Dealing with hostile public
76. Lack of devotion of employees
77. Accomplish the volume of work in the given time
78. Skill in making sound management decisions
79. Politics with the company (how they affect decisions)
80. Estimating time to perform work
81. Budget control and forecasting
82. In-house cost estimating/tracking
83. Purchasing policies
84. Interpersonal relations
85. Scheduling
86. Motivating others to contribute as a team toward a project goal
87. Database optimization and report use
88. Lack of supervisory training
89. Estimating engineering man hours required
90. Knowing what the boss really wants

Table 1

Sample of Verbatim Responses Regarding the Most Important Management-Related Problems Engineers Face *continued*

91. Meeting mandated deadlines
92. Motivating the people who work under you to try to achieve goals set
93. Upward communication
94. Business planning (growth projections, marketing plans, etc.)
95. Lack of initiative and curiosity
96. Understanding other people's work-related problems
97. Communications with upper management
98. Discipline (self and principles of application)
99. Financial management of firm
100. Time management
101. Work load distribution
102. Unions
103. System bureaucracy
104. Sales and marketing of services
105. Work appropriation
106. Performance evaluation
107. Keeping employees interested, enthusiastic, and committed to job
108. Salary adjustments
109. Scheduling individual items in a project so project is completed on time
110. Information collection and dissemination
111. Project management—getting a project to run smoothly
112. Developing people
113. Task prioritization
114. Performance/salary structure relationship
115. Engineer performance review
116. Selling ideas
117. Politics
118. Effective presentation of the results
119. Cost analysis/control
120. Monitoring jobs in progress
121. Effective communications with associates
122. Providing opportunities for advancement
123. The inability to rate people properly
124. Achieving desired end results
125. Making effective use of computer-based systems
126. Training
127. Lack of coordination of effort
128. Keeping projects within budget
129. Reducing duplication of effort
130. Cost awareness
131. Conveying concise direct ideas to engineers in written form
132. Inefficient budgeting and financial expertise
133. Not getting continual feedback on my performance—feel like a machine expected to do a task
134. Public speaking
135. Distribution of assignments
136. Transfer of knowledge
137. Meeting budgets
138. Correcting those I supervise
139. Written communication
140. Establishing priorities
141. Management at meetings
142. Decision making
143. Application of appropriate disciplinary actions
144. Long-range planning
145. Conducting effective presentations
146. Creating and controlling project budgets
147. Employee handling
148. Making the right decision based on facts
149. Cross training in other departments
150. Manpower projection
151. Financial control
152. Work flow between departments
153. Getting ideas across
154. Distribution and best use of manpower
155. Communications
156. Management perception of engineers as people vs. tools
157. Commitment and performance
158. Rating of subordinates
159. Convincing top management of your ideas
160. Preparation and management of budgets
161. Managing people
162. Manpower allotment
163. Meeting schedules that change rapidly
164. Evaluation of employees
165. Failure of those in management positions to take control
166. To communicate more effectively
167. Clear division of responsibility between groups
168. Negotiating
169. Documenting
170. Conducting effective meetings
171. Keeping projects on schedule
172. Project administration
173. Understanding financial management
174. Understanding leadership roles
175. Keeping a project within the cost restrictions
176. Delegation of authority as well as responsibility
177. Lack of honest constructive performance appraisal
178. Hiring/interviewing
179. Project work staffing
180. Counseling employees
181. Controlling employees
182. Supervisor does not aid me as he might in helping to pursue and achieve goals set down in annual performance review

The question was designed to gather some insights into the most common areas of management-related difficulties faced by all types of engineers. The question also specifically addresses the fourth research objective listed earlier: to determine the type of seminar topics that should comprise the certificate engineering management curriculum. A representative sample of the responses provided by the engineers to this question are listed in Table 1.

Questions

1. Establish what you believe would be a relatively exhaustive and useful set of codes that could be used to code the responses to the question and to answer the fourth objective for the study.

2. Use your *a priori* codes to code the verbatim responses listed in Table 1. Establish additional codes if needed to account for unanticipated categories of responses.

3. Summarize what the sample of data suggest about the problems faced by the engineers who responded to this survey. Recommend the types of seminars that should be included in the engineering management curriculum.

Case 5.2
Madison Gas and Electric Company (B)[1]

Madison Gas and Electric Company (MG&E) is a public utility serving the Madison, Wisconsin, metropolitan area. For a number of years, MG&E had extensively advertised the twin themes of energy conservation and electric and gas safety (see Madison Gas & Electric (A) for more detail). In 1983 the company was compelled to deal with a new Wisconsin law requiring that a public utility may not charge its ratepayers for any expenditure for advertising unless the advertising contained a verbal or written disclaimer that the expenditure will be charged to the utility's ratepayers. MG&E's management thought that the introduction of a disclaimer in the company's advertisements might have a negative impact on viewers' evaluation of the company's ads. As a consequence, a study was commissioned in which the influence of disclaimers on viewers' evaluations of MG&E's advertisements was to be examined.

Selection of Respondents

The research design to investigate the question of whether the disclaimer affected viewers' reactions to the ads involved exposing people to the ads and assessing their evaluations. More specifically, a sample of 450 subjects was selected, 150 subjects from each

---

[1]The contributions of Thomas Noordewier to the development of this case are gratefully acknowledged.

of the three main shopping centers serving the Madison area: East Towne, West Towne, and South Towne. All three centers were located on the outskirts of Madison. The West Towne center was located in a higher income area of the city and served primarily professionals and other white collar workers. The East Towne center was located in a lower income area and served primarily blue collar workers. The South Towne center served a mix of the two groups.

Subjects were selected in each mall according to the following procedure. Interviewers were assigned specific spots in the corridors and stopped adults going by at irregular intervals. Each adult was asked whether he or she had heard, seen, or read any utility advertising in the past few months and whether the household was a MG&E customer. Those that said yes to both questions were asked to participate in a study involving customer reactions to some selected commercials.

Treatment Conditions

Each qualified subject was assigned to one of three treatment conditions. In each treatment condition, the subject was exposed to four ads and was asked to rate each commercial immediately after seeing it using a scale that ran from "high rating" to "worst rating" on each of the attributes "helpful," "informative," "necessary," and "believable." Moreover, after viewing all four commercials, each subject was asked to provide an overall (summary) evaluation of the commercials, using "excellent" to "poor" descriptors. Subjects were also asked to indicate which ad they liked the "best" and the "least" and why. Finally, each subject was asked to respond to a set of demographic

---

Figure 1
Screening Questionnaire (asked of all three groups)

We're conducting research for a local utility company. Have you seen, heard, or read any advertisements from your gas and electric company in the past few months?

Where do you recall having seen, heard, or read the advertisements for your gas and electric company?

1. Radio
2. TV
3. Newspaper
4. Magazines
5. Billboards
6. Bill inserts
7. Other (specify)
8. Don't remember/don't know

Please tell me what those advertisements said. Tell me as many different things as you can remember. PROBE

If it is not clear that the person is an MG&E customer, ask if they are.

If not an MG&E customer dismiss. If MG&E customer but not at all aware of television advertising, dismiss.

Table 1
Summary of Treatment Conditions*

| | Shopping Center/Treatment Group | | | | | | | | |
| | South Towne | | | West Towne | | | East Towne | | |
Commercial Number	A	B	C	A	B	C	A	B	C
1	DW/O	DW	FW	EW/O	EW	FW/O	FW/O	FW	FW
2	EW/O	EW	DW/O	GW/O	GW	DW/O	DW/O	DW	DW
3	FW/O	FW	GW	DW/O	DW	GW	GW/O	GW	GW/O
4	GW/O	GW	EW/O	FW/O	FW	EW	EW/O	EW	EW/O

*The various symbols are:
   D: home energy audit ad;
   E: congratulations for conserving energy ad;
   F: gas safety ad;
   G: commercial energy audit ad;
   W: with the disclaimer;
   W/O: without the disclaimer.

and socioeconomic questions. See Figure 1 for a copy of the screening questionnaire and Figure 1 in the case, "Madison Gas & Electric (A)," for a copy of the viewing questionnaire (South Towne example).

The treatment conditions differed with respect to the presence or absence of the disclaimer; otherwise the ads in each treatment condition were the same. One ad involved the availability of a free home energy audit, another described a free commercial energy audit, a third was concerned with gas safety, and the fourth offered congratulations for conserving energy. All subjects in Treatment Condition A were shown videotaped television commercials without any disclaimers. All those in Treatment Condition B were shown the same four ads with the disclaimer "the cost of this message is included in MG&E's rates" inserted at the end of the message. Those in Treatment Condition C saw two ads with the disclaimer attached and two ads without the disclaimer. The ads to which the disclaimer was attached varied by shopping center, and the order in which the ads were seen also varied by shopping center. The complete design is displayed in Table 1. A complete list of the data is available from your instructor.

Questions

1. What is the impact of the disclaimer?
2. Are there differences in reactions to each of the four commercials by mall?

Case 5.3
WCOL-TV[1]

WCOL-TV is the local affiliate of the CBS network in Columbus, Ohio. The station is managed by Maurice Edward, who in 1986 commissioned an audience viewership study among the staff and students at Ohio State University. The study was done in November 1986 so as to coincide with the Nielsen and Arbitron ratings. The study was undertaken since these services, because of the transient nature of this community, did not include the university community in their viewership ratings of local news programs.

Edward believed that WCOL-TV had a much higher market share with its local news than either the ABC or NBC affiliates, particularly among university staff and students, and he commissioned the study to either support or refute this conjecture. If it was true, it would provide one more weapon in the station's arsenal when it came to selling advertising time. At the same time he wished to determine the features of each network's local news broadcast that were liked and disliked; the channel switching that occurs between the programs broadcast immediately prior to the 6:00 local news and during the local news; and the channel switching that occurs between the 6:00 p.m. news and the 11:00 p.m. news.

Research Method and Results

The self-administered questionnaire, developed by MEC Research Agency, by its owner and founder Mary Elizabeth Crosby to address Edward's concerns, was pretested on a judgment sample of staff and students. Other than rewording of some of the Likert-type statements regarding features, the questionnaire developed by the agency proved satisfactory. The final questionnaire was subsequently mailed to a sample of faculty, staff and students selected from the staff–student directory. The study team believed that this directory provided a reasonably good sampling frame, as it was published soon after fall registration.

The directory is organized into two parts, one listing faculty and staff and the other students; 79 percent of the listings are students and 21 percent faculty and staff. In order to select the desired sample of 800, a random start was generated and that name and every 80th name thereafter was used. This produced a sample of 170 staff and 630 students. Of the 800 questionnaires sent with self-addressed stamped return envelopes, 385 were returned.

The Likert-type statements on the questionnaire were coded 1–5, where 5 was assigned to the "strongly agree" response category. The means and standard deviations of the ratings for each of the three local news broadcasts are shown in Table 1. The ratings were generated by asking respondents "Which TV channel do you most often

---

[1]The location and channels for this case are disguised for proprietary reasons at the request of the sponsor.

Table 1
Mean Scores and Standard Deviations of Likert Statements Regarding Features

Statement	WCOL-TV Channel 12	WRXY-TV Channel 4	WKLM-TV Channel 2
1. Newscasts cover topics of viewer concern.	3.698(.7825)	3.886(.6402)	3.727(.7887)
2. Pace of newscast is slow.	3.294(1.0203)	3.365(1.0054)	3.273(.9684)
3. The weather reports are timely.	3.560(.9788)	3.515(.9483)	3.870(.9914)
4. The news team members take their work seriously and achieve credibility.	3.520(.9988)	3.788(.8323)	3.896(.7360)
5. The sports stories are up to date.	3.535(.7432)	3.743(.7075)	3.787(.7221)
6. The personalities frequently insert opinionated statements.	3.040(.9661)	3.154(.9929)	3.250(1.0344)
7. The friendliness of the personalities is evident.	3.770(.8501)	3.738(.8962)	3.724(.7933)
8. The weather report is not clear and understandable.	3.872(.8228)	3.721(.9395)	3.895(1.1025)
9. Newscasters and individuals interviewed are identified.	3.952(.6261)	3.976(.6982)	3.842(.6938)
10. Fastbreaking stories are given major importance in the newscast.	3.654(.8006)	3.721(.7563)	3.645(.8900)
11. The personalities are neatly dressed and have a well-groomed appearance.	3.866(.6565)	4.029(.6496)	4.000(.7297)
12. Field reports from the location of the news event are rare.	3.632(.9117)	3.743(.9202)	3.627(.7671)
13. The newscast mixes human interest stories with hard news (crimes, disasters).	3.748(.7450)	3.848(.5848)	3.649(.7908)
14. Newscast contains enough local news without undue emphasis on national news.	3.611(.9293)	3.713(.7528)	3.605(.8178)
15. There is too much emphasis on college sports.	3.177(1.1337)	3.419(.9485)	3.493(1.0827)
16. The news is presented in an easily understood language.	4.016(.5511)	3.981(.6502)	4.093(.5244)
17. The visual aids used in the weather report are readable.	3.635(.9087)	3.740(.8243)	4.000(.8736)
18. Newscasts report happenings at the university.	3.419(.8397)	3.667(.8397)	3.632(.9379)
19. Transitions between segments of the news program seem to be abrupt.	3.389(.8576)	3.467(.8443)	3.307(.8216)
20. The weather report is accurate.	3.220(1.0229)	3.375(.7782)	3.636(.8722)
21. On-the-scene film reports are frequent.	3.581(.8751)	3.600(.8390)	3.613(.7692)
22. The quality of operational and technical production is low.	3.240(1.0806)	3.333(.9268)	3.526(.9306)
23. There are too many commercials.	2.157(.9954)	2.667(1.0712)	2.421(1.1805)
Total number	97	95	58

Table 2
Response by Question

1. *On which of the following originating stations do you watch the 6 p.m. news?*
   - 97   12(CBS) WCOL-TV
   - 95   4(NBC) WRXY-TV
   - 58   2(ABC) WKLM-TV
   - 135   I do not watch the 6 p.m. news on television.

2. *Prior to the 6 p.m. news, do you watch?*
   - 129 12(CBS)—National news
   - 63   4(NBC)—National news
   - 44   2(ABC)—National news
   - 149   I do not watch the 6 p.m. news on television.

3. *On which of the following stations do you watch the 11 p.m. news?*
   - 69   12(CBS) WCOL-TV
   - 75   4(NBC) WRXY-TV
   - 57   2(ABC) WKLM-TV
   - 184   I do not watch the 11 p.m. news on television.

Table 3
Cross Tabulation of Question 1 versus Question 2

Station Watched Prior to 6:00 p.m. News	Station Watched for 6:00 p.m. News 12(WCOL-TV)	4(WRXY-TV)	2(WKLM-TV)	Do Not Watch	Total
12(WCOL-TV)	72	24	12	21	129
4(WRXY-TV)	4	48	8	3	63
2(WKLM-TV)	5	8	27	4	44
Do not watch	16	15	11	107	149
Total	97	95	58	135	385

Table 4
Cross Tabulation of Question 1 versus Question 3

Station Watched for 6:00 p.m. News	Station Watched for 11:00 p.m. news 12(WCOL-TV)	4(WRXY-TV)	2(WKLM-TV)	Do Not Watch	Total
12(WCOL-TV)	53	9	5	30	97
4(WRXY-TV)	6	48	11	30	95
2(WKLM-TV)	3	4	33	18	58
Do not watch	7	14	8	106	135
Total	69	75	57	184	385

watch for the news?'' and asking them to complete the scales with this channel in mind. The responses to the first three questions on the questionnaire and the questions that elicited these responses are contained in Table 2. Finally, Tables 3 and 4 contain, respectively, the cross tabulations of Questions 1 and 2 and of Questions 1 and 3.

Question

1. What would you tell Edward about how the local news on Channel 12 is perceived as opposed to perceptions of that on the NBC (Channel 4) and ABC (Channel 2) affiliates?

Case 5.4
Chestnut Ridge Country Club (B)[1]

For many years, Chestnut Ridge Country Club has been one of the most well respected country clubs in the Elma, Tennessee, area. It has one of the finest golf courses in the state, and its dining and banquet facilities are highly regarded. In addition, the club provides its members with outdoor tennis courts and a swimming pool. The country club's outstanding reputation is due in part to the commitment by the Board of Directors of Chestnut Ridge to keep attuned to the needs of current and potential club members. Recently, the board was concerned that applications for membership to Chestnut Ridge were declining. They believed a similar decline in applications was not occurring at the other country clubs in the area—Alden, Chalet, and Lancaster. As a result, the board contracted an outside research firm to survey members of the various clubs to see how Chestnut Ridge was perceived in comparison to the others (see Chestnut Ridge Country Club (A) for more background information and some summary results).

Currently the board is interested in determining what personal characteristics, if any, differentiate among members of Alden, Chalet, Chestnut Ridge, and Lancaster country clubs. The board wants to know if demographic factors such as age, sex, income, and so on, or club features themselves, bear any relationship to the decision to join one of the country club's in the area.

Methodology

To ascertain this information, the board surveyed a sample of randomly selected members of Chestnut Ridge. A number of questions were asked, including questions directed at member demographics and features that were influential in their decision to join a country club. The questions used to assess these two issues are shown in Figure 1. Ninety-three (93) questionnaires were mailed and 63 usable surveys were returned, for a response rate of 68 percent.

[1]The contributions of David M. Szymanski to the development of this case are gratefully acknowledged.

Figure 1

**Questions Used to Assess Demographic Characteristics and Influential
Features for Chestnut Ridge Country Club Members**

1. The following is a list of factors that may be influential in the decision to join a country club. Please rate the factors according to their importance to you with respect to your membership at Chestnut Ridge. Circle the appropriate response where 1 = not at all important and 5 = extremely important.

Golf facilities	1	2	3	4	5
Tennis facilities	1	2	3	4	5
Pool facilities	1	2	3	4	5
Dining facilities	1	2	3	4	5
Social events	1	2	3	4	5
Family activities	1	2	3	4	5
Number of friends who are members	1	2	3	4	5
Cordiality of members	1	2	3	4	5
Prestige	1	2	3	4	5
Location	1	2	3	4	5

2. *What is the approximate distance of your residence from the club (in miles)?*
   ____ 0–2 miles   ____ 3–5 miles   ____ 6–10 miles   ____ 10+ miles

3. *Age:* ____ 21–30   ____ 31–40   ____ 41–50   ____ 51–60   ____ 61 or over

4. *Sex:* ____ male   ____ female

5. *Marital status:* ____ married   ____ single   ____ widowed   ____ divorced

6. *Number of dependents including yourself?*
   ____ 2 or less   ____ 3–4   ____ 5 or more

The results of the survey of Chestnut Ridge members were to be used in conjunction with the responses to a similar set of questions asked respondents in a related survey. See Figure 1 in the case, "Chestnut Ridge Country Club (A)," for a copy of the questionnaires used for Alden, Chalet, and Lancaster members. In that survey, 87 randomly chosen members from each of the three clubs were mailed a questionnaire. Sixty-three (63) surveys from each member group were returned. In all, 252 survey responses were available for analysis, 63 from the Chestnut Ridge survey and 189 from the Alden *et al.* survey. A list of the data is available from your instructor.

Question

1. Are there any demographic factors or club features deemed influential in the decision to join a country club that differentiate among current members of Alden, Chalet, Chestnut Ridge, and Lancaster country clubs?

Case 5.5
Fabhus, Inc.

Fabhus, Inc., a manufacturer of prefabricated homes located in Atlanta, Georgia, had experienced steady, sometimes spectacular, growth since its founding in the early 1950s. In the late 1970s, and into the early 1980s, however, inflation coupled with extremely high interest rates on mortgage loans caused a severe decline in the entire home building industry.

In an attempt to offset the dramatic decline in sales, company management decided to use marketing research to get a better perspective on their customers, so that they could better target their marketing efforts. After much discussion among the members of the executive committee, it was finally determined that the following would be important questions to address in this research effort.

1. What is the demographic profile of the typical Fabhus customer?
2. What initially attracts these customers to a Fabhus home?
3. Do Fabhus home customers consider other factory-built homes when making their purchase decision?
4. Are Fabhus customers satisfied with their homes? If they are not, what particular features are dissatisfactory?

Method

The research firm that was called in on the project suggested a mail survey to past owners. Preliminary discussions with management suggested that Fabhus had the greatest market penetration near its factory. As one moved further from the factory, the share of the total new housing business that went to Fabhus declined. The company suspected this might result from the higher prices of the units due to shipping charges. Fabhus relied on a zone-price system in which prices were based on the product delivered at the construction site.

Local dealers actually supervised construction. Each dealer had pricing latitude and could charge more or less than Fabhus's suggested list price. Individual dealers were responsible for seeing that customers were satisfied with their Fabhus home, although Fabhus also had a toll-free number customers could call if they were not satisfied with the way their dealer handled the construction or if they had problems moving in.

Based on the potential impact distance and dealers might have, the research team believed it was important to sample purchasers in the various zones as well as customers of the various dealers. Since Fabhus's records of houses sold were kept by zone, and by date sold within zone, sample respondents were selected in the following way. First, the number of registration cards per zone were counted. Second, the sample size per zone was determined so that the number of respondents per zone was proportionate to the number of homes sold in the zones. Third, a sample interval, k, was chosen for each zone, a random start between 1 and k was generated, and every kth record was selected. The mail questionnaire shown in Figure 1 was sent to the 423 households selected.

Figure 1
Factory-built Home Owners Survey

1. *How did you first learn of the factory-built home that you bought? (check one, please)*

   ☐ Friend or relative   ☐ Direct mail
   ☐ Another customer   ☐ Newspaper
   ☐ Realtor   ☐ Radio
   ☐ Model home   ☐ TV
   ☐ Yellow pages   ☐ Don't remember
   ☐ National magazine   ☐ Other _____
                                         (please specify)

2. *Did you own the land your home is on before you first visited your home builder?*

   ☐ Yes   ☐ No

3. *How long have you lived in your home?* _____ years

4. *Where did you live before purchasing your factory-built home? (please check one)*

   ☐ Rented a house, apartment, or mobile home
   ☐ Owned a mobile home
   ☐ Owned a conventionally-built home
   ☐ Owned another factory-built home
   ☐ Other _____
            (please specify)

5. *Please rate your overall level of satisfaction with your home. (please check one)*

   ☐ Very satisfied
   ☐ Somewhat satisfied
   ☐ Somewhat dissatisfied
   ☐ Very dissatisfied

6. *How important to you were each of the following considerations in purchasing your factory-built home? (please check a box for each item)*

Considerations	Extremely Important	Important	Slightly Important	Not Important
Investment value	☐	☐	☐	☐
Quality	☐	☐	☐	☐
Price	☐	☐	☐	☐
Energy features	☐	☐	☐	☐
Dealer	☐	☐	☐	☐
Exterior style	☐	☐	☐	☐
Floor plan	☐	☐	☐	☐
Interior features	☐	☐	☐	☐
Delivery schedule	☐	☐	☐	☐

continued on next page

Figure 1
Factory-built Home Owners Survey *continued*

7. *Below, please list any other homes you looked at before purchasing the home you chose. Please state the reason you did not purchase the other home.*

Name of Home	Factory-built?	Reason for Not Purchasing
_____	☐ Yes ☐ No	_____
_____	☐ Yes ☐ No	_____
_____	☐ Yes ☐ No	_____
_____	☐ Yes ☐ No	_____

Now would you please tell us about you and your family.

8. *How many children do you have living at home?* _____ children

9. *What is the age of the head of your household? (check one please)*

☐ Under 20   ☐ 45–54
☐ 20–24   ☐ 55–64
☐ 25–34   ☐ 65 or over
☐ 35–44

10. *What is the occupation of the head of the household? (check one please)*

☐ Professional or official   ☐ Labor or machine operator
☐ Technical or manager   ☐ Foreman
☐ Proprietor   ☐ Service worker
☐ Farmer   ☐ Retired
☐ Craftsman   ☐ Other _____
☐ Clerical or sales   (please specify)

11. *Which of the following categories includes your family's total annual income? (check one please)*

☐ Under $6,000   ☐ $24,000–29,999
☐ $6,000–11,999   ☐ $30,000–35,999
☐ $12,000–17,999   ☐ $36,000–41,999
☐ $18,000–23,999   ☐ $42,000 or over

12. *Is the spouse of the head of the household employed? (check one please)*

☐ Spouse employed full-time
☐ Spouse employed part-time
☐ Spouse not employed
☐ Not married

One final question:

13. *Would you recommend your particular factory-built home to someone interested in building a new home?*

☐ Yes   ☐ No

Thank you very much for completing this survey.
Your help in this study is greatly appreciated.

A cover letter informing Fabhus's customers of the general purpose of the survey accompanied the questionnaire, and a new one-dollar bill was included with each survey as an incentive to respond. Further, the anonymity of the respondents was guaranteed by enclosing a self-addressed postage-paid postcard in the survey. Respondents were asked to mail the postcard when they mailed their survey. All of those who had not returned their postcards in two weeks were sent a notice reminding them that their survey had not been returned. The combination of incentives, guaranteed anonymity, and follow-up prompted the return of 342 questionnaires for an overall response rate of 81 percent.

A complete list of the data is available from your instructor.

Questions

1. Using the data provided by your instructor and analytic techniques of your own choosing, address as best you can the objectives that prompted the research effort in the first place.

2. Do you think the research design was adequate for the problems posed? Why or why not?

Case 5.6
McDougal, Johnson, and Demek[1]

Established in 1962, the firm of McDougal, Johnson, and Demek had consistently been the most profitable law practice in the small midwestern town where it was located. However, the number of new clients served had declined in recent years. This decline was of great concern to Joseph McDougal, president of the firm, who had planned to expand the firm within the next two years as a result of new client projections made at the beginning of the decade. Since the projections were made, however, the law industry had become increasingly competitive. The number of practices per capita had increased dramatically in the area served by McDougal's firm, and more firms were using the media to advertise services. (McDougal, Johnson, and Demek did not use the media to advertise services but instead relied upon personal references to attract customers.) McDougal believed it imperative that his firm take steps to become more competitive and reverse the downward trend in the number of new clients served.

After much discussion among the partners of the firm, it was decided that a marketing plan needed to be developed to help ensure the long-run viability of the practice. As a basis for developing such a plan, it was suggested that a study be conducted to determine the public's attitude toward lawyers. It was argued that the findings of such a study could benefit the firm in several ways. One, it might be possible to identify eligible clients, where one criterion for good prospects included those with misconcep-

---

[1]The contributions of David M. Szymanski to the development of this case are gratefully acknowledged.

tions or negative conceptions of lawyers. Two, it might be possible to determine the needs and expectations of the public regarding lawyers and to see if these needs and expectations coincided with the firm's perceptions. Three, the firm could determine if significant differences exist between the attitudes and demographic characteristics of users and nonusers of legal services. All of the above information could be useful for developing market segmentation strategies and formulating media campaigns, as well as

Figure 1
Lawyer Survey

	Strongly Agree	Slightly Agree	Neither Agree nor Disagree	Slightly Disagree	Strongly Disagree
1. Lawyers are usually good about getting things done.	——	——	——	——	——
2. Most lawyers have high moral standards.	——	——	——	——	——
3. Lawyers try to seem important by using language that laymen cannot understand.	——	——	——	——	——
4. Lawyers care genuinely about helping their clients.	——	——	——	——	——
5. Lawyers often keep clients in the dark about the progress of their cases.	——	——	——	——	——
6. Most lawyers can be trusted to keep their client's secrets.	——	——	——	——	——
7. Lawyers are generally honest in their dealings with clients.	——	——	——	——	——
8. Most people who go to lawyers are troublemakers.	——	——	——	——	——
9. Most lawyers do not care about the ethical ramifications of their work in court.	——	——	——	——	——
10. Most lawyers are only in the profession to make money.	——	——	——	——	——
11. I could find a lawyer easily if I needed one.	——	——	——	——	——
12. Most lawyers would engage in unethical or illegal practices to get their clients out of trouble in court.	——	——	——	——	——
13. Lawyers' fees are usually fair to their clients, regardless of how they figured them.	——	——	——	——	——
14. Most lawyers are concerned that other lawyers uphold ethical standards.	——	——	——	——	——
15. Lawyers spend a lot of time in community service.	——	——	——	——	——
16. Most lawyers are open in their dealings with their clients.	——	——	——	——	——
17. Lawyers have a very high reputation compared with other professionals in my town.	——	——	——	——	——
18. Most lawyers are loyal to their clients.	——	——	——	——	——
19. Most lawyers will take any case, even if they are not competent in that area of the law.	——	——	——	——	——
20. Lawyers tend to stretch the truth in court.	——	——	——	——	——
21. It is difficult to talk to most lawyers because I do not understand the terms they use.	——	——	——	——	——
22. People should go to lawyers only after they have exhausted every other possible way of solving a problem.	——	——	——	——	——

Figure 1
Lawyer Survey *continued*

	Strongly Agree	Slightly Agree	Neither Agree nor Disagree	Slightly Disagree	Strongly Disagree
23. Lawyers' fees are too high for the amount of work they do.	____	____	____	____	____
24. Most lawyers treat clients with consideration.	____	____	____	____	____
25. Most lawyers are competent to handle just about any kind of case.	____	____	____	____	____

The following questions are for classification purposes only:

26. Sex

____ Male   ____ Female

27. Age

____ 18–24   ____ 45–54

____ 25–34   ____ 55–64

____ 35–44   ____ 65 +

28. Race

____ White

____ Black

____ Other

29. Marital Status

____ Married

____ Separated

____ Divorced

____ Widowed

____ Never married

30. Family Income—Approximate Yearly Pretax Earnings

____ $7000 or less   ____ $20,000 to $29,999

____ $7000 to $9999   ____ $30,000 to $39,999

____ $10,000 to $19,999   ____ $40,000 or more

31. Highest grade of school completed

____ Grade school

____ Some high school

____ Finished high school

____ Some college

____ Bachelor's degree

32. Occupation

____ Blue collar

____ White collar

____ Unemployed

33. Have you consulted a lawyer for advice regarding any legal matter in the past two years?

____ Yes—once

____ Yes—more than once

____ No

for altering, if necessary, the firm's services to better meet the needs and expectations of the public.

After careful consideration, the partners of the firm unanimously approved the proposal and contracted an outside research company to conduct the study.

Method

It was determined that a mail survey was appropriate for measuring the public's attitude toward lawyers. A simple random sample of residents was drawn from the local telephone directory; 210 copies of the survey shown in Figure 1 were sent and 93 usable responses were received, for a 44.3 percent response rate. Because the anonymity of those surveyed was guaranteed, it was not possible to determine the identity of those responding, thus precluding a follow-up survey of nonrespondents.

A completed list of the data is available from your instructor.

Questions

1. What dimensions underlie people's attitude toward lawyers?

2. In general, are people's attitudes toward lawyers favorable or unfavorable?

3. Do people's attitudes toward lawyers differ by how often they use lawyer services?

Part 6

The Research Report and the Firm's Marketing Information System

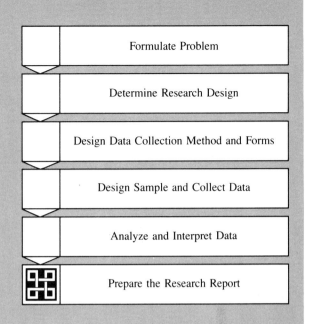

	Formulate Problem
	Determine Research Design
	Design Data Collection Method and Forms
	Design Sample and Collect Data
	Analyze and Interpret Data
	Prepare the Research Report

Part 6 consists of two chapters. In the first of these, Chapter 17, one of the most important parts of the whole research process, the research report, is discussed. The research report often becomes the standard by which the research effort is assessed, and it is important that the report contributes positively to the evaluation of the effort. Chapter 17 deals with the criteria a research report should satisfy and the form a research report can follow so that it contributes positively to the research effort. Chapter 17 also includes some of the graphic means that can be employed to communicate important findings more forcefully. In Chapter 18 the relationship between the project emphasis to research, stressed in this book, and decision support systems is discussed. Chapter 18 also discusses some of the more important issues that must be addressed when designing decision support systems.

Chapter **17**
The Research Report

A frustrated executive of a large corporation recently remarked that he is convinced reports are devices by which the informed ensure that the uninformed remain that way.[1]

If length were the criterion of importance of a chapter, there would be an inverse relationship between this chapter and the criterion. The chapter is short, but its subject is vital to the success of the research effort. Regardless of the sophistication displayed in other portions of the research process, the project is a failure if the research report fails. Empirical evidence indicates, for example, that the research report is one of the five most important variables affecting the use of research information.[2] The preceding research steps determine the content. The research report provides the form, and since the report is all that many executives will see of the project, it becomes the yardstick for evaluation. The writer must ensure that the report informs without misinforming.

The report must tell readers what they need and wish to know. Typically, executives are interested in results and must be convinced of the usefulness of the findings. They must be able to act on the report while recognizing the caveats entailed with the results. This means that they must have sufficient appreciation of the method to recognize its weaknesses and bounds of error. The researcher must convey the limitations and necessary details of the method to allow this appreciation. However, the researcher must do it in a way that is understandable and useful, and this is often easier said than done.

This chapter is designed to assist the researcher in this regard. The chapter itself is divided into four main sections: (1) the criteria by which research reports are evaluated, (2) the parts and forms of the written research report, (3) the oral report, and (4) some graphic means of presenting the results.

---

[1] Reprinted by special permission from William J. Gallagher, *Report Writing for Management,* p. 1, Addison-Wesley Publishing Company, Inc., Reading, Massachusetts, Copyright © 1969. All rights reserved. Much of this introductory section is also taken from this excellent book. See also Richard Hatch, *Business Communication,* 2nd ed. (Chicago: Science Research Associates, 1983).

[2] The other variables are the extent of interaction researchers have with managers, the research objectives, the degree of surprise in the results, and the stage of the product or service in its life cycle. See Rohit Deshpande and Gerald Zaltman, "A Comparison of Factors Affecting Researcher and Manager Perceptions of Market Research Use," *Journal of Marketing Research,* 21 (February 1984), pp. 32–38.

Research Report Criteria

Research reports are evaluated by one fundamental criterion—communication with the reader. The "iron law" of marketing research holds that "People would rather live with a problem they cannot solve, than accept a solution they cannot understand."[3] The reader is not only the reason that the report is prepared but also the standard by which its success is measured. This means, purely and simply, that the report must be tailor-made for the reader or readers, with due regard for their technical sophistication, interest in the subject area, the circumstances under which they will read the report, and the use they will make of it.

The technical sophistication of the readers determines their capacity for understanding methodological decisions, such as experimental design, measurement device, sampling plan, analysis technique, and so on. Readers with little technical sophistication will more than likely take offense at the use of unexplained technical jargon. "The readers of your reports are busy people, and very few of them can balance a research report, a cup of coffee, and a dictionary at one time."[4] Unexplained jargon may even make such persons suspicious of the report writer. Researchers must be particularly sensitive to this, because, being technical people, they may fail to realize that they are in fact using technical language and terms.

The readers' capacity establishes the technical upper limit of the report, while their interest, circumstances, and intended use restrict its level. These factors delineate individual preferences, and such preferences must be considered by the report writer.

Some executives demand a minimum report; they want only the results—not a discussion of how the results were obtained. Others want considerable information on the research methods used in the study. Many executives place a premium on brevity, while others demand complete discussion. Some are interested only in the statistical results and not in the researcher's conclusions and recommendations.

Thus, the audience determines the type of report. *Researchers must make every effort to acquaint themselves with the* specific preferences of their audience. *They should not consider these preferences as unalterable, but* any deviations from them should be made with reason and not from ignorance![5] *(emphasis added)*

The report writer's difficulties in tailoring the report are often compounded by the existence of several audiences. The marketing vice-president might have a different technical capacity and level of interest than the product manager responsible for the product discussed in the report. There is no easy solution to this problem of "many masters." The researcher has to be cognizant of the potential differences that may arise and must often use a great deal of ingenuity in reconciling them. This can sometimes entail the preparation of several reports, each designed for a specific audience, although it is

---

[3]Walter B. Wentz, *Marketing Research: Management, Method, and Cases,* 2nd ed. (New York: Harper & Row, 1979), p. 61.

[4]Stewart Henderson Britt, "The Communication of Your Research Findings," in Robert Ferber, ed., *Handbook of Marketing Research* (New York: McGraw-Hill, 1974), pp. 1–90.

[5]Harper W. Boyd, Jr., Ralph Westfall, and Stanley F. Stasch, *Marketing Research: Text and Cases,* 6th ed. (Homewood, Ill.: Richard D. Irwin, 1985), p. 665.

customary to satisfy the conflicting demands with one report containing both technical and nontechnical sections for different readers.

Writing Criteria

There are certain specific criteria the report should satisfy which enhance the likelihood that it will indeed communicate with the reader. In particular, the report should be complete, accurate, clear, and concise.[6] These criteria are intimately related. A clear report is an accurate report. For purposes of exposition, though, it is helpful to discuss the criteria as if they were distinct.

Completeness   A report is complete when it provides all the information readers need in language they understand. This means that the writer must continually ask whether every question in the original assignment has been addressed. What alternatives were examined? What was found? An incomplete report implies that supplementary reports, which are annoying and delay action, will be forthcoming.

The report may be incomplete because it is too brief or too long. The writer may omit necessary definitions and short explanations. On the other hand, the report may be heavy because it is lengthy but not profound. There is a tendency among report writers not to waste collected information. However, the presentation of information outside the interest of the intended readers may distract them from the main issues. If the report is big, it may discourage readers from even attempting to digest its contents. Readers are thus the key to determining completeness. Their interest and abilities determine what clarification should be added and what findings should be omitted. In general, the amount of detail should be proportionate to the amount of direct control users can exercise over the areas under discussion.

Accuracy   The previous steps in the research process are not the only determinants of accuracy. They are vital, to be sure, for a report cannot be accurate when the basic input is inaccurate. Given accurate input, though, the research report may generate inaccuracies because of carelessness in handling the data, illogical reasoning, or inept phrasing.[7]

An excellent example of inept phrasing and its consequences is provided by the experience of Jock Elliott, the chairman of the Ogilvy & Mather advertising agency; he writes:

Last month I got a letter from a vice-president of a major management consulting firm. Let me read you two paragraphs. The first:

"Recently, the companies of our Marketing Services Group were purchased by one of the largest consumer research firms in the U.S. While this move well fits the basic

---

business purpose and focus of the acquired MSG units, it is personally restrictive. I will rather choose to expand my management opportunities with a career move into industry.''

What he meant was: The deal works fine for my company, but not so fine for me. I'm looking for another job.

Second paragraph:

''The base of managerial and technical accomplishment reflected in my enclosed resumé may suggest an opportunity to meet a management need for one of your clients. Certainly my experience promises a most productive pace to understand the demands and details of any new situation I would choose.''

What he meant was: As you can see in my resumé, I've had a lot of good experience. I am a quick study. Do you think any of your clients might be interested in me?

At least, that's what I think he meant.

This fellow's letter reveals him as pompous. He may not be pompous. He may only be a terrible writer. But I haven't the interest or time to find out which. There are so many people looking for jobs who don't sound pompous.

Bad writing done him in—with me, at any rate.[8]

Inaccuracies also arise because of grammatical errors in punctuation, spelling, tense, subject and verb agreement, and so on.[9]

Clarity Clarity is probably violated more than any other principle of good writing. Clarity is produced by clear and logical thinking and precision of expression. When the underlying logic is fuzzy or the presentation imprecise, readers experience difficulty in understanding what they read. They may be forced to guess, in which case the corollary to Murphy's law applies, ''If the reader is offered the slightest opportunity to misunderstand, he probably will.''[10]

It is easy to say that the report should be clear. It is much more difficult to develop such a report. An absolute imperative is that the organization of the report is clear.[11] In

---

[8]Jock Elliott, ''How Hard It Is to Write Easily,'' *Viewpoint: By, For, and About Ogilvy & Mather,* 2 (1980), p. 18.

[9]Gallagher, *Report Writing,* Chapter 10, ''Reviewing for Accuracy: Grammar,'' pp. 156–177, has examples of how these inaccuracies can confuse and misinform. See also Charles T. Brusaw, Gerald J. Alred, and E. Watter Oliv, *The Business Writers Handbook,* 2nd ed (New York: St. Martins Press, 1982).

[10]Gallagher, *Report Writing,* p. 83.

[11]Kenneth Roman and Joel Raphaelson, *Writing That Works* (New York: Harper & Row, 1981). This book gives some excellent advice on how to write more effective reports as well as memos, letters, and speeches. See also Kenneth Roman and Joel Raphaelson, ''Don't Mumble and Other Principles of Effective Writing,'' *Viewpoint: By, For, and About Ogilvy & Mather,* 2 (1980), pp. 19–36. The little book by William Strunk, Jr., and E. B. White, *The Elements of Style* (New York: Macmillan, 1959), is a classic on how to write clearly.

order for this to happen, you must know yourself where you are going. Make an outline of your major points. Put the points in logical order and place the supporting details in their proper position. Tell the reader where you are going and then do what you said you were going to do. Use short paragraphs and short sentences. Don't mumble; once you have decided what you want to say, come right out and say it. Choose your words carefully. See *Research Realities* 17.1 for some specific suggestions when choosing words. Don't expect to get it right the first time. Expect to rewrite it, several times. When rewriting, attempt to reduce the length by half. That forces you to simplify and remove the clutter. It also forces you to think about every word and its purpose and what you are trying to say. Jock Elliott has some very pointed comments on writing clearly.

Our written and spoken words reflect what we are. If our words are brilliant, precise, well ordered and human, then that is how we are seen.

When you write, you must constantly ask yourself: What am I trying to say? If you do this religiously, you will be surprised at how often you don't know what you are trying to say.

You have to think *before you start every sentence, and you have to* think *about every word.*

Then you must look at what you have written and ask: Have I said it? Is it clear to someone encountering the subject for the first time? If it's not, it is because some fuzz has worked its way into the machinery. The clear writer is a person clearheaded enough to see this stuff for what it is: fuzz.

It is not easy to write a simple declarative sentence. Here is one way to do it. Think what you want to say. Write your sentence. Then strip it of all adverbs and adjectives. Reduce the sentence to its skeleton. Let the verbs and nouns do the work.

If your skeleton sentence does not express your thought precisely, you've got the wrong verb or noun. Dig for the right one. Nouns and verbs carry the guns in good writing; adjectives and adverbs are decorative camp followers.[12]

Conciseness Although the report must be complete, it must also be concise. This means that the writer must be selective in what is included. The researcher must avoid trying to impress the reader with all that has been found. If something does not pertain directly to the subject, it should be omitted. The writer must also avoid lengthy discussions of commonly known methods. Given that the material is appropriate, conciseness can still be violated by writing style. This commonly occurs when the writer is groping for the phrases and words that capture an idea. Instead of finally coming to terms with the idea, the writer writes around it, restating it several times, in different ways, hoping

---

[12]Elliott, "How Hard It Is to Write Easily," pp. 18–19.

Research Realities 17.1

Some Suggestions When Choosing Words for Marketing Research Reports

1. *Use short words*. Always use short words in preference to long words that mean the same thing.

Use this	Not this
Now	Currently
Start	Initiate
Show	Indicate
Finish	Finalize
Use	Utilize
Place	Position

2. *Avoid vague modifiers*. Avoid lazy adjectives and adverbs and use vigorous ones. Lazy modifiers are so overused in some contexts that they have become clichés. Select only those adjectives and adverbs that make your meaning more precise.

Lazy modifiers	Vigorous modifiers
Very good	Short meeting
Awfully nice	Crisp presentation
Basically accurate	Baffling instructions
Great success	Tiny raise
Richly deserved	Moist handshake
Vitally important	Lucid recommendation

Source: Excerpts on pages 7, 9, 10, 15 from *Writing That Works* by Kenneth Roman and Joel Raphaelson. Copyright © 1981 by Kenneth Roman and Joel Raphaelson. Reprinted by permission of Harper & Row, Publishers, Inc.

that repetition will overcome poor expression. Concise writing, on the other hand, is effective because "it makes maximum use of every word . . . no word in a concise discussion can be removed without impairing or destroying the function of the whole composition. . . . To be concise is to express a thought completely and clearly in the fewest words possible."[13]

One particularly helpful technique for ensuring that the report is concise is reading the draft aloud. This points out sections that should be pruned or rewritten.

---

[13]Gallagher, *Report Writing*, p. 87.

3. *Use specific, concrete language.* Avoid technical jargon. There is always a simple, down-to-earth word that says the same thing as the show-off fad word or the vague abstraction.

Jargon	Down-to-earth English
Implement	Carry out
Viable	Practical, workable
Net net	Conclusion
Suboptimal	Less than ideal
Proactive	Active
Bottom line	Outcome

4. *Write simply and naturally—the way you talk.* Use only those words, phrases, and sentences that you might actually say to your reader if you were face-to-face. If you wouldn't say it, if it doesn't sound like you, don't write it.

Stiff	Natural
The reasons are fourfold	There are four reasons
Importantly	The important point is
Visitation	Visit

5. *Strike out words you don't need.* Certain commonly used expressions contain redundant phrasing. Cut out the extra words.

Don't write	Write
Advance plan	Plan
Take action	Act
Study in depth	Study
Consensus of opinion	Consensus
Until such time as	Until
The overall plan	The plan

Silent reading allows him [the writer] to skim over the familiar material and thus impose an artificial rapidity and structural simplicity on something that is in reality dense and tangled. The eye can grow accustomed to the appearance of a sentence, but it is much more difficult for the tongue, lips, and jaw to deal with what the eye might accept readily.[14]

---

[14]*Ibid.*, p. 84.

Forms of Report

The organization of the report influences all the criteria of report writing. While good organization cannot guarantee clarity, conciseness, accuracy, and completeness, poor organization can preclude them. There is no single, acceptable organization for a report. The specific organization chosen depends on the reader. The following format is sufficiently flexible to allow the inclusion or exclusion of elements to satisfy particular needs.

1. title page
2. table of contents
3. summary
    a. introduction
    b. results
    c. conclusions
    d. recommendations
4. introduction
5. body
    a. methodology
    b. results
    c. limitations
6. conclusions and recommendations
7. appendix
    a. copies of data collection forms
    b. detailed calculations supporting sample size, test statistics, and so on
    c. tables not included in the body
    d. bibliography

Title Page   The title page indicates the subject of the report, the name of the organization for whom the report is made, the name of the organization submitting it, and the date. If the report is internal, the names of organizations or companies are replaced by those of individuals. Those for whom the report is intended are listed on the title page, as are the departments or people preparing the report. It is particularly advisable to list those who should receive a confidential report with intended limited distribution.

Table of Contents   The table of contents lists, in order of appearance, the divisions and subdivisions of the report with page references. In short reports, the table of contents may simply contain the main headings. The table of contents will also typically include tables and figures and the pages on which they may be found. For most reports, exhibits will be labeled as either tables or figures, with maps, diagrams, and graphs falling into the latter category.

Summary   The summary is the most important part of the report. It is the heart and core. Many executives will read only the summary. Others will read more, but even they will use the summary as a guide to those questions about which they would like more information.

The true summary is not an abstract of the whole report in which everything is restated in condensed form; neither is it a simple restatement of the subject, nor a brief statement of the significant results and conclusions. A true summary gives the high points of the entire body of the report. A properly written summary saves the time of busy executives without sacrificing their understanding. A good test of a summary is self-sufficiency. Can it stand on its own, or does it collapse without the full report?

A good summary contains the necessary background information, as well as the important results and conclusions. Whether or not it contains recommendations is determined to an extent by the reader. Some managers prefer that the writer suggest appropriate action, while others prefer to draw their own conclusions on the basis of the evidence contained in the study. Although the good summary contains the necessary information, it will rarely be broken down through the use of headings and subheadings. The summary that requires such subdivisions is, in all likelihood, too long.

The purpose of the introduction in the summary is to provide the reader with minimal background to appreciate the results, conclusions, and recommendations of the study. The introduction should state who authorized the research and for what purpose. It should state explicitly the problem(s) or hypotheses that guided the research. The problem as stated here should also guide the remainder of the report. No subject should be treated in the report if it is not anticipated here.

The results presented in the summary must agree, of course, with those in the body of the report, but only the key findings are presented here. A useful approach is to include one or several statements reporting what was found with regard to each problem or objective.

Conclusions and recommendations are not the same. A conclusion is an opinion based on the results. A recommendation is a suggestion as to appropriate future action. Conclusions should be included in the summary section. The writer is in a much better position to base conclusions on the evidence than is the reader, as the writer has greater familiarity with the methods used to generate and analyze the data. The writer is at fault if conclusions are omitted and readers are allowed to draw their own. Recommendations, though, are another matter. Some managers simply prefer to determine the appropriate courses of action themselves and do not want the writer to offer recommendations. Others hold that the writer, being closest to the research, is in the best position to suggest a course of action. For example, the Lipton Company has the philosophy that it is the responsibility of the marketing research people to interpret the findings. As Dolph von Arx, the executive vice-president comments: "We feel strongly that our market research people must go beyond reporting the facts. We want them to tell us what *they* think the facts mean—both in terms of conclusions, and, if possible, indicated actions. Those who are responsible for making the decisions may or may not accept those conclusions or recommendations, but we want this input from our Market Research people."[15]

[15]Dolph von Arx, "The Many Faces of Market Research," paper delivered at meeting of the Association of National Advertisers, Inc., New York, April 3, 1985.

Introduction   Whereas in the summary the readers' interests are taken into account, in the introduction their education and experience are considered. The introduction provides background information readers need to appreciate the discussion in the body of the report. Some form of introduction is almost always necessary. Its length and detail, though, depend upon the readers' familiarity with the subject, the approach to it, and the treatment of it.[16] As a general rule, the report with wide distribution will require a more extensive introduction than a report for a narrow audience.

The introduction often serves to define unfamiliar terms or terms that are used in a specific way in the report. For instance, in a study of market penetration of a new product, the introduction might be used to define the market. What products and companies were considered ''competitors'' in calculating the new product's market share?

The introduction may provide some pertinent history. What similar studies have been conducted? What findings did they produce? What circumstances precipitated the present study? How was its scope and emphasis determined? Clearly, if readers are familiar with the history of this project and related research or the circumstances that inspired the current research, these items can be omitted. A report going to executives with only tangential interest in the particular product or service dealt with would probably have to include them.

The introduction should state the specific objectives of the research. If the project was part of a larger, overall project, this should be mentioned. Each of the subproblems or hypotheses should be explicitly stated. After reading the introduction, readers should know just what the report concerns and what it omits. They should appreciate the overall problem and how the subproblems relate to it. They should be aware of the relationship between this study and other related work. And they should appreciate the need for the study and its importance. Through all of this, the introduction should serve to win the readers' confidence and dispel any prejudices they may have.

Body   The details of the research are contained in the body of the report. This includes details of method, results, and limitations.

One of the hardest portions of the report to write is that giving the details of the method. The writer has a real dilemma here. Sufficient information must be presented so that readers can appreciate the research design, data collection methods, sample procedures, and analysis techniques that were used without being bored or overwhelmed. Technical jargon, which is often a succinct way of communicating a complex idea, should be omitted, since many in the audience will not understand it.

Readers must be told whether the design was exploratory, descriptive, or causal. It is also necessary that they be told why the particular design was chosen. What are its merits in terms of the problem at hand?

Readers should also be told whether the results are based on secondary or primary data. If primary, were they based on observation or questionnaire? And if the latter, were the questionnaires administered in person or by mail or telephone? Once again it is important to mention why the particular method was chosen. What were its perceived

---

[16]Gallagher, *Report Writing,* p. 54.

advantages over alternative schemes? This may mean discussing briefly the perceived weaknesses of the other data collection schemes that were considered.

Sampling is a technical subject, and the writer cannot typically hope to convey all the nuances of the sampling plan in the body of the report but must be somewhat selective in this regard. At the very minimum, the researcher should answer the following questions:

1. How was the population defined? What were the geographical, age, sex, or other bounds?

2. What sampling units were employed? Were they business organizations or business executives? Were they dwelling units, households, or individuals within a household? Why were these particular sampling units chosen?

3. How was the list of sampling units generated? Did this produce any weaknesses? Why was this method used?

4. Were any difficulties experienced in contacting designed sample elements? How were these difficulties overcome, and was bias introduced in the process?

5. Was a probability or nonprobability sampling plan employed? Why? How was the sample actually selected? How large a sample was selected? Why was this size sample chosen?

The readers need to understand at least three things with respect to the sample: What was done? How was it done? Why was it done?

There is very little that can be said about the method of analysis when discussing research methods, since the results tend to show what has been done in this regard. It often proves quite useful, though, to discuss the method in general before detailing the results. Thus, if statistical significance was established through chi-square analysis, the writer might provide the general rationale and calculation procedure for the chi-square statistic, as well as the assumptions surrounding this test and how well the data supported the assumptions. This enables readers to divorce what was found from how it was determined. This can not only help their understanding but also prevent repetition. The procedure is outlined with its key components once and for all, and the results are then simply reported in terms of these components.

The results are the findings of the study, and their detailed presentation, with supporting tables and figures, will consume the bulk of the report. The results need to address the specific problems posed, and they must be presented with some logical structure.[17] The first requirement suggests that information that is interesting but irrelevant in terms of the specific problems guiding the research be omitted. The second requirement suggests that the tables and figures are not a random collection but reflect some psychological ordering.[18] This may be by subproblem, geographic region, time,

---

[17]Some of the many structures and the conditions under which they can be used are contained in Jessamon Dawe, *Writing Business and Economic Papers: Theses and Dissertations* (Totowa, N.J.: Littlefield, Adams, 1975), pp. 75–86.

[18]See Gallagher, *Report Writing*, pp. 50–68, for a discussion of the psychological order of things in research reports.

or other criterion that served to structure the investigation. Tables and figures should be used liberally when presenting the results. While the tables in the appendix are complex, detailed, and apply to a number of problems, the tables in the body of the report should be simple summaries of this information. Each table should address only a single problem, and it should be especially constructed to shed maximum light on this problem. There are several things researchers should do to accomplish this, including:

1. Order the columns or rows of the table by the marginal averages or some other measure of size. If there are many similar tables, keep the same order in each one.

2. Put the figures to be compared into columns rather than rows, and, if possible, put the larger numbers at the top of the columns.

3. Round the numbers to two effective digits.

4. Give brief verbal summaries of each table that guide the reader to the main patterns and exceptions.[19]

The figures should also address one and only one subproblem. Further, they should be chosen carefully for the type of message they can most effectively convey, but more on their choice later.

Although it would be nice to conduct the "perfect" study, this goal is unrealistic. Every study has its limitations. The researcher knows what the limitations of these efforts are, and he or she should not try to hide them from the reader. An open, frank admission of the study's limitations can actually increase, rather than diminish (as is sometimes feared) the readers' opinion of the quality of the research. If some limitations are not stated and readers discover them, they may begin to question the whole report and assume a much more skeptical, critical posture than they would if the limitations were explicitly stated. Stating them also allows the writer to discuss whether, and by how much, the limitations might bias the results. Their exclusion and later discovery allows readers to draw their own conclusions in this regard.

When discussing the limitations, the writer should provide some idea of the accuracy with which the work was done. The writer should specifically discuss the sources of nonsampling error and the suspected direction of their biases. This often means that the researcher provides some limits by which the results are distorted due to these inaccuracies. Readers should be informed specifically as to how far the results can be generalized. To what populations can they be expected to apply? If the study was done in Miami, readers should be warned not to generalize the results to the southern states or all the states. The writer should provide the proper caveats for readers and not make readers discover the weaknesses themselves. However, the writer should not overstate the limitations either but should assume a balanced perspective.

---

[19]See A. S. C. Ehrenberg, "Rudiments of Numeracy," *Journal of the Royal Statistical Society,* Series A, 140 (1977), pp. 277–297, and A. S. C. Ehrenberg, "The Problem of Numeracy," *American Statistician,* 35 (May 1981), pp. 67–71, for a particularly informative discusssion using examples of how adherence to these principles can dramatically improve readers' abilities to comprehend the information being presented in tables.

Conclusions and Recommendations The results precipitate the conclusions and recommendations. In this section, the writer shows the step-by-step development of the conclusions and states them in greater detail than in the summary. There should be a conclusion for each study objective or problem. As one book puts it, "readers should be able to read the objectives, turn to the conclusions section, and find specific conclusions relative to each objective."[20] If the study does not provide evidence sufficient to draw a conclusion about a problem, this should be explicitly stated.

Appendix The appendix contains material that is too complex, too detailed, too specialized, or not absolutely necessary for the text. The appendix will typically contain as an exhibit a copy of the questionnaire or observation form used to collect the data. It will also contain any maps used to draw the sample, as well as any detailed calculations used to support the determination of the sample size and sample design. The appendix may include detailed calculations of test statistics and will often include detailed tables from which the summary tables in the body of the report are generated. The writer should recognize that the appendix will be read by only the most technically competent and interested reader. Therefore, the writer should not put material in the appendix if its omission from the body of the report would create gaps in the presentation.

The Oral Report

In addition to the written report, most marketing research investigations require one or more oral reports. Frequently, they require interim reports regarding progress. Almost always they require a formal oral report at the conclusion of the study. The principles surrounding the preparation and delivery of the oral report parallel those for the written report.

The first imperative is to know the audience. What is their technical level of sophistication? What is their involvement in the project? Their interest? Once again, oral reports being delivered to those who are heavily involved or have a high degree of technical sophistication can contain more detail than reports to those only tangentially involved or interested. In general, it is better to err on the side of too little technical detail than too much. Executives want to hear and see what the information means to them as managers of marketing activities. What do the data suggest with respect to marketing actions? They can ask for the necessary clarification with respect to the technical details if they want it.

Another important consideration is the organization of the presentation. There are two popular forms. Both begin by stating the general purpose of the study and the specific objectives that were addressed. They differ with respect to when the conclusions are introduced. In the most popular structure, the conclusions are introduced after all of the evidence supporting a particular course of action is presented. This allows the presenter to build a logical case in sequential fashion. By progressively disclosing the facts,

---

[20]Boyd, Westfall, and Stasch, *Marketing Research,* p. 672.

the presenter has the opportunity to deal with audience concerns and biases as they arise and thus can lead them to the conclusion that the case builds.

The alternative structure involves presenting the conclusions immediately after the purpose and main objectives. The structure tends to involve managers immediately in the findings. It not only gets them thinking about what actions are called for given the results but also sensitizes them to paying attention to the evidence supporting the conclusions. It places them in the desirable position of wanting to evaluate the strength of the evidence supporting an action, since they know beforehand the conclusions that were drawn from it. The structure a presenter decides to use should depend on the corporate culture regarding which is preferred and the presenter's own comfort level with each organizational form. In either case, the evidence supporting the conclusions must be presented systematically, and the conclusions drawn must be consistent with the evidence.

A third important consideration for effective delivery of the oral report is the use of appropriate visual aids. Flip charts, transparencies, slides, and even chalkboards can all be used to advantage. It depends on the size of the group and the physical facilities in which the meeting is held. Regardless of which type of visual is used, make sure it can be read easily by those in the back of the room. Keep the visuals simple so that they can be understood at a glance. Use figures rather than tables to make the points, as figures are more easily understood.

Honor the time limit set for the meeting. Use only a portion of the time set aside for the formal presentation, no more than a third to a half. At the same time, don't rush the presentation of the information contained in the charts. Remember the audience is seeing them for the first time. Reserve the remaining time for questions and discussion. One of the unique benefits of the oral presentation is that it allows interaction. Use this potential benefit to advantage to clear up points of confusion, to highlight points deserving special emphasis, and so on by making sure there is enough time for interaction to occur. Adapt the presentation so that there is enough time to both present and discuss the most critical findings.

Finally, use the time-honored principles of public speaking when delivering the message. That means keeping the presentation simple and uncluttered so that the audience does not have to mentally backtrack to think about what was said. When writing out the presentation, choose simple words and sentences that are naturally spoken and expressed in your usual vocabulary.[21]

Graphic Presentation of the Results

The old adage that "a picture is worth a thousand words" is equally true for business reports. A picture, called a graphic illustration in the case of the research report, can indeed be worth a thousand words when graphic presentation is appropriate and a good design form is selected. When inappropriate or poorly designed, such a presentation

---

[21]There are a number of excellent books available on making effective oral presentations. See, for example, Dorothy Sarnoff, *Make the Most of Your Best: A Complete Program for Presenting Yourself and Your Ideas with Confidence and Authority* (Garden City, N.Y.: Doubleday, 1983).

may actually detract from the value of the written or oral research report. In this section, we therefore wish to briefly review when graphics are appropriate and the use of some of the more popular forms.[22]

As used here, graphic illustration refers to the presentation of quantities in graph form. Effective graphic presentation means more than merely converting a set of numbers into a drawing.

It means presenting a picture that will give the reader an accurate understanding of a particular set of "figure" information: a picture of the comparisons or relationships that he would otherwise have to search for—and perhaps fail to see. And if well done, it will give him this understanding more quickly, more forcefully, more completely, and more accurately than could be done in any other way.[23]

Graphic presentation is not the only way to present quantitative information, nor is it always the best. Text and tables can also be used. Graphics should only be used when they serve the purpose better than do these other modes. Textual material is generally the most useful in explaining, interpreting, and evaluating results, while tables are particularly good for providing emphasis and vivid demonstrations of important findings. Since some readers tend to shy away from graphic presentation as "too technical," it should be used with discretion and designed with care.

It used to be that graphic presentation was expensive and delayed the presentation of reports because the visuals had to be drawn by graphic artists. Computer graphics are changing that. The trends in the development of computer software for graphically portraying the results of a study now make the preparation of visuals fast and inexpensive. There is no longer any excuse for not using appropriately chosen graphics to make the points being studied.[24]

There are three basic kinds of graphics: charts that show how much, maps that show where, and diagrams that show how. Charts are the most generally useful of the three types, and the following discussion is restricted to some of the more common chart types.[25]

Pie Chart The **pie chart** is probably one of the more familiar charts. It is simply a circle divided into sections, with each of the sections representing a portion of the total.

---

[22]The presentation by no means includes all the graph forms that could be used, just some of the more common ones. Those interested in more detail should see Mary E. Spear, *Practical Charting Techniques* (New York: McGraw-Hill, 1969); Calvin F. Schmid, *Handbook of Graphic Presentation* (New York: Ronald, 1954); Paul Douglas, *Communication through Reports* (Englewood Cliffs, N.J.: Prentice-Hall, 1957); Robert L. Shurter, *Written Communications in Business* (New York: McGraw-Hill, 1957); and Edward R. Tufte, *The Visual Display of Quantitative Information* (Cheshire, Conn.: Graphics Press, 1983).

[23]American Management Association, *Making the Most of Charts: An ABC of Graphic Presentation,* Management Bulletin 28 (New York: American Telephone and Telegraph Company, 1960).

[24]See Hirotaka Takeuchi and Allan H. Schmidt, "New Promise of Computer Graphics," *Harvard Business Review,* 58 (January–February 1980), pp. 122–131, for discussion of the elements necessary for generating report graphics by computer and the development trends with respect to these elements.

[25]Although some general comments are offered regarding the usefulness of the various types, the serious reader will want to examine the empirical evidence that has been gathered regarding which form communicates best. See, for example, L. E. Sarbaugh, *Comprehension of Graphs* (Washington, D.C.: U.S. Department of Agriculture, Office of Information, 1961).

Figure 17.1

Personal Consumption Expenditures by Major Category for 1984

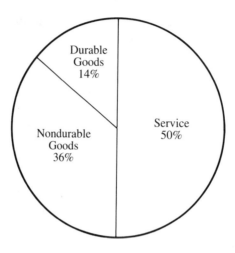

Since the sections are presented as part of a whole, the pie chart is particularly effective for depicting relative size or emphasizing static comparisons. Figure 17.1 (resulting from the data of Table 17.1), for instance, shows the breakdown of personal consumption expenditures by major category for 1984. The conclusion is obvious. Expenditures for services account for the largest proportion of total consumption expenditures. Further, expenditures for services and nondurable goods completely dwarf expenditures for durable goods.

Figure 17.1 has three slices, and the interpretation is obvious. With finer consumption classes, a greater number of sections would have been required, and although more information would have been conveyed, emphasis would have been lost. As a rule of thumb, no more than six slices should be generated; the division of the pie should start at the 12 o'clock position; the sections should be arrayed clockwise in decreasing order of magnitude; and the exact percentages should be provided on the graph.[26]

Line Chart   The pie chart is a one-scale chart, which is why its best use is for static comparisons of the phenomena at a point in time. The **line chart** is a two-dimensional chart that is particularly useful in depicting dynamic relationships such as time-series fluctuations of one or more series. For example, Figure 17.2, produced from the data of Table 17.2, shows that, for 1970–1984, new car sales of imports were subject to much less fluctuation than were domestic sales.

---

[26]Jessamon Dawe and William Jackson Lord, Jr., *Functional Business Communication,* 3rd ed. (Englewood Cliffs, N.J.: Prentice-Hall, 1983).

Table 17.1
Personal Consumption Expenditures for 1970–1984 (Billions of Dollars)

Year	Total Personal Consumption Expenditures	Durable Goods			Nondurable Goods				Services
		Total Durable Goods	Motor Vehicles & Parts	Furniture & Household Equipment	Total Nondurable Goods	Food	Clothing and Shoes	Gasoline and Oil	
1970	621.70	85.20	36.20	35.20	265.70	138.90	46.80	22.40	270.80
1971	672.20	97.20	45.40	37.20	278.80	144.20	50.60	23.90	296.20
1972	737.10	111.10	52.40	41.70	300.60	154.90	55.40	25.40	325.30
1973	812.00	123.30	57.10	47.10	333.40	172.10	61.40	28.60	355.20
1974	888.10	121.50	50.40	50.60	373.40	193.70	64.80	36.60	393.20
1975	976.40	132.20	55.80	53.50	407.30	213.60	69.60	40.40	437.00
1976	1,084.30	156.80	72.60	59.10	441.70	230.60	75.30	44.00	485.70
1977	1,204.40	178.20	84.80	65.70	478.80	249.80	82.60	48.10	547.40
1978	1,346.50	200.20	95.70	72.80	528.20	275.90	92.40	51.20	618.00
1979	1,507.20	213.40	96.60	81.80	600.00	311.60	99.10	66.60	693.70
1980	1,668.10	214.70	90.70	86.30	668.80	345.10	104.60	84.80	784.50
1981	1,849.10	235.40	101.90	92.30	730.70	373.90	114.30	94.60	883.00
1982	1,984.90	245.10	108.70	94.40	757.50	392.80	118.80	90.40	982.20
1983	2,155.90	279.80	129.30	104.10	801.70	416.50	127.00	90.00	1,074.40
1984	2,341.80	318.80	149.80	117.00	856.90	443.60	140.20	91.40	1,166.10

Source: Economic indicators.

The line chart is probably the most commonly used chart. It is typically constructed on graph paper with the X axis representing time and the Y axis values of the variable or variables. When more than one variable is presented, it is recommended that the lines for different items be distinctive in color or form (dots and dashes in suitable combinations) with identification of the different forms given in a legend.[27]

Stratum Chart   The **stratum chart** is, in some ways, a dynamic pie chart, in that it can be used to show relative emphasis by sector (for example, quantity consumed by user class) and change in relative emphasis over time. The stratum chart consists of a set of line charts whose quantities are aggregated (or a total that is disaggregated). For example, Figure 17.3 (again resulting from the data of Table 17.1) shows personal consumption expenditures by major category for the 15-year period 1970–1984. The lowest line shows the expenditures just for durable goods; the second lowest line shows the total expenditures for durable goods *plus* those for nondurable goods. Personal consumption expenditures for nondurable goods are thus shown by the area between the two lines. So it is with the remaining areas. We would need 15 pie charts to capture the same information, and the message would not be as obvious.

---

[27]Dawe and Lord, *Functional Business Communication.*

Figure 17.2
Retail Sales of New Passenger Cars

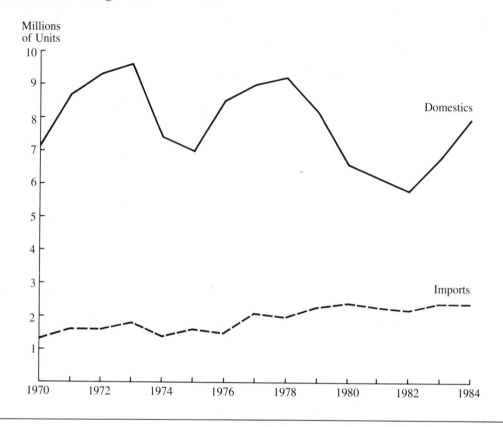

Table 17.2
Retail Sales of New Passenger Cars (Millions of Units)

Year	Domestics	Imports	Total
1970	7.10	1.30	8.40
1971	8.70	1.60	10.30
1972	9.30	1.60	10.90
1973	9.60	1.80	11.40
1974	7.40	1.40	8.80
1975	7.00	1.60	8.60
1976	8.50	1.50	10.00
1977	9.00	2.10	11.10
1978	9.20	2.00	11.20
1979	8.20	2.30	10.50
1980	6.60	2.40	9.00
1981	6.20	2.30	8.50
1982	5.80	2.20	8.00
1983	6.80	2.40	9.20
1984	8.00	2.40	10.40

Source: Economic indicators.

Figure 17.3
Personal Consumption Expenditures by Major Category, 1970–1984

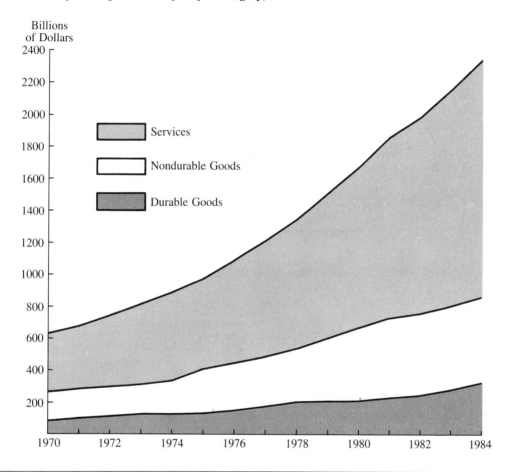

The *X* axis typically represents time in the stratum chart, and the *Y* axis again captures the value of the variables. The use of color or distinctive cross-hatching is strongly recommended to distinguish the various components in the stratum chart. As was true for the pie chart, the number of components distinguished in a stratum chart should not exceed six.

Bar Chart   The **bar chart** can be either a one-scale or two-scale chart. This feature, plus the many other variations it permits, probably accounts for its wide use. Figure 17.4, for example, is a one-scale chart. It also shows personal consumption expenditures by major category at a single point in time. Figure 17.4 presents the same information as Figure 17.1 but is, in at least one respect, more revealing; it not only offers some appreciation of the relative expenditures by major category, but it also indicates the

Figure 17.4

Personal Consumption Expenditures by Major Category for 1984

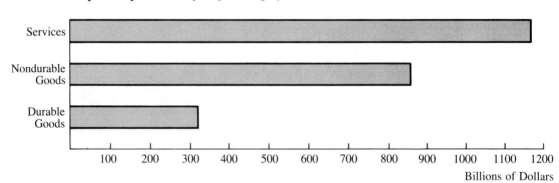

magnitude of the expenditures by category. Readers could, of course, generate this information from the pie chart, but it would involve some calculation on their part.

Figure 17.5, on the other hand, is a two-scale bar chart. It uses the data contained in Table 17.2 and shows total automobile sales for the period 1970–1984. The Y axis represents quantity, and the X axis time.

Figures 17.4 and 17.5 should illustrate the fact that the bar chart can be drawn either vertically or horizontally. When emphasis is on the change in the variable through time, the vertical form is preferred with the X axis as the time axis. When time is not a variable, either the vertical or horizontal form is used.

Bar Chart Variations   As previously suggested, bar charts are capable of great variation. One variation is to convert them to **pictograms.** Instead of using the length of the bar to capture quantity, amounts are shown by piles of dollars for income, pictures of cars for automobile production, people in a row for population, and so on. This can be a needed change of pace if there are a number of graphs in the report.[28]

A variation of the basic bar chart—the grouped bar chart—can be used to capture the change in two or more series through time. Figure 17.6, for example, shows the change in consumption expenditures by the three major categories for the period 1970–1984. Just as distinctive symbols are effective in distinguishing the separate series in a line chart, distinctive coloring and/or cross-hatching is equally helpful in a grouped bar chart.

There is also a bar chart equivalent to the stratum chart—the divided bar chart. Its construction and interpretation are similar to those for the stratum chart. Figure 17.7,

---

[28]Pictograms are especially susceptible to perceptual distortions. Report users have to be especially careful when reading them so that they are not misled with respect to the correct conclusions. See Patricia Ramsey and Louis Kaufman, "Presenting Research Data: How to Make Weak Numbers Look Good," *Industrial Marketing,* 67 (March 1982), pp. 66, 68, 70, 74.

Figure 17.5
Total Automobile Sales, 1970–1984

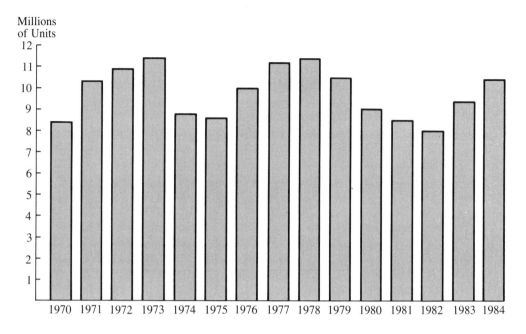

Figure 17.6
Personal Consumption Expenditures by Major Category, 1970–1984

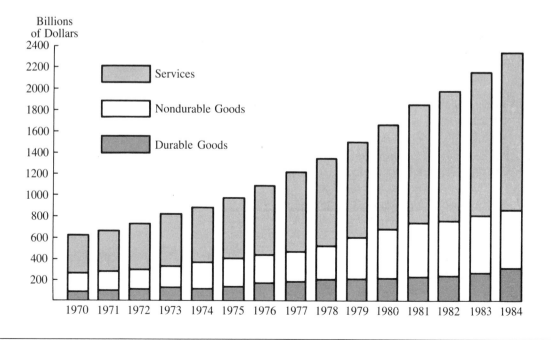

Figure 17.7

Personal Consumption Expenditures by Major Category, 1975–1984

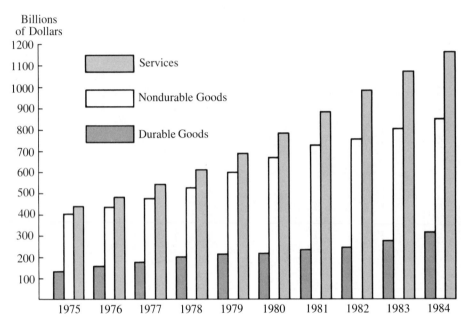

for example, is a divided bar chart of personal consumption expenditures by major category. It shows both total and relative expenditures through time. It, too, makes use of distinctive cross-hatching for each component.

Summary

The research report was discussed in this chapter. Four emphases were evident: the criteria for evaluating research reports, the elements of a written research report, the delivery of an oral report, and the graphic presentation of results.

The fundamental criterion for the development of every research report is the audience. The reader's interest, capabilities, and circumstances determine what goes in the report, what is left out, and how that which finds its way into the report is presented. The other criteria that need to be kept in mind in preparing the report are:

1. **Completeness**—does it provide all the information readers need in a language they understand?

2. **Accuracy**—is the reasoning logical and the information correct?

3. **Clarity**—is the phrasing precise?

4. **Conciseness**—is the writing crisp and direct?

There is no standard form for a research report since this, too, depends upon the preferences of the reader. Nonetheless, a "standard" report form that can be adapted to suit specific preferences was offered. It included a title page, table of contents, summary, introduction, body, conclusions and recommendations, and appendix. The main items contained in each section were highlighted.

The first rule when preparing oral reports is also to know the audience. It is better to present too little detail in an oral report than too much. It is useful to begin oral reports by stating the general purpose of the study and the specific objectives. The remainder of the presentation needs to systematically build on the evidence so that logical conclusions are drawn. Visual aids used in an oral report should be easily understood and easily seen by those in the back of the room. The time limit set for the meeting should always be honored, and only a portion of the allotted time should be used for the formal presentation. The remainder should be set aside for questions and discussion. The words and sentences used in the oral report should reflect natural-sounding speech, the presenter's usual vocabulary, and simple phrases.

Graphic presentation is often the best way to communicate those findings that require emphasis. Three main forms were discussed: the pie chart, the line chart, and the bar chart. The pie chart is a one-scale chart that is particularly effective in communicating a static comparison. The bar chart can be either a one-scale chart or a two-scale chart, while all the other types are basically two-scale charts. The two-scale chart can show the relationship between two variables and is often used when one of the variables is time, in which case time is captured on the X axis.

Questions

1. What is the fundamental report criterion? Explain.

2. What is meant by the report criteria of completeness, accuracy, clarity, and conciseness?

3. On the one hand, it is argued that the research report must be complete and, on the other, that it must be concise. Are not these two objectives incompatible? If so, how do you reconcile them?

4. What is the essential content of each of the following parts of the research report?
   (a) title page
   (b) table of contents
   (c) summary
   (d) introduction
   (e) body
   (f) conclusions and recommendations
   (g) appendix

5. What are the key considerations in preparing an oral report?

6. What is a pie chart? For what kinds of information is it particularly effective?

7. What is a line chart? For what kinds of information is it generally employed?

8. What is a stratum chart? For what kinds of information is it particularly appropriate?

9. What is a bar chart? For what kinds of problems is it effective?

10. What is a pictogram?

11. What is a grouped bar chart? When is it used?

Applications and Problems

1. The owner of a medium-sized home building center specializing in custom-designed and do-it-yourself kitchen supplies requested the I & J Consulting Firm to prepare a report on the customer profile of the kitchen design segment of the home improvement market. Evaluate the following sections of the report.

    The customer market for the company can be defined as the do-it-yourself and kitchen design segments. A brief profile of each follows.

    The do-it-yourself (DIY) market consists of individuals in the 25–45 age group living in a single dwelling. DIY customers are predominantly male, although an increasing number of females are becoming active DIY customers. The typical DIY customer has an income in excess of $20,000 and the median income is $22,100 with a standard deviation of 86. The DIY customer has an increasing amount of leisure time, is strongly value and convenience conscious, and displays an increasing desire for self gratification.

    The mean age of the custom kitchen design segment is 41.26 and the annual income is in the range of $25,000 to $35,000. The median income is $29,000 with a standard deviation of 73. The custom kitchen design customers usually live in a single dwelling. The wife is more influential and is the prime decision maker about kitchen designs and cabinets.

2. Discuss the difference between conclusions and recommendations in research reports.

3. The management of the Canco Company, manufacturers of metal cans, presents you with the following information.

The Canco Company
A Comparative Statement of Profit and Loss for the Fiscal Years 1982–1986

	1982	1983	1984	1985	1986
Net sales	$40,000,000	$45,000,000	$48,000,000	$53,000,000	$55,000,000
Cost and expenses					
Cost of goods sold	$28,000,000	$32,850,000	$33,600,000	$39,750,000	$40,150,000
Selling and admin.					
expenses	4,000,000	4,500,000	4,800,000	5,300,000	5,500,000
Depreciation	1,200,000	1,350,000	1,440,000	1,590,000	1,650,000
Interest	800,000	900,000	960,000	1,060,000	1,100,000
	$34,000,000	$39,600,000	$40,800,000	$47,700,000	$48,400,000
Profits from operations	6,000,000	5,400,000	7,200,000	5,300,000	6,600,000
Estimated taxes	$ 2,400,000	$ 2,160,000	$ 2,880,000	$ 2,120,000	$ 2,640,000
Net profits	$ 3,600,000	$ 3,240,000	$ 4,320,000	$ 3,180,000	$ 3,960,000

(a) Management has requested that you develop a visual aid to present the company's distribution of sales revenues in 1986.

(b) You are requested to develop a visual aid that would indicate the change in the net profit level to the change in the net sales level.

(c) The management of Canco Company wants you to develop a visual aid that will present the following expenses (excluding COGS) over the five-year period: selling and administration expenses, depreciation and interest expenses.

(d) The management has the following sales data relating to their two major competitors.

	1982	1983	1984
The We-Can Co.	$35,000,000	$40,000,000	$42,000,000
The You-Can Co.	$41,000,000	$43,000,000	$45,000,000

	1985	1986
The We-Can Co.	$45,000,000	$48,000,000
The You-Can Co.	$46,000,000	$48,000,000

You are required to prepare a visual aid to facilitate the comparison of the sales performance of Canco Company with its major competitors.

Chapter 18
The Research Project and the Firm's Marketing Intelligence System

The subject of marketing research can be approached in a number of ways. The perspective used in this book is primarily one of a *project emphasis*. We have focused on the definition of a problem and the research needed to answer it. At this point, the whole research process may appear to be a number of disconnected bits and pieces because of the necessity of separating it into logical components so that the design issues that arise at each stage could be highlighted. As mentioned in Chapter 2, however, the research process is anything but a set of disconnected parts. All the steps are highly interrelated, and a decision made at one stage has implications for the others as well. To show how this functions, the research process and some of the key decisions that must be made will be reviewed in this chapter.

A research project should not be conceived as the end in itself. Projects arise because managerial problems need solving. The problems themselves may concern the identification of market opportunities, the evaluation of alternative courses of action, or control of marketing operations. Since these activities, in turn, are the essence of the managerial function, research activity can also be viewed from the broader perspective of the firm's marketing intelligence system. The second part of this chapter, therefore, focuses on the nature and present status regarding the supply of marketing intelligence.

The Research Process Revisited

Marketing research was defined as the systematic gathering, recording, and analyzing of data about problems relating to the marketing of goods and services, and it was pointed out that these activities are logically viewed as a sequence of steps called the research process. The stages of the process were conceived of as follows:

1. formulate the problem;
2. determine the sources of information and the research design;
3. prepare the data-collection forms;
4. design the sample and collect the data;
5. analyze and interpret the data; and
6. prepare the research report.

The decision problem logically comes first. It dictates the research problem and the design of the project. However, the transition from problem to project is not an automatic one. There is a good deal of iteration from problem specification to tentative research design to problem respecification to modified research design and back again. This is natural, and one of the researcher's more important roles is to help to define and redefine the problem so that it can be researched and, more important, answers the decision maker's problem. While this might appear to be simple in principle, the task can be formidable because it requires a clear specification of objectives, alternatives, and environmental constraints and influences. The decision maker may not readily provide these, and it is up to the researcher to dig them out in order to design effective research. Perhaps research is not even necessary. If the decision maker's views are so strongly held that no amount of information might change them, the research will be wasted. It is up to the researcher to determine this before rather than after conducting the research. This often entails asking "what if" questions: What if consumer reaction to the product concept is overwhelmingly favorable? What if it is unfavorable? What if it is only slightly favorable? If the decision maker indicates that the same decision will be made in each case, there are other objectives that have not been explicitly stated. This is a critical finding. Every research project should have one or more objectives, and one should not proceed to the other steps in the process until these can be explicitly stated.

Here it is also important to ask whether the contemplated benefits of the research exceed the expected costs. It is a mistake to assume that simply because something might change as a result of the research, the research is called for. It may be that the likelihood of finding something that might warrant a change in the decision is so remote that the research still will be wasted. Researchers constantly need to ask: Why should this research be conducted? What could we possibly find out that we do not already know? Will the expected benefits from the research exceed its costs? If the answers indicate research, then the question logically turns to: What kind?

If the problem cannot be formulated as some specific "if–then" conjectural relationships, exploratory research is in order. The primary purpose of exploratory research is gathering some ideas and insights into the phenomenon. The output of an exploratory study will *not* be answers but more specific questions or statements of tentative relationships. The search for insights demands a flexible research design. Structured questionnaires or probability sampling plans are not used in exploratory research, since the emphasis is not on gathering summary statistics but on gaining insight into the problem. The personal interview is much more appropriate than the telephone interview, and that in turn is more appropriate than a mail survey, since the unstructured question is most useful in the experience survey. Interviewees should be handpicked because they can provide the wanted information, and thus a convenience or judgment sample is very much in order here, whereas it would completely out of place in descriptive or causal research. Focus groups can be productive for gaining important insights. A survey of the literature and an analysis of selected cases can also be used to advantage in exploratory research, particularly if the researcher assumes the correct posture of seeking rather than finding. The analysis of sharp contrasts or striking features in published data or selected cases is particularly productive of tentative explanations for the occurrence of the phenomenon.

Given that the exploratory effort has generated one or more specific hypotheses to be investigated, the next research thrust would logically be descriptive or causal research. The design actually selected would depend on the conviction with which the tentative explanation is held to be *the* explanation and the feasibility and cost of conducting an experiment. While experiments typically provide more convincing proof of causal relationships, they also usually cost more than do descriptive designs. This is one of the reasons why descriptive designs are the most commonly employed type in marketing research.

Whereas exploratory designs are flexible, descriptive designs are rigid. Descriptive designs demand a clear specification of the who, what, when, where, how, and why of the research before data collection begins. They generally employ structured questionnaires or scales because these forms provide advantages in coding and tabulating. In descriptive designs, the emphasis is on generating an accurate picture of the relationships between and among variables. Probability sampling plans are desirable, but if the sample is to be drawn using nonprobabilistic methods, it is important that a quota sample be used. Descriptive studies typically rely heavily on cross-tabulation analysis or other means of investigating the association among variables, such as regression analysis or discriminant analysis, although the emphasis can also be on the search for differences. The great majority of descriptive studies are cross-sectional, although some do use longitudinal information.

Experiments are the best means we have for making inferences about cause and effect relationships, since, if designed properly, they provide the most compelling evidence regarding concomitant variation, time order of occurrence of variables, and elimination of other factors. A key feature of the experiment is that the researcher is able to control who will be exposed to the experimental stimulus (the presumed cause). This allows the researcher to establish the prior equality of groups by randomization, either with or without matching, which in turn allows the adjustment of the results to eliminate many contaminating influences. Sampling plays little role in experiments other than in selecting objects that are to be assigned randomly to the treatment conditions. Because the emphasis is on testing a specific relationship, causal designs also demand a clear specification of what is to be measured and how it is to be measured. Structured data collection instruments should be used, and, although structured questionnaires and scales are often employed, experiments also rely heavily on the observational mode of data collection because of the typically more objective, more accurate information obtained this way. The major thrust in the analysis of experimental results is a test for differences between those exposed to the experimental stimulus and those not exposed; although the analysis-of-variance procedure is most often employed, other techniques (for example, the t test for the difference in means of independent or correlated samples) are used as well.

The previous paragraphs should indicate how significantly the steps are interrelated and, in particular, how the basic nature of the research design implies a number of things with respect to the structure of the data collection form, design of the sample, collection, and analysis of the data. A decision about appropriate research design does not completely determine the latter considerations, of course, but simply suggests their basic nature. The analyst still has to determine their specific format. For example, is the structured questionnaire to be disguised or undisguised? Is the probability sample to be simple, stratified, or cluster? How large a sample is needed? Does the data collection instrument dictate a data analysis procedure for nominal, ordinal, interval, or ratio data? These questions, too, will be determined in large part by the way the research question is framed, although the ingenuity displayed by the designer of the research will determine their final form. The researcher will have to balance the various sources of error that can arise in the process when determining this final form. In effecting this balance, the researcher must be concerned with assessing and minimizing total error; this often means assuming additional error in one of the parts of the process so that total error can be decreased.

The Research Project and the Marketing Intelligence System

It was suggested very early in this book that the fundamental purpose of marketing research is to assist marketing managers with the decisions they must make within any of the domains of their responsibilities. As directors of firms' marketing activities, marketing managers have an urgent need for information or marketing intelligence. They might need to know about the changes that could be expected in customer purchasing patterns, the types of marketing institutions that might evolve, which of several alternative product designs might be the most successful, the shape of the firm's demand curve, or any of a number of other issues that could affect the way they plan, solve problems, or evaluate and control the marketing effort. We suggested that marketing research is traditionally responsible for this intelligence function. As the formal link with the environment, marketing research generates, transmits, and interprets feedback originating in the environment regarding the success of the firm's marketing plans and the strategies and tactics employed in implementing those plans.

The project emphasis to research emphasized in this book is just one of the ways though by which marketing intelligence is provided. Two other ways are through marketing information systems (MIS) and decision support systems (DSS).[1] The purpose of this section is to provide some appreciation for the differences between the project emphasis to research highlighted throughout this book and these alternative schemes for providing marketing intelligence. The difference in perspectives was highlighted years ago in a useful analogy comparing a flash bulb and a candle.

The difference between marketing research and marketing intelligence is like the difference between a flash bulb and a candle. Let's say you are dancing in the dark. Every 90 seconds you are allowed to set off a flash bulb. You can use those brief intervals of intense light to chart a course, but remember everybody is moving, too. Hopefully, they'll accommodate themselves roughly to your predictions. You might get bumped and you may stumble every so often, but you can dance along.

On the other hand, you can light a candle. It doesn't yield as much light but it's a steady light. You are continually aware of the movements of other bodies. You can adjust your own course to the courses of others. The intelligence system is a kind of

---

[1]Information systems can be discussed at both the functional and corporate levels. When discussing corporate information systems, MIS stands for *management* information system, and it is understood that DSS refers to the structure of the decision support system for the whole company. Since our interest is marketing intelligence, we will use the term MIS to refer to the *marketing* information system and DSS to refer to the structure of the information system to support marketing decision making.

candle. It's no great flash on the immediate state of things, but it provides continuous light as situations shift and change.[2]

Historically, one of the problems of the research project emphasis has been its nonrecurring nature. A project is often devised in times of crises and carried out with urgency, and this has led to an emphasis on data collection and analysis instead of the development of pertinent information on a regular basis. One suggestion for closing the gap is to think of management in terms of an ongoing process of decision making that requires a flow of regular inputs rather than in terms of waiting for crisis situations to arise. Both MIS and DSS represent ongoing efforts over the last two decades to provide pertinent decision-making information on a regular basis to marketing managers. The essential thrust of these approaches can be appreciated from this forward-looking scenario that was first presented in 1969.

The year is 1988. The place is the office of the marketing manager of a medium-sized consumer products manufacturer. The participants in the following discussion are John, the marketing manager; Bill, the director of marketing science; Rod, Bill's assistant, who specializes in marketing research; and Scott, the sales manager for the company. The scene opens as Bill, Rod, and Scott enter John's office.

John: Good morning, gentlemen. What's on the agenda for this morning?

Bill: We want to take a look at the prospects for our new beef substitute.

John: What do we have on that new product?

Rod: We test-marketed it late in 1987 in four cities; so we have those data from last quarter.

John: Let's see how it did.

(All four gather around the remote console video display unit. John activates the console and requests it to display the sales results from the most recent test market. The system retrieves the data from random access storage and displays the information on the video device.)

John: That looks good! How does it compare to the first test?

(The console retrieves and displays the data from the first test on command from John).

Rod: Let me check the significance of the sales increase of the most recent test over last year's test.

(Rod requests that the system test and display the likelihood that the sales increase could be a chance occurrence.)

Rod: Looks like a solid sales increase.

Bill: Good! How did the market respond to our change in price?

(Bill commands the system to display the graph of the price–quantity response based upon the most recent test data.)

John: Is that about what our other meat substitute products show?

(John calls for past price–quantity response graphs for similar products to be superimposed on the screen.)

---

[2]Statement by Robert J. Williams, who was the creator of the first recognized marketing information system at the Mead Johnson division of the Edward Dalton Company. ''Marketing Intelligence Systems: A DEW Line for Marketing Men,'' *Business Management* (January 1966), p. 32.

John: Just as I suspected—this new product is a bit more responsive to price. What's the profit estimate?

(John calls for a profit estimate from the product-planning model within the system.)

John: Hmm . . . $5,500,000. Looks good. Is that based upon the growth model I supplied to the model bank last week?

Bill: No. This is based upon the penetration progress other food substitutes have shown in the past as well as the information we have on the beef substitute from our test markets.

John: Let's see what mine would do.

(He reactivates the product-planning model, this time using his growth model. The profit implications are displayed on the console.)

John: Well, my model predicts $5,000,000. That's close. Looks like my feelings are close to the statistical results.

Bill: Let's see if there's a better marketing strategy for this product. We must remember that these profit estimates are based on the preliminary plan we developed two weeks ago.

(Bill calls for the marketing mix generator to recommend a marketing program based upon the data and judgmental inputs which are available in the data bank's file on this product.)

Bill: There, we can increase profit by $700,000 if we allocate another sales call each week to the new product committees of the chain stores.

Scott: I don't think our salesmen will go along with that. They don't like to face those committees. The best I could do is convince them to make one additional call every other week.

John: What would happen in that case?

(The marketing mix generator is called with the new restriction on the number of calls.)

John: Well, the profit increase is still $500,000; so let's add that call policy recommendation to our marketing plan. I'm a little worried about our advertising appeals, though. Can we improve in that area?

Bill: Let's see what the response to advertising is.

(The video unit shows a graph of the predicted sales–advertising response function.)

Bill: If we changed from a taste appeal to a convenience appeal, what would the results be, John?

John: I think it would look like this.

(John takes a light pen and describes a new relationship on the video unit based upon his judgment of the effectiveness of the new appeal.)

Rod: Let me check something.

(Rod calls for a sample of past sales–advertising response curves of similar products using the convenience appeal.)

Rod: I think you are underestimating the response on the basis of past data.

John: Well, this product is different. How much would it cost for a test of this appeal?

(Rod calls a market research evaluation model from the console.)

Rod: It looks like a meaningful test would cost about $5,000.

Bill: Wait! Hadn't we better check to see if the differences between these two advertising response functions will lead to any differences in profit?

(The marketing mix model is called for each advertising function.)

Bill: Looks sensitive to the advertising response, all right. There's a $900,000 differ-
ence in profit.

John: I wonder what risk we'd run if we made a decision to go national with the
product right now. What are the chances of a failure with this product as it stands if
we include this morning's revisions to the marketing mix?

(A risk-analysis model is called on the system.)

John: Looks like a 35 percent chance of failure. Maybe we'd best run further tests in
order to reduce the risk of failure. What's next on the agenda this morning?[3]

Marketing Information Systems

The earliest attempts at providing information so that the above scenario could become
reality focused on **marketing information systems, (MIS)** which were defined as "a
set of procedures and methods for the regular, planned collection, analysis, and presentation of information for use in making marketing decisions."[4] Note that this definition
is very similar to our definition of marketing research as the systematic gathering, recording, and analyzing of data related to the marketing of goods and services. The key
difference in the definitions is the word "regular," since the emphasis in MIS is the
establishment of systems that produce information needed for decision making on a
recurring basis rather than on the basis of one-time research studies.

The thrust in designing marketing information systems is a detailed analysis of each
decision maker who might use the system in order to secure an accurate, objective
assessment of each manager's decision making responsibilities, capabilities, and style.
The analysis typically focuses on securing answers to such questions as:

1.   What types of decisions is each decision maker regularly called upon to make?

2.   What type of information is needed to make these decisions?

3.   What types of information does the decision maker regularly get?

4.   What types of special studies are periodically requested?

5.   What types of information would the decision maker like to get but is not presently
     receiving?

6.   What information should be received daily, weekly, monthly, yearly?

7.   What magazines and trade journals should be received regularly?

8.   What types of data analysis programs would the decision maker like to receive?

9.   What improvements would the decision maker like to see made in the current in-
     formation system?[5]

---

[3]David B. Montgomery and Glen L. Urban, *Management Science in Marketing,* © 1969 pp. 1–3. Reprinted
by permission of Prentice-Hall, Englewood Cliffs, New Jersey.

[4]Donald F. Cox and Robert E. Good, "How to Build a Marketing Information System," *Harvard Business
Review,* 45 (May–June 1967), pp. 145–154.

[5]Philip Kotler, "A Design for the Firm's Marketing Nerve Center," *Business Horizons,* 9 (Fall 1966), pp.
63–74. See also William R. King, "Developing Useful Decision Support Systems," *Management Decision,*
15 (Fall 1978), pp. 263–273.

Research Realities 18.1

Sales Analysis and Sales Expense and Margin Reports in a Consumer Food Products Company

Report Name	Purpose	Frequency	Distribution*
A. Sales Analysis Reports			
Region	To provide sales information in units and dollars for each sales office or center in the region as well as a regional total	Monthly	One copy of applicable portions to each regional manager
Sales Office or Center	To provide sales information in units and dollars for each district manager assigned to a sales office	Monthly	One copy of applicable portions to each sales office or center manager
District	To provide sales information in units and dollars for each account supervisor and retail salesperson reporting to the district manager	Monthly	One copy of applicable portions to each district manager
Salesperson Summary	To provide sales information in units and dollars for each customer whom the salesperson calls upon	Monthly	One copy of applicable portions to each salesperson
Salesperson Customer/Product	To provide sales information in units and dollars for each customer whom the salesperson calls upon	Monthly	One copy of applicable portions to each salesperson
Salesperson/Product	To provide sales information in units and dollars for each product that the salesperson sells	Quarterly	One copy of applicable portions to each salesperson

*To understand the report distribution, it is useful to know that salespeople were assigned accounts in sales districts. Sales people were assigned one or, at most, a couple of large accounts and were responsible for all the grocery stores, regardless of geography, affiliated with these large accounts, or they were assigned a geographic territory and were responsible for all of the stores within that territory. All sales districts were assigned to sales offices or sales centers. The centers were, in turn, organized into regions.

Given these information specifications, designers would then attempt to specify, get approval for, and subsequently generate a series of reports that would go to the various decision makers.[6] Research Realities 18.1, for example, shows the types of sales analysis reports and sales expense and margin reports developed for a sales information system for a consumer food products company for which the author served as consul-

[6]See Raymond McLeod, Jr., and John Rogers, ''Marketing Information Systems: Uses in the Fortune 500,'' *California Management Review,* 25 (Fall 1982), pp. 106–118, for the results of a survey conducted among the executives of the Fortune 500 that highlights the relative emphasis on marketing information systems and their use by management in the reporting firms.

Report Name	Purpose	Frequency	Distribution*
A. Sales Analysis Reports continued			
Region/Product	To provide sales information in units and dollars for each product sold within the region. Similar reports would be available by sales office and by district.	Monthly	No general distribution; used for special sales analysis when needed
Region/Customer Class	To provide sales information in units and dollars for each class of customer located in the region. Similar reports would be available by sales office and by district.	Monthly	No general distribution; used for special sales analysis when needed
B. Sales Expense and Margin Reports			
Salesperson Compensation and Expense Report	To provide a listing of salesperson compensation and expenses by district	Monthly	District managers
Salesperson Sales Expense Report	To provide comparative information regarding the ability of the salespeople to manage their expenses	Monthly	District managers
Salesperson Margin Report	To highlight the contribution of profit being made by the various salespeople	Monthly	District managers
Sales Office and Center Margin Report	To highlight the profitability of the various districts within a sales office or center	Monthly	Center mangers
Region Margin Report	To highlight the profitability of the various centers within a region	Monthly	Region managers

tant. As might be obvious from Research Realities 18.1, the purpose and form of each report typically meant designing it so that it might serve a number of managers with similar job titles. System support people spent a lot of time working with individual decision makers to develop good report formats and efficient systems for extracting and combining information from the various data banks, a typical occurrence when designing MIS's. It is not unusual to have separate data banks for general sales data, market data, product data, sales representative data, and consumer data in an MIS.[7]

---

[7]See Van Mayros and D. Michael Werner, *Marketing Information Systems* (Radnor, Penn.: Chitton, 1982), for detailed list of the data elements that might go into each one of these data banks.

To use an MIS on the introductory scenario, it would be necessary to anticipate the various information Bill, John, Rod, and Scott might want when making the decision on the new beef substitute and the form in which they could best use that information. Then it would be necessary to specify the data that would need to be in the system, how that data could be secured, how the data should be stored, how the data in separate data banks should be accessed and combined, and what the report formats should be like. Once these analysis and design steps were completed, the system would be constructed, which is essentially a programming task. Programmers would write and document the programs that would make data retrieval as efficient as possible with respect to the use of computer time and memory. When all the procedures were debugged so that the system was operating correctly, it would be put on line. Once implemented, decision makers like John and Scott could ask for any of the previously defined reports. In the early days of MIS, these requests would go through the computer or information systems departments, which would issue a hard copy or printed report. In later years, managers could access these reports directly through a computer terminal that might be sitting on their desks.

Decision Support Systems

When they were first proposed, MIS's were held up as an information panacea. The reality, however, often fell short of the promise. The primary reasons are as much behavioral as they are technical. People tend to resist change, and with MIS the changes are often substantial. Many decision makers are reluctant, for example, to disclose to others what factors they use and how they combine these factors when making a decision about a particular issue, and without such disclosure it is next to impossible to design reports that will give them the information they need in the form they need it. Even when managers are willing to disclose their decision-making calculus and information needs, there are problems.

Different managers typically emphasize different things and, consequently, have different data needs. There are very few report formats that are optimal for different users. Either the developers have to design ''compromise'' reports that are satisfactory for a number of users, although not ideal for any single user, or they have to engage in the laborious task of programming to meet each user's needs, one at a time. Sometimes top management provides less than enthusiastic support for the changes that necessarily accompany MIS, a condition that seems to be particularly common among the more unsuccessful attempts to develop MIS's. Equally troublesome, though, have been the problems associated with underestimating the costs and time required to establish such systems, caused by underestimating the size of the task, changes in organizational structure, key personnel, and electronic data processing systems they require. By the time these systems can be developed, the personnel for which they are designed often have different responsibilities or the economic and competitive environments around which they are designed have changed. Thus, they are often obsolete soon after being put on line, meaning that the whole process of analysis, design, development, and implementation has to be repeated anew.

Another fundamental problem with MIS is that the systems do not lend themselves to the solution of ill-structured problems, which are the most common kind of problems managers face. The notion of ill-structured problems can be understood through

Simon's[8] description of decision making as a process involving the three stages of intelligence, design, and choice.

Intelligence refers to the gathering of information from the decision-making system's environment and exploring that information in an effort to recognize the existence of problems. Design refers to the clarification of a problem, to the creation of potential solutions to the problem, and to the assessment of a potential solution's feasibility. Finally, the choice stage involves the act of choosing one of the feasible solutions and investigating the implementation of that solution. . . . If a problem encountered in decision making cannot be fully clarified and if the exploration of potential solutions cannot be completed before a choice must be made, then the problem is said to be ill-structured. Otherwise, the problem is well-structured and can (in principle, at least) be programmed.[9]

Many of the activities performed by managers cannot be programmed, nor can they be performed routinely or delegated, because they involve personal choices.[10] Since a manager's decision making is often *ad hoc* and addressed to unexpected choices, standardized reporting systems lack the necessary scope and flexibility to be useful. Nor can managers, even if they are willing to, specify in advance what they want from programmers and model builders, because decision making and planning are often exploratory. As decision makers and their staffs learn more about a problem, their information needs and methods of analysis evolve. Further, decision making often involves exceptions and qualitative issues that are not easily programmed.

As these problems with MIS became more apparent, the emphasis in supplying marketing intelligence on a more regular basis changed from the production of preformatted, batch reports to a **decision support system (DSS)** mode, where a DSS has been defined as ''a coordinated collection of data, systems, tools, and techniques with supporting software and hardware by which an organization gathers and interprets relevant information from business and environment and turns it into a basis for marketing action.''[11]

A DSS concentrates on the design of data systems, model systems, and dialog systems that can be used interactively by managers. See Figure 18.1.[12] The **data system** includes the processes used to capture and the methods used to store data coming from marketing, finance, and manufacturing, as well as information coming from any number of external or internal sources. Marketing research as discussed in this book would

---

[8]Herbert A. Simon, *The New Science of Management Decisions* (New York: Harper & Row, 1960).

[9]Robert H. Bonczek, Clyde W. Holsapple, and Andrew B. Whinston, ''Developments in Decision Support Systems,'' undated manuscript, Management Information Research Center, Krannert Graduate School of Management, Purdue University, pp. 3–4.

[10]P. G. Keen and G. R. Wagner, ''DSS: An Executive Mind-Support System,'' *Datamation,* 25 (November 1979), pp. 117–122.

[11]John D. C. Little, ''Decision Support Systems for Marketing Managers,'' *Journal of Marketing,* 43 (Summer 1979), p. 11. See also John D. C. Little, Lakshmi Mohan, and Antoine Hatorin, ''Yanking Knowledge from the Numbers: How Marketing Decision Support Systems Can Work for You,'' *Industrial Marketing,* 67 (March 1982), pp. 46, 50–56.

[12]Figure 18.1 and this surrounding discussion are adapted from the excellent treatment of the subject by Ralph H. Sprague, Jr., and Eric D. Carlson, *Effective Decision Support Systems* (Englewood Cliffs, N.J.: Prentice-Hall, 1982), Chapters 1 and 2.

Figure 18.1
Components of a Decision Support System

The DSS

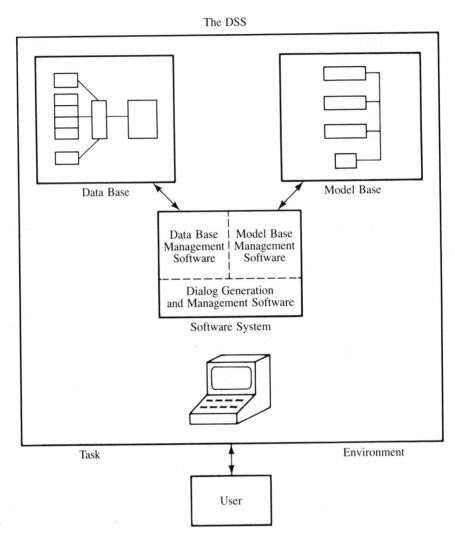

Source: Adapted from Ralph H. Sprague, Jr., and Eric D. Carlson, *Building Effective Decision Support Systems,* © 1982, p. 29. Adapted by permission of Prentice-Hall, Englewood Cliffs, New Jersey.

typically supply some of the information input to the data system. Other inputs might come from purchase of syndicated commercial marketing information services like National Panel Diary or Nielsen Retail Index. Still other information input to the data bank would come from the sales function via invoices or perhaps from salesperson call reports that detail which accounts salespeople are calling upon and how frequently. In sum, the data system would hold data from a variety of sources and in a variety of forms. The fundamental criterion as to whether a particular piece of data might find itself in the data bank is whether it is useful for marketing decision making, and the basic task of a DSS is to capture relevant marketing data in reasonable detail and to put that data in a truly accessible form. It is crucial that the data base management capabilities built into the system can logically organize the data the same way a manager does, regardless of the form that organization assumes.

The **model system** includes all the routines that allow the user to manipulate the data so as to conduct the kind of analysis the individual desires. Whenever managers look at data, they have a preconceived idea of how something works and, therefore, what is interesting and worthwhile in the data. These ideas are called models.[13] Most managers also want to manipulate data to gain a better understanding of a marketing issue. These manipulations are called procedures. The routines for manipulating the data may run the gamut from summing a set of numbers to conducting a complex statistical analysis to finding an optimization strategy using some kind of nonlinear programming routine. While many sophisticated techniques are available and can be useful for some purposes, "the most frequent operations are basic ones: segregating numbers into relevant groups, aggregating them, taking ratios, ranking them, picking out exceptional cases, plotting and making tables."[14]

The **dialog systems,** which are also called language systems, are the most important and clearly differentiate DSS from MIS. The dialog systems permit managers, who are not programmers themselves, to explore the data bases using the system models to produce reports that satisfy their own particular information needs. The reports can be tabular or graphical, and the report formats can be specified by individual managers. The dialog systems can be passive, which means that the analysis possibilities are presented to the decision makers for selection via menu, a few simple key strokes, light pen, or a mouse device, or they can be active, requiring the users to state their requests in a command mode. A key feature is that managers, instead of funneling their data requests through a team of programmers, can conduct their analyses by themselves (or through one of their assistants) sitting at a computer terminal using the dialog system. This allows them to target the information they want and not to be overwhelmed with irrelevant data. Managers can ask a question and, on the basis of the answer, can ask a subsequent question, and then another, and another, and so on.

With the right DSS, for example, a marketing VP evaluating the sales of a recently introduced test instrument could "call up" sales by month, then by the year, breaking them out at his option by, say, customer segments. As he works at his CRT terminal, his inquiries could go in several directions depending on the decision at hand. If his train of thought raises questions about monthly sales last year compared to forecasts he wants his information system to follow along and give him answers immediately.

He might see that his new product's sales were significantly below forecast. Forecasts too optimistic? He compares other products' sales to his forecasts, and finds that the targets were very accurate. Something wrong with the product? Maybe his sales

---

[13]John D. C. Little and Michael N. Cassettari, *Decision Support Systems for Marketing Managers* (New York: American Management Association, 1984), p. 14.

[14]*Ibid.*, p. 15.

department is getting insufficient leads, or isn't putting leads to good use? Thinking a minute about how to examine that question, he checks ratios of leads converted to sales—product by product. The results distrub him. Only 5% of the new product's leads generate orders compared to the company's 12% all-product average. Why? He guesses that the sales force isn't supporting the new product enough. Quantitative information from the DDS perhaps could provide more evidence to back that suspicion. But already having enough quantitative knowledge to satisfy himself, the VP acts on his intuition and experience and decides to have a chat with his sales manager.[15]

From the previous discussion, it should be obvious that DSS and MIS are both concerned with improving information processing so that better marketing decisions can be made. DSS differs from MIS, though, in a number of ways.[16] First, DSS tends to be aimed at the less well-structured, underspecified problems that managers face rather than at those problems that can be investigated using a relatively standard set of procedures and comparisons. Second, DSS attempts to combine the use of models and analytical techniques and procedures with the more traditional data access and retrieval functions. Third, such systems specifically incorporate features that make them easy to use in an interactive mode by noncomputer people. These features might include such things as menu-driven procedures for doing an analysis and graphical display of the results. Regardless of how the interaction is structured, these systems have the ability to respond to users' *ad hoc* requests in "real time," meaning the time available for making the decision. Fourth, they emphasize flexibility and adaptibility. They can accommodate different decision makers with diverse styles as well as changing environmental conditions.

An analysis of the current status of DSS suggests that there are probably three types of systems currently in place—data retrieval, market analysis, and modeling systems.[17] Data retrieval systems represent the most elementary DSS. They allow decision makers to extract, sort, summarize, and list data from any of a number of existing data files. Data retrieval systems are quite useful in helping managers answer the question "What has happened?" Managers usually want to know more, though. Good managers like to find out "Why did so-and-so happen?", which is typically found by analyzing expected relationships between the phenomena of interest and other marketing variables. Systems capable of addressing the why question are called market analysis systems. The most sophisticated systems currently in place are able to go beyond analysis and are able to address questions of the sort "What would happen if?" Many of these systems, called modeling systems, currently rely on electronic spreadsheet programs like Visicalc or Lotus 1–2–3 or on one of the financial planning programs especially designed for handling modeling issues. More powerful computer packages are being developed every day, and one would expect that many managers will gravitate to these powerful mod-

---

[15]Michael Dressler, Ronald Beall, and Joquin Ives Brant, "What the Hot Marketing Tool of the '80s Offers You," *Industrial Marketing,* 68 (March 1983), pp. 51 and 54.

[16]For discussion of the features that differentiate DSS from MIS, see Sprague and Carlson, *Effective Decision Support Systems;* and Bonczek, Holsapple, and Whinston, "Developments in Decision Support Systems."

[17]See Richard D. Canning, "What's Happening with DSS?" *EDP Analyzer,* 22 (July 1984), pp. 1–12, for further discussion of the three types of systems.

eling programs as they become more comfortable interacting directly with computers and as these packages are made easier to use. The scenario for the new beef substitute involving Bill, John, Rod, and Scott represents a true, modeling DSS.

Summary

This chapter had two purposes: (1) to increase the appreciation of the interrelationship of the stages in the research process; and (2) to provide some awareness of the purposes and current status of other means for providing marketing intelligence.

The first part of the chapter, therefore, was a review of the stages in the research process and a demonstration of how a decision with respect to the problem determines the basic nature of the research design, and further, of how a decision with respect to the research design in large part dictates the type of data collection instruments that should be used, the type of sample that should be employed, and even the type of analysis that might be conducted.

Marketing intelligence systems owe their existence to the development of high-speed computing machinery. The difference between the project emphasis to research assumed in this book and marketing information system (MIS) or decision support system (DSS) emphases is that both of the latter rely on the continual monitoring of the firm's activities, competitors, and environment, while the former emphasizes the in-depth, but non-recurring, study of some specific problem or environmental condition.

A marketing information system was defined as a set of procedures and methods for the regular, planned collection, analysis, and presentation of information for use in making marketing decisions. The thrust in designing MIS is the detailed analysis of each decision maker who might use the system in order to secure an accurate, objective assessment of each manager's decision making responsibilities, capabilities, and style, and most important, each manager's information needs. Given the specification of information needs, system support people develop report formats and efficient systems for extracting and combining information from various data banks. In the early days of MIS, information requests would go through the computer department, which would issue a hard copy or printed report. More recently, managers could get a copy of one of the standard report formats directly on a computer terminal.

While MIS did provide more regular marketing intelligence than had been true when firms relied on marketing research projects, such systems also suffered from some other problems. They required managers to disclose their decision making processes, which many managers were reluctant to do. Further, the report formats were typically compromises that tried to satisfy the different styles of the different users. Also, the development time required for these systems often meant that they quickly became obsolete.

DSS are replacing MIS in many companies. A DSS is a coordinated collection of data, systems, tools, and techniques with supporting software and hardware by which an organization gathers and interprets relevant information from business and environment and turns it into a basis for marketing action. A DSS concentrates on the design of data systems, model systems, and dialog systems. The data systems include the processes used to capture and store information useful for marketing decision making. A marketing research project might be one input to a data system. The model system includes all the routines that allow users to manipulate data to conduct the kinds of analyses they desire. The dialog systems are most important and most clearly differentiate DSS from MIS. They allow managers to conduct their own analyses while they or one of their assistants sit at a computer terminal. This allows managers to analyze problems using their own personal views of what might be happening in a given situation, relying on their intuition and experience rather than on a series of prespecified reports. This not only eliminates a lot of irrelevant data, it also saves time because they can program the analysis themselves rather than waiting for the computer department to process their request for some specific information.

Questions

1. What is a marketing information system? How does a project emphasis to marketing research differ from an information systems emphasis?

2. What are some of the basic questions that need to be answered in designing a marketing information system?

3. What are the main differences between a marketing information system and a decision support system?

4. In a decision support system, what is a data system? A model system? A dialog system? Which of these is most important? Why?

Applications and Problems

1. Twenty years ago the Marketing Information System was emphasized as being the solution to a host of problems arising from irregular research efforts. The promise was never realized and current emphasis is on the design of Decision Support Systems rather than Marketing Information Systems. How do you account for the gap between the promise and delivery of MIS? Do you think DSSs will suffer the same fate as MISs? Why or why not?

Appendix

Table 1
Cumulative Standard Unit Normal Distribution

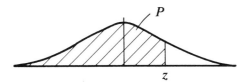

Values of P corresponding to Z for the normal curve. Z is the standard normal variable. The value of P for $-Z$ equals one minus the value of P for $+Z$, (e.g., the P for -1.62 equals $1 - .9474 = .0526$).

Z	.00	.01	.02	.03	.04	.05	.06	.07	.08	.09
.0	.5000	.5040	.5080	.5120	.5160	.5199	.5239	.5279	.5319	.5359
.1	.5398	.5438	.5478	.5517	.5557	.5596	.5636	.5675	.5714	.5753
.2	.5793	.5832	.5871	.5910	.5948	.5987	.6026	.6064	.6103	.6141
.3	.6179	.6217	.6255	.6293	.6331	.6368	.6406	.6443	.6480	.6517
.4	.6554	.6591	.6628	.6664	.6700	.6736	.6772	.6808	.6844	.6879
.5	.6915	.6950	.6985	.7019	.7054	.7088	.7123	.7157	.7190	.7224
.6	.7257	.7291	.7324	.7357	.7389	.7422	.7454	.7486	.7517	.7549
.7	.7580	.7611	.7642	.7673	.7704	.7734	.7764	.7794	.7823	.7852
.8	.7881	.7910	.7939	.7967	.7995	.8023	.8051	.8078	.8106	.8133
.9	.8159	.8186	.8212	.8238	.8264	.8289	.8315	.8340	.8365	.8389
1.0	.8413	.8438	.8461	.8485	.8508	.8531	.8554	.8577	.8599	.8621
1.1	.8643	.8665	.8686	.8708	.8729	.8749	.8770	.8790	.8810	.8830
1.2	.8849	.8869	.8888	.8907	.8925	.8944	.8962	.8980	.8997	.9015
1.3	.9032	.9049	.9066	.9082	.9099	.9115	.9131	.9147	.9162	.9177
1.4	.9192	.9207	.9222	.9236	.9251	.9265	.9279	.9292	.9306	.9319
1.5	.9332	.9345	.9357	.9370	.9382	.9394	.9406	.9418	.9429	.9441
1.6	.9452	.9463	.9474	.9484	.9495	.9505	.9515	.9525	.9535	.9545
1.7	.9554	.9564	.9573	.9582	.9591	.9599	.9608	.9616	.9625	.9633
1.8	.9641	.9649	.9656	.9664	.9671	.9678	.9686	.9693	.9699	.9706
1.9	.9713	.9719	.9726	.9732	.9738	.9744	.9750	.9756	.9761	.9767
2.0	.9772	.9778	.9783	.9788	.9793	.9798	.9803	.9808	.9812	.9817
2.1	.9821	.9826	.9830	.9834	.9838	.9842	.9846	.9850	.9854	.9857
2.2	.9861	.9864	.9868	.9871	.9875	.9878	.9881	.9884	.9887	.9890
2.3	.9893	.9896	.9898	.9901	.9904	.9906	.9909	.9911	.9913	.9916
2.4	.9918	.9920	.9922	.9925	.9927	.9929	.9931	.9932	.9934	.9936
2.5	.9938	.9940	.9941	.9943	.9945	.9946	.9948	.9949	.9951	.9952
2.6	.9953	.9955	.9956	.9957	.9959	.9960	.9961	.9962	.9963	.9964
2.7	.9965	.9966	.9967	.9968	.9969	.9970	.9971	.9972	.9973	.9974
2.8	.9974	.9975	.9976	.9977	.9977	.9978	.9979	.9979	.9980	.9981
2.9	.9981	.9982	.9982	.9983	.9984	.9984	.9985	.9985	.9986	.9986
3.0	.9987	.9987	.9987	.9988	.9988	.9989	.9989	.9989	.9990	.9990
3.1	.9990	.9991	.9991	.9991	.9992	.9992	.9992	.9992	.9993	.9993
3.2	.9993	.9993	.9994	.9994	.9994	.9994	.9994	.9995	.9995	.9995
3.3	.9995	.9995	.9995	.9996	.9996	.9996	.9996	.9996	.9996	.9997
3.4	.9997	.9997	.9997	.9997	.9997	.9997	.9997	.9997	.9997	.9998

Source: Paul E. Green, *Analyzing Multivariate Data* (Chicago: The Dryden Press, 1978).

Table 2
Selected Percentiles of the χ^2 Distribution

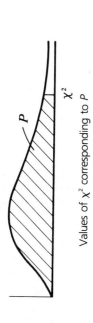

χ^2

Values of χ^2 corresponding to P

ν	$\chi^2_{.005}$	$\chi^2_{.01}$	$\chi^2_{.025}$	$\chi^2_{.05}$	$\chi^2_{.10}$	$\chi^2_{.90}$	$\chi^2_{.95}$	$\chi^2_{.975}$	$\chi^2_{.99}$	$\chi^2_{.995}$
1	.000039	.00016	.00098	.0039	.0158	2.71	3.84	5.02	6.63	7.88
2	.0100	.0201	.0506	.1026	.2107	4.61	5.99	7.38	9.21	10.60
3	.0717	.115	.216	.352	.584	6.25	7.81	9.35	11.34	12.84
4	.207	.297	.484	.711	1.064	7.78	9.49	11.14	13.28	14.86
5	.412	.554	.831	1.15	1.61	9.24	11.07	12.83	15.09	16.75
6	.676	.872	1.24	1.64	2.20	10.64	12.59	14.45	16.81	18.55
7	.989	1.24	1.69	2.17	2.83	12.02	14.07	16.01	18.48	20.28
8	1.34	1.65	2.18	2.73	3.49	13.36	15.51	17.53	20.09	21.96
9	1.73	2.09	2.70	3.33	4.17	14.68	16.92	19.02	21.67	23.59
10	2.16	2.56	3.25	3.94	4.87	15.99	18.31	20.48	23.21	25.19
11	2.60	3.05	3.82	4.57	5.58	17.28	19.68	21.92	24.73	26.76
12	3.07	3.57	4.40	5.23	6.30	18.55	21.03	23.34	26.22	28.30
13	3.57	4.11	5.01	5.89	7.04	19.81	22.36	24.74	27.69	29.82
14	4.07	4.66	5.63	6.57	7.79	21.06	23.68	26.12	29.14	31.32
15	4.60	5.23	6.26	7.26	8.55	22.31	25.00	27.49	30.58	32.80
16	5.14	5.81	6.91	7.96	9.31	23.54	26.30	28.85	32.00	34.27
18	6.26	7.01	8.23	9.39	10.86	25.99	28.87	31.53	34.81	37.16
20	7.43	8.26	9.59	10.85	12.44	28.41	31.41	34.17	37.57	40.00
24	9.89	10.86	12.40	13.85	15.66	33.20	36.42	39.36	42.98	45.56
30	13.79	14.95	16.79	18.49	20.60	40.26	43.77	46.98	50.89	53.67
40	20.71	22.16	24.43	26.51	29.05	51.81	55.76	59.34	63.69	66.77
60	35.53	37.48	40.48	43.19	46.46	74.40	79.08	83.30	88.38	91.95
120	83.85	86.92	91.58	95.70	100.62	140.23	146.57	152.21	158.95	163.64

Adapted with permission from *Introduction to Statistical Analysis* (2d ed.) by W. J. Dixon and F. J. Massey, Jr., McGraw-Hill Book Company, Inc., 1957.

Table 3
Upper Percentiles of the *t* Distribution

ν \ $1-\alpha$	.75	.90	.95	.975	.99	.995	.9995
1	1.000	3.078	6.314	12.706	31.821	63.657	636.619
2	.816	1.886	2.920	4.303	6.965	9.925	31.598
3	.765	1.638	2.353	3.182	4.541	5.841	12.941
4	.741	1.533	2.132	2.776	3.747	4.604	8.610
5	.727	1.476	2.015	2.571	3.365	4.032	6.859
6	.718	1.440	1.943	2.447	3.143	3.707	5.959
7	.711	1.415	1.895	2.365	2.998	3.499	5.405
8	.706	1.397	1.860	2.306	2.896	3.355	5.041
9	.703	1.383	1.833	2.262	2.821	3.250	4.781
10	.700	1.372	1.812	2.228	2.764	3.169	4.587
11	.697	1.363	1.796	2.201	2.718	3.106	4.437
12	.695	1.356	1.782	2.179	2.681	3.055	4.318
13	.694	1.350	1.771	2.160	2.650	3.012	4.221
14	.692	1.345	1.761	2.145	2.624	2.977	4.140
15	.691	1.341	1.753	2.131	2.602	2.947	4.073
16	.690	1.337	1.746	2.120	2.583	2.921	4.015
17	.689	1.333	1.740	2.110	2.567	2.898	3.965
18	.688	1.330	1.734	2.101	2.552	2.878	3.922
19	.688	1.328	1.729	2.093	2.339	2.861	3.883
20	.687	1.325	1.725	2.086	2.528	2.845	3.850
21	.686	1.323	1.721	2.080	2.518	2.831	3.819
22	.686	1.321	1.717	2.074	2.508	2.819	3.792
23	.685	1.319	1.714	2.069	2.500	2.807	3.767
24	.685	1.318	1.711	2.064	2.492	2.797	3.745
25	.684	1.316	1.708	2.060	2.485	2.787	3.725
26	.684	1.315	1.706	2.056	2.479	2.779	3.707
27	.684	1.314	1.703	2.052	2.473	2.771	3.690
28	.683	1.313	1.701	2.048	2.467	2.763	3.674
29	.683	1.311	1.699	2.045	2.462	2.756	3.659
30	.683	1.310	1.697	2.042	2.457	2.750	3.646
40	.681	1.303	1.684	2.021	2.423	2.704	3.551
60	.679	1.296	1.671	2.000	2.390	2.660	3.460
120	.677	1.289	1.658	1.980	2.358	2.617	3.373
∞	.674	1.282	1.645	1.960	2.326	2.576	3.291

ν = degrees of freedom

Source: Table taken from Table III of Fisher and Yates: *Statistical Tables for Biological, Agricultural and Medical Research* published by Longman Group Ltd. London (previously published by Oliver and Boyd Ltd, Edinburgh) and by permission of the authors and publishers.

Table 4
Selected Percentiles of the F Distribution

$$F_{.90(\nu_1, \nu_2)} \quad \alpha = 0.1$$

ν_1 = degrees of freedom for numerator

ν_2	1	2	3	4	5	6	7	8	9	10	12	15	20	24	30	40	60	120	∞
1	39.86	49.50	53.59	55.83	57.24	58.20	58.91	59.44	59.86	60.19	60.71	61.22	61.74	62.00	62.26	62.53	62.79	63.06	63.33
2	8.53	9.00	9.16	9.24	9.29	9.33	9.35	9.37	9.38	9.39	9.41	9.42	9.44	9.45	9.46	9.47	9.47	9.48	9.49
3	5.54	5.46	5.39	5.34	5.31	5.28	5.27	5.25	5.24	5.23	5.22	5.20	5.18	5.18	5.17	5.16	5.15	5.14	5.13
4	4.54	4.32	4.19	4.11	4.05	4.01	3.98	3.95	3.94	3.92	3.90	3.87	3.84	3.83	3.82	3.80	3.79	3.78	3.76
5	4.06	3.78	3.62	3.52	3.45	3.40	3.37	3.34	3.32	3.30	3.27	3.24	3.21	3.19	3.17	3.16	3.14	3.12	3.10
6	3.78	3.46	3.29	3.18	3.11	3.05	3.01	2.98	2.96	2.94	2.90	2.87	2.84	2.82	2.80	2.78	2.76	2.74	2.72
7	3.59	3.26	3.07	2.96	2.88	2.83	2.78	2.75	2.72	2.70	2.67	2.63	2.59	2.58	2.56	2.54	2.51	2.49	2.47
8	3.46	3.11	2.92	2.81	2.73	2.67	2.62	2.59	2.56	2.54	2.50	2.46	2.42	2.40	2.38	2.36	2.34	2.32	2.29
9	3.36	3.01	2.81	2.69	2.61	2.55	2.51	2.47	2.44	2.42	2.38	2.34	2.30	2.28	2.25	2.23	2.21	2.18	2.16
10	3.29	2.92	2.73	2.61	2.52	2.46	2.41	2.38	2.35	2.32	2.28	2.24	2.20	2.18	2.16	2.13	2.11	2.08	2.06
11	3.23	2.86	2.66	2.54	2.45	2.39	2.34	2.30	2.27	2.25	2.21	2.17	2.12	2.10	2.08	2.05	2.03	2.00	1.97
12	3.18	2.81	2.61	2.48	2.39	2.33	2.28	2.24	2.21	2.19	2.15	2.10	2.06	2.04	2.01	1.99	1.96	1.93	1.90
13	3.14	2.76	2.56	2.43	2.35	2.28	2.23	2.20	2.16	2.14	2.10	2.05	2.01	1.98	1.96	1.93	1.90	1.88	1.85
14	3.10	2.73	2.52	2.39	2.31	2.24	2.19	2.15	2.12	2.10	2.05	2.01	1.96	1.94	1.91	1.89	1.86	1.83	1.80
15	3.07	2.70	2.49	2.36	2.27	2.21	2.16	2.12	2.09	2.06	2.02	1.97	1.92	1.90	1.87	1.85	1.82	1.79	1.76
16	3.05	2.67	2.46	2.33	2.24	2.18	2.13	2.09	2.06	2.03	1.99	1.94	1.89	1.87	1.84	1.81	1.78	1.75	1.72
17	3.03	2.64	2.44	2.31	2.22	2.15	2.10	2.06	2.03	2.00	1.96	1.91	1.86	1.84	1.81	1.78	1.75	1.72	1.69
18	3.01	2.62	2.42	2.29	2.20	2.13	2.08	2.04	2.00	1.98	1.93	1.89	1.84	1.81	1.78	1.75	1.72	1.69	1.66
19	2.99	2.61	2.40	2.27	2.18	2.11	2.06	2.02	1.98	1.96	1.91	1.86	1.81	1.79	1.76	1.73	1.70	1.67	1.63
20	2.97	2.59	2.38	2.25	2.16	2.09	2.04	2.00	1.96	1.94	1.89	1.84	1.79	1.77	1.74	1.71	1.68	1.64	1.61
21	2.96	2.57	2.36	2.23	2.14	2.08	2.02	1.98	1.95	1.92	1.87	1.83	1.78	1.75	1.72	1.69	1.66	1.62	1.59
22	2.95	2.56	2.35	2.22	2.13	2.06	2.01	1.97	1.93	1.90	1.86	1.81	1.76	1.73	1.70	1.67	1.64	1.60	1.57
23	2.94	2.55	2.34	2.21	2.11	2.05	1.99	1.95	1.92	1.89	1.84	1.80	1.74	1.72	1.69	1.66	1.62	1.59	1.55
24	2.93	2.54	2.33	2.19	2.10	2.04	1.98	1.94	1.91	1.88	1.83	1.78	1.73	1.70	1.67	1.64	1.61	1.57	1.53
25	2.92	2.53	2.32	2.18	2.09	2.02	1.97	1.93	1.89	1.87	1.82	1.77	1.72	1.69	1.66	1.63	1.59	1.56	1.52
26	2.91	2.52	2.31	2.17	2.08	2.01	1.96	1.92	1.88	1.86	1.81	1.76	1.71	1.68	1.65	1.61	1.58	1.54	1.50
27	2.90	2.51	2.30	2.17	2.07	2.00	1.95	1.91	1.87	1.85	1.80	1.75	1.70	1.67	1.64	1.60	1.57	1.53	1.49
28	2.89	2.50	2.29	2.16	2.06	2.00	1.94	1.90	1.87	1.84	1.79	1.74	1.69	1.66	1.63	1.59	1.56	1.52	1.48
29	2.89	2.50	2.28	2.15	2.06	1.99	1.93	1.89	1.86	1.83	1.78	1.73	1.68	1.65	1.62	1.58	1.55	1.51	1.47
30	2.88	2.49	2.28	2.14	2.05	1.98	1.93	1.88	1.85	1.82	1.77	1.72	1.67	1.64	1.61	1.57	1.54	1.50	1.46
40	2.84	2.44	2.23	2.09	2.00	1.93	1.87	1.83	1.79	1.76	1.71	1.66	1.61	1.57	1.54	1.51	1.47	1.42	1.38
60	2.79	2.39	2.18	2.04	1.95	1.87	1.82	1.77	1.74	1.71	1.66	1.60	1.54	1.51	1.48	1.44	1.40	1.35	1.29
120	2.75	2.35	2.13	1.99	1.90	1.82	1.77	1.72	1.68	1.65	1.60	1.55	1.48	1.45	1.41	1.37	1.32	1.26	1.19
∞	2.71	2.30	2.08	1.94	1.85	1.77	1.72	1.67	1.63	1.60	1.55	1.49	1.42	1.38	1.34	1.30	1.24	1.17	1.00

ν_2 = degrees of freedom for denominator

Table 4 (continued)
Selected Percentiles of the F Distribution

$F_{95}(\nu_1,\nu_2)$ $\alpha = 0.05$

ν_1 = degrees of freedom for numerator

ν_2 \ ν_1	1	2	3	4	5	6	7	8	9	10	12	15	20	24	30	40	60	120	∞
1	161.4	199.5	215.7	224.6	230.2	234.0	236.8	238.9	240.5	241.9	243.9	245.9	248.0	249.1	250.1	251.1	252.2	253.3	254.3
2	18.51	19.00	19.16	19.25	19.30	19.33	19.35	19.37	19.38	19.40	19.41	19.43	19.45	19.45	19.46	19.47	19.48	19.49	19.50
3	10.13	9.55	9.28	9.12	9.01	8.94	8.89	8.85	8.81	8.79	8.74	8.70	8.66	8.64	8.62	8.59	8.57	8.55	8.53
4	7.71	6.94	6.59	6.39	6.26	6.16	6.09	6.04	6.00	5.96	5.91	5.86	5.80	5.77	5.75	5.72	5.69	5.66	5.63
5	6.61	5.79	5.41	5.19	5.05	4.95	4.88	4.82	4.77	4.74	4.68	4.62	4.56	4.53	4.50	4.46	4.43	4.40	4.36
6	5.99	5.14	4.76	4.53	4.39	4.28	4.21	4.15	4.10	4.06	4.00	3.94	3.87	3.84	3.81	3.77	3.74	3.70	3.67
7	5.59	4.74	4.35	4.12	3.97	3.87	3.79	3.73	3.68	3.64	3.57	3.51	3.44	3.41	3.38	3.34	3.30	3.27	3.23
8	5.32	4.46	4.07	3.84	3.69	3.58	3.50	3.44	3.39	3.35	3.28	3.22	3.15	3.12	3.08	3.04	3.01	2.97	2.93
9	5.12	4.26	3.86	3.63	3.48	3.37	3.29	3.23	3.18	3.14	3.07	3.01	2.94	2.90	2.86	2.83	2.79	2.75	2.71
10	4.96	4.10	3.71	3.48	3.33	3.22	3.14	3.07	3.02	2.98	2.91	2.85	2.77	2.74	2.70	2.66	2.62	2.58	2.54
11	4.84	3.98	3.59	3.36	3.20	3.09	3.01	2.95	2.90	2.85	2.79	2.72	2.65	2.61	2.57	2.53	2.49	2.45	2.40
12	4.75	3.89	3.49	3.26	3.11	3.00	2.91	2.85	2.80	2.75	2.69	2.62	2.54	2.51	2.47	2.43	2.38	2.34	2.30
13	4.67	3.81	3.41	3.18	3.03	2.92	2.83	2.77	2.71	2.67	2.60	2.53	2.46	2.42	2.38	2.34	2.30	2.25	2.21
14	4.60	3.74	3.34	3.11	2.96	2.85	2.76	2.70	2.65	2.60	2.53	2.46	2.39	2.35	2.31	2.27	2.22	2.18	2.13
15	4.54	3.68	3.29	3.06	2.90	2.79	2.71	2.64	2.59	2.54	2.48	2.40	2.33	2.29	2.25	2.20	2.16	2.11	2.07
16	4.49	3.63	3.24	3.01	2.85	2.74	2.66	2.59	2.54	2.49	2.42	2.35	2.28	2.24	2.19	2.15	2.11	2.06	2.01
17	4.45	3.59	3.20	2.96	2.81	2.70	2.61	2.55	2.49	2.45	2.38	2.31	2.23	2.19	2.15	2.10	2.06	2.01	1.96
18	4.41	3.55	3.16	2.93	2.77	2.66	2.58	2.51	2.46	2.41	2.34	2.27	2.19	2.15	2.11	2.06	2.02	1.97	1.92
19	4.38	3.52	3.13	2.90	2.74	2.63	2.54	2.48	2.42	2.38	2.31	2.23	2.16	2.11	2.07	2.03	1.98	1.93	1.88
20	4.35	3.49	3.10	2.87	2.71	2.60	2.51	2.45	2.39	2.35	2.28	2.20	2.12	2.08	2.04	1.99	1.95	1.90	1.84
21	4.32	3.47	3.07	2.84	2.68	2.57	2.49	2.42	2.37	2.32	2.25	2.18	2.10	2.05	2.01	1.96	1.92	1.87	1.81
22	4.30	3.44	3.05	2.82	2.66	2.55	2.46	2.40	2.34	2.30	2.23	2.15	2.07	2.03	1.98	1.94	1.89	1.84	1.78
23	4.28	3.42	3.03	2.80	2.64	2.53	2.44	2.37	2.32	2.27	2.20	2.13	2.05	2.01	1.96	1.91	1.86	1.81	1.76
24	4.26	3.40	3.01	2.78	2.62	2.51	2.42	2.36	2.30	2.25	2.18	2.11	2.03	1.98	1.94	1.89	1.84	1.79	1.73
25	4.24	3.39	2.99	2.76	2.60	2.49	2.40	2.34	2.28	2.24	2.16	2.09	2.01	1.96	1.92	1.87	1.82	1.77	1.71
26	4.23	3.37	2.98	2.74	2.59	2.47	2.39	2.32	2.27	2.22	2.15	2.07	1.99	1.95	1.90	1.85	1.80	1.75	1.69
27	4.21	3.35	2.96	2.73	2.57	2.46	2.37	2.31	2.25	2.20	2.13	2.06	1.97	1.93	1.88	1.84	1.79	1.73	1.67
28	4.20	3.34	2.95	2.71	2.56	2.45	2.36	2.29	2.24	2.19	2.12	2.04	1.96	1.91	1.87	1.82	1.77	1.71	1.65
29	4.18	3.33	2.93	2.70	2.55	2.43	2.35	2.28	2.22	2.18	2.10	2.03	1.94	1.90	1.85	1.81	1.75	1.70	1.64
30	4.17	3.32	2.92	2.69	2.53	2.42	2.33	2.27	2.21	2.16	2.09	2.01	1.93	1.89	1.84	1.79	1.74	1.68	1.62
40	4.08	3.23	2.84	2.61	2.45	2.34	2.25	2.18	2.12	2.08	2.00	1.92	1.84	1.79	1.74	1.69	1.64	1.58	1.51
60	4.00	3.15	2.76	2.53	2.37	2.25	2.17	2.10	2.04	1.99	1.92	1.84	1.75	1.70	1.65	1.59	1.53	1.47	1.39
120	3.92	3.07	2.68	2.45	2.29	2.17	2.09	2.02	1.96	1.91	1.83	1.75	1.66	1.61	1.55	1.50	1.43	1.35	1.25
∞	3.84	3.00	2.60	2.37	2.21	2.10	2.01	1.94	1.88	1.83	1.75	1.67	1.57	1.52	1.46	1.39	1.32	1.22	1.00

ν_2 = degrees of freedom for denominator

Table 4 (continued)
Selected Percentiles of the F Distribution

$$F_{.975}(\nu_1, \nu_2) \qquad \alpha = 0.025$$

ν_1 = degrees of freedom for numerator

ν_2	1	2	3	4	5	6	7	8	9	10	12	15	20	24	30	40	60	120	∞
1	647.8	799.5	864.2	899.6	921.8	937.1	948.2	956.7	963.3	968.6	976.7	984.9	993.1	997.2	1001	1006	1010	1014	1018
2	38.51	39.00	39.17	39.25	39.30	39.33	39.36	39.37	39.39	39.40	39.41	39.43	39.45	39.46	39.46	39.47	39.48	39.49	39.50
3	17.44	16.04	15.44	15.10	14.88	14.73	14.62	14.54	14.47	14.42	14.34	14.25	14.17	14.12	14.08	14.04	13.99	13.95	13.90
4	12.22	10.65	9.98	9.60	9.36	9.20	9.07	8.98	8.90	8.84	8.75	8.66	8.56	8.51	8.46	8.41	8.36	8.31	8.26
5	10.01	8.43	7.76	7.39	7.15	6.98	6.85	6.76	6.68	6.62	6.52	6.43	6.33	6.28	6.23	6.18	6.12	6.07	6.02
6	8.81	7.26	6.60	6.23	5.99	5.82	5.70	5.60	5.52	5.46	5.37	5.27	5.17	5.12	5.07	5.01	4.96	4.90	4.85
7	8.07	6.54	5.89	5.52	5.29	5.12	4.99	4.90	4.82	4.76	4.67	4.57	4.47	4.42	4.36	4.31	4.25	4.20	4.14
8	7.57	6.06	5.42	5.05	4.82	4.65	4.53	4.43	4.36	4.30	4.20	4.10	4.00	3.95	3.89	3.84	3.78	3.73	3.67
9	7.21	5.71	5.08	4.72	4.48	4.32	4.20	4.10	4.03	3.96	3.87	3.77	3.67	3.61	3.56	3.51	3.45	3.39	3.33
10	6.94	5.46	4.83	4.47	4.24	4.07	3.95	3.85	3.78	3.72	3.62	3.52	3.42	3.37	3.31	3.26	3.20	3.14	3.08
11	6.72	5.26	4.63	4.28	4.04	3.88	3.76	3.66	3.59	3.53	3.43	3.33	3.23	3.17	3.12	3.06	3.00	2.94	2.88
12	6.55	5.10	4.47	4.12	3.89	3.73	3.61	3.51	3.44	3.37	3.28	3.18	3.07	3.02	2.96	2.91	2.85	2.79	2.72
13	6.41	4.97	4.35	4.00	3.77	3.60	3.48	3.39	3.31	3.25	3.15	3.05	2.95	2.89	2.84	2.78	2.72	2.66	2.60
14	6.30	4.86	4.24	3.89	3.66	3.50	3.38	3.29	3.21	3.15	3.05	2.95	2.84	2.79	2.73	2.67	2.61	2.55	2.49
15	6.20	4.77	4.15	3.80	3.58	3.41	3.29	3.20	3.12	3.06	2.96	2.86	2.76	2.70	2.64	2.59	2.52	2.46	2.40
16	6.12	4.69	4.08	3.73	3.50	3.34	3.22	3.12	3.05	2.99	2.89	2.79	2.68	2.63	2.57	2.51	2.45	2.38	2.32
17	6.04	4.62	4.01	3.66	3.44	3.28	3.16	3.06	2.98	2.92	2.82	2.72	2.62	2.56	2.50	2.44	2.38	2.32	2.25
18	5.98	4.56	3.95	3.61	3.38	3.22	3.10	3.01	2.93	2.87	2.77	2.67	2.56	2.50	2.44	2.38	2.32	2.26	2.19
19	5.92	4.51	3.90	3.56	3.33	3.17	3.05	2.96	2.88	2.82	2.72	2.62	2.51	2.45	2.39	2.33	2.27	2.20	2.13
20	5.87	4.46	3.86	3.51	3.29	3.13	3.01	2.91	2.84	2.77	2.68	2.57	2.46	2.41	2.35	2.29	2.22	2.16	2.09
21	5.83	4.42	3.82	3.48	3.25	3.09	2.97	2.87	2.80	2.73	2.64	2.53	2.42	2.37	2.31	2.25	2.18	2.11	2.04
22	5.79	4.38	3.78	3.44	3.22	3.05	2.93	2.84	2.76	2.70	2.60	2.50	2.39	2.33	2.27	2.21	2.14	2.08	2.00
23	5.75	4.35	3.75	3.41	3.18	3.02	2.90	2.81	2.73	2.67	2.57	2.47	2.36	2.30	2.24	2.18	2.11	2.04	1.97
24	5.72	4.32	3.72	3.38	3.15	2.99	2.87	2.78	2.70	2.64	2.54	2.44	2.33	2.27	2.21	2.15	2.08	2.01	1.94
25	5.69	4.29	3.69	3.35	3.13	2.97	2.85	2.75	2.68	2.61	2.51	2.41	2.30	2.24	2.18	2.12	2.05	1.98	1.91
26	5.66	4.27	3.67	3.33	3.10	2.94	2.82	2.73	2.65	2.59	2.49	2.39	2.28	2.22	2.16	2.09	2.03	1.95	1.88
27	5.63	4.24	3.65	3.31	3.08	2.92	2.80	2.71	2.63	2.57	2.47	2.36	2.25	2.19	2.13	2.07	2.00	1.93	1.85
28	5.61	4.22	3.63	3.29	3.06	2.90	2.78	2.69	2.61	2.55	2.45	2.34	2.23	2.17	2.11	2.05	1.98	1.91	1.83
29	5.59	4.20	3.61	3.27	3.04	2.88	2.76	2.67	2.59	2.53	2.43	2.32	2.21	2.15	2.09	2.03	1.96	1.89	1.81
30	5.57	4.18	3.59	3.25	3.03	2.87	2.75	2.65	2.57	2.51	2.41	2.31	2.20	2.14	2.07	2.01	1.94	1.87	1.79
40	5.42	4.05	3.46	3.13	2.90	2.74	2.62	2.53	2.45	2.39	2.29	2.18	2.07	2.01	1.94	1.88	1.80	1.72	1.64
60	5.29	3.93	3.34	3.01	2.79	2.63	2.51	2.41	2.33	2.27	2.17	2.06	1.94	1.88	1.82	1.74	1.67	1.58	1.48
120	5.15	3.80	3.23	2.89	2.67	2.52	2.39	2.30	2.22	2.16	2.05	1.94	1.82	1.76	1.69	1.61	1.53	1.43	1.31
∞	5.02	3.69	3.12	2.79	2.57	2.41	2.29	2.19	2.11	2.05	1.94	1.83	1.71	1.64	1.57	1.48	1.39	1.27	1.00

ν_2 = degrees of freedom for denominator

Table 4 (continued)
Selected Percentiles of the F Distribution

$F_{.99}(\nu_1, \nu_2)$ $\alpha = 0.01$

ν_1 = degrees of freedom for numerator

ν_2 \ ν_1	1	2	3	4	5	6	7	8	9	10	12	15	20	24	30	40	60	120	∞
1	4052	4999.5	5403	5625	5764	5859	5928	5982	6022	6056	6106	6157	6209	6235	6261	6287	6313	6339	6366
2	98.50	99.00	99.17	99.25	99.30	99.33	99.36	99.37	99.39	99.40	99.42	99.43	99.45	99.46	99.47	99.47	99.48	99.49	99.50
3	34.12	30.82	29.46	28.71	28.24	27.91	27.67	27.49	27.35	27.23	27.05	26.87	26.69	26.60	26.50	26.41	26.32	26.22	26.13
4	21.20	18.00	16.69	15.98	15.52	15.21	14.98	14.80	14.66	14.55	14.37	14.20	14.02	13.93	13.84	13.75	13.65	13.56	13.46
5	16.26	13.27	12.06	11.39	10.97	10.67	10.46	10.29	10.16	10.05	9.89	9.72	9.55	9.47	9.38	9.29	9.20	9.11	9.02
6	13.75	10.92	9.78	9.15	8.75	8.47	8.26	8.10	7.98	7.87	7.72	7.56	7.40	7.31	7.23	7.14	7.06	6.97	6.88
7	12.25	9.55	8.45	7.85	7.46	7.19	6.99	6.84	6.72	6.62	6.47	6.31	6.16	6.07	5.99	5.91	5.82	5.74	5.65
8	11.26	8.65	7.59	7.01	6.63	6.37	6.18	6.03	5.91	5.81	5.67	5.52	5.36	5.28	5.20	5.12	5.03	4.95	4.86
9	10.56	8.02	6.99	6.42	6.06	5.80	5.61	5.47	5.35	5.26	5.11	4.96	4.81	4.73	4.65	4.57	4.48	4.40	4.31
10	10.04	7.56	6.55	5.99	5.64	5.39	5.20	5.06	4.94	4.85	4.71	4.56	4.41	4.33	4.25	4.17	4.08	4.00	3.91
11	9.65	7.21	6.22	5.67	5.32	5.07	4.89	4.74	4.63	4.54	4.40	4.25	4.10	4.02	3.94	3.86	3.78	3.69	3.60
12	9.33	6.93	5.95	5.41	5.06	4.82	4.64	4.50	4.39	4.30	4.16	4.01	3.86	3.78	3.70	3.62	3.54	3.45	3.36
13	9.07	6.70	5.74	5.21	4.86	4.62	4.44	4.30	4.19	4.10	3.96	3.82	3.66	3.59	3.51	3.43	3.34	3.25	3.17
14	8.86	6.51	5.56	5.04	4.69	4.46	4.28	4.14	4.03	3.94	3.80	3.66	3.51	3.43	3.35	3.27	3.18	3.09	3.00
15	8.68	6.36	5.42	4.89	4.56	4.32	4.14	4.00	3.89	3.80	3.67	3.52	3.37	3.29	3.21	3.13	3.05	2.96	2.87
16	8.53	6.23	5.29	4.77	4.44	4.20	4.03	3.89	3.78	3.69	3.55	3.41	3.26	3.18	3.10	3.02	2.93	2.84	2.75
17	8.40	6.11	5.18	4.67	4.34	4.10	3.93	3.79	3.68	3.59	3.46	3.31	3.16	3.08	3.00	2.92	2.83	2.75	2.65
18	8.29	6.01	5.09	4.58	4.25	4.01	3.84	3.71	3.60	3.51	3.37	3.23	3.08	3.00	2.92	2.84	2.75	2.66	2.57
19	8.18	5.93	5.01	4.50	4.17	3.94	3.77	3.63	3.52	3.43	3.30	3.15	3.00	2.92	2.84	2.76	2.67	2.58	2.49
20	8.10	5.85	4.94	4.43	4.10	3.87	3.70	3.56	3.46	3.37	3.23	3.09	2.94	2.86	2.78	2.69	2.61	2.52	2.42
21	8.02	5.78	4.87	4.37	4.04	3.81	3.64	3.51	3.40	3.31	3.17	3.03	2.88	2.80	2.72	2.64	2.55	2.46	2.36
22	7.95	5.72	4.82	4.31	3.99	3.76	3.59	3.45	3.35	3.26	3.12	2.98	2.83	2.75	2.67	2.58	2.50	2.40	2.31
23	7.88	5.66	4.76	4.26	3.94	3.71	3.54	3.41	3.30	3.21	3.07	2.93	2.78	2.70	2.62	2.54	2.45	2.35	2.26
24	7.82	5.61	4.72	4.22	3.90	3.67	3.50	3.36	3.26	3.17	3.03	2.89	2.74	2.66	2.58	2.49	2.40	2.31	2.21
25	7.77	5.57	4.68	4.18	3.85	3.63	3.46	3.32	3.22	3.13	2.99	2.85	2.70	2.62	2.54	2.45	2.36	2.27	2.17
26	7.72	5.53	4.64	4.14	3.82	3.59	3.42	3.29	3.18	3.09	2.96	2.81	2.66	2.58	2.50	2.42	2.33	2.23	2.13
27	7.68	5.49	4.60	4.11	3.78	3.56	3.39	3.26	3.15	3.06	2.93	2.78	2.63	2.55	2.47	2.38	2.29	2.20	2.10
28	7.64	5.45	4.57	4.07	3.75	3.53	3.36	3.23	3.12	3.03	2.90	2.75	2.60	2.52	2.44	2.35	2.26	2.17	2.06
29	7.60	5.42	4.54	4.04	3.73	3.50	3.33	3.20	3.09	3.00	2.87	2.73	2.57	2.49	2.41	2.33	2.23	2.14	2.03
30	7.56	5.39	4.51	4.02	3.70	3.47	3.30	3.17	3.07	2.98	2.84	2.70	2.55	2.47	2.39	2.30	2.21	2.11	2.01
40	7.31	5.18	4.31	3.83	3.51	3.29	3.12	2.99	2.89	2.80	2.66	2.52	2.37	2.29	2.20	2.11	2.02	1.92	1.80
60	7.08	4.98	4.13	3.65	3.34	3.12	2.95	2.82	2.72	2.63	2.50	2.35	2.20	2.12	2.03	1.94	1.84	1.73	1.60
120	6.85	4.79	3.95	3.48	3.17	2.96	2.79	2.66	2.56	2.47	2.34	2.19	2.03	1.95	1.86	1.76	1.66	1.53	1.38
∞	6.63	4.61	3.78	3.32	3.02	2.80	2.64	2.51	2.41	2.32	2.18	2.04	1.88	1.79	1.70	1.59	1.47	1.32	1.00

ν_2 = degrees of freedom for denominator

Glossary

Absolute Precision
Degree of precision in an estimate of a parameter expressed as within plus or minus so many units.

Accuracy
Criterion used to evaluate a research report according to whether the reasoning in the report is logical and the information correct.

Administrative Control
Term applied to studies relying on questionnaires and referring to the speed, cost, and control of the replies afforded by the mode of administration.

Analysis of Selected Cases
Intensive study of selected examples of the phenomenon of interest.

Analysis of Variance (ANOVA)
Statistical test employed with interval data to determine if $k(k \geq 2)$ samples came from populations with equal means.

Area Sampling
Form of cluster sampling in which areas (for example, census tracts, blocks) serve as the primary sampling units. The population is divided into mutually exclusive and exhaustive areas using maps, and a random sample of areas is selected. If all the households in the selected areas are used in the study, it is

one-stage area sampling, while if the areas themselves are subsampled with respect to households, the procedure is two-stage area sampling.

Attitudes/Opinions
Some preference, liking, or conviction with regard to a specific object or idea; a predisposition to act.

Awareness/Knowledge
Insight into or understanding of facts about some object or phenomenon.

Bar Chart
Chart in which the relative lengths of the bars show relative amounts of variables or objects.

Bayes' Rule
Formal mechanism for revising prior probabilities in the light of new information.

Bayesian Probability
Probability based on a person's subjective or personal judgments and experience.

Behavior
What subjects have done or are doing.

Blunder
Error that arises when editing, coding, key-punching, or tabulating the data.

Branching Questions
A technique used to direct respondents to different places in a questionnaire based on their response to the question at hand.

Brand-Switching Matrix
Two-way table that indicates which brands a sample of people purchased in one period and which brands they purchased in a subsequent period, thus highlighting the switches occurring among and between brands as well as the number of persons that purchased the same brand in both periods.

Causal Research
Research design in which the major emphasis is on determining a cause and effect relationship.

Census
A complete canvass of a population.

Central-Limit Theorem
Theorem that holds that if simple random samples of size n are drawn from a parent population with mean μ and variance σ^2, then when n is large, the sample mean $\bar{x}$ will be approximately normally distributed with mean equal to μ and variance equal to σ^2/n. The approximation will become more and more accurate as n becomes larger.

Central Office Edit
Thorough and exacting scrutiny and correction of completed data collection forms, including a decision about what to do with the data.

Cheating
Nonsampling error that arises because interviewers do not actually conduct interviews among designated respondents but instead fabricate some or all of the answers.

Chi-square Goodness of Fit Test
Statistical test to determine whether some observed pattern of frequencies corresponds to an expected pattern.

Clarity
Criterion used to evaluate a research report; specifically, whether the phrasing in the report is precise.

Classical Probability
Probability determined by the relative frequency with which an event occurs when an experiment is repeated under controlled conditions.

Cluster Analysis
Body of techniques concerned with developing natural groupings of objects based on the relationships of the p variables describing the objects.

Cluster Sample
A probability sample distinguished by a two-step procedure in which (1) the parent population is divided into mutually exclusive and exhaustive subsets, and (2) a random sample of subsets is selected. If the investigator then uses all of the population elements in the selected subsets for the sample, the procedure is one-stage cluster sampling; if a sample of elements is selected probabilistically from the subsets, the procedure is two-stage cluster sampling.

Coding
Technical procedure by which data are categorized; it involves specifying the alternative categories or classes into which the responses are to be placed and assigning code numbers to the classes.

Coefficient of Concordance
Statistic used with ordinal data to measure the extent of association among $k(k \geq 2)$ variables.

Coefficient of Determination
Term used in regression analysis to refer to the relative proportion of the total variation in the criterion variable that can be explained or accounted for by the fitted regression equation.

Coefficient of Multiple Correlation
In multiple regression analysis, the square root of the coefficient of multiple determination.

Coefficient of Multiple Determination
In multiple regression analysis, the proportion of variation in the criterion variable that is accounted for by the covariation in the predictor variables.

Coefficient of Partial Correlation
In multiple regression analysis, the square root of the coefficient of partial determination.

Coefficient of Partial Determination
Quantity that results from a multiple regression analysis, which indicates the proportion of variation in the criterion variable not accounted for by the earlier variables that is accounted for by the addition of a new variable into the regression equation.

Coefficient of Partial (or Net) Regression
Quantity resulting from a multiple regression analysis, which indicates the average change in the criterion

variable per unit change in a predictor variable, holding all other predictor variables constant; the interpretation only applies when the predictor variables are independent, as required for a valid application of the multiple regression model.

Cohort
The aggregate of individuals who experience the same event within the same time interval.

Communality
Quantity resulting from a factor analysis that expresses the proportion of the variance of a variable extracted by m factors, where m can vary from one to the total number of variables; the communalities help determine how many factors should be retained in a solution.

Communication
Method of data collection involving questioning of respondents to secure the desired information using a data collection instrument called a questionnaire.

Comparative Rating Scale
Scale requiring subjects to make their ratings as a series of relative judgments or comparisons rather than as independent assessments.

Completely Randomized Design
Experimental design in which the experimental treatments are assigned to the test units completely at random.

Completeness
Criterion used to evaluate a research report; specifically, whether the report provides all the information readers need in a language they understand.

Completeness Rate (C)
Measure used to evaluate and compare interviewers with respect to their ability to secure needed information from contacted

respondents; the completeness rate measures the proportion of complete contacts by interviewer.

Conciseness
Criterion used to evaluate a research report; specifically, whether the writing in the report is crisp and direct.

Conditional Association
Association existing between two variables when the levels of one or more other variables are considered in the analysis; the other variables are called control variables.

Conditional Opportunity Loss
Measure of the opportunity foregone if any decision other than the optimal one for a given state of nature is made; it is calculated from the payoff table by subtracting each payoff entry from the entry corresponding to the optimal act for each possible state of nature.

Conditional Probability
Probability that is assigned to an Event A when it is known that another Event B has occurred or that would be assigned to A if it were known that B had occurred.

Confusion Matrix
Device used in discriminant analysis to assess the adequacy of the discriminant function or functions; the confusion matrix is essentially a cross-classification table, in which the variables of cross classification are the actual group membership categories and the predicted group membership categories and the entries are the number of observations falling into each cell.

Conjoint Analysis
Technique in which respondents' utilities or valuations of attributes are inferred from the preferences they express for various combinations of these attributes.

Constant Sum Method
A type of comparative rating scale in which an individual is instructed to divide some given sum among two or more attributes on the basis of their importance to him or her.

Constitutive (Conceptual) Definition
Definition in which a given construct is defined in terms of other constructs in the set, sometimes in the form of an equation that expresses the relationship among them.

Construct Validation
Approach to validating a measure by determining what construct, concept, or trait the instrument is in fact measuring.

Contact Rate (K)
Measure used to evaluate and compare the effectiveness of interviewers in making contact with designated respondents. K = number of sample units contacted/total number of sample units approached.

Content Validity
Approach to validating a measure by determining the adequacy with which the domain of the characteristic is captured by the measure; it is sometimes called face validity.

Contingency Coefficient
Statistic used to measure the extent of association between two nominally scaled attributes.

Contingency Table
Statistical test employing the χ^2 statistic that is used to determine whether the variables in a cross-classification analysis are independent.

Controlled Test Market
A market in which an entire marketing test program is conducted by an outside service.

Also called a forced distribution test market.

Convenience Sample
Nonprobability sample sometimes called an accidental sample because those included in the sample enter by accident, in that they just happen to be where the study is being conducted when it is being conducted.

Convergent Validity
Confirmation of the existence of a construct determined by the correlations exhibited by independent measures of the construct.

Cophenetic Value
Level at which a pair of objects or classes are actually linked in cluster analyses.

Correlation Analysis
Statistical technique used to measure the closeness of the linear relationship between two or more intervally scaled variables.

Criteria of Simple Structure
Set of criteria employed in factor analysis to depict the conditions a factor solution should satisfy so that the factors are most interpretable.

Cross-Sectional Study
Investigation involving a sample of elements selected from the population of interest at a single point in time.

Cross Tabulation
Count of the number of cases that fall into each of several categories when the categories are based on two or more variables considered simultaneously.

Cumulative Distribution Function
Function that shows the number of cases having a value less than or equal to a specified quantity; the function is generated by connecting

the points representing the given combinations of X's (values and Y's (cumulative frequencies) with straight lines.

Cutting Score
Term used in discriminant analysis to indicate the score that divides the groups with respect to their respective discriminant scores; if the object's score is above the cutting score, the object is assigned to one group, while it is assigned to the other group if its score is below the cutting score.

Data System
The part of a decision support system that includes the processes used to capture and the methods used to store data coming from a number of external and internal sources.

Decision Support System (DSS)
A coordinated collection of data, system tools, and techniques with supporting software and hardware by which an organization gathers and interprets relevant information from business and environment and turns it into a basis for marketing action.

Decision Tree
Decision flow diagram in which the problem is structured in chronological order, typically with small squares indicating decision forks and small circles chance forks.

Dendrogram
Treelike device employed to interpret the output of a cluster analysis that indicates the groups of objects forming at various similarity levels.

Dependence Analysis
Problem in multivariate analysis in which one (or more) of the variables is to be considered separately and the emphasis is on investigating how it (or they)

depends (depend) upon the other variates.

Depth Interview
Unstructured personal interview in which the interviewer attempts to get subjects to talk freely and to express their true feelings.

Derived Population
Population of all possible distinguishable samples that could be drawn from a parent population under a specific sampling plan.

Descriptive Research
Research design in which the major emphasis is on determining the frequency with which something occurs or the extent to which two variables covary.

Determinant Attribute
Characteristic of an object that is important to the individual and that also differentiates one object from another.

Dialog System
The part of a decision support system that permits users to explore the data bases by employing the system models to produce reports that satisfy their particular information needs. Also called "language systems."

Dichotomous Question
Fixed-alternative question in which respondents are asked to indicate which of two alternative responses most closely corresponds to their position on a subject

Discriminant Analysis
Statistical technique employed to model the relationship between a dichotomous or multichotomous criterion variable and a set of p predictor variables.

Discriminant Validity
Criterion imposed on a measure of a construct requiring that it not correlate too highly with measures from which it is supposed to differ.

Disguise
Amount of knowledge concerning the purpose of a study communicated to the respondent by the data-collection method. An undisguised questionnaire, for example, is one in which the purpose of the research is obvious from the questions posed, while a disguised questionnaire attempts to hide the purpose of the study.

Disproportionate Stratified Sampling
Stratified sample in which the individual strata or subsets are sampled in relation to both their size and their variability; strata exhibiting more variability are sampled more than proportionately to their relative size, while those that are very homogeneous are sampled less than proportionately.

Double-Barreled Question
A question that calls for two responses and thereby creates confusion for the respondent.

Dual Questioning
Procedure used to assess determinant attributes; the procedure entails asking respondents two questions with respect to each attribute of an object, one to assess how important the attribute is to them and the other to assess their perceptions of how competing objects differ with respect to the attribute.

Dummy (or Binary) Variable
Variable that is given one of two values, 0 or 1, and that is used to provide a numerical representation for attributes or characteristics that are not essentially quantitative.

Editing
Inspection and correction, if necessary, of each questionnaire or observation form.

Element
Term used in sampling to refer to the objects on which measurements

are to be taken, such as individuals, households, business firms, or other institutions.

Equal-Appearing Intervals
Self-report technique for attitude measurement in which subjects are asked to indicate those statements in a larger list of statements (typically 20–22) with which they agree and disagree; subjects' attitude scores are the average score of the scale values of the statements with which they agree.

Equivalence
Measure of reliability that is applied to both single instruments and measurement situations. When applied to instruments, the equivalence measure of reliability is the internal consistency or internal homogeneity of the set of items forming the scale; when applied to measurement situations, the equivalence measure of reliability focuses on whether different observers or different instruments used to measure the same individuals or objects at the same point in time yield consistent results.

Expected Opportunity Loss
Number given by the product of the probability of a wrong decision times the amount lost by making the incorrect choice.

Expected Value
Value resulting from multiplying each consequence by the probability of that consequence occurring and summing the products.

Expected Value of Perfect Information
Difference between the expected value under certainty and the expected value of the optimal act under uncertainty.

Expected Value of a Research Procedure
Value determined by multiplying the probability of obtaining the kth research result by the expected value of the preferred decision given the kth research result and summing the products.

Expected Value under Certainty
Value derived by multiplying the consequence associated with the optimal act under each possible state of nature by the probability associated with that state of nature and summing the products.

Experience Survey
Interviews with people knowledgeable about the general subject being investigated.

Experiment
Scientific investigation in which an investigator manipulates and controls one or more independent variables and observes the dependent variable for variation concomitant to the manipulation of the independent variables.

Experimental Design
Research investigation in which the investigator has direct control over at least one independent variable and manipulates at least one independent variable.

Experimental Mortality
Experimental condition in which test units are lost during the course of an experiment.

Exploratory Research
Research design in which the major emphasis is on gaining ideas and insights; it is particularly helpful in breaking broad, vague problem statements into smaller, more precise subproblem statements.

External Data
Data that originate outside the organization for which the research is being done.

External Validity
One criterion by which an experiment is evaluated; the extent, to what populations and settings, to which the observed experimental effect can be generalized.

Factor
Linear combination of variables.

Factor Analysis
Body of techniques concerned with the study of interrelationships among a set of variables, none of which is given the special status of a criterion variable.

Factor Loading
Quantity that results from a factor analysis and that indicates the correlation between a variable and a factor.

Factorial Design
Experimental design that is used when the effects of two or more variables are being simultaneously studied; each level of each factor is used with each level of each other factor.

Field Edit
Preliminary edit, typically conducted by a field supervisor, which is designed to detect the most glaring omissions and inaccuracies in a completed data collection instrument.

Field Error
Nonsampling error that arises during the actual collection of the data.

Field Experiment
Research study in a realistic situation in which one or more independent variables are manipulated by the experimenter

under as carefully controlled conditions as the situation will permit.

Field Study
In-depth investigation of a few cases typical of the target population, emphasizing the interrelationship of a number of factors.

Fixed-Alternative Questions
Questions in which the responses are limited to stated alternatives.

Fixed Sample
Sample for which size is determined *a priori* and needed information is collected from the designated elements.

Focused Group Interview
Personal interview conducted among a small number of individuals simultaneously; the interview relies more on group discussion than on a series of directed questions to generate data.

Frequency Polygon
Figure obtained from a histogram by connecting the midpoints of the bars of the histogram with straight lines.

Full Profile
An approach to collecting respondents' judgments in a conjoint analysis in which each stimulus is made up of a combination of each of the attributes.

Funnel Approach
An approach to question sequencing that gets its name from its shape, starting with broad questions and progressively narrowing the scope.

Fusion Coefficients
In linkage cluster analysis, the numerical values at which various cases merge to form clusters. Also called amalgamation coefficients,

they can be read directly from a dendrogram.

Galvanometer
Device used to measure the emotion induced by exposure to a particular stimulus by recording changes in the electrical resistance of the skin associated with the minute degree of sweating that accompanies emotional arousal; in marketing research the stimulus is often specific advertising copy.

Goodness of Fit
Statistical test employing χ^2, to determine whether some observed pattern of frequencies corresponds to an expected pattern.

Graphic Rating Scale
Scale in which individuals indicate their ratings of an attribute by placing a check at the appropriate point on a line that runs from one extreme of the attribute to the other.

Halo Effect
Problem that arises in data collection when there is carry-over from one judgment to another.

Histogram
Form of bar chart on which the values of the variable are placed along the abscissa or X axis and the absolute frequency or relative frequency of occurrence of the values is indicated along the Y axis or ordinate.

History
Specific events external to an experiment, but occurring at the same time, which may affect the criterion or response variable.

Hypothesis
A statement that specifies how two or more measurable variables are related.

Implicit Alternative
An alternative answer to a question that is not expressed in the options.

Implied Assumption
A problem that occurs when a question is not framed so as to explicitly state the consequences, and thus it elicits different responses from individuals who *assume* different consequences.

Index of Predictive Association
A statistic used to measure the extent of association between two nominally scaled attributes.

Information Control
Term applied to studies using questionnaires and concerning the amount and accuracy of the information that can be obtained from respondents.

Instrument Variation
Any and all changes in the measuring device used in an experiment that might account for differences in two or more measurements.

Intention
Anticipated or planned future behavior.

Interdependence Analysis
Problem in multivariate analysis to determine the relationship of a set of variates among themselves; no one variate is selected as special in the sense of the dependent variable.

Internal Data
Data that originate within the organization for which the research is being done.

Internal Validity
One criterion by which an experiment is evaluated; the criterion focuses on obtaining evidence demonstrating that the variation in the criterion variable was the result of exposure to the treatment or experimental variable.

Interval Scale
Measurement in which the assigned numbers legitimately allow the

comparison of the size of the differences among and between members.

Interviewer–Interviewee Interaction Model
Model that attempts to describe how an interviewer and a respondent could be expected to respond to each other during the course of an interview; it is helpful in suggesting techniques by which response errors can be potentially reduced.

Item Nonresponse
Source of nonsampling error that arises when a respondent agrees to an interview but refuses or is unable to answer specific questions.

Itemized Rating Scale
Scale distinguished by the fact that individuals must indicate their ratings of an attribute or object by selecting one from among a limited number of categories that best describes their position on the attribute or object.

Judgment Sample
Nonprobability sample that is often called a purposive sample; the sample elements are handpicked because they are expected to serve the research purpose.

Kolmogorov–Smirnov Test
Statistical test employed with ordinal data to determine whether some observed pattern of frequencies corresponds to some pattern; also whether two independent samples have been drawn from the same population or from populations with the same distribution.

Laboratory Experiment
Research investigation in which investigators create a situation with exact conditions so as to control some, and manipulate other, variables.

Latin-Square Design
Experimental design in which (1) the number of categories for each extraneous variable we wish to control is equal to the number of treatments, and (2) each treatment is randomly assigned to categories according to a specific pattern. The Latin-square design is appropriate where there are two extraneous factors to be explicitly controlled.

Leading Question
A question framed so as to give the respondent a clue as to how he or she should answer.

Line Chart
Two-dimensional chart constructed on graph paper in which the X axis represents one variable (typically time) and the Y axis another variable.

Literature Search
Search of statistics, trade journal articles, other articles, magazines, newspapers, and books for data or insight into the problem at hand.

Longitudinal Study
Investigation involving a fixed sample of elements that is measured repeatedly through time.

Mail Questionnaire
Questionnaire administered by mail to designated respondents under an accompanying cover letter and its return, by mail, by the subject to the research organization.

Market Test
Controlled experiment, done in a limited but carefully selected sector of the marketplace; its aim is to predict the sales or profit consequences, either in absolute or relative terms, of one or more proposed marketing actions.

Marketing Information System (MIS)
Set of procedures and methods for the regular, planned collection, analysis, and presentation of information for use in making marketing decisions.

Marketing Research
Systematic gathering, recording, and analyzing of data about problems relating to the marketing of goods and services.

Maturation
Processes operating within the test units in an experiment as a function of the passage of time *per se*.

Maximum Chance Criterion
Decision rule used in discriminant analysis to develop a comparison yardstick for assessing the predictive accuracy of the discriminant function; the maximum chance criterion holds that an object chosen at random should be classified as belonging to the largest size group.

Measurement
Rules for assigning numbers to objects to represent quantities of attributes.

Method Variance
The variation in scores attributable to the method of data collection.

Model System
The part of a decision support system that includes all the routines that allow the user to manipulate the data so as to conduct the kind of analysis the individual desires.

Motive
Need, want, drive, wish, desire, or impulse, or any inner state that energizes, activates, or moves and that directs or channels behavior toward goals.

Multichotomous Question
Fixed-alternative question in which respondents are asked to choose the alternative that most closely corresponds to their position on the subject.

Multicollinearity
Condition said to be present in a multiple-regression analysis when the predictor variables are not independent as required but are correlated among themselves.

Multidimensional Scaling
Approach to measurement in which people's perceptions of the similarity of objects and their preferences among the objects are measured, and these relationships are plotted in a multidimensional space.

Multivariate
Problem of analysis in which there are two or more measures of each of *n* sample objects, and the variables are to be analyzed simultaneously.

Nominal Scale
Measurement in which numbers are simply assigned to objects or classes of objects solely for the purpose of identification.

Noncoverage Error
Nonsampling error that arises because of a failure to include some units, or entire sections, of the defined survey population in the actual sampling frame.

Nonobservation Error
Nonsampling error that arises because of nonresponse from some elements designated for inclusion in the sample.

Nonparametric Tests
Class of statistical tests, also known as distribution-free tests, that are applicable when the data reflect nominal or ordinal measurement or when the data reflect interval measurement but the assumptions required for the appropriate parametric test are not satisfied.

Nonprobability Sample
Sample that relies on personal judgment somewhere in the element selection process and therefore prohibits estimating the probability that any population element will be included in the sample.

Nonresponse Error
Nonsampling error that represents a failure to obtain information from some elements of the population that were selected and designated for the sample.

Nonsampling Errors
Errors that arise in research that are not due to sampling; nonsampling errors can occur because of errors in conception, logic, misinterpretation of replies, statistics, arithmetic and errors in tabulating or coding, or in reporting the results.

Not-at-Home
Source of nonsampling error that arises when replies are not secured from some designated sampling units because the respondents are not at home when the interviewer calls.

Observation
Method of data collection in which the situation of interest is watched and the relevant facts, actions, or behaviors recorded.

Observation Error
Nonsampling error that arises because inaccurate information is secured from the sample elements or because errors are introduced in the processing of the data or in reporting the findings.

Office Error
Nonsampling error that arises in the processing of the data because of errors in editing, coding, tabulation, or in some other part of the analysis.

Open-Ended Question
Question characterized by the condition that respondents are free to reply in their own words rather than being limited to choosing from among a set of alternatives.

Operational Definition
Definition of a construct that describes the operations to be carried out in order for the construct to be measured empirically.

Ordinal Scale
Measurement in which numbers are assigned to data on the basis of some order (for example, more than, greater than) of the objects.

Outlier
Observation so different in magnitude from the rest of the observations that the analyst chooses to treat it as a special case.

Overcoverage Error
Nonsampling error that arises because of the duplication of elements in the list of sampling units.

Pairwise Procedure
A method of structuring the stimuli that respondents need to evaluate in a conjoint analysis that treats two attributes at a time but considers all possible pairs.

Panel (Omnibus)
Fixed sample of respondents who are measured repeatedly over time but on variables that change from measurement to measurement.

Panel (True)
Fixed sample of respondents who are measured repeatedly over time with respect to the same variables.

Parameter
Fixed characteristic or measure of a parent or target population.

Parametric Tests
Class of statistical tests used when the variable (variables) is (are)

measured on at least an interval scale.

Part-worth Function
Function that describes the relationship between the perceived utilities associated with various levels of an attribute and the objective or physical levels of the attributes (for example, utilities associated with various prices).

Payoff Table
Table containing three elements: alternatives, states of nature, and consequences of each alternative under each state of nature.

Performance of Objective Tasks
Method of assessing attitudes that rests on the presumption that a subject's performance of a specific asigned task (for example, memorizing a number of facts) will depend on the person's attitude.

Personal Interview
Direct, face-to-face conversation between a representative of the research organization (the interviewer) and a respondent or interviewee.

Personality
Normal patterns of behavior exhibited by an individual; the attributes, traits, and mannerisms that distinguish one individual from another.

Personal (or Subjective) Probability
See Bayesian Probability.

Physiological Reaction Technique
Method of assessing attitudes in which the researcher monitors the subject's response, by electrical or mechanical means, to the controlled introduction of some stimuli.

Pictogram
Bar chart in which pictures represent amounts — for example, piles of dollars for income,

pictures of cars for automobile production, people in a row for population.

Pie Chart
Circle, representing a total quantity, divided into sectors, with each sector showing the size of the segment in relation to that total.

Plus-One Dialing
Technique used in studies employing telephone interviews in which a single randomly determined digit is added to numbers selected from the telephone directory.

Population
Totality of cases that conforms to some designated specifications.

Power
Function associated with a statistical test indicating the probability of correctly rejecting a false null hypothesis.

Pragmatic Validity
Approach to validation of a measure based on the usefulness of the measuring instrument as a predictor of some other characteristic or behavior of the individual; it is sometimes called predictive validity or criterion related validity.

Precision
Desired size of the estimating interval when the problem is one of estimating a population parameter; the notion of degree of precision is useful in determining sample size.

Pretest
Use of a questionnaire (observation form) on a trial basis in a small pilot study to determine how well the questionnaire (observation form) works.

Primary Data
Information collected specifically for the purpose of the investigation at hand.

Primary Source
Originating source of secondary data.

Probability-Proportional-to-Size Sampling
Form of cluster sampling in which a fixed number of second-stage units is selected from each first-stage cluster. The probabilities associated with the selection of each cluster are in turn variable because they are directly related to the relative sizes of each cluster.

Probability Sample
Sample in which each population element has a known, nonzero chance of being included in the sample.

Projective Method
Term used to describe questionnaires containing ambiguous stimuli that force subjects to rely on their own emotions, needs, motivations, attitudes, and values in framing a response.

Proportional Chance Criterion
Decision rule used in discriminant analysis to develop a comparison yardstick for assessing the predictive accuracy of the discriminant function; the proportional chance criterion holds that the percentage of objects likely to be classified correctly by chance alone equals $\alpha^2 + (1 - \alpha)^2$ where α equals the proportion of objects in Group 1 and $1 - \alpha$ the proportion of objects in Group 2.

Proportionate Stratified Sampling
Stratified sample in which the number of observations in the total sample is allocated among the strata in proportion to the relative number of elements in each stratum in the population.

Psychographic Analysis
Technique that investigates how people live, what interests them,

and what they like; it is also called lifestyle or AIO analysis since it relies on a number of statements about a person's Activities, Interests, and Opinions.

Q-Sort Technique
General methodology for gathering data and processing the collected information; the subjects are assigned the task of sorting a number of statements by placing a specific number of statements in each sorting category; the emphases are on determining the relative ranking of stimuli by individuals and in deriving clusters of individuals who display similar preference orderings of stimuli.

Quota Sample
Nonprobability sample chosen in such a way that the proportion of sample elements possessing a certain characteristic is approximately the same as the proportion of the elements with the characteristic in the population; each field worker is assigned a quota that specifies the characteristics of the people he or she is to contact.

Random-Digit Dialing
Technique used in studies employing telephone interviews in which the numbers to be called are randomly generated.

Random Error
Error in measurement due to the transient aspects of the person or measurement situation.

Randomized-Block Design
Experimental design in which: (1) the test units are divided into blocks or homogeneous groups using some external criterion, and (2) the objects in each block are randomly assigned to treatment conditions. The randomized-block design is typically employed when there is one extraneous influence to be explicitly controlled.

Randomized Response Model
Interviewing technique in which potentially embarrassing and relatively innocuous questions are paired, and the question the respondent answers is randomly determined.

Ratio Scale
Measurement that has a natural or absolute zero and therefore allows the comparison of absolute magnitudes of the numbers.

Recall Loss
A type of error caused by a respondent forgetting that an event happened at all.

Refusals
Nonsampling error that arises because some designated respondents refuse to participate in the study.

Regression Analysis
Statistical technique used to derive an equation that relates a single criterion variable to one or more predictor variables.

Relative Precision
Degree of precision desired in an estimate of a parameter is expressed relative to the level of the estimate of the parameter.

Reliability
Similarity of results provided by independent but comparable measures of the same object, trait, or construct.

Research Design
Framework or plan for a study that guides the collection and analysis of the data.

Research Process
Sequence of steps in the design and implementation of a research study, including problem formulation, determination of sources of information and research

design, determination of data collection method and design of data collection forms, design of the sample and collection of the data, analysis and interpretation of the data, and the research report.

Response Latency
The amount of time a respondent deliberates before answering a question.

Response Rate (R)
Measure used to evaluate and compare interviewers with respect to their ability to induce contacted respondents to participate in the study; R = number of interviews/number of contacts.

Sample
Selection of a subset of elements from a larger group of objects.

Sample Survey
Cross-sectional study in which the sample is selected to be representative of the target population and in which the emphasis is on the generation of summary statistics such as averages and percentages. Also called a field survey.

Sampling Control
Term applied to studies relying on questionnaires and concerning the researcher's dual abilities to direct the inquiry to a designated respondent and to secure the desired cooperation from that respondent.

Sampling Distribution
Distribution of values of some statistic calculated for each possible distinguishable sample that could be drawn from a parent population under a specific sampling plan.

Sampling Error
Difference between the observed values of a variable and the long-run average of the observed values in repetitions of the measurement.

Sampling Frame
List of sampling units from which a sample will be drawn; the list could consist of geographic areas, institutions, individuals, or other units.

Sampling Units
Nonoverlapping collections of elements from the population.

Scanner
Electronic device that automatically reads imprinted Universal Product Codes as the product is pulled across the scanner, looks up the price in an attached computer, and instantly prints the price of the item on the cash register tape.

Secondary Data
Statistics not gathered for the immediate study at hand but for some other purpose.

Secondary Source
Source of secondary data that did not originate the data but rather secured them from another source.

Selection Bias
Contaminating influence in an experiment occurring when there is no way of certifying that groups of test units were equivalent at some prior time.

Self Report
Method of assessing attitudes in which individuals are asked directly for their beliefs about or feelings toward an object or class of objects.

Semantic Differential
Self-report technique for attitude measurement in which subjects are asked to check which cell between a set of bipolar adjectives or phrases best describes their feelings toward the object.

Sentence Completion
Questionnaire containing a number of sentences that subjects are directed to complete with the first words that come to mind.

Sequence Bias
Distortion in the answers to some questions on a questionnaire because the replies are not independently arrived at but are conditioned by responses to other questions; the problem is particularly acute in mail questionnaires because the respondent can see the whole questionnaire.

Sequential Sample
Sample formed on the basis of a series of successive decisions. If the evidence is not conclusive after a small sample is taken, more observations are taken; if still inconclusive after these additional observations, still more observations are taken. At each stage, then, a decision is made as to whether more information should be collected or whether the evidence is sufficient to draw a conclusion.

Simple Random Sample
Probability sample in which each population element has a known and equal chance of being included in the sample and where every combination of n population elements is a sample possibility and is just as likely to occur as any other combination of n units.

Simple Tabulation
Count of the number of cases that fall into each category when the categories are based on one variable.

Simulated Test Marketing
Test marketing done by firms in shopping malls or consumers' homes as a prelude to a full-scale marketing test for the product.

Snake Diagram
Diagram (so called because of its shape) that connects with straight lines the average responses to a series of semantic differential statements, thereby depicting the profile of the object or objects being evaluated.

Snowball Sample
Judgment sample that relies on the researcher's ability to locate an initial set of respondents with the desired characteristics; these individuals are then used as informants to identify still others with the desired characteristics.

Spearman's Rank Correlation Coefficient
A statistic employed with ordinal data to measure the extent of association between two variables.

Spurious Correlation
Condition that arises when there is no relationship between two variables but the analyst concludes that a relationship exists.

Spurious Noncorrelation
Condition that arises when the analyst concludes there is no relationship between two variables but, in fact, there is.

Stability
A technique for assessing the reliability of a measure by measuring the same objects or individuals at two different points in time and then correlating the scores; the procedure is known as test–retest reliability assessment.

Standard Error of Estimate
Term used in regression analysis to refer to the absolute amount of variation in the criterion variable that is left unexplained or unaccounted for by the fitted regression equation.

Standard Test Market
A market in which companies sell their products through normal distribution channels.

Stapel Scale
Self-report technique for attitude measurement in which the respondents are asked to indicate how accurately each of a number of statements describes the object of interest.

Statistic
Characteristic or measure of a sample.

Statistical Efficiency
Measure used to compare sampling plans; one sampling plan is said to be superior (more statistically efficient) to another if, for the same size sample, it produces a smaller standard error of estimate.

Statistical Regression
Tendency of extreme cases of a phenomenon to move toward a more central position during the course of an experiment.

Storytelling
Questionnaire method of data collection relying on a picture stimulus such as a cartoon, photograph, or drawing, about which the subject is asked to tell a story.

Stratified Sample
Probability sample that is distinguished by the two-step procedure where (1) the parent population is divided into mutually exclusive and exhaustive subsets, and (2) a simple random sample of elements is chosen independently from each group or subset.

Stratum Chart
Set of line charts in which quantities are aggregated or a total is disaggregated so that the distance between two lines represents the amount of some variable.

Stress
Measure of the ''badness of fit'' of a configuration determined by multidimensional scaling analysis when compared to the original input data.

Structure
Degree of standardization imposed on the data collection instrument. A highly structured questionnaire, for example, is one in which the

questions to be asked and the responses permitted subjects are completely predetermined, while a highly unstructured questionnaire is one in which the questions to be asked are only loosely predetermined and respondents are free to respond in their own words and in any way they see fit.

Summated Ratings
Self-report technique for attitude measurement in which the subjects are asked to indicate their degree of agreement or disagreement with each of a number of statements; a subject's attitude score is the total obtained by summing the scale values assigned to each category checked.

Syndicated Research
Information collected on a regular basis that is then sold to interested clients (for example, Nielsen Retail Index).

Systematic Error
Error in measurement that is also known as constant error since it affects the measurement in a systematic way.

Systematic Sample
Probability sample in which every kth element in the population is designated for inclusion in the sample after a random start.

Tabulation
Procedure by which the number of cases that fall into each of a number of categories are counted.

Tachistoscope
Device that provides the researcher timing control over a visual stimulus; in marketing research, the visual stimulus is often a specific advertisement.

Telephone Interview
Telephone conversation between a representative of the research organization, the interviewer, and a respondent or interviewee.

Telescoping Error
A type of error resulting from the fact that most people remember an event as having occurred more recently than in fact is the case.

Testing Effect
Contaminating effect in an experiment due to the fact that the process of experimentation itself affected the observed response. The *main testing effect* refers to the impact of a prior observation on a later observation, while the *interactive testing effect* refers to the condition when a prior measurement affects the test unit's response to the experimental variable.

Thematic Apperception Test (TAT)
Copyrighted series of pictures about which the subject is asked to tell stories.

Total Association
Association existing between the variables without regard to the levels of any other variables; also called the zero order association between the variables.

Turnover Table
See Brand-Switching Matrix.

Type I Error
Rejection of a null hypothesis when it is true; also known as α error.

Type II Error
Failure to reject a null hypothesis when it is false; also known as β error.

Unbiased
Used to describe a statistic when the average value of the statistic equals the population parameter it is supposed to estimate.

Univariate
Problem of analysis in which there is a single measurement on each of n sample objects or there are several measurements on each of

the n observations, but each variable is to be analyzed in isolation.

Validity
Term applied to measuring instruments reflecting the extent to which differences in scores on the measurement reflect true differences among individuals, groups, or situations in the characteristic that it seeks to measure, or true differences in the same individual, group, or

situation from one occasion to another, rather than constant or random errors.

Variable Transformation
Change in scale in which a variable is expressed.

Varimax
Angle-preserving rotation of a factor-analytic solution done to facilitate substantive interpretation of the factors.

Voice Pitch Analysis
Type of analysis that examines changes in the relative frequency of the human voice that accompany emotional arousal.

Word Association
Questionnaire containing a list of words to which respondents are instructed to reply with the first word that comes to mind.

Zero Order Association
See Total Association.

Index

Note: The lowercase n after a page number indicates the information can be found in a footnote or source note on that page. The lowercase c after a page number indicates the information can be found in the case section to a specific part of the book.